Strategies for
African Development

Strategies for African Development

Edited by
Robert J. Berg
Jennifer Seymour Whitaker

A Study for the
Committee on African
Development Strategies

Sponsored by the
Council on Foreign Relations and the
Overseas Development Council

UNIVERSITY OF CALIFORNIA PRESS
Berkeley · Los Angeles · London

University of California Press
Berkeley and Los Angeles, California

University of California Press, Ltd.
London, England

1 2 3 4 5 6 7 8 9

LIBRARY OF CONGRESS CATALOGING-IN-PUBLICATION DATA

Main entry under title:

Strategies for African development.

    Includes index.
    1. Africa—Economic policy—Addresses, essays,
lectures. I. Berg, Robert J. II. Whitaker, Jennifer
Seymour, 1938–   . III. Committee on African
Development Strategies (U.S.). IV. Council on Foreign
Relations. V. Overseas Development Council.
HC800.S76   1986   338.96   85-23304
ISBN 0-520-05784-8 (alk. paper)
ISBN 0-520-05782-1 (pbk. : alk. paper)

Contents

Foreword

The work of the Committee on African Development Strategies came to fruition first in its report and recommendations, "Compact for African Development," released in December 1985. In pursuing its work, the Committee commissioned a set of studies, of which most are published in this volume.

Authors were asked to suggest policy and sectoral strategy guidance not only for Africans, but for their economic development collaborators. Most of the papers were discussed in full meetings of the Committee. In each case a dialogue of African and American experts was involved in these discussions.

The authors and a large number of other experts we consulted found a variety of internal and external factors requiring serious attention by African states and the major states interacting with Africa. In fact African authorities are actively re-examining their development options and this creates an almost unparalleled opportunity to enter into discussions on broad, fundamental issues as well as specific internal and external changes necessary for improved development performance.

Both African and external development experts agreed on the need for internal reforms supported by long-term, larger and qualitatively better external aid. The critical issues are the content of the reforms, their timing and whether sufficient political and social sense is brought to the process. Moreover, once better policies are adopted, and indeed much is changing in Africa along recommended lines, there are still major questions of sectoral strategy on which too little discussion has taken place. It is here where many of the authors of this volume were asked to make their main contributions.

There is some hope now that African economies can recover from the famine and economic depression of these past years in a way which can enable a range of sectoral strategies to be pursued. The reforms now taking place in a large number of countries are showing positive effects. Continuing external problems such as market access and relatively high interest rates may prove difficult to systemically correct, even if they are the culprits causing some of Africa's problems. National economic policy and institutional performance are the ingredients in their destiny Africans ought to be best able to affect.

The stark crisis in Africa—the starvation and displacement of peoples—has elicited an impressive nationwide response in America. Yet those who want to help must be concerned not only with ending the current crisis, but with preventing future crises. The challenge is to find a way of translating their concerns and questions into significant future action. We believe a way can be found to help create self-sustaining, prospering societies in Africa, but it will take deep commitment—particularly from Africa, but also from its friends.

Just as African development needs qualitative improvement, so must donors improve the quality and quantity of their aid if the prospects for Africa's development are to be greatly improved. Too often donor aid has served narrow political and commercial ends rather than being rigorously tied to development performance. The effectiveness of aid to Africa also is undercut by poor coordination among the donors and, in this time of rehabilitation of economies, by its being tied to new purchases rather than to fostering existing investments. Given its key position among donors and the influence of its policies in world aid, debt and trade discussions, we see an especially pivotal role for the United States in helping Africa to help itself. Stronger U.S. leadership is required even during this time of domestic budgetary stringency.

The Committee we chair represents a wide spectrum of backgrounds and viewpoints. Its members come from business, universities, media, voluntary organizations and political life. We are grateful for their active participation and informed advice. When we began this inquiry, the members of the Committee saw these issues as important; today, leaders across America are recognizing them as urgent and must also speak out to help effect the changes discussed in this volume.

We are also grateful to the Council on Foreign Relations and the

Overseas Development Council for suggesting the creation of this Committee and for supporting its work, and to Senior Fellows Bob Berg of the Overseas Development Council and Jennifer Seymour Whitaker of the Council on Foreign Relations for their able direction of the Committee.

We particularly appreciate the financial support of the Carnegie Corporation of New York, the Ford Foundation, the Ford Motor Company, the W.K. Kellogg Foundation, the Rockefeller Brothers Fund, and the Rockefeller Foundation. Most of their support was given prior to the general awareness of the crises in Africa, demonstrating the critical and farsighted roles so often played by private foundations.

In the course of our work, we have benefited from the thoughts of officials from African countries, the United States, and the international institutions who served in an ex-officio capacity during the discussion phase of the Committee's work.

The Committee on African Development Strategies neither proposes nor expects panaceas. Our recommendations, appended in this volume, are a set of actions the U.S. and other donors need to take in concert with African actions. The Committee proposed a considerable amount of additional aid because it felt the basis of a compact for African development existed: improved performance in Africa supported by enhanced levels of aid. The costs may seem high now, but the financial, political and human costs of not facing issues squarely will be incalculably greater.

This Committee is aware that setting out its recommendations for public consideration has only initiated the broader, longer term review of Africa's dilemmas and U.S. policy that we see as necessary. It will take hard work by Africans and their friends in the United States and other donor countries to bring about the long-term changes recommended. For our part the Committee will be working with public and private leadership groups across the United States to increase awareness of the need for action on the issues discussed in this volume. Efforts to become better informed on these issues cannot but help. And acting on these issues may well be the key to a more secure Africa and relationships between Africa and the United States built on the confidence of peoples living with dignity and progress.

Lawrence S. Eagleburger   *Donald F. McHenry*
Co-Chairman   Co-Chairman

January 1986

Acknowledgments

To the many colleagues who generously shared with us ideas and counsel we offer warm thanks. We wish particularly to express our appreciation to Wayne Fredericks, who played a major role in the inception of this project and in bringing the Council on Foreign Relations and the Overseas Development Council together to carry it through; to David Hamburg, whose insights inspired us along the way; and to John Sewell and Paul Kreisberg, who supported and guided our efforts within our two Councils. Val Kallab skillfully guided the Compact to publication. This book itself owes much to Margaret Novicki. It would have taken twice as long to produce—and to read—had it not been for her knowledgeable and adroit editing. The ingenious and thorough coordination and copy-editing of Meg Hardon and the keyboard wizardry of Terry Calway and Alice McLoughlin were also invaluable. Finally, David Kellogg's creative and unstinting marshalling of all our forces was central to producing this book.

R.J.B. and *J.S.W.*

The Policy Setting: Crisis and Consensus

Jennifer Seymour Whitaker

Over the past several years, Africa's economic crisis has generated a growing body of analysis and prescription on what has gone wrong and what should be done. This rethinking of African development policies has proceeded on parallel tracks in primary donor countries and the World Bank. It has sometimes converged, and sometimes clashed, with the anxious stock-taking of African officials and scholars. As usual, the Westerners are drawing sweeping conclusions about *what Africa ought to do*. And, as usual, the Africans have neither the flexibility nor the wherewithal to either reject the advice totally or follow through on it fully. But the heightened concern and intellectual energy focused on the crisis, both within and outside of Africa, provide at least the initial condition for change.

The Committee on African Development Strategies was created to study what makes sense for Africa's longer-term development, and how U.S. policy can best support that development. The present volume of papers commissioned by the Committee represents a concerted effort by experts on African systems to seek remedies for obviously grave dilemmas. As it evolved, we realized how far a number of our conclusions fit into a kind of consensus that has grown among Western donors and the World Bank since the extremity of Africa's problems became clear early in this decade. From this recognition springs both hope and wariness. Viewed most positively, general agreement brings hope for concerted action. On the other side of the coin, orthodoxy can inhibit our own best efforts and those of Afri-

1

cans. Therefore, we need to consider both the utility of the consensus and its limits.

The outlines of Africa's current economic crisis are well known. While recognizing the perils of generalizing about an area as vast and diverse as sub-Saharan Africa, this analysis will focus on the widely visible problems and patterns of causality that have given rise to current conclusions on policy.

Africa's problems did not start with the oil price hikes of 1973 and 1979. At independence, African governments inherited gerry-built institutions staffed by a thin layer of trained personnel. During the preceding decade, high commodity prices financed accelerated expansion of education and health care systems and creation of infrastructure, easing the transition from colonialism and raising expectations about upward mobility.

During the 1960s, Africa's average per capita growth was steady though modest (at about 1.5%, it lagged behind most of the developing world). But with the oil shocks and the deepening international recession, international terms of trade in Africa's main commodities fluctuated widely and eventually fell decisively; the prices of African minerals and agricultural commodities deteriorated while oil prices rose sevenfold, grain rose fivefold and manufactures rose proportionately to Western inflation. In addition, in the early seventies and then in the eighties, drought desiccated first the Sahel regions of Western and Central Africa and then an arc of countries from West Africa to the Horn of Africa and into southern Africa. Burgeoning population growth, a result of successful development programs, further strained land resources while increasing urban food needs.

The 1973 jump in oil prices created a series of external and environmental shocks that, in combination with poor domestic economic management, brought stagnation or decline in the growth of per capita national income—particularly in agricultural productivity—in many African countries. Political instability also exacerbated weaknesses in economic institutions.

From 1970 onward, per capita agricultural production for the continent as a whole fell about one percent a year. African shares in the international trade of many agricultural and mineral exports—affecting more than half of Africa's main commodities exports—declined. At the same time, food imports rose from previously low levels to a point where one in three Africans is dependent on imported food. The cumulative effect of rising import costs and falling export revenues led to growing balance of payments deficits, amounting to $7.9 billion in 1984.

Unable or unwilling for both political and economic reasons to cut expenditures as fast as revenues were falling, governments resorted to deficit financing. In these circumstances, it is not surprising that Africa's debt increased by an average 22 percent a year from 1973 to 1983, greatly exceeding the growth of output or exports. As total debt rose, the level of net capital inflows to low-income Africa, from public and private sources, dropped sharply—by 45 percent between 1980 and 1983. By the end of 1986, payments required to service African debts are projected to equal two-thirds of all aid receipts.

In addition to the rising debt service ratios, Africa's gross foreign exchange reserves have fallen overall to the equivalent of only four to five weeks of imports, and many countries are in arrears on current obligations. In countries that cannot pay their bills, current productive capacity is being wasted and continues to deteriorate.

Since the late 1970s, policymakers and scholars have been debating the relative importance of external and internal causes of Africa's problems, notably in the World Bank's *Accelerated Development in Sub-Saharan Africa*[1] (produced by a team led by Elliot Berg and popularly known as the "Berg Report"), with its focus on shortcomings of African economic policies, and the Organization of African Unity's *Lagos Plan of Action*,[2] with its emphasis on the adverse effects of international trends on African development. The debate cannot be entirely resolved; the skeins of causality are, finally, impossible to clearly disentangle. On one hand, it seems clear that the macroeconomic policies of African governments, which discouraged exports, were a primary cause of Africa's declining trade shares. On the other hand, government policies responded to crises engendered by adverse external trends. In addition, declining maintenance of infrastructures and cutbacks in essential government services—at least in part the result of the foreign exchange shortfalls—eroded effective implementation of policy. All of these unremittingly negative indicators accelerated the flight of capital from Africa.

In this volume, Stephen Lewis enters the debate most directly. He points (in Chapter 17) to evidence on both sides of the debate, asserting that economic performance in Africa could have been better—by a couple of percentage points a year—if either the external environment had been more helpful or African governments had implemented better policies. Most of the authors in this book, however, focus on internal performance—both policy and institutional effectiveness. Within this context, data showing the positive effects of specific policies—particularly on exchange rates and import-export balances[3]—offer modest grounds for optimism. National economic policy and institutional performance are ingredients in their economic destiny that Africans ought to be best able to affect.

WHAT WENT WRONG

As noted above, Africa sustained major external shocks in the 1970s and early 1980s. However, it is also clear that African economic and political behavior played a major role in the continent's economic decline. As Crawford Young argues in Chapter 1, in many instances African leaders inherited an authoritarian state model, with a tradition of strong government control over the economy. As popular expectations of modern economic life rose and governments had to draw on state resources to secure political control, demands on state economic resources burgeoned.

From the time of independence, government policies in many countries eroded incentives for economic growth, and particularly for agricultural production. With declining per capita growth in agriculture, after two-and-a-half decades much of Africa still relies almost entirely on agriculture for its export income, and four-fifths of its people depend on farming for their livelihood. For Africa's increasingly dependent economies, the most promising area for import substitution now is in food crops. Yet, on average, governments have invested a meager five percent of annual expenditures in agriculture, have held down agricultural prices and distorted markets to the disadvantage of farmers. Moreover, as Jane Guyer explains in Chapter 14, government extension, credit, and technical assistance programs have largely bypassed the women farmers who grow some 70 percent of the continent's food.

Both Africa's loss of trade share and the dramatic fall in rates of return on investment within most African countries—to about half of that in developing countries as a whole—point to poor economic management. African governments have pursued a wide variety of policies, but some generally counterproductive patterns have become discernible. Low prices to farmers—to raise government revenues on export crops and keep down food prices to urban consumers; severely overvalued exchange rates; and cumbersome trade regimes favoring import substitution and luxury consumption were the main culprits.

These policies—exchange rates, tariff and tax structures, import control systems and macroeconomic policies affecting the balance of payments—are integrally related to international trade. And for Africa's small, open economies they create the context for domestic productivity.

Too often exchange rates, tariff structures and credit allocations have favored import substituting industrialization over agriculture, and urban over rural well-being. Low food prices and artificially high values of national currencies favored imports of components for manufacturing, as well as food and even luxury goods. Perhaps most fundamental, inexperienced and sometimes venal leadership lacked the ability to analyze and change policies, and few African governments succeeded in maintaining balances between resource inflows and expenditures from fat times to lean ones.

POLITICAL INSTABILITY

In many countries, political instability has also severely inhibited economic development. Expressing the relationship between political and economic development in terms of its least common denominator, political stability is a necessary—though not sufficient—condition for economic progress. On the most basic level, insecurity about the future inhibits investment in African economies—both by citizens and foreigners. Looking at the African countries which have done comparatively well at building relatively more solid bases for growth—including Ivory Coast, Cameroon, Botswana, Malawi, and Kenya—they have almost without exception enjoyed strong continuous leadership, sometimes incorporating peaceful transfers of power.

Striking negative examples, on the other hand, include Ghana and Uganda, where, in countries blessed by rich human and material resources, continuous political upheaval has left infrastructures in ruins and caused increasing numbers of people to take refuge in the subsistence and "informal" sectors, largely outside government regulation. Again, the countries waging long continuing conflicts with their neighbors or with internal insurgents—including Chad, Ethiopia, Sudan, Somalia, Angola and Mozambique[4]—have heavily mortgaged their economic growth and in almost every case are among the chief victims of devastating famine. Nigeria's civil war also left a legacy of high societal costs. Obviously, expenditures on arms and armies drain scarce resources and war destroys infrastructures basic to production, marketing, and distribution.

Most African countries today are not fighting with their neighbors or with organized insurgent movements, but have been prey, since independence, to abrupt regime changes, usually via military coup. Only twelve countries in sub-Saharan Africa have not succumbed to military coups and at least half the countries of Africa today live under military rule. The consequences of military rule for development have been often, and inconclusively, debated.[5] In fact, the civil servants who run the economy under a military government are usually the same people who would do so in a civilian government. Moreover, the same economic and political motives—for growth, on the one hand; and for personal gain, patronage, urban order, revenue extraction, on the other, appear to drive military and civilian leaders alike. Ultimately, therefore, it has proved difficult to measure differences in performance. What has declined under the repressive regimes often characteristic of military rule is the ability to offer alternatives, to debate the necessity for change in policies.

In fact, regime weakness and its corollary—the use of state economic resources to bolster incumbent governments—have profoundly affected economic performance in most African countries.[6] Rational calculations about economic policy are often based on political rather than economic goals.[7] The more extensive the state's involvement in the economy, the more emoluments will be available to insure loyalty and reward constituents. Apart from draining national resources, constituency building through patronage fosters a variety of economic distortions.

Job creation through expanding bureaucracies is the most obvious distortion. This action has proven highly costly. First of all, the burgeoning state payrolls themselves drain resources: in the 1980s, government consumption has taken a higher percent of GDP in contemporary Africa than in all other developing regions save the Middle East and North Africa. African governments, moreover, spend an unusually large portion of recurrent costs simply covering wages and salaries of their employees: about thirty percent in the 1974–80 period, compared to roughly twenty percent in the Latin American/

Caribbean Region and about fifteen percent in Asia and the Middle East.[8]

Second, state-run corporations often have tended to regard profit as secondary to other non-economic goals—including employment creation—and their balance sheets have reflected this. Further, the channelling of virtually all larger investments through government, and complex licensing and allocation of foreign exchange often create rewards for loyal allies and windfalls for the government officials who administer them. Regulating international commerce and investment becomes a major source of revenue for individual bureaucrats as well as for the state itself.

ETHNICITY

Ethnicity also profoundly affects economic performance. Clearly, ethnic ties often constitute a major element in constituency-building and patronage relationships in national politics. But ethnic support networks starting at the village level also fundamentally shape economic decision making. As Goran Hyden argues in Chapter 2, ethnic and community links, often strongly held between rural and urban areas, lead to investment patterns aimed at diversifying and sharing risks, often by solidifying group ties.[9] What this means is: (1) profits and savings are often invested in enterprises aimed at securing ethnic links and security but unlikely to earn a *monetary* profit, such as village real estate, education and sustenance of kinfolk, installation of group members in high places, cultivation of "big men"; (2) whatever the stated aim of African businessmen, their enterprises are likely to respond first of all to communal pressures—principally job creation—and only secondarily to profits and growth.

Most important, ethnic ties supersede national allegiance for many, perhaps most, Africans. Thus the state's resources are not seen primarily as the common property of all citizens, but rather as fair game for ethnic groups building their own bases of support. The state is, in fact, regarded as the primary source of available resources. In these circumstances, public attitudes about government officials' accountability for national monies become somewhat ambivalent. Insofar as they think of themselves as citizens of a nation-state, everyone is opposed to corruption, but on the deeper level where they identify with particular groups, they do not question the legitimacy of taking their share. Rather than worrying about how the state has encroached on the private sector, one African scholar declared ironically that the state *is* often, in fact, a private fiefdom whose resources belong to a few powerful individuals rather than the citizenry as a whole.[10]

In sum, meager resources, scarce qualified manpower, weak governance and confused institutional goals have left African governments peculiarly unprepared to run command economies where virtually all decisions and allocations are made by government officials. Most African states have been living beyond their means, both in failing to push the exports necessary to finance growth, and in building state structures whose size has grown in inverse proportion to their effectiveness in fostering economic productivity.

THE ROLE OF DONORS

Looking at the record of donor aid over the last several decades, it is clear that development assistance has both helped and hindered African development. Donor programs have made important contributions in infrastructure, but as Timberlake and Guyer show (and Berg summarizes more comprehensively) donors have often been insensitive to fundamental environmental and social questions. Fluctuating fashions in aid levels and rationales—from "take-off," through integrated rural development, through basic human needs, to privatization—have sent conflicting signals from donors to recipients and increased problems in carrying out effective development. Complex donor interventions, in societies where the effects of external actions are not well understood, have often proved burdensome to weak African institutions.

Non-developmental objectives have all too often dominated donor priorities, with security and political interests skewing U.S. resource allocations in particular. Turf battles among donors and the tying of aid to exports also worked to distort assistance programs. Coordination among donors, or by African governments, has been poor. In its absence, proliferating and overlapping projects have drained the administrative energies of African officials and raised recurrent costs. Aid has in fact sometimes provided a negative model for African governments in emphasizing planning and building, without maintenance and follow-through. For the United States, the year-by-year

Congressional appropriations process has exacerbated endemic difficulties with longer-term planning.

THE CONSENSUS

The broad outlines of this analysis, accepted almost without exception by the contributors to this volume, lead to a set of conclusions on policy reform, which are also widely shared, both within this volume and among Western policymakers and scholars. The following, in summary, express the consensus:

First, agriculture is central: as the main present base for productivity in all African countries except the mineral exporters, and the main source of income for most people in all countries, it must receive priority attention and investment from both African governments and donors.

Second, policy changes within Africa are key to building African agriculture and diversifying Africa's productive base. Specifically, African governments should eliminate the bias toward import dependence inherent in past strategies of import substituting industrialization.

Third, effective African utilization of scarce available resources will be fostered by the reduction of excessive state controls which discourage private economic initiatives, and the streamlining of government bureaucracies.

Finally, donors should use the leverage inherent in development assistance to work with African recipients toward the achievement of appropriate reforms. This means, paradoxically, that donors must now use increasing African dependence to press African governments to take more responsibility—to become more accountable for both aid and national resources. Non-project aid, involving more direct transfers of financial resources and fewer schemes for complex new systems or institutions requiring ongoing maintenance expenditures, can provide needed leverage and avoid additional burdens on weak African governments.

Anyone familiar with the history of development assistance over the past 20 years must regard the emergence of a new consensus with some skepticism. How did the analysis evolve and who disagrees? How enduring is the strategy likely to be? Will the present reaction against strongly state-centered economic investment be followed by an equally strong swing back in the other direction? How can those who support the basic policy avoid the overcorrection that will produce its own reaction?

DEBATE ON POLICY

The first major component of the current consensus came in 1981 with the Berg Report. Commissioned at the request of the World Bank's African Directors, the study generated considerable debate, both within Africa and among Africanists. Elliott Berg laid out therein the now standard critique of African policy, emphasizing that the primary cause of Africa's malaise lay in African countries' failure to provide incentives for the agricultural exports which bring in the bulk of their earnings. He also asserted the need for loosening government controls and fostering a greater role for the African private sector.

The Report's critics took issue with Berg and the Bank on a number of issues. Some, like Gerald Helleiner, argued the importance of external shocks to Africa's plight and sought to demonstrate that the crucial variable in adjustment was maintaining imports.[11] Others, including, notably, a group of scholars at the University of Sussex's Institute of Development Studies (IDS), questioned the feasibility of Berg's prescriptions. Generally known for their advocacy of a strong state role in the economy, the Sussex scholars questioned particularly the importance of market forces or "getting the prices right" for agricultural products. They also pointed out that increasing output could further erode commodity prices. For their part, African commentators criticized the report's assumption that African countries should continue their excessive reliance on an export-led strategy. They also seized on the report's neglect of food production in the face of Africa's increasing dependence on imported food.

Three years later, the subsequent World Bank report on Africa: *Toward Sustained Development: A Joint Program of Action For Sub-Saharan Africa*[12] reiterated the need for policy reform but also took account of the reactions to Berg. It laid out a more nuanced strategy, with due regard for the difficulties involved in implementation and a more downbeat view of African prospects.

From the early 1980s, U.S. AID was also beginning to advocate "policy dialogue." This was, in effect, both a push for reform and an assertion of donor leverage over recipients' use of resources. After the Americans had been reiterating this theme for several years, the European Community more timidly initiated its own negotiation on the relationship between aid and performance, in its third five-year agreement on aid and trade with African, Pacific and Caribbean countries, at Lomé. While the Americans and Europeans put varying emphases on the need to strengthen the African private sector, they agreed on the importance of macroeconomic policy in stimulating productivity.

Significantly, many of the Berg Report's critics agree on the need for "structural adjustment" of African economies and other elements of the World Bank/U.S. prescription. At the same time, however, they take issue with aspects of the "privatization" analysis which they see as sweeping and inaccurate. In an important compilation of European views published in the fall of 1985, leading IDS scholars and others continued to point out the hazards in applying macroeconomic panaceas in Africa.[13] Here and elsewhere[14] they expressed continuing concern about the effects of increasing competition on the welfare of weaker members of society and of open markets in increasing the dependency of economies already highly vulnerable to forces beyond their control. They generally declined to defend the state's role in African economic development with any zeal, however, and in many instances agreed on the need for policy reform.

The main African counterpart to these Western intellectual trends, the Lagos Plan, was published a year before the Berg Report. In the Plan, African leaders proposed a development strategy emphasizing national self-reliance to be fostered through regional linkages. While acknowledging economic mismanagement, they placed most of the onus for declining African performance on the hostile external environment. Reiterating the need for industrialization, they also emphasized the importance of agriculture but principally in terms of food self-sufficiency.

Five years later, African and Western views appear somewhat closer. The ambitious goals of the Lagos Plan have been deeply shadowed by harsh present prospects. At the 1985 OAU summit, Africa's leaders declared that agriculture is the major economic problem facing the continent today, and that burgeoning populations and environmental deterioration threaten all development gains. They also acknowledged that solving Africa's economic problems largely depends upon African performance. At least on the level of ideas, many Africans are considering reforms that would run counter to the centralized economic controls they inherited at independence and have worked to expand. More than 15 African countries have instituted stabilization programs geared to IMF and donor recommendations. In the crisis, African leaders are casting about—often Westward—for new solutions.

IMPLEMENTING POLICY REFORM

In implementation, the current consensus is no more likely to provide easily applied answers than previous attempts to design wholesale solutions. Nonetheless, the converging analyses of what has happened in Africa since the early sixties and what resources may realistically be available to re-start African economies are likely to provide a strong continuing impetus for policy reform.

Without reiterating the analysis, it is clear that government policies—especially on agriculture—offer much room for improvement. But policy dialogue means different things to different people, and the great variations in African policy suggest the need for quite different prescriptions to be undertaken by African governments within their various contexts. Not surprisingly, advocates of conditionality vary widely in their approaches.

Until recently the IMF based its remedies for African debt on fairly strict application of neo-classical nostrums—particularly devaluation and elimination of consumption subsidies. On privatization, some analysts, including influential officials within the current U.S. Administration, advocate divestiture of government-run enterprises (widely known as parastatals) to private purchasers. Others, including Benno Ndulu and David Leonard in this volume, support early devolution of the economic activities which may be best handled privately—including transport and marketing—so that the state can perform its essential tasks more efficiently. Still others advocate a cautious approach to the largely inchoate African private sector (composed mostly of subsistence farmers and mini-enterprises), but push for macroeconomic policies favoring exports. Stephen Lewis, while strongly advocating price and exchange rate adjustment to correspond to international levels, carefully qualifies his call for liberalized trade, pointing out that some protection is necessary if African aims of diversifying production and exports are to be achieved. Jane Guyer cautions that decontrol of some agricultural prices could cut production if cheap imports are not restricted.

On agriculture, most of the contributors to this volume join a broad consensus advocating support for smallholder farming as Africa's only viable agricultural basepoint for development. Bruce Johnston and others concur on the need to shift the bias in exchange and interest rate policies as well as investment—where these favor import-substituting industry (and capital-intensive farming)—to benefit small farmers. Jane Guyer points out that decontrol of markets will not help small farmers unless institutionalized discrimination against them, affecting, for example, market access, market taxes, police controls, vehicle taxation, is addressed.

David Leonard argues that agriculture in Africa is at a crossroad as land limits are being reached in a number of countries, while sharp population growth is predicted everywhere. In his view, this will necessitate transformation from extensive production to a more intensive system and far more attention to rural institutions capable of stimulating and servicing science-based agriculture. Given the weaknesses of central government management, this leads him to support the transfer of many of these services into private or governmentally decentralized hands.

Discussing potential industrial development, on the other hand, Helmboldt et al. (in Chapter 12), Liedholm and Mead (in Chapter 11), and Hawkins (in Chapter 10) also emphasize that industry must build on agricultural expansion. Helmboldt, et al., argue as well that both African and foreign private investors can accommodate regulations in an environment in which regulations are fairly and predictably enforced. Reviewing the trade policies of a number of states, Hawkins analyzes the drawbacks of industrialization based on import substitution, but like the other authors, recognizes that some infant industry protection will be necessary for the export- and resource-led industrialization which is Africa's best bet for development of manufacturing. Liedholm and Mead point to the vitality of enterprises within the "informal, non-agricultural sector," which lies largely outside government purview, and show how it has been systematically discriminated against in access to credit and foreign exchange. They endorse more equal treatment and generally advocate reduced government regulation as a sine qua non for the emergence of entrepreneurship.

EXTERNAL TRENDS

In all its variations, the drive for policy reform is likely to endure because, simply speaking, there are few credible alternatives in view.

In the short and medium term, Africa's crisis is unlikely to be ameliorated by a significant improvement in external factors. Terms of trade for the continent's main commodities are not projected to change for the better during this decade. And although improved patterns of rainfall obviously will increase crop production in many instances, burgeoning populations and the associated continuing deterioration of the natural resource base will continue to increase pressures on arable land. Further, while concerted international efforts to relieve Africa's debt burden will release resources needed for development, without significant changes in present trends aid levels cannot be expected to rise sufficiently to maintain external resource inflows at the level of the seventies. For the past decade AID has financed about 40 percent of Africa's imports and nearly half its gross domestic investment. However, from 1980–84 external aid to Africa declined in absolute terms from $8.5 to $6.7 billion. In all these areas, then, it is evident that the rehabilitation and regeneration of African economies cannot depend upon improvements in the international environment.

HOW DURABLE THE CONSENSUS

This conclusion has been very little disputed. Its corollary, that economic progress in Africa must be based on far-reaching internal reforms and much more cost-effective use of resources by both Africans and donors, is more controversial. Nonetheless, it is difficult to evade the recognition that policy reform and institutional change constitute the main factors within human control to foster growth in Africa. Looking at institutions, it is particularly risky for donors to draw up blueprints for systems that Africans must build and run. Yet, it is clear enough that whatever the balance between state and private control, enterprises charged with productive use of African resources must emphasize the bottom line: they simply do not have the wherewithal to ignore profit and loss calculations.

Surveying African countries individually, it is apparent that those which have supported smallholder agriculture, like Zimbabwe, Malawi, Kenya and the Ivory Coast, and tried to keep imports generally in line with export revenues have done better than others. Minerals exporters such as Botswana and Cameroon have adjusted particularly well to external shocks by adroit fiscal management, prudently husbanding export revenues to compensate for shortfalls in diamond and oil prices as well as recurrent drought. Moreover, reforms now being undertaken in a number of countries have shown some positive results.

Looking at the effect of policy changes on overall performance, some proponents of privatization argue, at least tentatively, that separating economic institutions from the state could mitigate some negative effects inherent in weak government accountability. First of all, occasions for corruption would be reduced as state controls over allocation of economic opportunities diminished. And second, the profit motive might give concern for efficiency some edge over patronage in the management of enterprises.

Turning to donor policies, the environment of international and African resource scarcity also creates a context powerfully supportive of policy reform. For reasons of domestic politics as well as development objectives, donors must use assistance as effectively as possible to support improvements in African economic performance. This is not a new idea. But the current emphasis on "conditionality," on linking aid and policy reforms, represents a marked difference in the degree if not the kind of donor commitment to reform and results. In the African context, the importance of conditionality for donors is not likely to disappear with next year's aid program. Whether it involves policy reform, institutional management, high standards of accountability and policing of corruption, getting the desired effect from "policy dialogue" between donors and recipients will be a long-term process. But the present and enhanced commitment can only be justified if donor countries feel that their aid has helped spur successful African performance.

REALISM ABOUT POLICY REFORM

Because it will take a long time, realism about what is involved in implementing policy reform is imperative. In itself, the consensus on policy reform and dialogue can take us only so far. For the immediate and longer-term period, several central problems must also be faced. First, the squeeze on African imports and capital investment will decrease the flexibility of African governments. As Chandra Hardy shows clearly in Chapter 16, Africa's debt, increasing at 24 per cent per annum between 1973 and 1984, threatens to siphon off a major share of export revenues and mortgage all future investable resources. While the debt grew (by $21 billion between 1979 and 1983), the level of net inflows to Africa increased by only $1 billion, and between 1980 and 1983 net capital inflows to Africa declined markedly—with commitments from private sources falling from $1.5 billion to $137 million and official commitments dropping by 31 percent. Although, as Carl Eicher argues (in Chapter 9), African economies have often failed to absorb aid flows productively, it is also evident, as Helleiner posits, that the African countries most successful in adjusting to international economic crises have been those with sufficient resources to maintain needed levels of imports. During a transitional period, significant debt relief will be required to get African economies moving again.

Secondly, African countries must strengthen their physical, technical, institutional and human infrastructures significantly before their efforts to increase productivity can be expected to bear abundant fruit. As Eicher points out, Africa lags far behind Asia and Latin America in trained scientific and managerial manpower. Although some experts see Africa's technical lag as a failure to use existing technologies, Eicher and Dunstan Spencer (in Chapter 8) argue that the existing technical stock cannot provide the basis for the needed surge in agricultural productivity. Eicher estimates that it will take about fifteen to twenty years to develop technical inputs needed to accelerate agricultural productivity. Spencer underlines the need to strengthen the systems that provide farming technologies within African countries. At the same time, deteriorating and inadequate roads as well as marketing and storage facilities must be improved to increase the security of African farmers who will be taking risks on new technologies, and to facilitate the entry of private entrepreneurs into the marketing and transport business.

Third, many of our authors emphasize what is probably the most serious ongoing problem threatening Africa's future economic viability: population growth. As Fred Sai shows in Chapter 5, the size of Africa's population threatens to double within ten years. In many countries this means that traditional methods of expanding agriculture through the cultivation of surplus lands are no longer possible. Thus, the exploding populations place significant pressures on Africa's ecology, leading to deterioration and erosion of fragile soils and the denuding of forest areas.

In addition, continued urbanization has outpaced the capacity of governments to provide a bare minimum of social services in the cities. Moreover, as David Court and Kabiru Kinyanjui show in

Chapter 13, education systems energetically built up since independence are increasingly overloaded, with already evident declines in
quality, and probable decreases in overall proportions of educated
manpower. As Kenneth King argues in Chapter 15, policy issues
affecting manpower and training urgently need to be reformulated.
Specific and concerted attention to both education and health are
needed, not only to build the African work force but to create a base
for dealing with fundamental ecological problems. In their turn, population and environment will profoundly affect policy and institutional reforms.

Both Lloyd Timberlake's analysis of environmental problems (in
Chapter 4) and Fred Sai's on population bring home again the need
for African governments to plan with donors for the long term.
Results of environmental programs are unlikely to be visible in three-
to-five year time frames, and indeed in many instances unlikely to
materialize at all unless effort is sustained for a much longer period of
time.

In addition, progress particularly on population but also on environmental problems seems to entail an emphasis on equity and local
participation which figures infrequently in current policy dialogues.[15]
Beyond the generally observed demographic effects of improvements in social welfare, dealing with both population and environmental problems requires people at the village level be able to see
how their own interests are served by family planning and conservation of natural resources. It also requires that they help to shape
programs affecting them.

Fourth, donors must assess the feasibility of specific policy reforms
with African governments within the political contexts of their countries. Because the consolidation of power often depends on direct
government control of economic benefits, austerity and structural
adjustment programs that threaten the emoluments of elites or the
cost of living of city dwellers may seriously undermine regimes. Liberia's 1979 rice riots, which led eventually to the overthrow of the
Tolbert regime, and the 1985 coup in the Sudan were triggered by
highly resented government attempts to "get the prices right." In
seeking reforms, then, the IMF, the World Bank, and bilateral donors
must proceed with a sensitive concern for the political realities affecting the African governments involved.

Further, as David Leonard suggests in Chapter 7, both donors and
African governments should seek alternative economic payoffs for

African constituents that will not obstruct productivity as subsidies and patronage have done. For example, Leonard proposes that road and infrastructure building projects employing seasonal labor represent a form of distributable economic goods that avoids the permanent drain on government revenues inherent in expanding employment in government bureaucracies.

Fifth, policy reform will impinge on current methods of taxation and thus on revenues available to finance government payrolls and programs. Cutting duties and lowering government's share of agricultural prices may seriously deplete domestically generated government resources in the absence of income or sales tax systems. When government salaries fall in real terms, incentives for job performance also drop and incentives for corruption increase. Thus donors, with African governments, will have to take account of financial trade-offs involved in reforms.

Sixth, African efforts to increase trade and decrease dependence will ultimately hinge, in great part, on the development of intra-African trade links and, eventually, a continental market. In the past, donors have been tempted to move ahead of Africans in promoting regionalism, and experiments with regional economic institutions within Africa have shown little success. Reducing interstate barriers will require vision and political courage on the part of African leaders that will probably remain in short supply while the economic crisis continues. Although the economic viability of the continent over the long term demands regional efforts, heavy national agendas will come first.

Donors have taken little interest in regional schemes since the demise of the East African community. They can now, however, encourage intra-African links, by aid to communications and transport infrastructures. As Stephen Lewis suggests, they can also provide credits to assist with financing African exports to other parts of the continent and support currency clearing arrangements.

In sum, the road to African development cannot be seen as a straightforward drive to policy reform. The map will inevitably be much more complicated: African governments (supported by donors) must enable their people to better plan family size, arrest the corresponding erosion of the environment, and strengthen the productive sinews of their societies while simultaneously instituting more rational macroeconomic policies. Only with due attention to the other problems may the macroeconomic policies be expected to work.

Correspondingly, only with workable macroeconomic policies can African states expect to generate revenues to sustain domestic investment in the needed infrastructures and improve the quality of people's lives. Finally, only by strengthening regional links will Africa begin to experience the stimulus to productivity of a large continental market.

IMPLICATIONS FOR DEVELOPMENT ASSISTANCE

The Committee on African Development Strategies' Report (Appendix II) reiterates the need to incorporate longer term development objectives into the immediate focus on survival and then on rehabilitation. Given the need to move forward on several fronts simultaneously, the transition to self-reliant growth in Africa will take a considerable amount of time, leadership, and resources. If amassing the technical inputs necessary to spur African agriculture will take at least 15 years, a generation will be needed to educate the scientists, technicians, and managers who must staff modernizing African economies. At best, the most difficult transition—changing attitudes about fertility, including the relationship between childbearing and economic well-being—will take at least that long.

During this time, pushing through these changes will require an unparalleled order of effort and commitment from both African government leaders and donors, and both African and Western private sectors. It is likely that while some African countries will produce the leader or leaders able to mobilize the polity in an all-out effort, others will not. Thus, the performance of African countries will be increasingly differentiated according to the human resources at the top and in other levels of society.

For their part, donors must stand ready to adjust their course in response to perceived results within Africa, adopting what Robert J. Berg, in Chapter 18, calls the "learning model approach." This implies a highly flexible form of conditionality, involving an attentive policy dialogue and a willingness to commit aid on the basis of development performance. As the process continues, donors will have to differentiate in order to encourage success, measured variously in: upping productivity, building infrastructure, curbing population growth, fostering private initiatives.

What does all this imply for donor planning, regarding levels of resources and kinds of assistance? In the view of the Committee, immediate relief requirements—regarding debt and food aid increases in response to population growth—will place significant demands on Western coffers over the next one to two decades. If African states are to rehabilitate and build their infrastructures, significant new monies must also be available. For the Committee, this implies a need for a doubling of total bilateral and multilateral aid to Africa to a level of $16 to $20 billion a year over the rest of this century, including a tripling of U.S. aid to Africa. Building and maintaining support for aid at these levels is, realistically, a very tall order, calling for reallocations within existing programs and raising of new resources. However, attaining the desired results without it is not a realistic prospect.

Well-nigh universal agreement exists on the need to minimize distortions caused by aid, and particularly to counteract the debilitating effects of dependency. Both for this reason and because of Africa's acute balance-of-payments crisis, most of our authors concur on the desirability of non-project aid financing, in some cases involving balance-of-payments support and in others direct aid to particular sectors. In his analysis of aid programs over the past several decades (in Chapter 18), Berg agrees on the current imperative for direct resource transfers, but argues that project aid is particularly required for the transfer of technical and managerial knowledge and for larger capital project activities needed to lay a base for long term growth. And for this a variety of reforms are necessary to improve the quality of their programs.

Other authors also differ on the question of recurrent costs, with Eicher vehemently disparaging support for ongoing costs while others, led by Berg, defend the assumption of costs generated by assistance programs. Surely a symptom of dependence, donor responsibility for some recurrent costs is justified in the current crisis as the only way of protecting expensive—and necessary—investment. On the other hand, cutting way back on separate projects and initiating them in coordination with African governments should reduce problems of maintenance and recurrent costs.

Again, in all of this, the aim will be to reduce distortions generated by donor interventions, and support African institution building that donors see as potentially productive. Direct financial assistance conditioned on policy or institutional goals now seems to offer the most leverage and thus the most promise.

However, certain donor interventions appear essential for the growth of African technical capabilities. For the time being, research on plant varieties and farming systems within Africa require a great many Western scientists. Almost inevitably, a heavy research effort will involve a number of quasi-Western enclaves within African systems. Eventually, these must and will be staffed by Africans, but the research effort cannot wait until they are. With skill, the progressive integration into African systems that Dunstan Spencer calls for in Chapter 8 will enable the technical inputs to be integrated into African farming.

Each of these factors clearly will affect the record on policy reform in Africa. With the need to work on so many fronts simultaneously, the going will not be easy. If the commitment to policy reform falters, however, good alternatives may be hard to find. As has been argued, in a time of resource scarcity this set of policies offers the best hope and leverage for better use of those resources. Moreover, within Western countries, it is difficult to visualize alternative strategies which might be embraced *with enthusiasm* by publics being called upon for significant development assistance allocations. The release of private initiative offers an ideal that is congruent with the major donors' ideologies. Aid aimed at improving central government control over African economies—or at direct donor social engineering—does not. Thus it is to be hoped that African governments and donors will be able to stay—and skillfully tack—along the course now being set. The specifics may sound quite different ten and twenty years hence, but an unwavering commitment by both Africans and donors to effective investment of available resources will continue to be the sine qua non for a productive African future.

NOTES

1. World Bank, *Accelerated Development in Sub-Saharan Africa: An Agenda for Action* (Washington, D.C.: The World Bank, 1981).

2. Organization of African Unity, *Lagos Plan of Action for the Economic Development of Africa, 1980–2000* (Addis Ababa: OAU, 1980).

3. David Wheeler, "Sources of Stagnation in Sub-Saharan Africa," *World Development* 12 (1): 1–23 (1984).

4. Like the rest of South Africa's neighbors, Angola and Mozambique will be vulnerable to Pretoria's attempts to destabilize their governments and interdict ANC activity until the end of the apartheid system.

5. See Henry Bienen, *Armies and Parties in Africa* (New York: Africana

Publishing, 1978); also R. D. McKinlay and A. S. Cohan, "A Comparative Analysis of Political and Economic Performance of Military and Civilian Regimes," *Comparative Politics* 8 (1) (October 1975).

6. For a classic account of African styles of governance, see Robert H. Jackson and Carl G. Rosberg, *Personal Rule in Black Africa: Prince, Autocrat, Prophet, Tyrant* (Berkeley: University of California Press, 1982).

7. For an impressively full account of the interplay between political and economic decision making, see Robert H. Bates, *Markets and States in Tropical Africa: The Political Basis of Agricultural Policies* (Berkeley: University of California Press, 1981).

8. David Abernethy, "Bureaucratic Growth and Economic Stagnation in Sub-Saharan Africa." Paper presented at the American Political Science Association meetings, September 1984.

9. For an excellent account of how ethnic and family relationships among a group of Nigerian Yorubas affect economic choices, see Sara S. Berry, *Fathers Work for Their Sons* (Berkeley: University of California Press, 1985).

10. Ali Mazrui at the October 23, 1984 meeting of the Committee on African Development Strategies, Washington, D.C.

11. G.K. Helleiner, "Outward Orientation, Import Instability and African Economic Growth: An Empirical Investigation." Paper prepared for the Paul Streeten Festschrift, to be edited by Sanjaya Lall and Frances Stewart, April 1984.

12. World Bank, *Toward Sustained Development in Sub-Saharan Africa: A Joint Program of Action* (Washington, D.C.: 1984).

13. The World Bank, Tore Rose, ed., *Crisis and Recovery in Sub-Saharan Africa* (Paris: OECD, 1985).

14. See, for example, Manfred Beinefield, "The Lessons of Africa's Industrial 'Failure'," IDS Bulletin 16 (3) (1985): 69–87 (Sussex: Institute of Development Studies).

15. Edward Green, "U.S. Population Policies, Development and The Rural Poor of Africa," *Journal of Modern African Studies* 20 (1) (1982), p. 55.

PART I

MANAGING AFRICAN ECONOMIES

CHAPTER ONE

Africa's Colonial Legacy

Crawford Young

Impasse, crisis, decline—a grim vocabulary has come to dominate discourse on African development. From the hope and optimism that prevailed in the 1960s to the unease and apprehension of the late 1970s, the mood in the 1980s has shifted to acute anxieties and forebodings. The annual reviews of African affairs published by *Foreign Affairs* have captured this shift—an optimistic tone still pervades the 1980 summary, written by Andrew Young, but by 1982, John de St. Jorre speaks of a "loss of confidence," and in 1983, Jennifer Whitaker writes of a struggle for survival.[1]

The impasse in the development process evident today is inextricably linked to a crisis of the state. A state in disarray cannot perform the firm tutelary role which was central to the major developmental success stories of the late 1970s—the newly industrializing countries (NICs)—a category notably missing in Africa. In turn, deteriorating economies deny states the resources to carry out such missions, intensifying pressures toward further decline.

On the developmental side, the dismal litany is sufficiently familiar to require little elaboration. However, it is striking that much of the debate in developmental circles assumes that Africa's crisis has shallow historical roots, using the 1970s as the chronological baseline. A deeper historical perspective is indispensable for grasping both the political and economic dimensions of the present crisis.

The character of the contemporary African state has been determined by its colonial origins. The colonial state legacy in turn has been altered in crucial and often negative ways since political independence was achieved. While all trends in contemporary Africa cannot be simply laid at the door of the former colonizers, neither has the development crisis arisen simply from flaws in the post-colonial African ruling class. Rather, some patterns of state behavior and structure that arose out of the character of the colonial state and the ways in which the post-colonial state adapted its colonial legacy contribute toward an understanding of the dimensions of the present crisis.

DEFINITION OF THE STATE

Classical political theory defines the state[2] in terms of territoriality, sovereignty, institutions of rule, nationality, and law. Contemporary schools of analysis view the state in terms of the forces and interests it is presumed to serve: For liberal pluralists, these are competing interest groups; for Marxists, the ruling class; and for dependency theorists, the "international capitalist system." In this analysis, the state is viewed as an autonomous actor in the political and economic realms, and the prime determinants of state behavior can be summarized as hegemony, security, autonomy, legitimation, and revenue. Whereas these different imperatives often push the state in contradictory directions, they can help illuminate patterns of state behavior over time.

Hegemony, the first imperative of a state, reflects the need to establish the supremacy of government's laws and its authority over its territory and civil society. The full force of state power will descend upon individuals and groups who openly flout its authority. Security is a second state imperative, often taking priority in state revenue allocation, with the agencies that enforce internal security and external defense at its core.

Autonomy is a third imperative. The doctrine of sovereignty asserts that independence is a fundamental norm of true statehood, undaunted by the impossibility of its full realization. Internally, states assert their autonomy from particular interest groups through the claim to serve a broad "national" or "public" interest.

Legitimation, the fourth imperative, is a fundamental need in accumulation of power and effective exercise of authority. Civil society will usually offer voluntary compliance to authority which is perceived as legitimate in origin and behavior. Fear and force are sometimes used, but in the absence of legitimacy, recourse to such tactics can be costly. Lastly, the quest for revenue is a constant imperative of statecraft. As the resources necessary to satisfy the other imperatives must, in the last analysis, be derived from civil society, the state's revenue drive is a source of ceaseless tension with its citizenry.[3]

Before tracing the evolution of the African colonial state, some of its special characteristics must be outlined. Sovereignty was held by the occupying power and its prerogatives were delegated to the colonial administration. For the most part, colonial administrations held untrammelled authority to rule and to dispose of land, resources, and subjugated peoples—rights derived in conquest. Colonial territories were invariably endowed with a financial and legal personality separate from that of the metropole.

Although the colonial administration was designated by and hierarchically responsible to the metropolitan state, in practice, it enjoyed wide latitude in the exercise of its rule. Its personnel enjoyed a scope of arbitrary authority and could assume a social distance from their subjects unimaginable at home. A distinctive code and culture of rule emerged, carried out by an official class professionally specializing in colonial service. The colony was a state-like entity, though with special characteristics—alien to the core, erected upon a command relationship, and shaped by its vocation of domination.

CONSTRUCTION OF THE COLONIAL STATE

For simplicity of analysis, the African colonial state will be viewed in three epochs: construction, institutionalization, and decolonization. In the first stage, extending from the late 19th century partition until World War I, the most salient imperatives governing colonial state building were hegemony and revenue. The need to establish hegemony was particularly pressing because of the intensely competitive nature of the African partition and the determination of metropolitan finance ministries to force self-sufficiency upon the newly conquered domains.

With few exceptions, the use of European armies for conquest was far too expensive, as the Algerian experience had amply demonstrated. Cost-effective techniques were developed in India in the 18th century, based upon the organization of indigenous peoples under European officers, weapons, doctrine, and discipline. Particularly with the availability of the Maxim gun from 1889, such armies could defeat much more numerous resisting forces with relatively small losses.

While military superiority was a necessary condition for establishing hegemony, it had to be secured through institutionalization—by identifying and enlisting networks of collaborating indigenous intermediaries. Doctrines justifying their role differed, reflecting divergences in the state doctrines of various European powers, the strategic thinking of particular proconsuls, and local circumstances. The fledgling colonial state thereby acquired a rough-hewn apparatus of control, permitting the sparse band of soldier-administrators to claim that a framework of rule existed.

Mechanisms for economic intermediation were also required. For its own sustenance, the colonial state needed to gain leverage over the indigenous economy and acquire instrumentalities for its redirection. Many different groups took on these functions: long-established mercantile communities in coastal West Africa;[4] Zanzibari and Swahili planters in coastal East Africa;[5] and Mediterranean and other Indian sub-continent immigrants in a number of areas. At the upper end of the hierarchies of economic intermediation were large metropolitan trading houses, and, in some countries, settlers, plantation enterprises, and mining ventures entered the scene. Generally, the new colonial economy required destruction of intra-African trading systems which were not Europe-oriented and the capture of their resources.

Efforts toward gaining legitimation of the colonial state were directed at the metropolitan governments and societies and the European concert of states. In European parliaments, segments of the official community, and portions of the public up until the 1890s, there was substantial opposition to colonial conquest. Advocates of empire were forced to justify their actions by citing the benefits of colonialism in terms of strategic advantages, markets, and religious missions. The crucial bargain struck with critics of imperial conquest, however, was the pledge by all save the Italians that the metropolitan treasury would be guaranteed against any but temporary colonial expenditures. This pact of legitimation, therefore, imposed fiscal self-sufficiency upon the new colonial states.

Squeezed between the hegemony and revenue imperatives, the colonial state faced excruciating dilemmas. The harsh reality in much of the continent was that no revenue source was available, or at least nothing comparable to land in India, the highly valued exports of the

Dutch East Indies, the sugar of Caribbean slave plantation colonies, or the precious metals of Peru or Mexico. In Africa, the few exceptions were Islamic northern Nigeria, with a developed fiscal base that needed only to be directed to colonial purposes; coastal West Africa with some taxable external trade; and the southern African colonies after gold and diamond discoveries.

But much of the continent offered no evident fiscal resources, a fact that had often inhibited pre-colonial state-building as well. Therefore, the revenue imperative directed colonial states to their sole exploitable resource, African labor. Capitalization of African human resources was accomplished in several ways: direct taxation, labor conscription for infrastructural construction and transport services, and service on plantations and mines whose output could be subjected to state rents. Lastly, labor was compulsorily directed into crops such as cotton which were taxable on export.

The basic character and daily operation of the colonial state was thus profoundly shaped by its response to the twin exigencies of hegemony and revenue. Much of its early law hinged upon these requirements, as an ample arsenal of arbitrary ordinances empowered state agents to dominate and extract. By World War I, the basic framework of the colonial state was in place, but the infrastructure of military, political, economic, and cultural hegemony was far from complete, as the classic non-confrontational tactics of evasion, dissimulation, passive resistance, and private ridicule provided Africans with opportunities to preserve zones of autonomy, as Hyden has eloquently argued.[6] However, the scope of domination achieved by the colonial state was sufficient for its own ends and its agents acquired the conviction that their hegemony was entrenched for as far as one could peer into the future.

INSTITUTIONALIZATION OF THE COLONIAL STATE

Institutionalization, the second phase of the colonial state, covered the years between the first and second world wars. Whereas the 1920s were years of global prosperity, the depression and the following decade brought about severe pressures for revenues, with the head tax and labor service in kind again becoming crucial to state consumption after customs taxation had shown signs of providing an adequate fiscal base in the 1920s. Overall, the colonial state sought to consolidate its resources for the long haul.

In this second phase, the constant use of brute force was no longer required, as hegemony had been routinized. The skills and knowledge of the agents of the colonial state were upgraded through professionalization of the career service, raising entry requirements, and providing specialized training. Ad hoc strategies of domination were replaced by elaborate doctrines of colonial rule. Literacy and competence, along with ancestry and obedience to colonial authority, became criteria for the employment of African intermediaries.

The framework of the colonial state underwent significant change, as "development," "trusteeship," and "good government" entered colonial vocabulary. Albert Sarraut, French colonial minister from 1920–24, tirelessly propagated the notion of "mise en valeur" as a duty of the international community. Britain, newly conscious of the strategic asset the "undeveloped colonial estates" represented, symbolically offered a similar statement through the 1929 Colonial Development and Welfare Act, although this remained a largely unfunded metaphor until World War II.

Colonial state ideology allowed for the prudent management of the colonial realm by professionalized cadres who applied scientific methods. As trustees for a civil society lacking the capacity to articulate its own desires, colonial officialdom claimed to supply impartial adjudication of conflict and economical governance in the "paramount interest" of the subjugated.

However, static colonial revenue flows did not permit very extensive implementation of these new state doctrines. In rare cases, such as the Gold Coast, exceptionally favorable revenues from rising cocoa export taxes, along with an energetic governor personally committed to these concepts, did provide some momentum to welfare development. But much of the welfare responsibility remained with ancillary private agencies of the colonial domain—mission societies and, occasionally, corporations. During the depression, shrinking revenues restricted state operations to the reproduction of entrenched structures of hegemony.[7]

DECOLONIZATION

In the final stage of the colonial state, decolonization, dating from the close of World War II, the determinants of state behavior were altered significantly. Hegemony and legitimation took on new meaning; autonomy and security became important; and, for a period, revenue became an invitation to state expansion rather than a constraint. At the outset, no one foresaw how short the timetables of transition would be, nor the real nature of their outcome. Gradually, weakening colonial hegemony in most instances contributed to its own demise. The seeming inevitability of power transfer fostered by failed colonial military campaigns in Vietnam, Indonesia, Algeria, and later the Portuguese territories weighed heavily in the calculus of the withdrawing powers.

The imperative of hegemony was totally changed by the unfolding perspective of power transfer. The colonial state had to remain intact, yet both colonizer and nationalist wanted its internal structures of hegemony to be gradually Africanized. But Africanization of the colonial state was not enough, as formal recognition of the civil society was required. Some compact had to be devised whereby subjects were to become citizens. Here the constitutionalist ideology of the metropolitan state had a crucial impact. Withdrawal, it was said, had to be carried out with honor, which required replication of the metropolitan state organization as the exemplary model of the ideal polity.

For the nationalist political class, the metropolitan state was seen as an acceptable model, partly because of the prestige the metropolitan institutions commanded. For the nationalist forces, its representative and constitutional structures were also vehicles by which they could challenge colonial domination and accelerate its demise.

The constitutional blueprint for the post-colonial state was in profound contradiction to the entire colonial state heritage. Deeply embedded in the autocratic legacy of the colonial system was a concept of the state as the institutionalization of an alien command, reflected in its laws, routines, and mentality. The chasm that separated these two models of state was much wider than was appreciated at the time.

Undeterred by such gloomy thoughts, the colonial state set about unveiling the secrets of hegemony and encouraging the emergence of an array of associations—unions, cooperatives, and local government councils. In this new pedagogical role, the colonial official class and metropolitan state continued to assume ongoing proprietary rights. Decolonization was not to be a rupture of relationships, but rather a redefinition that would guarantee senior partner status to the metropole and its interests. The withdrawing colonizer frequently retained the capacity to orchestrate the decolonization process sufficiently to exclude from power its most intransigent adversaries.

As an African political class gained ascendancy within the institutions of power transfer, autonomy became a major preoccupation. The new leaders sought to sharpen the territorial personality of their own state, emphasizing differences with contiguous political units and redefining anti-colonial African nationalism into an exaltation of nationhood. Diversifying external links to escape the encompassing shadow of the metropole began to be discreetly supported.

Doctrines of legitimation required complete redefinition. Common ground was found between the colonial official class and the nationalist leadership around the themes of development and welfare. The promise to deliver rapid and tangible improvement in material conditions became crucial to the ability of the colonial state to retain tutelage over the decolonization process and to control its timetable. Nationalists were required to promise rapid delivery of material benefits to the rank and file in order to activate a mass clientele who could gain control over representative institutions and bring pressure for acceleration of power transfer.

This conjunction of the legitimation drives by the colonial official class and the nationalist elite gave dramatic impetus to state expansion. The construction of a developmental welfare state proceeded with remarkable speed. On the colonial side, from a skeletal pre-war base, large technical and specialized services were created, a veritable "second colonial occupation."

Although nationalists denounced the belated and insufficient efforts of the terminal colonial state to become preoccupied with subject welfare, there can be no doubt as to the efficacy of its welfare and developmentalist thrust in the final years. In the Belgian Congo, what had been a rudimentary educational system until the last colonial phase became a huge network enrolling 70 percent of school-age children by independence. In the 1920s, no real medical service for Africans existed; by 1960, the Belgians could boast that their health service was "without doubt the best in the whole tropical world."[8] Economies flourished in the 1950s, an era of rising real wages and prosperity in which the rural populations also shared. Although not noted at the time, the 1950s became a retrospective golden age and later came to serve as the yardstick for the performance of the post-colonial state.

The surge in welfare and development expenditures was remarkable. In the Belgian Congo, state outlays rose eleven-fold between

1939 and 1950, then tripled in the final colonial decade. In the last decade of British rule in the Gold Coast, public expenditures multiplied ten-fold; in the preceding 35 years, they had merely doubled. These patterns were characteristic.

This swift rise in state consumption was made possible by an exceptionally fortunate conjuncture on the revenue front. The prolonged commodity boom, extending through the Korean War, brought windfall gains to the colonial state. The state's capture of the profits from the price boom was facilitated in many instances by new public institutions created for wartime purposes that controlled marketing and export of agricultural crops. At the same time, driven by the new legitimation requirements, the metropolitan state for the first time was willing to undertake substantial public investment in the colonial territories. Rising levels of economic prosperity, in part fostered by expanding state investment and activity, further enlarged the fiscal potential.

In the field of revenue generation, colonial state behavior exhibited a striking continuity with its earlier forms. Rural taxation was heavily utilized, though the patterns of extraction had changed. In its first phase, the colonial state financed hegemony and conquest by rudimentary methods of transforming African labor into state cash flow. Now the revenue devices were far more subtle: taxation through export commodity price regulation; export taxation levied particularly upon African crops; marketing board monopolies whose surpluses were in effect transferred into the state capital account; discriminatory schedules of rail freight charges; and differential customs duties on imports mainly consumed by Europeans and those destined for African markets.

The older head tax became much less significant, though in many territories it remained an important revenue source well into the second phase of colonial state development. Data from Uganda in the 1950s demonstrated that real taxation rates for peasant households were well over 50 percent, vastly higher than fiscal rates affecting wealthier strata, immigrant or African.[9]

Overall, the African colonial state differed in significant ways from its analogues in other regions.[10] Although there were harsh periods, plundering episodes, and disruptive intrusions in other areas of the world, the colonial state elsewhere was much less dependent upon subjugated civil societies. Although its period of rule was brief compared to Asia and Latin America, the African colonial state was implanted in a highly competitive environment where consolidation of its rule was an immediate requirement.

The European state from which doctrines of rule were derived was a much more sophisticated and elaborated structure than in early phases of imperial expansion into Asia and the Americas. The colonial class had a more profound conviction of its cultural, biological, and technological superiority, and a more systematically negative view of its subject population than was the case elsewhere. The subjugation and exclusion of civil society was particularly thorough. The difficulties of adapting this state to the new circumstances of political sovereignty were bound to be enormous.

NATURE OF THE POST-COLONIAL STATE

The post-colonial state operated within a profoundly different framework, as entirely new threats to hegemony appeared. The legitimacy born out of the process of power transfer proved evanescent, and more enduring doctrines were as necessary as they were elusive. Autonomy and security as driving forces in state behavior became much more important. The revenue-fed momentum of state expansion of the 1950s continued, but was progressively undermined by a growing disequilibrium between state consumption and its resource base. By the late 1970s, a revenue crisis was at hand.

But in the triumphant mood of the early 1960s, these patterns were much less visible than the seeming success of the colonial state in organizing its own metamorphosis, with the important exception of the revolutionary cases. The keys of the kingdom were handed over in a veritable orgy of self-celebration, but the institutional synthesis upon which decolonization was founded proved exceedingly short-lived.

In its last years, the colonial state had institutionalized open political competition and a constitutionalized state-civil society relationship. While this formula provided adequate legitimation for the power transfer process itself, it swiftly decomposed in the post-independence environment. It soon ran afoul of the more enduring autocratic and hegemonic impulses of the colonial state. Only in Botswana and Mauritius can it be said that the power transfer pact in its original form still exists.

SECURING POWER

The issues of competition and alternation did not arise in the colonial state, as the ultimate arbiter and repository of sovereignty was the metropole. Governors might come and go, but the colonial state was a permanent structure and its agents, in large measure, interchangeable parts. But decolonization placed political agents in command of the state who had a different perspective, animated by the innate incumbent propensity to perpetuate their hold on power.

More was involved than a primal lust for power or the monarchical germ within every ruler's breast. Many of the nationalist generation regarded themselves—with some justification—as bearers of an unique historical mission of liberation and uplift. Sanctioned by a special mandate as founders of new polities, they viewed their task as requiring an enduring tenure to secure the fledgling state against its innumerable potential enemies, foreign and domestic.

Radical nationalist movements, such as the Parti Democratique de Guinee (PDG) or the Convention People's Party (CPP) of Ghana, regarded themselves as having earned permanent entitlement to rule through their aggressive and confrontational posture toward colonial authority and the enthusiasm which their aggregation of grievances and expectations had engendered. In some instances, this conviction was reinforced by their belief that they were launching an ideological project of socialist construction, which required assurance of protection against reversal or subversion by the menacing forces of international capitalism.

The insulation against threats from outside the colonial framework provided by the metropolitan security organizations was removed, and new states were at once subjected to the competitive environment of the Cold War. The Central Intelligence Agency, the KGB, and kindred agencies seeking a foothold in Africa recruited local clients, activities which by no means passed unnoticed.

Particularly in the early years of independence, the former metropole sought to preserve bastions of influence within the post-colonial state and to exclude the new intruders. These global rivals, each pursuing its own manichean security imperatives and entitled position in the newly sovereign domains of Africa, stalked each other through the corridors of power. The new rulers endeavored as best they could to avail themselves of services that could be extracted from external actors, while at the same time becoming acutely conscious of their vulnerability to penetration and the disposition of global powers to impose solutions favorable to their own strategic concerns.

Internal enemies soon became apparent to new rulers, often rendered all the more deadly—and illegitimate—by their potential access to external support. Additionally, open political competition in the terminal colonial epoch had amply demonstrated its potential for politicizing cultural cleavages within civil society. During the anticolonial struggle, nationalist movements had propagated the concept of subjugated civil society as a "nation-in-the-making"—an historically ordained collectivity in which ethnicity was a dangerous and reactionary force. The swiftening pace of decolonization had triggered new apprehensions among many about the perceived risk of domination by particular groups and the ethnic allocation of postcolonial resources.

The politically ambitious had discovered that crystallizing ethnic consciousness was the swiftest and surest way to attract a political clientele. The unfamiliarity of the electoral process itself reinforced the intensity of ethnic politics, escalating fears and insecurities, and lending an apocalyptic aura to competitive balloting. Set against the demon of politicized cultural pluralism, national integration was represented as the consummate good, not only by ruling elites but by expert opinion of all stripes, not least in the earnest prescriptions of the social science literature of the day. By this logic, restraint of political competition was both morally imperative and a convenient pretext for political monopoly.

Added to these factors propelling rulers toward restoration of the autocratic hegemony of the colonial state was a more curious belief that collective public energies were an inherently limited good which was distributed in zero-sum fashion. Whatever effort was dedicated to political competition was subtracted from the available quantum of developmental energies. Thus political competition was inherently wasteful and a luxury that could not be afforded.

Finally, beyond impulses to power innate in humans as political animals, more sordid attractions swiftly became apparent. In his deft critique of political monopoly two decades ago, Arthur Lewis encapsulates this dimension: "Personifying the state, ministers dress themselves up in uniforms, build themselves palaces, bring all other traffic to a standstill when they drive, hold fancy parades and generally demand to be treated like Egyptian pharaohs. . . .There are also vast opportunities for pickings in bribes, state contracts, diversion of public funds to private uses, and commissions of various sorts. To be a minister is to have a lifetime's chance to make a fortune."[11]

SINGLE-PARTY STATE

From the moment of independence, these pressures combined to yield a new form of political monopoly that reproduced the autocratic heritage of the colonial state—the single-party state. Only thrice in post-colonial African history has a change of incumbents come about through the electoral processes—Somalia, by parliamentary vote in 1967, Mauritius in 1982, and—ambiguously, with military interregnum—Sierra Leone in 1967–68. After independence, through coercion and cooptation, de jure or de facto one-party regimes spread throughout the continent.

When it became apparent that political monopolies guaranteeing incumbents indefinite prolongation of their mandates were becoming the rule, disaffection flowed into new channels, particularly the military. Although initially not perceived as such, the trend of the military coup as a vehicle for ruler displacement began in Egypt in 1952, moved to Sudan (1956), occurred half-heartedly in Zaire (1960), Benin (1963), and Togo (1963), and then became an institutionalized pattern with a rapid-fire sequence of putsches in 1965–66 (Algeria, Zaire, Nigeria, Ghana, Central African Republic, Benin). While displacement of incumbents to remedy their abuses served as entry legitimation for military regimes, longer-term power retention required other justifications. Military regimes themselves—with Egypt again as pioneer—adopted single-party ideologies and constructed monopolistic institutions for permanent legitimation of rule.

The single party has tended to combine populist rhetoric with exclusionary practices. Considerable energy and resources are devoted to the ritualization of legitimacy through ceremony, spectacle, and periodic plebiscitary elections. Within the single-party framework, some interesting experiments pioneered by Tanzania have been undertaken to improve the credibility and responsiveness of the party through competitive elections for legislative representatives, but not for the ruler. But the basic fact of political monopoly remains.

Political monopoly, however, solved only part of the problems facing rulers, merely offering a pre-emptive hegemony. There remained the challenge of assuring ruler ascendancy over the state apparatus and preventing hostile combinations from forming within it. The colonial official class was disciplined and controlled through the formal hierarchy, administrative regulation, and deontological code. Whereas informal clans founded on religious, ideological, or linguistic orientation might be found, especially in the French and Belgian cases, overall the colonial state bent to the will of its over-layer.

PATRIMONIAL RULE

Abstract bureaucratic jurisprudence no longer sufficed after independence. Hostile cliques and conspiracies had to be pre-empted by ensuring placement of personnel at critical points in the state apparatus whose fidelity to the ruler was not simply formal, but immediate and personal. Thus rulers constructed an inner layer of control—key political operatives, top elements in the security forces, top technocrats in the financial institutions—whose fidelity was guaranteed by personal fealty as well as by hierarchical subordination. The surest basis for such fidelity is affinity of community or kinship. Close scrutiny of the inner security core of the state will usually disclose such connections in states as diverse as Toure's Guinea, Nyerere's Tanzania, or Mobutu's Zaire.

Beyond and often in addition to affinity, personal interest is the most reliable collateral for loyalty. Accordingly, rulers must reward generously and impose severe sanctions for any weakening of zeal. Thus public resources become a pool of benefits and prebends, while dismissal from office, confiscation of goods, and prosecution face those who show slackness in their personal fidelity. Holders of high office individually tend to become clients of the ruler and collectively a service class. This process of patrimonialization of the state has been elegantly characterized as "personal rule" by Jackson and Rosberg, "a system of relations linking rulers not with the 'public' or even with the ruled (at least not directly), but with the patrons, associates, clients, supporters, and rivals who constitute the 'system.'"[12]

LEGITIMACY

The post-colonial state required new doctrines of legitimation, as the older colonial themes of trusteeship and good government were no longer serviceable. However, the terminal colonial ideology of development and welfare could be retained, joined to a populist discourse and nationalist vocabulary which promised an acceleration of momentum and a reinterpretation of its content. State-directed change would be rapid, Africa-centered, and mass-directed.

The new state began the era of independence with a substantial capital of legitimacy. In many countries, the nationalist platform generated vast enthusiasm, particularly among the young. Despite its vulnerability to the nationalist assault, the colonial state also had some elements of legitimacy which it bequeathed to its successor—an image of competence in execution of its mandate, some degree of trust as arbiter of conflicts, and the indisputable material accomplishments of its final decade.

Over time, the reservoir of legitimacy dissipated, due in part to performance. Disappointment came quickly, even though retrospectively in the 1960s, economic progress was generally respectable. But extravagant promises had been made and hopes unleashed which could not be met. As economies stagnated in the 1970s and decayed in the 1980s, the public mood turned skeptical. As governments' populist discourse lost its credibility, their exclusionary character became more resented.

Political succession through coups resulted in the long-term delegitimation of the state; each new regime sought entry legitimacy by erecting a veritable "black legend" around its predecessor. The venality of the previous rulers was exposed to public view and a catalogue of nefarious misdeeds compiled: extravagance, incompetence, ethnic favoritism, subservience to foreign interests, even treason. Cumulatively, the "black legend" came to encompass past, present, and future leadership.

AUTONOMY

The autonomy imperative has been a source of deepening frustration for the post-colonial state, as the developmental impasse has made its realization ever more remote. The colonial state had pursued a contradictory policy of, on the one hand, promoting privileged economic links with the metropole in which the latter's interests were naturally paramount, and, on the other, forcing autonomy on the colonies to avoid metropolitan subsidies. At independence, major enterprises were invariably owned by metropolitan capital, and trading relations were dominated by the colonizer. The lack of autonomy was greatest in the former French colonies that remained subordinated to the franc zone and relied upon undeniably efficient French security services, not only through defense pacts, but also through more informal intelligence support.

Today, the autonomy imperative is articulated in a commitment to non-alignment, formation of an African bloc in international agencies, and involvement in the network of Third World groupings, including the Group of 77 and the non-aligned, which have sought a "new international economic order" since 1973, though with little success. The emphasis on self-reliance and internally directed development in the OAU's conceptual response to the economic crisis—the creation of the 1980 Lagos Plan of Action—resonates with the autonomy imperative.

For the weaker states in an international system dominated by the strong, diversification of external linkages is one means of protection. In the economic realm, most states have sought to terminate the proprietary claims of the erstwhile colonizer. This has been particularly apparent in nationalization or indigenization measures which peaked in the early 1970s. These were invariably directed at colonial corporations or Mediterranean and Asian economic intermediaries who fashioned their niche under the protection of the colonial state.

Success was by no means certain in autonomy-driven assaults on colonial economic interests. In all but liquidating French interests save for one bauxite enterprise, Guinea brought about a prolonged decline in almost all spheres except bauxite mining because of its inability to successfully manage a large socialized sector. The state found itself singularly dependent upon this single source of external revenue and the French, American, and Soviet mining enterprises. Zaire, whose epic struggle with the arrogant colonial giant, Union Miniere du Haut-Katanga, seemed to end in triumph in 1967, wound up paying a very high price in management fees, compensation, and, arguably, global market shares.

THE SECURITY IMPERATIVE

By the 1980s, the growing costs upon the post-colonial state which the security imperative had slowly imposed had become substantial. In the colonial era, after the initial period of conquest, security demands weighed lightly on the state, save for the sacrifices resulting from involvement in the two world wars and for those colonial situations which degenerated into revolutionary liberation wars. Colonial constabularies, designed solely for internal security, were composed of small and lightly armed infantry units.

A number of factors brought security and defense preoccupations to the forefront during the independence era. Since 1966, 40 to 50 percent of the regimes in the continent have been military in origin, and in states not under military rule, intervention by the security forces remains a tangible threat. The armed forces have therefore become a potent corporate interest in the struggle for state resources.

The intensely competitive international environment plays its part, with major powers' ceaseless quest for allies and clients on the one hand, and African states' search for external patrons and protectors on the other. The provision of weapons, necessitating continuing supply of logistics, training, and spare parts, is particularly useful for the external state. Commercial motivations are also significant for a number of suppliers; France, the Soviet Union, Israel, and Brazil in particular depend heavily on the foreign exchange generated by weapons sales. The very competitive nature of these relationships, both political and mercantile, tends to drive African states to higher levels of armament.

A seemingly inexorable rise in levels of conflict in Africa set in after independence, gaining momentum in the 1970s. Several regional theaters of tension emerged—the Horn, the Middle East, the Western Sahara, Chad, and southern Africa—each setting in motion an arms race within its zone of impact. By the 1980s, it had become clear that liberation or dissident movements which succeed in building an internal zone of support and some access to external supply could sustain themselves virtually indefinitely, forcing the states involved to devote the greater part of their available resources to security (e.g., Angola, Morocco, Ethiopia).

The consequence is that security-driven state consumption is rapidly increasing. The minor role of security imperatives in the final phases of the colonial state meant that outlays for the armed forces were remarkably modest. From 1960 to 1980, however, for the developing world as a whole, there was a 117-fold increase in defense expenditures.[13] Research now in progress by Robert West demonstrates that in recent years for African states, real military expenditures as a percentage of government expenditure have been increasing faster than in any other group of countries, substantially exceeding economic growth rates. For small, low-income countries, military expenditures today constitute a higher effective burden than the security costs of the major world powers.[14]

OTHER STATE CONSUMPTION PRESSURES

Security has been far from the only factor exerting pressure on state consumption. Social expenditures driven by the legitimation imperative have also risen rapidly, a carry-over from terminal colonial patterns and external donor philosophy in the 1970s. The claims of the educational sector were especially powerful, as the perceived link between educational opportunity and social mobility became anchored in the popular consciousness. Even if they were so inclined, states find it difficult to arrest such expenditures.

More significant, efforts to match quantitative enlargement with qualititative performance or transmission of technical and vocational skills have fallen far short of the most modest expectations. The correlation between provision of education and economic growth has been axiomatic in developmental theory and appears validated in such exemplary success stories as Japan, South Korea, and Taiwan. In Africa, however, the relationship is much less clear; the more immediate results of education seem to have been increasing pressures for public employment and rural exodus.

Another potent factor in the growth of state consumption has been the trend to vest the accumulation function in parastatal agencies, a tendency visible across the ideological spectrum. For socialist states, the construction of a sprawling state sector corresponded to a blueprint of non-capitalist development; in the Tanzanian case, Reginald Green, economic adviser and partisan of the socialist strategy, was able to boast that by the mid-1970s, in the pursuit of state socialism, 80 percent of medium and large-scale economic activity was located in the public sector, a figure which exceeded that of Soviet bloc states at a comparable time period.[15] But parastalization of the economy did not require the stimulus of socialist doctrine; in Ivory Coast, the exemplary center of African capitalism, the number of parastatals grew from six in 1960 to 84 in 1977 (since somewhat trimmed back). Of the 54.6 percent of the industrial sector in Ivorian hands in 1977, 90 percent was held by the state.[16]

As economic entities, parastatal organizations are not necessarily inefficient; one recent study provides evidence that Brazilian public sector enterprises have played a major part in national growth.[17]

Singapore has a number of big public corporations that have contributed to its remarkable growth. Egypt generates $1 billion yearly from its parastatal Suez Canal Corporation. But overall, state enterprise performance in Africa has been dismal; one finds only a few contrary examples. All too characteristic is the Ghanaian Cocoa Marketing Board, which in the early 1980s employed 105,000 persons to export a crop half the size as that handled more efficiently by 50,000 employees in 1965. The ultimate necessity for the state to make good parastatal deficits and to resupply operating capital is a major factor contributing to swollen state consumption.

An important factor behind rising state expenditures has been increasing public sector employment. In Kenya, public sector employment rose from 188,000 in 1965 to 390,000 in 1978; the civil service alone expanded from 14,000 in 1945 to 45,000 in 1955 and 170,000 by 1980. In Senegal, those employed by the government swelled from 10,000 on the eve of independence to 61,000 in 1973.[18] In Congo (Brazzaville), the state agricultural extension service multiplied by 10 from 1960 to 1972, reaching a level where salaries exceeded the total cash income of the nation's 600,000 peasants; worse, this expansion was accompanied by a decline in output of most crops they endeavored to service.[19] In 1967, state consumption as a percentage of GDP was less than 15 percent for Africa as a whole, and often well below 10 percent in the 1950s. By the 1980s, it exceeded 40 percent for many countries.

African state revenues tend to be tightly bound to returns from price-volatile primary commodity exports. The post-colonial state has exhibited a formidable capacity to instantly transform a momentary revenue windfall into recurrent expenditure obligations, especially salaries. Nigeria, for example, converted virtually all of its oil revenues in 1973 and 1979 into state consumption. Government outlays ballooned from N997.4 million in 1971, to N17,513.1 in 1980.[20] Indeed, the trend toward state pre-emption of societal resources may be greater than official figures suggest. For most African states, most of the budget goes for wage and salary payments and the purchase of goods for state use; "government" thus enters national income accounts at factor cost, irrespective of its "product."

SOURCES OF REVENUE

The revenue imperative thus weighed heavily in state behavioral choices. Three basic strategies had emerged, which by the 1980s had proved harmful. Firmly established from the beginning of the colonial state, the pattern of relentless fiscal pressure upon the peasant sector was maintained and reinforced, producing demoralization, disaffection, and disengagement by the countryside. Second, the state sought to enlarge its rents from the former colonial sectors through diverse formulas of parastalization. There were some successes here, particularly in the mineral sphere; in the short run, for example, both Zaire and Zambia greatly increased their fiscal cut in copper proceeds. Over time, however, this strategy has been progressively undermined by the dispiriting performance of the state sector. Finally, states sought revenue relief from external sources. Initially, this seemed deceptively effective, as during the honeymoon years, foreign aid both from the former metropole and from the new entrants—United States, Soviet Union, Israel, China, Scandinavia— rose rapidly and was often on a grant basis. As Robert Berg points out, per capita official aid was higher to Africa than to any other region.[21]

However, very soon state consumption increases ceased to be matched by expansion in external aid. In the early 1970s, a new phase of external resource acquisition—borrowing—emerged. The period 1970–75 was extraordinarily propitious for public and private external borrowing. The major international financial institutions had large liquidities, and industrial world lending was relatively unpromising. Lending to less developed countries seemed attractive, as interest premiums could be charged. African debt burdens were then small, and, in practice, Western governments and the International Monetary Fund (IMF) were viewed as collectors of the last resort guaranteeing the loans. For African states, borrowed funds seemed an appealing and painless mechanism for overcoming short-term foreign exchange pressures. Further, real interests rates were at record lows, at times even negative, and the borrowed funds seemed a bargain.

By the late 1970s, all three of these avenues for revenue expansion were not only blocked, but had clogged channels of fiscal access. Rural populations turned to smuggling their crops or redirected their efforts to farming, artisanal, or commercial activities outside the reach of the public realm. Rather than replenishing public coffers, the deficitary parastatal sector put new pressures on the treasury. By the late 1970s, external lenders had become extremely wary of African exposure and instead concentrated their efforts on collection. The foreign exchange bind intensified by debt service burdens forced recourse to the IMF, with its battery of standard remedies, their inevitable political costs in delegitimation, and distant and speculative returns.

WEAKNESS IN ECONOMIC MANAGEMENT

The debt crisis has especially highlighted basic infirmities in state economic management. The permeability, weakness, and often venality of the state apparatus rendered it peculiarly vulnerable to colossal misestimates of project viability. In particularly pathological cases, such as Zaire, external borrowing patterns seem to closely approximate Issawi's calculations for the debts accumulated by Egypt, Tunisia, Morocco, and the Ottoman Empire in the late 19th century (leading in the first three cases to loss of sovereignty). In the Ottoman instance, no more than 5 percent of the funds obtained were placed in ventures that could be amortized.[22]

Looseness of control within a swelling state sector fragmented by the proliferation of parastatals was one factor. In countries as diverse in management reputation as Ivory Coast and Zaire, there was an identical pattern in the phase of debt run-up, wherein parastatal agencies engaging the credit of the state made substantial commitments without central bank knowledge. Thus, when consciousness of a debt problem suddenly dawned, neither state financial officials nor the external lenders initially had clear knowledge of what the debt was.

A recurrent pattern in the interaction between the state and external capital finds state agents and external interests with a common interest in structuring the arrangements so that each can secure a profit on the transaction. External capital offers turnkey projects, management services on contract, and technology, but avoids equity commitments. The entire risk is borne by the state and must ultimately be extracted from civil society. Examples are the $1 billion Ivory Coast sugar disaster and the equally costly Zaire Inga-Shaba power line. Within the state apparatus, the very nature of the project review process and its structural irrationalities leave the state prone to highly risky choices.

Out of these patterns of state behavior over the post-independence years has come a perplexing and difficult state-civil society relationship, which itself troubles and probably obstructs the development process. There may be both powerful continuities with the colonial state and new aspects flowing from characteristics of the post-colonial state of contemporary origin. The developmental impasse is reflected in the state-civil society nexus as both cause and effect.

The relationship between civil society and the post-colonial state is profoundly contradictory. The state remains deeply marked by the hegemonial pretensions and authoritarian legacy of the colonial state. In innumerable ways, the peremptory, prefectoral command style of the colonial state remains embedded in its successor. The citizenry lack empowerment, whether the ideology of the state is Leninist or capitalist. Civil society remains an aggregate of subjects confronted with the state.

Yet there is a crucial difference in the operation of the post-colonial state. The colonial state, in its second and third stages, had aggregated its authority and built reservoirs of institutional competence to a point where it had the capacity to accomplish a number of its goals at considerable cost to its subjects, upon whose shoulders the colonial state was able to place the entire burden of its hegemony. The appearance of "hardness" inherited from the mentalities and routines of the colonial state was sapped from within by the inner "softness" inherent in the process of patrimonial and clientelistic politics, by which civil society was able to penetrate the state, deflect its authoritarian strictures, and ultimately transform its despotic surface into a hollow shell.

As Hyden concludes: "The mechanisms of the soft state are the antithesis of the type of economic efficiency that is necessary for growth and development. The 'soft' state phenomenon is particularly harmful in Africa because of the wide scope of the public sector. The state apparatus is not limited to the provision of basic public services, levying taxes, maintaining law and order, but extends its tentacles to embrace broad economic activities with often catastrophic consequences."[23]

In his lament concerning the infirmities of the socialist orientation, Iliffe adds that African states have demonstrated their ability to block capitalism, but have not exhibited a capacity to find an alternative formula for releasing the social energies of their populace.[24]

A little noted but important field in which this shrinkage of institutional capacity has occurred is at the local government level. In many countries, the structures of intermediation, which the colonial state had carefully nurtured, have been corroded by a self-defeating compulsion of the central institutions to extend their own hegemony to the local level and the attendant suspicion of them as chiefly instruments of colonial control. Local government bodies have lost their revenue base, the effective support of regional state authorities, and their standing with the citizenry.[25] A survey of three Nigerian universities concerning attitudes about public servant integrity showed an overwhelming percentage of respondents (90 per cent) believed that relatively few civil servants in most African countries are capable of putting national interests ahead of their own interests.[26]

POLICY IMPLICATIONS

What then is to be done? Eight prescriptive reflections are put forward with a hesitancy borne of the conviction that the current African development impasse is not only far-reaching, but historically rooted. No handful of facile formulas can overcome Africa's travail. No single observer is likely to have sufficient breadth of perspective or vision to propound a definitive charter for future resurrection, nor are the thoughts that follow translatable into immediate operational directives.

• If not arrested, the present trends in African development and the nature of the post-colonial state condemn Africa to long-term marginalization and pauperization. There might be solace in the thought that only 15 years ago, African prospects still seemed encouraging, while Asia represented the crisis region of the world.[27] The Asian developmental configuration has changed beyond recognition, but the NIC pathway thorough which a number of Asian states have emerged as stellar-performance political economies requires a highly efficacious state. The contemporary African state is absolutely incapable of producing a NIC.

• If there are any grounds for subdued optimism at the present time, they are to be found in the growing recognition within and without Africa of the dimensions of the problem and the willingness to contemplate a reconsideration of the state which would have been unthinkable five years ago. Emblematic of courageous and forthright new patterns of state thought is the excellent contribution in this volume by a leading Tanzanian economist, Benno J. Ndulu, who notes the urgency of dismantling state controls and the need to reconstruct state institutions embued with greater accountability and competence.[28]

The 1982 Ndegwa Committee Report undertaken for the Kenyan

government is equally remarkable for its candor and the scope of its prescriptions. The scale of the adjustments that African states are called upon to make go far beyond the selective rollback of the "welfare state" which is occurring in a number of advanced Western industrialized states. Only state authorities' recognition that elemental survival overrides the other imperatives of state behavior which led to the present impasse can rally the "official mind" behind remedies as far-reaching and, in the short run, risky.

• The present impasse is far more than economic in nature. Thus, it will not readily yield to purely economic prescriptions. Herein lies the major difficulty with reform programs promoted by international financial institutions. Their mandate is essentially limited to the economic realm, and thus their remedies are incomplete. Directly political conditionality is doubtless unfeasible. However, "structural adjustment" programs need to include acknowledgement of their implications for the state: whether, given the nature of the state, they are realistically sustainable and whether they contribute toward the reorientation from control to service and from exclusion to accountability.[29]

• The basic texture of the state-civil society relationship is antithetical to development and requires restructuring. Efforts in this direction must be founded upon a realistic grasp of the nature of civil society and its divisions. The post-colonial state cannot sustain either the "hardness" of the bequeathed style of colonial state hegemony, nor the "softness" that undermines its efficacy. The empowerment of civil society in order to impose higher levels of accountability upon the state requires acceptance of spheres of autonomous operation for such diverse bodies as unions, cooperatives, churches, and local governments. Enlargement of the scope of private markets is another path to reinforcing civil society in its interaction with the state. In the longer run, a stronger civil society is not antithetical to a restructured and stronger state, better able to fulfill its role of guidance and orientation of the development venture.

• The legitimation imperative can no longer be met by ideological formulas, or by "mobilization" from above, be it Leninist or personalist. Self-celebratory state ritual and ceremony has lost all semblance of credibility. Performance is the key to recapturing the confidence of the populace. This standard cannot be met by the hypertrophic, over-extended contemporary state.

- Levels of state consumption far exceed resource possibilities and now constitute a veritable engine of underdevelopment. At present consumption levels, the revenue imperative drives the state into a confrontation with the rural sector that it is too weak to win. The state is also driven into debilitating recourse to external sources. Survival and self-reliance dictate load-shedding, particularly of the deficit-ridden parastatal sector.

- Consideration of the disabilities of the contemporary African state must incorporate international system factors. In innumerable ways in the pursuit of short-term advantage, public and private external actors have contributed to the African developmental impasse. Great power competition and arms sales have played a part in inflating military outlays. An honest inquest into the poor performance of external donor agencies is only beginning; organizational self-protection impulses obstruct. Full and public self-criticism by the external partners is a necessary accompaniment to the internal African process of rethinking the state.

- A major, long-term commitment to external assistance must accompany African efforts at overcoming present weaknesses of the state. Recent trends are in the opposite direction. Even more ominous is the possibility that stagnating levels of available aid resources are committed to security-driven objectives of external actors and the growing number of disaster relief and refugee crises which present trends in demography, climate, conflict, and economic decline make likely.

The reconsideration of the state now in progress and its adaptation to the reality of parallel economies and peasant disengagement involve a momentous process. The great challenge to developmental statecraft is to find creative and positive means to transcend the present impasse. No one can contemplate a mere perpetuation of present patterns far into the future. Existing trends evoke chilling visions of Africa's rendezvous with the 21st century.

NOTES

1. Andrew Young, "The United States and Africa: Victory for Diplomacy," *Foreign Affairs* LVIX, (3)(1981): 648–66; John de St. Jorre, "Africa: Crisis of Confidence," *Foreign Affairs* LXI, (3)(1983): 675–91; Jennifer Whitaker, "Africa Beset," *Foreign Affairs* LXII, (3)(1984): 746–76.

2. The term has been employed in innumerable ways; one author identified no less than 145 different meanings of the concept. A more elaborate explanation of our approach will be found in the introductory chapter to Crawford Young and Thomas Turner, *The Rise and Decline of the Zairian State* (Madison: University of Wisconsin Press, 1985).

3. The centrality of this factor is given powerful demonstration in the influential study by Robert H. Bates, *Markets and States in Tropical Africa* (Berkeley: University of California Press, 1981).

4. The importance of this petty mercantile class is well documented by A.G. Hopkins, *An Economic History of West Africa* (New York: Columbia University Press, 1973).

5. Frederick Cooper, *From Slaves to Squatters: Plantation Labor and Agriculture in Zanzibar and Coastal Kenya 1890–1925* (New Haven: Yale University Press, 1980).

6. Goran Hyden, *Beyond Ujamaa in Tanzania* (Berkeley: University of California Press, 1980).

7. In the welfare realm, state action was most visible in the public health field. Here the stimulus was not simply trusteeship obligations, but also more elemental revenue-imperative calculus. In many areas, the conviction grew that African populations were declining, endangering the fiscal base of the colonial state.

8. Jean Stengers, "La Belgique et le Congo," *Histoire de la Belgique Contemporaine* (Brussels: La Renaissance du Livre, 1974).

9. The calculations were made for Bwaamba, but we believe they are applicable to many, if not most, areas; E.H. Winter, *Bwaamba Economy* (Kampala: East African Institute of Social Research, 1958), pp. 34–35. Vali Jamal, "Taxation and Inequality in Uganda, 1900–1964," *Journal of Economic History* XVIII, (2)(June 1978): 418–38, shows the pervasive discrimination in import and excise taxes against rural households.

10. This argument is developed at greater length in Crawford Young, "The Colonial State and its Connection to Current Political Crises in Africa," Colloquium paper, Woodrow Wilson International Center for Scholars, Washington, May 1984.

11. W. Arthur Lewis, *Politics in West Africa* (New York: Oxford University Press, 1965), pp. 31–32.

12. Robert H. Jackson and Carl G. Rosberg, *Personal Rule in Black Africa* (Berkeley: University of California Press, 1982), p. 19.

13. Ruth Leger Sivard, *World Military and Social Expenditures 1982* (Leesburg, Va: World Priorities, 1982), p. 26.

14. Robert C. West, "National Security Provision in African Countries: Military Expenditures in the 1970s," typescript, 1984.

15. Bismarck Mwansasu and Cranford Pratt, eds., *Towards Socialism in Tanzania* (Toronto: Univeristy of Toronto Press, 1979), pp. 19–45.

16. Sheridan Johns, "Reform of State Enterprises in the Ivory Coast: Reform and Redirection," annual meetings, African Studies Association, Washington, D. C., November 1982.

17. Thomas J. Trebat, *Brazil's State-Owned Enterprises: A Case Study of the State as Entrepreneur* (New York: Cambridge University Press, 1983).

18. David B. Abernethy, "Bureaucratic Growth and Economic Decline in sub-Saharan Africa," paper presented to Annual Meetings, African Studies Association, Boston, December 1983.

19. Hugues Bertrand, *Le Congo* (Paris: François Maspero, 1975), p. 188, p. 256.

20. Sayre P. Schatz, "The Inert Economy of Nigeria," *Journal of Modern African Studies* XXII, (1)(1984): 19; Pauline H. Baker, *The Economics of Nigerian Federalism* (Washington, D.C.: Battelle Memorial Institute, 1984); Richard A. Joseph, "Affluence and Underdevelopment: The Nigerian Experience," *Journal of Modern African Studies* XVI, (2)(1978), pp. 221–40.

21. Robert J. Berg, "Foreign Aid in Africa: Here's the Answer, Is It Relevant to the Question?" paper for Committee on African Development Strategies, September 1984.

22. Charles Issawi, *An Economic History of the Middle East and North Africa* (New York: Columbia University Press, 1982), p. 63.

23. Goran Hyden, *No Shortcuts to Progress* (Berkeley: University of California Press, 1983), p. 63. The "soft state" concept was originated by Gunnar Myrdal, *Asian Drama* (New York: Pantheon, 1968), I, p. 66.

24. John Iliffe, *The Emergence of African Capitalism* (Minneapolis: University of Minnesota Press, 1984).

25. This topic deserves closer attention than it has received. For a careful inquest into the demise of local government in Ghana, see Anthony A. Edoh, *Decentralization and Local Government Reform in Ghana*, doctoral dissertation, University of Wisconsin—Madison, 1979. His findings are applicable to many countries.

26. Paul Beckett and James O'Connell, *Education and Power in Nigeria* (London: Hodder and Stoughton, 1977), p. 148.

27. Donald K. Emmerson, "Pacific Optimism," University Fieldstaff International, Fieldstaff Reports, 1982.

28. Benno J. Ndulu, "Economic Management in Sub-Saharan Africa: Key Issues, Experiences, and Prospects," paper for Committee on African Development Strategies, April 1985.

29. David K. Leonard, "Developing Africa's Agricultural Institutions: Putting the Farmer in Control," paper for Committee on African Development Strategies, January 1985.

CHAPTER TWO

African Social Structure and Economic Development

Goran Hyden

Independent Africa was born into a world characterized by its strong faith in progress. Captivated by scientific and technological advances, the post-war generation in both East and West dismissed all references to man's natural limitations as unfounded pessimism. In the West, as Albert Hirschman reminds us,[1] development economics spearheaded the effort to bring about an emancipation from backwardness. Coming to power in this intellectual climate, African leaders shared the spirit, if not the methodology of this positivist philosophy. From their no less ahistorical perspective, they viewed the attainment of political independence as merely a prologue to other victories.

Whether inspired by the "modernization" or "social transformation" paradigms, post-independence development strategies called on Africa to adopt contemporary models with historically alien antecedents. Consequently, pet notions from both East and West—many not fully understood even in their country of origin—were applied in Africa in order to bring it into the mainstream of international development. As Carl Eicher points out, development theorists drew heavily not only on Europe and North America, but on Asia and Latin America—particularly China and India—for their assumptions about agrarian institutions, economic behavior, and empirical evidence about the development process.[2]

As a result, the last 25 years have been a period of endless and sometimes shameless experimentation in Africa. In this atmosphere, governments and donors alike have ignored the narrow margins of survival that characterize African countries at all levels. Above all, they have failed to adequately look for African solutions to African problems.

African public institutions have run on imported energy rather than on domestically available resources. As Hart argues,[3] "development" in Africa is a process in which words and numbers bear little relationship to the material and social realities of the continent. Africa has been brought to adulthood with little respect for its own dynamics and abilities. No wonder, therefore, that it has taken so little time to bring it to its knees.

At long last, Africa is beginning to realize the shortcomings of past development strategies. Without suggesting that the continent can manage without foreign assistance, a growing number of policymakers and intellectuals concede that it has been a waste, as a senior Kenyan official puts it, "to apply half-baked theories, which find favor in their countries of origin, to countries where economic and social structures are completely different."[4]

It is high time, therefore, that the present crisis in Africa is recognized to a very large extent as the product of human arrogance and impatience in years past. Africa's problems are not primarily its backwardness and poverty, but rather the unwillingness of those concerned to accept that the continent is caught in its own historical process of development. Such an awareness requires patience, humility, and respect for those institutions that already serve the continent's peoples. Provided on conventional terms, money and expertise from abroad will not solve Africa's problems.

Rather, the entire agenda of the debate about African development must be recast and intellectual horizons must be broadened. Existing schools of thought and paradigms are unlikely to be very useful guides for that exercise. This chapter is an attempt to take stock of those features peculiar to Africa's political economy and to suggest actions for governments and donors in order to render their interventions more attuned to local needs, capacities, and processes.

AFRICA'S HISTORICAL SPECIFICITY

As the dust of the debates on development that raged in the 1960s and 1970s finally settles, it is possible to identify those factors that differentiate Africa from other continents.

THE ABSENCE OF INTERMEDIATE TECHNOLOGY

Unlike in other continents, there was no indigenous tradition of land alienation and concentration in Africa. Only in colonial times did such tendencies emerge, becoming prominent primarily in those territories with a considerable number of European settlers, such as Kenya and Rhodesia. Nowhere in Africa did truly feudal societies develop, nor the highly regimented small-scale agriculture that permitted the rise of the great civilizations of Asia. Precolonial agriculture in various parts of the continent remained technologically simple, characterized by limited scope for surplus extraction. Although colonial authorities turned the majority of African peasants into commodity producers, causing considerable changes in farming systems, agriculture remained largely controlled by peasants with access to their own land at the time of independence.

To be sure, both in precolonial and colonial days, social differentiation led to apparent differences in wealth, but this process was very feeble. A major reason for the virtual absence of land alienation and concentration in sub-Saharan Africa is that societies did not acquire the technological means to realize it. As Jack Goody has argued, in the absence of wheel, plow, and other "intermediate technology" for agricultural development, sub-Saharan Africa was unable to match the improvements in skill and productivity and hence changes in specialization and stratification that marked agrarian societies in medieval Europe or the Far East.[5]

Africa's failure to acquire technological advances cannot be explained by the denial of such innovations by other powers, because in those days Africa had a number of empires and kingdoms. But its rulers sustained their regimes not by advancing agriculture but by appropriating surpluses from long distance trade.[6] As a result, African societies south of the Sahara never developed the institutional mechanisms that tied rulers to a system based on the exploitation of land. Being almost exclusively dependent on long distance trade, their fortunes and power waned with its decline.

While African farmers today are engaged in commodity production, usually for world markets, their systems and modes of production remain precapitalist in nature, characterized by low productivity levels per unit of land. Unlike capitalist production units, activities are not differentiated according to a strategy of specialized production, nor is labor specialized; hence money wages are still a marginal phenomenon in Africa's rural economies.

The low productivity of peasant agriculture is manifested in the discrepancy between rates of output on the continent and those achieved elsewhere. While world output of cereals averages about 2000 kg per hectare, Africa's average is only half that figure and the gap is widening.[7] These discrepancies reflect at least in part the lag in productivity-increasing agricultural research, particularly with regard to local varieties and conditions that Eicher has pointed out.[8]

Compared with Asia, African agriculture remains extensive. As a result, economic behavior tends to differ from that assumed in conventional household economics which postulates that as the size of farm-households increases, net farm production surpluses shrink. To the contrary, where land is not an immediate constraint and extensive cultivation is still possible, as in many parts of Africa, farm-households with larger labor forces tend to produce greater crop surpluses. Moreover, micro-economic studies of rural Africa indicate that peasant farmers have been quite quick to adopt agricultural innovations under certain circumstances, although attempts by public authorities to increase per hectare productivity have been largely unsuccessful.[9] In other words, productivity gains are not necessarily translated into a greater willingness to engage in surplus agricultural production. Instead, labor savings on the land have normally led to a reallocation of household labor to off-farm activities.

THE RELATIVE AUTONOMY OF THE PEASANT
PRODUCER

Compared to peasant producers in other parts of the world, most African farmers enjoy a relatively high degree of autonomy from other groups and institutions in society. The main reason for this is the prevalence of rudimentary production technologies, in spite of many innovations. Because there is virtually no product specialization, there is a very limited exchange of goods between various units of production and no structural interdependence that brings them into reciprocal relations. Consequently, the scope for a refinement of the means of production is quite small. The limited product variety of households means that members are primarily engaged in socially necessary labor. In addition to tilling the land, rural labor forces do a great many other things both during the farming seasons and after it.

The fragmentation and autonomy at each level of production is reinforced by the absence of independently systemized knowledge to underpin prevailing modes of production. The necessary knowledge is in the producer's head and is normally transmitted from one generation to another through apprenticeship rather than formal training.

One significant illustration of structural autonomy is the method by which the surplus output is appropriated. Under feudalism and capitalism, for example, such appropriations are made in the context of either the landed estate or the factory. In such systems, the state is functionally and structurally linked to the productive demands of the economy and can be used by the rulers to run and control society. The submerged classes have no recourse but to respond to the dictates of the system at large. Where independent producers prevail, however, this relationship is qualitatively different.[10] Appropriations by those in control of the state have to be made in the form of taxation and as such are simple deductions from an already produced stock of values.[11]

To the independent peasant producer, the state is structurally superfluous and most public policy actions aimed at improving agriculture are viewed as having little or no value beyond any possible immediate gains to the producer himself. Because the peasant so extensively controls his own production, he is able to escape government policy demands to an extent that is certainly denied a tenant under feudal rule or a worker under capitalism. There is growing evidence that peasants in Africa use this "exit" option, particularly when policies are viewed as a threat or as devoid of any apparent benefits.[12]

What emerges from this analysis is that African governments are structurally less well-placed to influence agricultural development than governments in Asia or Latin America. Access to the peasant producer is limited and often must be accepted on the latter's terms. The notion that agricultural productivity can be markedly enhanced by "fine-tuning" the organizational instruments of government or by evolving new approaches to training the farmer is a costly illusion in most parts of Africa today. The African peasant producer is structurally less integrated in the wider economic system than his counterparts in Asia or Latin America, making him a particularly unpredictable actor. It also explains why so many policies based on official perceptions of "farmers' needs" have failed on the continent.

NO AGRICULTURAL SURPLUS LABOR

Another unique aspect of African history is that urbanization and industrialization have occurred without a concomitant "freeing up" of agricultural surplus labor in the rural areas. Between 1960 and 1980, Africa's rural-urban migration rate was the world's highest. From less than 20 percent in 1960, Africa was nearly 30 percent urbanized in 1980—an annual growth rate of about 5 percent or almost double the growth rate of total population.[13] Urban migrants almost invariably claim that they plan to retire in their home villages, consequently remitting considerable amounts of money not only to sustain the family members left on the land but also to invest in agricultural expansion and improvement.[14]

Because towns are only a place to live, but not home, the social and political orientation of most of Africa's urban residents has remained rural. Thus, Elkan's observation in 1960 that it is wrong to equate the growth of Africa's towns with the emergence of an urban proletariat seems equally valid today.[15] Certainly, when compared to the colonial days, Africa's urban centers have become increasingly ruralized in the process of accepting an accelerating influx of immigrants from the countryside. Hence, the distinction between rural and urban life has become less clear. Modes of interaction and of conducting business have increasingly taken on indigenous and rural characteristics.

The influx into the urban areas of both rich and poor who, through ownership and access to land, maintain a rural orientation, and the absence of a firmly established ruling class and thus an elite culture, give an inevitably populist character to African society. Strong informal ties and linkages between town and village exist that are rarely found in societies where productivity gains in agriculture have rendered a growing proportion of the labor force on the land superfluous. Because these ties are largely invisible—they do not show up in official statistics—and thus difficult to quantify, they tend to be ignored by economic analysts and policy-makers.

THE ECONOMY OF AFFECTION

The cellular character of agricultural systems and the rudimentary means of production, together with the extension of rural households to the urban areas, provide the African political economy with its historical peculiarity. The internal dynamics of the household and the relations they give rise to[16] constitute economic systems of their own within which members protect and promote their own interests, often at the expense of the larger system.

The economy of affection denotes networks of support, communications, and interaction among structurally defined groups connected by blood, kin, community, or other affinities such as religion. In this system, a variety of discrete economic and social units which in other respects are autonomous are linked together. The economy of affection is the articulation of principles associated with "peasant" or "household" economics as developed since the days of Chayanov, the intellectual forerunner of this school.[17] Chayanov argued that a peasant household would apply its own labor to farming in accordance with its internal equilibrium, determined by equating family demands and needs with the time required to meet them, not in terms of maximizing monetary profit. In this scheme, returns to family activities could not be broken down into components of wages and other factor payments. Rather, non-market aspects of both production and consumption were stressed and household decisions were based on use values rather than exchange values.

Chayanov recognized that the consumer/worker ratio within each household would vary according to its own development cycle, that is, as children grew older and could participate in production, the ratio improved and permitted greater consumption. He also accepted that within the household was the possibility of developing various forms of cooperation to enhance production efficiency. He also assumed, however, that the amount of land available to any household was given, in line with land tenure laws that prevailed in pre-revolutionary Russia. Thus, as its members increased, households had to make more intensive use of their time in order to meet consumption needs. These latter assumptions do not seem immediately applicable to Africa where land use is still extensive. Nor did Chayanov consider the possibility of members of rural households migrating to the towns and making their contribution to the household from an urban-based occupation. These two factors, however, have tended to enhance the autonomy of households vis-à-vis the "system," thus making household economics particularly relevant and influential.

The economy of affection is premised on the presence of structural opportunities for development through horizontal expansion, both economically and socially, within known and acceptable networks.

Although urban-rural remittances are generally less extensive in Latin America than in Africa, studies from that continent show how the economy of affection provides the basis for survival strategies of the poorer segments of the population.[18] With the exception of remittances by overseas workers, such transfers are also less important in the economies of Asia. But as in Latin America, they do form a regular part of the income of many poorer households.[19]

The single best contemporary example of both the strengths and weaknesses of the economy of affection is Lebanon, where economic prosperity was based on the institutionalization of economic and social forms of organization within each religious and ethnic community. Thus, business was typically conducted through family associations, and the political framework that was created permitted the spin-off effects of their activities to bolster the development of the country as a whole. Although the constitutional setup began to crack in the mid-1970s with the fragmentation of the political base, its affective components, because of their strong internal solidarity, survived and continued to provide the economic means to sustain military imperatives.

The Lebanese example shows that societies organized along the lines of an economy of affection can achieve quite impressive economic results but that their social and political fabrics tend to be fragile and, if torn, hostility among groups is likely to be both strong and difficult to overcome. In spite of Lebanon's current grave predicament, the country is one of the best examples outside of Africa of how an economy of affection can be made to work. Of particular relevance is the evolution of indigenous modes of economic organization and cooperation and their integration into a national economy that was able to attract large quantities of foreign capital, making it a show-case for the rest of the Middle East.

The motto of the economy of affection may be summarized in the words: "Diversification pays!" Whether applied by the household unit or the budding business firm, the strategy is the same. This inclination to spread the risks or maximize the opportunities for gains best summarizes the prevailing philosophy among Africans. The ability of the household to practice the economy of affection is a major reason why official development strategies have been contradicted or have failed altogether at the implementation stage.

In Africa, where the urban migrant usually does not lose his right to land, the introduction and adoption of improved technology may not arrest the movement from on-farm to off-farm employment but rather reinforce it, as Low has demonstrated with reference to southern Africa.[20] From an agronomic and development theorist point of view, more labor-intensive husbandry is a necessary corollary to the adoption of yield-increasing technologies. Yet, this is not happening on the average peasant farm in Africa. Instead, the acceptance of new technologies is accompanied by the use of less intensive cropping methods. In other words, rather than being the victims of the practices that pave the way for a more intensified capitalist penetration, the rural households manipulate the official innovations to their own advantage. The household can produce more food for itself using less time while still retaining the benefit of supplementary off-farm income to meet its cash needs.

To some extent, this discrepancy may be particularly acute in southern Africa because of the relatively low prices at which staple foods are available on the open market. Yet, it is also evident elsewhere if for no other reason than that urban wages have often been kept so high that male heads of rural households find it economically more rational to go off to the towns in search of additional income. It is no coincidence that the problem of an urban influx is less serious in Malawi because it is one of the few countries on the continent that has kept urban wages at a relatively low level.

The economy of affection does not disappear with increasing social differentiation. Organizations based on lineage and extended family connections have been significant in helping local entrepreneurs succeed in both West and Central Africa.[21] The age grade system has often served as a valuable substitute in East Africa.[22] Accumulation and social differentiation tend to be contained within the economy of affection and, as Sara Berry has shown in a study of Nigeria,[23] they run contrary to a strategy of economic development still predominant on the African continent which is based on centralizing investment decisions.

As Africa's answer to the attempt to impose other economic systems on the continent, the economy of affection reflects the self-help and harambee traditions so closely associated with the continent's peoples. Although not fought in those terms, the anti-colonial struggle was very much an expression of the sustenance of the principles of affection underlying African economics. The ability of leaders to mobilize the relations of affection for political purposes made a difference in the long run in the struggle against colonialism. As Hodgkin[24] and later Skinner[25] showed, urban-based welfare associations in West Africa were not only created to cope with the social and economic problems facing urban migrants, but developed into political tools used to fight the colonial presence.

Cliffe's review[26] of the emergence of anti-colonial movements in rural Tanzania also stresses the importance of mobilizing support through the unofficial channels of the economy of affection. These and other examples show that, under stress, the scope of this type of economy can be extended to incorporate relations that may not be considered under normal circumstances. Criteria of affinity are redefined and in a battle against an external enemy, a person from a very different community is accepted as "brother."

The ability of the economy of affection to open its doors to assist persons in stress makes it a very convenient weapon in political struggles and in self-defense against natural calamities. A foremost case in point is the armed independence struggle which was facilitated or in some instances made possible only due to the fighters' ability to make use of their relations of affection, thereby not only enhancing military effectiveness, but also popular support. The economy of affection served as their hinterland base for attacks on the colonial fortress.

Paradoxically, in post-independence Africa, the values and principles for which much of the anti-colonial struggle was fought run contrary to those underpinning the operations of the state machinery. Because the economy of affection does not presuppose appropriation of a surplus outside the context of given relationships, it is by definition hostile to formal bureaucratic principles common to Western societies. Relations of affection are constantly used to divert public funds for other purposes more in accordance with the ethos of the economy of affection. As a result, the state in Africa has increasingly lost its efficiency and effectiveness.[27] In much of Africa today, a "silent" guerrilla war has developed against those who in the name of "efficiency" or "socialist revolution" have tried to extend an impersonal bureaucratized state control over society. Using the peculiar structural safeguards of the economy of affection, these silent fighters are likely to outlast those in control of a sinking state.

Rights and obligations are still defined primarily in relation to the precapitalist structures associated with a system of smallholder production. The state is generally regarded as an arena to make gains if possible to enhance the relations of affection. It is the prevalence of this orientation that gives African politics its peculiar character. Politics of affection—or "clan politics" as Cruise O'Brien terms it[28]—continue where social differentiation has not yet crystallized into a distinct division between those who own the means of production and those who serve as workers. At present, Africa is witnessing only the early vibrations of its social transformation, tending to remain encapsulated in the communal relations sustained by the economy of affection.

Unlike their counterparts elsewhere, African leaders are not effectively in charge of a "system" in which policy instruments can be used to realize their private and public interests. Peasants can escape their demands and, therefore, they must be induced to serve the interests of government. As Sara Berry has noted,[29] accumulation strategies in Africa tend to be directed toward exerting power over resources rather than increasing their productivity. Whether the country is capitalist or socialist, property rights are politicized rather than privatized and used by the budding bourgeoisie to safeguard its own position.

The result is that the politics of affection is characterized by investments in patronage relations at all levels. The head of the household invests in the purchase of land for his wives and offspring even if this means ownership of many small plots operated at low productivity. If new land is unavailable, existing plots are subdivided or off-farm employment is sought to achieve the same end. Similarly, in order to safeguard his own position and respond to the affective pressures of his home community, the business entrepreneur tends to invest in many small enterprises which absorb labor at low levels of productivity rather than in the improvement of productivity within one or two operations.[30]

While the manager of a public enterprise may be bound more tightly by official regulations, he is not free from the pressures of affection, responding by steering investments to his home area and hiring people to whom he has an obligation. Even the civil servant finds it difficult to escape these pulls, particularly if he has to serve a politician whose legitimacy is almost wholly dependent on bolstering relations of affection.

With the investment of considerable sums of public money in "political maintenance," it is no surprise that public finances are in disorder. Problems of financial management on the continent are not due to lack of talent and experience, but rather originate in the emphasis

of the politics of affection on channeling public funds to loc
uencies, irrespective of considerations of efficiency and effec\
In the absence of countervailing pressures, efforts to impr
management of public finance in African countries are likely t(.c
futile.

SHORTCOMINGS OF EXISTING
DEVELOPMENT STRATEGIES

The peculiarity of the contemporary African political economy stems from low levels of technology in the peasant agricultural sector, giving rise to individual household strategies aimed at diversifying and maximizing economic gains within known social networks. While such a system has its own development potential, strategies adopted by governments and donors to date have failed to transform it or enable it to develop on its own terms.

Post-independence efforts in most African countries have separated state and society rather than bringing the two closer. Today the state sits suspended in mid-air above society, unable to break up existing networks and incapable of providing individuals with a means of transcending the narrow and often parochial confines of the economy of affection. Development strategies have failed to have an impact in most African countries because they have been formulated using criteria applicable to more technologically advanced systems.

The development strategies that have been adopted in the past have several major shortcomings. First, the inclination to tie strategies to specific target groups, notably the poorer segments of the population, overlooks the question of how to create self-sustaining development at the national level in economies that are still dependent on peasant producers using rudimentary technologies. The target group approach erroneously presupposes that systematic linkages exist for the transfer of resources to the poorer groups in society. In Africa, these linkages are either weak or non-existent, particularly where the official economy has more or less collapsed. Where the majority of rural producers enjoy an unusually high degree of autonomy from other groups in society, programs targeted on the rural poor are likely to have few systematic benefits. Thus, development aid has been placed in the proverbial cart without sufficient recognition that in order to move forward, it must be tied to a strong and healthy horse. Only in countries where the peasantry is increasingly "captured" (i.e., dependent on the macro-economic system for its own reproduction) will programs targeted on the poor begin to have an impact.

Second, there has been a tendency to develop programs and projects that bear little relationship to available management capacity. The Integrated Rural Development Program, so avidly endorsed by the World Bank and many bilateral donors, is one example. In addition to failing to benefit the poor, these programs have not succeeded in changing prevailing administrative practices and orientations, as a recent study of the IRDP in Sri Lanka shows.[31] In Africa, the IRDP has typically become a loose assemblage of individual projects run by single government departments. Attempts to add a planning structure to achieve integration have generally produced few results. Rather, these programs have limited government's operational flexibility and exacerbated red tape.

Third, the pressure on donors to spend large sums of money has resulted in projects that are overly complex in design and expensive to implement. In the case of urban housing, for example, the constraints of a time schedule and donor-approved standards that must be met make the completed schemes far too expensive for the average urban resident and thus wholly inadequate in dealing with urban housing needs. A recent survey completed in Nairobi indicates that there are three formal housing projects addressing the needs of the "low-income" residents, but at the same time there are least 20 squatter camps expanding much faster.[32]

Fourth, there is the notion that development problems can be solved if resources are concentrated in the most critical sector. Given the plausibility of the notion that the poverty and hunger of the rural poor can be best tackled if their agricultural yields are increased, it is not surprising that agriculture as the priority sector is embraced by all members of the donor community, including the international financial institutions. But in a situation where the peasant producer is not yet effectively captured by the official economic system, there is no assurance that he will respond in the expected manner. Furthermore, agricultural policy cannot be isolated from measures affecting job opportunities and wage levels in the urban areas. Sector-specific outlooks that have been so characteristic of the development debate in Africa have made the pendulum swing too far in either direction, overlooking the inevitable links between urban and rural development and agriculture and industry.

Although donors play a prominent role in determining African development strategies, it would be wrong to absolve the recipient governments, which have reinforced the above shortcomings and contributed their own. One is the notion that economies can be developed like armies under a single command. Relatively autonomous institutions like cooperatives and elected district councils have been subsumed under central government control. Kenya, Zambia, and Tanzania are only a few of the countries to have applied this notion, but as the Tanzanian experience suggests, mobilization and management of scarce economic resources requires a different approach.

A second shortcoming of African governments has been their tendency to view development as a collection of things to produce. They have almost totally ignored the fact that development is a do-it-yourself process, as all of today's highly developed economies were once backward. The prevailing illusion in Africa and in many other places (e.g., Iran under the Shah) is that development can be bought with revenue from oil or with aid. One of Africa's particular problems is the absence of an indigenous artisanal tradition from which to develop technology. The result is limited indigenous capacity for such key tasks as research, development, repair, and maintenance, creating the embarrassing paradox that industries begun only a few years ago remain inoperative or operate only at minimal capacity levels, while African governments continue to press for investments in new ventures.

Closely related to this orientation has been the belief that the continent's backwardness can be reversed by ready-made schemes for predetermined choices of products developed with assistance from the industrialized countries. Rather than encouraging trade within Africa, governments continue to pay primary attention to the dead-end trade with the more advanced economies. Instead of developing linkages between the cities and their rural hinterlands, the strategy pursued so far has left African countries as supply regions for the industrial world. Import-substituting schemes have been priced out of international markets and unlike efforts of a similar kind in Southeast and East Asia, imported industries have failed to break out of their limited domestic market.

The diversification of the economies of Kenya and Zimbabwe due to the presence of settler minorities made those countries structurally better equipped to make progress on their own. The same point is more applicable to South Africa, whose economic strength and growing role as a regional power is not only the result of exploiting cheap black labor or its position as a supply source for the industrialized countries.

A LOOK TO THE FUTURE

Because so many mistakes have been committed in the past two decades, it is easy to conclude that the outlook for Africa is a gloomy one. Gloom, however, is not necessary if governments and donors agree that conditions in Africa are different. It is easy to argue that pricing policies are wrong, that subsidies should be abandoned, or that excessive protection for local manufacturing is harmful to economic development. In Asia, for example, correcting failures in these areas produced positive results. Economies in Africa, however, are still such that they must be made better equipped to take on the challenge. Development is not merely a matter of choosing between a market of a planned economy. The conditions for the pursuit of these policies have yet to be created out of what remains a precapitalist base. African policy-makers are caught in structures and processes that place definite limits on what they can realistically accomplish, yet recognition of this point is absent in virtually all documents produced for consideration by African governments. Neither the Lagos Plan of Action nor recent World Bank reports on African development acknowledge it.

To develop a more balanced and realistic perspective on African development, it is necessary to accept what exists on the ground in African countries, starting from the premise that the fragile state of the African political economy creates pressures on leaders to centralize control and rule society through expensive gestures of state patronage. The preference for state control and direction cannot be explained by reference to African leaders' socialist inclinations. The prime rationale for such an approach is that it provides a better means of social control in a fluid political setup than does a market economy. The validity of this point is demonstrated in countries like Mozambique and Tanzania where socialist policies have not created socialism, but have only reinforced precapitalist forms of social and economic organization.

This statist orientation has also delayed or prevented the growth of an indigenous manufacturing and merchant class with power to act independently and demand policies that serve their interests. Even in West Africa where a merchant tradition has been kept alive, development policies have generally ignored the role of indigenous traders and in several cases treated them as pariahs. While a market economy approach seems more appropriate in contemporary Africa than one based on central planning, the legacy of the past cannot be ignored: Africa lacks the principal carriers of such an approach; the state is controlled by the volatile politics of affection; and rural producers remain constrained by rudimentary technologies, labor shortages, and a philosophy that puts higher premium on diversifying investments than intensifying agricultural production.

But if there are no shortcuts to progress, what are the ingredients of a development strategy more in tune with Africa's own social and material realities? In attempting to answer that question, consideration should be given to four principal propositions, each relating to choices of emphasis that will have to be made between elite and masses; town and village; government and non-governmental organizations; and direction and spontaneity.

STRENGTHEN AFRICA'S BOURGEOISIE

Africa's greatest shortcoming is its shortage of people with the creative capacity and power to set long-term development processes in motion. The bureaucratic bourgeoisie—politicians, administrators, and professionals in public institutions—may have the nation's interests at heart, but their efforts are hampered by cumbersome rules and regulations. African managers recruited by multinational companies, on the other hand, may possess the economic know-how and achievement orientation associated with entrepreneurship, but their impact is constrained by considerations of rates of return and other corporate principles guiding business ventures.

The historical artificiality of Marxism-Leninism in the contemporary African context is increasingly obvious even to leaders of states which continue to be categorized as such—far too simplistically—in Western media. Pressures to generate a bourgeoisie may in fact be strongest in those countries where the contradiction between political rhetoric and material reality is particularly striking. If these leaders find it difficult to retreat from a strategy of state control, it is less because of their belief in Marxist philosophy than their fear of political disunity caused by the economy of affection. Consequently, even in capitalist Kenya, for example, pressures toward political centralization and state control are also evident.

Africa's primary challenge is how to break out of its precapitalist cocoon. History suggests that the most probable strategy is to strengthen the bourgeoisie by encouraging the establishment of indigenous manufacturers and merchants. Liberals and socialists ought to have no difficulty in agreeing on such an approach, for only a strong bourgeoisie will overcome the constraints inherent in current primitive accumulation approaches and thus facilitate a sustained domestic capital formation. Without creative and productive talent of that kind, the African bourgeoisie will remain unable to protect and defend the continent against efforts by others to determine its course. Only a wholesome bourgeoisie will be able to create economic and political structures that eliminate the uncertainties associated with an economy of affection and without it, the evolution of durable socialist forms and relations on the African continent is likely to remain a faint possibility.

What is being proposed here has nothing to do with the assertion made in neo-liberal economic circles that capitalism is superior to socialism. Rather, the rationale behind a greater scope for capitalist principles in Africa today is their role in paving the way for a necessary transformation of prevailing precapitalist structures. In other words, capitalism must create the conditions under which it may prove its competitiveness with socialism in Africa.

What should African governments and donors do? Clearly, strategies must extend beyond the notion that multinational or state investments in agricultural and industrial development are the keys to progress. Incentives and support must be provided for the development of an indigenous corporate class. For example, special incentives could be provided for public servants to facilitate their move into private business without resorting to dishonest means to accumulate capital for such a purpose. Multinational companies could assist local managers in setting up their own businesses. By sponsoring local manufacturers in sub-contracting roles, foreign corporations could contribute to an improved business climate in Africa.

Another approach is based on the sister-industry concept, whereby small-scale manufacturers in Europe or the United States assist African entrepreneurs to set up similar businesses and provide them with access to export markets. Governments and donors should pay more attention to the local support structures required to facilitate entrepreneurship, such as credit institutions, technical assistance, and management training programs. Private capital must be allowed to work under conditions that facilitate rather than preempt local development.

DEVELOP A COMPREHENSIVE STRATEGY BASED ON THE CITY

History shows that cities, not national governments, are the power-houses of economic development. The development of constructive relations between the urban centers and the hinterlands is at the heart of successful national economies. Compared with other continents, Africa lacks a tradition of city development. While cities existed in precolonial Africa, they were not productively linked to their rural hinterlands, flourishing instead on long-distance trade. Colonial rulers did little to change the situation, creating cities as intermediary links between Europe's financial and commodity markets and primary producers in Africa. The artificiality of African cities was further reinforced by economic subsidies provided by the colonial authorities as a means of attracting a permanent indigenous workforce to the newly built towns.

In the post-independence period, Africa's economic development efforts started with the double handicap of lacking cities integrated with their local countryside and citizens able to tap the full potential of urban centers. The growth of a bureaucratic bourgeoisie lacking the ability to develop new linkages between the towns and villages has only reinforced this handicap in recent years. Given the present crisis in the agricultural sector, efforts to improve rural productivity are legitimate but, as Jane Jacobs reminds us,[33] evidence from other parts of the world shows that sustained improvements in rural productivity have been possible only when cities have begun to replace imports with cheaper domestic innovations. Evidence tends to confirm Jacobs' thesis that both rural welfare and national wealth are proportionate to the economic vitality of cities. Urban residents' remittances to their home villages in the context of the economy of affection are significant contributions to rural development.[34] Private investments in agriculture by urban residents are particularly important where the prospects for agricultural improvement are good.

The differences between Kenya and Tanzania's economic performances since independence are less likely to be the result of their ideological approaches to development than the ability of the former to develop creative linkages between town and countryside.[35] Kenya's

sustained economic growth has been in part due to its encouragement of the urban-based Asian minority to redirect its merchant capital into productive investments, thus gradually replacing imports
and facilitating African capital's entry into commerce and industry.
Tanzania, on the other hand, discouraged private capital from establishing more productive linkages between town and countryside,
leaving the task to inefficient state enterprises.

Governments and donors must accept that any future development strategy requires a more systematic focus on the role of cities in
rural development. Although it may sound paradoxical, the roots of
Africa's present crisis are urban rather than rural. African cities lack
the local manufacturers and merchants with ambition and ability to
improvise and innovate. Urban consumers are subsidized at unrealistic prices and urban wages render local goods uncompetitive with
imports. Because productivity-increasing innovations in African agriculture are unlikely to curb the influx to towns and may indeed encourage it, governments and donors have little choice but to pay
closer attention to urban issues, in particular how town and countryside can be linked more productively.

As part of encouraging the growth of local entrepreneurs, the bureaucratic bourgeoisie should be cut to size through various privatization measures, including incentives for public servants to start private business, as suggested earlier. Other interventions should aim at
reducing the privileged and protected status of African cities. Lowering real wage income for urban residents is necessary to make local
products more competitive, to limit the scope of the economy of
affection, and to make income differentials between urban and rural
areas less apparent.

Many economists would argue that the urban-rural equation cannot be satisfactorily resolved unless measures are taken to enhance
rural productivity. While in the long run such an approach makes
sense, it is unlikely that prime attention to rural productivity—at the
expense of urban issues—will yield any developmental benefits.
While peasant farmers may respond to better prices by producing
more of a particular crop, they may not be able to enhance productivity due to labor and other physical constraints. Nor is increased support for research likely to have immediate payoffs in Africa's locale-
specific and rainfed agricultural system. A green revolution is
impossible as long as developing Africa's agriculture is a more risky
strategy than diversification into various off-farm activities.

The backbone of the economy of affection needs to be broken, and the only groups strong enough to perform this painful function are businessmen and manufacturers who from a city base can articulate their demands for policies that enhance productivity or efficiency both at micro and macro levels. It is these people rather than government officials or development workers in the rural areas who are best placed to foster progress. For instance, much of the well-intended ingenuity that goes into developing "appropriate technology" is a waste of time. These solutions should be developed in conjunction with urban-based technicians and businessmen, as they are best placed to assess the marketability of the innovation. If the product proves successful initially, these marketing agents will ensure that the word of its success spreads into even the remotest village.

Town and village must also be considered together when setting food prices. As Low has shown in reference to southern Africa,[36] food price policies aimed at stimulating domestic production must take into account not only retail prices, but the implications of altering the availability and prices of imported foodstuffs. Raising retail food prices and reducing food aid and commercial imports in order to stimulate domestic production measures involve political risks. Such measures reduce the real income of net consuming households, adversely affecting the nutritional status of poorer households. So far, low-income households have remained unaffected by macro-economic measures because they have had access to the economy of affection as a safety valve. If on the other hand, policies are to be more than welfare measures, instead designed to enhance the capacity of African economies to stand on their own feet, the conflict between production and welfare goals will be intensified in the future. Well-developed cities, with productive linkages to their rural hinterlands, are a precondition to affording subsidies and other welfare programs.

DIVERSIFY INSTITUTIONAL RESPONSIBILITIES

Without a creative bourgeoisie in the driver's seat and productive cities as the powerful engine, Africa will become a perpetual "welfare" case. The rest of the world will have to pump endless amounts of money into the continent to stem misery and death. If the two propositions suggested above are taken seriously, there is at least a chance that the problem of human and social welfare on the continent will prove manageable. This strategy would provide options with a potential to make a difference.

Social development in post-independence Africa has lacked consideration of its long-term economic and political implications. For example, education has expanded without limit because it has proved popular and there is nothing wrong with providing new knowledge to people. Whereas basic health facilities have not been in as great demand as education, their provision has been a prominent part of Africa's development strategies to date, viewed as a "basic need" by donors. Both education and health projects are popular with politicians because they make for good political patronage. Even when these facilities have involved an element of self-help, they have been far less controversial with the local people than projects involving improvements in agricultural practices.

Thus, it is no coincidence that self-help efforts organized by political leaders have tended to focus on the social rather than economic aspects of life.[37] Whereas the provision of a school or health center makes a politician look responsible and concerned, insistence on agricultural improvements makes him a colonial taskmaster in the eyes of the local people. The result is that African countries today are saddled with a social welfare sector that the state is unable to handle. Unless something drastic is done, education, health, and other social sectors will decline, making African societies unmanageable entities.

In order to salvage the situation, African governments have little choice but to diversify institutional responsibilities by encouraging local communities, elected local councils, and voluntary agencies to play a greater part in running the country. Thus far, policy has been outright hostile toward these bodies with the result that people have lost the interest and motivation to participate in development programs and have been left with no venue to express their views. As long as a volatile economy of affection sets the stage for politics, there will be resistance to any change away from this pattern.

There is evidence, however, that its limits are increasingly being realized. Even those who do not necessarily favor the emergence of institutions independent of the state are ready to accept that government cannot do everything and that non-governmental organizations (NGOs) are needed to help carry out public responsibilities.

Although the door is being opened to the private and voluntary sectors, there has been little thought of what their contributions to development should be. Policy questions requiring attention at this stage include to what extent responsibility for primary education, basic health, and local water supply can be transferred to local authorities and voluntary or private agencies. Delegating responsibility for such tasks would be a meaningful step toward the establishment of more democratic forms of government, particularly if the responsibility is located at the community or village level rather than the district.

The district councils set up by the colonial powers were justified on the grounds of economy of scale. They operated in a satisfactory manner as long as they were under the tutelage of colonial officials, however, after independence they quickly fell into disrepute because they lacked accountability to the local communities and thus became arenas for indiscriminate dispensation of patronage by individual councilors. Any future local government system should be built from below, involving viable local communities in tasks meaningful to their own development.

Africa also lacks strong indigenous voluntary agencies, despite a deeply ingrained spirit of self-help. Most voluntary groups on the continent remain small-scale and unofficial and thus invisible to policy-makers and donors. A challenge therefore is how to mobilize the voluntarist spirit toward broader development goals. Best placed to perform this role are the many intermediary, often church-based organizations, which have become increasingly concerned with development issues in recent years. They are in close contact with local people, enjoy their confidence, and can usually rely on their voluntary contributions. Although they often lack management capacity, they are more likely to achieve results than heavy-footed public bureaucracies.

What then can African governments and donors do? In many countries, a first step would be to investigate the policy issues involved in a broader delegation of responsibilities to local governments and NGOs. Their role in domestic resource mobilization should be fully assessed in the context of national development strategies. Donors must increase their funding flexibility, no longer taking refuge behind avowals that they can only give funds to governments. Agreements must be reached with African governments to allow the flow of direct aid to NGOs.

Donors and African governments should pay greater attention to private and voluntary organizations because they demonstrate that development can be promoted more efficiently and effectively than through official channels. Investments to improve them are more likely to have tangible benefits than similar efforts in public bureaucracies. Second, governments will not be able to deal adequately with poverty alleviation in Africa for the foreseeable future. The only way to avoid a catastrophe is to engage the NGOs more directly in this task, as they have the flexibility and the contact with poverty groups that governments lack. They can develop and incorporate into their programs non-conventional solutions to poverty remediation issues.

In other parts of the world, poverty alleviation was handled almost exclusively by non-governmental agencies. The successful institutionalization of these measures subsequently paved the way for government to take over these functions once its revenue base permitted. It has been a tragedy that in Africa, governments and donors have continued to see poverty remediation as a state responsibility, particularly since government machineries are so ill-equipped to handle the task. Poverty remediation issues in Africa should not continue to be seen in contemporary Western terms.

Third, NGOs deserve increased support because, by becoming stronger, they will facilitate implementation of government programs and hold public officials more accountable for their actions. At present, many government programs achieve very little because there are no developed structures into which government agencies can plug their own operations. By strengthening these organizations, donors can indirectly help improve public management and promote democratic forms of governance. Because NGOs tend to cut across the narrow bonds of the economy of affection, they are important mechanisms for overcoming its often parochial outlook.

ADOPT A "GREENHOUSE" APPROACH

Given the positivist spirit that rapidly evolved in post-independence Africa, it is not surprising that policy-makers espoused a strong faith in planning and proper project designs and in their ability to contribute to the development process. Themselves captive of the positivist era, donors were only too eager to endorse this approach. To enable the state to perform its developmental role, it was necessary to enhance planning capacity at various levels and through the assistance of technical advisers, to ensure that individual projects were adequately prepared on the drawing board, with or without prior testing.

While careful programming and design may be of utmost importance in technical projects where variables can be manipulated at will, such an approach is inherently limited when applied to development efforts that depend on human resolution and will. For many years, Africans and donors alike attributed the inability to reach anticipated development objectives to insufficient planning skills, faulty programming methods, or inadequate project preparation, proposing more training, better programming, and fuller preparation as remedies.

This "blueprint" approach has an appealing sense of order because of its concentration on clearly defined activities with discrete and visible outcomes.[38] It also elevates the professional to a superordinate role in the development process. However, it presupposes a stable and predictable environment in which variables can be satisfactorily controlled and manipulated. For infrastructural projects, for example, tasks are defined, outcomes terminal, the environment stable, and costs consequently predictable. In Africa's predominantly rural environment, however, the situation is the opposite. Policymakers do not have control of their environment. In the typical rural setting, it is the peasant rather than the government officer who makes the ultimate decision on how factors of production like land, water, labor, technology, and capital are being utilized. The notion of the uncaptured peasant is particularly applicable to Africa where his marginal incorporation into a market economy and continued dependence on a simple technology leave officials with few strings to pull in order to influence his behavior.

The frustration of failing to control peasant production has caused many governments to resort to capital-intensive, large-scale farming or complex settlement schemes in which producers are treated as tenants. Direct government involvement in development projects of this kind, however, has generally proved no more successful, as even in these production settings, and the "autonomous" peasant has prevailed.[39]

The almost blind application of the blueprint approach has decreased confidence in public institutions' abilities to bring about progress. Today, citizens show great reluctance to participate in new government schemes, and scarce human resources are being wasted. For this reason, African governments and donors must consider alternatives that can restore human motivation to contribute to national development.

An appropriate alternative, the "greenhouse" approach is based on the assumption that people will organize and accomplish tasks of common concern if provided with the stimuli and incentives. Rather than organizing people for purposes beyond their comprehension and interest, the greenhouse approach focuses on factors that help local efforts grow on their own. True to its name, it provides a hospitable climate for growth even in otherwise adverse circumstances. For example, rather than implanting organizational models in the cooperative sector, the greenhouse approach starts with what already exists and encourages organizational development from below or within. It tries to accelerate progress on the basis of what society already offers.

Local savings efforts are cases in point. Studies show that "informal" credit and savings efforts are widespread in Africa and recent efforts in Kenya and Zimbabwe to recognize their role in rural development are beginning to pay off in increased income generation. The greenhouse approach would help strengthen local efforts by facilitating expansion beyond the parochial boundaries of small communities. While this approach recognizes that fostering progress in Africa involves much more than the application of capitalist principles, the latter are an integral part because only through an "open economy" policy will it be possible to accelerate a transformation of the continent's still predominantly precapitalist economies. Governments and donors will have to recognize and support institutions that address the issue of how the poor in the urban and rural informal sectors can become respected and meaningful participants in development.

A corollary of such a strategy would be to encourage alternatives to government involvement in economic activities. More scope must be given to improvised solutions such as the development of extension services organized by private, voluntary, or cooperative institutions. A plan must be devised for the reduction and reallocation of official manpower resources to NGOs. If such institutions do not already exist, policies that encourage their creation and growth must be adopted.

In short, the greenhouse approach enables governments and donors to discover how Africa's own wheels of progress can move faster and ultimately replace the foreign wheels which, because of their size and inappropriate construction, inevitably destroy the African terrain.

CONCLUSIONS

In 1973, the All-Africa Conference of Churches' call for an aid moratorium, based on its view that the spirit of self-reliance in Africa was undermined by ill-conceived aid projects that often preempted rather than facilitated local development, was not taken seriously. With the number of aid programs that have ground to a halt, it is tempting to agree with the AACC.

However, the prospects for African development have deteriorated considerably over the last decade and ceasing aid at this point is a much more controversial proposition. What is required is a retreat from the notion that Africa can be treated like any other Third World region because its historical circumstances are different. Even a market economy approach, which is favored in this chapter as the most effective way of transforming the precapitalist economy of affection, cannot harvest any easy victories in Africa, and is rather justified to prepare the ground for future productivity gains and social progress.

Africa needs to develop on its own terms. Its current crisis cannot be blamed simply on factors such as corruption and inefficiency because, thus far, African countries have been forced to progress on terms foreign to their own material and social realities. They deserve the benefit of a home game. African leaders, though very slowly, are gradually getting ready for such a game. Are the donors ready to adjust their strategies?

NOTES

1. Albert Hirschman, "The Rise and Decline of Development Economics," in *Essays in Trespassing: Economics to Politics and Beyond*. New York: Cambridge University Press, 1981, pp. 1–24.

2. Carl Eicher, "West Africa's Agrarian Crisis," paper presented to the Fifth Bi-Annual Conference of the West African Association of Agricultural Economics, Abidjan, Ivory Coast, December 7–11, 1983, pp. 19–26.

3. Keith Hart, *The Political Economy of West African Agriculture*. London: Cambridge University Press, 1982, p. 105.

4. J. G. Karuga, Permanent Secretary in the Ministry of Energy and Regional Development, quoted by *The Standard* (Nairobi), 7 July 1984.

5. Jack Goody, *Technology, Tradition and The State in Africa*. Oxford: Oxford University Press, 1971, p. 71.

6. See, for instance, Robin Law, *The Oyo Empire c. 1600–c. 1836: A West African Imperialism in the Era of the Atlantic Slave Trade*. Oxford: Clarendon

Press 1977; Richard Roberts, "Long Distance Trade and Production: Sinsani in the Ninetheenth Century," *Journal of African History* 21(2) (1980).

7. Economic Commission for Africa, *ECA and Africa's Development 1983–2008: A Preliminary Perspective Study*. Addis Ababa: Economic Commission for Africa, April 1983, p.9.

8. Eicher, op. cit., p. 10.

9. Particularly extensive and interesting materials are provided by Allan Low, *Agricultural Development in Southern Africa*. London: James Curry Publishers, 1985, especially Chapters 11–13.

10. In my own writings, I usually refer to existing pre-capitalist modes of production in Africa under the common label of the "peasant" mode, the reason being that those who appropriate the surplus are themselves dependent on the peasant producers and lack the means of effectively enforcing their own will on these producers. The dominant culture, therefore, also tends to reflect peasant values rather than forming a distinct "high culture" that is associated with more deeply stratified class societies.

11. This point is further elaborated by Barry Hindess and Paul O. Hirst, *Pre-Capitalist Modes of Production*. London: Routledge & Kegan Paul, 1975.

12. Evidence is provided by Sara S. Berry, "Agrarian Crisis in Africa? A Review and an Interpretation," paper presented for the Joint African Studies Committee of the Social Science Research Council and the American Council of Learned Societies, September 1983, p. 4.

13. Economic Commission for Africa, op. cit., p. 7.

14. Compare, for example, John O. Caldwell, *African Rural-Urban Migration: The Movement to Ghana's Towns*. New York: Columbia University Press, 1969; John C. Mitchell, ed., *Social Networks in Urban Situations*. Manchester: Manchester University Press, 1969; Joyce Moock, "The Content and Maintenance of Social Ties Between Urban Migrants and Their Home-Based Support Groups: The Maragoli Case," *African Urban Notes* 3 (Winter 1978–79); Thomas Weisner, "The Structure of Sociability: Urban Migration and Urban Ties in Kenya," *Urban Anthropology*, 5 (1976); and Richard Sandbrook, *The Politics of Basic Needs: Urban Aspects of Assaulting Poverty in Africa*. London: Heinemann, 1982.

15. Walter Elkan, *Migrants and Proletarians: Urban Labour in the Economic Development of Uganda*. Oxford: Oxford University Press, 1960.

16. For a useful overview of intra-household processes and the place of households in the context of community structures, see Jane I. Guyer, "Household and Community in African Studies," *African Studies Review* 24(273) (1981): 87–138.

17. A. V. Chayanov, *The Theory of Peasant Economy*. Homewood, Ill.: Richard D. Irwin for the American Economics Association, 1966.

18. See, for example, Dani Kaufmann, "Social Interactions as a Strategy of Survival Among the Urban Poor: A Theory and Some Evidence," Ph.D. dissertation, Harvard University, 1981.

19. See Mary Hollnsteiner, "Reciprocity in the Lowland Philippines," in F. Lynch and A. Gusman, eds., *Four Readings on Philippine Culture*. Manila: Ateneo de Manila University Press, 1973.

20. Low, op. cit., Ch. 11.

21. See, for example, Polly Hill, *Migrant Cocoa Farmers in Southern Ghana*. Cambridge: Cambridge University Press, 1963; John M. Janzen, "The Cooperative in Lower Congo Economic Development," in David Brokensha and Marion Pearsall, eds., *The Anthropology of Development in Sub-Saharan Africa*. Lexington, Ky.: Society for Applied Anthropology, 1969, Monograph 10, pp. 70–76; William Ogionwo, *Innovative Behavior and Personal Attitudes: A Case of Social Change in Nigeria*. Boston: G. K. Hall & Company, 1978.

22. Peter Marris and Anthony Somerset, *The African Entrepreneur: A Study of Entrepreneurship and Development in Kenya*. New York: African Publishing Corporation, 1972; Kenneth King, *The African Artisan: Education and the Informal Sector in Kenya*. London: Heinemann, 1977.

23. Sara S. Berry, "Oil and the Disappearing Peasantry: Accumulation Differentiation and Underdevelopment in Western Nigeria," unpublished manuscript, Boston University, 1984.

24. Thomas Hodgkin, *Nationalism in Colonial Africa*. London: Frederick Muller, 1956.

25. Elliot P. Skinner, "Voluntary Associations in Ouagadougou: A Reappraisal of the Function of Voluntary Associations in African Urban Centers," *African Urban Notes*, Series B, No. 1 (Winter 1974/75).

26. Lionel Cliffe, "Nationalism and the Reaction to Enforced Agricultural Change in Tanganyika during the Colonial Period," paper presented to the East African Institute of Social Research Conference, Makerere University, Kampala, December 1964.

27. The concept of the "soft" state was first coined by Gunnar Myrdal in his *Asian Drama: An Inquiry into the Poverty of Nations*. New York: Twentieth Century Fund and Pantheon Books, 1968.

28. Donal B. Cruise O'Brien, *Saints and Politicians: Essays in the Organization of a Senegalese Peasant Society*. Cambridge: Cambridge University Press, 1975.

29. Berry, "Agrarian Crisis in Africa?, op. cit., p. 67.

30. See, for example, ibid, and Glen Norcliffe, "Operating Characteristics of Rural Non-Farm Enterprises in Central Province, Kenya," *World Development* II (11) (1983).

31. Report on the Integrated Rural Development Programme in Sri Lanka, quoted in *Kenya Times* (Nairobi) 14 June 1984.

32. Graham Adler, advisor to National Cooperative Housing Union in Kenya, personal communication, July 3, 1984.

33. Jane Jacobs, *Cities and the Wealth of Nations: Principles of Economic Life*. New York: Random House, 1984, pp. 151–53.

34. Paul Collier and Dipak Lal, "Poverty and Growth in Kenya," Staff Paper No. 389, Washington, D.C.: The World Bank, 1980, p. 35.

35. It should be pointed out that within Tanzania, the situation of Dar es Salaam stands in contrast to the northern town of Arusha which has quite successfully developed a productive relationship with its rural hinterland and as a consequence has been prospering in spite of the country's general economic decline.

36. Low, op. cit., pp. 312–18.

37. For a discussion of this issue, see Frank Holmquist, "Class Structure,

Peasant Participation and Rural Self-Help" in Joel D. Barkan and John J. Okumu, eds., *Politics and Public Policy in Kenya and Tanzania*. New York: Praeger, 1979, pp. 129–53.

38. This approach is reviewed and analyzed by David Korten, "Community Organization and Rural Development: A Learning Process Approach," *Public Administration Review* 40(5) (1980): 481–511.

39. Robert Chambers, *Settlement Schemes in Tropical Africa: A Study of Organizations and Development*. London: Routledge & Kegan Paul, 1969.

CHAPTER THREE

Governance and Economic Management

Benno J. Ndulu

Whereas the magnitude of the economic crisis that has afflicted Africa over the last decade has varied from country to country, a consensus has developed concerning both the external factors and internal policies that have contributed to the current stagnation. Domestic economic management policies are increasingly drawing the attention not only of donors and international institutions, but also of African governments themselves.[1] Pan-African organizations have also begun to reassess economic policies and institutional structures in order to address the current crisis.[2] This new introspection has stemmed from a realization that the impact of external shocks can be minimized by sound economic management and that economic structures can be strengthened by a more efficient use of development resources.

THE POLITICAL-ECONOMIC CONTEXT

Development planning and economic management in Africa involve a careful balancing of different and often conflicting interests. The assumption implicit in liberal economic theory–that the state is a "neutral" and even benevolent arbiter whose role is to further the national interest in economic growth, efficiency, and social welfare–is not borne out in practice (Sandbrook, 1982, p. 77).

In most African political systems, whether civilian or military, the majority of the population is politically impotent, the power of the government is implicitly acknowledged, and elites cater to some of the demands of their "clients," while assuring that these demands do not reach levels requiring severe structural reforms. As a result, policies reflect in part the interests of the national elites, and in part, those of the population at large (Cleaves, 1980, p. 25). In the absence of more open political systems, in which organized interest groups can thrash out their differences, the state's involvement in resource allocation is more pronounced and often used as a means of balancing different interest groups and maintaining patron-client networks.

Another dominant characteristic of African regimes is the close link between the state bureaucracy and the private sector, both foreign and indigenous. Elites use state power either independently or in conjunction with private entrepreneurs to enter into the business sphere,[3] tending to create a strong symmetry of interests between the private sector and the state bureaucracy. As some price distortions, such as lowered tariffs for imports and subsidized capital, have benefited private and public sector interests at the expense of an overall efficient allocation of resources, they represent among the more formidable constraints to the implementation of lasting reforms.

Although the above characterization of African political structures seems to be generally applicable, there are important distinctions between the various regimes that are relevant to the analysis of macro-economic management. On one end of the spectrum are regimes with liberal open economies, in which foreign private sector interests dominate and national elites are weak, such as Ivory Coast, and on the other, states with strong "nationalistic" interests, such as Tanzania. Between these extremes, there are wide variations in the extents to which the state intervenes and to which non-economic goals are pursued.

It is in terms of the link between state-society power relationships and macro-economic management policies pursued that three regime typologies can be broadly defined.[4] The first, liberal economies, are characterized by an open door foreign investment policy and by a national elite and state machinery which play a secondary role in resource allocation. Such regimes allow for relatively free inflows and outflows of resources. State intervention in the markets for goods and resources is minimal. Development strategies aim at achieving maximum growth rates, while income distribution and equity are secondary concerns. The state's primary economic function is to maintain adequate infrastructure and a stable and attractive environment for foreign private capital. State intervention is confined for the most part to the domestic food markets where foreign private capital interests are not strong. While Ivory Coast is the best example of this regime typology, others might include Senegal, Niger, Chad, and Malawi.

Whereas development planning in these countries is indicative of the economic direction the country is pursuing, it is neither binding nor specific in allocation of resources. Over time, however, pressures have grown in these countries for indigenization of both the management and ownership of foreign capital. As a result, the public sector has expanded via equity state participation or new investments wholly owned by the state. The indigenous private sector has also grown, as has its involvement in large-scale agriculture.

The second typology includes those countries such as Nigeria, Ghana, Zambia, Botswana, and Kenya with strong "nationalistic" regimes, where the interests of the national elites take precedence over foreign private capital. National interest groups are strongly represented and have some influence on the state machinery and bureaucracy. In this type of regime, sometimes referred to as "state capitalist," the state plays a key role in allocating resources and controlling the development process. State participation in and control over directly productive sectors, either through wholly owned enterprises or partnerships with private capital, are consistent with the goals of economic nationalism and with public officials' own sense of identity with the state (Bienen and Diejomaoh, 1980, p. 138).

Economic growth is a key objective, but structural adjustment strategies and the indigenization of economic activities are also national priorities. Consequently, partial nationalization of foreign interests, expanded state investments, and encouragement of domestic private investment are part of the accumulation process. Not only are foreign capital inflows channeled through and controlled by the state, but resources are allocated either directly through the state budget or indirectly through commodity and price controls. Price distortions, however, are more severe than in the liberal economies because of the controls, while at least at the rhetorical level, distributional and equity issues are addressed in development planning.

The third typology, the "national-collectivist" system, includes those countries aspiring to socialism such as Tanzania, Mozambique, Angola, and Ethiopia. Rather than focusing on economic growth, these regimes make serious efforts to tackle issues of distribution and equity. While many features of the second typology apply here, the extent of government intervention in investment and marketing is greater. Public spending on social programs as a percentage of available resources is higher than in the other typologies. Although the use of price controls is more prevalent, the private sector's contribution to national output is nonetheless strong.

These distinctions between regimes are useful to our analysis because the extent to which the state intervenes and non-economic issues are considered in policy formulation has a bearing on the constraints to economic adjustment and stabilization measures. In the second and third typologies, more cautious approaches to such policy reforms will have to be adopted because of the more active involvement of domestic interest groups in the political arena and of the state in resource allocation.[5] By contrast, regimes in the first category face less political risk in implementing economic reforms. Given fewer controls and thus distortions in these economies, the political and financial costs associated with shifting resources are negligible. The sheer size of foreign private capital interests constitutes a formidable "voting" bloc that most often favors reforms, as "weak" national elites cannot ignore the threat of foreign sector withdrawal.

KEY ISSUES IN ECONOMIC MANAGEMENT: PROBLEMS AND PROSPECTS FOR REFORMS

The key issues in African economic management are the role and size of the public sector, the level of state intervention in resource allocation, and the use of counter-cyclical economic policies. While each of these issues will be addressed, it is necessary first to outline the climate in which reforms in these areas will take place, as it will have a bearing on the degree to which they are accepted and implemented by concerned governments.

Despite the political constraints on economic adjustment outlined here, recent developments have decreased the risk of implementing reform. The growth of parallel markets and corruption has, in effect, given impetus to some adjustments, eroding state control over markets. The black markets in foreign exchange and imports have indirectly increased domestic prices of scarce commodities and have undermined government subsidies on foodstuffs. When shortages occur, goods obtained at official subsidized prices are resold in parallel markets. In effect, this erosion of state control has significantly altered the political calculus of economic adjustment.

Reducing or eliminating food subsidies at a time when consumers are already purchasing more than 70 percent of their supplies from parallel markets at prices often more than double the official rate may be more acceptable than prior to the existence of such markets, when subsidized prices were maintained by using food imports to make up for shortages. Similarly, requiring that the costs for public services that were previously free be shared should be politically easier in a period when both the quantity and quality of free services are declining.

A more favorable attitude toward economic reform in sub-Saharan Africa has resulted not only from external economic pressures, but also from perceptions of the growing costs of ineffective state control over the economy and of the detrimental effects of economic deterioration on various interest groups. These elements have a bearing on the extent to which a government can politically and economically accommodate the burdens of adjustment.

It is still too early to judge whether the current willingness on the part of African governments to undertake reform can be sustained once economic conditions improve, or whether it is a temporary phenomenon. More detailed studies on the impact of economic retrenchment on interest groups and on state-society relationships will be required. It would appear, however, that sustainable reform will hinge upon the strengthening of institutional structures capable of defending the resultant changes. Further, it must be recognized that the causes of the current economic deterioration are long term, and that structural adjustment rather than short-term stabilization is the central issue. Therefore, this chapter will focus on the institutional aspects of reform which constitute the focal point of sustained change.

THE SIZE OF THE PUBLIC SECTOR
RELATIVE TO EFFECTIVE MANAGERIAL
CAPACITY

Over the past two decades, the public sector in sub-Saharan Africa has grown very rapidly. Governmental activities have expanded into the productive and commercial spheres through commercial enterprises, and the governmental sector itself (public administration) has also grown. The public sector now accounts for an average of over 50 percent of total wage employment, growing faster than the private sector partly because of changes in ownership, through nationalizations and majority equity participation, and partly because of an absolute rise in public sector activities. Other indicators, such as the growing share of public sector expenditures in the national accounts, corroborate this observation.

The expansion and diversification of activities of the public sector have seriously overtaxed management capacities. In addition to macro-economic management, the public sector is also responsible for the supply of economic and social infrastructure and management of commercial enterprises. The performance of the public sector relative to the share of national resources available to it is weak, both in terms of output and cost-effectiveness. Although a few public enterprises–notably those involved in extractive industries, financial intermediation, and manufacturing–have generated surpluses, others, especially in the agricultural marketing sector, have become a financial burden, requiring subsidization or loans from the domestic banking system.

Managerial capacity is poor in sub-Saharan Africa due to insufficient training and supportive infrastructure such as data bases and hard and software. Whereas many countries have made advances in education and training, the supply of skilled managers remains short of requirements. Most countries are still dependent on foreign technical capacity for the formulation of investment programs, the preparation of investment projects, and even the design of development plans and policy reviews. This shortage is evidenced by the widespread involvement of the World Bank and bilateral donors in the formulation of sectoral programs, and of foreign companies at the enterprise level.

Reliance on foreign technical capacity has given rise to several problems. First and foremost is the absence of a unified managerial system. The multiplicity of technical groups operating in a given country has frequently led to a situation where national investment programs have become a catch-all for projects originating from different sectors and enterprises. Balancing macro-economic resources, therefore, has been difficult, often resulting in capacity underutilization and high opportunity costs when expensive resources are left idle.

Second, given the differing and changing perspectives of the technical groups, discontinuity in economic management has become the norm over time, sometimes leading to drastic changes in development strategies. Third, costly time lags between formulation of programs and their implementation develop, partially because of lack of follow-up from the technical teams who often consider the program document their final task. Since the participation of local technical cadres in the preparation of programs has been limited, time is wasted over simply digesting the key facets of the programs to be implemented.

Effective economic management has also been hindered by the scarcity and poor quality of data required for planning and policy formulation. Information is not only essential for technical policy analysis and projections, but also for generating confidence in and gaining acceptance of projects. Unsupported by hard data on their likely impact on the economy and interest groups, reforms have a poor chance of gaining acceptance. Statistical bureaus in many countries are short of both qualified personnel and support systems for collecting and processing data. Whereas some ministries with independent sources of finance have tried to develop their own statistical base and some research institutions have become involved in statistics compilation, what often results is a multitude of disorganized and contradictory data.

The overcentralization of the state and the expansion of its activities have diluted its ability to focus on priority areas. However, many administrators believe that decentralization would relegate authority to inadequately trained, incompetent, and dishonest cadres (Jones, 1982, p. 557). While there is some basis for this perception, thinly spreading the more competent managers would not suffice either. Moreover, job accountability is not improved when bureaucratic structures are so encumbered with layers that locating the source of a decision or action is virtually impossible. Since 1972, several countries, including Tanzania, Sudan, and Senegal, have attempted government decentralization. These efforts, however, have increased administrative costs and have proven ineffective in expanding domestic participation in economic planning (Rondinelli, 1981, case of Sudan; N. Blues and Weaver, 1977, case of Tanzania).

Two approaches to correcting the problems presented above are proposed: first, reducing the size of the public sector and decentralizing management responsibilities to lower levels of government and to community groups; and second, strengthening local technical managerial expertise through training and improved data collection and dissemination systems.

REDUCING THE SIZE OF THE PUBLIC SECTOR

Reducing the size of the public sector can be accomplished by its withdrawal from certain commercial and production activities, specifically agricultural marketing, industry, and road transport.

Agricultural Marketing   Public sector withdrawal from agricultural marketing would have high payoffs. However, the lack of adequate infrastructure is a critical constraint. Transportation, storage, and information systems are prerequisites to efficient marketing, yet they have received less attention than the existing marketing institutions. Second, many countries have undergone a number of changes in their marketing arrangements since independence, from control by private interests to cooperatives to parastatals, creating an uncertain atmosphere for producers. As a result, any new changes should be carefully considered.

Not only do parastatals represent a budgetary burden on the state, but they have also become increasingly ineffective, as their share of marketed output, particularly in foodstuffs, has declined over time. Parallel markets that offer higher prices and prompt payment have rendered parastatals non-competitive.[6] Even as the volumes handled by parastatals have declined, their size has remained the same, causing unit overhead costs to shoot up. Hence, substantial losses were incurred. Food marketing parastatals, therefore, have benefited neither the producer nor the urban consumer, as they are unable to deliver the required quotas at the subsidized prices.

Private marketing agents and voluntary cooperatives could fill the gap created by public sector withdrawal from marketing, as both existed in many countries prior to extensive government intervention. The role of private agricultural marketing agents has grown with the development of parallel markets, which in some countries, channel as much as 70 percent of food supplies.[7] Historically, the development of indigenous private agricultural marketers has faced a number of constraints. Under colonial rule, foreign companies, notably Lebanese and Asian, dominated agricultural marketing. Indigenous private traders were largely confined to localized trade in perishables and suffered from lack of access to credit.[8] Only through registered producer cooperatives were Africans able to make any headway in agricultural trade. As a result, at independence, private agricultural trading capacity was underdeveloped.

In the immediate post-independence period, "nationalistic" regimes sought to replace the "alien" or foreign private traders with either government-initiated cooperatives or state/parastatal agencies, further impeding any development of indigenous private trading institutions. However, with increasing food shortages and the apparent inefficiencies of the parastatals, "clandestine" markets in which both operating costs and profits are high have attracted indigenous traders to agricultural marketing both at the local and national levels.

In the early 1970s, official consumer prices were maintained by importing food to meet excess demand, but this is no longer feasible as limited foreign exchange reserves have necessitated reductions in imports. The market share of parastatals in export crops has remained high, however, because of the lack of internal parallel markets for these goods, although there has been some smuggling across borders.

In the area of export trade and bulk handling, therefore, governmental control is likely to continue. As most large processing plants that serve several regions are publicly owned, expertise in procuring export crops from both private marketers and cooperatives will take some time to develop. Due to the critical importance of foreign exchange earnings in public sector allocations, governments will be loathe to relinquish control over these functions.

Short of a complete state withdrawal from agricultural marketing, a possible interim measure calls for the coexistence of marketing parastatals, cooperatives, and private agencies, each specializing in different areas. Streamlined marketing parastatals might concentrate in productive areas where infrastructure is poor, transport costs are too prohibitive for profit-motivated private agencies, and cooperatives are not yet well-formed. Where cooperatives are strong and members have autonomous control, the need for private and public agencies would be negligible. For their part, private marketing agencies might concentrate in easily accessible areas where cooperatives do not exist or are weak, and, at the national level, in interregional trade of foodstuffs. As infrastructure and training are gradually improved, cooperatives and private trading agencies will replace public marketing enterprises on the primary levels. The growth of independent marketing cooperatives should be encouraged for two reasons. First, strong cooperative societies and unions in agricultural marketing provide an organized forum for rural communities and represent a political force to be reckoned with (Lofchie and Cummins, 1982, p. 24), making it difficult for policy reforms to be reversed once economies are beyond the crisis period (Bates, 1983, chapter 5).[9] Second, strong marketing cooperatives prevent the development of private local marketing monopolies. Voluntary cooperatives can be used as a means of expanding the free market in mixed economies, provided they are able to cut loose from governmental control (Andreou, 1977, p. 70).

Appropriate pricing policies and adequate infrastructure are critical to the efficient operation of cooperatives and private marketing agencies. Food prices should be decontrolled and trading channels opened. The state's regulatory role should be confined to preventing monopolies from forming and to guaranteeing minimum prices to stimulate food production in areas that face severe infrastructural bottlenecks. Exchange rates must be adjusted to compensate for domestic inflation and to prevent the erosion of real producer prices for export crops.

Lastly, while improvements in marketing and thus prices for crops will encourage higher output levels, the use of advanced technologies in crop husbandry must be similarly encouraged. A second important function of marketing agents, therefore, is to ensure a smooth and cost-effective supply of production inputs. Given the relationship between the timely supply of inputs and increased productivity, a much more flexible supply system than that of the parastatals is required. If input distribution costs are decreased, profitability and hence productivity will increase.

Industrial Sector   The benefits of public sector withdrawal from the industrial sector are less apparent, given that activities in this domain are generally large-scale and private foreign capital involvement is limited. Considering foreign capital's perceptions of the high political risks associated with investment in industry and the limited availability of private local capital, the gap left by public sector withdrawal would be difficult to fill.[10]

In small- and medium-scale industries, however, there is room for a gradual expansion of local private business, with the public sector concentrating on large-scale industrial activities. Upgrading the performance of public industrial enterprises requires improved project appraisal and a national structure allowing for more operational autonomy and accountability in these enterprises. However, the shortage of skilled personnel remains a problem in both private and public sectors.

Operational autonomy of public industrial enterprises is critical to their commercial viability. While many enterprises are run according to legal charters defining the limits of their commercial activities, the line of accountability is firmly tied to the central authorities in parent ministries, allowing for frequent interference of a non-commercial nature. As a result, management cannot be held directly accountable for overall performance and lack of initiative is a common problem. In addition, channels of communication and overhead costs have been burdened unnecessarily by the proliferation of holding companies, which have expanded rapidly and exhibit monopolistic behavior.

Therefore, public sector industrial enterprises must be streamlined, granted autonomy over their own operations, and held accountable for their performance. Enterprises that cannot perform competitively should not be subsidized or otherwise protected.

Road Transport   African governments are heavily involved in the road transport sector, as public transport companies service most major cities, in some cases as monopolies. They also operate freight and passenger services interregionally, but often in competition with the private sector. Public transport and freight/passenger companies have been operating at losses for many years. Subsidized fares have led to real declines in revenues, generating budgetary deficits. Lacking surpluses, these companies rely heavily on government revenues to replace and expand their fleets. Although the urban transport companies offer subsidized services, their performance has deteriorated. Those public companies involved in cross-country freight and passenger services face the additional problem of servicing regions with poor roads, yet the rates they charge are significantly below the operating costs commensurate with road conditions. Private sector transport services, on the other hand, have fared comparatively better, concentrating in areas with better roads; when they do operate in poor road areas, they are able to charge higher rates.

Liberalization of urban transport services is underway in many countries, such as Tanzania and Zambia, and should be supported. Private companies are working with the public sector, charging higher rates, and the availability of services has improved noticeably. To keep pace with expansion in demand, the size of fleets will have to be increased by both types of operators. Public transport companies should be allowed to charge competitive rates, so that they can develop self-financing capabilities. For freight and passenger services operating in areas with poor road conditions, both public operators and cooperative transport companies will have to continue to play the developmental role until such time as road infrastructure is improved.

DECENTRALIZING ECONOMIC MANAGEMENT

If the responsibility for infrastructural services such as primary health care and education, feeder roads, and primary agricultural support services is shifted to local governments and communities, much of the pressure on centralized management can be alleviated. This is not a new idea–local government existed under British colonial rule and during the early independence period. The dismantling of these local structures and centralization of management was aimed at gaining control over national development under the leadership of newly independent states in order to build national cohesion (Jones, 1982, pp. 553–54).

Whereas this pattern of state control allowed for the pooling and allocation of national resources irrespective of the ability of specific areas to raise their own revenues, it also removed from local communities a sense of accountability for resource use and hence increased the level of dependency on the "omnipotent" government, stifling community initiative. Long lines of communication developed in administration, causing costly delays in decision-making and inflexibility in action. At the top levels of management, attention to priority areas was distracted by the necessity of routine supervision of activities which could have been handled effectively at the subordinate level.

Administrative decentralization and strengthening the role of local governmental structures are essential, given the failure of central governments to develop and maintain primary level services, and in view of the budgetary pressures on central government. Reintroducing the concept of local government can allow for a more appropriate linkage between infrastructural expansion and maintenance on the one hand, and resource mobilization capacity on the other, fostering a spirit of self-help and accountability in local communities. Decentralization also frees the central planning authority to concentrate on priority areas of national development.

STRENGTHENING AND STREAMLINING OF MACRO-
ECONOMIC MANAGEMENT CAPABILITY

A key deficiency in economic management in Africa is the insufficiency of competent local planners with experience in policy analysis, project formulation, and balancing of resources. While formal training must continue, the provision of practical experience, through apprenticeships with foreign specialist teams, has a high rate of return in terms of skills imparted and continuity in programs that have been implemented.

In addition to personnel training, efforts should be directed at encouraging policy analyses and research in independent research institutions, including universities. These institutions can provide the structural loci for more serious and focused studies which short-term specialists and ministries may not be able to undertake. African planning agencies' capacities and stature should be enhanced. As most have been involved mainly in the elaboration of medium-term plan documents, they have not been able to play an effective role in scrutinizing and evaluating projects from the ministries. The overriding sway of technical and financial ministries in determining the future of a particular plan must give way to permit planning agencies to contribute advice and program analyses. Development of a strong data base and dissemination system is a critical prerequisite for sound policy analysis and effective planning. Statistical bureaus must be strengthened in manpower, authority, data collection and analysis, and supportive infrastructure.

STATE MARKET INTERVENTION AND PRICE DISTORTIONS

The manipulation of prices to facilitate allocations of resources has been a common practice of many sub-Saharan African governments. Although the extent to which price controls are used varies according to the degree to which the state intervenes in the markets, in general, such practices have generated price distortions that result in inefficient use of resources. Allocations to unproductive sectors have engendered even greater dependence on subsidies and have stifled growth in key productive areas such as agriculture. Significant negative correlations have been demonstrated between price distortions and growth (World Bank, 1983, p. 63).

With the decline in state control over economic spheres and the rise in "unofficial" mechanisms over the last five years, the merits of manipulating prices to influence political interest groups have diminished. Moreover, price controls often have unintended results. Maintaining overvalued currencies, for example, has offset the degree of protection afforded by tariffs; consumer subsidies, though moderat-

ing pressures for higher wages and protective of real wage levels for
urban workers, have been inflationary. While low interest rates and
subsidies for transportation and inputs have been maintained to raise
rural incomes, these are more than counterbalanced by low producer
prices linked to overvalued exchange rates.

In order to eliminate price distortions, actions will have to be taken
with regard to all key prices which create biases against trade and
agriculture. Regular adjustment of the exchange rate to reflect
changes in inflationary conditions and the availability of foreign exchange; raising real interest rates to encourage savings; reducing
trade restrictions and relying more on indirect taxation for revenues;
and removing tax structures which distort resource allocation at the
production level are required.

Current price distortions are the result of cumulative interventionist actions of the past; therefore, alleviating the distortions will be a
long-term process. A gradual and sustained correction will involve
lower adjustment costs and produce less political opposition to reform.

EXCHANGE RATES

Average effective exchange rates in sub-Saharan Africa appreciated by 44 percent between 1973 and 1981 (World Bank, 1983, p. 58),
with the sharpest increase occurring after the second oil shock in
1979. Governments failed to respond with counter-cyclical adjustments in spending (see Wheeler, 1984, p. 11, fig. 3 for cases of Tanzania, Mali, Ghana, Uganda, Zaire, and Somalia), and the overvalued
currencies undercut increases in producer prices, resulting in declining export earnings and ultimately, reductions in exports.

Real producer prices for agricultural exports had begun to fall before 1978, due to export taxes and growing parastatal costs, but in the
high inflation period that followed, the situation was severely aggravated by non-adjustment of exchange rates. Some governments resorted to deficit financing, but the results of raising prices paid to
producers included accelerating rates of inflation and further declines
in real incomes. In effect, maintaining overvalued exchange rates
penalized those sectors dependent on exports, such as tourism and
manufacturing, and made imports more attractive. Excess domestic
demand, generated by below-equilibrium prices for foreign exchange, has had to be curbed through the application of import re-

strictions, fueling corruption, diverting the efficient allocation of resources, and reducing flexibility in resource allocations (Wheeler,
1984, p.12).

Exchange rate adjustments are an important instrument in stimulating trade and agriculture, and in reducing governmental budgetary
pressures. There is widespread skepticism on the short-term benefits
of devaluing exchange rates, given the limits to import reductions
and the slow-responding export sector. However, if exchange rate
adjustments are viewed as part of the long-term structural adjustment process, the systemic bias against trade and agriculture can
ultimately be removed. Protection of agricultural incomes and increases in the profitability of exports represent incentives in revitaliz-
ing the economies and fostering sustained economic growth.
Whereas devaluations tend to be inflationary in impact, in many
countries dependence on government subsidies, overvalued currencies, and recurrent budget deficits have been no less inflationary and
counter-growth.

TRADE RESTRICTIONS

Trade restrictions have also been widely used in sub-Saharan Africa, primarily as a means of protecting nascent industries against
foreign competitors. In a study of 31 developing countries, the World
Bank (1983, p. 63) found that in the subset of nine African countries,
four exhibited high distortions from protecting their domestic manufacturing sectors, with only two countries registering "low" distortions. By contributing to overvalued exchange rates, certain restrictions have also indirectly discouraged exports and agricultural
output.

Most countries invoke the "infant industry" argument in defense
of trade restrictions, as, ideally, these measures would allow for the
development of integrated industrial linkages. But recent experience
shows that in many instances, permanent infancy results from increased protection. Indeed, removing trade barriers alone does not
necessarily open domestic markets to foreign competition. The current limits on import capacity are sufficient to insulate a number of
domestic enterprises from foreign competition.

Import substitution industries, providing higher cost commodities
relative to unrestricted alternative supplies from foreign sources, depend upon transfers from other sectors—in effect, subsidies or foreign

capital inflows. With the decline of both of these areas, these industries are seriously jeopardized. More emphasis must be placed on raising domestic productivity and on reducing the costs of production. The latter can be accomplished through opening up markets to foreign competition by lowering tariffs and levying sales taxes for revenue purposes. In order to increase productivity, improvements will have to be made in training, management capacity, and infrastructure, including transport, power systems, and water.

Another aspect of trade liberalization involves reductions in import controls that have been imposed as a result of declining foreign exchange reserves. In the past, the artificially low cost of imports, due to overvalued exchange rates, produced severe excess demand for foreign exchange. As a result, rationing schemes were introduced by governments attempting to balance supply and demand pressures for foreign exchange (Wheeler, 1984, p. 9). While all countries have a policy on the allocation of foreign exchange earnings, in general, allocations have favored imports of capital goods, food, and raw materials.

In the face of foreign exchange shortages, many economies were slow in adjusting to the need to restrain import allocations. When they did, sizeable backlogs in applications for import licenses resulted, leading to crisis-oriented allocations and the proliferation of corruption. Whereas adjustment of the exchange rate will contribute toward reducing excess demand, recent experiences in Uganda have shown that flexible exchange rates do not alone produce desired development goals under conditions of extreme structural deterioration. The structure of imports favors luxury goods and flight of foreign exchange may result. Infrastructural support services, raw materials, and other basic goods needed for revamping the agricultural sector do not receive adequate allocations. Therefore, during the recovery period, some aggregate allocations will have to be made to stimulate growth in these priority areas. Once such allocations have been made, detailed controls should not be necessary as the adjusted exchange rate is allowed to affect the markets.

INTEREST RATES

Another problem widely cited is the effect of fairly constant or marginally rising nominal interest rates in the face of high inflation. Negative real interest rates have been prevalent in several countries, including Tanzania, Kenya, Ghana, Zaire, and Nigeria. These distortions have discouraged domestic savings and encouraged subsidization of investment, particularly in industry.

In tandem with overvalued exchange rates and low tariffs on capital goods imports, depressed real interest rates have fostered capital-intensive techniques and excess demand for credit. In those countries where excess demand for investments was met by foreign private capital or foreign aid, over time, the lack of recurrent resources to maintain capacity utilization resulted in declining returns on investment and in falling productivity rates.

In a study of 16 eastern and southern African countries (Gulhati and Datta, 1983), declines in investment rates and productivity were reflected in falling rates of growth. Furthermore, savings rates in these countries fell from the median level of 11.7 percent in 1973 to 7.7 percent in 1978. Although foreign capital inflows rose as a percent of total investment, as national savings dropped, investment growth slowed to 2.4 percent a year on average after 1973, from 6.4 percent prior to 1973. Incremental capital-output ratios (ICOR) increased from a median level of 4.3 for the period up to 1973, to 5.2 in the 1973–79 period. In a subset of countries including Ethiopia, Somalia, Zaire, Madagascar, Uganda, Zimbabwe, and Zambia, the median ICOR rose from 5.7 to 24.3, while Zaire, Uganda, and Zimbabwe registered negative ICORs.

For low income African countries, the rate of return on investment (the reciprocal of ICOR) declined from an average 24.6 percent in the 1960–70 period to an average of 10 percent in the following decade (World Bank, 1983, p. 38). Capacity underutilization, stemming from infrastructural constraints and inadequate supplies of raw material imports, was the key factor behind declines in investment productivity.

While positive real interest rates empirically failed to mobilize domestic savings in sub-Saharan Africa in the decade up to 1973 (income levels and financial intermediation at the margin were found to be more significant factors), when they turned negative in the high inflation period that followed, savings rates declined (Rwegasira, 1983, pp. 89–90). Low interest rates encouraged excessive borrowings, and mounting debt burdens, as governments attempted to bridge domestic financing gaps. Raising real interest rates will suffice to at least reduce the number of projects undertaken, particularly those with low rates of return.

COUNTER-CYCLICAL MANAGEMENT

Proper macro-economic management requires long-term measures that address issues of growth and development, and short-term counter-cyclical or stabilization policies that redress sudden fluctuations or shocks in the domestic market. Such demand management policies have been sorely underused in Africa over the past decade. In the steady growth period of 1960–70, few pressures warranted such measures. Most stabilization efforts were directed at offsetting losses in the mining and agricultural sectors due to climate-related declines in output or depressed world prices. Prior to 1970, many countries ran fiscal surpluses and inflation rates averaged 2.7 percent a year, with the terms of trade growing an average of 1.8 percent a year (World Bank, 1983). After the second oil price hike, world recession and declining terms of trade called for counter-cyclical demand management policies; in their absence, many of the effects of external shocks have been exacerbated.

The current situation is complex, as both structural adjustments and stabilization measures are required, but resistance to such reforms is widespread and implementation is difficult.[11] For example, while increased government spending is needed to break up bottlenecks, stabilization programs call for reducing fiscal deficits. In view of the weakened revenue base and rising debt-servicing obligations, it is no wonder that cutting budget deficits has proven to be the most difficult requirement of stabilization programs (Nelson, 1984, p. 991).

While government spending rose sharply when prices for primary commodities boomed in the mid-1970s, it failed to be adjusted downward in the bust period, adversely affecting the oil-importing countries in sub-Saharan Africa (World Bank, 1983, p. 22). As a result, governments resorted to financing their spending by borrowing, running deficits, or both; inflation rates accelerated as money supply expanded rapidly and production stagnated.[12]

Recurrent budget deficits as a percentage of GDP rose from –3.3 percent in 1972 to –5.9 percent in 1981 on average for all countries in sub-Saharan Africa (World Bank, 1983, p. 88). Subsequently, there have been numerous debt reschedulings in several countries. Overexpansionary fiscal policies can be attributed at least in part to the support of foreign donors who made resources available, often in grant form. In some instances, investments were unproductive as recurrent resources for maintaining capital utilization were unavailable. "White elephants" were the result.

Improved counter-cyclical management calls for restraining spending and building reserves during upswings, and reducing expenditures to levels that reflect available resources during downswings. Through such demand management policies, inflationary pressures and expectations can be moderated.

THE ROLE OF DONORS IN REFORMS

International organizations and bilateral donors have an important role to play in the initiation and implementation of policy reforms in Africa and have recently sought more direct involvement through their training programs, technical assistance, and policy dialogues (Nelson, 1984, p. 990). The current urgency of policy reform and the more favorable environment offer the best opportunity for these organizations to cooperate with specific countries in undertaking the necessary changes. In view of the vast sums these creditors have committed, it is imperative that they become involved in efforts to efficiently use the resources. However, it is absolutely necessary that the key "initiator" role be assumed by the concerned governments if reforms are to be sustained.

Bilateral and multilateral aid agencies have initiated reforms through two main channels: policy dialogues and conditionality. Both instruments have merits and shortcomings in achieving the desired results. Policy dialogues have been deemed to be politically preferable, as they involve less "interference" and recognize the government's ability to undertake independent action. However, in the absence of consensus, dialogues have produced delays. Given the depth of the current crisis, conditionality–"rewarding" those who undertake specified reforms–has increasingly become a means of instigating changes in policy. But conditionality should not be considered a substitute for the will and commitment to change if reforms are to be sustained. Purely imported reforms have limited effectiveness (Callaghy, 1984, p. 76). Moreover, the supervision costs to donors could be extremely high and frustrating if reforms are undertaken in an environment of unwillingness.

While conditionality in aid disbursements can be used to encourage change, the main impetus to reform must come from concerned governments. Working cooperatively rather than admonishing is central to donors' success in speeding up the process of economic change. The current situation calls for more active donor participation in policy formulation, but not as a substitute for local efforts and commitment.

Apart from the traditional areas of support–technical assistance and training–there is an increased need to support institutional reform. There is also a need to coordinate aid disbursements in order to ensure a balance between expanded capacities and recurrent resource availability. Available resources must also reach national priority areas and be efficiently utilized. This will require donor support for the improvement of technical capacity of ministries, and the channeling of their resources into programs that have already been adopted. Providing aid for projects that fall outside the accepted framework encourages irresponsible spending by local independent institutions, undermining the entire planning exercise and the efficient use of resources.

On the other hand, however, donors must agree on proposed programs. This can be achieved through coordinated dialogues with concerned governments on policy frameworks and determination of priority areas. Increased use of joint analysis with the host country can help thrash out key areas of disagreement. However, once an agreement is reached, donors and governments must abide by it, with flexibility limited to mutually agreed upon changes.

The success of policy reform in the long run depends on achieving some immediate results if political support is to continue. The process of getting prices right and removing structural bottlenecks and institutional barriers to growth and development will take a long time to bear results. To arrest further deterioration in the short term, therefore, a substantial injection of resources will be required. Such infusions will generate support for reform. Import capacity must be raised, and agricultural inputs, capital goods for industry, spare parts, and machinery for the rehabilitation and maintenance of infrastructure are needed to speed the process of structural adjustment. The required resources will depart from the traditional project-tied aid, supporting the utilization of current capacity, with new investments limited only to a few areas such as transport and storage (World Bank, 1984, p. 44).

SUPPORTING INSTITUTIONAL REFORMS

Donor support of reforms in agricultural marketing could be channeled toward strengthening voluntary cooperatives in marketing skills, financing, and training. It is critical that aid to these societies come from non-governmental sources in order to prevent the reemergence of government control. In addition to supporting cooperatives, donor assistance could be directed at expanding the ability of private traders to handle bulk volumes to promote economies of scale.

It is critically important that assistance be provided to improve infrastructure, especially transport, storage, and information collection and dissemination. By and large, infrastructural improvements will remain the responsibility of the state, but self-help schemes could be sparked by the provision of technical assistance at community levels. Continued support of industrial promotion institutions will help expand the activities of small-scale industries. Where cost considerations allow, construction of industrial estates for rental could be supported. Increased access to credit and the banking system, as well as support for the procurement of materials and marketing of products, would promote the development of more labor-intensive private or voluntary cooperative small-scale industries.

One important change in the disbursal of assistance is necessary if decentralization is to be achieved. The majority of aid thus far has been channeled through the central governments. However, there is a need to develop outlets through which assistance to non-governmental institutions, such as individual communities and organizations, can be provided. While the administrative cost advantages of dealing with one central institution, the Treasury, for example, are obvious, the independent development of non-governmental sectors can best be achieved if assistance to them is free of government control. In some cases, it might even be possible to offer assistance to cross-national and intercommunity programs, such as "sister city" projects, where urban councils or local government authorities in donor and recipient countries exchange ideas on how to raise revenues or manage expenditures.

Although donor support has to be focused on rehabilitating and increasing the utilization of installed capacity, some project-based support is still necessary in the area of infrastructure. Improvements in rural roads, development of small-scale irrigation schemes, and expansion of agricultural extension services are critical for increased agricultural productivity. Another area for productive project support is reforestation to curb the rapid deterioration of the environment, and especially desertification, which is progressing rapidly in both arid and semi-arid areas of the continent.

SUPPORT IN THE BUILD-UP OF TECHNICAL CAPACITY

Training and technical assistance must continue, but they should be reoriented toward a building of local capacity. As mentioned earlier, apprenticeships are an effective way of imparting practical skills, as well as providing local participants with insights into political-economic constraints.

It is also important that assistance be given to building local research capacity. Collaborative research with institutions in donor countries would complement traditional funding support. Statistical bureaus require support in the training of technical staff and infrastructural facilities for collection, compilation, and dissemination of data. In most cases, continuation of support by various international and bilateral agencies in setting up a national statistical system is required. There is also the need to acquire hard and software for analysis of data and to reduce the time lag between completion of surveys and the publication of results. Many countries still depend on facilities abroad for policy and planning purposes.

In order to provide more continuity and effectiveness in practical training of various technical cadres, specialists working for donor agencies could be given longer assignments. This would help them to acquire a better feel for political-economic conditions, and thus increase their potential effectiveness in advisory roles.

CONCLUSIONS

The current economic deterioration in sub-Saharan Africa has partly been caused by internal economic mismanagement. Wide state intervention in the productive spheres and in markets for resources and products has led to inefficient use of scarce resources not only in the "Pareto efficiency" sense, but also in relation to the development goals adopted by those countries. Serious biases against the development of the export and agricultural sectors have produced stagnant economic growth, arrested social development, increased dependence on food imports, and debt burdens requiring frequent reschedulings. Indeed, the current balance of payments crisis prevailing in African economies, rooted in this structural bias, has been exacerbated by the external shocks of the late 1970s and early 1980s. Protected import substitution industries have not produced the anticipated results, as resource constraints became binding and productivity declined. Instead, the process of industrialization has generated debt burdens and fueled inflation.

Economic deterioration has also undermined state control over economic spheres. Price controls and quantitative restrictions have become increasingly superfluous as parallel markets and corruption are rampant. Rapid expansion of public enterprises is not sustainable as they have become budgetary burdens and a damper on growth. Expansion in public sector employment now faces serious constraints due to reductions in transfer resources from the key productive sectors and foreign aid. Thus the very basis on which patron-client political networks were traditionally served has been undermined.

It is in light of these experiences that policy change is inevitable. The current political-economic situation is not sustainable, but political constraints to change do exist. Nevertheless, the professed distribution of resources and power among various groups has been eroded and a more malleable situation has emerged as unofficial adjustments are being made by different groups in reaction to changing conditions. The changing political calculus is not, however, uniform across the countries. In those countries in which there is little state intervention, fewer changes will have to be made. Structural reforms are less drastic and elites are invariably more accommodative to the recommendations of international financial institutions. For those countries in which state management of markets and participation in productive spheres has been more intensive, departures from the status quo are more dramatic on the surface, but, nevertheless, unofficial activities have largely begun the process of reform.

The main changes required are getting prices right, undertaking institutional reforms, and reducing the size of the public sector to a level commensurate with effective state managerial capacity. Structural adjustments of these economies are long-term undertakings and although stabilization efforts are currently required, they should not form the backbone of reform.

An appreciation of these points will help governments carry out sustained reform programs without necessarily raising high expectations for spectacular short-term results. However, there is a need for some immediate resources and efforts to arrest the trend of deterioration and to reduce hostility and political constraints to reform. This is an interim measure since sustained growth can only be achieved through structural adjustment.

The role of donors in reform efforts includes providing an "interim" injection of resources to raise import capacities, supplying technical and training assistance, and supporting policy and institutional reforms through advice and dialogue with specific governments. The catalytic role in initiating and sustaining reforms is as important as the traditional supportive role as long as it remains clear that the main actor in the process of change is the concerned country. Better coordination among donors will ensure more rational and efficient use of resources and strengthen consistency in planning. Project support by donors in infrastructure, especially in the rehabilitation of the transport system and basic social infrastructure, is of critical importance for revamping the agricultural sector and increasing productivity of investment.

As the UN's review of the "Critical Economic Situation in Africa" (1984:44) suggests, "It will now be necessary to move forward from reflection to concrete action. In this transition, Africa should not stand alone: Its economy is still too fragile to withstand the enormous stresses of moving from crisis to reconstruction and development."

NOTES

1. The World Bank's 1981 report, Accelerated Development in Sub-Saharan Africa, and Toward Sustained Development in sub-Saharan Africa (1984), have placed much emphasis on internal policy reforms to correct structural deficiencies and to reduce negative impacts of external shocks. David Wheeler's study (1984) has attempted to estimate the costs of internal mismanagement for several economies in sub-Saharan Africa and provides strong statistical evidence of significant foregone growth exceeding 2 percent per annum for 16 out of 24 countries studied. There is also a general consensus among bilateral and international aid agencies that improved efficiency and effectiveness in macro-economic management would significantly increase resource productivity.

2. Structural issues have been stressed in the joint report by the African Development Bank and the Economic Commission for Africa (1984), ECA study (1983) and by several specific studies commissioned or undertaken by individual countries, such as the Structural Adjustment Programme (Tanzania Government, 1982), Sessional Papers no. 10, and the more recent no. 4 of 1982 (Kenya Government).

3. In his study of Ivory Coast, Cohen (1974) concludes that access to government is very critical in the accumulation of private property and power.

4. Sandbrook (1982) distinguishes three main typologies prevalent in Africa: neo-colonialist regimes (e.g., Ivory Coast) dominated by foreign capital interests with a relatively weak role for domestic interest groups; "nationalist" regimes with dominant domestic/national interests and a mixture of

private and state capitalism; and "national collectivist" regimes aspiring to transition to socialism.

5. Nelson (1984), citing case studies of Ghana, Kenya, and Zambia among others, stresses the important role political cost/benefit of economic reforms plays in both the "will" to initiate and sustain reform programs.

6. In a report by Club du Sahel/CILSS, "Marketing Price Policy and Storage of Food Grains in the Sahel," for example, it is pointed out that despite government efforts to dominate food marketing through parastatal monopolies in Mali, Senegal, Niger, Chad, and Burkina Faso, these monopolies actually handle only a third or less of food produced and marketed domestically. Similar proportions were obtained in Tanzania (Ellis, 1982).

7. See note 6 above.

8. Barbara Lewis (1980, p. 115) emphasizes this point in her paper when she writes that the origin of barriers to private sector development in agricultural marketing (in West Africa) predates national independence. Colonial policy and practice favored French commercial houses and Lebanese merchants and also set up public institutions which limited the scope of private African merchants. The following independence governments expanded the role of public agencies reducing private traders' market share, at times reducing them to largely clandestine activity. Thus private trading systems remained underdeveloped in terms of specialization, quality control, and market integration. The situation in East Africa was quite similar under colonial rule.

9. Lofchie and Cummins (1982, p. 24) argue that one of the most important problems confronting peasant movements in Africa is to overcome rural-urban conflicts over food policies. The realization of (organized) power would assist in the creation of effective channels of communication with government agencies, and with organizations representing the interests of the urban-based social classes.

Again, Grindle and the Temples (in Grindle, 1980) agree separately that the most promising means of increasing the ability of popular sectors to receive benefits from public policies is through direct organization.

10. The potential of indigenous private industrial entrepreneurship is still largely unknown. Although case studies are available on small-scale private industries, the capacity of the indigenous private sector to undertake large-scale ventures remains unassessed. It is also not clear whether the private sector would escape the political, social, and ethnic calculus which has impinged on efficiency in the public sector.

11. Nelson (1984, p. 989) makes the same point when she writes that exogenous shocks and cumulative ill effects of domestic policies have been concentrated in the decade since 1974 with implications of complex and difficult policies. The fairly brisk growth of the first decade of independence has not provided experience on stabilization management.

12. UNECA, "Survey of Economic Conditions in Africa 1979–80" puts the average annual rate of increase in money supply in the post-1972 period at 25.8 percent per annum compared to the average of 13.6 percent during 1967–72. Given deceleration in real growth, this higher rate of monetary expansion fueled inflation.

REFERENCES

ADB and ECA. 1984. *Economic Report on Africa, 1984.*

Andreou, P. 1977. "An Economic Appraisal of the Role of Cooperative Institutions in Different Economic and Political Systems," in Andreou, P.
(ed.), *Cooperative Institutions and Economic Development in Developed and
Developing Nations: Selected International Readings in the Economics, Marketing and Management of Cooperative Institutions and Their Role in Economic
Development.* Nairobi: East African Literature Bureau.

Bates, R. H. 1981. *Markets and States in Tropical Africa.* Berkeley: University of
California.

Bates, R.H. 1983. *Essays on the Political Economy of Rural Africa.* Cambridge:
Cambridge University Press.

Beveridge, W.A and M. R. Kelly. 1980. "Fiscal Content of Financial Programs
Supported by Stand-by Arrangements in Upper Credit Tranches, 1969–
78," *IMF Staff Papers* (June) 7 (2).

Bienen, H. and V. P. Diejomaoh, eds. 1980. *The Political Economy of Income
Distribution in Nigeria.* New York: Holmes and Meier Publishers.

Blues, N. and J. H. Weaver. 1977. "A Critical Assessment of the Tanzanian
Model of Development." *Agricultural Council Reprints.*

Callaghy, Thomas M. 1984. "Africa's Debt Crisis," *Journal of International
Affairs* 38: 61–79.

Cleaves, S. 1980. "Implementation Amidst Scarcity and Apathy: Political
Power and Policy Design," in Grindle, M.S., ed., *Politics and Policy Implementation in the Third World.* Princeton: Princeton University Press.

Cohen, M. 1974. *Urban Policy and Political Conflict: A Study of Ivory Coast.*
Chicago: University of Chicago Press.

Delancey, M. W. 1980. "Cameroon National Food Policies and Organizations: The Green Revolution and Structural Proliferation." *Journal of African Studies* 7(2).

ECA. 1981. "Survey of Economic Conditions in Africa 1979–80." Freetown.

ECA. 1983. *ECA and Africa's Development 1983–2008: A Preliminary Perspective
Study.* Addis Ababa.

Ellis, Frank. 1982. "Agricultural Price Policy in Tanzania," *World Development*
10(4).

Grindle, S., ed. 1980. *Politics and Policy Implementation in the Third World.*
Princeton: Princeton University Press.

Gulhati, R. and G. Datta. 1983. "Capital Accumulation in Eastern and Southern Africa: A Decade of Setbacks," *World Bank Staff Working Papers,* no.
562.

Jones, D.B. 1982. "State Structures in New Nations: The Case of Primary
Agricultural Marketing in Africa," *Journal of Modern African Studies* 20(4).

Kuria, M. Chege. "The Role of Cooperatives in Agricultural Development of
Small Scale Farmers," in Andreou, P., ed. op. cit.

Lewis, Barbara C. 1980. "Political Variables and Food Price Policy in West
Africa," paper prepared for the USAID.

Lewis, S., Jr. 1984. "Africa's Development and the World Economy," background paper prepared for the Committee on African Development Strategies.

Lofchie, M. and K. Cummins. 1982. "Food Deficits and Agricultural Policies in Tropical Africa," *Journal of Modern African Studies* 20(1).

McKinlay, R. and A. Cohan. 1975. "A Comparative Analysis of Political and Economic Performance of Military and Civilian Regimes," *Comparative Politics* (October) 8(1).

McKinlay, R. and A. Cohan. July 1976. "The Economic Performance of Military Regimes: A Cross-National Aggregate Data Study," *The British Journal of Politics* (July) 6(3).

Nelson, J. M. 1984. "The Political Economy of Stabilization: Commitment, Capacity, and Public Response," *World Development* 12(10).

Reichmann, T. and R. Stillson. 1977. "How Successful are Programs Supported by Standby Arrangements," *Finance and Development* (March) 14 (1).

Rondinelli, D. A. 1981. "Administrative Decentralization and Economic Development: The Sudan's Experiment with Devolution," *Journal of Modern African Studies* 19(4).

Rwegasira, R. 1983. "Adjustment Policies in Low-Income Africa: An Interpretation of the Kenyan and Tanzanian Experiences, 1974–78," IMF mimeo.

Sandbrook, R. 1982. *The Politics of Basic Needs: Urban Aspects of Assaulting Poverty in Africa*. London: Heinemann.

Stewart, B. A. 1980. "Peanut Marketing in Niger," *Journal of African Studies* 7(2).

Wheeler, D. 1984. "Sources of Stagnation in Sub-Saharan Africa," *World Development* 12(11).

World Bank. 1981. *Accelerated Development in Sub-Saharan Africa: An Agenda For Action*. Washington, D.C.: The World Bank

World Bank. 1983. *World Development Report, 1983*. Oxford: Oxford University Press.

World Bank. 1984. *World Development Report, 1984*. Oxford: Oxford University Press.

World Bank. 1984. *Toward Sustained Development in Sub-Saharan Africa: A Joint Program of Action*. Washington, D.C.: The World Bank.

PART II

THE PEOPLE AND THE LAND

CHAPTER FOUR

Guarding Africa's Renewable Resources

Lloyd Timberlake

By mid-1985, a continent-wide calamity had left some 30 million Africans in 20 nations unable to feed themselves and had forced 10 million people to leave their homes in search of food and water. While often described as "environmental," the crisis was largely the result of poor policy decisions on the part of both African governments and donor and aid agencies.

In nations where over half of the population lives in the rural areas, governments have invested disproportionate amounts of financial support in the cities and their inhabitants. Examples abound. In Ghana and the Gambia, 64 and 82 percent of their populations, respectively, live in the countryside. Yet between 1978 and 1982, domestic agricultural spending in both countries declined by more than 10 percent a year (FAO, 1983).

An FAO study which looked at domestic per capita spending on agriculture found that for 17 African countries, such spending declined by 0.1 percent per year over 1978–82, whereas in all other regions of the developing world, it rose—by 7.3 percent in the Far East, by 3 percent in Latin America, and by 1.9 percent in the Near East (FAO, 1984).

Institutionalized rural poverty has played a major role in the so-called environmental crisis. Rural populations, with little to invest, have been depleting the natural resource base faster than it can be regenerated. The poor impoverish the land and the poor land further impoverishes those who rely upon it. This downward spiral has led

111

to environmental bankruptcy in some regions of Africa.

Describing Africa's "renewable resource" crisis poses a semantical problem. Environmentalists refer to the crisis as "environmental," while agronomists and others refer to it as "agricultural." Both are correct. While few of Africa's farmers are purely in the subsistence sector—completely uninvolved in the marketplace—the vast majority survive on the "environment" or the renewable resource base.

Most of a family's food comes directly from the ground, and perhaps some from livestock. Its energy comes from the ground in the form of fuelwood. [Trees supply well over 90 percent of the total energy used in poorer countries and 80 percent even in oil-rich Nigeria (Timberlake, 1985).] Its water comes directly from the ground or from streams and lakes—all of which rely to some extent on the protection afforded by trees and other greenery.

In Africa, the environmental crisis, renewable resource crisis, and agricultural crisis are one and the same, resulting in a threat to survival. Governments have tended to emphasize the gross national product rather than the "green national product," little of which is ever figured into the official GNP, but which is actually more important to the lives of most citizens. Efforts to put Africa's agriculture on a sustainable basis amount to steps toward preserving the environment. More important, conservation of environmental resources is a first step toward sustainable agriculture.

DESERTIFICATION

Resource degradation in Africa is often equated with "desertification." A number of ecologists and geographers are losing patience with this term because it is scientifically imprecise. A recent World Bank report defines it simply as "a process of sustained decline of the biological productivity of arid and semi-arid land" (Gorse, 1985). Most of Africa's arable land is semi-arid (Avery, 1985).

Since the UN Environment Programme's 1977 Conference on Desertification, most definitions of desertification emphasize the human role in causing it. Indeed, the recent World Bank report took the position that "desertification is a complex, still poorly understood process. . .caused by interactions between drought and human abuse of the environment." British environmentalist Alan Grainger put even more blame on human actions: "Drought triggers a crisis, but does not cause it. Overcultivation and overgrazing weaken the land, allowing no margin when drought arrives. Thus high human pressure will continue during the drought, leading ultimately to even greater and more visible damage to the land and the deaths of large numbers of people" (Grainger, 1982). This view suggests that while the roots of Africa's crisis may not be environmental, environmental degradation deepens any crisis and makes people more vulnerable to the next natural shock.

In 1984, UNEP assessed progress in countering desertification and found virtually none. Desertification of rainfed croplands and dry forest woodlands was accelerating across the Sudano-Sahelian region, while accelerating or continuing in the region's rangelands and irrigated lands. South of the Sahel, desertification was accelerating in rangelands, rainfed croplands, and woodlands, and holding constant at best in irrigated areas. Nowhere was there progress in containing desertification over a wide area (Walls, 1984).

Equally disturbing, the assessment was largely guesswork because so few nations had any idea of the rates at which they were losing productive lands, despite considerable investment in such studies by the UN. UNEP Executive Director Mostafa Tolba complained: "Assessments of the problem have generally not been made nor have national priorities been established" (UNEP, 1984).

Harold Dregne (1983) summed up the political approach to desertification: "Governments do not see desertification as a high priority item. Rangeland deterioration, accelerated soil erosion, and salinization and waterlogging do not command attention until they become crisis items. Lip service is paid to combating desertification but the political will is directed elsewhere. There seems to be little appreciation that a major goal of many developing nations—food self-sufficiency—cannot be attained if soil and plant resources are allowed to deteriorate."

The direct causes of desertification are usually identified as overgrazing, overcultivation, and deforestation. Yet poorly planned and maintained irrigation schemes can also cause desertification as land becomes waterlogged and salinized. While this problem is not extensive in Africa—evident only in Egypt, South Africa, and Sudan, with more than one million irrigated hectares each—it is a big problem in terms of wasted money and opportunities. In 1982, more than one-sixth of all project aid to the Sahel was going for irrigation, yet irrigated land was going out of production due to salinization and water-logging as fast as new land was being irrigated (Grainger, 1982).

SOIL CONSERVATION AND THE REALITIES OF AID

Many solutions to overcultivation focus on intensification of agriculture—getting more produce from a given area of land—in a continent where most systems have traditionally been extensive and where rapid population growth has spilled over to more marginal land. Irrigation offers hope only for the very long term because of problems of high initial investment, recurrent costs, and demographic mismatches—the densest rural populations are often far from areas that can be irrigated.

A World Bank report found that 20,000 new hectares a year could be irrigated effectively in the Sahel and Sudano-Sahelian zones by the mid-1990s, but the number of farming families that would be accommodated by this extension would equal only one-half of the current annual population growth rate in the region (Gorse, 1985).

Getting more without overtaxing the land will depend on individual farmers finding solutions they can afford, such as no-till or low-till cropping, mixed cropping, agro-forestry techniques, water-harvesting, small-scale irrigation, and efficient recycling of crop residues and dung. Many of these technologies are widely tested and understood, though all will need more reserach before being of use in many locations in Africa.

Constraints to on-farm research into these techniques tend to be political rather than scientific. After the 1968–73 Sahel drought, Sahelian and donor governments agreed on food self-sufficiency as a national goal. Yet of the over $11 billion in development aid which went into the region between 1974 and 1982, only 4 percent went to rainfed food crops, and only 1.5 percent went to projects for soil and water conservation and ecological stabilization which would make food self-sufficiency a realistic goal (Giri, 1984).

Governments often appear to be working toward short-term goals which can never be realized because of degraded resource bases. Many African government have relied on exports of agricultural commodities to earn foreign exchange and balance budgets, while the soil is gradually losing its fertility. Egyptian biologist Mohammed Kassas, former president of the International Union for Conservation of Nature and Natural Resources (IUCN), has found that measures to fight desertificaiton are simply incompatible with "rational" financial strategies. In Egypt, the reclamation of one hectare of desertified land costs about $13,000. Yet if deposited in a bank, such a sum of money could earn about $1500 per year in interest. Land "can never give those returns," Kassas noted (Timberlake, 1984).

Donors are no less short-sighted. Though their provision of aid increases purchases by African countries of donor countries' goods, the nature of aid programs per se does little to improve the ability of countries to buy. Britain cut bilateral aid for projects of direct benefit to African agriculture by about one-third in real terms between 1979 and 1984, while maintaining aid to rural road-building and power projects which may benefit agriculture indirectly but benefit British suppliers and contractors directly (All Party Parliamentary Group on Overseas Development, 1985).

In 1985, Canada was tying 80 percent of its bilateral aid to the purchase of Canadian products and was working to increase this figure (Sabatier, 1985). While generous with relief aid, the United States focused more aid where there were "free market" approaches, for military support, or for politically motivated reasons (Shepherd, 1985). Aid for agriculture and rural development from all the Organization for Economic Cooperation and Development nations fell by 20 percent in real terms between 1980 and 1983 (Madeley, 1985).

There are other constraints to investing in the environment. British development analyst Piers Blaikie has compiled a list of essential elements of conservation programs, comparing each item on his list with the realities of the ways in which aid agencies and recipient governments approach such programs. The two columns line up as opposites. Conservation requires efforts over many years, perhaps a decade, but aid-financed or government-run conservation projects require measureable benefits within three to five years. Success in conservation requires diverse, timely, and highly coordinated inputs, but projects usually work through only one ministry. The output of a successful conservation project will be diffuse and difficult to measure, but executing agencies must have quantifiable benefits predicted at the proposal stage. Success requires sustained political will by the central government; projects on the other hand are run through short-term consultancies, usually one to three years (Blaikie, 1985).

One program which has recently been praised in development circles is soil conservation efforts undertaken by the Swedish International Development Authority (SIDA) in Kenya. Having allegedly benefited half the farmers in Kenya, this program has been underway for 10 years, a time frame over which most other Western development agencies will have changed their fashions, philosophies, goals, and even country emphases several times.

WHERE ARE THE ANTHROPOLOGISTS?

Anthropologists have been underutilized in development efforts because their views are often an embarrassment. They are prone to look carefully at the socio-political realities of a project and offer a reasoned explanation of why a project is unlikely to work. In reality, aid project documents typically begin with a page uncritically praising a given recipient government's dedication to rural development and people, and then launch into the technicalities of the project.

Anthropologists and sociologists often feel "that their findings are cast in a negative light—that certain conservation measures will not succeed or will actually do harm—and also that they are frequently overridden or relegated to writing a disparate chapter in a project document or report entitled 'Social constraints to soil and water conservation'" (Blaikie, 1985). Sociologists are often forced into the role of public relations officers, required to persuade the local population to go along with something forced upon them from outside.

Two senior workers at Britain's Overseas Development Administration identified ignorance of what farmers were doing and their motives for doing so as the major causes of disappointing results after a decade of work on integrated rural development projects across Africa (Morris and Gwyer, 1983). The two offer many examples, but in projects in Malawi, Swaziland, and Tanzania, research into local farming methods was not begun until after the projects were initiated.

The science of anthropology is not a cure-all for development mistakes. In fact, natural scientists are justified in complaining that anthropologists spend too much time on marriage customs and kinship links and not enough on current problems, and that they often avoid political realities.

Yet an anthropologist's approach—rooting change in already existing human resources—seems to be the soundest way to bring about change. It has proven very difficult to get farmers to suddenly begin planting trees in large numbers. One of the most successful of such efforts was carried out in Haiti by an anthropologist who, in his own words, "did not know which end of the tree to put into the ground." Former attempts to implement afforestation programs had failed. Paid to plant trees, farmers let their goats eat them so they would be paid to plant more. Told that the government owned all the trees, farmers cut them so the government would have no claim to their land.

Anthropologist Gerald Murray studied Haitian smallholders. He found that farmers owned their own land, even though their plots were small. He found that most were engaged in small-scale market gardening and sold small quantities of beans or corn. He also found a large national market for charcoal. He suggested that trees be encouraged as a cash crop. Put in charge of the program by the Pan American Development Foundation, Murray set up a distribution system, giving trees to peasants who planted at least 500. His workers advised on species and intercropping techniques, but left technical choices to the peasants, only encouraging them to cut and sell for cash after about four years (Timberlake, 1983). Between 1981 and 1984, 20,000 farmers planted 13 million trees, and it was expected that 16 million, double the original goal, would be planted by the project's end (International Task Force, 1985).

One does not need to be an anthropologist to base one's actions on local human resources. One of the most often cited tree-planting successes in Africa, funded by the private voluntary organization CARE, involved the planting of 400 kilometers of double-row windbreaks to protect some 4000 hectares of cropland from wind erosion. These trees not only conserve soil, but provide fuelwood and building poles when pruned. The project was initiated in 1974 by a Nigerien forester and a Peace Corps volunteer; the forester had been the area's forestry extension agent for years. CARE established nurseries, dug wells, purchased fencing, and paid people to guard young trees from livestock for the first three years after planting. The labor was done by farmers, principally traditional young men's groups called "samaria." Initial studies of the project suggest it has increased grain yields by 23 percent.

CARE attributes success (which took some eight years) to several factors: the forester's rapport with the villagers; the backing of local authorities; the project's response to a problem the villagers had identified themselves; and its small scale, expanding only after initial encouraging results (Kramer, 1985). CARE did not list among these factors choice of species or expertise in forestry and soil conservation techniques.

In fact, the much-praised success of many private voluntary organizations (PVOs) in Africa is based on an anthropological approach: cooperation with local people, basing projects on farmers' perceived needs, changing plans according to local priorities. In praising PVOs as the most effective agencies in the campaign against desertification, UNEP said in 1984: "Their high record of success is related to the small-scale and local direction of their projects and the requirements for local community participation, as well as their flexibility in operation and their ability to learn from earlier mistakes. The dominance of field activities gives these actions an impact out of proportion to the money invested" (UNEP, 1984).

According to this description, governmental and multilateral development agencies suffer from overly large scales, direction by outsiders, lack of local participation, inflexibility, and an inability to learn from mistakes. The only way to resuscitate the environment is through individual farmers. Until large aid agencies can include anthropologists, or better still, soil, water, and forestry technocrats who are willing to implement their projects with local people, little aid will get to the grass roots upon which African agriculture is based.

TREES FOR THE FORESTS

Trees outside of those in forests provide most of Africa's fuelwood, and thus most of Africa's energy for cooking and heating. Often described as "bush" or "scrub" of "open forest savannah," these trees tend to be omitted in official accounts because they are not in forests. There was a time when they were classified by foresters in West Africa as "brousse inutile"—useless bush. These trees not only play a role in conserving soil and water, but also provide considerable amounts of food and fodder, and thus are under pressure both from fuelwood cutting and from clearing land for agriculture.

Improved woodburning stoves may make homes safer and healthier, but a study by Earthscan raises serious questions as to whether they are likely to save many trees (Foley et al, 1984). Farming families have little incentive to buy stoves as long as the three-stone fire and its fuel—wood and crop residues—remain free. As local wood supplies dwindle, people use wood more sparingly for fires. Metal stoves tend to be too expensive for agencies to give away, while mud stoves tend to fall apart in six months to a year.

Yet, given the difficulties in getting farmers to conserve fuelwood or plant trees for fuelwood, it becomes increasingly clear how important fuelwood is as a determinant of carrying capacity in dryland areas. A World Bank report (Gorse, 1985) has concluded that in the Sahelian climatic zone—defined here as the northern limit of cultivation south to the 350mm rainfall isohyet—the sustainable human population in terms of crop and livestock production is seven people per square kilometer. The sustainable population in terms of fuelwood production, however, is only one person per square kilometer. In the Sudano-Sahelian belt (350 to 600mm of rainfall per year), crop and livestock production can sustain 15 people per square kilometer, but fuelwood can sustain only 10 people per square kilometer. The report finds that "the natural forest cover is therefore the most vulnerable part of the ecosystem."

Farmers are more easily persuaded to plant trees for agricultural purposes than strictly for fuelwood purposes. The development of various types of agroforestry for specific locations—alley cropping, intercropping, contour rows of trees, and even more effective forest fallow systems—will spur such agriculture-related tree planting. Of course, a side benefit of the conservation is increased supplies of fuelwood and building poles.

The loss of enclosed forests, especially the moist tropical forests of West Africa and the Zaire basin, is a different problem. The major cause of losses here is not fuelwood gathering, but mismanagement of logging, unsustainable rates of logging, and clearing for agricultural land. Only in exceptional cases such as central Tanzania where fuelwood is needed for tobacco curing are forests disappearing to provide energy. Ivory Coast, Africa's biggest timber exporter, saw the area of its closed forest decline by two-thirds between 1956 and 1977, with agriculture destroying 4.5 times more than logging, a ratio which may be similar in other forested parts of Africa (Timberlake, 1985). Ivory Coast's timber exports, which earned foreign exchange worth over $300 million in 1980, are expected to begin to fall before the end of the decade. Nigeria was once a timber exporter, but has now banned exports and may have to start importing to meet domestic needs. Cameroon is logging at a rate which would clear its forests in 90 years, but there are plans to double this rate.

There is hope for the future as governments realize that overlogging their forests is bad business, and that there is more long-term profit to be made from sound, sustainable management. Techniques for such management exist, and there are signs that they are being adopted. Over the past two decades, Zambia has established industrial plantations which it believes can meet its projected industrial timber needs through the end of the century. By 1983, over 45,000 hectares of plantations, mainly pines and eucalyptus, were established, helping "to reduce pressure on the country's diminishing natural forests and developing a highly productive source of round-wood needed in its copper mines and other industries" (International Task Force, 1985).

Another hope is that African governments and foreign agricultural advisers will learn and then stress the value of natural forests in watershed protection and thus to agriculture near these forests. Perhaps the most spectacular example of such natural protection is in Rwanda, Africa's most densely populated country. Efforts by international conservation groups to save the 12,000-hectare Parc des Volcans on the Zaire border centered around convincing Rwandans of the role these forested mountains play in soaking up annual rainfall and releasing it slowly for agricultural use. Clearing would have led to cycles of flood and water scarcity below the mountains, and would have provided enough agricultural land to support only two months' national population increase.

Yet governments have been slow to learn. In early 1985, Kenya's minister of environment and natural resources announced that 17,000 hectares of Kenya's natural forests in 10 districts would be cleared for government tea plantations. Some of this clearing was to be done on the slopes of Mt. Kenya, and foresters were predicting erosion and reduced groundwater on and below those slopes. Kenya already suffers severe fuelwood deficits, and only 3 percent of the nation remains under natural forest (*New Scientist*, 1985).

Unsustainable rates of logging and land clearances raise the suspicion that the exploitation of natural resources by some African states may be due in part to high debts and the desperate need for foreign exchange. If true, a charitable approach to Africa's debt burden may be one of the most effective ways in which donor governments can help Africa safeguard its natural resources. Other ways include education in sound forest management and techniques of watershed protection and rehabilitation.

THE HERDS AND HERDERS

Some 15 to 24 million people in Africa depend on livestock-based incomes. Most of them inhabit the drylands—across the Sahel and through the Horn of Africa to the semi-arid lands of East and southern Africa. The vast majority of these people rely on natural forage rather than on cultivated fodders and pastures, and in the drylands they must move to keep their herds supplied with food.

The nomadic pastoralist system makes a tremendous amount of sense. In areas where natural resources are scarce, the system allows humans to move through those resources, harvesting them and "storing" them in the bodies of their mobile livestock. It may be the only and the most effective way of making a living in land too dry for cropping. Kenyan ecologist David Western has conducted studies in southern Kenya which suggest that nomadic pastoralism is a more efficient way of exploiting dryland savannah than the as-yet unrealized potential of "game ranching." "Contrary to commonly held views, the results do not show natural wildlife ecosystems to be more efficient than pastoralist-dominated systems; quite the opposite in fact. Both appear more efficient than commercial systems" (Western, 1984).

Yet no sector of African agriculture has been as badly treated by development efforts as nomadic pastoralism. African governments find nomads difficult to tax, educate, draft into the armed services, and generally to control. They are suspicious of large numbers of people who traditionally travel armed and who have more respect for ecosystems than for national boundaries. Countries such as Niger have traditionally suspected "nationalistic tendencies" on the part of the Fulani people.

The wet years in the early 1960s, before drought set in, encouraged settled farmers to migrate northward from their usual zones in the south. When drought began in the late 1960s, nomads found their usual refuges in the wetter south blocked by settled agricultural development. Other types of agricultural development took rangelands from herders elsewhere in Africa. For example, the development of the Awash River basin in Ethiopia for cash crops in the late 1960s led to widespread famine among the Afar pastoralists in both 1973–74 and 1984–85.

Because there has been very little offtake from the nomadic herds in terms of increasing GNP or providing domestic protein intake or beef exports, pastoralists have had very low standing with both their governments and aid agencies. Together with other factors, this has led to a widespread policy of "sedentarization"—the encouraged or enforced settlement of nomads.

If nomads settle, but maintain their large herds in dry areas, rapid desertification often results, and when drought occurs, large losses of livestock are incurred because of starvation rather than lack of water. After studying the effects of sedentarization, UNESCO's Integrated Project on Arid Lands in northern Kenya concluded that "it will only be possible to increase human welfare of pastoralists and to stop desertification if the mobility and dispersion of livestock can again be increased considerably, and if overall numbers of livestock can be better controlled through a greatly improved marketing system" (Lusigi and Glaser, 1984).

Fitting pastoralist societies into national development strategies will pose a problem for governments. Solutions will depend on their willingness to decentralize their authority to more traditional social organizations. Work by British rangeland expert Jeremy Swift and USAID's Niger Range and Livestock Project has shown that pastoralist societies can be organized into collectives that are responsible for the bulk purchasing of essential goods that link pastoralist groups to the local government.

Improved beef marketing systems are not likely in the near future. Pastoralists will have little reason to sell large numbers of animals until the consumer items they require are made available to them. With the large distances between nomadic pastoralists and trading centers, governments may have to settle for the more realistic goal of keeping citizens healthy and employed in livelihoods in regions where no other economic strategies work.

International aid agencies and the UN system have made a sudden about-face in their views of pastoralists. The 1968–73 Sahel drought caused agencies to focus on developing herds with the hope of turning the Sahel into a "meat-basket" for the region. The failure of these ambitions is documented by the abandoned abattoirs and fattening pens that litter the region. The confusion of agency goals were summed up by Dr. Michael Horowitz of the State University of New York in 1979: "Livestock projects have been supposed, simultaneously, to increase productivity, reverse the ecological deterioration of the range, shift production from dairy to a beef orientation, improve producer income and quality of life, maintain a regular supply of cheap meat for the internal market, and increase the supply of high-quality meat to the export market" (quoted in Timberlake, 1985).

Subsequently, agencies acted as though the large herds did not exist, or that they were a major cause of desertification. Recently, agencies have shown an understanding of the need to return to basic principles. In 1985, USAID set up a committee of rangeland experts to try to determine what was not known about African rangeland management, and what the research priorities were.

CONSERVATION

While it may seem trivial to consider the problems of Africa's national parks and other protected areas at a time when human lives and livelihoods are threatened, the issue of wildlife conservation raises some principles that apply to resource protection in general. First, conservationists' arguments that wild areas must be preserved because of the "genetic resources" they contain or may eventually be found to contain do not impress Africa or other Third World governments. Governments are being asked to spend money on conserving species which primarily benefit industrial countries.

Indonesia's vice-president, Adam Malik, perhaps best summed up the Third World view when he asked: "How much land for the hungry today? And how much for genetic resources to be preserved for tomorrow? In the past, we have neither received a fair share of the benefits, nor have we received a fair share of assistance—other than inexpensive advice or even more inexpensive criticism—in the efforts to save the common global natural heritage. Unless such responsibilities are equally shared, all our good intentions will only lead to global environmental destruction" (Malik, 1982).

Although much of the encouragement and cash for basic wildlife conservation in Africa will have to continue to be provided by the North, African governments have been willing to invest in conservation when it is connected to tourist revenue. As a result of the influx of tourists, however, the fauna of some of the popular parks are under pressure. In preserving areas for tourism, governments have posted armed guards to keep out the locals, and revenues generated by these areas go into national coffers.

The few experiments so far attempted at directing this revenue to local people—giving them a direct stake in protecting the parks—have borne fruit and suggested ways to proceed. The Zimbabwe government developed an anti-poaching scheme called "Operation Windfall" in Chizaria National Park and the Chirisa Safari Area west of Harare. Basically, the proceeds of elephant culling—sales of meat and ivory—were diverted to two local councils who used it as they saw fit—for schools, clinics, and local transport. Between early 1981 and June 1982, the councils received $960,000. Elephant poaching dropped so dramatically that the parks department found it no longer necessary to post wardens in the areas (Side, 1982).

A complex agreement between the Kenyan government and the Maasai herders who have traditionally depended on the Amboseli National Park for dry season grazing gives the Maasai some tourist revenue from the park, compensates them for cattle lost to wild predators, and has established watering points outside the park for the Maasai livestock. The effort, though it continues to be adjusted and refined, is credited with doubling the rhino population in the park between 1977 and 1983, and increasing the number of elephants, buffalo, and many migratory species.

BUT IS THERE TIME?

Much of the above argument appears to have proceeded on the assumption that the rapid degradation of Africa's natural resource base can be reversed. In many areas, it is admittedly not clear that this is the case.

Can sustainable agriculture really continue given the acceleration and continuation of desertification in all agricultural sectors of the Sudano-Sahelian region, considering that the population of that region has risen from 191 million to about 236 million in the seven years from 1977 to 1984 (Berry, 1984)?

Doubts about the long-term viability of the region are heightened by evidence that human activities actually may be changing the climate for the worse. There are three main ways that this could be happening. Stripping vegetation from the land, through deforestation, cultivation, and overgrazing, increases the reflectivity of the planet's surface, bouncing more solar heat back into the atmosphere and preventing the formation of rainclouds.

Loss of vegetation also means there is less evapotranspiration from plants and less moisture in the soil, so less moisture gets into the sky to return as rain. Finally, the increasing amounts of dust blown aloft from cleared ground may also prevent the formation of rainclouds. Increasing levels of atmospheric carbon dioxide around the planet, released by the burning of carbon fuels, are beginning to have their predicted "greenhouse effect," trapping solar radiation and changing weather patterns to make a drier Sahel (see Hare, 1984).

But the evidence for these changes comes mainly from computer models. Given that substantiating these claims requires conducting experiments, the lack of controls means that Sudano-Sahelian governments are unlikely to have proof of permanent climatic change in time to undertake any massive, planned transmigration projects to try to move their people south to more favorable areas. With rapid population growth rates, poor infrastructure, and inadequate organizational capabilities, it is also unlikely that such a scheme will be at all feasible in the near future, or that it could be guaranteed to do more good than harm. Finally, the people are likely to "vote with their feet" before any such scheme is organized. Though not very well documented, there appears to have been a steady movement southwards in the region for some time.

The question of whether the climate is changing raises other issues of a political and almost psychological nature. Travelling in the Sahel today, one hears many politicians and administrators throw up their hands and say, "What can we do? The climate is changing."

A growing number of geographers feel that concentrating on climatology per se is attention and funding misdirected. Kenneth Hewitt goes so far as to maintain that contemporary natural disaster research, with an emphasis on climatology and geophysics, has "become the single greatest impediment to improvement in both the understanding of natural calamities and the strategies to alleviate them" (Hewitt, 1983).

This is not to write off studies of climate, especially of rainfall and hydrology, as a waste of time. Hare (1984) points out that meteorological and hydrological services have severely deteriorated in recent years in arid zones, in part because adverse climate has reduced governments' ability to support them. But then these have more to do with weather and water availability than with climate, and have a part to play in any attempts to improve rural people's abilities to cope. Expensive computer climate models and satellite surveys have less to offer farmers.

Hare concludes that there are no "big science" answers available to the Sahel such as cloud seeding or other forms of weather modification. Though a climatologist, he sees what hope there is in agricultural and political responses. Control of land use, protecting it from livestock, reducing cultivation, planting trees and shrubs can protect the "micro-climate" at ground level upon which agriculture depends. He also recommends that vulnerable nations equip themselves with drought plans to protect people, land, and resources against future droughts. Whether the climate is changing or not, there will be future droughts.

A U.S. MODEL?

In the mid-1930s, a drought struck the Great Plains in the United States at a time when gross farm income was low and falling, and farmers were "overcultivating" to keep up. There was severe wind damage to desiccated soil and almost one in 10 farmers gave up and sold their farms. The period and the area affected became known as the "Dust Bowl" (Warrick, 1984).

The U.S. government did not respond by rounding up Oklahoma farmers and organizing them into gangs to plant huge tree belts across the state. There were no calls for in-depth studies of the climate of the Great Plains as a response to the crisis. What happened instead was that the government set up a framework, based on the needs and capacities of the farmers, encouraging them to take measures in their own individual interest to resuscitate the natural resource base. Organizations such as the Federal Crop Insurance Corporation, the Soil Conservation Service, and the Agricultural Stabilization and Conservation Service were established. There was frantic activity at the local level to conserve water and protect its sources, to encourage contouring, terracing, leaving fields fallow, using drought-resistant varieties, and to enforce land use regulations.

Similar sorts of activities have been tried in Africa, but in the United States, the emphasis was first on the farmers and their farms. The goal was to keep impoverished farmers in the economic and political systems of the nation for the sake of the nation. A side effect of this emphasis was that farmers were given both the incentives and the means to restore their environmental resource base. Also, the burden of the crisis was shared throughout the nation, in the form of taxes paid by people in cities and far from the drought areas.

It would be impossible for Africa to copy the U.S. response. But the response to the African crisis on the part of both foreign and African experts tends to focus too much on ecosystems, crops, trees, terraces, structures, wells, etc.—too much on things rather than people. One general cause of the African crisis is the tendency of many governments to leave its poor farmers outside of national economic and political systems. Instead of spreading the burden throughout a nation, governments have tended to focus the burden on those least able to bear it—the drought and famine victims themselves.

Donor governments, multilateral agencies, and African governments seem to have passed beyond the era of the "big fix" in Africa: continent-girdling tree belts and regional plans for livestock production and marketing. But they have not yet found the means of getting "development" to the majority whose ability to survive depends on the renewable resource base. Doing so will mean radical changes in the way donors operate, and even more radical changes in the ways in which most African governments operate. For the latter, it will mean finding ways of politically enfranchising their poorest and most powerless, and offering them hope that efforts to protect their environment will bring returns.

Unless these changes occur, once "renewable" resources will be squandered past renewing over large parts of the continent, and Africa's crisis will change from acute to chronic.

REFERENCES

All Party Parliamentary Group on Overseas Development. 1985. *UK Aid to African Agriculture*. London, Overseas Development Institute.

Avery, Dennis. 1985. *Potential for Expanding World Food Production by Region and Country*. Washington, D.C.: Bureau of Intelligence and Research, U.S. State Department.

Berry, Leonard. 1984. "Desertification in the Sudano-Sahelian Region, 1977–1984," in *Desertification Control Bulletin*, No. 10 (May). Nairobi: UNEP.

Blaikie, Piers. 1985. *The Political Economy of Soil Erosion in Developing Countries*. Burnt Mill, England: Longman.

Dregne, Harold. 1983. *Evaluation of the Implementation of the Plan of Action to Combat Desertification*. Nairobi: UNEP.

Eckholm, Erik, et al. 1984. *Fuelwood: The Energy Crisis That Won't Go Away*. London: Earthscan.

FAO. 1983. *Preliminary Report on Public Expenditure on Agriculture in Developing Countries*. Rome: FAO.

FAO. 1984. *How Development Strategies Benefit the Rural Poor*. Rome: FAO.

Foley, Gerald, et al. 1984. *Stoves and Trees*. London: Earthscan.

Giri, Jacques. 1984. "Retrospective de l'economie Sahelienne." Paris: Club du Sahel.

Gorse, Jean, et al. 1985. *Desertification in the Sahelian and Sudanian Zones of West Africa*. Washington, D.C.: The World Bank.

Grainger, Alan. 1982. *Desertification: How People Make Deserts, How People Can Stop and Why They Don't*. London: Earthscan.

Hare, F. Kenneth. 1984. "Recent Climatic Experience in the Arid and Semi-Arid Lands" in *Desertification Control Bulletin*, No. 10 (May), Nairobi: UNEP.

Hewitt, Kenneth. 1983. "The Idea of Calamity in a Technocratic Age," in K. Hewitt, ed., *Interpretations of Calamity*. Boston: Allen & Unwin.

International Task Force. 1985. *Tropical Forests: A Call for Action*. Washington, D.C.: World Resources Institute.

Kramer, John Michael. 1985. "Testimony before U.S. House of Representatives Subcommittee on Natural Resources, Agriculture, Research and Environment" in *Congressional Record* for 23 October, Washington, D.C.

Lusigi, W. J. and G. Glaser. 1984. "Combating Desertification and Rehabilitating Degraded Production Systems in Northern Kenya: The IPAL Project," in Di Castri et al., eds., *Ecology in Practice*, Vol. 1 (Ecosystem Management). Paris and Dublin: UNESCO and Tycooly Press.

Malik, Adam. 1982. Speech delivered to Third World National Parks Conference, Bali, Indonesia.

Madeley, John. 1985. *International Agricultural Development*. Vol. 5, No. 5.

Morris, J. and G. Gwyer. 1983. "UK Experience with Identifying and Implementing Poverty-related Aid Projects" in *Development Policy Review*, 1.

New Scientist. 1985. 21 February.

Sabatier, Renee. 1985. "In Canada, The Business of Aid is Business," *Earthscan Feature*, July 1985. London: Earthscan.

Shepherd, Jack. 1985. "When Foreign Aid Fails," *Atlantic Monthly*, April.

Side, Dominique 1982. "How to Stop Poachers," *Earthscan Feature*, September.

Timberlake, Lloyd. 1983. *The Improbable Treaty: The Cartegena Convention and the Caribbean Environment*. London: Earthscan.

Timberlake, Lloyd. 1984. "Alone in the Wastelands," *Earthscan Feature*, June 1984. London: Earthscan.

Timberlake, Lloyd. 1985. *Africa in Crisis: The Causes, the Cures of Environmental Bankruptcy*. London: Earthscan.

UNEP. 1984. *General Assessment of Progress in the Implementation of the Plan of Action to Combat Desertification*. Report of the Executive Director. Nairobi: UNEP, UNEP/GC.

Walls, James. 1984. "A Summons to Action," in *Desertification Control Bulletin*, No. 10 (May).

Warrick, Richard. 1984. "Drought in the U.S. Great Plains," in K. Hewitt, ed., *Interpretations of Calamity*. Boston: Allen & Unwin.

Western, David. 1984. "The Environment and Ecology of Pastoralists in Arid Savannahs," in *Development and Change* 13:183–211.

CHAPTER FIVE

Population and Health: Africa's Most Basic Resource and Development Problem

Fred T. Sai

With a land area two and a half times larger than the United States, sub-Saharan Africa, a region including 45 countries, is considered among the least developed areas in the world. As measured by basic development indicators, much of the continent has regressed over the last 30 years. After growing at an average of 3.8 percent per year between 1960 and 1970, gross domestic product grew at an annual average rate of only 3.0 percent between 1970 and 1982.[1] And as Africa's population growth rates have increased steadily from an annual average of 2.4 percent in the 1960s to a rate of 3.2 percent today,[2] per capita GDP has dropped markedly: from an annual average of 1.4 percent between 1961 and 1970, to 0.4 percent between 1971 and 1979, to –3.6 percent in the early 1980s.[3] Unfortunately, many of Africa's development problems defy rapid solution, as they have no historical precedent.

While Africa lags far behind the rest of the world in its level and rate of economic development, there is one area in which the continent takes the lead—the rate of growth of its population. Africa's future will be profoundly influenced by the demographics of its population, such as birth and mortality rates, as well as by internal and external migration and health and nutritional issues. These questions will continue to interact with other aspects of underdevelopment to make solutions to the continent's economic problems even more intractable.

Africa's population could well double by the end of the century.[4]

Infant mortality rates now average about 125 deaths per thousand births. The percentage of the population living in urban areas has just about doubled since 1960,[5] and this continued rural-urban migration has outstripped the capacity of governments to provide the bare minimum of social services in the cities. Basic health and nutritional problems remain widespread, despite improvements in medical research and technology elsewhere in the world and in places in Africa itself.

Because the present economic crisis has drastically limited the financial resources available to African governments for the future, it is paramount that African governments and foreign donors alike come to grips with the continent's troublesome population trends. What are the policy options that can effectively address these critical issues? In what manner can African states and foreign donors coordinate their efforts to assure the most economic, yet comprehensive approaches? These questions must be addressed now—for their answers will most certainly determine Africa's capacity for sustainable economic and social development in the future.

Major shifts in both policy and in budgetary allocations are required to address the critical questions of population, health, and nutrition. Such changes will occur, however, only by increasing governmental and public awareness of the dangers of neglect in these areas and by by generating sufficient political will on the part of governments. Additionally, increases in foreign assistance, improvements in health education, and a serious commitment to a regional or subregional approach to these questions are needed. This chapter will examine Africa's demographic features and its health and nutrition problems, and conclude with recommendations for African policy-makers and donors, particularly the United States.

AFRICA'S DEMOGRAPHY

The population of Africa south of the Sahara is estimated at over 450 million, with an average density of 18 persons per square kilometer. Given the land area of the region, the size of the population cannot be considered too great. However, a high population growth rate becomes a problem when it surpasses a nation's aspirations and the capacity of that nation's resource base to meet increasing demands. With an annual average population growth rate of 3.2 percent, the number of people in Africa will continue to exceed the support capacity of their economies unless serious efforts at the governmental level are undertaken to attain and maintain economic growth with a better distribution of national wealth (see Tables 5.1 and 5.2).

A number of demographic considerations indicate a worsening of Africa's population problem in the years ahead. First, the African population is very young, with some 19 percent under five years of age and 45 percent under age 15. This indicates that even if the fertility rate were to be lowered considerably, the population would continue to grow through "demographic inertia."[6] The next generation of parents has already been born. Moreover, Africa's population exhibits the highest dependency ratio in the world. The dependency ratio compares the number of very young and very old to those of labor force age who are capable of supporting them.

The consequences of high population growth rates and the age structure of the population are felt most immediately in increased demand for food, education and health services.[7] While in the rest of the world, the growth of food production has remained slightly ahead of population growth, this has not been the case in sub-Saharan Africa. Whereas food production and population in sub-Saharan Africa both grew at a rate of about 2.4 percent in the 1960s, by the 1970s, the population growth rate of 2.8 percent was far ahead of a food production growth rate of only 1.4 percent. While Africa was basically self-sufficient in food in 1970, today more than one-third of its peoples are fed in some part by imports, thus reducing already scarce foreign exchange reserves.[8]

The young and rapidly expanding population in sub-Saharan Africa means increased demands on already inadequate education and health care systems and implies little likelihood of much improvement in the quality of either. Countries already beset by slow economic growth will be hard-pressed to supply job opportunities to all the new entrants into the labor market. Agriculture offers limited prospects for new employment under current and prospective technologies, as land limits are being reached in a number of countries, creating pressure to leave rural areas. The rapidly growing urban areas have not been able to supply employment to a large share of job seekers. For governments then, the net result of the high dependency ratio is to increase the amount of the national product that goes to consumption, leaving fewer resources for productive investments in other sectors of the economy.

TABLE 5.1
SUB-SAHARAN AFRICA: POPULATION ESTIMATES, MID-1984

Country	Population Estimate mid-1984 (millions)	Persons per sq. km.	Birth rate (per 1000 population)	Death rate	Natural increase (percent annually)	Infant mortality rate[a]	Life expectancy at birth (years)
Sub-Saharan Africa, Total	433.5	18	48	17	3.1	112	49
Western Africa	162.3	26	49	18	3.1	120	47
Benin	3.9	35	51	22	2.9	145	43
Burkina Faso	6.8	25	48	22	2.6	145	43
Gambia	0.6	55	48	28	2.0	189	36
Ghana	13.0	54	47	14	3.3	96	53
Guinea	5.3	22	47	23	2.4	155	41
Guinea-Bissau	0.9	25	41	21	2.0	140	44
Ivory Coast	9.5	30	46	18	2.8	119	48
Liberia	2.1	19	48	17	3.1	109	50
Mali	7.8	6	50	22	2.8	145	43
Mauritania	1.8	2	50	20	3.0	134	45
Niger	5.9	5	51	22	2.9	137	43
Nigeria	92.0	100	50	17	3.3	111	49
Senegal	6.4	33	48	21	2.7	138	44
Sierra Leone	3.5	49	47	29	1.8	196	35
Togo	2.8	49	45	16	2.9	110	49

Eastern Africa	174.3	20	49	17	3.2	108	49
Burundi	4.5	161	47	20	2.7	134	45
Djibouti	0.4	18	47	21	2.6	—	—
Ethiopia	35.4	29	49	21	2.8	140	44
Kenya	19.8	34	55	14	4.1	79	54
Madagascar	9.7	17	44	16	2.8	65	50
Malawi	6.8	58	52	19	3.3	161	46
Mozambique	13.7	17	44	16	2.8	107	50
Rwanda	5.9	227	51	16	3.5	107	50
Somalia	5.4	8	46	21	2.5	140	44
Sudan	20.9	8	45	17	2.8	115	48
Tanzania	21.7	23	50	15	3.5	96	52
Uganda	15.2	64	50	14	3.6	91	53
Zambia	6.4	8	48	15	3.3	98	52
Zimbabwe	8.5	22	47	12	3.5	67	56
Middle Africa	60.7	9	45	17	2.8	117	48
Angola	8.5	7	47	22	2.5	145	43
Cameroon	9.5	20	43	17	2.6	114	49
Centr. Afr. Repub.	2.5	4	45	21	2.4	140	44
Chad	4.9	4	44	21	2.3	140	44
Congo	1.7	5	44	18	2.6	121	47
Equatorial Guinea	0.4	14	42	21	2.1	134	45
Gabon	1.1	4	35	18	1.7	109	50
Zaire	32.1	14	45	15	3.0	104	51

TABLE 5.1 (Continued)

SUB-SAHARAN AFRICA: POPULATION ESTIMATES, MID-1984

Country	Population Estimate mid-1984 (millions)	Persons per sq. km.	Birth rate (per 1000 population)	Death rate	Natural increase (percent annually)	Infant mortality rate[a]	Life expectancy at birth (years)
Southern Africa							
Botswana	36.2	13	40	14	2.6	91	54
Lesotho	1.0	2	50	12	3.8	77	55
Namibia	1.5	50	41	16	2.5	107	50
South Africa	1.5	2	45	17	2.8	112	49
Swaziland	31.6	26	38	14	2.4	89	54
	0.6	35	47	17	3.0	126	49

[a] Infant mortality rate = deaths under age one per 1000 live births in the same year.

SOURCES: Population estimates: United Nations, Population Division, Estimates and Projections Section, *Demographic Indicators by Countries as Assessed in 1982*, medium variant, New York, December 14, 1983, computer printout; Land area: World Bank, *World Development Report 1984* (New York: Oxford University Press, 1984), Table 1 and p. 276; 1983 per capita GNP: World Bank, *1984 World Bank Atlas* (Washington, D.C.: The World Bank, 1985).

Africa's total fertility rates (the average number of lifetime births per woman) are among the highest in the world. The average is 6.6 births per woman[9] (almost double the average of the world as a whole), though in Kenya the number is as high as 8.1. The continent's mortality rates are also high, with an average crude death rate of 17.3 per thousand;[10] only in a few island states is mortality less than 10 per thousand.

What is worrisome about this trend is that it is largely among the very young that the high death rate prevails. Infant mortality rates are still over 100 per thousand live births and in some rural areas, as high as 250. These figures range from 5 to fifteen times the rate in industrialized countries. A high infant mortality rate contributes to overall high fertility rates by encouraging "replacement births" and also by shortening the period of lactation, during which a woman is less likely to conceive. In Africa, death rates of children aged one to four range from 13 to 50 per thousand, with an average of 23, which is some 20 to 50 times that in the United States, where the rate is 0.8 per thousand and the most common causes of death are accidents or congenital abnormalities.[11] The rate of maternal mortality—death directly related to childbearing—is 300 to 600 per 100,000 live births in Africa, as compared to less than 10 per 100,000 in the industrialized world.

INTERNAL AND EXTERNAL MIGRATION

Africa's cities are growing faster than those in any other region of the world, many at a rate of 7 to 10 percent per year[12] (in Nairobi, the figure is as high as 13 percent). This rapid rate of urbanization poses yet another demographic problem for Africa. Concurrent with this population movement are three negative trends: the development of large shanty towns, or bidonvilles, within and around the major cities which pose serious public health threats; increased unemployment as largely unskilled rural laborers seek work in the cities; and along with the unemployment, an upsurge in crime and drug usage, and a concommitant deterioration of the cities.

Rural-urban migration is not a new phenomenon, but its rate of growth is. Africa is still the least urbanized region in the world. But since 1960, the percentage of urban population has almost doubled from 14 to 25 percent today. With the advent of independence and with efforts to expand social amenities, more work became available in and around the major towns, attracting rural residents to the cities.

TABLE 5.2
POPULATION GROWTH AND PROJECTIONS

	Average annual growth of population (percent)			Population (millions)		
	1960–70	1970–82	1980–2000	1982	1990	2000
Angola	2.1	2.5	2.8	8	10	13
Benin	2.6	2.7	3.3	4	5	7
Botswana	2.6	4.3	3.6	1	1	2
Burkina Faso	2.0	2.0	2.4	7	8	10
Burundi	1.4	2.2	3.0	4	5	7
Cameroon	2.0	3.0	3.5	9	12	17
Central Afr. Rep.	1.6	2.1	2.8	2	3	4
Chad	1.9	2.0	2.5	5	6	7
Congo	2.4	3.0	3.8	2	2	3
Ethiopia	2.4	2.0	3.1	33	42	57
Gabon	0.4	1.4	2.6	1	1	1
Gambia, The	2.2	3.2	2.3	1	1	1
Ghana	2.3	3.0	3.9	12	17	24
Guinea	1.5	2.0	2.4	6	7	9
Guinea-Bissau	..	..	2.3	1	1	1
Ivory Coast	3.7	4.9	3.7	9	12	17
Kenya	3.2	4.0	4.4	18	26	40
Lesotho	2.0	2.4	2.8	1	2	2
Liberia	3.2	3.5	3.5	2	3	4
Madagascar	2.2	2.6	3.2	9	12	16
Malawi	2.8	3.0	3.4	7	8	12
Mali	2.5	2.7	2.8	7	9	12
Mauritania	2.3	2.3	2.6	2	2	3

Mauritius	2.2	1.4	1.6	1	1	1
Mozambique	2.1	4.3	3.4	13	17	24
Niger	3.4	3.3	3.3	6	8	11
Nigeria	2.5	2.6	3.5	91	119	169
Rwanda	2.6	3.4	3.6	6	7	11
Senegal	2.3	2.7	3.1	6	8	10
Sierra Leone	1.7	2.0	2.4	3	4	5
Somalia	2.8	2.8	2.4	5	5	7
Sudan	2.2	3.2	2.9	20	25	34
Swaziland	2.7	3.2	3.9	1	1	1
Tanzania	2.7	3.4	3.5	20	26	36
Togo	3.0	2.6	3.3	3	4	5
Uganda	3.0	2.7	3.4	14	17	25
Zaire	2.0	3.0	3.3	31	40	55
Zambia	2.6	3.1	3.6	6	8	11
Zimbabwe	3.6	3.2	4.4	8	11	16

SOURCE: Derived from World Bank, *World Development Report, 1984*, Oxford: Oxford University Press, 1984.

Since the early 1970s, however, much migration has been the result of economic crisis in the countryside, as two decades of governmental neglect of rural develpment needs has made itself felt. Those with initiative rush to the cities to find work and a better life, but they often find their hopes dashed, at best finding low-paid jobs, but most of the time joining the vast number of unemployed in the towns.

Intra-African migration has also become a problem. Whenever opportunities for employment have presented themselves, such as in Nigeria during the oil boom or during Ivory Coast's agricultural expansion, workers from neighboring countries, usually semi-skilled, but sometimes professional and technical, have migrated in large numbers, creating a politically sensitive problem for the recipient country. Refugees from warfare or drought and famine are also part of intra-African migration. Africans account for about half of the world's estimated 10 million refugees.[13] Despite the hospitality of African governments that spend scarce resources to shelter them, most of the refugees live close to the margin of existence and at times contribute to political instability in their host countries. However, external migration is not confined to within Africa; many Africans— sadly, among the best educated in their countries of birth—leave the continent for better opportunities in Europe and the United States.

HEALTH AND NUTRITION PROBLEMS

Africa's main health problems—related to fertility, nutrition, and communicable diseases—continue to plague its population even when technological advances have been able to control or eradicate these same problems elsewhere in the world.

Fertility-related problems for women—hemorrhage and eclampsia, pre-eclampsia, anemia, and kidney conditions leading to hypertension—result from the prevalence of early pregnancies, closely spaced childbirths, late childbearing, and poor maternity care. Childbearing for African women begins in adolescence—from 15 years old—and may continue until about 50. Women who have more than five children, who continue bearing children into their late 40s, and whose pregnancies are spaced closer than two years are endangering their health and their lives as well as those of their babies. Further, each time a woman become pregnant, she suffers a decrease in her immune reaction, particularly to malaria. Both spontaneous and induced abortions and complications that follow from them are also common and dangerous threats to women's health.

The biological, social, and economic problems associated with adolescent childbearing have not been adequately recognized until recently. Extramarital pregnancies are increasing, causing high school dropout rates and other social problems. In many cases those who have children at a very young age are not provided with any opportunities for resuming their education or for acquiring other skills which would make them economic assets to their communities.

The health needs of infants and young children also require substantially increased investments. Africa's high overall death rates are due in part to the disproportionately high mortality rates of infants and young children. In some regions of Africa, children under five constitute about 20 to 25 percent of the population, but contribute 50 to 80 percent of the annual mortality toll, compared to about 3 percent in Western Europe. Diseases with often fatal results which affect children include diarrhea, pneumonia, malaria (responsible for the deaths of over 1 million children annually), measles, and whooping cough. All of these illnesses are even more hazardous to children's health when they combine with marginal or severe malnutrition. For an estimated cost of only $1.20 per child (not including transportation and administration costs), African children could be innoculated against the six most dangerous childhood diseases: measles, diptheria, whooping cough, tetanus, tuberculosis, and polio as part of a major effort to make low cost health care more widely acceptable.

Adults are subject to vector-borne, food-borne, and environment-related diseases which have largely been eradicated or controlled in other parts of the world. Several diseases commonly afflict a single patient, and the so-called apathy of African workers may simply be attributable to poor health and malnutrition. The mosquito vector carries malaria, filiariasis, and yellow fever which still reach epidemic proportions in areas of Africa. The black fly carries onchocerciasis, or river blindness, making many tracts of fertile land, particularly in West Africa, uninhabitable and unproductive. Trypanosomiasis (sleeping sickness), which attacks both humans and animals, is also a hazard to health and agriculture. Bilharzia, carried by snails, has not yet been controlled, and entire villages can be rendered unproductive by guinea worm.

There are also many endemic food-borne diseases—salmonellosis, shigellosis, and cholera—which are transmitted by the house fly or through poor food handling. Introduced in Africa in 1970, cholera has become endemic because of poor environmental sanitation and water and food control, which have facilitated its easy transmission. Polio-myelitis, infectious hepatitis, and various forms of dysentery are also caused by poor sanitation or poor food handling. Hookworms, asca-ris, and other nematodes also afflict all age-groups. Tropical ulcers are also common.

Tuberculosis and leprosy are among the more chronic adult dis-eases in Africa. Tuberculosis is common in cities and industrial estab-lishments, especially in the mining areas, and poor labor health poli-cies encourage its spread to rural areas. Agriculture, the principal occupation of some 70 percent of the population, also carries with it many health hazards. Apart from accidents resulting from improper use of implements, snake bites and tetanus are frequent afflictions of farmers.

NUTRITIONAL PROBLEMS

Sub-Saharan Africa is the only region in the developing world where nutrition has worsened in recent years (food consumption per capita has actually declined in the last 20 years). In late 1984, the FAO reported that 190 million people in 19 countries were still suffering from one of the worst droughts in Africa's history. But apart from such climate-induced fluctuations, the Sahelian region suffers from almost annual food shortages just before the harvest. These annual shortages lead to weight loss in both children and adults, causing such energy depreciation that adults cannot perform the full amount of work required to prepare for the next sowing season.

Protein calorie malnutrition, resulting in kwashiorkor and maras-mus, is one of the most serious nutritional problems in Africa, pri-marily affecting infants and children. Surveys have indicated that 2 to 10 percent of all children aged 1 to 4 suffer from overt protein calorie malnutrition, and 30 to 50 percent of those under five show a weight deficit which can be considered as clinical malnutrition, often result-ing in stunted growth.

Protein calorie malnutrition is associated with very high mortality. Without treatment, kwashiorkor may result in 20 to 50 percent mor-tality. When malnutrition begins in utero, it is known to affect the psychomotor and mental development of the infant, perhaps irre-versibly. Kwashiorkor also mentally retards children, and unless re-habilitative measures are undertaken to encourage mental develop-ment, the damage can be permanent.

Various degrees of protein calorie malnutrition have been noticed in adult women as well, particularly pregnant and lactating women. Anemia, resulting from iron and/or folic acid deficiencies, is so common as to occur in 20 to 80 percent of all women and in some men as well. Deficiencies of riboflavin, a member of the vitamin B group, are also common, leading to angular stomatisis, cheilosis, changes of the tongue, gum disease, and consequent tooth loss.

Vitamin A deficiency, affecting the eyes, is the most worrisome, causing xerophthalmia, which if untreated, can result in blindness. Its actual extent is not known and a study of its prevalence is needed. In some parts of the continent, goiter, resulting from inadequate iodine supplies, is a major problem. Goiter can cause foetal deficiency in pregnancy; iodine deficiency in the mother can result in cretin births.

POLICY IMPLICATIONS:
POPULATION AND DEVELOPMENT

The problems of population, health, and nutrition are interrelated in sub-Saharan Africa. In fact, the problems of population and development as a whole are linked. An ongoing debate has continued—particularly since the U.S. policy statement to the International Population Conference in August 1984—over the question of which has a greater impact on reducing fertility: economic development or family planning. Many have argued that family planning programs can have no effective impact until a certain level of development has been reached. In fact, some have gone to the extreme of declaring that economic development is the best contraceptive. Historical evidence shows that development, particularly if well ordered and the fruits reasonably spread, can be followed by fertility decline. On the other hand, evidence exists on the impact of well planned, well implemented family planning programs on fertility.

But examples have shown that even in countries such as Mexico with high levels of development as measured by per capita GNP, there have not been the expected reductions in fertility rates. Edward Green has argued that this is because the majority have not enjoyed the benefits of that development and still regard more children as an asset.[14] Therefore, a more equitable economic development is needed before this can have the desired effect on population growth.

By the same token, a reduction in the population growth rate is needed for more equitable development. Green further notes that rapid population growth further exacerbates the disparities between rich and poor. It leads to increased land values, more fragmentation of property, higher rents, and lower wages. Those who already own land and capital grow richer, while the poor get poorer. High population growth generally inhibits efforts to more equitably distribute resources, because it is difficult to improve the lot of the poor while trying to cope with a heavy rise in the total population. As Maudline and Laphan have demonstrated, good family planning programs together with good development programs have the most impact on fertility when working together. The effect of each by itself can be considerable too.

Arguments about either development or population control are likely to prove futile. Both are required. Without active measures to curb population growth rates the fruits of development will prove inadequate for the peoples' needs. The social burden will fall heavier on the very poor and the disparities between the rich and the poor will be exacerbated.

Baum and Tolbert [15] have stated that the main cost of rapid population growth is borne principally by the poor in the lost opportunities for improving their lives. They advance several reasons for this:

1. Rapid population growth slows development by exacerbating the choice between higher consumption now and larger investment towards future benefits for many.

2. In economies (like those of Africa) dependent on agriculture, population growth threatens the balance between people and scarce natural resources.

3. Rapid population growth makes it difficult to manage the adjustments necessary to promote economic and social change.

It needs to be remembered that whereas economic development brings about many improvements in health the direct application of bio-medical technologies help to provide faster and larger improvements; family planning technologies have to be looked at in the same way.

Africa remains far behind other continents in population and family planning programs, as its leaders have inadequately addressed the linkage between population questions and other development issues. At the time of the Bucharest Population Conference in 1974, only Mauritius, Kenya, and Ghana had evolved policies aimed at decelerating population growth rates and providing education and access to health services. Only Mauritius had instituted programs that were readily accessible to the majority of the population.

However, in 1981, eight countries formed the African Regional Council of the International Planned Parenthood Federation. Through their efforts and those of the UN Fund for Population Activities and other agencies, the relationship between population and other developmental issues began to be recognized at the governmental level. By 1984, eight African countries had formulated population policies, and some 24 others have family planning programs.

The tremendous change in perceptions of the issue of population at the governmental level has been brought about in a relatively short period of time. Still, even in those countries where there is sensitivity to population and family planning issues and where policies have been formulated, programs have had little impact. This is due to several factors.

As previously noted, the fertility rate remains high in Africa. Whereas it has fallen everywhere else in the world, it has remained, at least for the last 25 years, at 6.6 in Africa. There are a number of cultural and socioeconomic factors associated with the still high fertility rate on the continent. The Caldwells have extensively documented many of these factors.[16] For example, they have found that many African women still want more children, regardless of how many they already have (a finding confirmed by The World Fertility Survey). This is attributable in part to the great horror of terminal barrenness among women. Men are marked by an equal fear of impotence and both would seem to stem from the fact that having children is in many cases the supreme mark of manhood or womanhood. A woman's prestige is tied up with her children.

However, attempts to find explanations for Africa's continued high fertility err in imposing uniform explanations—usually of an anthropological nature. Essentially the high fertility relates to the socio-economic levels and conditions. At comparable stages in other people's histories they had high fertility too. It was perhaps never as high because external factors—biomedical technology in particular— were not as favorable as they are now.

While there is a great fear of barrenness, that alone does not explain the desire for large numbers of children. This is probably due first to the fact that the family is the agrarian production unit; and secondly in response to the perceived insecurity of a child's life due to high infant and childhood mortality rates.

There are other issues as well. In some societies where land was communally owned, the only investment that could be made was in children. Marriage in many societies was more a contract between families than individuals, and the bride price was understood to be a payment for reproductive and work capacity.

The Caldwells have found that among many Africans, it is thought that contraceptives are evil; they are feared to cause congenital defects, multiple births, barrenness, sterility, or illness. It is also commonly held that they will cause female promiscuity. In fact, they found that in places such as Nigeria, where contraceptives are used with greater frequency, the primary reasons are to reduce the period of sexual abstinence between births (but still not have births too close together), and to allow for extramarital relations.

Nearly universal distrust of contraceptives is fuelled by religious dogma and, recently, by Western (U.S.) policy. Yet the need for family planning is increasingly obvious as the rising rate of abortion shows.

The Caldwells note that in the past, many governments have derided population programs as examples of imperialist or neo-colonial plots to keep Africa down. But they say that this is not the real problem. Rather, these governments know that population programs run counter to the basic spiritual beliefs and emotions of many African societies.

Julian Conde has suggested historical reasons for the continued high fertility rates.[17] He notes that factors such as the slave trade, wars, natural disasters, and epidemics including plagues and yellow fever, have decimated and in some cases depopulated whole regions of Africa. He feels that "the need to make up for these losses experienced in the past may perhaps unconsciously prompt Africans to reproduce more readily than others."

There are, in addition, more practical reasons for the low success rates of family planning attempts. Many programs and personnel are urban-oriented, which means that the rural areas where the bulk of the population lives are often excluded. Further, the health delivery system in most African countries was inherited from the metropolitan power. Hospitals and health centers serving relatively large populations are the focal points of the system, meaning that health care is available to 20 to 25 percent of the population on a periodic basis. But the remainder of the population is required to travel long distances for treatment or make do with untrained or traditional birth attendants and healers. Further, urban-oriented health systems utilize some of the most advanced technology, creating a budgetary burden which constrains efforts to expand health care to the entire population. In Ghana, for example, hospital services take 80 percent of the health budget, while serving only 20 percent of the population.

IMPROVED PRIMARY HEALTH CARE AND FAMILY PLANNING PROGRAMS

Since the World Health Organization's 1978 Alma-Ata conference, many African countries have affirmed their commitment to extending primary health care to the entire population. However, translating their rhetoric into action has not been easy. The existence of fully staffed and equipped hospitals which take about 75 to 85 percent of the annual health budget makes it difficult to allocate sufficient resources to primary health care. Health services for all will be almost impossible to achieve without a shift of priorities away from prestigious, urban hospital-based care, which caters to the politically important urban population, toward rural services.

A major question, therefore, is to what extent governments can reallocate budgetary resources. If it is not possible to do so, it may still be feasible to increase the overall amount going to primary health care or preventive services. Apart from reordering priorities within health budgets, however, it is important to remember that only 5 to 7 percent of total annual budgets are spent on health. Health care cannot be improved unless the political will to free the necessary funds exists.

Only through national public awareness and pressure will such a policy and budgetary shift come about. And unless governments make a conscious change in policy toward focus on primary health care, no amount of external assistance will make a difference. Each country should have a primary health committee or council at the highest levels to collaborate with and coordinate the activities of the ministries of health, community development, economic development, education, and information.

Another priority is to involve women more directly in the entire development process. Providing women with access to both formal and health care education is critical. Educating women is also the surest way of bringing about declines in rates of fertility. As women are involved in about 80 percent of the continent's food production and handling, little can be achieved to improve health and nutrition for children without their involvement. In this context, special attention must be devoted to fostering breast feeding. Fortunately, in rural areas, breast feeding is the rule rather than the exception, and only a small minority of women—primarily working women—bottle-feed their children. However, there is the need to encourage prolonged breast feeding in all health improvement programs.

In other areas of primary health care and communicable disease control, efforts at oral rehydration for children with diarrhea, expanded immunization programs, and weight surveillance should be implemented both at the national and community levels. Focusing on eradication of a single disease or concentrating on a single sector will not serve to solve Africa's health problems. When a disease is a public health menace and the technology to control it is available at little cost, there is no reason why such a disease should not be attacked. Yet unless the people recognize the other factors—poor sanitation, poor nutrition, lack of education—which contribute to the spread of disease, the simple application of technology to cure it will represent only a short-term solution.

Family planning programs must be emphasized and supported, but this will not happen unless African governments accept that this area must be a priority, that such projects are implementable, and that they can yield results. Both autonomous family planning activities and those that form a part of overall health services are important and should be expanded. Autonomous family planning projects have proved useful in stimulating other aspects of the health care system in many communities. Pharmacies in many big cities find the demand for contraceptives to be substantial; however, because of legal restrictions, many methods of birth control are not available to the women who need them. There are few social marketing programs and few community-based distribution outlets for contraceptives.

Access to contraception needs to be expanded, with the medical system providing backup care, referral, and education on its use. However, a single-minded approach to family planning as the major solution to Africa's development problems, as was advocated in the 1960s and 1970s, should be avoided. This attitude sufficiently alienated many Africans as to make the implementation of family planning activities very difficult.

Food and nutritional problems are more intractable, and perhaps the best that can be hoped for at this stage is identification of the groups at risk. Identification and treatment of the more seriously malnourished can help reduce the level of malnutrition at the community level while education and food production programs take hold. But again the political will must be there if lasting changes are to be effected. Government policies which subsidize food prices, political and military conflict, and traditional agricultural practices also represent barriers to increasing food production. These factors are greatly exacerbated by the alarmingly accelerating rates of deforestation and desertification taking place in sub-Saharan Africa and the lack of attention to rainfed agriculture in research.

REGIONAL SOLUTIONS AND
GLOBAL PARTICIPATION

In addition to efforts at the individual government level, African countries must cooperate regionally to address issues of population and health. Unfortunately, neither the Organization of African Unity, the UN Economic Commission for Africa, nor the World Health Organization's regional offices have provided adequate leadership on these issues. For many years, these organizations regarded family planning and population activities as too sensitive to be advocated publicly. Of late, advances have been made in data collection, population censuses, and the training of demographers. But it is troubling that the continent's health authorities have not advocated family planning as part and parcel of efforts to improve the overall health and general living standards of the population. Even maternal and child health care services have not had the requisite support at national or regional levels.

The 1984 World Population Conference in Mexico City, preceded by the Second Africa Population Conference in Tanzania, have shown that there is sufficient interest in issues of health, population, and family planning on the part of African governments. Perhaps the continent's regional organizations can join together and begin to take a much more active role in advocating support for population and health programs by exchanging information, documenting experiences, and identifying programs that have worked and under what circumstances. Exchange programs and workshops at which African experts and health care workers can analyze the issues involved in the implementation of population and health policies of relevance to their people should be supported at the national, regional, and international levels.

A joint food and nutrition commission of the OAU, FAO, and WHO has existed for many years in Accra, Ghana, but at no time in its existence has it been adequately financed. Its primary tasks should be to analyze the food and nutrition situation both regionally and at the country-specific level, to help formulate food and nutrition strategies, and to put the issues before the international community to seek financial assistance. If strengthened, the commission could play a role in sounding alerts on famines as they develop and in identifying appropriate strategies to address them.

The opportunities for research through regional instruments and for regional collaboration are vast but as yet untapped. Efforts at regional economic cooperation are reviving and perhaps through organizations such as the Economic Community of West African States and the Southern African Development Coordination Conference, issues of population and health can begin to be addressed.

For international donors, and, in particular, the United States, there first needs to be a clearer understanding of region-wide and national health and population problems in Africa and institutional capabilities that exist and those that need to be created to deal with them. In these efforts, the important role played by non-governmental organizations and universities should not be forgotten. In addition, U.S. leaders should enter into a policy dialogue with African leaders in order to obtain an accurate assessment of how they perceive the issues of population and health.

The real potential of the communities—human resources that can be mobilized—must be explored. Equally, the limitations of the budgetary and financial allocation processes must be understood. This kind of expertise must be gained by visits to the countries and communities, but probably above all through seminars and workshops of U.S. and African experts. These workshops should aim at identifying solutions to Africa's health problems and examining approaches that have already been tried and failed. The scientific community in the United States can work with African scientists in these endeavors.

Human resource development and institution-building should be another area for emphasis. Many of the continent's institutions which have been founded in the post-independence period have not demonstrated any real relevance to Africa's development problems. Medical schools and institutions, for example, have not devoted adequate attention to developing approaches for expanding health care and services to the rural poor. Perhaps the United States could collaborate with the World Health Organization in improving the involvement of African universities in rural health care. A similar approach should be taken to schools of engineering and agriculture. Scholarship monies in the health field should not be spent only in U.S. institutions, but rather they should be granted for research in Africa on African health problems.

African universities and faculty focusing on agriculture are virtually isolated from the practical agricultural problems the continent is facing. Further, social sciences departments which should be in the forefront of studying the interaction of society and technology and innovation are not seriously addressing these issues. If these universities can be encouraged through outside support to involve themselves in non-traditional areas rather than strictly academic areas, they may be able to play a more significant role in Africa's development needs. Some American foundations and universities could break new ground in making African universities more relevant to development issues.

The United States government has recently expressed doubts about the merits of family planning as a separate program in development efforts and about whether the use of artificial contraceptives should be encouraged. It is unfortunate that the United States, which once stood for freedom of choice in personal decision-making, should be interfering in some of the most personal and critical areas of human life. The American government should realize that its policies toward international family planning organizations are dangerous and community and government leaders should speak out against them.

The American government has removed support from the International Planned Parenthood Federation because it spends less than one-fourth of 1 percent of its funds on abortion and related activities, such as medical meetings in which abortion is a topic of discussion. This will have disastrous consequences on family planning in Africa. The IPPF pays between 60 to 100 percent of the cost of family planning programs in some 25 African countries and without that support, or even less support, these services will collapse and institutions that have taken 15 or more years to develop will disappear. A bipartisan approach to health and population issues is required.

The low level of education for girls and women is one of the more intractable developmental problems Africa faces. Support must be mobilized for an assault on illiteracy and for the provision of reading materials for the literate population. While the overall adult literacy rate has nearly tripled (15.7 percent to 42.9 percent) since 1960,[18] the progress made by women has not been nearly as remarkable (literacy among women averages 20 percent).[19] Likewise, whereas 77.6 percent of all school age children attend secondary school, only 9.5 percent of girls do. Perhaps American women's organizations could commit themselves to literacy programs for African women.

The appropriateness of health technology in meeting Africa's needs should be studied. A center to evaluate health technologies and to adapt them to rural needs should be established. Regional centers to train personnel and to research and adapt appropriate health technology should be considered. In this regard, developed countries share the responsibility for having pressured developing countries to use their scarce resources on costly technology of marginal relevance to the problems they face.

The problems faced by the African continent have no historical precedent. The current rate of population growth is unprecedented. At its most rapid period of growth, the rate in Europe never reached above 1.6 percent per annum. A doubling of Africa's population by the close of the century poses very grave problems in the areas of education, health, and employment.

Technologies which can be applied in Africa are available for health and family planning provided the right choices of both the technology and their methods of delivery are made. Unfortunately, Africa has inherited expensive and irrelevant delivery models which have deluded it into becoming dependent on expensive high technology with limited applications.

The time has come for the United States to send a team of experts to Africa to examine, with African experts within each country, the continent's needs in health and population. During the visit or visits efforts should be made to identify individuals and institutions which could play a role in any effort to reverse the decline in Africa. The needs of such individuals and institutions should be first priority in any strategy, as it is from their success that major lessons will be learned. Special attention should be paid to the identification of women in leadership roles and to plan for their further training and critical development. Such women could be encouraged to travel extensively and be assisted in increasing their role in national affairs. Around them stronger women's groups should be created.

Efforts to get regional consensuses on health and population should be intensified. WHO, ECA and others should be assisted in undertaking an analysis of strategies for Africa in health and population, and set out programs and targets with interested nations. The problems are immense. Solutions will take a long time, and both donors and African governments should gear themselves up for long dedicated searches and applications.

Governments are responsible for the education, health, and welfare of all their citizens. The communications revolution has opened Africa to the rest of the world and has made it possible for African leaders to become aware of the technological advances which may be attractive, but of dubious relevance to their countries' economic development. The U.S. media should play a role in responsibly educating Americans as to the continent's needs and Africans to the opportunities. African governments are prepared for genuine dialogue and cooperation. The United States must evolve approaches with as little political partisanship as possible if long-term collaboration is to be assured.

NOTES

1. "Toward Self-Sustained Development in Sub-Saharan Africa: A Joint Program of Action," Washington, D.C.: The World Bank, September 1984, p. 58.

2. Ibid., p. 82.

3. "The Challenges for Sub-Saharan Africa," speech by Robert S. McNamara, November 1, 1985, p. 36.

4. *World Population Prospects*, New York: United Nations, 1985, p. 146.

5. *World Tables*, Washington, D.C.: The World Bank, 1983, p. 142.

6. "Population and Poverty in Sub-Saharan Africa" by Margaret Wolfson, in *Crisis and Recovery in Sub-Saharan Africa*, Paris: OECD Development Centre, 1985, p. 96.

7. Ibid., p. 97.

8. *World Tables*, p. 486.

9. Ibid., p. 142.

10. Ibid.

11. "Black and White Children in America: Key Facts," Washington, D.C.: Children's Defense Fund, 1985, p. 85.

12. "Compact for African Development Strategies," Council on Foreign Relations/Overseas Development Council, New York and Washington, D.C., December 1985. See Appendix II of this volume.

13. Ibid.

14. "U.S. Population Policies, Development, and the Rural Poor in Africa," Edward Green, *Journal of Modern African Studies*, 20 (I) (1982).

15. Warren C. Baum and Stokes M. Tolbert, *Investing in Development: Lessons of the World Bank Experience*, Oxford: Oxford University Press, 1985, pp. 213–14.

16. John C. Caldwell and Pat Caldwell, "Cultural Forces Tending to Sustain High Fertility in Tropical Africa," 1984 draft of an unpublished paper.

17. Julian Conde, "The Demographic Situation in Africa and its Effect on Economic and Social Development," OECD Development Centre, October 1984.

18. *World Tables*, p. 158.

19. *Women of the World: Sub-Saharan Africa*, Washington, D.C.: Department of Commerce, August 1984.

PART III

AGRICULTURE

CHAPTER SIX

Governmental Strategies for Agricultural Development

Bruce F. Johnston

Africa's recurring food crises have forced governments and donor agencies to search for more effective strategies for agricultural and rural development. Increasing food imports to meet the growing gap between demand and domestic production cannot be sustained over the long term. In order to accelerate the growth of agricultural output, a shift from traditional resource-based agriculture to a science-based agriculture will be required, involving the utilization of more productive technologies and increasing quantities of fertilizers and other manufactured inputs.

The predominantly agrarian structure of the economies of tropical Africa and rapid growth rates of population and labor force have critically important implications for the choice of a strategy for agricultural development. Because of Africa's unique demographic features, countries confront a choice between a "bimodal" (dualistic) pattern, in which resources are concentrated in large and capital-intensive farms, or a broadly based "unimodal" pattern of agricultural development. There is now considerable consensus concerning the advantages of agricultural strategies that foster the progressive modernization of small farm units in economies where 50 to 80 percent of the total population and labor force are still dependent on agriculture (Mellor and Johnston, 1984).

Africa's development problems require attention to the following goals: accelerating the rate of output growth; expanding farm and non-farm employment opportunities; reducing the most serious manifestations of poverty, particularly malnutrition and disease; and slowing rates of population growth. Over the next 30 to 40 years, small farm development strategies involving labor-intensive, capital-saving technologies represent the most economical approach to achieving these goals.

However, the diversity of agroclimatic and socioeconomic conditions, even within relatively small countries, is such that a variety of small-farm strategies will be required. For example, farm equipment innovations based on animal draft power are not feasible in tsetse-infested areas; even in savanna regions the feasibility and profitability of achieving wider, more efficient use of animal-powered implements will vary substantially.[1] Indeed, the diversity of environmental conditions in sub-Saharan Africa poses special problems in fostering technological progress and accelerated growth of agricultural production.

THE CHOICE OF AN
AGRICULTURAL STRATEGY

Agriculture's heavy weight in the economic structure is common to all African countries. Fifty to 80 percent of the population and labor force are still dependent on agriculture for employment and income. Rapid population growth ensures that agriculture's large share in the total labor force will continue and that the absolute size of the farm population and labor force will increase for at least several decades. Although between 1960 and 1984, the percentage of the population in urban areas doubled—from 11 to 22 percent—the farm labor force has continued to increase at an annual rate of approximately 2 percent (Gusten, 1984, p. 12).[2]

Because of those structural and demographic features, the countries of tropical Africa confront an unavoidable choice between an emphasis on agricultural strategies that promote large-scale farms and give rise to a "bimodal" (dualistic) pattern of agricultural development or small-farm development strategies leading to a "unimodal" pattern of development. The rapid growth of the farm population in recent decades has already created conditions of land scarcity in a number of African countries. Of more general significance, however, is the "purchasing power constraint" that characterizes a country where the domestic commercial market for agricultural products is small relative to the large number of farm households. The farm units that comprise a large-scale subsector are able to escape that sectorwide purchasing power constraint because they account for the lion's share of commercial sales. That means, of course, that for the great majority of farm households, the purchasing power constraint is intensified.

The widespread tendency to favor large-scale farm enterprises is often related to the vested interests of those who own or manage the farms, whether as private or state enterprises. This bias toward large farms or estates is, however, based upon a belief in the importance of economies of scale in agriculture. A treatise on the political economy of West African agriculture by Keith Hart provides an example of the view that the establishment of "large, capital-intensive estates" (publicly or privately owned) offers the only effective approach to achieving "a long-run dynamic of economic development through labor specialization, capital investment, and productive innovation" (Hart, 1982, pp. 154, 157).

A pervasive belief in the importance of economies of scale (or of farm size) has been reinforced by the experiences of the United States and other industrialized countries where agricultural productivity has grown on increasingly large farms using ever larger quantities of farm machinery and other purchased inputs. Theoretical analysis and empirical evidence, however, point to the existence of significant diseconomies as well as economies of scale.

Evidence of a decline in output per unit area as the total size of farm units increases—an "inverse relationship" between farm size and output—indicates, however, that in countries where labor is relatively abundant, the diseconomies typically outweigh the economies of farm size. The forces that give rise to this inverse relationship derive from what Binswanger and Rosenzweig (1983) refer to as "behavioral and material determinants of production relations in agriculture."

The principal diseconomies of farm size result from the fact that the costs associated with hiring labor exceed the cost of labor supplied directly by the family members of farm households. Because family members have a claim on the net income of the farm enterprise, their self-interest provides an incentive to seek to maximize the farm's profits by hard work, by acquiring technical knowledge and skills, and by exercising initiative and judgment in carrying out their tasks.

Because agricultural production is subject to the uncertainties of weather and other factors, a variety of "on-the-spot supervisory decisions" must be made (Brewster, 1950). The consequence is that various forces act to raise the cost incurred by employers of farm workers and to reduce the net income realized by wage laborers (Johnston and Tomich, 1984, pp. 43–64).

The technical characteristics of certain crops may give rise to genuine economies of scale. Sugar cane is perhaps the best example. Tea was long considered to be the plantation crop par excellence because of the need for close coordination between plucking the leaves and processing them in fairly large factories. However, the institutional innovation represented by the Kenya Tea Development Authority (KTDA) provided a mechanism for coordinating the collection of tea leaves and their prompt delivery to factories. As a result, small farms have been able to compete successfully with estates in the production of tea (Lamb and Muller, 1982).

It is often asserted—or assumed—that economies of scale are so important in agriculture that a small-farm development strategy is bound to be inefficient and can only be justified by invoking non-economic arguments related to income distribution or nutritional improvement. In fact, there is abundant evidence that small farm development strategies can be a more economical approach to achieving sectorwide expansion of agricultural production than a large-farm strategy when the opportunity cost of farm labor is low because of the lack of off-farm employment opportunities. When structural transformation and economic development reach a point where the relative availability and prices of capital and labor warrant a shift from labor-using, capital-saving technologies to labor-saving, capital-using technologies, then the economies of farm size become significant and small- farm development strategies cease to be appropriate.

In brief, historical experience and logic indicate that there are highly significant economic and social advantages in achieving a transition from resource-based to science-based agriculture by implementing small-farm strategies that lead to unimodal patterns of agriculture development. This does not mean that farms should be uniformly small or that different farms and areas should be expected to advance at the same rate.

Japan's experience is of considerable interest in demonstrating the feasibility and desirability of a unimodal pattern of agricultural development. Some 75 percent of the total labor force was employed in agriculture as late as 1880; and the impressive increases in agricultural productivity that played such an important role in the economic development of Japan were achieved among the small owner-cultivators and tenant farmers who continued to dominate Japanese agriculture until the post-World War II period.

As another example, Taiwan was one of the first developing countries to experience the rapid decline in mortality and "explosive" growth of population and labor force that have become commonplace in the decades since World War II. It was not until the late 1950s that the absolute size of the agricultural labor force in Taiwan began to decline, and during the preceding half-century, the farm workforce had doubled. Although that increase was much less than the fourfold increase projected for Kenya over the same period, it meant that Taiwan's farm units became smaller and smaller until the processes of demographic change finally led to a decline in the absolute and relative size of the farm labor force.

It would be absurd to suggest that Japan and Taiwan provide a "model" that can be emulated by African countries. In fact, a major theme of this chapter is that the physical environment for agriculture in sub-Saharan Africa provides a number of unique characteristics including the predominance of rainfed agriculture and an exceptional diversity of agroclimatic and soil conditions. Nevertheless, the experiences of Japan and Taiwan illustrate the critical ingredients of success—each country created an efficient agricultural research system, a good rural infrastructure, an efficient system for the distribution of farm inputs, and a broad educational system.

Impressive increases in agricultural productivity and output were achieved by gradually expanding the use of purchased inputs such as fertilizers that were capable of being used efficiently by small farmers and which enhanced the productivity of a large labor force rather than displacing farm labor prematurely when alternative employment opportunities were not available. Although the post-World War II land reforms in those countries reinforced their unimodal development, the basic patterns of agriculture were set much earlier when land ownership was highly skewed.

The experience of the Asian countries also points to the fallacy in the simplistic but widely held view that African countries are experiencing food problems because land and resources are devoted to production of export crops instead of food crops. In Taiwan, the expansion of export production enabled the country's small farmers to increase their cash incomes more rapidly than would have been possible if demand had been limited to subsistence requirements plus sales to a relatively small domestic commercial market (Johnston and Kilby, 1975, Chapters 6 and 7). The contribution of those exports to foreign exchange earnings also benefited the farm population, directly by financing imports of fertilizers and other essential farm inputs and indirectly by facilitating the expansion of output and employment opportunities in the nonfarm sectors so as to initially slow the increase in the size of the farm labor force and to eventually permit a reduction in its absolute size.

Under a bimodal pattern of agricultural development, the benefits from export expansion are likely to be restricted to the large-scale subsector. Indeed, it appears that the rapid growth of export production in Malawi between 1964 and 1980 was not only confined to the estate sector, but was in large measure financed at the expense of the country's small-scale farmers (Kydd and Christiansen, 1982).

The fundamental reason why small-farm strategies have significant economic advantages is because of the fit between the resource requirements of such strategies and the resource endowment that characterizes late-developing countries where the bulk of the population still depends on agriculture for employment and income. Since the agricultural sector in African countries is subject to a severe cash income or purchasing power constraint, the extent to which expansion of agricultural output can be based on increased use of purchased inputs is limited. This underscores the importance of the forces that determine the rate and "bias" of technical change (i.e., whether the innovations that become available induce the adoption of labor-using, capital-saving technologies or technologies that are capital-using and labor-saving). Hence, generating and diffusing innovations that are complementary to the existing on-farm resources of labor and land are of decisive importance in minimizing the cost of sector-wide expansion of farm output and also in determining the "pattern" of agricultural development.

In brief, the economic advantages of achieving widespread increases in productivity among a country's small-farm units derive from the fact that they are the most feasible and cost-effective means of attaining the multiple objectives of development—the growth of output, expansion of opportunities for productive employment, narrowing income differentials, reducing malnutrition and excessively high rates of infant and child mortality, and slowing the rate of population growth.

The key to the effectiveness of small-farm development strategies in contributing to the attainment of those multiple objectives lies in its potential for achieving a rate of expansion of employment opportunities, farm and nonfarm, that exceeds the rate of growth of the population of working age. The tightening of the supply/demand of labor that results represents the most reliable means of increasing returns to labor because of its combined effect on reducing underemployment and increasing the "price" of labor, including the implicit price of the unpaid labor of family members working on their own farm units.

The employment-generating potential of small-farm development strategies derives from their reliance on labor-using and capital-saving technologies. Such strategies make it possible to increase farm output by fuller and more efficient utilization of the large and growing farm labor force that characterizes African countries—the key to minimizing the agricultural sector's requirements for the particularly scarce resources of capital and foreign exchange. Past expenditures for tractors and tractor-drawn implements have often contributed to severe shortages of capital and foreign exchange; frequently this has meant that the great majority of farm households have not had satisfactory access to hoes and other basic farm implements.

Further, a successful unimodal pattern of agricultural development helps to encourage more rapid expansion of nonfarm output and employment opportunities. Broadly based agricultural development fosters positive interactions between agricultural and industrial development that stimulate more rapid growth of nonfarm output and employment than can be realized under a bimodal pattern of agricultural development. The pattern of rural demand for farm inputs and consumer goods that is associated with widespread increases in farm productivity and incomes fosters the dispersed growth of small- and medium-scale manufacturing firms that use relatively labor-intensive technologies and rely mainly on indigenous resources of labor and raw materials.

But a bimodal pattern of development tends to be associated with a growth in demand for more sophisticated consumer goods and farm inputs (e.g., automobiles and tractors) instead of bicycles and improved animal-powered agricultural implements. The rate of expansion of firms responding to the pattern of demand associated with bimodal agricultural development is inevitably more constrained by the scarcity of capital and foreign exchange than is the expansion of the smaller firms that are stimulated by widespread increases in in-

come under a successful unimodal pattern of agricultural development. The more rapid growth of off-farm employment opportunities
that results is also more important in slowing the rate of growth of the
farm work force, thus minimizing the adverse effects of diminishing
returns to labor as growth of the rural workforce puts pressure on the
arable land available for expanding the cultivated area.

Erroneous perceptions about the importance of economies of scale
and failure to recognize the extent to which emphasis on large-farm
strategies and the effective implementation of small-farm strategies
represent mutually exclusive alternatives have no doubt contributed
to the failure of virtually all African countries to achieve successful
unimodal patterns of agricultural development. The need for a choice
between small-farm and large-farm development strategies has been
emphasized because successful implementation of small-farm strategies leading to a unimodal pattern requires a conscious commitment
to the sustained and difficult effort required to achieve broad-based
agricultural development.

More direct obstacles to the successful implementation of small-
farm strategies have been related to macro-economic policies that
have adverse effects on the agricultural sector in general but especially on small farmers. Weak supporting services for agricultural
research, extension, credit, and programs for the construction and
maintenance of roads and other rural infrastructure have also been
responsible for generally ineffective implementation of small-farm
strategies. Excessive investment of scarce resources of money and
labor in promoting a subsector of large-scale farm units is only one of
a number of reasons for the weakness of those supporting services.

ACCELERATING AGRICULTURAL DEVELOPMENT: MACROECONOMIC POLICIES AND TECHNOLOGICAL PROGRESS

MACROECONOMIC POLICIES

Many critics of the agricultural strategies pursued by African governments come close to suggesting that "getting prices right" is all
that is needed to overcome the food and agricultural problems that
have become so serious during the past two decades. Some suggest
that the difficulties can be attributed to the failure of independent

African governments to manage their economies efficiently.[3] Reality is more complex. For most African countries, it is not accurate to describe the agricultural sector as "stagnant." Many countries have been expanding total agricultural production at rates that are impressive relative to those that were achieved by the industrialized countries, including Japan. But rates of increase of output of some 2.5 percent have been outpaced by population growth rates of 3 to 4 percent per annum.

There is no doubt that many macro-economic policies have had adverse effects on agriculture in Africa. This has probably been due as much to neglect of agriculture in resource allocations as to price distortions. Deficiencies in research and other support services and inadequate finance for the construction and maintenance of rural roads and transport have been very important factors in unsatisfactory rates of output growth.

Macro-economic policies that have adversely affected agriculture have usually included highly protectionist import-substituting industrialization, although other forces that have often led to high rates of inflation and overvalued exchange rates have also been significant. Budget deficits that fuel inflation are also a result of the failure to enlarge tax revenues in keeping with the expansion of government expenditures.

High tariffs and import quotas to protect a "modern" industrial enclave increase the price of most imports and of locally manufactured products and turn the terms of trade against agriculture by raising the cost of farm inputs and consumer goods. Overvalued exchange rates further worsen the terms of trade, especially for producers of export crops. In addition, governments often fix food prices at artificially low levels for the benefit of urban consumers, thus depressing producer prices and weakening their incentive to expand output.

Government measures to offset these negative effects are almost always concentrated on a subsector of relatively large-scale farmers. For example, financial institutions are often directed to make credit available at artificially low interest rates to farmers and manufacturing firms, leading to an "excess demand" situation as the low interest rates stimulate demand for credit while ceilings on the interest paid on deposits discourage savings. The result is administrative rationing of credit from institutional sources. Invariably, the larger and more influential farmers receive the bulk of the subsidized credit. Subsidized distribution of fertilizer has a similar effect in creating an "excess demand" situation.

Policies that enable large farmers or state farms to acquire tractors at artificially cheap prices have particularly adverse effects. Although tariffs on imports are generally very high, tractors and other capital goods are often allowed to enter duty-free. Given an overvalued exchange rate, the price of this imported equipment is already artificially low. When large farmers have access to subsidized credit, the acquisition of inappropriately capital-intensive, labor-displacing farm equipment is encouraged. In addition, government purchases of imported tractors have often been encouraged by the availability of loans under foreign aid programs which temporarily remove the foreign exchange constraint.

Many of these macroeconomic policies were probably adopted initially without recognition of the consequences. Donor countries have encouraged faulty decisions, such as the purchase of tractors, by offering concessional loans. However, such policies are adopted and maintained because they are beneficial to certain powerful group interests. A regime may attach a great deal of importance to strengthening its hold on power by securing the support of large and influential farmers, the bureaucracy, industrialists, and workers in the modern enclaves created by protectionist policies and other preferential measures (Bates, 1981, 1983).

TECHNOLOGICAL PROGRESS: OBSTACLES AND
OPPORTUNITIES

Strengthening National Research Systems   Deficiencies in both the level and orientation of investment in agricultural research have very likely been the single most important factor behind inadequate rates of technological progress and growth of agricultural production in Africa. Among the factors responsible for those deficiencies are overly optimistic expectations about the availability of profitable technical innovations adapted to Africa's diverse environmental conditions and impatience for quick results. These have encouraged large investments by governments and donors in area- or commodity-based development programs that typically have little impact on productivity and output because the "technical packages" on which they are based did not yield the expected returns.

This over-optimism about the potential for direct technological transfer has been influenced by a common misinterpretation of Asia's experience with the Green Revolution. IRRI and CIMMYT played a critical role in the development of semi-dwarf varieties of rice and wheat that spread so rapidly in the mid-1960s. Their role, however, was to support, not substitute, for national agricultural research programs. The point that bears emphasis is that the Asian countries that have benefited from the Green Revolution have had the indigenous research capability to follow up on the direct "material transfer" of high-yield varieties of rice and wheat with the second and third stages of technological transfer—"design and capacity transfer" (Hayami and Ruttan, 1984). Thus they have been able to utilize imported "prototypes" of genetic material and equipment, a growing body of scientific knowledge, and effective methodologies for experimental work, enabling them to develop crop varieties and agronomic practices adapted to local ecological and socioeconomic conditions.

The indigenous research capability in the countries of South and Southeast Asia is the result of a long-term process of institution-building. This process was strengthened considerably in the 1950s, and the result has been a substantial increase in the supply of well-trained agricultural scientists, social scientists, agricultural administrators, irrigation engineers, and other specialists. Indeed, the agricultural progress achieved since the mid-1960s would not have been possible without this augmented supply of scientists and administrators. The development of a network of agricultural universities in India during the 1950s is the most notable example, but similar progress has been made in many other Asian countries which benefited greatly from foreign aid programs with a high priority on the long-term process of institution-building. AID and other bilateral aid agencies provided major support in sustained technical assistance for the new educational institutions and in foreign training of the nationals who now staff university teaching and research programs. Programs of the Rockefeller and Ford Foundations and the relatively modest but strategic efforts of the Agricultural Development Council also made notable contributions to the strengthening of indigenous capabilities for research and administration of agricultural programs.

While similar programs have been carried out in Africa, they began later and the efforts were more limited and of shorter duration. The tragedy is that African countries, which had the greatest need for sustained programs to support institution-building for agriculture, did not begin to receive significant levels of foreign aid until after aid policies had shifted away from institution-building to new priorities such as "integrated rural development," "basic needs strategies," and preoccupation with "the poorest of the poor." And the "extension bias" that has led to a misallocation of resources in all developing regions appears to have had especially unfortunate consequences in Africa (see Evenson, 1978). Substantial domestic and external resources have been devoted to the creation of sizeable agricultural extension programs which have generally been quite ineffective because they have had so little to extend.

Strong agricultural research programs must be supported by an informed constituency which holds the programs responsible for worthwhile results. During the colonial period, such a constituency existed for export crops, but not for food crops. Kenya and Zimbabwe were the principal exceptions because politically influential European farmers were engaged in production of both.

It is noteworthy that Kenya's impressive progress in promoting smallholder agriculture has been concentrated in "high potential areas" and based mainly on high-value export crops. Prior to 1954, African farmers had not been permitted to grow certain high-value crops, ostensibly because they would compromise the reputation for quality of coffee and other export crops grown on European estates. In fact, Kenyan African farmers' production of high quality coffee and tea and management of high quality "grade" cattle for milk production has been very impressive. The success of that program and continued expansion following independence depended in considerable measure on the fund of knowledge accumulated by Kenya's research stations and in the trial-and-error learning by European farmers over many years. Progress in the "high potential" areas suited to those crops was rapid because the knowledge and experience to provide a basis for technically sound plans for accelerated agricultural development already existed (Heyer et al., 1976).

Widespread adoption of hybrid maize in parts of Kenya also demonstrates the readiness of African farmers to innovate when feasible and profitable innovations are available (Gerhardt, 1975). Mazabuka district in Zambia is another area where success has been achieved in introducing high-yield maize varieties among smallholders. To date, however, the success stories are very much the exception; and the lack of an adequate "research base" appears to be the most common cause of limited technological progress (Anthony, 1979, Chapter 5).

African countries face the difficult challenge of simultaneously increasing the effectiveness of their research programs and securing more sustained support for agricultural research. Limited experience with successful agricultural research programs makes it more difficult to mobilize the needed political and financial support for strengthening research both directly and indirectly through graduate training of future agricultural scientists and other specialists. At the same time, however, there is an important opportunity for donors to make a significant contribution in supplementing domestic financial and trained labor resources. Moreover, cost-effective methods for making agricultural research more relevant to the needs of small farmers who are subject to severe cash constraints are also needed.

"Farming Systems Research"   During the past decade, there has been considerable consensus that Farming Systems Research (FSR) represents an appropriate response to the problem of making research relevant to the needs of small farmers operating under the very heterogeneous conditions that characterize rainfed agriculture. Recent papers by Collinson (1982), Byerlee, Harrington, and Winkelman (1982), and CIMMYT economists (International Maize and Wheat Improvement Center, 1984) represent an important advance, for they emphasize "on-farm research with a farming systems perspective" rather than attempts by formal research programs to develop and diffuse complete farming systems. There are especially serious disadvantages in attempting to promote rigidly defined "technical packages" in heterogeneous environments. Indeed, even identifying appropriate components for farmers to fit into their farming systems requires a focus on specific "recommendation domains" that are reasonably homogeneous in terms of their physical environment, major socioeconomic constraints, and the main features of the prevailing farming systems.

Devising better methods to exploit the complementarity between formal experiment station research and farmers' local knowledge and capacity for "adaptive management" represents an especially important challenge in Africa, given the scarcity of agricultural scientists with the training and capacity for the diagnostic analysis required for FSR. As a recent study by Tomich (1984) has shown, farmers are capable of modifying technologies and adapting them to difficult and extremely heterogeneous conditions. Thus, the task of FSR becomes much more feasible.

The opening speech at a "networking workshop" held in Swaziland in October 1983 is of considerable interest in its emphasis on the need to "investigate and diagnose the constraints under which the majority of small farmers operate." The speaker also noted that it is important for social and technical scientists to work together: "Technical solutions to production problems devised by researchers will only be of any value if farmers can put them into practice given the socioeconomic circumstances in which they operate." He further emphasizes that the blame for farmers' failure to follow recommended practices "does not lie with the farmers, but with the recommendations themselves" (Dlamini, 1983).

A well-documented analysis of government interventions in Uganda by Stephen Carr (1982) emphasizes that the extremely limited impact of research on increasing farm productivity over a period of some 60 years is explained by its concentration on individual crops grown under experiment station conditions rather than by alleged stubbornness of farmers in refusing to adopt new practices. Indeed, more carefully designed trials have demonstrated that under actual farming conditions, the practices followed by farmers were superior to the recommended "improved practices."

In general, the potential yield increases that can be obtained from the introduction of high-yield, fertilizer-responsive crop varieties are considerably less under rainfed conditions than those possible with irrigation and greatly increased application of fertilizers. In Africa, however, it is often feasible for small farmers to increase their output by enlarging the area under cultivation as well as by increasing crop yields. Moreover, it is often necessary to improve soil and water management by better tillage methods in order to realize the yield potential of improved varieties. But it is not possible to expand the acreage cultivated per worker or to adopt improved tillage methods when farming depends entirely on the hoe and human labor.

Animal Draft Power and the Evolution of Farming Systems   Price distortions that make tractors artificially cheap and a tendency to view tractors as a symbol of "modernity" have diverted attention away from efforts to promote the adoption of a wider range of animal-powered farm equipment. Historical experience in Asia and recent developments in Africa suggest that for small farmers with limited cash income, wider and more efficient use of animal-powered equipment is a feasible option to increase area under cultivation and crop yields by soil- and moisture-conserving tillage practices and by improving the precision with which planting and other operations are carried out. Tractor-based technologies may appear to be attractive because of their power and speed, but they represent a large investment not feasible for small farmers.

The presence of tsetse is only one of a number of factors that determine whether animal draft power should be introduced in different farming regions in Africa. The recent work of Hans Binswanger and Prabhu Pingali (1984) is a valuable contribution in understanding the conditions under which a shift from handhoes to animal draft power and other aspects of intensification is encouraged. Population growth, increased off-farm demand for agricultural products, and reduced transportation costs are among the important factors that induce such changes. In a companion paper, Pingali and Binswanger (1984) stress that animal traction becomes important only with the intensification from bush fallow to short fallow systems or annual cropping.

The pattern of evolution of technologies in tropical agriculture is also associated with changing soil preferences that lead to a movement away from lighter soils that are easy to cultivate by hand but risky, toward bottom lands. The soils in bottom lands are hard to prepare by hand, but are more responsive to intensification with animal traction, land improvements, and application of manure and fertilizers.

With increasing population density, it becomes more feasible to undertake labor-intensive investments in irrigation, drainage, and stump removal. Trypanosomiasis and other diseases are minimized as intensification leads to a marked reduction in the density of trees and bush. Binswanger and Pingali (1984, p. 28) further note that tractor cultivation requires more complete and costly destumping than animal traction, which is one of the reasons for their conclusion that "it is almost impossible to bypass the animal traction stage and move directly to tractors."

The role of publicly supported research programs in farm equipment innovations is controversial. Historically, most of the research and development that has led to mechanical innovations has been carried out by manufacturers, often small rural-based workshops that have worked closely with farmers in identifying needs and designing implements that met the local requirements as economically as possible.

An important conclusion from the research by Binswanger and

Pingali is that "traditional" farmers "have responded to changes in population densities and external markets with changes in farming systems, land use patterns and technological change along systematic and predictable patterns" (Pingali and Binswanger, 1984, p. 336). Better understanding of those "systematic and predictable patterns" should increase the effectiveness of FSR researchers in facilitating adaptive learning by farmers as they make the transition to science-based farming systems. It is essential, however, for farmers to be involved from the beginning in what is bound to be a fairly time-consuming learning process. A recent study by William Jaeger (1984) documents the fact that it takes several years for farmers to achieve a rate of utilization of animal-powered equipment that ensures a satisfactory return on their investment.

Irrigation   Given the frequency and seriousness of drought in Africa, interest in irrigation as a means of accelerating the growth of agricultural production has increased. Ian Carruthers (1983, p. 12) has rightly warned against being seduced by the "power of a vision of a transformed, controlled, green, fertile desert." With the exception of Madagascar and Sudan, irrigation is currently of such limited importance that expansion of area under irrigation cannot be expected to contribute very much to the growth of agricultural production in the next two or three decades. It is estimated that on from 1 to 5 percent of the cultivated area in sub-Saharan Africa, some form of water control is utilized, ranging from conventional irrigation schemes to traditional "flood recession farming" (using residual moisture) and swamp drainage. (See Eicher and Baker, 1982, pp. 133–39 for an excellent review of the literature on irrigation in Africa.)

A broad consensus has emerged that most large-scale irrigation investments have proven to be expensive, inefficient, and poorly managed and maintained. After the early 1970s, additions to the irrigated area resulting from construction of new facilities were more than offset by others that had to be abandoned or required rehabilitation. Also, because water control is not complete or is poorly managed, not all developed areas are farmed (World Bank, 1981, p. 76). The expected high yields are not being obtained, technical problems continue, planning has been inadequate, health problems are created, and financing of operations and maintenance is woefully inadequate.

Evidence suggests that small-scale, farmer-initiated irrigation efforts are likely to be more beneficial than large-scale public schemes (Carruthers, 1984). These informal schemes have made greater contributions to food production than the larger ones and use rural labor and local materials. In contrast, conventional irrigation schemes are very costly, requiring an investment of some $5000 to $20,000 per irrigated hectare. Skilled management and further financial resources are needed to operate them effectively. The opportunity cost of capital and managerial staff is very high. Thus there is a very real danger that undue emphasis on irrigation will divert scarce resources from the less glamorous but vastly more extensive rainfed sector.

In the long run, irrigation will undoubtedly become more important. There is reason to believe, however, that natural conditions in Africa are less favorable for reliance on irrigation than in Asia. The great rivers of Asia get much of their water and alluvium from headwaters outside the tropics and carry a richer load of nutrient-bearing silt. The permanent snow cover of the Himalayas also represents an enormous resource for recharging underground aquifers, whereas the high rates of evapotranspiration in sub-Saharan Africa reduce significantly available water surpluses. The main economic potential of the Congo and other rivers in the high-rainfall basin is as a source of hydroelectric power. Studies in Kenya, which is probably more typical, suggest that the potential for expanded irrigation is limited (Eicher and Baker, 1982, p. 134).

Clearly, there is a major need for research to guide future irrigation development in Africa, including studies of the economies of rainfed versus irrigated agriculture as a basis for determining development priorities in individual countries. It seems likely that in much of Africa, it will be desirable to utilize water resources selectively, for example, for supplementary irrigation and for high-value crops, including dry season production of fruits and vegetables. Attention should also be given to improving water supplies for domestic use in order to reduce the enormous amount of time spent by women and children in carrying water long distances.

ORGANIZATIONS AND RURAL DEVELOPMENT

More efficient organizations and managerial procedures are of great importance in achieving better implementation of agricultural and rural development programs. In Africa, there appears to be a particular need for a more pragmatic, pluralistic approach to such issues. Emphasis on the competing "isms"—socialism versus capitalism or "the magic of the marketplace"—tend to polarize the development debate and divert attention from the more mundane but critical choices. In brief, a "shift in focus to technological and institutional details is long overdue. . .the most serious problems lie not in the grand design, but in what has the superficial appearance of details" (A.K. Sen as quoted in Hunter, 1978, p. 37).

The "institutional details" are critical because economic progress requires "a continually widening network of larger, specialized units of collective action" (Brewster, 1967, p. 69). Those "specialized units of collective action" can include private firms and cooperatives and other types of local organizations as well as government agencies. It is useful to view organizations as a framework for calculation and control through which individuals determine what each should do and seek to ensure that each does what is expected.[4] Those social techniques of calculation and control fall into four categories: "hierarchical techniques" on which governments must rely but which are also employed by large private corporations; "exchange techniques" epitomized by price and market mechanisms but which also include patronage systems; "polyarchical techniques" that provide for some degree of accountability, (e.g., through elective local councils and various systems of voting); and the "bargaining techniques" that are so important in small, local organizations such as cooperatives or irrigation associations.

There is now a growing recognition in African countries that the proliferation of parastatals has been a major source of inefficiency and a serious obstacle to agricultural progress. They are also an important symptom of a common problem in developing countries—an imbalance between the responsibilities taken on by the public sector and the resources available for fulfilling them. The imbalance between the responsibilities assigned to African parastatals and their limited administrative capacity has been particularly serious when they have been given operational responsibilities for the production and marketing of food crops.

A blanket condemnation of parastatals is as counterproductive as excessive reliance on such organizations. For example, the Kenya Tea Development Authority has performed a useful role in carrying out functions to facilitate rapid expansion of tea production by smallholders. S. Olayide and Francis S. Idachaba (1983) make the valid point that a parastatal has somewhat greater flexibility than a government ministry (e.g., in being able to pay more attractive salaries). They also suggest, however, that there is a need for a transition from "parastatals that engage directly in farm input supply and food marketing" to "facilitating institutions" which undertake more limited but crucial functions such as providing market information and coordinating price policies.

John K. Galbraith, who is certainly not an ideologue of the price system, has emphasized that market mechanisms "economize on scarce and honest administrative talent," whereas reliance on detailed planning and administratively determined prices jeopardizes the prospects for rapid and efficient growth. "The consequence—reliance on a large centrally planned and administered public sector—is that the greatest possible claim is placed on the scarcest possible resource. That is, administrative talent, with its complementary requirements in expert knowledge, experience, and discipline" (Galbraith, 1979, p. 111).

Discussions on the privatization of functions such as distribution of inputs or marketing of farm products in Africa often stress the weakness and venality of existing private firms. The important point, however, is that it is inherently more difficult for government agencies than for private firms to efficiently carry out essentially commercial operations. A government or quasi-governmental agency such as a grain marketing board must rely on the "discipline" of bureaucratic regulations to limit graft and corruption. Such regulations reduce flexibility and increase costs, although the patronage role of parastatals is also important in inflating their overhead and operating costs. The more general point is that government operations and controls that confer arbitrary and discretionary power inevitably create "rents" because they give certain officials and other favored individuals control over scarce resources. Literature on "the political economy of rent seeking" emphasizes that when government policies and programs create rents, there will invariably be public officials and private firms that engage in rent-seeking activity regardless of whether this involves illegal practices (Kreuger, 1974).

Needless to say, private traders and other entrepreneurs will frequently charge "exorbitant" prices or pay "unfair" prices (e. g., by using scales that underweigh produce delivered by farmers). Playing a regulatory role to minimize fraudulent practices is clearly a valuable one for governments. Competition, however, provides the most important discipline over private firms, spurring them to efficiency and curbing tendencies to cheat farmers or consumers. In isolated rural areas, however, private firms may be relatively immune from competition. Efficient distribution of farm inputs is likely to be especially difficult in the early stages of commercialization when the volume of transactions is low. A parastatal organization for input distribution may therefore play a useful role until the level of demand is sufficient to attract competing private firms and independent cooperatives.

Negative attitudes toward private firms and the price and market system derive in part from "the autocratic legacy of the colonial system" and "the control orientation of the colonial approach to agriculture" (Young, 1984, p. 16; Leonard, 1984, p. 20). Furthermore, it was expected that an activist, independent state would bring the good things of life to the people; the surge in development expenditures at the very end of the colonial period made that hope and expectation seem credible. Post-colonial African states have tended to equate "development and welfare" with direct government involvement in commercial operations as much as in the provision of "public goods" such as education, agricultural research, and health services. This was often reinforced by the very understandable resentment of the extent to which trade was dominated by Asians, Lebanese, or Europeans.

What are the prospects for a more pragmatic approach to the complex and difficult issues of choosing appropriate organizational structures and social techniques of calculation and control? The recent enthusiasm in development literature for "participation" has been a move in the right direction. There has been an unfortunate tendency, however, to take a narrow view of participation, equating it exclusively with "participatory organizations" in which elected officials and members rely on the social techniques of bargaining and voting in carrying out the tasks of calculation and control.

Local organizations such as marketing cooperatives and irrigation associations can perform valuable functions. But it is important to realize that such organizations impose substantial costs on their members in time and energy and they often fail, in part because benefits to be gained are not sufficient to induce the time and effort required for effective participation. Fortunately, fulfilling the two essential functions of participation—providing feedback based on direct, local knowledge and performing a watchdog function against arbitrary abuses of power—does not necessarily depend on the creation of formal membership organizations.

This broader view of participation has been emphasized by Grace Goodell, an anthropologist with extensive experience in developing countries, who focuses on the importance of "routine fields of interaction." Goodell argues that these fields of interaction, which result from frequent contacts between individuals engaged in economic transactions, are "the real locus of initiative and risk-taking, saving and investment, habits of work or laziness, decisions to link with one another for any common endeavor" (Goodell, 1983, p. 9). She emphasizes that it is within such fields of interaction that predictability—so important for rational allocation of resources—becomes possible.

Goodell also notes that predictability and the rational and innovative behavior which it engenders also depend on "the security of bonding" (i.e., the mutual confidence that derives from repetitive contacts and transactions among those who make up a "field of interaction" which becomes a "system"). That system is made up of individuals, firms, rules of behavior, channels, and specific institutions, which are more likely to be informal than formal. The evolution of savings institutions from informal savings clubs in Africa are an interesting example cited by Leonard (1984, p. 24).

These three prerequisites of sustained and vigorous development—rationality, predictability, and bonding—are jeopardized when participants in local fields of interaction are subject to arbitrary action by outsiders. However, as local "systems" emerge and grow more complex, the participants may gradually become sufficiently numerous and well-organized to act as a pressure group against arbitrary actions by government. In African countries, however, the ubiquitous involvement of government in commercial operations has created an environment hostile to such an evolution. Little progress has been made toward creating the positions that make for predictability, rationality, and bonding. To a large extent, economic development has been dependent on government action instead of being generated by the energy and initiative of individual farmers, traders, and a host of other small- and medium-scale entrepreneurs in positions to identify and act upon opportunities for economic and technical innovations.

Much has been learned since the era when the dictum that the government is best which governs least was advanced. We now know that there are many ways in which governments can play a catalytic and facilitating role in fostering economic and social progress. In particular, direct government action is indispensable in making available important "public goods." Because of the nature of public goods such as police protection and education, it is inefficient and inequitable to rely on markets and the response of private firms to demands for such services: They will simply not be made available at socially optimal levels without interventions by publicly supported organizations. In fact, one of the most powerful reasons for reducing government involvement in what are essentially commercial operations is to permit a concentration of its limited administrative capacity on "only those components which are not likely to be undertaken without planned public intervention" (Lele, 1979, p. 191).

Agricultural research systems and extension programs and investments in roads and other rural infrastructure are examples of public goods important to agricultural development. Public support for health, education, and family planning programs are equally important to the broader goal of rural development. Although public health activities have already brought about a drastic reduction in crude death rates, infant and child mortality rates are still excessively high.

It is beyond the scope of this paper to pursue the important issues of health, nutrition, and family planning. Nevertheless, it needs to be emphasized that expanding agricultural output sufficiently to permit improvements in per capita food consumption will become increasingly difficult and eventually insoluble unless progress is made in bringing birth rates into a more manageable balance with the sharply reduced death rates that now prevail. Otherwise, "equilibrium" may be reestablished through a tragic increase in death rates, as growing population pressure on the land and degradation of land resources lead to increasingly frequent and serious food crises.

POLICY IMPLICATIONS

The issues of agricultural and rural development in Africa are enormously complex. In the future as in the past, attempts to find "new" solutions that will be easy and quick will only result in frustration and waste of scarce resources. The compelling need is for determined and sustained efforts to move toward macro-economic policies that are less damaging to Africa's farmers and to accelerate technological progress among small farmers that will predominate in Africa until well into the 21st century. Because of the structural and demographic characteristics of African economies, there is no realistic alternative to an emphasis on small-farm development that will achieve increases in productivity and output based on labor-using, capital-saving technologies. This is not based on some romantic notion that "small is beautiful." Rather, it represents the most economical and realistic means of furthering the multiple objectives of development with which African countries must be concerned.

In the analysis of the problems of agricultural and rural development in the preceding sections, a number of policy recommendations have been implied. The most important of those policy implications are summarized below:

- Strengthening national research systems and increasing the relevance of research to the needs of small farmers is probably the most fundamental requirement in implementing small farm development strategies and in making the needed transition from resource-based to science-based agriculture.

- Farming systems research is certainly no panacea, but it appears to offer promise as a means of taking advantage of the potential complementarities between formal experiment station research and the local knowledge of farmers for adaptive management in modifying their farming systems. On-farm research in collaboration with farmers thus appears to be the most efficient approach to generating sequences of location-specific innovations that will be feasible and profitable given the constraints that small farmers face, including the lack of cash income that limits their reliance on purchased inputs.

- The difficulties of strengthening national agricultural research systems are compounded by the heterogeneity of the rainfed agriculture that predominates in Africa and by severe shortages of trained personnel. Donors have a particularly significant role to play in helping to expand the supply of agricultural scientists, administrators, and other specialists by providing sustained support for long-term institution-building and well-qualified foreign scientists to offset present shortages. The small size of so many African countries complicates these problems because of limited tax bases and special difficulties in overcoming labor shortages. Thus there appears to be a particular need for foreign aid to strengthen national programs and International Agricultural Research Centers with headquarters or regional programs in Africa. A number of countries contain areas with similar agroclimatic conditions which means that external assistance can play a critical role in facilitating the diffusion among countries of scientific knowledge and technical innovations.

- Because of the overwhelming importance of rainfed agriculture in Africa, priority must be given to increasing its productivity rather than making costly investments in expanding irrigation. Small-scale, locally controlled irrigation or drainage schemes appear to be more cost-effective than large-scale conventional projects. Assistance to large-scale projects should concentrate on rehabilitating and improving the management of existing schemes. There is also a need for research on surface and ground water resources and on the economics of rainfed versus irrigated agriculture in individual countries.

- Successful implementation of agricultural programs in Africa will require a realistic and pragmatic approach to overcoming weakness in administration. Those weaknesses represent what Jon Moris (1983) has aptly termed a "systemic problem." In addition to their adverse effects on farmer incentives and on resource allocation for agriculture, macro-economic policies have led to acute shortages of foreign exchange and revenue crises that have exacerbated the difficulty of achieving efficient administration of agricultural programs. For example, shortages of fuel and spare parts often make it impossible for field staff to make field visits. Those same shortages also have adverse effects on road maintenance and on the availability of farm inputs and the consumer goods that influence farmers' decisions to expand production.

- In addition to the need for improvements in macro-economic management, there is a need to achieve a better balance between governmental responsibilities and resources. The common practice of creating parastatals to perform essentially commercial operations has aggravated this imbalance. Better understanding of the strengths and weaknesses of alternative "social techniques of calculation and control" could lead to more realistic and more pragmatic decisions about activities that demand direct government action. In the provision of "public goods" such as agricultural research, roads, rural infrastructure, education, and social services programs related to health and family planning, direct government action is indispensable. There is a need, however, for a greater emphasis on administrative decentralization and on the role that local organizations can play in the planning and implementation of agricultural and rural development programs. It is also important to recognize that participation and accountability can often be ensured by price and market mechanisms: Private firms or independent cooperatives are inherently more efficient than government agencies in carrying out essentially commercial activities such as distribution of farm inputs or the marketing of agricultural products.

• Frank and well-informed policy dialogue between policy-makers and donors is probably the most feasible way to promote needed improvements in national strategies for agricultural and rural development and in donor policies and programs. Fruitful policy dialogue, however, requires strengthening indigenous capacities for policy research and analysis, which underscores the importance of the institution-building task emphasized above. It also requires a greater donor effort to recognize the weaknesses of past policies and operating procedures and to achieve a better understanding and a workable consensus concerning the priority needs for external assistance in the future.

ACKNOWLEDGMENT

I am indebted to Elizabeth Foster and Harriet Johnston for research and editorial assistance.

NOTES

1. The introduction to the valuable survey of research on agricultural development in sub-Saharan Africa by Eicher and Baker (1982) contains a useful summary of the major ecological regions and agricultural systems found in the 41 countries included in their survey. See also Johnston (1958) and Ruthenberg (1980).

2. The implications for the choice of an agricultural strategy of this "arithmetic of population growth and structural transformation" are so significant that it is useful to spell out the relationships. The rate of structural transformation (RST) in a country, defined as the absolute increase in the share of nonfarm labor in the total labor force, depends on the existing share of nonfarm labor in the labor force (Ln/Lt), the rate of increase in the nonfarm labor force (Ln'), and the rate of increase in the total labor force (Lt'). Thus:

$$RST = Ln/Lt \, (Ln' - Lt').$$

It is readily apparent from this equation that the rate of structural transformation will tend to increase gradually as Ln/Lt increases (from just over .1 to .35

in the Kenya projections) and also as Ln' increases or Lt' declines. However, a decline in the rate of growth in the total labor force cannot be expected to occur in less than, say, 30 to 50 years because there will be a time lag of 15 to 20 years before a decline in fertility will be reflected in a reduction in Lt'. An even longer time will be required to reach the turning point when the absolute size of the farm labor force begins to decline.

3. In a fine journalistic report on hunger in Africa, David K. Wills reports: "In Mali alone," says a senior (World Bank) official in Washington, "there's potential to feed all of the Sahel. The problem isn't money. That's available. The problem is management. Projects are simply being abandoned" (*Christian Science Monitor*, Nov. 28, 1984, p.23). Management is indeed a problem. But there is reason to doubt whether it is *the* problem—and also whether the "evidence" underlying the assertion that Mali could "feed all of the Sahel" is any better than the evidence that encouraged the French to make huge investments in the Office du Niger irrigation project that was a disappointment for decades before independence.

4. This section draws heavily on William C. Clark's chapter on "Organization Programs: Institutional Structures and Managerial Procedures" in our joint book (Johnston and Clark, 1982, Chapter 5). The view of alternative social techniques of calculation and control derives from Dahl and Lindblom (1953).

REFERENCES

Anthony, K. R. M., B. F. Johnston, W. O. Jones and V. C. Uchendu. 1979. *Agricultural Change in Tropical Africa*. Ithaca: Cornell University Press.

Bates, R. 1981. *Markets and States in Tropical Africa*. Berkeley: University of California Press.

Bates, R. 1983. *Essays on the Political Economy of Rural Africa*. Cambridge: Cambridge University Press.

Binswanger, H. P., and J. McIntire. 1984. "Behavioral and Material Determinants of Production Relations in Land Abundant Tropical Agriculture." Report No. ARU 17. Research Unit, Agricultural and Rural Development Department, Operational Policy Staff. Washington, D.C.: The World Bank.

Binswanger, H.P., and P.L. Pingali. 1984. "The Evolution of Farming Systems and Agricultural Technology in Sub-Saharan Africa." Report No. ARU 23. Research Unit, Agriculture and Rural Development Department, Operational Policy Staff. Washington, D.C.: The World Bank.

Binswanger, H. P., and M. R. Rosenzweig. 1983. "Behavioral and Material Determinants of Production Relations in Agriculture." Report No. ARU 5, Revised October 5, 1983. Research Unit, Agriculture and Rural Development Department Operational Policy Staff. Washington D.C.: The World Bank.

Brewster, J. M. 1950. "The Machine Process in Agriculture and Industry," *Journal of Farm Economics* 32(1) (February): 69–81.

Brewster, J.M. 1967. "The Traditional Social Structures as Barriers to Change," in H. M. Southworth and B. F. Johnston, eds., *Agricultural Development and Economic Growth*. Itahca: Cornell University Press.

Byerlee, Derek, Larry Harrington and Donald L. Winkelmann. 1982. "Farming Systems Research: Issues in Research Strategy and Technology Design," *American Journal of Agricultural Economics* 64(5) (December): 897–904.

Carr, S. 1982. *The Impact of Government Intervention on Smallholder Development in North and East Uganda*. A. D. U. Occasional Paper No. 5. Wye, England: Agrarian Development Unit, Wye College.

Carruthers, Ian. 1983. "Irrigation Investment: A Problem, Palliative or Panacea for Agricultural Development?," Ian Carruthers, ed., *Aid for the Development of Irrigation*. Paris: OECD.

Carruthers, I. and A. Weir. 1976. "Rural Water Supplies and Irrigation Development," in J. Heyer, J. K. Maitha and W. M. Senga, eds., *Agricultural Development in Kenya*. Nairobi: Oxford University Press.

Collinson, M.F. 1982. *Farming Systems Research in Eastern Africa: The Experience of CIMMYT and Some National Agricultural Research Services, 1978–81*. MSU International Development Paper No. 3. East Lansing: Michigan State University, Department of Agricultural Economics.

Dahl, R. A. and C. E. Lindblom. 1953. *Politics, Economics and Welfare*. New York: Harper & Brothers.

Dlamini, Gilbert. 1983. Opening remarks at "Networkshop on Draught Power and Animal Feeding in Eastern and Southern Africa." Networking Workshops Report No. 2. Mbabane, Swaziland: CIMMYT Eastern and Southern Africa Economics Programme.

Eicher, C. K. and D. C. Baker. 1982. *Research on Agricultural Development in Sub-Saharan Africa: A Critical Survey*. MSU International Development Paper No. 1. East Lansing: Michigan State University, Department of Agricultural Economics.

Evenson, R. E. 1978. "The Organization of Research to Improve Crops and Animals in Low Income Countries," in T. W. Schultz, ed., *Distortions in Agricultural Incentives*. Bloomington and London: Indiana University Press.

Galbraith, J. K. 1979. *The Nature of Mass Poverty*. Cambridge, Mass.: Harvard University Press.

Gerhardt, J. 1975. *The Diffusion of Hybrid Maize in Western Kenya-Abridged by CIMMYT*. Mexico City: Centro Internacional de Mejoramiento de Maize y Trigo.

Goodell, G. 1983. "The Importance of Political Participation for Sustained Capitalist Development." Cambridge, Mass.: Harvard Law School.

Gusten, P. 1984. "Agriculture in Sub-Saharan Africa." Washington, D.C.: The World Bank.

Hart, K. 1982. *The Political Economy of West African Agriculture*. Cambridge: Cambridge University Press.

Hayami, Y. and V. W. Ruttan. 1984. *Agricultural Development: An International Perspective*. 1984 manuscript copy; to be published in 1985 by the Johns Hopkins University Press.

Heyer, J., J. K. Maitha and W. M. Senga, eds. 1976. *Agricultural Development in Kenya: An Economic Assessment.* Nairobi: Oxford University Press.

Hunter, Guy. 1978. "Report on Administration and Institutions." Asian Development Bank. *Rural Asia; Challenge and Opportunity,* Supplementary Papers, Vol. IV, *Administration and Institutions in Agricultural and Rural Development.* Manila: Asian Development Bank.

International Maize and Wheat Improvement Center. 1984. "A Report of a Networkshop on Draught Power and Animal Feeding in Eastern and Southern Africa." Report No. 2. Mbabane, Swaziland: CIMMYT Eastern and Southern Africa Economics Programme.

Jaeger, W. 1984. "Agricultural Mechanization: The Economics of Animal Traction in Burkina Faso." Ph.D. dissertation, Stanford Unviersity.

Johnston, B. F. 1958. *The Staple Food Economies of Western Tropical Africa.* Food Research Institute Studies in Tropical Africa. Stanford: Stanford University.

Johnston, B. F. and W. C. Clark. 1982. *Redesigning Rural Development: A Strategic Perspective.* Baltimore: Johns Hopkins University Press.

Johnston, B. F. and P. Kilby. 1975. *Agriculture and Stuctural Transformation: Economic Strategies in Late-Developing Countries.* New York: Oxford University Press.

Johnston, B. F. and T. P. Tomich. 1984. "The Feasibility of Small-Farm Development Strategies." Paper prepared for the AID/PPC. Washington, D.C.: AID.

Jones, W. O. 1972. *Marketing Staple Food Crops in Tropical Africa.* Ithaca and London: Cornell University Press.

Kozlowski, Z. 1975. "Agriculture in the Economic Growth of the East European Socialist Countries," in L. G. Reynolds, ed., *Agriculture in Development Theory.* New Haven and London: Yale University Press.

Krueger, A. O. 1974. "The Political Economy of the Rent-Seeking Society," *American Economic Review* LXIV(3) (June): 291–303.

Kydd, J. G. and R. E. Christiansen. 1982. "Structural Change and Trends in Equity in the Malawian Economy, 1964–80." University of Malawi, Centre for Social Research, Income Distribution Project, Working Paper No. 2.

Lamb, G. and L. Muller. 1982. *Control, Accountability and Incentives in a Successful Development Institution: The Kenya Tea Development Authority.* Staff Working Papers No. 550. Washington, D.C.: The World Bank.

Lele, U. 1979. *The Design of Rural Development: Lessons from Africa.* Baltimore and London: Johns Hopkins University Press.

Leonard, D. K. 1984. "Developing Africa's Agricultural Institutions: Putting the Farmer in Control." Berkeley: University of Calfornia, Department of Political Science.

Mellor, J. W. and B. F. Johnston. 1984. "The World Food Equation: Interrelations Among Development, Employment, and Food Consumption." *Journal of Economic Literature* 22(2) (June): 531–74.

Moris, J. R. 1983. "What Do We Know About African Agricultural Development? The Role of Extension Performance Reanalyzed." Draft No. 1.

Washington, D.C.: Bureau of Science and Technology, Agency for International Development.

Olayide, S. O. and F. S. Idachaba. 1983. "Input Supply and Food Marketing Systems for Agricultural Growth: A Nigerian Case Study." Paper presented at the International Conference on Accelerating Agricultural Growth in Sub-Saharan Africa. International Food Policy Research Institute, Victoria Falls, Zimbabwe. August 29–September 1.

Pingali, F. L. and H. P. Binswanger. 1984. "Population Density and Agricultural Intensification: A Study of the Evolution of Technologies in Tropical Agriculture." Report No. ARU 22. Washington, D.C.: Research Unit, Agriculture and Rural Development Department, Operational Staff, World Bank, October 17.

Ruthenberg, H. 1980. *Farming Systems in the Tropics*. 3rd ed. London: Oxford University Press.

Shah, M. M. and F. Willekens. 1978. *Rural-Urban Population Projections for Kenya and Implications for Development*. Laxenburg, Austria: International Institute for Applied Systems Analysis.

Tomich, Thomas P. 1984. "Private Land Reclamation in Egypt: Studies of Feasibility and Adaptive Behavior." Ph.D. dissertation. Stanford University.

World Bank. 1980. *World Development Report, 1980*. New York: Oxford University Press.

World Bank. 1981. "Accelerated Development in Sub-Saharan Africa." Washington, D.C.: The World Bank.

World Bank. 1984. *World Development Report, 1984*. New York: Oxford University Press.

World Bank. 1984. "Toward Sustained Development: A Joint Program of Action for Sub-Saharan Africa." Washington, D.C.: The World Bank.

Young, C. 1984. "The African Colonial State and Its Developmental Legacy." Madison: University of Wisconsin, Department of Political Science.

Putting the Farmer in Control: Building Agricultural Institutions

David K. Leonard

Looking to the future of African agriculture, debates about the causes of current food shortages lose relevance.[1] Rather, what is important is that African agriculture is at a turning point in terms of the structure of production itself. This structural shift will be caused by two factors. First, the African land frontier soon will be exhausted. In many areas, no significant opportunities remain for adding crop land without irrigation, and in only a few places, such as southern Sudan and parts of Zaire, does it seem that the frontier will extend well into the future. The existence of fallow land should not deceive us into thinking that land is still available. Under current production conditions, Africa's fragile tropical soils require as long as 15 years to recover their fertility after they have been farmed. Already the beginnings of a shift toward increasing output through improvements in productivity rather than land expansion is evident (Berry, 1983, p. 50), and the era of growth through extensive agriculture will have to be replaced by intensification (Eicher and Baker, 1982, pp. 110,116).

The second factor affecting the structure of agricultural production is the high rate of Africa's population growth, which will increase both the demand for food and the numbers working in agriculture. Under the most optimistic assumptions, agriculture will continue to absorb increased absolute numbers of workers for at least another 30 years.[2] This factor will combine with the shortage of new land to create pressures and opportunities for the intensification of produc-

tion that have been absent in Africa's traditionally labor-scarc
culture (Hart 1982, p. 133). Demand pressures on food product
will also be accentuated. Since very few African states have the capacity to control food prices, a shift in the domestic terms of trade toward
food crops can be expected which will support and finance an intensification of production. These trends are also likely to encourage intensification of export crop production, making land more valuable
and labor more abundant.

As a result of population growth and land shortage, commercial
food production will become increasingly important. Demand will
come not only from the growing urban areas but also from the landless and near-landless whose numbers are increasing and who will no
longer be able to survive solely by subsistence efforts. Second, agriculture will make much more intensive use of land and labor. In most
places, the land frontier will cease to exist and the rural poor will have
to work for others in order to make ends meet. Third, profits will
increase sufficiently to make science-based agriculture and the use of
purchased inputs much more attractive for food crops.

This shift in the structure of production will not overtake all of
Africa at once, as there is great diversity in African agriculture (Berry,
1983, pp. 9–11). Nonetheless, with such a widespread and significant
structural shift will come a host of new problems and opportunities to
which African governments and donors will need to respond. A great
many of the insights developed over the years on the behavior of the
continent's farmers are beginning to lose relevance.

THE DYSFUNCTIONS OF THE CONTROL MODEL

To date, most efforts to promote agricultural production in Africa
have relied heavily on instruments of control. Some public agency or
private firm arrogates monopsony power over a crop and closely
supervises its growers (i.e., a monopoly is exercised over purchase).
If credit is to be extended for inputs, it is provided in kind and payments are deducted at the monopsony point of sale. This strategy
aims at bringing subsistence producers under state control and ex-
tracting resources from agriculture for other sectors of the economy
(Hart, 1982, pp. 88–90; Heyer, Roberts, and Williams, 1981, p. 10).

This particular method was based on two assumptions, however,

The first is that African smallholders are too
 ̷et forces to achieve the commodity quality,
 ̷ment level desired. The second is that only a
 ̷ating organization can assure the simultaneous
 ̷necessary requirements of commercial produc-
 ̷ ed African economies.

̷ may have been some basis for assuming farmer
insensi.. ̷ ̷ ̷narket, given the availability of land, and the fact
that the economic survival of smallholders was not dependent on the
market, and the weak price signals given by the commercially underdeveloped colonial economies. In this sense, farmers were autonomous, and administrators who were desperate to establish a rural
presence and to finance the state would have felt driven to establish
whatever controls they could (Hyden, 1980).

This assumption of price-insensitive producers was probably always overstated, however, and is doubtful today. As commercialization has progressed, evidence of price responsiveness has become
striking (Eicher and Baker, 1982, pp. 28–30).[3]

The other assumption undergirding the traditional control approach was a much stronger one. Commercial, science-based agriculture must be supported by an elaborate infrastructure. It is necessary
to assure the simultaneous and timely presence of seeds, fertilizer,
credit, extension, roads, transport, and markets. Traditional subsistence agriculture did not stimulate adequate supply of any of these
services. Therefore, the only way to achieve a breakthrough to commercial production was for all of the services to be provided by a
single organization integrated either vertically around a single crop or
horizontally for a particular region. Monopoly and monopsony are
not intrinsic to this solution—the purpose is to assure that at least one
of each service is present, but not only one. In practice, however,
monopoly is the result, in part because the assumption of price insen-
sitivity, which encourages control, comes to be mixed in with it. The
temptation to use profits from marketing to cross-subsidize the other
services makes it unprofitable for private traders to compete against
the subsidized services and makes monopsony necessary for the
profitable ones. These integrating organizations therefore are generally constructed around marketing monopsonies for a crop or region.
These monopoly powers then make it possible for socially uneconomic agencies to survive.

The integrating organization has a powerful logic and has produced many famous successes, such as Ethiopia's CADU, Malawi's

Lilongwe, and the Kenya Tea Development Authority (Lele, 1975). For a variety of reasons, however, it is now counterproductive for agricultural development in most of Africa. First, this method of promoting agriculture tends to create a fragmented and segregated series of support organizations. The integrating organization provides services for only one crop or region and leaves others totally unserved. Ultimately, these integrating organizations inhibit the development of a well-articulated national economic infrastructure, one in which all the parts can relate to one another and have the fluidity to move into whatever promising openings emerge.

Second, the specialized integrating organization approach is prejudicial to the support of food production. It is extremely difficult to enforce monopsony for commodities that are primarily consumed in mass domestic markets. Thus integrating organizations avoid them or support them only when the farmer also has an export crop (the anchor or security crop concept), which is prejudicial to the poorer farmers who grow only food. Both approaches severely inhibit the emergence of good support services for locally consumed crops because they skim off much of the most profitable business with their specialized focus.

Third, monopolies and monopsonies are dangerous if administrative performance is problematic. When an organization that is the sole provider of an essential service delivers inadequately or late, the entire crop will be threatened, even if all the other services are present. Management standards are not high in most of Africa today. Where recurrent finances are in jeopardy, tendering procedures are tangled, personnel administration is hampered by patronage, staff are underpaid and demoralized, or management by crisis is the rule, single channels for supply of services are a recipe for failure. Where several of them must interact for agriculture to progress, the probability of success is very low (Leonard, 1984). Overlapping, competing organizations—public, private, cooperative, or some mixture—provide the reliability of support which is required in an agricultural infrastructure and are thus the ideal (Landau, 1969).

IMPLICATIONS FOR GOVERNMENTAL ACTIVITY

Most African farmers now need a structure of businesses and other organizations which serves the national economy as a whole, rather than in regional or product-specific fragments. African producers, as consumers, are able to choose and coordinate the support services they require by purchasing them in an open market rather than having the decisions imposed by bureaucrats who are all too often distant and ill-informed (Bottrall and Howell, 1980, p. 150). Achieving this new economic infrastructure will require a concentration on institutional development, involving dismantling current monopolistic controls, facilitating the growth of smaller entrepreneurs, promoting improvements in retrenched public agencies, and financing the construction and maintenance of the necessary physical infrastructure. Such changes will have to be phased in gradually and will require only a modest increase in governmental and donor resources.

Much of the required changes are in the area of public policy and a large part of external assistance will be of the non-project variety. By no means will all activity be of this character, however. A simple dose of privatization and getting prices right will not solve the continent's agricultural problems. The problem in the agricultural sector is more the anti-market and control orientation of the state than its presence. The objective is to move it from a control to a service role which promotes a highly competitive private and cooperative sector.

Since the present policies and structures are deeply rooted in the political sociology of contemporary Africa, such institutional changes will be difficult to achieve and will require considerable amounts of project assistance focused on institutional development. Conditions attached to economic support funds may be useful in bargaining over major policy decisions, but they are too blunt an instrument for the finer, day-to-day operations of government agencies, where much of the reform is needed. Institutional change is never easy and only a small part of the process is the initial decision by government leaders that it would be desirable. A great deal of what appears to have been won at the policy level is lost during implementation.

Institutional development requires a good deal of patient waiting and a long time-horizon. More narrowly focused projects may produce quicker results that can be credited to visible, specific donors, but institution-building is the only way to create a set of structures that will sustain dynamic, national agricultural development. It is institutional structures that distinguish Africa's agriculturally successful nations, not the volume of their project activity.

Donors will not have to wait long to begin institutional reform and development. The first openings already exist. The world recession, the African drought, and the recent changes in the development community's analysis of the continent's problems have combined to produce quite dramatic changes in the receptivity of African governments to institutional reform. Nonetheless, these first openings are only the start of a long, difficult process that will take many years and much patient searching for strategic opportunities.

THE MARKETING OF SUPPLIES AND PRODUCE

Science-based agriculture depends upon on a strong set of market institutions. Fertilizer, improved seed, and other inputs have to be bought and produce has to be sold to pay for these purchases. The establishment of these markets is often very difficult in the early stages of commercialization, for the volume of transactions is so small that profits are low for the trader and prices are unattractive to the farmer. Traders are discouraged from developing these markets and farmers from selling. Thus volume remains low and the trade that exists is frequently monopolistic, making prices still worse. Integrating government corporations have often been created to speed the breaking of this vicious circle. The problem is that these organizations tend to become monopolies and eventually exploit producers with poor prices or bad service, as they have little incentive to perform efficiently.

There are other solutions to the vicious circle problem. The development of roads and the improvement of transportation greatly reduce trading costs, boosting prices and competition. Access to credit and other forms of assistance may also help to bring in new entrepreneurs and lower their operating costs. Governments also may encourage the development of larger wholesale commodity markets in some towns (Jones, 1980, pp. 337–39). Trader exploitation of farmers is best prevented by competition, government broadcasting of price information, and regulation of weights and measures. The available evidence indicates that rural traders, being small and competitive, operate on low margins (Lele, 1981, p. 59). Providing roads and assistance to transporters and traders has the additional advantage of being popular with groups that are politically powerful in most African countries.

Despite the general attractiveness of the small trader option, it has not been judged viable in the past. Government marketing operations are acceptable and cooperative ones can be encouraged as long as they do not result in monopoly. African farmers' most effective power is the ability to withdraw their business. When monopoly deprives them of this exit option, they are quickly exploited. African marketing cooperatives performed quite well in the 1950s when they were struggling for their existence, but have done badly since they began to enjoy official protection, as they have been made instruments of government programs and are not permitted to fail. If the weak cooperatives were allowed to go under, incentives for good management would improve dramatically. The major issue is not a public versus private structure for markets but rather a monopolistic versus a competitive one (Peterson, 1982a).

The opening of new markets is not the only reason for government marketing corporations. They have also been used to tax exports and to even out extreme fluctuations in commodity prices. Revenues must be raised from the rural sector in these predominantly agricultural economies, and export producers tend to be the more affluent farmers. Thus the tax function of public corporations is legitimate, although many African states have so overdone it as to harm the very export crop production on which they depend (World Bank, 1981, Chapter 5).

The dampening of price fluctuations is also a legitimate public function, although it is more often proclaimed as a justification than actually practiced. During the commodity boom of the 1950s, this argument was used to withhold full payments from West African producers, but the funds were diverted and the argument was then forgotten when prices turned down. The restriction of price extremes for food grains requires considerable storage facilities, as stocks must be bought in the good years and sold off in the bad. Very few African countries have the storage capacity to even attempt the exercise. Given the likelihood of recurring drought, the expansion of such facilities is worthy of consideration for those countries that do sometimes produce surpluses.

While there is a case for state intervention in produce marketing, it is not an economic one. Taxes have to be raised and welfare needs are often quite pressing. Whether these justifications are sufficiently persuasive to outweigh their economic costs will depend on the particular circumstances of each country.

Nonetheless, none of the arguments for state participation requires intervention in local markets. The state need only be a buyer of last resort to ease price fluctuations or to provide food security. The taxation of export crops can be done at the point of shipment. Ivory

Coast has the most efficient cocoa marketing structure in West Africa because its government marketing corporation never handles physical delivery of the crop, confining its role to regulating and taxing private trade (Gbetibouo and Delgado, 1984, p. 120). In this way the burden that the government places on agriculture is explicit, intentional, and directly benefits the Treasury, rather than acting as a hidden weight on agriculture through inefficient operations that benefit only the patrons that use them to provide jobs.[4]

The logic of the argument for less direct state involvement in the marketing of inputs and outputs is persuasive, but it will not be easy to achieve where a presence has already been established. Once these government corporations exist, they are hard to dismantle, for the political cost of dismissing employees is high. It is easier to reduce their monopoly powers, although even there resistance is fierce.

For most of Africa, food marketing is the main area where it will be possible to limit the role of the state, because its control has always been marginal, and the main task will be to resist its encroachment on these commodities. Since this is the area where the largest proportionate increase in commercial transactions will occur as the continent's agriculture undergoes its structural shift, this segment of the market is no small matter. Food crops are also the easiest for which to stimulate purely indigenous trading activity and are an important focus of market activity for women, especially in West Africa. It should not be difficult to build strong, private, locally controlled marketing systems for food, as long as governments provide infrastructure and some encouragement.

CREDIT AND SAVINGS

Across the continent, the provision of subsidized credit has been one of the most popular methods of inducing agricultural innovation. Its use has been based on the assumption that capital is scarce in the rural areas and that cheap credit can be used to reduce the costs and risks of new investment. Generally, most of the credit has been provided in kind in the form of inputs, and collections have been made when the farmers sell their produce to monopsonistic marketing organizations. The need to provide security for such formal credit has been one of the primary rationales for the registration of land ownership as well. Such credit schemes have been attractive to African governments because they provide a visible and popular way to "do something" for farmers, and donors have supported them because they provide a vehicle through which large amounts of capital can be moved quickly. Nonetheless, virtually every aspect of this traditional approach to rural credit is flawed.

First, it is unclear that capital really is scarce in rural Africa (Hill, 1970; Donald, 1976, p. 164). Although money often is unavailable for needed agricultural investments, rural dwellers can find capital to pay for school fees and for investments in transport and commerce. Instead, the problems are that investments in agriculture have not been sufficiently profitable and rural savings have been poorly mobilized.

Frequently, subsidized credit has been used to induce changes in small farming that are only weakly profitable or even sometimes detrimental (Heyer, Roberts, and Williams, 1981, p. 7; Donald, 1976, p. 36). Credit then is a substitute for improvements in the profitability of a particular crop by raising its sale price or lowering the cost of its inputs. The available evidence suggests that input subsidies provide much stronger incentives to adopt a new technology than do low interest rates (Adams and Graham, 1981, p. 354). They are also more efficient, as they affect a larger portion of the farm population, whereas subsidized credit is likely to be restricted to the most influential.

Furthermore, it is likely that there are substantial untapped sources of savings in the rural areas (Lele, 1975, p. 97) and that access to them is actually being damaged by subsidized credit programs. Not only does such credit divert attention from the task of building rural savings institutions, but it also decreases the incentive to save and so depresses savings. Thus the leading experts on rural financial markets recommend that savings mobilization should come before emphasis on credit in the early stages of rural development (Adams and Graham, 1981, pp. 351, 356).

Second, it has been presumed that the high interest rates charged by traditional money-lenders are usurious and that low-interest government loans will stimulate development. The available evidence indicates that money-lenders' charges are high because of the costs and risks associated with making loans to small borrowers, not because of exploitative profits. Small farmers are frequently prepared to pay this price for the ease of traditional borrowing, for they often choose it over low-interest government-sponsored credit laden with formal procedures. Indeed, artificially low government interest rates are dysfunctional, depressing the incentive for savings and resulting in most of the loans going to the influential. Thus subsidized interest rates neither stimulate rural development nor help the poor. The general consensus today is that credit should carry market interest rates and that subsidies should go instead into the administrative costs of making savings and credit available to the smallholder (Peterson, 1982a, pp. 90–95).

Third, the form in which agricultural credit has been provided traditionally has been dysfunctional. Arising out of the control orientation of the colonially inspired approach to agriculture, farmers are not trusted to make their own investment decisions and are provided with credit in kind. One disadvantage is that this inhibits the use of loan funds for labor costs and so discourages the very intensification of agriculture that is desired. Another disadvantage is that using the capital for non-agricultural purposes is made difficult. Very often a farmer's most pressing need for capital is not for his crops, but for food, school fees, or attractive commercial opportunities (Chambers, 1983, pp. 117–319). The farmer will go to great lengths to convert the in-kind loan into cash (at a discount to its value) in order to meet other pressing needs. As a consequence, the loan will not benefit the farmer as much as it should, it will not lead to increased production, and it probably will not be repaid (for no new income is produced and the farmer will recognize that he or she will not get another loan without evidence of higher yields).

Several of the leading figures in the field now urge that the use of credit for consumption purposes should be accepted as legitimate and that loans should be untied (Adams and Graham, 1981, p. 355; Lipton, 1980, p. 243). Such a policy actually leads to a significant improvement in loan repayment rates, as farmers are extremely anxious to protect their access to general, untied credit sources (Lele, 1975, p. 94; Leonard, 1984a, p. 183). Thus general rural savings and credit institutions, not ones that are tied narrowly to agriculture, should be promoted. Such a strategy would support broad economic development in the rural areas and would probably support agriculture better than the specifically agricultural credit institutions, as farmers would increasingly use loans for agricultural purposes once they have met their other pressing credit needs. Improved functioning of rural financial markets would also result from the higher use and repayment rates.

The fourth disadvantageous aspect of existing agricultural credit policy is methods of assuring repayment. The most common has been to loan only to farmers who grow cash crops that will have to be sold through a monopsonistic outlet and to collect at the point of sale. There are several problems with this "security crop" method: It imposes a known disability on farmers as a condition for a benefit that is not enjoyed by all; it denies credit to those who produce only food; it makes women's access to credit more difficult, as men generally control export crop revenues while women control the production of food crops; and finally, it doesn't work. Once a credit system begins to break down, farmers have proved remarkably adept at getting around their obligations, even with monopsonies. They change their names, sell to other producers for resale, bribe receiving agents, etc. (Leonard, 1984, p. 183).

The other traditional method of assuring repayment is to require that individually owned and registered land be used as collateral, but this has disadvantages as well. The costs of registering land are much higher than the likely benefits of the credit system that will use it. Creditors, particularly governmental ones, also find it difficult and costly to foreclose on land-secured loans. Further, reliance on land as collateral denies women access to credit. Finally, the system encourages central governments to take control of land use and tenure away from local communities.

The most reliable and viable methods for assuring high loan repayment rates are the borrower's knowledge that he or she will need to use the credit system again, and the sanctions of the borrower's neighbors. The first is most readily assured through a general rural credit system. Virtually all rural dwellers have recurrent needs for consumption credit and will go to considerable lengths to protect their access to it. If formal credit institutions were less rigid about tying their loans and if all creditors (traders, money-lenders, banks, and government agencies) communicated with one another about defaults, farmers would have a powerful incentive to repay their debts and to maintain their credit ratings.

The creation of local sanctions for repayment could be highly complementary with the stimulation of rural savings. Informal savings clubs are extremely widespread in Africa, especially among women (Miracle, Miracle and Cohen, 1980, p. 701). With care, these clubs could be developed into small credit unions and could provide the base for small, cost-effective credit operations through links with more formal banking institutions.

Thus the development of effective rural financial markets need not involve the creation of a new set of credit institutions. What is needed instead is assistance with the extension of the functions of an indigenous social institution and its linkage with commercial banks. This would involve subsidies for administrative costs, but not for interest rates. Although it is important that these clubs initially focus on savings, they can evolve into associations in which rural dwellers are lending their own money to one another, thereby having a considerable stake in assuring repayments (Bottral and Howell, 1980, p. 159). The eventual goal would be a well-articulated, integrated banking system, linking rural and urban sectors. Farmers would continue to save but they would also be able to draw on the larger capital resources of urban residents and entrepreneurs (Donald, 1976, p. 95).

This type of credit system is quite different from the usually unsuccessful marketing cooperative credit schemes. The latter associations are not face-to-face institutions, so that people do not know one another well and cannot apply effective social sanctions. Marketing coops also handle the funds they on-lend in such a way that members rarely feel that losses are coming out of their own pockets (even when they are). As a result, there has been room for considerable exploitation in cooperative credit schemes. All of these unfortunate attributes probably could be avoided in the credit union clubs, with the expectation of quite different results. For example, the savings clubs tend to evolve on lines that are rather homogeneous socio-economically (Muzaale and Leonard, 1985). As long as steps are taken to encourage the availability of clubs to even the poorer members of rural society, the homogeneity of the clubs could help to assure that the more influential do not dominate them and use them to exploit the less advantaged, as they have in the marketing cooperatives (Peterson, 1982b). The experience of the Cameroon Cooperative Credit Union League, the Zimbabwe Rural Savings Clubs, and group credit in Malawi are encouraging examples of what can be achieved (Von Pischke and Rouse, 1983, pp. 27–33).

Although not everyone will be able to save or have access to credit through such a system, in practice only a minority have access to loans now. For those who are left out of the rural financial markets, off-farm employment opportunities are needed. The creation of rural financial markets is important precisely to foster such employment generation. State-sanctioned credit is generally directed too narrowly to meet farmers' strong demands for diversifying their investments and strengthening the rural off-farm economy. All of these steps will take much less capital than has been customary in past donor activity and much more patience and investment of time and local energy in building self-reliance. These institution-building investments have a major, albeit indirect, economic rate of return.

RESEARCH AND EXTENSION

Research and extension are essential to science-based agriculture and are necessary areas for state activity; however, research has not received the priority it deserves in Africa. Investments in this area return benefits only over the long term and are therefore easily neglected by governments that are overwhelmed by pressing needs.

Improvements in the quality and quantity of research are needed and here the farming systems approach has a particularly important contribution to make. Many technical innovations have been stillborn because they were inappropriate to the actual conditions of typical small farmers. Farming systems research can make plant breeders, entymologists, engineers, and others aware of the real constraints that smallholders in various ecosystems are facing and so direct their attention to innovations that will relieve them. The task of "on-farm research with a farming systems perspective" is to assist in the feedback and technical development process by making agricultural scientists aware of what farmers' problems really are (Johnston, 1984). Once research breakthroughs have expanded the range of feasible and profitable options, it can be left to smallholders themselves to decide how best to use them.

Extension has a significant role to play in the development and dissemination of appropriate innovations. Researchers cannot possibly be aware of all the intricacies of farm-level problems and must rely on feedback from the extension agents. Unfortunately, Africa's extension systems are deficient and in need of improvement.

Africa's extension services have been built on quite a different model from the American one, which has well-trained professionals serving a sophisticated and condensed farm population. Instead, African systems have a large number of moderately trained paraprofessionals at its base, serving a mass of smallholders. A system based on paraprofessionals is quite difficult to run, for they need to be organized, motivated, and kept informed to a degree that professionals do not (Leonard, 1977; Leonard and Marshall, 1982, p. 9).

The World Bank's Training and Visit (T&V) system represents the best available solution to these management demands, taking a highly disciplined approach to extension management. A set of formal groups is created, among which the extension agent circulates in a regular, predictable, and readily supervised manner. It is also quite systematic in arranging for the monthly training of extension staff by professional specialists and creating opportunities for problems to be discussed, providing feedback to the research system (Benor and Harrison, 1977; Benor and Baxter, 1984). T&V is not without problems but it has achieved successes in an area in which failure is more common.

At the paraprofessional level, improvements in the quality of training are in order. There are several reasons for wanting to hold back on the numbers of staff at the base of the extension pyramid at this stage. First, expenditures on extension can only be justified when there are profitable innovations to diffuse. A higher quality extension service is justified for it will improve feedback and adaptation, however, and thus improve the quality and appropriateness of research. Second, most of the continent's extension systems have suffered from the under-supervision of junior staff, so it is appropriate to hold back on lower-level numbers in order to restore balance. Third, the usual argument for increases in extension is based on the ratio of farmers to agents, which assumes that farmers must be under the continual supervision of government staff who "know better" if production standards are to be maintained. This degrading image of the farmer is inappropriate. Instead, extension should be conceived of as dealing with a chain of farmer groups which are taught innovations in succession, thus obviating the need for agents to be available to all farmers at all times. Governments are often receptive to donor offers to expand extension services even when they are unpersuaded of their economic value, for they see them as a way to relieve the pressure of unemployed school leavers. When good agricultural research is not available, this is not a cost-effective way of dealing with this pressure, especially when Africa's public payrolls are already overburdened (World Bank, 1981, p. 42).

Government and donor support for agricultural research and extension is therefore needed. The priorities should be expanded research, improvements in the appropriateness of innovations through farming systems work, tightened management of extension services by the application of Training and Visit system reforms, and enhanced quality for agricultural education.

LAND

Traditional land tenure systems in Africa were corporate. Land was held collectively in family, kinship, clan and tribal units, and allocated to individual households for their personal use who lost rights to it if they ceased to occupy it. The collectivity periodically distributed land to new claimants. The view is widely held that this type of tenure pattern inhibits economic development. It is believed that it is inflexible in the face of change as it does not permit sale, and that smallholders are reluctant to adopt innovations that would enhance the value of their land, for fear of losing the benefits in redistribution. Thus it is often argued that centrally imposed individualization and registration of land ownership is necessary for agricultural development (Cohen, 1980, pp. 353–55).

It is now clear that these conceptions greatly underestimate the adaptability of collective land tenure systems. Wherever there has been land pressure, individualization has tended to emerge and with it the de facto selling and renting of land rights (Cohen, 1980, pp. 365–61). Thus these "traditional" systems have not in fact inhibited agricultural development. At the same time, the persistence of collective tenure has permitted communities to regulate their own membership, to react to challenges to their common interests, and to assure some minimal degree of welfare for their poor.

Thus there are few costs and many benefits to land tenure systems under the control of local communities. Communities can guide themselves through the evolution of land law with greater flexibility and sensitivity to local conditions than national authorities can. Communities are willing and able to exercise these responsibilities and would be strengthened in doing so if national governments gave legal authority and other support. The greatest threats to land rights occur when individuals within the community use outside institutions to enforce traditionally unacceptable claims or when outsiders begin to encroach on the community's lands. The latter is a particular problem for pastoralists. Often their ability to dry-season graze on land that is marginal for crops is essential to their use of large amounts of other land with no crop potential. These are instances in which central government support is often needed to protect a community's ability to effectively control and adjudicate over its own land.

The argument made for land ownership systems here is an extension of the case made for seeing African farmers as responsible and ready to take charge of their own economic and social fate, this time through communities' legal control of their own tenure systems. This right is fundamental to a community's ability to define and control its own identity.

IRRIGATION

To date, the experience with irrigation schemes in Africa, particularly large-scale ones, has not been happy. Their effect on income distribution has often been negative (Barnett, 1981, p. 323). They also rarely pay for themselves or have economic rates of return competitive with other investments in agriculture (Stryker, et al., 1981, p. 1). Thus major irrigation schemes are not a near-term priority.

Nonetheless, with African agriculture at a turning point irrigation will soon begin to be more attractive. The land frontier is nearing exhaustion; rural population pressure makes intensification inevitable; and the marketing of food is growing and already accounts for a significant portion of production and consumption.

Most of the major irrigation projects that have been attempted in Africa so far have been built on rigid control models, with the state managing every detail of production. Experience with irrigation on the left bank of the Senegal River is instructive. Two successive attempts at centrally controlled systems, based on Asian models, were dismal failures. Yet when local communities were involved in the construction and management of the operation, productivity was greater and the costs of construction were substantially lower, making the project an economic success (Diallo, 1984). The possibilities for local involvement are greatest on small projects; on large systems local control is feasible only at the turnout level.

The geography of the area in which a system is being constructed largely determines its type, but there is still considerable scope for small-scale irrigation projects in Africa (Stryker, et al., 1981, pp. 30, ii). These units will have economic rates of return in the near-term, whereas large systems will generally become attractive only at the turn of the century. Small-scale irrigation has the added advantage of being amenable to labor-intensive construction methods, which pump money into the rural economy where it can be used to finance agricultural innovations.

OFF-FARM RURAL EMPLOYMENT

The generation of increased off-farm employment is vital to the promotion of rural development. It will be especially important to create jobs for marginal groups. The commercialization of agriculture and the disappearance of the land frontier will lead to a growth in rural inequality. Those with access to land, capital, family labor, and entrepreneurial skill are better placed to take advantage of the new opportunities. Already a significant portion of rural dwellers are dependent on employment by other farmers in order to purchase at least some of their food. The rural poor also are short of capital and find it difficult to borrow, making it hard for them to purchase the inputs that would enable them to make the most out of the land.

Thus for the poor it is especially important that agricultural development be accompanied by increases in rural employment opportunities, for their existence will otherwise be even more marginal than it is now. It is also particularly valuable if these jobs are off-farm and concentrated in the seasons in which agricultural work is slack. Not only does such work have direct welfare benefits, but it also contributes to the productivity of the farms of those who are land-poor or have difficulty raising capital. It gives them a source of funds for investment in crop inputs and provides them with the financial breathing space to work their own farms fully.

RURAL ROADS

Attention to the construction and maintenance of rural roads is one of the more important ways in which the state can stimulate agriculture. It also can assist with rural commerce and off-season employment. Of course, road construction by itself will not produce development; it must be accompanied by an economic infrastructure that can deliver inputs and market surpluses (Devres, 1980, pp. 47,54,20,55).

Labor-intensive methods of road construction obviously have the greatest effect on employment and also have a larger impact on community welfare, as the skills demanded are less sophisticated and are more likely to be available locally. USAID's labor-intensive rural roads project in Kenya has been extremely creative in building small, dirt roads with a minimum of heavy equipment.

Road maintenance is at least as important as construction, as dirt roads deteriorate quickly. Both Kenya and Tanzania have had experience with donor-constructed roads that have had to be completely rebuilt because of lack of maintenance. This task can be performed easily by local residents working under the supervision of a government field engineer.

The biggest problems with road maintenance are financial, not technical. Rural roads have a low political priority for national governments once they have been built. Frequently, donors and governments have expected feeder roads to be maintained by local self-help activity. This has been unsuccessful and was unrealistic in the first place. Poor communities are often willing to contribute funds and labor for the construction of new projects, but they find it almost impossible to raise resources for the recurrent costs of public goods on a volunteer basis (Ralston, et al., 1983, pp. 42-43). These have to be paid out of some form of taxation instead. This could well be a purely local tax, for communities are aware of the benefits of infrastructure such as roads, but the authority for its assessment and enforcement must be available.

LIVESTOCK PRODUCTION

Africa's livestock industry is probably best dealt with in two parts—that which is a part of small, mixed farming operations and that which is pastoral. While many donors and African governments expect nomadic stock-keeping to be swept away with the future tides of development, such an attitude is misguided. Pastoralism makes productive use of an environment that is unsuited for any other form of agriculture given current technology (Horowiz, 1979, p. 32). When crop producers do displace pastoralists, their activities generally are marginal, making them especially vulnerable to variations in rainfall. Furthermore, nomadic stock-keeping persists to this day in the western United States and the eastern U.S.S.R. and should not be seen as "unmodern" (Sanford, 1983, p. 31). The issue then is what can be done to improve its productivity.

The record of recent attempts to improve nomadic livestock production is extremely poor. African pastoralists know more than anyone else about their particular type of herding, and efforts to import scientific approaches from the semi-arid areas of the United States and Australia have been a failure. The reasons are simple. Ranchers in the latter areas are concerned solely with beef production and with maximum returns on investments. African pastoralists are operating a dairy system which is designed to support the largest possible human population on the land, and beef production is only a sideproduct.

Nonetheless, African pastoralism does have problems and assistance in resolving them could improve its productivity. First, the pressure of human and cattle populations on the range has increased dramatically since the turn of the century and ecological damage from overgrazing is sometimes a problem. More serious is the problem of overgrazing in the sense of higher than economically optimal stocking levels. When many herders share a common range, they have an incentive as individuals to stock beyond the ideal carrying capacity of the range (Jarvis, 1984).

Much of this overgrazing has been created or exacerbated by past government efforts to assist pastoralists by construction of new watering points. Traditionally, although African pastoralists have considered the range a common resource, they have treated watering points as the property of well-defined social groups. Access to water effectively determines whose livestock can use a particular segment of the range. Once public watering points were introduced, this traditional mechanism of control broke down. Opening new range by the drilling of boreholes is desirable, but it should be done as a loan to specific social groups, so that traditional methods of ownership and grazing control are reinforced rather than undermined (Horowitz, 1979, p. 40).

A second problem concerns the frequent weakness of the markets serving pastoralists. Almost all of Africa's nomadic herders are involved to some degree in the long-distance movement and sale of stock. The primary function of their herds is to provide for family subsistence needs, however. For East Africa, it has been estimated that an average family needs 30 to 35 adult cattle for this purpose (Horowitz, 1979, pp. 57–58). It is only as these requirements are exceeded that substantial trade in beef becomes a real possibility. The recognition of these needs will foster a more realistic perspective on the limits to commercial beef production in the semi-arid and arid areas. The problem with markets is most serious in times of drought when the prices offered for livestock are so low as to discourage even distress sales. This exacerbates the grazing pressure on the range and raises the family's general calculation of the stock numbers needed in normal times to assure its survival in the harsh ones. State-subsidized market outlets for drought periods may well be appropriate both from a welfare point of view and to support the commercialization of pastoralism.

The third problem for pastoralists is disease control. They are keenly aware of this problem and frequently administer modern veterinary medicines themselves. Given the economics of most contemporary pastoral production, however, sophisticated veterinary services are only justified for disease prevention at present, not for curative treatment. Prevention and the control of outbreaks cannot be made profitable for private practitioners. Thus the veterinary medicine made available to pastoralists must be provided by the state, even if its costs are recovered through taxes on cattle production. Since disease outbreaks often have international implications in Africa, support for government veterinary services is a particularly appropriate area for donor activity.

Livestock production on small, mixed farms has very different requirements from those of pastoralism. Small stock (sheep, goats, pigs, and poultry) are found on small holdings throughout Africa. Most farms in eastern and southern Africa keep at least one cow as well, primarily as a source of milk. Experience in central Kenya indicates that smallholder dairy production can be quite sophisticated. A science-based livestock industry is feasible and economically attractive in many parts of Africa. The requirements for its support are: research, particularly on improved breeds of small ruminants and on disease control; veterinary services; extension on improved feeding and management practices; and improved milk markets. The time is particularly ripe for the development of private curative veterinary practices (Leonard, 1984b).

DECENTRALIZATION

The agricultural development strategy presented above is a decentralized one—but of a complex variety. Central governments on the continent have over-extended themselves. Instead of trying to do and control everything themselves, they need to decentralize many functions to other entities and concentrate on supporting them to perform well. Only rarely does this involve the classic pattern of devolving authority to elected units of local government. There are many differrent forms of decentralization and agricultural development in Africa requires that almost all of them be used (Leonard and Marshall, 1982, Chap. 1).

For marketing functions, the needed form of decentralization is to make a multiplicity of smaller businesses the primary carrier of services, giving farmers control in their customer role. A similar movement to the private sector is appropriate for agricultural services, such as curative veterinary care and plowing.

Credit involves another form of privatization—the organization of small, face-to-face groups of friends and neighbors to save together, to lend to one another, and to serve as guarantors on each other's loans. This network of alternative local organizations would be linked to the banking system for its larger savings and credit needs. The role of stimulating and supporting the local groups would fall either to government or to international voluntary organizations. Both have demonstrated expertise in handling this linkage function in different parts of Africa and it would depend on the country as to which would do the job better.

The effective operation of an agricultural extension system requires deconcentration of authority to the central government professionals working in the field. Only they are close enough to the farmer to be able to make the adaptations to technical advice that Africa's large ecological diversity requires and only they can provide the feedback to the research system that will make it responsive to these local conditions.

Land use, tenure, and water rights are the areas for which devolution of authority to local governments is most needed. The appropriate place for such jurisdiction is with the entities that traditionally controlled land use, which generally are smaller than the district (anglophone) or department (francophone). Often the authority of these local governments has eroded and would have to be rebuilt by central government support. For irrigation systems, such local government entities would have to be created de novo, since the function usually is not a traditional one and would have to be structured specifically around the system itself.

Rural road construction and maintenance were often handled by district and department governments in the colonial period. Frequently the function was then centralized because local governments were diverting resources from roads to health and education. If special taxes were authorized for roads, local governments would perform this function well.

THE POLITICS OF ALTERING
AGRICULTURAL STRATEGY

African governments should accept the consequences of the inevitable commercialization and intensification of agriculture, should abandon their traditional control-oriented strategy of development, and should concentrate on fostering private firms that would compete with one another and with state institutions whose services to small farmers would be coordinated through the operations of the market. But is it politically feasible for African governments to relinquish their direct involvement in and control over much of the agricultural economy? To answer this question, the character of the African state and the alternative ways in which its needs can be met must be considered.

The state is a particularly fragile institution in most African countries, threatened with military coups and ethnic secessions. African elites also are linked to particularly large networks of social obligation. The egalitarianism of pre-colonial African society and the relatively meritocratic character of upward mobility in the late colonial and independence periods have produced African leaders and managers with large numbers of poor relatives and strong ties to disadvantaged communities. The values of the social exchange systems that villagers employed to insure themselves against risk are still strong (Hyden, 1983). Consequently, Africans have major patronage obligations to poorer peoples and feel strong moral pressures to fulfill them. For these reasons and for selfish ones that are far more universal, state organizations in Africa are used extensively to pursue the informal, personal goals of their managers rather than the collective ones that are formally proclaimed.

The relationship of African states to their rural economies is both close and exploitative. The continent's governments spend large amounts of money on programs of direct support to agricultural producers, but all too often they simultaneously do damage that far outweighs the good by imposing inefficient marketing organizations and extractive prices on the farm economy. At first this seems surprising, particularly given that the credit and subsidized input programs into which the money is poured are ineffective and the negative consequences of poor marketing are dramatic.

Robert Bates has demonstrated the political rationality that underlies the frequent economic irrationality of these activities. Positive acts of support for farmers bring gratitude and can be directed to the clients of a politician or civil servant, thereby bolstering the legitimacy of the regime and strengthening the patronage networks of those who work with it. Although good prices are seen by farmers as positive, they produce no patronage. From the point of view of the government, the economic and political costs of creating marketing boards that effectively tax agriculture are more than offset by the political benefits of the jobs and "free goods" which they indirectly finance (Bates, 1981). Even Tanzania, which has resisted the creation of personalized patron-client networks, has felt it necessary to extract a dysfunctionally large surplus from agriculture in order to finance expansions in social services and formal sector jobs.

Escape from the unproductive growth of the state will require something more subtle than laissez-faire economics. The performance of public organizations is poor because few of their participants are committed to their formal, stated goals, and are rather pursuing individual or village interests. To propose the discipline of the free market as a cure for this problem amounts to calling for the imposition of a new method of pursuing the national interest. It is true that the market can achieve this end with a smaller number of consenting actors than a hierarchy. (Marris and Somerset, 1971, have shown that African small businessmen start pulling away from social obligations under the pressures of market discipline.) Ultimately, however, why should the politicians who use their hierarchical positions to pursue narrow interests now undertake the difficult task of turning to the market for the sake of the national interest?

It is essential to the survival of their regimes and the interests of their political leaders that African governments produce visible, distributable benefits. African politicians must have projects and patronage to distribute if they are to survive. The priority therefore is not to dismantle the state but to redirect its activities into areas that combine some economic returns with high political pay-offs. If the latter are high enough, it may be possible to contain pressures for still greater state expenditures, thereby preserving incentives for vigorous growth. It is unlikely that the extraction of resources from agriculture to support urban and elite interests will cease. We can aspire, however, to a structure in which resources are extracted and used relatively efficiently, thereby lessening the net burden on farmers.

One way to raise political returns while lowering economic costs is for benefits to be provided in such a way that they can be given again, rather than constituting a permanent drain on resources. The granting of a job has a relatively low level of political productivity, for once it is bestowed the salary will have to be paid for another 30 years while the recipient's gratitude will not last a tenth that long. In contrast, a labor-intensive rural roads project has a much higher political pay-off. From an economic point of view, roads improve access to producers and rural markets, thereby lowering the costs of trade and improving the chances of competition without imposing government controls that could become exploitative. Simultaneously, roads are very popular with rural constituents and when they deteriorate, their construction can be undertaken again. If those employed are drawn from the local area, the jobs given are a limited act of patronage that can be repeated with new jobs in the future.

Innovative thinking is needed about how vital rural services can be provided in ways that will make them politically productive and self-managing, while not becoming a permanent drain on the Treasury. For example, a subsidy could be paid to set up a veterinarian or paramedic in a private rural practice (perhaps by providing housing, equipping the lab, and maybe giving a cash grant). Even if only one out of two of these practitioners worked out, services in the rural areas would be expanded, government would not be left paying for those who do not work, and both communities and practitioners would be grateful for the initial subsidy. The introduction of private practice makes it more likely that competition will develop, lessening the exploitative potential that goes with public and private monopoly.

In this regard, the high failure rate of loans given to new, small, indigenous businessmen in Africa should be re-evaluated. The political returns on these "grants" is quite high, particularly as this social group is much more influential in politics than workers or small farmers. Small, indigenous businesses are particularly valuable in building a strong, rural, commercial infrastructure and in expanding off-farm employment. The cost to the government of such attempts to expand the economy is certainly less than the permanent drain presented by government corporations. Also, even badly administered loans and grants are less damaging to the economy than the manipulation of protective tariffs and licenses. The development community needs a realistic acceptance of the political and economic benefits of support to African small industry and commerce.

The thrust of the foregoing analysis is to identify those aspects of the agricultural development strategy advocated in this chapter that have potential political returns. The state can then use the pay-offs to buy the room within which the other needed policies can be implemented. Although this will not be easy, it is possible. If it is done, more positive forces of economic growth will be set in motion and resources for still more political favors will be generated, permitting an upward spiral that can be followed as long as these resources are used in ways that are both politically and economically productive. It is unlikely that this strategy will produce economic optimality, but then a government's uncompromising pursuit of that ideal is likely to result in a coup attempt.

SPECIAL CONSIDERATIONS FOR DONORS

African governments have been treated as the primary client for the rural development strategy presented in this chapter. Donors have a significant role to play in African development, but it is a supportive one. The policies that the donors should pursue in Africa are the same ones recommended for the continent's governments. Nonetheless, change cannot be forced on an unwilling society. Donors can try to persuade host countries of the wisdom of their advice; they can and should refuse to support policies and projects they believe are misguided. They can keep a sharp eye out for those moments in which an official in some part of a government seems to be moving in the right direction and to single out those programs for special support. If they try to impose their vision of the future, however, the result will probably be counter-productive, for a program that is unwillingly implemented has almost no chance of success.

Nonetheless, this strategy has specific implications for donors, as it is an institution-building approach to agricultural development. As such, it requires that donors see their interventions in light of their impact on the economy's institutions as a whole and not focus narrowly on specific changes in production that can be credited as "their own successes."

Institutional reform and development also require patience, experimentation, and adaptation. There can be no blueprint for progress in this area. A learning process must be created, requiring that the principal actors come to know one another well, assimilate the unanticipated lessons that their experience produces, and make new and adaptive responses (Korten, 1980). None of this can be done in a short period of time. Perhaps the most destructive of American contributions to international development has been the two-year contract. Agencies of social change within the United States consider such a period too brief for a manager to make a significant contribution. How much longer it must take to do something meaningful in a society one must first learn to understand! If donors are serious about influencing public policies in Africa, they will have to find ways to keep their personnel in the field for at least five years and to make it possible for those who have proven themselves particularly adept in a society to return to work in it again.

Once donor representatives can be kept in place long enough to have true insight into their host societies, they should be given substantially greater discretion than they currently have. An adaptive approach to development requires that those who are doing the learning be given the opportunity to experiment. This suggests that country representatives be given greater influence in the selection of projects and that they have discretionary funds for small opportunities with high marginal productivity. At the moment, one of the great problems of development is that whereas good large projects are hard to develop and justify, there is almost no end to small ways in which monies could be spent to overcome bottlenecks in critical institutions and to exploit fast-breaking opportunities. Money could be well spent quickly if the bureaucratic red tape were cut.

Finally, donors must recognize that strong economic institutions depend for their effectiveness on political stability. Many of the economic policies that donors are recommending for Africa today are politically difficult to implement. Much of the needed policy reform can be achieved only if donors assist governments on the continent to deliver at least some projects with a wide political appeal. Thus although donors may be primarily concerned with narrowly defined economic goals, it is important that they remain involved in the areas of education and health. These "old," "soft," and humanitarian basic needs projects have precisely the political attractiveness needed to sweeten the bitterness of much of the laissez-faire medicine being delivered today.

These kinds of trade-offs will not be easy for donors. The idea that a project in one sector might be undertaken in order to make a policy change in another sector possible implies a considerable amount of cooperation among specialists in the donor agency and a willingness to have progress on one's project dependent on progress outside one's primary area of concern. It also implies that a portion of a donor's portfolio would be tied up in projects that did not appear to reflect the agency's top priorities. Obviously this would be difficult for a donor, but then so are the reforms that are expected of African governments. Is it unreasonable to ask for institutional change on both sides of the Atlantic?

African agriculture is at a turning point and is about to enter an era of intensification and commercialization. This change will make the long-awaited wide-spread shift to science-based agriculture feasible and makes it possible to achieve the increases in food production that are needed to stay ahead of population growth. These structural shifts require a fundamental change in the character of the institutions serving African production. The traditional control approach to the continent's farmers is now inappropriate and dysfunctional. Monopoly and centralization are the most destructive forces at work in Africa's rural areas today. What is required, instead, is a new network of overlapping, competing public and private organizations that will provide reliable services and put the farmer as consumer firmly in control. It is to the politically difficult task of creating this new institutional framework that the efforts of African governments and donors must now be bent.

ACKNOWLEDGMENT

I would like to express my appreciation to Julie Howard for her invaluable comments and research assistance and to the Institute of International Studies of the University of California, Berkeley, for its partial funding of this study.

NOTES

1. It is widely assumed that the present shortages of food are a problem of production, that agricultural growth is no longer keeping pace with increases in population (e.g., World Bank, 1981, p. 45). We don't actually know that this is true, however; the aggregate data for Africa is so weak and the variation shown by the good micro studies is sufficiently great that such continent-wide conclusions are subject to legitimate scepticism. The current shortages in food could be caused by marketing, distribution, or weather problems instead (Berry, 1983, pp. 1–5).

2. Such a result is based on the unrealistic presumption that recent trends in urban population growth reflect increased employment opportunities. Some sources put the present rate of growth of formal non-farm employment below that of population, which would increase labor in the agricultural sector ad infinitum (Johnson and Clark, 1982, pp. 39–44; World Bank, 1981, pp. 176–79; UN, 1981).

3. It is true that much of this evidence concerns specific commodities and is inconclusive about the price responsiveness of aggregate farm production (Berry, 1983, pp. 24–25). The latter depends on the development of a research base and an economic infrastructure that permits farmers to expand their

investments rather that shift them from one crop to another. Precisely such an infrastructure is now or can soon be in place in most of Africa, however, rendering outmoded the traditional assumptions about price behavior.

4. The taxes imposed are believed by many experts still to be too high (J. Peberdy, private communication), but the burden would be even greater under a different structure.

REFERENCES

Adams, Dale and Douglas Graham. 1981. "A Critique of Traditional Agricultural Credit Projects and Policies," *Journal of Development Economics* 8: 347–66.

Barnett, Tony. 1981. "Evaluating the Gezira Scheme: Black Box or Pandora's Box?" In J. Heyer, P. Roberts and G. Williams, *Rural Development in Tropical Africa*. London: Macmillan.

Bates, Robert H. 1981. *Markets and States in Tropical Africa: The Political Basis of Agricultural Policies*. Berkeley: University of California Press.

Benor, Daniel and Michael Baxter. 1984. *Training and Visit Extension*. Washington, D.C.: The World Bank.

Benor, Daniel and James Q. Harrison. 1977. *Agricultural Extension: The Training and Visit System*. Washington, D.C.: The World Bank.

Bergman, Kenneth. 1983. "Climate Change," *International Journal of Environmental Studies* 20: 91–101.

Berry, Leonard and Mustafa Khogali. 1981. "The Physical Resource Background to African Development." Paper presented to The Committee on African Development Strategies.

Berry, Sara S. 1983. "Agrarian Crisis in Africa? A Review and Interpretation." Paper presented to the Joint African Studies Committee. New York: Social Science Research Council and the American Council of Learned Societies.

Bottrall, Anthony and John Howell. 1980. "Small Farmer Credit Delivery and Institutional Choice." In Howell, 1980.

Chambers, Robert. 1983. *Rural Development: Putting the Last First*. London: Longman.

Cohen, John M. 1980. "Land Tenure and Rural Development in Africa." In R. Bates and M. Lofchie, eds., *Agricultural Development in Africa: Issues of Public Policy*. New York: Praeger.

Devres, Inc. 1980. *Socio-Economic and Environmental Impact of Low-Volume Rural Roads—A Review of the Literature*. Program Evaluation Discussion Paper No. 7. Washington, D.C.: United States Agency for International Development.

Diallo, Thiousso. 1984. "Participation Villageoise au Développement Hydro-Agricole de la Vallée et du Delta du Fleuve Sénégal (Rive Gauche)." Unpublished paper. Davis, Cal.: University of California.

Donald, Gordon. 1976. *Credit for Small Farmers in Developing Countries*. Boulder: Westview Press.

Eicher, Carl K. and Doyle C. Baker. 1982. *Research on Agricultural Development in Sub-Saharan Africa: A Critical Survey*. East Lansing: Department of Agricultural Economics, Michigan State University, MSU International Development Paper No. 1.

Gbetibouo, Mathurin and Christopher L. Delgado. 1984. "Lessons and Constraints of Export-Led Growth: Cocoa in Ivory Coast." In I.W. Zartman and C.L. Delgado, eds. *The Political Economy of the Ivory Coast*. New York: Praeger.

Hart, Keith. 1982. *The Political Economy of West African Agriculture*. Cambridge: Cambridge University Press.

Heyer, J., P. Roberts and G. Williams. 1981. *Rural Development in Tropical Africa*. New York: St. Martins.

Hill, Polly. 1970. *Studies in Rural Capitalism in West Africa*. Cambridge: Cambridge University Press.

Horowitz, Michael M. 1979. *The Sociology of Pastoralism and African Livestock Projects*. Program Evaluation Discussion Paper No. 6. Washington, D.C.: United States Agency for International Development.

Howell, John, ed. 1980. *Borrowers and Lenders: Rural Financial Markets and Institutions in Developing Countries*. London: Overseas Development Institute.

Howell, John. 1984. "Conditions for the Design and Management of Agricultural Extension." Agricultural Administration Network Discussion Paper No. 13. London: Overseas Development Institute.

Hyden, Goran. 1980. *Beyond Ujamaa in Tanzania: Underdevelopment and an Uncaptured Peasantry*. Berkeley: University of California Press.

Hyden, Goran. 1983. *No Shortcuts to Progress: African Development Management in Perspective*. Berkeley: University of California Press.

Jarvis, Lovell S. 1984. "Overgrazing and Range Degradation: Is There Need and Scope for Government Control of Livestock Numbers?" Paper presented to the Conference on Livestock Policy Issues. Addis Ababa: International Livestock Center for Africa.

Johnsen, S.J., W. Dansgaard, and H.B. Clausen. 1970. "Climatic Oscillations 1200–2000 AD," *Nature* 227 (August 1): 482–83.

Johnston, Bruce. 1984. "Agricultural Development in Tropical Africa: The Search for Viable Strategies." Paper presented to The Committee on African Development Strategies. Washington, D.C. Overseas Development Council.

Johnston, Bruce and William Clark. 1982. *Redesigning Rural Development: A Strategic Perspective*. Baltimore: Johns Hopkins University Press.

Jones, William O. 1980. "Agricultural Trade Within Tropical Africa: Achievements and Difficulties." In R. Bates and M. Lofchie, eds., *Agricultural Development in Africa: Issues of Public Policy*. New York: Praeger.

Katz, Richard W. 1977. "Assessing the Impact of Climate Change on Food Production," *Climate Change* 1: 85–96.

Kleemeier, Lizz Lyle. 1984. "Integrated Rural Development in Tanzania: The Role of Foreign Assistance, 1972–1982." Ph.D. dissertation submitted to the Department of Political Science, University of California, Berkeley.

Korten, David C. 1980. "Community Organization and Rural Development: A Learning Process Approach," *Public Administration Review* 40(5): 480, 512.

Landau, Martin. 1969. "Redundancy, Rationality and the Problem of Duplication and Overlap," *Public Administration Review* 29(4).

Lele, Uma. 1975. *The Design of Rural Development: Lessons from Africa*. Baltimore: The Johns Hopkins University Press.

Lele, Uma. 1981. "Cooperatives and the Poor: A Comparative Perspective," *World Development* 9: 55–72.

Leonard, David K. 1977. *Reaching the Peasant Farmer: Organization Theory and Practice in Kenya*. Chicago: University of Chicago Press.

Leonard, David K. 1984a. "Disintegrating Agricultural Development," *Food Research Institute Studies* XIX (2).

Leonard, David K. 1984b. "The Supply of Veterinary Services." Paper presented to the Conference on Livestock Policy Issues. Addis Ababa: International Livestock Center for Africa.

Leonard, David K. and Dale Rogers Marshall, eds. 1982. *Institutions of Rural Development for the Poor: Decentralization and Organizational Linkages*. Berkeley: Institute of International Studies, University of California.

Lipton, Michael. 1980. "Rural Credit, Farm Finance and Village Households." In Howell, op. cit.

Marris, Peter and Anthony Somerset. 1971. *The African Businessmen*. London: Routledge and Kegan Paul.

Miracle, Marvin P., Diane S. Miracle, and Laurie Cohen. 1980. "Informal Savings Mobilization in Africa," *Economic Development and Cultural Change* 28(4).

Muzaale, Patrick and David K. Leonard. 1985. "Women's Groups in Agricultural Extension and Nutrition in Africa: Kenya's Case," *Agricultural Administration* 19(1).

Nicholson, Sharon E. 1978. "Climatic Variations in the Sahel and Other African Regions During the Past Five Centuries," *Journal of Arid Environments* 1: 3–24.

Peterson, Stephen B. 1982a. "Government, Cooperatives and the Private Sector in Peasant Agriculture." In Leonard and Marshall, 1982.

Peterson, Stephen B. 1982b. "Alternative Local Organizations Supporting the Agricultural Development of the Poor." In Leonard and Marshall, 1982.

Peterson, Stephen B. 1982c. "The State and the Organizational Infrastructure of the Agrarian Economy: A Comparative Study of Smallholder Agrarian Development in Taiwan and Kenya." Ph.D. dissertation submitted to the Department of Political Science, University of California, Berkeley.

Ralston, Lenore, James Anderson, and Elizabeth Colson. 1983. *Voluntary Efforts in Decentralized Management: Opportunities and Constraints in Rural Development*. Berkeley: Institute of International Studies, University of California.

Sanford, Stephen. 1983. *Management of Pastoral Development in the Third World*. Chichester: John Wiley and Sons.

Stryker, J.D., C.H. Gotsch, J. McIntire, and F.C. Roche. 1981. "Investments in Large Scale Infrastructure: Irrigation and River Management in the Sahel." Washington, D.C.: United States Agency for International Development.

United Nations. 1981. *Statistical Yearbook*. New York: United Nations.

Von Pischke, J.D. and John Rouse. 1983. "Selected Successful Experiences in Agricultural Credit and Rural Finance in Africa," *Savings and Development* 1(7).

World Bank. 1981. *Accelerated Development in Sub-Saharan Africa*. Washington, D.C.: The World Bank.

CHAPTER EIGHT

Agricultural Research: Lessons of the Past, Strategies for the Future

Dunstan S.C. Spencer

Sub-Saharan Africa is the only region in the developing world in which per capita food production has declined during the last two decades, with only Rwanda, Central African Republic, Swaziland, Ivory Coast, Mauritius, and Cameroon showing any positive trends. West Africa has exhibited the slowest growth rate in total food production of all regions, as per capita production of all crops, with the exception of rice, has declined. Slight annual increases in total food production are attributable almost exclusively to increases in area under cultivation, indicating that technological change has had little impact on Africa's food production.

Africa's economic crisis has sharply limited governments' abilities to finance essential capital goods imports and recurrent expenditures, such as fertilizers and irrigation systems, needed to increase agricultural production (OAU, 1980). Poor economic management, inefficient parastatals, and misguided pricing policies have undermined the agricultural sector, particularly export crop production, in which Africa's comparative advantage is the strongest (World Bank, 1981, 1984a, b). Less often considered, however, are environmental constraints and a lack of appropriate technologies, which have also played a significant role in bringing about the decline in the agricultural sector. While better internal policies and a more favorable external economic climate might have delayed the current crisis, they would not have prevented it.

Although agricultural research has come up with some answers to environmental and other agricultural development problems, these solutions have not been transferred to farmers because of bottlenecks such as poor extension systems, inadequate pricing policies, and ineffective and inefficient seed multiplication programs and marketing parastatals. Environmental and other constraints on farmers have not been adequately taken into account in research. New technologies rarely correspond to farmers' changing needs and fail to bring about sustainable growth in aggregate output. This chapter will review strategies for Africa's agricultural development and the performance of earlier agricultural systems, and concludes with a critical evaluation of a modern agricultural research strategy.

AFRICAN AGRICULTURAL DEVELOPMENT STRATEGIES: THE IMPLICATIONS FOR RESEARCH

Ruttan (1980) has provided a useful outline of agricultural development models, some of which are relevant to agricultural development and research in sub-Saharan Africa.[1] In the "frontier model," agricultural development involves expanding area under cultivation in order to increase overall output. While available statistics show that the small increases in Africa's total agricultural output during the last two decades were brought about by expansion of areas cultivated (Paulino, 1983), the increases were not sufficient to keep up with population growth rates. As a result, the frontier model is of little relevance to sub-Saharan Africa, particularly as new, productive lands open for settlement are lacking.[2]

According to the "conservation model," agricultural output is increased by recycling plant nutrients through organic manures and by labor-intensive methods of drainage, irrigation, and other physical facilities, thus more effectively utilizing land and water resources. There is ample scope for this model in many sub-Saharan countries, as substantial areas are unsuitable for cultivation or other human and animal uses due to desert conditions, rock outcroppings, periodic flooding, or diseases such as bilharzia, trypanosomiasis, and onchocerciasis (Matlon and Spencer, 1984).

Second, there is a high degree of micro-variability in land quality and the better soils are often already under cultivation. Third, soils are unstable, requiring a high ratio of fallow time relative to cultivation. In addition, the rapid growth of the African rural population over the last 30 years has led to intense cultivation of land, resulting in stagnant or declining crop yields and a degradation of the land base. Therefore, soil conservation measures are needed to prevent further deterioration in the land base and to increase agricultural productivity.

As Berry and Khogali (1984) point out, two-thirds of Africa's land area is classified as arid, semi-arid, or dry sub-humid. It is ironic, therefore, that the existing surface and ground water resources have remained largely untapped. Despite recent investments in large-scale irrigation in West Africa, only about 3 percent of the land is currently under irrigation (FAO, 1978). Unfortunately, however, assessments of the large-scale irrigation projects have usually revealed economic losses or non-competitive returns (Sparling, 1981). The evidence strongly suggests that in the absence of long-term and highly subsidized donor commitments which include substantial investments in the training of local workers, it is unlikely that large-scale irrigation schemes will play an important role in improving Africa's ability to meet its food needs in the future.

On the other hand, small-scale, labor-intensive projects managed and operated by family and/or community groups have demonstrated attractive returns on investment (Eicher and Baker, 1982). Agricultural development policy will therefore need to focus on dryland agriculture in the short run, while a mixed strategy which also emphasizes irrigated agriculture is appropriate over the longer term.

The loss of vegetation, (i.e., grasses and trees) is another aspect of the deterioration of the environment, as Berry and Khogali (1984) have also pointed out. Livestock productivity is declining because of the degradation of pastures, while reduction of the forest cover is causing profound changes in soil productivity and probably also in the climate. Therefore, sub-Saharan African countries should pursue a development strategy which includes reforestation and maintenance of livestock herds particularly in semi-arid zones. While it is clear that a rigorous application of the conservation model of agricultural development could reverse the downward trend in Africa's agricultural output, it is not likely to bring about rates of growth needed to match projected increases in aggregate demand.

Due to the limitations of the above models, a number of new ones have emerged since the late 1960s. T.W. Shultz (1964) put forward what Ruttan has called the "high pay-off input model," in which investment to make modern high pay-off inputs available to farmers is the key component in transforming traditional agriculture.[3] Hayami and Ruttan (1972) extended this framework by developing the "induced innovation model," in which indigenous technical change is central to the development process. This model is attractive because it clearly shows that improvements in agricultural productivity "can only be made available by undertaking investment in the agricultural research capacity needed to develop technologies appropriate to the countries' natural and institutional environments and investment in the physical and institutional infrastructure needed to realize the new production potential opened up by technological advances" (Ruttan, 1980).

The institutional capacity to generate technical changes adapted to local resource endowments must be in place and there must be a heavy emphasis on a science-based system of agriculture, since there is only limited scope for a natural resource conservation policy to bring about much increase in agricultural output. While many attempts have been made over the last decade to develop models based on African resource endowments and institutions[4], this chapter will focus on two contemporary issues: whether development strategies in sub-Saharan Africa should emphasize small or large-scale farming and export or food crop production.

LARGE-VERSUS SMALL-SCALE FARMING

Available data shows that small-scale farming has a number of advantages over large-scale farming in Africa. Timmer, Falcon, and Pearson (1983) have stressed the need for broadly based programs for small farm households in most food production strategies. Likewise, Mellor and Johnston (1984) have provided strong theoretical arguments for "unimodel" or focus strategies that emphasize small-scale farming. Dualistic strategies, based on rapid modernization of large-scale, capital-intensive farm units together with capital-intensive industrialization, have not worked in many developing countries because they do not take into account the countries' resource endowments. Agricultural development in sub-Saharan Africa is only likely to succeed by gradually increasing the productivity of small farmers through innovations appropriate to their factor proportions.

EXPORT VERSUS FOOD CROP PRODUCTION

The controversy surrounding export versus food crop production is based on the contention of the World Bank and other international organizations that Africa should specialize in export crops in which it enjoys a comparative advantage, and because its agricultural labor productivity is generally substantially higher in export than in food crop production.[5]

John Mellor succinctly summarized the counter-argument as follows:

> First, given the risk aversion common to farmers, the extent to which they are willing to put their resources in export crop production is determined by their ability to produce adequate home food supplies. Thus, food production and export production may be complementary, not competitive. Increased productivity of the former allows increased production of the latter.
>
> Second, a substantial proportion of African labor resources are already in food production. Failure to substantially raise the productivity of these resources in food production means leaving large numbers of people in poverty and malnutrition for the decades required to facilitate a shift to alternative production and distribution systems. Third, and leaving behind the second point, there is great variability from place to place in the food production resource base in Africa. Although the comparative advantage argument against food production may apply in some areas, it seems unlikely in others. Fourth, no government, given reasonable prospects of success in domestic food production, will import the bulk of its basic food sustenance (Mellor, 1984, p. 4).

In addition to the above points, specialization in export crop production with concomitant increases in food imports would require an accelerated change in food preferences in Africa. Rice, wheat, and maize, which are readily available on the world market, would almost completely replace millet, cassava, and other root crops. There would also need to be a significant increase in transportation facilities, including ports, marketing, and storage infrastructure. While the case for substantially increased investment in food crop production is much stronger than that for specialization in export crops, the latter also need to be increased if foreign exchange is to be earned to finance other essential imports (e.g., petroleum) that cannot be produced domestically. A mixed strategy with major emphasis on food crop production is therefore required.

IMPLICATIONS FOR RESEARCH

The main implications for research of the discussion on agricultural development strategies are:

• Sustained agricultural development will result only if technological and institutional innovations are appropriate to the continent's resource endowments. Therefore, research is needed to provide a thorough understanding of the natural resource, institutional, and socio-economic constraints on sub-Saharan African agriculture.

• There is still scope to increase agricultural productivity by conservation of natural resources, especially land and water resources, particularly in semi-arid zones. To this end, research is needed to develop soil conservation, irrigation, and reforestation technologies.

• Given high population growth rates and the poor quality of most land resources, development strategies and research that focus on small-scale farming should be emphasized.

• While attention should be given to increasing export crop production, particularly where there is clear evidence of comparative advantage, major emphasis should be on food crop production and research.

PAST PERFORMANCE OF AGRICULTURAL
RESEARCH SYSTEMS: THE COLONIAL
PERIOD

Colonial governments did not neglect agricultural research; between 1900 and 1920, at least one agricultural research station was established in virtually every country in sub-Saharan Africa (McKelvey, 1965). These research stations, however, concentrated almost exclusively on export crops such as oil palm, cocoa, coffee, and groundnuts, and yielded rather substantial returns. Hybrid oil palms were developed that contributed significantly to the growth of agricultural exports between 1940 and 1960 (Abaelu, 1971), outyielding local wild palms by 500 to 700 percent in West Africa (Eicher, 1967). Research on cotton began in Uganda around 1904 and spread to northern Nigeria and the French colonies in the 1920s and 1930s. In Burkina Faso, for example, substantial yield increases were obtained by applying the results of cotton research under farm conditions (Delgado, 1981). Similar successes were obtained with cocoa due to research which began in West Africa in the 1920s, and to a lesser extent with groundnuts.

Hybrid maize in Kenya and Zimbabwe was the only food staple to which substantial research efforts were directed during the colonial period. Launched in Zimbabwe in 1932 and Kenya in the mid-1950s, these long-term research programs have yielded substantial returns (Eicher, 1984). Otherwise, there has been a near total lack of research on the major food staples (Collinson, 1983).

While most of the colonial research programs on export crops relied heavily on the successful transfer of materials from other regions of the world—plant-breeding materials for oil palm from Asia, cotton from the United States, and coffee from South America—unfortunately, this successful technology transfer was not repeated in food crop research.

As Judd, Boyce, and Evenson (1984) and Oram and Binglish (1984) have shown, investments in agricultural research as a percentage of total agricultural production were much lower in sub-Saharan Africa than in other developing and developed countries. Thus, although there was considerable investment in export crop research during the colonial era, in absolute terms, it proved insufficient to guarantee the long-term profitability of cash crop production.

In the years following independence, public sector expenditures on research increased significantly. Judd, Boyce, and Evenson (1984) estimate that agricultural research expenditures in East and West Africa in constant 1980 U.S. dollars increased from about $57 million in 1959 to $280 million in 1980, while manpower increased from 1636 scientist man-years to 4100. Over the same time period, public sector expenditure as a percentage of the value of agricultural output rose from about 0.37 percent to about 1.19 percent in West Africa and from 0.19 percent to 0.81 percent in East Africa.

These commendable increases have not produced a commensurate growth in research output. The lack of productive agricultural research in post-colonial sub-Saharan Africa can be approached by a review of the operational difficulties that have been encountered by national research systems and an evaluation of the stock of technologies that have been produced.

OPERATIONAL DIFFICULTIES OF NATIONAL RESEARCH SYSTEMS

In order to function effectively, an agricultural research system needs trained personnel, adequate funds to cover fixed costs (e.g., building of laboratories and purchase of equipment), and operating costs, (e.g., purchases of fuel, fertilizers, and chemicals), and payments of laborers. While there has been a substantial increase in the number of agricultural research workers, statistics do not reflect their levels of qualification or competence. In many national research institutions, many researchers hold only bachelor of science level qualifications and at best can only be expected to perform routine experiments and analysis. As a result, many experiments are repeated year after year, long after they have lost any significance. It often takes a team of outside consultants to suggest new areas of research!

Qualifications levels of researchers in many national programs must be raised. Donor agencies sometimes encourage the tendency to staff national research systems with unqualified people by insisting on training counterparts in externally funded short-term research projects. Those with B.S. level qualifications work with expatriate Ph.D. researchers for one to three years; then they are left on their own to carry on and modify the research programs as necessary. Another constraint is the lack of operational funds and poor financial and research management.

The situation has recently been described as follows:

> The effectiveness of research, extension, and training institutions is impaired by the lack of operating resources needed to function as they should. Yet, all too frequently, governments continue to expand programs, hiring more personnel instead of providing necessary resources to those already on the payroll. Poor performance and effectiveness thus go beyond the simple lack of resources. They arise from poor development administration and financial management.
>
> Poor personnel management and work discipline, lack of performance incentives and professional advancement, inadequate operating funds to do a good job, all discourage highly motivated researchers, trainees, and extension agents. The resulting high staff turnover disrupts research programs and institution-building efforts so necessary for creating effective indigenous national research and extension systems. Until these problems are addressed, zonal research and networking programs will not achieve their full potential.
>
> Untimely budgetary allocations frequently disrupt production campaigns, agricultural experiments, and data collection activities throughout the Sahel. Experiments sometimes must be abandoned or curtailed half-way through the season, or are not properly tended because of a lack of gasoline, vehicles, or other resources, or because of the inability to control implementing staff.
>
> Partly these problems arise from unpredictable budgeting exercises over which research and extension institutions have little control.

Partly they arise from legal structures that severely constrain the institutions' ability to control and allocate resources put at their disposal. Partly they arise from poor internal planning and management of resources in the face of what is obviously a highly unstable and unreliable resource situation. Unless these kinds of institutional constraints are appropriately identified, analyzed, and resolved, we risk spending another 10 years making little progress toward increasing agricultural production. . . .(Lebeau, et al., 1984, pp. 5–6)

EVALUATION OF NEW TECHNOLOGICAL OPTIONS

Matlon and Spencer (1984) have recently examined some of the current stock of technological innovations in terms of their appropriateness to small-scale farming. With regard to land and water management, improved systems in the humid tropics—light clearing, in situ burning, and intensive use of surface mulch in combination with herbicides and minimum or zero tillage—which are being developed by the International Institute of Tropical Agriculture (IITA), have yet to prove effective in on-farm testing. Moreover, chemical weed control methods and small-scale equipment for use in low tillage systems pose more immediate research problems (ter Kuile, 1983).

In the semi-arid zones, tied ridges have dramatically reduced runoff and increased yields in on-station trials in both East and West Africa (Ruthenberg, 1980; ICRISAT, 1981), yet the extensive use of this approach remains doubtful due to its substantial labor costs and yield gaps. Because of increasing demands on crop residues for livestock feed, fuel, and other purposes, the potential extensive use of mulches in sorghum and millet production is limited. On the other hand, tests conducted in Burkina Faso have concluded that the introduction of dirt anti-erosion dikes constructed on the contours of farmers' fields has significantly increased short-term yields (ICRISAT, 1983).

Mechanization schemes using tractors have met with limited success in the humid tropics due to the high capital costs relative to available resources, the scale of farmers' operations, and the lack of know-how in equipment use and maintenance. In addition, the potential yield and labor-saving benefits of animal-powered cultivation practices, repeatedly measured at experimental stations, have rarely been confirmed under farmers' management (Sargeant et al., 1981).

Despite the generally poor chemical composition of most African soil and its rapid depletion under continuous cultivation, the use of chemical fertilizers in sub-Saharan Africa has been minimal. This is due to the high cost of fertilizers, low and extremely variable technical response rates, and the need for complementary applications of large quantities of organic matter to achieve and maintain the potential response to chemical fertilizers over the long run (IFDC, 1976; ICRI-SAT, 1983; Pichot et al., 1981).

With regard to crop improvement, it is clear that with few exceptions such as hybrid maize in Zimbabwe and Kenya, programs concerned with the genetic improvement of food staples are relatively new and have had little success. Although on-station results have often been promising, when most new varieties are cultivated by farmers, yield gaps of up to 60 percent have consistently occurred (ICRISAT, 1980/83). Unacceptable taste and processing and storage problems are also commonly encountered. As a result, probably less than 2 percent of total sorghum, millet, and upland rice area in West Africa is sown with cultivars developed through modern genetic research.

REASONS FOR FAILURE TO PRODUCE APPROPRIATE
NEW TECHNOLOGIES

From the previous review, it is clear that the response of new production technologies to the continent's evolving needs has been inadequate. To a large extent, failures stem from two causes: inadequate understanding of small farmer goals and resource limitations. A glaring example of where research objectives were very different from those of its potential clientele is the case of intercropping. Numerous studies have shown that apart from some small areas in East and southern Africa, intercropping is vastly more important than monocrop systems, occupying over 90 percent of cropped area in most countries. Although there was some work done in the 1930s (Belshaw, 1979), it was only in the 1970s that any serious research on intercropping in sub-Saharan Africa began to be undertaken.[6] Even today, less than 20 percent of all agronomic research in the region addresses the issue, yet what little research has been done shows that intercropping is often much more efficient and less risky than monocropping even from the agronomic point of view.

The second major cause was the colonial period's over-reliance on the diffusion or technology transfer of export crop materials from other countries. With the Green Revolution's success in spreading wheat and rice varieties developed by the International Maize Improvement Center and the International Rice Research Institute to Latin America and Asia, the technology transfer model of agricultural development took firm root in sub-Saharan Africa.

Not only was the model adopted by national research systems, which had few alternatives as shortages of staff and funds prevented them from doing more fundamental research, but regional and international research centers also adopted it as a modus operandi. Thus the West Africa Rice Development Association (WARDA) was founded to conduct rice research, development, and training activities in West Africa on the principle that importing varieties from other parts of the world, testing them for adaptability, and selecting the suitable ones was all that was needed in varietal research (Lewis, 1982). Initially, ICRISAT's Africa program relied very heavily on material transfers from Asia, placing scientific staff in one or two-man teams in national programs (CGIAR, 1978).

The extent to which technical solutions developed elsewhere can be imported into Africa is quite limited because of the continent's higher rate of demographic change and more difficult physical conditions which determine technical potential. Consequently, success has been lacking to date in the direct introduction of exotic high-yielding cultivars, with the exception of irrigated rice where the environment can be modified to suit the crop. ICRISAT has had little success in introducing Indian sorghum and millet varieties to West Africa (Matlon, 1983), and after 10 years of variety trials in which over 2000 imported varieties were tried in the mangrove swamps of West Africa, WARDA found only two varieties that performed as well as the best local varieties (WARDA, 1984). As a result, international and regional centers have learned some lessons from these experiences[7] and some national programs are concentrating on the development of local materials to the extent that their resources permit.

ELEMENTS OF A MODERN AGRICULTURAL RESEARCH STRATEGY FOR SUB-SAHARAN AFRICA

POLICY RESEARCH

As suggested earlier, most recent reviews of Africa's economic situation have highlighted the fact that governmental economic policies have been faulty. Effective agricultural policy-making is a complex activity, encompassing efforts to influence and direct actions of millions of producers, consumers, and marketing agencies in order to meet broad social objectives. This process necessarily requires trade-offs which are not always readily apparent. As a result, there is a critical need to examine the potential costs and benefits of alternative agricultural policies on different segments of the population.

Before this can be accomplished, however, a rather large data set is needed.[8] Data is needed on the consumption patterns of urban and rural households in order to identify the numbers and locations of poor and malnourished elements of society who should be the target of food policy, and to determine aggregate demand parameters in order to trace the effects of various price and income policies. Data is also needed on farming systems in order to better understand the characteristics of production systems in terms of seasonality of supply, distribution of output, the decision-making environment of farms, and the potential sources of technological change.

Similarly, information is needed on markets and marketing institutions—storage, processing, and transportation of agricultural commodities—and on exchange rate functions and price formation. There is a general consensus that agricultural marketing parastatals have largely failed in sub-Saharan Africa. But in order to objectively determine what can replace them, more analysis and information on alternative marketing systems are needed. Lastly, data is needed on the relationship between agricultural systems, the macro-economy, and international markets.[9]

In no African country is there an adequate data base to allow for effective and comprehensive agricultural policy analysis. At the very best, the available data allows only partial analysis of the potential impact of alternative policies. Policy-making therefore continues with an inadequate information base. The situation described by (Stolper, 1969) in *Planning Without Facts* still exists 15 years later in virtually all sub-Saharan African countries.[10] At present, policy-making is based more on "gut feelings"—that private enterprise is intrinsically better than parastatals—than on hard empirical evidence. There is no guarantee that many of the current policy prescriptions which lack empirical evidence will be any more successful than the experiments of the past.

Therefore, given the current confusion, analyses of agricultural and particularly food policies need to receive top research priority.

Initially, emphasis must be placed on collecting primary data, as policy researchers in Africa cannot rely as much on secondary data as in other continents. Therefore, most policy analysis will have to be done by local university researchers and associates and other institutions that have a long-term commitment to the continent. Most Western consulting firms employing short-term consultants do not have the necessary expertise or time to first collect the necessary primary data, then to perform the multifaceted analysis required.

RESEARCH WITH A FARMING SYSTEMS PERSPECTIVE

One of the basic flaws in agricultural research in the region over the last three decades has been the omission of resource and other constraints on small-scale farmers who are the clientele of the research. To overcome this problem, agricultural research must be conducted with a farming systems perspective that views the farm in a holistic manner as it interacts within the larger system (CGIAR, 1978). The major objective of this approach is to increase the productivity of farming systems by generating appropriate new technology. It includes location-specific on-farm research with a short-term objective of developing improved technologies for target groups of farmers, as well as longer-term research at experiment stations to overcome the farming systems' major limitations (Byerlee, Harrington, and Winkelmann, 1983; Gilbert, Norman, and Winch, 1980).

On-station research is an integral part of research with a farming systems perspective.[11] Through such research, new technological components—crop varieties, herbicides, and new cropping methods—are developed, screened, and tested on a pilot scale. Unfortunately, by emphasizing the crucial role of on-farm research, most of the literature erroneously gives the impression that such research can stand on its own and that experiment station research has at best a rather unimportant role to play.[12]

In the last five years, a number of farming systems research teams have been set up all over Africa, supported by finance and technical assistance from external donors. National research programs are also being urged and assisted to launch large farming systems research (i.e., on-farm research efforts).[13] These efforts are likely to bring to the attention of researchers and policy-makers the true problems faced by small farmers. While it will be clear that ready solutions to the problems are not yet available, there is a grave danger that research will not move beyond that point if equal emphasis is not placed on necessary experiment station research. Given their poor reputation, these stations now run the risk of being starved of necessary funding and staffing.

CHARACTERISTICS OF NEW TECHNOLOGIES
NEEDED IN SUB-SAHARAN AFRICA

In order to increase Africa's agricultural productivity, new biological, chemical, and mechanical technologies that would allow intensification of agriculture are needed. In addition, new soil and water conservation techniques must be developed. Biological technology adaptable to local conditions is needed; there are very clear indications that varieties of sugar cane, wheat, and rice suitable to Latin America and Asia have limited adaptability in sub-Saharan Africa.

Given small-scale farmers' limited capital resources and input distribution problems, recommended varieties should be highly responsive to low levels of inputs such as fertilizers. Varieties are needed that perform as well or slightly better than farmers' traditional varieties under traditional levels of management, but yield substantially more under slightly improved management. Too many improved varieties require levels of management beyond farmers' existing capabilities before their full potential is realized.

Several corrective prescriptions can be suggested. In the semi-arid tropics, for example, moderate yield increases with substantially greater stability could be achieved through breeding for improved seedling vigor, drought resistance, and resistance to the most common pests and diseases. The development of varieties with different agronomic characteristics, such as shorter crop cycles or modified plant structures, could also increase farmers' management options, such as intercropping or permitting late planting without yield loss (Stoop et al., 1981).

With regard to new chemical technologies, material inputs such as fertilizers should be derived as much as possible from local sources in order to reduce transportation costs. This calls for substantial research on new plant designs and processes that would allow more economical production of phosphate fertilizers from domestic rock phosphate. Given the labor bottlenecks at weeding time in many countries and the demonstrated yield-reducing effects of weeds in many farming systems, cheap, effective, and easily applied herbicides are urgently needed.

Although sub-Saharan Africa can be defined as land surplus, capital-intensive methods of cultivation cannot substitute for labor in a big way. Mechanical technologies, such as processing machines, cannot economically replace hand labor (Timmer, 1973; Byerlee, Eicher, Leidholm, and Spencer, 1983); animal traction or mechanized land cultivation has had only limited success. Nonetheless, labor productivity is quite low compared to that of Asia (Mellor and Johnston, 1984) and there are often severe labor bottlenecks. Therefore, research on appropriate mechanization technology that is within farmers' reach is needed.

Cooperative ownership and management of agricultural machinery has not worked in sub-Saharan Africa, nor have government tractor hire schemes. It appears then that the only open avenue is research on the improvement of farmers' existing tools and equipment. A hand weeder that allows a farmer to weed twice as fast as existing weeding devices would have a big impact on labor productivity. The International Livestock Center for Africa (ILCA) recently designed an animal yoke that allows the traditional Ethiopian plow to be pulled by one instead of two oxen. This innovation is likely to have more of an impact on agricultural productivity in the Ethiopian highlands than all the mechanization research over the last 30 years, which concentrated on replacing traditional cultivation methods with mechanized methods rather than on improving existing ones.

Therefore, research on improvement of farmers' hand tools and equipment, unglamorous as it might seem, is needed. For example, hand-held equipment—not scaled-down models of equipment used in developed countries—is needed for minimum tillage in the humid zones.[14]

In order to identify appropriate technologies, a research strategy that emphasizes in situ development of new plant materials, local sources of chemical and biological fertilizers, and improved hand tools and animal traction is needed. Combined into simple technological packages which would be adopted in stages by small-scale farmers, these improvements would substantially increase rural incomes.

SOIL, WATER, AND FOREST CONSERVATION RESEARCH

Efforts to conserve soil, water, and forest resources will allow for some gains in productivity. Again, research is needed on improved conservation practices that could be profitably adopted by small farmers. In semi-arid zones, immediate attention should be given to research aimed at improving the management of existing large-scale irrigation schemes. Soils research is also needed to develop economical ways of maintaining or increasing water infiltration and reducing run-off in semi-arid areas. Also, high priority should be given to research which undertakes to develop economical crop rotations including tree crops, leguminous species, and mixed farming.

Reforestation is included under the general concept of conservation because of the alarming rates at which losses in the forest cover are occurring both in the arid zones where desertification is increasing and in humid zones where climatic changes are taking place. There is little hope of reducing firewood demand either by substitution with other fuels or by police actions or taxation. Efforts must be made to increase fuel wood supplies while maintaining the forest cover.

In the past, reforestation programs have relied too heavily on imported tree species and techniques which have rendered projects hopelessly uneconomic (Taylor and Soumare, 1983). Rather, emphasis should be placed on improving traditional forest species and on the identification of fast-growing trees for humid areas as well as those suited to harsh semi-arid conditions. Research into the incorporation of trees into crop and animal production systems should be given high priority.

LIVESTOCK RESEARCH

An important part of farming systems, particularly in the semi-arid zones where crop production takes place alongside rangelands, livestock production requires research, especially on control of livestock diseases. During the colonial period, livestock research was mainly veterinary. Such early endeavors, together with recent work by the International Laboratory for Research into Animal Diseases (ILRAD) and other international organizations, have yielded economical control measures for most of the important diseases except trypanosomiasis.

The available literature on livestock production and productivity[15] shows that unreliable feed supply is probably the most limiting factor on animal production. But there is limited scope for profitably increasing feed supplies by rangeland pasture improvement (Ruthenberg, 1974; Doppler, 1980). As a result, substantial increases in live-stock productivity will have to await increased crop production. Supplementary livestock feeding can then be based on crop residues or on feed specifically grown for livestock. Fortunately, increased demand for livestock products is likely to occur only after substantial increases in demand for staple food crops, (i.e., cereals, roots, and tubers) (Mellor and Johnston, 1984).

RESEARCH RESOURCE ALLOCATION

In a world of limited resources, decisions on allocation necessarily imply some trade-offs. Given agriculture's contribution to African economies, the amounts invested in agricultural research are inadequate and should be increased. But even if resources increase, decisions will need to be made as to which of the many areas of research covered in this study should be given priority. Should the emphasis be placed on crop or livestock research, on soil conservation research or genetic improvements, on export or cash crop research, on the Sahel or humid zone?

In identifying priorities, it is often argued that research resources should be allocated where the probability for success is highest. However, breakthroughs in agricultural research are often a result of past research in which a great deal of work has already been done and in which many of the elements of the problem have been identified. Minor investments in new research may yield quick and high returns; the probability of success is highest where there is an existing knowledge base.

Second, there is no a priori basis to argue that research in areas in which there is a high probability of success are those that are likely to have significant effects on agricultural productivity or on equity. Therefore, considerations of probability of success in agricultural research should be put aside in favor of areas of need when allocations of resources are determined.

Research resources should be allocated between various competing needs within a logical framework. Sub-Saharan Africa can first be divided into sub-regions or zones[16] determined by climatic, economic, administrative, or other factors, assuming that research conducted in one sub-region has little relevance for another. Consequently, physical and climatic factors should probably be used as the main criteria in making the divisions.[17] Once established, these demarcations can provide the basis for allocation of resources between the regions and among commodities and research topics.

As a simple rule of thumb, commodity and regional research allocations should be proportional to the share of the commodity or region in the total value of output (Boyce and Evenson, 1975; Ryan, 1978). M. von Oppen and J. Ryan (1981) have proposed a list of 10 criteria, using elements that affect the efficiency of agricultural research and the likely equity implications. They provide a composite numerical index which uses all 10 criteria to derive the required allocation of resources for an international agricultural research center.

Unfortunately, no comprehensive study has been undertaken of research resource allocations between commodities and livestock or between sub-regions in terms of the congruence between the actual and ideal allocation. Neither is it possible to perform such an analysis in the context of this chapter. We must therefore rely on indirect and partial analysis.[18]

From such a preliminary evaluation, the following points emerge:

- Diets in sub-Saharan Africa are dominated by consumption of cereals, roots, and tubers. While cereals account for 60 to 75 percent of the caloric intake in the Sahel, roots and tubers are most important in Central Africa, accounting for 50 to 65 percent of caloric intake. In humid West, East, and southern Africa, cereals account for between 20 and 35 percent. Livestock thus contributes less than 25 percent of total caloric intake. As expansion of livestock output is highly dependent on increased crop production, there is a strong case for placing primary emphasis on crop research in the short to medium term. Investment in livestock research should probably be maintained at present levels. Research in the Sahel should focus heavily on cereals, while roots and tubers should receive most emphasis in Central Africa.

- In terms of volume of production, the most important cereals in sub-Saharan Africa are maize, sorghum, millet, and rice, in order of importance. The most important root and tuber is cassava. While per capita food production has declined significantly in the past two decades, growth rates for cereals as a whole have been lower than for pulses or roots and tubers. Among cereals, the growth rates have been particularly low for millet and maize. As a result, the current allocation of available research funds between commodities is not optimum. In particular, there appears to be an insufficient allocation of available resources to millet and sorghum research.

• While population growth rates are uniformly high in sub-Saharan Africa, it is clear that agricultural research resource allocations to the Sahel should receive highest priority, followed probably by West and Central Africa.

• Consideration of allocations on a sub-regional basis and among areas of research underlines the inappropriateness of generalizations. Rather, decisions must be made in relative terms. Broadly speaking, more emphasis should be placed on soil, water, and forest conservation research than on genetic improvement in the Sahel. Conversely, in the more humid areas of West Africa where these factors are less constraining, the reverse is probably true.

THE RESEARCH SYSTEM AND TIME FRAME FOR AGRICULTURAL RESEARCH IN SUB-SAHARAN AFRICA

There is no substitute for national agricultural research. Countries that have made the most progress in agricultural development are also those that have established efficient and effective agricultural research systems (Mellor and Johnston, 1984; Evenson, 1981). Even if a national research system does not conduct "basic research," a substantial investment in national capacity is needed in order to gain access to and effectively use the advances in knowledge (Schultz, 1979; Ruttan, 1983).

While strengthening national research systems should therefore be given highest priority, these systems in sub-Saharan Africa face many operational problems. Oram and Binglish point out in a forthcoming study that many of the smaller African countries, and in Central America and the Caribbean, would not be able to support a national system capable of handling all their potential agricultural research needs even at a substantially higher rate of expenditure. Therefore, the efforts of national systems must be supplemented in the short to medium term by a system of sub-regional and international research centers.

These centers, in turn, should concentrate on research problems common to several countries. But because of variations in environment and natural resources and other constraints already discussed, individual programs will need to be at the most sub-regional in character. For example, sorghum improvement programs should be designed differently for the Sahel and for southern Africa.

If there is one thing that is clearly evident from reviews of research in sub-Saharan Africa, it is that the successful programs have been those that have not only been well-managed, but have also been long-term in nature (Eicher, 1984). Agricultural research must be cast within 10 to 20 year time frames, rather than the two to five years common in the past.

THE ROLE OF EXTERNAL ASSISTANCE

The primary responsibility for economic development in any country lies with its national government. However, many countries in sub-Saharan Africa would not be able to have sufficiently large national systems even if they increased research expenditures significantly. Prospects for domestic financing of research are even worse with the current dismal budgetary situation of many governments. Unless substantial assistance is forthcoming, agricultural research in Africa will be starved of funds, making it impossible to develop the technology on which future growth and development depend.

Indeed, given that the failures of agricultural development projects over the past decade were partly due to the inadequate stock of technologies ready for adoption by farmers, a major shift in donor resources away from extension or production projects and in favor of agricultural research is justified. This shift, however, should not affect emergency aid needed to combat the present famine and to help cover expected food deficits in the immediate future.

Donors should invest in human capital development as part of assistance to agricultural research. With a comparative advantage in high-level formal education and training at the masters and Ph.D. level, Western donors can help improve the quality of staff in national programs and build a stock of trained researchers. In this regard, it should be stressed that the number of people to be trained ideally would exceed the number of positions that must be immediately filled, as provision must be made for unavoidable losses to organizations and private enterprises.[19]

THE ROLE OF THE PRIVATE SECTOR

As the private sector is profit-oriented, industrial firms will undertake only strictly applied research in which they can expect to derive quick results. The private industrial sectors of most African countries are very small, as are the amounts that can be invested, compared to the magnitude of resources needed for agricultural research. Further, because of the long gestation period of agricultural research and the uncertainties of success, multinational corporations cannot be expected to engage in this activity in a big way.

As stated by Schultz (1979): "The only meaningful approach to modern agricultural research is to conceptualize most of its contributions as public goods. As such they must be paid for on public account, which does not exclude private gifts to be used to produce public goods" (reprinted in Eicher and Staatz, 1984, p. 337).

CONCLUSIONS

The dismal record of agriculture has contributed greatly to the poor economic performance of sub-Saharan African countries in the post-independence period. Domestic and international agricultural research systems must share the responsibility, as they have not produced a large enough stock of technological innovation capable of ensuring sustainable growth in aggregate agricultural output.

Researchers have had an inadequate understanding of small farmer goals and resource limitations, resulting in incompatible recommendations. In addition, an over-reliance on the technology transfer model has discouraged work on improving locally available plant materials and farming systems.

To improve the situation and lay the groundwork for future agricultural growth and development, an increase in investment in agricultural research and a change in the direction of research are required. Major increases in agricultural productivity can only be expected from investment in the agricultural research capacity which is needed to develop technologies appropriate to the region's natural and institutional environment.

Since agricultural development can only be brought about by widespread but gradual increases in productivity by small farmers adopting innovations appropriate to their factor proportions, research must concentrate on developing appropriate technologies such as crop varieties that are adaptable to limited areas and respond well to low doses of inputs such as fertilizers. Material inputs should be derived mainly from local sources and mechanization research should concentrate on improving hand tools and animal traction.

Major emphasis should be placed on soil, water, and forest conservation, and particularly on research to develop economical crop rotations including tree crops, leguminous species, and mixed farming. Top priority should be given to food crop research on sorghum and millet in particular. Although an increase in export crop research may be justified in some countries, present levels of investment in livestock research need not be increased until substantial gains have been made in crop output levels. Because many policy decisions are made with an inadequate knowledge base, policy research which includes substantial primary data gathering should be given high priority.

Major emphasis will also need to be placed on developing and increasing the efficiency of national research systems. But in the short to medium term, regional and international research centers must continue to play an important role in agricultural research in sub-Saharan Africa. Substantial donor assistance will be required in the short to medium term to ensure that these centers and national research systems receive adequate funding. Lastly, investment in research must be cast within a longer time frame than has been common in the past. These allocations must reflect a farming systems perspective and embrace the development of human capital.

NOTES

1. There is a substantial literature on this topic, starting with Lewis (1955) and including Ranis and Fei (1961, 1964), Jorgenson (1961), etc. For a review of the application of these and similar models to African countries, see Eicher and Baker (1982), pp. 30–35.

2. The onchocerciasis areas of the Volta River valley being opened up by control of the blackfly will permit limited application of the frontier model in the next two decades. But this will not make much impact on aggregate agricultural output.

3. These inputs were classified according to three categories: the capacity of public and private sector research institutions to produce new technical knowledge; the capacity of the industrial sector to develop, produce, and market new technical inputs; and the capacity of farmers to acquire new knowledge and use inputs effectively (Ruttan, 1980).

4. See Eicher and Baker (1982), Chapter II, for a review of theoretical perspectives.

5. To ensure success in these areas, considerable policy reforms particularly in marketing and pricing policies are counselled by the IMF and World Bank.

6. Three researchers played an important role in regenerating interest in intercropping research in sub-Saharan Africa. David Norman's farm surveys in northern Nigeria in the 1960s demonstrated the importance of the system

(Norman, 1974), while agronomic research, also in Nigeria, by Bede Okigbo and D.J. Andrews gave professional prominence to intercropping research (Andrews, 1972, 1974; Okigbo and Greenland, 1977).

7. For example, ICRISAT has reorganized its sub-Saharan African research program into one regional center in Niamey, Niger, three sub-regional teams in Zimbabwe, Burkina Faso/Mali, and Malawi, and one bilateral program in Mali (ICRISAT, 1984) and WARDA has established special research projects to do more fundamental research (WARDA, 1984).

8. For a good text on the techniques of food policy analysis, see Timmer, Falcon, and Pearson (1983).

9. The need for food policy analysis to consider these macro as well as micro issues is often neglected by many policy analysts.

10. As an example, the Central Bank of Nigeria's new report on the economy could give no figures on total crop production or on crop losses, etc. (Derrick, 1984).

11. Referred to as "upstream research" by Gilbert, Norman, and Winch (1980).

12. See, for example, the manual by Shaner, Philipp, and Schmehl (1982) which gives an otherwise excellent treatise on the methods and modalities of on-farm research.

13. See, for example, the large U.S.-funded Senegalese program with ISRA and the planned Malian program.

14. Perhaps a good example of the inappropriateness of this scaling-down approach to machinery development is the recent series of equipment developed for zero tillage in the humid tropics. To use the equipment requires land clearing techniques not found on small farms. The equipment can thus only be used by large farmers, yet it is billed as small farm equipment.

15. See Eicher and Baker (1982), Chapter VI, for a review of social science research in this area.

16. For allocation of national research resources, analogous subdivisions of a country could also be made.

17. Sub-Saharan Africa could for example be subdivided into Sahel, East, Central, and southern Africa (USDA, 1981).

18. Every research institution or donor agency should systematically examine its research resource allocation between commodities, programs, and regions, as has been done by ICRISAT (Ryan, 1978, von Oppen and Ryan, 1981, and ICRISAT, 1984).

19. Losses could of course be reduced by setting up attractive incentive schemes for researchers. But donor agencies could do little in this regard except try to convince national governments of the need to attract and keep trained researchers at their jobs.

REFERENCES

Abaelu, John. 1971. "The Nigerian Oil Palm Sector and Social Returns From Hybrid Palms." Agricultural Economics Seminar Paper. Chicago: University of Chicago, Department of Economics, January.

ADB/ECA. 1984. *Economic Report on Africa*. African Development Bank and Economic Commission for Africa.

Andrews, D. J. 1972. "Intercropping with Sorghum in Nigeria." *Experimental Agriculture* 8:139–50.

Andrews, D. J. 1974. "Responses of Sorghum Varieties to Intercropping." *Experimental Agriculture* 10(1): 57-63.

Berry, L. and M. Khogali. 1984. "The Physical Background to African Development." Background Paper, Committee On African Development Strategies, Washington D.C.: Overseas Development Council.

Belshaw, D. G. R. 1979. "Taking Indigenous Technology Seriously: The Case of Intercropping in East Africa." *IDS, Sussex Bulletin* 10:24–27.

Binswanger, H. P., and J. G. Ryan. 1977. "Efficiency and Equity Issues in Ex Ante Allocation of Research Resources," *Indian Journal of Agricultural Economics* 32:3.

Boyce, J. K. and R. E. Evenson. 1975. *National and International Research and Extension Programs*. New York: ADC.

Byerlee, D., C. K. Eicher, C. Leidholm and D. S. C. Spencer. 1983. "Employment-Output Conflicts, Factor-Price Distortions and Choice of Technique: Empirical Results from Sierra Leone." *Economic Development and Cultural Change* 31(2): 315-36.

Byerlee, D., L. Harrington, and D. L. Winkelmann. 1983. "Farming Systems Research: Issues in Research Strategy and Technology Design." *American Journal of Agricultural Economics* 64(5): 897–904.

CGIAR. 1978. Farming Systems Research at the International Agricultural Research Centers. Rome: TAC Secretariat.

CGIAR. 1978. Report of the TAC Quinquennial Review Mission to the International Crops Research Institute for the Semi-Arid Tropics (ICRISAT). Rome: TAC Secretariat.

Collinson, M. 1983. "Technological Potentials for Food Production in Eastern and Central Africa." Paper presented at the Conference on Accelerating Agricultural Growth in Sub-Saharan Africa, Victoria Falls, Zimbabwe, August.

Delgado, C. 1981. "Price Policy, Returns to Labor and Accelerated Food Grain Production in the West African Savannah," in *Food Policy Issues and Concerns in Sub-Saharan Africa*. Washington, D.C.: IFPRI, pp. 103–18.

Derrick. 1984. "Decline of Agriculture Shows No Sign of Slowing," *African Business* 76:17.

Doppler, W. 1980. *The Economics of Pasture Improvement and Beef Production in Semi-Humid West Africa*. Eschborn: German Agency for Technical Cooperation.

ECA. 1983. *ECA and African Development, 1983–2008*. Addis Ababa: Economic Commission for Africa.

Eicher, C. K. 1967. "The Dynamics of Long-Term Agricultural Development in Nigeria." *Journal of Farm Economics* 49:1158–70.

Eicher, C. K. 1984. "International Technology Transfer and the African Farmer: Theory and Practice." Working Paper, University of Zimbabwe, Dept. of Land Management, March.

Eicher, C. K. and Doyle C. Baker. 1982. *Research on Agricultural Development in*

Sub-Saharan Africa. East Lansing: Michigan State University International Development Paper, No. 1.

Eicher, C. K. and J. M. Staatz, eds. 1984. *Agricultural Development in the Third World*. Baltimore: Johns Hopkins University Press.

Evenson, R. E. 1981. "Benefits and Obstacles to Appropriate Agricultural Technology." *The Annals of the American Academy of Political and Social Sciences* 458 (November): 54–67.

FAO. 1974. "Provisional Food Balance Sheets, 1972–74." Rome: Food and Agricultural Organization.

FAO. 1978. *Regional Food Plan for Africa: Report of the Tenth FAO Regional Conference for Africa, 18–29 September, 1978, Tanzania*. Rome: Food and Agricultural Organization.

Gilbert, E. H., D. E. Norman and F. E. Winch. 1980. *Farming Systems Research: A Critical Appraisal*. East Lansing: Michigan State University, Dept. of Agricultural Econ., MSU Rural Development Paper No. 6.

Hayami, Y. and V. W. Ruttan. 1971. *Agricultural Development: An International Perspective*. Baltimore: Johns Hopkins University Press.

ICRISAT. 1980–83. *Rapport Annuel*. Ouagadougou, Burkina Faso: Programme Cooperatif. International Crops Research Institute for the Semi-Arid Tropics. ICRISAT/Burkina Faso, 1980, 1981, 1982, 1983.

ICRISAT. 1984. *A Long Term Plan for Developing International Cooperation*. International Crops Research Institute for the Semi-Arid Tropics, October.

IFDC. 1976. *Etude sur les engrais en Afrique de l'ouest*. International Fertilizer Development Center. *Muscle Shoals, USA*: Volume 1.

Jaeger, W. 1984. "Agricultural Mechanization: The Economics of Animal Traction in Burkina Faso." Ph.D thesis, Stanford University.

Jorgenson, D. W. 1961. "The Development of a Dual Economy." *Economic Journal* 71: 309–34.

Judd, M. A. L., J. K. Boyce and R. E. Evenson. 1984. "Investing in Agricultural Supply." *Economic Development and Cultural Change* (in press).

Lebeau, F. J., R. F. Chandler, C. E. Fergusson and T. Zalla. 1984. "Assessment of Agricultural Research Resources in the Sahel." USAID, May.

Lewis, W. Arthur. 1955. *The Theory of Economic Growth*. London: Allen and Unwin.

Lewis, J. K. D. 1982. *West Africa Rice Research and Production: One Crop, Fifteen Nations, and Multiple Ecologies*. Project Impact Evaluation, Washington, D.C.: USAID.

Matlon, P.J. 1983. "The Technical Potential for Increased Food Production in the West African Semi-Arid Tropics." Paper presented at the Conference on Accelerating Agricultural Growth in Sub-Saharan Africa, Victoria Falls, Zimbabwe.

Matlon, P. J. and D. S. C. Spencer. 1984. "Increased Food Production in Sub-Saharan Africa: Environmental Problems and Inadequate Technological Solutions." *American Journal of Agricultural Economics* (in press).

Mellor, J. 1984. "The Changing World Food Situation—A CGIAR Perspective." Paper presented at the International Centers Week, November 5–9, IFPRI, Washington, D.C.

Mellor, J. and B. F. Johnston. 1984. "The World Food Equation: Interrelation

Among Development, Employment, and Food Consumption." *Journal of Economic Literature* 22: 532–74.

McKelvey, J. J., Jr. 1965. "Agricultural Research" in R. A. Lystad, ed., *The African World: A Survey of Social Research*. New York: Praeger, 317–51.

Norman, D. W. 1974. "Rationalizing Mixed Cropping Under Indigenous Conditions: Example of Northern Nigeria." *Journal of Development Studies* 11: 3–21.

Oram, P. and V. Binglish. 1984. "Investment in Agricultural Research in Developing Countries: Progress, Problems, and the Determination of Priorities." IFPRI (forthcoming).

OAU. 1980. *The Lagos Plan of Action for the Implementation of the Monrovia Strategy for the Economic Development of Africa*. Lagos: OAU.

Okigbo, B. N. and D. J. Greenland. 1977. "Intercropping Systems in Tropical Africa" in R. I. Papendick, P. A. Sanchez and G. B. Tyiplett, eds., *Multiple Cropping*, Madison, Wisconsin: American Society of Agronomy, 63–101.

Paulino, L. 1983. "The Evolving Food Situation in Sub-Saharan Africa." Paper presented at the Conference on Accelerating Agricultural Growth in Sub-Saharan Africa, Victoria Falls, Zimbabwe.

Pichot, J., M. P. Sedogo, J. F. Poulain and J. Arrivets. 1981. "Evolution de la Fertilité d'un Sol Ferrugineux Tropical sous l'Influence des Fumures Minérales et Organiques." *Agronomie Tropicale* 36 (2): 122–33.

Ranis, G. and J. C. H. Fei. 1961. "A Theory of Economic Development." *American Economic Review* 51(4): 533–46.

Ranis, G. and J. C. H. Fei. 1964. *Development of the Labor Surplus Economy: Theory and Policy*. Homewood, Ill.: Richard D. Irwin.

Ruthenberg, H. 1974. "Artificial Pastures and Their Utilization in the Southern Guinea Savanna and the Derived Savanna of West Africa. Tour d'Horizon of an Agricultural Economist." (Two Parts). *Zeitschrift für Ausländische Landwirtschaft* 13(3): 216–31.

Ruthenberg, H. 1980. *Farming Systems in the Tropics*. 3rd ed. Oxford: Oxford University Press.

Ruttan, V.W. 1980. "Models of Agricultural Development" in Eicher and Staatz, eds., *Agricultural Development in the Third World*. Baltimore: Johns Hopkins University Press, 38–45.

Ruttan, V. W. 1983. "The Global Agricultural Support System." *Science*: 222.

Ruttan, V.W. and Y. Hayami. 1972. "Strategies for Agricultural Development," Food Research Institute, 9(2): 129-48.

Ryan, J. G. 1978. "Agriculture and Research in the Semi-Arid Tropics." Economics Program, ICRISAT, Hyderabad, India.

Sargent, M. J. Lichte, P. Matlon and R. Bloom. 1981. "An Assessment of Animal Traction in Francophone West Africa." East Lansing: Michigan State University, Department of Agricultural Economics, African Rural Economy Working Paper No. 34.

Schultz, T.W. 1964. *Transforming Traditional Agriculture*. New Haven: Yale University Press.

Schultz, T.W. 1979. "The Economics of Agricultural Research," In C. K.

Eicher and J. M. Staatz, eds., *Agricultural Development in the Third World*. Baltimore: Johns Hopkins University Press, 1984, 335–47.

Shaner, W. W., P. F. Philipp and W. R. Schmehl. 1982. *Farming Systems Research and Development*. Boulder: Westview Press.

Sparling, E. W. 1981. "A Survey and Analysis of Ex-Post Cost-Benefit Studies of Sahelian Irrigation Projects." Department of Economics, Colorado State University (mimeo).

Stolper, W.F. 1969. *Planning Without Facts: Lessons in Resource Allocation From Nigeria's Development*. Cambridge, Mass.: Harvard University Press.

Stoop, W. A., C. Pattanayak, P. J. Matlon, and W. R. Root. 1981. "A Strategy to Raise the Productivity of Subsistence Farming Systems in the West African Semi-Arid Tropics." *Sorghum in the Eighties*, 519–26, ICRISAT, Hyderabad, India.

Taylor, G., and M. Soumare. 1983. "Strategies for Forestry Development in the Semi-Arid Tropics: Lessons from the Sahel." Paper presented at the International Symposium on Strategies and Designs for Afforestation, Reforestation and Tree Planting, Waageningen, September 19–23.

ter Kuile, C.H.H. 1983. "Technological Potentials for Food Production in Humid and Sub-Humid Tropics of Africa." Paper presented at the Conference on Accelerating Agricultural Growth in Sub-Saharan Africa, Victoria Falls, Zimbabwe.

Timmer, C.P. 1973. "Choice of Technique in Rice Milling in Java." *Bulletin of Indonesian Economic Studies* 9(2): 57–76.

USDA. 1981. *Food Problems and Prospects in Sub-Saharan Africa: The Decade of the 1980's*. ERS, Foreign Agriculture Research Report No. 166. Washington, D.C.: United States Department of Agriculture .

Von Oppen, M. and J. Ryan. 1981. "Determining Regional Research Resource Allocation at ICRISAT." Economic Program. Hyderabad, India: ICRISAT

WARDA. 1984. Programme Achievement, Contribution to and Impact on Rice Development in West Africa. West Africa Rice Development Association, WARDA/84/STC-14/17. Monrovia, Liberia.

World Bank. 1981. *Accelerated Development in Sub-Saharan Africa*. Washington, D.C.: The World Bank.

World Bank. 1984a. *World Development Report, 1984*. Washington, D.C.: The World Bank.

World Bank. 1984b. *Toward Sustained Development in Sub-Saharan Africa: A Joint Program of Action*. Washington, D.C.: The World Bank.

CHAPTER NINE

Strategic Issues in Combating Hunger and Poverty in Africa

Carl K. Eicher

"Since most Africans are farmers, raising the productivity of farmers is a sine qua non of raising the African standard of living."—W. *Arthur Lewis*, 1955

Hunger and poverty in sub-Saharan Africa are two fundamental problems that are morally unacceptable to Africans and to world opinion. Hunger is especially intolerable in a world "awash with grain," where North America, the EEC, and Japan are competing for Third World markets and where enough food is produced each year to provide every person with 3000 calories.

Sub-Saharan Africa[1] is a vast continent that defies easy generalizations. But amid its diversity and complexity, two important facts stand out: Many African states have slowly lost the capacity to feed their people, and Africa is the poorest continent in the world economy. In 1985, Africa's famine captured world attention and resulted in a tripling of the 1983 level of food aid to 7 million tons of grain. But both the Sahelian famine of the early 1970s and the Ethiopian famine of 1985 are dramatic manifestations of longer-terms problems that have been building up for two decades—increasing rates of population growth, lagging food production, malnutrition, and pervasive poverty (Eicher, 1982).

African states are now receiving generous advice from many quarters on what needs to be done to solve hunger and poverty, but much of it is based on confusion over the causes of Africa's agrarian crisis. There is little understanding of the technical and institutional requirements for agricultural change and a tendency to underestimate the gestation period required to develop human capital, managerial skills, and bio-chemical technology—the prime movers of agricultural change.

This chapter is devoted to a discussion of the strategic issues in combating hunger and poverty in sub-Saharan Africa over the medium term (3 to 5 years) and long term (5 to 15 years); the nature of the problem and the required long-term response; the hunger and poverty battle; the role of agriculture in the macro-economic strategy of African states; the prime movers of agricultural development; food security policy dilemmas; and the role of foreign assistance in African agriculture under conditions of limited absorptive capacity.

THE NATURE OF THE PROBLEM AND THE REQUIRED LONG-TERM RESPONSE

Because the food outlook is bleak for many African countries, additional resources are being mobilized by private groups, charities, and donor agencies. However, before additional funds are pumped into African agriculture, it is important to examine the nature of the problem—the causes of hunger and poverty—and the required long-term response.

Africa-wide generalizations about rates of growth of population, food production, and per capita income tend to cloud many of the remarkable achievements of individual countries. Although Africa's economic performance has been poor, there are bright spots. For example, "Many countries, both middle-income (e.g., Ivory Coast, Cameroon, and Botswana) as well as some of the poorest (Rwanda and Malawi) have performed well for some time, achieving real average annual growth rates from about 5 percent to over 12 percent between 1970 and 1982" (Jaycox, 1985). Life expectancy has increased by 20 percent from around 39 years in 1960 to 47 in 1983.

What are the prospects for Africa's future economic performance? As a general rule, economic projections, even for individual African countries, should be made cautiously. In 1960, Africa was basically self-sufficient in staple foods, and some countries, such as Senegal and Nigeria, were significant exporters of groundnuts to Europe. In the 1960s, Africa's population growth rate was modest—1.5 to 2.0 percent—and new land was more or less automatically brought under cultivation by subsistence farmers without foreign aid-financed food production projects. However, Africa's rapid population growth since independence has raised some important issues. Food production has grown at half the population growth rate since the 1970s. Thus, one of the two core problems examined in this chapter is the food production-population battle.

THE FOOD PRODUCTION—POPULATION BATTLE

The starting point for understanding the food production-population battle is the rate of population growth—not the population density or the total size of a nation's population. In Africa, current rates of population growth of between 2.5 to 4.4 percent are extremely high by historical standards and imply a population doubling over a period of 15 to 25 years. A comparison between Africa and Japan is instructive. Japan is a textbook case of how a country with a poor natural resource base skillfully mobilized smallholder agriculture to finance its structural transformation from a feudal power in 1878 to an industrial nation by 1912. The agricultural sector made a strategic contribution to national development through a land tax that financed 63 percent of the national budget until 1902. Moreover, thanks to improved rice varieties and steady domestic terms of trade, the agricultural sector grew 2.3 percent per year, outstripping the population growth rate of around 1.0 percent over the 1878–1912 period.

In Africa, agricultural output grew by 1.7 percent between 1970 and 1985—a respectable rate in comparison with Japan's 2.3 percent over the 1878–1912 period (Ohkawa and Rosovsky, 1964). But Africa's population is currently growing at roughly triple the rate in Japan over the 1878–1912 period. Hence, there is a significant difference in one of the "initial conditions"—the population growth rate—in the early stage of Japan's modern economic growth and contemporary Africa. Kenya's annual population growth rate of 4.4 percent will require a doubling of food production in 16 years—a rate unprecedented in the early history of Japan and other industrial countries.

One of the simplest measures of population growth is the total fertility rate—a rough proxy for the average number of lifetime births per woman. Currently, the total fertility rate in Africa is 6.9 compared with 1.8 in the United States. But unlike in China, where there is concerted campaign to implement the "one family, one child policy,"[2] there is little debate in Africa today—even among academics—overpopulation and family planning, let alone political support for measures to reduce the average number of children per family from seven to five.

Today, demographers generally agree that family planning programs have been ineffective in Africa in the last 25 years, and that "no nation displays any significant sign of fertility decline" (Caldwell and Caldwell, 1984). Africa's population explosion will result in a doubling of population in 15 to 20 years in most countries, thus increasing pressure on land and natural resources, such as fuel wood, grazing areas, and national parks.[3]

It is time to shelve the misleading cliche that Africa is a land-abundant continent. Because of unequal population distribution in relation to agricultural potential and political barriers to international migration to land-abundant countries, calculating Africa's total food production potential is irrelevant to the ability of a sub-region such as the Sahel or a country such as Kenya to feed its population. The long-term trend is toward increasing population pressure on land and natural resources and growing food dependence on industrial countries (FAO/UNFPA/IIASA, 1982). Three policy implications emerge from this analysis. First, assuming that there will be no significant reduction in fertility over the next 10 to 15 years, the food needs of many African states will have to be partially met through food imports for the next 10 to 20 years, just as India drew on food aid for 15 years from 1956–71. Second, to double food production over the coming 15 to 20 years, many African governments will have to place substantially higher priority on the agricultural sector for several decades—not for one year as President Moi did when he declared 1984 the "Year of Implementation" in Kenya. Third, Africans cannot ignore population growth as they turn to industrial countries for food aid. Food aid and population control measures should be viewed as two sides of the same coin in policy and foreign assistance negotiations.

A PERSPECTIVE FROM INDIA ON THE TIME FRAME

India responded to Ethiopia's 1985 famine by donating 100,000 tons of food grain, but, surprisingly, this generous gift was not picked up by the media—perhaps because there is a perception in Europe and North America that India is still a food aid client of the West. India's achievement of a reliable food surplus in 1980 after two decades of pro-agricultural policies is of broad significance to African governments and donors as they start to pump additional aid into African agriculture.

Thirty years ago, India suffered poor harvests in two successive years, and the food emergency was met by a vast inflow of food aid, primarily from the United States, that extended for 15 years. India's food crisis of the mid-1950s shattered the heavy industry development strategy that was being pursued on the recommendation of the Indian mathematician, Professor P.C. Mahalanobis, head of the Indian Statistical Institute. Mahalanobis' heavy industry model reflected his pessimistic view of the ability of India's peasantry to mobilize agriculture as a leading sector of development, and his admiration for Russia's emergence as a world industrial power in one generation.

The seeds for the "long view" of agricultural reform were planted by a team of American agricultural scientists under the sponsorship of the Ford Foundation. The team's influential study, *Report of India's Food Crisis and Steps to Meet It* (India, 1959), made the case for long-term investments in human capital, research, irrigation, and infrastructure as the foundation for modernizing Indian agriculture; they argued that industrial development would founder without a reliable food surplus. India's policy response to its food crisis of the mid-1950s and bad harvests of 1965–67 led to a deemphasis on heavy industry and increased public investment in the agricultural sector over two decades. The United States and several other key donors linked expanded food aid to basic agricultural reforms.[4]

India became self-sufficient in food production in the early 1980s. But two decades after its concerted drive to modernize agriculture and achieve self-sufficiency in food grain, India has eliminated neither hunger nor poverty. A quarter to a third of the rural population lacks either access to land or income to buy enough calories. India is taking vigorous steps to deal with hunger through rural works programs, fair-price shops serving the urban labor classes, and carefully targeted food subsidies.

What can African states and donors learn from India's experience? There is no single answer, except what can be gleaned from a mosaic of interrelated factors: four decades of political stability without a coup; the skillful use of massive food aid shipments for 15 years until Green Revolution wheat and rice varieties gained widespread adoption; sound and consistent macro-policies for agriculture; investment in agricultural research, rural roads, and irrigation; and the introduction of a new institution—state agricultural universities—modeled on the U.S. system of land grant universities.[5] Although foreign aid to India amounted to a substantial $14 billion over the 1951–70 period, per capita aid was only $1.50 per year (Mellor, 1979, p. 89)[6]—an extremely modest amount compared to Africa today, where aid flows to some West African states are $50 to $75 per capita a year.[7] The main lesson for African states and donors, however, is not the role of aid in India's development, but the concentration on macro-economic policies favoring agriculture, technology generation, human capital, and strengthening agricultural institutions—over 25 years. One of the most painful lessons that has been learned about agricultural development in Africa is that it takes time to develop stable political structures, a competent civil service of high integrity, an indigenous scientific capacity, locally financed agriculture research, biologically stable and economically profitable technology for rainfed farming, and the development of local Masters and Ph.D. training programs to reduce dependence on expatriate assistance. The accumulated evidence of the 25 years since colonial rule suggests that the required response to hunger and poverty in Africa should be conceptualized in a time span of several decades, a period that makes a mockery of donors who are peddling projects—particularly institution-building projects—with three to five-year time spans.

THE HUNGER AND POVERTY BATTLE

Hunger is the lack of adequate nutrition on a temporary or chronic basis. Because there is no accepted agreement on the quantitative cut-off point between adequate nutrition and malnutrition, there is no consensus among specialists and international agencies on the number of hungry and malnourished in Africa. A conservative estimate is that about one-fourth of the African people or about 100 million were hungry and malnourished in 1985.[8] A decade ago, it was commonly assumed that protein shortages were the dominant cause of malnutrition, but recent research has shown that the key to good nutrition for most people is getting enough calories from several different sources.

A great deal has been learned over the past decades about the complex linkages between hunger and poverty. Hunger and malnutrition are caused primarily by one or more of the following: low productivity of family labor on subsistence farms; unstable output levels due to drought; lack of access to land; and lack of income to purchase adequate food on a timely basis. Expanded food production alone, however, will not eliminate hunger and malnutrition, as although the United States and India are self-sufficient in food, neither country has solved its hunger and malnutrition problems. There is increasing recognition that hunger is a function of multiple causes and that the hunger-poverty battle is a complex political struggle over how a society deals with poverty—the root cause of hunger in industrial and Third World countries.

Pervasive in Africa, poverty is a major cause of hunger because it prevents people from purchasing a calorie-adequate diet. The majority of the poor in Africa are subsistence farmers who are producing food at low levels of labor productivity. One of the most effective ways of raising real incomes of subsistence farmers in the short run is to increase the productivity of their main enterprise, staple food production. This can increase the per capita availability of home-produced foods, raise cash incomes through the sale of staple food, or enable family food needs to be produced with less land and labor, thus freeing these resources for other income-earning activities such as cotton production or off-farm employment (see Chapter 11). Historically, however, the only proven long-term solution to rural poverty is economic development, a process that absorbs some farm labor in rural small-scale industry and induces the migration of rural people to the industrial and service sectors.[9]

A few African states and donors are discarding the appealing but potentially misleading concept of food self-sufficiency, replacing it with "food security" as a strategic goal of national development. Food security is defined as the ability of a country to ensure that its population has access to a timely, reliable, and nutritionally adequate supply of food on a long-term basis (Eicher and Staatz, 1984).

THE ROLE OF AGRICULTURE IN THE MACRO-ECONOMIC STRATEGY OF AFRICAN STATES

The neglect of agriculture in most African states since independence raises two basic questions. First, has agriculture been neglected because policy-makers are ignorant about the strategic role of a reliable agricultural surplus as a foundation of industrial development? Second, has agriculture been neglected because policy-makers and researchers are confused about how to solve the dilemma of investing in agriculture to expand its future productivity, while having to tax it to develop other sectors of the economy?

With the growing consensus on the importance of agriculture to African development, one can conclude that agriculture has not been neglected in African policy circles because of ignorance. The second question, on the other hand, has to be answered partially in the affirmative because most policy-makers, civil servants, and donors are confused over how to find the proper balance between investing in and taxing the agricultural sector. This problem has plagued Western development economists for 30 years.[10]

The following illustrates why it is difficult to get African leaders to accept the view that the agricultural sector can be a motor of change in the overall economy:

- In the absence of the petroleum, minerals, or other non-agricultural sources of government revenue and foreign exchange, how does a government accelerate national development from an agrarian base when international trade in agricultural commodities cannot be counted on as a long-term engine of growth?[11]

- How does a government generate consistent political support among urban and military leaders for long-term investment in agriculture when a succession of coups and counter-coups "force" political leaders to emphasize crash programs "to get agriculture moving"?

- How does a government use agricultural pricing policies to achieve multiple objectives? For example, how does a government resolve the dilemma of raising producer prices to stimulate food production in the long run, when higher prices will make it more difficult for net food buyers (e.g., landless and urban poor) to meet their minimum nutrition needs in the short run?[12]

- How does a government promote structural change (e.g., Tanzania's Ujamaa resettlement program and Zimbabwe's land transfer program) without a large loss of production in the short run?

- What are the relative roles of technology policy, price policy, and institutional reform in bringing about increased farm production?

The following country illustrations highlight some successful and unsuccessful attempts at finding a meaningful role for agriculture in macro-economic strategies over the past 25 years. During the first two decades of independence, many African scholars and planners looked to Israel,[13] Yugoslavia,[14] China,[15] and other countries for successful development models that could be imported to assist in the "catching up" process. These imported models invariably failed. The failure of many ranches, state farms, settlement schemes, and government tractor hire schemes over the past two decades was partially a function of the inexperience and incompetence of political leaders and their foreign advisers. As President Nyerere of Tanzania recently reported: "There are certain things I would not do if I were to start again. One of them is the abolition of local government and the other is the disbanding of cooperatives. We were impatient and ignorant" (Nyerere, 1984, p. 828).

An important lesson that has been learned is that whether capitalist or socialist, the ideology of development cannot in and of itself generate agricultural development, as in both systems there have been many failures. Agricultural development is too complex to be a function of any single factor such as climate, ideology, or appropriate technology. Nevertheless, in terms of agricultural production goals, capitalism has proven to be a more reliable strategy than socialism at this stage of Africa's economic history. After 25 years of independence, there are no models of agrarian socialism in Africa that have produced a reliable agricultural surplus. At this early stage, most low-income African states lack the skilled managers and the vast information network required to manage state farms, plantations, or ranches with a high degree of efficiency. Tanzania's experience with agrarian socialism is instructive.

Despite Tanzania's well-publicized pro-agriculture strategy following the 1967 Arusha Declaration, the government compelled farmers to abandon their individual farms and to live in villages while quietly turning the price and income terms of trade against them. In fact, in 1980, farmers received 36 percent less for their food and export crops in real terms (after correcting for inflation) than in 1970 (Ellis, 1982, p. 272). After two decades of promises to get agriculture moving, President Nyerere retired in October 1985 leaving behind the legacy of a stagnant agricultural economy. Tanzania's inability to feed itself is the fundamental reason why African states no longer emulate Tanzania as a model of development.

On the other hand, Malawi, Cameroon, and Zimbabwe are the agricultural success stories of the 1980s. With consistent governmental support for agriculture over several decades, smallholders in Malawi have responded and produced a maize surplus in 8 of the past 10 years. Also minister of agriculture, President Banda systematically makes two "crop inspection" trips throughout the country each year at planting and at harvest time. Even during the 1984 drought year, Malawi produced a large maize crop and sold 50,000 tons to neighboring countries.

Cameroon is another under-reported agricultural success story. President Ahidjo and his successor President Biya have repeatedly emphasized that "the soil is the first and most dependable employer," earning more than 80 percent of the country's foreign exchange. Agricultural achievements in Malawi, Zimbabwe, and Cameroon have given political leaders and policy-makers a feeling of self-confidence. There is a growing sense within Africa that policy-makers should draw on their own experiences to solve their problems—a spirit of collective self-reliance at the heart of the Lagos Plan of Action. It is time to refocus the study of African agriculture, drawing lessons from African successes[16] and failures, as well as from India, Hungary, Brazil, Australia, China, and other countries.

A common denominator in Africa's post-independence history is political instability, which adds to the difficulty of developing and implementing a long-term agricultural development strategy. For example, Nigeria's six coups over the past 19 years have each been followed by a knee-jerk food production campaign under the banner of the Green Revolution and Accelerated Food Production.

PRIME MOVERS OF AGRICULTURAL DEVELOPMENT

Agricultural production must be doubled in many African states in order to catch up with the population growth rate. However, no amount of political will, policy reform, or change in relative prices of single commodities will achieve this unless policy-makers and donors concentrate on the prime movers of agricultural change over the medium to long-term:

- New technology that is produced by public and private investments in agricultural research.
- Human capital and managerial skills that are produced by investments in schools, training centers, and on-the-job experience.
- Accretionary growth of biological capital investments (e.g. improving livestock herds, planting, spraying, pruning and main-

taining cocoa and coffee trees) and physical capital investments in infrastructure such as small dams, irrigation, and roads.

• Improvements in the performance of institutions such as land tenure, marketing, credit and national agricultural research, and extension services.

• Favorable economic policy environment.

The first four of the prime movers require long gestation periods of from five to 25 years. For example, experience has shown that it takes 10 years of research on the average to produce a new plant variety, and another five to eight years in which to gain widespread farmer acceptance. It takes 10 to 15 years of graduate study and on-the-job training for an agricultural research scientist to be productive. Donors, however, are avoiding the long gestation investments required to develop indigenous scientific, managerial, and technical capacity. The World Bank has financed showcase components of human capital projects such as buildings for the faculties of agriculture at the University of Zambia, University of Nairobi, Rural Development Institute in Senegal, and the Kolo School of Agriculture in Niger. The EEC recently provided a $12 million loan for a new building for the Faculty of Veterinary Medicine, University of Zimbabwe, while Japan is financing a $6 million Veterinary Medicine Building at the University of Zambia. Buildings, vehicles, and equipment also weigh heavily in foreign aid loans and grants for agricultural research projects. For example, the World Bank is allocating roughly two-thirds of its $19 million loan to Senegal over the 1982–88 period to develop and rehabilitate six research stations, including laboratories and office space, and 106 houses on the stations; and to purchase 11 trucks, 20 tractors, 27 tillers, 205 vehicles, and 105 motor bikes. But delivering vehicles and constructing buildings can be completed in two to three years. Who will train the research staff after the present multi-donor-financed project is completed in 1988? Who will help the young Senegalese researchers gain experience and maturity in developing new varieties of millet, sorghum, maize, and cowpeas over the next 10 to 15 years?

The preference of donors and African states to finance buildings and equipment illustrates their poverty of thinking in the critical area of institutional development. It reflects a lack of understanding of the accretionary process of human capital formation and institution-building. The second characteristic of the prime movers is their complementary nature. Payoffs to investment in applied agricultural re-search will be low unless there is an effective extension service to diffuse the new technology. Likewise, payoffs to investing in agricul-tural extension services in Africa have generally been low because many research services have had little to offer to extension agents. Let us turn to the first prime mover—agricultural research to generate new technology.

TECHNOLOGY GENERATION

Africa has an under-reported colonial history of crop improve-ments such as cotton in Sudan, Mali, and Senegal; oil palm in Zaire and Nigeria, and hybrid maize in Zimbabwe and Kenya (Eicher and Staatz, 1985). But with the exception of a few crops such as maize, research in food crops was modest relative to export crops during the colonial period. This neglect is easily explained because with low rates of population growth and densities, African farmers could meet increased family food needs by bringing more land under cultivation.

With a few notable exceptions such as maize in eastern and south-ern Africa and cassava in West Africa, farmer-tested food crop tech-nology is almost non-existent in Africa. New production technology for food crops, export crops, and livestock can be an important means of generating income for farmers, allowing them to purchase an im-proved diet for their families. In short, hunger can be combatted by expanding export crops, livestock, the sale of food, and rural off-farm employment.

USAID has announced an innovative long-term plan to strengthen national agricultural research services and faculties of agriculture in Africa (AID, 1985b). Ideally, the World Bank and other donors will cooperate with AID and work closely with African states in strength-ening national research services and regional research networks and improving the linkages between these institutions and the interna-tional research centers. As a first step, donors should design agricul-tural research and faculty of agriculture projects with a ten-year life of project and fold many existing farming systems projects into broad-based efforts to strengthen national research services.

HUMAN CAPITAL AND MANAGERIAL SKILLS

By any yardstick—literacy rates, percentage of school-age popula-tion in secondary school and universities, or percentage of expatriates in scientific, managerial, and academic staff positions—Africa is at the bottom of the human resource scale in the Third World. What has been the response of donors? The World Bank approved two education projects for Africa totalling $24 million in 1984, representing 3.6 percent of its worldwide education portfolio of $694 million (World Bank, 1984). Currently, USAID has around 650 bilateral projects in 38 countries (AID, 1985c). Three of the 650 projects are supporting undergraduate and higher degree programs in agriculture in Cameroon, Uganda, and Zimbabwe, and 250 African students are being supported in long-term training (B.S., M.S., and Ph.D.) in various agricultural disciplines (AID, 1985b)—modest responses by two major donors to Africa's crushing human resource problems.

Kenneth Shapiro (1985) recently reported that the stock of human capital in scientific fields per million people in Africa in 1980 was about one-fourth the relative scientific strength of Asia in 1970. The quality and relevance of agricultural training in Africa's universities are coming under increasing scrutiny. Tanzania's bold decision to establish a new agricultural university—the Sokoine University of Agriculture—in 1984 was an outgrowth of President Nyerere's 1981 visit to the Punjab Agricultural University, one of India's 20 state agricultural universities established in the 1960s and modeled after the U.S. Land Grant System. The faculty of agriculture at the University of Dar es Salaam has formed the nucleus of the new university at Morogoro. But Tanzania is ill-prepared to finance a second university at a time when its treasury is almost empty.

Nobel Laureate T.W. Schultz recently reflected on the United States' leadership role in financing human capital in India and its record in Africa to date: "The role that U.S. foreign aid and that of American leadership. . .played in establishing the agricultural universities in India stands as a major achievement of permanent value. It was not a short-term undertaking. It entailed building a new institution (the state agricultural university) for the long-term. But regrettably, U.S. aid has failed to undertake any corresponding enterprises since then; to wit our dismal record throughout most of tropical Africa" (Schultz, 1983, p. 464).

At present, there appears to be little agreement among the departments of education and agriculture within UNDP, USAID, SIDA, FAO, FAC, the African Development Bank, and the World Bank on how foreign assistance can most effectively assist in strengthening Africa's indigenous capacity in food and agriculture. In the 1970s and early 1980s, major donors and U.S. foundations have retreated from investment in human capital. Having allocated 10.6 percent of its Africa budget to education in the 1960s, the World Bank reduced this to 4.1 percent in 1980–84 (Lele, in press).

RURAL CAPITAL FORMATION

In industrial countries, agricultural development was fueled by the mobilization of family labor for clearing land, picking stones, and building fences—an accretionary type of capital formation whereby land and livestock productivity improved over generations. Security of tenure plays a strategic role in converting family labor into capital formation because, with security, farm improvements can be passed on to the next generation. In Africa, there is a tendency for donors to concentrate on financing new agricultural projects while overlooking how to help African farmers and rural communities mobilize savings to finance their own investments.

RURAL INSTITUTIONS

The fourth prime mover is strengthening the performance of rural institutions from land tenure systems to farmer irrigation associations. Not only is there a paucity of literature on how to strengthen rural institutions such as national agricultural research, credit, and extension services, but this topic falls outside the realm of economics—whether neoclassical, political economy, dependency, or marxist. Research, pilot projects, seminars, and workshops are urgently needed to strengthen basic agricultural institutions over the next 10 to 15 years (Bonnen, 1982).

ECONOMIC POLICY ENVIRONMENT

A favorable economic policy environment, the fifth prime mover, is crucially important to facilitate the implementation of the four prime movers already mentioned. Policy dialogue and pricing policies have replaced basic human needs as code words in development circles in the 1980s. For example, Ernest Stern, vice-president of the World Bank, recently challenged the view that drought is the cause of African stagnation, asserting that "it was not nature, but policies which reduced Ghana's cocoa exports from 380,000 tons in 1973 to

160,000 tons 10 years later" (Stern, 1985, p. 5).[17] Aid administrators have commonly focused on policy reform as the fundamental issue in restarting African economies. Several donors have reported that pricing reforms have boosted the production of commodities such as maize in Zambia, sorghum in Somalia, and cocoa in Ghana by 30 to 50 percent. But the crucial point is not what happens to a single commodity but to aggregate farm production. There is solid evidence that favorable pricing policies are a necessary but not sufficient condition for boosting total agricultural production in the long run.[18]

Unfortunately, single commodity responses to higher prices oversimplify and mask the complex set of parallel actions that must be taken to boost the production of a broad range of commodities. For example, smallholders dramatically cut back on cotton production in Uganda in 1983–85 because they had waited for up to one year for the government cotton board to pay them for their crop. Instead, they used their land and labor to produce sunflower for cooking oil and maize for home consumption and export to neighboring countries. Therefore, it is time to shift the debate to the difficult art of gaining national political commitment and consistent donor support for the five prime movers as a policy package.

This analysis has highlighted the strategic importance of long-term investments in the prime movers of agricultural development in order to strengthen the productive capacity of the agricultural sector in the medium to long term. Food aid can be used to buy time until investment in these prime movers pays off. Donors need to come to grips with long gestation investments by making an explicit, up-front commitment to financing human capital and institutional development projects for 10 to 15 years; and by designing, implementing, and evaluating these institutional investments as a "core policy package" under the aegis of a consultative group of donors. But in the final analysis, donors will probably swing their weight behind the prime movers before African states do because the ruling elite in many African countries do not view agriculture as a motor of change. Hence, they are reluctant to shift gears from short-term projects with short-term political results to the prime movers as a coordinated national effort.

FOOD SECURITY POLICY DILEMMAS

As the food production and population race and the hunger and poverty battles are complex and inter-related, they must be analyzed within the political economy framework of specific countries. Neither slogans such as "Food First" nor computer scenarios can identify the complex trade-offs and consequences on production, consumption, nutrition, foreign exchange earnings, and government revenue of pursuing specific food security policies. Country-level research on the interaction between technology, institutions, and macro-economic policies is urgently needed to help resolve some of these policy dilemmas. The first step is to distinguish between food self-sufficiency and food security.

DEFINITIONS OF FOOD SELF-SUFFICIENCY AND FOOD SECURITY

The concept of food self-sufficiency implies the ability of a country to meet all its staple food needs with domestic production and storage under all weather conditions. Food self-sufficiency has a built-in supply (production) bias—increasing the production of food and the reliability of forecasts by installing early warning systems, and increasing grain storage as a hedge against drought and the uncertainty of buying food in international markets.

Food security is defined as the ability of individuals and households to meet their staple food needs on a year-round basis from home production, the domestic market, or imported food. Food security analysis deals with supply issues as well as with a wide range of factors that affect demand for food. A major premise of food security policy is that poverty or the lack of effective demand (purchasing power) is a major cause of hunger and malnutrition. Hence, food security researchers spend considerable time addressing demand factors such as policies and projects for generating income and employment, and income distribution policies that help the poor secure adequate calories. Demand factors are important because even if a country is self-sufficient in food, people can die if there are landless or poor who cannot translate their food needs into access to resources to produce or to buy enough calories to survive.

It is time to discard food self-sufficiency as a policy objective and to replace it with food security. Food self-sufficiency fails to address what combination of home production, domestic storage, food imports, and distribution programs is needed to meet the food needs of all members of society. As a policy goal, food security means that food policies of African governments and donors should not be limited to food production per se, but should encompass a broad range of policies to help rural and urban people increase their incomes and access to a reliable supply of food at all times. But gaining political and technical support for food security as a policy goal will take time.

The influential Berg Report on Africa (World Bank, 1981) helped shift the debate from equity issues to economic growth. Many econo- mists now contend that expanded growth and international trade are key to increasing food security because the benefits from faster growth will "trickle down" to all members of society, thus enabling them to purchase their foods needs. But others believe that it will take too long for an increased rate of economic growth to trickle down to help the poor in the Sahel and northeast Brazil or the landless and unemployed in India. For example, Amartya Sen of Oxford Univer- sity argues that India's food self-sufficiency is a hollow achievement relative to Sri Lanka and China where political priority has been given to the food needs of the poor. As a result, "the average Sri Lankan or Chinese can expect to live about a decade and a half longer than the average Indian" (Sen, 1984, p. 82).[19]

Many African nations have adopted explicit food security strate- gies and have prepared food security plans. The strategies of Senegal, a food-deficit state, and Zimbabwe, a food exporter, will be examined briefly to illustrate some of the complex food security policy dilem- mas.[20]

SENEGAL AND ZIMBABWE

In recent years, Senegal has imported about half its annual cereal consumption. If present production and population trends continue, it may import about two-thirds of its food grain needs by the year 2000 (Abt Associates, 1985, p.iii). Senegal currently imports about 1000 tons of rice a day, mostly broken rice from Thailand at a relatively low price. Broken rather than long grain rice is the preferred staple of many Senegalese because it is cheap and it absorbs cooking oil during the preparation of the national dish, rice and fish. The Senegalese government is faced with several tough questions: How can food production be increased on rainfed and irrigated land? What role should international trade play in achieving an assured food sup- ply—especially for urban consumers? What are the interactions be- tween short-run and long-run policies to achieve food security? How can urban consumers be encouraged to consume more locally pro- duced millet and sorghum and less imported wheat and rice? How will the food import bill be paid?

Since the 19th century, Senegal has followed a policy of agricultural specialization, exporting groundnuts and importing broken rice to supply both the urban and rural areas. Historically, the state has played a direct role in agricultural trade, legally monopolizing the groundnut trade, rice imports, and, until 1980, grain marketing. Over the past 15 years, drought has reduced domestic food grain and groundnut production. In the early 1980s, the combined effects of drought, a depressed world market for groundnuts, and the worldwide recession forced the government to review its agricultural strategy. To address the worsening food situation, the government announced a "New Agricultural Policy" in 1984 that called for: increased food grain self-sufficiency, primarily through irrigated rice production in the Senegal River Valley in northern Senegal, and millet and sorghum production in the Groundnut Basin; a greatly expanded role for private trade and farmers' cooperatives in input and output marketing; and a reduction in the activities of state-managed regional development authorities and parastatals. The new policy aims at production of 75 percent of the nation's food grain consumption by 2000 (Senegal, 1984, p. 6c).

In implementing the New Agricultural Policy, the government has had to face competing objectives—paying higher prices to farmers to encourage them to produce more and cushioning urban consumers from higher food prices—and the difficulty of developing private trade after years of state marketing. In launching the new policy, the price of imported rice was raised over 20 percent to reduce the budget deficit and to stimulate production of locally produced millet, sorghum, and rice. Yet, when the consumer price of millet and sorghum also rose, some government officials called for strict price controls on these cereals to help protect urban consumers.

The use of pricing policies to increase local food production is producing mixed results. For example, the cost of irrigated rice production on the large government-managed farms in the Senegal River Valley is extremely high by world standards (Ndiame, 1985). Government investment in these perimeters has reduced funds available for the development of rainfed crops such as maize in higher rainfall areas. Because traditional millet and sorghum varieties respond only modestly to fertilizer, an increase in the domestic supply of these food grains in response to higher relative prices is likely only at a high marginal cost. In addition, lacking clearly defined rules, private traders have been hindered from playing the role envisaged of them in the New Agricultural Policy (Sow and Newman, 1985). Senegal's agricultural research system is weak and has generated almost no improved food crop technology for farmers. This experience demonstrates the fallacies of depending almost totally on pricing policy to increase food production both in the short and long term. Senegal is a high cost food producer partially because its technology package is empty and partially because of ineffective government support services. A nationwide survey in 1984 revealed that the government fertilizer agency delivered fertilizer to farmers after 90 percent of them had completed millet planting and 38 percent had finished planting peanuts (Crawford, et al., 1985).

Senegal's failure to get its agriculture moving during the 20 years of Senghor's regime and the five years under President Diouf has imposed a severe hardship on the welfare of the population and has been a severe brake on the entire economy. Senegal is one of the few African countries where per capita incomes were about the same in 1985 as at independence in 1960. Ongoing food security studies suggest that Senegal should abandon its long-run goal of 100 percent food grain self-sufficiency. Since Dakar is a major seaport, it may be more efficient to try to assure food security by importing relatively low-cost broken rice while increasing millet, sorghum, and maize production for rural people. Alternatives to rice production in the irrigated perimeters of the north (e.g., vegetables and tomatoes for canning factories) should be considered as Senegal seeks more cost-effective ways of assuring its food security.

At independence in 1980, Zimbabwe inherited a dual agrarian structure of roughly 5000 large commercial farms and 700,000 smallholders. The fundamental problems in agriculture were the low productivity of smallholders, widespread poverty and malnutrition among commercial farm workers, a large landless population, and a rural infrastructure that had been battered by the guerrilla war (Blackie, 1981). In 1981, the government identified the "achievement and maintenance of food self-sufficiency and regional food security as an important national objective" (Zimbabwe, 1981). One of the fundamental policy dilemmas the Mugabe government has skillfully addressed is the redistribution of land and income to the urban and rural poor while maintaining the productive capacity of its commercial agricultural sector—a major earner of foreign exchange.

Despite poverty and malnutrition among smallholder families and workers on commercial farms, Zimbabwe has maintained its dual production structure in the short run. In 1985, commercial farms produced about 50 percent of cotton and the marketed surplus of maize, and 99 percent of the tobacco crop. The government has tried to improve the food security of the rural poor by raising the minimum wage of farm workers and by purchasing commercial farms on a "willing buyer-willing seller" basis, in order to transfer land to the landless. At the same time, aggressive steps are being taken to help smallholders expand rainfed crop production, especially cotton and maize, and to promote smallholder irrigation.

The government has followed pricing policies which favor agriculture, even though this may have increased the food insecurity of the urban poor in the short run. In 1983/84, the government eliminated Z$100 million in consumer subsidies on wheat bread, meat, dairy products, and refined maize flour—the staple food of civil servants. In an attempt to lessen the impact of these changes on the urban poor, subsidies were retained on their staple, coarse maize meal, and the minimum wage was increased. Following a three-year drought, the government raised maize producer prices 28.5 percent in June 1984,[21] four months before planting time for the 1984/85 crop. With favorable weather, farmers responded with a record maize crop, a large percentage of which came from smallholders. Zimbabwe is now developing inter-African trade agreements to sell its maize surplus.

Although Zimbabwe's experience is frequently cited as an example of the successful use of pricing policies to stimulate maize and cotton production, not all the increase in production should be attributed to higher prices and good weather. Zimbabwe's farmers are able to respond to favorable prices because they have access to well-functioning input and output markets, a seed coop supplied by a network of 200 commercial seed growers, an extension system that has given increasing attention to smallholders in recent years, and one of the strongest agricultural research services in Africa.

In 1949, Zimbabwe became the first country after the United States to develop hybrid maize varieties after 17 years of research (Eicher, 1984). Subsequent research led to the development of a long-season hybrid for commercial farmers—SR52—that can be called the green revolution of southern Africa. Although several hybrid varieties were developed specifically for smallholder growing conditions and made available to them in the mid-1970s, it was only with improvements in the marketing, credit, and extension systems, expansion of private fertilizer distribution facilities, and an end to the disruption caused by war that smallholders rapidly adopted the new varieties. The government of Zimbabwe is skillfully using pricing and technology policy as a package because it has a backlog of proven maize and cotton varieties for both smallholders and commercial farmers and it realizes that pricing and technology policies are complementary. In 1985, smallholders produced 50 percent of the maize and cotton marketed, up from 10 percent at independence in 1980.

Zimbabwe is one of Africa's agricultural success stories of the 1980s. The government has concentrated on the prime movers of agricultural development, walked a tight rope on efficiency and equity issues, devalued its currency to promote industrial and agricultural exports, and harnessed its agricultural sector as an engine of economic change. In spite of its success in increasing total food production and becoming a maize exporter, Zimbabwe's long-term food security also depends on its ability to deal with periodic drought, its rapid rate of population growth, and land hunger in a dual agrarian society.

FOREIGN ASSISTANCE UNDER
CONDITIONS OF LIMITED ABSORPTIVE
CAPACITY

Calls for more aid to Africa are gaining momentum. Music benefits raised $54 million for Africa in three months in mid-1985. The World Bank's Special Facility for sub-Saharan Africa—to compensate for the shortfall in the resources of the International Development Association (IDA), the Bank's concessionary affiliate—began operation on July 1, 1985. While hunger and famine are powerful magnets for resource transfers, it is important to keep in mind that:

- Although Africa has 16 percent of the population of Asia, Africa received more official development assistance (ODA) ($8 billion) in 1982/83 than Asia received.

- Although Tanzania consumed $2.7 billion of ODA over the 1973–82 period, its economy is stagnant, and Nyerere, like Nkrumah, will be viewed as a failure in domestic economic management.[22]

- Senegal has received a high aid allocation—about twice the level of ODA per capita of other African countries and four to five times higher per capita than Asian countries. However, after 25 years, Senegal's per capita income is about the same as it was at independence. In 1981 and 1982, official aid transfers amounted about one-fifth of Senegal's GDP.

- "The technological basis for increased production on the majority of Sahelian farms does not exist" (AID, 1985a, p. 9).
- In many countries, more aid cannot be absorbed in irrigation, rainfed farming, and livestock projects "with integrity" because of absorptive capacity problems, lack of improved technology, etc.
- African states are flooded with project aid which co-opts scarce human capital, such as African scientists and managers (Morss, 1984). Kenya had 1000 projects in all sectors in 1985; 40 of the 1000 were agricultural research projects or research components in agricultural and rural development projects.
- Technical assistance (expatriate advisers) is being increasingly questioned by Africans because of its cost ($80,000 to $150,000 per person per year), mediocre quality, and frequent turnover.

From this brief overview, foreign aid is faced with a number of serious challenges. The starting point is to examine how efficiently foreign assistance has been absorbed by African states.

ABSORPTIVE CAPACITY

In the 1950s, the phrase "absorptive capacity" emerged "as a rough measure of a society's ability to employ efficiently additional capital resources" (Rostow, 1985, p. 47). Constraints on absorptive capacity were repeatedly flagged during the 1960s because most countries had small pools of skilled personnel to staff their research stations, hospitals, and schools.[23] One of the most perplexing problems that African planners and foreign advisers have grappled with over the past 25 years is how to realize the desire of African political leaders to "catch up" with the industrial world given the modest capacity of most states to absorb available ODA[24] and foreign private investment. Problems of absorbing and using aid efficiently became especially acute when aid was doubled in real terms in just six years from 1975 to 1981.

Following the 40 percent compound rate of growth of foreign aid inflows to the Sahel over the 1971–78 period (Berg, 1983, p. 45), questions were raised about aid absorption. For example, the inspector-general of USAID questioned the Sahel's ability to absorb development assistance at the 1981 level (AID, 1981). Three years later, another team visited the Sahel and reported: "In project after project, one also found that AID project designers overstated the capabilities of the host governments to implement the projects. Despite nine years' experience, this continued to occur. Consequently, the host governments, unable to implement, were overwhelmed and the projects were ineffective" (AID, 1984, p. 20).

The reasons for the chronic absorptive capacity problems in Africa are directly linked to the colonial policies of under-investment in human capital and the failure of foreign assistance to strengthen indigenous training and research institutions while flooding Africa with project aid requiring local managerial capacity to implement, monitor, and meet the audit requirements of donors. Although donors have trained tens of thousands of Africans overseas since independence, this type of training is not a substitute for building local institutions to develop indigenous scientific and managerial capacity. Accordingly, from evidence across Africa, the absorptive capacity problem has been underestimated and skirted by both African states and donors for several decades. This problem should be addressed squarely before additional aid is pumped into African agriculture in the next few years, especially given the hundreds of organizations that are trying to help Africa under the banner of famine prevention.

OBJECTIVES OF FOREIGN ASSISTANCE AND
STANDARDS OF PERFORMANCE

The volume of foreign assistance transferred to Africa overshadows the quality of aid in comparative assessments of donor performance. Why is this the case? Many donors incorrectly assume that the primary objective of aid is to transfer resources from rich to poor countries and that the largesse of a particular industrial country can be ranked by the percentage of its GNP allocated to aid for the Third World. However, the correct criterion is to assure that the absorptive capacity is expanded and matched by the availability of capital for development programs which are in appropriate sectoral balance (Rostow, 1985, p. 330). This leads us directly to issues of absorptive capacity and recurrent cost and the standards of performance used by donors.

The absorptive capacity problem is being studiously avoided by most African states, by donors who typically equate the volume of resource transfers with "helping" Africa,[25] and by some donors who tolerate lower standards of performance in Africa. Edward V.K. Jaycox, vice president of the eastern and southern Africa department of the World Bank, recently reported that perhaps the most important reason for the high failure rate of projects in Africa is the fact that "African countries have not been held to the standards of performance common elsewhere in the world, including other low income countries" (Jaycox, 1985).

RECURRENT COSTS

Recurrent costs are an integral part of the absorptive capacity problem. A few years ago, many donors started to pay the recurrent costs of agriculture and health projects in Africa because of the devastating drought in the Sahel from 1968–73, the oil price shocks, and the general shift in donor priorities to helping the poorest of the poor. Donors' soft position on recurrent costs has been a major mistake because: it artificially elevates the number of projects beyond the ability of African states to manage them and it makes it difficult, if not impossible, to achieve effective donor coordination;[26] it takes the pressure off African states to mobilize rural resources to pay for water supplies, agricultural extension, agents and health services; and it promotes a delusional system of shadow government agencies, offices, titles, and local perquisites that can never be financed by domestic resources after foreign aid is phased out.[27]

A recent study in the Gambia showed that if all donor-financed agricultural projects were continued after their scheduled termination date (normally in three to five years), the operating budget of the ministry of agriculture would have to be increased by 70 percent (Tyner and Billings, 1984). Since the Gambia—like many other countries—is being pressed by the IMF, World Bank, and some bilateral donors to trim budgets and reduce the role of the state, a large percentage of the agricultural projects are likely to be picked up by other donors[28] or will fade away after donor assistance is phased out. The issue raised in the pioneering study by Tyner and Billings is fundamental: Is there a life after donor-financed projects? Addressing the recurrent cost problems at both sectoral and national levels is a major challenge for African states and donors. Most African states are treating the recurrent cost problem casually because they realize that donors have a penchant for starting new projects. As a result, it is relatively easy to repackage projects and get new donors to pick up where others have left off.

TECHNICAL ASSISTANCE: COST, QUALITY,
AND TURNOVER

There is no exact figure on the number of expatriate advisers, teachers, scientists, and planners in public agencies in Africa, but the figure is in the tens of thousands. Technical assistance is coming under increasing attack in Africa because its costs are too high, its quality uneven, and its rapid turnover detrimental to institution-building. African states are increasingly using some of their international loans and grants to purchase three person-years of technical assistance from Third World countries for the cost of one person-year from industrial countries.

U.S. FOREIGN ASSISTANCE AND AFRICAN
AGRICULTURE

Since the United States is a large bilateral donor in Africa, it is important to examine what it is doing to combat hunger and poverty. In 1985, USAID channeled about $1 billion to 35 African countries through bilateral assistance and numerous regional programs. This figure does not include the emergency food assistance the United States provided to Africa in calendar year 1985. AID has dramatically reduced the number of its projects from about 900 to 1000 in 1984 to 650 in mid-1985 (AID, 1985c).

The number of African countries assisted by USAID has varied widely over the past 20 years. In 1966, USAID had technical assistance programs in 35 African countries. In the mid-1960s, under pressure from Senator Fulbright to reduce the number of "potential Vietnams," President Lyndon Johnson requested the American ambassador to Ethiopia, Edward M. Korry, to review the U.S. aid program in Africa. The "Korry Report" of 1966 recommended that the United States concentrate its aid program in Africa on a few "development emphasis countries" and lend its support to the World Bank for coordination of external aid.

In 1967/68, AID adopted a new policy that reduced its regular bilateral assistance programs to 10 countries (AID, 1967), following the guidelines of the Korry report. A number of regional programs— some hastily designed—were introduced as a way to channel U.S. assistance to small countries such as Benin, Botswana, and Swaziland. But the number of AID bilateral programs increased rapidly in the mid-1970s, partially in response to the Sahel drought[29] and the emergence of southern Africa as a policy priority. The USAID regional program for Botswana, Lesotho, and Swaziland was replaced by bilateral programs. But 20 years after the Korry Report, the number of AID bilateral programs is back to the 1967 level—35—and the same question remains: Can AID's technical staff and contractors (U.S. universities and consulting firms) in food and agriculture do a credible job in managing agricultural programs and projects in 35 countries?

Some hard choices now confront USAID, Congress, and the Executive branch. But, unfortunately, Congress is not getting sound counsel. The recent Office of Technology Assessment report on Africa is the product of a hurried effort by a team that assembled many facts but glossed over the tough technical, institutional, and political issues in getting African agriculture moving (OTA, 1984). USAID is scattering its limited technical staff across too many projects and too many countries to make a "significant difference" in combating food and poverty in Africa. Moreover, most U.S. ambassadors and their counterparts in other diplomatic missions in Africa are pressing for foreign aid projects that will produce what one U.S. ambassador recently described as "high visibility and quick returns." Currently, USAID is being forced to reduce the number of permanent staff in Africa as part of the budget reduction exercise of the federal government.[30] Unless basic issues of time frame, absorptive capacity, and strengthening the technical capacity of USAID programs are squarely addressed , U.S. foreign assistance in Africa will not achieve its full potential.

AID is now in the process of consolidating its Sahel program (AID, 1985a), reducing the number of projects in Africa, and implementing an innovative plan to strengthen national agricultural research services and faculties of agriculture over the next 20 years (AID, 1985c). Nevertheless, USAID will find it difficult to deliver on its present food and agriculture programs in 35 countries unless its agricultural staff (career and contractors) is increased in quality. AID currently does not have a full-time irrigation specialist in the bureau for Africa in Washington or in its regional offices in Abidjan and Nairobi.

CONCLUSIONS

While famine has faded from much of Asia since the mid-1970s, famine and chronic hunger have become more prominent in Africa, leading not only to massive short-term relief efforts, but also to crash programs to increase food production. In dealing with hunger and poverty in Africa, it is important to recognize that many of the hungry, particularly the chronically hungry, are malnourished not because the aggregate supply of food is inadequate, but because the poor lack the purchasing power to buy a calorie-adequate diet. Improving the food security of the poor requires measures to increase their purchasing power. Food security should replace food self-sufficiency as a policy goal for African states and become the focal point of donor assistance to food and agriculture in Africa.

Further, it is time to stop thinking of Africa as a land-abundant continent. Because of vastly different rainfall levels and patterns and availability of locally adopted technology, there are better prospects for food production outstripping population growth in the temperate climates in southern Africa than in the semi-arid zone of Sahelian West Africa. The message is clear—it is time to focus on sub-regions and examine the problems unique to each region rather than discussing Africa in homogenous terms.

In the long run, given appropriate policies and investments in the prime movers of African agriculture—human capital, agricultural research, bio-physical capital, and strengthened rural institutions—most countries have the physical capacity to feed themselves. But in the short to medium term, population growth is generating food needs in many countries that cannot be met except through food grain imports. Just as India did, African states should learn how to increase the efficiency of food aid. Donors should link long-term food aid to tough policy reforms, including a fundamental reordering of development priorities in favor of agriculture. But this will require a degree of donor coordination that has not been achieved in Africa over the past 25 years.

The issue of aid and African agriculture has raised some fundamental problems that require further analysis, debate, and change. Donors—large and small, bilateral and multilateral—do not have a coherent plan to assist Africa in combating hunger and poverty in the 1980s and 1990s. In many sectors—rainfed farming, irrigation, and livestock—additional aid cannot be absorbed given Africa's limited capacity, lack of profitable technical packages, the project mode of delivering aid, and lip service to donor coordination.

Donor attention should shift from short-term pricing policy reforms to a number of complex and parallel investments in the prime movers of agricultural development. Each must be examined as part of a core investment package covering a period of 10 to 20 years.

It is time to jettison donors' preoccupations with increasing the quantity of resource transfers to Africa. Immediate priority must be given to increasing the efficiency of existing foreign assistance-financed programs and projects. As part of this process, the following problems should be addressed: absorptive capacity, indigenous scientific and managerial capacity, recurrent costs, standards of performance, donor coordination, and marshalling donor support for the prime movers of agricultural development. The large volume of aid enables African political leaders to avoid some hard decisions on food and agriculture. Finally, while the U.S. Congress has encouraged USAID to operate bilateral programs in 35 African countries, unless USAID concentrates on the prime movers of agricultural change over the next 10 to 15 years, the United States will not make a significant difference in helping African countries tap their large agricultural potential.

ACKNOWLEDGMENT

The research supporting this chapter was financed by the U.S. Agency for International Development, Bureau for Science and Technology and Bureau for Africa, under a "Food Security in Africa" cooperative agreement with the Department of Agricultural Economics, Michigan State University.

NOTES

1. Hereafter referred to as Africa.

2. Reports from rural areas of China indicate that there is strong resistance to this policy and a failure of some local authorities to enforce it.

3. In Zimbabwe, the National Park Service is examining how farmers surrounding national parks can harvest some of the game on the edge of the parks while retaining the basic integrity of the parks. Large game have to be culled in Zimbabwe's parks and boreholes supply water at critical times of the year in order to maintain the animal herds for tourists.

4. For two accounts of the constructive role played by donors in bringing about agricultural policy reforms in India in the 1960s, see Rostow (1985, pp. 176–78) and Paarlberg (1985, pp. 143–70).

5. See Mellor (1979); Sen (1981); and Lele (1984).

6. To put this figure of $1.50 per capita aid in perspective, it is worth about $4.00 to $5.00 in 1985 prices.

7. In 1981, the eight countries in the Sahelian region of West Africa, with a total population of 34 million, received $1.96 billion in Official Development Assistance (ODA) or $56 per capita (AID, 1985a).

8. Based on unpublished data from FAO, Rome, June 1985.

9. In China, there is nearly complete prohibition of rural to urban migration. Permitting migration would imply that industrialization and urbanization would eliminate rural poverty instead of the official self-reliance strategy which challenges farmers to escape from poverty by increasing farm productivity and encourages villages to improve social services to hold people in rural areas (Perkins and Yusuf, 1984, p. 200).

10. For a synthesis of agricultural development ideas in historical perspective, see Staatz and Eicher (1984). See Delgado and Mellor (1984) for an analysis of required structural changes in African agriculture.

11. See World Bank (1983) and Duncan (1984).

12. See Timmer, Falcon, and Pearson (1983) for a seminal analysis of the food price dilemma.

13. Chief Akin Deko, then minister of agriculture, Western Nigeria, led a delegation to Israel in 1959 to study Kibbutz and Moshav settlements. Based on their favorable impressions, Nigeria imported the Moshav model and spent about $50 million before the schemes collapsed in the late 1960s.

14. A team of planners in Yugoslavia prepared Ethiopia's first development plan and sent the plan to Addis Ababa via the diplomatic pouch.

15. A steady stream of African heads of state, including President Mobutu of Zaire, visited China to find the key to agricultural development. When President Mobutu returned to Zaire, he declared agriculture to be the "priority of priorities" for 1974. In Kinshasa in 1974, civil servants spent Saturdays tending their gardens and farm plots following directives from the Presidency.

16. See Lamb and Muller's (1982) account of the highly successful Kenya Tea Development Authority, a parastatal that assists 18,000 smallholders in tea production, processing, and marketing.

17. Stern's comments are echoed by a plea for policy reform by the Nordic countries (Nordic Delegation, 1984). For an influential study of the political rationale for seemingly irrational agricultural policies, see Bates (1981).

18. The late Raj Krishna (1982) of Delhi University contends that if price policy alone is used as the sole instrument to raise agricultural output in the long run, the inflationary effects would be untenable on both economic and political grounds. Krishna is of the opinion that "a balanced policy should stress a technology policy more than price policy, while the price environment is kept as favorable as possible" (p. 256).

19. The 1983 life expectancy is as follows: India, 55; China, 67; Sri Lanka, 69 (World Bank, 1985a).

20. This section draws on Eicher and Staatz (1984).

21. Since inflation was running about 20 percent per annum, the real price increase received by farmers was positive.

22. But the donors are an integral part of Tanzania's stagnation. T.W. Schultz contends that "the relationships among the official foreign aid donors of the high income countries are all too cozy. . . .For example, a compe-

tent analysis of the actual harm that has been done by the aid of the World Bank, the IMF, and other multilateral UN agencies to the economy of Tanzania, would be exceedingly instructive" (Schultz, 1983, pp. 460–61).

23. For example, in 1964, there were only three African scientists in all of the agricultural research stations in East Africa (Kenya, Tanzania, and Uganda), (Johnston, 1964, p. iii).

24. ODA refers to concessional transfers for development purposes with a grant element of at least 25 percent.

25. The concept of "moving money" has been used as a proxy for "helping the Sahel." The Club du Sahel, OECD, Paris, reports that "with respect to the volume of donor assistance to the Sahel, it is possible to make a specific assessment of the Club's contribution. Donor flows have clearly increased since the creation of the Club du Sahel in 1975. In 1976 , ODA commitments for Sahel countries were $817 million. Soon after the Club's inception, donor commitments began to grow, rising from $817 million in 1975. . .to $1.9 billion in 1981" (De Lattre and Fell, 1984, p. 80).

26. For example, in the Eastern region of Burkina Faso in March 1981, there were 10 different donor projects providing credit funds to the government extension agency: USAID, 4; UN, 3; France, 2; and the Swiss, 1. Moreover, the quantum jump in donor assistance for integrated rural development projects increased the number of extension agents in the region from 24 in 1978 to 149 in 1981. In Kenya, there are roughly 20 different kinds of water pumps in rural areas that have been supplied by donors. Getting spare parts is a nightmare.

27. For example, the World Bank has established a "shadow" statistical organization in Nigeria to collect data for Bank-financed agricultural projects.

28. Since Italy is a relative newcomer in the donor community in Africa, it is common knowledge that it has taken over many marginal projects that other donors have "shed" from their portfolios.

29. For example, in Burkina Faso, the United States opened a small bilateral aid mission after independence but terminated it in the mid-1960s. In 1973, the United States provided $12 million of emergency food relief and launched 16 short-term recovery and relief projects totalling $3.2 million. In September 1974, USAID opened a small Country Development Office and began to implement larger-scale, longer-term development projects. In May 1978, with the increased scale of development programming, the Country Development Office was turned into a full USAID bilateral mission. But in 1985, USAID is cutting back its program in Burkina to a skeleton operation because of policy differences with the Burkina government.

30. USAID is planning to reduce its worldwide direct-hire (career) staff in 1986 and again in 1987.

REFERENCES

Abt Associates. 1985. *Senegal Agricultural Policy Analysis*. Report to USAID/ Senegal. Cambridge, Massachusetts.

AID. 1967. *U.S. Foreign AID in Africa*. Washington, D.C.: Agency for International Development.

AID. 1981. *Improvements Must be Made in the Sahel Regional Program*. Washington, D.C.: The Inspector General, March 10.

AID. 1984. *Inadequate Design and Monitoring Impede Results in Sahel Food Production Projects*. Washington, D.C.: The Inspector General, January 31.

AID. 1985a. *Sahel Development Program: Annual Report to the Congress*. Washington, D.C., March.

AID. 1985b. *Plan for Supporting Agricultural Research and Faculties of Agriculture in Africa*. Washington, D.C., May.

AID. 1985c. *Agriculture and Rural Development: Functional Review FY 1978–86*. Washington, D.C.: Africa Bureau, Office of Technical Resources, Agriculture and Rural Development Division, July.

Bates, Robert. 1981. *Markets and States in Tropical Africa: The Political Basis of Agricultural Policies*. Berkeley: University of California Press.

Berg, Elliot. 1983. *Absorptive Capacity in the Sahel Countries*. Paris: OECD, Club du Sahel, April.

Bingen, R. James. 1985. *Food Production and Rural Development in the Sahel: Lessons From Mali's Operation Riz-Segou*. Boulder: Westview Press.

Blackie, Malcolm. 1981. "A Time To Listen: A Perspective on Agricultural Policy in Zimbabwe." Harare: University of Zimbabwe, Department of Land Management, Working Paper 5/81.

Bonnen, James. 1982. "Technology, Human Capital and Institutions: Three Factors in Search of an Agricultural Research Strategy." East Lansing: Michigan State University, Department of Agricultural Economics, Ag. Econ. Staff Paper No. 82-117.

Busch. L. and W. Lacy, eds. 1984. *Food Security in the United States*. Boulder: Westview Press.

Caldwell, John C. and Pat Caldwell. 1984. "Cultural Forces Tending to Sustain High Fertility in Tropical Africa." Australian National University (draft).

Carter, Gwendolen and Patrick O'Meara, eds. 1985. *African Independence: The First Twenty-Five Years*. Bloomington: Indiana University Press.

Chigaru, P. R. N. 1984. "Future Directions of the Department of Research and Specialist Services, Ministry of Agriculture, Zimbabwe." Harare: Ministry of Agriculture, Department of Research and Specialist Services, November.

Crawford, Eric, Curtis Jolly, Valerie Kelly, Philippe Lambrecht, Makhona Mbaye and Matar Gaye. 1985. "A Field Study of Fertilizer Distribution and Use in Senegal, 1984: Final Report." Dakar: Institut Sénégalais de Recherche Agricole.

DeLattre, Ann and Arthur M. Fell. 1984. *The Club du Sahel: An Experiment in International Cooperation*. Paris: OECD.

Delgado, Christopher and John W. Mellor. 1984. "A Structural View of Policy Issues in African Agricultural Devlopment," *American Journal of Agricultural Economics* 66(5):665-70.

Duncan, Ronald, ed. 1984. "The Outlook for Primary Commodities, 1984 to 1995." Staff Working Paper No. 11. Washington, D.C.: The World Bank.

Eicher, Carl K. 1982. "Facing up to Africa's Food Crisis." *Foreign Affairs*, Fall.

Eicher, Carl K. 1984. "International Technology Transfer and the African Farmer: Theory and Practice." Harare: University of Zimbabwe, Department of Land Management, Working Paper 3/84.

Eicher, Carl K. 1985. "Agricultural Research for African Development: Problems and Priorities for 1985–2000," paper presented at a World Bank Conference at Bellagio, Italy, February 25–March 1.

Eicher, Carl K. and Doyle C. Baker. 1982. *Research on Agricultural Development in Sub-Saharan Africa: A Critical Survey*. MSU International Development Paper No. 1. East Lansing: Michigan State University, Department of Agricultural Economics.

Eicher, Carl K. and John M. Staatz, eds. 1984. *Agricultural Development in the Third World*. Baltimore: The Johns Hopkins University Press.

Eicher, Carl K. and John M. Staatz. 1985. "Food Security Policy in Sub-Saharan Africa," paper presented at the XIXth Conference of the International Association of Agricultural Economists, Malaga, Spain, August 25–September 5.

Ellis, Frank. 1982. "Agricultural Price Policy in Tanzania," *World Development* 10(4).

Evenson, Robert E. 1984. "Benefits and Obstacles in Developing Appropriate Agricultural Technology." in Eicher and Staatz (1984), pp. 348–61.

FAO/UNFPA/IIASA. 1982. *Potential Population Supporting Capacities of Lands in the Developing World*. Report of Project INT/75/P13, Land Resources for Populations of the Future, FAO, Rome.

FAO. 1984. *SADCC Agriculture: Toward 200*. Rome.

Higgins, Benjamin. 1959. *Economic Development: Principles, Problems and Policies*. New York: Norton.

India, Ministry of Food and Agriculture. 1959. *Report on India's Food Crisis and Steps to Meet it*. New Delhi.

Jaycox, Edward V. K. 1985. "Africa: Development Challenges and the World Bank's Response." Lecture, Woodrow Wilson International Center for Scholars, Smithsonian Institution, Washington, D.C., August 6.

Johnston, Bruce. 1964. "The Choice of Measures for Increasing Agricultural Productivity: A Survey of Possibilities in East Africa," *Tropical Agriculture* 41(2):91–113.

Kerr, Richard. 1985. "Fifteen Years of African Drought," *Science* 227 (March 22).

Krishna, Raj. 1982. "Some Aspects of Agricultural Growth, Price Policy and Equity in Developing Countries," *Food Research Institute Studies* 38(3):219-60.

Lamb, Geoffrey and Linda Muller. 1982. *Control, Accountability and Incentives in a Successful Development Institution: The Kenya Tea Development Authority*. Washington, D.C.: World Bank, Staff Working Papers, No. 550.

Lele, Uma. 1984. "Rural Africa, Modernization, Equity and Long-Term Development," in Eicher and Staatz, pp. 436–52.

Lele, Uma. In Press. "Growth of Foreign Assistance and Its Impact on Agriculture," in Mellor, Delgado and Blackie.

Lewis, W. Arthur. 1955. "The Economic Development of Africa," in *Africa in the Modern World.* Calvin W. Stillman, ed. Chicago: University of Chicago Press, pp. 97–112.

Lewis, John P. 1985. "Aid, Structural Adjustment and Senegalese Agriculture." Princeton: Princeton University, Woodrow Wilson School (draft).

Mellor, John W. 1979. "The Indian Economy: Objectives, Peformance and Prospects." *India: A Rising Middle Power,* ed. John W. Mellor. Boulder: Westview Press, pp. 85–110.

Mellor, John W., Christopher Delgado and Malcolm J. Blackie. In Press *Accelerating Food Production Growth in Sub-Saharan Africa.* Baltimore: The Johns Hopkins University Press.

Morss, Elliott. 1984. "Institutional Destruction Resulting from Donor and Project Proliferation in Sub-Saharan African Countries," *World Development* 12(4): 465–70.

Ndegwa, Philip. 1985. *Africa's Development Crisis and the Related International Issues.* Nairobi: Heinemann.

Ndiame, Fadel. 1985. "A Comparative Analysis of Alternative Irrigation Schemes and the Objective of Food Security: The Case of the Fleuve Region in Senegal," unpublished M.S. thesis, Department of Agricultural Economics, Michigan State University.

Nordic Delegation. 1984. "Policies in Agriculture and Rural Development: A Nordic View," Nordic position paper, SADCC conference, Lusaka, 1–3 February.

Nyerere, Julius. 1984. "Interview," *Third World Quarterly* 6(4):815–38.

Office of Technology Assessment, U.S. Congress. 1984. *African Tomorrow: Issues in Technology, Agriculture and U.S. Foreign Aid; A Technical Memorandum.* Washington, D.C.

Ohkawa, Kazushi and Henry Rosovsky. 1964. "The Role of Agriculture in Modern Japanese Development," in *Agriculture in Economic Development,* eds. Carl K. Eicher and Lawrence Witt. New York: McGraw-Hill, pp. 45–68.

Paarlberg, Robert L. 1985. *Food Trade and Foreign Policy: India, the Soviet Union, and the United States.* Ithaca: Cornell University Press.

Perkins, Dwight and Shahid Ysuf. 1984. *Rural Development in China.* Baltimore: The Johns Hopkins University Press.

Reutlinger, Shlomo. 1984. "Project Food Aid and Equitable Growth: Income-Transfer Efficiency First," *World Development* 12(9):901–11.

Reutlinger, Shlomo and Marcelo Selowsky. 1976. *Malnutrition and Poverty: Magnitude and Policy Options* (World Bank Staff Working Paper No. 21). Baltimore: The Johns Hopkins University Press.

Rostow, W. W. 1985. *Eisenhower, Kennedy and Foreign Aid.* Austin: University of Texas Press.

Schuh, G. Edward. 1985. "Strategic Issues in International Agriculture." Washington, D.C.: World Bank, Agriculture and Rural Development Department, draft.

Schultz, T. W. 1983. "A Critique of the Economics of U.S. Foreign AID," in *Issues in Third World Development,* eds. K. C. Nobe and R. K. Sampath. Boulder: Westview Press.

Sen, Amartya K. 1981. *Poverty and Famines: An Essay on Entitlement and Deprivation*. Oxford: Clarendon Press.

Sen, Amartya K. 1984. "Food Battles: Conflicts in the Access to Food," *Food and Nutrition* 10(1):81–90.

Sénégal, République du. 1984. *Nouvelle Politique Agricole*. Dakar: Ministère du Développement Rural, Mars–Avril.

Shapiro, Kenneth. 1985. "Strengthening Agricultural Research and Educational Institutions in Africa." Hearings, the Subcommittee on Foreign Operations, the Senate Committee on Appropriations, U.S. Senate, Washington, D.C., March 26.

Sklar, Richard. 1985. "The Colonial Imprint on African Political Thought," in Carter and O'Meara, pp. 1–30.

Sokoine University of Agriculture. 1985. *The Mission of Sokoine University of Agriculture*. Morogoro: Tanzania, April.

Sow, P. Allansane and Mark D. Newman. 1985. "La Réglementation et l'Organisation des Marchés Céréaliers au Sénégal: Situation des Campagnes de Commercialisation 1983:84 et 1984:85." Dakar: ISRA/BAME Document de Travail 85-2.

Staatz, John and Carl K. Eicher. 1984. "Agricultural Development in Historical Perspective." in Eicher and Staatz, pp. 3–30.

Stern, Ernest. 1985. "Speech at the Overseas Development Council," Washington, D.C., February 20.

Timmer, C. Peter, Walter P. Falcon and Scott R. Pearson. 1983. *Food Policy Analysis*. Baltimore: The Johns Hopkins University Press.

Tyner, Wallace and Martin Billings. 1984. "Recurrent Costs of Agricultural Sector Projects in the Gambia." Abidjan: USAID, November.

Valdes, Alberto, ed. 1981. *Food Security for Developing Countries*. Boulder: Westview Press.

World Bank. 1981. *Accelerated Development in Sub-Saharan Africa: An Agenda for Action*. Washington, D.C.

World Bank. 1983. *The Outlook for Primary Commodities*. Washington, D.C.: Staff Commodity Working Papers, No. 9.

World Bank. 1984. *Annual Report, 1984*. Washington, D.C.

World Bank. 1985a. *Ensuring Food Security in the Developing World: Issues and Options*. Washington: Agriculture and Rural Development Department, November 15.

World Bank. 1985b. *World Development Report 1985*. Washington, D.C.

Zimbabwe, Government of. 1981. *Growth With Equity*. Harare.

PART IV

INDUSTRY

CHAPTER TEN

Can Africa Industrialize?

A.M. Hawkins

"Industrialization is the main hope of most poor countries trying to increase their levels of income." Expressed 30 years ago by Hollis B. Chenery, this view continues to hold sway among economists, planners, and policy-makers for whom industrialization and economic development are synonymous. The development of a dynamic manufacturing sector has typically marked a country's transition from low to intermediate income levels. However, since the 1950s, only a handful of countries—the so-called newly industrializing countries (NICs) of East Asia and Latin America—have achieved such a change in status. In sub-Saharan Africa, only Zimbabwe, where manufacturing output contributes one-quarter of the gross domestic product (GDP), comes close to having attained such a transformation.

Africa lags far behind the rest of the developing world in industrial development. Although the share of manufacturing in sub-Saharan Africa's GDP has risen since 1960, it remained under 10 percent by 1980—well below the average share of other developing regions. To some extent, the rising share of manufacturing actually reflects sluggish agricultural performances rather than vigorous industrial expansion, as taxation and subsidies have artificially shifted price factors in favor of manufacturing. On the other hand, however, existing data almost certainly understates the extent of industrialization in Africa, as official statistics do not include most small-scale manufacturing industries which account for an estimated 20 percent of Africa's total manufacturing output.

While Africa's share of the world's manufacturing value added
(MVA) rose by 32 percent, from 0.41 percent in 1963 to 0.54 percent in
1981, and its share of MVA in all developing economies rose slightly
from 9.5 percent in 1963 to 10.4 percent in 1983, a closer look at the
geographic distribution behind these figures reveals an uneven pattern. In 1981, five sub-Saharan African countries—Nigeria, Zimbabwe, Ivory Coast, Ghana, and Kenya—accounted for more than 60
percent of MVA; 21 countries accounted for 7 percent of the region's
MVA; and the remaining 17 countries, 31.5 percent.

While MVA in all developing countries, excluding the least developed, grew an average 8 percent a year in the 1963–73 period, falling
to 5.1 percent in the next decade period (1973–82), in sub-Saharan
Africa, MVA in constant terms (1975 base year) rose 8.5 percent a year
through the 1960s, slowing to just over 5 percent per annum in the
1970s. Furthermore, out of a total set of 40 African countries, per
capita MVA between 1973 and 1981 declined in more than half.

The 1975 conference of the United Nations Industrial Development Organization (UNIDO) established the Lima Target by which
developing countries' share of global industrial production was to
reach 25 percent by the year 2000. In 1983, however, the UNIDO
Secretariat estimated that developing countries were unlikely to exceed a 13.5 percent share by the turn of the century, with Africa's
share amounting to no more than 1.2 percent. While per capita MVA
in Africa in 1980 was comparable to the rates of South and East Asia,
UNIDO projects that by the end of this century, Africa's MVA will be
less than half that of Asia (UNIDO, 1984a).

Industrialization has barely begun in many sub-Saharan African
countries, particularly as low incomes and populations in small countries and high costs associated with transportation and other distribution sectors in larger economies effectively limit market size, discouraging industrial investment as economies of scale cannot be
achieved. Moreover, in contrast to Chenery's view, there is a host of
evidence to support the argument that manufacturing is unlikely to
become a self-propelling and leading economic sector in countries
that lack certain "threshold" levels of per capita income.

SOURCES OF INDUSTRIAL GROWTH

The three traditional sources of industrial growth are: production
for export, including the processing of primary products; production

for domestic markets; and production to replace imports, or import substitution. Africa's share of world exports, falling from 2.7 percent in 1970 to 1.9 percent in 1983, is both small and restricted to a limited range of primary commodities (UNCTAD, 1984). Rather than diversifying its export base, the continent has become increasingly dependent on exports of primary products for its foreign exchange earnings. Whereas in 1970, 68 percent of Africa's exports were resource-based, by 1978, this figure had risen to 72 percent. For developing countries as a whole, the comparable figures were 53.3 percent and 53.1 percent (UNIDO, 1983a).

Africa's share of world exports of manufactured goods, estimated at 0.36 percent in 1980, has been falling despite rising levels of output, while its share of total world industrial output increased from 0.83 percent in 1970 to 0.97 percent in 1980. These UNIDO calculations suggest that the main impetus to increased manufacturing output has been growing domestic demand, including import substitution industries, rather than exports. As manufacturing valued added per capita was growing faster than GDP per capita until the mid-1970s, import substitution was the more significant source of demand expansion.

Reinforcing the observation that import substitution industries provided the main stimulus to industrial growth, data for 5 countries confirms that, with the exception of Nigeria, import-substituting industries contributed to at least one-third of industrial growth rates in the 1970s. If the five countries are at all representative, then Africa appears to have been more reliant than average on import substitution as a source of demand growth.

STRATEGIC OPTIONS

To date, the three main strategies to industrialization have been the import substitution option; the export orientation option, including the further processing of primary products; and the agricultural demand-led option. Although these options are not necessarily mutually exclusive, there is evidence that import substitution as a strategy for industrialization has jeopardized and delayed the development of export industries and could also have adverse effects on the agricultural demand-led approach.

African manufacturing is dominated by firms producing simple consumer goods import substitutes—notably foodstuffs, beverages, and tobacco, accounting for 31 percent of MVA, followed by clothing

and textiles, contributing 21 percent (Table A.2 in Appendix I). The
concentration on products that are income inelastic in demand partially explains the slowdown in industrial growth during the 1970s.
Once the initial "easy" phase of import substitution was completed,
countries experienced difficulties in either expanding their import-
substituting bases or entering the world export markets. Unfortunately, industries with low income elasticities of demand—food, beverages, clothing and textiles, wood and furniture products, and
paper products—are the sub-sectors in which less developed countries (LDCs) clearly have a comparative advantage as they are labor-
intensive and low-skilled industries.

Contributions to total manufacturing growth in world markets
were dominated by skills-intensive industries between 1960 and
1980. The expansion of the chemicals and machinery industries accounted for 63 percent of world manufacturing growth in the 1966–73
period and 70 percent between 1974 and 1980, while industries such
as foodstuffs and clothing accounted for only 7 and 12 percent, respectively. Heavy industry and high-tech industries are expanding
more rapidly than light industries, with adverse implications for the
LDCs in terms of increasing their share of world manufacturing value
added and employment, given the capital-intensive nature of the
faster growing industrial sub-sectors.

IMPORT SUBSTITUTION VERSUS EXPORT ORIENTATION

The debate on import substitution versus export orientation has
dominated contemporary discussions on African development strategies. But the impressive growth performance of the handful of
newly industrializing countries in the 1960s and early 1970s has
spawned the new conventional wisdom that export-led growth is
likely to be the more efficient path for sub-Saharan Africa.

The shortcomings of the import substitution strategy in Africa
have been documented, and the experience of Kenya, regarded in the
1960s and 1970s as one of the continent's few economic success stories, underlines the validity of this assessment. Between 1964 and
1978, Kenya's real industrial output grew at an average 9.5 percent a
year, outstripping annual real GDP growth rates of 5.9 percent. Similarly, wage employment in manufacturing doubled between 1966–
1978 to 130,000.

Advances in industrial growth stemmed from heavy protectionist policies, such as foreign exchange quotas, licensing, and tariffs, resulting in local manufacture of simple import substitutes, particularly those goods consumed by middle and upper-income groups. The primary beneficiaries were not Kenyan firms, but foreign multinationals who were assisted by direct loans and equity capital contributions from the government, access to foreign exchange at an overvalued exchange rate, and bureaucratic encouragement.

As a result, manufactured goods imports as a percent of total domestic supplies fell from 44.3 percent in 1972 to 31.5 percent in 1978, while exports of manufactured goods as a percent of gross output were more than halved. Further, value added dropped as a percent of gross output from 28 percent in 1972 to 18.2 percent in 1978. Essentially, the "easy" phase of the import substitution strategy had wound down by the end of 1970s, confronting the government with the necessity of either breaking into export markets or developing an expanded import substitution base, including intermediate goods and capital equipment.

The pattern of industrial growth was strongly biased against export expansion because high protection levels made import replacement substantially more profitable than exporting, especially given the requirement that exporters use high cost and often sub-standard local inputs. Low (1979) notes that the export food processing sector had to pay high prices for local packaging materials, a sugar price twice as high as world prices because of unrebated excise taxes, and in some instances higher prices for raw materials.

Alluding to the Kenyan experience, the World Bank found the import control system "complex, cumbersome, and inconsistent," with a "wide latitude for abuse." Furthermore, the effects of import restrictions on local prices were found to be "uniformly upward" (Low, 1979, p.410). The agricultural sector suffered from negative protection "to the extent that almost all the locally manufactured items the farmers buy are protected"; the Kenyan motor vehicle assembly plants undoubtedly raised the cost of transportation in the country (p.415).

More significant perhaps, protectionist policies in Kenya have favored large-scale and often foreign firms. As a result, the industrialization process has been skewed toward capital-intensive techniques and the production of goods more appropriate to higher income markets.

Import-substituting strategies that include protectionist policies have encouraged a pattern of industrial growth that precludes export expansion. Evidence from a number of countries, including Nigeria and Zimbabwe, illustrates that import substitution tends to shift the pattern of imports away from final consumption items to raw materials and intermediate and capital goods, rather than reducing dependence on imports altogether. As a result, the degree to which a country can compress its imports is reduced, giving rise to the mounting adjustment problems since 1974, and the necessity of depressing consumption, income, output, and employment.

The manufacturing industry in Africa has also been a formidable net user of foreign exchange. This sector has contributed to a nearly fivefold increase in import elasticity of GDP in the last two decades. The African Development Bank (1985) notes that the manufacturing industry in a majority of sub-Saharan countries is "overly dependent on imports and sometimes structurally inefficient."

Import substitution policies also require detailed and efficient administration. As Galbraith has argued (1979), while market mechanisms "economize on scarce and honest administrative talent," interventionist strategies, such as operating a complex system of import licensing, place "the greatest possible claim on the scarcest possible resource."

BEYOND IMPORT SUBSTITUTION

Three key prerequisites for African economic growth for the remainder of the century will be increased savings ratios, higher returns on investment, and substantially enhanced net foreign exchange inflows. Industrialization programs will have to focus on savings of foreign exchange, the creation of new jobs, and the achievement of increased per capita incomes along with a more equitable pattern of income distribution. In light of the region's poor economic performance since 1973, it is argued that emphasis should be placed not on income redistribution now, but on policies designed to raise average incomes and above all policies that generate employment, as these will indirectly improve income distribution. Given the record of import substitution not only in Africa but in LDCs as a whole, it is clear that a new approach must be taken.

Export-led industrialization has been widely acclaimed to provide a more sustainable basis for efficient economic growth in sub-Saharan Africa. The rapid growth rates of the newly industrializing countries (NICs) during the 1960s and 1970s, and their apparent ability to weather two oil price rises have been "somehow closely related to factors associated with the rapid growth of exports" (Krueger, 1984). Economic growth rates in the NICs accelerated appreciably after export-oriented policies were undertaken and were clearly not the consequence of one-shot injections of resource allocations. Switching to an export orientation not only accelerates industrial expansion, as Krueger argues, but it can lead to major new primary exports, as has been the case in Brazil, reducing dependence on capital inflows and foreign borrowing—the so-called "indebted industrialization" that has contributed to the current debt crisis (OECD, 1984).

Theoretically, export-led growth improves the efficiency of allocations and increases the supply of foreign exchange, paving the way for more liberal and sustainable import regimes. Moreover, it has been shown to be more labor-intensive than production for domestic consumption, with the unskilled labor component estimated to range between 50 to 100 percent higher than in import-substituting industries.

Although export growth stimulates overall output levels and incomes, thereby generating additional employment, a number of resource-based industries, particularly those in basic processing and exports of minerals, are not labor-intensive. These activities often require significant capital outlays to sustain relatively few jobs. Rather, an indirect stimulus occurs as the subsequent increase in foreign exchange allows for looser import controls and therefore higher output levels and job creation elsewhere in the economy.

When export-led industries draw on unskilled and semi-skilled labor, they have a direct impact on primary as well as secondary employment. It is precisely because they have a comparative advantage in labor-intensive manufactures that developing countries show positive employment trends in their export-led industries. In addition, an emphasis on export-led growth has encouraged transfers of technology. Korean industry, for example, enjoyed "virtually free access" to technological and managerial information through foreign buyers who were the most important source of information on product development and who contributed to improved production and managerial techniques (World Bank, 1983a).

THE VIABILITY OF EXPORT-LED GROWTH

Even if the rationale underlying export-led growth is acceptable, its applicability to sub-Saharan Africa is less certain. Hypothetically, if all LDCs exhibited similar export intensities to those of Singapore, Hong Kong, Korea, and Taiwan, this would translate into a 700 percent increase in manufactured exports from developing countries, increasing their share of industrial countries' import markets from 16.7 percent in 1976 to more than 60 percent. In effect, as Cline concludes, the Asian export-led growth pattern cannot be replicated "without provoking a protectionist response ruling out its implementation" (1982, p. 89).

Further, the rapid export growth of the NICs in the 1960s and 1970s coincided with a period of sustained, rapid expansion in world trade—a phenomenon unlikely to be repeated in the next 10 to 15 years. The slowdown in world trade since the late 1970s and the rise in protectionism in developed economies suggest that export-led growth will be more difficult to achieve in coming years, particularly as protectionism is most evident in labor-intensive manufactures— precisely the area in which LDCs have comparative advantage (Baldwin, 1970).

Compounding the problem of entry into markets are advances in technology. In several industries such as electronics, transnational firms have been able to relocate production to final markets rather than maintain presences in developing countries (Kaplinsky, 1984, pp. 79–84). A recent UNIDO study acknowledges these barriers to export-led strategies, urging industrialized countries to grant favorable quotas to the LDCs to enable them to secure a market foothold. Given high levels of unemployment in many industrial economies, however, this suggestion is likely to meet with strong opposition. No less contentious is UNIDO's companion recommendation that the NICs relinquish their efforts in labor-intensive manufactured exports and venture into more technologically advanced export areas.

More fundamental questions arise as to the ability of low-income African economies to replicate the Asian model, given small domestic markets and therefore high unit costs, inadequate access to technology, and limited entrepreneurial capacities.

RESOURCE-BASED INDUSTRIALIZATION

The popularity of a variant of the export-led model—resource-based industrialization—has dwindled in recent years given the sluggish performance of primary product prices on world markets. Natural resource exploitation, particularly of minerals and petroleum, has often created export enclave economies characterized by a high-wage, capital-intensive sector with limited employment as an island of prosperity in a sea of underemployment, unemployment, and rural poverty. Dependence on a single resource has also encouraged governments to neglect their agricultural sectors and to maintain overvalued exchange rates, which militate against industrial growth and deter much-needed export diversification.

There are, however, some instances where resource-based industrialization has been successful—Ivory Coast, Malawi, and Zimbabwe are examples. In each case, industrialization has been partially encouraged by protectionist strategies and agriculture has played a critical role either as the primary foreign exchange earner or as creator of a market for the outputs of domestic industry while simultaneously earning foreign exchange from raw material or semi-processed exports.

The drawbacks of resource-based industrialization, however, are vulnerability to exogenous shocks, such as international prices for exports and adverse weather conditions. However, this strategy is more attractive than import substitution or dependence on export of manufactures because it exploits comparative advantage; it can be highly labor-intensive; and it does generate net foreign exchange revenues.

AGRICULTURE-LED GROWTH AS AN ALTERNATIVE

If both import substitution and the export orientation are ruled out, is there a third way? Adelman (1984) has advanced the agricultural demand-led approach to industrialization as a means of "buying time" to enable the industrial countries to overcome protectionist pressures and open the door to renewed growth in manufactured exports by NICs.

To be adopted by those LDCs that have few or no prospects for developing or expanding non-traditional exports, that are net food importers, or that have an already established industrial base, this strategy is based on the underlying assumption that a domestic mass market will develop as a result of increased agricultural productivity. Small-scale and medium-sized farmers, many of whose inputs can be supplied by domestic industry, will produce goods that can be processed by manufacturers and rising incomes will generate further demand for local goods. Again, the pitfalls of this approach, similar to those of import substitution, concern the ability of domestic industry to provide inputs at competitive prices and to thrive either domestically or in foreign markets without government subsidies.

But recent experience in Zimbabwe lends some support to this strategy. Government supply-side policies aimed at increasing productivity particularly among small-scale farmers included improved access to farm credits; investment in boreholes, marketing depots, roads, bridges, and irrigation schemes; incentive pricing; and expanded extension services. As a result, there was a substantial increase in smallholder cotton and maize output in the 1984/85 season; the cotton is ginned locally and about 30 percent is absorbed by domestic clothing and textile manufacturers, with the balance exported as lint. Similarly, maize is milled domestically and the surplus is exported. As the Standard Chartered Bank of Zimbabwe reports, increases in production of consumer goods in 1984 reflected rises in the spending power of peasant farmers.

THE POLICY DEBATE

As the foregoing review of various options indicates, the debate on appropriate strategies of industrialization is far from closed. Although in theory, it might be possible to proceed simultaneously on all three strategies, practical obstacles to such a comprehensive approach are formidable. For example, export promotion in practice implies some degree of discrimination against industries producing for the domestic market; protecting manufacturing activities breeds high cost export sectors; and strong domestic markets encouraged by the agriculture-based strategy conflict with the development of export markets since it is more profitable to engage in manufacturing for the home market.

Since the 1960s, economic policy in Africa has largely focused on macro-economic planning without due consideration to micro-economic issues. Successful economies, like sound businesses, are essentially those that have a diverse portfolio of investments. Rather than basing decisions on artificially high rates of return that are a function of import barriers, insulated monopolies, subsidized interest rates, or other investment incentives, they should reflect the perceived net economic worth of projects. Accordingly, a broadly neutral economic environment is desirable, in which policy-makers can encourage savings and investment in various sectors of the economy.

Such a purely neutral approach to economic planning, however, is unlikely to be adopted in Africa, given a strong commitment to state intervention reflecting a belief that political independence is meaningless without economic self-determination and self-sufficiency. Realistically, the smaller the market, the greater the likelihood of state participation in any major venture. In those cases where the limits of import substitution have been reached, some degree of public sector intervention must come into play if incentives to exports and agricultural output are to be implemented.

Given the varying levels of industrialization in Africa, gross generalizations on policy initiatives are dangerous. But in effect, small, least developed economies have few options other than to retain the infant industry protection they already enjoy, while endeavoring to eliminate discrimination against small-scale, labor-intensive, or export-oriented industries. In these countries, import substitution is a dead-end strategy since the smaller the domestic market, the faster the saturation point will be reached and the greater the danger of establishing high-cost inefficient industries. The Malawian model, with its emphasis on self-sufficiency in foodstuffs and agricultural exports as a springboard for resource-based industrialization, is commendable from the viewpoint of small, resource-poor nations.

In larger, relatively more prosperous countries such as Nigeria, there is a dire need to shift focus from import substitution to agricultural rehabilitation, which in the long run will enhance the competitiveness, viability, and growth prospects of existing industries. This will involve temporarily downgrading the role of manufacturing in the economy, along with the implementation of policies designed to restructure incentives toward an outward-looking bias.

Experience over the last decade suggests that African policy-makers are reluctant to undertake such a corrective strategy until it is forced upon them by crisis conditions. But the longer the policy transition is delayed, the more difficult it will be to achieve.

The typical policy package involves devaluation of the currency to bring domestic prices more in line with those on world markets; gradual removal of quantitative restrictions on imports and other non-tariff barriers and their replacement with tariffs; a general reduction in the average tariff level; and a move toward tariff uniformity that no longer favors the importation of intermediate and capital goods. Such a policy package is more likely to be implemented successfully, however, if linked to balance of payments support from donors.

EXPORT INCENTIVES

As tariffs will have to be maintained during the transitional period, it will be necessary to provide counterbalancing export incentives. The typical export incentive program embraces preferential credit lines and access to foreign exchange for imports of industrial inputs, tax concessions to industries promoting exports, outright subsidies and exemptions from import duties for exporters, and provision of subsidized export supplier credits to exporters of machinery and capital equipment. These programs, however, should be seen as ancillary rather than mainstream efforts to increase foreign exchange earnings. Specific incentives to boost exports have been found to be less effective than the creation of an economic climate that encourages efficiency and competitiveness. In a study of 27 LDCs, Love (1984) concludes that successful export programs depended significantly on supply side variables in all but four countries, rather than on export incentives per se.

Further, domestic monetary and fiscal policies should be reformed to eliminate biases against labor-intensive industries and against small-scale enterprises. In the past, policies such as tax concessions on new investment, minimum wage legislation, restrictions on the "hire and fire" policies of private companies, and the encouragement of investment by means of negative real interest rates have distorted factor prices in such a way as to lead industrialists to adopt capital-intensive techniques.

TECHNOLOGY

Two distinct problems arise with regard to transfers of technology to Africa. First, there is a need to ensure that appropriate technologies are adopted in industry, and, second, that more rapid technological progress be made in order to avoid the danger of African industry being left behind and forced to compete, using outmoded technologies, in the mature, slow-growth sub-sectors.

The trade regime adopted by a country has a significant bearing on productivity, growth, and technological advance. Import substitution programs tend to dissuade technological advance when they allow highly concentrated or monopolistic industries to form. Operating at low capacity, these industries generate a cost-permissive atmosphere of "x-inefficiency," in which goods are produced at high costs because industrialists are free of open market competition. International competition, on the other hand, induces a "challenge response" mechanism whereby efforts to minimize costs lead domestic industry to adopt more efficient new technologies (Nishimizu and Robinson, 1984).

Foreign exchange constraints similarly deter technological transfers, as modern capital equipment and intermediate inputs become more costly. Policies that promote export-led expansion through easier access to foreign exchange can lead to higher productivity through increased availability of imported technology, economies of scale, and competitive incentives.

At the same time, appropriate technologies have been found to be both available and viable in LDCs. The Pickett study of choice of technologies in 12 industries concluded that a significant range of efficient technologies existed in virtually all the industries under review, and in some instances were labor-intensive. In those instances where labor-intensive techniques were used but were less than optimal, the opportunity costs were found to be invariably small. For 430 of the 486 technologies studied, the net present value, at a 10 percent discount rate, of the most labor-intensive technology was within a mere two percent range of the most profitable technique, implying that the rate of return from a sub-optimal technology is only slightly below the profit-maximization technique.

These and other research findings suggest that choices of technology in LDCs are often sub-optimal, reflecting lack of familiarity with available techniques; a tendency to imitate developed economies in their choice of technologies; the inclination of transnational corporations to employ the same techniques they use at home; a distorting structure of incentives—negative real interest rates, subsidized loans, and tax incentives—and the over-pricing of labor. Although well-intentioned, many industrial relations policies, including minimum wage levels, raise the implied cost of labor by restricting the private sector's freedom to manage its employment policy.

The solutions to these problems must include measures to eliminate biases against labor-intensive techniques and to encourage entrepreneurial decision-making in choosing appropriate technologies.

State intervention in this field is desirable, given its access to the requisite data.

THE ROLE OF FOREIGN INVESTMENT

Transnational corporations remain the most effective means of transferring technology across international borders. With the slow-down in foreign direct investment since the 1970s and Africa's deep-ening liquidity crisis, there has been a renewed interest in foreign private investment on the part of African governments. As a result, two negative trends have become apparent. First, countries have begun to compete against one another for new investments, with the result that concessions granted have reduced the value of the project in terms of tax revenues, net foreign exchange earnings, etc. Second, fierce competition for new investment has led to the implementation of inappropriate projects.

The main advantage of direct foreign investment is not the inflow of funds, which in net terms has been substantial in only a relatively small number of LDCs and very few in Africa, but its associated benefits in transfer of skills and technology and access to world mar-kets.

Over the last decade, joint ventures in which foreign equity does not exceed 50 percent have been on the increase. Indeed, a number of contractual arrangements now involve some investment by the for-eign firm, but no equity participation at all. Turnkey operations, sub-contracting, licensing arrangements, management, service and pro-duction-sharing contracts are examples.

These new forms of investment offer potential advantages to host governments concerned about limiting the foreign presence in their economies and their dependence on foreign capital, management, and technologies. They offer the host country increased control over investment decisions, job creation, technology choice, and exports, without the disadvantages of foreign ownership and control.

The issue of dependency is central to an industrialization strategy for sub-Saharan Africa. Five forms of dependence can be identified: market dependence, technological dependence, managerial depend-ence, dependence on foreign capital, and economic inflexibility (Roemer, 1981). Industrialization strategies in Africa in the past have reflected efforts to reduce such dependencies; import substitution was seen as an obvious way to reduce dependence on foreign trade while indigenization decrees were adopted to increase the authority of local management.

However, the record of the last 25 years shows that not only has a new kind of foreign trade dependence arisen in the form of import dependence, but reliance on foreign capital—indebted industrialization—has also increased. Technological and labor dependence remains acute, as does economic inflexibility as evidenced in the severe difficulties in adjustment to external shocks.

Trade, aid, and investment underline international interdependence in economic relationships. Economic interdependence for developing countries is primarily vertical—volumes of north-south trade, aid, and investment are much more substantial than south-south flows. Given the weaknesses of export-led growth, it is imperative that sub-Saharan Africa develop south-south trading links with other developing economies. But for the remainder of this century, opportunities created by access to industrial country markets, capital, technology, and expertise must be exploited. The challenge for African governments is to design a framework within which foreign investment will take place on a substantial scale, but without setting off fierce competition between host countries.

EMPLOYMENT

Industry's contribution to job creation in most LDCs has been disappointing; its share of the total labor force has averaged 14 percent in low income countries and an estimated 12 percent in sub-Saharan Africa (Squire, 1979). In contrast, in the United Kingdom in the mid-19th century, 40 percent of total employment was provided by the manufacturing sector. With some notable exceptions in East Asia, the insignificant role of industry in employment generation in developing economies reflects an emphasis on capital-intensive techniques (World Bank, 1982).

Between 1960 and 1980, industrial employment in sub-Saharan Africa grew by 4.5 percent per year, exceeding the estimated 2 percent annual growth rate of the labor force. However, even if the growth rate in industrial employment were to double, manufacturing's share would amount to only half of the growing labor force. As a result, manufacturing alone is unlikely to solve Africa's growing unemployment crisis.

Nevertheless, small-scale enterprise is considerably more labor-intensive than medium and large-scale businesses. Accordingly, policies should promote the small-scale sector wherever possible. Second, the labor intensity of exports of manufactures has been found to be greater than that of producing for the domestic market or for import substitution. Export-oriented policies stimulate industrial employment, as higher profits in the export sector lead to increased investment, employment, and output levels throughout the economy. Third, increased industrial employment yields external economies in the form of higher productivity per worker than in agriculture or services, along with improvements in the quality of labor that arise from skills acquired on the job.

It is clear that the region faces a deepening unemployment crisis resulting from rapid population growth and low levels of investment. It is essential therefore that policy should be directed at raising capital-labor ratios in existing enterprises and ensuring that, where possible, new investment should be labor-intensive. Getting prices right for capital and labor is an obvious step in the right direction.

WAGES

Labor in sub-Saharan Africa is generally considered to be overpriced. Historically, high wage levels were the consequence of colonization which imported wage structures from the metropole. Structurally, rapid productivity growth in enclave export sectors, such as copper in Zambia and Zaire and oil in Nigeria, gave rise to a distorted wage structure, as average wages throughout the economy were linked to those in the export sector. A third reason has been income redistribution goals of African governments, who often use statutory minimum wage policies toward this end.

High wage levels—partially a result of overvalued exchange rates—and lower productivity have deterred employment growth and undermined Africa's relative comparative advantage in labor-intensive activities (Table 10.1). If Africa is to replicate the experiences of certain Asian and Latin American countries that have attracted foreign investment in assembly plants, for example, a more comparative cost advantage in wages is essential. But it would be wrong to place undue emphasis on the role of low wage levels in attracting industrial investment. UNIDO describes average wage levels as at best ambiguous determinants of industry location or in the prediction of changes in world industry. Recent advances in the microelec-

TABLE 10.1
AVERAGE WAGES IN MANUFACTURING: SELECTED COUNTRIES

Country	Average Wage per Month US $ (1980)
Pakistan	60
Tanzania	71
Ghana	130
Nigeria	170
Kenya	174
Singapore	215
Zambia	229
Korea	242
Zimbabwe	325
United States	1,250

SOURCE: International Labor Organization. *Yearbook*, Geneva, 1984.

tronics industry and in robotics have enabled firms in the developed economies to overcome unfavorable wage differentials through a combination of increased productivity and quality improvements.

Nevertheless, appropriate labor pricing remains important. Continued distortions which extend beyond explicit wage costs to industrial relations policies will adversely affect choices of technologies and encourage capital-intensive methods at the expense of creating jobs.

CAPITAL UTILIZATION

In sub-Saharan Africa, capital utilization rates tend to be very low in comparison with other LDC regions, with industry largely dependent on imports of raw materials, intermediate goods, and spare parts, and on small, low income domestic markets. To a large extent, underutilization of capital stems from industrial capacity growth rates that outstrip both the supply of imported inputs and domestic demand. Encouraged by high profits in protected and uncompetitive domestic markets, the rapid expansion in industrial output ceased in the late 1970s when imports became too costly or simply unavailable. As a result, industries became unprofitable, operating at high unit costs but at low levels of capital utilization. The situation was exacerbated on the demand side by falling per capita incomes in a number of countries.

The importance of capital utilization cannot be stressed enough. Low rates not only mean low returns on capital, thereby discouraging new investment, but also wasted resources. Raising capital utilization rates is both a quick and an inexpensive way of increasing output, productivity, and employment without new net investment, freeing savings for investment elsewhere in the economy. In addition, such a policy works well in tandem with export-led growth. Given the relatively high costs of inputs and limited domestic markets, companies operating with substantial excess capacity—for example, the manufacturing industry in Nigeria was operating at only 50 percent capacity in 1984—can increase their output for export purposes with no additional investment.

Winston (1984) has shown that high capital utilization rates are determined in part by wages, interest rates, and technology. Negative real interest rates and high wages encourage large-scale, capital-intensive investments that will tend to have low utilization rates. Positive real interest rates and market-determined wages on the other hand will force companies to utilize their capital more efficiently, resulting in higher employment and output per unit of capital.

In the near-term, donors will continue to have an important role to play through commodity import programs, which have, for example, contributed significantly to maintaining output and employment in Zimbabwean industry since 1983. Donor countries should consider program aid which enhances utilization of existing capacity as part of a general policy reform package, in preference to project aid designed to create new capacity.

In the medium-term, efforts must be made to expand export markets and to develop stronger domestic markets, tapping local sources for input supplies. This will require adjusting overvalued exchange rates and imposing tariffs on imports of raw materials and intermediate goods.

STATE-OWNED ENTERPRISES

In the post-independence period, Africa's public sector has grown rapidly, extending into the mining, manufacturing, and services sectors. The record has not been a happy one, as Killick (1983) notes: "A large industrial public sector will contribute little to dynamic industrial growth, will tend to become a drain on public finances, will require a net inflow of resources to cover its capital requirements, and will discourage the growth of private industry."

In a sample of 70 developed and developing countries, Africa's public sector contributed an average 33 percent of investments in the 1970s, against 16.5 percent in the other countries (Short, 1984). Even these statistics, however, understate the role of government in a typical African economy. Governments exercise far-reaching controls over their economies by way of regulations governing the private sector, such as import restrictions, monetary and fiscal policies, labor and wage legislation, and indigenization decrees.

Although less than in the utilities and mining sectors, the share of public ownership in the industrial sector has exceeded 25 percent in many sub-Saharan African countries (Table 10.2). State-owned enterprises are found to use both more capital and labor than private companies for the same or even lower outputs. In Tanzania, for example, the more capital-intensive public sector has had slightly lower output per worker and lower productivity of capital, while in Ghana, labor productivity in public enterprises was only 55 percent that of the private sector in 1969/70 (Killick, 1983).

Nevertheless, the privatization of industrial ownership must be approached cautiously, as inefficiencies are not a result of public ownership per se, but rather a function of the degree to which the state interferes in daily decision-making, the degree of decentralization of decision-making, the flexibility of management structures, and the policy environment in which public enterprise operates.

There is a danger that privatization strategies will merely shift ownership and control from one inefficient management to another, given scarce managerial and entrepreneurial skills. As long as the policy environment is hostile to business efficiency, as long as managerial and entrepreneurial skills are scarce, and as long as there is overt political interference including a requirement to satisfy non-commercial goals, enterprises will remain inefficient regardless of ownership.

Above all, state-owned enterprises cannot be assessed on purely economic criteria, but rather must be judged against the social and political goals they are required to attain. It has been argued that a more practical policy goal in Africa would be to make the public enterprise sector more efficient and development-oriented rather than reducing its size.

State-owned enterprises were established because of a perceived

TABLE 10.2

PUBLIC AND PRIVATE SHARES IN MANUFACTURING VALUE ADDED: PERCENTAGE FOR SELECTED COUNTRIES

Country	Early/Middle 1960s	1969	1972–73	1979–80
Ghana				
State-Owned	13.3	16.0	17.2	27.1
Joint Ventures	7.9	19.7	18.0	25.6
Private	78.9	64.5	64.8	47.3 [a]
Zambia				
Public/Parastatal	n.a.	n.a.	53.2	56.4
Private	n.a.	n.a.	46.8	43.6
Tanzania				
Parastatal	5.0	22.5	33.2	31.0
Private	95.0	77.5	66.8	69.0
Kenya				
Public	15.5	13.2	18.0	n.a.
Private	84.5	86.8	82.0	n.a.

[a] consisted of 25.7% private Ghanaian, 12.7% private foreign and 12.7% private mixed (domestic and foreign).
SOURCE: W. F. Steel and J. W. Evans: *Industrialisation in Sub-Saharan Africa.* Technical Paper No. 25 (Washington, D.C., The World Bank, 1984.)

need to gain control of strategic sectors and to become involved where private enterprise was either unwilling or unable to launch a new venture, and where entrepreneurial know-how was absent. State participation was often required by foreign investors as a means of gauging creditworthiness and ensuring security for foreign sector interests.

In the mid-1970s, the budgetary burden of public enterprise deficits in Africa averaged 3.3 percent of GDP, reaching 10 percent in Zambia (1978/80) and 4 percent in Tanzania (1974/77) (Short, 1984). These public sector deficits have contributed to balance of payments problems because they are partially financed from foreign borrowings, thereby increasing the debt-servicing burden, and because of the sector's high propensity to import. Financing their deficits from domestic bank credit has clearly been an important factor contributing to high rates of money supply growth and therefore high inflation rates.

Given the disappointing performance of the state sector, most African governments have been reluctant to launch new parastatals and a number of countries—Ghana, Nigeria, and Zambia—have adopted a privatization approach. In May 1985, Tanzanian President Julius Nyerere was quoted as saying that sisal plantations will be returned to private ownership, as production had fallen from 220,000 tonnes in 1970 to 47,000 tonnes in 1984.

Whether the solution lies in this approach or in better management of public sector enterprises remains to be seen. In any event, privatization will not be a viable option unless public enterprises are seen by the private sector as potentially profitable. It is doubtful whether private sector funding exists in most countries to take over state-owned enterprise. A more promising approach would be to restructure economic policy along market-oriented lines and to revise the guidelines within which public enterprises will operate in the future.

FINANCE AND CAPITAL MARKETS

Efficient capital markets, in which interest rates and yields on financial assets are determined by competitive supply and demand forces, are central to industrial development. Pegging interest rates below rates of inflation in order to control the cost of credit and encourage investment has often been counterproductive, in effect deterring savings and generating excess demand for credit. This in turn requires direct control over bank lending policies which tend to favor large rather than small enterprises and which frequently allocate funds to inefficient low-return investments while encouraging capital-intensive projects.

Efficient capital markets on the other hand increase both savings and investment, channeling them to productive uses throughout the economy on the basis of the highest rates of return, and ultimately generating employment and overall economic growth.

Unfortunately, governments in many developing countries have placed their emphasis on attracting foreign investment via investment codes and incentives to multinational corporations rather than on developing efficient capital markets which would to some extent reduce dependence on foreign capital.

Reviewing the development programs of 16 sub-Saharan countries, the African Development Bank concludes that dependence on foreign capital is as high as 80 to 100 percent for some of the least developed states, averaging 56 percent for the entire sample. Only Guinea, Sudan, Uganda, Botswana, and the Gambia had investment plans where the bulk of financing was to be met from domestic sources. Furthermore, the bank found that domestic savings ratios have stagnated, except in oil-exporting countries, and investment rates have declined. Net investment as a percent of GDP is reckoned to have been below the 15 percent gross investment ratio of GDP estimated for 1984 because of the serious deterioration of capital stock in many parts of the region.

In the low income countries, the domestic savings ratio fell from 10.9 percent in the 1960s to 8.8 percent in the 1970s, and is expected to drop to an average of 8.6 percent over the next decade (ADB, 1985). Although partially explained by stagnating real income levels, this trend also reflects policies and institutional structures that are not conducive to savings and investment. Structural deficiencies in the banking systems also explain the failure to mobilize even low levels of savings and to channel these funds into productive investment. In terms of investment, low rates of return on capital in manufacturing and problems within the investing institutions themselves, such as development banks, are among the more glaring shortcomings.

Suffering from lack of resources, development banks have been hard hit by the international debt crisis and the subsequent reluctance on the part of international lenders to invest in Africa. Further, bottlenecks in some countries have arisen at the project proposal stage. When submitted to development banks and other investing institutions, proposals have been found to be so poorly prepared that their chances of acceptance are considerably reduced (UNIDO, 1984b).

Although provision of long-term finance for capital investment is not within the domain of commercial banks, they could assist the development process by providing working capital which can be the critical factor in the success or failure of the small-scale enterprise sector. The deterioration of the fiscal balance in the region poses another on-going problem. Large fiscal deficits mean that a substantial proportion of available savings is being absorbed by the public sector—partly to finance the deficits of state-owned enterprises—which reduces the availability of capital for investment in manufacturing and indirectly imposes a severe balance of payments strain since a fiscal deficit is frequently mirrored by an external payments deficit.

ENTREPRENEURSHIP

African governments have justified nationalization of industry on the basis of a lack of indigenous entrepreneurship, and an ADB/OAU/ECA report supports this claim, stating that entrepreneurial ability is probably "the most important scarce skill in sub-Saharan Africa." Although this may be true, the environment in which policies are made—high rates of domestic inflation, overvalued exchange rates, and lack of access to technology—have made it more attractive for entrepreneurs to engage in the trade and services sectors such as transport, than in manufacturing. It is therefore arguable that Africa's problem is not a shortage of entrepreneurs, but of industrial entrepreneurs.

Governmental ambivalence toward private enterprise has also contributed to the lack of private participation. Whereas in some francophone countries, leaders have openly stated a preference for foreign investors over local entrepreneurs because they come equipped with finance, foreign exchange, technology, expertise, and market access, other governments have actively discouraged private enterprise. However, government regulations and restrictions have both discouraged indigenous enterprise and favored the larger firms which are invariably foreign-controlled.

Efforts to indigenize foreign-owned businesses have tended to create a small new elite or have further enriched the existing military or bureaucratic elite. The Kenyan government's drive to reduce the Asian presence in the economy in the early 1970s was unsuccessful because, as a Kenyan minister subsequently conceded, "We didn't have enough financial backup, nor did we have the management skills to operate the shops we pushed the Asians out of." Ten years later, Asian entrepreneurs were estimated to account for one-quarter of Kenya's GDP, 55 percent of manufacturing output, and three-quarters of retail activities (Baker, 1983).

While there is no easy solution to this problem, there is room for improved business education and extension programs for manufacturing industries. However, as long as the public sector and international companies continue to offer greater security and financial remuneration, they will attract the best entrepreneurial talent. As most indigenization efforts have failed, African governments should exploit the entrepreneurial talents of the "permanent" expatriate community—the Asians in East Africa, the Lebanese in West Africa, and the whites in southern Africa. The most promising policy would be to focus on education, training, and extension along with access to credit and technology that are designed to help the successful small-scale manufacturers make the difficult transition to medium-scale activities.

FUTURE POLICY

That the onus for reversing the current trend in African economies rests squarely with the governments and people of the continent is widely recognized. The assistance that the donor community can realistically be expected to provide is limited, given the disappointing results of the substantial aid flows over the last two decades. Numerous studies, including those undertaken by African institutions, emphasize the need for improved policies, management, and institutions within the continent itself. This will require, first and foremost, a restructuring of the domestic policy environment.

POLICY REFORM

Stated time and again by multilateral agencies such as the World Bank and International Monetary Fund, policy reform must include a system of incentives that is as uniform as possible across different sectors. Such a neutral policy environment allows industrialists to make decisions on the basis of perceived long-term returns rather than on the basis of a protected domestic market or tax holiday. While laissez-faire policies cannot be embraced totally or import-substituting policies completely relinquished, it will be necessary to move gradually toward a uniform incentive package, counterbalancing the existing biases by special incentives to export industries as well as agriculture. Future industrial investments will be determined by the country's resource endowment and its comparative advantage.

Even if a restructuring of incentives, including the adoption of a realistic exchange rate policy, fails to stimulate export-led expansion, investments in import-substituting activities or those aimed at satisfying domestic demand will be more soundly based and more efficient than under a system of high levels of effective protection.

Effective supply-side strategies that eliminate existing obstacles to investment and growth are also needed. These include the creation of essential infrastructure, access to credit, supply of complementary inputs—raw materials, intermediate items, skilled personnel, technology, marketing expertise, and entrepreneurial capacity—and legislative, monetary, and fiscal policies that combine to create a positive environment for investment. Moreover, political stability is required to create a conducive investment climate. Above all, African governments can stimulate industrial growth by accentuating incentives and curbing regulatory and restrictive programs.

TRADE RATHER THAN AID

The donor community's most valuable contribution to industrialization in sub-Saharan Africa would be to remove protectionist and particularly non-tariff barriers to trade. According to a GATT estimate, about 35 percent of world trade is subject to non-tariff barriers of some kind, while the Leutwiler Committee's report (Leutwiler, 1985) calls for fairer and clearer rules in agricultural trade in order to allow efficient agricultural producers to compete.

In effect, policies such as the EEC's Common Agricultural Policy discourage exports in LDCs and fuel skepticism over the viability of an export-led growth strategy. If donors wish to see economic policy reform in Africa, they should reverse the present trend toward protectionism and provide balance of payments and technical support to help countries through the difficult period of adjustment toward an outward-looking industrial strategy. It is pointless for bilateral and multilateral donors to insist on conditionality for financial support during a period of structural adjustment, if export market opportunities are restricted by protectionism.

Second, given excess capacity in sub-Saharan industry, donors should focus their efforts on provision of commodity import assistance and balance of payments support rather than on aid for new industrial capacity. Third, Western donors are particularly well-placed to assist developing countries in the screening of new projects, in building African capacity in negotiating skills with transnational corporations, in providing technological guidance and advice, and in offering business school training to entrepreneurs and managers.

Donors also have a responsibility to improve communications between African governments and business on the one hand, and their own multinational corporations on the other. Donors can help promote investment opportunities, draw attention to market openings, and use moral suasion against implementation of inappropriate projects and techniques on the part of LDCs. It is in the interests of the countries in the region to terminate competition for new investment.

Firms in the Western countries are the foremost source of technology and donor governments should take steps to speed up the rate of technology diffusion, while ensuring that transfer costs are minimized. Lastly, Western businesses could provide direct assistance in entrepreneurship development by offering on-the-job training to African managers or by seconding staff to operate extension services in the region. Such technical assistance will yield greater rewards than expertise at the macro-economic or planning level.

CONCLUSIONS

In the mid-1980s, it is apparent that many of the ambitious targets outlined in the Lagos Plan of Action are unlikely to be achieved. Given the weak performance of agriculture, it is unfortunate that the Lagos summit designated the 1980s as the "Industrial Decade for Africa," as industrial expansion will continue to be hampered by a weak agrarian base. The Lagos Plan of Action's emphasis on self-reliance and self-sustained growth is ironic because agricultural failure has made sub-Saharan Africa more rather than less dependent on developed market economies for aid, capital, skills, and even food.

For at least the remainder of this decade, the manufacturing sector will be secondary to agriculture in most of the continent. Therefore, priorities should be redirected toward agriculture as the continent's leading sector. Further industrialization should be dependent either on domestic market growth resulting from rising farm output and incomes, from export expansion, or preferably from a combination of the two. Manufacturing value added is likely to grow as a result of increased production for domestic demand, renewed emphasis on resource-based industry, and, it is hoped, increased exports, primarily to other developing countries, but also to the developed market economies.

Although self-reliance and self-sufficiency in agriculture and resource-based industrialization are worthy objectives, no country or trading bloc can claim to be self-sufficient in a world of increased economic interdependence. Further, the danger is that the quest for self-reliance and self-sufficiency will spark another round of inward-focused industrialization based on comparative disadvantage rather than advantage, with adverse effects on efficiency, growth, exports, employment, and income distribution.

The strength of an outward-oriented economic strategy lies in its reliance on market signals to achieve an efficient or at least more efficient allocation of economic resources. In the long run, an agriculture-led growth strategy, accompanied by national economic policies which provide incentives and limited restrictions, is more likely to enhance economic stability and flexibility in sub-Saharan Africa, reducing the degree to which countries are dependent on foreign aid and capital.

REFERENCES

Adedeji, A. 1982. "Development and Economic Growth in Africa to the Year 2000," in Timothy Shaw, ed., *Alternative Futures for Africa*. Boulder: Westview Press.

Adelman, Irma. 1984. "Beyond Export-Led Growth," *World Development* 12(9) (September).

African Development Bank. 1985. *Annual Report 1984*. Addis Ababa.

Baker, Pauline. 1983. "Obstacles to Private Sector Activities in Africa." Report for the U.S. Dept. of State (mimeo).

Baldwin, R.E. 1970. *Non-Tariff Distortions in International Trade*. Washington, D.C.: Brookings Institution.

Cline, W. R. 1982. "Can the East Asian Model of Development be Generalised?," *World Development* 10(2).

Financial Times. 1985. "Why Steps are Needed to Safeguard Free Trade." *Financial Times*, March 28, 1985.

Fransman, M. 1984. "Explaining the Success of the Asian NICs: Incentives and Technology," *IDS (Sussex) Bulletin* 15(2).

Galbraith, J. K. 1979. *The Nature of Mass Poverty*. Cambridge, Mass.: Harvard University Press.

Kaplinsky, Raphael. 1984. "The International Context for Industrialisation in the Coming Decade," *Journal of Development Studies* 21(1) (October).

Killick, Tony. 1978. *Development Economics in Action: A Study of Economic Policies in Ghana*. New York: St. Martin's Press.

Killick, Tony. 1983. "The Role of the Public Sector in African Developing Countries," *Industry and Development* 7. New York: UNIDO.

Krueger, Anne. 1983. *Trade and Employment in Developing Countries*. Chicago: University of Chicago Press.

Krueger, Anne. 1984. "Comparative Advantage and Development Policy Twenty Years Later," in *Economic Structure and Performance, Essays in Honor of Hollis B. Chenery*. Orlando: Academic Press.

Leutwiler, Fritz. 1985. *Trade Policies for a Better Future*. Geneva: GATT.

Livingstone, Ian. 1984. "Resource-based Industrial Development: Past Experience and Future Prospects in Malawi," *Industry and Development* 10. New York: UNIDO.

Love, J. 1984. "External Market Conditions, Competition, Diversification and LDC Exports." *Journal of Development Economics* 16(3).

Low, F. 1979. "Export Potential in the Kenyan Fruit and Vegetable Processing Sector." Nairobi (mimeo).

Nishimizu, M. and S. Robinson. 1984. "Trade Policies and Productivity Change in Semi-Industrialised Economies," *Journal of Development Economics* 16(1-2) (September-October).

OECD. 1984. *New Forms of International Investment in Developing Countries*. Paris.

Organisation of African Unity, African Development Bank, Economic Commission for Africa. (undated). *Accelerated Development in Sub-Saharan Africa: An Assessment by the OAU, ADB AND ECA Secretariats*.

Pickett, J. 1979. "A Consistent Approach to the Choice of Technology," *World Industry Since 1960*. New York: UNIDO.

Roemer, Michael. 1981. "Dependence and Industrialisation Strategies," *World Development* 9(5).

Schaatz, S. P. 1977. *South of the Sahara; Development in African Economies*. Philadelphia: Temple University Press.

Shirley, M. M. 1983. "Managing State-Owned Enterprises." Staff Working Paper No. 577. Washington, D.C.: The World Bank.

Short, R. P. 1984. "The Role of Public Enterprises: An International Statistical Comparison," in *Public Enterprise in Mixed Economies*. Washington, D.C.: IMF.

Squire, Lyn. 1979. "Labour Force, Employment and Labour Markets in the Course of Economic Development." Staff Working Paper No. 336. Washington, D.C.: The World Bank.

Standard Chartered Bank. 1984. *Zimbabwe Economic Bulletin* (November). Harare, Zimbabwe.

Steel, W. F. and J. W. Evans. 1984. "Industrialisation in Sub-Saharan Africa." Technical Paper No. 25. Washington, D.C.: The World Bank.

UNCTAD. 1984. *Handbook of International Trade and Development Statistics.*

UNIDO. 1979. *World Industry Since 1960.* New York.

UNIDO. 1981. *World Industry in 1980.* New York.

UNIDO. 1983a. *Industry in a Changing World.* New York.

UNIDO. 1983b. "A Strategy of Industrial Development for the Small Resource-poor, Least-developed Economies," *Industry and Development* (8).

UNIDO. 1984a. *A Statistical Review of the World Industrial Situation in 1983.* New York.

UNIDO. 1984b. *The Role of National Development Financial Institutions in Organisation of the Islamic Conference Countries in Promoting Industrial Development.* (mimeo).

Winston, G. 1984. "The Utilisation of Capital in Developing Countries." UNIDO working paper (mimeo).

World Bank. 1982. *Trade and Development Policies for Industrial Development.* Washington, D.C.

World Bank. 1983a. *World Development Report 1983.* Washington, D.C.

World Bank. 1983b. *Kenya: Growth and Structural Change. Vol. 2.* Washington, D.C.

World Bank. 1984a. *Towards Self-Sustained Development in Sub-Saharan Africa.* Washington, D.C.

World Bank. 1984b. *World Development Report 1984.* Washington, D.C.

Zimbabwe Banking Corporation. 1985. *Economic Newsletter.* Harare.

CHAPTER ELEVEN

Small-Scale Industry

Carl Liedholm and Donald C. Mead

The role of small-scale industries in African development has recently emerged as an important concern among policy-makers, international donors, and researchers. The Lagos Plan of Action, for example, argues that as part of their industrial strategies, countries should aim at creating "a network of small and medium-scale industries as well as actively promoting and encouraging the informal sector." Even today, however, relatively little is known about these activities in Africa.[1] Consequently, policy-makers and planners charged with formulating programs to assist small-scale industry are frequently forced to make decisions "unencumbered by evidence."

This chapter aims to help fill the knowledge gap by setting forth what is known about small-scale industries in sub-Saharan Africa and the implications of these findings for policies and programs. Our coverage of industry includes manufacturing (ISIC codes 31–39), as well as the repair of manufactured goods (ISIC code 951), a treatment consistent with most manufacturing censuses and studies.[2] "Small-scale" is defined as those establishments with less than 50 workers. Although somewhat arbitrary, such a limitation excludes most foreign-owned firms and those with more modern and sophisticated management skills, more capital-intensive production techniques, and greater access to capital, technical assistance, and government incentive schemes.

DESCRIPTIVE PROFILE

OVERALL MAGNITUDE AND IMPORTANCE

The available evidence indicates that small-scale firms are a signifi-cant if not dominant component of the industrial sectors of most African countries. Not only are the overwhelming majority of indus-trial establishments small, but they account for the vast bulk of indus-trial employment. Small-scale firms in countries with the required data generally account for two thirds or more of total industrial em-ployment; indeed, for one country, Sierra Leone, with quite complete and accurate data, the figure is 95 percent. Moreover, most of the employment is concentrated at the smallest end of the size spectrum, with relatively less employment found in firms in the 10 to 49 worker size range. Small-scale firms also generate an important portion of the value-added of Africa's industrial sectors, although their share of value-added is not as great as their employment contribution.

COMPOSITION

An examination of available data indicates that clothing produc-tion—primarily tailoring—predominates in most countries, ranging from 25 percent of all establishments in rural Burkina Faso to 52 percent in Nigeria. Wood production—primarily furniture-making—follows, with metal-working (usually blacksmithing), food produc-tion (primarily baking), and vehicle, shoe, electrical, and bicycle re-pairs also found with some frequency. In the rural areas of several countries, such as Burkina Faso and Botswana, beer brewing is a dominant activity, usually undertaken by women. In general, small-scale firms are involved in the production of "light" consumer goods—clothing, furniture, simple tools, food, and drink.

LOCATION

A surprising yet significant finding is that, in most countries, the vast majority of small industries are located in rural areas.[3] Moreover, employment in small rural manufacturing industries often exceeds that generated by all urban manufacturing firms. In Sierra Leone, for example, 86 percent of total industrial sector employment and 95 percent of industrial establishments were located in rural areas

(Chuta and Liedholm, 1985). Similar findings have been reported elsewhere in Africa and in other parts of the world (see Liedholm and Mead, 1985). These figures may actually understate the true magnitude of rural industry because country censuses often fail to register the smallest of the rural industries.[4]

SIZE

The overwhelming majority of these firms are very small, with most employing fewer than five persons. Studies in Nigeria (Aluko, 1972), Sierra Leone (Chuta and Liedholm, 1985), and Ghana (Ghana, 1965) have found that 95 percent or more of the small-scale firms employ fewer than five individuals. Many are simply one-person enterprises. In rural Burkina Faso (Chuta and Wilcox, 1982), for example, 52 percent of the small-scale firms were one-person activities, while in Sierra Leone (Liedholm and Chuta, 1976), the figure was 42 percent. Such findings indicate that most small-scale industrial firms in sub-Saharan Africa are tiny. In view of their large numbers and generally low incomes (see Chuta and Liedholm, 1985), they constitute a potentially important target group for policy-makers concerned with the poor.

OWNERSHIP

The available evidence indicates that the overwhelming majority of small firms are organized as sole proprietorships. In Nigeria (Aluko, et al., 1972), Sierra Leone (Chuta and Liedholm, 1985), and Burkina Faso (Chuta and Wilcox, 1982), for example, over 97 percent of the small firms are set up in this fashion. Female sole proprietors dominate certain small industries in a number of countries, such as beer brewing in Burkina Faso (Chuta and Wilcox, 1982), Botswana (Haggblade, 1984), and Ghana (Steel, 1981), gara dyeing in Sierra Leone (Chuta and Liedholm, 1985), and clothing production in Ghana. There are a few limited liability companies, partnerships, and cooperatives, but almost no small enterprises in the public sector. Indeed, the vast majority of the private industrial establishments in sub-Saharan Africa are small scale.

LABOR AND CAPITAL

A review of the available data, which is summarized in Table 11.1, indicates that hired labor is generally a minor component of the labor force in small enterprises. An interesting finding is that apprentices play a dominant role in parts of West Africa (Nigeria, Ghana, and Sierra Leone), but are quite minor elements of the labor force in East

TABLE 11.1
LABOR FORCE CHARACTERISTICS OF SMALL-SCALE MANUFACTURING FIRMS
(PERCENTAGES)

Country (Area Covered)	Proprietors and Family Workers	Hired Workers	Apprentices
Sierra Leone entire country [1976]	41	17	42
Nigeria			
Western Region [1970]	39	11	50
Mid-West Region [1971]	30	7	63
Lagos [1971]	33	10	57
Ghana			
Kumasi [1975]	29	6	65
Accra [1972]	39	9	52
Burkina Faso			
Eastern ORD [1980]	94	2	4
Tanzania Dar and 20 townships [1967]	52	41	7
Kenya Rural industries (RIDC clients) [1977]	20	69	11

SOURCES: Sierra Leone: Liedholm and Chuta, 1976; Nigeria: Aluko, et al., 1972; Kumasi: Aryee, 1977; Accra: Steel, 1979; Burkina Faso: Chuta and Wilcox, 1982; Tanzania: Schadler, 1968; Kenya: Child, 1977.

Africa, where the tradition of an organized, indigenous apprentice-ship system is lacking. Proprietors and family workers play a key role in small-scale industries. Most entrepreneurs have little formal education, have learned their technical skills as apprentices in other small-scale enterprises, and lack extensive training in marketing, financing, or management (see Chuta and Liedholm, 1985).

The overwhelming source of capital, either for establishing or expanding firms, is personal savings, relatives, or retained earnings (Table 11.2). In these countries, less than 4 percent of the funds come from formal sources such as the commercial banking system or the government.

GROWTH

Although systematic information on industrial growth is limited, available evidence indicates that small-scale industrial activity in Africa has been increasing. Small-industry employment, for example, grew at a 6 percent annual rate during the 1960s in Ghana (Steel, 1981), and at the same rate over the 1974–80 period in Sierra Leone (Chuta and Liedholm, 1982). Whether small-scale industry has been increasing at a faster rate than large-scale is not clear. In Sierra Leone, small-scale employment grew at a faster rate than large-scale, but in Ghana, the opposite pattern occurred.[5] Nevertheless, since small-scale industries account for such a large portion of industrial employment, even if small producers were to grow at slower rates than the large, the absolute increases in small-scale employment could still be substantial. In Ghana during the 1960s, for example, small-scale industries absorbed five times as many workers as the large-scale firms, although the latter grew at a faster rate.

What kinds of small-scale enterprises are growing the most rapidly? By firm size, limited evidence from Sierra Leone and from other developing countries outside of Africa indicates that one-person firms are increasing the least rapidly (indeed, in Sierra Leone they were declining), while those in the 10 to 49 size group are growing the fastest.[6] The number of and employment in small firms appear to be growing the most rapidly in the urban areas. In Sierra Leone, for example, small-industry employment grew at a 6 percent annual rate from 1974 to 1980 in urban areas, but at less than half that rate in rural areas.

By enterprise types, food-related activities (such as baking and

TABLE 11.2

SOURCES OF FINANCE FOR INITIAL INVESTMENTS BY SMALL ENTERPRISES IN SOME AFRICAN COUNTRIES

(Percentage of Initial Investment by Source)

	Nigeria							
Source	Western State	Mid-West State	Kwara State	Lagos State	Tanzania	Sierra Leone	Uganda
Own savings	98	88	96	98	78	60	78
Relatives	2	10	[a]	2	15	20	—
Banks	[a]	[a]	2	[a]	1	1	1
Government	—	—	2	[a]	1	—	—
Money lenders	[a]	1	—	[a]	—	1	—
Other	—	1	—	—	6	18	21

[a]less than 1 percent

SOURCES: Nigeria: Aluko, et al., 1972; Tanzania: Schadler, 1968; Sierra Leone: Liedholm and Chuta, 1976; Uganda: Bosa, 1969.

milling), tailoring and dressmaking, furniture-making, and metal-working have generally grown rapidly, even after large-scale domestic factory production in these sub-sectors has begun. Moreover, several newer activities, such as bicycle, auto, and electrical repair, have grown especially rapidly. On the other hand, activities such as spinning and weaving, shoe and leather goods production, and pottery generally appear to have been declining in importance. These differential growth patterns are important in designing policies and programs directed toward small-scale enterprises.

DETERMINANTS OF THE ROLE OF SMALL-SCALE INDUSTRY

DEMAND PROSPECTS

What is the major source of demand for the products of small-scale industry in sub-Saharan Africa? The overwhelming bulk of products made in small firms are simple consumer goods that cater primarily to the needs of relatively low income urban and rural households. Consequently, a key issue is whether the demand for these products increases as local incomes increase. Most entrepreneurial surveys in Africa indicate that lack of demand is an important constraint facing most small firms. Although some have argued that these types of products are inferior (i.e., demand for them would decline as incomes increase), the few empirical studies indicate that there is a strong, positive relationship between local income and demand for small-scale industry products.

In Sierra Leone, for example, King and Byerlee (1978), on the basis of their pioneering survey and analysis of rural expenditures, reported that an income increase of 10 percent would increase the demand for the products of small-scale firms by almost 9 percent. Consequently, the growth of demand for small-scale industry products would appear to be closely linked to corresponding increases in household incomes, particularly among the rural and low-income segments of the population.

Are there important sources of demand for small-industry products that stem from their backward and forward production linkages with other segments of the economy? In general, these sources of demand appear to be less developed in sub-Saharan Africa than in other parts of the developing world. The strongest of these production linkages in sub-Saharan Africa, however, are found in the agricultural sector, where the processing of several crops, such as rice and oil palm in West Africa (see Spencer, et al., 1976, and Miller, 1965), and the production of implements for traditional agriculture (see Chuta and Liedholm, 1985) are frequently undertaken by small-scale firms. Production linkages with large-scale industry appear particularly weak in sub-Saharan Africa; very few sub-contracting relationships between large and small industrial firms appear to have been developed as yet.

Further, foreign demand for small-industry products is relatively small, limited to a few specialty products such as gara-dyed cloth from Sierra Leone (Chuta and Liedholm, 1985) and baskets from Botswana (Haggblade, 1984).

SUPPLY FACTORS

Small-scale industries are generally more labor intensive than their larger-scale counterparts. Since in sub-Saharan Africa, capital and foreign exchange are relatively scarce, and labor, particularly unskilled, is relatively abundant, those firms that generate more employment per unit of capital would appear to represent activities or techniques most appropriate to the country's factor endowments. Both aggregate and industry-specific data consistently show that small firms in sub-Saharan Africa generate more employment per unit of scarce capital than their larger-scale counterparts (see Chuta and Liedholm, 1979, and Page and Steel, 1984).

A key related issue is whether these same labor-intensive small-scale firms use the scarce factor of capital more effectively than their larger-scale counterparts. Aggregate data are limited and do not show consistent results. A few industry-specific studies have been completed in which firms in the same industry are grouped together. The findings from these studies indicate that small-scale firms in these industries generate more output per unit of scarce capital than their larger-scale counterparts.

Do these same small enterprises also generate a higher rate of "economic profit" than their larger-scale counterparts? The economic rate of return to capital, a measure that reflects profit when all inputs including family labor and capital are valued at their opportunity cost, may be a better measure of economic efficiency or total factor productivity than the output-capital ratio, which assumes that labor and other factor inputs have a "shadow price" of zero. Although economic profitability data are limited, the available results are consistent with the previous capital productivity findings: small-scale firms generated higher "economic" rates of return to capital than their larger-scale industrial counterparts. While not conclusive, these findings do indicate that in several lines of activity, small-scale industries are economically efficient.

POLICY AND PROJECT ISSUES

The preceding discussion makes clear that small enterprises are widespread and diverse in sub-Saharan African economies and that they are apparently quite efficient in their use of resources. In view of their potential contribution to future growth in income and employment, they should be the target of policy and project-focused attention from African governments and donors. A focus on small producers also corresponds with the U.S. Agency for International Development's current interest in private enterprise, one of the "four pillars" of emphasis in current aid programs.

However, questions arise concerning the design and implementation of policies and projects to support the growth of small producers. In this section, we make a distinction between policies which are designed to affect broad classes of producers on the one hand, and projects which are based on a patron-client relationship to provide assistance to particular designated firms, on the other. For each of these, it is helpful to separate policies and projects that operate on the "supply side" (i.e., which focus on the availability of inputs and production conditions), as distinct from those whose major focus is on demand considerations.

POLICIES

Industrialization was a major development goal in virtually all sub-Saharan African countries in the immediate post-independence period. In large measure, this meant an emphasis on large-scale firms, generally using the most modern technology with a high level of capital intensity and an import substitution focus (see Ewing, 1968). This approach subsequently came under attack on two related counts: it often involved considerable economic inefficiency in resource use; and it led to only minimum absorption of labor in the manufacturing sector (see Frank, 1968, and Morawetz, 1974). The result was a widespread disillusionment with large-scale industrialization as a central focus for development policy.

This disillusionment also led to a renewed interest in exploring the possibilities of industrialization through small enterprises. While most governments in sub-Saharan Africa have stated that they favor and support the growth of small producers (see, for example, OAU, 1982), there are only few policies that might be considered as directly supportive of the growth of small firms. In fact, the most pervasive impact of current government policies on small producers arises from their unintended side-effects. In large measure, the central impact of these policies on small producers is negative, operating in ways which discriminate against them rather than encouraging their development. First, a considerable amount of assistance is provided to large producers through policies that are restricted in their design and specification. A typical example is the Development Ordinance enacted in Sierra Leone in 1960, which gave income tax holidays and import duty exemptions to firms planning to invest $50,000 or more in plant and equipment, but no comparable assistance to smaller firms. (Chuta and Liedholm, 1985).

Second, even for policies which in principle apply equally to all types of enterprises, implementation is often undertaken in such a way as to have strongly differential impacts on producers of different types and sizes. In Rwanda, for example, small enterprises generally do not import their inputs directly, but buy them from local importers, who are subject to higher tariff rates. In a similar way, in other countries, small firms find it difficult if not impossible to act as suppliers to the government, since the procurement packages are too large and there are no provisions for partitioning of contracts. In this situation, the most important first step in instituting a policy regime supportive of small enterprise growth is to eliminate the existing policy biases against the small producer.

SUPPLY SIDE POLICY ISSUES

There are a number of different policy areas that concern the availability and costs of inputs and related questions pertaining to the production process. The first of these relates to credit. Interest rate ceilings are an important area where policies have a major impact on small enterprises. Studies suggest that it generally costs more per dollar lent to process loans to small compared to large borrowers; risks of default may also be higher than for more established firms. In such a situation, interest rate ceilings may make it unprofitable for financial institutions to lend to small producers at all. The result is that small enterprises are often forced to turn for their credit needs to informal sources that generally charge much higher interest rates.

In Sierra Leone, for example, the maximum official interest rate in 1974 was 12 percent, but the informal market rate was over 160 percent (Byerlee et al., 1983). Official interest rate ceilings in Africa generally run from 10 to 20 percent, while informal rates frequently are 100 percent or more (see Chuta and Liedholm, 1979). Therefore, efforts to protect small borrowers from bearing the full costs of their credit needs means that they are forced to rely on even higher cost alternative credit channels.

The policy implications here are straightforward. It is important to work toward the elimination of interest rate ceilings as a move toward ensuring that interest rates more closely approximate the opportunity costs of capital for small borrowers.

Second, small producers often find themselves at a disadvantage in access to foreign exchange. Obtaining an import license often requires skills and contacts with government bureaucracies which small firms do not have. Beyond this, tariff rates are generally set in a decision-making context based on a response to pressures; small firms often find that they do not have the requisite influence. In the case of tariffs on textile machinery in Sierra Leone, for example, large garment producers were covered by the country's industrial incentive package and were able to import their machines duty-free; small tailors, by contrast, found that the sewing machine, their basic capital input, was classified as a luxury consumer good and taxed accordingly with no duty relief. Similarly, dyes used in large-scale textile firms were admitted duty-free, while the dyes used in the making of gara cloth were subject to the full import tariff (Chuta and Liedholm, 1985). Such differential treatment of large and small firms with respect to foreign exchange access and tariffs should be eliminated.

As a third supply-side policy issue, governments in many countries exercise extensive control over the distribution of industrial inputs. This may reflect a suspicion of unscrupulous merchants and their excessive mark-ups or it may be a part of a policy aimed at the control and regulation of supplies of imported inputs. There is often a bias in favor of the larger producers in the implementation of such controls.

Unless the government makes a conscious effort to ensure that these inputs are equally available to smaller firms, the larger producers will generally end up benefiting from the controlled markets. These problems arise most clearly in relation to imported inputs handled by public sector distribution systems; they also appear for local products distributed through public sector channels. In both cases, the most common picture involves unequal access to inputs between the large and small users. The most effective way of removing this bias is to work toward a system based on reduced governmental control and intervention in the distribution system.

A fourth area of concern relates to governmental rules and regulations. There has been considerable interest in exploring the position of a category of small producers referred to as the "informal sector" in Africa. While we have not found this categorization to be particularly helpful, it has one important characteristic related to government regulations (Page, 1979). In many ways, small producers fall outside government assistance programs, but also outside taxation, regulation, and control mechanisms. In some cases, the laws explicitly state that they do not apply to small producers (small firms are not required to obtain certain kinds of licenses, to obey certain labor regulations, or to pay certain types of taxes). In many other cases, however, the laws are written as if they apply to all producers regardless of size. This is often the case even when all agree that enforcing the laws for very small producers is quite unrealistic.

Stating the law in broad terms but then interpreting it more restrictively has not only bred contempt of the law, but has also exposed small producers to threats that unless they "pay off" the appropriate officials, the law in question will be put into effect against them with the risk that they can be put out of business. Frequently, the implementation of such laws for small producers is highly arbitrary and erratic, making it virtually impossible to engage in sensible business planning. Industrial regulations should be screened carefully to ensure that there is a workable and equitable way of implementing them for small producers or that these small producers are explicitly exempted from coverage.

DEMAND SIDE POLICY ISSUES

Numerous studies have made clear that perhaps the single most important constraint facing small producers, particularly in the rural areas, is the problem of finding markets for their output. Many of these producers sell only in local or regional markets. Conversely, a significant share of the low-cost consumer goods sold in such rural markets are produced by small enterprises located in the same region. This means that policies supportive of increasing income in rural areas will have significant multiplier effects through expanding demand for the output of small manufacturers. Probably the most important set of policies for the encouragement of small manufacturers particularly in rural areas concerns the expansion and equitable distribution of agricultural incomes. Policies slanted against agricultural development lead not only to a stagnant agricultural sector, but also to stagnant demand for products of rural small manufacturers.

PROJECTS

Until recently, most of the attention of African governments and donor agencies on small enterprise development has been focused not on the overall policies that affect small businesses generally, but on targeted projects or programs that involve some form of patron-client relationship with individual establishments. In the 1950s and early 1960s, most of these projects in Africa focused on the provision of an integrated package of inputs to a relatively limited number of "modern" small businesses, following the "Indian model" developed and applied earlier in Asia and Latin America by the Stanford Research Institute and the Ford Foundation (see Staley and Morse, 1965).

After a hiatus of about a decade, interest in small industry in sub-Saharan Africa reemerged under the guise of appropriate technology and the informal sector. Currently, most of this interest surrounds firms at the lower end of the size spectrum, typically with a rural orientation and involving subsidized assistance for a small minority of producers. Perhaps reflecting the normal lag between theory and practice, however, many projects are still designed on the earlier model, with relatively high cost assistance being provided to a relatively small number of firms.

SUPPLY SIDE PROJECTS: CREDIT AND TECHNICAL ASSISTANCE

In recent years, credit projects have been the most common method of providing direct assistance to individual small enterprises in sub-Saharan Africa. These programs have been designed to overcome small firms' lack of access to formal credit sources (Table 11.2)—the greatest "perceived" constraint as viewed by the producers themselves. A number of countries in sub-Saharan Africa, such as Cameroon, Zambia, and Kenya, have designed special credit programs aimed specifically at the small producers (Kilby and D'Zmura, 1985). Very often, though, they have been directed toward the top end of the small enterprise sector, leaving the smaller producers with limited access to institutional credit. These programs are often based on a tranche of funds from outside donors lent to a certain category of borrowers at subsidized interest rates. These below-cost interest rates also raise the potential danger of spreading to small producers the same perverse excessive capital intensity which has often characterized the larger firms. They also make it unlikely that local funding agencies will step in to continue this credit flow when external assistance is no longer available.

Only a few of these credit projects in sub-Saharan Africa have been evaluated. It is frequently argued, however, that the administrative costs and risks of lending are much higher for small than for large firms (see World Bank, 1978). Concern is also expressed regarding the extent of small industry's demand for credit and the effectiveness of the delivery channels. Two recent reviews of several small industry credit schemes such as the Partners for Productivity Rural Enterprise Development Project in Burkina Faso indicate that several have been successful, generating benefit-cost ratios consistently above one, and frequently with administrative costs and arrears rates below 10 percent of the loan value (Kilby and D'Zmura, 1985, and Liedholm, 1985).

Most of the successful projects have some common characteristics that should be considered when designing new schemes. First, they have primarily provided working capital rather than the fixed capital that is the focus of most lending schemes,[7] consistent with the findings of most recent small industry studies that point to the lack of working capital as a primary financial constraint facing most small-scale firms.

Second, the delivery mechanisms of these successful credit projects differ markedly from the standard credit schemes. Loans are screened on the basis of character rather than on project feasibility and/or collateral. Moreover, the institutions are locally based with decentralized decision-making; the initial loans are small for short periods; and loan volume per loan officer is high. Finally, interest rates are high enough to cover operating expenses including the cost of funds. In several countries, formal credit institutions, including commercial banks, have been able to modify their loan procedures to meet these characteristics.

Two steps may be taken to encourage formal sector financial institutions to lend to small firms. One would be to pay a share of the administrative costs for commercial banks or other financial institutions, and provide loan guarantees. This could be done on a temporary basis, with the share of costs covered from outside and/or the magnitude of the guarantee declining over time. Second, consideration might be given to providing technical assistance to financial institutions to enable them to develop lower-cost screening mechanisms for lending to very small producers (Liedholm, 1985).

Technical and managerial assistance schemes have also been a popular method of providing direct project support to small firms in sub-Saharan Africa. As early as 1962, industrial development centers designed to provide technical and managerial assistance to small businesses were established in Zaria and Owerri, Nigeria, with USAID assistance. Similar centers were subsequently established in many other African countries, including Ghana, Botswana, Tanzania, and Kenya (Livingston, 1977). Although there have been a few evaluations of individual centralized assistance centers (see, for example, Hawbacker and Turner, 1972), there has not yet been a systematic analysis of their experiences or of the effectiveness of technical assistance schemes for sub-Saharan Africa. It is frequently argued, however, that business' demand for such services is very small.[8] Another often-heard criticism is that such programs have ended up concentrating a large volume of resources on a relatively limited clientele and that their delivery costs per client are therefore unduly high (see Kilby, 1982).

A review of a number of projects in sub-Saharan Africa makes it possible to isolate several common characteristics that seem to accompany successful technical assistance activities. First, these projects tend to be industry- and task-specific, such as the highly regarded training program in Botswana that imparted joinery skills to carpenters to enable them to produce coffins for the local markets (Haggblade, 1982). Second, these projects addressed situations where only a single "missing ingredient" needed to be supplied to the firm rather than an array of ingredients.[9]

The Botswana mud oven training course, which was designed to teach women to make mud ovens and bake bread for sale, provides a graphic example. The women in the scheme who previously had baked other products for sale were able to increase their incomes substantially, while those women without any prior commercial baking experience failed because there were too many "missing ingredients" (Haggblade, 1982). Projects assisting existing firms are therefore more likely to be successful than those that attempt to establish new firms.

Third, before successful projects were launched, prior surveys of industries had been undertaken to uncover the demand for the activity and the number and type of "missing ingredients." Such surveys are important because evidence is accumulating that the constraints facing small-scale industries in sub-Saharan Africa vary significantly from country to country and from industry to industry (see Chuta and Liedholm, 1979).

Finally, successful projects tend to be built upon proven existing institutions. Although these may often be formal institutions, existing informal institutions should not be overlooked. The apprenticeship system is an example of an informal institution that can provide a low-cost alternative for the delivery of technical and management assistance to small firms in sub-Saharan Africa. One of the striking features of the labor market in West Africa, illustrated in Table 11.1, concerns the central role of the apprenticeship system in the training of workers in small enterprises. The contrast with East Africa (as well as with most other countries of the world) is quite marked. Thus in East Africa, government training programs play a particularly important role in supplying skilled personnel to the small enterprise sector.

Care is needed to ensure that training programs are designed with the needs of smaller producers in mind. Beyond this, the expansion of apprenticeship systems in East and West Africa should be explored. A comparison of apprenticeship systems and government vocational training programs demonstrates that the former can be far more effective—and particularly more cost-effective (Mabawonku, 1979). Policies aimed at encouraging the expansion of apprenticeship systems might include rewarding their graduates in public and private sector hiring practices; regularizing the terms of service; and recognizing the implications of their activities (i.e., those who provide the training cannot always capture its benefits, since trained workers are free to move to a different employer). Other types of training programs might also be instituted through the apprentice-ship system, particularly to help develop managerial skills among small producers.

In a number of African countries, a key aspect of small enterprise development policy has centered around industrial estates, provid-ing construction of sheds with basic utilities which are then rented or sold to small enterprises. Two arguments have been advanced to justify the construction of such facilities. First, currently available space with the required utilities is inadequate; in some cases, this is explained in terms of problems of establishment of clear land titles. Second, grouping firms together in such an estate makes it possible to provide common trading programs and facilities, such as machine shops, (i.e., various types of industrial extension services.)

While these arguments sound convincing, in practice most indus-trial estates have proven to be an expensive means of subsidizing the work-space costs of a limited number of existing enterprises (see, for example, Kilby, 1982). They have also been ineffective in facilitating the development of new firms. For the firms they do help, their assistance is high cost, involving a wide range of assistance, much of which will not be needed by the client firms. In general, industrial estates have not proven to be effective channels for providing assist-ance to small enterprises in sub-Saharan Africa.

DEMAND-SIDE PROJECTS: MARKETING ASSISTANCE

One common characteristic of small producers in Africa and else-where is that they are often more skilled in production than in prod-uct design and marketing. As a result, they often produce standard-ized products for sale in local markets that may be growing only slowly. In such situations, an appropriate focus would be to assist small producers to establish more effective links to outside markets. This could be done through sub-contracting arrangements, either with larger manufacturers or with merchants.

Sub-contracting arrangements among producers are said to be rel-atively rare in Africa, although arrangements based on contracts be-tween small producers and merchants or traders can be found in some African countries, often for the marketing of craft products. An excellent example is Botswanacraft, which in the 1970s provided the single missing marketing link that was needed to support the com-mercial production of basketmaking in the rural areas (see Haggblade, 1982). Where they are effectively carried out, such contract production and sub-contracting systems can play an important role in establishing linkages between isolated producers and more dynamic markets. Consideration should be given to exploring ways of expanding the nascent role of sub-contracting in sub-Saharan Africa (Mead, 1985).

IMPLICATIONS FOR AFRICAN
GOVERNMENTS AND DONOR AGENCIES

Small enterprises are of considerable importance as sources of employment and income in sub-Saharan Africa today. This importance is likely to increase over time, as population growth puts strains on available cultivable land, and as the number of people seeking work outside agriculture exceeds the absorptive capacity of large-scale industrial and service enterprises. This discussion has suggested a number of measures to facilitate the expansion of small enterprises and to channel this expansion in productive directions.

Three major conclusions can be drawn concerning small enterprise policies, the ways these policies currently impinge on small producers, and the need for more effective policy support in the future. The first is that the impact of current policies on this group of enterprises has generally been negative, resulting in discrimination against small producers and in favor of their larger-scale and better-connected competitors. This discrimination arises both from the ways in which laws are written and the ways they are implemented. African governments and donor agencies need to better understand the ways in which existing policies operate in practice, with the aim of eliminating this discrimination and establishing more equal competitive conditions for large and small enterprises.

The second major conclusion is that the key constraint hindering the growth of small enterprises, particularly in rural areas, is related to a deficiency of demand. The government's overall development policies can play a key role in overcoming this deficiency. In particular, agricultural policies aimed at a rapid growth of rural incomes are important not only in their own right, but also because they contribute in a major way to the growth potential of non-agricultural, rural small enterprises.

Efforts to establish pricing systems that provide incentives to farmers to increase their output, to encourage the development of effective marketing systems for selling their products, and to institute agrarian reform leading to an equitable sharing of the benefits of increasing agricultural output can all contribute in important ways to the potential for growth among small non-agricultural producers.

The third major point, closely related to the previous two, involves a recognition that, in thinking about the effects of policies on small producers, African governments and donor agencies must adopt a comprehensive view, looking far beyond the traditional sphere of industrial policy to agricultural pricing and income policies and the general foreign exchange regime of the country.

Projects or client-specific programs in sub-Saharan Africa have primarily focused on eliminating or reducing supply constraints. African governments and donor agencies have a useful continuing role in this area. The majority of projects directed at the support of small enterprises have been in the area of credit, partly reflecting the fact that many small enterprise projects are best designed as small projects, requiring only limited amounts of funding. However, donors are often under pressure to "move money," and one of the few ways of doing so in significant volume is through concentration on credit activities.

A review of successful credit projects suggests the following guidelines to facilitate the growth of small enterprises in sub-Saharan Africa as elsewhere in the world: concentrating on working capital rather than fixed capital; screening of loans based on the character of the applicant rather than the characteristic of the project; decentralizing decision-making to local institutions and local individuals; and granting loans in small amounts, for short periods, to encourage and facilitate high repayment rates.

Among the key findings concerning small enterprise projects in areas other than credit, the following may be singled out as being of primary importance in the design and implementation of future projects. First, useful projects will generally be carefully targeted to a limited range of enterprises, probably in one or a few closely related industries. Second, projects are more likely to succeed if they can be targeted to deal with one or a limited range of missing components, rather introducing a complex range of changes all at once. Third, it is generally advisable to start from existing institutions, rather than attempting to begin from scratch with a new locus and staff. Fourth, projects aimed at establishing more effective links between dispersed producers and more dynamic and often more distant markets can provide useful contributions. Fifth, there is a need for careful field research to determine the needs of small producers in particular situations so that projects are effectively targeted.

POLICY REFORM AND IMPLEMENTATION ISSUES

The process of policy reform is a complex one, involving pressure groups and compromises which are difficult for an outsider to understand, much less lead. Experience suggests some rules about the most effective way of working toward policy change. First, policy change is generally a long-term process. Almost any change will mean that some groups benefit while others lose. Efforts to move things too rapidly can cause great social turmoil, during which all possibilities of improvement may be frozen.

Second, the most effective route to policy reform often involves participation by actual and potential policy-makers in analyses of the ways in which policy currently works and how alternative policy configurations might operate. Well-focused policy-oriented studies can provide important insights into the ways policies are currently working, thereby supplying a firmer base of understanding for those who wish to effect changes. With judicious governmental policies and carefully formulated direct assistance measures, the already sizeable contribution of small-scale industries to sub-Saharan African development can be further enhanced.

NOTES

1. For a review of existing studies, see Liedholm (1973), Page (1979), and Page and Steel (1984).

2. Mining, construction, trading, and transport are not included in this review.

3. The UN definition of rural localities with fewer than 20,000 inhabitants is used in this chapter. The conclusions do not change markedly if other definitions are used.

4. Rural manufacturing employment had been underestimated in Sierra Leone by almost one-half (Liedholm and Chuta, 1976).

5. In Tanzania, it appeared that small industry's share of industrial output fell from 1966 to 1974 (Wynne-Roberts, 1980).

6. In Sierra Leone, over the period 1974–80, one-person firms were declining at a 4 percent annual rate; firms in the 2 to 9 workers category increased at a 3.5 percent annual rate; while those firms with from 10 to 49 workers increased at a 12.7 percent annual rate (Chuta and Liedholm, 1982).

7. The emphasis on fixed capital stems from aid donors' interest in lending schemes with high foreign exchange components, an orientation of academic economists toward fixed assets, and a paucity of requisite statistics.

8. See, for example, Page and Steel(1984) and Liedholm and Chuta(1976) and the Economic Commission for Africa (1982), which states that "it must be kept in mind that most small-scale enterprises are unaware of the need for these services."

9. Peter Kilby (1982) developed this notion when reviewing ILO/UNDP small-enterprise projects worldwide.

REFERENCES

Aluko, S. A., O. A. Oguntoye and Y. A. O. Afonja. 1972. *Small Scale Industries: Western State Nigeria*. Ile-Ife: Industrial Research Unit, University of Ife.

Aryee, George. 1976. "The Inter-Relationships Between the Formal Sector and the Informal Manufacturing Sector in Kumasi, Ghana." Geneva: ILO.

Bosa, George R. 1969. *The Financing of Small Scale Enterprises in Uganda*. Nairobi: Oxford University Press.

Byerlee, D., Carl Eicher, Carl Liedholm, and D. Spencer. 1983. "Employment-Output Conflicts, Factor Price Distortions, and Choice of Techniques: Empirical Evidence from Sierra Leone." *Economic Development and Cultural Change* 31(2): 315–36.

Child, Frank C. 1977. *Small Scale Rural Industry in Kenya*. Los Angeles: UCLA, African Studies Center, Occasional Paper No. 17.

Chuta, E. and Carl Liedholm. 1979. "Rural Non-Farm Employment: A Review of the State of the Art." East Lansing: Michigan State University, MSU Rural Development Paper No. 4.

Chuta, E. and Carl Liedholm. 1982. "Employment Growth and Change in Sierra Leone Small-Scale Industry, 1974–80." *International Labour Review*. 121(1) (January–February): 101–13.

Chuta, E. and Carl Liedholm. 1985. *Employment and Growth in Small-Scale Industry: Empirical Evidence from Sierra Leone*. London: Macmillan Co.

Chuta, E. and D. Wilcox. 1982. "Employment in Rural Industries in Eastern Upper Volta." *International Labour Review*. 121(1) (July–August): 455–68.

Economic Commission for Africa. 1982. *Programme for the Industrial Development Decade for Africa*. New York: ECA/OAU/UNIDO.

Ethiopia, Government of. 1980. *Statistical Abstract, 1980*. Addis Ababa: Central Statistics Office.

Ewing, A. F. 1968. *Industry in Africa*. London: Oxford University Press.

Frank, Charles. 1968. "Urban Unemployment and Economic Growth in Africa." *Oxford Economic Papers*. 20(2) (July): 250–74.

Ghana, Government of. 1965. *Area Sampling Survey of Small Manufacturing Establishments-1963*. Accra, Ghana: Central Bureau of Statistics.

Haggblade, Steve. 1982. *Rural Industrial Officers' Handbook*. Volume II, District Planning Services, Ministry of Commerce and Industry, Gaborone, Botswana.

Haggblade, Steve. 1984. "The Shabeen Queen." Ph.D. dissertation, Department of Economics, Michigan State University.

Hawbacker, George and H. Turner. 1972. "Developing Small Industries: A Case Study of AID Assistance in Nigeria, 1962–1971." Washington, D.C.: AID.

Kilby, Peter. 1982. "Small Scale Industry in Kenya." East Lansing: Michigan State University, MSU Rural Development Paper #20.

Kilby, Peter and John D'Zmura. 1985. "Searching for Benefits," AID Evaluation Special Study No. 28, Washington, D.C.: USAID.

King, Robert and D. Byerlee. 1978. "Factor Intensities and Locational Linkages of Rural Consumption Patterns in Sierra Leone." *American Journal of Agricultural Economics* 60, (2): 197–201.

Liedholm, Carl. 1973. "Research on Employment in the Rural Nonfarm Sector in Africa." East Lansing: Michigan State University, African Rural Employment Paper No. 5.

Liedholm, Carl. 1985. "Small Scale Credit Schemes: Administrative Costs and the Role of Inventory Norms." East Lansing: Michigan State University, MSU International Development Working Paper (forthcoming).

Liedholm, Carl and Enyinna Chuta. 1976. "The Economics of Rural and Urban Small Scale Industries in Sierra Leone." East Lansing: Michigan State University, African Rural Economy Paper No. 14.

Liedholm, Carl and Donald C. Mead. 1985. "Small Scale Enterprises in Developing Countries: A Review of the State of the Art" (draft).

Livingston, Ian. 1977. "An Evaluation of Kenya's Rural Industrial Development Programme." *Journal of Modern African Studies* 15: 494–504.

Mabawonku, Adewale. 1979. "An Economic Evaluation of Apprenticeship Training in Western Nigerian Small Scale Industries." East Lansing: Michigan State University, African Rural Economy Paper No. 17.

Mead, Donald C. 1985. "Subcontracting Systems and Assistance Programs: Opportunities for Intervention." East Lansing: Michigan State University, MSU International Development Paper (forthcoming).

Miller, W. L. 1965. "An Economic Analysis of Oil Palm Fruit Processing in Eastern Nigeria." Ph.D. dissertation, Michigan State University.

Morawetz, D. 1974. "Employment Implications of Industrialization in Developing Countries: A Survey." *Economic Journal* (84): 491–592.

Norcliffe, G. B. and Freeman. 1980. "Non-farm Activities in Market Centers of Central Province, Kenya." *Canadian Journal of African Studies* 14(3): 503–17.

Organization of African Unity. 1980. *Lagos Plan of Action for the Economic Development of Africa, 1980 to 2000*. Addis Ababa: OAU.

Page, John. 1979. "Small Enterprise in African Development: A Survey." Staff Working Paper No. 363. Washington, D.C.: The World Bank.

Page, J. and W. Steel. 1984. *Small Enterprise Development: Economic Issues from*

African Experience. Technical Paper No. 26. Washington, D.C.: The World Bank.

Spencer, Dunstan, I. May Parker, and Frank Rose. 1976. "Employment Efficiency and Income in the Rice Processing Industry in Sierra Leone." East Lansing, Michigan: Michigan State University, African Rural Employment Paper No. 15.

Staley, Eugene and Richard Morse. 1965. *Modern Small Industry for Developing Countries*. New York: McGraw-Hill.

Steel, William F. 1977. *Small-Scale Employment and Production in Developing Countries: Evidence from Ghana*. New York: Praeger Publishers.

Steel, William F. 1979. "The Urban Artisanal Sector in Ghana and the Cameroon: Comparison of Structure and Policy Problems." *Journal of Modern African Studies* 17(2): 271–84.

Steel, William F. 1981. "Female and Small-Scale Employment Under Modernization in Ghana." *Economic Development and Cultural Change* 30(1) (October): 153–67.

World Bank. 1978. "Employment and Development in Small Enterprises." Washington, D.C.: The World Bank.

Wynne-Roberts, C. R. 1980. "Small Scale Industry Development in Sub-Saharan Africa." Washington, D.C.: The World Bank (mimeo).

CHAPTER TWELVE

Private Investment and African Economic Policy

Niles E. Helmboldt, Tina West, and Benjamin H. Hardy

The achievement of self-sustained economic development in Africa depends on the policy decisions of its governments. The policies of the United States or any other outside party, although they can be a help or hindrance to development, are secondary. Without an appropriate, consistent set of economic policies that favor the growth of local, private production to meet local and external demand, African governments will find only temporary escape from the conditions that constitute the African economic crisis. Harnessing the energies of the private sector to help Africa achieve its development objectives seems to be the appropriate strategy.

The choice of a particular development strategy, particularly one as heavily laden with ideological connotations as the free market, is a political decision. This chapter does not presume to direct national leaders on how to decide these issues. However, given recent efforts of a number of governments to revitalize their economies—including giving a larger role to the free market—we can point to various practical steps that can increase the benefits and perhaps diminish the ills of this approach.

The focus of this chapter is on actions African governments can take to achieve their goal of self-sustained growth. Current policies that constrict the growth of the domestic private sector seem an easier obstacle to address than those presented by the structure of international trade. This is not to deny that factors beyond the control of African governments—weather, the slow growth of world trade, and weak commodity prices—have played a large role in causing their economic problems. While African officials have been calling for the industrialized countries to create a more favorable trading environment, current trends of protectionism and political conservatism in the United States and elsewhere make such action unlikely in the near future.

Our analytical schema addresses near-term prospects—two to four years—for investment in Africa, mobilized both domestically and from abroad. We make three basic points. First, little new capital, especially foreign private capital, will be available for Africa during this period, for reasons largely related to African government policies. Therefore, reforms in these policies may help make Africa more attractive to capital investors, particularly over the medium to longer term.

Second, even in the absence of new capital, Africa can begin to recover and to generate new economic development because development does not depend on capital alone. The apparent disarray of African economies often blinds us to existing resources both in the modern and the traditional sectors. Investments already made in manufacturing and commercial agriculture need only foreign exchange for rehabilitation, or, in many cases, removal of the controls and disincentives that currently limit productivity. Small farmers, small entrepreneurs in the informal sector, and small manufacturers already possess the capacity to increase production and the demand for goods exists.

While it is reasonable to assume that the private sector is the most significant source of investment capital, incentive structures in many African countries have not encouraged the private sector to take investment risks. Again, short-term policy reforms can produce salutary results quickly. Governments can stimulate production by reallocating resources to improve the productivity of their own capital investment and by removing some of the existing disincentives to private sector investment. They can also increase the private sector's access to foreign exchange.

The third point is addressed to the U.S. government and the international donor community, which can lend support to African governments in these efforts by their advice on policy and by standing ready to help in practical ways. If promotion of the private sector is not to become another development fad, donors must assist in African governments' efforts to resolve the political problems which can result from economic policy reform and with the pervasive problems of foreign exchange shortages. Structural adjustment will be achieved not only by advocating theories, but by devising creative solutions to practical problems.

THE SHORT-TERM INVESTMENT OUTLOOK

PRIVATE CAPITAL INFLOWS AND FOREIGN PRIVATE INVESTMENT

Unless Treasury Secretary James Baker's initiative is fully implemented, which now seems unlikely, external capital is unlikely to increase from any private source over the next several years, given changed institutional outlooks on the part of banks and multinationals and the investment climate to which African government policies have contributed.

The most authoritative projection of near-term external capital flows to sub-Saharan Africa is contained in the World Bank's *Toward Sustained Development in Sub-Saharan Africa*. Net capital inflows are forecasted to drop from an annual average of $10.8 billion during 1980–82 to $5 billion for 1985–87. Gross capital flows from official and private sources (excluding the IMF) remain roughly the same, at $8.9 billion and $4.2 billion, respectively, but debt amortization payments increase from $2.3 billion to $8 billion—$5 billion of which is owed to private sources.[1]

Although the gross figures imply that repayment of private loans is a major problem, most African countries rely far more on official grants and loans. Based on the data in the 1985 edition of *World Debt Tables*, at end-1983 official lending to 36 sub-Saharan countries made up more than 75 percent of total public or publicly guaranteed debt, including undisbursed debt.[2]

Private and official debt are roughly equal in only two countries, Benin and Congo, with only four countries more heavily indebted to private lenders: Gabon (67 percent), Ivory Coast (59 percent), Nigeria (80 percent), and Zimbabwe (64 percent). Private borrowings by these four countries amount to $20.6 billion, or 71 percent of the total of $29.2 billion in private external lending to sub-Saharan Africa. Similarly, debt service payments of these four countries constitute the bulk of repayments to private lenders—74 percent of the total due between 1985 and 1987. For the remaining countries, new inflows depend largely on their relationships with official lenders.

Our observation that new investment from the industrialized

countries is unlikely to increase substantially in the next few years is confirmed by available data on private sector investment. Although measuring the value of total foreign private sector investment is an inherently difficult process,[3] the OECD Development Assistance Committee (DAC) has compiled a time series that is reasonably consistent.[4] Direct investment by DAC members in sub-Saharan Africa (excluding South Africa) grew from approximately $4.9 billion in 1967 to $7.1 billion in current dollars in 1972—an average annual growth rate of 7.7 percent in nominal terms. By the end of 1981, investment totaled about $11.6 billion, and the annual rate of increase had slowed to 5.6 percent.

However, the average annual growth rate of investments in all developing countries between 1970 and 1981 was 10.7 percent, suggesting that DAC-member investment is increasing more slowly in sub-Saharan Africa than in other developing areas.[5] If these growth rates were adjusted for inflation, they would probably show very little increase in the value of DAC-member investment in Africa.

Investment in Africa from newly industrialized countries, particularly Brazil and India, is increasing more rapidly than that of DAC members. Brazilian companies have invested widely in Nigeria (telecommunications and ethanol) and in the Lusophone countries, while Indian companies have invested in paper and machine tool manufacturing in Kenya. Africa ranked second as a recipient of Indian foreign investment in 1980, according to data quoted in Wells (1983).[6]

The bulk of new investment from industrialized countries is coming from companies that already have long-term commitments in Africa—the 1983 Heinz purchase in Zimbabwe being one of several exceptions. Such companies are more likely to seek funding for new investments than those with no previous experience in Africa. African governments, leery of dishonest investors, can take some comfort in dealing with firms that have established track records. During good times, committed companies are likely to reinvest a significant portion of their profits. Goldsbrough (1985) reports that in a group of developing countries, reinvested earnings averaged 39 percent of recorded investment during 1973–1982, noting that over 50 percent of direct investment from the United States and the United Kingdom was in the form of reinvested earnings.[7]

Although these companies form a hardy band of long-term investors, many others have become disillusioned with their investments in Africa. The Japanese withdrawal from SODIMIZA—a joint copper mining venture with Zaire—and the closing of the American Motors assembly operation in Kenya are recent examples.

A potential source of investment, though not of foreign exchange, is blocked currency held by external private investors and trade creditors. Halting the legal repatriation of funds is a disincentive to new investors. However, a number of governments have already blocked repatriation of large sums, including dividends and short-term trade debt. This money, which the central bank usually declares to be temporarily nonconvertible, may remain blocked for many years. If governments can persuade foreign investors and debt holders to continue holding these blocked funds in local currency, however, the money can become a source of new investment.

While most foreign creditors and investors have no interest in using their blocked funds to invest in a country, others may consider the cost of waiting to be higher than the risks of investing. Several governments are designing incentives to encourage these companies, such as allowing access to the foreign exchange earned by new exports. Although if these investors undertake new projects, they will probably bring in only the minimum amount of additional foreign exchange needed for the project, the investments are otherwise similar to direct foreign investment projects.

By declaring that these foreign investments will be treated as new direct foreign investments, governments may enable investors to obtain insurance or other guarantees from their home country. In African countries where there is a bilateral investment agreement, American investors can obtain OPIC coverage on the same terms as new investment. The foreign government approval letter need only state that the investment from blocked funds will be treated as new investment.

DECLINING FOREIGN INVESTMENT:
CAUSES AND REMEDIES

There are a number of reasons why prospects for foreign capital inflows are poor today. African governments can address the internal problems more effectively than the external ones. New policies might well improve the investment climate and its attractiveness to foreign investors in particular. In the text below, we outline prescriptions for policy reform; they are, however, intended for governments that have already decided to increase the scope of the private sector in their economies.

EXTERNAL FACTORS

Bank Lending   Increased lending from private commercial banks is unlikely. After peaking at $8.6 billion in 1981, new commitments from private creditors dropped to $5 billion in 1983, according to the *World Debt Tables*.[8] Probably they declined further in 1984 and 1985.

Commercial banks are reluctant to lend to Africa for reasons not necessarily related to African economies. Major American banks with international portfolios are currently reviewing their exposures, particularly those in energy, agriculture, and other weak spots in the domestic economy, as well as in Latin America. Under these circumstances, they are not aggressively seeking new lending opportunities in developing countries. Lending within the United States is more profitable than it has been for some time thanks to a larger than usual spread between the prime rate and the cost of funds. A recent estimate shows that U.S. bank lending abroad dropped by $13 billion during 1984.[9] Reinforcing bankers' reluctance to add significantly to their Third World lending is the fear that it would send up a red flag to Wall Street financial analysts, adversely affecting bank stock prices. Given the poor profit performance of some of the largest banks over the past three years, analysts are now especially watchful.

Regional banks in the United States that participated in syndicated loans in the boom years are more unhappy about reschedulings than are the money-center banks that have long-term commitments to African markets. The regional banks would like to get their money out and stay out. By contrast, a few money-center banks are willing to maintain their exposures and will increase their lending again when African opportunities become relatively attractive. Among their clients are multinational companies, many of which are also in Africa for the long haul. By staying in Africa, these few money-center banks have remained close to opportunities for collateral business, such as deposits from customers and fees for letters of credit and funds transfers. However, both European and American banks are looking for guarantees from their export credit agencies or at least for the comfort of World Bank and IMF programs which impose financial discipline on creditor governments.

Private Investment   In a parallel change in institutional perceptions, multinational investors from industrialized countries are increasingly unwilling to set up operations in the low and middle-income developing countries if more prosperous and stable countries are available. Even if it is more expensive to locate and operate a plant in Australia, for example, rather than Jamaica, Thailand, or Kenya, many investors are taking the safer route.

For their part, Africans no longer have high expectations of foreign investment. Each side has been hurt by abuses of trust. International contractors have delivered shoddy products, including entire turnkey projects; corrupt or capricious African officials have milked contractors or thwarted programs. It will take time to undo this damage; investors who have been burned once will not clamor to return at the first sign of reform.

INTERNAL FACTORS

Investment Climate   Perceptions of high risk act as a barrier to new foreign investment and are based on the entire economic picture, especially the investment climate. For private investors, the sine qua non of their involvement is profitability as measured by return on capital. They perceive Africa not only as a place where business costs are high, but also as a relatively unpredictable environment.

Ultimately, the investment climate reflects investors' perceptions of the government's ability to maintain stable policies that allow viable, prudent investments to operate profitably. Such confidence is more a function of the government's reliability over time than its ideology; some socialist governments have excellent reputations for dealing fairly and effectively with foreign investors.

That the investment climate in African countries is a specific deterrent to foreign investment is clear from surveys of potential foreign investors in DAC-member countries. Baker (1983) estimated that as of 1982, American investment in sub-Saharan Africa totaled less than $6 billion—about 3 percent of total U.S. foreign investment.[10] Baker's survey of U.S. investors reveals that their attitudes toward African risk are shaped not only by structural and environmental factors, but also by more immediate, day-to-day operational problems.

She reports that investors who had decided not to invest in Africa gave six major reasons: markets were too small, the response of the host governments was too slow or requirements were too complicated, the ideology of the host country government seemed hostile to private investment, there were prospects for political instability, credit-worthiness (as indicated through mounting debt, a shortage of foreign exchange, sudden import bans) was lacking, and government intervention in the economy was excessive. It is significant that very few firms indicated that they were concerned with nationalization or expropriation. Instead, companies seem to realize that indigenization is likely to be undertaken by countries seeking greater control of their economy and that insurance can be obtained against nationalization. Hence, in evaluating political risk, "the trend is away from studying macro-political stability to studying a country's regulatory process and its likely choices."[11]

Baker also found that the complaints most frequently voiced by firms already in or planning to operate in Africa had to do with the inefficiency, capriciousness, and/or corruption of bureaucratic processes and government decision-making.[12] A crucial step toward improving the investment climate lies in streamlining government procedures where they touch upon routine relationships with business.

For example, some central banks have worsened their relations with private lenders and damaged their credit standings through slow, inefficient procedures, clerical mistakes, and what appears to lenders to be a reluctance to cooperate. A poor reputation with creditors decreases the ability to obtain loans on the lowest terms. In some countries therefore, central bank efforts to improve debt administration would yield large benefits at relatively modest cost.

Domestic investors also find arbitrary regulations a major obstacle. One successful African entrepreneur told us recently that half his time is spent dealing with government bureaucrats rather than on managing his operations. Uncertainty about changes in regulations limits the amount of investment he is willing to undertake.

Legal Climate   Investor confidence in the rule of law is perhaps the most important single determinant in any investment decision. Legal protection is one area in which the government's performance must match that of other countries if the nation wishes to compete successfully in attracting investors. It is in the government's interest to provide and adhere firmly to a legal code that provides fair and equitable treatment to all businesses. In particular, multinational firms invest widely throughout the industrial world where legal protections are routinely available; such firms expect developing countries to replicate that legal environment as closely as possible.

Unquestionably, the government has the right to demand that foreign and domestic businesses conform to its laws. However, investors compensate for uncertainty by increasing the threshold rate of return required to elicit a positive investment decision. In uncertain environments, they require high short-term profits that may not be in the country's long-term interest. The investor is as concerned with consistency of application as with the content of laws. A foreign investor can live with a wide range of "rules of the game," but prefers to locate a project in a country where arbitrary changes in economic or legal policies do not occur. They want to be assured that the government will treat them fairly, and they want a number of explicit legal guarantees. Among these are equitable and prompt compensation in case of nationalization; the same protection for patents, trademarks, and designs that industrial nations offer; equality before the law for domestic and foreign-owned firms; and clearly agreed upon processes for resolving disputes with the government.

The Investment Code   The legal system and governmental policies concerning private sector investment meet in the investment code. The investment code should clearly specify the laws with which the investor must comply—indigenization schedules, local equity provisions, local value added requirements, labor laws—so that the investor can include the cost of compliance in the calculation of expected profitability. As far as possible, the code should contain or identify clearly all the information the investor needs for these calculations, and should make clear what the government expects from the investor.

Both governments in search of foreign exchange inflows and investors looking for more certain profits may take actions that are not justified by their economic return. While highly desirable from the investor's point of view and cheap to grant on the government's part, protection from competition distorts the economy. Tariff exemptions encourage investment in capital-intensive, import-dependent enterprises. Attempts to compete with the financial incentives—such as tax holidays and free land—of other developing countries may raise costs to the government without attracting any more investment than market opportunities warrant already.

Baker and other scholars have found that foreign investors weigh the overall investment climate far more heavily than financial incentives in their decisions.[13] Surveys of investors over the past 30 years have consistently found that legal guarantees are more important than special financial incentives.[14] Guarantees of the investor's right to repatriate investment capital and dividends, interest on approved loans, and expatriate salaries are also major primary concerns.

Foreign vs. Domestic Investment African governments may be tempted to view these issues as relevant to only a small group of foreign actors whose role in the domestic economy is limited and who must be restrained in any case. What troubles us more than the slowdown in foreign investment is the slow growth of investment in manufacturing by African investors. While foreign investment has the drawback of using substantial amounts of foreign exchange, there are others as well, such as the use of inappropriately capital-intensive technology, or the difficulties of linking imported enterprises with the local economy. While foreign capital should not be discouraged, in many cases its contribution to development is not as substantial or permanent as the growth of the informal sector and increased domestic investment in light manufacturing would be. However, the same disincentives to investment that frustrate foreigners also discourage Africans.

REINVIGORATING AFRICAN PRODUCTION

We disagree with the African finance minister who recently said, "A developing country always finds itself in a vicious circle. There is no development without investment, no investment without equipment, and no equipment without getting indebted."[15] The implicit assumption is that development is imported and that it stops when the ability to borrow or attract equity investment is curtailed. This statement overlooks the potential for increased productivity that African economies already possess. African countries can begin moving now toward the Lagos Plan of Action goal of building self-reliance independent of massive foreign capital.

THE NEED FOR FOREIGN EXCHANGE

The most serious constraint today on the growth of the private sector is the lack of foreign exchange—needed less for new investment than to preserve the capacity to import essential goods for maintaining production. Without policy changes, the private sector appears unlikely to generate sufficient foreign exchange because of weak international demand for most of Africa's major exports, heavy debt service burdens, large food and fuel import bills, and a myriad of smaller bills for imported goods and services needed to keep the economy from deteriorating further.

The public sector continues to absorb the major share of foreign exchange. Over the years, governments, mainly through foreign borrowing and aid, have undertaken massive capital investment programs, many of which are perpetual foreign exchange drains, as they often rely heavily on imports for production and maintenance. These projects seldom produce exportable goods and services, thus generating no foreign exchange themselves. Some private investment projects share these characteristics, and although others provide net foreign exchange inflows, all make some demands on foreign exchange for dividends and loan repayments.

Both African governments and foreign investors have borrowed heavily abroad to finance projects. Only when projects generate foreign exchange through new exports or save it through import substitution is there a net foreign exchange gain. Certainly, inflows of direct foreign investment and foreign loans initially ease the balance of payments deficit, but their long-term benefits depend on the project's net foreign exchange effects, which take some time to be felt. Only if the project's foreign exchange earnings or savings exceed repatriated flows will it contribute toward a favorable balance of payments. On the other hand, where foreign borrowing fails to generate increased foreign exchange earnings, foreign exchange shortages are exacerbated.

If foreign exchange is insufficient, existing capital is underutilized. Factories that depend on imported raw materials or spare parts often operate at 10 to 20 percent of capacity or shut down altogether. Lack of imported agricultural inputs reduces yields and increases the difficulties of harvesting and processing crops. The continuing shortage of foreign exchange must cause a shake-out of those organizations most dependent on imports, although some public sector organizations performing vital economic and social functions will correctly be protected from market forces. For the private sector, governments can make access to foreign exchange the incentive to find local substitutes and to export. As has been demonstrated in Zambia, such an incentive increases both production and investment.

Improving access to foreign exchange can be the most powerful incentive currently available to governments to encourage investment. Zambia's provision of foreign exchange incentives over the last 18 months demonstrates the value of such an approach. Extremely limited since the end of the copper boom in 1975, the private sector's access to foreign exchange was expanded in July 1983, with the central bank's announcement that exporters of agricultural goods would be allowed to retain 50 percent of their foreign exchange earnings and use them for goods imported under valid import licenses. The government later extended the incentive to all exporters, except those of minerals. The private sector's response was a marked increase in activity; farmers found markets for fruit and vegetables in Europe and beef in other African countries. Manufacturers found new markets for textiles, uniforms, bicycles, and pottery in neighboring countries. Foreign-owned companies with large blocked local currency holdings began to search for profitable export-oriented investments in manufacturing and agricultural processing.

DEVELOPMENT WITHOUT FOREIGN CAPITAL

During the 1960s, many development economists assumed that scarcity of capital was the critical constraint to growth in developing countries.[16] However, countries that increased capital stocks without achieving much growth have demonstrated that the role of capital is more complex. In his classic article, "The Place of Capital in Economic Progress," Cairncross avers that "the biggest single influence on capital formation is market opportunity."[17] He suggests that rapid growth of investment and income can arise from the same set of favorable circumstances and that indeed growth in income can precede growth in investment.

The point is relevant to Africa today. Government economic policies that encourage production in the private sector can initiate growth. Productive units in the private sector include small farms, small enterprises in the informal sector, and larger, privately owned manufacturing, service, commercial agriculture, and agricultural processing firms. Under-used productive capacity in all segments of the private sector, combined with existing demand and fueled by increased agricultural incomes, could produce a fairly rapid increase in incomes and output. It should in turn encourage successful producers to expand in response to opportunities. African countries have succeeded in adding to both their physical and human capital stocks during the past 25 years; what is needed now is to make fuller use of them.

In Africa's present circumstances, the dearth of foreign investment capital need not preclude economic development. Economic development is measured not only by rising national income but also by increased capacity for self-sustained growth. Development is a process of augmenting the ability to add value, and it results from new combinations of existing natural resources, labor, capital, and ingenuity to produce needed goods and services. It is not a checklist of investment projects or heavy industries, and it cannot be bought.[18] While shortages of investment funds increase difficulties, they need not bring development to a stop.

If African governments encourage the productive sectors in their economies, working with rather than against them, development will take place. Private producers need consistent economic policies. These include realistic exchange rates that favor local production and exports over imports; positive real interest rates that ration scarce capital and encourage domestic savings; some immediate access to foreign exchange so that the lack of a $50 spare part does not shut down production for a month; and government regulations that promote open and competitive markets and minimize bureaucratic delay and arbitrary enforcements.

MOBILIZING DOMESTIC CAPITAL

Fostering existing productive capabilities in agriculture, the informal sector, and manufacturing involves a somewhat different set of governmental responsibilities. African governments have tried to shoulder the major responsibility not only for directing their economies toward long-range goals, but also for acting as the main engine of economic development. The Chinese have found that governments cannot afford to do it all, that centralized decision-making becomes inefficient, and that therefore it makes sense to harness private energies to help in the effort. Governments should encourage the growth of competitive markets in goods and services by reducing the number of state-owned monopolies, but they should retain (and in some cases strengthen) their role as arbiter of last resort on issues of economic power and justice.

Governments can see the effects of their economic policies in the behavior of their citizens. If it is more profitable to import than to produce locally, few citizens will invest in production. If trading produces a more secure and reliable income than manufacturing, most people will become traders. If it is more profitable to invest in real estate or abroad than in factories, farms, or services at home, money will flow into buildings and foreign bank accounts. Where officials' speeches contradict their policies, the people will respond to the realities, not to the rhetoric. National economic priorities must be reinforced with real incentives that reward desirable economic behavior and make undesirable behavior unprofitable.

CREATING OPTIONS FOR DOMESTIC INVESTORS

Investment Funds   African governments limit opportunities for domestic private sector investment by constricting the supply of funds. Sources of investment capital for the modern private sector are limited to bank lending, foreign investors, and self-financing. The mobilization of investment funds through domestic capital markets is not possible today, as the only formal capital markets are in Kenya, Nigeria, Ivory Coast, and Zimbabwe, and these are stagnant, if not contracting.

Without functioning capital markets, investors who might be willing to take an equity position in another firm have no assurance that they can sell that position when they so desire. The inability to "cash out" at will reduces the number of potential investors and forestalls the development of venture capital activities. Governments should encourage the creation of capital markets and provide the oversight necessary to prevent their abuse.

Government interference in financial markets also reduces the supply of funds and investor options. When governments raise money by issuing bonds with negative real interest rates, the purchasers tend to be only those who are legally obliged to hold a portion of their assets in government bonds, primarily insurance companies and pension funds. The bonds thus represent a subsidy by the holders to the government—not an attractive investment alternative—while holding government bonds also reduces funds available to the private sector. Finance ministry officials should price bonds so as to provide real rates of return, thus encouraging the development of a free market in government securities.

Similarly, government ceilings that hold bank interest rates lower than the inflation rate eliminate bank savings accounts as an economically rational alternative, preventing banks from playing their traditional intermediary role between savers and investors. Artificially low interest rates create a demand for loans that cannot be met. Banks or government agencies then control the allocation of loans, usually with the result that large borrowers find it easier to raise funds than small ones, and foreign firms are preferred over indigenous ones. Again, bank interest rate levels should move freely or at least be set with the objective of creating a modest real rate of return to encourage savers.

African businesses rightly complain that they have less access to bank loans than the government and foreign firms. In our experience, banks have turned to the smaller businesses only when more secure opportunities have dried up, preferring the lower risk of lending to government agencies and foreign multinationals. However, a higher level of savings would force banks to put their funds to work. One result would be an interbank market in which banks with lending opportunities borrow from banks with surplus funds. Another would be a wider range of acceptable borrowers. Improving smaller business access to loans can be accomplished by increasing savings levels, which encourages banks to make riskier and more profitable loans, and by encouraging small cooperative lending schemes.

Investment Choices   Domestic entrepreneurs in search of profits have only three choices—to go into business for themselves, to invest in real estate, or to invest abroad, which often entails using illegal means to get their money out of the country. Despite vigorous efforts, governments have not succeeded in preventing transfers of funds abroad. As in many other economic contexts, the regulated are better at finding loopholes than the regulators are at designing controls.[19] This problem stems in part from overvalued exchange rates. Not only do they drive domestic capital out of the country, but they also allow foreign goods to compete unfairly, undermining local production and precluding otherwise profitable enterprise, especially in manufacturing. Governments can allow exchange rates to reach realistic levels and then maintain them there.

Without reforms, few citizens will invest in manufacturing because it takes a relatively long time to produce a return, it demands a substantial initial investment, and its operations are highly vulnerable to disruption. As a Nigerian journalist has written, "The logic of

investing in productive industry is considered warped in the face of
the ability of a trader with much less capital to turn over so much
money as to make the return on investment for the industrial entrepreneur seem pitiful."[20]

Lastly, in many parts of Africa, there is no commonly shared set of
business practices which would provide a basis for mutual trust. For
example, young, foreign-educated MBAs have little in common with
wealthy traditional landowners, although as business partners, they
could accomplish much. An important task for African governments
and business communities is to develop a business code that reinforces the legal code of ethical behavior. Clearly, the responsibility for
forging such a consensus lies with Africans, not outsiders, but it is
necessary if the private sector is to thrive.

THE DOMESTIC PRIVATE SECTOR AS AN ENGINE OF GROWTH

The largest and possibly the only short-term sources of increased
production and investment are the three productive segments of the
existing domestic private sector. Smallholder agriculture accounts
for the bulk of the population's employment, the informal sector for
the major share of employment in manufacturing, and the larger
enterprises for a substantial portion of GDP. In the aggregate, each
sector's economic decisions are crucial to the overall health of the
economy.

CALLING EXISTING CAPACITY BACK INTO PRODUCTION

Like the modern manufacturing sector, the agricultural and informal sectors are producing at less than capacity. In agriculture, unused capacity can be defined in terms of the ability to increase overall
production at a given market price using existing farming methods.
Unused capacity in the informal sector is even more difficult to quantify, but the availability of appropriately skilled labor and its ability to
respond quickly to increased demand are rough measures.

Increasing production by putting existing productive capacity to
work does not require large amounts of investment capital, but rather
working capital and market opportunities, coupled with the producer's efforts. Some working capital can be supplied in domestic
currency through credit institutions. Foreign exchange auctions al-

low manufacturing firms to purchase (albeit at a premium) those items vital to profitable production and those using mainly local inputs needing only modest amounts of foreign exchange have an advantage over firms that have to import most of what they use. This system can stimulate firms to find local substitutes or to do more local processing.

Structural adjustment is called for when the existing capital stock does not match opportunities and new investment capital is required to expand existing capacity, or to create new capacity. Here, governments should favor private activity that yields early, high output-to-capital ratios. Africa's private agriculture and light manufacturing accomplish this better than the public sector which is concentrated in utilities, public works, and heavy industry. When the economy is stagnant, stimulating the private sector and postponing all but the most urgent capital-intensive public investments may be the best way to get the economy moving again. This is not to suggest that the government should neglect social welfare programs in favor of the private sector, but rather that heavy industry, public building, and major dams and irrigation projects must wait.

A recent study by two IMF economists supports a strategy of encouraging the private sector in developing countries. Blejer and Khan (1984) analyzed the behavior of public and private investment between 1971 and 1979 for a varied group of 24 developing countries.[21] Their preliminary findings suggest that developing countries which allowed the private sector a relatively large investment role achieved higher levels of overall savings and higher average rates of growth. They found clear evidence that the level of private investment varies with the flow of credit to the private sector, and that short-term government investment tends to crowd out private investment, while long-term government investment in infrastructure encourages it.

Such government investment can achieve multiple objectives. Rural infrastructure development projects making use of local labor during slack seasons can increase rural incomes and achieve improved output-to-capital ratios. The highly successful Kenyan Rural Access Road Program, for example, has built roads with high engineering standards at low cost for 15 years. Forty-two local construction units supervise road building in their areas, providing training, hand tools, and guidance to seasonally available workers. The program's diverse group of foreign donors minimizes demands on the government's administrative resources by setting standardized procedures and meeting annually to review progress.

SMALLHOLDER AGRICULTURE

The potential for increasing small farm productivity is limited at present to what can be achieved with existing technology. Farmers could certainly benefit from better availability of inputs—credit, seed, pesticides, and fertilizers—but there are no economical, high-tech, quick fixes because technological breakthroughs for rapid increases in the production of African food crops (other than maize) have yet to be made. At the same time, there is no doubt that African smallholders respond swiftly to price incentives.

In Zambia, the small farmers of Central Province clearly understand that payment now is worth more than payment later. Normally, maize is a slightly more profitable cash crop than cotton, which is much more labor-intensive. Cotton production, however, is expanding rapidly. Farmers choose cotton partly because of its resistance to drought, but more because the cotton parastatal takes only three weeks to pay, while the maize parastatal takes three months. Here, where farmers are powerless to make their own selling arrangements, the incentive is the relative efficiency of one parastatal over another. This arbitrary situation does not reflect a conscious policy decision by the government, and it may not correspond to the needs of the economy.

Our recommended strategy to increase investment is to increase market opportunities. Many governments have already committed themselves to increasing producer prices for agriculture and to foreign exchange rate devaluation. A healthy agricultural sector is the foundation upon which to rebuild, as it relieves foreign exchange shortages to the extent that domestic foodstuffs replace imports and agricultural exports increase. It provides purchasing power to the largest segment of the population and when they buy locally manufactured goods, they create opportunities for farsighted, energetic local businesspeople.

That agricultural policy affects the growth rate of the entire economy is evident in a recent FAO comparison of nine African countries between 1970 and 1981. The four countries whose domestic terms of trade were relatively most favorable to agriculture (Malawi, Kenya, Ivory Coast, and Cameroon) had rates of agricultural and GDP growth at 4.2 percent and 6.0 percent, respectively—higher than the five remaining countries (Ghana, Tanzania, Ethiopia, Senegal, and Nigeria), whose growth rates averaged 1.3 percent and 2.7 percent, respectively.[22]

Since 1981, many governments have changed their pricing policies. While some have seen positive results, drought has obscured the effects in other cases. Even if harvests improve, farmers and governments will face bottlenecks in harvesting, transport, and storage. The United States should be prepared to provide funds temporarily, as a logical extension of drought relief, for the purchase of spares, tires, and fuel for transport, bags for harvesting, and temporary storage, including tarpaulins and sheds. African governments and local private firms should carry out these activities in the future.

African governments have an important role to play as guarantors against the exploitation of smallholders and as providers of infrastructure. It is not enough for governments to increase prices for food and export crops in order to stimulate smallholder production. They must also take steps to ensure competitive markets that provide the farmers with an adequate flow of inputs, services, and consumer goods, allowing the private sector to provide the credit, seed, fertilizers, pesticides, and other goods. The new system must leave the bulk of the profits from agricultural sales in the producers' hands, in order to encourage expansion. Otherwise, from the small farmer's point of view, it makes no difference whether his profits go to the marketing board or to the local trucker or retail store. If retail prices rise because farmers with higher incomes seek more non-agricultural goods, middlemen's efforts to re-stock will ensure that wholesale prices also rise, increasing manufacturers' incentives to produce more goods. There must be competition among traders if higher agricultural prices are to stimulate long-lasting increases in farm output.

In a free market, farmers need information about prices if they are to hold their own against traders and transporters. The government can provide this through radio broadcasts,[23] in which regular bulletins announce prices prevailing in various regions. This device will work only if there are competing buyers and sellers of goods and services.

Farmers' needs for additional sources of funds must be met. At present, commercial banks find rural lending unprofitable because small loan administration is prohibitively expensive. Therefore rural lending schemes are good sources for this money. Farmers and small businessmen, particularly in West Africa, have developed their own credit schemes.[24] Government or PVO-funded lending is yet another alternative to commercial banking. In their analysis of five small enterprise lending projects, Kilby and D'Zmura (1984) report that these are among the most successful of all foreign aid projects, generating exceptional rates of economic return if loan administration is kept simple, local, and inexpensive. They find that the simplest systems are the most effective; technical assistance often adds more cost than benefit.[25]

THE INFORMAL SECTOR

Outside of the so-called modern sector—commercial agriculture and manufacturing based on imported technology—there is a broad range of small-scale, non-farm economic activities, including trading, crafts, simple manufactures, and services, which comprise the informal sector. Those activities in which investment would raise overall output are those which produce goods and services, and not those performed by middlemen. Sharing many of the problems of the small farmer, entrepreneurs in the informal sector would benefit similarly from the policy changes already discussed. In this sector, which employs so many workers and facilitates the spread of skills, the growth in the number of enterprises and their income levels can serve as an important measure of economic development.[26]

Page and Steel (1984), using another way to differentiate traders from producers of goods and services, define an informal sector micro-enterprise as one characterized by some barriers to entry, but too small to have access to bank finance or public agency programs.[27] These barriers may be limited capital or skill requirements. Such an enterprise avoids management and organizational issues because it is small enough to be run by one person. Its size precludes participation in industrial estates or other government assistance aimed at larger enterprises. Therefore, the best way to help the small entrepreneur, like the small farmer, is to change the general economic environment.[28]

As they stand today, government policies tend to discriminate against informal producers. A government that rations imports rather than devalues favors large firms over small ones, as do artificially low interest rates; in both cases, the small firm is crowded out. Burdensome regulations and taxes encourage the informal enterprise to operate in the gray market, outside the official nets (both the tax net and the safety net of social services). The informal entrepreneur operates on the fringes of legality, harassed or victimized by the police. A simple tax system, minimal regulation, and an end to harassment would allow the informal sector to grow in response to increases in rural demand and to contribute to government revenues.[29]

Bank lending to the informal sector faces the same obstacle as lending to small farmers: administrative costs per loan are too high to allow profits. However, loans that provide working capital to buy the inputs needed for production can contribute importantly to growth. The same lending schemes recommended for small farmers can serve the urban informal sector. African governments should encourage the formation of informal sector lending projects.

The U.S. government could also expand funding to lending schemes administered by PVOs or local groups, some of which have developed good banking mechanisms.[30] However, training in simple banking techniques should accompany funding to PVOs. In at least one of the cases studied by Kilby and D'Zmura, untrained expatriate administrators wasted resources and time reinventing workable systems.[31] Assuring repayment is not necessarily a problem, but strict sanctions against delinquents remain essential.[32]

THE MEDIUM- AND LARGE-SCALE MANUFACTURING SECTOR

The existing modern manufacturing, service, and agribusiness sectors have been among the focal points of development efforts in most countries. Ownership is shared to varying degrees between the public and private sectors and within the private sector, between foreign, immigrant, and African investors. The performance of many firms has fallen short of both government and investor expectations. Well-run, profitable parastatals are rare. Firms granted protection from competition have failed to produce goods at competitive prices. Development of local intermediate inputs has been slow. In countries where policy reformers choose to expand the private sector, market forces ultimately must sort out the viable enterprises from those which can only operate with subsidies or protection.

Private Sector Response to Incentives   The Zambian foreign exchange retention incentive mentioned earlier has dramatically improved the investment climate because it addressed a number of problems simultaneously. It has encouraged increased use of local inputs and has created new demand that mobilizes local funds for investment. It has also encouraged producers to learn to compete effectively in international markets.

With a radical change in the attitudes of the local business community in Zambia, an interest group may be created which, having benefited from economic change, will support further reform. The central bank has provided a valued incentive, and has ensured that exporters face a minimum of red tape and have unimpeded access to their foreign exchange entitlements. This incentive alone will not solve all of a country's problems, but it is a simple, pragmatic step to encourage growth, an opportunity made possible by the economy's own distortions. It is not a complete solution, but it is an encouraging move toward diversifying exports and increasing productivity.

In a number of African countries, the private sector has demonstrated its ability to respond to opportunities created by changes in government policies. As the response of medium and large-scale entrepreneurs has been less well-documented than that of the smallholder agricultural and informal sectors, we present below a few examples from our experience.

In 1978, the government of Zaire ended Air Zaire's monopoly on domestic air passenger and freight service. As a result, there are now several new, profitable airlines offering scheduled service between Kinshasa, Lubumbashi, Goma, and Kisangani. These successful companies are either solely owned by private Zairean businesses or are joint ventures with foreign partners. Private air transport in Nigeria has been similarly successful, with recent foreign joint venture partners providing equity contributions. By contrast, despite rising tourist demand for air safaris, Kenya's sales tax and customs duties, which nearly double the cost of aircraft, have stifled the growth of private air transport and postponed the replacement of aging aircraft.

The Nigerian government has acted to increase returns on large-scale agriculture and has forced manufacturers to try to develop local raw material inputs. A startling new phenomenon—the Lagos lawyer or accountant turned farmer—has recently appeared; these would-be entrepreneurs are attracted by promising profit potential created by the military government's policy changes. Manufacturers now receive import licenses only for production of essential goods with high local content.

In sum, Africa's private manufacturing sector is dynamic enough to respond to opportunities if the government is willing to change its economic policies. The costs will include a painful shake-out among the medium- and large-scale enterprises, hardships for urban workers, and some loss of direct control over economic resources by the government. The benefits of increased growth accrue to both the private sector and the government. The government will begin to show its people that earlier social welfare promises can be made good, and the success of the private sector will gradually relieve the pressure on government to employ more people than it needs. As private sector activity increases, its skills and its ability to meet new demands increase as well. This rocky road can lead to self-sustained growth.

IMPLICATIONS FOR U.S. POLICY

The most appropriate short-term investment strategy for Africa today requires policy reform in four broad areas:

- The removal of barriers and uncertainties to doing business in the domestic economy.
- Encouragement of the growth of competitive markets in goods and services, reducing the number of state-owned monopolies, but retaining or even strengthening the government's role as arbiter of last resort on issues of economic power and justice.
- Encouragement of economic activity that yields early, high output-to-capital ratios.
- Maintenance of a flow of real credit to private investors and directing government investment as much as possible to infrastructure.

Even in the expected absence of large private capital inflows from overseas, these reforms will soon yield economic benefits because they call into production existing capital resources—idle plant and skilled labor.

The United States can play a useful role in bringing about these reforms. At a time when past economic policies are being questioned, some African governments are ready to experiment with new approaches. However, the reforms must show benefits quickly—within one or two years—and they must not threaten the existing political order.

The United States should provide concrete financial assistance during the period of transition. The most important first result of increasing production from re-employed resources will not be wealth, but the restoration of hope; a substantial surplus for economic development will come later. Two recommendations made earlier for harvest support and assistance in creating small lending schemes can have the speedy results that are urgently needed.

Foreign aid will have to continue indefinitely. As domestic production increases, moreover, the need for basic infrastructure and social services will increase. African government will have to coordinate multilateral and bilateral aid in support of these essential activities.

During 1985, the United States provided more than $1 billion in emergency drought and famine relief, over and above the $1.166 billion in non-military aid. Even if the emergency conditions abate, the administration should request that Congress continue this assistance. The economic justification for continuing assistance is that growth in Africa will contribute to greater world trade, providing new markets for American goods. From an ideological standpoint, a program of policy-based assistance that encourages economic development through free market mechanisms is likely to appeal to the administration, the Congress, and the electorate. On humanitarian grounds, those who have supported famine relief should also support assistance that will help to prevent a recurrence of famine.

We advocate deemphasizing new American private investment in Africa until there are genuine opportunities on the appropriate scale. Rather, the role of the United States should be that of adviser and supporter of the free market system, the success of which will call forth increasing investment from all sources. AID economic support funds must continue as a means of persuading African leaders to adopt economic reforms and rewarding those who do so. The African Development Foundation can assist Africans at the village and community levels in development projects that will contribute to productivity and Congress should ensure that the Foundation is adequately funded. As Treasury Secretary James Baker explicitly recognized at Seoul in October 1985, the United States should support the funding of World Bank and other multilateral programs that promote policy reforms intended to increase the scope of private economic activity.

In addition to providing policy-based aid, the U.S. government can help simply by maintaining existing institutions that foster American investment, lending, and trade in Africa. The Export-Import

Bank, the Overseas Private Investment Corporation, USAID's Bureau for Private Enterprise, and similar entities can facilitate private American activity that supports expansion of the private sector in Africa. As part of its general campaign against protectionism, the administration should resist pressures to erect trade barriers to new African manufactures and semi-processed goods.

The easiest element of the American role is advocacy. Since the Reagan administration has a strong ideological commitment to the free market, it should not be difficult to find spokesmen who can argue tactfully and persuasively and who can give cogent advice about the economic effects of specific steps. Advocacy and advice should be provided in the person of a temporary special ambassador—a highly visible public official who can concentrate the energies of the United States on practical action. This person should be an experienced Africanist and a strong advocate of productive free enterprise. He or she should concentrate on devising appropriate ways for American foreign assistance programs to reinforce positive steps toward building the private sector.

NOTES

1. World Bank, *Toward Sustained Development in Sub-Saharan Africa* (Washington, D.C.: The World Bank, 1984), p. 47.

2. World Bank, *World Debt Tables: External Debt of Developing Countries*, 1984–85 Edition (Washington, D.C.: The World Bank, 1985), pp. 26–119.

3. For a good discussion of the difficulties, see Reginald Herbold Green, "Foreign Direct Investment and African Political Economy," in Adebayo Adedeji, ed., *Indigenization of African Economies* (New York: Africana, 1981).

4. The 1967 and 1972 figures are quoted in Helge Hveem, "The Extent and Type of Direct Foreign Investment in Africa," in Carl Widstrand, ed., *Multinational Firms in Africa* (Uppsala: Scandinavian Institute of African Studies, 1975), p. 83. The 1981 figure is from OECD, *Investing in Developing Countries* (Paris: OECD, 1982), p. 25. It assumes that investment in sub-Saharan Africa continued to represent 75% of total investment in Africa, as was true for the 1967 and 1972 DAC estimates.

5. OECD, op. cit., p. 22.

6. Louis T. Wells, Jr., *Third World Multinationals: The Rise of Foreign Investment from Developing Countries* (Cambridge, Mass.: MIT Press, 1983), p. 169.

7. David Goldsbrough, *Foreign Private Investment in Developing Countries*, Occasional Paper No. 33 (Washington, D.C.: IMF, 1985), p. 6.

8. World Bank, *World Debt Tables*, op. cit., p. 26.

9. *The Economist* 294(7382) (February 23, 1985): 84.

10. Pauline H. Baker, *Obstacles to Private Sector Activities in Africa*, unpublished, prepared for U.S. Department of State, January 1983, p. 6.

11. Ibid., p. 50.

12. Ibid.

13. Among those who make this point are Richard D. Robinson, *National Control of Foreign Business: A Survey of Fifteen Countries* (New York: Praeger, 1976); Isaiah Frank, *Foreign Enterprise in Developing Countries* (Baltimore: Johns Hopkins, 1980); and several studies quoted in Alice Galenson, *Investment Incentives for Industry: Some Guidelines for Developing Countries* (Washington, D.C.: The World Bank, 1984). This last is an excellent discussion of African investment incentives and their economic effects.

14. The above group; also Jurgen Voss, "The Protection and Promotion of Foreign Direct Investment in Developing Countries: Interests, Interdependencies, Intricacies," *International and Comparative Law Quarterly* Volume 31 (October 1982), pp. 686–708.

15. Michael Griffin, "Madagascar's Finance Minister Reflects on the Economy," *African Business* (April 1984): 29.

16. UN, ECAFE, *Programming Techniques for Economic Development* (Bangkok: 1960), quoted in Gerald M. Meier, ed., *Leading Issues in Economic Development*, 4th ed. (New York: Oxford University Press, 1984), p. 219.

17. A.K. Cairncross, "The Place of Capital in Economic Progress" (1955), quoted in Meier, op. cit., pp. 225–229.

18. Jane Jacobs, *Cities and the Wealth of Nations* (New York: Random House, 1984), p. 119. She is not alone in describing development as a process, but her description of the organic growth of new skills from older work is particularly clear.

19. Jonathan David Aronson in *Money and Power: Banks in the World Monetary System* (Beverly Hills: Sage, 1977) gives the example of the U.S. banks' ability to circumvent U.S. regulation in order to enter the Euromarket.

20. Pat Utomi, "Nigerian Bankers Prefer Trade to Industry," *African Business* (May 1984): 61.

21. Mario I. Blejer and Mohsin S. Khan, "Private Investment in Developing Countries," *Finance and Development* (June 1984): 26–29. (None of the countries in the sample is African; the sample is clearly not random and the results are not necessarily representative of developing countries as a group.)

22. Food and Agriculture Organization of the United Nations, "Agricultural Price Policies in Africa," paper for the Thirtieth FAO Regional Conference for Africa held in Harare, Zimbabwe, July 16–25, 1984, p. 19.

23. David K. Leonard also makes this point in Chapter 7.

24. Marvin P. Miracle, Diane S. Miracle, and Laurie Cohen, "Informal Savings Mobilization in Africa," *Economic Development and Cultural Change* (August 1980) 28:4.

25. Peter Kilby and David D'Zmura, "Searching for Benefits," unpublished, May 1984, pp. 2–4.

26. We thank Peter Kilby and John Harris for this measure of growth.

27. John M. Page, Jr., and William F. Steel, *Small Enterprise Development:*

Economic Issues from African Experience (Washington, D.C.: The World Bank, 1984), p. 11.

28. Ibid., pp. 37–39.
29. Ibid.
30. Miracle, Miracle, and Cohen, op. cit.
31. Kilby and D'Zmura, op. cit., p. 21.
32. Ibid., pp. 125–27.

PART V

HUMAN RESOURCES

CHAPTER THIRTEEN

African Education: Problems in a High-Growth Sector

David Court and Kabiru Kinyanjui

In a continent characterized by tumult and change, the persistent and seemingly insatiable public demand for formal education has been one fascinating constant. The abiding faith of African governments and individuals in education as a means of advancing economic and social well-being has been found to be well-placed, since, in the absence of other modernizing institutions, schools have been found to have more profound beneficial implications than earlier recognized.[1]

From this perspective, low levels of investment in human resources must account in part for the apparent stagnation and decline of African economies. While the need for more education is thus accepted, urgent questions remain. What kind of education should be provided? What policies should govern its provision? What means are available for its finance?[2] These concerns are significant in the calculations of individuals, governments, and international agencies which place education at the center of the debate about fostering development in Africa.

THE HISTORICAL CONTEXT OF EDUCATION IN AFRICA

The educational systems inherited by the newly independent African nations in the early 1960s were designed to serve colonial and minority interests. Overall provision of education was grossly inadequate given the needs of modern nationhood, with enrollment of the relevant age groups little more than one-third in primary schools, less than 3 percent in secondary schools, and a minute fraction in the few institutions of higher education that then existed on the continent.[3]

In countries with colonial settlements, education systems were characterized by racially segregated structures and by corresponding imbalances in patterns of expenditure. Educational opportunities were unevenly spread within countries and dependent on proximity to areas of colonial settlement, missionary presence, and levels of economic development. Curricula were infused with European content, practice, and ethos and were administered and largely taught by expatriates at the secondary levels. There was little technical or agricultural education and girls were hardly represented at all at secondary and higher levels.

Given that these systems were ill-designed for the economic and social needs of newly independent African countries, achievements in the field of education since 1960 have been truly dramatic. From a small base, enrollment in primary education is virtually universal in many countries, accompanied by more extensive secondary enrollments (Table A.3 in Appendix). This expansion reflects the removal of racial structures and the incorporation of groups that previously had no access to formal education and was made possible by the allocation of sizeable public funds and community efforts.

Accompanying the quantitative expansion were important qualitative improvements, including the adaptation of inherited structures and content to reflect national circumstances and culture, first at the primary level and more recently in secondary schools. In many countries, a variety of educational and training institutions has been created to meet the growing need for skills and services. Adult education has become an important component and in several countries, such as Tanzania and Ethiopia, massive and repeated national campaigns have succeeded in reducing illiteracy.

Increased attention has been given to agricultural education through, for example, the expansion of farmer training centers. The greater emphasis on technical training is evident in the establishment of polytechnics and a range of technical and professional courses under private and government auspices. Most African countries have established at least one national university, but several have developed multi-layered systems of higher education.

The localization of staff has proceeded apace. Educational administration and the teaching force at the primary and secondary levels are now almost entirely in national hands, while the number of expatriates in tertiary education has been steadily reduced. At the same time, attention has been given to improving the qualifications of educators. Research to further understanding of the functioning of educational systems in Africa has expanded. Most countries have become more adept at monitoring increasingly complex systems of education. In particular, systems have been sustained by the dedication of innumerable teachers who are improving the lot of the next generation, often through improvisation in the face of diminishing resources.

Great strides in improving the external efficiency of education systems are evident in the extent to which staffing targets have been met and in the less tangible but no less important benefits that accrue to a nation that increases its literate population. These socio-economic outcomes of education are difficult to quantify, but there is increasing recognition of the wider impact of education on development, beyond staffing provision. It is clear that one of the most important effects of expanded education has been to foster achievement which in turn has helped to hold the nation-state together throughout most of the continent.[4]

DIMENSIONS OF THE CURRENT SITUATION

Despite the impressive achievements that have been made in education systems in many African countries, the present situation provides little grounds for complacency. Symptoms of decline are evident throughout the continent. The central problem is that the expansion of enrollments has exceeded the capacity of African economies to sustain their educational systems. After a period of advance, the efficiency of educational provision and the quality of instruction are deteriorating in most African countries. Several broad dimensions of the problem can be identified.

First, the overall provision of education in Africa remains inadequate in terms of both economic requirements and issues of equity (Table A.3). There is a growing consensus that the low level of human resource development in Africa relative to other inputs accounts for poor economic conditions in most of the continent. Empirical evidence substantiates this claim. Throughout Africa, institutions and projects are languishing or inoperable for lack of trained personnel to run them.

Moreover, research on the economic benefits that result from extended education in the form of greater agricultural productivity, labor efficiency, and so forth supports this observation.[5] Education also produces major non-economic benefits in improved community health, nutrition, fertility control, and general responsiveness to technological innovation.[6]

Second, due to rising numbers of students, a sizeable part of the primary and much of the secondary school sectors have degenerated into little more than facades of learning institutions.[7] Many such schools have large classes—often of 100 students—and no desks, chairs, chalk, blackboards or other teaching aids. Textbooks are unavailable or inappropriate and untrained teachers are common. Grade repetition and drop-out rates are high. Although evidence is scanty, it is almost certain that average academic performances have declined because of deteriorating facilities, declining resources, and admissions of disadvantaged groups.

More serious than the presence of untrained teachers is the decline in teacher morale. While in the past, teachers enjoyed great status in the community and the profession was a sought-after one, today teachers are a beleaguered and dispirited force. Those that cannot leave the profession seek ways of supplementing their incomes, adversely affecting the quality of their instruction.

Associated with the decline in the quality of the state system is the erosion of public confidence. Those with resources opt out of the system at all levels from nursery school to university, with an increasing number of children being sent to Europe or America for secondary and higher education.

Third, access to educational opportunities in most countries is still not evenly distributed across the sexes and across regional and social groups, and sharp differences in performances on national examinations have been observed. Educational policy in the early years of independence tended to ignore these types of disparities, thereby reinforcing them. Correcting the imbalance was not viewed as a priority because of the absolute shortage of those with educational qualifications and the need to fill positions in the expanding economy which led to an emphasis on secondary and higher education for those who were already in the system.[8]

Regional inequalities in the provision of education assume a particularly critical importance in Africa because they tend to be synonymous with ethnic differences. Especially at the secondary and higher levels, several countries have been forced to adopt regional quota systems as a way of responding to the threat to national integration posed by differing educational access. However, even in those countries that have made major efforts to restructure their societies along egalitarian lines, data suggests that regional inequalities have persisted and indeed increased.[9]

Data concerning access to education of different social groups is less conclusive. Initially, systems were relatively "open" in terms of affording opportunities to children from rural or poor areas. However, with the increasing differentiation of African societies resulting from the spread of monetary economies, a corresponding differentiation of schools has resulted and socio-economic factors are becoming more important in determining access to better education and subsequent mobility.

From a developmental standpoint, the most important aspect of present inequalities in education concerns the restricted opportunities for girls, particularly at the higher levels. At the primary level, the number of female enrollments has risen substantially—from 24 percent of the age group in 1960 to approximately 60 percent in 1985—with an increase at the secondary level from 3 to 15 percent. However, there are notable differences in these ratios in the various countries. The need remains to increase enrollments in those countries where it is low in the first cycle.

However, the more fundamental problem of gender inequality has to do with the limited access of girls to quality secondary schools, universities, science and certain professions, and training opportunities and scholarships of all types. Research shows that the education of women outweighs all other factors, including income, in its beneficial impact on a range of development-related areas such as childcare, nutrition, and health.[10] Thus, continuing restrictions on educational opportunities for women are not only a matter of inequity, but a serious impediment on national development.

The dramatic expansion in formal education was a response to a shortage of middle-level personnel, but ironically its most visible consequence has been the "school-leaver problem." Graduates of primary and secondary schools have faced increasing difficulty in finding employment in the modern wage economy, as the number of students in the system has surpassed the capacity of African economies to provide the kind of employment school-leavers had been led to expect.[11]

The pressure was felt first by primary school students whose certificates no longer guaranteed employment. Following a period in the mid-1960s when a period of shortage of those with secondary school education merged with an equilibrium in supply and demand, unemployment among some secondary school-leavers was noticeable for the first time in the mid-1970s.

As the jobs for which school-leavers felt prepared were in the towns, urban migration became an integral part of the problem. Worsening employment prospects have intensified rather than reduced the demand for education and triggered the now-familiar phenomenon of qualification escalation. This is a rational response to an educational structure in which students must complete one level before being allowed to enter the next and to a social structure where there are few alternative channels for mobility. Since only a minority of students can pass from one stage to the next and the rewards to gaining entry are high, the result is a system characterized by competition and exclusion. With the majority at each level of the hierarchy unable to proceed with further education, schooling is inevitably geared to the interests of the minority.

At the lower end of the scale, only about half of African youth complete the basic seven-year cycle of primary education, of which approximately 23 percent continue on to any kind of formal secondary level education. Consequently, most of Africa's youth are left at an early age to fend for themselves in small-scale farming and rural enterprises. The challenge for the school systems is to find ways of preparing them for productive lives in the rural sector.

For those at the upper end of the hierarchy, the expansion has not produced self-sufficiency in high-level personnel in most African countries. A shortage of highly trained people, especially in the scientific and technical fields, continues to plague most countries and, as a result, many remain dependent upon outside professionals.

A final consequence of the growing number of students is the strain on management capability. Keeping the system afloat, much less making qualitative reforms of curricula or structures, has become the all-consuming preoccupation of ministries of education. Compounding management problems are incomplete, unreliable, or unavailable data bases that are essential for effective management and reform. Nor is there the necessary research expertise for making good use of existing data.

From an educator's viewpoint, the critical problem facing Africa at present is the poor quality of education available for society in general and the shortage of those highly trained individuals who can be the designers, implementors, and catalysts of development policy. Quality improvements and cost-saving innovations—central to any educational strategy for Africa—require sustained attention to improved planning, analysis, and management capacity.

NATIONAL POLICY RESPONSES

Three distinct responses to the problems just described are discernable in the educational policies of African nations over the last 25 years: adaptation of the inherited structure, creation of a parallel system, and rejection and transformation of the old system.

In the first group are those countries which have kept the structure of the system inherited at independence largely intact and have concentrated on adapting it to meet new circumstances and on nationalizing its content and personnel. Characteristic of these systems are a retention of a metropolitan language, a stress upon examinations, international standards, higher education, and overseas training, and a relative lack of emphasis on adult literacy and the incorporation of previously neglected groups. These systems are highly academic and elitist and do not cater to the employment and skills needs of large segments of the population.

The perception in many countries that the formal system of education was not providing the relevant skills and values needed for employment and economic development led to the growth of parallel structures of non-formal education. A variety of out-of-school learning activities exists in most countries in sub-Saharan Africa. Sponsored by a host of non-governmental agencies, they include literacy classes, vocational skills, agricultural extension, paramedical training, and a number of other skill-imparting programs.

In many cases, these training programs provide a valuable means of improving the lives and employment opportunities of participants and have been especially successful in developing community leadership and social mobilization. They also provide an ideal alternative to conventional schools for organized learning. Yet surprisingly little is known about the efficiency and cost-effectiveness of individual programs. Where assessments have been made, the record is mixed. The varied learning activities carried on outside the formal school system have proven to provide neither alternative education nor a short-cut to rapid education. As a result, the parallel structures have remained a second-best choice in the eyes of the population.[12]

The third type of response, based on a fundamental questioning of the appropriateness of inherited structures to African circumstances, is an attempt to replace them with a different and more relevant system. In some cases, the radical critique and the formulation of alternatives emerged during the struggle for liberation from the colonial power. Necessitated by conditions of the struggle, such changes were part of a larger rejection of the type of society that was seen as embodying the oppression of Africans, as was the case in Mozambique, Guinea-Bissau, and Zimbabwe.[13] In Tanzania and Ethiopia, on the other hand, reformulation and experimentation were the result of the state's ideological premises and policy positions.[14]

In both cases, however, the reform of education was part of a wider effort to transform the economic and political structures of the society. Education was expected to develop a new consciousness and new skills that would contribute to this transformation. Emphasis was therefore placed on mass education—both adult and primary— rather than on secondary and higher levels, and extensive use was made of literacy campaigns. Educational content stressed political understanding, practical experience, and a pedagogical approach to productivity in agriculture, health, and nutrition. Prominent among the structural emphases were the importance of integrating schools into the surrounding community, collective decision-making, the utility of manual labor, and the necessity of educating women.

A critical assessment is long overdue of the experiences of countries that have attempted fundamental educational change in face of economic or political circumstance. In several instances, these countries have anticipated educational emphases that other countries have come to recognize as important, such as the significance of women's education, productive work, and local culture. Second, the experiences of those countries that have recently emerged from a liberation struggle are relevant to the future experiences of Namibia and South Africa that have yet to attain majority rule. Third, it is clear that whatever their political orientation, governments are grappling with issues of general concern to the continent. Because their experiences are instructive, they should not be ostracized by Western donors on political grounds.

THE CONTEXT OF THE POLICY RESPONSE

Before turning to some of the specific critical issues in education, it is necessary to identify the particular features of the socio-political environment that most condition the formulation of educational policy. Africa has the highest fertility rates and the fastest rate of population growth of all regions in the world. The population is expected to double its present size shortly after the turn of the century. This increase will exacerbate the pressures already described by raising the demand for education and intensifying the pressure on limited resources.

By the year 2000, children in the 5–14 age group will account for one in seven of the population in the industrial world, but one in four in Africa. This suggests that "not only is there a bigger school expansion job to be done in Africa, but that there are proportionately fewer people in the working population to carry the burden of that schooling."[15]

The pressures created by population growth are intensified by economic crises. The recent economic recovery seems to be bypassing African countries and a rapid improvement in economic conditions cannot be expected. As a result, public spending on education relative to numbers of students or in absolute terms is unlikely to increase. Many African countries are already spending as much as 20 percent of their national budgets on education. The pressure on educational budgets comes not only from the per capita decline in available resources, but also from escalating costs. Further, the current expansion of education systems is occurring at the post-primary level, requiring more expensive teachers, plant, and equipment than at lower levels.

Another less obvious but harmful constraint on quality improvements stems from the political context. Twenty-five years after independence, there are few governments in Africa that are not still striving to create a sense of nationhood and to break down the parochial ties that threaten national unity.

The paramount preoccupation is establishing a unified economic and social system and synthesizing traditional and modern administrative institutions. Lacking a unified economic and political base, governments are required to invest large amounts of productive capital in institutions that hold society together.[16] Among the most important of these institutions, schools are the focal point for divergent political interests. As education at the upper levels is regarded as a means of attaining future status, schools are an important arena for political competition.

Uneven distribution of educational facilities in African countries is therefore a considerable source of political vulnerability and finding ways of reducing these disparities is a continuing preoccupation. Another pervasive feature of the socio-cultural context in which educational policy is made is the loosely termed phenomenon of "tribalism," which has more aptly been characterized as the "economy of affection."[17] This system of reciprocal relationships based on kinship, residence, and religion tends to override other loyalties, constituting a powerful social force which penetrates all spheres of life. Its impact on education has been positive, providing the driving force to act collectively, raise resources, and build and run schools in homogeneous communities.

The impact of the economy of affection in the national context is less positive, however. The strength of established familial loyalties tends to weaken the legitimacy of national institutions assigned to develop educational policy. For example, individuals and groups in which the economy of affection is strong have tended to direct public resources to private and community purposes.[18] Institutions become subject to patterns of conflict between interest groups and positions within them become part of localized power struggles that have little to do with the qualities required for a particular job. Frequently, actors in key policy positions are moved in or out with little regard for the health of the institution.

In its broader manifestation, the economy of affection leads to styles of decision-making, attitudes toward authority, assumptions about community, and notions of merit that heavily constrain management and can render ineffective otherwise productive inputs of skills and training. In this climate, Western notions of management are not easily introduced, explaining the ineffectiveness of so many aid projects that are predicated upon management styles and assumptions about the behavior of bureaucracies that simply do not apply in the African context.[19]

The varied participation of donors in the development of African education has created a relationship with recipient ministries that heavily conditions the formulation of policy. Aid has undoubtedly made massive contributions to the development of African education, but some of its effects have been less noteworthy. Problems have arisen from the volume of aid and the multiplicity of donors, each with its own style, timetable, project orientation, information requirements, and demands for accountability.

By definition, the aid relationship is an unequal one. The volume of external funds creates a dependency relationship in which the "real" preferences of countries rarely emerge. The willingness of some African countries to adopt external models and experimental projects that were preordained to be irrelevant or inadequate in terms of any conceivable national purpose is explained largely by ministries' weak bargaining position in the aid negotiation process.

Moreover, the different styles and information requirements of various donors pose an immense burden on recipient ministries.[20] Servicing these diverse needs frequently absorbs most of the time of scarce ministry talent. Common to many donors is the desire to make a quick and distinctive impact. This dissuades support for the simple, routine, and the proven, and encourages buildings and bounded projects rather than long-term measures involving recurrent costs. Africa has been host to innumerable projects, experiments, and models which in some cases reflect the wholesale transplant of established foreign models—Swedish folk development colleges, Cuban agricultural schools, British libraries, Canadian technical colleges—and, in others, reflect the powerful and often passing fashions of donor conviction. Consequently, in many African countries, the national system of education is a patch-work quilt of semi-autonomous projects of diverse national hue.

While donor agencies proclaim their commitment to project replication, in practice they often pay insufficient attention to the relevance of a project to the wider system. Indeed, in response to management problems, donors have emphasized the autonomy of their projects. While additional aid is undoubtedly part of the solution to some of the educational problems of Africa, past aid has been part of the problem. Rationalizing aid coordination, practice, and style can improve the situation, as can efforts to increase the capacity of African nations to participate more "equally" in the negotiations that determine aid patterns and practice.

CRITICAL ISSUES IN EDUCATIONAL POLICY

While greater investment in Africa's human resources is needed, governments lack sufficient funds to finance the development or even maintenance of their school systems. This is because education is highly subsidized and the proportion of the total budget allocated to education is already high, with unit costs of further expansion likely to be greater than before. In permitting further expansion of education to proceed unquestioned in response to popular demand, there is a danger that the steady deterioration of facilities, the demoralization of teachers, and the ritualization and impoverishment of the learning process already evident in several countries and many schools will continue. New ways of organizing resources and channeling demand are therefore essential.

Modifying demand for education so that it accords more with social needs and with what is financially feasible is a major challenge. Demand for education has evidently not been weakened by those who have been unable to get the high-paying jobs they had hoped for. Demand is sustained by the high rewards that are rigidly tied to educational attainment and by the propensity of employers to consistently upgrade the qualifications required for any given job level. As long as one type of formal schooling monopolizes access to positions of prestige, influence, and wealth, demand for that type of education is unlikely to be altered by exhortation, curriculum change, or the mere provision of other types.

Eventually, unemployment among the educated may reach a level where people will begin to doubt the wisdom of their investment in education. But until that point is reached, the only way to modify demand is to alter the incentive structure in order to bring private calculations of the costs and benefits of education more in line with social benefits.[21] One means to this end is to transfer more of the cost of education from the state to the individual and to reduce the pay differentials that are currently tied to higher level qualifications.

Adjusting public sector salary structures as a means of modifying educational demand is fraught with political implications, as it involves a self-denying ordinance on the part of civil servants. A more practical approach is to seek new sources and patterns of finance.

In most African countries, the national educational system is heavily subsidized by the state at all levels. Based on studies of the rates of return, primary education has relatively greater social benefits than secondary and higher levels.[22] Therefore, in terms of both equity and cost considerations, reducing subsidies to secondary and higher level education and channeling the saved resources to primary education is desirable. It is not yet clear how shortfalls at the upper levels can be met, but imposing tuition fees and charges for accommodation and food, providing student loan programs, developing private schools, and involving the private sector in the provision of bursaries are suggested.[23] Another method that has been successful in several countries is the development of productive activities in schools— particularly farm production—as a means of supplementing diets and offsetting food costs.[24]

An additional means of expanding resources available for education is to use existing facilities more efficiently. Establishing economies of scale—increasing class size, raising student-teacher ratios, expanding the school day, using new technologies such as the radio, teaching fewer subjects, taking advantage of alternative types of schools such as Koranic schools, and modifying the school calendar to accord with seasonal changes—provide a few options.[25]

Cost reduction must be accomplished with an eye to the effect on quality. Research findings show that factors inside the school—curriculum, facilities, qualifications of teachers—are more important determinants of student achievement than in the industrialized world where social factors have more influence.[26] Therefore, given the poverty conditions of most African classrooms, simple improvements have an inordinate effect on quality.[27] Measures that are especially beneficial include raising the morale and knowledge of teachers and providing textbooks and examinations.[28]

The link between schooling and jobs in the wage economy has forced educational planners to reexamine the purpose of education to see how it can anticipate the conditions of rural life that most students will encounter. As the ratio of students to job opportunities has risen, a new rationale for schooling other than preparation for a paid job must be developed. Anticipating self-employment has become one of the most popular re-interpretations of the purpose of schooling in Africa.[29] The expectation is not that schools can create self-employment any more than they can create paid jobs, but that they can improve the quality and variety of the skills that students bring to their rural communities. Three concepts have emerged among African educational planners: terminal education, vocationalization, and productive school work.

Recognizing that most African youth will be exposed to no more than the basic cycle of primary education, some planners believe that primary education should be complete and terminal in itself. It should stress the skills needed by the terminating majority rather than the requirements of those continuing on to secondary levels.

The major problem with this approach is in determining which skills are most relevant to self-employment in agriculture and petty trading and which school subjects can provide them. Defined in such terms as the provision of "survival skills" and "basic competencies," the essential cognitive prerequisites for agricultural productivity and productive self-employment are not yet known.[30] Two equally questionable experiments in African countries have been expanding the number of subjects studied in the hope that broad coverage will include items of relevance, and increasing the vocational and practical content of the curriculum.[31] To date, however, there is little evidence to suggest that these responses will provide useful skills to students.

Achieving terminal education is not simply a question of finding the right curriculum and combination of subjects. More fundamentally, it requires de-linking primary and secondary schools in the minds of students and the general populace. As long as secondary education is perceived to be the route out of rural poverty and into the security of an urban wage-paying job, it will be difficult to replace the lure of secondary education with the notion of terminal primary education.

In the search for relevant schooling, a number of African countries are integrating productive work activities into the more academic aspects of the school syllabus.[32] The rationale is partially economic— to recover some costs through the sale of produce or the production of food—but it also involves helping to ease the move from school to work by beginning the transition at school. However, the socialization goals of school production have proved less easy to accomplish due to the difficulty of reconciling the pedagogical and economic aspects of productive work.[33]

Perhaps the most common response of ministries of education to the widening gap between students and jobs is the increasing emphasis on the vocational aspect of education.[34] Structures parallel to the academic system—technical, agricultural, and industrial schools which provide intermediate level skills for the wage economy—are one example. A second approach has been to set up a compulsory vocational training component in the curriculum to encourage acquiring employment skills. In a third approach, vocational education occurs in non-formal, post-primary training programs.

A central aspect of colonial policy, vocational training has also received substantial resource commitments from post-independence governments and has been a central plank of much donor assistance.

Ironically, the current drive toward vocational and technical training coincides with emerging research results which reveal that they are more expensive than general education and do not seem to achieve the economic and labor market goals that are sometimes claimed.[35] Although there may be strong political grounds for emphasizing vocational education at all levels, the economic and financial constraints argue against such an approach.

When attempting to increase the relevance of education, a distinction must be made between two types of knowledge and skills as the content of basic education. On the one hand are those skills which need to be acquired by all and can be prescribed centrally—literacy, numeracy, and a common level of political knowledge. In a different category are more specific skills which relate to the dominant economic activities in a local setting. The latter at the very least should be identified and implemented by the local community. In practice, however, it is difficult to distinguish between the different types and consequently to decide how much time should be allocated to each.

Finding an appropriate balance between local and national learning needs is complex and can be illustrated by the running debates over teaching foreign languages in primary schools and the proportion of school time which ought to be devoted to practical and farm work. In most African countries, an international language—English, French, or Portuguese—is taught to all students, although for most it is a second or third language with little immediate relevance to rural life. It is argued that this requirement burdens young pupils and introduces the risk that the international language and the culture it embodies will foster an external perspective inimical to the development of locally relevant skills and frames of reference. Others maintain that to abolish it would deprive the majority of students of access to an inestimable store of knowledge and medium of communication which may be relevant in the long-term to the goals of improved rural development.

If the language question poses the danger that access to the outside world may detract attention from local realities and priorities, emphasizing practical work and farm production raises the opposite concern. Excessive attention to meeting school production targets or assisting with community work may detract from the minimum amount of classroom time needed for long-term self-education and hence contributions to rural development. The general dilemma, then, is that of finding a balance in curriculum content and allocations which ensures that long-term intellectual development is not sacrificed on behalf of a spurious short-term practicality.

At the heart of the need for a balanced approach to local and national learning requirements is the issue of administrative responsibility for education.[36] It is one thing to acknowledge that community participation in educational decision-making requires decentralization of administration and quite another to effectively divide responsibilities between the capital and the regions.

In most countries, the administration of education is highly centralized because of earlier efforts to train high-level personnel and relate it to national economic plans, a belief in the need for a uniform curriculum both to ensure minimum national standards and encourage desired socialization, and a view of educational resources as political assets. The dilemma resides in the fact that effective educational reform demands localization as an objective and centralization as a mechanism.

Examinations are an effective instrument that can be utilized by ministries of education to control, direct, and monitor quality, while encouraging the development of locally relevant self-employment skills and knowledge. In most African countries, national examinations are held at each level, in effect weeding out the majority of students. With opportunities decreasing sharply at each successive stage and a small number of wage-earning jobs, the selection process based on a national examination system is inevitable in a pluralistic context where it is essential to have a procedure appearing "objective."[37]

In resource-poor countries, it is important that those selected for further education and training are those best equipped to make good use of it. Consequently, the selection function of education tends to dominate the broader goals of schooling. Subjects taught heavily reflect the contents of the examination rather than the nominal syllabus or the broad ideals of society. Nevertheless, the power of examinations over teaching staff and pupils can be used to influence what is taught in a positive direction.

By careful analysis, it is possible to ascertain which concepts and skills are being mastered by most pupils and which present difficulty. Teachers who are especially effective in passing on difficult skills can be identified. Because the examination is standardized and national, it can be used for important diagnostic and monitoring purposes both over time and between areas. This capacity for analysis and diagnosis is complemented by a feedback system in which schools and teachers are informed of which areas require further work.

It is therefore possible to use an examination not only for identifying an elite through selection, but also for developing skills and competence among the school-going population. It is also possible to focus attention on curriculum content relevant to terminal primary education irrespective of individual motivations for secondary education. Examinations provide a means of defining, encouraging, and evaluating quality.

While needing to respond to the circumstances and development goals unique to African countries, the educational systems must also maintain and encourage internationally acceptable standards. This issue is significant at every stage of the education system, but it is encountered perhaps most acutely at the university level in the debate over appropriate structures and practices for the national versus universal role of universities.[38]

The debate about the internationalism of African education has been clouded by perspectives on both extremes. One argument posits that whether international standards are a product or a cause of the technological dominance of the industrial world, their mastery is a prerequisite for understanding and dealing with that world. The opposite view holds that to aspire to foreign standards is to perpetuate Africa's cultural and technological dependency and to ignore the needs of the majority of people.

In reality, this is not an "either-or" situation. Some educational practices and goals—particularly those involving a technology of research and teaching in languages, science, and engineering, for example—seem to be universally applicable and useful. Others, such as Western concepts of medical qualifications, may be inappropriate to African circumstances and needs. The question should be what to borrow in the light of associated costs.

At this historical juncture, isolationism in education cannot be Africa's creed. The challenge is how to develop a cadre of scientists, professionals, researchers, and managers who reflect the best skills that international training has to offer, but who are also committed to the development of their own societies.

The role of universities has been a central issue in the debate about the contribution of education to national development.[39] In the 1970s, national leaders and international agencies had high expectations and stressed the singular responsibility of the university to serve society in direct, immediate, and practical ways that would improve the well-being of the national population.[40]

Despite efforts at reform, universities in general remain in financial and political trouble. Criticisms have increased that universities are not justifying their high costs by either a corresponding contribution to the improved well-being of their people or to the transformation of their societies. Their adherence to the metropolitan model was seen to inhibit their ability to respond to the needs of their own societies, leaving them as detached islands in a sea of poverty.

As cost-benefit analyses showed relatively greater returns from other forms of education, the tide of assistance turned against universities and toward primary, secondary, and technical education.[41] At the same time, the expansion of lower levels of education has brought about irresistible pressure for more places at the university which in turn produces overcrowding and the inevitable dilution of quality.

Government pressure on universities to emphasize vocational and professional courses runs up against university concerns over autonomy and scholarship. In the face of increasing student dissension, insistence on higher levels of political conformity and on government involvement in university decision-making has fostered even greater staff demoralization. This is further exacerbated by financial pressures which keep salaries at declining values and in many cases deprive universities of the very tools of their existence such as books, journals, and paper.

It is clear that the expectations that universities would transform their societies were inflated and misplaced. In the 1970s, the newly established universities were preoccupied with institution-building and were in no position to address complex developmental tasks. Nor are universities the most appropriate institutions for providing vocational training or leadership in developmental projects. Critics have tended to lose sight of the contributions universities have actually made, judging them by their failure to realize a set of preconceptions that may have had limited applicability in the first place.

The main achievement of African universities has been to establish their legitimacy as valued institutions by improving the relevance of teaching and research to the national environment and by training their own staff. From being based largely on imported texts and theories, curricula have now developed a degree of autonomy and research is now an integral part of the university purpose. Now that questions of staffing and institutional identity have been resolved, universities are able to assume a role in development based on commitment, conviction, and consensus rather than as an artificial response to governmental or external expectations. The challenge of the 1980s is for universities to convince their governments and national populace that beyond meeting staffing targets, they have a responsibility to train the minds that can advance development.

The challenge for donors is to support this purpose. Universities in Africa are languishing for want of resources and new sources need to be found. For all their problems, universities remain the principal means of regenerating scientific and professional expertise and represent one of the few havens of reflection and critical thought in Africa. Donor agencies helped to bring them into being and for those from societies where universities are part of the national fabric to conclude that similar institutions in Africa are irrelevant luxuries on the basis of their brief history is to condemn the continent to perpetual intellectual dependency.

RESEARCH ON EDUCATION

Implicit in much of what has been said is the need for additional and improved research on education. The development of Africa's universities is the most significant institutional advance from the perspective of research over the last ten years. Despite the need for constant refurbishment, universities in the major countries of the region have developed to the point where they represent a significant resource and source of expertise.

Concomitantly, national research units in governments and parastatals have emerged, including research and evaluation units in ministries of education, central statistical bureaus, and national councils of science and technology. The emergence of these research institutions has been followed by the formation of national educational research associations in various countries.

An important outgrowth of the national institutions is the spread of regional networks for research on education where the region's leading educational researchers meet periodically to review research findings and methodologies. By identifying and assessing research that is not generally accessible in international publications, they help to correct the imbalance between north and south in research on African education. Another important institutional development has been the increasing interest of a variety of non-governmental organizations—notably religious and women's organizations—in establishing an improved research base for their work in education and rural development.

Despite the vigor and depth of the research infrastructure, some significant problems remain.[42] Poor research, particularly from the education departments of colleges and universities, is common. The very few able researchers are scattered among different institutions, affecting the depth of overall research capability. Further, educational research has been beset by isolationism and territoriality. Researchers have shown little inclination to move beyond issues of classroom pedagogy; therefore, links with corresponding institutions in community health, agriculture, and population are virtually nonexistent. There is thus an overriding need to strengthen local institutional capacity for research and analysis in education and for better research focusing on the relationship between education and different aspects of economic and social development.

Considering the amount of public and external funds allocated to education, the proportion dedicated to research and to research training is minuscule. External support for doctoral work overseas has declined, adversely affecting the regeneration of the educational research community. However, the U.S. Agency for International Development's (USAID) interest in education and training appears to be growing. Described in the USAID policy paper, "Basic Education and Technical Training," a strategy is set forth which calls for the "institutionalization and long-range improvement of the indigenous information base and the strengthening of LDC capability for analysis, resource allocation, and policy determination."[43]

USAID has recently announced a ten-year commitment to improve the efficiency of education and training systems in five countries—Niger, Somalia, Liberia, Botswana, and Cameroon. This project will support research, planning, and analysis of education, build host country capacity to undertake these activities, and focus initially on the formal primary system. A network for both information exchange and cooperation with other agencies is expected to emerge from this undertaking.[44]

The International Working Group on Education (formerly the Bellagio Group) has also been notable in developing and utilizing research on education in Africa. Held annually to bring together the representatives of the main donor agencies supporting work on education, meetings of this group have provided an opportunity for exchanges of information and for concentrated attention on important themes such as literacy, the financing of education, and basic education. During the past three years, "new" donors—particularly the Scandinavians, Dutch, and Germans—have joined the group, as have more African educationists.

The relationship between education on the one hand and agricultural productivity and other developmental indicators such as health, nutrition, and fertility on the other is one of the most important areas in which research is needed. While it is acknowledged that education has some bearing on economic and social development, the mechanisms that account for its impact remain unclear.[45] The next step is to clarify how the process of schooling affects an individual's later ability to adapt to the technological requirements of agriculture, health, and other development domains.

A second area requiring urgent research are the impediments to and development consequences of women's education. Similarly, investigations of those factors that influence student achievement and of policy options that can improve it are needed. Research is also needed on the financing and administration of educational systems. Expanding enrollments have placed a heavy financial burden on central government, causing it to devolve some of the costs upon local communities. Therefore, both new forms of educational finance and major reorganizations of administrative structures and loci of control will be required.

STRATEGIES FOR ACTION: THE ROLE OF NATIONAL GOVERNMENTS

African governments remain the prime movers in their nations' economic development, and particularly in educational development, because their decisions not only shape the direction, utilization, and management of available resources, but also determine the parameters for action by local communities, non-governmental agencies, and donors. Given the state's central role in the operation of educational systems, several strategies can be identified.

- One of the most urgent priorities of national governments is to improve the management and administration of the ministries of education. This task involves the exploitation of available technologies such as more efficient information systems and better use of research. More attention must be paid to the human resource side of management, which is currently characterized by a disregard for professional knowledge, unplanned and ill-formed interventions, expenditures without justifiable benefits, arbitrary staff transfers, and a consequent instability in the system as a whole. Improving utilization of human resources for increased professionalism in ministries requires a decision-making system that encourages participation and a reward system that encourages commitment on the part of a professional staff.

• The quality of management at the school level has a significant bearing on student and teacher motivation and hence on academic performance. Recruitment, salary, and promotion policies that encourage the most capable administrators and teachers, and in-service training that permits their constant refurbishment can go a long way in improving the quality of education. Along with such policies, measures to strengthen the sense of teacher accountability to parents, the community, and ministry officials are needed. Where morale is high and commitment strong, inspection and supervision are likely to lead to increased efficiency and accountability.

• In the last two and a half decades, ministries have been preoccupied with problems of quantitative expansion. With the current rate of population growth on the continent, the demand for education will intensify to the point where concern for quality is likely to be a secondary issue. However, if the current trend toward disillusionment with the state system and the emergence of a dual structures is not to become irreversible, ministries must take deliberate measures to ensure the quality of educational output and to strengthen the conditions that promote and increase high standards at strategic points within the public system.

• Growing demands for education pressure governments to allocate resources to education at the expense of other productive sectors of the economy. The expansion of education needs to be placed in the context of increased food production and employment creation. This is not simply a matter of balancing the allocation of resources between different sectors, but of fostering those types of education that have a demonstrated impact upon productive behavior in different development domains. Given the absence of such knowledge at present, it is advisable to pursue general education at the primary level rather than programs that target industrial, agricultural, or vocational goals.

• With the dominant role of national governments in education, there has been a lack of organized, alternative views that would invigorate debates on educational policies. Such debates are important for the development of sound strategies and require the encouragement and involvement of relevant interest groups, including teachers' unions, parent and student associations, and women's groups. Essentially, a democratization of the education system is called for, which would stimulate initiatives and experiments by non-governmental and community organizations.

• African governments today have a more qualified pool of professional talent that can be harnessed for improving education. However, policies in hiring, promoting, training, and utilizing this scarce resource often lead professionals to seek opportunities outside their country. Discriminating measures to identify and encourage high-level professionals need to receive more attention.

• The quality of governance is central to the likelihood of improved educational performance. The challenge is to encourage governments to take a hard look at the systems they have been operating for the last 20 years and to explore ways of making them more quality-oriented and rewarding to teachers and pupils. Financial stringency often deters change, but much can be achieved without incurring additional costs. In fact, the most effective changes are those concerned with improving existing practices rather than a radical transformation of existing structures. However, changes in social attitudes and behavior will be necessary before any reforms can be implemented successfully, and this challenge is primarily a political one.

STRATEGIES FOR INTERNATIONAL ASSISTANCE

The future of education in Africa ultimately depends on reducing the rate of population increase and reviving economic growth.[46] However, improving education both in qualitative and quantitative terms can further both these goals. While national governments are ultimately responsible for the contribution of education to national development, international assistance can facilitate and accelerate the process.

Donor agencies considering innovative strategies must take into account what has been tried in the past. Africa has a sorry history of educational innovations that were highly touted at the time of their inauguration, but are now commemorated in broken radios, missing batteries, dust-covered science kits, immovable tractors, unworkable lathes, and forgotten syllabi. The recent World Bank review, "Basic Education and Agricultural Extension," is an important reminder of the need to take account of historical experience.[47]

If we have learned anything about the development process in the last 20 years, it is that technological change is rarely a complete solution. Education is critical in improving the non-technical aspects of technological change, although education itself seems to be infertile terrain for technological interventions. Anderson's dictum of 10 years ago that "the educational process is unlikely to experience a major technological breakthrough" has been confirmed by donor experience since then.[48] For reasons spelled out recently by C.E. Beeby, improvements in education are more likely to occur as a result of incremental increases in understanding rather than from a sudden technological discovery.[49] New technologies such as micro-computers and cassette recorders can contribute to improvements in teacher training and the management of education systems, but it is unlikely that they can be of widespread use as classroom tools in systems that have trouble ensuring supplies of chalk, exercise books, texts, and chairs.

Swings in emphases in education have occurred over the years. Lifelong learning, non-formal education, community education centers, and education and production have come and gone with bewildering rapidity, illustrating a tendency to treat the part as a whole.[50] When a chosen route fails to achieve what was expected, attention shifts to another element that is not yet discredited. Within donor agencies, the broad problem of the African country becomes defined in terms of the narrow administrative category in which the agency works. The agency then becomes captive in its approach to a problem. Avoiding this requires a broad-gauged strategy of what one is trying to achieve and an underlying institutional philosophy demonstrating long-term commitment, permitting flexibility within a framework, and offering a coherent image to prospective beneficiaries of assistance.

Education systems do not exist in a vacuum, but are rather embedded in a web of values, interests, and institutional relationships. As agencies think about new forms of research and training, they need to take account of what exists in prevailing institutions, cultural styles, and incentive systems. For much of the 1970s, non-formal educational activities were viewed from outside the continent as a relatively cheap and more rapid means of "delivering" education, and substantial aid resources were devoted to this goal. Yet research and experience have not vindicated this approach—whereas these activities may be a useful supplement to formal education, they cannot replace it. The primary school remains the principal means of providing literacy and numeracy. Thus, donors could have a greater impact if reforms are directed toward the existing primary school system rather than alternative institutions or technology.

Another example of the benefits of building upon existing incentive structures is provided by the history of examinations in Africa. Looked at from the perspective of Dore's "diploma disease," examinations would not appear to be a very appropriate vehicle for donors in trying to improve the content and relevance of basic education.[51] Yet, examinations are and will remain a central part of the incentive structure in Africa. Donor attention to strengthening national examination councils in Africa could have a significant impact upon the quality of education in Africa. Reform has the most chance of succeeding if it is based on what exists and on what is important in the prevailing educational context.

National institutions for research and training fare better than regional ones. With one or two notable exceptions, the experience of donors has been that while economies of scale may frequently point toward regional centers of excellence, these have been extraordinarily difficult to sustain given problems of coordination and national sensitivity. However, the greater strength of national over regional institutions should not obscure the importance of seeking ways to foster regional interchange. Focused research in education is particularly necessary, as is the creation of networks that can provide a means for sharing regional experience.

There is a need to go beyond the ritualistic commitment to replication toward building a concern for system-impact into initial project designs. This will require some serious thinking about the long-term consequences of a given aid activity including the recurrent cost implications. More broadly, it may require new ways of organizing projects so that lessons are gained from the project experience.

In the past, some donors have tended to focus more on the end product of assistance—a well-prepared plan, a convincing evaluation, a well-constructed building, or an elegant curriculum—than on the process from which these products emerged. Lately, however, the importance of the empirical and analytical bases for policies has been acknowledged. Above all, research and training that can improve understanding of educational problems require the development of strong national and regional research institutions.

Local institutional capability is a prerequisite for effective educational reform and a priority in any assistance strategy. Local institutions are sensitive to the context of a problem and the likely consequences of proposed reforms. More important, however, it is imperative that the sense of dependence that currently inhibits self-motivated reform in Africa be reduced. A degree of achieved self-awareness and self-confidence is a necessity for effective educational reform.

A degree of local capacity in research policy and management is needed that can strengthen the recipient's ability to set priorities and argue counter-priorities and lead to policies that the people will accept. The strategy paper of the Africa bureau at USAID is notable for its recognition that universities offer one of the best sources for developing this skill.[52]

Another area in which aid can make a major contribution is in improving the data-gathering and processing capabilities of education ministries. In most African countries, there is an urgent need for the establishment of a system for the regular collection and publication of basic statistics. Part of this task is the development of management tools such as resource allocation criteria, indicators of performance, and principles of cost-effectiveness which lead to better administration of the system as a whole.[53]

Donors have emphasized quantitative expansion in education in keeping with the priorities of African governments. Now, however, more attention must be paid to what happens inside schools and how this relates to other dimensions of human welfare. It is clear that many of the central issues in education are questions of values and motivation rather than numbers. Hence, there is a need for new forms of research that focus on content, quality, and motivation—what is being learned and why—rather than on the numbers passing through.[54]

Closely related to new styles of research is the need for new forms of training. Donor agencies have supported training in the past, but it is clear that neither the right number nor the right type have been produced. There are some respected external training programs—the

IIEP in Paris, the EDI in Washington, and a number of university-based programs—which have provided adequate training in research methods. But some have been preoccupied with education system efficiency itself or with narrowly defined economic and political outcomes. To date, training of analysts and managers has not been concerned with the relationship between education and other aspects of human welfare, nor has it focused on identifying an appropriate balance between local and external training.[55] The problem is less a shortage of money than of good ideas and institutions with an appropriately trans-sectoral outlook.

In stressing the need for more and improved training, we need to guard against the notion that training alone can bring about institutional reform. It is common for returned participants in donor training programs not only to fail to bring about institutional reform, but to be constrained in their individual contribution because of the absence of a supportive infrastructure. However, it is now recognized that relatively modest resources made available to returnees and their institutions can help offset some of the constraints.

It has been fashionable outside the continent to deride African universities as irrelevant or expensive. But within the continent, they are valued and influential and will continue to be the principal source of local expertise for research and analysis. Given their importance, it is clearly unwise for donor agencies to view them as undesirable luxuries. Because they have an enormous potential influence over the rest of the education system, it is necessary to seek ways in which they can be assisted in providing the leadership and resources in research and training that they are uniquely placed to offer.

Resistance among African policy-makers to outside prescriptions on the treatment of women has been common. Consequently, donors must exhibit particular sensitivity in this area. The imperative of expanding educational opportunities for women comes as much from the goals of development as from concerns about equity. Supporting government plans for expanding educational opportunities for women is one of the single most important strategies for African development.

Williams has equated the "learning-resource famine" with more familiar food famine in the gravity of its impact upon Africa's future.[56] Aid agencies are in a good position to help resolve this type of famine because they can supply the foreign exchange needed to purchase equipment, books, paper, transportation, fuel and so forth which are crucial to the educational enterprise in Africa. Learning resources within schools, colleges, and universities must be strengthened to increase the possibilities for independent study.

There is an urgent need for greater coherence in the overall aid process; however, tension is inevitable between the priorities and styles of individual donor agencies and the goals of coordination. One area where greater coordination may be possible is in reducing the burden of information demands placed upon recipients by greater standardization in their requests. Another means is by structuring increased African participation in the inter-agency dialogues about aid that occur in a variety of gatherings such as the International Working Group on Education.

CONCLUSIONS

The essence of the problem facing education systems in Africa is that the expansion of enrollments is exceeding the capacity of African economies to maintain educational quality. The gap in learning achievements between African students and those of industrial countries is widening to unbridgeable proportions, threatening a condition of permanent dependency. Educational deficiencies have long-term implications for the health, fertility, as well as agricultural productivity of the African populace and therein lies much of its significance. The empirical relationship between educational attainment and the increase in human well-being and potential is now clear, but much remains to be discovered about the mechanisms which can strengthen it. Associated with the practical problems of inadequate mass education and research inadequacies is the shortage of trained analysts and researchers who can provide the problem-solving capability for African nations.

To restate the gravity of the problems facing education in Africa is neither to imply past failure nor to countenance despair for the future. The accomplishments of the past 20 years—increased literacy and enrollments, sacrifices made, and commitment demonstrated—give hope for addressing the challenges of the future. The new problem is how to accommodate the increasing numbers and how to relate education to improvements in the quality of life through better health and more productive self-employment.

Attention has been drawn to a series of issues that merit consideration by those who will frame responses to current problems. Above all, the primary school remains the best hope for providing the kinds of skills needed to equip people for meaningful lives. National and international resources should therefore be concentrated on methods of improving the quality of primary education. This can be done by the provision of books, the improvement of management, the involvement of communities, and the stimulation of teacher morale. Measures that stress the incorporation and education of girls are especially important.

It is doubtful that many of the new information technologies offer hopes of a breakthrough in improving cognitive attainment. However, they do hold the potential of complementing and enriching educational experience and merit continued systematic experimentation. The needs and opportunities for education to affect the well-being of the population are clear. Further improvement in the human resources of the continent is an urgent requirement. The challenge facing African governments and the international community is finding the finance and applying it strategically and imaginatively.

NOTES

1. This is the conclusion emerging from a series of research reviews and studies conducted by the World Bank. Many of the most significant pieces of work are reviewed in Steven Heyneman, "Research on Education in the Developing Countries," *International Journal of Educational Development* 4(4)(1964): 293–304.

2. G. Psacharopolous, "Education Research Priorities in Africa." Washington, D.C.: The World Bank, 1984.

3. D. Court and D.P. Ghai, *Education, Society and Development: New Perspectives from Kenya*. Nairobi: Oxford University Press, 1974.

4. P. Williams, "Education Priorities in Sub-Saharan Africa," paper prepared for Conference on Education Priorities in Sub-Saharan Africa, Windsor, 3–7 December 1984.

5. D. Jamison and L. Lau, *Farmer Education and Farm Efficiency*, Baltimore: Johns Hopkins University Press, 1982.

6. C. Colclough, "Primary Schooling and Economic Development: A Review of the Evidence," Staff Working Paper No. 399, Washington, D.C.: The World Bank, 1980.

7. K. King and D. Court, "The Interaction of Quantity and Quality in Primary Education," paper prepared for conference on Primary School Effectiveness, Arusha, Tanzania, 1982.

8. K. Kinyanjui, "The Distribution of Educational Resources and Opportunities in Kenya," Discussion Paper No. 208, Nairobi: Institute for Development Studies, 1974.

9. D. Court and K. Kinyanjui, *Development Policy and Education Opportunity: The Experience of Kenya and Tanzania*. Paris International Institute for Education Planning, 1978. D. Court, "The Education System as a Response to Inequality in Kenya and Tanzania," *The Journal of Modern African Studies* 14 (4)(1976).

10. J. Grant, *The State of the World's Children 1985*. New York: UNICEF, 1984.

11. K. King, "Education and Youth Unemployment: Some Propositions," paper presented at the Ninth Conference of Commonwealth Education Ministers, Nicosia, Cyprus, 23–26 July 1984.

12. D. Court, "Dilemmas of Development: The Village Polytechnic Movement as a Shadow System of Education in Kenya," *Comparative Education Review* 17(2) (1974).

13. C. Diaz, "Education and Production in Guinea-Bissau," *Development Dialogue* II (1978): 51–57. F. Ganliao, "The Struggle Continues: Mozambique's Revolutionary Experience in Education," ibid: 25–36. N. Shamuyarira, "Education and Social Transformation in Zimbabwe," ibid: 58–72.

14. J.K. Nyerere, "Education for Self-Reliance," Dar es Salaam, Government Printer, 1966.

15. P. Williams, op. cit., p.4.

16. G. Hyden, *No Shortcuts to Progress*. London: Heinemann, 1983.

17. G. Hyden, op. cit.

18. G. Hyden, op. cit.

19. J.R. Moris, "The Transferability of Western Management Concepts and Programs, An East African Perspective," in L.D. Stifel, et al., *Education and Training for Public Sector Management in Developing Countries*. New York: The Rockefeller Foundation, 1978, 73–83.

20. K. King, "Problems and Prospects of Aid to Education in Sub-Saharan Africa," paper presented at Conference on Education Priorities in Sub-Saharan Africa, Windsor, 3–7 December 1984.

21. E.O. Edwards and M.P. Todaro, "Educational Demand and Supply in the Context of Growing Unemployment in Less Developed Countries," *World Development* 1 (3 & 4)(1973).

22. G. Psacharopolous, "Returns to Education: An Updated International Comparison," *Comparative Education* 17: 321–41.

23. J.C. Eicher, "Educational Costing and Financing in Developing Countries: Focus on Sub-Saharan Africa," Staff Working Paper No. 655. Washington, D.C.: The World Bank, 1984.

24. D. Court and K. King, "Education and Production Needs in the Rural Community: Issues in the Search for a National System," Paris International Institute for Educational Planning, 1979.

25. J.C. Eicher, op. cit. A. Fowler, "Seasonal Aspects of Education in East and Southern Africa," Nairobi mimeo, 1982.

26. S.P. Heyneman, "Influences on Academic Achievement: A Comparison of Results from Uganda and More Industrialized Societies," *Sociology of Education* 49(3)(July 1976): 200–11.

27. S.P. Heyneman, "Research on Education in the Developing Countries," *International Journal of Educational Development* 4(4)(1984): 293–304.

28. S.P. Heyneman, "Improving the Quality of Education in Developing Countries," *Finance and Development* 20(1983): 18-21.

29. K. King, op. cit.

30. S.P. Heyneman, op. cit.

31. D. Court and K. King, op. cit.

32. K. King, *The Planning of Technical and Vocational Education and Training*, Paris International Institute for Educational Planning, 1984.

33. D. Court and K. King, op. cit.

34. K. Lillis and D. Hogan, "Dilemmas of Diversification: Problems Associated with Vocational Education in Developing Countries," *Comparative Education* 19 (1)(1983).

35. G. Psacharopolous and W. Loxley, "Diversified Secondary Education and Development," Report on the Diversified Secondary Curriculum Study, Washington, D.C.: World Bank, 1984.

36. D. Court and K. King, op. cit.

37. D. Court and K. Kinyanjui, op. cit.

38. The issue of the "academic gold standard" is reviewed at length in E. Ashby, *Universities British, Indian, African: A study in the Ecology of Higher Education*, Cambridge, Mass.: Harvard University Press, 1966. See also E. Shils, "The Implantation of Universities: Reflections on a Theme of Ashby," *Universities Quarterly*, XXII (2)(1968): 142–66, and T. Eisemon, *The Science Profession in the Third World*. New York: Praeger, 1984.

39. D. Court, "The Development Ideal in Higher Education: The Experience of Kenya and Tanzania," *Higher Education* 9(1980): 657–80.

40. J.K. Nyerere, "The University's Role in the Development of New Countries," opening speech, World University Assembly, Dar es Salaam, June 27, 1966. Aklilu Habte, "Higher Education in Ethiopia in the 1970s and Beyond: A Survey of Some Issues and Responses," in C. Ward, ed., *Education and Development Reconsidered*, New York: Praeger, 1974, pp. 214–40.

41. J.C. Eicher, "Education Costing and Financing in Developing Countries," Staff Working Paper No. 655, Washington, D.C.: The World Bank, 1984.

42. See S. Shaeffer and J. Nkinyangi, eds., *Educational Research Environments in Developing Countries*, Ottawa: IDRC, 1984.

43. USAID, "African Bureau Strategy Paper: Education and Human Development." Washington, D.C., 1984.

44. R.M. Morgan and V.J. Cieutat, "Improving the Efficiency of Educational Systems: Project Introduction and Summary." Florida State University, 1984.

45. D. Court, "Education and Socio-Economic Development: The Missing Link," mimeo, 1985.

46. P. Williams, op. cit.

47. H. Perraton, et al., "Basic Education and Agricultural Extension: Costs, Effects, and Alternatives," Staff Working Paper No. 564. Washington, D.C.: The World Bank, 1983.

48. C.A. Anderson, "Fostering Educational Research in the Third World," in F.C. Ward, op. cit.

49. C.E. Beeby, "The Quality of Education in Historical Perspective,"

paper presented at seminar on the Quality of Education, The World Bank, Washington, D.C., mimeo, 1983.

50. B. Robinson, "The Sector Approach to Education and Training." Nairobi: USAID, RESDO/ESA, 1984.

51. R. Dore, *The Diploma Disease: Education, Qualifications and Development*. Berkeley: The University of California Press, 1976.

52. USAID, op. cit.

53. P. Williams, op. cit.

54. F. Method, "National Research and Development Capabilities in Education," in F.C. Ward, op. cit.

55. J.L. Moock, "Overseas Training and National Development Objectives in Sub-Saharan Africa," *Comparative Education Review* 28 (2)(1984).

56. P. Williams, op. cit.

Women's Role in Development

Jane I. Guyer

Ten years ago, policy-making for African women's activities and concerns was necessarily "planning without facts." The fund of information on the status of women was thin and scattered, and in only a few countries were there organizations at the national and local levels with the expertise and political influence to articulate women's interests. As a result of a wide variety of efforts undertaken during the UN Decade for Women, this is no longer the case. There has been a great improvement in African women's access to education, and in the number, independence, and sophistication of women's organizations. For policy and aid purposes, there has been a major improvement in the documentation of women's economic and familial roles, and in understanding the obstacles in the path of policy implementation for women from the international to the local level.

This increased knowledge, experience, and organizational expertise suggests that development policies must build on women's potential and improve the conditions under which they work, or suffer losses and foregone opportunities which Africa cannot afford at this juncture. The fact that women's work is a crucial resource in African rural economies, particularly in food production, has been known for decades. What has been almost completely lacking, however, has been a long-term, sustained attempt to develop and implement an agricultural and social policy with this fact in mind.

It would be naive to suggest that the same set of policies could be pursued throughout such a diverse continent. Indeed, one of the central arguments of this chapter is the need to work with the differing national and regional realities in a flexible manner. There are, however, certain general guiding principles: first, we need to accept the fact that women's African agricultural production will continue to depend heavily on women for the foreseeable future; second, promote women's interests in the context of broader development objectives; third, shift the emphasis in policy-relevant work on women and by women, toward measures which go beyond the rubric of "the development project."

A strategy for the future must be based on the following principles:

- *Facts*: Women's enterprise is critical in Africa's agricultural economy, particularly in food production for domestic use and the home market, and in local and regional trade. Their successes have been achieved with negligible foreign or national aid, and with little political representation. Women's legal and practical disabilities are increasingly at odds with the urgent needs of economic and population policy.

- *Aims*: Optimal conditions for promoting welfare, employment, and technical innovation depend on the promotion of diversified regional economies in which opportunities for occupational specialization, income generation, and property-holding are available to women. Women's optimal participation in production and in family and national life depends on the protection and promotion of their legal rights and the recognition of their organizations.

- *Implementation measures*: There are three organizationally independent ways in which women's interests should be represented at national and international levels: a) policy research devoted to analyzing the effect of past and prospective social policy on women's activities, b) women's bureaus devoted to legal and political representation, and c) technical expertise on women's concerns represented in specific projects and policies within the specialist services or ministries.

The three parts of this chapter illustrate and expand on each of these arguments.

THE RECORD ON WOMEN IN ECONOMY
AND SOCIETY

AGRICULTURE AND RELATED ACTIVITIES

The majority of the African population continues to work in primary production, and, in almost all rural areas, women outnumber men.

Official figures compiled from official sources suggest that a little under half of the rural labor force in Africa is female (FAO, 1982; Dixon, 1982).Impressive as this may sound by world standards where the comparable proportion is about one-third, there are reasons to believe that this figure underestimates women's importance. For example, in Malawi, women constitute two-thirds of the full-time farmers (FAO, 1982), and their seasonal labor input is often more consistent and exacting than that of their male counterparts. In a Liberian study, men worked on the farm more than 80 percent of the available days only one month out of the year, whereas women worked beyond 90 percent capacity in five months (Carter, 1982, p. 103). And they often work longer hours in the fields; in a Burkina Faso study, women spent 80 percent more time than men in production, supply, and distribution (McSweeney, 1979, p. 381, see Appendix 1). This picture of hard work on an exacting daily and seasonal rhythm characterizes much of the African woman's productive labor.

Women's work is concentrated in certain tasks and crops. In a breakdown of 13 duties, from clearing new fields to provision of cooked food, women were found to provide half or more of the labor for 10 of those tasks (FAO, 1982, p. 4). Women provided 70 percent or more of the labor in hoeing and weeding, farm to village transport, storage, processing, and the provision of water and fuel. Men provided 70 percent or more of the work in cutting the forest, staking out fields, turning the soil, and hunting.

While men's tasks are declining in importance due to decreasing heavy forest cover and declining game resources, the tasks associated with female labor are becoming increasingly important. The re-cultivation of short-fallow land requires increased weeding; the increasing distance of fields from villages demands transport; and the growth of regional food marketing places a premium on processing and storage of the raw crops from the field. Therefore, even without male outmigration or male specialization in export crops, there is increasing pressure on the agricultural tasks associated with women. In areas where men migrate out to work, women are required to take over male tasks as well.

Women tend to specialize in food crops for home consumption or regional markets, whereas men concentrate in export crop production. This division is the most marked in the forest areas of West and Central Africa. In commercial tree crops, particularly cocoa and coffee, men provide 80 percent of the labor, while they do as little as 9 percent of the work in root crop cultivation for food. Figures from other countries, however, suggest a considerably higher women's contribution to export crop production; they provide 35 percent of the labor on tobacco in Swaziland, 47 and 37 percent in two different cases of cotton production in Malawi, and 70 percent in coffee production in Rwanda (FAO, 1982, p. 4). According to Rodriguez, "most cashew workers in Mozambique are women" (1983, p. 130).

Conversely there are some areas in which men produce food crops for the local market. In parts of Nigeria and Ethiopia men are the principal farmers. Men provide 36 percent of labor in hybrid maize production, and 45 percent in upland rice and 60 percent in swamp rice in Sierra Leone (FAO, 1982, p. 4).

In recent years, one important innovation has been truck farming of European vegetables, highly perishable fruits, flowers, and other fragile crops in the peri-urban areas. Women have figured prominently in this type of cultivation, for example, producing onions in Ghana and vegetables in Abidjan. Intensive farming requires relatively small areas of land and little clearing labor, and is therefore quite manageable by women when they have restricted access to resources.

Despite rising food imports, urban food supply in large parts of Africa is still ensured in the regional productive and trading economy. Throughout the continent, small-scale processing and trade is dominated by women, while men predominate in transport. Major cities such as Ibadan, Brazzaville, and Kinshasa have been fed through women's trade. In the 1950s and 1960s, economists P.T. Bauer (1954) and W.O. Jones (1972) found the food trade to be highly competitive and efficient within the restrictions imposed by poor infrastructure and access to capital.

Outside the coastal regions of West Africa where women have dominated trade for centuries, women's self-employment in processing and trade has been a fairly recent development. Since the rapid growth of urban areas after 1945 and particularly after independence in the 1960s, women have responded to the opportunities presented by expanding markets, in part as a result of income incentives, but also due to the exigencies of low incomes and insecure access earnings. According to Dixon, 43 percent of the workers in the self-employed sector in Africa are women (Dixon, 1982). Most urban centers are now heavily dependent on the services provided by these women.

THE FORMAL SECTOR

Information on women's formal sector employment has been gathered only very recently. As late as 1977, Lucas noted that the data were so poor and inconsistently collected that "generalizations about African women are scarcely possible" (p. 36). Studies now confirm what was intuitively clear—women's representation in formal sector employment is much lower than men's at all levels. At the top, there are a few highly educated women in law, politics, medicine, and other professions. Many of these women come from prominent families, however, and hardly represent the possibility of upward mobility for the brilliant girl from an ordinary background.

At a lower professional level, recent figures for Liberia, for example, show that 16.7 percent of the working male population were formal sector employees, as compared with 1.1 percent of working women (Carter, 1982, pp. 1–9). In Tanzania, women were 5 percent of the employed labor force in 1951, and 9 percent in 1974, a negligible increase when one considers the substantial shift in investment from large-scale agriculture to industry over the same period (Bryceson and Mbilinyi, 1978).

Some of the limitations on women's employment were set during the colonial period and, in some countries, the "traditional" Western female occupations are dominated by men. Nursing and midwifery are generally male occupations in francophone countries as a result of the military medical tradition of the colonial period. Domestic service is predominantly male in Zambia, again due to the colonial tradition (Hansen, 1984). There are more male school-teachers in Africa than in Europe.

When women do find steady employment, it therefore tends to be in unskilled jobs, for example in certain categories of plantation labor, such as tea-picking in the CDC plantations in Cameroon, ancillary work in rubber and oil palm estates in Liberia, and nursery work, weeding, mulching, and gathering in Kenya.

The overall pattern of women's employment reflect the following set of factors. First, women's educational levels have lagged far behind men's until very recently, so that women now in their productive years tend to have poorer formal sector skills, including mastery of the official language. Second, occupational structures were established fairly long ago, and under conditions of high unemployment, thus it is difficult for women to break into the old "preserves." Finally, in some places, there are the familiar cultural constraints on women in technical fields and managerial positions.

WOMEN'S EARNINGS

In the formal sector women earn lower wages than men. Steel and Campbell suggest that in Ghana, men's wages are as much as 90 percent higher than women's, largely due to women's over-representation in low status work (1982, p. 239). In agricultural labor, the differential is somewhat narrower; women on a Cameroon rubber plantation, for example, earn about three-fourths the salary of men (Koenig, 1977, p. 94). The differential, in earnings between men and women appears to be considerably higher, however, in the small-scale, self-employed or family labor sector than in formal sector agricultural wage labor.

Efforts to estimate returns to labor by sex in self-employment are fraught with methodological problems, but the critical factor in determining differentials appears to be access to resources. Certain crops, especially cocoa and coffee, provide much higher returns than others, and farming of these crops is almost universally male. The Liberian study showed that cocoa and coffee bring three or more times the returns per labor day as rice, and up to twice as much as cassava. Both men and women produce rice; cassava is cultivated predominantly by women (Carter, 1982, p. 113). In other words, the differential in returns is not a simple direct function of the gender of the farmer or trader. The returns to men's labor, however, are in a higher range even though there is considerable overlap. There can be as much as a 4:1 differential between men's returns from cocoa and women's from food crops, as was the case in southern Nigeria during the 1952 cocoa boom (Galletti et al 1956).

Women tend to control less capital than men, and this may account for their lower returns to labor in some cases. In the plow economies of southern Africa, where women have access to oxen only through men. In Botswana, Lucas reported that women's farms tend to produce similar yields per unit area as men's farms, but at a much higher labor cost (1979). Without timely use of the plow, deficiencies have to be compensated for by increased hand labor. The same pattern of increased labor to make up for disabilities to other inputs is evident in Kenya, where women farmers have suffered from limited access to official agricultural services, extension, credit, and improved seed (Staudt, 1982).

In the processing and trade sectors, women's enterprises tend to be somewhat smaller than men's, and their access to markets tends to be more geographically limited (Dulansey and Austin, 1985, p. 99). Given these restrictions, most of which are a function of lower status, it is not surprising that women's earnings are lower than men's.

PRODUCTIVITY, INNOVATION AND RESOURCE ACCESS

There is evidence that given the same resource endowments, women can be as productive and innovative in their work as men (Moock, 1976). Fortmann shows that women farmers are responsive to new techniques as men who grow the same crop (Fortmann, 1982). Muntemba relates how a Zambian production scheme for women "mushroomed" when it was provided with extension services (1982, p. 94). Women themselves have introduced various innovations independent of government, particularly in marketing organization. In Ghana and Nigeria, where women's enterprise has a long history and where women have developed their own credit organizations, many women have gained prominence as entrepreneurs.

There is nothing "natural" about the marginalization of women into low- status, poor return occupations. It is a question of resource control, itself a legal and policy issue which, in the past has been rendered unapproachable by the association of local practices with the idea of "custom."Closer examination shows that "customary" provisions can be quite recent inventions, often shaped by central policy. The effective exclusion of women from the planning machinery and the restriction of women's extension education to home economics in Malawi cannot conceivably be thought of as "African tradition" (Hirschmann, 1985). In some cases, the limitations on women's access to formal sector resources are even contrary to local "customary" practice. The various provisions that restrict women's access to capital, extension, and higher level decision-making must be seen as, in principle, changeable through the political process.

Beyond its effects on production, a further benefit from encouraging improved income and resource control for women is its influence on their patterns of consumption and savings. Women's interest in saving and in technical and productive investment may be greater than men's at the same income level. They appear to devote less money to social and ceremonial expenditures, due to their marginal position in local power structures. Women's credit associations have spring up when female incomes rise, offering credit and investment opportunities in those situations where women can translate improved incomes into increased resource control.

WOMEN, FAMILY WELFARE, AND POPULATION

African family structures present a different configuration of elements than those of Europe and Asia, with their own economic and demographic implications. Within the "extended family," there is a separation of functions. A child is socialized and fed within the very small unit centered around the mother, while at the same time being a full member of a larger group which provides a house site and ensures political, legal, and social support in relation to outsiders. Women's claims, like men's, are defined by this context, although generally through marriage rather than descent. Many of the characteristics of marriage derive from polygyny, even though the present rates of polygyny are much lower than in the past. A man assumes only certain defined responsibilities toward each wife and her children, and the wives themselves have both the right and duty to fulfill the others. Women therefore expect to support their own children within the mother-child unit which Ekejiuba has described as the "hearth-hold," to distinguish it from the household (1984).

When they search for ways of earning an individual income, women see themselves as pursuing their children's and broader familial interests. All sources suggest that the simplest answer to the classic question, "What do women want?" would include independent control of income. It is imbued in women that provision of their children's material needs rests largely with them. Their husbands are generally expected to pay for religious, political, and occupational education.

The combination of the two principles—nested familial structures and the relative economic autonomy of the hearth-hold—makes it imperative for women to earn an income. Studies have shown that women tend to choose a reliable source of personal income over uncertain access to a possibly larger sum in their husbands' or fathers' pockets. Dey quotes Gambian women rice farmers as preferring work on their own plots to their husbands', even for a wage (1981, p. 120). Jones shows that women in northern Cameroon shift their work from their husbands' to their own crops unless adequately rewarded (1972). Dupire describes women in Ivory Coast refusing to provide free porterage of their husbands' crops to market (1960, p. 14) and Obbo has written about women's "struggle for economic independence" in the urban setting of Kampala (1980).

This pursuit of individual income is a corollary of the division of labor, income, and responsibility between husband and wife. Under present conditions of insecurity, including probelms of resource access, high divorce rates, late marriage, or destitution at widowhood, there is an even greater incentive than in the past to insure such an income.

Besides providing for themselves, women's work and incomes are disproportionately devoted to children's nutrition and basic welfare. In the forest region of southern Cameroon, women provide most of the staples from their fields and devote up to three-fourths of their cash income to food supplements and household needs such as soap, matches, and kerosene (Guyer, 1984). In four ecologically different rural areas in Ivory Coast, Berio shows that "women supply between 48 and 63 percent of the most important food groups" (1983, p. 65).

In welfare terms, any deliberate or inadvertent measure which inhibits women's access to income and resources is likely to have swift effects, certainly on nutrition.

It would also affect fertility. In theory, women's employment is expected to provide anti-natalist incentives if work is in the formal sector and pro-natalist if it is in the informal and peasant sector. Neither correlation seems to hold true in Africa (Cain, 1984). Three West African studies find practically no reduction in desired or actual family size among women who work (Lewis, 1982; Fapohunda, 1982; Kollehlon, 1984). Rather, it is argued that fertility is likely to remain high wherever women have no alternative support in widowhood and old age (Cain, 1984). In this case, improving women's security of access to resources may be one plank of population policy. It certainly appears that demands for family planning are coming far more from women than from men.

WOMEN IN LAW AND POLITICAL LIFE

African nations have quite varied constitutional provisions and policies with respect to women's status, ranging from the militant promotion of women's equality in Mozambique (Urdang, 1984), to the exemption of family law and the position of women from the anti-discrimination clause of the new Zimbabwean constitution (May, 1982). Even where there is official support for women's organizations, as Feldman describes in Kenya, "economic and political crises. . .have tended to displace attention" (1984, p. 67). Foreign donors have shied away from the interventionist implications of taking a strong, explicit stand on a topic as imbued with passion and in some cases religious fervor as the position of women.

The record here is discouraging. First, in many African countries, it is unrealistic to call for increased participation of groups of citizens, whether male or female, because of political restrictions. Second, in some countries, there has been an effort to redefine "tradition" with respect to the position of women in quite misleading ways. Under Mobutu's ideology of "authenticity," the women's groups which sprang up after 1960 were banned, then selectively affiliated with the party. In the legal system, "the combination of the Belgian legal code and 'traditional' laws has resulted in a hodge-podge of some of the worst aspects of both" (Wilson, 1982, p. 164).

Finally, even with militant ideologies of one sort or another, all African countries recognize local "custom" with respect to family law. Rarely does the civil code cover all possible contingencies of marriage and inheritance. This means that even when a woman is married under the civil code and earns an income in the formal sector, her property rights may be subject to customary practice. The main points which need emphasizing here are that "custom" has often been reworked to serve particular interests and no longer bears a strict relationship to precolonial practice. The following are brief illustrations chosen to throw some light on women's legal problems.

In Kenya, land law has been changed in order to promote individual tenure. In the Luo region, men own the land, but women acquire permanent use rights by virtue of marriage. Individual tenure creates a whole series of unresolved problems in relation to women's rights, largely because inheritance is still judged in terms of "custom." The security of a woman's rights in case of inheritance, sale, or lease of the land on which she works, the right of an inheritor to dispossess his father's widow in favor of his own wife, and the rights of unmarried women to farm land are all ambiguous and disputable (Pala, 1980). While women provide the main agricultural labor force, their rights to the land are insecure.

In Zimbabwe, inheritance is governed by custom, which in this case means that if the children are minors, the entire estate goes to the brother or lineage next-of-kin. A widow who has worked to develop her husband's business, built and furnished his home, and educated the children can be left totally bereft (May, 1983).

In both these cases, as in many others, the version of customary law which has been sanctified over the years constitutes a barrier between the female producers and the incentives to production. Very few women serve as assessors on the tribunals through which "custom" is interpreted. Short of radical legal change, provisions to represent women's interests in these courts might provide means for local reforms and innovations.

Women's political organizations at the national level are quite varied in their power, representativeness and formal affiliation within the larger political arena. While one cannot be unrealistic about the possibilities they offer, they may be the only context in which women can rise to political prominence and in which women's issues can gain a national audience.

One encouraging prospect in women's rights is that education levels for females have greatly increased, especially at the primary level. The change is most striking for Tanzania, where the percentage of women aged 15 to 49 who have enrolled in primary school rose from 18 to 93 percent between 1960 and 1981 (Poats, 1984). The Sahelian countries remain at a lower level, but the increase is still significant (see Table A.3 in Appendix I).

The gains at higher levels and in adult education are less impressive. There are still very few women with technical expertise. Rural courses for women have tended to concentrate on home economics skills, instead of building on new levels of literacy to advance technical knowledge and accounting. At a Zambian farm institute studied by Muntemba, courses were given to 704 men and only 288 women, and most of the women's curriculum revolved around sewing and knitting (1982, p. 93). In a comparable case in Malawi, over half of the course hours for "farmers' wives" were devoted to home skills (Hirschmann, 1985).

The possibility of improvement on all social fronts has been strengthened by the expansion of women's organizations. Increased literacy and increased collective representation for women are the two conditions under which national debates about economic, welfare, and legal policy toward women can develop.

OBSTACLES TO WOMEN-IN-DEVELOPMENT POLICIES

The scope of the problems concerning women-in-development programs in donor countries can be indicated by Staudt's stark figures on the Women In Development Office (WID) of the U.S. Agency for International Development (U.S.AID), where "a million dollar budget (was) allocated to WID in a multi-billion dollar agency" (1985, p. 139). U.S.AID records show that projects in Africa which were women-specific or had women's components accounted for only 4.3 percent of regional bureau funding, and only four out of 45 agricultural projects mentioned women as beneficiaries (Staudt, 1985, pp. 97, 100). The 1982 report of the administrator of the United Nations Development Programme showed that between 1974 and 1980, only 4 percent of projects approved were considered to "involve women's participation," and in over half of these, the female participation was "minor" (1982, p. 4). On the list of recipients of projects involving women by continent, only the Arab states and Europe rated lower than Africa (1982, p. 7).

Given the importance of women's labor in African economies, why is it so consistently bypassed? One way in which African social change has been understood and its future projected is through a theory of social evolution. In this model, women's involvement in farming is considered "backward," to be replaced by peasant "household" production. By implication, women's farming and their independent enterprises are expected to disappear "naturally" and therefore neither is worth careful consideration or the investment of scarce resources. The way forward is thought to be promotion of large-scale enterprise in which Western scientific farming can be practiced without the intricate incumbrances of family law, women's time budgets, etc.

It is not the emphasis on plantation agriculture per se which is wrong with this theory, but rather the elimination from consideration of those currently farming the land and who will continue to do so barring massive urban migration, for the foreseeable future. In fact, the fragmentary evidence suggests that women's importance in rural economies continues to increase. It is not a question of whether women's farming will still exist in the year 2000 and beyond, but whether it will be carried out under optimal conditions. These would ideally include the use, by scientific research, of women farmers' expertise in managing a tricky environment.

Another view holds that as long as agriculture is associated with female labor, it will remain low in status, receive poor returns, and be relatively distant from the formal sector. This situation is perceived as alterable only by favoring the increased participation of men.

Both these views are outdated, based on simplistic assumptions that African development in the late 20th century will or can necessarily repeat the same "stages" as other parts of the world at other moments in history. Women's improved organization and modern education offers the possibility of lifting some of the restrictions on women's enterprise. The realization in development circles that indigenous farming techniques have great adaptive strengths, offers the possibility of productive engagement for the first time.

A third negative view might link the "crisis" state of African agriculture to female farming. In fact, there is no correspondence between areas in particular distress at the moment and the gender-specificity of food cultivation. As the current worst case, Ethiopia has plow cultivation systems run by men, which is otherwise quite unusual in sub-Saharan Africa. Depending on the traditional short-handled hoe, women's farming in southern Cameroon feeds its own rural population at close to adequate levels, and also urban centers from Gabon to eastern Nigeria. World Bank estimates of changes in productivity by crop over the past 20 years indicate that cassava, a crop grown almost entirely by women, has been the only staple to keep up with population growth (IBRD 1981, pp. 168–9).

These hidden erroneous assumptions prevent constructive consideration of possibilities for strengthening women's enterprise as a component in diversifying rural economies. Whereas women's farming, processing, and trade cannot be the entire answer to Africa's agricultural needs, neither are they the major source of the problem.

SUMMARY

The collected knowledge about women in Africa is not only a list of facts or an account book of successes or failures, but a collection of information in support of a set of complementary ideas. Development policies which fail to address women's current economic activities are running against the tide with respect to women's participation, and are potentially setting up serious ripple effects in children's welfare, fertility, and the poor use of development resources. Women's interests are optimally furthered when allied with general measures to to promote rural employment and strengthen regional diversity. Policies which support and promote women's activities have to be part of such a broad development strategy.

Policies promoting women must also be varied and flexible enough to address different constraints at the national level. No single policy can possibly apply everywhere; alternative routes and strategies must be available to circumvent particular setbacks and limitations in order to avoid abandonment of the goals themselves.

The work by and about African women has generated a far better-documented policy debate than was possible 10 or 15 years ago. This is a very short period of time in relation to the enormous breadth of the issues, and can only pay off in the longer term over an extended period of continued work and active experimentation.

STRATEGIES AND PRIORITIES

Framing a coherent approach to the role of women in African economies demands developing a set of goals, from the most general to the most particular. At the most general level, research on women's activities and incomes supports a development policy in which current indigenous practices and small-scale intensive enterprises are seen as a potential strength. To a considerable degree, the interests of women can be met within a "small-scale farmer" policy; by contrast, they are less likely to be served by large-scale, specialist commercial plantation agriculture or a strong export crop focus. The economic and welfare returns tend to be higher for more women when productive economies are diversified, where local and regional trade can develop, and where the avenues to diffusion of technologies are open.

A specific focus on women, however, considerably sharpens the parameters of such a policy. The following discussion outlines both the convergences between a general approach to diversification and an approach with women's concerns as the central focus, and the modifications which the latter imposes. It is critical that women-in-development advocates engage in the debate in this manner as both allies and critics, because the ultimate goal must be the promotion of greater general welfare and economic vitality.

INTERNATIONAL AND NATIONAL TRADE POLICY

African products have held a weakened position on world markets for some time. Rising food imports have caused particular concern since around 1975, when the combined effects of drought, escalating petroleum prices, and civil disturbances undermined the regional and urban-rural food trade. Since women figure prominently in the domestic food supply sector, they are deeply affected by the way in which this situation is managed. Research and political representation should be undertaken on this crucial issue by those concerned with women's economic interests.

Two main dangers are in evidence. First, at the international level, there is a possibility of state-subsidized competition for new grain markets by the farmers of the developed world. This has been advocated recently by Orville Freeman (1985). The argument that the de-control of African grain prices would lead to improved incentives for African farmers no longer holds if cheap imports are unrestricted. Trade is just as much a "woman's concern" as population policy or civil rights, since decisions on this matter will affect women's access to income.

Material and technical inputs for the productive processes are the more urgent imports. Small-scale industry and agriculture can be blocked by the lack of one particular ingredient required from abroad—chemicals for soap production, sheet metal for tool-making, spare parts for machinery, improved seed and planting materials, vaccine for livestock, solar pumps for irrigation, etc. If trade with Africa is to be promoted—as Secretary of State Shultz has suggested (1984)—it should be in types of goods which stimulate local enterprise and raise the productivity of both men and women, not in consumer goods which replace their products on the market.

Studies of income generation projects for women are unanimous in their findings that the high cost of imported inputs and the low cost of imported competing products militates very strongly against success (Buvinic, 1984, p. 2). Such projects cannot realistically be pursued without a supportive trade policy. Many of the so-called failures of women's projects may be due to the policy environment rather than the structure or purpose of the project itself.

At the national level, regarding staple grain markets, women will benefit most if the small-scale sector can strengthen its niche in the distribution system. At present, the small-scale parallel market is discouraged in a variety of institutionalized ways—through high vehicle taxation, discriminatory market access, market taxes, prohibition of inter-regional transport of certain crops, and police controls. In Guinea and Ghana, there has been outright hostility between the government and women traders. If these measures and attitudes are left unaddressed when markets are decontrolled, large-scale business will be greatly favored over the smaller scale operations which Bauer showed to be more competitive and efficient in their use of resources and in their ability to bring market incentives to relatively scattered rural producers. It is very important that the potential effects of decontrol on employment and incomes, as well as consumption, be examined under varying national conditions.

PROMOTION OF TECHNICAL CHANGE

Among those who advocate agricultural policies that favor the small-scale farmer, there seems to be quite profound disagreement over whether "technical solutions" for improving African agriculture already exist "on the shelf." Attention to the role of women in rural economies helps to focus the question. There are some known and successful technologies, particularly in the predominantly female spheres of processing, storage, small animal husbandry, and truck farming, whose diffusion is too slow. Although based on sophisticated scientific and technical research, they tend not to be of the "package" variety, but rather specific innovations. For example, animal vaccination removes a general constraint on husbandry; the introduction of intensive truck crops in peri-urban areas makes use of potentials for land and labor reallocation; and mills for processing cassava remove a particular labor and management bottleneck.

Information about new crops and methods has diffused across the continent throughout its history, and continues to do so. Staudt, for example, reports that "the diffusion of information was found to occur among women's networks" in Kenya (1982, p. 221). But much more work needs to be done to speed the adaptation of known technologies to local situations.

Experimentation and adjustment of appropriate technologies offer enormous potential in the medium-term, not solely by means of expanding adoption of such methods, but through the participation of the producers in making their own social and technical modifications. A graphic example of an effort to improve potato storage is given by Rhoades (1984). From one side of the globe to the other, farmers have incorporated the principle that storage in diffused light results in shorter sprouts and less weight loss than storage in darkness, although the techniques used to achieve this vary from place to place. Olga Linares provides the example of Diola rice farmers' rapid adoption of a rice variety with a sharp spike which inhibits pre-harvest losses to birds and releases the female and child labor otherwise devoted to bird-scaring.

The possibilities seem quite wide, but it remains largely a question of planning, orchestrating, and financing such a program of participatory information dissemination. Since women would be a major category of participants, the research on women suggests some of the constraints and possibilities.

Public Identification of Technologies   Studies by and about women identify problems of safety regarding the use of some technologies, particularly chemical poisons such as insecticides and herbicides, which must be spread under much more controlled conditions. Having such substances and their containers around in the environment of African villages, where the level of vigilance over children is low when all adults are working, poses serious public health problems. Technologies for diffusion should be low-risk in physical and financial terms in order to promote maximum experimentation with minimum damage.

With regard to other possibilities for lifting technical constraints, an analysis of work patterns suggests bottlenecks around particular tasks (Cloud, 1985). Women find it difficult to recruit extra labor (Johnny et al., 1981), and often rely on their children's help in solving the need to be in two places at once (Pala, 1979). Large-scale capital and technology does not lift these constraints and in fact often creates new ones. For example, when larger areas can be plowed by tractor, the weeding and harvesting are often left to women to manage with the old hand techniques (Boserup, 1970; Anderson, 1985). In the short to medium term, the "labor shortage" is task-specific and often associated with the availability of women's labor.

Technologies that remove particular constraints can promote expansion. For example, ILO studies of cassava-processing in southern Ghana show that even during economic crisis, diesel-powered graters are used and processing capacity now outstrips production (ILO, 1984, pp. 8, 272). In Central Africa, by hand-processing cassava, not only are women working extremely hard (Adam, 1980), but surplus production is often left in the ground unharvested. There is no point in lifting the production constraint if the processing constraint is not removed.

Many problems identified in artisanal processing are amenable to technical solutions already known. Some improved techniques are already employed, but again, in limited areas: solar driers for fish preservation, diesel mills for cassava-grating, energy-efficient stoves for cooking, and drying platforms for cassava flour (ILO, 1984).

Certain crops and cropping systems are particularly amenable to technical change through participatory dissemination. Truck farming for urban markets has spread quite widely, often with minimal needs for on-going intervention. Experimental systems, such as alley cropping developed at the International Institute for Tropical Agriculture in Ibadan, could be attempted throughout the humid zone. Leguminous trees are planted in widely spaced rows, and perform the dual function of maintaining soil fertility and providing mulch and fodder for animals. The system is well-suited to areas where the population density is too high to permit long fallow cycles. Such low-risk techniques could be attempted in a wide variety of social and ecological environments.

The choice of known technologies worth promoting must also include certain services which will only be available through the government, such as livestock vaccination. From women's perspective, particular attention should be given to small ruminants such as goats and sheep, since women more often own this kind of animal for both investment and food.

While the situation varies across Africa and the rest of the tropical world, it is hard to believe that a vast technical wisdom does not already exist with actual prototypes which could be tried out. The inventory of potential technologies needs to be matched with the actual bottlenecks in production and processing to serve as a basis for dissemination and comparison of results. It is not a question of doubting the importance of crop/fertilizer packages, but rather of placing them within the total labor and technology context. Far more can be done beyond developing new strains of crops, and many other innovations can directly address the constraints on women's work.

Formation of National and International Networks   Some form of organizational structure is required for semi-controlled dissemination of technology and for the collection and evaluation of results in different areas. No innovations can be diffused without channels of information, yet women have not been well represented in those channels in the past. Women's formal and informal organizations which exist almost everywhere in Africa may provide the conduit. Working with women's organizations ensures that where techniques apply to women's tasks and crops, women will be involved in the field trials. The experimental activity itself strengthens these organizations' interest and expertise in technical issues.

Outlets   Inexpensive inputs should be sold, with subsidies only for the cost of maintaining a broad enough inventory to allow for experiment. Studies in many regions show that as poor as people are, some resources do exist in the rural areas and savings and credit clubs are growing. Commercial sale of items such as seed, grinders, containers, and storage materials obviates the very difficult problems presented by formal sector credit—the small size of loans, the need for collateral, and the difficulty of enforcing repayment. For larger items, however, new forms of credit will have to be made available.

Credit   Lack of access to credit has been identified by a variety of sources as a major obstacle to the adoption of new techniques by women (ILO, 1984, p. 371; Loutfi, 1980, p.42, Fortmann, 1982, p. 193). Where credit is an essential component of a project or program, a means of extending it to women must be developed. Many of the barriers women face in this regard are due to their disabilities with respect to the sole source of collateral recognized by banks—title to property.

The provision of formal sector credit poses a problem both to customers and to the banks and parastatals which try to enforce repayment. More goods could be sold outright if retail outlets for productive inputs could be made a profitable endeavor, leaving the small-scale credit to local rotating credit associations. Whereas credit has been used for other purposes, such as tying farmers to monopsony purchasers of the product, parastatal control is likely to be limited in the future. Distribution of inputs through commercial outlets may provide women with better access than cooperatives because female membership in formal cooperative groups is limited.

Commercial access has often benefited women; in fact, the picture of women as "traditional" is far from accurate. Rural life is more commercialized in some respects than the stereotypical views suggest: The West African food processors studied by the ILO purchased 34 to 35 percent of their firewood (1984, p. 224), and a sample of Ghanaian female cocoa farmers hired 44.3 percent of the labor required on their farms, 10 percent more than their husbands (Okali, 1983, p. 85). Alternatives to "traditional" resource access tend to favor women, who often turn to the market with great alacrity.

Education/Extension   Women's access to extension services is poor in Africa. In general, women are less mobile than men, less able to set aside large blocks of time for training, and unable to spend long periods of time on the farm with a male extension worker. In addition to ensuring that women farmers are included in any extension network, some investment should be made in developing new means of transmitting technical information to them. Radio broadcasts in local languages are one possibility, but written material should not be ruled out altogether as female literacy rates rise. Training of women extension agents with levels of technical expertise comparable to men should be a priority in higher education.

RESEARCH

Processing and Storage   Reliable processing and storage are critically important in order to make full use of current production, especially since improved transport and infrastructure are unlikely to be affordable under present circumstances. If a policy focusing on small-scale farmers succeeds, it will eventually generate more marketable surpluses which in turn will place heavier demands on those who are primarily responsible for processing and storage, namely women.

In the short to medium term, improvements in processing techniques are of greater strategic importance than improvements in production itself. This is especially true for cassava, one of Central and West Africa's major staples. Cassava is highly perishable unless reduced to flour, which takes at least twice as much labor time as cultivation. Cassava could become price-responsive if processing techniques, market prices, and market access were more favorable.

An ILO study of cassava processing provided a number of useful observations. It found that women were not necessarily unreceptive to innovations which involved moving their activities out of the home; rather, they made an explicit trade-off between technical benefits and social losses (1984, p. 370). The group work which resulted from sharing expensive capital obtained higher levels of labor productivity.

At the moment, tons of fruit rot in all but the most efficiently commercialized or most densely populated rural areas. Fruit processing could generate employment for rural women. The enormous fruit surplus produced in the humid zone and the low level of fruit trade to the savanna is in part a problem of consumer tastes, as preserves and jams are not part of the diet, but dried fruit could be one alternative.

In other words, there are still unworked opportunities and women are not necessarily intransigently conservative. Present technologies may be programmed into a particular rhythm of daily life, but this does not mean that women are unwilling to change.

Agriculture   Research on women's work suggests several priority concerns in agriculture itself. First, a positive approach to multiple cropping and mixed farming is far more likely to benefit women farmers than crop-specific research for large-scale production. Intercropping has technical advantage in Africa and also fits in with the family dietary requirements which form the basis, though not the limit, of most women's farming.

Second, where women share tasks and fields with men, it is often the (misnamed) "secondary crops" which are controlled by the women. The importance of "secondary crops" cannot be overestimated. A study in Sierra Leone found on average 21 intercrop species per farm plot. "Crops in addition to the main crop (rice) accounted for 54 percent of the market value and 73 percent of the food energy value of the total output of such farms" (Richards, 1983, p. 27). Research to develop varieties for multiple-cropped fields, rather than for maximum production under controlled, monocropped conditions, has been promoted recently and should be further encouraged.

Despite men's association with monocropping and export crops, the barriers to women's development of monocropped fields have more to do with local and national discrimination against access to large stretches of land, capital equipment, and permanent trees than with the technical potential of the current division of labor by sex. Women's peri-urban market gardening can be very successful without running up against such barriers. Adaptation of truck vegetables to new environments, the diffusion of other tropical vegetables from tropical Asia, and development of indigenous vegetables are useful areas for research.

No major staple is more associated with women's cultivation and primary processing than cassava. Cassava has many assets as a crop: It is the staple whose productivity in Africa compares most favorably with yield levels elsewhere in the world; it is more nutritious than often asserted, especially if the leaves are eaten as a green vegetable; and it has always been marketed through the "private sector" at "free market" prices. Technical improvements in cassava cultivation would benefit women more than improvements in any other single crop. Research on cassava and other root crops has been carried out at the International Institute for Tropical Agriculture in Ibadan and should continue to be funded at a level comparable to the major cereal crops.

WOMEN IN LAW AND SOCIETY

As earlier stated, the record here is among the most discouraging. Women's access to and control of resources is consistently more limited than men's in projects, in legal statements, and in customary practice. Donors can exert influence in these areas by funding female students for higher and technical education; by developing equitable resource access in projects; by funding women's projects, networks, organizations, and publications; and by providing technical advice on civil rights and legal issues.

The major funding agencies do not have a good track record in any of these areas. Dey describes women who have been cut off from access to land as a result of development projects (1981); Conti shows how women assumed to be free of family labor (1979); and Rogers' book (1979) is a litany of the ways in which women have been sidelined, sometimes out of the sheer myopia of Western thinking. Policy can be at serious variance with the views of local men. Lapido, for example, quotes Yoruba farmers as being pleased "that something progressive might also reach their wives" (1981, p. 131).

While impressive gains were made in primary education during the 1970s, during the same period, the number of women trained by U.S.AID halved and over half of the remaining number were trained in population and health (Staudt, 1985, pp. 95-96). At the same time, there is a shortage of trained people to do technical work (ILO, 1984, p. 287) and of female teachers to work with female farmers and artisans on experimental trials of new technologies.

Critical legal work on women's status has been needed for a long time. Anomalies in current legal frameworks are sometimes glaring. Family law is the basic framework of any "peasant" or small-farmer strategy; continuing disputes about inheritance, the legitimacy of marriage, the seniority of children, the rights of widows and so on are debilitating and counter-productive (Okali, 1983). There are no simple answers here, but the lack of attention given to legal issues in recent years and the potential of drifting into de facto attenuation of women's rights is serious. Women's organizations within African countries need the resources to research and monitor their own situations and to implement policy reforms—as limited as ensuring female assessors on all customary tribunals or as radical as guaranteeing women's rights to land. This is not only an issue of civil rights, but a prerequisite for improving women's ability to respond to incentives.

IMPLEMENTATION STRUCTURES

In the past decade, the concern with women has been institutionalized in multi-purpose offices with the particular mandate to research and represent women within larger organizations. The Women In Development Office of U.S.AID and the UN Voluntary Fund for Women are two examples within the donor community. Some African countries have ministries or bureaus for women's affairs, while others have only a small understaffed office or committee. Most political parties have women's branches.

Over the years, the limitations of this approach have emerged. Staudt's book on the AID office shows that in terms of the numbers of projects concerned with women, the output has been disappointing. The WID endeavor has been poorly funded in terms of the resources of the agency. The UN fund is voluntary—not a regularly budgeted item—dependent on the annual commitments of individual countries. National organizations run into the same sort of problem—enough resources to function, but not effectively. They depend to a much greater degree than comparable organizations on voluntary labor (Buvinic, 1984, p. 22) and get stuck in small-scale, pilot-stage activities.

The lack of financial commitment is only one aspect of the problem. Some of the obstacles are clearly attitudinal: simple lack of interest on the part of the professional staff, a certain inertia in the organization of the field offices, and diffidence about "intervening" in family issues. Others include poor institutional links to technical sectors such as agriculture and lack of a firmly grounded disciplinary basis on which to evaluate results. Briefly put, "women's affairs" are susceptible to being relegated to an inconspicuous corner of the bureaucracy, with few connecting links of reporting or authority.

Regardless of existing institutional and personal resistance to a concern with women, it is clear from reports of those working within such structures that they are very awkward and perhaps unworkable. Women's issues span health, education, nutrition, and agriculture and yet the women's office has no authority with regard to projects funded in those areas. This may be one powerful reason why a great deal of recent successful work on women has focused on small-scale technology, an area not really captured by any other department and one which is slightly anomalous, neither industry nor agriculture.

Women's offices seem to have intrinsically incompatible aspects to their mandates. Research in technical areas, from tax policy to crop rotations, requires integration into the rest of the technical community. Political action, on the other hand, such as advocacy of a women's perspective within the organization as a whole, lobbying for more funding for women's projects, or the maintenance of links to other women's groups, demands cross-disciplinary organization and a somewhat more confrontational collective stance. Working on project administration involves yet another kind of structure defined by authority and cooperation. Individuals may be able to do all of these at once, but an organization runs up against the limits to flexibility in level of expertise, loyalty, collective morale, and so on. This is all the more problematic when the issue itself is as controversial as that of "women," and adversaries are looking for ways to avoid dealing with it.

Staudt suggests abandoning this overburdened, underfinanced, and understaffed type of organization in favor of a "loosely knit but diverse front" (1985, p. 139) of people located mainly within the technical sectors. Buvinic argues that the form of a "women's organization" should be retained, but used solely for research and evaluation (1984, p.22). Staudt adds that consultation with such an office ought to be a compulsory part of all project formulation and evaluation. In summary, a division of labor among those concerned with women's status should be actively sought.

At the very least, three functions are needed: broad policy research, representation, and technically specific expertise. Separation of these functions has the merit of improving organizational functioning and flexibility in the face of shifting politics and funding, and also achieves a critical transition from project-based to policy-based work. The broad question of women and development must be liberated from the tyranny of the "project."

Throughout this discussion, it has been implicit that those concerned with women's role in development can and should urgently address policy at the national and international levels as well as being involved with the formulation and implementation of development projects. Women gain and lose from trade and pricing policies, wage and benefit policies, changes in family law, and the narrow focus of agricultural research at the international centers. Local and international scholars and experts need to carry out the necessary research to suggest alternative courses of action. Ideally, there should be forums for local constituencies to comment on the implications.

Policy research shows that women's status can be addressed irrespective of the vexing problems of accessibility, obstacles to project organization, and the inertia of bureaucratic structures. The perception that "projects" have not worked very well for women is no valid reason for continuing to bypass the female side of economic and domestic life.

Projects themselves are likely to remain a major feature of aid—they are discreet, fundable, amenable to sub-contracting, and focus on measurable results. As pointed out in the introduction, there has been a significant improvement in the knowledge of why projects for women succeed or fail (see, for example, Overholt et al., 1985). The work of the next decade is to address the findings—that women tend to be second-class citizens with respect to access to resources for development, that they can, on the contrary, be highly effective as aid recipients, and that women's networks and organizations can function as sources and disseminators of information, promoters of credit associations, and potential lobbies for agricultural interests.

ACKNOWLEDGMENTS

The following people's suggestions and comments on earlier drafts are gratefully acknowledged, without committing them to any of the views expressed: Sara Berry, Christine Jones, Margaret Jean Hay, and Pauline Peters.

REFERENCES

Adam, Michel. 1980. "Manioc, Rente Foncière et Situation des Femmes dans les environs de Brazzaville (République Populaire du Congo)." *Cahiers d'Etudes Africaines* 20(1-2): 5–48.

Anderson, Mary B. 1985. "Technology Transfer: Implications for Women." In C. Overholt, et al., *Gender Roles in Development Projects*. West Hartford, Conn.: Kumarian Press, pp. 57–78.

Bauer, P.T. 1954. *West African Trade*. Cambridge: Cambridge University Press.

Berio, Ann-Jacqueline. 1983. "The Analysis of Time Allocation and Activity Patterns in Nutrition and Rural Development Planning." *Food and Nutrition Bulletin* 6(l): 53–58.

Boserup, Ester. 1970. "The Changing Role of Tanzanian Women in Production: From Peasants to Proletarians." Unpublished paper, University of Tanzania.

Bryceson, Deborah F. and Marjorie Mbilinyi. 1978. "The Changing Role of Tanzanian Women in Production: From Peasants to Proletarians." Unpublished paper, University of Tanzania.

Buvinic, Mayra. 1984. "Projects for Women in the Third World: Explaining their Misbehavior." Washington, D.C.: International Center for Research on Women.

Cain, Mead. 1984. "On Women's Status, Family Structure and Fertility in Developing Countries." Washington, D.C.: The World Bank.

Carter, Jeannette E., assisted by Joyce Mends-Cole. 1982. *Liberian Women, Their Role in Food Production and Their Educational and Legal Status*. University of Liberia: Profile of Women in Development Project.

Cloud, Kathleen. 1985. "Women's Productivity in Agricultural Systems: Considerations for Project Design." In C. Overholt, et al., op. cit., pp. 17–56.

Conti, Anna. 1979. "Capitalist Organisation of Production through Non-Capitalist Relations; Women's Role in a Pilot Resettlement in Upper Volta." *Review of African Political Economy* 15/16: 13–52.

Dey, Jennie. 1981. "Gambian Women: Unequal Partners in Rice Development Projects?" In Nici Nelson, *African Women in the Development Process*. London: Frank Cass, pp. 109–122.

Dey, Jennie. 1983. "Rice Farming Systems. Case Studies of Current Developments and Future Alternatives in Upland Rice and Inland Swamp Rice."

Expert Consultation on Women in Food Production. Rome: Food and Agriculture Organization of the United Nations.

Dixon, Ruth. 1982. "Women in Agriculture: Counting the Labor Force in Developing Countries." *Population and Development Review* 8(3): 539–66.

Dulansey, Marianne and James E. Austin. 1985. "Small Scale Enterprises and Women." In C. Overholt et al., op. cit., pp. 79–131.

Dupire, Marguerite. 1960. "Planteurs autochtones et étrangers en Basse-Côte-d'Ivoire orientale." In *Etudes Eburnéennes* VIII: 7–237.

Ekejiuba, Felicia. 1984. "Contemporary Households and Major Socio-Economic Transitions in Eastern Nigeria." Paper presented at the workshop on "Conceptualizing the Household: Issues of Theory, Method and Application." Cambridge, MA.

Fapohunda, Eleanor. 1982. "The Child-care Dilemma of Working Mothers in African Cities: The Case of Lagos, Nigeria." In Edna G. Bay, ed., *Women and Work in Africa*. Boulder, Colorado: Westview Press, pp. 277–88.

Feldman, Rayah. 1984. "Women's Groups and Women's Subordination: An Analysis of Politics Toward Women's Groups in Kenya." *Review of African Political Economy* 27/28: 67–85.

Food and Agriculture Organization of the United Nations. 1982. "Follow-Up to WCARRD: The Role of Women in Agricultural Production." Rome.

Fortmann, Louise. 1982. "Women Work in a Communal Setting: The Tanzanian Policy of Ujamaa." In Edna G. Bay, ed. op. cit., pp. 191–205.

Freeman, Orville. 1985. "Opening Markets for Food Abroad." *New York Times*, May 15th.

Galletti, R., K.D.S. Baldwin and I.O. Dina. 1956. *Nigerian Cocoa Farmers; An Economic Survey of Yoruba Cocoa Farming Families*. London: Oxford University Press.

Guyer, Jane I. 1984. *Family and Farm in Southern Cameroon*. Boston University, African Research Series #15.

Hansen, Karen Tranberg. 1984. "Negotiating Sex and Gender in Urban Zambia." *Journal of Southern African Studies* 10(2): 219–38.

Hirschmann, David. 1985. "Bureaucracy and Rural Women: Illustrations from Malawi." *Rural Africana* 21:51–63.

International Bank for Reconstruction and Development. 1981. *Accelerated Development in Sub-Saharan Africa* Washington, D.C.

International Labor Office. 1984. *Technological Change, Basic Needs and the Condition of Rural Women*. Geneva.

Johnny, M. M. P., J. A. Karimu and P. Richards. 1981. "Upland and Swamp Rice Farming Systems in Sierra Leone: The Social Context of Technical Change." *Africa* 51: 596–620.

Jones, Christine Winton. 1983. "The Mobilization of Women's Labor for Cash Crop Production: A Game Theoretic Approach." Unpublished Ph.D. dissertation, Harvard University.

Jones, W.O. 1972. *Marketing Staple Food Crops in Tropical Africa*. Ithaca: Cornell University Press.

Koenig, Dolores B. 1977. "Sex, Work and Social Class in Cameroon." Unpublished Ph.D. thesis, Northwestern University.

Kollehlon, Konia T. 1984. "Women's Work-role and Fertility in Liberia."
    Africa 54(4): 31–45.
Lapido, Patricia. 1981. "Developing Women's Cooperatives: An Experiment
    in Rural Nigeria." in Nici Nelson, ed., op. cit., pp. 123–36.
Lewis, Barbara. 1982. "Fertility and Employment: An Assessment of Role
    Incompatibility among African Urban Women." In Edna G. Bay, ed., op.
    cit., pp. 249–76.
Loutfi, Martha. 1980. *Rural Women, Unequal Partners in Development*. Geneva:
    International Labor Office.
Lucas, David. 1977. "Demographic Aspects of Women's Employment in
    Africa." *Manpower and Employment Research* 10(1):31–38.
Lucas, Robert. 1979. "The Distribution and Efficiency of Crop Production in
    the Tribal Areas of Botswana." African Studies Center Working Paper
    No. 20, Boston University.
McSweeney, Brenda Gael. 1979. "Collection and Analysis of Data on Rural
    Women's Time Use." *Studies in Family Planning* 10(11/12): 378–82.
May, Joan. 1982. *Zimbabwean Women in Colonial and Customary Law*. Gweru:
    Mambo Press.
Moock, Peter. 1976. "The Efficiency of Women as Farm Managers." *American
    Journal of Agricultural Economics* 58: 831–35.
Muntemba, Maud Shimwaayi. 1982. "Women and Agricultural Change in
    the Railway Region of Zambia: Dispossession and Counter-Strategies."
    In Edna G. Bay, ed., op. cit., pp. 83–104.
Obbo, Christine. 1980. *African Women: Their Struggle for Economic Indepen-
    dence*. London: Zed Press.
Okali, Christine. 1983. *Cocoa and Kinship in Ghana. The Matrilineal Akan of
    Ghana*. London: Kegan Paul International.
Overholt, Catherine, Mary B. Anderson, Kathleen Cloud and James E. Aus-
    tin. 1985. *Gender Roles in Development Projects: A Case Book*. West Hartford,
    Conn.: Kumerian Press.
Pala, Achola Okeyo. 1979. "Women in the Household Economy: Managing
    Multiple Roles." *Studies in Family Planning* 10: 337–43.
Pala, Achola Okeyo. 1980. "Daughters of the Lakes and Rivers." In Mona
    Etienne and Eleanor Leacock, eds., *Women and Colonialization: Anthropo-
    logical Perspectives*. New York: Praeger, pp. 186–213.
Poats, Rutherford. 1984. *Development Cooperation*. Paris: Organisation for Ec-
    onomic Cooperation and Development, Chapter 12.
Rhoades, Robert E. 1984. "Tecnicista versus Campesinista: Praxis and The-
    ory for Farmer Involvement in Agricultural Research." In P. Matlon, R.
    Cantrell, D. King and M. Benoit-Cattin, eds., *Coming Full Circle: Farmers'
    Participation in the Development of Technology*. Ottawa: International Devel-
    opment Research Centre, pp. 139–50.
Richards, Paul. 1983. "Ecological Change and the Politics of African Land
    Use." *African Studies Review* 26(2): 1–72.
Rodriquez, Anabella. 1983. "Mozambican Women after the Revolution." In
    Miranda Davies, ed., *Third World—Second Sex: Women's Struggles and Na-
    tional Liberation. Third World Women Speak Out*. London: Zed Press, 127–34.

Rogers, Barbara. 1979. *The Domestication of Women, Discrimination in Developing Societies*. New York: St. Martin's Press.

Shultz, G. 1984. The U.S. and Africa in the 1980s. Current Policy No. 549. February 15. Washington, D.C.: U.S. Department of State.

Staudt, Kathleen. 1982. "Women Farmers and Inequities in Agricultural Services." In Edna G. Bay., ed., op. cit., pp. 207–24.

Staudt Kathleen. 1985. *Women, Foreign Asistance and Advocacy Administration*. New York: Praeger.

Steel, William F. and Claudia Campbell. 1982. "Women's Employment and Development: A Conceptual Framework Applied to Ghana." In Edna G. Bay, ed., op. cit., pp. 225–48.

United Nations Development Program. 1982. "Integration of Women in Development." Report of the Administrator. New York.

Urdang, Stephanie. 1984. "The Last Transition? Women and Development in Mozambique." *Review of African Political Economy* 27/28:8-32.

Wilson, Francille Rusan. 1982. "Reinventing the Past and Circumscribing the Future: Authenticite and the Negative Image of Women's Work in Zaire." In Edna G. Bay, ed., op. cit., pp. 153–70.

Manpower, Technology, and Employment in Africa: Internal and External Policy Agendas

Kenneth King

The local and external agendas on the role of manpower in African development look very different. The external agenda is concerned with "getting the numbers right," the dangers of over-expansion and under-utilization of labor, and the training of very specific subgroups to address the problems of agricultural productivity, population control, and other development issues. The local manpower agenda, conditioned by the traditions of scarcity of skilled labor and exclusion from training that prevailed in the colonial era, is fundamentally suspicious of labor over-supply.

A comprehensive approach to manpower development is lacking both locally and among external donors. On the external side, this is partially due to donors' preoccupation with projects and their preference for building on their comparative advantage in particular sectors. Thus, one donor is concerned solely with increasing formal apprenticeship in industry and another with agricultural extension, the engineering faculty, or the training of rural artisans. The provision of manpower is invariably a justification for regional projects, but in practice, this amounts to little more than an assertion that national development is impeded by shortages of specialized manpower.

No less difficult to grasp, the local manpower agenda has little to do with whether the state does or does not have a ministry of manpower development or whether there is a tradition of carrying out manpower surveys. As is the case with the donor agencies, the implicit manpower assumptions of the state have to be deduced from a wide variety of sources, many of them far removed from the official manpower planning apparatus. The actual manpower policies of the state consist of many uncoordinated initiatives such as guaranteeing graduates employment, measures which favor science over arts in tertiary education, concern about the ratios of men to women in modern sector jobs, and others. These policies in turn determine the expansion of polytechnics, secondary schools, and universities.

Overlaying these forces, the official apparatus of manpower planning seeks to control the politics of the domestic manpower agenda. Manpower planning units have won few rounds in this contest over the last 20 years, but it is nevertheless useful to regard these official units as a negotiating forum between the external and internal agendas for manpower development. In many countries, the existence of an official apparatus represents the hope that if only the different categories of manpower could be ascertained, they could be scientifically managed.

ASPECTS OF THE LOCAL MANPOWER AGENDA

In the 1980s, local agendas continue to be preoccupied with expanding education at all levels. Since there are virtually no signposts from manpower planning ministries or elsewhere as to the appropriate size of secondary, polytechnic, or university education, the lure of universal primary education has given way to that of universal secondary, and eventually to open higher education.

Underlying increasingly open educational systems is the assumption that opening opportunities to compete for the few good jobs available is more equitable than shaping educational policy to the pyramid of well-paid jobs. Therefore there is little correspondence in size between the education and training system (the supply) and the wage and salary sector (the demand). The increasing determination of a number of African countries to build colleges of technology, polytechnics, and technological or agricultural universities in the face of strong negative pressure from external agencies illuminates the tensions between local and foreign agendas.

Countries are determined to provide access to scientific and technological careers, particularly during one of Africa's worst recessions. Consultants carrying out feasibility studies on the need for more polytechnic or university graduates are in a peculiarly difficult position. Investigating something that is already feasible in local eyes, they represent agencies that are skeptical of the country's ability to fund or absorb further graduates.

Nowhere is the conflict between manpower agendas more fierce than over the issue of pre-vocational skills for all. With their increasingly cross-national research base, donors believe that offering pre-vocational skills in general schools cannot succeed in developing countries. But what to external donors is yet another example of the vocational training fallacy is to local decision-makers a relevant and logical extension of educational opportunity.[1]

A corollary of the dispute over basic skills is the differing attitudes of donor agencies and national governments toward training in the informal sector of the economy. The ILO and other bodies were fascinated by the open access system of training and skills in the shanty towns, roadsides, and villages—local, low-cost skilled manpower development. By contrast, governments could barely be constrained from sweeping the informal sector out of sight, destroying shanty workshops, and in some cases trying to prevent young apprentices from developing their skills.[2]

While dramatic evidence of local manpower agendas is found in access to different levels of education, other elements in the informal manpower agenda concern the relationship between skills and scientific knowledge. Of particular importance are relations between artisans, technicians, scientists, and engineers in the industrial sector, and between the various grades of agricultural staff in the rural sector.

One example of the relationship between skills and knowledge is the application of the 1:5:30 ratio as suggested proportions of engineers, technicians, and artisans. While this ratio is widely argued over and has been used to support the expansion of technician and scientific careers, for all the decades of manpower planning, there has been no rule of thumb to give direction to university expansion. Ministers are guided by rather simple but compelling manpower agendas and not least by the evidence of massive social demand for higher education of the sort evident in Southeast Asia.

In many African countries, there are entire shadow university populations overseas that often exceed the number of home-based students. This is central to manpower planning, for very few of the shadow university students are on government scholarships. Unlike the home situation where there is some attempt to "get the numbers right" for arts, computer science, agriculture, and so on, in the shadow university system, tens of thousands of students are deciding their own course of study.

In the United States in 1983-84, at least half of the 330,000 foreign students chose just three disciplines: engineering, management, and computer science.[3] For the carefully controlled schools of engineering and computer science in a national university of an African country, the implications of these figures do not need much explanation. Therefore, African ministers are as much guided in their plans for local university expansion by the evidence of a 1:1 ratio between their home-based and overseas students as by donor arguments about the impossible costs of further higher education.

In Tanzania for almost 20 years, a very different educational model has been in operation—neither a pyramid nor a square, but a low, flat rectangle with a tiny, thin spire. President Nyerere has preached that secondary education is a privilege not a right, and that a poor country cannot afford to have more than 1 or 2 percent of its primary school leavers attend secondary school. In proportion to the number of children in primary school, Tanzania consequently has the smallest secondary school population in the world. This controversial model was widely praised by the donor community. Now, however, it must be admitted that this particular manpower approach is in ruins; there are shortages of educated people at all levels.[4]

Both Kenya and Tanzania's systems of further education were planned by a colonial power determined that higher education in Africa should not be influenced by the Indian model with its ever-expanding associated colleges.[5] Now, with more than 5000 East African students studying in Indian colleges and universities, African decision-makers are clearly impressed by India's claim to have the third largest contingent of scientific and technical manpower in the world, and have considerable admiration for the investment in science that they associate with India, Singapore, Hong Kong, and South Korea.

African policy on higher education for development is now at a peculiarly difficult crossroads. Lacking signposts, policy-makers have to fall back on very basic intuitions, of which the most compelling is the conviction that they have dramatically under-invested in science and technology since independence.

By contrast, many African countries have been content with Afri-

canizing the public service, approaching the localization of the industrial and extractive sectors with extreme caution. As a result, in the
mid-1980s, many of the scientific careers where Africa offers opportunities are still dominated by white science. Rangeland management,
ecology, archaeology, palaeontology, renewable energy, mining,
and specialized agricultural research are only a few of the fields
where technological capability is predominantly in expatriate hands.
It is not surprising, therefore, that at their recent Harare conference,
African ministers of education targeted science and technology education as the next great advance.

The real manpower agenda is increasingly determined to extend
provision of science and technology at all levels, as well as agricultural skills and sciences. Some argue that saturation with skills and
science is the only way around the dilemmas of scarcity, but whether
through mobility or misallocation, small cadres of trained people
have not utilized their skills in jobs for which they were trained.

A fundamental issue is identifying the local meaning categories of
skill and technical knowledge. The time-honored European distinctions between skilled and semi-skilled labor, between artisans, technicians, and scientists do not apply in Africa at all. Unlike the European and Asian skilled workers whose attitude to their craft has been
hardened by caste, community, or union traditions over many generations, the majority of African artisans, technicians, and scientists are
still first generation.

As a consequence, there is little disposition to think of these occupations as lifelong or family concerns. Polytechnic students are not
necessarily settling down to 25 years as contented technicians, any
more than technical or vocational school students are planning to stay
in skilled work throughout their lives. Assumptions about the connection between training facilities and subsequent careers seldom
take into account local perspectives. In reality, it is entirely possible
that some polytechnics are full of shadow university students, and
that some technical schools are full of students identical to those
found in the ordinary high schools.[6]

The lack of connection between the training facility and the category of work aspired to makes a good deal of difference to calculations of skilled manpower supply. Therefore, understanding how
skill and knowledge hierarchies are viewed locally is important for
any analysis of the need for middle-level manpower. A similar case
could be made for the distinctions between certificate, diploma, and
graduate qualifications in agriculture.

Another important element in gaining a sense of the local man-power agenda is the difference between the small number of modern sector paid jobs and work in subsistence agriculture or in the urban and rural informal sectors. In many African economies, only 10 percent of the labor force is employed in the paid wage and salary sector, with more than half of this number in the public service.

Workers in the modern sector are few and relatively privileged. In one sense, people inside this favored sector have more in common with each other than with the large majority who work outside, both in terms of different traditions of training and education and the jobs themselves. Thus a carpenter in the modern sector, employed by a multinational or the ministry of works, has more in common with a clerk or other middle-range civil servant than with a carpenter who is working on his own in the informal sector of the economy.[7]

The most dramatic examples of belonging to the fortunate few come from those very systems like Tanzania's where secondary school children are virtually guaranteed jobs because of the exclusion from government secondary school of 98 percent of primary school leavers. In this situation, whether students pursue agriculture or home economics in secondary school is of minimal importance when compared to those not in school at all. Loyalty to these "disciplines" is consequently very weak and it is therefore not surprising to find little correlation between education and subsequent employment. The rather high mobility among those who are inside the modern sector can foil attempts to relate training to job classifications.

A second very crucial aspect of the distinction between jobs and work is that the bulk of those practicing a particular trade—automobile mechanic, builder, carpenter—fall outside the modern sector and are not captured by statistics. This would not be significant if the modern sector was a self-contained system separate from the 90 percent working outside. The reality, however, is quite the opposite. The vast number of shadow artisans and workers in the informal sector are incorporated into the modern sector at many points. For example, it is common for formal sector construction companies to use low-paid, non-unionized labor from the informal sector in regular building contracts, having an obvious impact on the "demand" for formally trained artisans. This raises problems for approaches to manpower that treat the modern sector as independent from the larger system.[8]

A crucial element in the local manpower perspective is related to the moving educational frontier between "real" jobs and ordinary work. In a situation where only 10 percent of the workforce have real jobs, the universalization of primary or secondary education and the moves toward open higher education can have unforeseen consequences. In the inevitable democratization of primary education after independence, the marketability of the primary school certificate was devalued almost overnight. Consequently, following a short-lived political concern about the "educated unemployed" primary school leaver, new generations of secondary school graduates became the focus of political concern, giving way in turn to the higher secondary and college graduates. By the mid-1980s in many developing countries, primary school leavers could no longer be described as educated unemployed.

Primary school leavers were no longer seriously considered for modern sector jobs. Widespread concern about the political threat of several million "jobless" school leavers proved unfounded; the expected demoralization of youth did not materialize. As these school leavers lacked any incentive to register as unemployed, it became difficult to quantify them. They vanished back into the informal and unregistered occupations of their parents.[9]

The consequence of this moving educational frontier is that in many countries, primary and secondary school leavers are politically irrelevant, apart from some regular exhortations to use their school skills for self-employment. Only graduates are sufficiently politically important to warrant job-creation schemes. This does not necessarily mean that governments regard the eight or 12 years of education as wasted, but concern with how such education is being used is not very high on the manpower agenda. Where government ability to create jobs is restricted to the public service and parastatals, the most popular political alternative is to create educational opportunities to compete for these jobs.

ASPECTS OF THE EXTERNAL MANPOWER AGENDA

Although more is known about the external than the internal manpower agenda, the external map for particular countries is not clear. It can be deduced from the mass of official and voluntary projects and technology and investment decisions of foreign companies operating in the country.[10]

External agencies have strong views about their own comparative advantage in manpower training in Africa, tending to support a particular sector in a style peculiar to them. Some agencies are exclusively concerned with rural artisans, others with a particular type of agricultural extension or maternal and child health. While all provide training components in-country, overseas, and in third countries, except where donors share a sphere of influence, there is virtually no knowledge of what other donors are doing, or any attempt to coordinate.

THE TEMPTATIONS OF SCALE

Donors' interest in promoting manpower initiatives in Africa is due to the relative smallness of most of the countries. With single universities and polytechnics and easy access to most of the senior decision-makers, individual countries appear open to influence compared to South and Southeast Asia. External agencies seem to believe that the manpower situation can be corrected with the right delivery system. What cannot be grasped in a few weeks, however, even in a very small country with a handful of training institutions, is the local significance of skill and knowledge—a sense of how parents, pupils, and politicians are using particular institutions.

THE DESIRE FOR RATIONALIZATION

By the mid-1980s, even a country whose first trade school dates only from the 1920s is likely to have a whole range of government, private, parastatal, and NGO bodies involved in skills training at different levels. The donor community tends to think that this apparent duplication must be rationalized and coordinated. Given the highly political nature of many of these educational decisions, such demands for rationalization strike very close to local political nerves.

In the colonial period, independent educational initiatives were frequently halted. With independence, however, a number of African achievements in education and training have been treated with great skepticism by donors on pedagogical or fiscal grounds. External skepticism to measures in Kenya, for example, can be documented in the outright condemnations of the Harambee secondary school movement, free primary education to Standard Four, the development of some 15 Harambee institutes of science and technology, free primary education to Standard Seven, and many other educational initiatives.

By reason of its enormous commitment to the expansion of education, Kenya has encountered this clash between internal and external manpower agendas more than other nations. Yet even countries with quite different priorities, such as Tanzania, are frequently given recommendations for rationalization. The paradox of these recommendations is not only that there is virtually no rationalization of donor priorities, but that donor priorities often shift dramatically within the space of two or three years. Donors end up competing for projects they had earlier declared foolhardy, or deciding that local priorities they once admired are simply no longer tenable.

DIFFERENT MANPOWER RESEARCH AGENDAS

While there is no common external approach to manpower research, some of donor interests in this area are derived from fundamentally different concerns than local ones. The types of manpower research projects considered as important are often those that contrast the cost and effectiveness of two parallel "delivery systems" in technical, vocational, or agricultural education. The working assumption is that research may point to where rationalization is needed.

The temptation for external research to rationalize is particularly acute when four or five different institutions are involved with broadly similar types of training. But the "scientific" rationalization of what appear to be illogical LDC systems often fails to take account of the history and specificity of the institutions under review.[11]

Efforts to associate particular amounts of education with particular development outcomes are also common among external donors. Donors are preoccupied with identifying what increments to agricultural or industrial manpower can be derived from particular sequences of education. Possibly the single best known example is the assertion that four years of education is basic to worker productivity.[12] Some studies have been very influential within the donor community in making the case for increased support to basic education.

Donors' concepts of human resource development and deployment are a world apart from the local agenda on education and manpower. The commitment to universal primary or secondary education originates from quite different sets of assumptions in many

African countries. There are too few studies which look at the impact of three years of higher education on the nature of graduates' work, perhaps because research has been preoccupied with legitimizing the priority of primary education, rather than with analyzing what a country may hope to reap from its new generations of graduates.

Thus, one of the challenges to African researchers is to develop a local research agenda for education, manpower, and employment. On the external research agenda it is already clear that some priority research will be concentrated over the next decade upon clarifying how schooling affects an individual's later ability to adapt to the technological requirements of agriculture.[13] Based on their own insights into manpower policies, African researchers have the opportunity and obligation to lay out and implement a different set of solutions than those currently proposed.[14] In the absence of local initiative, the grounds on which manpower discussions take place in developing countries will be claimed by the Western research community.

MANPOWER POLICIES, UTILIZATION, AND
THE TECHNOLOGICAL ENVIRONMENT

Having sketched some features of the foreign and local manpower maps, it may be useful to look more closely at current manpower planning in some African countries and what new approaches are being developed. Regarding the protracted and unproductive debate about particular techniques for manpower planning, Hollister has summarized the present rather unimpressive state of the art admirably:

> In looking back over these (20) years, I am struck by how little progress seems to have been made: the literature on manpower planning seems little different to what was written two decades ago, and, more important, the practice of manpower planning seems hardly to have changed at all.
>
> It is my impression that the plans made by manpower planners have rarely had any effect on the policy decisions actually made. The methods used, however, have had the effect of discouraging the development of information which could have been used to improve the policy-making process.[15]

Given the amount of information actually collected by different agencies, it seems quite likely that under-utilization of existing information is as serious as the absence of information. However, a priority of any new approach to manpower must be a concern with utilization of existing personnel rather than quantitative projections of those who are not yet hired. Officials in manpower ministries often assume that if a manpower survey were available, the shortages and surpluses would be evident and it would then be simple to argue for more technicians (and in turn for more polytechnics), or more artisans (and more training schemes).

Nothing could be further from the truth. There is virtually nothing that can be deduced from knowing how many engineers, technicians, and artisans there are in a particular country. Instead, therefore, we shall explore a number of ways for looking at the complex issue of utilization, which itself is inseparable from the technological environment.

THE FARM, FIRM, AND FACTORY

A prerequisite for understanding how manpower is actually used in Africa is to examine a few case studies in the main sectors of the economy. For the purposes of illustration, three sectors—farm, firm/office, and factory—could be looked at in each of four modes: public, multinational, local, and informal.

Manpower surveys often concentrate on what is measurable, large-scale, and modern sector, routinely excluding the bulk of employment. It is critical that smaller local and informal sector enterprises are included in these case studies, because their pattern of labor use directly affects the pattern in the wage and salary sector. It is also critical to include the public sector (i.e., a ministry) because no less than half of the modern sector works for the government. The purpose of these case studies is to uncover different patterns of utilization of labor in different sectors, and to note how these are affected by education, training, and technology policies, as well as by elements in the two manpower agendas.

GOVERNMENT OFFICE OR MINISTRY

Understanding the labor process and the culture of the civil service is central to any broader goals of manpower analysis, since in several countries the state sector absorbs all the graduates of certain training institutions, and 75 percent of many crucial occupational groups, such as engineers. Among the more salient features of work organization are:

- The rise of oral decision-making and a measure of retreat from reliance on literacy. For field ministries like education and agriculture, the retreat from literacy has forced headmasters into headquarters and brought ministry officials to the province and district. It also dramatically reduces workloads for secretaries and typists. In addition, though French and English remain immensely popular in schools, they are not an easy or effective medium for many of the secretarial staff.
- Constant delegation of decision-making to higher levels has reduced the written output in lower professional cadres and the number of decisions made because of over-centralization.
- The absence of effective induction systems for new entrants can mean the destruction of the morale of both school and university graduates within a matter of weeks.
- The technological environment is not elaborate, but irregular supplies of paper, ribbons, servicing, and even electricity combine with unwieldy and ineffective filing and registry systems to make evaluations of office efficiency rather complex.
- Finally, the public sector alone offers scope for limited job creation within patronage systems; hence there is a greater expectation of over-staffing and under-utilization in ministries than in most other areas.

The colonial civil service tradition bequeathed to the continent has clearly undergone a major transition since Africa's independence, yet almost no thought has been given to the personnel implications of these changes. The civil service is more educated but less trained and skilled in some ways than it has ever been. Twelve years of basic education may now be the norm for civil service secretaries in many countries, but this does not necessarily translate into increased efficiency if education is underutilized on the job. The state of the civil service is part of a much wider set of political issues. No simple manpower formula for altering ratios of secretaries and professionals or exposing everyone to some system of management will do more than scratch the surface of the problem.[16]

The local and external manpower agendas converge at the level of the African civil service, which is likely to be a common point of conflict between the two. Donors perceive that their own manpower priorities in particular projects or programs have to be made system-proof by special executive committees or by expatriate teams. While one agency would reintroduce expatriate manpower, another believes that the introduction of new information technology might make manpower planning possible. While new technology may simplify the management task, it will have little or no success if one of the explicit manpower policies of the head of state is that all graduates must find work, if need be, in the civil service.

In this case study, it is clear that the techniques of manpower planning are not relevant, nor are improved national manpower surveys which identify crucial shortages and surpluses. Nothing is more important to the deployment and employment of technical manpower in a country than understanding the under-utilization of the still rather good general education of those who enter the nation's largest "firm."

SMALL-SCALE LOCAL ENGINEERING WORKSHOP

While local engineering firms differ dramatically from one country to the next with the salient features of manpower utilization altering accordingly, the following points might emerge from case studies of small-scale skilled engineering firms. First, this sector is still dominated by expatriates or non-African management. Second, in some cases it has the potential to make tools, dies, spare parts, and components of great variety, but it is plagued by low levels of capacity utilization.

Third, some of this under-utilization of capacity is directly linked to the technology policy of the state. The range of imported goods is so great that there is little incentive or comparative advantage to increasing local manufacturing. Thus, the investigation of under-utilization of manpower is sometimes inseparable from the under-utilization of capacity in the firm itself, which in turn is influenced by national policy.

Firms tend to use "shadow" technicians and artisans who are trained on the job by skilled European or Asian machinists, rather than hiring formally trained technical school and polytechnic graduates and/or utilizing the formal apprenticeship system. This strategy reduces the salary bill and the danger of poaching by providing limited skills to the African artisans. If such firms really wanted to enter the field of components manufacture, they would find that the new technologies and associated quality controls dictated by the industrialized countries require an investment in machine tools and a labor process that actually undervalues their existing improvisational skills.

The manpower analysis implications of these critically important small engineering workshops are complex. The concentration of skills in expatriate hands renders the pursuit of the ratio of engineer to technician to artisan meaningless. Informally trained technicians and artisans will not even show up in manpower surveys that assume that these categories can only be produced in formal training institutions. Hence, understanding the constraints of the small engineering sector is a precondition to interpreting any data that a wider survey of engineering manpower might produce.

The absence of trained African technicians and artisans in small-scale engineering workshops cannot be construed as a "demand" for such people, to be met by polytechnics or other formal training schools. On the surface, Africans who acquire a modicum of skills in expatriate engineering workshops would improve on their expertise by leaving and starting their own workshops. But for that to happen at the level of a skilled machinist, for example, access to capital and equipment is necessary, reinforced by a technology policy that makes local manufacture of spare parts and components worthwhile.

As an essential means for deciphering data collected on a wider scale, case study work on the labor process and work organization in one or two representative engineering firms should be conducted. In a 1982 manpower survey in Kenya, some 75,000 individual workers were interviewed and information about their work experience and training was collected. The titles used by the workers to describe their own positions were then "translated" into the numerical codes of the Kenya National Occupational Classification System.

Most of the classic problems of relating job titles in particular firms to larger occupational classifications can be presented in a small table relating to one category of engineering worker (Table 15.1).[17] It is virtually impossible to sort out the skilled from the semi-skilled workers because many semi-skilled machine operators are lumped in the same category as skilled machinists, turners, or fitters. A machine operator can be working on a machine which routinely punches out identical pieces of metal throughout the shift, or he can be on a machine where a great deal of skill is required.

Where coders translating worker titles into national codes do not know the engineering industry or do not have strong English skills, miscoding can take place. One indication is when the category "other worker" is preferred to a specific description. Another is when the very crucial distinction is missed between "tool maker" and "hand tool operator." Such surveys tend to aggregate findings so that all the specific job groups within different sectors are lost in a single category of production, maintenance, and factory workers. Even if education and training are cross-tabulated with this large work group, there is no way of knowing the different levels of education and training in each of the sub-groups. From a policy viewpoint, it would be important to know whether only in the multinational and parastatal sectors workers had completed secondary education and institutional training, or whether the level of certification was rising throughout the productive sectors.

TABLE 15.1
METAL WORKING MACHINE OPERATORS AND MACHINERY FITTERS

Code	Job Group	Number
7110	Leading hand	16
7121	Metal working machine setter/operator	116
7122	Lathe setter/operator/turner	119
7123	Milling machine setter/operator	22
7124	Planing machine setter/operator	12
7125	Boring machine setter/operator	5
7126	Tool sharpener, saw doctor	31
7129	Other machine tool setter/operator	339
7131	Machinery assembler (production)	5
7132	Machinery fitter/maintenance	153
7140	Hand tool operator	37
7150	Precision instrument maker/repair	10
7190	Other metalworking machine oper./ftr.	1698
Total in this sub-group		2556

THE MULTINATIONAL INDUSTRIAL SECTOR

Because the multinational sector is by far the most studied, we will focus on the way it is regarded by governments as the ideal representative of attitudes toward training and manpower utilization. The multinational sector is generally highly responsive to formal training, accepting regular apprentices, seconding them to the local training schools and later to polytechnics, and accommodating levy-grant schemes. It supports institutionalized training both at home and abroad and has the personnel and managerial capacity to organize in-house induction and training systems.

Large multinationals are naturally at the forefront of the local training lobby; they are represented on tripartite training committees and provide a very visible ideal that is hard to follow. Even governments find it difficult to emulate them, for although ministries are very responsive to demands for institutional training, they do not have the capacity to utilize productively the levels of training in which they invest so willingly.

Government technical ministries, parastatals, and multinationals account for almost all the apprenticeship places, scholarships, and sponsorships to national polytechnics, and main users of the levy-grant system where it operates. Therefore, almost all high quality, high cost training efforts are situated at the tip of the iceberg, reinforcing and legitimizing higher pay and benefits.

The danger of multinationals' "responsiveness" to those forecasting demand for formally trained technical labor is that it is easy to assume that other sectors should follow suit. Unlike the situation in Denmark, Scotland, or Germany, where rural workshops have regular apprentices, the imported apprenticeship system has no roots at all in the small urban or rural firms. Attempts to this end distract attention from existing and developing local systems of skill acquisition. The close liaison between the formal technical training system and this restricted group of parastatal, government, and multinational enterprises more importantly deflects attention from measures that would allow low-cost access to formal training and upgrading to firms that cannot afford sponsorship or day release.

THE SMALL AND MEDIUM-SIZED FARM

Numerous manpower studies address the size of various groups of graduates leaving the agricultural training system and the need for improved agricultural extension systems. However, there is little knowledge of the skill levels of those who run their own farms or are employed as small-scale farm managers, nor is there much sense of the availability of jack-of-all-trades workers who can weld farm equipment and do basic carpentry, building, and plumbing.

These skills are of crucial concern to many farmers, and it is quite possible that the specialized skills offered by the regular training institutions do not fit the bill at all. Formal agricultural skills are basically monopolized by the government, multinational estates, and agro-related industries, scarcely penetrating to the level of the local farm manager. Case studies of manpower utilization in the small and medium farm sector could provide some insights into the relationship between the formal training system and the utilization of agricultural skills in the rest of the farm sector. They might also be of value in considering the relationship between new systems of agricultural extension and the skill and knowledge needs of those running small mixed farms.

MANPOWER AND THE INFORMAL SECTOR

Most manpower surveys in Africa have assumed that for skills to be taken note of, they must be located in regular enterprises with a given minimum of employees. In many surveys of high- and middle-level manpower, skilled artisans were captured if they worked in modern sector firms and excluded if they worked elsewhere. In recent years, the manpower potential of the informal sector has come to the attention of national governments and has led to calls for productive self-employment. However, there is no clear pattern of how young people learn to become self-employed or how skills are acquired and extended in different fields. Fortunately, there is now a growing number of case studies from both francophone and anglophone Africa which could be taken advantage of by planners who wish to understand the dynamics of labor use and which could eventually begin to alter the local political rhetoric about education for self-employment.[18] Some of the lessons for manpower planners from this literature include the following:

• There is no such thing as a mass program of training for self-employment.

• It is exceedingly hard for governments (always so closely associated with the formal employment sector) to promote self-employment.

- NGOs, accustomed for decades to working on small budgets close to the grassroots, stand a better chance of developing small-scale programs in support of self-employment.

- In many cases the political rhetoric in favor of training for self-employment is a good deal stronger than government commitment to its development.[19]

It is exceedingly important that manpower analyses extend beyond matters of training and low-cost access to formal institutions to incorporate the technological dimension that is so vital to understanding capacity utilization in the small-scale industrial sector. In some ways, the rate of technological change has been more marked in the informal sector than in Africa's formal industrial estates. More work needs to be undertaken on the role of technology in labor processes. The external manpower agenda relating to the informal sector also needs to address the impact of basic primary education on informal productivity. If some causal connection can be found, this would certainly be valuable in maintaining external support to primary education.[20]

MANPOWER POLICIES IN EDUCATION, TRAINING, AND PRODUCTION: IMPLICATIONS FOR PLANNING

Having outlined some of the connections between technological change and particular patterns of labor utilization in different sectors, it may now be useful to underline some of the consequences of adopting these approaches. The challenge to planners working with manpower or human resource policies is that they must operate with a knowledge of the three crucial areas—education, training, and production.[21]

Traditional discussions about manpower have described the task of the planner as achieving a fit among these three spheres, yet they must also acknowledge that there are limitations on matching these three activities because of the powerful inherent differences in their modes of operation. For example, similar skills exist in each of the spheres, such as metal work, computing, or secretarial skills. For the planner, this situation has frequently been described as "substitutability"—that the welder trained on the job can replace the welder trained in a vocational training center, or someone who has picked up welding in the machine shop of a secondary school.

Obviously, this situation immensely complicates the task of anyone trying to work out the sources and quantities of expertise in different areas. The crucial point is that few skills are easily transferable. Agriculture, carpentry, or office practice learned in school cannot be compared with or substituted for similar disciplines offered in training institutions or acquired directly on the job. This is not to apply value judgments on school-based skills versus on the job skills, but rather to suggest that the context and "feel" of skills acquired in the areas of education, training, and production are significantly different.

In addition, therefore, to a concern about how labor is utilized, there needs to be an awareness of the environment in which the skill was first produced. Instead of totalling up mechanics or other trades coming out of secondary schools, trade schools, and industrial or parastatal training units, it is important to discern the different combinations of exposure to skills and specialized knowledge that young people can gain as they move through the spheres of education, training, and production.

In some situations, it may appear that a young person has been exposed three times (in school, training center, and in the firm) to what may sound like a similar skill, but the different contexts and purposes of the institutions concerned can mean that there is no redundancy. Identifying the various combinations and tracks that are favored by students, governments, and employers is probably more vital than head counting school graduates and seeing if they utilize their skills. The emphasis needs to be less on the title of the course or the skill and more on the specific contributions of the school or industry.

In some of the older studies based on assumptions of substitutability, the focus was on whether someone educated in technical studies or agriculture was in an occupation related to that discipline. Our present schema would be much more concerned with assessing the quality and specificity of the school's contribution before even deciding whether it could be legitimately traced from the world of education to the world of production.

This new approach to manpower not only appreciates what are likely to be the very different contributions of school carpentry courses, training center modules, and carpentry acquired in a furniture firm, but also the impact and the often unanticipated effects of government intervention in these three spheres of education, production, and training. There are also powerful political interventions within the three spheres to rearrange these patterns. Industry may be pressured to undertake a great deal more training, and schools may be required to undertake production or orient their students through more specific training for the world of jobs or self-employment.

Concern about unemployment usually is more evident in the sphere of education than in training or production because the state has more direct control over that sphere. Lacking the power to intervene very effectively in industry, it often seeks to affect employment or industry indirectly by directly affecting schools. There are therefore a series of interventions in many African states to reorder relationships among education, training, and production.[22] These are the cutting edge of the local manpower agenda. In relation to these initiatives, the primary task of the manpower analyst should be less to calculate how many thousands of fresh vocational graduates there might be than to study the way that innovations are incorporated and adapted by the larger system.

The process of incorporation eventually determines whether or not a political initiative for vocationalization of education gets turned into a routine school subject. This implies that the planner must be well aware of the local traditions of education, training, and production, if new attempts to rearrange the pattern of relations are to be set within this historical context. The nearer the planner gets to the local traditions of training, education, or production, however, the clearer it becomes that there is no such thing as a single training tradition or training lobby. The training sphere is itself an accretion of particular interest groups, institutions, and organizations whose origins often reflect a particular historical issue or negotiation.

African traditions of training, education, and production are also complicated by the legacies of colonial and post-colonial external manpower agendas. While the original rationale for their adoption has passed and they have been indigenized, they may still represent a particular training lobby of non-governmental organizations, specific donors, or local companies.[23]

From the perspective of the 1980s, while it may appear that there is no such thing as a national training system, but a bewildering array of semi-autonomous training initiatives, it would be premature to stress rationalization and reduction. One of the chief characteristics of the training systems in Africa is their smallness in numbers and coverage. National youth services, industrial vocational training centers, and polytechnics may well have only a few thousand students altogether.

The challenge to the planner is to uncover the logic of this scattered system—what determines its size, what are the advantages of fragmented bodies responsible for training, and what are its organizing principles. Planners must also understand the important relationship between manpower trained in the workshop and the informal sector on the one hand, and manpower produced in modern sector firms and their related training system on the other.

It must be acknowledged that the circle of production contains an enormously greater variation in a developing country than in a developed one. A majority of producers are located in subsistence self-employment or in petty production (which includes services, agriculture, and industry), while only an extremely influential minority are in the modern sector. After more than a decade of study on the informal sector, a great deal is known about the types of work, people, technologies, incomes, and training patterns in the informal sector.

As a result, the informal sector has finally become a policy item on the local manpower agenda; previously it was only part of an external agenda. This development merely underlines the gap between the formal and the informal sectors, as well as the difficulty of communicating to governments the complexity of the informal sector and its patterns of labor and technology utilization.

Tapping the informal sector as a means of solving unemployment is a compelling approach. There is an acute shortage of jobs, and the informal sector is mostly composed of the self-employed and seems able to expand. Therefore, if there is more education and training for self-employment in the school system, there will be less educated unemployment. The "logic" of this argument has led to attempts to reorient the education system with the insertion of a training function and sometimes even a production element.

MANPOWER POLICIES: THE METHODOLOGICAL CHALLENGE AND AN AGENDA FOR ACTION

Currently, the possibilities of producing a series of techniques that will facilitate manpower policy planning appear limited, while the constraints of research information in effecting change are also recognized. Following are some of the key areas for further analysis and action.

The relation of the local manpower agenda to a labor utilization perspective is most important. As we have defined it, the local manpower agenda is a composite of the interrelationship between local traditions in education, training, and production. These traditions are obviously dynamic, but typically involve generalizations about whether training is sponsored or open, whether local communities expect to build schools or have governments provide them, how parents and young people view the distinction between paid jobs and self-employed work, and so on.

The local agenda also includes political interventions in the spheres of education, training, and production, and the logic behind them. In many African states, these interventions are driven by concern over unemployment, tending to be system-wide initiatives based on snapshot insights into labor relations, as illustrated above.

The political agenda often includes such items as more primary school skills for self-employment; more science and technology courses in higher secondary and university; and more training facilities for middle-level technicians. It is important to stress that this type of political manpower agenda is not derived from the national plan (which is often written with an eye to the external manpower agenda), but from the priority interventions of government in these spheres.

Finally, by far the weakest component of the local agenda is the research wisdom of planners and analysts in ministries and in university research centers about human resource development strategies. This is not just a question of doing better research, but of closing the gap between the research culture on the one hand and the policy culture on the other. Although it is clearly possible at certain points to inform policy-makers, it must generally be acknowledged that the priorities of the world of policy are different from those of research. Hence, even if more analysis gets done within the framework we have been proposing, the process of translating it into policy will not be rapid or easy.

KEY ELEMENTS IN AN INTEGRATED LABOR
UTILIZATION PERSPECTIVE

Manpower utilization can be defined as the intersection point of education, training, and technology policies, as well as of part of the local and external manpower agendas. The explicit policies in each of these areas are relatively useless in analyzing labor use. Just as the local manpower agenda has never been stated explicitly but must be deduced and mapped out, so too the implicit policies of education, training, and technology must be laid bare if the nature of labor use in any particular sector is to be understood.

This requires looking at sector-specific utilizations of education, training, and technology. All sectors are likely to have some common job categories such as mechanics, clerks, and accountants, but it is unnecessary to total these up. Rather, what must be understood are the series of local negotiations about education, training, and technology that define differently these similar-sounding jobs in each sector, and how the local manpower agenda of the government has an impact on that firm-level negotiation.

In many countries, even a brief examination of these intersection points would reveal some very salient features of the local labor utilization systems. For example, there are local hierarchies of skill and knowledge, and local titles to define them in the different sectors; the ministry's hierarchy of labor classification is intimately connected to certification in the national polytechnic system, to which there is sponsored access; the small firm is resisting inclusion in the new training levy system; in the large farm, there has been no connection with any off-farm training except at the level of management. From this approach, a series of sector utilization studies can emerge, identifying the technical form of the large farm, the engineering shop, the technical wing of a ministry, or the urban informal repair sector, and so on.

SECTOR UTILIZATION STUDIES AND THE TWO
MANPOWER AGENDAS

Some essential differences between the local and external manpower agendas have been outlined; both are powerfully affected by political considerations, and in many ways are pulling in different directions. Therefore, it may be worth examining to what extent the proposed utilization emphasis can more creatively alter or build upon the two manpower agendas. The first advantage of the utilization approach is that it gives a sector snapshot of a particular set of interrelations. This could be extremely timely in small farm sectors affected by drought, or in giving an accurate reading of the mix of employment, education, and training policies as they affect the public sector employers.

Without some careful analysis of how farming and public service traditions are being affected by the local manpower agenda, it is easy for external actors to jump to conclusions about the need for more agricultural extension or for drastic steps against over-manning in the civil service. The second way that the approach could be incorporated by the two manpower agendas is where the two meet—for example, where there is a powerful local bid to expand higher technical education and the donor community is approached.

At present, this is typically a situation where the external agenda requires justification of the project through some manpower forecasting. Instead, there would be merit in looking at the utilization and non-utilization of certain groups of graduates from the existing polytechnics operating in the firms surrounding the proposed technical college. For example, clarifying why no small manufacturing workshop ever employs a polytechnic leaver or ever sponsors an employee to attend such a college is potentially more important than a general guesstimate about the need for ever more middle-level technician manpower.[24]

THE INTERDISCIPLINARY UTILIZATION ISSUE

The other methodological shift associated with this approach is that although manpower policy analysis is clearly a mix of education, training, technology, and employment policies, these disciplines are seldom integrated. In traditional employment missions, there may appear to be an interdisciplinary team, but educators look only at the schools, the training experts at the training system, and the economists at factories. In the approach we have proposed, the term "labor utilization" includes the utilization of school skills and knowledge from training centers, but it also involves understanding employer attitudes toward education and training, and how they relate to learning and available technology in the world of production.

Given the crucial separation between the spheres of education, training, and production, an interdisciplinary team would be able to guard against inappropriate evaluations, such as the use of school knowledge in firms as though it was designed to be vocational, and similarly with the training curriculum. Instead of researching what proportion of school math, science, or university engineering is actually used in industry or agriculture, an examination is needed of what relearning and adaptation has to take place in different sectors, what are the discontinuities between the culture of the school and that of the firm, and between school science and the presence or absence of an atmosphere of technological innovation.

ACTION AND ANALYSIS FOR THE EXTERNAL MANPOWER AGENDA

In the last few years, the manpower and human resource development theme has occupied an increasingly important place in donor planning—Britain's ODA has a new policy on its manpower assistance to Africa; Canada's CIDA has put human resources planning at the forefront; and the World Bank has devised a human resources agenda for action. However, as of yet, none of these external agendas for specific African countries have been analyzed. Individual projects are known, but their underlying assumptions have not been examined.

Advice to decentralize, reform the public sector, train management, privatize, and improve planning is abundant, but the different implicit agendas behind donors' fascination with manpower at this point are less clear. Some are of the view that African public sectors do not function effectively because of overmanning, nepotism, abandoned standards, or politicization. From these kinds of assumptions, policies aimed at increasing expatriate manpower and management training are derived.

But there are other assumptions based on the view that it may take at least 20 years for the corner to be turned on African management capacity in public administration and on research capacity in science, agriculture, and other fields—views which could result in a commitment to more training at every level. While some recommend training as near to the production site as possible, it is difficult to know whether this implies a disillusionment with the quality of higher education or merely a more rapid way of getting a project started.

Precisely because of the magnitude and complexity of the external manpower agenda, both governments and donors would benefit if there is a careful mapping of its contours. Currently, the project focus and special interests of each donor prevent a clear view of the overall picture. It would therefore be extremely timely if a map of where human resource development aid is going and why could be developed for two or three African states.

Such a review would reveal uneven emphases reflecting different aid traditions and particular preferences for relations between education, training, and production, as well as unpredictable political interventions in the scale and priorities of assistance in manpower development. If African manpower agendas appear irrational and overly political at times, the same can be said of the often unexplained shifts in aid policies.

It may also be useful to highlight a small number of activities that relate directly to the issue of manpower utilization. For example, several donor agencies might wish to support small-scale labor utilization studies for sectors in which they intend to invest. The precise method employed would depend on the sector and task, since, as Hollister has argued, "There is no uniform method applicable across the entire public sector, and the procedure should be to shape the analysis to the character of the manpower problems in each subsector. The character of the problems and the appropriate methods for analyzing them will vary substantially from one sub-sector to another."[25]

Although context-specific, undertakings by external agencies in the manpower field should address such salient themes as open and closed training, the science and technology content of key training courses, on-the-job training in key industrial and agricultural sectors, and the role of job recruitment and certification systems, such as trade testing or the public service commission. These issues affect a large number of jobs, and understanding them could provide useful insights into the local manpower utilization systems. Another high priority would be a review of the functions and leverage of the various manpower planning units in ministries such as agriculture, education, health, and finance—obvious foci of interest for any attempt to reshape the manpower analysis system.

REVIEW AND DISSEMINATION OF RESEARCH TO POLICY

Any review or revision of an approach to manpower must take the local and donor decision-making environments into account. Admittedly, the process of changing traditional attitudes to manpower assessment cannot happen overnight. The research community must take the first step, and there is now evidence of a shift in approaches by the very variety of perspectives on the manpower assessment task. There has also been an enlargement of the concept of manpower policy to include the role of science and technology, education, training, and employment policies.[26]

The new approaches will then have to be applied, for although the older manpower paradigms are in many ways discredited, the alternative methods have not yet been tried. The new methods could be implemented either at the sub-sector level, or could involve labor utilization studies in crucial sectors; analyses of key themes cutting across the local manpower agenda; mapping the external manpower agendas in selected countries; and reviewing current manpower planning units across ministries.

Since donors are more open to research findings than hard-pressed national governments and ministries, it is likely that some of the new approaches will first be adopted by the donor community. The World Bank's manpower research may eventually become part of discussions with lenders and other agencies. But progress in changing approaches to manpower training will be even slower when members of the national research community in developing countries seek to influence their policy-makers. Dissemination of relevant research to the policy-making community is not yet highly developed; hence, the time horizon for change will be very long.

In the meantime, the methodological challenge is to develop new tools and more appropriate concepts to describe African manpower issues. This will necessitate an understanding and incorporation of traditions of labor use in Africa, a clarification of the implicit relationship between education, training, production, and technology, and more coherent options for revisions of both the internal and external manpower agendas.

NOTES

1. K. King, "The Planning of Technical and Vocational Education and Training," IIEP, occasional paper, 1985, p. 35; P. Foster, "Some Policy Implications of the Tanzanian and Colombian Studies," Washington, D.C.: The World Bank, September 1984 mimeo.

2. K. King, *The African Artisan* (London: Heineman, 1977).

3. K. King, "Open and Closed Universities: North-South Contrast," Society of Hong Kong Scholars Conference: Current Development in Higher Education, January 1985, Hong Kong.

4. K. King, "The End of Education for Self-Reliance?" occasional paper, 1984, Centre of African Studies, Edinburgh University. Also, "Education

Research in Tanzania, Summary Comments," report of a seminar, August 1984, Dar es Salaam University, Department of Education.

5. Eric Ashby, *Universities, British, Indian, African. An Ecology of Higher Education* (London: Weidenfeld and Nicolson, 1966).

6. K. King, "Technology, Education, and Employment for Development (TEED). The Research Context and the Methodological Challenge," seminar paper, IDRC, Nairobi, January 1985.

7. K. King, "Education for Self-Employment" in IIEP (UNESCO), *Education, Work and Employment*, II (Paris: UNESCO, 1980).

8. K. King, *The African Artisan*, op. cit.

9. Ninth Conference of Commonwealth Education Ministers, "Education and Youth Unemployment: Some Propositions," working paper by K. King, Nicosia, 23–26 July 1984.

10. For a more detailed analysis of the ecology of aid, see K. King, "Problems and Prospects of Aid to Education in Sub-Saharan Africa," lead paper, Conference on Education Priorities in Sub-Saharan Africa, Windsor, England, 3–7 December 1984.

11. Jon Moris, *Managing Induced Rural Development* (Bloomington: University of Indiana Press, 1981) passim.

12. D. Jamison and L. Lau, *Farmer Education and Farm Efficiency* (Baltimore: Johns Hopkins University Press, 1982); D. Jamison and P. Mook, "Farmer Education and Farm Efficiency in Nepal: The Role of Schooling, Extension Services and Cognitive Skills," *World Development* 12, 1: 67–86.

13. S. Heyneman, "Research on Education in the Developing Countries," *International Journal of Educational Development* 4 (4) (1984): pp.301–302, quoted in K. King, "Technology, Education, and Employment for Development" op. cit., p. 5.

14. See K. King, "Technology, Education, and Employment for Development. The Research Context and the Methodological Challenge," op.cit.

15. Robin Hollister, "A Perspective on the Role of Manpower Analysis and Planning in Developing Countries," in "Manpower Issues in Educational Investment," Staff Working Paper No. 624 (Washington, D.C.: The World Bank, 1983), p. 59.

16. Jan Loubser, *Human Resource Development in Kenya: An Overview* (CIDA), Hull, November 1983, pp. 119ff. Also, Republic of Kenya, Working Party on Government Expenditures: Report and Recommendations, Nairobi, July 1982.

17. K. King, "Preliminary Reactions to the Interpretation of Manpower Data in Kenya: Toward a Qualitative Approach," 31.8.84, Nairobi, mimeo.

18. N. Ngethe et al, "Technology Policy and Planning in the Informal Sector" in Workshop on Technology Policy and Planning in the Informal Sector: the Case of Food, Agriculture and Energy in East Africa Sub-region, Economic Commission for Africa, December 1984. J. Odurkene, "Indigenous Apprenticeship and On the Job Training Practices in Uganda," paper to Workshop on Technology, Education, and Employment for Development, IDRC, Nairobi, January 1985. See also Workshop on the Informal Sector in Francophone Africa, University Institute for Development Studies, Geneva, March 1985.

19. K. King, "Planning of Technical and Vocational Education," op. cit., pp. 77–78. Also, Wim Hoppers, "Skill Training and Self-employment" (The Hague: CESO, 1983) mimeo.

20. Ongoing work by P. Moock on the informal sector in Peru, Washington, D.C.: The World Bank, Education Department.

21. For an elaboration, see K. King, "Education with Production: Approaches to a State of the Art" in Workshop on Education and Production in Theory and Practice (The Hague: CESO, 1985), reprinted in *Education with Production* (Gaborone) Autumn 1985.

22. For a valuable analysis of patterns of intervention in Latin America and the Caribbean, see Noel McGinn et al., "Recent Experiences in the Coordination of Education, Employment and Technology in Latin America and the Caribbean," draft mimeo, Harvard University Graduate School of Education, April 1, 1985.

23. See K. King, "Educational Transfer in Kenya and Tanzania," *Compare* 13 (1), (1983), pp.81–87.

24. For a similar perspective, see Robin Hollister, op.cit. pp. 72–74.

25. Ibid., p. 73.

26. See, for example, the series of workshops on Technology, Education, and Development organized by IDRC in East Africa, January 1983, August 1983, and January 1985.

PART VI

AFRICA AND THE WORLD ECONOMY

CHAPTER SIXTEEN

Africa's Debt: Structural Adjustment with Stability

Chandra S. Hardy

The crisis atmosphere that followed Mexico's moratorium on principal payments in 1982 has abated somewhat over the past three years with economic recovery in the industrialized world, stretched out repayment schedules for the major debtors, and the willingness of borrowers to undertake very tough adjustment policies. However, for most developing countries and especially those in sub-Saharan Africa, financing their external debt continues to pose very serious difficulties.

Estimated at around $100 billion, Africa's total external debt is not large, amounting to less than that of Brazil alone, but it is extremely burdensome. Comparable to those of the largest borrowers, debt service payments in Africa account for 50 to 60 percent of export earnings. In low-income Africa, total external debt amounts to more than half the value of output and six times the value of exports.

Despite these telling figures, Africa's debt has received less international attention than that of the major Latin American debtors, for example. Accounting for only 10 percent of total developing country debt and for less than 5 percent of debt owed to commercial banks, Africa's external debt is not perceived to pose any systemic risk. Significantly, however, the majority of those countries that have been accumulating arrears and rescheduling debt have been African. And despite repeated reschedulings, Africa's debt burden has increased rather than eased, suggesting that the problem is one of deep-rooted poverty and insolvency, not temporary illiquidity.

Few attempts have been made to devise a comprehensive solution to Africa's debt problems. This chapter reviews the nature and dimensions of the debt, recent economic conditions and future prospects, the inadequacy of rescheduling operations, and the role of the International Monetary Fund. It concludes with a recommended policy agenda.

GROWTH OF EXTERNAL DEBT

Between 1973 and 1983, Africa's debt increased six-fold, growing at an average annual rate of 22 percent, substantially in excess of the rate of growth in output or exports (Table A.5 in Appendix I). For low-income Africa, long-term indebtedness grew at a relatively more modest, but still alarming rate, increasing more than four-fold, from $5 billion to $22 billion.

Over 90 percent of Africa's debt is owed directly to or is guaranteed by official sources in the creditor countries (official debt). By the end of 1983, medium- and long-term debt in sub-Saharan Africa amounted to $58 billion.[1] Another $5 billion was owed to the International Monetary Fund (IMF), with short-term debt and arrears reaching $18 billion. By year-end 1983, therefore, total external debt amounted to $81 billion. Other estimates range from $107 billion to $150 billion, reflecting the inclusion of additional countries.

Over the same period, the structure and composition of Africa's external debt changed markedly. As a share of total outstandings, official and concessional loans declined, while private and commercial bank loans rose. For sub-Saharan Africa as a whole, concessional loans fell from 43 percent to 36 percent of total outstandings between 1973 and 1983, with loans carrying variable interest rates increasing from 9 percent to 22 percent of the total.

Whereas long-term debt owed to private creditors accounted for 40 percent of total outstandings in 1973, by 1983 it amounted to 46 percent. Behind this increase, the debt owed by the public sector to the financial markets rose nine-fold over the decade to $19 billion in 1983; its share of total outstandings climbing from 21 percent in 1973 to 33 percent in 1983. Of the long-term debt owed to official creditors, the portion owed to multilateral agencies rose from 27 percent in 1973 to 41 percent ten years later. More important, the share of "preferred creditors" (multilateral lenders and the IMF) in total long-term external liabilities grew from 18 percent in 1973 to 28 percent in 1983. In low-income Africa, this shift was more dramatic, rising from 18 percent to 37 percent.

The changes in the structure of external obligations are reflected in the hardening of the average terms. Maturities and grace periods on new commitments became shorter while interest rates rose over the decade. As a result, the grant element or degree of concessionality fell from 32 percent in 1973 to 16 percent in 1982.

Debt service payments grew rapidly from $1.2 billion in 1973 to nearly $6 billion in 1983. In effect, debt service payments increased at a slower pace than absolute debt levels because of an accumulation of payments arrears and reschedulings. In 1983, payments of interest and amortization amounted to only 40 to 50 percent of the total debt-servicing costs falling due that year. Further, with hardening terms, the composition of the debt service altered. Interest payments rose from 25 percent of the total debt service paid in 1973, to 39 percent in 1978, and to 43 percent in 1982. Interest payments continue to account for one-third of projected debt-servicing costs.

The increase in indebtedness over the past decade, however, has not been matched by an increase in Africa's capacity to pay. A look at the principal indicators of debt—the external debt/export ratio, the external debt/GDP ratio, and the ratio of interest and principal payments to total exports of good and services (debt service ratio)—reveals that in comparison to other regions, Africa and low-income Africa in particular is the most heavily indebted.

Over the past decade, all of these debt ratios deteriorated sharply in Africa. The debt service ratio jumped sharply from 9.2 percent in 1975 to 17.3 percent in 1981. In low-income Africa, this ratio rose from 9.2 percent to 22 percent over the same period. Moreover, these figures understate the true extent of the burden. Omitting short-term debt obligations and arrears and payments to the IMF, the data includes only the debt service that was paid on public medium- and long-term debt. When the former are taken into account, the debt service ratio exceeds 50 percent for sub-Saharan Africa overall and surpasses 100 percent for many individual countries. Even with an incomplete data base, the toll of debt-servicing costs on low-income African economies is apparent in the ratio of interest payments to GNP, amounting to 2.1 percent as compared to 0.3 percent for low-income Asia.

Another indicator of Africa's perilous financial situation is the drastic fall in the level of foreign exchange reserves. In 1982, Africa's gross foreign exchange reserves amounted to less than one month of substantially reduced imports, below their 1973 levels. In net terms, reserve levels were negative by several billion dollars. The lack of foreign exchange reserves heightens the continent's vulnerability to exogenous shocks. For example, even a slight delay in the receipt of export earnings can hold up food and oil imports since banks are unwilling to provide unconfirmed letters of credit, and can cause delays in payments to official creditors who in turn can suspend disbursements on existing loans.

The current situation is desperate and is not likely to improve without major and concerted action on the part of Africa's official creditors. Much of the recent increase in debt has been due to the capitalization of arrears—either unpaid interest payments are added to the stock of debt and thus "capitalized," or new loans are extended to cover unpaid interest and principal payments falling due—and declining net capital inflows. Between 1979 and 1983, outstanding debt grew by $20 billion, but net inflows rose by only $1 billion, and net transfers declined in nominal terms, implying an even greater fall in real terms (Table A.5 in Appendix I). The recent drop in net inflows reflects a rise in amortization payments and a decline in new commitments. In 1973, the ratio of scheduled principal payments to disbursements was 31 percent; by 1983 it had risen to 58 percent.

More ominously, between 1980 and 1983, new commitments to all developing countries fell by 21 percent, while those to low-income Africa plunged 45 percent, with commitments from private sources dropping from $1.5 billion in 1979 to just $137 million in 1983. The 31 percent decline in new commitments from official sources poses a more serious problem as these represent the principal source of funds for low-income Africa. The impact of falling levels of commitments is likely to be expressed in depressed net inflows, and debt service payments are expected to remain high. In 1983, net transfers from private sources to low-income Africa were negative by $300 million. Unless these trends in capital flows are reversed, net transfers from official sources will also be negative in a few years.

ECONOMIC SITUATION AND PROSPECTS

Declining output levels, rising inflation, and widening current account deficits are symptoms of the overall deterioration in economic activity in Africa over the past decade. Since 1974, per capita GDP has dropped nearly 1 percent per annum; inflation has jumped from an annual rate of 10 percent to over 20 percent in 1984; and the combined current account deficit has increased from $4 billion to $14 billion in 1984. These deficits were not financed by a net inflow of medium- and long-term debt, but rather by what are called monetary transactions—a build-up of short-term debt, a drawdown on reserves, purchases from the IMF, and the accumulation of payments arrears.

Africa's deteriorating economic situation is largely due to a series of shocks, each more devastating than its predecessor. Over the past decade, in addition to wars and two prolonged periods of drought, Africa has experienced a five-fold increase in the price of grain, a seven-fold increase in the price of oil, recession and inflation in the industrial countries, high and volatile interest and exchange rates, and a collapse in commodity prices.

Of these, the most adverse in scope and duration have been trends in the international economy. The sharp decline in output and accelerated rates of inflation in the industrial countries after the first oil shock resulted in reduced demand for Africa's exports and a weakening of commodity prices. As a result of low world demand for exports, declining terms of trade, and inelastic demand for imports of food, fertilizers, oil, and producer goods, African economies experienced widening current account deficits.

Domestic policies have also played a part in Africa's economic decline given weak institutional structures, overblown bureaucracies, and governments committed to overambitious spending programs that could no longer be funded by trade revenue. Unable and in some cases unwilling to cut expenditures to meet declining revenues, governments resorted to deficit financing, fueling the inflation created by acute shortages, particularly of imported goods.

The severity of the external environment can be gauged from the fact that income losses due to the deterioration in Africa's terms of trade were as much as 10 percent of GDP in 1974–75 and again in 1979–82. Some countries registered losses as high as 25 percent of GDP during the latter period. By contrast, the income loss to the industrial countries due to adverse terms of trade was 2 percent of GDP after each oil shock.

DOMESTIC POLICY ADJUSTMENT

Adverse terms of trade reduce the purchasing power of export earnings. As a result, incomes fall, costs rise, and larger current account deficits are incurred. In order to finance these deficits, reserves are drawn down and borrowings increase. In an effort to reduce the need for external financing, domestic policy adjustments are undertaken to reduce imports, increase exports, dampen consumption, and raise investment levels. In poor countries, however, the social costs of cutting public spending can be high and changing the structure of production is a lengthy process, requiring additional resources.

Adjustment in low-income Africa has largely entailed cuts in consumption and investment, causing higher rates of unemployment and falling real incomes and output.

Reductions in spending have often been accompanied by accelerated rates of inflation as the domestic prices of imports rise as a result of scarcity or devaluation. As a result, governments have been unable to cut spending at the same rates as declining revenues, leading to wider fiscal deficits financed by monetary expansion.

By the time a country requests assistance from the IMF, the financial situation is often desperate. The need for stabilization is thus not in question, but rather at issue are the scope and speed of adjustment and the required policy mix. Some key questions must then be asked: Do all domestic policy failures have to be corrected simultaneously? Must the time period required for assessing the success of stabilization periods be three years rather than five or 10 years? Can stabilization programs be designed that provide some minimum protection of basic human needs?

As most governments are unable to mobilize the political consensus needed to implement stabilization programs that require further cuts in living standards, an alternative policy package would include a higher level of net capital inflows needed to carry out structural change. In this way, the conditionality required by the IMF would be retained, but with greater flexibility in the prescribed period for achieving the targets and in the monitoring of performance criteria (Williamson, 1983). At present, the IMF does not have the resources needed to finance longer-term adjustment programs. Therefore, unless these funds come from other creditors, sooner or later drastic adjustments, perhaps including debt repudiation, will have to take place.

FOREIGN BORROWING AND ADJUSTMENT

The growth in external indebtedness in Africa may suggest that increased reliance on foreign resources was a means of avoiding adjustment. However, this is not the case. Many African countries adjusted by cutting imports and output growth, borrowing to maintain investment levels and to cushion the fall in consumption. In fact, borrowings proved insufficient to check a widespread erosion of the physical and human capital stock.

After the first oil shock, the international donor and financial communities responded promptly and generously to Africa's financing needs. The IMF established an oil facility and a trust fund to make concessional loans to low-income countries. However, increased borrowing from official sources was not sufficient to offset a decline in the purchasing power of exports, and thus to prevent a decline in imports and output growth.

In 1976–77, recovery in the industrial countries, a frost in Brazil that damaged its coffee crop, and good weather in many parts of Africa led to an increase in export volumes and prices and a modest decline in current account deficits (Table A.8 in Appendix I). But the recovery was unsustainable, and even before the second oil price increase in 1979, the terms of trade had started to deteriorate sharply.

Adjustment to the second oil shock was borne almost entirely by a reduction in imports and output. As the industrial economies fell into the worst recession since the 1930s, demand for Africa's exports collapsed and commodity prices plummeted to their lowest levels in 25 years in 1980. Although more severe than the first, the second oil shock met with a cooler official donor response. A number of countries scrambled for funds by resorting to government-insured or guaranteed funds from export credit agencies and banks. Facilitated by industrial countries' efforts to expand their exports, these suppliers' credits in effect financed the current account deficits after 1979, along with a further reduction in reserves and an accumulation of arrears.

Existing arrangements for meeting the financing needs of developing countries fail to recognize countries' unequal capacity to adjust to payments imbalances. The biggest debtors had enjoyed rapid growth rates before running into debt-servicing difficulties. Their economies are diversified; their domestic savings rates are high; and they have demonstrated the political and economic ability to run trade surpluses in the midst of a prolonged recession at home and abroad. Their weight in international financial markets has drawn attention to their problems; thus they and their creditors have cooperated to find imaginative and flexible solutions to their debt-servicing problems.

Although on the order of the major Latin American borrowers, Africa's debt burden has received less attention because it is not considered a threat to the international financial system (Table A.6 in Appendix I). However, Africa's debt problems warrant attention because its economies are more vulnerable to liquidity crises:

- Their share of trade to GDP and the ratio of debt to exports are much higher than for low-income Asia, and therefore they are more exposed to international fluctuations.

- African economies are predominantly agricultural and therefore more subject to climatic variations.

- Primary commodities account for nearly 80 percent of Africa's exports and primary commodity producers suffer sharper terms of trade swings than exporters of manufactured goods.

- Poorer economies are also less able to withstand shocks. Given rigid production structures, African economies cannot quickly move out of one kind of export to another when international prices deteriorate, nor can they reduce imports in favor of domestic substitutes. Unlike the major borrowers, African economies are less able to smooth adjustment to shocks by borrowing, as they lack access to balance of payments financing from banks; their quotas in the IMF are small; their net reserve levels are negative; and their administrative and institutional capacity for crisis management is weak.

FUTURE PROSPECTS

Even if there is a sustained recovery in OECD growth, most African economies are unlikely to see any improvement in living standards over the coming decade. Even given a modest improvement in the terms of trade, net annual inflows of 7 percent of GDP, and substantial increases in official development assistance (ODA) and commercial flows, low-income Africa is projected to show no increase in per capita GDP for the rest of this decade, according to the 1985 World Development Report.

In the absence of any remedial measures by the international community, the prognosis for Africa could be even worse. First, the international environment remains hostile. A set of unfavorable price trends, including high real interest rates, an overvalued dollar, and adverse terms of trade, greatly increases its real debt burden.[2] Real interest rates are at unprecedented levels in the United States, and when the nominal rates applicable to Africa are adjusted for the movement in real export prices, real rates of interest of 20 percent have been estimated.

The high value of the dollar in relation to the other major trading currencies adversely affects Africa's trade with Europe—its principal market—and its debt-servicing costs, as the loans are denominated in dollars.

World Bank projections indicate that even with faster growth in the industrial countries, commodity prices may only reach 1980 levels in 1995. Some commodities will show no recovery in real terms over the coming decade. However, a more disturbing development is the failure of commodity prices to revive with the U.S. recovery. In February 1985, the World Bank's commodity price index stood at 87.3 (1977/79 = 100), 13.5 percentage points below the level of a year ago and 1.4 percentage points below the level in October 1982, the bottom of the 1981–82 recession. In short, the combination of high borrowing costs and the collapse of commodity prices in spite of the U.S. recovery is not improving the manageability of Africa's debt burden.

Second, the trend in capital flows is not consistent with a recovery in African output. Since 1980, net lending to developing countries has been declining. In 1983, the net inflow was $1 billion and probably negative in 1984. The drastic decline in the level of commitments suggests that net lending will remain depressed.

Third, projected debt service on public and publicly guaranteed debt is estimated at $10 to 11 billion per annum through 1987, twice the level of the annual debt service paid in 1980–83, while repayments to the IMF are estimated at $1.2 billion per annum. There has been no progress in reducing trade arrears, estimated at $18 billion, and gross revenues are less than one month's imports.

DEBT RESCHEDULINGS

With balance of payments deficits amounting to 9 percent of GDP in 1984 and limited scope to correct these imbalances, Africa clearly requires higher levels of net capital inflows and longer periods for adjustment. To date, however, the policy response to Africa's debt-servicing problems has been short term and piecemeal, consisting largely of annual debt reschedulings which fail to address the need for additional aid.

Since 1975, 15 African countries have rescheduled debt in multilateral negotiations with official creditors or commercial banks on 47
occasions. An even larger number of countries are accumulating arrears on payments since not all with debt problems have requested or
been able to satisfy the conditions needed to obtain debt rescheduling. According to the IMF, Gambia, Ghana, Guinea, Mali, Sierra
Leone, Tanzania, Zaire, Zambia, Benin, Chad, Guinea-Bissau,
Mauritania, and Nigeria are all in arrears on payments, while a few
have also had debt reschedulings.

Reschedulings of debt to official creditors normally are discussed
under the auspices of the Paris Club, an ad hoc group of Western
creditor governments which has met under the chairmanship of the
French Treasury since Argentina's 1956 request to replace bilateral
negotiations with a multilateral meeting of its creditors. Over the
years, the Paris Club has evolved a set of unwritten governing procedures and practices which have also been adopted by the Bank of
England (London Club) and the OECD.

These procedures include agreement among creditors to meet only
after payments arrears have arisen and the debtor country has agreed
to an IMF stabilization program; only the principal creditors and the
debtor are invited to the meeting; relief is limited to officially insured
export credits and government loans; debt relief is limited to about 80
percent of the principal payments due over a three-year period; and
debts are rescheduled for three to 10 years at market interest rates.

Since 1979, the pace of debt reschedulings has accelerated. In the
period 1979–82, over half of the multilateral debt renegotiations (20
out of 38) were for African countries and 16 out of 17 which took place
at the Paris Club over this period were African. In addition, 11 countries have had to reschedule their commercial bank debt under separate agreements, including Ivory Coast and Nigeria, which had enjoyed high credit ratings in the mid-1970s.

The Paris Club mechanism has not been effective in easing Africa's
debt difficulties, as the relief provided has been too little and too
costly. Designed to keep debtors on a short leash, Paris Club procedures apply strict limits on the definition of debts eligible for relief.
Excluded are debts owed to Eastern Europe, the multilateral development banks and the IMF, debts previously rescheduled, interest payments, and arrears on short-term debt. As a result, more than half of
most countries' debts are ineligible. In addition, since the amount of

relief provided suffices only to ease liquidity problems for a year or two, repeated reschedulings have been common. Most countries have experienced three or more debt reschedulings over five years.

The effect of repeated reschedulings has been to increase the debt burden. While debt relief has been provided by stretching out maturities at market rates of interest, interest charges on debts incurred at original average interest rates of 6 percent have increased to an average 10 percent. As a result, interest payments have risen from $429 million in 1973 to an estimated $3.3 billion in 1984, with interest charges accounting for one-third of the debt service due over the next three years. The capitalization of overdue principal (and, in a few cases, interest charges) and short-term debts have added $21 billion to debt outstanding since 1979. Over the same period, net inflows increased by only $1 billion per annum.

Further, Paris Club reschedulings have failed to mobilize additional public and private funds for Africa. The existing arrangements for debt rescheduling thus point to an asymmetry in the treatment of large and small debtors. At the urging of the IMF, rescheduling packages and IMF assistance to the major debtors were contingent on "new" lending from existing creditors and a re-opening of short-term lines of credit. This approach has not been evident in the case of Africa's major creditors. While an IMF stabilization program is required before the Paris Club will reschedule debt, new aid and credits are not part of the Paris Club procedures.

The level of net inflows to Africa is largely decided by official sources, usually coordinated at aid group meetings. As a result, after 21 reschedulings since 1979, the level of net inflows of ODA declined from $12 billion to $6 billion in 1983, and net inflows from private sources have turned negative.

Paris Club reschedulings have also failed to normalize short-term trade financing arrangements. Official export credit agencies which provide guarantees on private sources of credit to developing countries go "off cover" for countries accumulating arrears or requesting debt reschedulings. While until about 1979, once a country had agreed to an IMF program and had rescheduled part of its long-term debt, its creditworthiness for some portion of insured credits was restored, this is no longer the case. Particularly in Africa, acceptance of an IMF program and restructuring debt at market rates only provide temporary relief and do not guarantee new trade lines of credit.

THE IMF IN AFRICA

Over the past decade, the IMF has helped African countries finance growing balance of payments deficits. In 1975, purchases from the IMF's oil facility furnished 53 percent of the total gross flows from the IMF to Africa, cushioning the impact of the first oil shock. In addition, the IMF used part of the profits from the sale of gold holdings to set up the Trust Fund and an interest-subsidy account to provide low-cost loans to its poorest members. After 1979, when commercial bank lending to Africa virtually dried up, the IMF became Africa's only source of balance of payments (non-project) financing.

Between 1979 and 1983, the average volume of IMF lending to Africa increased more than three-fold. By 1983, net purchases from the IMF were equivalent to 34 percent of net flows of public and publicly guaranteed debt. However, the nature of the support offered by the Fund was quite different after the first and second oil shocks. In 1975 and 1976, low conditionality funds accounted for 80 percent of Africa's purchases, but after 1977, higher conditionality lending steadily increased, amounting to 75 percent of IMF lending to Africa.

Another major change has been the reduction in Extended Fund Facility (EFF) arrangements or medium-term adjustment programs in favor of standby arrangements 12 to 18 months in duration. Despite the IMF Board's 1981 claim that "the adjustment process in many countries is under growing external pressure and longer periods of assistance under the EFF will continue to be increasingly important," the EFF has been used less and less. At the end of 1981, five African countries held EFF drawings, four of which were signed that year. That same year, however, three were cancelled. In 1982, two more African countries signed extended EFF agreements, but these were also cancelled a year later. Thus, of seven African countries which signed EFF agreements between May 1979 and April 1982, only Ivory Coast and Gabon retained the facility. At present, Malawi is the only African country to have an EFF agreement. Standby arrangements have been the far greater source of funds. In 1979, some 29 African countries had standby agreements; today only 13 are in effect.

In addition to its higher conditionality lending, the IMF has increasingly exercised a leadership role in the international financial community vis-à-vis Africa. A consensus has emerged among bilateral and multilateral donors and official export credit agencies that all financial arrangements now hinge upon recipients' adoption of an IMF adjustment program. Similarly, requests for debt rescheduling at the Paris Club are not approved unless the borrower has concluded an agreement with the Fund, and require continual satisfaction of IMF performance criteria. This enlarged IMF function has aroused a great deal of controversy; therefore it may be useful to briefly review the applicability of IMF operations to Africa's debt problems.

IMF OPERATIONS

The IMF's resources are held in a revolving fund that is augmented through periodic quota increases, the most recent of which was in 1981. Members of the IMF enjoy drawing rights—use of Fund resources—that are determined in relation to the size of their quotas. As of December 1984, the value of all quotas in the Fund was SDR 89 million ($91.5 million). The industrial countries accounted for 62.8 percent of all quotas; the non-oil developing countries accounted for 26.3 percent, and the oil-exporting countries for 10.9 percent. The IMF can also supplement its resources by borrowing from governments; the General Agreement to Borrow is one such means by which industrial countries agree to make additional funds available for special situations.[3]

Whereas the World Bank was established to help countries achieve longer-term economic growth, the Fund's task was to prevent member countries experiencing cyclical balance of payments problems from adopting the deflationary policies and competitive devaluations prevalent in the 1930s. To qualify for Fund assistance, a member was required to agree to correct its payments imbalance. Until the early 1970s, the principal borrowers from the IMF were the industrial countries.

As stated in a recent staff paper, the Fund's basic objectives are to promote economic growth, to reduce inflation, and to improve the current account position in the medium term. Consequently, IMF programs involve setting specific quantitative targets for output, inflation, and current account deficits; selecting the mix of instruments to achieve these objectives; and determining the intensity with which each instrument is used. While no two Fund programs are identical, the principal policy instruments generally involve exchange rate adjustment, credit controls, fiscal measures to reduce expenditure and increase taxes, and the removal of arrears.

Critics of the IMF contend that its prescriptions and funding are unsuitable for Africa. IMF programs stress demand management (expenditure cuts) to correct external payments imbalances. While measures to stimulate domestic production are included, they have lower priority when they conflict with the need to cut imports. However, after a decade of declining import and output growth rates, further belt-tightening measures are no longer viable solutions for Africa.

Second, critics argue that current Fund programs require countries to show improvements in their external payments position in three to five years, and, under standby arrangements, within one year. But the required structural reforms take time to implement and require additional investment. Third, IMF funds are costly—interest is slightly below market rates and repayment periods average five years.

Fourth, reaching agreement with the IMF does not ease the liquidity constraint. Very often net inflows from the IMF to Africa are zero or even negative during the course of a stabilization program. Moreover, the IMF does not play a catalytic role in mobilizing additional aid for Africa. In fact, since 1979 net ODA flows to Africa have declined by 50 percent and private flows have turned negative.

Lastly, the IMF's record of effectiveness as measured against its own agreed targets or results after the program has ended is not encouraging. After a decade of increasing IMF involvement, Africa has fallen deeper into crisis.

The IMF does not discriminate against Africa per se. Its policy prescriptions are the same for all its members, whatever their stage of development and causes of their external payments imbalance. Rather, criticism of the IMF rests on its generalized solution to a problem which cannot be generalized—the indebtedness of developing countries. Whatever the merits of the IMF's approach to the correction of payments imbalances, performance criteria should be tailored to the needs of specific countries. Africa needs longer-term structural balance of payments financing on concessional terms.

Conditionality itself is not the issue; urgent measures are needed to restore order to Africa's financial transactions. Rather, the controversy centers on how and over what time period these required policy measures can be put into effect. Whereas IMF programs are deemed successful if external account imbalances are reduced, unless structural reforms and some stimulus to production result, such balance of payments "improvements" are apt to be transitory. Structural transformation in Africa requires measures to raise the productivity of smallholder agriculture and increase export volumes. These reforms cannot be accomplished in the short run, nor can they be realized without higher levels of investment and agricultural imports.

Resources available from the IMF can only provide a fraction of Africa's needs for balance of payments financing. Africa accounts for only 3.3 percent of IMF quotas, and since the 1981 quota increase, access to the use of Fund resources has been reduced twice, from 150 percent to 95 percent of quotas under "normal" circumstances (115 percent in exceptional circumstances) and from 600 percent to 408 percent cumulatively. In net terms, sub-Saharan Africa has significantly lower access limits in 1985 than before the general quota increase. Access to the Compensatory Financing Facility has been reduced from 100 percent to 83 percent of quotas, and the practice that up to 50 percent of quotas was available on low conditionality terms has been withdrawn.[4]

Africa's total use of IMF resources cannot exceed $12 billion, or about 20 percent of its imports in 1980. As of January 1985, Africa's use of Fund resources totalled $5.1 billion, with much of the increase in lending taking place after 1979. Net IMF credit made available to Africa between 1979 and 1983 equalled $3.7 billion, sufficient to offset only about one-quarter of the cumulative shortfall in the purchasing power of exports resulting from the 20 percent deterioration in the terms of trade over this period.

Further, the use of Fund resources is too costly for Africa. Because of the rapid increase in its lending since 1979, the IMF has become one of Africa's main creditors, with repayments estimated at over $1 billion in 1984. The IMF was also owed 50 to 75 percent of the debt service paid in 1984.

Between 1985 and 1987, repayments to the IMF are projected at $1.2 billion per annum, in addition to the $10 to 11 billion per annum due on public and publicly guaranteed debt. If the average volume of purchases remains at the 1984 level of $1 billion, net transfers from the Fund will be negative by $200 million per annum over the next few years. The IMF will then become part of Africa's debt problem rather than part of its solution. Already, a few countries—Chad, Sudan, and Tanzania—are falling into arrears on their IMF loans and this trend is likely to continue unless action is taken to increase net official flows to Africa.

Expanded use of Fund resources did not prevent an overall decline in total resources available to Africa, and, given the short maturity and high cost of IMF loans, it is not surprising that the IMF's involvement in Africa has so far met with little success. An IMF staff review (Zulu and Nsouli, 1985) of programs in operation in Africa in 1980 and 1981 showed that the targets for output growth and reduction of fiscal and balance of payments deficits were met in 20 to 30 percent of the cases; the targets for reducing inflation and net credit expansion were met in 50 percent of the cases. The slippages in implementation were attributed to unforeseen developments, lack of political will, administrative weakness, over-optimistic targets, and delays or shortfalls in net inflows of development assistance.

CONCLUSIONS

While external debt is not the most serious problem confronting Africa, failure to resolve its debt-servicing difficulties limits the continent's ability to confront the more urgent problems of growing poverty and economic decline. Not only has the absolute level of external debt increased over the past decade, but the burden of financing increasingly nonconcessional and shorter-term loans has mounted. By 1982, the grant element on new borrowing had fallen to 16 percent from 32 percent in 1973, and debt service payments due had risen from $1 billion to $10 billion over the same period.

Africa's debt-servicing difficulties are evident in the rapid increase in arrears on payments and in the number of debt renegotiations. Between 1956 and 1974, there were 30 renegotiations for 11 countries, of which Ghana was the only African country, accounting for four renegotiations between 1966 and 1974. Since 1975, however, 15 African countries have rescheduled their external debt on 47 occasions, and payments arrears have approached an estimated $18 billion, about one-third of outstanding public medium- and long-term debt.

African countries could do very little about rising international interest rates, the appreciation of the U.S. dollar, the decline in aid flows, and adverse terms of trade movements. As a result, attention was focused on the decline in export volumes which was largely attributable to domestic policy failures—inefficient pricing and marketing arrangements, particularly those affecting agriculture. However, insufficient attention has been given to two additional constraints: Africa's high import dependence and its low level of agricultural productivity.

In relative terms, African economies exhibit higher import elasticities of demand than most other developing countries. Ratios of imports to GDP range from 19 percent to 30 percent, with both industry and agriculture highly dependent on imports of intermediate goods. The decline in export volumes should therefore be examined in the context of the 50 percent decline in intermediate goods imports over the past decade.

Second, while existing government structures and agricultural policies share part of the responsibility for the overall decline of this sector, it would be simplistic to view pricing and marketing measures as sufficient to reverse negative trends. The crisis in African agriculture preceded its financial and economic crisis and it is not easily overcome. Thus, while African countries exhibit short-term liquidity problems common to other countries with debt-servicing difficulties, these arise from structural weakness and require different solutions.

PATTERNS OF ADJUSTMENT

In contrast to the adjustments African countries were able to make to the first oil shock mostly by virtue of positive external factors, no comparable adjustment has taken place following the 1979 oil shock. Commodity prices continue to be depressed, weather conditions unreliable, and aid flows declining. The failure to provide Africa with the resources needed to offset the loss in income due to adverse terms of trade movements has led to widespread erosion of physical and human capital stock in every sector which, unless reversed, will adversely affect future growth rates.

The response to Africa's debt crisis has entailed a series of annual Paris Club reschedulings contingent upon agreement on a standby program with the IMF. The method and terms of these renegotiations, however, do not take into account Africa's requirement for long-term net resource inflows to halt the economic decline and stimulate a recovery in production. In addition, in many countries that have been unwilling or unable to reach agreement with the IMF, the crisis has deepened. Debt service payments are consuming an increasing share of Africa's declining export earnings and net capital inflows, despite the fact that almost the only debts currently being serviced are those to the World Bank and the IMF.

At present, the international environment remains unfavorable to Africa and prospects will not improve without a concerted effort by major creditor countries. According to World Bank projections, even with modest improvements in world commodity prices, a declining U.S. dollar, and renewed aid inflows, per capita income in 1990 may be no higher than in 1970, and the debt burden will remain high. Over the next several years, scheduled debt service payments are projected at nearly $10 billion per annum, with 70 percent of the debt owed to the IMF falling due over the next three to four years. Africa's export potential is insufficient to finance long-term development on conventional terms or even to service much of its existing ODA debt.

SUGGESTED POLICY AGENDA

There is an overwhelming need to approach Africa's debt problem with a more comprehensive consideration of both the financial and non-financial aspects of the problem. African debtors could be divided into many categories—oil exporters, low- and middle-income countries—to which different sets of policy could be applied. But such an approach is unnecessary because what is striking about Africa's plight is its universality. The same post-independence pattern of high growth, stagnation, and crisis has emerged in most countries because of the considerable homogeneity of African economies—small populations; tropical environments; dependence on commodity exports and on foreign trade; agrarian bases; and high infant mortality, low literacy, and low life expectancy.

Second, Africa's economic problems cannot be separated into the problems of food, population, ecology, refugees, debt, as all are aspects of the deep-seated obstacles to growth. Unless progress is made on all fronts, the achievements are likely to be few and ephemeral.

Third, Africa's payments problems cannot be divided into short-term balance of payments and liquidity issues and longer-term growth and development issues, and hence parcelled out among the relevant international institutions. Africa's balance of payments problems pre-date the oil price increases and other shocks of the 1970s. The continent's debt problem has been internationally recognized as one of long-term poverty and therefore must be addressed in that context. Against such a comprehensive and longer-term setting, special actions must be taken to reduce Africa's mounting debt burden, including some of the following.

Debt Cancellation   The most effective solution to Africa's debt problem would be to cancel its obligations. High debt service payments are in part due to the amortization of old debt. If all bilateral creditors adhered to UN resolution 165 of March 1968 to cancel or retroactively adjust the terms of past ODA debt, some needed relief would have been provided. Only a few countries—Canada, Sweden, Switzerland, and Holland—have fully complied with the agreement. While the United States has legislation in place that allows for conversion of debt into local currency, this has not been implemented.

A precedent for a more comprehensive debt write-off exists in the 1970 renegotiation of Indonesia's debt. On that occasion, all of Indonesia's obligations to Western creditors were rescheduled for 30 years at no interest. Repayments of interest on originally contracted debt were to begin during the latter half of the repayment period and the country was given the option of deferring principal payments due in the first 8 years to the last 8 years of the agreement for a modest charge. The agreement also provided for a review of these arrangements in 10 years, at which time the country's economic situation and debt-servicing ability would be reassessed.

For those lenders unwilling or unable to cancel debts, there are the options of allowing debts to be paid in local currency or refinancing existing debt on softer terms. Specific action, however, is needed by the IMF, World Bank, and regional development banks which account for almost half of the projected debt service. They are not allowed to reschedule debts and are permitted by other creditors to be excluded from debt rescheduling operations; hence their preferred creditor status. However, debt relief measures that apply to only 30 to 50 percent of the debt service due do not ease the liquidity constraint.

With 1984 trends indicating that the IMF is reducing its net exposure in Africa, not only will net transfers from the Fund be negative, but other sources of balance of payments financing will be needed if IMF debts are to be paid on time. If, on the other hand, IMF lending to Africa were to increase, it should be on concessional terms. A specially funded trust fund could be established that would both extend concessional loans and refinance IMF debts over the long-term, on the order of a similar IMF program after the first oil shock.

Multi-year Rescheduling   Repeated debt reschedulings will not adequately address Africa's debt problem. They have merely added to the debt burden, constrained access to trade financing, and failed to bring about an increase in import levels. In May 1984, the London Summit endorsed multi-year reschedulings, which have been acted upon for the major debtors and which allow for part of the debt owed to private sources to be rescheduled for 12 to 14 years at existing rates but with reduced spreads and fees. Applied to Africa together with an option to adjust payments in line with terms of trade movements, such an approach would ease immediate debt burdens. In recognition of the structural reforms needed, concessional debt relief could be considered a legitimate form of development assistance. To counter the argument that those countries that have borrowed the most would benefit most, measures could be instituted to ensure that such countries receive less additional aid. The total resource package would be determined by current needs and performance criteria, with debt relief only one component of the overall policy package.

It may also be more effective to alter the forum for debt rescheduling for the poorest countries from the Paris Club to aid group meetings. Since 15 of the 21 countries which rescheduled debts between 1970 and January 1983 were low-income countries, aid group meetings could have provided better multilateral forum for consideration of debt problems in relation to the minimum level of inflows needed to restore normal trade arrangements and import capacity.

Increased Aid   Higher levels of imports and investment are needed to restore Africa's productive capacity. The need for increased aid to Africa must be examined in the context of the significant decline in net inflows from official and private sources. Official flows declined by 25 percent in 1981 to below the 1979 level in nominal terms. Net transfers declined by 30 percent. Total commitments to low-income Africa fell by 42 percent in 1981. If these trends are not reversed, net flows and net transfers from officials sources may soon be negative. Net transfers from private sources have been negative since 1979, despite the accumulation of commercial arrears which can account for up to a year's export earnings, as in the case of Zambia and Tanzania.

For the future, Africa will not be regarded as creditworthy for commercial bank lending and will have to rely largely on official concessional aid. Given the small size of the markets, equity investment in non-extractive industries is not likely to be profitable unless governments provide high rates of protection. And increased reliance on suppliers' credits since the mid-1970s has contributed to the rapid increase in the debt burden and the proliferation of uneconomic projects. An additional $6 billion in annual ODA flows to the poorest countries could be achieved if bilateral donors complied with the multilaterally agreed target to raise their share of ODA from the current level of 0.08 percent to 0.15 percent of GNP. This could be achieved by a reduction in the share of ODA to middle-income developing countries.

Improved Aid Quality   It would be misleading to conclude from Africa's desperate economic situation that much of the aid it has received over the past decade has been wasted. There have been some success stories in some countries, in some sectors, and at different times. However, three years of drought at the end of a decade of shocks has created an unbearable burden and many distortions. Domestic policy failures and lack of effectiveness in some of the past aid to Africa, documented in many recent reports, further underscore the need for improvements in the quality of aid.

The need for domestic policy reforms must be continually stressed, but donors also need to take a number of measures that would improve aid effectiveness: bringing aid flows more in line with the current financing priorities of the recipients; raising investment and recurrent expenditures on agriculture; rehabilitating existing projects; and restructuring the debt more in line with its debt-servicing capacity. Other measures could include a decline in the number of projects, a reduction in tied aid, and increased financing of local currency and recurrent expenditures.

It is estimated that about one-half of bilateral ODA is tied to purchases in the donor country. Aid-tying can add up to 20 percent to the cost of projects in addition to creating projects that are not suitable to local conditions and also result in the lack of standardization of machinery and spare parts. Finally, many projects are started that place heavy demands on local currency and recurrent expenditures and intermediate goods imports. Donors' doubling of the share of existing ODA which goes to the poorest countries and implementation of measures to improve the quality of aid would produce enormous benefits at no additional budgetary costs.

Improved Debt Management   The debt crisis has exposed the need in all developing countries for better systems to collect and process debt information, and for closer coordination of the pattern of borrowing and investment. But African governments also need to consider that the risks of borrowing are greater for smaller, poorer, and heavily indebted regions, and special efforts need to be taken to control the growth and composition of future indebtedness. Good debt management is a part of good economic management and while better systems for controlling debt do not prevent crises from occurring, they do minimize the real economic burden of financial disruptions.

The following guidelines would contribute to improved debt management: utilizing available computer facilities to improve the recording and processing of data on all foreign exchange receipts and payments; establishing systems to coordinate the flow of the above information with decisions taken by the country's financial managers, especially at the Central Bank and the Ministry of Finance; giving final borrowing authority to a financial management team; foregoing borrowing for investment if the returns or requirements are questionable; limiting borrowing which is not long term and concessional; and recognizing that borrowing on market terms is especially hazardous for primary commodity producers.

SDR Allocation   In addition to increased resource transfers, Africa also needs a stable source of reserve creation and access to short-term trade financing. Its lack of liquidity is evident in the low level of gross reserves and the build-up in trade arrears. During the 1970s, the global need for liquidity was largely met through the dramatic increase in the price of gold and the expansion of commercial bank lending. These developments did not help the poorest countries, as their only source of balance of payments financing is the IMF. However, IMF quotas are very low. A special issue of SDRs is needed pending increased quotas and enlarged access to Fund resources. An agreement could also be reached by which the industrial and oil-exporting countries would forego their allocation of SDRs in favor of the poorest countries. Trade arrears could be taken up by the IMF and refinanced along with the debt owed to the IMF. Alternatively, the special SDR issue could be used to consolidate these arrears and replenish reserve levels. Africa's liquidity could also be enhanced by increased access to an enlarged Compensatory Financing Facility.

Existing arrangements for meeting the financing needs of developing countries are not adequate. At present, these arrangements are not working well for either creditor or debtor countries—a pre-condition for international monetary reform. However, even within the present unstable and risky framework, special attention needs to be given to the financing needs of the poorest countries which bear a disproportionate share of the burden of adjustment to global payments imbalances. They have experienced the biggest cuts in living standards and the decline in official flows is accelerating their economic decline.

NOTES

1. The data on Africa's debt is not complete. The data from the World Bank's Debtor Reporting System are the most comprehensive source, but they exclude IMF drawings, short-term loans, trade arrears to non-financial

enterprises, and private non-guaranteed borrowing. For many countries, these obligations are quite large.

2. The real debt burden is measured by the number of export units—tons of coffee, cotton, etc.—needed to meet a dollar of debt service.

3. Including use of the General Agreement to Borrow, whereby the industrial countries make additional funds available for special situations.

4. Access to the Compensatory Financing Facility has been reduced from 100 percent to 83 percent of quotas and the practice that up to 50 percent of quota was available on low conditionality terms has been withdrawn.

REFERENCES

Adedeji, A. 1984. "Foreign Debt and Prospects for Growth in the Developing Countries of Africa in the 1980s." Addis Ababa: United Nations.

Balassa, B. 1982. "Adjustment Policies and Development Strategies in sub-Saharan Africa, 1973-78." Discussion Paper No. 41. Washington, D.C.: The World Bank.

Balassa B. 1982. "Policy Responses to External Shocks in sub-Saharan African Countries." Discussion Paper No. 42. Washington, D.C.: World Bank.

Duncan, R. 1983. "Quarterly Review of Commodity Markets." Washington, D.C.: The World Bank.

Griffith-Jones, S. and R. H. Green. 1984. "African External Debt and Development: A Review and Analysis." Mimeo. Sussex, England: Institute of Development Studies.

Hardy, C. S. 1982. "Rescheduling Developing Country Debt, 1956-1981: Lessons and Recommendations." Monograph No. 15. Washington, D.C.: Overseas Development Council.

Helleiner, G. K. 1984(a). "Outward Orientation, Import Stability and African Economic Growth, and Empirical Investigation." Department of Economics, University of Toronto. Mimeo.

Helleiner, G. K. 1984(b). "Aid and Liquidity: The Neglect of the Poorest in the Emerging International Monetary System." Department of Economics, University of Toronto. Mimeo.

Hope, N. 1984. "Notes on the Debt and Debt Prospects for sub-Saharan Africa." World Bank. Mimeo.

Loxley, J. 1984. "The IMF and the Poorest Countries." Ottawa: North-South Institute.

Williamson, J., ed. 1983. IMF Conditionality. Cambridge: Institute for International Economics/MIT Press.

World Bank. 1981. Accelerated Development in Sub-Saharan Africa: An Agenda for Action. Washington, D.C.: The World Bank.

World Bank. 1983. World Development Report 1983. New York: Oxford.

World Bank. 1984. Toward Sustained Development in sub-Saharan Africa: A Joint Program of Action. Washington, D.C.: The World Bank.

World Bank. 1985. World Development Report 1985. New York: Oxford.

World Bank. World Debt Tables, 1984-85. Washington, D.C.: The World Bank.

Zulu, J. B. and S. M. Nsouli. 1985. "Adjustment Programs in Africa." Occasional Paper No. 34. Washington, D.C.: International Monetary Fund.

CHAPTER SEVENTEEN

Africa's Trade and the World Economy

Stephen R. Lewis, Jr.

Africa's relationship to the world economy over the past four centuries has failed to instill confidence in the workings of international trade. The first two centuries were dominated by the human plunder of the slave trade. Then, the 19th-century scramble for Africa by European commercial and political interests began, in some regions, an exceptionally exploitive system. The cash crop economy and African labor's involvement in production for the international market were expanded in the 20th century. But development was limited to primary production: Africa was to provide hewers of wood and drawers of water for the industrial world, and trade and international commerce often was controlled by foreign minorities. In the post-independence period, shocks from the international economy have reverberated more strongly in Africa than in other regions of the world.

Despite this rather dismal record of contact with the world economy, the small size of most African countries means foreign trade must play an important part in their development strategies, even for those countries whose long-term objective is to reduce their vulnerability to the international economy.

THE RECORD OF GROWTH AND TRADE IN AFRICA

FOREIGN TRADE

In the 1960s and through the commodity boom of the early 1970s, Africa's export performance was quite satisfactory, but after the first

476

oil shock, it slipped badly both absolutely and in comparison to other developing regions (Table A.9 in Appendix I). Low-income African countries have suffered a consistent deterioration in their external terms of trade since the mid-1960s (Table A.10). Overall, Africa's terms of trade have held fairly constant since the mid-1960s, reflecting a rise in the continent's oil exports.[1]

While Africa appears to have fared slightly better than "non-oil developing countries" as a group, it has coped less well with declining terms of trade than the low-income countries of Asia. The purchasing power of exports (the volume of exports adjusted for changes in the terms of trade) rose substantially in low-income Asia, but fell modestly in low-income Africa. While all non-oil developing countries experienced a 137 percent expansion in the purchasing power of their exports between 1967 and 1983, this indicator rose by only 36 percent in Africa.[2]

One possible reason for Africa's greater difficulties is the steeper decline in the terms of trade for low-income African countries in comparison with low-income Asia in the two recession periods of 1973–76 and 1979–82. Viewed over longer time periods, however, movements in the terms of trade in these two groups were much closer. Since external shocks hit poor countries harder, the sharper downward fluctuations contributed to the relatively poorer African showing. Consequently, short-term stabilization efforts may be more important for Africa than elsewhere.

A fairly consistent pattern of declining export shares of Africa's important commodities is shown in Table A.11. In four of the eight important metals and minerals (copper, zinc, tin, and lead), Africa's share of developing country exports declined between 1960 to 1978, and in two more (iron ore and bauxite), the share declined during the 1970s. For 10 important food commodities, African shares declined in six (cocoa, groundnut oil, palm oil, bananas, and maize) over the entire period, with its share of coffee falling during the 1970s. Further contractions in Africa's share of world exports occurred in timber, cotton, tobacco, rubber, and sisal over the longer period, with its contribution of hides and skins decreasing in the 1970s.

Had the decline in these export shares been associated with a concomitant rise in output of other commodities, there would have been little cause for concern. However, overall stagnant export performance (shown in Table A.9) and poor GDP growth rates indicate that other types of production were not increasing.

Import volumes have not suffered to the same extent as export volumes in Africa largely because of a rising share of capital inflows. However, both the variability of imports and the inadequate import growth rate (1 percent per year since 1976) have constrained growth in most African countries. The financing of imports, both on a long-term and on a counter-cyclical basis, is a matter of greatest importance to income growth and to trade policy reform.

CAPITAL FLOWS, DEBT, AND RESERVES

Capital inflows have become more important in Africa than in the low- and lower-middle income countries of the rest of the developing world. While Africa has suffered from foreign exchange constraints in recent years, its external debt build-up, most of which is long term and non-commercial, has been very substantial. Given slow growth in both GDP and exports, the rapid accumulation of debt even on concessionary terms will eventually prove to be a serious burden. Africa's debt service ratio has tripled over the past decade, with debt service payments in excess of a quarter of export earnings for a number of countries.

Insufficient liquidity to cope with external shocks such as changes in terms of trade or weather has imposed a certain inflexibility on governments, not only inhibiting economic growth,[3] but also forcing the adoption of import and foreign exchange control systems.[4] Thus, not only have African countries suffered from long-term shortages of foreign exchange, but they have also been confronted with critical day-to-day problems that inhibit sound decision-making.

CAPITAL FORMATION

Rates of capital formation and productivity of capital give particular cause for concern. Africa has a lower ratio of investment to GDP than other regions, although the ratio did rise modestly in the 1970s. Both the share of savings in GDP and the share of investment financed by domestic savings are low and deteriorating as compared with other regions. The rising deficits of domestic saving mirror the growing balance of payments deficits which must be financed by foreign capital.

Perhaps of greater importance, investment has failed to generate significantly higher levels of output and incomes. Marginally rising investment ratios and declining output rates in the 1970s strongly suggest that the productivity of new investment was negative. Rates of return on investment in low-income Africa fell dramatically as compared with other regions. Such low productivity of new capital inflows is a major cause for concern, especially when investment is financed by extended debt. If there is to be a brighter future for Africa, increasing the productivity of resources will have to form a major part of the solution. Africa cannot continue to require twice as much investment as other regions in the world to generate the same increase in incomes.

EXTERNAL FACTORS AND DOMESTIC POLICIES

DEBATE OVER THE PAST RECORD

Apportioning blame for Africa's poor economic performance has spawned a rather vigorous debate over whether the principal causes are beyond the control of African governments (i.e., the poor state of the world economy, associated declines in commodity prices, and drought) or due to adverse government policies on key issues such as exchange rates, imports, and pricing structures.

In reality, however, Africa's poor performance can be blamed almost equally on both factors. Its economic performance could have been substantially better over the past decade if either the exogenous environment had been more benign or if African governments had adopted more appropriate policies.[5] In fact, some studies suggest that, on average, African governments could have offset most of the adverse effects of the external environment of the 1970s by optimal policy choices.[6] Further, a good many of the external factors could have been mitigated by different policies on the part of industrial countries and international institutions. Since both external and domestic policies could be improved, there is some basis for optimism when considering the future prospects of the region.

ENVIRONMENTAL FACTORS

There is no doubt that African countries have been at a disadvantage due to poverty, characterized by low levels of literacy, less diversified economic structures, low savings rates, etc. These features of underdevelopment make it more difficult to respond to adverse exogenous trends such as drought, declining export prices, or increased energy prices. Further, Africa's relatively newer machinery of government has limited its ability to respond to the adversities of the 1970s. Many African countries have also had to confront the instability of domestic or international violence in the relatively short period since independence.[7]

The international economy has also had a substantially negative effect on Africa in the past two decades, particularly since the first oil price shocks. In the 1970s, greater fluctuations in primary commodity prices and a downturn in real prices (both associated largely with the performance of the OECD economies) made Africa's external economic environment exceptionally difficult. According to one estimate, only two variables—the growth rates in the OECD's imports and Africa's barter terms of trade—account for over 80 percent of the variations in Africa's growth rates over the two decades 1960–1980. From such evidence, many observers have concluded that environmental or external factors are the principal cause of Africa's poor performance.[8]

DOMESTIC POLICIES

The issue of domestic policies pursued by individual African countries is a complex one, often generating heated debates. The key policies include exchange rates, tariff structures, import and other direct control systems, government wage policies, pricing policies (especially for agricultural commodities and parastatal or government-owned corporations), and a variety of macro-economic policies, including adjustments to fluctuations in external conditions. To a large extent, the debate divides between those who advocate market-oriented and outward-looking policies, and those who suggest that reliance on market forces and greater involvement in international trade will inhibit equitable growth and increase Africa's political and economic vulnerability and dependence.

A balanced reading of the evidence suggests that domestic policies do play a major role. Studies by independent scholars and analyses by the IMF and the World Bank substantiate the view that certain measurable policies lead to improved economic performance. Specific policy measures that are conducive to improvements in overall economic performance include exchange rate adjustments to avoid excessive overvaluation,[9] altering import levels in response to changes in export earnings,[10] and adoption of more appropriate policies during adverse movements of foreign exchange reserves.[11]

On the other hand, overvalued currencies that discriminate against exports and import controls that starve key productive sectors of needed inputs appear to be major determinants in Africa's declining share of many commodity exports. Further, failure to maintain more balanced macro-economic management over the trade cycle has led to variations in import rates which have also detracted from economic performance.[12]

A quicker payoff from improved trade and macroeconomic policies is more likely to come in countries that have already reached a somewhat higher level of income and diversification, however, a point emphasized by Helleiner and by the IMF's 1983 studies.[13] Since African countries are predominantly lower income, the short-term benefit from adopting the "prescribed" policies could be less significant than elsewhere.

BALANCING ENVIRONMENTAL AND POLICY VARIABLES

David Wheeler (1984) presents some intriguing results that have a bearing on the current debate. "Environmental" variables—terms of trade, civil disturbances, presence of minerals, and lack of initial diversification—generally have a greater impact on performance than "policy" variables, such as exchange rate adjustment and adapting to changed circumstances. His calculations show what the performance of 24 African countries might have been had either the environmental factors or policy choices been "optimal."[14]

For the average country, the environmental cost on economic growth was about 3.3 percent per year, while the cost of non-optimal policy choices was about 2.4 percent per year. While environmental factors clearly dominate, a typical country could have eliminated over two-thirds of the costs imposed by external conditions by changing its domestic policies. Sixteen countries could have added at least 2 percent per year to their growth rates by changing policies, and in 11 countries, optimal policy choices would have more than offset the costs of adverse environmental factors. One factor classified by Wheeler as "environmental"—the presence of mining activities—

seems to me to be more policy related. The poor performance of mining economies is not purely a function of external factors, although the character of mining economics does present problems for policy makers.[15]

In sum, evidence suggests that despite the low-income nature of many African economies and the adverse external climate of the past two decades, it was within the power of African governments to significantly affect economic performance by appropriate policies on international trade—exchange rates, tariff and tax structures, import control mechanisms, and macro-economic policies bearing on balance of payments management.

OPPORTUNITIES AND CONSTRAINTS OF TRADE

DEVELOPMENT OBJECTIVES

Given low levels of per capita output in most African countries, raising output levels so that the average person will benefit directly must be the first major objective of policy reform. Maximizing GDP growth alone is not enough—growth must be broadly based and accessible to the currently disadvantaged—which in most African countries means the rural majority.

The scarcity of key factors, including arable land, capital, water, skilled labor, and foreign exchange (and the likelihood that these will remain key constraints in the coming decade) means that a second priority must be to increase the productivity of these factors. More output per unit is essential if there is to be a significant and sustained improvement in the level of well-being of the majority of Africans.

Third, with substantial excess capacity in many productive sectors—underutilized industrial and infrastructure projects and high unemployment and underemployment of labor—policies should aim at expanding output rather than reducing demand as a means of addressing balance of payments problems. While stabilization programs are important, they must exhibit a bias toward growth.

These three propositions are at the core of any search for improved policies and performance, regardless of judgments about likely levels of external assistance. Indeed, without higher productivity, there is little sense in borrowing larger volumes of external resources.

CONSTRAINTS AND OPPORTUNITIES

The constraints posed by international trade relate primarily to the traditional export commodities: these cannot provide for rapid growth of per capita income in Africa on a sustained basis. Fluctuations in international demand for African primary commodities will continue, and no demand projections suggest that a sustained and dramatic upward trend is likely. While some countries may yet be able to increase output and real incomes from growth of traditional commodities (including petroleum), traditional exports cannot be assigned a leading role in Africa's economic recovery.

Another source of constraints on international trade is inaccessible markets. Even if production meets competitive quantitative, qualitative, and pricing criteria, protection in the export markets of the developed or the developing world, credit terms, and lack of knowledge of overseas markets all present obstacles to growth through international trade. These constraints on trade tend to be stressed by opponents of "outward-looking, market-oriented" policies as a preferred regime.[16]

Nevertheless, it is virtually impossible for Africa to contemplate significant progress in economic development and genuine economic independence without exploiting more fully the opportunities offered by the international economy that complement domestic economic structures. These include access to cheap sources of products needed for development and profitable added markets for goods that can be produced at home. The key issue is not whether to trade, but rather what, how, and when to trade. What are the conditions under which the domestic economy should be linked to or integrated with the international economy? And when and how should portions be de-linked or partially or totally isolated from international trade?

Both the constraints and the opportunities inherent in the international economy express themselves largely in terms of price structures. While declining commodity prices or rising energy bills may represent a constraint on domestic policy, they also represent opportunities for converting domestic production of some commodities into domestic consumption of others at an attractive rate of exchange. A key issue is how to be certain that both the constraints on and the opportunities for national gains through trade are made apparent to domestic producers.

POLICY ALTERNATIVES AND EMPHASES

With nearly four-fifths of Africa's population dependent on agriculture for its livelihood, increased agricultural production is essential for any meaningful improvement in living standards. Given high rates of population growth, the size of farm populations will grow for the next 30 to 40 years even if there is an extraordinary growth in Africa's non-agricultural economy.[17] Growth in agricultural output and productivity as the sine qua non of development is substantiated by the experience of virtually every middle or upper-income country. Agriculture has provided the savings, foreign exchange, markets for new domestic manufactures, labor force for the towns, and food for the labor force over the history of virtually every developed country.

In addition, changing the industrial structure—in particular the manufacturing sector—is intimately related to overall economic development. Achieving structural change involves balancing incentives to, and investment in, agriculture and manufacturing. This question cannot be put in terms of import-substituting versus exporting industries: Excessive dependence on internal markets is a dead-end especially for small countries; and in virtually all successful cases, industries were established initially for a domestic market and later broke into exports. Therefore, the key issues are first balancing the incentives given to production for the home versus the export market both for agricultural and for manufactured goods, and then how to provide incentives for productivity growth that can lead to competitiveness in export industries.[18]

Finally, issues of trade orientation and agricultural growth have been linked in a somewhat pointless discussion over cash versus food crop production. Such a question cannot be answered in the abstract, as the right balance in agricultural production depends on the economics of producing specific commodities in a specific country and the markets for those commodities at home and abroad. It makes no more sense to encourage production of export cash crops that face declining prices abroad than it does to encourage production of food crops where the productivity of labor, land, capital, and water is relatively low. As markets and technology change, so do optimum cropping patterns. The objective should be the growth of farmers' real incomes and of the economy as a whole.

PRICING AND INCENTIVES

All developing countries must choose pricing incentives for producers, consumers, and traders. Since individuals and enterprises make most crucial decisions on the basis of prices, sound national economic management requires prices that promote sustained development. Pricing policies can adversely affect income distribution, production of both food and export crops, and employment opportunities in both agriculture and industry, but can also play a positive role. Evidence from Africa shows that peasant farmers are rational economic calculators, adjusting their behavior to react to changes in prices and known technologies, and to the uncertainties and constraints faced in their economic lives.[19]

In the industrial sector, response to price is less precisely established, but sectors with increased profitability and greater certainty of markets and profits have shown increased investment and output, while those that are discriminated against in terms of profits, prices, and certainty are less likely to expand. Even parastatal bodies (unless finance is no constraint) must pay attention to the prices of inputs and outputs, and must cover operating costs—thus they will enter production lines when they can be sure to influence the prices paid or received, and will not produce products or provide services where they are at substantial risk.[20]

DOMESTIC PRICING AND INTERNATIONAL TRADE

Domestic price structures should be based on an implicit cost-benefit calculation made from a national economic standpoint. Most resources have a variety of potential economic uses and international prices generally represent a set of opportunities for buying and selling which the country must accept as given.[21] Consequently, the national calculus should aim at producing those goods with the highest payoff in terms of the real value of domestic output, usually measurable in terms of net import savings or net export earnings.

The national calculus must also take into account international market conditions for major products, the necessity of learning by doing in newly developing sectors, and the value of diversifying away from traditional sectors. All these points are critical for African countries, as there are limits to the payoff from expanding traditional export products. Diversification both within agriculture and into other sectors is important to permit expansion of economic activities without facing market limitations and to reduce risks associated with concentration in a few products and markets.

As new activities often require higher start-up costs, a successful diversification program must aim at productivity growth rates and cost reductions that outpace those of traditional activities. Thus, uninhibited free trade, with a domestic price structure identical to world prices, is not the best policy, particularly for the lowest income countries.[22]

Nevertheless, domestic prices that deviate too drastically from international prices have been inimical to African development objectives. This is due in part to a failure to recognize one of the constraints of international trade: whatever domestic prices are set, the international price structure is what it is. Ostensibly protected against foreign competition, one local industry is simply favored over other local industries. Protection is a subsidy; consumers could have purchased the protected product more cheaply abroad, but were forced to trade with the domestic producer. As a result, income is transferred from the domestic consumer to the local producer.[23]

More important, the protected sector always appears to be saving more foreign exchange than is actually the case. Differences between apparent savings—after purchases of local inputs and income payments for wages and profits—and the amount actually saved must be made up by a subsidy payment exacted from the consuming sector.[24] In extreme cases, the contributions of protected industries can be negative, as the foreign exchange needed for inputs is greater than the foreign exchange value of the output. As a result, real national income falls and the balance of payments worsens although physical production increases.[25]

How long can such subsidies continue? As protected sectors grow, their needs for subsidies also mount unless their rate of productivity growth is very rapid. If the protected sectors grow more rapidly than those providing the subsidies (as has been the case in virtually all of Africa), then growing sources of transfers, such as agriculture, mining, and tourism, must be found. But with stagnant output in agriculture and mining, protected sectors have no source of subsidy to support their expansion.[26]

Capital inflows have also permitted protected domestic industry to make factor payments that exceed foreign exchange savings. Much of the non-agricultural growth in Africa in recent years has effectively been subsidized by rising capital inflows. This approach, too, is a dead-end unless there are rapid productivity increases in the protected sectors, both to remove the need for continued subsidy and to earn or save enough foreign exchange to repay the foreign loans.

Pricing structures adopted by many African countries have tended to favor protection for manufacturing industries that produce only certain goods, notably luxury and semi-luxury consumer goods, for the domestic market. Consequently, industries which manufacture exports, many essential import substitutes, and agricultural products all have been heavily penalized. In agriculture, pricing discrimination is evident not only for traditional exports,[27] but for new agricultural exports and food crops. The issue, then, is not merely sectoral discrimination, but also a systematic bias toward production of selected manufactured goods for the domestic market.

It has been argued that the scope for growth outside import-substituting industries has been negligible in most African countries which inherited monocultural economies, and, therefore, that there are no alternatives to subsidies for import-substituting industries. While there is some truth to this argument (production in a new industry is most likely to first serve the demands of the home market), in the absence of exceptionally rapid productivity growth, the present structure of incentives is both impossible to reconcile with development objectives and completely self-limiting. When industries producing manufactures for the home market are paid 10, 20, or 50 times as much as producers of agricultural goods in order to save foreign exchange, no reasonable productivity growth differential will eliminate the need for perpetual subsidies.[28]

African countries must encourage the expansion of non-traditional exports and the manufacturing sector. Modest amounts of protection for new products in the domestic market and modest assistance for new exports are justifiable as incentives when changing economic structures.[29] This point must be understood and accepted by Africa's trading partners, international institutions, and donors. But it is the extent of discrimination against all exports and against agriculture that has caused interventions in the pricing system to become pernicious rather than productive.

What products could be exported and to which markets? It is impossible to answer this question with any precision. The nature of diversified growth is that a variety of sectors and industries are engaged in producing for both the home and external markets. With balanced incentives, a wide mix of activities emerges, capable of satisfying both domestic and foreign demand.[30]

OTHER DOMESTIC POLICIES

In addition to pricing structures of internationally traded goods, domestic price distortions and overall fiscal and monetary policy can help or hinder growth and diversification of international trade. Domestic wage and parastatal pricing policies have adversely affected economic performance. With real wages in the modern sector much higher than in agriculture, for example, newer sectors have faced difficulties in becoming internationally competitive. When prices for the output of parastatals are kept low, shortages, under-investment, inefficient use of resources, and deficit operations result, adding to the burden on public financing.

Aggregate monetary and fiscal policies have also played a role. Currency overvaluation often can be attributed to excess money creation, as monetary authorities respond to the requirements of financing fiscal deficits. As public expenditures have risen faster than tax revenues, the public sector has borrowed from the banking system. As a result, excess demand has put pressure on domestic wages and prices. In the absence of exchange rate adjustments, domestic prices have risen above the domestic currency equivalent of similar goods traded internationally. The resulting balance of payments problems have accelerated the adoption of import control systems and tariff structures which discriminate against new exports and duty-free imports such as food.

OPTIONS FOR IMPROVED PERFORMANCE

As indicated earlier, Africa's economic performance could be considerably improved by actions undertaken by the countries themselves and by international institutions and donors. A number of suggestions are presented here.

THE ENVIRONMENT OF THE NEXT DECADE

The pattern of economic history suggests that world economic performance in the next decade is likely to be considerably better than in the preceding one. While a commodity boom is not likely in the next decade, commodity markets are expected to be healthier based on modest assumptions of growth in industrial countries and lower real interest rates. Further, I think that the current forecast of recovery in the OECD countries is too pessimistic. Given the close relationship between Africa's trade and growth prospects and OECD growth, the next decade should show improved African economic performance, even if policy changes are not undertaken by African governments or the international community.[31] Indeed, renewed growth of the OECD economies should help reduce current protectionist trends and provide opportunities for new African exports.

Having stated that African trade opportunities are expected to expand, it would be wrong to conclude that Africa will automatically reach an acceptable growth rate by virtue of the world recovery. African exports are primarily those commodities subject to the constraints of trade, and the need for diversification will remain. In most African countries, the opportunities for successful, low-cost import-substituting industrialization will not be sufficient to trigger output of non-traditional exports from agriculture and manufacturing on the required scale. Import substituting agriculture and non-traditional exports from agriculture and manufacturing are both essential and possible.[32]

Another lesson from the past is that volatility in primary commodity markets will continue. African governments must adopt policies and employ resources to buffer their economies from cyclical fluctuations more effectively than in the past.[33]

ACTION BY AFRICAN GOVERNMENTS

African government must review their price and tax structures to:

- eliminate major pricing anomalies, particularly of foreign exchange and basic foods, and excessive protection for import-replacement industries that result from import controls,
- provide modest discrimination in favor of exports and import replacement activities in manufacturing and agriculture,
- reduce the extent of discrimination against traditional exports,
- substitute sales and excise taxes for tariffs to ensure that consumption restraints and revenue needs do not result in unwarranted protection.

Countries need to improve their macro-economic management by adopting counter-cyclical balance of payments and budgetary policies in both upswings and downswings.

Administrative reforms are needed to encourage a more productive role for foreign trade, especially:

- minimizing administrative barriers to exporters,

- increasing encouragement of exports through provision of adequate credit, information on markets and procedures abroad, etc.,

- easing producers' access to imported components, spare parts, and capital goods.

The reform of price structures is a necessary, though not sufficient condition for improving Africa's economic performance. The pricing of foreign exchange is an extremely powerful policy tool and the incentive system is an effective means both of increasing agricultural output and shifting its composition toward productive use of resources. Excessive protection has also contributed to Africa's economic problems. The proposed agenda would first involve removing the most extreme distortions in each country. However, modest penalties are required on the production of most traditional export commodities and on other goods in which countries have established cost advantages.[34]

Restructuring prices should provide some advantage for the newer sectors of the economy. Modest levels of protection on all import-replacement activities and modest encouragement to all non-traditional exports are called for. To this end, relatively uniform tariff levels on different types of products and modest subsidies to new exports are recommended.[35]

There is always a concern that in restructuring prices, excessive demand for consumer goods, particularly luxuries, will be created. Countries should utilize sales and excise taxes, rather than tariffs and import controls, to regulate consumption. While reduced tariff and quota protection will mean lower prices to producers, higher sales and excise taxes will keep prices facing higher-income consumers at penalty levels.

Proposal pricing reforms are not new, but would provide greater incentives to agricultural production, increase the lowest income groups' share of GDP, and raise output from the agricultural sector, hence improving incomes, output, and the balance of payments. They would also restructure the output of manufacturing sectors toward lower cost industries. The success of countries such as Malawi and Ivory Coast in diversifying their economies and exports over the past decade highlights the positive use of incentives.

Improved macro-economic management is also a high priority, particularly in smoothing the peaks and troughs of international commodity markets. Most of the financing burden of this exercise should be underwritten by the international community, although individual countries must exercise monetary and fiscal restraint when commodity prices are relatively high, in order to conserve resources when they are low. The argument that developing countries can ill afford to keep resources "idle" in foreign exchange reserves is based on the assumption that the productivity of other uses of resources is greater than the use of resources to avert extreme restrictions when commodity prices decline. However, the evidence suggests that the damage done by severe restrictions is greater than the output foregone by building up modest international reserves.[36] Further, if countries had greater resources at the beginning of periods of stringency, the need to resort to extreme trade-restricting measures would be less likely.

Exchange rate adjustments are an essential element of reform, but adjustments made without budgetary and monetary discipline will simply feed inflation. And, such modifications must be part of long-term planning, not crisis management. In addition to better pricing of foreign exchange, tariff reforms, and modest subsidies to new exports, export activities require other types of support. In many African countries, despite the extreme scarcity of foreign exchange, it is almost as difficult to get permission to export as to import. Documentation requirements and other clearance procedures must be minimized, and export activities should receive preference in credit allocations as countries appraise private and parastatal projects.

Finally, a persistent problem in most of Africa is the import control and allocation system. Scarce imported goods often do not reach the sectors that could use them most productively. Exporters and producers of highly valued import substitutes, including food, are often starved of access to imported inputs and capital goods. To complement pricing structure reforms, greater flexibility in the allocation of imports is also needed.[37]

The suggested changes face a host of obstacles. Altering the pricing structure will change the distribution of rewards. In countries in

which the urban and often mining workers have benefited from the
policies of turning the domestic price structure against agriculture,
reforms which raise agricultural prices will meet objections from employed workers. Licensing systems have created their own circle of
wealth and privilege that will not easily be given up. Nor is it easy to
pursue budgetary and balance of payments management policies
which involve more restraint in cyclical booms in order to avoid the
stop-and-start effects that have had a negative effect on overall economic performance. Governments will need considerable support in
making these reforms, and the assistance of the international donor
community is essential.

Countries with already diversified economies may see the quickest
benefits from improved policies. But the need to realign the incentive
structures in the poorest and least diversified economies is equally
important, as the loss of real output from inefficient projects is more
critical in the low-income countries.[38] Stabilization policies to avoid
stop-and-start growth will improve the efficiency with which investment is used and increase growth rates for the poorest countries
which have no access to commercial capital for counter-cyclical financing.

ACTIONS BY THE INTERNATIONAL COMMUNITY

The following actions by the major donor countries and multilateral institutions are recommended.

Donor assistance should be shifted toward greater non-project financing by:

- Debt relief, particularly from bilateral donors,
- Increased non-project aid in support of reform programs under-
  taken by recipient countries,
- Increased resources for compensatory financing, either through
  the IMF or another source, operating on a more automatic basis for
  both drawdowns and repayments,
- Provision of new financing vehicles for non-traditional exports to
  African markets and elsewhere.

Industrial countries should continue to reduce tariff and non-tariff
barriers on African exports and should not retaliate when African
countries use modest subsidies on non-traditional exports.

The mix of external assistance should be shifted toward a higher share of non-project aid, as the perceived bias of donor agencies toward project assistance may have contributed to both the low productivity of new investment and the crisis management of the foreign trade sector in Africa. When countries are short of foreign exchange, they are likely to accept any donor-financed project. In providing the host country's contribution, domestic resources are then diverted from other uses irrespective of relative productivity. When completed, the project requires scarce resources for its operation, runs at less than its optimal level, and yields lower returns on investment.

Shifting the aid mix would make possible higher productivity of both existing and new projects and more rational macro-economic planning on the part of African governments. In addition, non-project aid could be budgeted to support the domestic policy reforms that must be undertaken if external assistance is to have improved productivity rates.

The shift to greater non-project assistance might take different forms, depending on the planning and implementation capacity and economic structure of the country. In a country with high debt burden and considerable planning and implementation capacity, a substantial debt rescheduling could provide enough resources and sufficient breathing space for needed reforms and recovery while other aspects of the aid and investment program remain unchanged. In other countries, greater use of structural adjustment loans and comparable aid from the bilateral donors might accomplish a similar goal, with somewhat more focus on sector policies and projects. And in a low-income country with fewer management capabilities, greater automatic compensatory financing to facilitate better macro-economic management over the trade cycle could greatly enhance aggregate performance.

Relieving the official external debt burden of low-income Africa in particular would free up much needed resources. A major advantage of debt forgiveness or of significant rescheduling is that the released resources are not tied to projects. While the multilateral institutions, particularly the IMF and the World Bank, do not reschedule or forgive obligations falling due, the bilateral donors could make a substantial contribution. Several billion dollars a year could be provided in this manner, augmenting Africa's "untied" aid substantially and possibly increasing net capital flows by 50 percent.[39]

Increased concessionary financing to facilitate reform of pricing and incentives is an essential component of the process of moving toward higher rates of output growth and productivity. The World Bank's structural adjustment loan program is a step in the right direction, but its resources are limited. Additional funds from bilateral donors would strengthen the impact on the overall development program and if such assistance were available on a continuing basis rather than only at time of crisis, the process of matching policy reforms with aid would be less politically charged than at present.

The IMF's short time horizon and the fact that it is usually called in when the situation is already desperate places too great a burden on the difficult process of policy reform. In such circumstances, discussions can be acrimonious and misunderstandings are common. If more development and stabilization assistance were put in a context of long-term policy reforms, less emphasis would be placed on meeting a particular condition by a specified date. Further, the entire process could be tailored to the particular needs of individual countries, rather than being bound by the IMF's relatively rigid rules.[40]

A third category of resources would be used for meeting cyclical fluctuations in commodity prices. Declining import capacity has directly retarded African development, and the policies adopted in times of crisis have made matters worse in the longer run. No less problematic have been cyclical management policies when commodity prices are on the upswing. Countries have been quick to spend increases in foreign exchange earnings, postponing the repayment of short-term stabilization funds that are borrowed on a fixed repayment schedule.

While holding higher average levels of reserves would be a good solution, this seems to be nearly impossible in most countries. As an alternative, the size of IMF compensatory financing arrangements could be increased and the terms modified. More financing would become available automatically when a country's major exports declined by specified amounts or when cereal or energy imports increased due to external factors.

Further, repayment would be scheduled over a relatively long period independent of the behavior of the major exports, but would be automatically converted to a shorter schedule if export earnings improved by a specified amount. The automatic allowance for larger drawings would remove some of the pressure on governments and central banks when export earnings are depressed or import payments surge. At the same time, with the automatic repayment schedule, there would be some assurance that countries would not become over-committed in times of temporary abundance.

The fourth set of measures involve aid flows aimed more directly at increasing Africa's non-traditional exports. Two elements are important in this effort. First, financing non-traditional exports from African countries, both to other African countries and to the rest of the world, would involve providing credit to central banks so that the exporter could extend normal trade credits. The central bank would provide credit to the exporter through normal banking channels which would be repaid by the exporter and by the central bank when foreign exchange was received from the importing country. The credit line could then be drawn down again for more non-traditional exports.

From a national point of view, there would be substantial interest in making sure such exports increased to assure that the credit lines to the central bank were fully tapped. The country would have the incentive to establish procedures that would be readily accessible to exporters and would improve on the competitiveness of African suppliers. It would also ensure that domestic credit favored export diversification and expansion.

Second, assistance to increase trade should include the extension of credit for regional payment clearing arrangements. The clearing arrangements of the Preferential Trade Area for East and Southern Africa provide for the central banks of the member countries themselves to extend credit and take the risk of receiving hard currency at the end of the settlement period. If financing were available for the settlement of such intra-African trade debts, countries would have a much more powerful incentive to utilize the exports of their neighbors. The small size of intra-African trade suggests a low cost to such financing; yet the small size of individual national markets suggests the potential from regional integration would be fairly large.[41]

Finally, the continued extension of preference for all exports from African countries to the United States and other OECD countries is an essential ingredient of any program to increase Africa's benefits from international trade. The size of African exports, under the most optimistic assumptions about export performance over the next decade, is so small that relaxation in the OECD countries could be accomplished without measurable hardship in those countries, while the benefits to Africa in terms of increased export earnings and output could be very substantial.[42]

ACTIONS BY GROUPS OF AFRICAN COUNTRIES

Cooperation among African countries in removing barriers to intra-regional trade is another imperative. Regional groupings represent the best vehicle if they work toward limited goals, such as reducing licensing requirements and improving payments clearing arrangements before dealing with tariff reductions, and not attempting to agree on "rationalization of industrial location." If the donor community provides funding to cover the foreign exchange risks of trade liberalization of trade among African countries, African governments would be more willing to engage in such practices. Since closer economic cooperation among African countries is an important principle throughout the continent and a key element in the Lagos Plan of Action, donors and African governments should work together to achieve a greater measure of cooperation in trade expansion.

CONCLUSIONS

Africa's record of economic growth has been dismal for the past decade or more. GDP growth has lagged, GDP per capita has fallen, export growth has been slow, the productivity of investment has declined, and dependence on capital inflows has risen, leading to sharply rising ratios of debt to both GDP and exports. Agriculture, in particular, has grown slowly, resulting in declining yields per hectare and output per capita.

The likely payoff of better domestic policies is quite high, and if combined with adjustments on the part of the industrialized countries, more rapid growth in Africa than is now forecast is possible. The package of policies for sustained growth involves actions by both the African countries and the donor community. African countries need to adopt reforms of exchange rates, import controls, and agricultural pricing systems to remove the extremes of subsidies and penalties inherent in their current arrangements. They must also adopt better counter-cyclical macro-economic management. An increase in non-project aid, such as the World Bank's structural adjustment loans, would be highly desirable to support such policy reforms.

Trade policies can play a key role in determining African economic performance. Genuine progress toward greater economic independence will only come through adoption of policies which lead to a more effective and efficient use of Africa's resources—land, capital, people, foreign exchange, water. Not only must policies maximize the opportunities inherent in international trade, but they must also limit the effects on domestic economies of adverse movements in foreign markets. The international donor community can assist in the process of reform both by directly financing reform efforts and by reducing trade barriers to African exports.

NOTES

1. Measurements of the terms of trade are more complex and difficult to interpret than many other economic magnitudes, whether for a particular country or a group of countries. While the basic notion is simple (the import purchasing power of a given volume of exports), measuring prices of non-standardized goods is difficult, and any significant change in the composition of either imports or exports raises questions about the weightings to be used. Since success in economic development implies that the composition of both imports and exports will change dramatically, the weightings will necessarily change rapidly, and fixed weight indices may give misleading results.

2. The data used in these comparisons are taken primarily from World Bank sources. IMF data are also used. Although the groupings of countries are slightly different between the two sources, the overall results as judged from the two institutions' data are not affected by the differences in coverage and definitions. Detailed information on definitions and on the classifications of the countries can be found in the various issues of the World Bank's *World Development Report*, or the IMF's *World Economic Outlook*.

3. Evidence on this point is provided by Helleiner (1984).

4. The sequence of foreign exchange crises leading to trade policy regimes of a highly restrictive and distorting nature is spelled out well by Bhagwati (1978) and Krueger (1977) and confirmed by case studies undertaken for their joint efforts, as well as in earlier comparative studies of Little, Scitovsky and Scott (1970) and Balassa and Associates (1971). Kenya's resort to controls in successive foreign reserve crises in the 1970s is a clear case of a control system that arose largely in response to short-term emergencies, and where the certainty of direct controls in restricting imports was a decisive factor in their adoption over other measures that were considered. However high the costs, industries that promised to "save imports" could successfully recommend that competing imports be banned.

5. This judgment refers to the two decades ending around 1980. The most recent two to three years have not yet been included in any rigorous statistical analysis.

6. Alternatively stated, in some of the cases of lowest economic perform-ance, the effect of an adverse external environment was made considerably worse due to the choice of policies by the countries involved.

7. Wheeler (1984) shows that lack of economic diversity and domestic political instability were major factors affecting the performance of African countries in the 1960s and 1970s, while Helleiner (1984) illustrates how im-port instability deteriorates economic performance in less diversified, low income countries.

8. Wheeler (1984) distinguishes between several measures of the quantity of OECD imports, using both simultaneous and lagged variables, and a single measure of the net barter terms of trade. The analysis is carried out for Africa as a whole, and there are numerous data problems in producing plausible variables for a diverse continent and its similarly diverse markets. However, the underlying relationships seem extremely strong, and the sig-nificance of each coefficient and the accuracy with which both the trend and the turning points of African growth are predicted are impressive.

9. The *World Development Report 1982* and *1983* both contain analyses pointing to the power of exchange rates in encouraging or discouraging economic performance; Balassa's (1983) work on Africa and on other coun-tries' responses to external shocks gives the same result. Wheeler's analysis of African countries points to the power of the exchange rate, as does the IMF's analysis in its *World Economic Outlook* in 1983.

10. Wheeler's studies as well as those of Balassa show that the ability or willingness to adjust to changed external circumstances is important in Af-rica. Note, however, Helleiner's cautionary note that the lowest income countries may be unable to adjust import levels without substantial penalty to economic activity. This important issue is discussed below.

11. Harberger and Edwards (1982) compared countries, including Afri-can countries, which had to deal with falling international reserves. They concluded that "crises countries" which adopted policies to deal with falling reserves too late in the cycle demonstrated worse economic performance than countries which managed reserves with better anticipation of the conse-quences, and took actions earlier to stabilize their external positions.

12. Helleiner's studies are a major source of evidence here, though he would stress the need for externally financed liquidity to allow countries to ride out the cycles.

13. The 1983 *World Economic Outlook* contained an analysis of the effects of exchange rate changes on the trade balance in various groups of developing countries. In general, significant improvements were found in the countries that depreciated their currencies, relative to those that appreciated, during periods of adjustment to crisis. The least significant relationship was for the low-income country groups.

14. "Optimal" values were determined from the economic performance *within the 24 African countries themselves*. Thus, the results are based solely on conditions and performance in seventeen low-income and seven lower-mid-dle-income countries of Africa. While Wheeler's results are extremely inter-esting and suggestive, they cannot be called definitive. For example, the civil

disturbance variable is a dummy variable used when there are coups or civil wars. The precise definition of any such variable is obviously a difficult empirical problem. The measurement of some of the other variables, too, such as those showing the ability to adjust to changed economic circumstances, could also be questioned. The effort is a most imaginative one, however, and is the best available.

15. I have described and analyzed elsewhere (Lewis, 1984) an "automatic adjustment mechanism" in mining economies. Based on the nature of mineral enterprises and the political economy of mining developments, the mechanism will tend to give mineral-rich countries a poorer record of performance than those without minerals. However, this mechanism can be circumvented to capture the potential gains from mineral developments (e.g., through preventing the effects of mineral export earnings from dominating the exchange rate, and ensuring that wage settlements in mining and government reflect conditions in the rest of the economy), rather than having them serve as a negative influence. I find it difficult to regard the presence of economically exploitable, non-renewable resources as necessarily retarding economic performance.

16. Such opponents often have other items on their agendas—for example, the conviction that such policies will retard the movement toward more economic independence and self-reliance, that market related solutions are inherently likely to generate unequal distributions of income, or that such policies are likely to lead to larger or more pernicious roles for transnational companies.

17. This general theme is elaborated in the recent survey of the world food equation by Mellor and Johnston (1984).

18. Achieving a better balance between export production incentives and import substitutes will not necessarily lead to a rising ratio of exports to GDP. As productivity rises, and real GDP per capita increases, domestic markets will grow. In some countries, prospects for substantial import replacement may exceed the prospects for major export growth, so that growth with more diversified output would result in a falling share of exports and imports to GDP. On the other hand, to the extent that there are substantial domestic spin-offs from a rapidly growing export sector, "export led" growth need not result in an increased ratio of exports to GDP either. Countries that have pursued a better balance of incentives have generally achieved more diversified economies, regardless of whether they have become more open or closed as measured by ratios of trade to growth.

19. Eicher and Baker (1982) point to over twenty studies (covering cotton, coffee, cocoa, palm oil and kernels, tobacco, rubber and groundnuts) which together provide "irrefutable evidence that smallholders are economic men," and incorporate price factors into production decisions (p. 90). They also conclude more generally (p. 30) that "there is unambiguous evidence that African farmers, traders and migrants will respond to economic incentives."

20. The growth of the manufacturing industry in Kenya in the 1970s was very closely related to the incentives provided by the tariff and import licens-

ing system. Indeed, the quickest and most accurate way of finding out what Kenya produces is to examine either the tariff schedule to identify the highest tariff rates or the import licensing schedules to see which goods are subject to the tightest restrictions.

21. When a country faces less than perfect elastic demand for its exports, then it is marginal revenues, not prices, which are given, and the country will affect its price by the quantities it attempts to sell. There are also circumstances, sometimes a matter of contract, where a country is limited in the quantity of the commodity it can sell at a given price. For relatively small producers, or for producers just entering a market, these constraints are less likely to apply.

22. In the strictest formal economic terms, if there were perfect capital markets and a variety of other condidtions, private decisions on profit maximization would lead to optimal investment patterns even for new industries with higher costs. Such conditions are not present in developing countries, particularly in Africa. Consequently, there is a strong case for government intervention in the pricing system.

23. After Ghana opted for heavily protected industrialization in the 1960s, for example, producers of all non-cocoa exports were being paid about one new cedi to earn a dollar, while they had to pay at least one and a half new cedis to purchase a dollar's worth of clothing produced by local industry.

24. This is a simple restatement of the principle of the effective rate of protection to an industry. For elaboration, and one of the first applications in Africa, see Steel's work (1972) on import substitution in Ghana.

25. Steel (1977) and Leith (1974) report cases in Ghana, Phelps and Wasow give examples in Kenya, and the World Bank gives an anonymous African example of such perverse results from excessive protection.

26. This factor is explicitly recognized by the Kenya government and is outlined carefully in the 1984 budget speech explaining the reform in tariff and indirect tax structure. Note that *if* productivity had grown rapidly, the new sectors could export and the problems of stagnation and balance of payments deterioration would be avoided.

27. *Some* discrimination against traditional exports is justified in many cases on both demand inelasticity and diversification grounds.

28. Ratios of this magnitude appear in a number of countries. The most well-documented cases are those reported by Leith, Steel, and Phelps and Wasow. Such relative rewards could not be defended in terms of differences in demand elasticities, either.

29. Note that discriminating modestly in favor of new import substitutes and new exports necessarily means modest discrimination against traditional exports in which a country has established cost advantages.

30. Botswana, which was dominated by mineral developments for fifteen years, has had growth rates of real manufacturing output and employment in excess of 10 percent per year throughout that period. The new industries sold partly in domestic and partly in export markets (primarily but not exclusively

regional). Botswana has the least restrictive import control system in Africa, and has provided little in the way of specific protection to new industrial activities until very recently, when a system providing equal incentive payments to import replacement and exporting industries was adopted.

31. The 1984 IMF *World Economic Outlook* and the World Bank's 1984 *World Development Report* both forecast recoveries in the OECD countries that are, in my view, a bit pessimistic. I think both fail to take account of the fact that many of the structural problems of the 1970s, including adjustment to a much higher level of energy prices and coping with some institutionalized aspects of inflation in the high-income countries, seem to be behind us. Since developments in the OECD countries are crucial to the forecasts for the developing countries, my view of the forecasts for the developing world is more optimistic as well. John Kendrick's recent article (1984) focusing on productivity growth in the United States articulates a number of reasons why the current forecasts of the OECD growth rates may be too pessimistic.

32. Eicher and Baker (1982) point out that the large volume of illegal and unrecorded trade among African countries is indicative of substantial potential trade if the penalties on international exchange were removed.

33. Neither the IMF nor the World Bank 1984 forecast addresses what, from Africa's viewpoint, may be a key issue: *Whatever* the trend in the next five to ten years, there is bound to be a cycle around it. Managing the cycles well is at least as important as the trend. The 1984 *World Development Report* (p. 31) also points to the serious consequences in Africa of poor management during the upswings of commodity markets in the 1970s.

34. "Modesty" may be in the eye of the beholder, but, in both penalties for traditional exports and protection for new industries, one should be skeptical of proposals for departing from international prices by more than twenty-five percent. I have no "scientific" basis for this, but the results of the comparative studies by Balassa and Associates (1971), Little, Scitovsky and Scott (1970), and Bhagwati (1978) and Krueger (1977) are suggestive of such limits.

35. It is important for the high-income countries to accept that some modest form of what appear to be subsidies will be required in most developing countries for their new exports. New activities have initially higher costs, and the tax, tariff, and exhange rate systems in Africa generally penalize domestic producers relative to world market prices. If the developed countries are serious about their desire to have Africa become more self-reliant, less dependent on aid, more attuned to using prices to guide their economies, and better able to buy exports from the industrial countries, then they will have to accept that African countries must give special encouragement to new exports aimed at all markets, and not retaliate with tariffs or quotas.

36. Helleiner's analysis stressing the importance of stability in import coefficients, and the adverse consequences of import instability adds strength to this point. Further, given the recent record in Africa on the productivity of investment, accumulation of reserves in order to avoid sharp reductions in imports would probably have resulted in more growth than the

use of those resources to undertake unproductive investments. If capital inflows had been aimed less at creating more projects and had been devoted instead to stabilizing import levels during low commodity prices, African economic performance would have been better over the past decade.

37. Zimbabwe's recent experience with a World Bank credit that provides for significantly easier access of exporters to necessary imports is a good example of one step toward administrative reforms that would support the objectives of using trade to promote growth. Zambia's experiment with allowing exporters to retain a portion of their foreign exchange to meet requirements for imports of raw materials and spare parts also appears to be quite successful.

38. The use of "efficient" here simply refers to the amount of real goods and services produced, as valued by the costs facing the country. Under exceptionally distorted pricing structures projects are chosen that simply deliver much less value for money from a national viewpoint, even if they are privately profitable (or, if undertaken by a parastatal, completely cost-covering). And, projects which would provide more real goods per unit of capital, foreign exchange, or highly skilled labor, are not taken up because they are not cost-covering (or privately profitable) at the existing set of prices.

39. In the early 1980s the gross capital flows to Africa were around $12 or $13 billion, of which $8 or $9 billion was from bilateral and multilateral grants and loans. Amortization was about $2 to $3 billion on total debt, but only around $0.5 to $1 billion on debt to bilateral and multilateral aid agencies. The amortization figure is rising rapidly, however, and in the next two or three years will rise to between $6 and $9 billion on total debt, and around $3 billion on aid to official agencies. It is this latter figure that could be significantly affected, and if it were to be done through forgiveness, the interest burden could be reduced as well. These numbers are based on IMF and World Bank sources.

40. Helleiner, one of the most persuasive of the critics of the IMF activities in Africa, has aimed much of his criticism at the Fund's failure to consider individual characteristics of the countries it is called to help. Having greater flexibility to craft the solutions to the problems would increase the likelihood that reforms would be entered into with greater conviction on the part of African governments.

41. There could be more elaborate forms of this payments clearing arrangement, which owes its concept to the European Payments Union and the mechanism for distributing assistance under the Marshall Plan. I have in mind something a good deal less elaborate, and, given the relatively small size of existing intra-regional trade, a good deal less expensive.

42. The World Bank reported that in the 1976–78 period the traditional primary commodities listed in Table A.3 (Appendix I) accounted for about 83% of Africa's total exports, leaving about US$4.5 billion in other exports. The total is not a great deal larger today, given the disastrous export performance noted earlier. This compares with a figure for 1982 imports into the industrial market economies of $US 1,200 billion.

REFERENCES

Balassa, Bela, and Associates. 1971. *The Structure of Protection in Developing Countries*. Baltimore: Johns Hopkins University Press.

Balassa, Bela, and Associates. 1983. "Policy Responses to External Shocks in Sub-Saharan African Countries," *Journal of Policy Modelling* 5(1)(March).

Bhagwati, Jagdish N. 1978. *Foreign Trade Regimes and Economic Development (XI): Anatomy and Consequences of Exchange Control Regimes*. Cambridge, Mass.: Ballinger.

Eicher, Carl K. and Doyle C. Baker. 1982. "Research on Agricultural Development in Sub-Saharan Africa: A Critical Survey," East Lansing: Michigan State University, International Development Paper, No. 1.

Gordon, David F. and Joan C. Parker. 1984. "The World Bank and Its Critics: The Case of Sub-Saharan Africa," Ann Arbor: University of Michigan, Center for Research on Economic Development Discussion Paper No. 108.

Harberger, Arnold C. and Sebastian Edwards. 1982. "Lessons of Experience Under Fixed Exchange Rates," in Mark Gersovitz, Carlos F. Diaz-Alejandro, Gustav Ranis and Mark R. Rosenzweig, eds., *The Theory and Experience of Economic Development: Essays in Honor of Sir W. Arthur Lewis*. London: George Allen.

Helleiner, G. K. 1983. "The IMF and Africa in the 1980s," *Princeton Essays in International Finance* 152(July).

Helleiner, G. K. 1984. "Outward Orientation, Import Instability and African Economic Growth: An Empirical Investigation," in Sanjaya Lall and Frances Stewart, eds., *Paul Streeten Festschrift*, forthcoming.

IMF. 1980. *World Economic Outlook*. Washington, D.C.

IMF. 1984. *World Economic Outlook*. Occasional Paper No. 27. Washington, D.C.

Kendrick, John W. 1984. "Productivity Gains Will Continue," *Wall Street Journal*, August 29.

Krueger, Anne O. 1977. *Foreign Trade Regimes and Economic Development (IX): Liberalization Attempts and Consequences*. Cambridge, Mass.: Ballinger.

Leith, J. Clark. 1974. *Foreign Trade Regimes and Economic Development (II): Ghana*. New York and London: Columbia University Press.

Lewis, Stephen R., Jr. 1984. "Development Problems of the Mineral Rich Countries," in M. Syrquin, L. Taylor and L.E. Westphal, eds., *Economic Structure and Performance: Essays in Honor of Hollis B. Chenery*. San Diego: Academic Press.

Lewis, W. A. 1980. "The Slowing Down of the Engine of Growth," *The American Economic Review* (4)(September).

Little, Ian, Tibor Scitovsky, and Maurice Scott. 1970. *Industry and Trade in Some Developing Countries*. Paris: Oxford University Press.

Mellor, John W. and Bruce F. Johnston. 1984. "The World Food Equation," *Journal of Economic Literature* XXII(2)(June).

Phelps, M. G., and D. Wasow. n.d. "Measuring Protection and Its Effects in Kenya." Working Paper No. 37. Nairobi: Institute for Development Studies.

Steel, W. F. 1972. "Import Substitution and Excess Capacity in Ghana," *Oxford Economic Papers* 24(2)(July): 212–40.

Steel, W. F. 1977. *Small-Scale Employment and Production in Developing Countries: Evidence from Ghana.* New York and London: Praeger.

Wheeler, David. 1984. "Sources of Stagnation in Sub-Saharan Africa," *World Development* 12(1)(January): 1–23.

World Bank. 1982. *World Development Report.* New York: Oxford University Press.

World Bank. 1983. *World Development Report.* New York: Oxford University Press.

World Bank. 1984. *World Development Report.* New York: Oxford University Press.

Foreign Aid in Africa: Here's the Answer—Is It Relevant to the Question?

Robert J. Berg

By almost any measure, sub-Saharan Africa is extraordinarily dependent upon the goods, services, and funds supplied by foreign aid. Except for the radical right and left, almost all analysts concerned with Africa's deep developmental crisis believe that future aid flows will be of continuing and perhaps growing importance. Africa's development partners have played an important role in the continent's economic development and must take both some of the credit and some of the blame for its current predicament. Africa is where it is today in part because of aid, and its future will be strongly shaped by what donors do and how they do it.

In this chapter, the effectiveness of aid to Africa will be described and recommendations will be made for increasing the benefits aid can bring to African development. While other chapters in this volume make recommendations on what development options present the most promise for Africa, this study is restricted to the mechanism through which many of these options are likely to be financed.

DESCRIPTION OF FOREIGN AID TO AFRICA

For decades, the developing countries have been the recipients of major flows of resources from the developed world, averaging over $100 billion per year in the last four years.[1] Nearly two-thirds has been nonconcessional and has recently included major roll-overs of past private debt. The remaining one-third is development assistance, of which about $35 billion a year is official aid and $2 billion a year from non-governmental organizations.

Africa is dependent upon the aid flows provided from official and private donors. Total financial flows to Africa are estimated to have averaged $13 billion in recent years, just over half of which has been concessional. While Africa's 369 million people constitute approximately 12 percent of the people in the developing countries,[2] Africa receives 22 percent of official development assistance (ODA).[3]

Twenty-five of the 45 countries in sub-Saharan Africa depend upon aid for over two-thirds of their total externally provided financial receipts. Of these, 15, including many of the smallest countries, are dependent by more than 90 percent on aid. According to the UN Economic Commission for Africa (ECA), aid to this area equalled almost 40 percent of its total imports and over half its total investment in 1981.[4]

In 1982, official aid averaged 5.85 percent of Africa's GNP[5] (excluding Nigeria, the average was 7.52 percent), although there were wide variations, running from .05 percent for Nigeria to 51.4 percent for Cape Verde. In 1982, ODA made up 19 percent of total gross domestic investment in all of sub-Saharan Africa. Excluding the oil-exporting countries, however, ODA was 44 percent of gross domestic investment.[6]

Africa's precarious international debt situation heightens the importance of foreign aid. No other part of the world has as serious a debt burden relative to GDP. While the total debt is relatively small compared to that of Latin America, Africa has beaten a path to the Paris Club to reschedule its debts with far greater frequency than any other area of the world.[7] Half of Africa's debt arises from past foreign aid, as compared to only 15 percent for Latin America.

While Africa's external finance situation is extremely serious now, barring unexpected changes in Africa's terms of trade, it is very likely that this situation will deteriorate. Without a major push, aid levels are likely to remain constant, while repayments from past loaned aid will rise. Hence, net aid levels are likely to decline over the rest of the decade. Similarly, substantial repayments to the IMF and commercial creditors are due in the short and medium term. New investment in Africa has tailed off in recent years and few expect much in the way of a recovery over the next several years.

Finally, it should be noted that Africa is far more dependent than any other part of the world on foreign sources for the goods and services most often required for development. Other parts of the world, reaping the benefits of their past development, can tap local sources of industrial and service production to a far greater extent. The need for a larger proportion of foreign exchange to carry out development initiatives and the absence of a strong and reliable export base has made Africa highly dependent upon foreign aid to finance its development efforts.

Aid is traditionally categorized by type: technical assistance, capital assistance (both project and non-project aid), and food aid. Capital assistance accounts for two-thirds of concessional aid to Africa, some $4.6 billion a year. This transfer of foreign goods to Africa is largely packaged in project aid. For many years, African officials have called for this aid to be switched to a non-project, budgetary support basis. To an increasing extent, this is occurring, but not to ease administration as much as to increase donor leverage in economic policy discussions.

Technical assistance is still of great significance in Africa; indeed, the area may receive up to 75 percent of all technical assistance provided by donors.[8] While the financial sum involved is large—about 25 percent of all aid to Africa[9]—what is of greater significance is the sheer number (perhaps 20,000) of resident foreign technicians in Africa, particularly in the francophone countries. While the days when major African development issues were decided solely by foreign-supplied technicians are largely over, the influence of foreign consultants is still great, particularly when new initiatives are designed or launched. And the costs are very large indeed—two to three times the cost in their home countries and 10 to 25 times the cost of sometimes comparable local experts.

Food aid to Africa normally amounts to about $650 million a year, but in the 1984–86 emergency, it is running at over $2 billion a year.[10] Emergency food programs have played a crucial role in meeting African food needs in the 1973–74 and current droughts, providing about half of total net cereals imports. Non-emergency food aid, used for school lunch and food-for-work programs, for example, has also been a continuing part of donor programs.

Because of this book's special interest in U.S. policy, it is worth paying particular attention to the size and composition of U.S. aid to Africa. Such assistance comes through bilateral aid channels and through major U.S. contributions to multilateral programs that benefit Africa. Bilateral U.S. aid to Africa has grown fairly rapidly in the last several years and now is over $1 billion excluding sizeable emergency aid (another $1 billion in 1985–86). The main components of this aid are noted in Table A.12 in Appendix I, showing changes since 1980. Military aid has been included in this calculation to indicate that along with Economic Support Fund assistance, the United States now gives about 46 percent of its non-emergency assistance to Africa for open political and military purposes.

TRENDS AND ISSUES IN AID TO AFRICA

Public and private international donors operate through or with the consent of national governments in developing countries. This is more than a diplomatic nicety to African governments: It is a sign that Africans want to be and in most cases are in charge of their development.

Donors have respected and helped to underwrite Africa's development goals, in part because donors have often participated in the planning process, but also because it is clearly in the donor's short-term political interest to support the development aspirations of local political leaders. With perhaps a stronger commitment to reinforcing national plans, multilateral donors have also strengthened and subsidized national planning efforts of African officials. Some continue to do so, but others, most notably the World Bank, have been seeking to modify national planning strategies. By and large, however, local development planning has been backed by donor finance. When planning has been good, this has been beneficial; when it has been incompetent or corrupt, the donor has been an accomplice.

DONOR TRENDS

The development aims of African governments have evolved from a post-independence preoccupation with basic infrastructure and institution-building to a more recent concern with the rural sector and its accompanying infrastructure and service needs.

Donors have not been passive observers of changes in development trends in Africa, however. They have their own agendas and interests which often change. Some of these changes have come about through normal learning and adjustment to new problems, but other shifts have resulted from changes in the donor's political environment, new personnel, the need to present a new face on programs to sell them to legislatures, or simple-minded impatience with existing programs.

Incomplete data from the Development Assistance Committee of OECD indicates some of the major changes that have occurred. Table 18.1 shows a major increase in support to agriculture over the past few years, sizeable increases in health and education, and a decline in general economic support, the latter having been reversed more recently. For the United States, the shifts from infrastructure and institution-building in the 1960s to basic human needs in 1973 and back to institution-building and policy reform in 1981 were far more abrupt than was warranted.

While in the past, these shifts in donor preferences have sometimes been at odds with African planners, in the last year a new pattern of convergence has occurred. The major donors and African planners agree at least rhetorically on the major priorities for Africa's development: emergency assistance now emphasizing food aid and debt reform; rehabilitation emphasizing balance of payments aid; and long-term development based on population planning, agricultural development (especially food self-sufficiency), and related supporting development of human resources and non-agricultural sectors. The agreed-on agenda contains a huge dose of policy and structural reform. All of this presents a tremendous opportunity to undertake reinforcing actions and to greatly increase the effectiveness of domestic and foreign development assistance.

In so doing, there are also very great opportunities to capitalize on the lessons of previous development experiences. The evidence of past experience is more readily available now than in any previous period, because in recent years donors have heavily invested in evaluation of their aid programs. A main question is whether policy-makers will consult this evidence as they consider and undertake policy changes, or operate in the absence of an informed reading of the past and future.

Donors influence the outcome of activities they support not only by choosing sectors and strategies, but by how they act individually and as a group. Over the last few decades the following has occurred in donor aid to Africa.

More Donors and Projects   There are many donors active in Africa now and there are likely to be more in the future. If it is hard to match

TABLE 18.1

SECTORAL ALLOCATION OF OFFICIAL DEVELOPMENT ASSISTANCE (ODA) TO AFRICA, 1978–82
(in current $ millions)

Sectors	1978	1979	1980	1981	1982	1978–82 Sectoral Total
Energy	137	221	534	267	287	1,446
Food & Agriculture	866	1,078	1,359	1,655	1,880	6,838
Health	158	281	266	414	543	1,662
Education	165	186	187	340	299	1,177
Social Infrastructure & Welfare	133	91	162	177	205	768
Transportation, Storage & Communication	833	827	981	811	990	4,442
Industry, Construction & Mining	126	89	215	138	276	844
Trade & Tourism	24	66	42	20	72	224
Gen'l Economic Support	1,650	1,054	1,509	1,229	1,157	6,599
Other & Unallocated	195	75	144	118	225	757
Total	4,287	3,968	5,399	5,169	5,934	24,757

SOURCE: Data from an unpublished study by OECD, Paris. Because of gaps in information relating to sectoral allocations, yearly aid totals from this table do *not* equal total ODA assistance to Africa.

program needs and donors now, it will be harder in the future, as donor-financed projects and entities continue to clutter the physical and public administration landscape.

More Field Staff   More donors are recognizing that international assistance cannot be administered solely from the home country with only infrequent trips to the field to consult with African governments. Placing more and better people in the field has enabled some donors to delegate more decision-making to their field staffs which often helps speed implementation.

Greater Flexibility in the Rules   Too much aid is tied to home-country procurement and legislated or administrative rules which seem reasonable in the abstract but are difficult to carry out in practice. In spite of almost interminable negotiations, the Development Assistance Committee of the OECD has failed to achieve landmark reforms. Some individual donors have increased their flexibility to permit more local buying and more ease in adjusting projects mid-stream. But there are disturbing counter-trends toward more tied aid, engendering more corruption and less value.

Some Softening of the Terms   Donors were slow to react to Africa's need for soft credit, but made generally appropriate changes in the 1970s. Some donors have even forgiven past ODA loans to the poorest countries, but the United States has refused to do so.

Increased Coordination of Aid   Efforts to coordinate African aid have been in direct response to the trauma of its crises. As a consequence of the 1973–74 drought, the Club du Sahel was created to coordinate donor work in the Sahelian states. A back-to-back grouping of Sahelian governments—the Permanent Interstate Committee for Drought Control in the Sahel—was also created to facilitate working with the donors. Both institutions have been useful and have worked together admirably. In the late 1970s, seven countries which account for some 65 percent of bilateral aid to Africa (Belgium, Canada, France, Italy, United Kingdom, United States, and West Germany) formed the Cooperation for Development in Africa to jointly analyze sectoral strategy questions and to coordinate their donor programs. In addition, since 1984, UN agencies have drawn closer together under the stimulus of the UN Secretary-General, and the World Bank has also been more active in coordinating donor assistance. More donors and

African governments now recognize that a better coordinated donor effort is required and the barriers to coordination are beginning to fall.

All of the above characteristics and trends greatly affect how well the donors are able to contribute to African development. At present, however, two major factors overshadow all others in their impact on African development today: the drought and how it has affected African needs and the consequent new demands on donors; and, second, a great shortage of recurrent finance and an absence of development finance generated from domestic sources. Host country counterpart staff and funds have always been in short supply. Now, where such staff are available, their salaries, fuel, and support rations have been cut so drastically that their effectiveness is greatly impaired. Donor agencies are faced with aiding institutions which do not have the financial capacity to undertake anything new. To a major extent, the donors inadvertently exacerbated the recurrent finance problem by shifting in the 1970s to types of development activities requiring large amounts of recurrent support. While in theory, major donors now are willing to finance more recurrent costs, in practice a major shift in financing formulas has not occurred.

U.S. AID IN PERSPECTIVE

Among the donor programs that have changed the most is that of the United States. While there has been some consistency of approach beneath changes in rhetoric (hence long-time programs in Liberia and Zaire and support to many institutions in Africa, and a consistency, at least on paper, in functionally concentrating on agriculture, health, education, and population), there has been a great amount of real shifting. The following are notable:

- A tilt toward Africa: more budget; an attempt to upgrade field leadership and staff in key Washington posts; more leadership internationally on some African development issues; and creation of the African Development Foundation to work with grassroots organizations.

- A more politicized program: Politically justified economic aid is not only 34 percent[11] of U.S. economic aid to Africa, but it is so mixed in with "Development Assistance" (non-political aid funds) in many country programs that the motives for the entire U.S. aid program have become confused. To an increasingly large extent, the quid pro quo for U.S. aid is political loyalty rather than economic performance. The United States' reluctance to respond quickly to emergency food needs in Ethiopia and Mozambique in 1983 is held up by the American religious and NGO communities as evidence of the heavy political basis of U.S. aid.[12]

• A major shift in content: From the concentration on basic human needs that was evident in the 1970s and remains at the core of USAID's legislative mandate, interest has now shifted to programs emphasizing the private sector and market forces, changes in developing country pricing policies, human resource development, and science and technology. While it has been argued that the shift was more in interpretation than in basic philosophy, the shift in rhetoric was major and a large number of USAID programs in Africa have been changed as a result.[13]

AID ISSUES RAISED BY THE WORLD BANK

In contrast to the U.S. program, which as of early 1986 had produced no clear, long-run game plan for aiding Africa, the World Bank developed a fairly clear program in 1981 on how it wished to assist African development. In its celebrated *Accelerated Development in Sub-Saharan Africa: An Agenda for Action*,[14] the Bank focused on a number of strategy issues. Uppermost were policy reform to provide more incentives for farmers and the private sector; emphasis over the medium term on agriculture for export; more efficiency in agricultural and human resources; reduced emphasis on industrialization; more efficiency and expansion of energy resources; and greatly increased aid levels in order to facilitate recommended policy reforms.

Public reaction to questions of policy reform recommended in the "Berg Report" has been so strong that its recommendations on aid have almost entirely escaped critical attention. The report implies that aid is perhaps the major vehicle for rich countries to help Africa. While the report did not analyze the effectiveness of past aid to Africa, it did offer several important suggestions on how aid can be made more useful in the future, some of which have been acted upon by the World Bank, others which have not. The suggestions include:

• Increasing assistance in formulating and supporting policy reforms through such mechanisms as technical assistance and non-project aid (acted upon).

- Continuing major reliance on project assistance (acted upon).
- More flexibility in project design and administration, including evolutionary design models such as pilot projects.
- Increasing local cost and recurrent cost financing over relatively longer periods of time.
- More harmonization of donor procedures and more donor coordination in general, although the report (p. 130) cautions that "some African governments are unenthusiastic. They fear 'ganging up,' as well as a loss of 'maneuverability'."
- Continuing substantial technical assistance to increase the local management of aid-funded projects.

These suggestions will be revisited after consideration has been given to a question that has been absent from many discussions on aid to Africa: How effective has aid been? In brief, is it an answer to the kinds of questions facing Africa?

HAS INTERNATIONAL ASSISTANCE BEEN EFFECTIVE IN AFRICA?

We can now answer the question better than ever before. Until recently, opinion on the effectiveness of aid was based on anecdotal evidence often collected by writers representing the political extremes. Evidence has also been provided from econometric studies such as the famous Bariloche model. In 1976, the Fundacion Bariloche concluded that aid was only modestly helpful in improving socioeconomic well-being, a finding that many intellectuals in developing countries interpreted to mean that aid was a luxury most countries could live without.

The Bariloche researchers asked the right question: Are countries better or worse off with aid? Unfortunately, this question cannot be answered for Africa in general since so few states have been without aid. Further, it would be meaningless to relate economic performance only to inflows of aid. The next best level of analysis would be to ask whether aided projects perform better or worse than unaided projects. This is possible in some African settings where larger portfolios of unassisted development projects exist, but little evaluative work has been done on them.

While whether or not aided projects and programs work may not be the most perfect question, for the first time donors are in a position to answer it. For over a decade, the World Bank has been collecting evaluative information on its portfolio. USAID has been conducting an important series of impact evaluations since 1977,[15] as have Canada, West Germany, Netherlands, United Kingdom, and the EEC. Some of the major NGOs also have evaluative information on their portfolios. In addition, the Western bilateral donors have begun to compare their evaluation results through the Evaluation Experts Working Group of the OECD's Development Assistance Committee.[16]

A number of the donors have recently begun to aggregate their findings in very useful ways. The available information permits a large number of observations about the effectiveness of aid in general and to Africa specifically.[17]

ECONOMIC AND SOCIAL RESULTS

The general economic setting of the past two decades is well-known: Although overall GNP growth rates are not very different from other regions of the world, Africa's tremendous increase in population has meant very slow growth and even declining per capita GNP. While we do not have the techniques to judge aid's effect on GNP growth, aid has been an important mainstay of development budgets and has been responsible for a great amount of new investment. As noted above, in 1982, for example, ODA represented 19 percent of overall gross domestic investment in Africa. Excluding the oil exporters, ODA was 44 percent of gross domestic investment.

Non-Project Aid   Donors have tried to influence the macro-picture through their overall aid programs, particularly through non-project aid, most of which has provided general budgetary support intended to foster specific reforms. This is a difficult type of intervention to evaluate since the donor's funds blend into general foreign exchange holdings and government budgets so the additional development uses cannot be traced. Even so, it is surprising that so little is known about the effectiveness of non-project aid, given the current emphasis on facilitating policy reforms through this mechanism.

Bilateral donors have not kept a very good evaluation record on their non-project assistance, as the Development Assistance Committee's evaluation group discovered. An exception is the USAID study of program aid to Zimbabwe in 1981, which found very efficient and effective use of post-independence funds provided by the United States to help meet a backlog of import needs.[18]

The World Bank's record of assessing its non-project lending is a good deal better, but much of it concentrates on South Asia.[19] The Bank's analysis claims that countries receiving major non-project Bank aid performed substantially better than non-recipients (e.g., a GDP growth rate of 4.5 percent in 1981–83 versus 2 percent for all other oil-importing developing countries, and a greater reduction in current account deficits than other countries).

Two recent studies shed additional light on non-project assistance. Innovative work by Joan Nelson[20] highlights the importance of taking national political and administrative features into account when crafting strategies of structural reform. Donors have not been sensitive enough to these factors.

In a review of the World Bank's structural adjustment program, former Bank official Stanley Please maintains that the Bank enjoys a comparative advantage over other donors in helping develop and negotiate policy reforms in such regions as sub-Saharan Africa.[21] He argues that Bank project lending often calls for the same kind of analysis given to non-project assistance, but that projects are an awkward way of achieving policy reforms and may indeed undercut simultaneously given non-project assistance. Please believes that the World Bank ought to concentrate far more on non-project assistance to achieve policy reforms. Other donors, he feels, are able to carry the bulk of project assistance needs.

The evidence from project lending bears this out to the extent that project outcomes are influenced by the sectoral and policy setting. Donors have frequently found that projects could not be effectively carried out while the sectoral setting was unfavorable or needed adjustment.

While there is a clear need for non-project aid in a large number of African settings due to urgent requirements for inputs and to help foster basic policy reforms, it is important to realize that the evidence of final impact of such lending is almost non-existent. It is simply an informed article of faith that the poor will be better off if non-project assistance is given rather than project aid. Such articles of faith are not permitted in project lending.

The question is whether the sole quid pro quo for aid ought to be policy adjustment or whether aid ought to accomplish more or other things. The case for more reliance on non-project assistance is considerably enhanced if there is proof that a government is able to administer programs well, delivers goods and services to those who need them, and even has the capacity to expand its administrative reach by undertaking new activities. This is a case which has long been made in India, but can be made only rarely in Africa. Indeed, it is project aid which can best build the administrative capabilities needed to be able to use non-project aid.

It is equally clear, however, that the project system upon which most donors will rely in Africa is not without its distortions of the macro-economic scene. Unlike non-project assistance, project assistance negotiated through the national government (the aid mode official donors and NGOs use) has drawbacks, as was pointed out in an EEC study of the results of four of its Africa programs. Project aid was bound to "fragment the development process, create development enclaves isolated from the economic, social, and administrative context, make it more difficult to carry out development experiments, particularly in rural areas, and make implementation of the national plans more hazardous."[22]

Thus, both non-project and project assistance have defects and advantages. Historically, there has been a pendulum swing between the two kinds of aid. We are now in a period where the swing is toward non-project aid. What kind of aid best suits Africa must be answered through country-specific analysis, but there are some relevant observations:

- Non-project aid may well be necessary for the short run due to the need for import finance and policy reform which should be instituted soon. In a well-ordered world, such assistance would be abundantly available under longer-term financing from the IMF. The argument by Please that the Bank has the ability to best argue through policy reform may be correct, but that ability ought to be more apparent in the IMF.

- The need for technical aid can in no way be met by non-project aid.

- The requirement for longer-term capital assistance can be supplied through non-project aid, but this takes very well-established administrative staffs. In Africa, there will still need to be a significant amount of project aid to help form and administer new and particularly larger development investments.

The bulk of aid to Africa now ought to be non-project, but ought to return soon to project assistance. There is no question that the relationship between the two kinds of aid must be more complementary. Good non-project aid ought to enable projects (however financed) to function well, and good larger projects ought to be crafted to reinforce the policy changes more centrally sought by non-project aid. Better coordination between donors and better collaboration with African states will improve the art of using these aid mechanisms.

Project Aid   For many years, it was thought unnecessary to compile evidence on the effectiveness of projects aided by donors. After all, ports, highways, universities, elementary schools, airports, health clinics, industrial plants are all in clear evidence, built, being used, and often accompanied by signs attributing the financing to specific donors. But some of the buildings are empty. And some of the trained staff are no longer around. And some projects didn't turn out the way they were intended and may unintentionally harm the well-being of people.

Most major donors conduct case study evaluations after the donor involvement in the project has ended. Critics have questioned the objectivity of evaluations prepared by the donors themselves, but in reality, the reports are often very hard-hitting and include discussions of "failures" which biased organizations would never circulate.

ECONOMIC RESULTS

The results of a large number of evaluations indicate that aid has generally been put to productive purposes, but that aid to Africa has yielded a lower economic return than in most other areas.

The World Bank has assessed a large number of projects in its Post-Project Audit Reports. These project evaluations pay particular attention to estimating the economic rate of return[23] of projects a year or so after the Bank has finished disbursing funds for the activity. IDA credits are particularly relevant to Africa.[24]

On the basis of discussions with other donors, it is fair to conclude that projects in Africa do not perform as well as projects in more robust economies. Aided projects generally do succeed in Africa—although not by as large a margin as in other parts of the world—but this relative success is not well appreciated.

The World Bank's reports are large enough in number to permit a useful analysis of economic results by sector of activity. The ex post economic rates of return for Bank projects started and completed in the 1961–81 period are shown in Table 18.2.[25]

There is not a sufficient volume of evaluation data from other donors to meaningfully aggregate African results by sector. But it is worth noting what is available. Canada has compiled the results of 62 project evaluations, 33 of which are from Africa. The summary results are shown in Table 18.3.[26]

The study of USAID data, using a 1-10 rating system (1 worst, 10 best), showed the sectoral results in Table 18.4.[27] From this data, one begins to gain a small idea of donor diversity and differences in sectoral performance. Perhaps surprisingly, agriculture in West Africa and transport in general come out well. Education projects are the best sector in AID's analysis, but are a source of problems to Canada (and are not assessed by the Bank in this analysis). The 92 IDA/IBRD West Africa projects score far higher than Latin America in three of four sectors, but East Africa projects score low in a number of sectors. USAID and World Bank data indicate that neither institution has had much success with potable water projects, perhaps because tracing their economic benefits is a complex business.

Other studies and an examination of individual reports illuminate the sectoral results more clearly.

Irrigation   A large number of the Bank's agricultural projects are in irrigation. Bank and USAID experiences are about the same: These projects are expensive, difficult to carry out, frequently have management problems, and yield less satisfactory results than other sectors.

Rural Development   World Bank results in Africa up to the late 1970s were mixed, averaging a 15 percent return, but have since deteriorated significantly, particularly in East Africa where fully half of Bank agricultural projects evaluated in 1974–85 were judged to be failures.[28] Integrated rural development projects have faced very tough problems everywhere, but they have not been replaced by a more logical theory of rural development.

Livestock   Almost all donors report major problems with livestock projects, particularly those aimed at improving the economic lot of nomadic herders in Africa, an area of work where social knowledge is particularly important and often lacking among donors. African livestock projects could be improved, however, by treating them as experiments—drawing them up and staffing them carefully and monitoring them closely.

TABLE 18.2

IDA/IBRD LOANS AND CREDITS: ECONOMIC RATES OF RETURN, 1961–81

(Average by Project Estimated at Audit)

Sector	East Africa	West Africa	Europe/ Middle E./ No. Africa	Latin America/ Carib.	East Asia/ Pacific	South Asia	Total	No. of Credits
Trans.	14.5	20.1	18.6	22.6	21.9	22.2	20.0	185
Agric.	9.7	15.4	18.0	12.7	21.7	27.7	16.8	221
Power	14.0	12.7	15.8	11.7	13.2	30.0	13.5	62
Indust.	3.0	—	16.3	13.6	25.0	14.3	14.6	21
Telecom.	14.0	—	26.0	18.0	19.1	19.9	19.9	28
Water	9.1	9.9	10.0	6.7	5.0	—	8.4	21
Total	11.7	17.4	17.6	15.8	20.1	23.7	17.3	538
No. of Credits	78	92	85	138	92	53	538	

SOURCE: World Bank data prepared by Clarence Gulick, Task Force on Concessional Flows, work in progress.

Agricultural Research and Extension   USAID's study of agricultural research programs showed relatively good results, as did a far more comprehensive Bank report of 128 projects in 10 countries, four of them in Africa.[29] Both studies indicate the need to carefully identify research priorities and to better link them with national agricultural planning and implementation. The USAID report stressed the value of a multi-disciplinary approach in planning such interventions (farming systems research).

Education   USAID studies corroborate World Bank and other findings that educational activities are often quite productive and satisfactory donor projects in Africa. The 1980 *World Development Report* concluded that investments in education were one of the highest pay-off options in the field of development.

TABLE 18.3
CANADIAN AID (CIDA) PROJECT EVALUATIONS: IMPACT ON TARGET GROUPS

| Sector | Projects | *Percentage of Total (234) Findings* | | |
		Positive	Mixed	Negative
Agric. & Rural Development	15	64	4	32
Water Supply	3	74	10	16
Forestry	3	89	—	11
Education	16	52	9	39
Health	3	62	13	25
Cooperatives	1	25	25	50
Energy	2	67	—	33
Transportation	4	62	3	35
Mining	2	33	33	33
Environment	2	88	—	12
Others	11	53	23	25
Total	62[a]	62	9	29

[a] 33 Africa; 18 Latin America; 11 Asia

Health and Population   Health and population interventions could benefit from greater systematic assessment. A frequent stumbling block for village health programs has been the inability to cover recurrent costs. Charging user fees for health and other social services may be one way out of the dilemma. Potable water is one of the very few areas in which comparative evaluative work has been done on all donors in one field. In a survey in Tanzania,[30] it was found that the Netherlands ran especially good programs, the Australians ran very costly and inappropriate programs, and nine other donors fell in between. The survey highlighted the great costs to a poor country of carrying multiple supply and maintenance systems instituted by donors using separate approaches and procurement channels. An out-

TABLE 18.4
OVERALL RATING OF U.S. AID PROJECTS BY REGION
AND SECTOR

Region/Sector	Rating[a]
Africa	6.45
Near East/North Africa	6.21
Asia	7.50
Latin America/Caribbean	7.88
Total	7.28
Agr. Research	7.37
Irrigation	6.55
Rural Elec.	7.82
Rural Roads	7.14
Education	7.99
Potable Water	6.60
Other	7.21
Total	7.28

[a]Scale: 1 (worst) to 10 (best)

come of this survey was the adoption of a national policy in Tanzania favoring low technology (hand-dug village wells) which can be maintained with locally available materials and skills.

Infrastructure   The record is mixed to good. Donors are generally skilled in planning the technical aspects of infrastructural projects. Donor-supplied contractors and/or supervisory services have assured the completion of many "concrete" projects throughout Africa. Numerous studies have emphasized the need to better maintain such projects, but the record of deterioration of Africa's infrastructure is more complex than what is apparent at first glance. It is easy to see if roads are used. But infrastructure projects have also brought a set of social and economic issues such as shifts in land holdings as greedy urbanites benefit from their knowledge of planned new roads by buying up rural land and displacing the planned beneficiaries (Liberia, 1981); or falling standards of living as useless trinkets from the urban economy reach rural residents while new ways of earning money to pay for these luxuries do not (Ethiopia, 1972). Infrastructure is often necessary, but inadequate by itself to improve standards of living. The political role infrastructure projects can play in linking parts of new nations together has not been well analyzed in donor evaluations, but ways of increasing the social and economic value of such projects are identified in these studies.

Food Aid   Assessments of food aid point to the particular importance of child feeding, emergency, and food-for-work programs in areas where food stocks are low to nonexistent or where the poor lack the purchasing power to obtain food. There has been difficulty, however, in effectively targeting the benefits from long-term projects aimed at improving the nutritional well-being of selected groups. Many improvements are needed in this area.[31] Chronic food shortages in Africa in recent years have made food aid a permanent feature of assistance to the continent.[32] Food aid has negative side effects on recipients, however, causing a shift in urban consumer tastes from indigenous to imported foods and, in turn, a foreign exchange drain in the future. Negative effects of bulk food aid are noted but are considered avoidable and not pervasive.[33]

This rapid survey has not covered evaluations published by the United Nations, which tend to be consistent with the findings of the bilateral and other multilateral donors. A word should be added about the evaluation evidence from non-governmental organizations (NGOs), particularly in view of the large number of American NGOs in Africa and the significant amount of funding handled by them. At best, NGOs display commendable economy of action, flexibility of implementation, and effective results with small, community-oriented projects. But these organizations can also be careless, easily over-extended, not well-coordinated with other activities, and economically inefficient. As with official donors, organizations have different strengths and the same organization can perform well in one area and very poorly in another.

SOCIAL RESULTS

While the previous section highlighted a part of the growing literature on the economic impact of assistance to developing countries, the equally important social results of foreign aid must also be considered.

Africa's economic woes are well-known, but its social situation is less well appreciated. A useful yardstick is the Physical Quality of Life Index (PQLI), an aggregate of infant mortality, life expectancy at age one, and literacy. It is clear that Africa has the greatest difficulty in meeting basic social needs of life, literacy, and health. The area with the highest PQLI is North America with 96, whereas Africa's PQLI is 43. A measure of closing the gap in the index, the Disparity Reduction Rate (the rate at which the disparity between a country's level of performance in the social indicators and the best performance expected anywhere in the year 2000 is being eliminated) shows a fair amount of progress over the period 1960–82: 1.6 percent per year for low-income Africa (versus 0.9 percent for low income Asia) and 1.4 percent per year for middle-income Africa (low in comparison with Asia and Latin America).

Despite this progress and the fact that many donor programs aimed at improving the quality of life have been implemented throughout Africa, a major deterioration in social gains has taken place recently given the severity of Africa's crises. Gains over the rest of this century in the Sahelian belt in particular will be very difficult.

Among the major donors, social concerns became more prominent in the early 1970s. Notable were the World Bank's policy changes announced by Robert McNamara in Nairobi in 1973 and the New Directions legislation for USAID in 1973, along with AID's subsequent requirement that each of its project feasibility studies include a social soundness analysis to assure that benefits go to intended recipients. During this time, major donors also became more concerned with bettering the condition of women, and very recently with setting goals for improvements in child well-being.

Donors have had difficulty in translating their concerns about equity into well-crafted programs, perhaps not realizing quickly enough that even in low-income countries, there is ample opportunity to divert intended benefits from the poor. Recent World Bank evidence indicates that where the poor have been especially targeted as beneficiaries of rural development projects, the overall economic results have been competitive with non-targeted projects, although the former required greater amounts of staff time for design and monitoring. As noted, education projects have had particularly important equity effects, particularly those which bring education to new areas and open up opportunities for girls and women.

But all is not positive in this area of concern. In fact, the EEC found that all of their agriculture projects produced gains in producers' incomes, but that most of these went to the male landholders. "Projects rarely aim at improving the welfare of the young or of women, and still more rarely achieve it."[34] And it can almost be categorically stated that donors find that the very poorest groups in countries are difficult to reach.

This is not to say that the means of enhancing the social effectiveness of projects are unknown. Greater participation by the poor in the design and implementation of projects has been shown to increase the effectiveness of aided projects[35], but the added costs entailed have discouraged donors from more widespread replication of these experiments.

Donors and African states have better technical than social knowledge. Since the on-board strength of social scientists in donor and recipient governmental organizations is low to non-existent, a turnaround in the mediocre social results of aided activities is not apt to come soon.

POLITICAL IMPACT

For the few donors, particularly the United States, which invest significant aid funds largely to yield political benefits, little evidence exists as to whether intended political payoffs actually materialize.

On the basis of scanty evidence, the following is put forth:

- Measureable political goals are seldom formulated and never articulated as part of a donor's development plans.
- Development initiatives funded with political monies are seldom specifically designed to achieve articulated political ends.
- Political aims are often shorter term, while development aid is a long-term proposition (projects take six to 10 years to show real impact, non-project aid two years); hence there is a risk of mismatching the demand and the supply.
- The greater the political urgency, the less rigorous the design of the development intervention, and the greater the chance that it will not succeed in its development objectives.

The net result is that development assistance aimed at political ends runs a high risk of failing to achieve both specific political desires and development goals.

EFFECTS ON INSTITUTIONS AND MANAGEMENT

There can hardly be any objection to Africans managing their own economies in more effective ways. Donors have had this high on their agendas both in recognition of the importance of managerial capacity in the development process and for the simple selfish reason that life is easier for the donor when a country has the ability to implement development projects.

The challenges in this field have been great. Evaluations of donor projects in Africa are replete with complaints about administrative problems. The few countries where donors find life easier in Africa seem to be ones that have given up some of their autonomy to troops of foreign advisers (e.g., Malawi, Botswana, Ivory Coast) who are often quite skillful in organizing information for donors.

It is almost impossible to gauge accurately whether institutional and managerial performance has improved in Africa, but a case can be made that it has. Independence brought new institutional needs and an exodus of important talent—two challenges which the new governments were poorly prepared to meet. Donors responded by providing tens of thousands of technicians and great volumes of technical assistance and institution-building projects. The impres sion is that the volume of such assistance has somewhat declined recently (although it is still notably high in francophone Africa). This assistance seems also to have changed in character as Africans have gained more experience in institutional management. The days when any and all technical advice was accepted are long over. African officials may need advice, but the needs are far more sharply and professionally defined and technical recommendations are more critically screened now than in the past. One very important factor is that the current crises have led to a new tone of realism about the policy environment in Africa. More African officials are discussing and acting on the kinds of administrative and policy reforms long advocated by many development observers and participants.

Donors have always been involved with institutional reform and growth in Africa, but in recent years, even greater attention has been given to this need, particularly by the World Bank and USAID. To what extent this new emphasis has incorporated lessons from past programs is not known.

The scoreboard from past programs has not been encouraging. Two major reviews of institution-building projects in Africa have been produced in recent years. USAID reviewed a sample of 183 of its Africa projects (active from 1974 to 1982) which had institution-building components.[36] While in about 50 percent of the projects, the positive findings outweighed the negative, fully 42 percent of the projects had negative results outweighing positive results (versus an average of 33 percent world-wide).

Results from a more thorough World Bank survey of 118 institutional development projects in Africa are even less positive.[37] Most of the projects had serious implementation problems; over half were considered to have had little or no impact; and only one in 10 was considered to have been very effective.

In a study of 62 projects, including 33 African projects, Canada's CIDA found that while 60 percent had improved managerial capabilities, fully two-thirds had not enabled the institution being helped to become significantly more self-reliant.[38] Indeed, evaluators of EEC aid stressed that it had to focus far more on creating the "capacity for self-development."[39] In view of this poor record, it is perhaps commendable that donors have maintained their technical assistance and institution-building programs, as the need has not evaporated. But there is little evidence that donors have changed the way they provide technical assistance. Repeated criticisms that experts float in and out, thereby precluding the possibility of sustained dialogues, that provision of expertise is very costly, and that foreign technicians are culturally insensitive, have not been acted upon. Nor has there been much creativity in providing management options for situations where a policy dialogue is useful but doesn't require full-time technical assistance.

Donors must also recognize that the donor mode of operation has negative institutional development effects. Donors have frequently end-run African institutions by creating special enclaves for their projects. What makes good sense in each individual project case creates cumulative chaos and undermines good public administration.[40] Thus donors are both part of the problem and given Africa's shortage of skills and resources, a necessary part of the solution to institutional and managerial reform.

Most basically, the need to help improve Africa's institutions and management demands a better calculus by donors as to whether foreign help or training of Africans will be most effective. There is little disagreement that training of Africans will be most effective and a far cheaper and more enduring solution to solving institutional problems in Africa. Why this solution is not turned to more often calls for a complex explanation involving such factors as real and perceived needs for quick fixes, the unavailability of candidates for training, and in some cases a subtle need to have troops of foreign technicians in order to justify high standards of living for African managers. Of course, there are urgent short- and medium-term institutional and management needs where foreign help will be very useful, but these must not preclude donors and Africans from placing greater emphasis on more enduring solutions. These solutions will undoubtedly involve heavy reliance on project aid, but also require better management of such aid by both sides.

REPLICATION AND SPREAD EFFECTS

Most often donor staff commence a program, policy, or project initiative with the idea that it will lead to a widespread ripple effect in the national application of a policy, replication by the government or private sector, or diffusion of the benefits. Unfortunately, evidence of project replication and spread in Africa is very scanty.

A vigorous private sector and a well-funded government are important catalysts in expediting the spread of social and economic innovations, but both institutions are weak in Africa. This explains in part the paucity of evidence on replication/spread in Africa today, but the complexity of gathering the evidence itself must also be recognized. Difficulties include the long time periods involved and problems associated with sorting out the many influences acting on project diffusion.

There is some hopeful evidence that even in Africa's difficult setting, diffusion of innovations can take place. Numerous simple technological innovations in agriculture, health, and education have spread well on a local or regional scale in Africa. Further, the literature on diffusion and spread indicates that projects and programs can be better designed to encourage ripple effects. Both experiences with small-scale diffusion in Africa and this literature have important implications in helping to design future assistance programs in Africa.

IMPLICATIONS: CAN PROJECTS IN AFRICA
COMPETE?

In this rapid review of aid effectiveness in Africa, it has been clear that aided activities in Africa perform less well than elsewhere. Economic rates of return are lower, failure rates are higher, management problems are greater, and the social context is less well understood and hence not handled well. The averages mask the losers which haunt aid officials—the white elephants, the "showpiece investments. . .made possible largely by generous financial support from the donor community,"[41] and the earnestly invested careers which have left little behind.

Contrast this with aid to South and East Asia—great results to impress parliaments, an easy lifestyle in the field, careers which are bound to look good. Why should donors bother with Africa? The wonder is that most still do and are increasing their concern and programs. But some are not, particularly those emphasizing the private sector and those normally drawn to larger infrastructural investments, areas where prospects in Africa are often regarded as poor.

If the shift by some donors away from Africa was the result of a rational thought process, this might be better understood. But where this has occurred, it is more because African projects do not compete as well as other options and hence a major strategic question is being decided in the absence of real policy discussion.

For those donors wishing to continue major activities in Africa, there is a tendency to mask the real problems by adding an extra dose of fiction to decisions that lead to commitments of new development investments, but also to quite unrealistic expectations and plans.

For both donors switching out of Africa with little hard thought and for those staying but with unrealistic expectations, the relevant question may well be: Should donors adjust their standards in order to respond to Africa's development needs with more candor? The embodiment of these standards is the economic rate of return. Is too much reliance being placed on this calculation in deciding whether and how to assist Africa?

These concerns are perhaps best illustrated by the case of the Manantale dam in the Senegal river basin, a major scheme to assist Senegal, Mauritania, and Mali by regulating the flow of the Senegal River and creating major opportunities to foster irrigated agriculture. After lengthy and expensive feasibility and environmental studies, AID and the World Bank decided that the project could not be supported. Although the need—regulating the supply of water in one of the most difficult and drought-prone areas in Africa—was great, the fatal fact was that the economic rate of return forecast for the $1 billion investment was zero. Yet Germany and several Middle East donors put up the money because they saw no other more feasible option for the area.[42]

The Manantale dam is a dramatic example of what donors face in Africa. The economic rates of return on past donor investments have been satisfactory, but future development investments look poor given clouded economic prospects in a number of countries. Donors are now faced with the choice between sticking with relatively stringent standards and shifting away from Africa, or staying in Africa but sitting out on tasks which someday must be undertaken, such as development of Africa's relatively few large-scale water resources. If donors are to effectively respond to Africa's long-term development crises, a fresh approach to project selection criteria is imperative. Donors must recognize that standard measures of feasibility such as rates of return are not accurate indicators of a project's importance to the development of a resource-starved area. The need for simultaneous development to raise the general level of economic performance means that if any given project is weighted by itself, it may not seem worthwhile. It may take a nexus of what now seem like marginal investments in order to create a renewed momentum to development in Africa.

RECOMMENDATIONS

How can Africa take advantage of more donor programs while avoiding the burden of a more chaotic development pattern? And what can donors do to be of better assistance to Africa? In this section, recommendations are addressed to donors and to African governments.

LEVELS OF AID

In both the short and longer term, aid will play a key role in Africa's development. External finance is critical to Africa's survival and growth, but most sources apart from aid are drying up. Trade prospects are uncertain, private investment has decreased, new net capital resources are unlikely, and domestic resources are shrinking and unlikely to recover soon. Short-term needs include food requirements not available on the continent, spare parts to restore existing production, and help to restore basic services.

At the same time, larger longer-term development investments are needed to lay a better base for agricultural production and many other fundamental building blocks of development. Again, no other resources, particularly from the foreign sectors, are in sight to provide major new funds for these purposes.

In the short run, Africans are faced with finding new aid resources and seeking debt forgiveness for past aid. It also may be possible for some donors to institute legislative changes permitting repayments of past aid loans to be cycled back to Africa.[43]

In the longer run, however, new donor funds might well come from switching of traditional aid allocations from other regions to Africa. The switching should come about naturally as currently aided countries in Latin America and other better off areas evolve into stronger trading and financial partners.

Some respected analysts of African development argue that Africa receives too much aid and is having difficulty absorbing the flow of resources it now receives. There are abundant problems which reinforce this viewpoint: Aid is poorly coordinated; African states are hard put to find counterpart funds and staff; and new long-term programs cannot easily take root in the midst of all the crises Africa is facing.

Attacking the constraints affecting the absorption of aid is needed and holds more hope for Africa's development. This view has shaped a number of the following recommendations. Simply put, it is very hard to see how Africa would be better off with less aid. The best solution would be more aid and much better quality in the handling of that aid by donors and African governments.

African states themselves can help to expand resources from donors. Better management of resources will attract more aid. In addition, African governments need to become more cognizant of donor interests and more proficient at marketing their own programs. Nevertheless, increasing aid levels obviously will be difficult. It will take concerted leadership by Africans, international organizations, and politicians in the donor community.

IMPLEMENTING FOR SURVIVAL AND FOR QUALITY

The prolonged development crisis in Africa dramatically highlights the most basic reason for aid to Africa—survival. This must be the first priority for donors and African states. There are three critical ingredients: balance of payments support to finance imports of critical goods necessary to keep economies afloat; assistance to maintain and restore the public infrastructure; and food aid.

Africa's current economic crisis requires an adjustment of the content and financial formulas of donor aid programs. The main requirement in Africa now is to keep the economies running instead of starting new projects. Spare parts and maintenance of infrastructure, industry, and services will be far more important in the next few years than financing new efforts.[44] Finance for foreign exchange and local currency recurrent costs is critically needed in many countries.

Because food aid is a special kind of assistance, a few added recommendations are in order. To plan effective short-term strategies, Africans require more assurance that food aid will be supplied by the donors in adequate volume and with sufficient logistical support to meet emergency needs. The food surplus countries have a special obligation, and the United States is in far better shape than other major supplier countries such as Canada, Australia, and Argentina. Non-governmental organizations have repeatedly pointed to the need not only for increased food supplies, but for financial support to provide in-country logistical support for food deliveries. Another improvement takes more political courage. Donors could help to reinforce local African markets by supplying food aid from local supplies when there is a surplus.

The crucial strategy decision for African governments and donors is how to carry out the survival tasks and still lay a basis for longer-term growth. Just as it would be wrong to continue putting the great bulk of resources in long-term development investments, it would be wrong to finance only short-term needs.

This chapter reviewed data showing that many kinds of aided activities perform satisfactorily. But it has argued that donor investment standards might have to be adjusted in order to permit some kinds of basic, needed initiatives to be carried out in Africa. Development in Africa must proceed on the assumption that the name of the game remains to implement for quality—reinforcing what works and weeding out or altering what doesn't.

The underlying recommendation is that African governments be assisted in gaining the capacity to fully manage their own development. It is worth reflecting on this goal in the context of improving the quality of development programs. Governments which implement for quality need the ability to judge how development is going in their country. An unbiased flow of information must be generated inside the government and must reach top political levels quickly. Some governments have impressive capabilities in these matters which ought to be studied. For example, the government of Sri Lanka's Ministry of Plan Implementation has been extremely resourceful in identifying bottlenecks holding up development projects across the country. Because the head of state holds the ministry's portfolio, there is an appropriate audience for key recommendations to enhance the quality of development.

African governments and donors can take a number of actions to improve public administration by helping create local monitoring and evaluation units (as is being done in a very few African countries now) to assess development performance and search for economical ways to reach desirable goals.

COORDINATION

Foreign aid will not be seen as an unqualified asset as long as there are mismatches between demand and supply and as long as the costs of dealing with donors continue to be so large. There is considerable agreement that foreign assistance requires better coordination to improve the quality of aid to Africa. The question is how best to do this. The problems seem to be field-centered and the solutions tried now generally are not.[45]

The largest donors will resist being coordinated and will need to be involved in sectoral strategy consultations with African states. This is appropriate since these donors can help underwrite entire sectoral strategies. African states and the World Bank have a special role in actively promoting this kind of consultation in the field. For the larger number of project-oriented, medium- and smaller-sized donors, field-centered options are needed which expedite coordination and are under the lead of African ministries, yet save time for officials on all sides. These ideas are suggested:

- Special coordination units could be formed on a sector-by-sector basis within each country. While there has already been some use of sector coordination committees, the concept could be expanded to make an entity the sole bargaining unit between all donors and a ministry. The unit would identify demands for donor involvement, help "recruit" donors, assign donors by geographic area, and negotiate master agreements with the ministry. The coordinating unit would then arrange a series of agreements with donors and would be the conduit to raise implementation issues/complaints/suggestions with the ministry for the set of donors involved. The unit might also be the holder of counterpart funds. This kind of unit could permit donors to staff projects for field duty instead of having to assign staff for capital city negotiations. The costs and staffing of such units would have to be carefully considered in order to be acceptable to all sides.

- Rather than sector-by-sector units, smaller countries might find it convenient to create one unit intended to be the intermediary for all but the largest donors. Such an entity might have sole responsibility for negotiating with donors which finance any project or program. An example is the Institute for Solidarity in Cape Verde which has been highly successful in attracting funds to the island republic.

- The soundest way, in theory, to consolidate initiatives by Africans and donors would be for almost all initiatives to be carried out under line ministry auspices. An alternative would be for the donors to pool funds for specific endeavors to be carried out under the leadership of one of them.

It will take political courage from all sides to effect better systems of coordination. Donors will need to suppress some of the ego value of

aid and African states will have to suppress their fears of being locked
into an unequal partnership.

CHOICES OF DONORS BASED ON MERIT

African states ought to be in a position to match development
financing needs to the abilities of donors in a specific area. African
officials should have access to the significant amount of information
available regarding which donors do what best. More candid exchanges of information can lead to useful mutual pressure to improve
performance and to allocate resources where donors can make the
most valuable contributions.

Bilateral donors also have a range of choices along the continuum
of channeling their aid through bilateral mechanisms or multilateral
institutions. Many of the bilaterals ought to be more supportive of the
multilateral agencies. A number of the bilaterals are not very competent donors and ought to recognize that their aid will continue to be of
inferior quality unless they make major improvements soon. Even
the largest bilaterals must concede certain advantages to the World
Bank, with its unique abilities and power, and to the International
Fund for Agricultural Development, UNICEF, and the UN Fund for
Population Activities, all of which are effective and germane to Africa. Bilaterals have been negligent in helping these institutions secure the funds to assist Africa now and into the future.

While the World Bank has its faults, the bilaterals can more quickly
effect instititutional changes there, given their powerful roles as Bank
executive directors, than they can change their own aid institutions.
A thorough review of evaluation information ought to help bilaterals
better decide where comparative advantages lie.

LEARNING MODEL APPROACH FOR DESIGN AND
IMPLEMENTATION

For some time, leading authorities have espoused the virtues of the
learning model approach for development. This approach emphasizes model and pilot projects as well as evolving designs of projects
during implementation. Evaluation evidence reinforces both the
need for this kind of approach and the value of making well thought-
out changes during the life of projects and programs.

A key implication of the learning model approach is the need for
more flexibility by governments and donors to permit mid-stream

project changes; in fact, such course corrections should be encouraged. Encouraging easy ways to make justified mid-stream changes is important and generally can be accommodated in bureaucracies. However, it is particularly difficult to alter a project at the very end of an agreement when the project reverts to a country's sole technical and financial care. During implementation, donors must focus more on whether a recipient country will be prepared to take over assisted endeavors when the donor funds expire and/or when foreign technicians leave. If it will take some additional input of funds or staff to assure a smooth transition to African management, the donor must be prepared to decide well in advance of termination dates so that all involved can plan accordingly.

In the private sector, financing changes during implementation is less of a problem. Corporations have contingency funds. Given the high frequency of cost and time overruns in Africa, it is a pity that donors have so far been unable to devise a similar mechanism of prudent management. In the absence of a quick-disbursing contingency fund, there is a premium on timing evaluation and monitoring teams at useful points and well enough in advance of key dates in order to be able to act prior to the dreaded cutoff date.

LEARNING MODEL IN POLICY AND PROGRAM DESIGN

Reference was earlier made to the large number of evaluation findings which are now being brought together more systematically by the major donors. Typically, these reports identify a large number of weaknesses in project designs which are translated into special sector reports and guidelines as to how to improve projects. While this may be necessary, it is far from a sufficient response.

Donors should take the evaluation evidence far more seriously. The most inexcusable donor action is to keep repeating mistakes. Some donors have instituted regular reviews of the findings of their own evaluations. It would be even more useful for donor executives to regularly review evaluation evidence generated from the wider donor community.

Meeting with African officials to review the validity and implications of major evaluation findings is also important. This would allow for a more "hands-on" approach to professionalizing staff and would emphasize that both sides must learn the lessons of experience.

In both African and donor establishments, development policy ought to evolve based on actual experience. Donors have an obligation to factor in African officials' participation when policy decisions are being considered. One looks to the day when donor coordination meetings will be run by African governments and will center on hard evidence from their own development experience along with analysis of its implications on development policy and donor assistance.

STAFFING FOR DEVELOPMENT

Staff composition in the donor organizations and within African governments must be looked at carefully. As there is a repeated finding that projects operate without accurate social and institutional knowledge, then it seems logical for African governments and donors to put more emphasis on hiring social scientists, institutional change experts, sector policy analysts, and implementation planning experts.

TERMS AND CONDITIONS OF ASSISTANCE

As donors contemplate future assistance to Africa, they will need to consider the terms of their assistance more carefully. Reviews of the effectiveness of past aid programs to Africa have already provided keys to needed improvements.

- Investment for the long haul is needed, particularly if spread effects, replication, and other diffusion are anticipated. A large proportion of assistance to Africa involves technical, managerial, and institutional development goals that require longer-term approaches. There must be recognition that in many kinds of programs, particularly agricultural development, a great deal of experimentation is needed. Carefully paced pilot, research, and model programs require time to be carried out and the assurance that, if they succeed, there will be a responsive follow-up.

- Any responsible review of Africa's financial situation will lead to the conclusion that only soft financial terms are appropriate. The only question is whether more donors can shift funds to a grant basis. Many already have.

- Both World Bank and USAID policy now recognize the need for more recurrent cost financing for developing countries.[46] The issue

is particularly germane since many analysts recommend that donors back existing activities rather than start new ones in Africa, in
recognition of the imperative of keeping the existing economies
going, of building from whatever strength exists, and of reinforcing existing institutions in preference to creating new ones. The
financial implication for donors is that such projects call for far
greater emphasis on recurrent and local cost financing. This type of
financing is never popular with donor treasuries and central
banks. Therefore, the decision to undertake more financing of existing activities is at root a political one.

• The "Berg Report" correctly recommends that donors harmonize
  their aid procedures.[47] Who could disagree, but who could be optimistic after the OECD Development Assistance Committee has
  tried unsuccessfully to do so for at least 20 years? From time to
  time, one or another of the major donors has unbashfully volunteered its own procedures as the standard to which others should
  conform, but there have been few if any takers. A solution, of
  course, is for donors to pay far greater attention to host country
  procedures and to harmonize around them to the greatest extent
  possible. In some cases, this is done, but in most cases donors
  seem completely unaware that the aid recipient has its own system
  of design or monitoring projects.

If a country lacks an adequate system for development management, then it is imperative that donors work to help recipient governments achieve this capacity. In the interim, donors can involve national officials far more in the routine tasks of project management,
(e.g., by including local officials in the reviews and evaluations of
donor-financed projects and by sending them copies of key donor
reports on that country's projects).[48]

LESSONS FROM THE EEC: LINKING AID AND TRADE

Through the Lome Agreements, the EEC states have entered into
comprehensive aid and trade relationships with a large group of African, Caribbean, and Pacific Basin states. The agreements offer some
examples of innovations in donor behavior well worth considering:

• The agreements are the products of negotiations that emphasized
  equal bargaining power on all sides. The renewable agreements

run for five years each. There is a strong feeling that the EEC has entered into predictable and responsible "contracts" for development with the African-Caribbean-Pacific states involved.

• The Lome Agreements link aid and trade, as does the U.S. Caribbean Basin Initiative. To a limited extent, the agreements also cover investment promotion. While U.S.-African trade ties are not strong, the reinforcing potential of coordinated trade-aid-investment policies can serve as a constructive dynamic in Africa's development and can effectively further longer-term U.S. interests. Aid has an important long-term development role which, if done well, can greatly increase the long-range potential for trade and investment. The long-term benefits of aided development should not be sacrificed to short-term considerations which leave little developmental residual. Aid should not be turned into front money for short-term trade and investment deals. The Lome Agreements, in financing trade promotion and a large number of other aid-trade linked ideas, point the way to a number of initiatives which are of longer-term value and which might be considered by other donors.

THE CONCEPT OF SHARED RISK

Africa is in a terrible plight. Given the bleak economic outlook and the lack of financial alternatives, aid flows are of fundamental importance to the survival of peoples and to prospects for their betterment. While the quantity of aid must be increased to brighten Africa's prognosis, so must its quality. Efforts to improve the quality of aided and unaided development have tremendous importance. The likelihood of huge increases in aid levels is not strong: More must be achieved with existing resources. In any case, a better quality performance will enhance the prospects for aid.

None of the recommendations in this chapter will be easy to bring about, but some seem simpler and will encounter less resistance than others.

The underlying theme of this chapter is that two kinds of risks are going to have to be taken in greater measure. First, African leaders and donors must take steps aimed at a more rational use of aid resources and at placing Africans more at the center of their own development. There must be a greater willingness to enter into coordination, to implement for quality, and to make decisions based more on actual performance.

The second kind of risk is to keep trying to do the difficult. No clear-eyed reading of the evaluation evidence would leave one sanguine about continuing current practices in fields such as livestock and institutional development. But does that mean that the donors should abandon such fields? To agree to this would imply ceasing to care about problems such as the fate of 30 million pastoralists in Africa.

It would be easy to improve the record by dropping the risky projects. The more responsible task is to recognize openly that in a number of areas, there are fairly high risks and that prudent management is imperative. Riskier programs and strategies raise questions about existing donor standards and they certainly entail higher overhead costs in design, supervision, and field management time. These projects and programs predictably will need to be changed and they often will be frustrating. They will probably be on the books longer than most projects and will have to withstand pressure for termination. But if the projects in risky areas are sensitively managed, they may prove far more valuable than standard approaches ploddingly carried out or bright fads that come and go with few lasting results.

It will take unusual political courage to bear the burdens of these kinds of risks. But if donors and African governments can work together more in a sense of partnership and with as much professionalism as possible, the burden of risk can be shared and peer support can be found to help see African leaders and their peoples through very difficult times.

ACKNOWLEDGMENT

I acknowledge with great thanks abundant help from Julie Howard and Marguerite Turner in preparing this chapter.

NOTES

1. In this chapter, "foreign aid" will refer to official flows from bilateral and multilateral sources and grants from private agencies (private aid). "Official flows" are composed of: (1) Official development assistance (ODA), that is, grants or loans; undertaken by the official sector; with promotion of economic development and welfare as main objectives; at concessional financial

terms (if a loan, at least 25 percent grant element); (2) Technical cooperation: grants or loans to nationals of developing countries receiving training abroad and to cover costs of developed country personnel serving abroad; and (3) Other official (non-concessional) flows.

2. Mid-1982 estimates from: United Nations, *Demographic Yearbook 1982*, New York, 1984. Department of International Economic and Social Affairs, Statistical Office. International Bank for Reconstruction and Development, *World Development Report 1984*, New York: Oxford University Press, 1984.

3. According to OECD's Development Cooperation 1984, in 1983, total ODA receipts for less-developed countries were $33.6 billion. For sub-Saharan Africa alone, ODA totalled $8 billion.

4. United Nations Economic Commission for Africa, *Survey of Economic and Social Conditions in Africa, 1982–1983*, Document E/ECA/CM.10/4, 9 March 1984.

5. Weighted by population.

6. World Bank, *Toward Sustained Development: A Joint Program of Action for Sub-Saharan Africa*, Washington, D.C., August 1984. Calculated from Table A.Z.

7. In the period 1975 through March 1984 there were 45 Paris Club debt reschedulings. Thirteen sub-Saharan African Countries accounted for 32 of these reschedulings. (Briefing paper prepared by L.M. Goreux of the IMF, April 30, 1984.)

8. Uma Lele, "Rural Africa: Modernization, Equity, and Long-term Development," *Science* 211 (4482) (February 6, 1982).

9. World Bank, *Accelerated Development in Sub-Saharan Africa*, op.cit., p. 165.

10. The average cost of providing U.S. food aid to Africa has been estimated at $300/ton (including transportation). Personal communication, USAID.

11. See page 9, "U.S. Official Bilateral Assistance to Africa," op.cit.

12. For example, see "Bread for the World Report on the U.S. Responses to the African Famine," released May 3, 1984.

13. There is some confusion in this. For example, recent Africa Bureau leaders in USAID have publicly called for a deemphasis in population programs in Africa while approving budget increases for such programs.

14. World Bank, 1981. The report was written by an African Strategy Review Group coordinated by Elliott Berg. It is often referred to as "The Berg Report."

15. I initiated this series in 1977 and managed it until 1982.

16. I chaired the predecessor of this group fropm 1980 to 1982.

17. Unfortunately, most of this information is not publicly available at this time. One can only encourage donors to release these analyses for public discussion. In any case, I am grateful to have been given access to much of the existing information.

18. Gary Wasserman et al., *U.S. Aid to Zimbabwe: An Evaluation*, AID Program Evaluation Report No. 9, August 1983.

19. "Structural Adjustment Lending-Progress Report," draft, April 1984.

20. "The Politics of Stabilization," in *Adjustment Crisis in the Third World*, Richard E. Feinberg and Valeriana Kallab, eds., Overseas Development Council, Transaction Books, 1984.

21. *The Hobbled Giant: Essays on the World Bank*. Boulder: Westview Press, 1984.

22. Commission of the European Communities, staff paper, "Initial Report of the Results of Overall Evaluation of Community Aid," SEC (81) 189, Brussels, February 1981.

23. The rate of return is the remuneration to investment stated as a proportion or percentage. The financial rate of return is the internal rate of return based on market prices; the economic rate of return is the internal rate of return based on economic values.

24. The International Development Association (IDA) is the World Bank's soft-loan window, providing most of its concessional finance for the poorest developing areas, including Africa.

25. World Bank, calculations prepared by Clarence Gulick, Task Force on Concessional Flows, 1984.

26. CIDA, "Bilan des Evaluations Bilaterales, 1981–83."

27. R. Cohen, op.cit.

28. See World Bank, "Rural Development Projects: A Retrospective View of Bank Experience in Sub-Saharan Africa" (Report 2242), 1978 and World Bank, "Tenth Annual Review of Project Performance Audit Report 1984," published 1985.

29. Josette Murphy, *Strengthening the Agricultural Research Capacity of the Less Developed Countries: Lessons From AID Experience*, U.S. Agency for International Development Program Evaluation Report No. 10, September 1983. World Bank, "Agricultural Research and Extension: An Evaluation of the World Bank's Experience," forthcoming.

30. Daniel Dworkin, *Rural Water Projects in Tanzania: Technical, Social, and Administrative Issues*, AID Evaluation Special Study No. 3, November 1980.

31. David E. Sahn and Robert M. Pestronk, *A Review of Issues in Nutrition Program Evaluation*, USAID Program Evaluation Discussion Paper No. 10, July 1981.

32. World Food Programme, *World Food Programme in Africa*, Rome, June 1984.

33. Edward J. Clay and Hans Singer, *Food Aid and Development: The Impact and Effectiveness of Bilateral PL480 Title I-Type Assistance*, USAID Program Evaluation Discussion Paper No. 15, December 1982.

34. Commission of European Communities, op.cit.

35. Kurt Finsterburch and Warren Van Wicklin III, "The Contribution of Beneficiary Participation to Development Project Effectiveness," a review of 52 USAID evaluations, draft, July 1985.

36. Barnett and Engel, *Effective Institution Building*, AID Program Evaluation Discussion Paper No. 11, March 1982.

37. World Bank, "Institutional Development in Africa" (report no. 5085), May 1984.

38. CIDA, op.cit.

39. Commission on the European Communities, op.cit., p. vii.

40. Robert J. Berg, "The Long-run Future of Donor Planning, Monitoring, and Evaluation," *Development* XXII, (2–3), 1980.

41. Uma Lele, op.cit.

42. Whether recessional agriculture depending on annual floods, dry land, or small irrigation systems would be more feasible is hard to tell particularly due to a poorer understanding of such systems among Western and Western-trained African technicians.

43. Debt forgiveness is an issue for the United States. It is legally permissable for the United States to forgive official debts to least developed countries, but this option has never been exercised perhaps out of fear that a precedent would be set for the huge debt owed by India and a few other major recipients of past USAID loans. But surely the crisis in Africa is of an order not faced by these other past recipients. Debt forgiveness for Africa and reinstituting the ability to use reflows to fund new aid programs would be very useful steps for the United States to take.

44. Reginald Herbold Green and Mark Faber, "Sub-Saharan Africa's Economic Malaise: Some Questions and Answers," *Journal of Development Planning*, forthcoming.

45. "Review of Coordination among Multilateral Agencies in Support of World Food Conference Objectives: Report by the Executive Director," World Food Council/1984/3, January 27, 1984.

46. The Bank and AID encourage recipients to finance recurrent costs out of user charges wherever possible. The point that user charges are often too low (see Jacob Meerman, "Minimizing the Burden of Recurrent Costs," *Finance and Development*, December 1983, pp. 41–43) is well taken, but in these years of crises it may be a poor time to rigorously institute that policy. See also "Recurrent Costs," AID Policy Paper, May 1982.

47. *Accelerated Development in Sub-Saharan Africa*, op. cit., p. 130.

48. A non-African example: Until the late 1970s, there was no donor contact with the highly professional evaluation staff of India's National Planning Commission, a staff which was established in 1952 and controls a professional network of 900 trained evaluators. The Indians were not asked to carry out, participate in, or read an evaluation prepared to meet a donor need. There are numerous parallels in Africa, but no African government has such a well-established evaluation system. Given other perceived priorities, it is unlikely that good monitoring and evaluation systems will be established in Africa in the absence of donor encouragement.

Tabular Appendix

TABLE A.1
LAND USE IN AFRICA
(As Percentage of Total Land Area)

	1967–71	1974	1977	1980
Arable and permanent crops	5.58	5.75	5.92	5.97
Permanent pasture	25.91	25.91	25.87	25.86
Forest and woodland	23.99	23.59	23.27	22.95
Other land	42.31	42.55	42.75	43.02

SOURCE: *FAO Production Yearbook 1981*, v. 35, p. 65.

TABLE A.2
DISTRIBUTION OF MVA IN AFRICA—1975
(Percentage)

Food, Beverages and Tobacco	31
Textiles, Clothing and Leather	21
Wood and Furniture	4
Paper, Printing, Publishing	5
Chemicals, Petroleum, Coal, Rubber and Plastics	16
Non-Metallic Minerals	5
Basic Metals	4
Fabricated Metal Products	13
Other	1

SOURCE: UNIDO (1983).

TABLE A.3

COMPARISON OF ENROLLMENTS AT DIFFERENT EDUCATION LEVELS FOR SUB-SAHARAN AFRICAN COUNTRIES, 1960–81

| | Number enrolled in primary school as percentage of age group | | | | | | Number enrolled in secondary school as % of age group | | Number enrolled in higher education as % of population aged 20–24 | |
| | Total | | Male | | Female | | | | | |
	1960	1981	1960	1981	1960	1981	1960	1981	1960	1981
Angola	21	—	28	—	13	—	2	—	(.)	(.)
Benin	27	65	38	88	15	42	2	18	—	1
Botswana	42	102	35	94	48	110	1	23	—	—
Burkina Faso	8	20	12	26	5	15	1	3	(.)	(.)
Burundi	18	32	27	40	9	25	1	3	—	1
Cameroon	65	107	87	117	43	97	2	19	—	2
Cent. Afr. Rep.	32	68	53	89	12	49	1	13	—	1
Chad	17	35	29	51	4	19	—	3	—	(.)
Congo	78	156	103	163	53	148	4	69	1	6
Ethiopia	7	46	11	60	3	33	—	12	(.)	1
Gabon	100	202	124	207	76	198	5	34	—	—
Gambia, The	12	52	17	67	8	37	3	14	—	—
Ghana	38	69	52	77	25	60	5	36	(.)	1
Guinea	30	33	44	44	16	22	2	16	—	5
Guinea-Bissau	25	101	35	141	15	61	3	20		
Ivory Coast	46	76	68	92	24	60	2	17	(.)	3
Kenya	47	109	64	114	30	101	2	19	(.)	1
Lesotho	83	104	63	84	102	123	3	17	(.)	2
Liberia	31	66	45	82	18	50	2	20	(.)	2

Madagascar	52	*100*	58	*—*	45	*—*	4	*14*	(.)	*3*
Malawi	—	*62*	—	*73*	—	*51*	1	*4*	—	*(.)*
Mali	10	*27*	14	*35*	6	*20*	1	*4*	—	*1*
Mauritania	8	*33*	13	*43*	3	*23*	—	*10*	—	*—*
Mauritius	98	*107*	103	*107*	93	*106*	24	*51*	—	*—*
Mozambique	48	*90*	60	*102*	36	*78*	2	*6*	—	*(.)*
Niger	5	*23*	7	*29*	3	*17*	—	*6*	—	*(.)*
Nigeria	36	*98*	46	*94*	27	*70*	4	*16*	(.)	*3*
Rwanda	49	*72*	68	*75*	30	*69*	2	*2*	—	*(.)*
Senegal	27	*48*	36	*58*	17	*38*	3	*12*	1	*3*
Sierra Leone	23	*39*	30	*45*	15	*30*	2	*12*	(.)	*1*
Somalia	9	*30*	13	*38*	5	*21*	1	*11*	(.)	*1*
Sudan	25	*52*	35	*61*	14	*43*	3	*18*	(.)	*2*
Swaziland	58	*110*	58	*111*	58	*109*	5	*40*	—	*—*
Tanzania	25	*102*	33	*107*	18	*98*	2	*3*	—	*(.)*
Togo	44	*111*	63	*135*	24	*87*	2	*31*	—	*2*
Uganda	49	*54*	65	*62*	32	*46*	3	*5*	(.)	*1*
Zaire	60	*90*	88	*104*	32	*75*	3	*23*	(.)	*1*
Zambia	42	*96*	51	*102*	34	*90*	2	*16*	—	*2*
Zimbabwe	96	*126*	107	*130*	86	*121*	6	*15*	(.)	*(.)*

NOTE: Figures in italics are for years other than those specified.
SOURCE: *Towards Sustained Development in Sub-Saharan Africa* (Washington, D.C.: The World Bank, 1984).

TABLE A.4
SUB-SAHARAN AFRICA: SHARE OF MANUFACTURING IN GDP 1981
(Percentage)

Zaire	2.5	Uganda	4.2
Angola	2.6	Namibia	4.4
Gambia	2.6	Lesotho	4.7
Guinea	3.1	Sao Tome & Principe	4.7
Reunion	3.5	Sierra Leone	4.8
Equatorial Guinea	5.1	Seychelles	6.6
Liberia	5.2	Sudan	7.1
Niger	5.3	Gabon	7.7
Benin	5.4	Chad	7.8
Cape Verde	5.4	Mali	7.8
Comoros	5.4	Mozambique	8.8
Botswana	5.6	Somalia	8.8
Nigeria	6.1	Tanzania	9.0
Togo	6.4	Cameroon	9.8
Madagascar	10.1	Cent. Afr. Repub.	13.5
Burundi	10.9	Burkina Faso	13.8
Ivory Coast	11.0	Ghana	13.9
Rwanda	12.7	Senegal	14.7
Kenya	13.3		
Malawi	15.2	Swaziland	24.3
Mauritius	15.5	Zimbabwe	26.5
Zambia	15.8		

SOURCE: UNIDO data base.

TABLE A.5
AFRICA: GROWTH OF INDEBTEDNESS
(U.S. $ billion)

	1973	1979	1983
Debt outstanding[a]	9.9	36.7	57.8
Disbursements	2.2	8.8	10.6
Net inflows	1.3	6.2	7.4
Principal repayments	0.9	1.6	3.1
Interest	0.3	1.3	2.6
Debt service	1.2	2.8	5.7
Net transfers	1.0	5.0	4.8
Exports	13.3	40.5	28.0
Debt-service ratio	8.8	7.0	20.3

[a] Public and publicly guaranteed medium- and long-term debt only.

SOURCE: *World Debt Tables*, The World Bank.

TABLE A.6
1983 DEBT INDICATORS
(percent)

Principal Ratios	Major Borrowers	Sub-Saharan Africa	Low-income Africa
Debt/export	167	197	598
Debt/GNP	29	32	37
Debt service/exports	22	20	31
Interest/GNP	2.3	1.5	0.9
Gross reserves (months)	3.2	1.5	3.3

SOURCE: *World Debt Tables, 1984*, The World Bank.

TABLE A.7

STRUCTURE OF THE LONG-TERM EXTERNAL DEBT OF SUB-SAHARAN AFRICAN COUNTRIES, 1973–1983

(U.S. $ billion)

	1973	1978	1979	1980	1981	1982	1983[a]
Total debt outstanding and disbursed	9.9	29.2	36.7	43.3	47.5	51.4	57.9
A. Public and publicly guaranteed	9.3	27.4	34.4	40.4	44.5	48.1	53.8
Official creditors	5.9	15.7	19.8	24.1	26.3	29.2	31.1
Multilateral, of which	1.6	5.6	6.7	8.4	9.8	11.4	12.6
Concessional	0.6	3.1	3.8	5.0	5.8	6.8	n.a.
Bilateral, of which	4.3	10.3	13.1	15.7	16.5	17.8	18.5
Concessional	3.7	8.0	8.9	10.2	10.9	11.6	n.a.
Private Creditors	3.4	11.7	14.6	16.5	18.2	18.9	22.7
Suppliers	1.3	3.5	3.7	3.5	3.5	3.4	3.8
Financial Markets	2.1	8.2	10.9	13.0	14.7	15.5	18.9

B. Private Nonguaranteed	0.6	1.8	2.3	2.7	3.0	3.3	4.1
Memorandum							
Concessional Loans %	43.4	38.1	34.6	35.1	35.2	35.8	n.a.
Variable Int. Rate Loans %	8.8	15.6	17.8	19.2	21.0	22.0	n.a.
Debt to preferred creditors	1.8	6.7	8.4	10.4	13.2	15.4	17.4
Multilateral[b]	1.6	5.4	6.7	8.4	9.8	11.4	12.6
Use of IMF Credits	0.2	1.3	1.7	2.0	3.4	4.0	4.8

[a] Estimates.
[b] Multilateral includes the IMF Trust Fund.
SOURCE: The World Bank.

TABLE A.8

AFRICA: SELECTED ECONOMIC INDICATORS, 1973–82[a]

	1973	1974	1975	1976	1977	1978	1979	1980	1981	1982
					(in percent)					
Economic growth	2.39	6.27	2.75	5.85	2.82	1.84	1.52	2.69	1.84	1.90
Inflation	9.86	17.07	15.84	16.63	24.30	18.95	22.32	23.29	25.84	16.25
Terms of trade	8.30	7.63	-12.19	7.16	17.64	-7.25	-0.35	-7.09	-6.21	-4.74
Ratio of external debt to GDP	24.90	25.87	27.50	32.82	35.10	36.90	38.96	42.36	23.41	50.63
Debt service ratio	—	8.00	9.50	9.50	11.40	15.00	15.50	17.20	20.50	27.40
					(in billions of U.S. dollars)					
Current account	-4.50	-4.00	-7.20	-6.50	-6.60	-9.40	-9.90	-12.90	-14.00	-13.20
Net official transfers	1.10	1.50	1.70	2.00	2.30	2.50	3.10	3.20	3.60	3.20
Net capital inflows	3.80	2.60	4.90	4.40	4.90	6.30	6.40	7.10	6.80	6.80
Overall balance of payments	0.50	0.30	-0.60	-0.10	0.70	-0.40	-0.20	-2.40	-3.60	-3.20
Total outstanding debt	11.60	14.75	18.40	23.40	30.22	37.20	45.54	57.23	61.84	67.70

[a] This follows the IMF's International Financial Statistics classification of the African countries. These include all the African member countries, with the exception of Algeria, Egypt, Nigeria, and Libya, which are classified under different headings. In this table, South Africa is also included.

SOURCES: IMF, Current Studies Division; *World Economic Outlook*, Occasional Paper No. 9.

TABLE A.9
EXPORT VOLUME GROWTH RATES

	1960–70	1970–79
All low-income countries	5.4	–1.0
All low-income excluding China and India	5.7	–1.1[a]
Low income Africa	5.3	–1.9
Semi-arid	5.9	4.4
Other	5.0	–2.7
All middle income countries	5.4	4.3
Oil exporters	4.4	2.6[a]
African oil exporters	6.6	–0.1
Oil importers	6.7	4.1[a]
African oil importers	7.1	–0.5
Sub-Saharan Africa	5.9	–0.8

[a] 1970–80

SOURCES: *World Development Report*, 1984, p. 234; *Accelerated Development in Sub-Saharan Africa*, 1981, p. 149; *World Development Report*, 1982, p. 124.

TABLE A.10
TERMS OF TRADE AND PURCHASING POWER OF EXPORTS
(Average Rates of Change)

	Terms of Trade		Purchasing Power of Exports	
	1961–70	1970–79	1961–70	1970–79
Sub-Saharan Africa	2.9	2.5	7.6	1.0
Oil exporters	1.2	14.7	7.7	12.6
Oil importers	3.4	–1.5	7.6	–2.7

SOURCE: World Bank, *Accelerated Development in Sub-Saharan Africa*, 1981, p. 18.

TABLE A.11
SUB-SAHARAN AFRICA'S SHARE OF DEVELOPING COUNTRY EXPORTS
OF SELECTED COMMODITIES
(Percentage)

	1960	1970–72	1976–78
Fuels			
Petroleum	0.3	7.6	8.6
Minerals and Metals			
Copper[a]	47.3	52.1	38.8
Iron ore[b]	10.8	30.3	19.7
Bauxite	5.7	4.7	31.7
Phosphate rock	0.6	13.3	14.3
Manganese ore[b]	22.2	53.1	36.9
Zinc[a]	27.7	25.9	18.7
Tin[a]	11.7	9.7	3.6
Lead[a]	12.9	19.4	6.6
Food and beverages			
Coffee[b]	19.3	29.3	29.1
Cocoa[a]	72.8	80.1	72.3
Sugar	4.6	5.6	11.0
Tea	7.1	15.7	19.4
Groundnuts[a]	87.1	74.8	63.5
Groundnut oil[a]	77.3	72.2	56.8
Beef	4.5	4.0	8.6
Palmoil[a]	65.7	22.6	6.7
Bananas[a]	11.3	7.2	4.9
Maize[a]	4.8	4.4	2.5
Nonfood			
Timber[a]	44.7	22.8	18.5
Cotton[a]	23.2	28.8	22.4
Tobacco[a]	40.6	25.4	19.4
Rubber[a]	7.4	7.9	4.9
Hides and Skins[b]	21.2	33.7	23.7
Sisal[a]	68.5	58.3	52.8

[a]Africa's share declined 1960 to 1976–78.
[b]Africa's share declined 1970–72 to 1976–78.
SOURCE: World Bank, *Accelerated Development in Sub-Saharan Africa*, 1981, p. 21.

TABLE A.12
U.S. OFFICIAL BILATERAL ASSISTANCE TO AFRICA
(Commitments, in $ millions)

	1980	1984	1985
Economic Assistance			
Development Assistance	282	349	356
Economic Support Fund			
(Economic aid given for			
political purposes)	133	338	425
P.L. 480	268	295	334
Emergency Food Aid	—	—	1,000 *est.*
Total Economic Assistance	683	982	2,115
Military Assistance	77	157	170
Total Assistance	760	1,139	2,285

NOTE: Military aid has been included in this calculation to indicate that along with Economic Support Fund assistance the U.S. now gives about 46% of its non-emergency assistance to Africa for open political and military purposes.

SOURCE: (Economic Assistance) USAID Policy Bureau Analysis, May 13, 1984; (Military Assistance) 1980: USAID, U.S. Overseas Loans and Grants, Washington, D.C., 1983; 1984 and 1985: Personal Communication, Bureau of Political Military Affairs, Department of State.

TABLE A.13
OFFICIAL DEVELOPMENT ASSISTANCE PER CAPITA BY REGIONS
(current dollars)

	1961	1971	1981	1982	1983
Africa	$4.21	$5.10	$20.27	$19.68	$19.10
Latin America					
(exclusive of W. Indies)	3.78	2.30	6.57	6.69	6.44
Asia					
(including China)	1.08	1.77	3.34	2.95	2.64
Asia					
(excluding China)	1.96	3.19	5.90	5.14	4.38

SOURCE: Overseas Development Council calculations based on OECD, *Development Assistance and Development Corporation,* 1964–1983; and United Nations, *Demographic Yearbook,* 1982.

Compact for African Development

Report of the Committee on African Development Strategies

CO-CHAIRMEN

*Lawrence S. Eagleburger
  Kissinger Associates, Inc.

*Donald F. McHenry
  Georgetown University

COMMITTEE MEMBERS AND
ENDORSERS OF THE REPORT

Morton Bahr
  *Communications Workers of
  America*

*Douglas J. Bennet, Jr.
  *National Public Radio, Former
  Administrator, USAID*

---

*Member, Committee on African
Development Strategies.
Affiliations are for identification
only. Committee members and
endorsers are acting in their
individual capacities.

*Elliot Berg
  Elliot Berg & Associates

*Louis Berger
  Louis Berger, Inc.

Marjorie Craig Benton
  Save the Children Federation

*Tom Bradley
  Mayor of Los Angeles

Andrew F. Brimmer
  Brimmer & Co., Inc.

*Robert S. Browne
  Economic Consultant

Prescott Bush
  Prescott Bush & Company

*Goler T. Butcher
  Howard University

William H. Bywater
  *International Union of Electronic,
  Electrical, Technical, Salaried and
  Machine Workers*

*Frank C. Carlucci
  Sears World Trade, Inc.

Joseph R. Daly
Doyle Dane Bernbach, Inc.

*John C. Danforth
U.S. Senate

*Ralph P. Davidson
TIME, Incorporated

Peter J. Davies
InterAction

John Diebold
Diebold Group, Inc.

*Julian C. Dixon
U.S. House of Representatives

Thomas R. Donahue
AFL-CIO

*Donald B. Easum
African-American Institute

*Thomas L. Farmer
Prather, Seeger, Doolittle, and Farmer

*Richard E. Feinberg
Overseas Development Council

*Louis B. Fleming
Los Angeles Times

*J. Wayne Fredericks
Ford Motor Company

*Paul Fribourg
Continental Grain Company

*David A. Hamburg
Carnegie Corporation of New York

*Niles Helmboldt
Equator Holdings Limited

*Jesse Hill, Jr.
Atlanta Life Insurance Co.

*Benjamin L. Hooks
National Association for the Advancement of Colored People

*Robert D. Hormats
Goldman, Sachs & Co.

Vernon E. Jordan, Jr.
Akin, Gump, Strauss, Hauer & Feld

*Elizabeth T. Kennan
Mount Holyoke College

*Paul H. Kreisberg
Council on Foreign Relations

*Carol Lancaster
Georgetown University

*Mickey Leland
U.S. House of Representatives

*John P. Lewis
Princeton University

George N. Lindsay
Debevoise & Plimpton

*Bruce Llewellyn
Philadelphia Coca Cola Bottling Co.

*C. Payne Lucas
Africare

*Alex Massad
Mobil Oil Corporation

*Paul F. McCleary
United Methodist Church

Robert S. McNamara

*William Grawn Milliken
Former Governor, State of Michigan

Erwin Millimet
Stroock & Stroock & Lavan

*Richard Moose
Shearson-Lehman, International, Inc.

Victor H. Palmieri
The Palmieri Company

Peter G. Peterson
The Blackstone Group

*Charles W. Robinson
Energy Transition Corporation

*Randall Robinson
TransAfrica

David Rockefeller
Rockefeller Brothers Fund

Fred Rosen
Fred Rosen Associates

SUMMARY

The drought, famine, and debt emergencies in Sub-Saharan Africa have demonstrated the depths of the continent's fundamental development crisis. Perhaps because of the crisis, African leaders and their donor friends in the Western world and the multilateral organizations have arrived at a new consensus about what needs to be done for Africa's development. This Committee strongly believes that this consensus creates an historic opportunity. Africa, the United States, and other nations of the world should now make a strong, long-term commitment to help Africa help itself.

Humanitarian and political interests require that the United States take a leading role in creating a Compact for African Development. The cost of such a compact, especially in a period of budget stringency, is significant: some $3 billion a year in long-term assistance from the American public and private sectors. But the costs later would be higher still if African economies were to slide into full-scale economic collapse.

The Compact requires a mutual undertaking: A U.S. commitment to long-term support in exchange for an African commitment to implement reforms and improve economic performance. Only such reforms can guarantee greater external support; yet greater resources must be made available before reforms can lead to growth.

A comprehensive approach for Africa's development must address remaining emergency needs, rehabilitation of economies, and longer-term development problems. The program set forth in this report addresses these needs. Specifically, the Committee on African Development Strategies recommends actions to:

MEET THE IMMEDIATE FOOD NEEDS OF HUNGRY
PEOPLE WHILE FOSTERING DEVELOPMENT

1. Using food from the United States and other donors, African states should
initiate food-for-work and other food programs to foster agricultural development and increase productivity.

2. The United States and other donors providing assistance should negotiate
longer-term food aid arrangements in Africa, covering up to five years at a
time and guaranteeing support—in the event of shortfalls during that
period—to those governments that are working vigorously to reform policy
and increase investment for higher agricultural productivity.

STOP THE DETERIORATION IN AFRICA'S
ECONOMIES

3. In exchange for the reaffirmation by African states of responsibility for
their debt, the United States government should re-program, or stretch out
over an extended period of time, its share of most African debt.

4. The United States should pledge $250 million to the World Bank's Special
Facility for Sub-Saharan Africa.

INITIATE STRATEGIES AND ACTIONS FOR THE
LONGER TERM

5. The United States should lead a drive for increased investment in environmentally sound African agricultural development, with special emphasis on
small farms and the women farmers who have previously been neglected by
aid programs.

6. In cooperation with African governments that are moving to increase
productivity, the United Stated should launch a major and sustained campaign in research and training to create the human and technical building
blocks needed for a "Green Revolution" in Africa.

7. The United States should work with the International Planned Parenthood
Federation and the United Nations Fund for Population Activities to institute
major population programs in each African country that has a bilateral U.S.
aid program.

8. The United States should help Africa unleash the creativity of its own
private sector through technical help, improved procurement practices, and
trade reform.

9. The United States should make a full contribution of $1.33 billion a year
over the next three years to the eighth replenishment of the International

Development Association (IDA), the "soft loan" window of the World Bank, to assure more adequate long-term multilateral financing for African development.

10. Congress should amalgamate security and development aid monies for Africa into a single account clearly designated for development purposes to demonstrate that U.S. assistance is geared to African development performance.

To support the U.S. commitment to the Compact for African Development, we propose:

11. Repayments from past U.S. foreign aid loans should be used to help finance new initiatives for Africa.

12. The United States should triple the long-term U.S. finance going to Africa through a combination of bilateral and multilateral programs to reach a new level of $3 billion per year.

We urge private groups to search for ways to be of help both in using their own resources and in advocating a greater public response. We also urge Congress and the Executive Branch to act with foresight to reflect our country's long-term interests in an Africa that can both survive short-term crises and assume its place as a full participant in the world economy.

COMPACT FOR AFRICAN DEVELOPMENT

Africa is suffering from an extraordinary crisis. Its proportions are mythic, its severity almost impossible for the rest of the world to imagine or comprehend.

Even though the worst of the recent famine is over, Africans will be struggling to survive for decades to come. Tens of millions of African children, if they live beyond their first year, may never know a decent, secure existence. Entire communities may perish while African and outside governments stand by helplessly. Unless new measures are adopted, some independent African countries may be doomed to live in a state of perpetual chaos, aggravated by combination of natural disasters, political upheaval, human failings, and financial ruin. Their governments will survive only by depending on others.

The causes of the crisis in Sub-Saharan Africa[1] are many and varied: some were visited upon the continent by outside forces, and some by Africans themselves. It is important to examine and understand those causes, but merely finding and identifying past errors will not guarantee a better future. Something more must be done urgently unless the cycle of catastrophe is to be repeated over and over again, with the bulk of African and outside energies spent on staving off disaster rather than building for the future.

Africa's situation is not hopeless. The continent can emerge from its current dire circumstances. First of all, Africa must help itself, but the international community must also take bold, dramatic steps to help Africa help itself.

The task will be difficult. It will require new approaches, drawing upon the lessons and mistakes of the past but avoiding dogma and narrow ideologies. Cooperative efforts must be undertaken among African states, among developed states, and between Africa and the developed world. Clear, long-term goals must be agreed upon and mutual obligations undertaken. Meaningful progress will require nothing less than a compact—a reciprocal commitment to make sacrifices and work toward lasting change.

Neither a formal covenant nor a legal agreement, the compact would be a mutual undertaking between the United States and other Western donors and African states that wish to take part. We foresee no new institution, but rather regular consultations between donors and African states about what needs to be done to sustain development.

On the African side, the compact calls for strong leadership to build productivity and accountability. From Western donors it will require consistent and selective support for effective African performance. Because U.S. initiatives can be successful only if they are paired with intensive African efforts, the mutuality expressed in the compact is indispensable to both maintaining U.S. commitment and ensuring that it results in self-reliant African development.

As the leader of international relief efforts, the United States has played a crucial, catalytic role in the recent crisis. But American and other Western donors must change their approach to Africa or they risk exacerbating the already serious situation. As a political, economic and technological world power, and as a nation with a history of deep commitments to helping those who help themselves, the United States has a unique potential and responsibility to work with the people and governments of Africa.

In formulating a compact for African development, we must look beyond the current emergency—to focus the attention of international leaders and the world public on the long-term problems of Africa and to help Africans and those that help them face up to their past mistakes. One basis for hope lies in the exceptions to Africa's overall picture of decline. Some African countries show remarkable survival powers amidst the crisis. These countries, relatively more market-oriented than others, tend to enjoy greater political stability. They have lessons to offer their fellow Africans.

In fact, the crisis itself has created an opportunity that must not be lost. Africans see this clearly, as evidenced by the Lagos Plan of Action drawn up in 1980, by the resolutions on development agreed to at the Organization of African Unity's summit in July 1985, and most emphatically in a declaration issued by their planning ministers last April: "What our governments are seeking is a complete restructuring of the African economies so that progress is based on the use of the region's own resources and potential." Western donors realize this too. And increasingly, the World Bank, in its reports on Africa, is stressing longer-term economic reform as a crucial element in African reconstruction efforts. This unique and timely conjuncture makes the compact all the more necessary and appropriate.

The need now is to move from analysis to action.

THE DEPTH OF AFRICA'S CRISIS

What has happened to Africa in the past two decades can be compared to the effects of a world war. Its crisis is different from anything found anywhere else in the world: no other continent is suffering such acute famine and environmental loss, and nowhere else do institutions and skills lag so far behind problems.

No other region of the developed or developing world finds itself in such a steep and steady decline as Africa. Economic growth rates in Africa have been consistently lower than those of other developing areas. The most optimistic current projection from the World Bank is that per capita income in Africa will decline slightly in the next ten years. But if interest rates are high and the industrial countries undergo another recession, African income will slip by at least another 5 per cent.

In Asia and Latin America, per capita food production is increasing and population growth rates are decreasing, while in Africa exactly the reverse is true; per capita food production is declining while population growth rates are soaring. Elsewhere, health improvements are taking place rapidly, but in Africa the famine had led to a dramatic deterioration in the health of its people, particularly its children and its elderly. Even these broad trends do not convey the debilitating effects of endemic diseases, especially malaria and diarrheal disease and widespread malnutrition, all of which exact a heavy toll on the quality of life and the productivity of huge numbers of Africans.

It sometimes seems meaningless to ask when things will begin to improve in Africa; a more basic question is when they will stop getting worse at such a rapid rate. As a matter of fact, Africa is fighting to hold on to what it has. Roads, educational systems, communications networks, and buildings are deteriorating rapidly, and enormous resources are needed just to maintain and preserve these past investments.

By 1985, the existence of some 150 million Africans—more than one in three people in Sub-Saharan Africa—depended partially or totally on imported food. But even with all this imported food, according to World Bank estimates, perhaps 60 per cent of the people who live in Africa consume fewer calories each day than are thought to be necessary for normal life. This helps to explain why five million children die in Africa every year and another five million are permanently crippled by malnutrition and hunger.

Africa's dramatic drought of the early 1970s, which took one hundred thousand lives, looks modest in comparison to recent events. The far more severe drought of the early 1980s, covering a much wider area, has taken an enormous—still uncounted—human toll. At least twenty-four African countries experienced catastrophic food shortages in 1984-85.

More than twenty of the world's thirty-four poorest countries are located in Africa. Their poverty has dimensions that are staggering:

- African agricultural growth has been based on opening up unused land. Now, as growing populations crowd available land, overuse is depleting the natural wealth of Africa's soils. Without new methods of cultivation, Africa will experience absolute declines in agricultural productivity. Also inhibiting output is the spread of livestock diseases. Some of the richest forests have been stripped of wood for fuel. As dryness has prevented the normal growth of plants and trees in recent years, ground water has evaporated more rapidly and soil erosion has become more severe. The specter of spreading desertification haunts Africa.

- Africa's population is growing faster than anywhere else in the world, and even the most optimistic projections of improvements in food production offer little hope of catching up. More than 400 million people live in Sub-Saharan Africa today; at an estimated overall population growth rate of 3.2 per cent a year, the figure could quadruple by the year 2025.

- Africans, because of poverty and adverse environmental factors, are more vulnerable to infectious diseases and other serious illnesses than any other people in the world. Poor sanitation severely limits ability to deal with these health problems. Despite significant improvements, infant mortality rates remain extraordinarily high and average life spans pathetically short.

- Africa is host to about half of the world's estimated 10 million refugees largely as a result of famines and wars, yet refugees in other areas have commanded greater international attention. Despite the hospitality of African governments that spend scarce resources to shelter them, African refugees live close to the margin of existence and often contribute to political instability in their host countries.

- Africa faces a critical shortage of professionals, technicians, and managers. Perhaps even more worrisome is the dearth of people educated to improve agriculture. Africa's shortage of health personnel, the most severe in the world, has been aggravated by a "brain drain" of young people who have been trained abroad. Many talented Africans who might contribute to development are unable to do so because of political differences or repression.

- Africa's urbanization is more rapid than that of any other region: many African cities are growing at a rate of 7-10 per cent a year; the figure may be as high as 13 per cent for Nairobi, the capital of Kenya. As a result, vast shantytowns have sprung up, where hunger, poor health, unemployment, and crime fester, as inadequate urban facilities are increasingly overtaxed.

- Africa's international debt is not as large as that of Latin America, but it is an enormous burden for countries that are living so close to the margin of survival. By the end of 1986, the payments required to cover the interest on Africa's debts will be equal to two-thirds of all the money the continent receives in aid, leaving very little for new development efforts. The continent's balance of trade is bleak; the deficit was up to $7.9 billion in 1984 and is getting worse all the time.

WHAT HAS GONE WRONG IN AFRICA

While generalizations about Sub-Saharan Africa's forty-six countries mask real differences in their development, no one doubts that things have gone awry in Africa. The continent has taken severe external blows and also wasted precious resources. What makes the continent's circumstances particularly disheartening to its friends, and even more intolerable to its own peoples, is the vast gap between the often unrealistic expectations that flourished at the time of independence and the somber reality that prevails today.

The period of decolonization was an especially heady time in Africa. The new regimes were expected, and tried, to provide a vast array of services to their people. They also embarked on the construction of state edifices and industries that would give dramatic, demonstrable reality to their political sovereignty. As long as the relatively favorable economic conditions of the 1960s lasted, all this seemed to be possible. During the early years of independence, plenty of rain and high commodity prices helped Africa sustain stable, if modest, growth. It was Asia that struggled with famine at that time, while Africa raised its nutritional levels.

The "oil shock" of 1973 was the first of a series of crises which introduced Africans to a harsh new reality. The same international economic trends that buffeted the developed countries and the rest of the Third World in the 1970s and early 1980s hit Africa with devastating force, reducing income from exports and raising the price of imports at the same time. Despite efforts of the Organization of Petroleum Exporting Countries (OPEC) to provide special concessional aid, the average loss of income in Africa as a result of skyrocketing energy costs was 10 per cent, and in some countries it was as high as 25 per cent. The purchasing power of African exports declined 30 per cent.

Opportunities for a better life faded with astonishing speed for the first generation of independent Africans. With harvests stunted by drought and overseas markets for crops severely reduced, livelihoods began to evaporate. Inflation caused the buying power of salaries to plunge; the deterioration of national economies caused many jobs to disappear altogether. Roads, lacking proper maintenance, broke up, and travel to the interior of some countries became more difficult. Vehicles rusted out and were often abandoned alongside deteriorating roads. In a number of countries, even the infrastructure inherited from the colonial era became unusable.

To design the remedial steps to be taken, analysis of what has gone wrong is essential. The easiest course—and it has been taken by many angry Africans—is to suggest that Africa is simply the unwitting and helpless victim of colonialism and of external factors such as the oil shocks and the adverse cycles of world economic conditions during the 1970s and 1980s. In fact, these are part of the problem. Africa inherited internal geographic boundaries and political dividing lines that once delineated European spheres of influence; they are now an economic liability.

At independence, colonial powers left African economies for the most part dependent upon a few commodity exports. New African regimes started out with few workable political institutions and had little training to run them. In the short period since independence they have struggled to build political and economic systems simultaneously.

These are the facts of Africa's life, and no programs for development can go forward without taking account of them. At the same time it is important to recognize the serious mistakes that Africans themselves have made in the past quarter-century:

- Agriculture has been severely neglected. Even now, when many countries are newly emphasizing agriculture, that emphasis is not always reflected in the allocation of resources. African states spend an average of only 5 per cent of their budgets on agriculture, whereas in Southeast Asia, the nations that lead in agriculture spend two or three times as much, with impressive results. Much of what is invested in agriculture overlooks the largest and most efficient group of African producers, the small-scale farmers (a very large proportion of whom are women) who grow some 70 per cent of the continent's food.

- The majority of African governments embarked on unwise and economically unfeasible industrial programs. State-controlled corporations were created to manage vast areas of economic activity, frequently with a high degree of centralization and costly government subsidies, and almost always without the skilled personnel that would give them a chance to work successfully. Many of these corporations regarded their main purpose as employment-creation, and burgeoning state payrolls only drained resources further.

- Poor governmental economic policies, particularly controlled prices, often restricted the creativity of Africans, weakening incentives for production and reducing efficiency. While keeping food cheap in the cities, these policies shortchanged the rural areas.

- Corruption has often distorted and sometimes replaced economic management. Governmental and private-sector elites have drained off a substantial percentage of national resources as well as outside aid.

- Many African governments have undertaken wasteful prestige projects— such as the construction of extravagant government office buildings, conference centers, and luxury hotels—that cannot be justified in terms of development priorities.

In many states, these mistakes have both contributed to and been accentuated by political instability. Africa's coup-per-country rate is the highest in the world. Indeed, only twelve African nations have survived since independence without undergoing a single coup, and today at least half of Africa's people live under military rule. Most African countries have failed to develop strong institutions that will help promote a reliable system of political succession. Too often this had led to the repression of opposition. Moreover, through the Organization of African Unity and other international forums Africans have projected an image of indifference to African abuses of human rights and civil liberties. All of this adversely influences the reputation of Africa in the world community, diminishing the believability of African rhetoric and potentially constraining the willingness of others to help Africans solve their problems.

But Africans alone are not to blame for their dismal situation. Usually well-intentioned outsiders have also contributed to the problems:

- Donor aid has often been short-term and uncoordinated. African governments have sometimes been induced to undertake projects simply because aid is available for them from certain countries. Frequently these projects end up interfering with priorities that should have been maintained.

- Some donors have encouraged Africans to undertake obvious white elephants—boondoggles that have less to do with generosity or with genuine development assistance than with domestic political and economic considerations in the country providing the money.

- Outside funds are often available only for purchases of new equipment—for example trucks—from donors. But the real need is for spare parts to maintain items already contributed by someone else or bought with precious foreign exchange, as well as training of Africans to repair existing equipment. The result of this mismatch is the creation of graveyards of unrepaired vehicles while new vehicles continue to be imported.

- Projects are often financed that support a donor's narrow political priorities—including competition between the superpowers and their recruitment of friends in the Third World—and this, too, skews the development priorities of recipient nations. Indeed, the donors' security concerns are occasionally disguised as development imperatives.

- In the heady days of recycling petro-dollars, commercial banks abandoned some of their usual caution and made funds available at bargain rates and in amounts that looked prudent. Some of these loans financed projects whose economic viability was highly questionable. Later, when real interest rates rose and commodity prices fell, these loans became unsupportable.

- Most donors, including international institutions, have jumped from one fad to another to justify development expenditures—from the support of infrastructure development, to a concern with basic human needs, to the most recent heavy focus on agriculture and encouragement of the private sector. In reality, a properly executed, long-term development process probably requires a balance of all these approaches and others.

On both sides, then, there have been ill-conceived policies, haphazard administration, and self-interested motives, but it is the African people who have suffered the consequences.

Outside donors, for all the money that they have poured into Africa since independence, have often made contradictory demands or imposed conflicting conditions on the beneficiaries of their largesse. Meanwhile, proliferating and overlapping projects have drained the administrative energies of African officials and left the continent's landscape strewn with rusted-out bright ideas.

Annual per-capita aid levels in recent years have been higher in Africa than in other regions of the Third World—reaching $20 per person per year by 1982—but the returns on capital investment have generally declined. Africa's ability to use its available resources productively increasingly has been called into question. African governments have lived beyond their means, postponing the day of reckoning to a moment that seemed unforeseeable but that is now upon us.

THE OPPORTUNITY IN AFRICA

The most recent drought and famine, tragic as they have been, have given both Africa and its donor friends an opportunity to start afresh, to correct some of the most grievous errors of the past, and to build a new, more secure future.

No one is more convinced of the need to change course on development than Africans are today. There is a new mood of realism in Africa—a willingness to enter into a tough analysis of past mistakes and present confusion, a sobriety that verges on humiliation. Africans are looking, frequently Westward, for new ideas. In some cases this is already leading to successful innovation.

Throughout Africa, more and more people are recognizing: the necessity of cutting back the role of the state in the economy, the urgency of emphasizing food production, and the gravity of the population problem.

With all its grave weaknesses, the African record so far also shows some striking strengths:

- Ten years have been added to average lifespans during the past three decades.

- Adult literacy has almost tripled, from 16 per cent in 1960 to 43 per cent in 1980, through the addition of thousands of schools and the doubling of primary school and quadrupling of secondary school enrollments in the past twenty years.

- Communication networks have been established, bringing some rural areas into much greater contact with African capitals and governments.

Thousands of miles of new roads and railroads were constructed, and energy consumption more than doubled.

- An impressive degree of nation-building has taken place, despite artificial boundaries and other inherited disadvantages, and despite the pressure created by unrelenting political turmoil.

- A few countries, for example, Malawi, Zimbabwe, and Ivory Coast have made significant strides in agricultural development while others, including Botswana and Cameroon, have shown excellent financial management, keeping imports within the limits imposed by export revenues. Others have begun to remove obstacles to productivity by raising farm prices, trimming state bureaucracies, lowering subsidies, and adjusting exchange rates.

- African people have made great personal sacrifices, willingly spending large proportions of their minimal incomes to educate their children, and often sharing what little they have with others who are more needy. They have, among other things, been uncommonly tolerant of refugee influxes.

Most important is the new attitude among Africans—among government officials, military officers, and the small but influential middle class—that the economic and political management of their nations must improve, that accountability must increase and corruption must decline, and that hard realities must be faced while greater outside interest and help are available. The key task is to take the necessary actions that flow from this frankness and self-criticism before this unique opportunity fades.

Although the economic trends give no grounds for optimism, determination and ingenuity can be combined to attack Africa's fundamental problems.

WHY AMERICANS MUST PLAY A ROLE

The hungry people of Africa are very far away from America in both miles and circumstances: even after seeing graphic films of their plight on television, few of us can imagine the conditions in which most Africans live. But there are strong moral and practical reasons why Americans cannot ignore Africa.

The song is right when it says, "We are the world." The United States and other wealthy societies share the planet with hundreds of millions of people who lack the most basic necessities of a decent existence. According to the tenets of all religions and most political philosophies, it is a fundamental responsibility of the rich to help the poor. It is also in the best American secular tradition to act boldly in such an emergency, to show humanitarian concern without being unduly preoccupied with geopolitical or strategic considerations. Vast numbers of people in Africa are not merely poor, but facing starvation and death; and their circumstances invoke that responsibility with particular urgency. The wealth of the United States and the poverty of Africa is shown in a few statistics: An average African's income is less than one thirtieth of an average American's income. If one adds up the gross national products of all forty-six Sub-Saharan African states, the total is less than 6 per cent of the U.S. gross national product. Africa must support 400 million people on an economy producing only as much as the state of Illinois.

The fact that millions of Americans responded as generously as they did in 1984 and 1985, with at least $170 million in donations to ease African misery, symbolizes the readiness of Americans to respond to human pain. And the fact that much of that money went to Ethiopia, now ruled by a harsh Marxist military regime bitterly critical of the United States, shows that principle can triumph over politics.

Apart from humanitarian considerations, there are compelling reasons for U.S. involvement in helping Africa today. America's economic interests on the continent, for example, go far beyond the concern about strategic minerals in South Africa and Zaire, or with oil in Nigeria. An Africa that is stable and develops in an orderly fashion may eventually be the source of other raw materials and an expanding market for industrial and other finished goods— a continent where normal trade can be conducted in a businesslike fashion to the benefit of both sides.

Indeed, there is an unprecedented opportunity to mobilize African enterprise to play a role in the continent's recovery. The stage can be set for an active African role in international commerce and investment, in which the United States can and should become involved.

Africa matters politically as well. If the United States genuinely cares about advancing the cause of freedom in the world, then Africa, with its dozens of separate, independent countries, certainly merits attention. In international forums, Africans are in a position to advance or impede peacekeeping efforts in the Middle East and other parts of the world. There are also realistic considerations of Western security that come into play in Africa. Turmoil arising from persistent economic chaos might be exploited by those interested in advancing narrow political, ideological, or military interests. In the unlikely event that much of Africa were to fall under the control of forces hostile to the West, the implications would be grave.

Moreover, gaps between rich and poor countries in the world continue to widen—with most of Africa at one extreme and the wealthy countries, especially the United States, at the other. Resentment of American indifference could be exploited, particularly by anti-Western fundamentalist movements whose use of terrorist force may seriously threaten future world order. U.S. commitment now to Africa's growth can help break down divisions that will only grow more rigid if allowed to persist.

International divisions may also cause division in this country. Hostility or desperation in Africa can affect racial feelings in the United States. African turmoil may find echoes here. In an interdependent world, it is important for the United States and for everyone else that Africa develop those human and physical resources that will promote the interests and the well-being of humankind. The world cannot truly advance as long as one of its parts—a huge continent—lags far behind.

Finally, the U.S. experience can help Africa. In the 1930s, America faced a depression in its Western and Southern farm belts similar to what we see in Africa now. That economic and environmental crisis was ended by years of long-term concessional finance, work programs, large-scale soil and water conservation projects, and extension services to help farmers cope with new challenges. U.S. expertise in solving a wide range of problems is probably the best available. Africa can use U.S. scientific capability in agricultural research, medicine, and information. Our Peace Corps, international business, consultants, and voluntary agency staffs offer a large bank of experience to draw upon.

CARRYING OUT THE COMPACT

Africans and those who would help them must act quickly, not only to alleviate the current crisis, but also to chart a long-term course for Africa's recovery and further development. These tasks go hand in hand. At the individual family level, it is clear that those who are starving need food, that they need to be able to regain useful productive lives, and that they then need to be able to improve their well-being through better technology and investment of additional resources. African nations face this same set of challenges. Coherent actions are needed to meet the emergency, rehabilitation, and growth requirements of the sub-continent.

In response to these needs, we are proposing a compact that is, above all, a mutual undertaking. Both Africans and those who want to help them are being asked to evaluate their past performance and make important philosophical and practical changes. The United States and other donor countries and agencies have many of the human, technical, and economic resources that can alleviate Africa's problems, but that alone is not the answer. The task cannot simply be performed or imposed by outsiders. Rather, Africa must be helped to help itself. This is the agenda:

I. MEET THE IMMEDIATE FOOD NEEDS OF HUNGRY PEOPLE WHILE FOSTERING DEVELOPMENT

The American record in providing food aid to Africa over the years has been outstanding. In the recent crisis, U.S. assistance, public and private, has provided half of the emergency famine relief. Indeed, the performance of the entire international community, particularly of the United Nations, in responding to Africa's anguish has been highly commendable; there has been a level and an intensity of involvement that far transcends anything done before. At the same time, the disappearance of prominent, daily news coverage of famine and drought should not allow us to overlook the fact that a crisis is still at hand—and that the long-term problems remain to be dealt with.

It will be necessary over the course of the next few years to maintain significant emergency levels of food aid to Africa. Food aid also will be needed over the longer run. The World Bank estimates that even if by 1988 Africa again benefits from normal rains—the right amounts in the right places at the right times—the continent will still need, as a result of population growth, the same amount of imported food that it received in the 1985 emergency. Given the poor prospects for earning enough foreign exchange to finance growing food import needs, donors and African states should anticipate large food aid programs to Africa for several more years. The question is how to structure this aid to ensure that it helps as much as possible to foster the only long-term solution that is viable: African self-sufficiency in food. Ways must be found to use food aid to promote development rather than dependency.

1. *Using food from the United States and other donors, African states should initiate food-for-work and other food programs to foster agricultural development and increase productivity.*

American food aid can be used to pay for development work. This has been done extensively in Asia, but not in Africa. It will require more oversight, but with American encouragement, African governments should use food aid to pay in cash or kind for rural labor to rehabilitate roads, earthworks, dams, and rural water supplies necessary for agricultural production and distribution as well as health. Other food-for-work programs should focus on soil conservation and reforestation. This will put income into the hands of farmers, enabling millions who have lived at the margin of relief to support themselves again, while giving a boost to those who are struggling to pay for the tools, seeds, and fertilizer needed to maintain or expand output. It will also emphasize the connection between food supplies and maintenance of the environment, establishing the need to prevent further erosion of Africa's productive land as a means of guarding against future famine.

The United States would, in effect, be working both sides of the supply-and-demand equation: reducing the demand by channeling food to the impoverished, while increasing the supply by channeling the local currencies generated by food aid to rural development and agricultural production activities. Local roads and communications will be improved in the process, and people will be given a more direct stake in their own development. To make these efforts effective, the U.S. government should rely more heavily on the private voluntary organizations working in Africa and switch some of its oversight of aid programs from capital cities to rural areas.

2. *The United States and other donors should negotiate longer-term food aid arrangements in Africa, covering up to five years at a time and guaranteeing support in the event of shortfalls during that period for governments that are working vigorously to reform policy and increase investment for higher agricultural productivity.*

In addition to the short-term relief required by African countries, there is a longer-term structural need for financial help to continue importing food to cover the shortfalls from production. Africa now imports 20 per cent of its food supply on a regular basis, and this is apt to increase until the time when the continent becomes significantly more capable of raising its own food supplies.

While this recommendation carries certain burdens for the American public purse, it would also have clear advantages: there would be fewer last-minute dashes to Congress for supplemental appropriations to meet unanticipated needs and a more assured market for U.S. farmers; further, the U.S. government could buy the food it is going to use for aid in a more orderly manner, probably at lower cost. African governments, knowing they could depend on American assistance, would have added incentives to undertake reforms that often involve political risks. No one wants to foster dependency on food aid. Therefore this transitional aid must be structured to achieve steady progress toward local food security for African peoples.

II. STOP THE DETERIORATION OF AFRICA'S ECONOMIES

Before Africa can truly make progress toward self-sufficiency, some of the terms of its current dependency must be altered and greater generosity and patience will be required on the part of those who are already helping.

Africa's debt problem is due not merely to a bad cash flow, but to deep-rooted poverty and insolvency. Until recently, the international community tended to ignore the debt because it apparently did not present a threat to the world financial system. At about $100 billion today, African debt still accounts for only 10 per cent of the world total for developing countries and less than 5 per cent of the debt owed to commercial banks.

But for Africa, the debt burden is staggering. On the average, more than half of all export earnings are now required to service foreign loans; for some countries, debt service actually exceeds export earnings. In 1983, Africa paid $300 million more to private banks than it received from them. As a consequence of this and other factors, the foreign-exchange reserves of most African countries have declined precipitously. At the end of 1984, reserves covered only 27 days' worth of imports, compared with 93 days' worth for Asian countries and 113 days for those of Latin America. Africa is unable to repay its debt and have any margin for progress. Now several African countries are in arrears to the International Monetary Fund. The inability of some to repay or even service their debt has serious implications for the international financial system.

After the 1973 oil price shock, the IMF set up special arrangements to help the poorer countries maintain their energy imports. But after the 1979 oil shock, African borrowing—encouraged by commercial banks and the IMF—led to vast increases in African debts bunched for repayment in the 1985-87 period. A large number of African states simply cannot meet their debt payments. There are two choices: African debts can be stretched out substantially, or huge new amounts of aid can be pumped in just to help pay the debt. Otherwise, Africa literally must take funds that are needed for food and fuel imports and use them to pay off the banks, the IMF, and other official lenders.

The cost to Africa of this debt problem goes far beyond money; it drains valuable human energies that could be devoted to more productive tasks. One of the poorest nations on the continent complains that it took the key people in its government six months just to negotiate a twelve-month extension of debt payments.

Economic stabilization programs of the kind frequently recommended by the IMF can be useful in eliminating wasteful practices. However, when pursued in a short-term manner, compressed reforms are liable to erode further the capacity for recovery in Africa. Drastic cuts in expenditures have high political and social costs in such poor countries, and changing the structure of production takes a long time and requires additional resources. More systematic solutions must be found; in the meantime, intermediate steps can be taken.

3. *In exchange for the reaffirmation by African states of ultimate responsibility for their debt, the United States government should re-program, or stretch out over an extended period of time, its share of most African debt.*

Until now, Americans have lagged behind the Europeans in offering relief from official debt to Africa. The United States must, by law, suspend all aid to any country, whatever its circumstances, that is more than six months overdue on repaying official U.S. loans; the entire U.S. aid program to Tanzania was jettisoned over this very point.

The cost of making such a concession to all African countries that are in debt to the United States government is relatively small—approximately $20 million a year—but such a move would demonstrate American flexibility in an important area. In return, the African countries involved should reaffirm ultimate responsibility for their debt and should commit themselves to reforms that will increase their productivity and, therefore, their ability to pay.

Another option is for the U.S. government to accept repayments of African debt in local currency using the repayments for financing development programs.

Beyond changing repayment terms, new finance must be found during the next few years to help keep African economies afloat. This will require some $5-6 billion per year. Because new commercial lending and investment are unlikely for some time, the only possibility to meet this need is through a combination of debt refinancing and new aid.

The United States took an important step regarding debt refinancing at the October 1985 IMF/World Bank meetings in Seoul, Korea, when it advocated the use of funds being repaid to the IMF Trust Fund (largely from other countries) to refinance IMF lending to Africa on longer terms. This action should enable the most hard pressed African states to remain current with the IMF and thereby preserve the possibility of debt financing from others. In advocating a resumption of Trust Fund operations, the United States was using its position as the largest shareholder in the IMF to assert real leadership on an issue that threatened to undermine a great many IMF operations.

It also expressed a willingness to explore additional development finance for Africa. This kind of leadership is needed at the World Bank, where the United States is also the largest shareholder.

The debt issue facing Africa needs more than stop-gap measures and the rejuggling of funds and agreements. It requires enough additional capital to enable Africa to grow its way out of debt. This issue can be faced now at some cost or later at considerably greater cost.

Thus we wish to emphasize the need for significant amounts of new money to help meet a fair share of the internal finance gap facing Africa. We believe this should involve tripling the long-term U.S. assistance going to Africa through a combination of bilateral and multilateral programs to reach a new level of $3 billion per year.

4. *The United States should pledge $250 million to the World Bank's Special Facility for Sub-Saharan Africa.*

Contributions of more than $1 billion have been committed by other nations, including several close U.S. allies, to the key international effort organized to address Africa's need for financing imports of critical goods and services. For the first time, the United States has not been in the lead on such a multilateral finance effort—indeed, this is the first time that others have gone ahead without Washington's participation. A contribution from the United States would greatly strengthen this important international initiative to help African nations restart their economies.

The United States should continue the Economic Policy Initiative launched last year with a five year program, averaging $100 million/year, to reward policy reform in Africa with extra assistance. This is a useful effort. But the needs require a greater U.S. response. We also need a channel where larger sums of money are combined for more effective coordination of aid and policy signals to African states during these critical times. Improvements in aid coordination are imperative and can best be accomplished by multilateral institutions in concert with African governments.

An American contribution to the new World Bank effort will underscore the utility of multilateral assistance that is not tied to specific projects, as well as show Africans that Americans understand the depth of their crisis and are willing to be flexible.

III. INITIATE STRATEGIES AND ACTIONS FOR THE LONGER TERM

Sub-Saharan Africa is now suffering an economic depression. Drought and debt have enforced an austerity that has profound consequences for daily life: massive unemployment; less food and less nourishment; the deterioration of roads, bridges, farms, and industry; declining health services; and, in schools, crowded classrooms, poorly paid and trained teachers, and a few books. In some countries, it is only Africa's strong cultural tradition of communal support that has allowed large numbers of people to survive.

Where should donors place their priorities in trying to help Africans increase productivity and achieve long-term development? It seems clear now that except in the few favored African countries that can count on substantial income from the export of oil, agriculture must serve as the base for all forms of economic progress. With populations increasing dramatically, the central challenge for African countries is to feed themselves. They must be helped to do so and encouraged to emphasize small, efficient farms over large, inefficient ones; to explore new marketing alternatives that avoid excessive centralization; and to improve technical higher education that might help bring Africa its own "Green Revolution."

5. *The United States should lead a drive for increased investment in environmentally sound African agricultural development, with special emphasis on small farms and the women farmers who have previously been neglected by aid programs.*

U.S. policy should reinforce the growing conviction of African governments and multilateral institutions, including the World Bank, that Africa must succeed in the agricultural domain before it can move on to other areas. A hopeful sign was the commitment of Africa's heads of state at their July 1985 summit to increase gradually the share of agriculture in national public investment to 20–25 per cent by 1989. Agriculture is the engine of nonagricultural growth, and more and more Africans are coming to recognize and act on this economic fact. Moreover, the potential for agriculture is great throughout almost all of Africa. But it will often be politically risky for African governments to turn their emphasis away from the cities and industry. The United States should strongly support those governments that are willing to face up to these risks in the long-term interest of their economies.

Addressing the rural political economy also involves challenges. Without question, large-scale progress in African agriculture will only come about when programs focus on small farms, which are the source of subsistence for the vast majority of African families and which produce most of Africa's food. And the majority of the food producers are women. Technologies, services, and resources must be structured to serve the real producers of food in Africa. Fostering agricultural development also requires improving collection, storage, processing, transport to market, and distribution—all of which hold promise for more involvement by the growing local private sectors. All these changes will require a reorientation of programs.

If rural development is to be self-sustaining, maintaining and restoring Africa's natural resource base will be necessary. Technologies and methods suited to the local environment are essential. Africa's Green Revolution will not be like Asia's, where a few breakthroughs had widespread applications. Africa's complex environment requires a broad variety of approaches.

Dealing with environmental problems will require integrating soil, water, and forest management issues into all agricultural sector planning. Only within the past few years have African leaders begun to acknowledge the importance of maintaining their land resources; for many years, conservation had been deemed an alien or "colonial" cause. As with population, U.S. officials need to reiterate the central importance of the environment in general discussions with African officials. The United States should also contribute use of its unique satellite capabilities to help set up climate research and early-warning systems for drought. It should also support mass communications efforts to educate farmers on cost-effective ways to safeguard their natural resource base.

There are no panaceas for restoring the natural resource base in Africa. The best way to get better results than in the past will be seriously to rethink approaches, to recruit staff combining social and environmental expertise, and to involve local peoples and institutions in essentially local activities.

American private voluntary organizations have a special role to play at the village level in Africa, by working directly with agricultural producers as individuals and in community groups. At the same time, American universities and the U.S. private sector can contribute meaningfully to this effort, by applying their talents in agricultural research and management and helping Africans make further progress themselves.

One effective international organization that can help with this effort is the International Fund for Agricultural Development (IFAD), a specialized multilateral bank to which the United States belongs and which has pioneered many approaches to helping the small farmer in the Third World. IFAD has helped the World Bank and other major groups recognize the value of working directly with small farmers: higher productivity, better repayment records, and greater social impact than can be expected from programs that deal exclusively with large-scale agriculture. The United States should work to assure funds so that IFAD can continue and greatly expand its role in African agriculture.

Turning to human resources, it is clear that progress in African development requires far more trained managers and decision makers. Training in administration should be part of the professional preparation of Africans in a wide variety of disciplines. At the same time, the relationship of human resource development and agricultural production in Africa must be a special concern.

6. *In cooperation with African governments that are moving to increase productivity, the United States should launch a major and sustained campaign in research and training to create the human and technical building blocks needed for a "Green Revolution" in Africa.*

Most African countries lack the in-country research capabilities that are necessary for any breakthrough in agriculture comparable to the ones realized by India during the early 1970s. They also lack productive agricultural training facilities to keep a stream of talent going into research, extension services and agricultural management.

Although women account for 70 per cent of the food production in Africa, to date, research has largely neglected the food crops most commonly grown by African women—tubers, sorghum, and millet, which provide the staple diet for more than half of Africa's people—and it has failed to develop technologies for simplifying food processing. Indeed, the United States, other Western donors, and the World Bank have invested only meager amounts of money in education and training for agriculture.

It may take twenty-five years to see sustained results in this area, but the investment would be worthwhile. What is required is a long-term partnership in which African and American institutions work together, for example, to apply the new lessons of biological, genetic research. U.S. institutions must be willing to provide incentives to encourage good researchers to make time commitments for Africa's needs. African governments also will have to be willing to make commitments to research efforts that may take many years to pay off. In some smaller countries, it may be necessary to sacrifice national prestige and rely upon regional research centers.

7. The United States should work with the International Planned Parenthood Federation and the United Nations Fund for Population Activities to institute major population programs in each African country that has a bilateral U.S. aid program.

African states, fearing that the continent's population, according to some projections, could approach 1 billion by the year 2000, have come to recognize the problem—in some cases, belatedly—and have recently made clear that rapidly increasing population is now a priority concern. This has taken political courage in a setting of great sensitivity. But leaders now recognize that Africa has a far better chance to feed itself at some point in the foreseeable future if it reduces its population growth rates.

At the same time, the United States, acting in response to domestic political considerations, has cut back its important support to the two organizations that have the best outreach in Africa and are in the best position to tailor population programs to particular economic, cultural, and social needs. These cutbacks must be reversed. New programs should be started, with these organizations and others established in the field working with country leaders. Otherwise, the prospects for an effective approach to one of Africa's most serious problems will be imperiled.

A related concern is the health of Africa's people. Here there is room for optimism. A decade ago, the World Health Organization succeeded in eliminating smallpox not just in Africa, but in the entire world. Very low-cost changes in health care being promoted by UNICEF could save millions of infants and young children.

Vaccination, if universal in Africa, would also make a vast difference. Inoculating an African child against measles, diphtheria, whooping cough, tetanus, tuberculosis, and polio would cost only $1.20 per child (exclusive of salaries and transport for medical personnel who would administer the programs). All of Africa's children could thus be vaccinated and millions of young lives saved at a cost of $120 million for vaccine.

New medical discoveries will soon make it possible to vaccinate against the deadliest forms of malaria. Additional health breakthroughs also should be fostered. The United States should pool the medical knowledge developed by its private and public sectors that is of special relevance to Africa and make it available at little or no cost.

American firms doing research on vaccines and treatment methods often come across findings that would be of use to Africa, but they do not develop them because Africa is deemed to be too poor a market. Similarly, federal agencies like the U.S. Public Health Service interpret their mandates narrowly and often fail to direct their efforts toward health problems that plague Africa. Greater public- and private-sector cooperation to help Africa in the health field would be useful and could make an enormous difference. For example, the Public Health Service could become a repository of health knowledge of relevance to Africa developed in the private sector and a focal point for scientific cooperation. The United Nations has had success with simply packaged health innovations, and there is no reason why the United States cannot do the same.

For Africans, health breakthroughs may come faster than population breakthroughs. But health programs can support population policies by providing family planning services within health programs, as well as by actively promoting maternal and child health care, thereby increasing confidence of parents that more of their children will survive.

An improvement in African health services would not only alleviate the miserable lives that so many people on the continent endure, but would also contribute to solving several other problems. It would, for example, bring the welfare of rural areas more into line with that of the cities. Progress on Africa's main health problems could bring major opportunities. Vast areas of cultivable land would open up that remain unsettled because of severe health problems. Assuring clean water supplies can reduce debilitating chronic diseases and thereby increase labor productivity.

But technology alone will not do the job. In many countries, it will be necessary to reorient health-service delivery to reach the majority rather than just urban elites.

8. *The United States should help Africa unleash the creativity of its own private sector through technical help, improved procurement practices, and trade reforms.*

From rural marketplaces to businesses that are national in scope, Africans demonstrate their interest and ability in private enterprise. Now their governments must create conditions that will give internal and external parties confidence that they can invest and trade with the knowledge that payments will be made, agreements will be honored, and legal mechanisms will be available to enforce contracts if necessary. U.S. technical assistance could be helpful in proposing reforms that reflect the realities of the marketplace.

The United States and other donors can also stimulate local private markets by making a special effort to buy local goods and services in carrying out aid programs.

Americans can help to foster trade on the buying side. The United States should review the trade barriers that affect African products, with a view toward lowering them. Admittedly, some particularly sensitive areas are involved, but they warrant exploration. African states tend not to be strong enough politically or well enough organized to request tariff relief from the U.S. government, but this is a field in which the Executive Branch could take initiatives that would have a real impact on African economies.

Trade cooperation within Africa is also desirable. African governments should be encouraged to take advantage of every opening for regional cooperation. Such fundamental areas as easing the convertibility of currencies and lowering trade barriers offer opportunities. The United States cannot get out in front of Africans on these matters, but it should be ready to reinforce whatever progress is made through technical help and political support of regional linkages.

9. *The United States should make a full contribution of $1.33 billion a year over the next three years to the eighth replenishment of the International Development Association (IDA), the "soft loan" window of the World Bank, to assure more adequate long-term multilateral finance for African development.*

Assured World Bank finance for Africa is a critical part of any reasonable approach to Africa's future growth. The Bank is in the lead in discussions concerning strategy and donor coordination, two topics of pervasive relevance to future development. IDA, the part of the World Bank intended to help the poorest countries through long-term concessional loans, requires new funding, and discussions are under way for its eighth three-year replenishment. For the sixth replenishment, the agreed level was $12 billion. The Bank asked for $16 billion for the seventh replenishment, but the United States insisted that the level be $9 billion. It was this inadequate funding that forced the Bank to organize a special program for Africa (see Recommendation 4) to meet current needs. For the next replenishment, a level of $16 billion would be in order, of which 25 per cent would go to Africa. The U.S. share would be about $1.33 billion annually for the next three years. This kind of contribution would create helpful leverage to obtain three times this amount from many other countries and would underline the leading role of the World Bank in the reforms and growth strategies necessary for Africa's future development.

10. *Congress should amalgamate security and development aid for Africa into a single account clearly designated for development purposes in order to demonstrate that our assistance is geared to African development performance.*

Currently, half of U.S. economic aid for Africa comes from Development Assistance funds, which are allocated on the basis of need and tests of economic, social, technical, environmental, and financial feasibility. The other half is in the form of Economic Support Fund activities, formerly known as Security Assistance; this money is allocated more along political lines—in effect as a reward for a country's friendship with the United States. Whereas the first category invokes a rigorous test of development performance, the second can be used more loosely, to finance struggling nations' balance of payments and other kinds of non-project needs that are vital during this period of African rehabilitation. One problem is that economic support funds can be redirected to other parts of the world to meet short-term political needs; thus African countries cannot always count on getting the money they were expecting.

With some African countries getting half of their U.S. aid from each of these programs, it is often unclear whether the central goal of U.S. assistance is development performance or whether it is political support regardless of development needs and performance. It would be useful to clarify this issue by creating a combined fund for Africa to be administered for development purposes. The creation of such a fund, while denying some flexibility to the State Department, would stress the point that the security problems in Africa that overshadow all others are problems of *economic* security.

This step would protect against raids on money designated for Africa, provide the flexibility to meet rehabilitation needs now and development needs later, and reinforce those who wish to operate American assistance programs on more professional and less political lines. For Africa, it would be a clear signal that the real condition for American aid is development performance. Programs that are based on political attachments would not be ruled out, but the recipients would know that something more than rhetoric or a U.N. vote is expected in return.

IV. FINANCIAL AND POLITICAL IMPLICATIONS

The bulk of Africa's development inevitably will be paid for by Africans through improved productivity and through the development of their own resources. But the program presented in this report has clear financial implications for donors, particularly for the United States. The cost to the United States of the steps we recommend would be some $2 billion a year over and above the $1 billion of official U.S. funds already devoted to Africa's long-term development. In addition, there are significant opportunities for the American private sector, including the non-profit sector, to contribute to Africa's long-term development.

The threefold increase of support recommended for the public sector may seem large, but it adds up to approximately $7.50 per African—or less than 1 per cent of the per-capita aid level that the United States currently extends to a single country, Israel, which receives $1000 for every one of its citizens, and just over 12 per cent of the current aid to Egypt, which receives $60 per capita.

Not all of this increase need come from new money. Reallocations within the current $15-billion aid program are possible, and use of past foreign aid loan repayments should be mandated.

11. *Repayments from past U.S. foreign aid loans should be used to help finance new initiatives for Africa.*

Added stability of funding for African development could be obtained by channeling repayments from past aid loans directly to the African development account rather than to the Treasury, as in current practice. Until about a decade ago, repayments from past foreign aid were earmarked for new aid programs. Under the arrangement proposed here, Congress would have to compensate Treasury for the payments, but funding for African development would gain in stability. The amount of such repayments from 11 economic programs is about $500 million per year and rising.

A major benefit of this recommendation is that it would permit the United States to demonstrate to Africans that it seriously contemplates a long-term commitment of funding for African reform and development.

12. The United States should triple the long-term U.S. finance going to Africa, through a combination of bilateral and multilateral programs, to reach a new level of $3 billion per year.

Commitment to establish larger and firmer aid programs for Africa also should be sought from other major donors. In this regard, it should be noted that the European states, in their recent Lomé III agreement with African, Pacific, and Caribbean nations, entered into a five-year commitment on aid, trade, and commodity prices, but without increasing aid levels. There is a great deal more that Europeans can do to provide additional support for African development. Japan has pledged to increase its total foreign aid to $40 billion over the next seven years. As part of a shift of its aid to more developmental purposes, Japan should significantly increase its aid program to Africa. While U.S. support along the lines suggested in this report will be essential to help Africa, it should be part of a program of help in which other major industrial countries do their share, too.

At the same time, the compact proposed here will require a willingness on the part of African countries to institute the kinds of changes that they have already agreed—among themselves and with donors—are necessary. African leaders must recognize that failure to follow agreed-upon policies will undermine, and perhaps make impossible, a significant and coordinated program of long-term assistance.

CONCLUSION

In calling for the Compact, we are suggesting that substantial new funds—some $3 billion per year, a tripling of the current level—be committed to long-term development in Africa. This will be seen as a difficult, if not impossible, feat for the United States at a time of budget stringency. It would be easier to settle for the current program of assistance, which is limited in scope and effect, whose sale to Congress and to the American public already presents a great challenge. But such is the magnitude of Africa's crisis that a much more ambitious and imaginative effort must be mounted. The problems facing Africa will only become more expensive later if they are not realistically addressed soon. It is far easier to rescue economies from further decline than it is to rebuild them from scratch.

America has an opportunity to use publicly supported bilateral and multilateral programs, together with its universities, foundations, corporations, and private voluntary organizations, to help Africa in a coherent, lasting way. We urge private groups to marshal their own resources and to advocate a greater public response. We urge Congress and the Executive Branch to act with forsight to express our country's long-term interests in an Africa that can both survive short-term crises and assume its place as a full participant in the world economy.

COMMENTS BY COMMITTEE MEMBERS

ELLIOT BERG:

The report properly stresses the desperate economic circumstances prevailing in much of Africa, but it paints an excessively bleak picture.

The report does not take adequate account of the fact that policy reform has been a major feature of donor policy for three years at least.

Africa needs plenty of aid money, especially in the next few years, but the report should say more about what it is to be used for. Food-for-work programs cannot absorb much. Agriculture can, but mostly in big dam projects, some of which are of dubious priority. Americans should be willing to spend more money on African aid, but they will want some indication that it will be spent productively, and not repeat the errors of past aid flows.

The report is far too negative about IMF stabilization programs, many of which have positive supply-side effects.

The report contrasts too sharply the "development" impacts of Development Assistance versus the Economic Support Fund. The argument that the aid relationship should be non-political is unrealistic, and if adopted would be counterproductive. Development performance should be one condition, but if it is to be given heavy weight, then why any aid to most African countries? The consequence would not only be a reallocation within the region, but probably less aid to Africa as well.

ROBERT S. BROWNE:

Recommendation 3: The implications of Africa's external debt, both for itself and for its creditors, are currently being examined in various fora. There are, however, clear indications that—even under the most optimistic of assumptions—the economies of several of the African countries may never be able to retire their international debt, and that the consequences of being obliged to attempt to do so may merely destroy these societies without reimbursing the creditors. Some European countries have already chosen to forgive a portion of their African debt, and the United States may well find it in its interest to follow suit. In any case, recommendation 3, by failing to recognize that non-payment is a possible option, is overly restrictive and could prove to be highly unrealistic as well. (Goler T. Butcher and Donald B. Easum wish to be associated with this comment.)

Recommendation 8: The thrust of the recommendation is commendable. Inasmuch as this is the only recommendation that mentions trade, however, it seems the appropriate place for a clear expression of disapproval of protectionism. The text that accompanies the recommendation is entirely too weak and implicitly accedes to a continuation of trade barriers in the very areas of major interest to some African countries. (Goler T. Butcher wishes to be associated with this comment.)

Recommendation 9: Although I vigorously support recommendation 9, I feel that Africa's regional development bank, The African Development Bank/African Development Fund (ADB/ADF), merits an equal measure of attention and support for its important work. The ADB/ADF is currently operating a $1-billion annual development program that is highly appreciated on the continent. Its work deserves to be better known in the donor community. Recommendation 9 should be amended to call for substantially enhanced funding for the forthcoming ADF replenishment. (Goler T. Butcher wishes to be associated with this comment.)

GOLER T. BUTCHER:

Recommendation 5: Regarding this recommendation, I believe that all aided projects in the agricultural sector should be oriented to help small farmers, particularly women.

FRANK C. CARLUCCI:

I agree with the need for substantially increased resources but believe that the precise amount can only be determined by more detailed analysis, including weighing African imperatives against other national priorities—a task which was obviously beyond the scope and capacity of the Committee.

SENATOR JOHN C. DANFORTH:

Recommendation 7: Although this recommendation does not imply support for abortion programs, I wish to be unambiguously clear that I could not support any association of U.S. funding for such activities in Africa or elsewhere.

CAROL LANCASTER:

It may be difficult for the United States to provide decisive support for African development alone. The U.S should actively explore ways to involve other donors as the Compact for African Development evolves.

NOTE

1. The Committee has not addressed the extremely complex questions involved in South Africa in this report. In its first twenty-five years of independence, Africa has been concerned with decolonization and development. Decolonization is all but complete, except in Namibia.

In South Africa, the internal disparities dictated by *apartheid*, the rigid and abhorrent system of racial separation, and the likelihoodof continuing unrest and upheaval threaten to undo economic progress for all races, guaranteeing political and social chaos.

Both Namibian independence and *apartheid* remain major concerns of African countries on their merits. These unresolved issues directly affect the economic development of the other countries of southern Africa that sometimes host South Africans opposed to *apartheid*. South Africa's continuing destabilization of its neighbors and the presence of large refugee populations have led to a diversion of resources and to some destruction of already meager infrastructure.

Notes on Contributors

ROBERT J. BERG is co-director, Committee on African Development Strategies, and Senior Fellow, Overseas Development Council.

DAVID COURT is Regional Representative, The Rockefeller Foundation, Nairobi.

CARL K. EICHER is Professor of Argicultural Economics, Michigan State University.

JANE I. GUYER is Associate Professor of Anthropology, Harvard University.

BENJAMIN H. HARDY is Vice President, Equator Holdings Limited.

CHANDRA S. HARDY is Senior Economist, Eastern and Southern Africa Programs, The World Bank.

A.M. HAWKINS is Dean of the Faculty of Commerce and Law, University of Zimbabwe.

NILES E. HELMBOLDT is President and Chief Executive Officer, Equator Holdings Limited.

GORAN HYDEN is Visiting Fellow, Department of Government, Dartmouth College.

BRUCE F. JOHNSTON is Professor of Agricultural Economics, Food Research Institute, Stanford University.

KENNETH KING is Senior Fellow, Centre of African Studies, Edinburgh University.

KABIRU KINYANJUI is Director, Institute of Development Studies, Nairobi University.

DAVID K. LEONARD is Associate Professor of Public Administration, University of California, Berkeley.

STEPHEN R. LEWIS, JR., is Chairman, Department of Economics, Williams College.

CARL LIEDHOLM is Professor of Economics, Michigan State University.

DONALD C. MEAD is Professor of Agricultural Economics, Michigan State University.

BENNO J. NDULU is Professor of Economics, University of Dar es Salaam.

FRED T. SAI, M.D., is Senior Population Adviser, The World Bank.

DUNSTAN S.C. SPENCER is Principal Economist, International Crops Research Institute for the Semi-Arid Tropics, Sahelian Center, Niger.

LLOYD TIMBERLAKE is Editorial Director, Earthscan, International Institute for Environment and Development, London.

TINA WEST is consultant to Equator Holdings Limited.

JENNIFER SEYMOUR WHITAKER is co-director, Committee on African Development Strategies, and Senior Fellow, Council on Foreign Relations.

CRAWFORD YOUNG is Chairman, Department of Political Science, University of Wisconsin.

Index

Abaelu, John, 220
Abidjan, 267, 396
Abortion, 149
Absorptive capacity, 263–264
Accelerated Development in Sub-Saharan Africa: An Agenda for Action, 3, 513
Accelerated Food Production, 251
Accra, 148
Adam, Michel, 410
Adams, Dale, 192, 193
Adelman, Irma, 287
Adult education, 362
Africa: African solutions for, 53; aid to, 44; and balance of payment deficits, 3; causes of malaise of, 10, 16; debt burden of, 44; deficit financing and, 3; development policies for, 1, 3, 53; dilemmas of, 1; diversity of sub-Saharan, 2; drought in, 2; economic crisis of, 1–3; economic development of, 52–77; economic management in, 81–104; economy of affection in, 57–63; expenditures in, 42–43; external environment in, 3; flight of capital from, 3; foreign exchange reserves of, 3; governance, 81–104; growth of, during the 1960s, 2; at independence, 2; low levels of technology in, 63; optimism regarding, 25; pessimism regarding, 25; policy implications for, 47–49; policy reforms for, 99; political instability in, 2; population of, 124; population growth in, 2; problems

of, 2, 3, 47–49; renewable resources of, 111–128; size of, 2; social structure of, 52–77; socialism and, 46; *See also* Agricultural institutions; Agricultural research; Agriculture, in Africa; Debt, in Africa; Donor countries; Economic development, in Africa; Economic management, in Africa; Education, in Africa; Foreign aid, in Africa; Governance, in Africa; Government strategies for agricultural development; Industrialization, in Africa; Investment, in Africa; Managing African Economics; People, the, and the land of Africa; Population; Poverty and Hunger in Africa; Small-scale industry; Social structure and the economic development in Africa; Trade; Women
African bloc, 40
African Development Bank (ADB), 254, 284, 300, 301
African Development Foundation, 354
African Development Strategies: Committee on, 1, 19–21; governmental, for agriculture, 155–183;
African governments: and authoritarian state model, 4, 8; and confused goals, 8; and economic development, 162–163, 172, 297, 301, 331, 335, 343, 349, 353; and education, 2, 381–383; and external shocks, 10, 14; and health care systems, 2; at inde-

589

Compositor: The Seven Graphic Arts, New York
Printer: Vail-Ballou Press
Binder: Vail-Ballou Press
Display: Palatino
Text: 10/13 Palatino

CALIFORNIA UNDER SPAIN
AND MEXICO

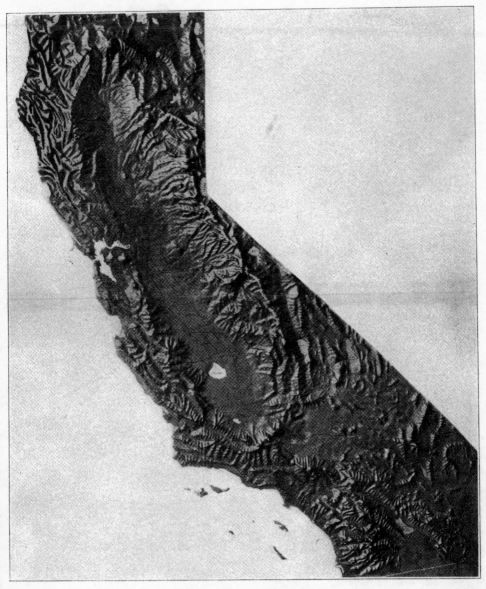

I. RELIEF MAP OF CALIFORNIA

CALIFORNIA UNDER SPAIN AND MEXICO

1535-1847

A CONTRIBUTION TOWARD THE HISTORY OF THE
PACIFIC COAST OF THE UNITED STATES, BASED
ON ORIGINAL SOURCES (CHIEFLY MANU-
SCRIPT) IN THE SPANISH AND
MEXICAN ARCHIVES AND
OTHER REPOSITORIES

BY

IRVING BERDINE RICHMAN

WITH MAPS, CHARTS, AND PLANS

COOPER SQUARE PUBLISHERS, INC.
NEW YORK
1965

Published 1965 by
Cooper Square Publishers, Inc.
59 Fourth Avenue, New York, N.Y. 10003

Library of Congress Catalog Card Number: 65-22549

Printed in the United States of America

PREFACE

THE present book, fruit of two years' investigation in California and of much research elsewhere, is designed both for the general reader and for the special student. Its object, first, is to provide, from the original sources, a readable yet concise narrative of the history of California under Spain and Mexico (1535–1847), and second, to equip the narrative with a sufficient apparatus of citation and criticism.

The Atlantic Coast of North America has been dealt with in works elaborate and minute. The Pacific Coast, on the contrary, is as yet nearly a virgin field, few critical monographs having been devoted to it. The consequence is that in this field it is necessary for the historical writer to use the sources directly; and these sources are almost wholly manuscript.

They are contained in two principal repositories, — the National Archives of Spain at Madrid and Sevilla, and the Central Archives of Mexico in Mexico City. For documents pertaining to navigation and exploration, the supreme repository is the General Archives of the Indies at Sevilla, and for documents pertaining to internal administration, the Archivo General, the Museo, and the Biblioteca Nacional of Mexico. In the case of the Spanish Archives, the writer has had the benefit of a tabulation of California materials prepared at Sevilla in 1910, at the instance of Dr. Francis S. Philbrick of the University of Nebraska, and Dr. H. Morse Stephens of the University of California. In the case of the Mexican Archives, he has had the benefit of a systematic search conducted in 1907 and 1908, through the courtesy of the Carnegie Institution of Washington, by Dr. Herbert E. Bolton (now) of Leland Stanford University. Over three thousand index cards to documents bearing upon California were made by Dr. Bolton, and of the documents themselves the most important were copied in full.

Some manuscript material (copies) has been gathered from the British Archives (Public Record Office), through the courtesy of Dr. Ephraim D. Adams of Leland Stanford University, and much from national and private collections in the United States. The Library of Congress (Lowery Collection, New Mexico Documents, and Map Division) has proved rich in the extreme; and the same may be said of the Library of Harvard University (Sparks Collection), of the Lenox Library (Rich Collection), and of the Edward E. Ayer Collection in the Newberry Library in Chicago.

With regard to the collection gathered by Mr. Hubert Howe Bancroft of San Francisco, and now the property of the University of California, there is need of a special word. This unique mass of material affects not alone the history of California, but that of Louisiana, Texas, New Mexico, Arizona, Utah, Washington, Oregon, Old Mexico, Central America, and the Hawaiian Islands. For California its chief sources are: (1) Copies (largely abridged) of the early Spanish Archives of the state, in 69 volumes; (2) the Vallejo Collection of twenty thousand original letters and papers, in 36 volumes; (3) the Thomas O. Larkin private correspondence, in 9 volumes, and correspondence as United States Consul at Monterey, in 2 volumes; (4) the private papers of prominent Californians, such as José de la Guerra of Santa Bárbara, Manuel Castro of Monterey, Juan Bandini, José Ramón Pico and the Estudillos of San Diego, and others; (5) copies of Mission records and papers,

the most extensive being the records of Santa Bárbara, in
12 volumes, and of the California Archbishopric, in 5 volumes; (6) copies of diaries of northern navigation (*Viajes
al Norte*), copies of diaries and of miscellaneous documents
gathered by M. Alphonse Pinart, under the title, *Papelas
Varios*, the Mayer manuscripts (copies), and manuscript
translations of the histories and papers of the Russian-
American Company.

The serviceability of the Bancroft Collection, so far at
least as California is concerned, is in a measure impaired
by the circumstance that Mr. Bancroft and his corps of
assistants used it well-nigh to exhaustion. Within the
range of its materials, not much can be added to what
the Bancroft History itself discloses; yet, despite size and
value, the collection is limited in range and unsymmet-
rical in character. Neither by himself, nor through others,
did Mr. Bancroft make any examination of foreign
archives, — Mexican, Spanish, or British; and but little
examination of foreign private manuscript collections or of
domestic collections outside of California. For the period
of early voyages and exploration in the Pacific, and of the
occupation of California (1535–1770), the collection is very
incomplete; and for subsequent periods it lacks, in whole or
in part, many sets of documents of the first importance.
These *lacunæ*, it is but just to observe, are better known
to the curator of the collection than to any one else, and
are being rapidly overcome by the addition of transcripts
from the archives of Spain.

In the present book, the new materials for California
history — those gleaned by the writer from foreign
sources, and from home sources other than the Bancroft
Collection, and such as have been gleaned by a careful re-
examination of the Bancroft Collection itself — are in the
case of each chapter listed and cited in notes at the end

of the volume. Many of the most valuable sources used in the Bancroft History are cited in it as "MS." These sources, when cited in the notes, are assigned by volume and page to their place in the Bancroft Collection.

Attention is directed not alone to the text and notes, but to the accompanying maps, a list of which follows the table of contents. The map and the diagram ("Spanish and American Trails of the Southwest affecting California," and "Secularization in Alta California") and the chart of galleon routes in the Pacific have been prepared by special hands under the direction of the writer.

It has been said that by reason of the virgin character of the field, and of the lack therein of critical monographs, a writer upon Pacific Coast history is compelled to use his materials directly. Scattered as these are throughout the archives and collections of Europe and America, the task is not inconsiderable, for while much rewards him, much eludes his quest.

For services many and unwearied, the writer would express hearty acknowledgment to Miss Anna M. Beckley, head of the reference department of the Public Library of Los Ángeles. He is also especially indebted to Miss Nellie M. Russ, librarian of the Pasadena Public Library, and to Miss Eudora Garoutte, head of the historical department of the California State Library at Sacramento. Others who have rendered aid are Dr. James A. Robertson of the Philippines Libraries, Manila, P. I., Dr. James R. Robertson of Berea College, Kentucky (author of the as yet unprinted monograph, "From Alcalde to Mayor"), Miss Emma Helen Blair of Madison, Wisconsin (co-editor, with Dr. James A. Robertson, of the "Philippine Islands" series), Mr. Zoeth S. Eldredge of San Francisco (author of studies of the Anza routes), Fr. Zephyrin Engelhardt, O. F. M., of Santa Bárbara, Mr. A. S. Macdonald of

Oakland, Mr. Charles F. Lummis and Mr. George L. Lawson of Los Ángeles, Mr. Frederick J. Teggart, curator of the Bancroft Collection, Mr. George Parker Winship, librarian of the John Carter Brown Library, Providence, Rhode Island, Mr. Reuben G. Thwaites of the Wisconsin Historical Society, Miss Ernestina López of San Gabriel, Mr. Byron Olney Lovelace, head ranger of the San Jacinto Forest Reserve, and the librarian and staff of the Public Library of Muscatine, Iowa.

I. B. R.

Muscatine, Iowa, March 1, 1911.

CONTENTS

CONTENTS

LIST OF MAPS, CHARTS, AND PLANS

MAP II. INDIANS OF CALIFORNIA BY LINGUISTIC GROUPS

CALIFORNIA UNDER SPAIN
AND MEXICO

**Persistence of the Idea of North America
as a Group of Islands:
In two Plates, 1502 - 1622.
Plate II, 1529 - 1622**

Verrazzano Map (1529). Type of Map-Group
including Maiollo Map (1527) and Agnese Map (1536).

Gastaldi Map (1554). Type of Small Map-Group
including Lok Map of 1582.

Kaspar van Baerle (Herrera) Map (1622). Type of Map-Group
possessing many Representatives Down to 1746.

Alaska as an Island.
J. von Staehling Map, 1768.

JAPAN

JAPAN

JAPAN

BACALAR
(Labrador)

FLORIDA

ISABELLA
(Hispaniola)

CUBA

**Persistence of the Idea of North America
as a Group of Islands:
In two Plates, 1502 - 1622.
Plate I, 1502 - 1514**

Da Vinci Map (1514).
Type of Map-Group A.
{ Cantino Map, 1502
Ruysch Map, 1508
Lenox Globe, 1508, 1511
Sylvanus Map, 1511

Nordenskiöld Gores
(1511-1515).
Type of Map-Group B.
{ Waldseemüller Map, 1507
"Tross Gores," 1515-1518
Schöner Globes, 1515,1520
Frankfort Globe, 1520
Münster Map, 1532

Stobnicza Map (1512).
Type of Map-Group C.
{ Admirals' Map, 1513
Reisch Map, 1515

CALIFORNIA UNDER SPAIN AND MEXICO

CHAPTER I

DISCOVERY

THE discovery of California — Lower and Upper (Baja and Alta) — was a result of the idea that North America constituted a group of islands — an archipelago — near the coast of Asia, screening the latter with its silks and porcelains from European observation and approach.[1]

Of this idea, sixteenth-century cartography from 1501 to 1520 shows in numerous instances the prevalence and persistence. In the Ruysch map of 1508, "Spagnola" is represented as off the coast of "Tebet Magni"; in the Sylvanus map of 1511, Cuba, Hayti, and Labrador not only lie off the Asiatic coast, but are near one another; in the Da Vinci map of (circa) 1514, the group of islands consists of Cuba, Labrador, and Florida; while on the Nordenskiöld Gores of 1511–15 and the Schöner globes of 1515 and 1520, Cuba forms a group with Japan. And when, for certain regions, the idea in question had to be abandoned, cartography shows that it was abandoned reluctantly. The areas that once had been islands now were joined, but by bands tentative and easily to be sundered. On the Ptolemic map of 1530 and the Ruscelli map of 1544, Labrador and Florida are united by a slender isthmus, an isthmus that in the Münster map of 1545 significantly gives place to a strait bearing the legend: *Per hoc fretu iter patet ad Molucas.* It is true that in the Castillo map of 1541, and other maps down to 1622, California is set down as peninsular, but in a whole series of maps dated between 1622 and 1746 the peninsula is replaced by an island.[2]

North America, then, while a barrier to Asia, was a barrier to be penetrated, and by the close of the first quarter of the sixteenth century various attempts to this end had been made: by John Cabot in 1497; by Gaspar and Miguel Cortereal in 1500–02; by Giovanni da Verrazzano in 1524. But the only attempt that thus far could in any wise be accounted successful was by Fernão de Magalhães (Magellan) in 1520, and it was by way, not of North America, but of the continent to the south.

The fact, however, that one strait from sea to sea had unquestionably at last been found, stimulated search for another, and among those most ardent in this search was Hernán Cortés. In his *Carta Cuarta* (Fourth Dispatch) to Charles V, dated October 15, 1524, Cortés ventures the opinion that a strait will be discovered "on the Florida [Atlantic] Coast, running into the South Sea [Pacific]"; and that "if found according to a true chart [which he has] of that part of the sea near the archipelago which Magellan discovered, it seems that it [the strait] must issue very near there [the archipelago]. . . . If," he continues, "it please our Lord that the said strait joins there, the voyage to the Spice Islands will be so convenient for these your Majesty's dominions that it will be two thirds shorter than the present course,[3] and without any hazard to the ships in going or coming; for the voyage will be entirely among states and countries [large and rich] belonging to your Majesty. Therefore," concludes Cortés, "acquainted as I am with your Majesty's desire of knowing this strait, . . . I have laid aside all other profits and advantages . . . in order to follow entirely this course." [4]

And follow it the Spanish leader did with characteristic determination. In 1526 he made ready to send a fleet from Zacatula, but was prevented by a royal order diverting the vessels to the relief of the missing navigator Jofre de Loaysa. In 1532 he did send (from Acapulco) Diego Hurtado de Mendoza and Juan de Mazuela with two ships; and in 1533 (from Tehuantepec), Diego Bezerra de Mendoza and Hernando de Grijalva with two ships. By the first expedition nothing of importance was accomplished; but by the second, — or rather by Bezerra's ship, after the latter through a mutiny had passed under the control of Fortuno Ximénes, chief pilot, — Lower California was discovered at Santa Cruz Bay.

Here was something tangible both towards "large and rich countries" (the bay was reputed rich in pearls) and towards new islands and straits (the spot was reached by sailing away from the mainland), and Cortés resolved to inspect it personally. He set forth in 1535, and on May 3 anchored at Santa Cruz (La Paz). It was while here, between 1535 and 1537, endeavoring to found a colony, that the Spanish leader, according to the historian Herrera, called the waste about him California; and that, according to Bernal Díaz, he and his island (*su isla*) were heartily cursed by his followers, — a starving band.[5]

Cortés in 1540 returned to Spain, but meanwhile (1539) one of his captains at La Paz (Francisco de Ulloa) explored the Gulf of California to the mouth of the Colorado River, proving as conclusively as ineffectually that California was not an island.[6] Meanwhile, also, Don Antonio de Mendoza, Viceroy of New Spain, and Pedro de Alvarado, Governor of Guatemala, allured by a fabulous tale of treas-

ure to the northwest, — the tale of the Seven Cities of
Cibola, — prepared, each, an expedition to fare in quest
of it, — the Coronado-Alarcón expedition of Mendoza, and
the so-called Navidad expedition of Alvarado. By the one,
or rather the Alarcón part of it, the Gulf of California
(Domingo del Castillo, *piloto*) was reëxplored and its shores
charted.[7] By the other there was brought to notice the
Portuguese navigator, Juan Rodríguez Cabrillo.

It is to Cabrillo that the discovery and exploration of the
California of to-day — the California that forms a part of
the American Union — was due. This captain had been
hired by Alvarado for his projected expedition to the north,
and upon the death of the latter, which occurred in 1541,
Cabrillo was confirmed in employment by Mendoza. He
was intrusted with two small ships, — the San Salvador
and the Victoria, — and with them sailed from La Navidad
on June 27, 1542. On September 28 he came to anchor in
San Diego Bay, at the southwestern extremity of Upper or
Alta California, and on October 18 landed at San Miguel
Island. Here he had the misfortune to fall and break his
arm near the shoulder. On January 3, 1543, Cabrillo died
from the effects of his broken arm, at San Miguel, where
his ships had temporarily returned, and the command
devolved on Bartolomé Ferrelo, a native of the Levant.
Before expiring, Cabrillo had given orders that the work
of discovery was in nowise to be intermitted because of
him; and under Ferrelo it was carried (by March 1) as far
north as 42°, — the latitude of the boundary line, as later
established, between California and Oregon.

It will thus be seen that by the expedition under Juan
Rodríguez the entire coast line, or western boundary, of
Alta California was traversed. Nor was the task inade-
quately performed. The ships crept warily along from

point to point, anchoring at night and exploring by day.
So progressing, it was noted that just below San Diego the
bare, sandy land which had extended from "the extremity
of Lower California [Cape San Lucas] to this place," gave
way to "a country of beautiful vegetation"; that the
course of the ship was closely watched by the Indians, for
"great signal smokes were kindled on shore"; that, indeed,
Indians could be induced to come on board, and that they
spoke of "men like us traveling in the interior," — men
"with beards, and armed with cross-bows and swords, and
riding on horseback"; that lying off the coast were a number of large islands, — Las Islas de San Lucas, — the
islands of the Santa Bárbara Channel; that near Punta de
Arenas there were visible "grand sierras covered with
snow," and that northward from Cape San Martín "all the
coast is very bold with mountains that rise to the sky, and
against which the sea beats, and which appear as if they
would fall upon the ships," — La Sierra Nevada. It moreover was noted that around Cape Mendocino (not then
named) the winds were boisterous and the sea high, so
that, "coming from many parts and breaking over the
ships," it forced the seamen as good Spaniards and devout
Catholics to "commend themselves to our Lady of Guadalupe" and to "make their wills." [8]

By way of boundary for Alta California on the east,
naught in the sixteenth century existed, save, to the north,
mountains, and to the south, desert and the Colorado
River. Of these the mountains stood in a grandeur as yet
unlooked upon; while the desert and the river had been
scanned, the former by Friar Marcos and the followers of
Coronado, and the latter by Ulloa and Alarcón. Yet, undefined as the eastern boundary of necessity was, there lay
between it (in the course that one day it was to take) and

the Pacific a world of natural wonders, — wonders of topography, of climate, and of living things.

In the topographical domain came first the Coast Range,
extending from the present Oregon to Point Conception,
and attaining an elevation of between two thousand and
eight thousand feet. Below Point Conception this range
was broken by small, fertile valleys, drained seaward by
slender rivers. Above the Point, the range near its centre
gave way suddenly to the passage since known as the
Golden Gate; [9] while north of its centre it was pierced
by deep canyons conducting rivers that were turbulent
and swift. Next came the Sierra Nevada Range, mingling
with the Coast Range at the north, and then, after a sharp
divergence to the east, extending south for some four hundred miles, to mingle again with the latter at Tehachapi
and the heights of San Rafael, — a conjunction serving
later to demark Northern from Southern California.

The Sierra Nevada Range, steep on its eastern face,
comprehended the most imposing examples of North
American scenery. Two of its peaks (Whitney and Shasta)
peered sublimely down 14,522 and 14,440 feet. One of
its valleys (Death Valley) crouched 200 feet below sea
level. Its passes averaged 11,000 feet. One of its waterfalls (the Yosemite) plunged to a death in spray at 2600
feet. Its forests contained the largest and oldest of growing things on earth, — trees 300 feet high and over 30 feet
in diameter; trees between three thousand and five thousand years old, — older than the Spanish monarchy and
all Christendom; while from an altitude of 8000 feet, more
than a thousand lakes mirrored the clouds and flashed back
the sun.

Separating the Coast Range and that of the Sierra
Nevada, lay a great plain, four hundred miles long and
between thirty-five and sixty miles wide; [10] and this, from

the north and south respectively, was drained by two
partially navigable streams (the Sacramento and the San
Joaquín), which poured their combined waters into the
sheltered básin now known as San Francisco Bay. Nor
was this all, for, skirting the base of the Sierra Nevada,[11]
there stretched to the Colorado River miles upon miles of
alkaline desert, — desert sought valiantly to be reclaimed
by sentinel yucca and sprawling cactus, but everywhere
white, sun-tortured, and drear.

In respect to climate, Alta California presented that
diversity which might be looked for in a region extending
through nearly ten degrees of latitude, and composed of
seacoast, mountain, valley, and plain. A cold current
washed the coast as far south as Point Conception, — a
current attended by fogs and humidity; but below the
Point the coast was deflected sharply to the eastward.
This deflection gave to the southern part immunity from
cold on the west; while the Sierra Nevada on the northeast
was a great wall shielding that part from continental
rigors, and husbanding its sunshine.[12] Here in summer the
winds prevailed from the northwest, bringing drought; and
in winter from the southeast, bringing rain; and with the
rain came, first, greenness, and then, throughout all the
valleys and to the summits of the hills, a riotous proces-
sion of the flowers, — golden poppies, buttercups, daisies,
pinks, nemophilas, roses, violets, larkspurs, and lilies;
purple pressing hard upon gold; blue upon purple; and
pink and white upon blue.[13] The land, withal, at least
in the coast valleys, was vexed by no violent storms of
thunder and lightning, though there were not infrequent
shocks of earthquake.

Last of the wonders mentioned as embraced within the
limits of California at the time of the discovery were living
things; and these were as varied as the topography and the

climate. Along the coast might be found the whale, the
sea-otter, and the seal; in the mountains, the grizzly and
the brown bear, the puma, the wildcat, and the mountain
sheep; in the forests and opens, the elk, the black-tailed
deer, and the antelope. The thickets and streams swarmed
with grouse, geese, and ducks. The air harbored the
eagle, the vulture, song-birds, butterflies, and bees. On
the desert, lending in a literal sense piquancy to the sands,
there lurked the rattlesnake, the gila monster, the scor-
pion, and the tarantula.

Man alone among the sentient orders seemed inferior
in his rôle. The California Indian — he of the typical
eighteen small tribes of central California (and excepting
always the Athapascán of the extreme northwest, the
Shoshone and Yuma of the southeast, and the Chumash
of the Santa Bárbara Channel coasts) [14] — was short in
stature, dark of color, flat of nose, filthy in habit, a laggard
in war, and a poor hunter. He dwelt near the water-
courses in villages (rancherías) of dome-shaped huts of
reeds, fed upon acorns and seeds, and painted his body.
His female was skilled in mats and basketry; but male or
female he, ethnically considered, was so far inchoate as
to be without the totem, without clan organization. His
religion, too (as discriminated from his philosophy), was
Shamanism, — wizardism; a religion rendering him a facile
dupe to the conjurations of the medicine man. In temper
he was docile, and he eschewed the tomahawk, the taking
of scalps, and the torture of prisoners; yet, for these very
reasons, when compared on the one hand with the Iroquois
or Dakota of the north, or on the other with the Apache,
Navajo, Mojave, or Yuma of the south, he revealed a
paucity of vigor — physical, mental, and spiritual — that
was palpable. [15]

But concerning Alta California from the point of view of

its natural wonders, for the present enough. It has been the object of this chapter to show how the early Spaniards in North America, partakers of the spirit of Spain under Charles V, were led in their quest (on the course to Asia) for golden isles and treasured cities, to explore the western, and in part the eastern confines of the California region. It will be the object of the next chapter to relate how this region came to be visited with a view to its permanent occupation.

CHAPTER II

THE discovery by Magellan (1521) of an archipelago near China (the Philippine Islands) effectually disposed of the theory that North America was merely a group of outposts to Asia; but room was left for the belief that the land, though a continent, was traversed by an interoceanic strait, later called Anian,[1] connecting the Gulf of St. Lawrence with the North Pacific Ocean.

If such a strait existed, the fact was important to Spain, for by means of a passage the sea route from Spain to Asia would, as Cortés himself was to point out, be vastly shortened. Spain, however, having at last finished the work of Columbus and discovered the "Western Islands" (the Philippines), was for the moment too deeply engrossed in seeking to confirm her conquest, to bestow much thought upon Anian; a mental state which in the somewhat curious course of its working-out gave rise to a first attempt to occupy Upper California.

Magellan's expedition came to an end with the return to Spain, in 1522, of one ship, the Victoria. In 1525 García Jofre de Loaysa was sent to continue the work of Magellan, but his ships met with disaster. In 1526 Sebastian Cabot was sent on a like errand, but he got no farther than the coast of South America at the mouth of the Río de la Plata. Hereupon (1526) Cortés, who had been diligently building ships with which to discover "rich countries" (insular, Amazonian, or what not), together with that strait which he was convinced issued "very near" Magellan's archipelago, was directed by Charles V to send ships

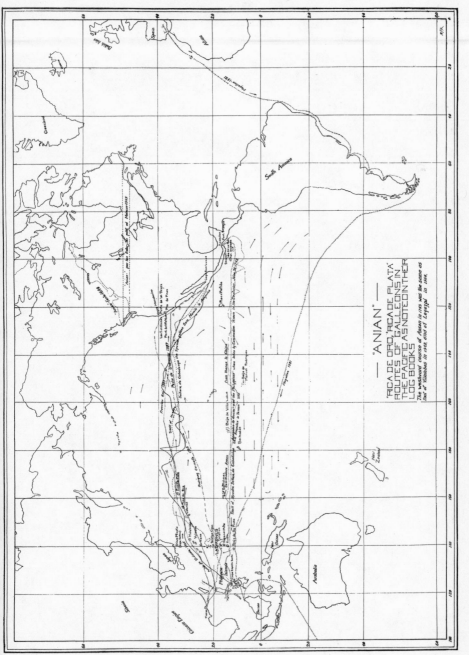

— "ANIAN" —

"RICA DE ORO", "RICA DE PLATA"
ROUTES OF GALLEONS IN
THE PACIFIC AS NOTED IN THEIR
LOG BOOKS

The westward course of Anian in 1743 was the same as
that of Villalobos in 1542 and of Legaspi in 1564.

CHART I

to glean news of Loavsa and Cabot. This expedition (under Álvaro de Saavedra) was no more successful than had been its predecessors, and so matters remained until 1542. By that time Coronado and Alarcón, by fruitless journeyings northward, had destroyed Spanish faith in the "Seven Cities," and shaken it in Anian. When, therefore, upon Alvarado's death, it fell to the lot of Mendoza to take entire command, he sent (under Cabrillo) only two ships to survey the California coast; while, under Ruy López de Villalobos, he sent six across the Pacific to "note the products of the Western Islands." Villalobos set sail in November, and on reaching the Western Islands, so called, rechristened them Las Philippinas. Otherwise he effected nothing lasting.[2]

Then came 1556. In that year Charles V abdicated his throne, kingly and imperial, and Philip II, so far as in him lay, succeeded to the kingly part. To this time the Moriscos (Christianized descendants of the Moors, and ever in Spain the most valued element industrially) had carried on in comparative peace their varied vocations. In the Alpujarras, southeast of Granada, they cultivated the fig, the pomegranate, and the orange, as also hemp and the cereals. Here was grown the mulberry for its silk; and here, in the valleys and alpine pastures, were herded great flocks of merino sheep for their wool. Through the Moriscos, the cities of Spain (Córdova, Toledo, Segovia, Sevilla, Valencia, Valladolid, Granada) were become centres of manufactures and of trade. Córdova was famed for its leather, and Toledo for its blades. As late as 1552 Segovia employed thirteen thousand men (mostly Moriscos) in the woolen manufacture; and after Philip's accession a like number were employed in Sevilla in operating her sixteen thousand looms for wool and silk.[3]

For the products named, and for others, an important

outlet was New Spain. Ever since Cortés in 1519 had established in Mexico the port of Vera Cruz, supplies of all kinds — food, wine, clothing, implements, accoutrements, arms — had annually been sent hither and exchanged for the precious metals. And the cargoes had constantly become greater. The stock of gold rifled by Spain from the Indians had not lasted long,[4] but with the discovery in 1545 of the Peruvian silver-mines of Potosí, and in 1548 of the Mexican mine of Zacatecas, — the former the *raison d'être* for the Panama town of Porto Bello, — silver bullion to the amount of 11,000,000 *pesos* per annum[5] had in considerable part been available to colonial Spaniards for the purchase of those silks, velvets, laces, ribbons, buttons, and gewgaws, which, originally the habit and fancy of the hated Moor, had now become indispensable to the Spaniard himself.

But under Philip II not alone in the Atlantic did commerce thrive between Spain and the New World. It came into existence in the Pacific. At last the Philippine Islands were beginning to pay tribute. In 1564 — twenty-two years after the fruitless expedition of Villalobos — Miguel López de Legazpi was commissioned by Luis de Velasco, successor in the viceroyalty to Mendoza, to subdue the Philippines, and in seven years he performed the task of founding Manila and of establishing trade with Mexico.[6] Little was discovered in the islands that could with advantage be sent to New Spain, but China, Molucca, and Siam were near, and soon the luxurious taste of the conquerors drew from these flowery realms a multitude of costly products: from China, raw silk and velvets, "brocades of gold and silver upon silk," "stuffs of all colors," musk, ivory, cushions, carpets, "caparisons for horses," "preserves of oranges and peaches," "very fine capons," nutmegs, ginger, nuts, "fine thread," writing-boxes, "gilt seats," "caged birds which talk and sing," beads, precious stones, and porcelain; while from Japan were derived "smart screens," cutlery, caskets of wood, and wheaten flour; from Molucca, cotton cloths, muslins, cloves, cinnamon, pepper, amber, "rich hangings and coverlets," jewels, needlework, and lace; and from Siam, ivory, rhinoceros horns, rubies, and sapphires. "Of these goods," says Antonio de Morga (secretary to the governor of the Philippines from 1595 to 1603), "the Spaniards made purchases and shipments for New Spain." In the new moon of March the islands were visited by squadrons of Chinese junks. Late in June a ship, or two ships (at first small, afterwards of galleon size), laden with wares brought by the junks, and with native cinnamon and wax, set sail for Mexico.[7] In the autumn they reached the port of Acapulco, and straightway there was held a thirty days' market.[8]

This, however, was subsequent to 1573. Prior to that year the voyages had not been distinctively commercial. The main object of them had been to find, from Manila eastward, a safe and convenient route. Passing by the north equatorial current readily westward from Acapulco, navigators down to 1565 (Saavedra and Villalobos) had not been able to reverse the process.[9]

The first to trace back a route from Asia were Alonso de Arellano (one of Legazpi's captains) and Andrés de Urdaneta, an Augustinian friar, Legazpi's pilot.[10] Their course, in order to gain a wind, was laid (June, 1565) to the northward of that of Legazpi; and therein they were followed by navigators for twenty years. But the winds upon the new course proved often baffling, and in 1584 Francisco de Gali, under orders from Viceroy Contreras to discover a better course, laid one yet farther north, thereby haply striking the great Japan current, — "a very hollow water and stream running out of the north and northwest," — which carried him "seven hundred leagues," or to within "two hundred leagues" of the coast of Alta California off Cape Mendocino: a point sighted, though not named, by Ferrelo; a point which it is possible that Urdaneta or Gali did name; one from which, in any event, Gali made his way down the California coast to Cape San Lucas and Acapulco.[11]

Gali's route was that afterwards regularly taken by galleons from the Philippines,[12] but important as it was, the voyage was of inordinate length, sometimes 204 days. It was beset by the harassments of vermin, dysentery, beriberi, and scurvy; and, near Cape Mendocino, by those of cold, fogs, and tempests,[13] — conditions which made this cape one as much to be dreaded as formerly had been Bojador on the coast of Africa. Indeed, so formidable to sixteenth-century craft was the Alta California coast along its upper stretches, that in 1595 the galleon San Augustín, pursuing explorations under Sebastián Rodríguez Cermeño, was driven behind Point Reyes into a bay called by Cermeño San Francisco, and wrecked.[14] Still the perils of the California landfall and the distresses of the Manila-Acapulco passage were not without compensation, for they prompted Philip of Spain to reflect upon Alta California as a region (because of probable bays of refuge) first to be carefully surveyed, and then permanently occupied.

But to reflection upon Alta California Philip was prompted by yet another consideration.

A revival of interest in Anian had begun. In 1542 Ferrelo had mistaken the drift from the mouth of some river (not impossibly the Columbia) for a discharge from Anian, and in 1561 Urdaneta, inditing a memorial to the King, had asked what there might be in the rumor that the French had discovered a westward route "between the land of the Baccalos [Labrador] and the land north of it."

Furthermore, in 1584 Gali had thought the deflection of the Japan current, near the California coast, an indication of a "channell or straight passage betweene the firme lande of Newe Spaine and the countreys of Asia and Tartaria." The queries of Ferrelo and Urdaneta (now that Spain was in the Philippines, — now that the East had actually been gained by sailing west) may be regarded as stimulated by the belief that, as all nature abhorred a vacuum, so equally all nature "cried aloud for a Northwest Passage"; but not so the query of Francisco de Gali. Behind it lay a fact of far-reaching import.

England, under Elizabeth, was attaining to national self-confidence upon the sea. In 1545 the tonnage of the island, according to the seventeenth-century London merchant, Sir Joshua Child, "had been inconsiderable, and the merchants very mean and few." But, after 1560, owing to the effect, in combination, of an economic dislocation of classes and of the allurements of Spanish treasure, English maritime activity had risen rapidly. In 1562 John Hawkins of Devonshire, by a slaving voyage, had "opened the road to the West Indies." In 1572 Francis Drake (Hawkins's kinsman) had surprised a Spanish caravan on its way from Panama to Nombre de Dios, and carried away gold, jewels, and silver bars. In 1578–79 the same Francis Drake had passed the Strait of Magellan, sailed up the South American coast, captured vessels little and big, including a Philippine galleon, and stowed the hold of his own ship, the Golden Hind, with silver bars "the bignes of a brick-bat eche." The adventurous Englishman had sought a route homeward by the Northwest Passage, but, failing to find it "where the north and northwest winds send abroad their frozen nimphes to the infecting the whole aire with insufferable sharpnesse," had run down the coast of California, called by him New Albion, to

Francis Drake's Bay (the San Francisco Bay of Cermeño),[15] overhauled there his ship, and reached Plymouth by way of the Cape of Good Hope in 1580.

Although Drake had not found Anian, the fact of his appearance in the Pacific at the sources of Spanish wealth (Peru and Mexico) was startling to thoughtful Spaniards. The English seaman had got safe home with half a million of treasure. What might not happen if Anian not only should be found, but be found by the English? As if to meet this reflection, Urdaneta's query of 1561 and Gali's of 1584 were revived in 1586. In that year a memorial to Philip II was prepared and signed by the members of the Royal Audiencia of the Philippine Islands, voicing, among other recommendations, this: That China be immediately occupied by Spain in order to "forestall the danger that the French and English and other heretics and northern nations will discover and navigate that strait which certainly lies opposite those regions, — that of Labrador, as those people say." [16]

Not yet, however, was Philip sufficiently roused with regard to Anian to give specific orders for the occupation of Alta California, the land (supposedly) of its western outlet. A more drastic stimulus than a memorial was required, and this was supplied by the Englishman Thomas Cavendish. He set sail with three small ships from Plymouth, in 1586, and reached the Pacific in February, 1587. Having harried the coast of Mexico, he passed with two ships to Cape San Lucas, in October, and there lay in wait for the annual Philippine galleon. The galleon of 1587 was the Santa Ana, described by Domingo de Salazar, Bishop of the Philippines, as "the richest ship to leave these islands," — a ship laden with "a thousand *marcos* of registered gold" and as much unregistered; with "twenty-two and one half *arrobas* of musk, an abundance of civet, many

pearls, and the richest of silks and brocades." All this
merchandise, with the ship itself, fell into Cavendish's
hands after a fight of five hours. The prize was brought to
shore, and, the best of the cargo having been appropriated,
she was set on fire and left to her fate. Cavendish with
one ship, the Desire, returned home, as had Drake, by way
of the East Indies.[17]

Prior to the expedition of Drake, protection for the silver
ships from Mexico had, even in the Atlantic, not been
for Spain a serious problem; [18] and prior to the expedition
of Cavendish, protection for the Philippine galleons had
not even been thought of. It is true that after the return of
Hawkins from the West Indies in 1564, the dispatches
of De Silva (Spanish ambassador at London), recounting
Hawkins's proceedings, had wrung from Philip startled
interjections of "*Ojo! Ojo!*" But, down to 1587, so certain were the governors of the Philippines that naught of
evil could befall in the Pacific, that, as Santiago de Vera
wrote after the capture of the Santa Ana, "As no other
ships but ours have ever been sighted on this voyage,
which is through so remote regions, they have always
sailed with little or no artillery and with as little fear from
corsairs as if they were on the river of Sevilla." [19] Rude,
therefore, was the awakening by Cavendish; so rude that
surprise is hardly felt when Salazar complains to Philip
that "an English youth of but twenty-two years, with
a wretched little vessel and forty or fifty companions," has
wrought vast damage and got away "laughing."

Cavendish's voyage performed, the culmination of the
Anian question — the question of an interoceanic strait
capable of seizure by the English — was rapid. Interest,
between 1587 and 1592, led to the claim by various pilots
(Maldonado and Juan de Fuca) of having passed through
the strait. One memorial in particular invites attention.

It was prepared at Manila in 1597 by Hernando de Los Ríos Coronel, advocated a search for Anian, and in due time was placed in the hands of Philip.[20] But already (at last) that procrastinating ruler had been made alive to the reasons for the occupation of Alta California, — reasons alike of maritime need and colonial defense, — and had permitted to be sent northward Sebastián Vizcaino.

Of Vizcaino we hear first in 1593. In that year he, an humble trader, applied to Viceroy Luis de Velasco for permission to engage in the pearl-fishery in the Gulf of California. Accordingly in 1594 there was revived to him, with certain partners (Gonzalo Rodríguez Calvo, Mateo de Solís, Melchor de las Roclas, and others), a twenty-year *merced* (license) issued by the Archbishop of Mexico, on August 7, 1585, to another company (Hernando de Santotis and partners). Under the license, the company grantee might, on payment of the usual royalties, "fish for pearls, cod, sardines," etc., on the coast of the South Sea, "from la Navidad to California." The company was to choose one of its members as captain, and the latter was to take with him two padres of the Order of Jesus. At some point of the coast, island or mainland, a fort was to be constructed "whereby there could be defended the whole coast where the Englishman Don Tomás [Cavendish] had captured and robbed the ship Santa Ana from China." By Vizcaino's contract, which was to date from March 1, the privilege of the pearl-fishery was to continue, as originally specified, for four years, but thereafter it was to be limited to a district of ten leagues on the California coast to be designated by the company. In 1595 (August) additional concessions were sought, — the loan of a ship, and the privilege of holding in *encomienda* all natives converted to the Catholic faith, except one fifth to the Crown.[21] In

1595–96 ratification was obtained from the Conde de Monterey, successor to Velasco in the viceroyalty,[22] and in August, 1596, Vizcaino set sail. Owing to fierce northwest winds, he succeeded in doing little save effect a landing at the Santa Cruz of Cortés, — a spot which, from the docility of the natives, he rechristened La Paz.[23]

Vizcaino's first voyage, even as a private venture, had proved a failure; but in 1598 Philip II died, and was succeeded by his son Philip III. Searching among the papers of his late father, the third Philip came upon two documents. The first was a dispatch from the Conde de Monterey, dated the 26th of November, 1597, inclosing a memorial from Vizcaino, asking to be allowed to make a voyage with the object of exploring "the whole bight and gulf of Californias," the same to be taken possession of for the King, "turning over to the royal crown seaports, heads of departments, and cities, — all in a most quiet way, and without working any wrong to the natives." And the request was emphasized by the Viceroy, who reminded the King that with the loss of the San Agustín "the exploration of all the southern coast, which is of interest in connection with the ships from the Philippines . . . came to an end."[24] The second document was the memorial of Hernando de Los Ríos on the subject of Anian.

His imagination fired (especially by the Ríos document), the King carefully examined the latter in September, 1599, and in a fortnight a *cédula* was issued directing the Conde de Monterey to undertake yet again "a discovery and settlement in California"; a *cédula* whereof the Count took prompt advantage by commissioning Vizcaino captain-general for a second California voyage.[25]

"To-day, being Sunday the 5th of May, 1602," wrote the captain-general to the King, from Acapulco, "I sail at five o'clock, in the names of God and his Blessed Mother, for the discovery of the harbors and bays of the coast of the South Sea as far as Cape Mendocino." There were four vessels, two of them (the San Diego and the Santo Tomás) ships; the third (the Tres Reyes) a *barcolongo;* and the fourth (not named) a *lancha.* They carried two hundred picked men under Commander Toribio Gómez de Corván, Lieutenant Martín Aguilar and Chief Navigator Francisco de Bolaños. They carried also the friars (Carmelite) Andrés de la Asunción, Tomás de Aquino and Antonio de la Ascensión, and a cosmographer, Gerónimo Martín Palacios. After a severe battle of six months with northwest winds, and after passing and naming the Todos Santos and Coronados Islands, the expedition landed, November 10, in Cabrillo's harbor of San Miguel, — a harbor compared by Vizcaino to that of San Lúcar in Spain, and named by him San Diego in honor of his flagship.

Quitting this point on November 20, Santa Catalina, Santa Bárbara, and San Nicolás islands were sighted and named; the Santa Bárbara Channel (now for the first time, so called) was traversed; Point Conception, the Sierra de Santa Lucía, and Río Carmelo were named; and on December 16, Point Pinos having been rounded, anchor was cast in "a noble harbor," which in honor of the ruling Viceroy was called Monterey. Here (Mass first having been said by Ascensión under a spreading oak) Vizcaino lingered a fortnight. He took note of the region as convenient for the Philippine galleon, with its "infinite number of very large pines, straight and smooth, fit for masts and yards"; its "oaks of a prodigious size proper for building ships"; its *rosas de Castilla*, large clear lagoons, fine pastures and arable lands; and last, but by no means least, with its shell-fish, its sea-fowl, its huge bears, its horned mountain sheep, and its good-natured, "well-looking and affable people."

Having dispatched the Santo Tomás to Acapulco with

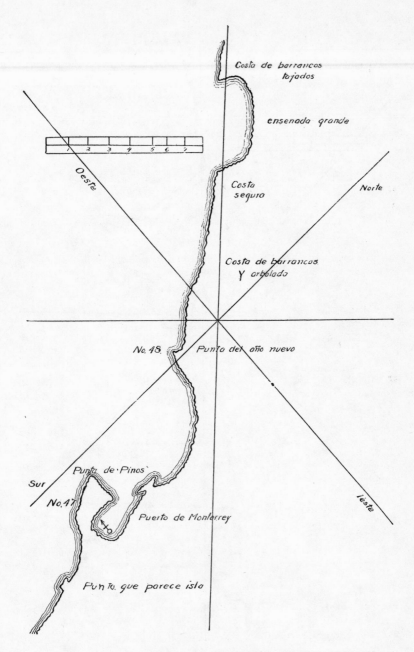

Costa de barrancos
tajados

ensenada grande

Costa
segura

Norte

Oeste

Costa de barrancos
y arbolada

No. 48.   Punta del año nuevo

Punta de Pinos

Sur

No. 47

Puerto de Monterrey

Ieste

Punta que parece isla

CHART II, PLATE 1. PORT OF MONTEREY. BY VIZCAINO, 1603
(*Hitherto unreproduced*)

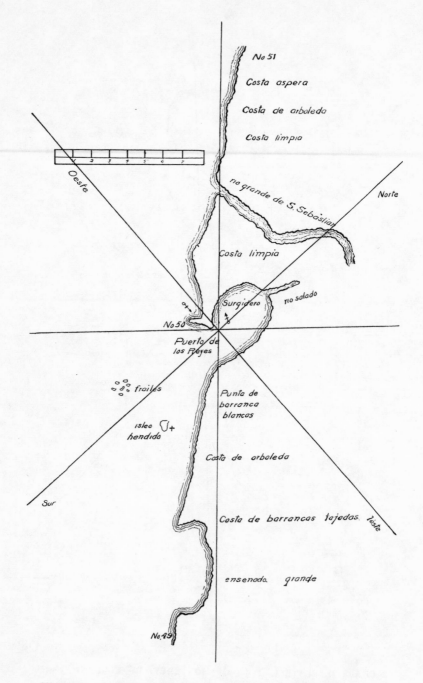

No 51

Costa aspera

Costa de arboleda

Costa limpia

rio grande de S. Sebastian

Norte

Oeste

Costa limpia

Surgidero   rio salado

No 50

Puerto de
los Reyes

frailes

Punta de
barranca
blancas

isleo
hendido

Costa de arboleda

Sur

Costa de barrancas tajadas.   Ieste

ensenada grande

No 49

CHART II, PLATE 2. SAN FRANCISCO BAY OF CERMEÑO (PUERTO
DE LOS REYES). BY VIZCAINO, 1603

(*Hitherto unreproduced*)

his sick, the captain-general on January 3, 1603, continued his voyage northward. About January 7, he, with the San Diego, passed the Farallones and reached Francis Drake's Bay (the San Francisco Bay of Cermeño), which he called the Puerto de Don Gaspar or Puerto de los Reyes. Here he looked in vain for traces of Cermeño's unfortunate San Agustín, and then, pressing further, passed Cape Mendocino on the 12th. Both the San Diego and the Tres Reyes attained the latitude of the present Cape Blanco, but about January 19 were forced by cold and illness to retrace their course to Acapulco, where, after vicissitudes many and distressing, they arrived, the Tres Reyes in February, and the San Diego in March.[26]

The second voyage of Vizcaino made it clear that there were at least two good harbors for galleons above Cape San Lucas, — San Diego and Monterey. But with respect to Anian (the inciting cause, under Hernando de los Ríos's memorial, of any voyage at all at this time) the voyage cleared up nothing. It indeed was of reactionary effect. Already in 1554 Jacobo Gastaldi and in 1582 Michael Lok, ignorant of Castillo's chart of 1541, had issued maps depicting California (Lower and Upper) as a single great peninsula, joined at its northern extremity to the American continent by a slender isthmus. Antonio de la Ascensión of Salamanca (cosmographer-assistant to Palacios) now went a step further. He asserted that not only was the mouth of the broad river, which Aguilar (like Gali) had distinguished by its drift, the outlet of Anian, but that the Gulf of California was a sea opening into this outlet. "I hold it," he said, "for certain that this sea [the Gulf of California] communicates with the Strait of Anian, and by the latter with the Sea of the North [the Atlantic Ocean]"; an assertion which, if true, abolished the Gastaldi-Lok isthmus, and left California a body purely insular.[27]

Though California might be insular, it none the less (through Anian) commanded "against those demons of English and Dutch heretics" the western littoral of North America, a fact emphasizing the need for the occupation of such a harbor as Monterey. In 1606 therefore, on the 19th of August, Philip III gave to the Viceroy of Mexico (the Marqués de Montesclaros) an urgent command to look for Vizcaino, whose whereabouts had been lost, and to intrust to his capable hands a third expedition to California; this time with the express object of "making a settlement at the said Puerto de Monterey and thus introduce the touching [of the galleons] at that port." 28

But just here a sudden change was made in the royal plans, — a circumstance which carries us back a little in our narrative.

Sometime between September 25, 1584, and May 10, 1585, Fray Andrés de Aguirre (companion of Urdaneta in 1565) wrote to the Archbishop of Mexico, Pedro de Moya y Contreras, who lately had been made Viceroy, a letter urging upon his attention the need of a refitting station for the Philippine galleons after their long voyage across the Pacific. The idea of course was not new. Over and over had Legazpi been charged in official instructions from Valladolid not to delay among the Western Islands trading and bartering, but to return immediately to New Spain, "as the principal reason of this expedition is to ascertain the return voyage." And by sending back Urdaneta the charge had been complied with. Urdaneta's voyage, however, had been most unfortunate, for his pilot, his master, and fourteen of his men had died. Then had come the voyage of Gali. But while both voyages had served to point the need, between Manila and Acapulco, of a station for refitting, neither had accomplished anything toward finding a suitable spot. Under these conditions it was, and while contemplating sending Gali on a search for such a spot, that Contreras received the letter of Aguirre.

Aguirre told of a communication from a Portuguese captain which had been shown to him in 1565 by Urdaneta. It described two large islands, nine days to the eastward of Japan, in a port of which the captain had been forced to take refuge from a storm; islands rich in "silver, silks, and clothing," which, out of compliment to an Armenian merchant sailing with the Portuguese captain, had been named "Isles of the Armenian." [29]

Gali, as it chanced, was not sent on a voyage of search by Contreras. Instead, there was sent in 1587, in the ship Nuestra Señora de la Esperança, a navigator of Macao, Pedro de Unamunu, who on returning reported no such "isles" as those of the Armenian, or of Rica de Oro and Rica de Plata, their equivalent, to exist. [30] But Unamunu reported further:—

From the latitude of the Island of Armenio, as they call it (which is 35⅓°), we sailed on August 26 east by north and to the northeast in search of the country of Nueva España, intending to reach it at as high a latitude as we could. . . . We sailed as far as the latitude of 39°, [but] on September 3 [by reason of wind and cold and broken mainmast] we came back to the latitude 32½°. . . . Sailing on various courses . . . we succeeded in reaching the latitude of somewhat above 35½° on the 17th October. . . . On this day land was seen. . . . At the first watch we turned away from it [on account of fog]. Heading northeast . . . we encountered two little islets adjoining the mainland. . . . On Sunday the 18th at daybreak we made the shore of the land, and God, giving us the light of day, we saw toward the north a country that was elevated with only three pine trees on the highest point, which served as a landmark. . . . On the north a headland extended apparently northwest and southeast. Inside this headland appeared a bay broad toward the east, in which there seemed to be harbors. . . . When we reached it we saw toward the east a sandy beach of considerable extent and moderate breadth. We steered for that place and cast anchor . . . in twenty-seven fathoms of water. . . . We cast anchor in the said harbor on the 18th of October, the day of Saint Luke; and because it was that saint's day, the name of Puerto de San Lucas was given to the place. Here in this harbor there is an infinite number of fish of various kinds; and there are trees suitable for a ship's masts, and water and firewood, and many shell-fish, — a place where any one can, when in need, obtain supplies of all these things. . . . We took observations of the sun and found that the said harbor lies in a little more than 35½° of latitude. . . . I landed on the shore with twelve soldiers wearing their mail-coats and carrying their arquebuses. In front of us was Father Martin Ynacio de Loyola bearing a cross in his hands, with some Indians from Luçon armed with swords and bucklers. . . . On the northeast side [of a hill] we saw a river of considerable size descending through a plain below, and many well-worn roads going in various directions. . . . We tasted the water of the said river and found it very good; it flowed down the said river through sand. Thence the ascent of the river was made by way of an upward slope toward the north, where the said river formed a large lake; we concluded that some bar and harbor would be there, since the sea was so near. When we reached it we saw that it was water held back from the said river, and that its way to the sea was obstructed by a great quantity of sand. All this river, on both sides, is well shaded by willows and osiers of considerable size, with other and lofty trees which look like the ash; there are also many fragrant plants, such as camomile, pennyroyal and thyme.

. . . As a matter concerning the demarcation and crown of the King Don Felipe, our sovereign, I took possession in the said name by Diego Vazquez Mexia, one of the alcaldes appointed for this purpose. In this act he was supported, as he was a magistrate, in due legal form by planting a cross . . . and cutting branches from the trees that grew about the place.[31]

On October 21, after a conflict with Indians, Unamunu set sail for Acapulco, because "the wounded were in very bad condition," and because, "from the island of Cedros to the port of Acapulco, the whole coast had been discovered for a long time."

From the islands of Babuyanes, Unamunu observes, we sailed one thousand eight hundred and ninety leagues, on varying courses according as the weather favored us, — although a straight course would make about one thousand five hundred and fifty leagues. At that latitude and by that route there is very good navigation, better for health and shorter than it is in lower latitudes. From the said port of Saint Lucas to Cape Sanct Lucas, which has a latitude of nearly twenty-three degrees, the distance is two hundred and ninety leagues, about half of the way on a southeast course, and the other half sailing southeast by south. From this cape Sanct Lucas to the port of Acapulco it is about two hundred and sixty leagues, sailing half the way southeast, and the rest southeast by east.

Puerto de San Lucas, discovery of which is thus announced by Unamunu, was not improbably Monterey Bay. It was in a latitude "above 35½°"; its "landmark" was "three pine trees on the highest point"; on the north "a headland extended apparently northwest and southeast"; inside this headland "appeared a bay broad toward the east," and into the bay there flowed "a considerable river" (the Salinas?). But to Viceroy Contreras, bent upon the discovery, for refitting stations, of treasure islands (Isles of the Armenian or what not), Unamunu's report was little significant. It was consigned to oblivion, and the first occupation of Monterey was, and is, ascribed to Vizcaino.

It was in 1607 that the Isles of the Armenian (or rather of Rica de Oro and Rica de Plata) claimed attention again. On May 24 Viceroy Montesclaros, acknowledging receipt of the royal order of August 19, 1606, for the dispatch of Vizcaino for the settlement of Monterey, represented to Philip III that the occupation of the port in question, for a way station, would be ill advised. The most difficult part of the Manila-Acapulco passage, it was observed by Montesclaros, was not the stretch across the

North Pacific, nor yet the run down the coast of the Californias, but the devious way from Cape Espiritu Santo on the island of Manila, all along the chain of the Ladrones to the east point of Japan, called Cape Sestos (Shiwo Misaki); a way necessarily taken by the galleons, in order to gain, in the proper latitude, an offing. Galleon upon galleon, bravely cleared from Manila with music and dancing, had either been wrecked outright on the shoals and rocks of Japan, or forced reeling back to port, dismasted and forlorn. What, therefore, argued the Viceroy, was needed for the galleons was not a port-of-call in California, at the end of a voyage, but such a port off Cape Sestos at the beginning, — a need for the satisfaction of which there happily existed "two islands in latitude thirty-four or thirty-five, named Rica de Oro and Rica de Plata." [32]

Accordingly in 1608 (September 27), the King gave orders to Viceroy Luis de Velasco that Sebastián Vizcaino, instead of proceeding to occupy and settle Monterey as commanded in 1606, should go to the Philippine Islands, and "with two small and lightly laden ships" return thence for "the discovery, settlement, and opening to navigation of a harbor in one of the said islands Rica de Oro and Rica de Plata"; and that, meanwhile, "the opening to navigation and settlement of the harbor of Monterey should be suspended." [33]

Vizcaino, so far as known, did not go to the Philippines, but in 1611 he went, as admiral, in the galleon San Francisco, to Japan.[34] For Rica de Oro and Rica de Plata he sought, we are told, with extraordinary diligence throughout two hundred leagues. But the sailors having elicited from the *piloto-mayor* the statement that, in his opinion, "there were no such islands in the world" (*no había tales islas en el mundo*), a mutiny was threatened and the search abandoned. Vizcaino was yet in Japan in 1613, and, as

late as 1620, Hernando de los Ríos Coronel was urging
upon the King that a small vessel be sent from Manila to
explore the island of Rica de Plata, — an island described
by him as over one hundred leagues in circumference, and
as "placed midway the Pacific like an inn." [35]

With Monterey suspended as to settlement, attention
(1615–94) was directed to the task of gaining a foothold
at Cape San Lucas, or La Paz. In 1629 Padre Ascensión
recommended the occupation of the cape. Thus not
merely might California itself be peopled, but thus might it
be ascertained whether by the Sea of California one could
pass to the Estrecho de Anian; at what point might be
located the famous city of Quivira; where the river Tizón
entered; where lay the pearl island of Giganta, and what
parts were peopled by a white race. Ascensión's views
were approved by the royal purser, Martín de Lezama, a
son-in-law of Vizcaino, but by Henrico Martínez (royal
cosmographer) they were subjected to criticism. Great
riches and an extended population in California, Martínez
did not believe to exist. As for a lake of gold (laguna de
oro), described by Padre Ascensión, — a lake from which
the Indians drew vast treasure, — common sense, he declared, denied it reality. Occupation of the cape, moreover, was not necessary to afford refuge to the Philippine
galleon; for was not the latter wont to reach Acapulco
without even sighting California? As for occupation to
forestall an enemy, one could never reach the coast, so
great was the distance to be traversed; and if traverse it an
enemy should, why there could be done to him "as Pedro
Melendes did to the French in Florida, and as Fadrique de
Toledo did to the Hollanders of San Salvador and the
coast of Brazil." [36]

The views of Ascensión none the less prevailed, and by

1694 expeditions into the California gulf (most of them, like the first expedition of Vizcaino, for pearls, but with settlement as at least an ostensible object) had been undertaken by nine different adventurers: Tomás Cardona, Juan de Iturbe, Francisco de Ortega, Luis Cestín de Cañas, Porter y Casanate, Bernardo Bernal de Piñadero, Lucenilla y Torres, Isidro Otondo (under whom, April 5, 1683, the peninsula was formally named Santísima Trinidad de las Californias), and Francisco de Itamarra.

If in the seventeenth century (upon the failure of the search for Rica de Oro and Rica de Plata, and during the period of the gulf expeditions), Spain had persisted in her original plan, — the settlement of Monterey, — the opportunity so far as her enemy England was concerned was quite at hand. James I sat upon the English throne, and the spacious days of great Elizabeth — the days of the Hawkinses and the Drakes — were replaced by the petty days of the Stuarts. In 1604 the Constable of Castile had negotiated with James a treaty by which the latter had agreed "not to allow English ships to trade in the Indies"; and long thereafter the successive Spanish ambassadors at London — Zúñiga, Velasco, Gondomar — held English policy much in their own keeping.

Yet, despite favorable conditions, Spain now (1600-1700) was so broken, — the Spanish Cæsar become so utterly a simulacrum, a mere painted Jove, — that Alta California was not visited once. Its sierra slumbered in the skies, and its valleys gave subsistence to wild creatures, all amid a loneliness as profound as that before the days of Cabrillo. A single time each year, as the Philippine galleon (foul with scurvy yet towering nobly at poop and prow, and with silken cargo redolent of musk) sighted Cape Mendocino or Santa Lucía Peak, was the region glimpsed by the eye of civilized man.

CHAPTER III

THE MISSION

Siempre habían producido mejores efectos las adquisiciones que se hacían lentamente por medio de los Misioneros que las conseguidas a fuerza de armas. — Viceroy Bucarely to the King, October 27, 1772.[1]

DOWN to 1694, the year of the last expedition to the California peninsula (that of Itamarra), the means relied upon for the "reduction" of California, says the Jesuit historian Miguel Venegas, were "arms and power. . . . But," he continues, "it was the will of Heaven that the triumph when it came should be owing to the meekness and courtesy of God's ministers, to the humiliation of his cross, and the power of his word."

The singular efficacy of the Cross in the subjugation of men is a thing which historians have had occasion to remark; and it is true, as we are reminded by Venegas, that Lower California became the scene of another of its triumphs. Whether the reduction of Alta California might not have been accomplished in the time-honored secular way, by force, had it not been that in the eighteenth century the Spanish Government, though in process of rehabilitation, was extremely poor, is a question. At all events, in 1769 danger to New Spain by way of the California coast again arose; and, in the dearth of money, there was left to Spain but one tried, strong, and effective instrument of defense, — the Mission.

First, a word with regard to the danger itself; and, next, with regard to the remarkable instrument by which it was sought to be averted.

I

Under the last of her Austrian kings, Charles II (Charles
the Bewitched), who died in 1700, Spain touched the lowest point of demoralization, political, industrial, and commercial, which she was destined to reach. With the accession of the Bourbons, in the person of Philip V, a slight
recovery of power was to be observed; especially after the
political reins, in 1714, had passed into the deft hands of
Giulio Alberoni, successively priest, prime minister, and
cardinal. Moreover, as the eighteenth century brought
renewed activity for Spain in Europe, so, likewise, it
brought for her renewed activity in the Indies.

In 1680 rumor declared that the English were to be expected soon again in the Pacific. In the words of Spanish
merchants, writing to their Panama correspondents,
"There would be English privateers that year in the West
Indies, who would make such great discoveries as to open
a door into the South Seas." The first to appear (albeit a
trifle belated) was "Captain Swan." In 1686 he entered
the California gulf with one ship, carrying as pilot and his-
toriographer William Dampier, a navigator actuated by a
restless ambition "to get some knowledge of the northern
parts of this continent of Mexico." After Swan it was
Dampier himself who, with his "knowledge," next sought
to open a door into the South Seas for Englishmen. In December, 1704, he attacked with a single ship the Manila
galleon of the year, below Cape San Lucas, but was beaten
off. Then in 1709 came Captain Woods Rogers with two
ships, piloted by the indefatigable Dampier. As a passenger in one of them was Alexander Selkirk, the true
Robinson Crusoe. But though "Crusoe" joined against
the galleon, the English, after a combat near the cape,
were again worsted.[2]

Each of the adventurers, Swan, Dampier, and Rogers, believed in Anian (a route to the happy regions of the galleons and gold which he knew must be shorter than that around Cape Horn), and no one of them, except Rogers, was prepared to deny that California was an island. It was in 1620, by Antonio de la Ascensión, Vizcaino's assistant cosmographer, that, as noted in the last chapter, the insular hypothesis for California was revived. The hypothesis proved strong enough, be it added, to withstand distinct proof in contravention of it obtained through explorations to the Colorado River, in 1701, 1702, and 1706, by the Jesuit missionary Eusebio Francisco Kino.[3]

Some years after the Woods Rogers attack (1717), Cardinal Alberoni sought to forestall danger to New Spain from the English on the California coast. But Alberoni's tenure of power proved brief, and in 1721 Captain George Shelvocke appeared off Cape San Lucas with evil intent. He accomplished nothing, and soon departed for Canton.[4] No other Englishman of note followed him till 1740, when Captain George Anson lay long off Acapulco in wait for a galleon, finding reward at last in a richer vessel near the Philippines.[5]

After 1740 it was from a fresh quarter that danger from the English arose. The Hudson's Bay Company (organized in 1670) was operating under a charter reciting that a main consideration for the instrument was "The Discovery of a New Passage into the South Sea." Here obviously was a command to seek Anian (and hence California) from the east. But as late as 1740 it was averred by Arthur Dobbs, an enthusiastic Irishman, that no serious effort at discovery had been made by the company; wherefore in 1742 Dobbs undertook the task himself. His expedition failed to disclose an exit westward from the bay; yet so persistent was he that in 1745 he induced Parliament to vote £20,000 as a contingent reward for a further expedition. Prosecuted by the Dobbs Galley and the California, this likewise was a failure and came to an end in 1746.[6]

Meanwhile for a hundred years Russia had slowly, but with glacier-like inexorability, been moving eastward toward the only real Anian, the strait dividing Siberia from the present Alaska, and by 1706 had reached Kamtchatka. By 1728 Vitus Behring had drifted through the strait; by 1741 North America had been sighted; by 1745 a descent had been made upon the Aleutian Islands; and by 1760 a Russo-American trade in otter-skins had been opened.[7]

II

The Mission — instrument in Spanish hands (so far as the Californias were concerned) for the safeguarding of the Philippine galleon and for the control of Anian — was the result of two interacting human passions, — Religious Propagandism and Avarice. The second is the more primitive passion of the two, and it is to the credit of Spain that in the settlement of the Indies, Avarice, triumphant at the beginning, waged on the whole a losing battle with Propagandism.

The root of the Spanish propagandist passion was largely the Spanish temperament, but present and abetting were two specific influences: (1) The Bull of Pope Alexander VI, of date May 3, 1493, awarding to Spain, "in the fulness of papal apostolic power, and of the vicarship of Jesus Christ on earth," the New World, on condition that there be sent thither "worthy, God-fearing, learned, skilled, and experienced men, in order to instruct the inhabitants in the Catholic faith; [8] and (2) the personality of Queen Isabella, who so felt the responsibility of the papal injunction, that in her will (1504) leaving to Ferdinand the regency of Castile, she charged that what was commanded by the

Pope as to the Indians, "be not infringed in any respect" (*no se exceda cosa alguna*).[9]

It is with the avarice side of the account, "Spain in the Indies," that we are concerned first.

Neither Queen Isabella nor King Ferdinand saw reason why the Indians, while undergoing conversion, should not respond by the payment of reasonable tribute, provided the same were exacted from them as from other freemen and not as from slaves. But in the application of this idea (even when sought to be applied justly), there was difficulty. In 1503 Nicolás de Ovando, Governor of Hispaniola, wrote with undoubted truth that the Indians would not work even for wages, and that, indeed, they shunned the Spaniards in every relation. The reply of the monarchs was, that contact with the Indians was indispensable for ends religious as well as secular, and that Ovando, therefore, might assemble them in villages, upon lands which they could not alienate, and under a protector, and so compel them to consort with the Spaniards; he paying them such wages as he might deem fit. Nevertheless (so the monarchs insisted), what was required of the Indians should be required of them "as free persons, as they are, and not as slaves." [10] Thus enjoined, Ovando proceeded to inaugurate a system of *encomiendas* — a kind of New World feudal system. "To you," ran the deed apportioning the Indians among their *encomenderos* or protectors, " are given in trust [*se os encomiendan*], under Chief So-and-so, fifty or one hundred Indians, with the chief, for you to make use of them in your farms and mines; and you are to teach them the things of our holy Catholic faith." [11] In theory the system was not necessarily bad. What in practice it became is well known. It became slavery and robbery, and not seldom it became also murder.[12]

But what, meanwhile, of those "worthy, God-fearing,

learned, skilled, and experienced men," who, according to
the Papal Bull, were to be ever present in the Indies
to instruct the inhabitants in Christianity, — men wholly
other than the *encomenderos* themselves, who, ninety-nine
times in a hundred, were fortune-seekers of the worst type,
the very incarnation of Avarice? Here there arose a fresh
difficulty. The secular Catholic clergy of the day, especially the Spanish branch of it, — that is to say, the Spanish bishops and priests, — were worldly to the core. Said
Cortés to Charles V in that famous *Carta Cuarta* of his,
already cited: "If there be [sent to the New World] bishops
and other prelates, they cannot but continue the habit, to
which for our sins they are now given, of disposing of the
goods of the Church, which is to waste them in pompous
ceremonies and in other vices, [and] in leaving entails to
their sons or relations; and should the Indians learn that
such were ministers of God, and should see them given
over to the vices and irreverence that are practiced in our
day in those realms, it would cause them to undervalue
our Faith and hold it to be a matter of jest." [13]

Seculars, however, it was who (greedy, lustful, indolent)
were at first sent by Spain in fulfillment of the great proviso in the Bull of 1493. But regulars — the friars — an
order of ministers armed against temptation by ample
vows of poverty and chastity — soon followed, and the
Pope's behest for the conversion of the Indians was given
effect.

In 1510 a band of Dominican monks, under their vicar
Pedro de Córdova, landed in Hispaniola. They perceived
that the *encomienda* was both a fraud upon the will of the
monarchs and destructive to the Indian, and forthwith
they proceeded, through one of their number, Antonio de
Montesino, to raise against it a vehement protest. The
matter was carried to King Ferdinand, and on Decem-

ber 27, 1512, there was promulgated by him a series of
decrees (conceived under the influence of Bishop Fonseca)
called the Laws of Burgos.[14] By these laws *encomiendas*
were modified and regulated, but they were not condemned. Among those who in 1512 went to Spain, because of the controversy provoked by the words of Brother
Montesino, was Pedro de Córdova himself. He examined
the Laws of Burgos, disapproved of them, and expressed
his disapproval to the King. "Take upon yourself then,
father," said the King, "the charge of remedying them;
you will do me a great service therein." But the vicar,
declining the task as beyond his province, took upon him
work of greater moment, — the propagating in the New
World of the plan of the Mission.

It was the conviction of Córdova that the Indian, so far
from being dealt with for the good of his soul while in
encomienda, — while within exploitation range of the
conscienceless gold-seeking Spanish adventurer, — should
be so dealt with only when in segregation, when organized
apart from the lay Spaniard altogether. He, therefore,
while in Spain, obtained from King Ferdinand a license to
occupy with his Dominican brethren a portion of *Tierra
Firme* (mainland of New Spain), there to labor with the
Indians free from lay supervision and interference. Piritú
de Maracapána, near Cumaná (the earthly Paradise of
Columbus and Cortés),[15] was the spot chosen, and the
experiment was full of promise, when suddenly it was cut
short by a raid of pearl-fishers. The raiders carried away
the cacique of the locality, thus rousing against the friars
a suspicion of connivance, — a suspicion which brought
about the death of two of the latter, though not of Córdova, who as yet had not quitted Hispaniola.

At this juncture there appeared Bartolomé de Las Casas.
A bachelor of Salamanca, he had arrived in the Indies

with Ovando, and, becoming an *encomendero* in Cuba, had
heard, in Hispaniola, Montesino's denunciation of the
encomienda system. By 1514 he, too, was ready to de-
nounce it, and by the autumn of 1515 to go to Spain to try
to secure a radical revision of the Laws of Burgos under
which the system derived sanction. Montesino accompanied him, and by help of Cardinal Ximénez de Cisneros
(regent to Ferdinand's successor, young Charles V), they
succeeded in raising the whole question of Indian slavery
and spoliation. Ximénez himself was a bold defender of
Indian freedom, and in Council it was repeatedly proposed
to abolish the *encomienda* and require of the Indians payment of a capitation tax to the Crown. This proposal was
negatived by the fact, reluctantly admitted, that "the
Indians had no real inclination to Christianity, and when
left to themselves soon relapsed into heathen beliefs." [16]
As for the Córdovan idea, — the idea of the Mission, —
the idea that the way to convert the Indian was to segre-
gate him, — it did not occur to the Council, was not suggested by Las Casas, and in any event would have been
deemed too paradoxical for adoption.

With Pedro de Córdova, however, it was the Mission
idea that remained uppermost, and in 1518 he sought at
the hands of Charles V a grant of one hundred leagues
around Cumaná, as a field for work according to the Mission plan. But in 1521 Córdova died, and there were left
only Montesino and Las Casas to take resolutely a stand
in behalf of the Indian. The one hundred leagues (enlarged to two hundred and fifty leagues) which had been
desired by Córdova were obtained by Las Casas; but the
latter, instead of organizing at Cumaná an Indian religious
retreat, — a place from which the lay Spaniard was excluded, — planted the usual mixed colony, and with the
usual disastrous result.[17] Depressed by failure, Las Casas

in 1523 became a monk in Hispaniola, and the *encomienda* flourished.

Yet, despite all, the Córdovan idea — the idea of the Mission — the one workable idea for conserving and converting the Indian — gained gradually a wider acceptance. By 1531 one hundred friars (Dominicans and Franciscans) were in New Spain. In 1531 an *oidor* (judge) of the Audiencia for Mexico, Licenciate Quiroga, earnestly recommended to the Council of the Indies that the Indian youth of the country, reared in the various monasteries, should be settled in pueblos, "at a distance from other pueblos," and under the guardianship of "three or four religious, who [might] incessantly cultivate these young plants to the service of God." [18] What was more, Las Casas himself, now (1535) out of retirement, had advanced very nearly, if not quite, to the position of Córdova. Relying no longer on secular means for Indian conversion, he wrote a treatise in Latin (*De Unico Vocationis Modo*) in support of the thesis that men were to be brought to Christianity by persuasion.[19] Indeed, on May 2, 1537, he entered into a specific compact with Alonzo Maldonado, lieutenant to Pedro de Alvarado, Governor of Guatemala, to demonstrate by actual test that the wildest tribes of the New World could be pacified and converted without the use of force.

The people selected for the test were those of the Guatemalan province of Tuzulatlán, — a people so fierce that their land, whence thrice the Spaniards had been thrust in defeat, was a place of terror, one known as Tierra de Guerra, — Land of War. Into this land, between 1537 and 1539, Las Casas sent Fray Luis Cáncer (Alférez de la Fé), with such success that soon the province became more widely renowned as Tierra de Vera Paz (Land of True Peace) than it had been as Tierra de Guerra.[20] But, apropos of the development of the idea of the Mission, the

point especially to be observed is, that when Las Casas
made his compact with Lieutenant-Governor Maldonado,
he insisted upon the following concessions: (1) That neither
then, nor at any future time in Tuzulatlán, might Indians
be given in *encomienda;* and (2) that for five years access to
the province should be interdicted to every lay Spaniard,
excepting only the governor, Alvarado himself.[21]

From 1539–40 to 1544 Las Casas was kept in Spain by
Charles V, who was meditating his celebrated mandatory
letters, "The New Laws"; and in 1543 the letters were
printed. Under the Indian Code of Spain, as perfected by
"The New Laws," it was provided that the Indians should
dwell in civil (not distinctively religious) communities,
choosing their own *alcaldes* (magistrates) and *regidores*
(councilmen). But provisions useful for Mission ends were
not lacking. (1) No Indian might be held as a slave;
(2) no Indian might live outside his village; (3) no lay Spaniard might live in an Indian village; (4) no lay Spaniard
might tarry in an Indian village overnight, unless he were
ill or were a merchant, when, if a merchant, he might remain three nights; and (5) the Indian was to be faithfully
instructed in religion. As for the *encomienda*, it was abolished; but in 1545, in response to colonial demands, it had
to be restored to its former (1536) validity for two lives.[22]

The Spanish Indian Mission — witness to the triumph,
through Córdova and Las Casas, of Propagandism over
Avarice,[23] and fostered, through Charles V, by the Laws
of the Indies — was to show in the course of its development some variation. As viewed by the Spanish Government, its object was the Christianizing (and that speedily)
of the Indian, in order to civilize him. As viewed, on the
other hand, by the friars, its object was the Christianizing
of the Indian to save his soul, — a process which might be

accomplished speedily, or which might require an indefinite period. A clash at times ensued with regard to the segregating of the Indian. What the government understood by "segregation" was (1) the exclusion of lay Spaniards from Indian settlements; and (2) the ministering spiritually to the natives in their own abodes.[24] What the missionaries understood by the term was not alone the exclusion from Indian settlements of lay Spaniards, and the ministering spiritually to the Indians in their own abodes, but the gathering of Indians from far and near into and about a central establishment (a mission), where they as wards or protégés might be governed in respects temporal as well as spiritual.[25]

In central Mexico, where the natives (already at the conquest not uncivilized) were mild of disposition, the clash above referred to did not occur, for segregation as understood by the government was sufficient for objects both political and religious. But in north Mexico (Upper Sonora and Nueva Vizcaya, — the borders of Apachería), a district warlike and uncivilized, necessity compelled the adoption of segregation as understood by the missionaries. This the government, amid controversy, alternately tolerated and discountenanced through the power of the *Patronato Real*.[26]

It was in Paraguay that the Spanish-Indian Mission prospered most. Introduced by the Jesuits between 1586 and 1612, it made of each village a theocratic centre — a centre civil, religious, and even military — under a missionary father.[27] In the Philippine Islands, where the Mission was introduced by the Augustinians under Legazpi in 1564, the form was less specialized. The degree of specialization attained in Alta California, where, as against the English and Russians, the Mission was employed as an instrument of state in and after 1769, will be shown in the sequel.

CHAPTER IV

CALIFORNIA NO ES YSLA

THE Mission, pending its use in 1769 as a Spanish instrument of state in Alta California, was subjected to yet a further test.

Eusebio Francisco Kino was born at Trent in the Austrian Tyrol in 1640. First a professor of mathematics at the University of Ingolstadt in Bavaria, and next a Jesuit, he crossed to Mexico in 1680. Here his labors were those equally of missionary and royal cosmographer. As missionary, his zeal spurred him to the frontier; and as cosmographer he was sent in 1683, with Isidro Otondo y Antillón, to California on the expedition which gave to the peninsula the name Santísima Trinidad de las Californias. In 1685 he was compelled to leave California because of the recall of Otondo to convoy the Philippine galleon past Dutch buccaneers to Acapulco. But so deeply had the spell of this land of Cortés been laid upon him, that ever afterwards he was eager to return and make converts of its people.[1]

"The enterprise of the conquest and conversion of California having been suspended [by royal order in 1685]," writes Kino in 1698, "I asked of the provincial (at that time Padre Luys del Canto) license to come to these Gentile people of these coasts nearest to the said California [Upper Sonora or Pimería]. . . . The fiscal of His Majesty (may God guard Him), D. Pedro de la Portilla, asserted that from these coasts there would be the greatest opportunity possible to continue . . . the conquest and conversion of

California. I set out from Mexico on the 20th of November, 1686, and arrived at Guadalaxara, whence I set out on the 16th of December [arriving at Oposura in February]." [2]

In 1687, on March 13, Kino founded the mission Nuestra Señora de los Dolores (about 120 miles south of the present Tuçón), and between 1687 and 1690, in conjunction with Padre José de Aguilar, he founded the establishments San Ignacio, San José de los Imuris, and Nuestra Señora de los Remedios. But in Mexico ill reports regarding the Pimas had been spread, and in 1690 there was sent to Sonora as *visitador* the *asistente* at Las Chínipas, Juan María de Salvatierra. Born in Milan, Italy, November 15, 1644, a sometime student at the Seminary of Parma, and since 1675 a Jesuit in Mexico, Salvatierra was an emissary strong in body, firm in resolve, prudent in judgment, and of endearing gentleness of bearing. Accompanied by Kino, he visited each of the Pimería missions in 1690 and 1691, and "in all of these journeys," writes Kino, "the Father Visitador and I talked together of suspended California, and we agreed that these so fertile lands and valleys of this Pimería would be the remedy for the scantier and more sterile lands of California." [3]

On coming to Mexico, Kino had believed California to be a peninsula. But in the account of Oñate's New Mexican expedition of 1604–05 it was intimated that the *adelantado*, proceeding westward, had reached the South Sea in 37°; moreover, most of the cosmographers now represented California as insular; and as noted by Kino himself the currents of the gulf were those rather of a strait; so he had changed his opinion. [4] As for Salvatierra, his views were those of his coadjutor. Indeed, on taking leave of the cosmographer, Salvatierra counseled him to reduce the Sobaipuris of the north and Sobas to the west, and — "in

order to go [thence] to California — to build a small bark." [5]
Accordingly in 1692 (August to September), Kino, with
fifty beasts of burden, his servants and some Indians, went
to the Sobaipuris, and at the *ranchería* of San Xavier del
Bec displayed a map of the world by which he showed
"how the Spaniards and the faith had come by sea to Vera
Cruz and had gone to Puebla, to Mexico, to Guadalaxara,
to Sinaloa, to Sonora, and now to the lands of the Pimas."
And in December, 1693, still mindful of the advice of Salvatierra, he went with Padre Agustín de Campos and
Captain Sebastián Romero to the Sobas. "After about
eight leagues journey," he relates, "we came to a little hill
which we named El Nazareno, and from its summit, on the
15th of December, we saw clearly more than twenty-five
continuous leagues of the land of California, for it is not
more than fifteen or eighteen leagues across to the principal *rancherías*. And . . . we named the spot La Concepcion de Nuestra Señora del Caborca." [6]

Nor was the building of a ship forgotten; for in July
Kino went with Lieutenant Mateo Manje (*alcalde-mayor*
and *capitán-á-guerra* in Sonora) to the Sobas at Sonoydag,
and began the construction of "a bark twelve varas [eleven
yards] long and four varas [three yards] wide, cutting
the timbers and keel-beams; the rest of the framework, the
flooring and the futtocks, being made here in Nuestra
Señora de los Dolores, with the idea of carrying this whole
bark in four parts to the sea by mules, and there to put it
together, nail it, calk it, and to pass to the near-by California." [7]

But for use of the bark opportunity was delayed, and in
1694 (February) Kino, with Manje, went again to "the
waters of the Sea of California." "We saw very clearly,"
he says, "the same California and its principal and larger
hills. We named them San Marcos, San Mateo, San

Juan (for San Lucas is already the name of the Cape of California), and San Antonio, as may be seen from the map." The trip was repeated a few months later (June), resulting in the discovery of "the good port of Santa Sabina." [8]

In November, Kino visited the Casa Grande of the Gila, near which, in the *rancheria* of El Tusonimo, he said Mass, and in November, 1695, he set forth by leave of his provincial for Mexico, to discuss with the latter and with the Viceroy the "conversion of California." Arriving at the capital on January 8, 1696, whom should he meet but Salvatierra, who the same day had reached the city by another road.[9]

It was during the reign of Charles II (the Bewitched) that Kino adventured to Mexico; but for the "conversion of California" the time was inopportune, for it fell within the interval of national depression when Monterey as a port-of-call for the galleon had been abandoned in favor of the islands (one or other) Rica de Oro and Rica de Plata; an abandonment emphasized by the royal *cédula* of 1685 suspending California expeditions.

Kino was back at Dolores by the middle of May, but he had left Salvatierra in Mexico; and in 1697, on the coming of Conde de Moctezuma as viceroy, the failure of 1696 was retrieved. By Salvatierra there were won to the California cause not only the Society of Jesus, hitherto reluctant, but the Audiencia, and, last, the Viceroy himself; and on February 5 there was issued a license authorizing Kino, jointly with Salvatierra, to undertake the reduction of the Californias on two conditions: first, that reduction be at their own expense; second, that it be effected in the name of the King.[10] Salvatierra raised by subscription an endowment fund (*Fondo Piadoso*) of 47,000 *pesos*,[11] and appointed as *procurador* (financial agent) the rector of the

Jesuit College of San Gregorio, Juan Ugarte. Then, leaving Kino in Sonora, where his presence was said to be worth "a well-regulated presidio," he set sail, October 10, 1697, from Yaqui for the California coast. Comprising the expedition were a *lancha* containing six Spanish soldiers and three Indians, and a *galeota* containing six sailors, all under command of Juan María Romero de la Sierpe. Says Salvatierra, writing on Christmas Day, 1697, to the Bishop of Guadiana (Durango): —

From Hiagui [Yaqui] the currents drifted me near Sal si puedas and we took shelter at Concepcion, 25 leagues from San Bruno, the same bay where the Spaniards wintered two years, upon another attempt. . . . Having lost the launch with six men, in a storm, and not hearing anything of them for several days after, and finding ourselves in danger on account of the exposed situation of San Bruno, we drew lots, in the name of the Holy María, as to where we should go, the sailors being acquainted with some of the beaches. Our lot fell upon the Harbor of San Dionisio, and we set sail in the vessel and landed here.

The place appears to me a good one. It is a plain of some ten leagues in circumference, with good pastures and an abundance of mesquit and other trees, canebrakes, and good water. We were kindly received by the people, who begged us to continue with them. We landed our goods and provisions, and I took possession of a level piece of tableland on top of two of the highest hills on the large plain, abounding in springs of fresh water and a large reservoir of the same at the foot of the hill, for animals. We threw up our breastworks for fortifications, as best we could, having only six Spaniards, two Indians from Sonora, and another Indian. The vessel returned to Hiaqui and we few conquerors remained alone. We were in imminent risk of our lives for three whole weeks, because the cupidity of the Indians was tempted by our corn and flour, and they wished to kill us all and obtain booty. . . .

About midday, on St. Stanislaus Kostka Day, four squadrons belonging to four tribes — the Edues, Didues, Laymones, and Moquies Tapioses — charged down upon our intrenchments, with arrows, stones, and earth. They fought until the sun went down, having made several attacks, but the Virgin prevailed over the powers of Hell; the Great Madona was triumphant and victorious. Many of them fell on all sides, while I and my companions escaped unhurt. . . . The battle resulted in our favor, they humbled themselves, and we made peace with them. They are now obedient and a great many people come to learn the doctrine, and thus with a few Spaniards has this land been conquered.

We have subsequently discovered the yuca here, from the root of which the casave is made, an article of food in many of the kingdoms of America. We learned of it the day after our victory. Two days later, the launch, with the six men which were lost, appeared here. About this time also, the vessel, which it was also thought had been lost on account of accidents and getting ashore at Hiaqui, arrived, and brought me great relief from Father Francisco María Picolo, which aid, in a great measure, is due to your Reverence.

Thus on October 25, on the heights above San Dionisio, there was founded in commemoration of Our Lady of Loreto, Loreto de Concho, the first mission of Lower California.[12] Between 1697 and 1769, the year of the founding of San Diego de Alcalá, — the first Upper California mission, — there were planted in the peninsula eighteen missions,[13] all, save San Fernando de Velicatá, by the Jesuit Order. The powers conferred in the license issued by Moctezuma were to enlist, pay, and discharge soldiers for guard purposes, and to appoint proper persons for the administration of justice. In other words, the powers conferred were those which pertained to the Mission as such, whether conducted by Jesuits, Franciscans, or Dominicans; powers the outgrowth of the experience of Pedro de Córdova and Las Casas; powers sanctioned under the Laws of the Indies; powers whereby a community of Indians might be secluded from lay Spanish contact, and governed apart from lay Spanish interference, to the end that it might not be demoralized and exploited out of existence through lay Spanish avarice.[14]

For the exercise of such powers there proved to be need in California as elsewhere. Salvatierra's six recruits had all mutinied on learning that there was to be permitted no fishing for pearls, — a form of treasure-seeking wherein the earlier adventurers in the gulf had maltreated the Indians; and in 1700 the repressive attitude of Salvatierra was made matter of formal complaint by Antonio García de Mendoza, captain of the mission guard.[15]

Moreover in 1705 the vice-regal government, actuated by a belief (in which it was sustained by Madrid) that the secular authority in California was too much subordinated to the sacerdotal, proposed establishing a presidio at a point on the peninsular coast suitable for the galleon. The plan, had it been carried out, would have exposed California to the evils perpetrated in Hispaniola in the sixteenth century, — evils which the Mission had been created to forestall; and Salvatierra, now provincial of his Order, met the crisis with a successful protest.[16]

But to recur to Kino. Eager for California, he "set out," as he records, —

on the 22d of September [1698], from this pueblo of Nuestra Señora de los Dolores, with Captain Diego Carrasco, the [Indian] governor of this place, and with seven others, my servants, traveling with more than 60 sumpters toward the north and northwest to the Rio [Gila] and Casa Grande. . . . Afterwards we set out for the south and southwest and to the west about 80 leagues journey, and, arriving at the Sea of California under the lee of the estuary of the Rio Grande, we found a very good Port or Bay, in 32 degrees elevation, with fresh water and timber; and it must be the Port which ancient Geographers called the Puerto de Santa Clara; it has a southwest-northwest entrance and a sierra to the West. We came reconnoitring the whole coast from the northwest, from the Rio Grande to La Concepcion [del Caborca], which is more than 90 leagues long from north to south.[17]

Salvatierra was aroused by this *entrada*, and on March 28, 1699, he wrote to ask of the cosmographer "what sign there is on that [the Pimería] side whether this narrow sea is landlocked," and to propose a joint voyage of discovery along the inner California coast northward of 36 degrees.[18] But already Kino was on the march. On February 7 (1699), he with Padre Adamo Gilg, Lieutenant Manje, his servants, and "more than 90 sumpters," had set out for San Marcelo del Sonoydag near the port of Santa Clara. Proceeding down the Río Grande, which he and Padre Gilg now named Río de los Santos Apóstoles, the party came at San Pedro to the Cocomaricopas, from whom they learned of "the very populous Colorado, near by," where dwelt the Yumas. They, moreover, were presented by the Cocomaricopas with some curious shells of a heavenly blue (*conchas azules celestes*) which, observes Kino, "so far as I know, occur only on the opposite coast of the West of California." [19]

By the shells there was afforded Kino ground of conjecture not only that California was not an island, but that the sea dividing it from Sonora was of extent so limited that presumably the head lay not far to the west; yet at the door of discovery, — or rather rediscovery, for, from the time of the voyages of Ulloa and Alarcón to that of the voyage of Vizcaino, the limited extent of the Sea of California was known to cosmographers, — Kino was blind. That the blue shells were an indication of peninsularity was obvious, but to use his own words: —

I penetrated 170 leagues to the northwest and went beyond 35° latitude with Father Adamo Gilg and Captain Mateo Manje . . . and came almost to the confluence of the Rio Grande de Gila and the Colorado, and the natives gave us some blue shells, and still it did not occur to us that by that way there was a land passage to California, or head of its sea; and only in the Road when

we were returning to Nuestra Señora de los Dolores did it occur
to me that said blue shells must be from the opposite Coast of
California, and the South Sea, and that by the route by which
they had come from there hither we could pass thither from here,
and to California; and from that time forward I ceased the
building of the bark . . . which we were building at Concepcion del Caborca near the Sea of California and here at Nuestra
Señora de los Dolores, to carry it all to the sea afterward.[20]

The "heavenly blue shells" of the South Sea, these now
(1700) became for Kino talismanic. At San Xavier del Bec
(April 26 to May 2), he catechized "the principal governors and captains from more than 40 leagues distance, to
find out whether the blue shells came from any other region
than the opposite coast of California." And to every inquiry the answer was the same, that the shells "came from
that sea ten or twelve days' journey farther than this
other Sea of California, on which there [were] shells of
pearl and white and many others, but none of these blue
ones which were given us among the Yumas." "I thank
Your Reverence for . . . the sending of the blue shells,"
wrote Padre Antonio Kappus, rector at Matape. "I am
very strongly of the opinion that this land in which we are
is terra firma with that of California. . . . If Your Reverence accomplishes the *Entrada* by land into California, we
shall celebrate with great applause so happy a journey
whereby the world will be enlightened as to whether it be
an Island or a Peninsula, which to this day is unknown."
And the rector of Oposura (Padre Manuel Gonzáles)
wrote: "A Statue Rich and Famous we must erect to you,
if you do this [make a California *entrada*]; and if it [the
way] be short, there will be two statues." [21]

Starting from Los Remedios on September 24, 1700,
Kino descended the Gila to its junction with the Colorado,
where he arrived on October 7.

I ascended [he says] a Ridge to the Westward, where we knew how to sight so as to see the Sea of California, and looking and sighting toward the West and Southwest, with a telescope and without a telescope, [we beheld] more than 30 leagues of level lands without any sea.

And on the 9th he adds:—

Having set out from San Dionisio, and from the confluence of the two rivers, we arrived in the afternoon at the Paraje de las Sandias where was our relay; and we passed on two leagues farther to a *ranchería* where they gave us much fish; and we ascended another, a higher Hill, whence at sundown we sighted plainly many lands of California, and [perceived] that the two rivers (after their confluence) ran about 10 leagues to the west, and that afterward, turning southward about 20 leagues, they emptied into the Head of the Sea of California.[22]

The problem was practically solved. California could hardly be insular. Between it and Pimería there lay but the barrier of what Kino describes as the "very full-flooded, very Populous and very fertile Rio Colorado, which without exception is the Greatest [river] that all New Spain has; is that which Ancient Cosmographers called the Rio del Norte; is very probably from La Gran Quivera." But doubters there were, and to silence them it remained to confirm the fact of peninsularity by an expedition which, starting from Los Dolores, should reach Loreto by land.

In 1701 the California establishments were in sore need of chocolate and tobacco, and about February 20, Salvatierra crossed to Pimería. He reached Dolores, from Yaqui, with ten Sonora soldiers and six California Indians, and having been joined at San Ignacio by Lieutenant Manje, and at Caborca by Kino, the entire party, on March 10, with forty loads of provisions, bent their steps California-ward along the coast of the gulf. They bore aloft a picture of Our Lady of Loreto, and before it the very trail itself

broke forth into "pleasantness and beauty of roses and
flowers of different colors," as, "praying and chanting
praises of Our Lady in Castilian, in Latin, in Italian, and
in the California language," the pilgrims made their way.
On March 15, at San Marcelo del Sonoydag, letters were
received from Ugarte on the way to California from
Mexico, and on the 18th, at El Carrizal, there came
messages, how the Quiquimas who dwelt beyond the
Colorado, and who were the first objective of the expedition, were awaiting its arrival "anxiously and lovingly." [23]

But straightway the problem of the desert arose.
Should the expedition pursue a course west across the
sands, rounding the head of the gulf; or should it "ascend
to the northwest, circling the very great sandy waste of the
Head of the Sea of California, and ascending to the Rio
Grande and Rio Colorado by the circuit by which [Kino]
had already come in 3 other times?" Manje favored the
Gila-Colorado route; but it was decided to "travel by the
road shortest and most directly westward." For fifteen
days men and animals pushed on over sand-dunes and
lava-beds, stopping at water-holes, and making the most
of the scant pasturage till they reached Pitaqui (La
Petaca). "Here," says Kino, "from a little ridge which we
ascended, taking with us the Picture of Our Lady of Loreto,
we plainly sighted California and the great Sierra called
Sierra del Mescal, and the other called Sierra Azul, and
the Closing in of Both Lands of this New Spain and California." But it was declared by Indians of the locality
that "to penetrate to the Quiquimas of California there
lay still 30 leagues, or three days' journey, of stretches
of sand so great as to be without water or pasturage;
whereupon," Kino continues, "Padre Salvatierra determined that we should return, and we planned that I,
on another more favorable occasion, should penetrate in

higher latitude by way of the confluence of the Rivers and by San Dionisio." [24]

Kino's conviction that California was not an island was not only not fully shared by Lieutenant Juan Mateo Manje: it was not so shared even by Salvatierra. On May 16 (1701), the latter wrote to his friend, assuring him of "benedictions" for his journey and discovery "from afar" that New Spain was conjoined to New California, but stating that rejoicings at Loreto were "much greater that [his] Reverence [had] means and desires to examine at close range what on distant view might be misleading." [25] The uncertainty felt by Manje arose from the circumstance that, "from a point about 3 leagues farther to the west than the Ridge from whence we returned," there could be descried a bay of limits undefined.[26] To meet this objection, and at the same time others, there was for Kino but one way, — to pass personally into the peninsula by land. Between November 3 and December 8 he penetrated to the Gila-Colorado junction at San Dionisio, descended the east bank of the Colorado among natives amazed at the speed of the horse, — an animal never before seen by them; was ferried across the stream on a raft by the Quiquimas, and so set actual foot upon the soil of a California which, in recognition of the fact that it lay a day's journey above the head of the gulf, was given by Kino the designation of Alta.[27] The Colorado had now been crossed, but its course to the gulf had not been fully traced. This task was reserved for the year 1702. Setting out, on February 5, with Padre Visitador Manuel Gonzáles (who, ill at starting, died on the completion of the trip), Kino, in March and April, descended the river along its eastern bank to tide-water. Here, as later by the intrepid Garcés, the night was passed, and here, in Kino's words, "the full sea rose very near our beds." [28]

On this *entrada* our cosmographer was accompanied neither by Manje nor by Salvatierra, yet by it the doubts of the twain with respect to peninsularity were sensibly diminished.

I have reached and seen [Manje certified on May 15] the Arm of the Sea of California at three distant places in various altitudes of the North Pole. In that of 28 degrees I have seen and observed exactly, with mathematical Instruments, that said Arm of the Sea is no more than twenty-six leagues; and at . . . 32 degrees only twenty leagues; and at 31 degrees, where I saw it the last time, said sea has only the inconsiderable width of twelve leagues, which measures and observations testify that the nearer one approaches the said Arm of the Sea to the North-west, the more and more does its width diminish; and in order to find out if it ended higher up to the Northwest, the said Father Euzevio Francisco Kino set out on the *Entrada* to which Reference is made. And His Reverence informed me with hon-esty [he has] been at the Head of the said Arm of the Sea, and saw that the land of the Pimería joined with California, and states confidently [that] it is a Peninsula. . . . I have not seen [all] to certify it here with the verisimilitude which the case requires; only I assert confidently that it is a Relation of a fervid Minister to whom has been given entire Credit, as above I stated.[29]

The testimony of Salvatierra was penned March 3, 1703, and is as follows: —

I received the [letter] of Your Reverence accompanied by the Map of the Discovery of the Landlocked Strait which is so much doubted, whereupon I have been no little weighed down. But . . . there is no reason to be discouraged, but to try well with the Superiors to make another journey, in which this truth shall be found out, this time with evidence. . . . With it, so many New Map-Makers will be silenced, for they are not going to be silenced until they see themselves confuted [*concluidos*].[30]

But be the testimony of Manje and Salvatierra what it might, Kino's faith that California was not an island was fixed, and upon it there was reared by him a great conception. To Salvatierra peninsularity meant chiefly a stable means of food-transportation to Loreto. To Kino it meant more. It meant a crossing to "the opposite coast of the Sea of California, to its Cape Mendocino, [and] to the Harbor of Monte Rey"; for the climate of California, was it not "like to that of Castilla, to that of Andalusia, to that of Italy, to that of France"? Withal, to Kino, peninsularity meant "the removing of great Errors and Falsehoods": as of "a Crowned King carried in a Litter of Gold"; of "a lake of quicksilver and of another lake of gold"; of "a walled city with Towers"; of "the Kingdom of Axa"; of "the Pearls, Amber, Corals of the Rio del Tizon," etc. Finally (so Kino argued), might not peninsularity signify that the strait of Anian itself had no more foundation than this "Arm of the Sea" which made of California an island, — the true way from Japan being by Cape Mendocino, whence "might be brought to these Provinces of Sonora the goods of the very Rich Galleon from the Philippines." [31]

But the sun of the cosmographer of Ingoldstadt was beginning to decline, and in 1711 he died among the Pimas, at the age of seventy-one years. Never after 1702 did he visit the Colorado; yet he made other journeys, and in 1706 twice penetrated to the shore of the gulf. Of these visits the first (January) resulted in the discovery of an island named by Kino Santa Inés, and of a California cape named by him San Vicente.[32] The second visit was more memorable.

General Jacinto de Fuens-Zaldaña of the *compañía volante* for Sonora was friendly to Kino, and in October sent him forth to the Sea of California attended by persons who, if California really were peninsular, could bear convincing testimony to Viceroy and King. The expedition, besides the necessary *vaqueros* and *arrieros* with pack-train and cattle, consisted of Lieutenant Juan Mateo Ramírez, Corporal Juan Antonio Durán, and a Franciscan padre, Manuel de la Ojuela y Velarde, who had come north soliciting alms for the Franciscan establishment at Guadalajara. Seemingly it was intended to round the head of the gulf, thus completing the attempt made by Kino and Salvatierra in 1701; for word was sent in advance to the Indian governor of Sonoydag that by that way two padres and two soldiers would make *entrada á la California* by land. But on reaching Sonoydag, on November 2, no Quiquima guides had appeared, and it was decided to climb Santa Clara Mountain and take an observation from its summit.

Santa Clara Mountain — a cluster of the Gila Range — is described by Ojuela as "grand in the extreme." From the midst rose three heights pyramidal in form, one to the south, one to the east, and one to the west, forming a triangle. To look downward inspired terror, the sand-hills so simulating the sea that the latter, though more than nine leagues away, seemed to surge against the base. The foot of the pile was gained on the afternoon of the 5th, and here, at a tank in the rocks, all partook of meat and drink. Then, with Durán in charge of the sumpters and relays, and with the best mules as mounts, the ascent of the south peak was begun. When the task was finished, it was sundown. "We saw," says Ojuela, "the Sea of California, its mountains and the great sandy beach in which the said Sea ends. . . . We could not," he adds, "discern with perfect distinctness, for straightway night fell upon us, and here we slept." With the dawn, Ojuela hastened down the south peak in order to ascend that to the west, which was yet higher, and from its summit what he saw (and that clearly) was "a port three or four leagues in circuit; . . . a great sand beach covered, for more than sixty leagues, with box [sage-brush], wherein the port and sea termin-

ated"; and last "the disemboguement of the full-flooded
Colorado" in an estuary "great enough, perchance, to float
ships of the royal navy. . . . Wherefore," affirms he, "*no
es Ysla la California sino solo Peninsula*, — the truth of
which the Padre Eusebio Kino, who has said and written
it many times, had brought us to confirm."

The same day, concludes Ojuela, "we descended the two
eminences; saddled our mules; rode to the tank where we
had left our sumpters and relays; heard the padre [Kino]
say Mass; ate; mounted our horses and began the return to
San Marcelo [del Sonoydag]." [33] — "And Moses went up
from the plains of Moab unto the mountain of Nebo, to the
top of Pisgah, that is over against Jericho. And the Lord
shewed him all the land of Gilead, unto Dan; and all
Naphtali, and the land of Ephraim, and Manasseh, and
all the land of Judah, unto the utmost sea; and the south,
and the plain of the valley of Jericho, the city of palm trees,
unto Zoar. And the Lord said unto him, This is the land
which I sware unto Abraham, unto Isaac, and unto Jacob,
saying, I will give it unto thy seed: I have caused thee to
see it with thine eyes, but thou shalt not go over thither."
That while Kino (a Jesuit) surveyed from afar the land of
promise which he was not to enter, there should have stood
beside him a Franciscan father, — one of a holy Order
which later was to subdue the land and possess it even
"unto Cape Mendocino and the Harbor of Monterey," —
is not the least exceptional incident of this exceptional
entrada of 1706.

Meanwhile, the California missions (there at length
were two, — Loreto and San Xavier) were kept alive
with difficulty. On quitting Loreto for Pimería in 1701,
Salvatierra had left Piccolo as vice-rector. On returning, he found Ugarte, and by the firmness of the latter

he was prevented from abandoning the peninsula in bitter tears. But, on July 17, Philip V (King of Spain since 1700) issued three *cédulas* conferring on the missions of California an annual stipend of 6000 *pesos*.[34] Piccolo at the time was in Mexico, but in 1702 he returned with the first year's stipend and with private gifts to the Pious Fund from the Marqués de Villapuente and Nicolás de Ortega and wife, of 40,000 *pesos*.[35] Moreover in 1703 this stipend of 6000 *pesos* was ordered by the King increased to 13,000.[36] At intervals between 1702 and 1711 the Crown, as represented by the Duque de Albuquerque, sought to substitute a military occupation for an occupation exclusively or dominantly sacerdotal. But the attempt was not prolonged, and California exploration and settlement were carried forward by missionaries on the Mission plan.

In 1717, on July 17, Salvatierra, while on a journey to Mexico, died at Guadalajara, at the age of seventy-three.[37] But Ugarte as yet was only fifty-seven, and in 1721, in a ship built by him at Mulegé, and named significantly El Triunfo de la Cruz, he fared to the mouth of the Colorado, testing for himself the soundness of Kino's views on the peninsular question.[38] Ugarte himself, however, died in 1730, and four years thereafter (1734) Lower California was swept by an Indian uprising provoked by a Mission order against polygamy. From this revolt, during which two padres were killed and an attack was made upon a shore party from the Philippine galleon San Cristóbal, it resulted that the Spanish Government, reverting to the idea of secular control, established at San José del Cabo a presidio for the convenience of the galleon, now regular in its stops at Cape San Lucas. The presidial commander withal was made free from missionary supervision, but the change led to disorders among the soldiery, and in 1738 the old system was restored.[39] Crowning all, there appeared in

1747, on December 4, a royal *cédula* which sanctioned for the reduction of the Californias the exact plan of Kino. Pimería Alta (the scene of Kino's labors) was to be occupied; a presidio was to be established on the Gila River; and Alta California was to be entered by way of the Arizona desert.[40]

To settle finally the question of peninsularity, Fernando Consag, a Jesuit, had in June, 1746, been sent by his provincial, Cristóbal Escobar, to the mouth of the Colorado. In due course he had made report,[41] and in the decree above cited, Ferdinand VI of Spain (successor to Philip V) pronounced that California *"no es Isla* [but] *una tierra firme,* bordering, in its upper or northern part, on New Mexico." Anian, however, was still to be reckoned with. Was there not, asked Miguel Venegas in his *Noticia de la California,* printed in 1757, a chance that the strait might be discovered by the English through the efforts of some disciple of Arthur Dobbs? As for the Russians, it was Venegas's claim that already they had taken surveys of their own coasts on the South Sea; had sailed as far as the islands of Japan, and had landed in several parts of Spanish America. Therefore, continued the Jesuit historian, emphasizing the Spanish Government's indorsement of Kino's far-reaching conception, "the missions must . . . be joined to the rest with New Mexico, [and] extended from the latter beyond the rivers Gila and Colorado to the furthest known coasts of California on the South Sea, — to Puerto de San Diego, Puerto de Monterey, the Sierras Nevadas, Cape Mendocino, Cape Blanco, or San Sebastián, and to the river discovered by Martín de Aguilar in forty-three degrees." [42]

California must be joined to Mexico not alone by way of Sonora (Pimería) but by way of New Mexico, — so

declared Ferdinand VI and the historian Miguel Venegas.
The idea had already been entertained by Kino.

In 1699 Kino described Pimería as extending "almost to
the Province of Moqui"; and in April, 1700, when at San
Xavier del Bec questioning "the principal governors and
captains" about the heavenly blue shells, he said: "We
also discussed what mode there might be of penetrating to
the Moquis of New Mexico," a distance, as he conceived,
of but sixty or seventy leagues. And in 1708 it was Kino's
statement that "with these new conversions one can trade
by sea and by land with . . . remote provinces and nations
and kingdoms; with all Nueva Galicia, and with Nueva
Vizcaya; with Moqui and with New Mexico, which shall
be able to come to join hands with these Provinces of
Sonora, and even with New France."

Little, however, was done for New Mexico, under Jesuit
auspices, until 1743. In that year Padre Ignacio Keller
was permitted to start for Moqui, and in 1744 Padre
Jacobo Sedelmayr was allowed to do the same. The
former, by an Apache attack, was forced to return, but
the latter reached Bill Williams Fork. Sedelmayr as an
explorer possessed comprehensive ideas. Like Kino he
planned to make Pimería a base of operations northwestward as far as Monterey, and northward as far as Moqui.

"What of his Majesty having charged upon us the reconquest
of Moqui?" asked Sedelmayr of the Viceroy from Tubutama on
January 25, 1751. "Must we not first reduce the nations of
the Gila and Colorado, through whose lands Moqui [and Upper
California are] to be reached? . . . True is it that there are
needed eleven or twelve missions to control the administration of
so many nations, — Pimas, Cocomoricopas of the Gila, Cocomoricopas of the Colorado, Yumas Cuhana, Guicama, all in the
valley of these rivers. . . . True is it that there will be required
a presidio more numerous than the others, but by locating it on
that part of the River Gila not very distant from Apachería, it

will operate, concurrently, almost to surround the Apaches; . . .
and in such case the [other] presidios will be relieved. If the
Seris be subjected, the presidio of San Miguel de Horcasitas will
be relieved, and it might be transferred to the River Gila." [43]

But while, as regards Alta California, the Mission was to
serve Spain effectively, it was not so to serve in Jesuit
hands. The Jesuits, barring a few exuberant spirits, had
never been enamoured of California. In 1686 they had
refused outright to attempt its conquest. In 1697 they
had recalled their refusal with hesitation. Later, under
Albuquerque, Salvatierra even had offered to give up the
conquest. So solitary amid rocks and thorns was Mission
life on the peninsula, and withal so fruitless, that it bred
melancholy. [44] Communication with Europe required two
and even three years, and with Mexico many months; while
as for Indian conversion (or rather "reduction"), despite
the padres it had become a process in which the disease
of syphilis, [45] spread by the presidial soldiery, had wasted
a population originally twelve thousand souls to 7149. [46]

In 1766 relinquishment was once again proposed, and,
as it chanced, with augmented reason, for the Jesuit Order
was tottering to its fall. Known throughout the world
for chastity and obedience, the Jesuits had failed to win
recognition for poverty. Neither mendicant nor lowly,
they, both in Europe and Paraguay, were deemed to have
heaped up unto themselves riches, and to have grasped at
power. Be the truth concerning them in these respects
what it may, they of a certainty had gained neither riches
nor power in California. Relief came to them in 1767. At
Loreto, on the 17th of December, they were formally notified by Gaspar de Portolá, in the name of Charles III (King
of Spain since 1759), of their expulsion from all the Spanish
dominions. [47]

CHAPTER V

REOCCUPATION OF MONTEREY, AND DISCOVERY OF THE BAY OF SAN FRANCISCO

WITH the Mission, — Spain's sword of the Spirit, — tested and tempered by use in the Philippine Islands, in Paraguay, and, last, in Lower California, the conquest of Alta California was undertaken by Spain through the Franciscan Order of missionary friars, in the year 1769.

Of the religious Orders active in New Spain for the propagation of the Gospel, the Franciscans were by far the most popular, alike with the Spanish Government and with the Indians. The soul of their character was disinterestedness and self-abnegation. Their vows of chastity and obedience (at least since the reforms of Cardinal Ximénes) were well observed.[1] But their supreme merit was their observance of the vow of poverty, — the particular vow in respect to which the Jesuits as an Order were so signally to fail. The Franciscans at the beginning of their labors had in one point been inferior to the Dominicans. In Hispaniola they had not been unequivocally for freedom for the Indian. They had not joined with Pedro de Córdova in denunciation of the *encomienda*. But as time passed, they became so far liberalized that it was with difficulty that any inferiority to the Dominicans could be pointed out.[2]

The Order made its appearance in Mexico in 1524.[3] It came in response to royal commands and papal Bulls, issued respectively by Ferdinand (1508), by Leo X (1521), and by Adrian VI (1522); and it came in characteristic

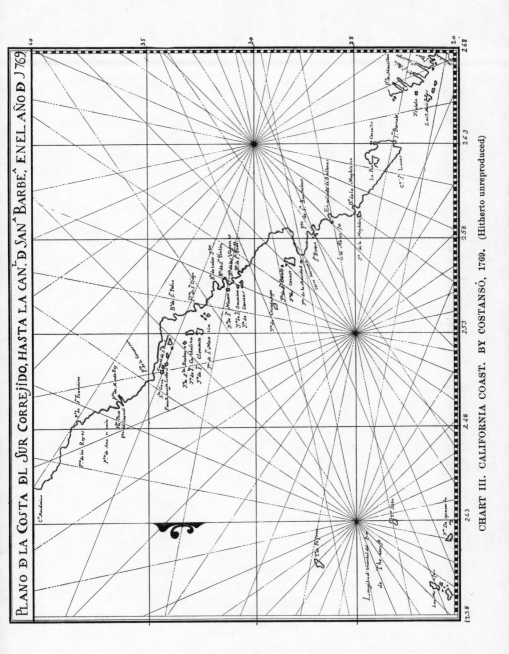

PLANO Đ LA COSTA ĐL SUR CORREJIDO, HASTA LA CAN.ᴸ Đ SANᵗᵃ BARBEᵃ, EN EL AÑO Đ 1769.

CHART III. CALIFORNIA COAST. BY COSTANSÓ, 1769. (Hitherto unreproduced)

guise. Sandal-shod and in flowing gowns of sackcloth, the Franciscans, a band of twelve, the apostolic number, arrived in the capital on May 13, and were reverently greeted by Cortés, who, abasing himself at the feet of their superior, Martín de Valencia, humbly kissed his garments. Almost immediately (July 2) the *Custodia del Santo Evangelio de Propaganda Fide en la Nueva España y Tierra de Yucatán* was established, with the capital as a base; and apostolic colleges or missionary training-schools were formed at Querétaro, Zacatecas, and elsewhere, points convenient for supplying missionaries for the spirtual conquest of outlying provinces.[4]

One of the colleges so formed (1734) was that of San Fernando.[5] It was located at the capital, and in 1767 (June), on the enforcement in New Spain of the expulsion decree against the Jesuits, was assigned the duty of taking charge of the missions (soon to be vacated) of Lower California. Five of the members — among them the Mallorcans Juan Crespi and Fermín Francisco Lasuén — were in the Sierra Gorda, a district of the province of Nueva Galicia near the Gulf of Mexico. These now were recalled, and having been joined by eleven from the college, — among them the Mallorcan Francisco Palou, — the entire band was placed under the presidency of another Mallorcan, himself of distinguished service in Sierra Gorda, — Junípero Serra.[6] The band took ship from San Blas on March 13, 1768,[7] and on April 1 they reached Loreto. But the substitution by the government at Madrid of Franciscans for Jesuits as guardians in the peninsula was significant of more than at first appeared.

Charles III (successor in 1759 to Ferdinand VI) ascended the Spanish throne under favorable conditions. It was his good fortune to have had in Ferdinand a predecessor who loved peace, founded libraries and academies, encouraged the useful arts, and laid up money. To Charles there were bequeathed a National Library, an Academy of History, fifty ships of war, over fourteen thousand silk looms, and three millions in cash, — an accumulation of resources unparalleled since the days of the Moriscos. Withal under the new king there took place a revival of interest, economic and political, in New Spain, — a revival not unlike that provoked under Philip III by the memorial of Hernando de los Ríos, and under Philip V and Ferdinand VI by the ideas of Eusebio Kino. What, however, made the new revival distinctive was the confirmation thereunder of the policy of the ministers Aranda, Campomanes, and Floridablanca, who sought to curb the priesthood, — a course which in Alta California (*vide* chapter VII) was destined to be pursued by its chief lawgiver, Felipe de Neve.

In 1761 José de Gálvez of Malaga, a son of the people,[8] was sent to Mexico as *visitador* (inspector) general. In 1764 he was vested with powers well-nigh supreme, and in 1766, still further to strengthen his hands, Carlos Francisco de Croix, scion of a family illustrious in Flanders, was appointed viceroy. Shortly after the coming of Croix, war with the Indians (Apaches, Seris, Pimas) broke forth in Sinaloa and Sonora, and the Viceroy, finding his resources taxed, took earnest counsel with the *visitador*. The result (January 23, 1768) was a joint dispatch to the King, — a dispatch fundamental in the history of California, — in which it is stated that, in view of the remoteness of Sonora, Sinaloa, Nueva Vizcaya, and the peninsula of California, and of their unsettled condition, it has been decided, in council, that Gálvez shall visit these provinces, establish in them pueblos, and regulate their government. Further reasons assigned for the visit of Gálvez are: (1) Attempts for two centuries by France and England to discover the Strait of Anian; (2) the recent conquest of Canada by England, — "a nation that spares neither expense, diligence, nor fatigue in advancing her discoveries"; and (3) the efforts of Russia, by trading expeditions from Kamtchatka to the Aleutian Islands, to penetrate "our new Indies" by way of the sea of Tartary.

The joint dispatch says: —

It is known to our court by the voyages and narratives that have been published in Europe that the Russians have familiarized themselves with the navigation of the sea of Tartary, and that (according to a well-founded report) they already carry on trade in furs with a continent, or perhaps island [Alaska], distant only eight hundred leagues from the Western Coast of the Californias, which extends to the capes Mendocino and Blanco.

And again: —

It admits of no doubt that from the year 1749, [sic] when Admiral Anson came to the western coast of this kingdom, to the time of the seizure of the Port of Acapulco [by the Dutch], the English and Dutch have acquired a very particular knowledge of the ports and bays that we hold on the South coast, especially the peninsula of the Californias; so that it would be neither impossible, nor indeed very difficult, for one of these two nations, or the Muscovites, to establish, when least expected, a colony in the port of Monterey. Wherefore [the dispatch concludes], it behooves us, taking matters in time, to put in force what means are possible for warding off the dangers that threaten us. And — the peninsula of the Californias disembarrassed, and its population increased by help of the free commerce which ought to prevail between it and this kingdom — it will be easy to transport a colony to the port of Monterey by the same ships that we already have in the South Sea,—ships constructed for the purposes of the expedition to Sonora against the Indians.[9]

On this same 23d of January, 1768, the date of the above dispatch by Croix and Gálvez, it chanced that the Spanish Government itself, aroused by the voyages of the Russians eastward from Kamtchatka, was inditing a dispatch. It

was addressed to the Viceroy, and commanded him to
warn the newly appointed governor of the Californias —
Gaspar de Portolá, occupant of the peninsula since November 30, 1767 — against Russian attempts; attempts
which if possible he was to frustrate. This dispatch,
received by Croix in May, was acknowledged by him on the
28th of the month, with the statement that he had communicated its contents to Gálvez, who since April 9 had
been on the way to the peninsula, and that he (Gálvez)
had resolved to effect a reconnoissance of the important
port of Monterey for the purpose of establishing there a
presidio.[10]

When the *visitador* reached Lower California (Cerralvo
Inlet, near La Paz) it was the 5th of July.[11] He was met
by the captain of the presidio of Loreto, Fernando Xavier
Rivera y Moncada, and headquarters were assigned him at
the hacienda of Manuel Osio [12] in the royal mining-camp
of Santa Ana. The problems which confronted him were
three: (1) The establishing of Indian pueblos; (2) the promotion of colonization by Spaniards; and (3) the expedition to Monterey. By the first problem Gálvez was not
a little perplexed. He had come expecting to find a set of
mission establishments well regulated and with a clientage
of natives passably broken to civilization. What he in fact
found was a set of establishments, — the spiritualties in
charge of Serra and his Franciscans, the temporalties
in charge of soldiers (*comisionados*) appointed by Portolá,
— with a native clientage, if clientage it might be called,
half-fed, wholly naked, devoured by syphilis, and wandering in the mountains.

The *visitador* first dismissed the *comisionados* and restored the system of the Mission, by bestowing upon the
Franciscans the temporalties.[13] Next, he addressed himself to the Indians. For feeding the wretches, he brought

whole *rancherías* from the north, where population exceeded the means of subsistence, to the less burdened south. For clothing them (a point upon which he insisted as one indispensable to civilization), he made requisition for bales of cloth; and for weaning them from the mountains, he sought to establish them in *pueblos formales*, or regular towns, "giving them houses and lands to be inherited by their sons." [14] Finally, in order that his efforts might be promptly seconded by the padres, he proclaimed that Spanish honor was at stake. Very soon there were to arrive in the peninsula six French Academicians, accompanied by two officials of the Spanish marine, to observe the transit of Venus. What if these learned foreigners were to behold there "the sad sights and depopulated places that [he] had beheld four months before"? What if they should cause it to be published in their reports that "in the Californias the greatest and most pious monarch of the world was lord only of the deserts, and had for vassals wandering Indians living like wild beasts"? [15] Colonization by Spaniards was also a problem of difficulty. Solution was attempted by the *visitador* through a decree (August 12, 1768) offering Crown lands and military rights.[16]

But it was the expedition to Monterey (his own conception) that claimed the heart of Gálvez. It claimed also the heart of Croix; and, straightway it was known, the heart of Junípero Serra. An unusual group — one unusual even for New Spain — were the three men, José de Gálvez, *visitador;* Francisco de Croix, viceroy; and Junípero Serra, president of the California missions: Gálvez, — honest, masterful, and bluff; Croix, — honest, discerning, and diplomatic; Serra, — a seraphic spirit, a later Salvatierra, a New-World Francis of Assisi; post-mediæval, yet not belated for his task; beholder of visions, believer in miracles, merciless wielder of the penitential scourge; [17] yet through simple purity of heart, possessed of a courage not unequal to labors the most arduous, and of a wisdom not unequal to situations the most perplexing. When, therefore, two from the group (Gálvez and Serra) met under the sanction of the third (Croix), as they did at Santa Ana on October 31, 1768, to confer regarding the exact means and course for reaching Monterey, activity was assured.[18]

There was to be an expedition, Indian auxiliaries included, of about 225 men in four divisions, — two by sea, and two by land.[19] Among the transports plying between San Blas (Spanish naval base for the Northwest), San José del Cabo, and Guaymas, were the Lauretana, the Sinaloa, the Concepción, the San Carlos, and the San Antonio or Príncipe. Of these the first three were used by Gálvez to bring supplies to La Paz, while the other two (brigantines) were appointed by him to take, each, from that point a division of the expedition. Northwestern navigation in 1768 was no less formidable than in the days of Vizcaino, and from the moment that the *visitador* charged himself with the fate of these vessels he scarcely slept. "Both the San Carlos and Príncipe may reach La Paz between the 20th and 25th of this month," he writes to Serra on September 15, "but if retarded, the months of October and November will be suitable for sailing, as then, according to a Filippine pilot, there prevail winds favorable for Monterey." [20] On October 7, he writes: "I long with eagerness for the coming of the packet-boats, and, as I am persuaded that at San Blas the Equinox is passed, I conceive them as already this hour on the sea. God grant that they come soon to La Paz!" [21] Four days later he has heard that in a tempest on the 29th of September the Lauretana and Sinaloa were driven aground but have escaped damage. "Implore our patroness Lady of Loreto," he adjures Serra, "that she bring safely the packet-boats, for without them everything will be undone." [22] At length (November 12) word comes of the arrival at Cape San Lucas of the San Carlos, and the vessel is impatiently ordered by Gálvez to hasten to La Paz.[23]

From the elaborate and somewhat costly vestments and silver utensils (censers, candlesticks, chalices) with which the Jesuits had provided the peninsular churches of La Pasión, San Luis, and Todos Santos, the *visitador* has been making requisitions for the north. "I think," he writes to Serra on October 11, "that we shall not be able to establish more than three missions right away, and to each of these we can assign six sets of vestments; while as for the utensils, they are being cleaned and repaired by the official silversmith." [24] Names for the new establishments had been considered on September 15. The ancient discoverers had given the name San Diego to a port where one of the new missions was to be placed. There should be no change. To another famous port they had given the name of the glorious patriarch San Francisco. Here especially no change should be made, as by the intercession of so great a father there would be facilitated the founding of a mission at Monterey. As for the intermediate mission, let it, in order to share the intercession, be called San Buenaventura; while as for the fort and pueblo to be erected at Monterey, no name should be considered but San Carlos, — name at once of "our beloved sovereign, of the Prince of Asturias, and of the Viceroy of New Spain." [25] Then there were other matters: bells (three of five belonging to La Pasión and San Luis) to be unhung and packed, and a supply of sour fruits ("precious against scurvy in latitude 30° and beyond") and of oil, dates, wine, brandy and vinegar, to be collected. "So infinite is my business, so many are the things to be seen to by me at one time," exclaims Gálvez in distraction, "that even though my ardor rises with my difficulties, my days not merely are consumed, but in great part my nights!" [26]

Meanwhile the San Carlos (brigantine of eleven sails), on arriving at La Paz, had been found unseaworthy, had been careened, and was being thoroughly overhauled both as to her keel and sides. The work, closely supervised by the *visitador*, was finished on December 27, and although performed with scant resources, was pronounced excellent in character. [27] The day fixed upon for sailing — whether the Príncipe (San Antonio) should be come or not — was January 8, 1769. Besides the church furniture, the oil, the dates, the wine, etc., already mentioned, there were on board meat, fish, maize, lard, wood, coal, sugar (white and brown), figs, raisins, salt, red pepper, garlic, flour, bread, rice, chick-peas, water, cheese, chocolate, hams, smoked tongue, lentils, candles, bran, beans, hens, a few live cattle, and 1000 *pesos* in money. There also was on board a carefully chosen company: Captain Vicente Vila (Andalusian) of the royal navy, with a mate (Jorge Estorace) and crew of twenty-three sailors and two boys; Cosmographer Miguel Costansó, — an engineer already distinguished, and destined to become yet more so in connection with notable undertakings in Mexico; Surgeon Pedro Prat of the royal navy; Lieutenant Pedro Fages, with twenty-five volunteers from the Catalan company serving in Sonora; four cooks; two blacksmiths; and last a chaplain, Hernando Parrón, one of Serra's Franciscans. [28] Serra himself, as well as Gálvez, was present at the departure. [29] " *Oratio brevis*," the latter writes to Palou, on January 9, from La Paz, "the San Carlos is just sailing from this port for the Sacred Expedition. . . . The twelve

[Indian] boys whom you sent have pleased me much. I turned them over to the priest here to aid in the confessions and to assist at the ceremony of blessing the packet-boat and banners, — a ceremony performed by the Father-President. Then *I* preached, the worst of all."

Gálvez in the Concepción accompanied the brigantine as far as Cape San Lucas, alike to observe her behavior and to intercept, near the cape, the San Antonio (unable, it was thought, to reach La Paz), and to send her forward as division two of the Sacred Expedition. Solicitous at first, as he watched the San Carlos, his own handiwork, meet the seas, the *visitador* quickly gained a joyous confidence.

We cast anchor on the 14th [he wrote to Serra, from the cape, on January 26] and in truth might have come in two days, had I put myself in the San Carlos; for, to keep in convoy the Concepción, which carried full sail during the voyage, the blessed packet-boat carried only her fore-topsail and her main-topsail half lowered. In short, the San Carlos, with a moderate wind, growing fresh as on the second day we left the island of Cerralvo, went six knots an hour. It may be imagined how she would have sped if she had been free to use but half her sails. Your Reverence may offset with this truth (which all have noted with admiration) the infamous lies which are spoken of the packet-boat, — a vessel, without exaggeration, one of the best possessed by the King in his armadas.

And he adds: —

Joachín Robles, and all the old sailors who came in the Concepción, exclaimed constantly in benedictions and praises of the San Carlos, and say that she is worthy to be enchased in gold. Your Reverence may conceive the satisfaction of those sailing in her, and my satisfaction to see falsified all the coward prognostications of the distrustful, and my own projects realized, which, undertaken with constant faith and a pure heart, God has willed should find complete fulfillment in this voyage to the cape.[30]

But concerning the voyage of the San Carlos, let us be advised by the log of her commanding officer: —

Noon of Monday, January 9, *to noon of Tuesday, January* 10, 1769. — At midnight, with a shore breeze (cat's paw) south-southwest, hove anchor [from La Paz], and with everything set and launch at prow prepared to sail. Tide contrary and so strong as scarcely to be stemmed. At one o'clock (wind seaward northwest) anchored in mid-channel in three fathoms of water, mud and sand. At midday, hoisted jib, fore-topsail and spanker; the launch with a kedge doing all possible, by way of towing, to give us an offing.

Tuesday, 10, *to Wednesday,* 11. Continued kedging till half-past four in the afternoon, when cast anchor almost in the mouth of channel, for already the tide was rising. At half-past six in the morning set topsails, wind brisk from the southwest. At this hour descried the packet-boat standing out with flag at main-mast, the Most Illustrious Señor Visitador-General on board, bound for Cape San Lucas and the Bay of San Bernabé. At half-past seven, passing [the packet-boat] to starboard, lowered topsails and saluted by hail and by the six guns which were mounted, keeping in convoy. At midday saw Cerralvo Island to southeast six or seven leagues, finding myself still in channel between Point San Lorenzo and the island of Espiritu Santo. . . . The bottom of the channel, which sounds four, five, or six fathoms, is clear, consisting of sandbanks and stone, with some mud. And it is said by coast pilots that these banks bear pearl-producing shells.

Wednesday, 11, *to Thursday,* 12. . . , Sunrise: the coast and smoky horizon gave no sign of the Concepción or Comandante till nine o'clock, when boat was sighted in-shore to starboard, and I shortened sail to wait for her. . . . Made out the island of Cerralvo to the northwest and Cape Pulmo to the southeast.

Thursday, 12, *to Friday,* 13. Followed, with moderate wind, on lookout for Pulmo, topsails lowered, to avoid passing the Concepción, till four in the afternoon, when, coming within hail, his Excellency ordered me to press sail, as he wished to see the packet-boat [San Carlos] show her speed. At sunset, being about a league from the Comandante, furled all light sail and lowered the great sails, continuing with the topsails. . . . At Angelus, two huge fires seen on Pulmo. At midnight, hove to off Cape Porfía to await Comandante, and at four in the morning proceeded in convoy.

Friday, 13, *to Saturday*, 14. Continued in convoy of Comandante, wind contrary with moderate sea, etc. At eleven o'clock, Comandante passed. Kept in wake on lookout for Cape San Lucas.

Saturday, 14, *to Sunday*, 15. Followed Comandante, wind moderate, sea calm, to within a league of the coast, all sail set. At four o'clock in the afternoon, a league and a half from the bay of San Bernabé, wind almost calm, the Comandante lowered and sent ashore a boat. At Angelus, Comandante, with our ship alongside, anchored in twenty fathoms. At eight o'clock, went to kiss the hand of his Excellency, and at nine returned on board. Night passed in calm, and at half-past seven in the morning his Excellency came on board with his suite and the crew of the Concepción. Mass over, his Excellency said farewell to all, giving orders in particular that without loss of time I should sail for my destination, governing myself exactly by the instructions already given me.[31]

Stopping at San Lucas only long enough to take fresh water, and hay for the cattle, the San Carlos, on the night of January 15 stood for the South Sea. And here occurred a thing not unmixed with pathos. For four days there prevailed light and contrary winds, with opposing currents of the ocean, and on each of the four days the *visitador*, from a high hill (*cerro eminente*), watched with anxious gaze the far-off and baffled ship. But on the 20th good breezes sprang "from the east and southeast," and "straightway the San Carlos disappeared." The founding of Alta California was indeed begun. The first division of the expedition to that end had been dispatched. "The Lord conduct it prosperously, the undertaking is all his!" prayed Gálvez.[32]

The San Antonio (which on January 15 had reached La Paz, despite efforts by Gálvez to intercept her off Cape San Lucas) dropped anchor at the cape on the 25th, and at once was beached and overhauled "from keel to pennant." More heavily provisioned even than the San

Carlos, and with a crew of twenty-eight men, she was got
to sea, under Juan Pérez (Manila *piloto*), Miguel del Pino
(master's mate), and Chaplains Juan Vizcaino and Francisco Gómez, on February 15. The day was further made
memorable by the arrival at the cape of the San José, a
new packet-boat especially built at San Blas for Monterey
uses. "We blessed the ships and standards," facetiously
writes the *visitador* on February 20, "by the help of four
friars, two cannon, and a homily by me *á la burlesca*, as at
La Paz. . . . It will be said that in the Californias there
is verified *la comedia del Diablo Predicador*, and I shall
laugh that so they call me, if only we gain the blessed
object of our enterprise. . . . But," he continues, "the
tongue, in my preachments, but spoke the feelings of my
heart, which had gone in the ships, I not being able myself
to go with them."

Thus was dispatched the second division of the expedition to Monterey. And all the while the heart of Gálvez
grew lighter, for the winds continued to set from the south
and southeast. "We have not had a day of northwest,"
writes the *visitador* (February 20), "since the sailing of the
Príncipe (San Antonio); the winds have been so favorable
that we all deem the ships as already at the doors of San
Diego, and even as at anchor in that port. Both sail like
birds." And two days later: "I have no doubt that the
San Antonio is in San Diego, as the south and southeast
winds have continued." [33]

There remained the two divisions by land to be dispatched, — divisions three and four of the expedition.

In these Gálvez put not the same trust as in the divisions
by sea, as in his opinion they had not been undertaken
with the same *viva fé*. But he wrought valiantly by exhortation to set them in motion. Of the first division Rivera y
Moncada was commander, and by him, from and after

September, 1768, there were gathered (originally at Santa María, the most northerly of the peninsular missions, but afterwards at a point of good pasturage eighteen leagues further north) supplies of cattle (200 head), horses (38 head), mules (144 head), pack-saddles, leather bags, sides of leather, bottles, wheat, flour, dried meat, lard, sugar, figs, raisins, and wine.[34] And now that the San Carlos and San Antonio both had sailed, there was need that camp be broken by the land force. On February 20, therefore, Gálvez sent to Rivera a peremptory order to advance, expressing the wish that "God might lend wings to the bearer"; for was not news soon expected that "the packet-boats were lording it in that *famoso puerto* which had cost so many expeditions and anxieties"?[35] The division having on March 22 been joined at Velicatá by Padres Crespi and Lasuén (the former to accompany it and the latter to bless its departure), the captain, at four o'clock of the afternoon of the 24th, guided by the cosmographer, José Cañizares,[36] and at the head of 25 cuirassed men from the garrison of Loreto, 42 Christianized Indians, and three muleteers with 188 mules and horses, took up his march.

The fourth division (second of the two by land) had been mustered at San Juan de Dios, a spot some six leagues to the north of Velicatá, and on May 21 it followed Rivera. It was led by Governor Portolá himself (Catalan officer of dragoons, forty-seven years old),[37] a man laconic to the point of dropping his *h*'s, but honest withal and circumspect. Comprised in it were 10 soldiers (cuirassiers) of the presidio of Loreto, under a stout sergeant, José Francisco Ortega; 44 Christianized Indians; four muleteers with 170 mules; and two servants.[38] The division was accompanied by Junípero Serra, president of the new establishment, who had joined it on May 5, and one of the servants was

for him. In the winter of 1749–50, the year of his arrival
in Mexico, Serra, alive to the observance of Franciscan
austerities, had insisted on proceeding from Vera Cruz to
the capital on foot. A part of the way was infested with
mosquitoes, and, sleeping one night in the open air, one of
his ankles had been cruelly stung. The wound, envenomed
by scratching and neglect, had developed into an ulcer,
and but for his servant's help the Father-President would
have been unable to mount his mule.[39] "Although it is
an act of temerity," Gálvez had written him on March 28,
"for you to set forth on a journey so great and labor-
ious with your foot inflamed, I have no doubt that midway the fatigue it will grow better, and even well; for so
the Lord rewards the *viva fé* of his followers who look to him
as physician sovereign and unique." [40] For some weary
leagues Serra proceeded under the inspiration of the words
of the *visitador*. Then he had recourse to muleteer's oint-
ment, a remedy by which speedily he found relief.

On May 1, the *visitador* himself had sailed for Sonora.
The things upon which, when leaving, he had insisted
were (barring the Monterey expedition) those upon
which he had insisted when he came: Indian pueblos
and colonization by Spaniards. As the site for a pueblo,
Loreto had been designated. Hither were to be brought
from the other peninsular missions one hundred families
to dwell in whitened adobes, on tree-shaded streets, about
a plaza. The youth were to be instructed in the propagation of the cochineal; while pearl-fishing, which, as sought
to be practiced by the Spanish soldiery, had so plagued
Salvatierra, was now to be conducted humanely under
missionary superintendence.[41] But ever present to the
mind of Gálvez, as prerequisite for the civilization of the
California Indian, was that he be clothed, — "the men
and boys in jackets and trousers, and the women and girls

in chemisettes and skirts"; and this, too, before the spectacle of their nakedness should, to the scandal of Church and State, be revealed to the French Academicians shortly to arrive at Cape San Lucas. To this end, therefore, and to forward supplies by the San José, Francisco Palou was delegated by Serra to remain at Loreto as peninsular mission president *pro tempore*.[42]

Spanish colonization had received from Gálvez an impulse through a decree for a Spanish settlement; [43] but it was not until May 14 that a final matter of importance was carried out. For the support of the three establishments to be planted in the north (San Diego, San Buenaventura, and San Carlos), it had early been decided by the *visitador* to plant three between Santa María and San Diego. Of these the first (and, as it proved, also the last) was founded with appropriate ceremonies, on the date named, at Velicatá, — the mission of San Fernando.[44]

The objective of the Gálvez expedition was Monterey (Vizcaino's haven), but the four divisions had been ordered to rendezvous at San Diego, and here, by favor of the spouse of Our Lady of Loreto (St. Joseph, patron of the undertaking),[45] and by virtue of propitiatory litanies and Masses, the San Carlos, the San Antonio, Rivera, and Portolá were all arrived by July 1.

The division first to arrive had been the San Antonio. Keeping an inside course, the vessel had proceeded north to 34°. Thence turning southward she had sighted Vizcaino's Isla de Gente Barbada, which she had renamed Santa Cruz, and with two dead from scurvy had cast anchor on April 11.

As for the San Carlos, she had not only been behind the San Antonio, but far behind. By February 15 she had reached Guadalupe Island in 29°. By the 17th she had passed northward, encountering northwest winds with fog, rain, and heavy seas, and on the 26th had sighted the California mainland. For nearly a fortnight she had surveyed the coast for a watering-place, but without success; and on March 7 had stopped at the island of Cerros (Cedros). On the 26th (the northwest winds becoming "northwesters"), a sheltered course had been sought between Cerros Island and that of Natividad, and for the first time scurvy had appeared. By the 18th of April, twenty-two seamen and ten of Fages' squad were incapacitated, and the coxswain, Fernando Álvarez, had died. On the 24th, all the sick, even those not reconciled with the Church, had confessed and received the Sacrament, and there had died the coast pilot, Manuel Reyes. On the 26th, the San Carlos being within sight of Point Conception, Vila had decided to change his course to the southward. Inland rose "lofty sierras all covered with snow, like the Sierras Nevadas of Granada as seen along the Mediterranean on the coast of Motril and Salobreña," — an indication of the Santa Lucía Range at which the Philippine galleons were wont to alter direction for Acapulco. From Point Conception, down through San Pedro Bay (where anchor was dropped) to the Coronados Islands, the San Carlos under press of canvas, but with what were indeed "a ghastly crew," had reached San Diego near sundown on April 29.[46]

But what meanwhile of the divisions by land? On May 28, Serra records: "Until now we had not seen any woman among the Indians; and I desired for the present not to see them, fearing that they went naked as the men. When amid the *fiestas* two women appeared, talking as rapidly and vivaciously as this sex knows how and is accustomed to do; and when I saw them so honestly covered that we could take it in good part if greater nudities were never

seen among the Christian women of the missions, I was
not sorry for their arrival." And on June 24: "We slept
under a very corpulent oak, and here we lacked the privilege of Lower California of the exemption from fleas, for we
were covered with them and some ticks." On July 3 the
Father-President records further: "About midway from
Velicatá the valleys and rivers began to be delightful. We
found vines of a large size and in some cases quite loaded
with grapes. We also found [and here a touch that en-
dears Serra to all lovers of California] in water-courses
along the way . . . besides grapes, *varias rosas de
Castilla.*" Already on June 2 he had noted: "Flowers
many and beautiful, . . . and to-day we have met the
queen of them all [*Reyna de ellas*], the rose of Castile. As
I write, I have a branch before me with three full-blown
roses, others in bud, and six unpetaled." [47]

The first land division (Rivera's) had made camp on
May 14, and the second (Portolá's) on June 28; and in
point of spirits and health both were unexceptionable.
Serra, even, was cured of his lameness. Camp made, however, the scene beheld by the newcomers was most pite-
ous.[48] Addressing the guardian of San Fernando on June
22, Crespi says that twenty-three persons (two of them
Catalan volunteers) have died.[49] Portolá's account, sent
July 4, is even more discouraging. Of the sea divisions,
"all without exception," he declares, "seamen, soldiers,
and officers, are stricken with scurvy, — some wholly
prostrated, some half disabled, others on foot without
strength, until the total number of dead is thirty-one." [50]

Vila, under orders issued by the *visitador* on January 5,
was to proceed with the San Carlos, Fages and his men
on board, at once from San Diego to Monterey. But this
was conditioned upon the presence of the land division

under Rivera. Should Rivera be anticipated by the San
Carlos in arriving, the vessel was to wait for him twenty
days and then proceed to Monterey, the San Antonio
accompanying her if at that time in port.[51]

As we know, the San Antonio in fact reached San Diego
before the San Carlos, but this was of little moment. What
was of moment was the prevalence of the scurvy. By it the
whole expedition was deranged. Seamen there virtually
were none, and if Monterey was to be occupied at all, it
must be by a force by land. Word (July 9) was sent to the
Viceroy; the San Antonio, with five men and such of the
sick as were able to be transported, was dispatched to San
Blas for fresh crews for herself and the San Carlos; and, on
July 14, the expedition — Portolá, Rivera, Fages, Ortega,
Costansó, Crespi, and Gómez, 27 cuirassiers, 8 volunteers, 15 Christianized Indians, 7 muleteers, and 2 body-
servants, 67 persons — again set out for the north.[52]

At San Diego — to found the mission of San Diego de
Alcalá and to speed to Monterey the San José — there
were left Vila, Serra, Vizcaino, Parrón, Cañizares, Prat, a
blacksmith, a carpenter, and forty-five or fifty sailors and
soldiers, mostly ill. The founding, the principal ceremony of which was a Mass by Serra under a great cross,
was effected on July 16;[53] but as for the San José, she
never came. Dismasted in the gulf in the year 1769, she, in
May, 1770, sailed for the north and was lost.[54]

All the way from Velicatá the natives had been docile,
but San Diego was in a Yuma district, a district of robbers, and in resisting depredations from certain of these
on August 15, a fight was precipitated by the guard. Three
Yumas and one Spaniard were killed, — the latter by an
arrow in the throat; while Fray Vizcaino was disabled by
an arrow in the hand.[55]

The Monterey party (to recur now to the expedition)

depended chiefly for guidance on two books in the hands of Miguel Costansó: the *Noticia de la California* of Venegas, which contained the account, from Torquemada, of Vizcaino's voyage of 1602–03, and a manual of navigation by the celebrated galleon pilot, Cabrera Bueno, printed at Manila in 1734.[56] The manual placed the far-famed port in 37°, and to the attainment of this latitude the party looked forward with eagerness. Their route lay by the seashore past San Clemente and Santa Catalina Islands to the site of the present city of Los Ángeles; thence through the San Fernando Valley to the headwaters of the Santa Clara River; thence, by the river valley, to the sea again; thence past Points Conception and Sal to the extremity of the Santa Bárbara Channel; thence inland to the site of the mission of San Luis Obispo; thence through the Cañada de los Osos to the sea at Morro Bay, and up the coast till progress was barred by the Sierra de Santa Lucía at Mount Mars. The sierra crossed (*camino penoso*), the route lay by the Salinas River Valley to the sea; and so to Point Pinos, which, according to Cabrera Bueno, was the index of Monterey.[57]

At the head of the party [writes Costansó] went Portolá with most of the officers, the six [eight] men of the Catalonian Volunteers, and some friendly Indians with spades, mattocks, crowbars, axes, and other pioneering implements, to chop and open a passage wherever necessary. Then came the pack-train in four divisions, each with muleteers and an escort of soldiers. The rear was closed by the remainder of the troops under Rivera y Moncada, who convoyed the horse-drove and the mule-drove for relays. By the necessity of regulating marches with reference to watering-places [Costansó continues], camp was pitched early each afternoon, so that the land might be explored one day for the next; and at four-day intervals more or less general fatigue, or the recovering of animals stampeded by a coyote or the wind, compelled a halt more protracted.[58]

Adventures were few. The party culled roses, — troops of them; fed on antelope; felt, near the present Los Ángeles, — a spot described by Crespi as "possessed of all the resources required for a large town,"[59] — *horrorosos temblores*, or frightful shocks of earthquake; noted springs and streams of sweet water; saw Indians, — the males "totally naked (*totalmente desnudos*) like Adam in Paradise before the fall"; remarked the number, stature, intelligence, and skill in canoe-building of the tribes along the Santa Bárbara Channel coasts; killed bears (*brutos ferocísimos*) in the Cañada de los Osos; gazed in discouragement from Santa Lucía Peak, 3000 feet high, on a foreground and background billowy with mountains; suffered from scurvy; and on October 1 (1769) gazed joyfully from a hilltop out over the bay of their search, indicated, as the histories said, by a beautiful point of pines.[60] But where was the harbor, the *puerto?* What was to be seen was simply an open roadstead. *Ni Puerto de Carmelo, ni de Monterei*, sorrowfully records Portolá.[61]

There remained, however, a point to be considered. The party as yet had not quite reached latitude 37°. So, after a council of officers and padres, at which it was agreed to find (by God's aid) Monterey with the San José there in waiting, or perish in the attempt, they on October 8 started again northward. Food ran short; scurvy reappeared; men had to be borne in litters; three cuirassiers received extreme unction; Portolá and Rivera themselves fell ill.[62] But at length rains came and all the sick recovered. Amid trials Crespi notes: "We came (October 10) on some tall trees of reddish-colored wood of a species unknown to us, having leaves very unlike those of the Cedar, and without a cedar odor; and as we knew not the names of the trees, we gave them that of the color of the wood, *palo colorado* (red wood)."[63] By the 1st of November the party reached

Point San Pedro, and from a hill (first of a series which barred further passage) saw before them in the distance Point Reyes, and at its base, extending toward the northeast, — six or seven *farallones* in its mouth, — the San Francisco Bay of Cermeño, — in a word, the present Bay of Francis Drake.[64]

Costansó, with his Cabrera Bueno, found little trouble in identifying the bay; but, to make fully certain, Ortega was sent by Portolá to examine Point Reyes, and during his absence (November 2) a thing occurred which caused perplexity. Some soldiers, climbing the hills to the northeast in pursuit of deer, came suddenly in sight of a new Mediterranean, the great inland sea now known as San Francisco Bay. How so extensive a body of water had hitherto escaped observation — the observation of Unamunu, of Cermeño, of Bueno, and of other northern navigators — was the question.[65] It was not answered, for Ortega, cut off from Point Reyes by the channel of the Golden Gate,[66] soon returned with a report by Indians of a ship anchored at the head of the newly discovered sea, — a ship which might be the long-expected San José. Upon search, however, no ship was found, and on November 11 Portolá, convinced that Monterey either had been passed in the fog, or long since had been obliterated by sand, started with his command, short of rations, back to Point Pinos, where he arrived on November 28.[67]

Monterey, not recognized by the explorers on the way north in October, was not recognized by them on the way south in November; and, having on December 10 erected as declaratory of their visit two great crosses, — one on the shore of Carmelo Bay, and the other on that of the very bay of which they were in quest, — they on December 11 pressed forward, reaching San Diego on the 24th of January, 1770.

For a little time the fate of the Gálvez expedition, and with it that of Alta California, trembled in the balance. At San Diego there had been many deaths, — fifty up to February 11, 1770; thirteen of them from Fages's band of Catalans alone.[68] Moreover, there was great scarcity of food. On January 28, Portolá calculated that the quantity on hand (maize, flour, etc.) would last fifty-four persons and fourteen Christianized Indians (his entire land force) twelve and one half weeks. Accordingly, March 20 was fixed upon as the latest date to which, with safety, a return of the expedition to Velicatá might be deferred. The gloom was general and it was deep. On February 11, Rivera with twenty-two men was sent to Velicatá to fetch north the cattle gathered there, and a sharp lookout was kept for the San Antonio, the return of which with supplies and a crew for the San Carlos was hoped for rather than expected.[69] Summing up, on February 9 and 11, to the *visitador* and Viceroy, respectively, the results of the Monterey adventure, Crespi and Portolá put stress upon the bright side. "I am not at all chagrined," writes the former, "that we failed to hit upon the port of Monte Rey; . . . and if in time we still fail of it, we possess of a certainty and as an actuality the Port of San Francisco." "To me," writes Portolá, "there remains the consolation that by this expedition there has been lost nothing but our great labor in the six months and a half that it has consumed. Exploration has been carried to the very precincts of San Francisco. The spirit of the *gentilidad* has been tested. The infinity of the population of the Channel of Santa Bárbara has been made known. The illusion that Monterey exists has been dispelled." [70]

But though Portolá might be convinced that Monterey no longer existed, and though Crespi might entertain as to its existence some doubt, Serra, who had remained at San

Diego, was firm in faith to the contrary, and made, according to Palou, a compact with Vila of the San Carlos to go in search of the port by sea, on the coming of the San Antonio, even though Portolá should on March 20 abandon the country. All day long on March 19 (St. Joseph's own day), the Father-President and his coadjutors prayerfully strained their eyes seaward for a sail. One appeared toward evening, but vanished with the fall of night. It nevertheless brought hope. Portolá deferred his departure, and five days later the San Antonio, under Pérez, sailed into port. When sighted she had been on her way with supplies to Monterey, under the belief that San Diego had already been visited by the San José. Landing near Point Conception for water and to regain a lost anchor, it was gleaned from the natives that the Monterey party had withdrawn, and course was at once changed to the southward.

The coming of the San Antonio, falling as it did on the day of St. Joseph, was taken for a strong omen by Portolá. It in fact quite roused his mind. Persuaded now that to fail in his undertaking would be disloyalty á Dios, al Rey, á mi 'onor, and remembering that on leaving the peninsula he had resolved "to perform his commission or to die," he took counsel with Pérez, with the result that on April 16 the San Antonio, carrying Pérez, Serra, Costansó, and Prat, was dispatched up the coast; while on the day following, Portolá with seven cuirassiers, Fages with twelve volunteers, and Crespi with five Christianized Indians, followed by land. Pérez was to proceed first to the estuary seen of the deer-hunters on the second of the preceding November (the present San Francisco Bay), where exploration was to be made by Costansó for a port and for a mission site. Next, the San Antonio was to go in search of the port of Monterey, — a spot which, although not found by land, might, as Gálvez had intended, be found by sea.

As a common rendezvous Point Pinos was selected. Thus, in the discovery of Monterey (if the port existed), the land force might participate with the ships. If, however, Monterey no longer did exist, a mission and presidio were to be established in whatever good port might be chanced upon, — perhaps the port of San Francisco; for the farther north such outposts were established, the farther north would be extended the dominions of the King.[71]

The land party reached Monterey Bay on May 24, and Crespi and Fages, attended by a soldier, at once hastened to the cross which had been erected. At its foot they found arrows, feathers and offerings of meat and fish. They then turned to the beach. The day was clear; the great bay lay like a lagoon between Points Pinos and Año Nuevo; and within it, at play, were to be seen numberless seals and two great whales. A few steps more, and the bay assumed the form of a vast O. With one voice the three men exclaimed: "This is the port of Monterey which we seek, in form exactly as described by Sebastián Vizcaino and Cabrera Bueno!" On the 31st, Monterey was reached by the San Antonio, which, although having attained the latitude of the estuary, had not stopped to explore it; and on June 1, Portolá received the embraces and congratulations of Fages and Crespi.[72]

With the occupation (under Gálvez) of Monterey by Serra and Portolá, — an occupation destined to be permanent, — there were brought to an end two hundred and thirty-five years of effort on the part of Spain to possess herself of California; effort at no time designedly relinquished, save during the years 1607 to 1612, when interest in Anian lay dormant, and when, as a substitute for Monterey as a port-of-call, the islands Rica de Oro and Rica de Plata were vainly sought, amid storm and stress, by Sebastián Vizcaino off the coasts of Japan.

But occupation as a feat was not permitted to overshadow occupation as an event. Recognizing with respect to California a vital nexus between the days of Philip III (1606) and those of Charles III (1770), Gálvez had enjoined occupation under penalty (in case of failure) of offense "to God, the King, and the country"; and under requirement (in case of success) of suitable and stately observances. The latter, participated in by the chief functionaries of Church and State, were now (June 3) duly celebrated.

On the beach, near Vizcaino's oak, there was erected an altar equipped with bells and surmounted with an image of Our Lady. Before it (President Serra in alb and stole representing the Church) the assembled company chanted in unison, upon their knees, the beautiful *Veni Creator Spiritus*. The President then, amid din of exploding arms on land and ship, blessed a great cross and the royal standards of Castile and León. He next sprinkled with holy water the beach and adjoining fields, "to put to flight all infernal enemies," recited the Mass, and preached. With a *Salve* to the image of Our Lady, and with the singing by the company of *Te Deum Laudamus*, the religious ceremony was brought to a close. It was followed by a ceremony on the part of the State. Here as representative, the governor, Gaspar de Portolá, officiated. In his presence the royal standards were again unfurled, grass and stones were wrenched from the earth and scattered to the four winds, and the varied proceedings of the day were made matter of record.

It had been the express order of Gálvez that *Te Deum* be sung at Monterey. And, in order that the hymn might be repeated in Lower California and in Mexico, proclaiming there the glad northern tidings, he had directed that word of the occupation be dispatched southward as rapidly as possible. Intrusted to a cuirassier (Joseph Velásquez), who left Monterey on June 15, it reached Todos Santos on August 2. Meanwhile, on July 9, the mission and presidio San Carlos Borromeo de Monterey having been founded as described, and duly christened, Portolá turned over to Fages the military command, and with Costansó and Pérez sailed in the San Antonio for San Blas. Arriving August 1, he at once sent a courier to the Viceroy, announcing his intention to rest at Tepic and then personally to present himself at the capital. This news, anticipating that borne by Velásquez, was received by Viceroy Croix on August 10.[73] It was heralded, first, by the bells of the city cathedral,[74] and then, responsively, by those of the churches. A solemn Mass in thanksgiving was attended by the government dignitaries, and on the 16th the news was spread throughout New Spain by an official proclamation.

In these rejoicings the *visitador*, who, victim of vast exertions, had for the greater part of the year 1769 lain prostrate of fever at Álamos,[75] was happily able to take part. At the viceregal palace, in company with Croix, he was made the recipient of hearty congratulations.

The Sacred Expedition was ended. Its fruits were yet to be gleaned. By the letters of Crespi, written in 1769 and 1770 from San Diego to his superior and to Gálvez, it became evident that six new California missions — three for the peninsula north of Santa María and three for Northern California — would not meet the needs of the dense population which had been encountered: ten thousand souls, it was estimated, along the coasts of the Santa Bárbara Channel alone. Indeed, as early as March 28, 1769, Gálvez had expressed to Serra the hope that the fleet which had sailed from Cádiz on November 4, 1768, would bring at least part of an expected reinforcement of Franciscans.[76] On June 8, 1769, the *visitador* had written from Álamos to Guardian Fray Juan Andrés, to send to the Californias all the *operarios* possible;[77] and two days later he had expressed to Croix the hope that, "of the forty-five friars levied from Spain, some had come in the present fleet." Forty-five, under Fray Rafael Verger as superior, ultimately did come, and on November 12, 1770, Gálvez and the Viceroy signified to Serra and Palou: (1) That five new establishments (San Gabriel Arcángel, San Luis Obispo, San Antonio de Padua, Santa Clara and San Francisco de Asis) were to be planted in the upper land under ten of the forty-five friars; and (2) that five other new establishments were to be planted in the peninsula, north of Santa María, under twenty of the same band.[78] They stated also that henceforth in California, as Gálvez had confided to Serra, missions would be founded and missionaries paid from the proceeds of the Pious Fund; the Indians themselves not being required, as by the Jesuits, to contribute.[79] For founding a mission, the allowance would be 1000 *pesos;* and for the salary of a missionary, 275 *pesos*.[80] In conclusion, attention was called to two sets of vestments contributed by the Viceroy, — one set, "very rich," for Loreto; and the other, "sumptuous" and "complete," for Monterey.

By the Monterey contingent of friars, after the arrival, May 21, 1771, of the ten from Spain, the missions San Antonio de Padua and San Gabriel Arcángel were established on July 14 and September 8, respectively. In 1772 (September 1) the mission San Luis Obispo de Tolosa was founded. San Carlos itself was not permitted to retain its original site, but, church, storehouses, and magazine, was reërected before the end of December, 1771, in an attractive spot in the Carmelo Valley.[81]

CHAPTER VI

Á la que estoy del Río Colorado no hávia pasado hasta hoy la tropa de
S. M. — Juan Bautista de Anza to Viceroy Bucarely, February 9, 1774.[1]

IN 1771, both Viceroy Croix and Visitador Gálvez were
recalled to Spain.[2] Each had deserved well of his country, and each was to be suitably rewarded. Croix was made
viceroy and captain-general of the kingdom of Valencia,
and Gálvez was made *ministro universal* (general minister)
of the Indies. Serra, alone of the remarkable trio, remained
in Alta California to face in the field the problems to which
the occupation was fast giving rise. To sustain him in his
task there was the tradition of Croix-Gálvez pro-mission
methods, but this might be little regarded by a viceroy
personally or officially hostile.

Serra's presidency of the missions of Alta California
(terminated only by his death in 1784) outlasted the
natural life of Croix's immediate successor, Antonio María
Bucarely y Ursúa, and the official life of the first governor
and comandante of the soon-to-be-created Provincias
Internas, — Teodoro de Croix.[3] It was marked, moreover,
by events of the highest importance: The transfer, in 1772,
of Lower California to the Dominicans; the establishment,
in 1773, of a *modus vivendi* or working arrangement between
the mission authorities (the padres) and the comandante
and his subordinates; the overland expeditions, between
1774 and 1777, of Captain Juan Bautista de Anza, resulting
in the founding of the presidio and mission of San Francisco; the dispatch northward, between 1774 and 1779, of

three maritime parties in search of the Russians; the establishment, in 1777 and 1781, respectively, of the pueblos San José and Los Ángeles; and the attempted founding, between 1780 and 1782, of "pueblo missions" on the River Colorado. Of these events the present chapter will deal with the first three.

The transfer of the peninsular missions to the Dominicans was the outcome, first, of a plea by the Order itself, made in 1768 to Charles III, for a license to found establishments on the west coast of California; and, second, of a suggestion to the Viceroy, made in December, 1771, by the guardian of the College of San Fernando, that the Dominicans, or some other Order, take in charge seven of the establishments already controlled by the Franciscans.[4] The project, from fear of a clash between the Orders, was opposed by Croix and Gálvez;[5] but in 1770, by a royal *cédula* of date April 8,[6] a division of territory was commanded, and on April 7, 1772, there was signed a *concordato* fixing at fifteen leagues below San Diego the line of apostolical demarcation between the two Californias.[7] This act was followed in 1773 (August 19) by the erection on a high rock, by Palou, of a wooden cross bearing the inscription: *División de las Misiones de nuestro Padre Santo Domingo y de nuestro Padre San Francisco, Año 1773.*[8]

It will be remembered that on receipt of the news of the founding of San Carlos, five new missions for Alta California were planned by Gálvez and Croix. One was to be located between San Buenaventura and San Diego; two were to be located between San Buenaventura and Monterey; and two north of Monterey. This requirement, so far as the interval between San Buenaventura and Monterey was concerned, had by 1772 been met by San Antonio de Padua and San Luis Obispo; and, with respect to the interval between San Buenaventura and San Diego, by San Gabriel Arcángel; but as yet San Buenaventura itself had not been founded. The cause was scarcity of soldiers for guard purposes. As early as August, 1770, Serra had been advised by Matías de Armona (successor to Portolá as governor of the Californias)[9] that the "vehement desire" of his Reverence to establish missions additional to those of San Diego and Monterey was, in the dearth of troops, nothing less than a *tentación del demonio*.[10] But orders from the Viceroy (November 12, 1770), not only to found San Buenaventura, but to survey the port of San Francisco and found there at least one mission, as an outpost against the Russians, were urgent; [11] and to the time of the founding of San Gabriel (September 8, 1771) Comandante Fages had sought diligently to execute them. To replace the twelve volunteers lost by scurvy, Viceroy Croix had sent to the comandante twelve men from Guaymas, and there had been transferred to him by Felipe Barri (successor to Armona) twenty cuirassiers of the peninsular force under Rivera.[12] Thus encouraged, he, on July 18, 1771, had made known to Croix from San Diego, whither, with Serra, he had come from San Antonio, his determination to found San Buenaventura immediately after San Gabriel.[13] What had prevented was a conflict with the Indians just after the San Gabriel founding; an affair which more than ever impressed Fages with the need of strong guard detachments for the missions.[14]

By the failure to found San Buenaventura in 1771, Serra, who deemed the caution of Fages unnecessary, was much exasperated.[15] But something was to arise by which he was to be exasperated still more. In 1770, in Lower California, Palou, through Padre Dionisio Basterra, had complained to Visitador Gálvez of a disposition on the part of the governors of the peninsula to assert control of the temporalties and to treat the padres as subalterns.[16] In 1771–72 a like disposition became manifest in Fages. He meddled in the discipline of neophytes; he withheld and opened letters; he appropriated the mission mules; he diverted mission supplies; and he refused to retire soldiers for bad conduct. The last act perhaps gave most serious offense, for by reason of it the men were more or less protected in their illicit relations with Indian women, — relations which, aside from the effect in neutralizing the moral teaching of the padres, were laying the basis for a wide infection of the northern Indians with the same disease which had wrought havoc in the south.

By the course of Fages, there was raised for Alta California the whole question of the Mission. Was State Sacerdotal to control State Secular, or to be by it controlled? As developed by Córdova and Las Casas (1518–43), the Mission involved for the Indian, during tutelage, segregation under missionary supervision. As further developed by Kino and Salvatierra (1697), the Mission involved for the missionary the right to "enlist, pay and discharge soldiers of the guard." Before 1697 the Mission in Paraguay had assumed to control secular agencies, including the military; but despite this fact, and the fact of such control in Lower California by the Jesuits, Serra and Palou had not come to Monterey advised by a consistent practice on the part of the Spanish Government. What they could aver was, that in 1747, in the Sierra Gorda, under Lieutenant-General José de Escandón, it had been found necessary, after five or six years of secular control of temporalties, to intrust to the Franciscans both temporalties and spiritualties, — a course which in twenty-three years had brought about secularization; and that in the peninsula the same thing, after the expulsion of the Jesuits, had been found necessary by José de Gálvez.[17]   This accordingly Serra did aver; and, to make his words the more effective, he set out in September, 1772, for Mexico, to wait personally upon Viceroy Bucarely.

Antonio María Bucarely was a lieutenant-general of the royal forces, a knight commander in the Order of St. John of Malta, and a great viceroy. He was descended, on both the paternal and maternal sides, from Italian and Spanish families illustrious through popes, cardinals, and dukes; and before coming to Mexico had been governor of Cuba. When, therefore, Serra arrived in Mexico in February, 1773, he met a chief capable of understanding and appreciating the Croix-Gálvez tradition. The President's grievances were heard, and he was asked to digest them in a memorial. He prepared two papers, March 13 and April 22, embodying in all thirty-three representations. Of these the most important were the complaints against Fages.[18] But there were two others of much importance: first, that the method of sending northward mission supplies by sea from San Blas (the Gálvez method) be not discontinued, as was proposed, in favor of a system of mule caravans from Lower California; and, second, that, looking to the future, supply routes be explored, first, from Sonora, and then from New Mexico; routes to be secured by a chain of missions past the head of the California gulf, as designed by Kino.[19]

Over Fages the triumph of Serra (and hence of the Mission idea) was speedy and complete. His representations were reviewed by the Board of War and Finance (*Junta de Guerra y Real Hacienda*), and by this body it was decided that mission guards should be retired for irregular conduct, at the instance of the padres, without specification by the latter of the irregularity prompting the request. Furthermore (and herein lay a distinct recognition of the idea of the Mission), the missionaries might manage their establishments as *in loco parentis*, to wit, as a father would manage his family, — a procedure sanctioned by Spanish law since the conquest.[20] Finally, mission letters were not to be intercepted by the comandante, nor the mission supplies withheld. The action of the board was approved by Bucarely on May 12, and in August Fages was recalled.

Nor was Serra less fortunate with regard to San Blas as a supply station. Delay, suffering, and peril pertained to the sea. Not only had the San Carlos lost practically her whole crew by scurvy on the voyage to San Diego in 1769, but in February, 1771, she had been driven by fierce "northwesters" from San Blas nearly to Panama. Her rudder dangling by a single bolt, her casks drained, her decks blistered by a torrid sun, saved only by a timely flood of rain, she, as buffeted as the barque in "The Ancient Mariner," had reached Loreto on the 23d of August. Yet the Father-President was able to show that, to supply the new missions overland from the south, there would be required fifteen hundred mules and one hundred guards and muleteers, — an argument so forcible for San Blas and the sea, that it was approved by the Viceroy without a reference.[21]

In respect to details, — details both politico-military and financial, — Alta California was left to an expert, Juan José de Echeveste, forwarder of supplies. By him there was drafted a plan providing, in the case of the united Californias, for a governor at a salary of 4000 *pesos* with residence at Loreto; and, in the case of the non-peninsular division, for a captain, three sergeants, eighty soldiers, eight mechanics, two storekeepers, and four muleteers.[22]

The annual cost was to be 42,985 *pesos*. San Blas, with

a small transport fleet, was to be kept as a naval base, at a cost per annum of 63,907 *pesos*. The grand expenditure (Lower California at 12,450) was to be 119,342 *pesos*. To meet this total there were declared available (counting the proceeds of the Pious Fund, the yield of salt works near San Blas, and an annual subsidy of 33,000 *pesos* promised by the King in 1772) about 63,808 *pesos*. The deficit (nominally some 55,534 *pesos*) was to be made good by the royal treasury.[23]

Echeveste's plan, or *Reglamento* as it was called, went into effect January 1, 1774, and on May 25 of the same year Captain Rivera y Moncada succeeded Fages as northern comandante. Meanwhile Palou, having erected the cross of apostolical demarcation between Baja and Alta California, had by permission of his college made his way northward to Monterey, arriving in November, 1773. On May 11, 1774, the same point was reached by Serra. He came overland from San Diego, where he had arrived on the Santiago, a new ship commanded by Pérez, and brought, among other news, that of an increase, at the instance of Echeveste, of the annual stipend for each padre to 400 *pesos*.

But what of Serra's representation in favor of explorations for supply routes to Alta California by way of the present Arizona and New Mexico?

Here likewise his views were sanctioned. Whatever might be true of the California Indian as a being comparatively docile and inactive, the Apache — occupant, settled or nomadic, of the region east of the tributaries of the Gila to Moqui — had never been docile, and rarely inactive; and Christianity with him had made headway haltingly.[24] As late as 1773, the year of Serra's visit to Mexico, Kino's and Sedelmayr's dream of permanent missions on

the Gila and Colorado — links in a chain, Sonora to Moqui, and Sonora to the two Californias — remained to be
fulfilled.

But to go back a little.

In 1737 the presidio of Santa Rosa de Cordeguachi, or
Fronteras, a presidio of northern Sonora, was in charge of
Captain Juan Bautista de Anza, an officer in whom there
glowed something of the ardor of the *conquistadores* of old.
In 1732 it had been the duty of Anza to escort bands of
Jesuit padres to exposed points northward toward the Gila,
where missions were to be established. Later (1736) it became his duty to report upon the discovery, then recent,
of the Bolas de Plata mines. Unsettled still in 1737 was the
query, — Is California insular? And to this query there
was added by the mine discovery a further one: After all,
might not the Seven Cities of Coronado's time — with the
great Teguaio or Quivira at the head, and with the Strait of
Anian as a connecting highway — be more than a myth?
At all events, Spain had ever responded to the lure of souls
to be converted and of gold, silver, and pearls to be won.
Wherefore, on January 14, 1737, Anza urged upon Viceroy Juan Antonio that it were well that he (Anza) —
with a volunteer force of fifty or sixty men-at-arms, some
Pimas, two Jesuit padres, a train of horses, mules, and
cattle, carpenters for constructing canoes to cross the Gila
and Colorado Rivers, and gifts for the Indians — be commissioned to penetrate toward Quivira, and to establish
a *villa* on the Colorado.[25]

The plea was considered, and on June 13, 1738, was re-
ferred by the King to a *junta*, which (Anza falling by the
Apaches in 1739) was the last of it for thirty-four years.[26]
But the doughty commander of Santa Rosa had left a son,
— Juan Bautista. In what year Anza junior was born is
not known, but he grew to manhood imbued with the ardor

and ambition of his sire, and in 1772 commanded the presidio of Tubac.[27] By this time the traditions of Quivira and
Anian were a good deal faded, but between the desert and
the sea there still slept much of enticing mystery; and what
was more, the expedition of Gálvez to Monterey had
invested that mystery with a practical aspect. Could the
desert be crossed with a view to succoring the new establishments?

A request of Anza junior to be permitted to open communication between Sonora and Monterey was referred
to Viceroy Bucarely on May 2, 1772. It was based largely
upon an *entrada* made in 1771 to a point near the mouth of
the Colorado, by Francisco Garcés,[28] a missionary of the
College of Querétaro, who in June, 1768, had been appointed to San Xavier del Bec. "Padre Garcés and I are
persuaded," wrote Anza, "that the distance from Tubac
to Monterey is not so great as formerly was thought, and
that it may not be impossible to overcome it; . . . wherefore I hope that your Excellency will instruct the president
of these [the Querétaro] missions to permit the said padre
to accompany me. I consider October [1773] an opportune
time for an expedition, as then there can be spared from
my company 20 or 25 soldiers, a force which in my opinion
will be sufficient." [29]

As a skilled engineer, and as one of the party which had
just made the journey to Monterey, Miguel Costansó was
consulted by Bucarely, and his advice (the distance from
Tubac to San Diego being estimated at 180 "common
Spanish leagues," 473.4 miles) was that the request of
Anza be granted. Costansó, however, advised that two
soldiers from the Loreto garrison, who had been at San
Diego, be detailed to accompany Anza as guides.[30] And
by the governor of Sonora, who also was consulted, it was
suggested that, in order to avoid exciting the Indians,

Anza proceed to San Diego escorted only by Padre Garcés.[31]

It was with the Anza project at this stage that (February–March, 1773) Bucarely was waited upon by Serra. Garcés's diary of the *entrada* of 1771 was examined, and on September 17, the captain of Tubac was authorized to make a military reconnoissance to the establishments of Monterey.[32]

A start was effected on January 8, 1774. It was made from Tubac, at one o'clock of the afternoon after solemn Mass, and with the following troop: Captain Juan Bautista de Anza; two padres from Querétaro, — Francisco Garcés and Juan Díaz; twenty volunteer soldiers from Tubac presidio; one soldier versed in California routes; one interpreter of the Pima dialect; one Indian from Tubac presidio; five muleteers, and two servants. Good horses and pack animals were important for the expedition, and 130 of the former had been collected at Tubac. But just before the start they were stolen by Apaches, and it became necessary to proceed to the presidio of Altar, and make from that point, with other animals, very ill-conditioned, a start anew. At Altar, Anza added to his troop a useful member, Sebastián Tarabel, a neophyte of Lower California who had accompanied Portolá to San Diego, but who, later, attaching himself to the mission of San Gabriel, had deserted thence across the desert to Sonora.[33]

From Caborca Mission, district of Altar, Anza set forth on January 22 with 65 head of cattle, and with his saddle and pack animals recruited to 140. His course to the coast was to involve three well-defined stages: the first (January 22 to February 8), Altar northwest to the Gila-Colorado junction; the second (February 9 to March 10), the Gila-Colorado junction west to the foot of the San Jacinto Mountains; the third (March 11 to April 18), the San

Jacinto Mountains northwest to San Gabriel Mission, and north to Monterey. Stage one lay over desert, lava-bed and mountain, but it had been traversed by Kino in 1700 and by Garcés in 1771, to say naught of the crossing in 1540 by Coronado's hapless lieutenant, Melchior Díaz. At the Gila-Colorado junction the Yuma nation of Indians centred, and here Anza was met and welcomed by the Yuma chief Salvador Palma, with whom he had become acquainted at Altar, and whom he now, by a medal and an *alcalde's* staff, invested with authority under the King.[34]

It was stage two of the progress that developed a crisis, and proved the mettle of both leader and men. "Where I am," wrote Anza to Bucarely on February 9, "no troop of the King has ever passed the Colorado."[35] From the stream in question, which above its junction with the Gila was easily crossed by fording, there stretch to the Sierra Madre of Southern California hills of sand. Unstable as sea-billows, albeit often as gracefully curled, they harbor for the traveler bewilderment and death. To avoid these, Anza kept by the river-margin to Santa Olaya,[36] the last watering-place within the jurisdiction of the Yumas. Here Palma, who had been attending him, turned tearfully back, and he found himself in the country of the Cojats or Cajuenches.[37] By them he was welcomed, but he still was confronted with the sand-hills. Making into these on February 15, and soon deserted by the few Cojats who had proffered guidance, he was first compelled by the exhaustion of his mules to leave half of his baggage under guard at a place of brackish water (*La Poza de las Angustias* — Well of the Afflictions), and then to face the advisability of returning to the Yumas, of leaving with them half of his baggage and half of his men, and with the remainder pushing rapidly forward to California. To this plan Padre Díaz agreed, but Garcés was opposed, and the expedition held its course until, encountering a sand-hill too high to be surmounted, it became necessary to change direction to the south, where at no great distance rose a sierra.[38]

The mountains were gained at sundown, and the night was spent by Garcés in anxious quest for an Indian *ranchería* (San Jacome), which he was sure that he had visited hereabouts in 1771. Naught came of the search, and, as now many of the soldiers were on foot leading their jaded beasts, Anza gave orders for a return to Santa Olaya. This point, after the loss of a number of cattle and other animals, but with recovered baggage, was reached by the expedition in detachments between February 19 and 23. Palma cheerfully charged himself with the care of surplus articles and of seven of the men. With the remainder, all of whom expressed readiness to proceed *pie á tierras* if necessary, Anza on March 1 resumed his advance. On the 7th he came to a watering-place (Yuha Springs) recognized by Tarabel as one of the camping-spots of Portolá, and on the 8th reached the base of the mountains of San Jacinto.[39]

If stage one of the Anza progress may be called "Purgatorio," and stage two, "Inferno," stage three was indubitably "Paradiso." Entering, on March 11, the dry bed of the San Felipe River, the troop was cheered by news of a sea three days to the westward (*Océano de Filipinas*), and of people "like ours," — the dwellers at San Diego. On the 13th, amid the steeps of Coyote and Horse Canyons, grass and trees began to appear, and on the 15th running water. At 4700 feet a pass disclosed itself, named by Anza *El Real de San Carlos*,[40] and from it, as by a *coup de théâtre*, it was possible to descry beautiful, flower-decked plains and a white-capped sierra spiked with pines, oaks, and other trees native to cold lands. Here (just west of

Vandeventer Flat) the waters divided, running some
toward the Gulf of California, and others toward the
"Philippine Ocean"; a demonstration that the ridge in
question was a continuation of that of California Baja.
From San Carlos Pass the route led through Hemet Valley past Hemet Reservoir and along the San Jacinto River
to San Jacinto Lake; thence to the Santa Ana River; and
finally (on the 22d) to the mission of San Gabriel, which
was reached at sundown, and where the sturdy captain of
Tubac — worthy fulfiller of the ambition of a worthy parent — was received with rejoicing, with pealing of bells,
and chanting of *Te Deum*.[41]

During a stop at the mission of eighteen days, Anza
obtained supplies from the vessel Santiago, then at San
Diego, and sent back to the Yumas, at the Gila-Colorado
junction, Padre Garcés and all of his troop but six.[42] With
the latter he took on April 10 the road (Portolá's) for Monterey, where, despite great scarcity, he was entertained at
the presidio by Fages, and at the mission by the padres.
He left Monterey on April 22, accompanied by six of
Fages's men, to whom the way across the desert was to be
shown, and on the 27th, below San Luis Obispo, met Serra,
the Father-President, recently landed from the Santiago.
With him he tarried the night to relate the story of his
journey, and on May 1 was once again at San Gabriel.
Thence his course, save a stretch through the sands to
Santa Olaya, was that by which he had come. At the Gila-
Colorado junction he dismissed Fages's men, received from
Palma his own troop and baggage, and, having on the 21st
left Garcés on the Gila, seeking communication by letter
with Moqui, reached Tuçón on the 25th, and Tubac on the
27th.[43]

By the success of Anza (a success due in part to the presence of Serra in Mexico, in the spring of 1773) the work of Portolá was made sure of completion.

As yet no presidio and mission had been established at San Francisco. "Our father, St. Francis, is he to have no mission?" had anxiously been asked of Gálvez, by Serra, at La Paz. "Let him show us his port," the *visitador* had replied, "and he shall have a mission." [44] On November 21, 1770, Fages, with six soldiers (event hitherto unchronicled), had obtained a distant prospect of the present San Francisco Bay. This survey had been followed in 1772 (March-April) by one under Fages and Crespi, — a survey planned to include Point Reyes, in order to determine whether the estuary first seen by the deer-hunters in 1769, and again in 1770 by Fages's men, was a part of the Cermeño bay. But the Fages-Crespi party had reached only the mouth of the San Joaquín River, having been turned back by the waters and by news of starvation at San Diego. [45]

The truth is that until 1774, year of the Anza expedition, it had not so much as been settled where (strictly) lay that port of St. Francis at which there were ultimately to be planted two missions and a presidio, and at which the planting of at least one mission was deemed by Bucarely a present need. What, however, was presumed was, that the estuary of 1769 and 1770 (the present San Francisco Bay) was appurtenant to the old San Francisco Bay of Cermeño. Said Costansó in 1772, in a letter to the Viceroy: "On the fourth day of November [1769], following the eastern Shore or Branch of the Bay [*Estero*] (which we already called that of San Francisco), [46] we entered into a Sierra," etc. And on a map, with which the diary of the Portolá journey, as kept by Costansó, was supplemented, the present San Francisco Bay is called *Estero de S. Francisco*. [47]

To found San Francisco on the estuary,[48] therefore, would, it was adjudged, be admissible; and, in view of the fact that as yet Fages had not been furnished with soldiers sufficient for the founding even of San Buenaventura, there arose (apropos of the coming of Anza) the question: Could not men for the founding of San Francisco — and this, moreover, as suggested by Costansó accompanied by their families — be brought overland from Sonora? Furthermore, could not Kino's long-dreamed-of missions now be established on the Gila and Colorado Rivers? In a word, could not the views of Kino, Salvatierra, Sedelmayr, Anza (father and son), Serra, Costansó, and Bucarely be now, by what the secretary to the Viceroy happily called "a Sonora-Monterey hand-clasp," brought to a common fruition? [49]

Anza himself so believed. At Monterey he had proposed to Palou a chain of establishments "from these of California to the last of those of Querétaro in Sonora." He also (because of an Indian report that the estuary of San Francisco was connected by a branch of the Colorado River with the Gulf of California) had proposed that the annual Philippine galleon, stopping either at Monterey or at San Francisco, should there discharge Chinese goods for the benefit of Sonora and New Mexico.[50] But the determining consideration in favor of founding San Francisco on the estuary by men from Sonora, and of establishing missions on the Colorado to secure the Sonora connection, was the experience at Monterey of the new comandante, Rivera y Moncada.

Appointed successor to Fages on August 14, 1773, he had been instructed by Bucarely to explore the port of San Francisco for a mission site. Later (September) he had been notified of the expedition of Anza, for the guidance of which he was to furnish two soldiers. With fifty-one

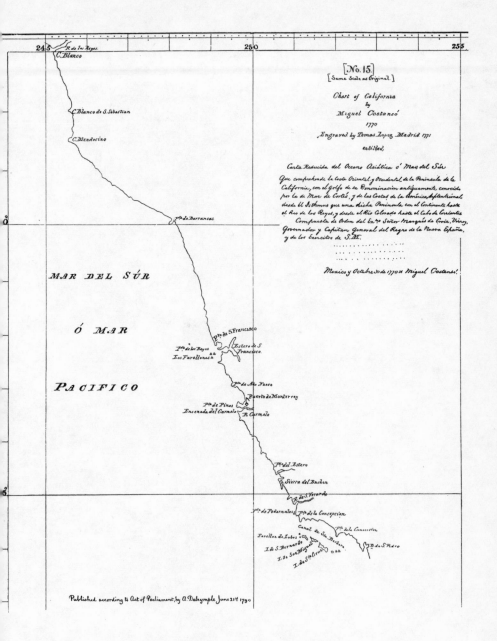

CHART IV. CALIFORNIA COAST. BY COSTANSO, 1770

persons (soldiers and their families) recruited in Sinaloa, Rivera reached the peninsula in March, 1774, but too late to furnish guides to Anza, or to join him. His assumption of duty at Monterey took place, as has been seen, on May 25, and in June there began to issue to Mexico a stream of plaintive dispatches: Supplies were scarce; arms were lacking or defective; Indians were vicious; desertions occurred. Regarding a San Francisco mission, he wrote to Bucarely on October 8, "Most excellent Señor, for founding a mission at San Francisco the number of soldiers is too small." [51]

Anza's project, in the broad view of it taken by Costansó, had been approved by the King on March 9,[52] and now (December) that communication with Alta California was actually open, a *junta* was called by the Viceroy. By this body it was determined: (1) That the port of San Francisco should be occupied by Anza with forty soldiers and their families, — soldiers chosen from the *Alcaldías* (alcalde districts) of Culiacán, Sinaloa, and Fuerte, where "most of the inhabitants were submerged in the greatest poverty and misery"; (2) that twenty-eight of the soldiers, under a lieutenant and sergeant, should be volunteers, and ten should be veterans of the reconnoissance; (3) that there should be chosen as lieutenant, either Joseph Joachim Moraga of Cordeguachi, or Cayetano Simón of Buenavista; and as sergeant, either Joseph Espinosa or Pablo Grijalva, both of Terrente, or Antonio Bravo of Buenavista; (4) that of the total cost of the expedition (computed at 21,927 *pesos* and 2 *reales*) the Pious Fund, "this one time only," should be called upon for 10,000 *pesos;* (5) that Padre Garcés should attend the expedition as far as the banks of the Colorado, there to await its return, and that Fray Pedro Font should attend it throughout; (6) that on his arrival at Monterey, Anza should turn over

to Rivera y Moncada the volunteers, and, having with
his own ten men aided in a survey of the *Río de San Francisco*, should return with them to Tubac.[53]

A start from Tubac was effected on October 23, 1775,
with a large company: forty soldiers under Anza as lieutenant-colonel,[54] Moraga as lieutenant, and Grijalva as sergeant; ninety-six soldiers' families and four other families;
three padres, — Garcés, Font, and Tomás Eixarch; one
purveyor, Mariano Vidal; fifteen muleteers; three herdsmen; three servants to the padres; four servants to the
comandante; five interpreters of the Pima, Yuma, Ca-
juenche, and Nifora idioms; 165 mules, 340 horses, and 302
cattle. Our Lady of Guadalupe, Saint Michael, and Saint
Francis of Assisi figured as patrons of the expedition, and
there was observed the following order on the march: four
scouts; Anza with a vanguard; Font with the settlers; a
rear-guard under Moraga; and last, in a long train, the
mules heavily packed, the horses, and the cattle. Each
morning the *Alabado* (Praise of the Sacrament) was sung
by the company, and it was sung by them again each evening on reciting their beads.

The route as at first taken (*via* San Xavier del Bec and
Tuçon) was more direct than that of the year 1774, but it
merged into the latter at Yuma, and thence so continued
to San Gabriel. On the present occasion, sand-hills were
not to give so much perplexity, and the watering-places
were known, but tribulations were not to be lacking. Between Anza and Font bickerings arose. The comandante,
so Font declared, wished him to receive no credit for taking altitudes; nor would he permit him to use a musical
instrument with which, for the edification of the Yumas, he
had provided himself. It was the rainy season, — November, December, January, — and in the mountains the rain
became snow, and strong winds blew. On December 17,

Moraga was stricken with deafness in both ears. On the 20th, when ascending the Baja-Alta California Cordillera, such cold prevailed that at night roaring fires were maintained at the cost of all sleep. At San Carlos Pass (the 26th) it rained, the storm culminating in a peal of thunder; and on issuing from the pass the sierra was beheld so covered with snow that its summits seemed the crested billows of the South Sea. To the women of the company, reared in a warm land, the sight though grand was disheartening, and they sorely wept. Moreover, cattle constantly perished, and there took place the last of eight childbirths, few of which had been achieved without *dolor violento*.[55]

The most significant incidents of the journey were a meeting with Palma on November 27, and an involvement in January (1776) occasioned by an uprising of the Indians at San Diego. As for Palma, he was the embodiment of cordiality, tendering his people as Spanish vassals, and his lands for missions. Informed by Anza that establishments on the Colorado could not at once be planted, he declared that on the return of the comandante he would accompany him to Mexico, there personally to make solicitation of the Viceroy.[56] Unable himself to stop with the Yumas, Anza left with them Garcés and Eixarch, commissioned to investigate what Dr. Elliott Coues characteristically renders "the animus and adaptability of the natives for the catechism and vassalage of the King"; and with the padres he left three interpreters, three servants, and supplies for four months. To Palma, to insure his goodwill, Anza presented a gift from the Viceroy, — a costume consisting of a shirt, a pair of trousers, a waistcoat yellow in front, a laced blue-cloth coat, and a gemmed and plumed black-velvet cap. This attention Palma reciprocated by a feast (served under a bower) of cakes, calabashes, corn, and watermelons.

San Gabriel was reached on January 4,[57] but the approach had awakened solicitude, for on January 1, it had been learned from three soldiers sent to the mission with dispatches for Rivera, that on the night of November 5, 1775, the mission at San Diego had been attacked and burned by conspiring bands of neophytes and Gentiles, and that Fray Luis Jayme had been killed.[58] The outbreak, as it proved, was an incident significant in two ways: the founding of San Juan Capistrano (an establishment authorized by the Viceroy in May, 1775, and begun by Lasuén and Lieutenant Ortega, of San Diego, in October) was suspended;[59] and the founding of San Francisco — that founding which, now that the estuary was deemed a part of the bay of Cermeño, was being more and more urged from Madrid — was deferred.

Anza, prevailed upon by Rivera (by whom he was met at San Gabriel)[60] to lend aid at San Diego, arrived with seventeen of his own men on January 11, and, between that date and February, supported the comandante in dispatching search-parties to the various *rancherías*. With Rivera, however, punishment of the Diegueños was but a secondary object. Opposed to any foundation at San Francisco, he yet was afraid that a foundation would be effected by Anza, and sought by dilatory action to detain the latter at San Diego in the hope that he would relinquish command of his soldier colony there, instead of at Monterey, and return to Sonora.

Every day [records Font] we talked a great deal about Monterey, and more yet of the San Francisco Port; the Señor Rivera ever saying that we could omit this trip, as we would not attain the object of it. . . . "What is your object in going there?" he would say. "To get tired out? I have told you that I have examined everything well, and have informed the Viceroy that there is nothing there suitable for that which he has planned." . . . "Friend," replied Señor Anza, ending the discussion, "I am going there, and if we find that river [of San Francisco], I shall draw a phial [*limeta*] of water, cork it well, have its genuineness certified by Fray Pedro here, and present it to the Viceroy." The Viceroy, Señor Anza declared, had ordered that if he did not find a fit site at the mouth of the port, the settlement should be established where it seemed best, even if that were some leagues away, — just so the port could be taken possession of by Spain.[61]

On February 3, word came from Moraga and Vidal, at San Gabriel, that the mission food-supply was becoming exhausted, and on the 9th, Anza, leaving at the mission ten of his men under Grijalva, set out with the remainder for San Gabriel, where he arrived on the 12th. From this point (Moraga with ten men first having been dispatched after some deserting muleteers) he on the 21st, with seventeen men, their families and his trains, started northward. On March 7, at San Antonio, he was rejoined by Moraga who had overtaken the deserters, and he reached Monterey on the 10th.[62]

At San Carlos Mission, Anza lay ill for a week of what seems to have been pleurisy; but on the 17th he was able to send to Rivera eight men from the presidio to relieve the ten left at San Gabriel under Grijalva; and on the 23d, with Moraga, Font, and eleven soldiers, started for the estuary, — henceforth by common consent called the Bay of San Francisco. In 1774 (November-December), Rivera with Palou and a guard — a fact adverted to by Rivera in the conversation with Anza — had skirted the estuary to Point Lobos, where Palou had erected a cross.[63] In 1775, night of August 5, Lieutenant Juan Manuel de Ayala of the royal navy, instructed to discover what connection there might be between the estuary and the bay of Cermeño,[64] had in the San Carlos passed the Golden Gate,[65] opposite which he had cast anchor at an island called by him

Isla de Los Ángeles.[66] Moreover, in September, the naval officer Bruno Heceta, likewise under orders for Anza's benefit, had with Palou penetrated by land to Point Lobos.[67] The advent of Anza to the bay, therefore, was to a water by no means uncharted,[68] and on March 28 he chose on a *cantil blanco* (white cliff), "where nobody had been," a site for a *fuerte* (Fort Point) and *nueva población;* and the next day, at a spot called by him from the calendar Los Dolores (Mission Bay), he chose a site for a mission.[69]

Regarding Fort Point, Font writes: —

The comandante decided to fix the holy cross, which I blessed after Mass, on the extreme end of the steep rock at the interior point of the mouth of the port; and at eight o'clock he and I went there with four soldiers, and the cross was fixed at a suitable height to be seen from the entire entrance of the port and from some distance. At the foot, under some rocks, the comandante left a report of his coming, and a plan of the port. On departing we ascended a short hill to a very green flowery tableland abounding in wild violets and sloping somewhat toward the port. From it the view is *deliciocisima.* There may be seen [not only] a good part of the port with its islands [but] the mouth of the port and the sea, whence the prospect ranges even beyond the *Farallones.* I judged that if this site could be well populated, as in Europe, there would be nothing finer in the world, as it was in every way fitted for a most beautiful city, — one of equal advantages by land or water, with that port so remarkable and capacious, wherein could be built ship-yards, quays and whatever might be desired. . . . I examined the mouth of the port, and its configuration, with the graphometer, and I tried to sketch it, and here I place the sketch.[70]

The squad sent south by Anza on the 17th had carried a letter to Rivera, requesting him to make known at once his intention with regard to the founding of San Francisco; but on Anza's return to Monterey on April 8 (a return effected by way of the present San José, Berkeley, and Monte Diablo), no reply had been received. Ill-con-

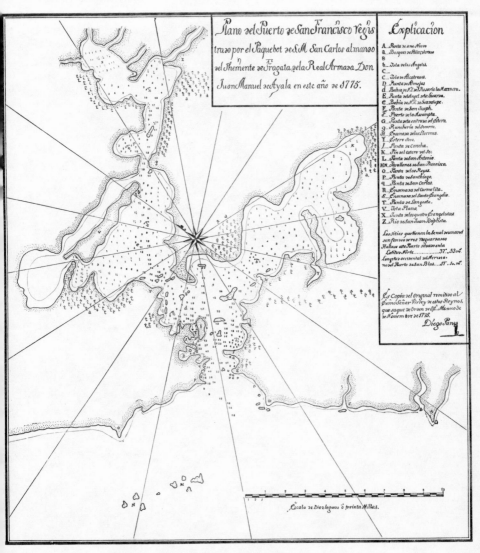

Plano del Puerto de San Francisco Regis
traso por el Paquebot de S.M. San Carlos al manso
del Theniente de Fragata de la Real Armada Don
Juan Manuel de Ayala en este año de 1775.

Explicacion

A. Punta de año Nuevo
a. Bosques de Palos colorados
B.
b. Isla de los Angeles.
C. Isla de Alcatraces.
D. Punta de Almejas
d. Bahia de N.ª del Rosario la Merced
E. Punta del Angel de la Guarda.
e. Bahia de N.ª de Guadalupe.
F. Punta de San Joseph.
f. Puerto de la Asumpta.
G. Punta de la entrada del Estero.
g. Ranchería del Berro.
H. Ensenada de los Berros.
I. Estero chico.
J. Punta de Concha.
K. Fin del estero del N.e.
L. Punta de San Antonio.
MN. Farallones de San Francisco.
O. Punta de los Reyes.
P. Punta de Anthinga.
q. Punta de San Carlos.
R. Ensenada del Carmelita.
S. Ensenada del Santo Evangelio.
T. Punta de Angosta.
V. Isla Plana.
X. Punta de los quatro Evangelistas.
Z. Rio de San Juan Baptista.

Los Sitios que tienen la Señal de nuard
son los que sirve de Guarniciones
Hallase este Puerto situado en la
Latitud Norte.............37°.53m.
Longitud occidental del Meridiano del Puerto de San Blas...11°.30.m.

Es Copia del Original remitido al Comodoro Perry de estos Reynos, que saque de Orden de S.E. Mexico de Noviembre de 1775.

Diego Panes

Escala de Diez leguas ó treinta Millas.

CHART V. PORT OF SAN FRANCISCO. BY AYALA, 1775

tent at the situation, and weak from his pleuritic attack,
Anza now sent word to Rivera by a sergeant (José María
Góngora) that he would meet him at San Diego on April
25 or 26, for consultation; and having turned over the
command of the colony to Moraga, set out on the 14th for
Sonora, — a day, by reason of the tears and farewells of

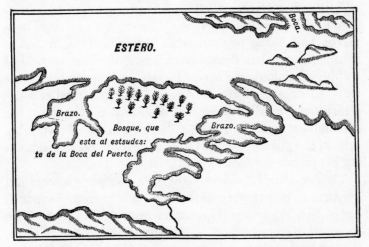

CHART VI. SAN FRANCISCO BAY, BY PEDRO FONT, 1776

the settlers, pronounced by the sturdy soldier the saddest
ever known at Monterey.

On the 15th, Anza, to his surprise, met Góngora returning with news that Rivera was just behind him. He had
come upon the comandante near San Antonio, and had
tendered him the letters in his charge. These Rivera had
declined to receive, bidding the sergeant retire. Afterwards he had consented to take the letters, and, thrusting
them unopened into his pouch, had, in exchange, handed
Góngora two communications for Anza, bidding him go in
advance and deliver them. "Señor," said Góngora (drawing Anza to one side), "my captain is either fatuous or

mad, and those with him say that he comes from San Diego Presidio excommunicated because of having taken from the church the Indian Carlos." [71]

Rivera was not mad, but he undeniably was fatuous; and the reason was twofold. He was envious of Anza; and he had involved himself in an uncomfortable tangle with the padres at San Diego. Of those conspiring against the mission but afterwards repenting, Carlos, a San Diego neophyte, had taken asylum from the military arm in the church. Rivera had demanded his rendition, and on refusal by the missionaries (Fuster, Lasuén, and Gregorio Amurrio) had dragged forth his victim. Ecclesiastical censure straightway had followed, and when met by Góngora, the comandante was, so to speak, bearing his head under his arm, in the guise of a missive from his tormentors announcing his graceless plight.

The communications brought by the sergeant were found by Anza to be curt refusals by Rivera to permit the founding of San Francisco. Thereupon resuming his journey he soon met Rivera himself. "He was wrapped," says Font, "in a blue blanket and wore a cap half covering his face, leaving visible no more than the right eye and a little of the beard, which he wore very long." Rivera complained of his health. "I am sorry you are ill," said Anza. "While at San Gabriel," replied the former, "I contracted a pain in this leg," pointing to the right one. He then took Don Juan's left hand, drew it over his right arm, said "*Á Dios,*" put spurs to his mule, and passed on. "You may reply to me at Mexico or wherever it pleases you," called Anza. "So be it," answered Rivera, and the colloquy ended.

Toward the comandante there now was assumed by Anza a punctilious reserve. The former proceeded to Monterey, was refused absolution by Serra until Carlos should be restored to his asylum, and on April 19, started

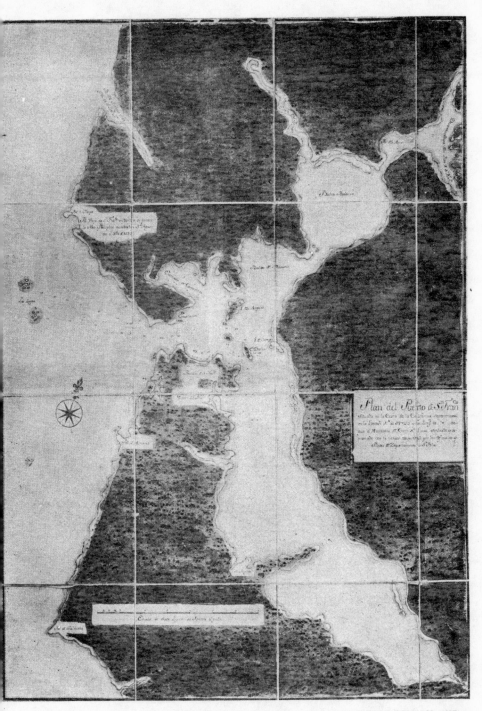

CHART VII. SAN FRANCISCO BAY SUBSEQUENT TO FOUNDING OF SAN FRANCISCO PRESIDIO AND
MISSION. BY SAN BLAS NAVAL OFFICERS. (Hitherto unreproduced)

for San Diego. At San Luis Obispo a letter of formal apology from him was delivered to Anza, and a meeting solicited; but the Sonora leader declined intercourse except in writing, and on May 2 set out for the Colorado; while, the next day, the way southward was resumed by Rivera. At Yuma (May 11), Anza was joined by Eixarch and by Palma, — the latter still resolute in his determination to go to Mexico to make in person submission to the Viceroy. As for Garcés, he was thought to be on the Colorado, three days to the northward of Yuma, among the Galchedunes. Dispatching him a letter, Anza on the 14th left by way of Sonora, Caborca, and Altar for San Miguel de Horcasitas, where he arrived June 1, and where at once he began preparations for a journey to the capital.[72]

The retreat of Garcés is presumed by Dr. Elliott Coues to have been near the present Needles. But what had been the course of this indefatigable man since December 4, 1775, — the date of the departure of Anza from the Gila-Colorado junction? And what was to be his course to September 17, 1776, the date of his return to his mission of San Xavier del Bec?

Provided with a banner, on one side of which was portrayed the Holy Mary, and on the other a lost soul, Garcés, by May 11, 1776, had penetrated to the mouth of the Colorado,[73] had revisited San Gabriel, and (near Bakersfield) had entered the Tulare, or great central valley of California, — the first Spaniard so to do save Pedro Fages, who in 1772 had pursued thither a party of deserters.[74] Thus much in fulfillment of the Viceroy's commission "to investigate the animus and adaptability of the natives on the Colorado for the catechism and vassalage of the King." But another commission of the Viceroy's demanded fulfillment, and by it the course of Garcés was determined to the time of his return to his mission.

Serra, in his memorial to Bucarely, March 13, 1773, had revived an idea broached by Kino and emphasized by Sedelmayr. He had not only recommended that communication be opened between Alta California and Sonora, but also between Alta California and New Mexico, — Santa Fé. "Let an order be given," the Father-President had said, "to some *jefe* (officer) of New Mexico"; and by the War Board it had been declared advisable that an expedition from New Mexico be conducted separately from that from Sonora.[75]

To the idea of a Santa Fé expedition to the coast, impetus had been given by the return of Garcés and Díaz from the first Monterey expedition of Anza, for it was undeniable that the Anza route was fraught with peril by its sands and lack of water. Even in Sonora, officials — notably the governor of that province, Francisco Antonio Crespo — were of the opinion that a route to Monterey, by way of Santa Fé, Moqui, and the Galchedunes, would be found preferable to Anza's route: first, because the region was more fertile, and second, because such a route would rend Apachería and bring about the reduction of Moqui, — a district defiantly independent. It was indeed the suggestion of Crespo, that until the route in question could be explored (by himself), it might be well to suspend the founding of San Francisco.[76] No exploration by Crespo, however, was authorized, and in 1775 the matter was taken in hand at Santa Fé. Here were two zealous Franciscans, Silvestre Vélez de Escalante and Francisco Atanasio Domínguez, — the former resident padre at Zuñi. After an *entrada* in June, the two padres, July 29, 1776, set forth northwestward, with eight men, for Monterey, and actually reached the vicinity of Great Salt Lake; but, provisions failing, they were forced to return, arriving at Zuñi on November 24.[77]

The viceregal commission to open communication with
Alta California by way of Santa Fé — a commission intrusted by Bucarely neither to Crespo nor yet to "some
jefe of New Mexico"; one, moreover, unsuccessful in the
hands of Escalante and Domíngue — was accomplished
by Garcés. Quitting the Tulare Valley on May 11–17, 1776,
he went east to the site of Fort Mojave on the Colorado
River, and thence again east by way of the Grand Canyon
(which he named *Puerto de Bucarely*) to Moqui.[78] Here,
despite the allurements of his banner, he (July 2) was but
coldly received, being given shift in a court-yard; and on
July 4, chagrined, he withdrew southward. Approaching
San Xavier del Bec, where, as stated, he arrived on September 17, his heart was cheered by greetings from the
Pimas (Kino's nation), who in affectionate drunkenness
assured him that they were "well," were "happy, knew
about God, and were the right sort of men to fight the
Apaches." [79]

San Francisco, meanwhile, had been founded at last.
On May 8, Rivera at San Diego, repentant (upon thought
of the Viceroy) of his peremptoriness in refusing to permit the founding, sent to Moraga instructions to establish
a presidio on the site chosen by Anza, but to defer the
establishing of a mission. The lieutenant, accompanied
by Padres Palou and Benito Cambón, at once went with
the Sonora colonists to the San Francisco peninsula, and
on June 27 camped near the spot called by Anza Dolores,
— a spot within easy reach of the presidio site. By help
of Cañizares and others of the crew of the San Carlos,
which came from Monterey in August with supplies, presidial quarters — chapel, comandante's dwelling, and warehouse, all of palisades with roofs of earth — were soon
ready; and on the 17th of September, day of the coming

of Garcés to San Xavier, the foundation was dedicated
with a Mass, a *Te Deum*, and with salvos of artillery.
At Dolores a settlement had grown up under Palou.
Moraga, regardless of Rivera's injunctions, now added a
church and a priest's dwelling; and on October 9 the whole
was formally dedicated as the mission (sixth in the Alta
California list) of San Francisco de Asís.[80]

Rivera himself was advised in July of a transfer of
Barri's successor, Felipe de Neve, to Monterey, and of his
own transfer to the peninsula as lieutenant-governor.[81]
In November, he paid to San Francisco an official visit
of inspection, and approved all that Moraga had done.
The spot, in April, 1777, was visited by Neve; and, on
October 10, the venerable Junípero Serra, gazing from
the *castillo*, beheld within the Golden Gate that which, in
measure more than sufficient, was a response to Gálvez's
demand that St. Francis disclose his port.[82]

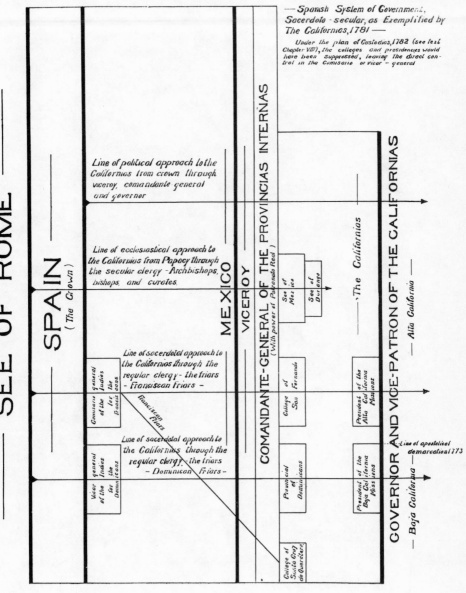

SEE OF ROME

SPAIN
(The Crown)

MEXICO

VICEROY

COMANDANTE-GENERAL OF THE PROVINCIAS INTERNAS
(With power of Patronato Real)

GOVERNOR AND VICE-PATRON OF THE CALIFORNIAS

— Baja California —   — Alta California —

—Spanish System of Government,
Sacerdota-secular, as Exemplified by
The Californias, 1781 —

Under the plan of Custodias,1782 (see text
Chapter VIII), the colleges and presidencies would
have been suppressed, leaving the direct control in the Comisario or vicar-general

Line of political approach to the
Californias from crown through
viceroy, comandante-general
and governor

Line of ecclesiastical approach to
the Californias from Papacy through
the secular clergy - Archbishops,
bishops, and curates.

Line of sacerdotal approach to
the Californias through the
regular clergy - the friars
- Franciscan friars -

Line of sacerdotal approach to
the Californias through the
regular clergy - the friars
- Dominican friars -

Comisario general
of the Indies
for the
Franciscans

Vicar general
of the Indies
for the
Dominicans

Franciscan
Friars

See of
Mexico

See of
Durango

The Californias

College of
San Fernando

Provincial
of the
Dominicans

President of the
Alta California
Missions

President of the
Baja California
Missions

College of
Santa Cruz
de Querétaro

Line of apostolical
demarcation 1773

CHAPTER VII

THE PROVINCIAS INTERNAS

LAST in the catalogue of Alta California notable events which took place in the lifetime of Junípero Serra, were the three anti-Russian maritime expeditions, 1774–1779; the founding (1777 and 1781) of San José and Los Ángeles; and the attempted founding (1780–1782) of pueblo missions.

On March 24, 1773, the Marqués de Grimaldi wrote to Viceroy Bucarely that the King had news that it was designed by the celebrated English navigator "Bings" to sail, in May, straight for the Pole, to ascertain if it might not be practicable to pass thence to the west, and so reach California. In case the design was carried out, and Monterey or other ports were visited, the ships were to be detained and their papers, maps, etc., seized under the Laws of the Indies. But this for the present aside.[1]

In 1773, on April 11, — San Francisco being yet unfounded, — there was received at Madrid, from the Conde de Lacy, Spanish minister at St. Petersburg, a hurried dispatch. It stated that in 1769 an official of the Russian navy, named Tscherikow, had, from Kamtchatka, undertaken for his country the task of exploration toward America; that in 1771 he had returned from his voyage, and that, leaving his crew in Siberia, he, early in 1772, had with his secretary reached St. Petersburg, where his papers had been deposited by the government in an archive sealed with three seals, and where he and his secretary had both been sworn to profound silence regarding his discoveries.[2]

On September 25, two other dispatches from Lacy were

received, — one stating that Russia was about to force the
Great Wall of China with 25,000 men, and then assail Japan
from Kamtchatka; the other, that the famous Albrecht von
Haller, professor in the Royal Academy at St. Petersburg,
had advised the sending of a Russian squadron by way of
the Cape of Good Hope to Kamtchatka, there to continue
the Russian advance toward America, — a land belonging
to Russia more than to any other power by reason of having originally been peopled from Siberia.[3]

Upon the Lacy dispatches, the first of which reached
Mexico in July, and the last in December, action by Bucarely was promptly taken. Juan Pérez, the naval officer
first with his ship at San Diego in 1769, was communicated
with; and by January 24, 1774, he, furnished with maps of
the routes of Behring and Tscherikow, with a ship's company of eighty-eight men, and with a ship itself of his own
selection (the Santiago), had set sail from San Blas. He
was required to follow the coast northward to latitude 60°,
the limit, according to Lacy, of exploration by Behring
and Tscherikow,[4] and everywhere, by religious ceremonies and the planting of great crosses, to take possession
in the name of Charles III. Pérez, in fact, — first stopping
at San Diego to put ashore Serra (vide chapter VI), and
then (May 23–June 11) at Monterey to receive as chaplains and diarists Padres Crespi and Tomás de la Peña, —
surveyed the coast, including Nootka Sound, from Mendocino to the extremity of Queen Charlotte Island in latitude 55°, and returned to Monterey on August 27.[5]

With the voyage of the Santiago (60 degrees not having
been attained, nor anywhere a landing effected) dissatisfaction was felt in Mexico, and on November 26, 1774, the
Viceroy advised the King of a second expedition, one designed to reach 65 degrees. Available for it were six naval
officers of ability from Cádiz and Ferrol, whose coming

had been announced the preceding August; among
them Lieutenants Bruno Heceta and Juan Francisco
Bodega y Quadra.[6] Under the former, with Pérez as *piloto*,
the Santiago in 1775 (March 16) sailed from San Blas.
She reached latitude 49° on August 11, and anchored at
Monterey on the 29th, having discovered the port of
Trinidad and, probably, the mouth of the Columbia
River.[7] As for Bodega y Quadra, assigned as second officer
to the Sonora (a schooner requisitioned by Heceta for the
exploration of ports and bays), and unexpectedly given
first place by the transfer of his superior Juan de Ayala to
the San Carlos, he in his cockle-shell, thirty-six feet "over
all," reached 58 degrees, discovered Bodega Bay, and anchored at Monterey on October 7.[8]

A deal of coast had been laid bare, but naught of the
Russians had been found, save, by Pérez, a bayonet and
part of a sword in the hands of Indians on Prince of Wales
or Queen Charlotte Island. In 1776, therefore, a third
expedition to the north, with Heceta and Bodega y Quadra
in command, was ordered by the King.[9] It was to take
place in 1777, and this for a specific reason. The rumor of
1773 — that the English under Admiral Byng were about to
seek California by way of the Pole — had proved false;
but in March (1776) it had come to the knowledge of Spain
that Captain James Cook — fulfilling Venegas's forecast of a
further search for Anian by a successor to Arthur Dobbs [10] —
was preparing with two ships, the Resolution and the Discovery, to sail for the South Sea and the Northwest Coast.
That Anian, whether as an outlet to the bay of James, of
Baffin, or of Hudson, was a myth, had been proved to the
satisfaction of Bucarely by the exploration of 1775; yet in
quest of it, and of possessory rights over the territory about
it, Cook evidently was coming; that, too, stimulated by a
Parliamentary grant of twenty thousand pounds contingent

upon success; and it behooved Spain to be represented in northern waters when he arrived.[11]

This project was prevented by lack at San Blas of a vessel that could be spared for the purpose, the Santiago being destined to Peru; and it was not until 1779, the year of Bucarely's death, that the expedition (two *fragatas*, the Princesa and the Favorita, built respectively at San Blas and Lima, and commanded, the one by Lieutenant Ignacio Arteaga, and the other by Lieutenant Bodega y Quadra) was able to set sail.[12] It quitted San Blas on February 11 under orders to reach latitude 70°; but having on July 1 attained about 60 degrees, was forced back by scurvy, making on the way an examination of Drake's Bay (the bay of Cermeño), and anchoring at San Francisco the middle of September.[13] Meanwhile (1778) Captain Cook, unchallenged, had visited the Northwest Coast, stopped long in Nootka Sound, and, striking across the Pacific to the southwest, had met death in the Sandwich Islands.

By the three expeditions of Pérez, Heceta, and Arteaga and Quadra, it became evident that the Russians, whatever their ultimate designs, were as yet making no southward encroachments. For delayed projects of a domestic nature, therefore, the time was opportune.

In 1768, in that dispatch, basic for the history of Alta California, wherein Gálvez and Croix had pointed out to the King the necessity, as against both the English and the Russians, of the occupation of the port of Monterey, something had been pointed out besides, to wit: the advisability (so assumed) of the creation in New Spain of a new territorial and administrative unit. As in the sixteenth, seventeenth, and eighteenth centuries, Spaniards of central Mexico — soldiers, priests, and miners — had fared constantly farther to the north, divers provinces had become delimited: Sinaloa, Nueva Vizcaya, Sonora, New Mexico, the Californias, Coahuila, and Texas. Because of remoteness from the capital, these provinces had early been called the Provincias Internas (Interior Provinces).[14] The meeting-ground of two of them — northeastern Sonora or southeastern Arizona, and southwestern New Mexico — had long been the roaming district of the Apaches; and here by 1768 two presidial groups were in existence: one, coastwise and linear from Guaymas to Pitic, including Horcasitas; the other, inland and wedge-shaped with Fronteras at the apex, including, besides Fronteras, Altar, Terrente, and Tubac. As for Nueva Vizcaya (Chihuahua) and New Mexico (central portion), a line, including Janos and Paso del Norte, connected San Buenaventura with Santa Fé; while in the Californias, to say nothing of posts in Coahuila and distant Texas, there was the presidio of Loreto.[15]

Control, from the capital, of military groups such as these was a task the difficulty of which had in 1768 been impressed upon *visitador* and viceroy alike by the war in Sonora.

If [so the dispatch recommending the formation of outlying provinces into a unit of separate administration had averred] from the glorious conquest, as achieved by Hernan Cortés, of these dominions that fall under the name of New Spain, it had been the practice of successors in the government to follow up and prosecute the high designs of that hero, there would have supervened the light of the Gospel and the dominion of the august kings of Spain to the ultimate bounds of this immense and unexplored continent. But as the spirit of activity and of conquest was quenched with the life of that inimitable man, so (with his death) there ceased the rapid progress made, until of late no one has sustained or conserved the possession of those rich territories on the frontiers of Sonora and Nueva Vizcaya. Of the decadence and veritable destruction which the unfortunate inhabitants of these provinces have suffered (with grave prejudice to the State) the exact causes are, in reality, the total neglect

with which the provinces in these last years have been regarded
from Mexico, by reason of the distance of more than six hundred
leagues from this capital at which they are situated; and the great
mass of occupations and cares, near at hand, which weigh upon
the attention of a viceroy of New Spain; since, destitute of subaltern aids, it is impossible that either his active dispositions or
the influence of his authority should reach to the remote confines
of an empire almost illimitable.[16]

The new administrative unit was to be a *comandancia-
general*, or military department, and not a second viceroyalty. Thus would be avoided "odious embarrassments"
sure to arise "between adjacent *jefes* when equal." It furthermore was to embrace only Sonora, Sinaloa, Nueva Vizcaya, and the peninsula of the Californias. Justice was to
be dispensed from Guadalajara, and it was suggested that
the capital be fixed either at Caborca Mission, or at the
confluence of the Gila and Colorado Rivers, so that, from
a point almost equidistant from the Californias and Nueva
Vizcaya, the governor might with facility pass to one or
the other. In respect to power, the *comandancia* was to be
invested with all that was required for keeping itself free
of the barbarians and for extending its territorial limits.
With reference to the viceroyalty, its subordination was to
be that only of making reports and of asking aid when
necessary.[17]

In 1776, on August 22, five years after Gálvez's return
to Spain, the Provincias Internas — in essential respects
as recommended in the dispatch of 1768, but including
Coahuila and Texas as well as the Californias — were created by royal decree an administrative unit, with capital
fixed at Arizpe in Sonora.[18] Of the department in question
— one where, if anywhere, it were needful "for the man
with the crucifix to be backed by the man with the musket"
— there was appointed as governor and comandante-general, with power of the *Patronato Real*,[19] Teodoro de Croix

(Caballero), native of Flanders and nephew of the Marqués de Croix, the predecessor of Bucarely. Croix reached Mexico in December, 1776, and Durango in Nueva Vizcaya (his provisional capital), in September, 1777. Fond of parade, he was disposed to claim as much equality with the Viceroy as possible, and forthwith contrived it that at low Mass his confession was received standing, and that at solemn Mass salutation was made to him by priest and deacons from the altar, — ceremonies permitted by the laws to none but the viceroys of Mexico and Peru.[20] With regard, however, to Alta California, the significant fact in connection with Comandante-General Croix is that he valued personally and supported officially the new governor, Felipe de Neve.

Neve, a major at Querétaro (originally from Sevilla), had on September 27, 1774, been sent as governor to Loreto, to compose bitter differences which had arisen in the peninsula between State Secular and State Sacerdotal, — the one as represented by Governor Barri, and the other by the Father-President of the Dominicans, Vicente Mora.[21] But in 1776 the Viceroy, in view of the outbreak at San Diego, was ordered by the King to transfer Neve to Monterey. Northern California was not an alluring field, and it was only after a second order from Madrid that Neve, on November 3, was constrained to manifest his submission to the royal will.[22]

Reaching Monterey on February 3, 1777, he was soon put in possession of two communications, the contents of which, as assimilated and carried into effect by his own strong intelligence, materially changed for Alta California the status civil and religious. The first, dated December 25, 1776, was a letter of instructions from the Viceroy. In it Neve was directed to give attention to four things: first, the strengthening of connection between Loreto, San Diego, and San Francisco by the erection of various missions, two, as Serra had long prayed, on the Santa Bárbara Channel, — Concepción and San Buenaventura, — and one to the north of San Carlos, — Santa Clara; second, the determining of the practicability of a connection with Mexico by way of San Gabriel through missions to be erected on the Gila and Colorado Rivers; third, a distribution of lands to colonists and soldiers with a view to rendering the province independent of the royal treasury; and fourth, the gaining of the Indians "by attention, love, and gifts, and not by rigor." [23] As for the second communication, which also was from the Viceroy, it notified Neve of the arrival in Mexico of Croix to take command in the Provincias Internas, — a *jefe* with whom, thereafter, he was to conduct all correspondence, except regarding supplies; [24] while as for the third (dated August 15, 1777), it was from Croix himself. It advised the Governor that by a royal order of March 21, 1775, the *Reglamento* of Echeveste was to be remodeled, and asked Neve to suggest what he could for its improvement. [25]

Hitherto in the Californias the subordination of State Secular to State Sacerdotal had been marked. It had been with comparative ease that Palou in the case of Barri, and Serra in that of Fages, had triumphed as to Mission control of the soldiery and Indians; and that Serra and his colleagues in the case of Rivera y Moncada had triumphed as to a mission at San Francisco and a course of mildness toward the revolted neophytes of San Diego, of whom the culprit Carlos was an example.

Neve, however, impressed with the injunction to render the province of Alta California self-supporting, resolved first to found two pueblos of Spaniards, — two communities for the exclusive support of the presidios; namely, San José on the Río Guadalupe near Santa Clara, and La

Reina de los Ángeles on the Río Porciúncula near San Gabriel.

Gathering fourteen heads of families, — nine of them presidial soldiers of Monterey and San Francisco, and five of them men from Anza's party (sixty-six persons), — the Governor, on the 29th of November, 1777, through his representative Moraga, laid the foundations of San José.[26] The town — a few houses of plastered palisades with flat roofs of earth — was constructed facing a plaza, and to each family there was assigned a *suerte*, or field, for the irrigation of which the waters of the Guadalupe were restrained by a dam. And for the present this was all that was attempted. If pueblos were to be founded, settlers of Spanish blood must be provided in numbers sufficient for the purpose. Anza had succeeded in transferring by the Colorado route a considerable company from Sonora to the north. But so far as Los Ángeles was concerned, the site selected lay far to the south, and might be reached either from Loreto or from the Colorado. Accordingly, in 1779 Lieutenant-Governor Rivera y Moncada was sent by Neve to Arizpe, to receive from Croix, as comandante-general of the Provincias Internas, instructions to escort to California from Sinaloa and Sonora a second body of Spanish colonists, — a body specifically for the founding of the pueblo Los Ángeles.[27]

This body was to consist of twenty-four families, each family to receive ten *pesos* a month and regular rations for three years, together with an advance of clothing, livestock, seed and implements, to be repaid from the yield of the soil. The quota must include a mason, a carpenter, and a blacksmith. With the whole there were to go as an escort, and for service in California, fifty-nine soldiers; and all, settlers and soldiers alike, were to be bound to remain at least ten years. By December, 1780, Rivera had secured fourteen families of settlers, and these, escorted by seventeen soldiers, he dispatched to San Gabriel by way of Loreto and San Diego.[28] He himself, with forty-two soldiers under Lieutenants Cayetano Limón and José Dario Argüello, and a train of 960 horses and mules, set out for the same point in the spring of 1781, by way of the Colorado River.[29]

It was August 18 when the settlers with their soldier escort reached San Gabriel, and on the 26th instructions for the founding of the new pueblo were issued, prepared by Neve, after a law for the Indies by Philip II.[30] It was to be located on high ground near the Porciúncula, from which, as from the Guadalupe at San José, irrigation was to be provided for a wide area. It was to centre in a plaza 200 by 300 feet, so quartered that the corners faced the cardinal points, and with each of the four sides intersected perpendicularly by three streets. The east side of the plaza was to be reserved for a church and royal buildings, and all house-lots were to be twenty *varas* in width by forty in depth.[31] As early as March 8, 1781, Neve had issued a *bando* (edict) specifying in minute detail the course to be pursued in the assignment of lands, and the conditions upon which they were to be held.[32]

The classes of lands recognized by Spanish law and custom were four: *solares* (house-lots), *suertes* (planting-lots, or fields, 550 feet square), *ejidos* (commons), and *propios* (income-producing lots for public uses).[33] Of these each settler was to be assigned (by lot) one *solar* and four *suertes;* two of the *suertes* being irrigable and two dry. No settler might sell any portion of his assignment, for "the lands, all and each, must be indivisible and inalienable forever"; nor might any portion be mortgaged, but it might by testamentary disposition be given to one child in preference to another. For five years settlers were to be exempt from all tithes and taxes; but within one year their houses must be wholly finished and provided with six hens and a rooster. Irrigating ditches must be opened within one year; within three years a public granary must be built, and within four years the royal buildings must be erected. Each settler must be provided with two horses, a saddle complete, a firelock and other arms. Animals must be marked and branded, and the brands placed of record. Patents of title to lands were to be issued, and of these also a record was to be made. Finally, the pueblo Los Ángeles, as likewise San José, "was to be given *alcaldes* (magistrates) of the first instance, and other officials of the *cabildo* (council), yearly," — officials who for the first two years were to be appointed by the Governor, but thereafter were to be nominated by the people and approved by the Governor.[34]

Los Ángeles was founded on September 4, 1781, with eleven families, — forty-six persons, — of whom only two even claimed to be of pure Spanish blood, the remainder being confessedly Indian and mulatto.[35] In the case of San José, the five-year probationary period expired in 1782, and in May, 1783, Moraga, as *comisionado* for the Governor, placed of record a plat of the town. The same service for Los Ángeles was performed in 1786 (September), by José Argüello as *comisionado*. Thus the plan of Neve for succoring the presidios was carried into effect.[36]

But from the point of view of the Mission, Spanish pueblos in a province like that of Alta California were an anomaly, and not unfraught with peril. If, as colonists, Spaniards were to be permitted to form themselves into communities autonomous and apart from the missions, to trade with the Indian (a being as yet nomadic or merely neophyte), and to exploit him, as Spaniards (laymen) in the New World were wont to do, what was to become of the great Mission idea, — the idea of Córdova and Las Casas? This query, between 1778 and 1782, had given pause to Serra, and had pointed his pen in an animated correspondence with Governor Neve.[37]

Nor as between State Sacerdotal and State Secular, under the *comandancia-general* in California, was this all. The College of San Fernando had early applied to Rome for a grant to Junípero Serra of the power to administer confirmation, — a power which had been granted to Jesuit superiors by a Bull of Pope Benedict XIV. The request had met with favor, and on July 16, 1774, the *comisario-prefecto* of the Franciscans in America (Juan Domingo de Arricivita of Querétaro) had been authorized to delegate the power in question to one friar in each Franciscan college. Delegation in the case of Serra — after approval by the Council of the Indies, the Audiencia of Mexico, and the Viceroy — had been made on October 17, 1777, and by the end of 1779 he had confirmed no less than 2431 souls. But about the middle of 1779, he had suddenly been required by Neve to cease confirming and to surrender his patent to Croix, as wielder of the *Patronato Real*, for inspection. In Serra's opinion, an ecclesiastical patent was something with which a comandante-general had no concern, and he continued to practice confirmation throughout the year 1780. The result had been that, after correspondence between the College of San Fernando and the Viceroy, Serra himself had sent the instrument to Croix, who, finding it regular, had returned it with orders to Neve to permit the Father-President to continue his administration.[38]

The course of Governor Neve with regard to San José and Los Ángeles was sanctioned by the King in the autumn of 1779; [39] but bearing in mind the need, according to royal behest, of a post and missions on the Santa Bárbara

Channel, — and not forgetting the request of the coman-dante-general for a new *Reglamento* for the Californias, — Neve, on June 1, 1779, had submitted to Croix a paper of high significance; a paper, which, approved by the latter in September, was approved by the King, under the hand of José de Gálvez, on October 24, 1781. As Article Fourteen, the *bando* on land-distribution was used. As Article Fifteen, five sections appeared, which fixed the number of Santa Bárbara Channel mission establishments at three, and directed that there be established, at from fourteen to twenty leagues to the eastward of the existing Alta California mission-chain, a second chain so contrived as to cover with its units the interstices of the first. Guards for the establishments of this second chain were to be provided by diminishing the escorts in the older establishments; padres, by gradually reducing the quota at each of the older establishments from two to one; and funds, by the saving effected in missionary salaries.[40]

Article Fifteen of the *Reglamento* of Neve was adverse to the plan of the Mission, and in that part of the Californias between San Diego and San Francisco it was nullified by the determined opposition of the College of San Fernando. But, for the present, to the Colorado.

Returning from the second Anza expedition, Garcés (January 3, 1777) prepared his diary for submission to the Viceroy. He indicated fourteen or fifteen points on the Gila and Colorado Rivers, as suitable for missions, but, assuming that the government would not care to found more than four, — two on the Gila, and two on the Colorado, — he advised suppressing the presidios, now disused, of San Miguel de Horcasitas and Buenavista and the founding of two new presidios of fifty men each, — posts whence a guard of ten men could be detailed for each of the river missions, "the surrounding nations being numerous, powerful, and warlike"; and in this advice Anza concurred.[41]

The question of Gila-Colorado missions at this time (1776–77) was one of extreme interest both to the Viceroy and to the King. But connected with it were at least three problems: Should establishments be placed on the Gila éxclusively? Should they be placed at the confluence of the streams, to wit, in Palma's country? And if placed at the confluence, should they be manned by Dominicans from the peninsula, or by Franciscans from Querétaro? [42]

It was the opinion of Padre Juan Díaz, who had been Garcés's companion to San Gabriel in 1774, that missions should be placed mainly if not exclusively on the Gila, because of aid often extended by the Gileño Pimas "to our arms against the Apaches"; because of the greater directness of the Pima-New Mexico route to Monterey; and because of the greater fertility of the Pima lands.[43] Governor Crespo of Sonora, Governor Mendinueta of New Mexico, and Comandante-Inspector Hugh Oconor were of a like opinion. Crespo recommended one mission "in Palma's country," but he laid much greater stress on the "reduction of the district between the junction of the rivers Gila and San Pedro and the presidio of Terrente." [44] As for Oconor, he ignored altogether the claims of Palma, but thought that by "three or four missionaries, picked and known for their talent and apostolic zeal," Sonora and Monterey might be conjoined through the medium of the hitherto intractable Moquis.[45]

On suppressing the presidios of San Miguel and Buenavista, Díaz and Crespo were in accord with Garcés and Anza.[46] They recognized the need of a presidio on the Colorado, but it should be placed some thirty leagues to the northeast of the confluence with the Gila; hence not in Palma's country (that of the Yumas), but above the entrance of Bill Williams Fork — the country of the Gal-chedunes.[47]

To Croix, however, the idea of Gila-Colorado missions was distinctly unattractive. Not so much that the coman-dante-general was opposed to occupation of the two rivers, — or of the Colorado, — but that, like Neve, unsympathetic with priests and beset by need of economy in administration, he was resolved to put in practice on the river boundary of Alta California a scheme of "reduction" still more emasculated than that which in Article Fifteen of the *Reglamento* Neve had outlined as for the future to be practiced on the coast boundary, — a scheme adumbrative of the plan of the *Custodia*, about to be tried in Sonora, an account of which will be given in chapter VIII.

Strange moreover to say, the attitude of Croix received countenance from within the cloisters of Querétaro itself. In 1777, Fray Juan Agustín Morfi, a *lector* (professor) of the college, to whom the Viceroy had submitted the diary of Escalante and Domínguez, condemned unsparingly the Escalante *entrada*, declaring that the padres had gone far astray, not knowing that Santa Fé and Monterey were in the same latitude. He even assailed missionary *entradas* in general. The object of them was to convert as many heathen as possible. They were made without instruments for taking altitudes, and in such haste that no sooner was one mission founded than it was quitted to found another deeper in the wilderness. The padres as they moved along depicted to the Indians the riches of the King of Spain in colors so brilliant that never afterwards was the government able, by its gifts, to meet the expectations so created. Instead of *entradas*, he advocated soldiers and war. Not even among the Yumas would he, for the present, establish missions. If war was to be waged, the best of the Yuma nation, as allies of the Spaniards against the

Apaches, would be absent on campaigns; so let the founding of missions be postponed until a general pacification, to wit, for two or three years.[48]

But if on the Colorado sham establishments only were to be erected, and these not for some years to come, the fault was not to be Palma's. He and his people had beheld too distinctly "the riches of the King of Spain" lightly to forego a bounty (beads, blankets, and tobacco) conditioned upon so simple a thing as baptism. The Yuma chief, a brother, and two others of his family, escorted by Anza as governor-elect of New Mexico, reached Mexico City on October 27, 1776. Palma on November 11 made, for his nation, submission both political and religious, and on February 13, 1777, after a season of catechism and regalement, was duly baptized under the name of Don Salvador.[49]

News of the submission having been received in Spain, the King on February 10, 1777, sent an order to the Viceroy and to Croix, that, in response to Palma's desire for "a presidio and mission in the heart of his country, there be given to these Indians missionaries and a guard of presidial troops."[50] The royal order was officially indorsed by Bucarely on May 16, and Palma, gratified, proud, and confident of speedy action, returned to the Yumas.

Months now passed, but from Croix, absent in Nueva Vizcaya, nothing was heard, and in March, 1778, Palma, a little anxious, made a visit of inquiry to Altar. Pacified with the excuse of Croix's absence, he returned home. More time elapsed, and the prestige of Palma, as the good friend of the rich king who evermore was to supply the Yumas with unlimited commodities, began seriously to decline. A second visit to Altar was essayed by Palma, and one to Horcasitas, the seat of military government for Sonora. Informed of these visits, and apprehensive of the effect of continued delay, Croix wrote from Chihuahua, in

February, 1779, to the Guardian of the College of Querétaro to ask that Garcés, with a companion, be sent to the
Colorado; and to the Governor of Sonora, to direct that
soldiers and supplies be furnished.[51]

With an escort of twelve men and a sergeant, all that
could be spared from the presidios of Altar and Tuçón
(Tuçón in 1776 having taken the place of Tubac), Garcés,
accompanied by Juan Díaz, started, August 1, 1779, for
the Gila-Colorado junction. Díaz and ten of the escort
were forced by lack of water to return to Sonoita to await
rains, but Garcés, in order not further to disappoint Palma,
pressed forward with two soldiers, reaching his destination
the last of the month. Palma's immediate followers he
found "jovial," but the others "restless and surly." Yet
remembering that "this was the first undertaking of the
comandante-general"; that, as a thing especially charged
upon him by the Court, it involved his honor; and that
"with God all is possible," he resolved to establish a mission. Success might not have been wanting had Croix
been sufficiently instructed, or prescient, to send with the
padres a supply of gifts. Palma in Mexico had been laden
with promises. With the coming of Spaniards to the Colorado, there was to begin for him, he was told, an era of
splendor and power hitherto unconceived. Accordingly,
when, on October 2, Garcés was rejoined by Díaz with his
ten men, expectation on the part of the Yumas was intense,
and the little band of white men was surrounded and
clamorously besought for trinkets, stuffs, and tobacco.

Unable to respond, yet alive to the dangers of refusal,
Díaz in November was sent to Arizpe to lay the matter
before Croix. The latter, forestalling the plan of the *Custodia*, met the case, March 20, 1780, by an order providing
for two settlements (pueblo missions) on the west bank of
the Colorado River, — La Purísima Concepción and San

Pedro y San Pablo de Bicuñer. Twenty families and twelve laborers were to be distributed, and lands were to be assigned as afterwards at San José and Los Ángeles. In each settlement two padres were to be stationed, — Garcés and Juan Antonio Barreneche at Concepción, and Díaz and Matías Moreno at San Pedro, — and their duties were to be twofold. To the Spaniards they were to minister as curates; but to the Indians they were to be missionaries, visiting them in their *rancherías* and effecting there their conversion. The converted, as neophytes, were to dwell in the settlements, and, stimulated by Spanish example, assume the ways of industry and civil life. No presidio was to be erected, but for the protection of the new pueblos a guard of ten soldiers was to be allotted to each.[52]

It was not until the autumn of 1780 that, escorted by Lieutenant Santiago de Islas, the aforesaid company of settlers, laborers, and soldiers actually arrived, and that Concepción and San Pedro y San Pablo were in fact founded. The settlers brought 192 head of cows and horses and 200 sheep, and the soldiers 42 riding animals. These, ranging along the river margin, were suffered, despite protests, to trample the corn-fields of the Indians. Then in June, 1781, Rivera y Moncada came with his 42 soldiers and 960 head of horses under Limón and Argüello. Most of the men, with the lieutenants, were sent forward to San Gabriel, but Rivera himself with a detachment of a dozen recrossed to the east bank of the Colorado to pasture his emaciated beasts. And here, as on the west bank, the animals wrought damage, destroying the mesquite plants. Finally, stocks and a whipping-post were set up, and while Ignacio Palma, brother to Salvador, was put by Santiago in the one for insolence, certain of Palma's compatriots were publicly castigated at the other for theft.

Deluded and bitterly disappointed, there lay before the Yumas the choice either of losing utterly their Colorado heritage or of smiting the dispossessor; and, led by Salvador Palma, the worst deluded yet most long-suffering of them all, they smote without relenting. San Pedro y San Pablo was attacked on the morning of July 17. Díaz and Moreno, the soldiers, and some of the settlers were killed. Others of the settlers were made prisoners, the church and adjacent buildings were burned, the sacred vestments stolen, and the images and ornaments hurled into the river. On the same day, at the same hour, an attack was made on Concepción. The soldiers and a few settlers were killed, but the padres were not molested, and at midday the Indians withdrew. This, however, was but to enable them to cross the Colorado and attack Rivera. The captain dug hurriedly a trench about his camp, and when on the next morning he was set upon by a "tumultuous throng," he and his few men with their firelocks fought to the end.[53] At Concepción, meanwhile, the survivors were disposed to congratulate themselves on a happy escape, but on the afternoon of the 18th the settlement was again assailed. The buildings were burned and many were killed, including Garcés and Barreneche, although there is evidence that death for the padres, especially Garcés, was contrary to the wish of Palma.

In the massacre on the Colorado, the Yumas, it is worthy of remark, glutted their vengeance exclusively on the male element of the population. There was no destruction of women and children. In the case even of the men, cruelty of a wanton sort was not practiced. The victims were dispatched as promptly as possible with the club.[54] As for the principal victims, — Rivera y Moncada and Garcés, — each met a death honorable to his calling. But while in the calling of the soldier Rivera was commonplace, in that of the priest Garcés was, exceptional. Compared with his prototype Kino, he was, if not so original a mind, fully as valiant an explorer. In him was the cardinal virtue of sincerity, and by Pedro Font, his colleague on the second Anza expedition, a spirited portrait of him has been sketched.

Padre Garces is so fit to get along with Indians, and go about among them, that he seems just like an Indian himself. He shows in everything the coolness of the Indian; he squats cross-legged in a circle with them; or at night around the fire, for two or three hours or even longer, all absorbed, forgetting aught else, discourses to them with great serenity and deliberation; and though the food of the Indians is as nasty and disgusting as their dirty selves, the padre eats it with great gusto, and says that it is appetizing and very nice. In fine, God has created him, I am sure, totally on purpose to hunt up these unhappy, ignorant, and boorish people." [55]

But what of the massacre on the Colorado as determining the practicability of Kino's design of uniting Sonora with California by a chain of missions northwestward past the head of the Gulf?

Here again an interesting contrast is afforded between Rivera y Moncada and Garcés. Rivera had ever been averse to communication between the Colorado River and the coast, — so averse that when Garcés, faring westward in 1776 from the Needles to San Gabriel, sought at the mission to obtain an escort wherewith to pass to San Luis Obispo as a starting-point for New Mexico, he was refused. The ground of the refusal was danger from the Yumas; and the massacre of 1781 would, had Rivera survived it, no doubt have been regarded by him as a confirmation of his fears. Still the establishments Concepción and San Pedro y San Pablo were not missions. With the plan of the Mission they stood at variance. There was no segregation of the Indians; the padres administered no temporalties; respect was inspired by no presidio. If, as recommended by Garcés and Anza, two garrisons, strong and mutually supporting, had been placed by Croix on the Gila and Colorado, and if, under cover of these, there had been placed on each stream two missions, — establishments to which the natives were solicited, or even compelled, to repair, and at which rewards and punishments were meted out to them, — there seems reason to believe, whatever the view as to the ultimate effect of the Mission upon native character, that the design of Kino might have been accomplished.[56]

"Drooped the willows; pale the poplars; sad the birds; fled the fish; shrouded the sun; horror-stricken all nature, the day that saw the dusk waters of the Colorado crimsoned by the innocent blood of our four beloved brothers," wrote Padre Francisco Antonio Barbastro of the College of Querétaro to Guardian Agustín Morfi, on September 25, 1781. "Yesterday a messenger sent by Palma came to this presidio [Altar] with a letter for the captain, asking pardon for what had been done. To-morrow there go from here troops destined for the Colorado."[57]

News of the massacre had reached Croix in August, at Arizpe, by way both of Tuçón and of Altar. A council of war had been held on September 9, and by its decision a force under Pedro Fages (lieutenant-colonel) was to be sent against the Yumas to chastize them as rebels and apostates. The expedition, 90 strong, started from Pitic on the 16th, passed by way of Altar, where it was reinforced to 110, and reached the Colorado on the 19th of October. Here, the ransom of 64 captives, mostly women, was effected by means of blankets, beads and tobacco. The expedition returned to Sonoita, whence the ransomed were dispatched to Altar. By November 30 Fages was at the Colorado again. At Concepción and San Pedro y San Pablo he recovered ten more captives, and secured certain church vestments and the bodies of the four missionaries and of the dead soldiers and settlers. But upon the Yumas, elusive as the wind, no distinct harm was inflicted, and early in 1782 Fages found himself back at Pitic with exhausted horses.[58]

Hope of chastisements nevertheless was not abandoned. On January 3, Governor Neve at Monterey was notified by Croix that Fages with 40 men would proceed to San Gabriel, and that Pedro Tueros, captain at Altar, would march to the Colorado. At the river, Tueros was to be joined by Neve with all the troops in California. Fages was met by Neve at San Gabriel on March 26, but, it being decided that the high water of the Colorado would be a hindrance, Tueros was informed of a postponement of action until September. On the new basis, which Croix approved, Captain José Antonio Romeu with 108 men reached the Colorado by September 16, and was there joined by Neve with 60 men, but unaccompanied by Fages. The latter had been turned back by orders received on the way; orders which directed that Neve proceed to Sonora to assume the office of inspector-general of the Provincias Internas, and that Fages proceed to Monterey to be installed as governor. As for Romeu, he conducted against the Yumas a campaign which resulted in 108 natives being killed, 85 taken prisoner, five Christians freed from captivity, and 1048 horses recovered. Otherwise the result was naught. "Neither then nor afterwards," declares the chronicle of Arricivita, "was subjection secured. Hope of reëstablishing the pueblos, or of reducing the Indians, none remained; and the expenditures incurred for communication between Sonora and Monterey by the Colorado River were wasted."[59]

As far back as June, 1777, Felipe de Neve had written to Viceroy Bucarely that, mindful of the ease with which the

CALIFORNIA ORGANIZED   139

eight or ten thousand Indians along the Santa Bárbara Channel might, if so disposed, interrupt transit to the north, he had decided to found, in addition to the terminal establishments San Buenaventura and Purísima Concepción, a central establishment to be called Santa Bárbara.[60] Until the coming, in the summer of 1781, of the 42 soldiers recruited by Rivera in Sonora, this had been impracticable. Meanwhile Croix had issued his decree for pueblo missions on the Colorado.

The provisions of this instrument, consonant as they were with the views of Neve, and to be carried out, as they were, within Neve's own province, may have suggested to the latter imitation with respect to the establishments for the Channel; especially as the Colorado Yumas and Channel Chumash were alike in being numerous and so located as to derive a regular subsistence from their trade of fishing. At all events, in 1782, on March 6, Neve issued to Lieutenant Ortega instructions that the establishments about to be erected as missions were to be operated as *hospicios*. The Canaleños were not to be withdrawn from their *rancherías* and put to agricultural and mechanical tasks, but to be converted by pastoral visitations.[61] On March 31, San Buenaventura — the mission beloved of Gálvez — was founded by Ortega in conjunction with Serra, and on April 21, Neve and Serra founded the presidio of Santa Bárbara.[62]

But, on August 23, 1779, the great Viceroy, Bucarely (deceased, April 9), had been succeeded by Martín de Mayorga, — a man imbued with the spirit of Neve and Croix. A field-marshal in Spain, Mayorga in America had been governor, president, and captain-general of Guatemala. Under him (December, 1780) the College of San Fernando, warned by the recent decree of Croix denying temporalties to Garcés and his companions, had consented to send six friars to the Channel, provided they were assigned two to a mission, and were allowed the usual vestments, bells, live-stock, implements, and funds for foundations. This offer Mayorga, on April 5, 1781, had rejected. Between College and Viceroy a deadlock thereupon had ensued, but news of it had not reached the Channel at the time of the founding of San Buenaventura Mission and Santa Bárbara Presidio.

With the creation of the district of Santa Bárbara, short by two establishments though it was, the organization of Alta California, secular and sacerdotal, became complete. Secularly there now were the four military districts, — San Diego, Santa Bárbara, Monterey, and San Francisco;[63] and the two pueblo districts, — San José and Los Ángeles. Sacerdotally there were the missions, — San Diego, San Juan Capistrano, and San Gabriel; Santa Bárbara and San Buenaventura; San Carlos Borromeo de Monterey, San Antonio de Padua, and San Luis Obispo; San Francisco and Santa Clara, — establishments where nineteen friars, charged with the care of 4000 neophytes, 4900 head of mules and horned cattle, and 7000 head of sheep, goats, and swine, were able to grow wheat, maize, and barley to the amount of a predictable annual yield of 22,500 bushels.

In Alta California, prior to 1781, the secular head was the *jefe militar*, or *comandante de armas*, to whom appeal might be taken from the presidio comandantes, and from the *cabos* (corporals) of the mission guards. Civil rule began with the introduction of the pueblo, with its *alcalde* and *regidores*,[64] — functionaries of great antiquity, especially the *alcalde*, who, an outgrowth of the Roman municipality, derived his designation from the *cadi* of the Moors.[65] Neve, the first Alta California political head (*jefe político*, or *gobernador*), was such not so much by his posi-

tion as by the fact that he founded two pueblos, from the
alcaldes and *cabildos* [66] of which (as also from his own *comisionados*) appeal to him might be taken; he in turn being
subject to be appealed from to the comandante-general or
Audiencia (Supreme Court) of Guadalajara.

As for the sacerdotal head, he was, prior to 1781, as
afterwards, the president of missions. From him appeal might be taken to the College of San Fernando,
and thence to the *comisario-general* of the Franciscans in
Spain. Withal, down to 1781, when the Californias became part of the diocese of Sonora, they had been part of
that of Durango; but this fact signified naught, for not
only were there no curacies in the province, but, from
regular to secular, from monk to bishop, there was no
appeal; save, perchance, in cases like that of the neophyte
Carlos, who by taking refuge in the mission church of San
Diego had raised the question of right of asylum.

Under the organization described, advantage lay (as ever
in the Spanish dominions) with State Secular; for while, as
between State Secular and State Sacerdotal, the former was
free from authoritative intervention by the latter, the reverse did not obtain. In criminal causes, the missions, as
has been seen, were subject to the governor; and in so far as
by a choice of Indian *alcaldes* and *regidores* the missions became pueblos, they were thus subject to the extent of the
governor's approval of the choice made. By virtue, moreover, of the *Patronato Real* the entire Spanish clergy, regular as well as secular, could (*vide* chapter III) be controlled in
everything save the internal regulation of their own corporations. [67] Advantage lay with State Secular, too, from the
broad circumstance, noted in chapter v, that Charles III
was king, and that during his reign Madrid, influenced by
rationalized France, had set out to curb the priesthood.

CHAPTER VIII

STATE SECULAR vs. STATE SACERDOTAL

BY the promotion of Neve on July 12, 1782, to the position of *comandante-inspector* in the Provincias Internas, Pedro Fages had become governor of the Californias. It now was thirteen years since, from his "high hill," near Cape San Lucas, José de Gálvez had watched the San Carlos vanish below the horizon of the South Sea; and the pioneers of the Sacred Expedition were beginning to pass away. On January 1, 1782, the diligent Juan Crespi had died at the age of sixty-one; and on August 28, 1784, he was followed, at the age of seventy-one, by Junípero Serra.

On the 18th of August, Palou (recalled to Monterey from San Francisco) found Serra, who lately had completed an arduous round of mission calls, suffering from trouble of the chest, and from a recurrence of his old trouble of the leg. He found him distressed also by rumors of an impending displacement of the Franciscans in Alta California by the Dominicans.[1] On the 27th, fever supervened, and at the church, attended by Indians and cuirassed men, the Father-President received the last Sacrament. On the 28th, the fever increasing, he was visited in the morning by Captain José Cañizares, whose ship lay at anchor in the bay; and between one and two o'clock in the afternoon, having drawn about him his cloak and composed himself on his bed-of planks, he resigned his spirit. His funeral, which took place on the 29th in the presence of mariners, soldiers, and neophytes, was conducted with solemn pomp. The body, covered with *rosas de Castilla* (token of 1769–70) and attended by guardsmen with lighted tapers, was borne amid chanting about the plaza to the church, where, in the presbytery on the epistle side, it was interred near that of Crespi.

> One sees the pulpit o' the epistle-side,
> And somewhat of the choir, those silent seats,
> And up in the aëry dome where live
> The angels, and a sunbeam's sure to lurk.

On September 4, Serra's garments were distributed as amulets, and on the 6th, Palou, writing to José de Gálvez in behalf of the nine missions of northern California, — "daughters of the fervid zeal of your Excellency," — set forth the incidents of which use has been made in the above account.[2]

It has been said in chapter v that Junípero Serra was seraphic in spirit, simple in faith, and pure in heart. That he was not unpossessed of shrewdness has there also been intimated. In 1781, in view of his course on the confirmation question, Neve, writing to Croix, charged upon him "unspeakable artifice," — a "pretended obedience to an authority [the government] which he in fact eludes." And in 1783, Fages found him "despotic" and opposed "to every government undertaking." In the larger sense, which also is the truer, Serra is not so much to be regarded as a person as a force, — a representative, less astute than Salvatierra, less even than Palou, of the idea of the Mission: in personal concernments, tractable to the point of humility; in concernments of faith, steadfast to the point of aggression.

Crespi and Serra were dead. Palou yet survived but was becoming infirm. Before the death of Serra he had applied to the King for leave to retire to San Fernando; but, pending the arrival at Monterey of Fermín Francisco Lasuén, who meanwhile had been named as Serra's successor, he was kept at the head of the Alta California establishments.[3]

On reaching his college (1786) he was made guardian, and
in 1787 he published his *Relación Histórica de la Vida* ...
del venerable Padre Fray Junípero Serra, a book of nearly
three hundred and fifty pages. It is agreeably written,
and bears as a frontispiece a portrait of its subject. The
original picture (a painting) was secured through the liber-
ality of former Guardian Verger, now Bishop of Linares.[4]

The Gálvez-Croix dispatch of 1768 declared, that

if from the glorious conquest (as achieved by Hernan Cortés) of
those vast dominions that fall under the name of New Spain, it
had been the practice of successors in the government to follow
up and prosecute the high designs of that hero, there would have
supervened the light of the Gospel and the dominion of the august King of Spain to the ultimate bounds of this immense and
unexplored continent.

But the "high designs" of Cortés had not been followed
up, and by way of remedy there was proposed a *comandancia-general* for the Provincias Internas. A system of *intendencias* was also proposed. Durango, Sonora, and the
Californias were to be placed, each, in charge of a *gober-
nador-intendente,* — an official who, with entire independence of initiative as to government, police, justice, treasury
and war, was to be subject to the Viceroy, or comandante-
general, and Audiencia, and to the *Superintendente de
Hacienda* (Secretary of the Treasury) on appeal.[5]

The problem which confronted Gálvez and Croix, however, was not alone one of administration. It was the problem, early noted by Gálvez,[6] of reduction of the natives to
civilized life. In the days of Cortés "reduction" had given
no serious trouble. It had been an incident of conquest.
Between 1530 and 1540, conversions in the City of Mexico,
in Texcuco, in Michoacán, and elsewhere — all, too, at
the hands of but sixty missionaries, — had amounted to

millions; and, upon conversion as a base, civil organization had straightway been engrafted. To-day in Sonora and Nueva Vizcaya conversions were not only few, but the converted remained civilly as "unreduced" as when they were infidels. Evidently something was required to meet the problem other than *comandancias-generales* and *intendencias*. Gálvez and Croix did not disclose this something, but by recalling the methods of Cortés, political and religious, they indicated it.

In 1772 (July 13), Fiscal Areche observed, that

to check decadence a new method of government, spiritual and temporal, was necessary. [In it] there should be digested all the rules of experience for erecting the missions in regular towns, and not in *rancherías* as most of them were; rules that would be useful for the good domestic government of the Indians, — for introducing among them family order, obedience to superiors, the practice of agriculture and commerce; rules that in the days of Cortés had been observed in Michoacán with a success such as to render its pastor and bishop, Don Vasco de Quiroga, worthy of a foremost place in the history of America.[7]

The same year, on November 15, Guardian Verger said: —

When Hernan Cortés entered these kingdoms, he found villages, towns, and pueblos already formed, civilized, and improved with everything necessary, as the histories say, excepting only the knowledge of the true God and of his Holy Law, by which they were to serve, love, adore, and reverence Him. But as for the Gentiles whom we are striving to conquer, they lack all of this, insomuch that for the most part they go naked, wandering in their intricate mountains and extended valleys.

Still, if it were desired to profit by Cortés's example, let it be remembered how, upon the coming of the first friars, he went forth to receive them in the Avenue of Tepayac (now called that of Guadalupe), and, kneeling in the dust, kissed the hand of each, and by his interpreter said to the Indians: —

Although I, in the name of the Emperor, govern the bodies of men, these fathers are come in the name of the head of the Church, which governs their souls, with authority from the same God whom we adore, to guide them to his glory. What the fathers command, obey even as ye have seen me obedient first.

By some *jefes* (so Verger affirmed) it was made their first business to tell the Indians that they need ask permission of the fathers in nothing; that "the fathers were not allowed to inflict punishments; that their authority extended only to the hearing of confessions and the saying of Mass."[8]

But on the question of the attainment of civil status for the Indian by a "new method of reduction," it was deemed well to obtain the opinion of Padre Antonio de los Reyes. His college (Querétaro) had in 1773 been emphatic in support of the plan of the Mission, but in 1776, Reyes, about to become Bishop of Sonora, had rejected this in favor of the plan of the *Custodia*, — the plan of "reduction" so successful under Cortés; one, withal, expressly sanctioned in 1686 by a Bull of Pope Innocent XI. Let the Provincias, said Reyes, be divided into *custodia* districts. In the head town of each district let there be established an *hospicio*, or "home," of six or more padres under a director responsible to the *comisario-general* of his order. From such *hospicio* — or, where desirable, from a sub-*hospicio* of three padres under a president — let the inmates go forth as missionaries to Spanish pueblos and mining-camps and to Indian *rancherías*. As for support, let it be obtained somewhat by royal donation, but chiefly by "the charity of the faithful." Only two *custodias* were contemplated for the entire Provincias: one, — including the missions of Parra nearest the Sierra Madre, of Toranmora Alta and Baja, of

Sonora and of the Californias, — with seat at Arizpe; the other,— including the missions of New Mexico, Chihuahua, Coahuila, and Texas, — with seat near the centre of the territory. To the general plan of Reyes assent had been expressed by the Franciscan *comisario-general*, Manuel de la Vega, in November, but Vega had suggested four *custodias* instead of two: one for New Mexico (La Concepción), one for Nueva Vizcaya (San Antonio), one for Sonora (San Carlos), and one for Alta California (San Gabriel).[9] Thus the matter stood on the advent of Fages to power, at Monterey, in 1782.

In 1783 (February 11), the three Franciscan missionary colleges — Guadalupe de Zacatecas for Durango, Santa Cruz de Querétaro for Sonora, and San Fernando de Méjico for Alta California — united in a determined protest against the whole *Custodia* scheme. The royal *cédula* enjoining it bore date May 20, 1782, and with the *cédula* there had come a Bull of sanction by Pope Pius VI and elaborate *estatutos* (ordinances) drafted by Manuel de la Vega. "The colleges," the protest confessed, "are overwhelmed with weight of authority, Pontifical, Royal, and Prelatical." But *custodias* — successful under Cortés among the semi-civilized nations of the South— could, it was averred, never be aught but a failure in the North. Success for the *Custodia* required clergy, convents, churches, money, — the incidents and appurtenances of a settled condition, — and it was notorious that a settled condition in the North did not obtain, but one of robbery and murder, as witness the four padres of Querétaro lately put to death on the banks of the Colorado River.[10] By Bishop Reyes the protest was pronounced full of *falsas suposiciones y expresiones injuriosas*, and on January 14, 1784, it was disallowed by the King. Yet it so far served its purpose that, whereas the *custodia* of San Carlos in Sonora was erected without delay, the erecting of the *custodia* of San Gabriel in Alta California was postponed; a postponement that proved a nullification, for in 1792 (August 17) the King decreed that even in Sonora the plan of the Mission should be resumed.[11]

But the *Custodia* was not the only means of "reduction," civilly, for the Indian to which, between 1776 and 1791, the government of the Provincias was to have recourse. By a Law of the Indies called the *alcalde* law (*vide* chapter III), Indians were required to dwell in pueblos, choosing for themselves *alcaldes* and *regidores*. As early as December, 1778, Neve instructed the San Diego and San Carlos padres to put neophytes through the form of choosing two *alcaldes* and two *regidores;* and the padres at San Antonio, San Luis, and San Gabriel to contrive an election of *alcaldes* and *regidores* in number proportioned to population.[12] In 1781, Comandante-General Croix revived viceregal decrees which required the furnishing of inventories and statistics to the Governor, and invoked the *Patronato Real* to the effect that, except for urgent cause, no padre might be transferred from one mission to another. By order of Neve in 1782 padres were forbidden military escort save when visiting a presidio or *ranchería* to hear confessions; and the same year, apropos of a *cédula* of 1776 directing the landing of the Philippine galleon at Monterey, it had been ordered that no priest should pass on shipboard.[13] The privilege, too, of franking letters had been abridged;[14] and not alone this, but padres wishing to retire to their college, or to Spain, were obliged to obtain a government permit.[15] Finally, there was the question of the employment by the padres of Indians as messengers and *vaqueros*, — of teaching the neophytes to ride. To control the military, as had been permitted the Jesuits in Paraguay, and the Franciscans in Lower California and in Texas, this was to wield temporal power indeed; and Neve, by his virtual interdiction of escorts, had, in the interest of State Secular, seen to it that such power was not wielded in Alta California.[16]

Promulgated by Neve and Croix, it was upon Fages that for the most part it devolved to put the foregoing laws and decrees into effect. And Fages, loyal to the government, yet mindful of his rustication in 1773 at the instance of Serra, found himself between two fires.

In vain did he protest to Palou that in the business of governing he had a partner, a veritable Jorkins. With the best intentions he dared not too much disregard orders, for his adjutant (Soler), animated by a keen desire to be governor himself, was "deadly at intermeddling." In vain did he modify a rule of Neve's that absconding neophytes were never to be brought back by the military.[17] His concessions — so, Hamlet-like, he averred to Father Cambón — were requited only by insult. Did he go half a league from San Carlos Presidio to greet Father Palou — he was rebuffed by scowls and taciturnity. Did he furnish the padre three attendants and three of his best horses, and direct in his honor a salute of two guns — Palou would not even break bread with him. Did he pay a visit to San Carlos Mission — Father Matías, in Palou's presence and by him abetted, stamped roundly his foot, and cried out upon him. Did he, at San Luis, ask from Father Caballer (Catalan like himself) an inventory, saying that inventories had been rendered at the other missions of the South — he was told to his beard that he would be believed when the documents were produced. His love for the padres had been such that it had gained for him the nickname of *frailero* (panderer to friars), yet the padres, even in their letters, denied him the courtesy of the usual forms of address, —

Muy Señor mio (My very respected Sir), and *Beso á Vd. su mano* (I respectfully kiss your hand). At such disrespect, he ("not as Fages but as governor") stood fairly aghast. Because he obeyed orders, he was said by the populace to be "persecuting the *frailes*," when, in truth, he had endured so to be dragooned by them that, looking within, he had been obliged to say to himself, "I am governor, not Fages." Distraught, however, though he was, and with the feet of their reverences the padres upon his very head, he was resolved to depart no jot from duty. So comporting himself he could not be put to blush, and would have his reward from conscience.[18]

The Governor by 1785 had determined upon a course of action, — an appeal to the Viceroy. Under date of September 26, the chief immediate grievances, — failure of the padres to perform chaplain duty at the presidios,[19] disregard of the *Patronato Real*, unwarranted charges for mission produce, refusal to render inventories, failure to solicit permission when quitting the province, — all had been formulated. The document was sent by the Viceroy (through the Audiencia) to the College of San Fernando, where Palou on his arrival in 1786 was intrusted with the task of reply.

Chaplain duty, said Palou, was by favor and not by requirement, and should be paid for. As for the *Patronato Real*, Fages, ignorant of its scope, made of it a cloak for despotism. As for the tariff of prices for produce (an attempt to regulate what should be left to demand and supply), it never had been sanctioned by the King. As for permission to retire, padres, by order of Viceroy Mayorga, were so permitted on exhibiting a license from their prelate. Palou said nothing as to inventories, but on the point (not raised by Fages) that under the new *Reglamento* but one padre was to be allowed at a mission, he pleaded an abrogation of the requirement by the King in his *cédula* of May 20, 1782.[20] By way of general counter-charge upon the Governor, Palou submitted that the *Reglamento* had not been published in the Californias until September, 1784,[21] when Fages's bill of grievances bore date, and that escorts had been withheld, to the crippling of the business of the Mission, temporal as well as spiritual.[22]

"State Secular *vs.* State Sacerdotal in Alta California" was thus ready for adjudication. But the points involved were delicate, and the Audiencia, glad of a chance to shift the responsibility of deciding them, referred the case to the comandante-general of the Provincias Internas, — Jacobo Ugarte y Loyola. On the appointment, in 1783, of Caballero de Croix to be Viceroy of Peru, Felipe de Neve, his comandante-inspector had been given the place of comandante-general. But Neve had died in 1784, and as no officer with adequate knowledge was available as a successor, a compromise was effected in 1785 by restoring to the Viceroy of Mexico (Conde de Gálvez) supreme authority as possessed by Bucarely, and by creating Ugarte y Loyola his subordinate. When, therefore, the Alta California case was received by Loyola, it was received reluctantly as by one without authority. In the emergency the Comandante-General applied for light to Lasuén, the new mission president at Monterey.[23]

The points which Lasuén emphasized were three which Fages did not make. "What I oppose and resist with my whole strength," he declared, "is being left alone in a mission. I offer myself for every kind of hardship (even unto death in these parts) at the order of my superior, but no man is able to convince me that I ought to subject myself to solitude in this ministry." The use of Indians as messengers and *vaqueros* he upheld as necessary, but the instituting of Indian *alcaldes*, — "lazy, overbearing, and conniving in dereliction," — he pronounced a legal formality, farcical, mischievous, and unseasonable.[24]

By Ugarte y Loyola the Alta California case was vouchsafed a determination no more definite than by the Audiencia. By both Audiencia and Comandante-General the finding was, that Mission and Government in Alta California — State Sacerdotal and State Secular — were to keep each within its own sphere and jurisdiction, observing *armonía y correspondencia*. If either litigant triumphed, it was the Mission rather than the Government, for the Audiencia explicitly recommended that the padres at San Francisco be paid for saying Mass at the presidio, and that on "indispensable journeys" the padres be furnished by the Government with escorts.

Regarding San José and Los Ángeles, as civic institutions under Fages, they were as uncomfortable a Neve heritage as the *Reglamento* itself. Both towns were fretted by disorders from three causes: gambling on the part of the settlers; immorality on the part of the settlers with the Indians; and horse-stealing on the part of the Indians. At San José, Ignacio Vallejo was *comisionado*, and at Los Ángeles, Vicente Félix; and in 1787 Fages found it necessary to furnish to the latter minute instructions as to police.[25] Through the pueblos, indeed, there was taking place the very thing which the Laws of the Indies, by strict prohibition of miscellaneous intercourse between Indians and whites, had sought to preclude, to wit, demoralization of the Indians by whites demoralized already. Lasuén, therefore, was justified when, alluding to San José, he said in his plea to Ugarte y Loyola that Gentile Indians (male and female), employed at the pueblo in tasks of house and field, were by their "scandals and libertinism" fast neutralizing the good done by the adjoining mission of Santa Clara.

Hurt by the projected *Custodia;* hurt by the enforced toleration of Indian *alcaldes* and *regidores;* hurt by fear of the *Reglamento;* hurt by need of interposing at Mexico and Arizpe defense against charges of insubordination; and hurt, lastly, by the presence, aggressive and unsavory, of the pueblos, there yet remained to State Sacerdotal a consolation. The missions of Santa Bárbara and La Purísima Concepción — desired by Serra and planned by Neve, but suspended in their founding by the refusal of the College of San Fernando to assign to them padres — both at length were to be erected. "You will oppose all innovation, and will refuse to supply priests on the Río Colorado method," wrote the Guardian of San Fernando to Lasuén on April 1, 1786; and the terms, perforce, had been accepted.[26] The day of founding for Santa Bárbara was December 4, 1786; for Purísima, December 8, 1787.[27] Nor were these foundings the only consolation of the time. To a recommendation made in November, 1787, by Nicolás Soler, who, besides being "deadly at intermeddling," was dominated by Neve ideas, that the missions straightway be dissolved and their lands granted in severalty, Fages interposed the pertinent comment, that as yet the Indians had not been weaned from their Gentile state, nor could they be addressed without an interpreter.[28]

By 1789, strife between the secular and sacerdotal elements in Alta California had, in obedience to the Audiencia, been suffered to become appeased. Not that bitterness was easily laid aside by Palou. Writing on January 28, 1781, to Comisario-General Manuel María Truxillo, the Guardian said: —

Little have the missions grown spiritually since my departure, — a backwardness due to the contrary attitude of that Señor Gobernador Don Pedro Fages, who in everything has set himself to impede the apostolical zeal of the missionaries; due also to the scandals committed upon the poor neophytes by subaltern officers; and due, finally, to the bad example of the soldiers. The said Don Pedro (always governor in fact) ruled at the beginning under the title of comandante, but the Venerable Father Junípero Serra, perceiving that the conquest was in nothing advanced but rather hindered, felt himself obliged to perform the task of coming to this court and making representations to the Most Excellent Señor Viceroy Don Antonio María Bucarely; whence it resulted that the said Fages was recalled and that straightway the conquest, spiritual and temporal, was advanced notably. But with the transfer, after a few years, of the Provincias Internas to the command of a comandante-general, separate and apart from the captaincy-general and viceroyalty of New Spain, there supervened the return of Don Pedro with more honor and with the title of governor. And, coming thus, he, as all the padres feel, has acted much according to his whim; either because of his nature, resentful of dependence, or by way of avenging himself for what, during his first incumbency, was accomplished by the report of the Venerable Father Junípero.[29]

But *pace* Palou. Fages, on May 18, 1790, was relieved of the office of governor at his own request. He was fifty-six years old, and for seven and a half years had faithfully served the King at Monterey. He left behind him nine missions in four presidial districts (an addition of two establishments, — Santa Bárbara and Purísima) and the two pueblos. Of San José, the population now was about 80, and of Los Ángeles about 140. In the latter were 29 adobe dwellings, an adobe town-hall, barracks, guard-house, and granary, all inclosed by a wall of adobes.

The new governor, a client of Viceroy Revilla Gigedo, was José Antonio Romeu. Fages was required to yield office to him at Loreto, and then proceed to Mexico to be invested with a colonelcy. The transfer was made, however, by José Joaquín de Arrillaga (lieutenant-governor) on April 16, 1791.[30] Romeu reached Monterey on October 13, and soon thereafter Fages set sail for San Blas. He had already dispatched south his wife, Doña Eulalia de Callis, with his children, and had brought to conclusion a series of intimate notes to his successor.

September 14, 1790. You will find in this *casa real*, which is sufficiently capacious, the necessary furniture; a sufficient stock of goats and sheep which I have raised; and, near by, a garden which I have made at my own expense, from which you will have fine vegetables all the year. *February* 26, 1791. Half a league from this post I made a garden in the year 1783. It is 308 *varas* long and 80 wide. There are in it grapes and about six hundred fruit trees, — pear, apple, peach, apricot, quince, etc. *May* 24, 1791. With the Dominicans I have had no serious trouble, but with the Fernandinos quarrels have arisen. They are opposed in the highest degree to the *Reglamento* and Government. That you will be able to endure their independent ways, I much doubt.[31]

But to partake of the fruits and vegetables of Fages's garden, or to match diplomacy with the friars, Romeu had little opportunity. He died on the 9th of April, 1792, and was buried at San Carlos Mission, — a spot, by its hallowed dust of saints and rulers, fast becoming a Santa Croce of the wild. Romeu's successor *ad interim* was Lieutenant-Governor Arrillaga, who held office until 1794, when he was replaced by a governor *proprietario*, — Diego de Borica.

The governors and comandantes of the Californias whom thus far in the course of narration we have met, have been seven: Portolá, Armona, Barri, Rivera y Moncada, Neve, Fages, and Romeu. Portolá was kindly but negative; while as for Armona and Barri, neither had passed north of the peninsula. It may be said of the one that, accomplished, and approved by Palou, he shrank before difficulties; and of the other, that, arbitrary in temper, a conspicuous trait was violence. In Rivera y Moncada hauteur was made grotesque by envy, but personality lacked interest through mediocrity. Neve and Fages remain, each a man of character, but, strange to say, only one (Fages) a man of personality. Neve, indeed, possessed so much character, was so imperturbable, kept so well his temper, wrought with an inexorability so final, as to be personally of scant account. Neve was the *Reglamento* and the *Reglamento* was Neve — little besides. Among early California rulers, therefore, it is upon Fages that personally the emphasis falls, for, to cite from New Netherland a parallel, Fages in whatever relation viewed was a veritable Peter the Headstrong.

According to Serra, with whom he had had trouble, he often had trouble with his men. Then there was his adjutant, Soler. With him, whom Neve had not found insupportable, he could do nothing. "The caviling spirit of our Don Nicolás disturbs me much," he writes in 1787. "He persists in transacting affairs, and in ventilating here and there his chimerical schemes, to the disquietude of all."

Last (and hereby a tale) there was the *gobernadora,* Fages's wife Doña Eulalia. We get a glimpse of her first in a letter from Fages to Father Morfi from Pitic, dated February 12, 1782: —

On June 10 last, I informed you of my arrival at Arizpe accompanied by my wife, Catalan servants, and soldiers. At the same time there was given me the satisfaction of an increase in my command, with whom God was pleased to rejoice us the night of the 30th of last May, and who was baptized on the 4th of June, the Señor Intendente, Governor Don Pedro Carbalon, being godfather. The child was named Pedro José Fernando, and I trust that your Reverence will be pleased to add him to the number of your children.

We get another glimpse on September 13, 1784: —

In the mission of San Francisco [writes Palou to Guardian Juan Sancho], we remained with the Governor more than four weeks.

Being on a visit to the presidio with his wife, he there awaited the birth to her of a child whom we baptized. The *señora* was pleased with our behavior, and was a notable example to the neophytes and soldiers. Much was accomplished by her bearing and presence.

But Doña Eulalia, delicately bred, was fearsome of the frontier. Her presence at Monterey had only been secured by repeated urgings from Fages, in which Neve and Romeu joined; and no sooner had she arrived (escorted by her husband, amid rejoicings, from Loreto) than she was eager for the latter to resign his governorship and return with her to Mexico. Means for accomplishing her will were few, but among them was one upon which she relied with confidence, — rigid exclusion of her consort from the conjugal couch. For three months, October, 1784, to February, 1785, this means was tried, but at the end of the term, the Governor's steadfastness continuing, Doña Eulalia was constrained to affect jealousy, — jealousy toward a servant of the house, a Yuma maid, Indizuela. Vowing divorce, she fled tempestuously her abode; and although dealt with by the padres, who enjoined seclusion and forbade the bruiting abroad of scandals against the governor, she became so violent as to provoke threats of castigation and handcuffs.[32]

Eulalia began divorce proceedings in April, 1785, before the Acting Comandante-General José Antonio Rengel, at Chihuahua, but Asesor (Solicitor-General) Galindo Navarro decided that, the case being one of divorce, its proper forum was the ecclesiastical court of the Bishop of Sonora. By advice of the *asesor*, however, an order was entertained for the removal of both Doña Eulalia and the maid Indizuela to "some house of honest matrons" in Sonora, and for a writ upon a third part of the salary of Fages, to enable the complainant to prosecute her suit. The Bishop, before whom the case came in November, spurned the interlocutory findings of the *asesor*—"eager to thrust his sickle in the grain"—as beyond the secular jurisdiction, and as, therefore, a reprehensible affront. But here censure and, as well, the suit were stayed; for in December it became known to Rengel that Fages and Eulalia had been reconciled in September.[33]

My family are well [writes Fages to Palou, on January 2,1787]. Suddenly one morning Eulalia with a thousand protests summoned me, and amid tears humbly sought pardon for all the past. She confessed that all had been pure illusion and falsity, and that she herself had suborned Indizuela to ensnare me. Afterwards she summoned Don Hermenegildo Sal [the paymaster], Vargas [the sergeant], and other persons, and told them the truth, that they might make it public in discharge of her conscience. *Gracias á Dios* that now we dwell in union and harmony![34]

What Fages did not write was that it was largely due to Nicolás Soler, "deadly at intermeddling," that the reconciliation had been brought about.

But, reconciled or no, Doña Eulalia did not abate her activity. Determined to exchange the barbarism and fogs of Monterey for the refinement and salubrity of Mexico, she in 1785 came near to proving a factor as fatal to her husband's governorship as Serra in 1773 had proved to his *comandancia*. In the year named, on October 25, Fages was compelled to notify the authorities at Chihuahua that his wife had petitioned the Audiencia for his transfer for health reasons, and to beg of them that the petition be disregarded.

CHAPTER IX

DOMESTIC EQUILIBRIUM

DIEGO DE BORICA — native of the Basque town of Vitoria, and Knight of the Order of Santiago — was the most sagacious and chivalric of the men sent by Spain to represent the King at Monterey. Under him old things in Alta California passed away, and many (if not all) things became new, — new, that is, by a reversion of conditions to what they were under Viceroy Bucarely. But this making of the province new, by causing it to revert to the old, signifies not that the early forces were controlled by the early minds. In 1794 Lasuén, a figure venerable and benign, still lived and wrought, but the grave had closed upon Crespi, Serra, and Palou, and (1787) upon José de Gálvez, and (1788) upon King Charles III himself. In part, the newness mentioned is to be ascribed to the withdrawal, in 1793, of the Californias from the jurisdiction of the Provincias Internas.[1] In part, also, it was due to the accession of Charles IV to the throne, representative in Spain of a European reaction (guillotine-bred) toward Absolutism and the Church.

But whatever its source, the newness prevailed, and its manifestations were dual: (1) a revival of interest in Anian, the English, and the Russians, — a revival involving undertakings which set Alta California before the world as an entity, a something with boundaries political as well as natural; a something, withal, through guns and fortifications, with power; (2) a culmination of the Mission dynamically, — a culmination marked on the one hand by additional Mission foundations, and on the other by a growing severity of attitude (reflex of Indian incorrigibility) by padres toward neophytes.

I

In 1778, men of Captain Cook's command, when at Nootka, obtained from the natives a number of skins of the sea-otter. These, while in the hands of the natives, had been used as garments, and had become infested with lice; nor was their condition improved by Cook's men, who used them in high latitudes as bed-coverings. But at Canton, in December, 1779, they fetched, the best of them, $120 each.[2] The Russians had for thirty years been selling otter-skins, obtained from the Aleutian Islands, to Chinese merchants at Kiakhta, and the English had for a like period been exporting to St. Petersburg, for Kiakhta delivery, skins of the otter and beaver from Hudson's Bay, — facts made known to the world in 1780 by William Coxe in a book entitled "Russian Discoveries."[3] Yet it remained for Cook's "Voyage," published in 1784, to create a world-interest in the Northwest fur-trade.

In August, 1785, Nootka was visited for furs by Captain James Hanna from Macao. In September of the same year, the Nootka region was sighted by two captains from England, both of whom had served with Cook, Nathaniel Portlock and George Dixon. Between June and September, 1786, the Northwest Coast, from Alaska down past Nootka to Monterey, was surveyed by the French navigator Jean François Galaup, Comte de la Pérouse; and in September, 1788, Nootka was made a rendezvous by two fur-trading vessels from Boston, the Lady Washington and the Columbia Rediviva.[4] Spain herself (in government circles at least) was roused to an interest in furs by the voyages of Cook; and in August, 1786, Vicente Basadre y Vega arrived at Monterey, as royal commissioner, to begin collecting skins of the otter and seal. He was met in Monterey by Pérouse, who records an anticipation by Spain of brilliant results from a trade in California furs with China by way of Manila. But the scheme, a government monopoly, lacked in enterprise, and in 1790 was abandoned.[5]

Just after the northern expedition of Arteaga and Cuadra, in 1780, Spain, satisfied that the Russians were making no dangerous approaches toward California, had ordered northern explorations to cease. But with the coming in 1786 of Pérouse, — co-religionist, accomplished scientist, and gallant gentleman, — fresh alarm was created. On December 18, Estevlán José Martínez, who had just returned to San Blas from a supply trip to Monterey, wrote to Viceroy Gálvez: —

On the 14th of September last, while at anchor in the port of Monterey, two *fragatas* were seen, distant about five leagues and making as though to enter the port. I observed that their flags were French, and concluded that the vessels must be those destined by His Most Christian Majesty for the work of discovery. . . . Said *fragatas* were the Brujula and Astrolabe, under command of the Conde de la Pérouse, etc. The Señor Conde assured me as a fixed fact that the Russian nation was in possession of the island of Oonalaska. . . . Not only were they in possession of the said island, but of portions of the coast that extends from 61° southwest; and their furthest establishment was in latitude 56°: 30'. The business of the Russians with the Indians, the Count assured me, was to exchange manufactured iron for otter-skins.[6]

Martínez in the Princesa, and López de Haro in the San Carlos, were sent in 1788 by Viceroy Manuel Antonio Flórez to make an investigation. They found the Russians on Kadiak and Unalaska Islands, the latter the largest of the Aleutian group, and heard of them on Cook's River.

Martínez wrote to Flórez on December 5, 1788: —

Eustrate Delarof [Russian factor at Kadiak] told me that as
a result of his having informed his sovereign of the commerce
which the English from Canton are carrying on at Nootka, he
was expecting four *fragatas* from Siberia to sail next year for the
purpose of making an establishment at Nootka. He assured me
that his sovereign had a better right to that coast than any other
power, on account of its having been discovered by the Russian
commanders Behring and Tscherkow, under orders from the
Russian Court, in the year 1741. It therefore seems to me advisable that an attempt should be made next year, 1789, with such
forces as you may have at hand, to occupy the said port and establish a garrison in it. . . . By accomplishing this we shall gain
possession of the coast from Nootka to the port of San Francisco.
I say this, at the same time offering myself to carry out the project; and to prove the feasibility of it, I will sacrifice my last
breath in the service of God and the King, if you approve.[7]

Here, bodily made manifest at last, were the Russians,
for whom since 1774 Spain had been probing with such
diligence the North; and, despite the decree of 1780, Flórez
felt warranted in heeding the request of Martínez and in
sending him, together with Haro, back to Nootka, in 1789,
to occupy the spot and to protect it with fortifications.
Martínez arrived in the sound on May 5, and discovered
there an American vessel, the Columbia, and an English
brig under Portuguese colors, the Iphigenia. The American craft was not molested, but between May 6 and July
14 the Iphigenia, her consort the Northwest America, and
the Argonaut (the latter under Captain James Colnett), —
all British vessels, — were seized by Martínez as poachers
on Spanish preserves. Spain afterwards made restitution,
but the matter was dwelt upon by Great Britain, and,
after much warlike demonstration, the two powers, on
October 28, 1790, ratified the Nootka Convention. By
this treaty Spain yielded claim of exclusive sovereignty
to the Northwest Coast, but obtained from her adversary an agreement "not to navigate or fish within ten

leagues of any part of this coast which Spain already occupied." [8]

But the treaty was not without ambiguity. It provided for a restoration of "buildings and tracts of land" to owners. The provision was a sequel to the fact (as claimed) that in 1788, — the year preceding that of the Spanish occupation of Nootka, — John Meares, instigator of the voyage of the Iphigenia, had built there a house and breastwork; acts which the British Government was not disinclined to regard as acts of occupation by the English.[9] On the part of Spain, it was not admitted that Nootka had been occupied in a jurisdictional sense by any power other than herself; and under Conde de Revilla Gigedo, appointed Viceroy in 1789, Nootka, abandoned for some unknown cause by Flórez, was reoccupied and refortified.[10]

Furthermore, through the gradual development of the fact that the Northwest Coast was skirted and masked by a narrow but complex archipelago, Spain saw fit between 1789 and 1793 to renew a search for Anian by way of the Straits of Juan de Fuca and Maldonado. In 1790, she sent out Salvador Fidalgo, Francisco Elisa, and Manuel Quimper; in 1789–91, Alejandro Malaspina; in 1792, Jacinto Caamaño; and in 1793, Dionisio Galiano and Cayetano Valdéz in the schooners Sutil and Mexicana. By the latter expedition — the last to the north of California undertaken by Spain — that government was able to confirm a growing conviction of the non-existence of an interoceanic passage below the Arctic regions, and to give to Anian its quietus.[11]

The situation, barring the Sutil and Mexicana expedition, was as described, when, in November, 1792, Captain George Vancouver arrived at Monterey. He came from Nootka, where he and Bodega y Cuadra, as commissioners for Great Britain and Spain respectively, had been trying to agree as to the meaning of the restoration clause of the Nootka Convention.[12] Vancouver had demanded a transfer of the port to Great Britain jurisdictionally. Cuadra, refusing, had nevertheless proposed, under instructions from Spain and the Viceroy, that Nootka be abandoned by both Spain and Great Britain, and that the northern boundary of California be fixed at the Strait of Fuca.[13] Nothing was effected, but ultimately (January 11, 1794) Great Britain and Spain entered into a convention, which was executed, that Nootka be transferred to the former, but that immediately the port be abandoned, and that thenceforth neither of the two powers claim therein any right of sovereignty or territorial dominion to the exclusion of the other.[14]

By the struggle for Nootka, — a struggle in which Spanish power to the northward in America met its term, not, as might have been expected, in the presence of Russia, but of England, — there was foreshadowed for Alta California its first political boundary.

The earlier incidents of the Nootka affair took place during the governorship of Pedro Fages and that of José Antonio Romeu. It was while Fages was governor (1786) that Monterey was visited by Comte de la Pérouse.

On the 18th of September [wrote Basadre y Vega], the Conde with all the scientists and people of both *fragatas* went to the mission of San Carlos, where they were received by the Reverend Father Fermín Francisco Lasuén, and three other religious, with choir-cape, cross, and candle-bearers, who ushered them into the church where *Te Deum* was sung. A repast followed, simple and frugal, as befitted the character of those who gave it. All these expressions of religion and affection were received by the French with demonstrations so extraordinary that I lack words for a sufficient account. The final acknowledgment proffered by the strangers was that they had gained the satisfaction of knowing and meeting men truly apostolical, followers of Peter and Paul in the life evangelical and in the work of reducing the Gentiles.[15]

But the attitude of Pérouse toward the California Mission as part of a system was that of José de Gálvez, of Neve, and of Fages.

I confess [he says], that, more a friend of human rights than a theologian, I could have wished in the case of the Indian that to the principles of Christianity there had been joined a legislation that by degrees should make citizens of men the condition of whom differs scarcely at all from that of the negroes of our own colonies. . . . I know that upon the Indian reasoning has no effect, that it is necessary to impress the senses, and that corporal punishments, with rewards of double rations, has up to the present been the only means adopted by his legislators. But would it be impossible for an ardent zeal and an extreme patience to make known to a small number of families the advantages of a society based upon human rights; to establish among them the right of property so attractive to all men; and, by this new order of things, to induce each one to cultivate his field with emulation, or else to devote himself to work of some other kind?[16]

Later, Monterey was visited by the Malaspina expedition. The visit took place during the term of Romeu (1791) but before Fages's departure; and to Lasuén, — of whom Pérouse had spoken as one whose *douceur*, whose *charité*, whose *amour pour les Indians*, are inexpressible, — Malaspina made a gift of cloth, of wine, of chocolate, and of wax.

As noticed in chapter VIII, José Joaquín de Arrillaga became acting governor of California on April 9, 1792. Under him therefore it was, though prior to his arrival from the south, that Monterey (as also San Francisco) was visited by Vancouver. The English captain was regaled with feast and frolic by Sal, the senior comandante, and at San Francisco was permitted with seven of his officers to penetrate inland to Santa Clara, and at Monterey to San

Carlos. But Spain, though disposed to be courteous because of the Nootka affair, desired to keep from the world, and especially from the English, knowledge of the weakness of the California defenses. Indeed, at the very moment of Vancouver's visit, Viceroy Revilla Gigedo (November 24) was cautioning Arrillaga to be on the watch for English vessels, so as to prevent the true state of the province from becoming known. Sal was accordingly rebuked for his hospitality, and right ruefully did he confess: "I had at San Francisco but one cannon, and it was out of commission." [17]

To be armed against the future, the Viceroy in 1793 resolved to fortify the port of San Francisco, to erect works at Monterey and San Diego, and to occupy Bodega Bay.[18] At Monterey there were "eight guns and three swivels, all in good condition"; at Santa Bárbara, "two guns and one swivel"; at San Diego, "three guns." But at Santa Bárbara and San Diego the guns were "dismounted and without artillerists." As for troops, Arrillaga could n't vouch for it, but he thought there might be thirty-five in each presidio. From these must be deducted the *habilitados* (paymasters), the surgeon, invalids, blacksmiths, masons, etc. He recommended a force of 264 men, to be allotted, 75 at San Diego and Monterey; 63 at Santa Bárbara; and 51 at San Francisco.[19]

The occupation of Bodega was designed to forestall England in any attempt to fix the northern boundary of California as far south as the mouth of the Bay of San Francisco. Herein Revilla Gigedo was governed by the motive which the year before had led him to favor Fuca Strait as a northern limit. But Fuca Strait was not Anian, and now (April 12) the Viceroy, narrowing his pretensions, urged that Spain cease straining toward the Pole and be content with a boundary at the Columbia River or Bodega Bay, either of which, assuming Anian to exist, might be its outlet. The Columbia was far to reach, so effort was concentrated upon Bodega. Lieutenant Juan Matute reached the bay with the Sutil in July; and on August 5 Lieutenant Felipe Goycoechea of Santa Bárbara was dispatched with a sergeant and ten men to open a road thither from San Francisco.

During the sixty-four days consumed in my voyage [wrote Matute to Francisco de Elisa, comandante at San Blas], I encountered no ship or foreign settlement. It is my conclusion that this was due to there being at Bodega no port deep enough for boats larger than the Sutil, and to there being, near the anchorage, neither timber nor firewood. For this cause, indeed, it was impossible for me to build there a house or to subsist myself. Signs of prior occupation of the bay there were none, save some sawed trees left by the Englishman Colner [Colnett], who was driven there in a tempest, and whose chart of the port (1790) has served all vessels commissioned to that destination up to the present. . . . I undertook an expedition, with the small boat of the schooner, to the southeast, to see whether there might not be disclosed the mouth of some river or estuary in the same roadstead exterior to Bodega. After three days of rather perilous search I came upon a *puerto nuevo* very good for boats of a draught of not to exceed fifteen feet, but, with the northwest winds, subject to be barred by sand.

On July 16, the *fragata* Aranzazu reached Bodega from San Blas, with soldiers, artisans, supplies, and tools. But as it was impossible to bring the vessel to a point near the *puerto nuevo*, she, together with her men and stores, was sent to San Francisco on the 24th. On August 8, Goycoechea arrived. He was shown the difficulties of the situation, and, a chart of the locality having been made, Matute on the 11th withdrew to San Francisco, where, falling ill, he contented himself, in view of the cost of other arrangements, with recommending that a *lancha* be constructed wherewith to reach the *puerto nuevo*, or Bodega, and that the points named be occupied by one or two missions. Bodega, suffice it to say, never again was sought to be made an ultimate outpost for California. In 1794, on June 9, the Viceroy informed Arrillaga that its occupation had been indefinitely postponed.[20] As for San Francisco, — the exposure of the innocuous condition of which had been the undoing of Sal, — the Governor on December 8 dedicated at Fort Point the Castillo of San Joaquín.

But the year 1794 was that of the advent of Borica. His appointment was of early date, and, setting out overland from Loreto on July 24, he arrived at Monterey on November 9. A lover of "Don Quixote," we find him, as we should expect, urbane and cultured, a man fond of society, of badinage, and of good Rhenish, port, and madeira. Should it be said of him that more than any of his predecessors he suggests Bucarely, — himself a master of urbanity and a connoisseur of vintages, — no injustice will be done to either. His family (by whom he was accompanied) consisted of his wife, Doña María Magdalena de Urquides, and a daughter of sixteen, Josefita, who was accounted beautiful. He brought with him a valet, a maid, a cook, and a negro page. From Loreto he had written on May 15: —

Monday at 3 P. M. we arrived in the Peninsula. María Magdalena and my daughter were quite seasick. They disgorged, among other things, ire. Narciso [his valet] and Juan José [the cook] did not lift their heads till they went ashore. The little negro was quite seasick, but he was the only one able to prepare for the rest a little chocolate, garlic soup, and some stew. Don Andrés and myself kept firm. The trip to Monterey will be by land, as the Señoritas are horror-stricken at the mere thought of the sea.[21]

But now that Monterey had been reached, whom should Borica meet but Vancouver? In 1793 the English captain had visited San Francisco and Monterey a second time, but Arrillaga himself had been at the capital, and the privileges conceded had been few. "With the Señores Vancouver, Peter Puget, and others," writes the new Governor on November 13, "I am waging a contest. None of them can beat me over a dozen of wine. . . . This is a great country, neither hot nor cold. One finds good bread, the finest of meats, dainty fish, and (best of all) *bon* [*sic*] *humeur*." In other letters, Borica describes California as a land where the general fecundity extends even to the people. "We are all beginning to look like Englishmen. . . . To live long and without care, one must come to Monterey." Vancouver sailed for England on December 2. "We did not give him time," wrote the Governor, "to observe again certain things of which it were well that he remain ignorant."[22]

That, prior to Borica, Alta California should practically have been without defenses is upon the whole little surprising. Down to 1769 there had in the local sense been no California north of the peninsula. The predatory visits of Drake and Cavendish, of Swan, Dampier, and Woods Rogers (1578–1709), and of Shelvocke and Anson (1721–1740), were to Alta California — the California of 1794 — as though they had never occurred. In 1780 and 1781 excitement had risen at Monterey upon a warning to beware of English war-ships; and like excitement had risen at San Francisco in 1789, upon the receipt of orders to seize the American ship Columbia, "belonging to General Washington."[23] In other respects quiet had ruled until 1793, when war (offspring of the French Revolution) had been declared by Spain against France.

Borica assumed office with hostilities as something seriously to be reckoned with; nor throughout his incumbency did foreign relations improve.[24] In 1796 war was declared by Spain against England. In 1799 Spain became embroiled with Russia, and Alta California was admonished to be prepared for invasion by way of Kamtchatka; while, between 1797 and 1800, a rumor, pronounced by Borica purely Platonic [speculative], became rife that all New Spain was about to be invaded from the United States.[25]

The Conde de Branciforte, successor to Revilla Gigedo in 1794, referred the question of fortifications for Alta California to Miguel Costansó. In the opinion of the veteran engineer, to fortify would be to entail an expense altogether insupportable. The English were a people skilled, intrepid, audacious; their acumen in things relative to navigation was consummate; they were successful, and how? By colonies and commerce. Therefore instead of forts, let Spain place at San Diego and Monterey groups of settlers, and establish with Alta California relations that were commercial. Thus only could the province be retained.[26]

But in 1795 war with France made armament indispensable, and by a war board, of which Costansó was a member, batteries and cruisers were authorized. During 1796 and 1797 there arrived at Monterey and San Francisco a company of Catalan volunteers, seventy-five strong, under Lieutenant-Colonel Pedro Alberni, an artillery detachment of eighteen under Sergeant José Roca, and (with the artillerists) the engineer Alberto de Córdoba. The latter inspected the fortifications and found them all worthless, not excepting the new Castillo of San Joaquín. He nevertheless established at San Francisco (Black Point) the supplementary battery of Yerba Buena. Having constructed a battery at San Diego and made a map of the country, Córdoba in 1798 was recalled.[27]

The views of Costansó as to the need in Alta California of Spanish colonists, while of necessity deferred, were not disregarded. Were not his the views of Gálvez, of Anza, of Neve? It was proposed to erect a settlement, which, though a municipality, should at the same time be a fortress, — in other words, a *villa*, a town palatine. In 1780–81 there had, in the case of the Indians, been tried upon the Colorado the pueblo mission. In 1789 there had, in the same case, been tried in Sonora, at Pitic, the *villa*. Now, therefore, — not in the case of the Indians, who had given no trouble, but in that of whites upon the coast, who had, — it was designed to try the *villa* in Alta California. Organized as a presidio under a comandante subject to the Audiencia of the district, the *villa* was designed to become as rapidly as possible a pueblo; armed, it is true, but ruled by *alcaldes* and *regidores*.[28] Preparations for the California *villa*, called Branciforte, were made by Borica and Córdoba with enthusiasm.

But could the province endure another pueblo? Already there were San José and Los Ángeles; and their condition, — what was it? At neither did the settlers do aught but gamble, strum the guitar, and trifle with the Indian women. Said Father Isidro Alonso Salazar to Viceroy Branciforte in May, 1796: —

The two towns founded twenty years ago have made no advancement. The people are a set of idlers. For them the Indian is errand-boy, *vaquero*, and digger of ditches, — in short, general factotum. Confident that the Gentiles are working, the settlers pass the day singing. The young men wander on horseback through the *rancherías* soliciting the women to immorality.[29]

And the same month José Señán declared: —

In Alta California the pueblos hardly deserve the name, so formless and embryonic is their state. The cause is scant relish for work on the part of the settlers. One is more likely to find in their hands a deck of cards than the spade or the plow. For them the Gentile sows, ploughs, reaps and gathers the harvest. Debased, moreover, by the bad example of his white associates, the Gentile continues in the darkness of heathenism, when from distant *rancherías* many are won to the fold of Holy Church.[30]

That Branciforte might ever come to the condition of San José and Los Ángeles, — Branciforte, the pride of the Viceroy, — was a thought not to be entertained. "Don Alberto Córdoba" (so, on November 18, 1795, it was ordered) "was to proceed to the port of San Francisco and locate the *villa* so as to give it connection with the battery, and make it defensive of the coast, — a sally-port against disembarkations; the engineer availing himself of the rules of fortification wherein he [was] well versed."[31] The environs of San Francisco were decided to be unfit for the new establishment, but between San Francisco and Monterey on the Río San Lorenzo, at a spot accessible from the sea, — a spot where the mission of Santa Cruz had been founded on September 25, 1791, — conditions were excellent.[32] "This locality," Palou had written in 1769, "is not only sufficient for a village but for a city. Not a single necessary thing is lacking. Fine lands, water, pastures, firewood, timber, — all are close at hand in abundance. The bay of Monterey is at a short distance, and the town could be located . . . not more than one fourth of a league away."

So by the river, opposite the mission, on the site of the present town of Santa Cruz, the *villa* Branciforte, with plazas, streets, churches, and government buildings, — all as at Pitic, — was to be founded. Its garrison was to be the Catalan company under Alberni, and Alberni himself might be made lieutenant-governor. Its citizens, "Christian in conduct," were to be recruited chiefly in Mexico. Among its officers and officials (who were to dwell in flat-roofed houses), Indians who were captains of *rancherías* were to be invited to dwell in like houses, — a Pitic custom. Such was the dream.[33]

The first colonists (nine families — seventeen persons — from Guadalajara) arrived at Monterey in 1797 on May 12. On May 26, Corporal Gabriel Moraga, son of the

founder of San Francisco, was ordered by Borica to build
for their accommodation wooden structures each capable
of holding fifteen or twenty families, and the colonists were
sent to their destination. Instructions, wherein doubt
as to the Christianity of the *villa* founders may be dis-
cerned, were issued on July 17. There was to be neither
gambling, drunkenness, nor concubinage. On days of
obligation, all were to attend Mass under penalty of three
hours in the stocks. Returning from work, the men were
to recite the rosary of the Blessed Virgin in the guard-
room. Lent was to be rightly observed, and of such right
observance a certificate was required. With the Indian
rancherías there was to be no communication by day or
night. On Sundays a general inspection of trappings,
arms, and implements was to be held, and stolen articles
were then to be returned to their owners.[34]

A few years, and the Christianity of the Branciforteans was in doubt no longer. In 1798–99 the colonists
were rebuked for laziness; some were threatened with irons
for desertion, and all were forbidden trips to San José —
the Monte Carlo of the province. By 1800 they had so far
degenerated as to be arraigned before the Viceroy as not
alone a scandal for immorality, but as would-be assassins
in the bargain, for one had attempted the life of the
lieutenant at Monterey, and another that of Borica himself.[35] But long ere 1800 the *villa* as such had disappeared.
On staking it out in the summer of 1797, Córdoba had
estimated its cost at 23,405 *pesos*, an estimate so disheartening that straightway (October 24) the Governor
had issued an order for the suspension of all work.[36]

Gone was the *villa*, but not the Branciforteans. To provide such of them as were unmarried with wives, Borica in
1797 asked the Viceroy for women "young and healthy,"
each provided with "a woolen skirt, a coarse *rebozo*, a

bodice, two sets of muslin underwear, a pair of coarse stockings, and a pair of heavy shoes." But for bachelor maids the allurements of California in the eighteenth century were not great, and none responded to the appeal.[37] In 1800, when San José boasted of a population of perhaps 170, and Los Ángeles of perhaps 315, Branciforte (any comparison of which with the two pueblos would in 1795 have been regarded by Borica as presumption) could claim in all — guard, retired soldiers, and original colonists — 66 souls.

II

Of Mission progress under Borica, — a progress so considerable as to mark in Alta California the culmination (dynamically) of the institution of the Mission, — the beginnings are to be sought under Romeu. In 1791, on September 25, there was founded, as already noted, the mission of Santa Cruz. But the same year yet another mission was founded, — Nuestra Señora de la Soledad, — Our Lady of Solitude. La Soledad, though circumscribed by the Coast Range, was designed as the first of the second or interior chain of establishments planned by Neve in his *Reglamento*. It covered the interval between San Carlos and San Antonio; and the early padres, Mariano Rubí and Bartolomé Gili, were priests of the Order of Friar Tuck.

In this asylum of San Fernando, where, upon reaching New Spain, these padres withdrew themselves [records Guardian Tomás de Pangua on September 13, 1793], they passed the day in sleep and idleness and the night in outrages, disturbing the repose of those that having spent the day in work must needs sleep at night. They behaved, indeed, like sons of darkness, forcing bolts to rob the supply-room, breaking the jars where the chocolate of the community was kept, stealing the chocolate-pots to beat them for drums; and, appropriating the balls which were kept by the community for the recreation of the religious, bowled them through the dormitories at unseasonable hours of night, with result to the religious of terror and confusion.[38]

Besides La Soledad, the establishments of the second mission chain were San José, covering the interval between San Carlos and San Francisco; San Juan Bautista, covering that between San José and San Carlos; San Miguel Arcángel, that between San Antonio and San Luis Obispo; and San Fernando Rey de España, that between San Buenaventura and San Gabriel. But San José, San Juan Bautista, San Miguel, and San Fernando (Borica foundations of the year 1797) were as little free of the Coast Range as was La Soledad.[39] A final Borica establishment — a mission for closing the gap between San Juan Capistrano and San Diego — was San Luis Rey de Francia, founded in 1798.

The total number of Alta California missions was now eighteen, and the disposal of them was varied. Above the sea and dominating it stood San Diego and Santa Bárbara; beside the sea and greeting it, San Juan Capistrano, San Buenaventura, and Santa Cruz; aloof from the sea yet with observant eye upon it, San Luis Rey, La Purísima Concepción, San José, San Carlos, and San Francisco. As for San Gabriel, San Fernando, San Luis Obispo, San Antonio, San Juan Bautista, Santa Clara, — they were inland, but pleasantly accessible amid spaces purple-girt and parked with liveoaks. Only two establishments were gloomy and remote. These — situated in the throat of a valley long, level, windy, and arid; often hot, ever alone — were La Soledad and San Miguel. Special interest attaches to one mission — La Purísima. Placed at the mouth of an *arroyo* leading to the clustered heights of San Rafael, it served to mark that line of cleavage which, as noted in chapter I, Nature in Alta California had traced between the northern and southern portions.

In 1798 the problems of Mission management in Alta California were many. Neophyte population was mounting past the thirteen-thousand mark; [40] and of artisans to give instruction in blacksmithing, carpentering, bricklaying, mill-making, tanning, shoemaking, weaving, and saddlery, the need was urgent. So far as this need had existed in 1787, Fages had sought to supply it by the introduction of convict artisans; and the idea being approved by Borica, some twenty-two such were obtained. But respectable craftsmen were preferred, and, as early as 1795, twenty had been brought from Mexico. Thenceforth, at the principal missions, the wool of the province was woven into coarse cloth, and the hides were converted into rude shoes and saddles. [41] Soap and pottery were made, and water-power and horse-power mills erected. Moreover, in 1795 at San José the cultivation of flax and hemp was undertaken.

Then there were the old problems. Padres still clamored for escorts, and the rigid rule of Neve, forbidding guards at a mission to sleep outside the mission walls, was in a degree modified. [42] As for the election of Indian *alcaldes* and *regidores* under the Laws of the Indies, — a practice which the padres had avoided since 1792, — it was ordered by Borica in 1796 to be resumed, but with the proviso that these functionaries were to be under missionary supervision, except in causes of blood, wherein they were to be under the supervision of the mission corporal. [43] Apropos of one instead of two padres at a mission, it was conclusively demonstrated in 1797 by Pedro Callejas, Guardian of San Fernando, that the two-padre plan was sanctioned alike by precedent and by royal order. "To the profound speculative wisdom of the Señor Don Felipe de Neve," exclaimed Callejas, "this apostolical college opposes the profound practical knowledge of all the missionaries who in all times have protested against solitude."[44]

But of all problems under Borica, that of most importance was the problem of disciplining the neophytes.

As early as 1771, Guardian Verger (vexed at Gálvez) had declared, with regard to the missions of the peninsula, that "they never had been, were not, and never would be complete pueblos";[45] and in 1796 Borica had averred, with regard to those of Monterey, that "at the rate they were then moving, not in ten centuries would they be out of tutelage."[46] It was twenty-five years since the first establishments had been planted in Alta California, and according to what had been achieved in the Sierra Gorda in twenty years, to say naught of what had earlier come to pass under Cortés in ten, civilization on the part of the California native was something the Spanish Government had reason to expect. That the expectation was not being met was proof that it was likely never to be met; but so to admit would be to confess the Mission in Alta California a failure.[47] What the padres did, therefore, was to strive to stimulate the native in religious observances, and in the performance of tasks of house and field, by the hobble, the stocks, shackles, and the lash.[48]

On the right to flog, provided the punishment was moderate, State Sacerdotal and State Secular were agreed. On that memorable day in 1524 when Cortés had abased himself in the dust before Martín de Valencia, the great *conquistador* had also submitted his back to the lash. In 1772 and 1780 Verger and Serra had mentioned the conduct of Cortés, and an act of the Lima Council whereby it had been determined that, "for the Indian, correction by words was not sufficient."[49] For Alta California the question had been settled by the *junta* of 1773, which had decided that it belonged to the padres to "educate and correct" the natives, just as to a natural parent it belonged to educate and correct his sons, — a decision the obligation of which had been recognized even by Neve. Nor did Borica dispute it. Twenty-five lashes he pronounced to be a moderate punishment.[50] But in 1795 neophytes in large number (280) deserted the mission of San Francisco, and the question presented itself: Was the general treatment of the Indians there that of a parent or of an exacting task-master ?

At San Francisco, in 1796, Father Antonio Dantí was succeeded by Father José María Fernández; and the latter, convinced that the desertions of 1795 had been due to harshness by Dantí, so informed Borica. Upon investigation the charge of Fernández was substantiated, and the Governor admonished Lasuén to effect a reform. Almost at once, however, the chivalric spirit of Borica asserted itself, for, on receipt of word from the Father-President that reform would be attempted, he wrote: "If I use strong language, it is but to inspire those who have the power to do good. I am a soldier, and thou a holy father. It is natural that the one, full of fire, should desire the other to imitate him in zeal that may be precipitate."[51] The charge by Fernández proved to be but the prelude to charges more vigorous and sustained.

When in 1795, Estaván José Martínez, hero (or culprit) of the Nootka affair, was returning from Spain to Mexico, there came with him to Vera Cruz a friar, — Antonio de la Concepción. In 1797, Concepción was sent to Alta California, where in company with Buenaventura Sitjar, a missionary of long service at San Antonio de Padua, he was assigned by Lasuén to the new establishment of San Miguel Arcángel. He reached his post in July, but hardly was he settled ere he began to manifest the mental disorder called megalomania. On arriving at the College of

San Fernando, he had laid claim to the position of *maestro de ceremonias*, an office unknown to apostolical colleges; and on arriving at San Miguel he assumed the air and port of a dictator. Having ostentatiously made his hard Franciscan couch comfortable with blankets, his first act was to compose himself for a prolonged siesta. The same day he boisterously indulged in criticism of Mission management, and the day following, during a walk with Sitjar, wrought himself to such frenzy over the "tyranny" of certain padres that with shaking body, hands smiting the breast, face discolored, and froth covering the lips, he declared: "Little lacked it last night that I took a course with the Father-President that would have resounded in the land."

His foremost grievance was that padres did not compel neophytes to speak Castilian; and, as Sitjar was of those who connived at the use of the native idiom, he took occasion in his first sermon to proclaim to the Miguelinos that they must discard it, and that the Spaniards "as lords and judges" had come to see that discard it they did. For twenty-seven days Concepción girded at the mission servants, issued orders to the guard, anon fell silent, and anon broke into peals of witless mirth, when, a general horror of him seizing upon neophytes and guard alike, it became necessary to appeal to Lasuén.

The latter, upon whom Sitjar waited at Santa Bárbara, ordered Concepción taken to Monterey to be dispatched (with Borica's consent) to Mexico, as one demented. The padre's chest, containing various *cédulas* on the use of Castilian, and a brace of pistols, was sent in advance, and on September 13 the Governor wrote to the Viceroy that having found the padre a "braggart" and of "imperfect judgment, qualities prejudicial to his calling," and having *con arte* secured his pistols, he had sanctioned Lasuén's order.

Back at his college, Concepción, on July 12, 1798, sent a memorial to the Viceroy. The document embraced five charges; to wit: that the Indians of Alta California, contrary to royal order, were taught the *Doctrina* in their own tongue; that they were baptized without previous instruction; that they were permitted to return to the mountains, and sometimes, after several years, were baptized a second time; that the missionaries, though possessing more or less wealth, and spending hundreds for liquor, were unwilling to give wine for the Mass; that in business they disregarded the tariff of prices fixed by the *Reglamento;* and finally, that they treated neophytes in ways "the most cruel that history records," visiting the slightest delinquencies with shackles, with the stocks, and with stripes. It was because of exposure of practices such as these, Concepción explained, that he had been accused of dementia, and he asked that he might finish his ten years of required missionary service in the province of Michoacán, model "reduction" under the conquest. The plea for a transfer was not granted, but early in 1799 Concepción was sent to Querétaro. As for his charges, they were submitted by the Viceroy to Borica for serious investigation on August 31, 1798.

Borica's report, accompanied by special reports from Argüello, Sal, and Goycoechea,[52] — comandantes at San Francisco, Monterey, and Santa Bárbara, — was ready by December 31. It stated that while Concepción's charges as to the neglect of Castilian, as to baptism without instruction, and as to permission to wander in the mountains, were not to be seriously taken, the charge of illtreatment was in the main well-founded. At the same time, it must not be forgotten that reform could not be effected through the Governor, as his authority over Mission affairs was little or nothing. Even in respect to temporalties he might not intervene. At a year's end he knew nothing as to the condition of the Mission exchequer. It probably was richer than was supposed.

The King — so Borica thought — should issue an *instrucción breve*, prescribing in the case of Mission establishments rules for the construction of lodgings and infirmaries; for the assignment of tasks and the fixing of hours of performance; for the selection of work to be undertaken; for the choosing of pastimes; and for fixing the punishments which the padres might inflict for delinquencies outside the royal jurisdiction. Furthermore, presidents of missions should be made subject to local prelates, as were priors or guardians in their convents.

The cause of Concepción against the Order of St. Francis in Alta California had made thus far no small progress. Indeed, so much progress thus far had it made that the Viceroy, suspecting the matter might be becoming one-sided (Concepción, moreover, having returned from Querétaro, where, in the archiepiscopal palace, he had been denied a claim to the high privileges of preacher and confessor), appealed on September 12, 1799, to the Guardian of San Fernando — Miguel Lull. The honor, *fama y estimación pública* of an entire college, Lull replied, were at stake. Concepción's *denuncia* was full of "grave deceptions," "manifest falsehoods," and of "accusations blackening, opprobrious, offensive, and defamatory." Nor did the chivalric Borica himself escape defiance. He was taunted by the Guardian with "bloodying his pen" and "voiding his venom" against the Alta California missionaries in respect to their entire "conduct, management, and procedure."

It was resented in particular by Lull that Borica should have intimated that the exchequer of San Fernando was in some wise rich. The books of the college, certified by the *aviador* and *síndico*, showed, he said, that as late as July 7,

1799, there stood to the credit of the Alta California establishments a total of only 12,279 *pesos*, as against liabilities of over 14,000; the annual cost of maintenance being about 26,000 to 27,000. "I pray and entreat," exclaimed the Guardian with indignation,

that the Señor Gobernador abstain (as commanded by Law 73 of Book I of Title 14 of the *Recopilación*) from prosecution of the missionaries on idle grounds, as otherwise padres cannot be kept in the Alta California field. And I supplicate that your Excellency be pleased either to intrust the reductions there to other hands, or else that before the King our sovereign, the public his vassals, and all the world, the honor, credit, and good name of the individuals of this college, and the fame and reputation of our sacred habit, be wholly cleared and vindicated, — a right which we cannot forego, and one that before all tribunals we shall ever maintain.

Henceforth the cause of Concepción waned. On June 19, 1801, Lasuén (who next was consulted by the Viceroy) defended the missionaries in a plea eloquent and extended. As for flogging, said the Father-President, the Indians were flogged, — and wherefore not? They were "a people without education, without government, without religion, and without shame. . . . Accustomed to avenge injuries with death, they were addicted also to lasciviousness and theft. Men of this quality we are commanded "to correct and punish." Yet the watchword was ever "patience." Only twenty-five lashes were permitted, and these "with an instrument that caused no blood or noticeable contusion"; while as for the women, they were beaten apart from the men, and by one of their own sex. The desertions from San Francisco complained of by Fernández had been from fear of contagion, not from fear of the lash. All missionaries, it was true, were not alike. Some had more virtue than others, more prudence, more gentleness, more zeal, more knowledge; but the Father-President had known none that "could be called hard, much less cruel." Let it not be forgotten by the government that "with the aid of but six soldiers the padres had reared amid the *gentilidad* a Christian pueblo [Loreto]. They had sustained, nurtured, and brought it to a condition so flourishing that, as a fruit of their labors, the happy stability and useful blessings of human society, of the Christian religion, and of *el vasallaje Español* were assured."

The charges of Concepción were reviewed in 1804 by Borica's successor Arrillaga. Not in an experience of seven years, averred the new Governor, had a single complaint of cruelty come to him. Padres he thought likely to err toward the Indians in indulgence rather than in rigor, even though occasionally excessive rigor might be practiced. Father Concepción ought to remember that what he considered cruelty and tyranny had been the way in the peninsula since its reduction, — more than a hundred years, — and that of all the California governors, presidents, and missionaries in that time, he only had been censorious.

Upon Arrillaga's verdict the *odiosa causa* was brought to an end. In 1805, on April 15, the fiscal certified that the representations of Concepción were false, and that naught remained but to restore the missionaries to their good name and credit, a restoration which was declared effected. As for Concepción himself, he in 1801 had been pronounced by the physician of San Fernando a hypochondriac who ought to be sent to Spain; and in 1804, with the consent of the Viceroy and the Council of the Indies, he was placed on shipboard. When last seen he was being conducted to his province from Madrid, after a season at Aranjuez, where in the royal audience chambers he had sought to attract notice by ringing a hand-bell and uttering pious ejaculations. "Such," wrote the Guardian to the Viceroy in 1805, "is he who denounced us." [53]

It was on January 16, 1800, that Borica, after six years
of service as governor of the Californias, was permitted by
Viceroy Azanza to retire. Of his wife, Doña María Magdalena de Urquides, and of his daughter Josefita, nothing,
after their arrival at Monterey, has been recorded. What
Borica himself accomplished for the defense of his province,
and what for the advancement therein of the Mission, has
in the main been told. As comandante, he sought to revive the old projects of direct communication with New
Mexico and Sonora;[54] and as *jefe político* he wrought hard
for secular education, establishing primary schools at the
presidios and pueblos, and making attendance compulsory.[55] Of the revenues secular and ecclesiastical, — derived from a poll-tax, a tax on tobacco, postal charges,
sales of indulgences, and tithes, — Borica was a faithful
guardian. An important change which he advocated was
the separation of the Californias into distinct provinces.[56]
Through the Nootka affair, a political boundary for Alta
California had been foreshadowed on the north. Separation
from the peninsula would determine a like boundary on the
south. Under Borica, Alta California, founded by priests
for the glory of God, and organized by Neve for the glory
of the King, became so far unified in its elements as to
settle measurably into equilibrium.

CHAPTER X

THE PROBLEM OF SUBSISTENCE

ON June 26, 1803, there died Fermín Francisco Lasuén. He was buried in the mission church of San Carlos, near Crespi and Serra. In March, 1769, Lasuén had pronounced the blessing upon Rivera's men as they broke camp for the journey to Monterey. By 1786 he had attained the dignity of president of the Alta California establishments, and of *vicario* with power to confer all the sacraments, including that of confirmation. His successor was Estevàn Tapis, who held office until 1813. From 1804 to 1814 the governor of Alta California was José Joaquín de Arrillaga. The period of Tapis and Arrillaga, as between State Sacerdotal and State Secular, was one of substantial equilibrium; but outwardly it partook of the fear of England and Russia incident to Borica's rule.

In west and northwest America, at this time, the problem was one of subsistence. From San Diego to Monterey there was for the Spaniard need of manufactured goods, especially clothing; and at Kadiak, Behring's Bay, and Sitka there was for the Russian need of food-stuffs. A determined effort on the part of Spaniard and Russian alike to supply his respective needs, gave to the period its character. But, first, a word with respect to the problem of subsistence in Alta California from the beginning.

For four years the first missions were almost wholly dependent for supplies (grain included) upon Mexico. The transports, of which annually there were two, brought maize, wheat, beans, lentils, hams, sugar, chocolate, olive oil, wine, and brandy. In 1772, however, the San Antonio and San Carlos were unable to reach San Diego until late, and failed of Monterey altogether, and both points were threatened with famine. At Monterey, indeed, Fages in desperation formed a party for a bear hunt in the Cañada de los Osos.[1] And about the same time, at San Diego, Crespi wrote to Palou: —

Though his Majesty has put his hand to so much new Christianity as is here, what are we to do if there is not wherewith we can maintain ourselves? If the escort for a long time is maintaining itself with the sole ration of half a pint of corn, and of only twenty ounces of flour, daily; and the Fathers the same with a little milk — how are they able to endure? . . . God grant that Father Dumetz arrive promptly with the succor for these missions, and that the Barque bring it to us. For otherwise we are lost.[2]

It was Monterey that in the prevailing scarcity suffered longest, for, as Palou wrote to Guardian Verger in November, 1773, the *pilotos*, after making San Diego against fierce head-winds, were loath to protract the voyage, against still fiercer head-winds, to the north.[3] As late as April, 1774, when Anza on his reconnoissance reached Monterey, padres and soldiers were weak from hunger, a condition relieved only by the coming of the Santiago in May. After 1774 famine no longer threatened, but the founding of San Francisco was the more readily conceded by Bucarely to Serra, in view of the practicability (assumed to have been demonstrated by Anza) of provisioning the post overland from Sonora.

Trade as a means of succor was an idea scarcely entertained.[4] To private ships, trade was forbidden; and to private persons it was permitted only under heavy restrictions through the medium of the San Blas transports. Respecting the Manila galleon, which, in the days when California consisted of the peninsula, had been wont to touch for fresh provisions at Cape San Lucas, Viceroy

Bucarely in 1774 reminded the King that "continually
from the date of the conquest of the Philippine Islands,
there had been sought on the north coast of California
a port that might serve as a refuge to the galleons that
came to this New Spain." And on May 16, 1776, the King
ordered that henceforth these vessels ascend to the latitude of Gali's course, for the purpose of making port
at either San Francisco or Monterey.[5] But while in 1782
the order was enforced by a penalty of 4000 *pesos*, trade
with the galleon was as much interdicted as it had been
when the port-of-call was Cape San Lucas.[6]

In 1786 trade by the transports was freed from restrictions for five years, and in 1794 this concession was renewed for a decade; but it is significant that in 1791 Fages
condemned the freedom as conducive to luxury,[7] and that
in 1797 pleas for commerce by Borica and Manuel Cárcaba,
— the latter paymaster-general at San Blas, — met with
no response.[8]

José Joaquín de Arrillaga (born in 1750 at Aya, Spain, in
the province of Guipúzcoa) became governor *proprietario*
of the Californias on November 16, 1804. The problem of
subsistence had already asserted itself in a revival of two
projects which had given solicitude to Borica, — a division
of the Californias, and a route overland from Santa Fé.
The division project was the result of a general desire for
simplified administration. Delay incident to the approval
at Monterey of *memorias* exclusively for Loreto, could no
longer be endured, and, as elsewhere pointed out, division
was effected in 1804 on August 29.[9] As for the project of a
Santa Fé route, there was not the unanimity of approval
of earlier years. In 1796 Borica had urged the dispatch
of a party of Indian explorers to Santa Fé from Santa
Bárbara. He had learned from Fernando de la Concha,

retiring governor of New Mexico, that there were in New Mexico some fifteen hundred *gente de razón* useless from lack of employment. Why might they not be transferred to the coast? But Lasuén feared evil from contact between the neophytes and the Indians of the Tulares, and Pedro de Nava, comandante-general of the Provincias Internas, deprecated any attempt to withdraw population from a land where, as he maintained, abandoned settlements were about to be reëstablished.[10]

Divided Californias and a Santa Fé route were means for solving the subsistence problem which may be classed as direct. Further direct means were certain proposed community colonies and certain actual royal farms or *Ranchos del Rey*, the chief of which was located at the present Salinas City near Monterey, with a flourishing branch at San Francisco.[11]

The first colony to be mentioned is one that in 1788 was proposed for the island of "Owyhee" (Hawaii). When seeking Russian settlements near Nootka Sound, Martínez met in Cook's River a Scotch navigator, William Douglas, who had had in his ship an Hawaiian, — King Tayana, — whom he had afterwards restored to his country. The Indian had spoken much of the fruitfulness of Hawaii in cassava, sugar-cane, and watermelons, and had said that foreign vessels on their way to Nootka always supplied themselves with these foods. "I conclude from this," Martínez wrote to Viceroy Revilla Gigedo, "that it would be useful to form in Hawaii an establishment of our nation, in order that the Indians there may be 'reduced,' and that foreigners may be deprived of a port of refuge, where their commerce is nourished, and their passage to our 'coasts of Californias' facilitated." For meeting the cost of an Hawaiian establishment, Martínez suggested the formation of a commercial company in Mexico, with exclusive right for fifty years to deal in otter-skins, and to export tropical woods to Canton. But the Viceroy, though impressed with the usefulness of Hawaii as a port-of-call for the Philippine galleon, had not deemed its exploitation practicable.[12] Then, in 1797, Padres Mugártegui and Peña (retired) had proposed founding a Carmelite convent of twelve priests at San Francisco "for the cultivation of the soil" and the rendering of "great service to God, the King, and the Public," — a convent that "by its domes and towers should give a favorable impression to foreign navigators."[13]

But the most pretentious colony of a community kind projected for Alta California was one for which Luis Pérez de Tagle of Manila solicited permission in 1801. The plan, Tagle said, of compelling the Manila galleon to stop at Monterey, in order to lure the Indian to the coast, had notoriously failed. He (Tagle) would therefore beg, if haply the King might so far condescend, that the government of the port and coast of Monterey be conferred upon him. In return, he would engage to bring from Manila his family and others, including artisans, for the improvement of the country. Thus by a colony of "culture and commerce" the Indian would be led to know his King and to eschew fraudulent commerce with the English. Tagle's scheme found favor with Arrillaga, but it came to naught under the scrutiny of the Viceroy and the Crown.[14]

As between the two classes of means, direct and indirect, for meeting the problem of subsistence for Alta California, the indirect means were most in evidence; and of these smuggling was the chief.

Few trading craft of any nationality touched upon the coast prior to the arrival at Monterey, on October 29, 1796, of the Otter of Boston, commanded by Ebenezer Dorr. The publication of Cook's "Voyage" in 1784 had led to the sending to Nootka from Boston, in 1788, of the Lady Washington and Columbia Rediviva. Throughout the remainder of the eighteenth century, and down to the year 1812, Boston fur-trading vessels flocked to the Northwest. Outnumbering by many to one the vessels of other nations, they extended their operations above and below Nootka, gathering from the Indians rich cargoes of furs, which were taken to China and exchanged for teas, nankeen, and lacquers. The Russians, who claimed sovereignty southward of Kadiak, met the American intruders with protests; but the Spaniards, who but yesterday had yielded claim to sovereignty over the whole South Sea, met them with artillery. For a time, knowledge of the strict non-intercourse trade regulations of the Spanish Government, coupled with a plentiful supply of the best otter in northern waters, deterred Bostonians from smuggling operations below San Francisco. But as the northern and better otter became scarce, and knowledge of the ineffective nature of the California defenses became more definite, the Americans grew bolder.[15]

The Otter (despite her name) does not seem to have visited California with intent of unlawful trade, but of American vessels between 1801 and 1810 — the Lelia Byrd, the Alexander, the Hazard, the Enterprise and the O'Cain — as much may not be said. Spanish comandantes, therefore, whether at San Francisco, Monterey, Santa Bárbara, or San Diego; and Spanish padres, whether at the points named or at others, found themselves beset with temptation and behaved each according to his cloth. If comandante, he frequently, though not always, accepted a bribe; if padre, he usually — in pursuance of a custom which made of him a general importing agent — sold otter-skins to the foreigner.[16]

Ventures by American craft were many, but the boldest

was one made in March, 1803, by the Lelia Byrd under
command of William Shaler, with Richard J. Cleveland as
mate. Hearing at San Blas — where, on a voyage round
the Horn, they had contrived to purchase a quantity of sea-
otter skins — that a further quantity might be obtained at
San Diego, Shaler and Cleveland, on March 17, brought
the Lelia Byrd to anchor there on the regulation plea of
need of supplies. The comandante, Manuel Rodríguez,
was approached but proved non-corruptible, and placed on
board the ship a guard of five men. Don Manuel, moreover, was resourceful. He set decoys, and certain of the
crew of the Lelia Byrd, who while bartering were entrapped, were thrust by him in bonds and paraded on the
beach. They were liberated by Cleveland under cover of
pistols, and the Lelia Byrd, shipping her port battery of
three 3-pounders to the support of the 3-pounders of her
starboard side, put to sea past the Spanish defenses, —
a battery (*relict* of Alberto de Córdoba) of some six or
eight 9-pounders. Between shore and ship a fiery interchange took place, the ship receiving damage aloft and a
shot between wind and water; and the Spaniards, during
the hottest of the engagement, fleeing nimbly to cover. It
is related that so terror-stricken were Rodríguez's guard
on board the absconding vessel, first from flying iron, and
next from thought of expatriation, that being set on shore
(once the vessel was well past Point Guijarros), they celebrated their deliverance by falling on their knees, crossing
themselves, and shouting, *Vivan, vivan, los Americanos!* [17]

But what, meanwhile, of the problem of subsistence, as
at Kadiak, Behring's Bay, and Sitka it confronted the
Russians? A potent figure in Russian America — an
elemental man, one prodigious for energy, wondrous for
fidelity — was Alexander Baránoff. In 1790, Gigor Ivan-

ovich Shelikof, projector of the principal Russian-American trading company of the time, made Baránoff his agent, and when in 1799 the Russian-American Company itself was chartered, Baránoff became administrator. His abiding care was the providing of food. Each year in March there occurred a run of herring announced by the presence of sea-gulls; and from this time to the end of November edible fish of divers sorts were more or less to be obtained. But in the winter, eagles, crows, devilfish, mussels, seals, and sea-lions, with for tidbit an occasional halibut, were what the larder must welcome.[18]

Baránoff had sought to bring food from Chile, the Sandwich Islands (Owyhee), and even Manila, and was still sorely perplexed for it, when in October, 1803, he met at Kadiak Captain Joseph O'Cain. Of the captain's vessel (called by him the O'Cain, and by the Russians the Boston) Abel and Jonathan Winship of Boston were owners. The first American "trader" to visit Kadiak had been the Enterprise (April 24, 1799), with O'Cain as mate; and Baránoff, reviving acquaintance with the latter through a purchase of goods, entered into a compact by which the captain, seconded by a company of Aleutian Islanders, was to go southward and take otter for himself and Baránoff.[19] Under O'Cain, the Winships, and others, Russo-American otter-hunting expeditions along the California coast, from Trinidad Bay to Todos Santos Islands and into the very estuary of San Francisco, — expeditions in which the Russians furnished the hunters, and the Americans the equipment, — remained a feature of California annals down to 1815.

It, however, was not so much the coast of California as California itself, — land of flocks, of herds and yellow grain, — to which instinctively the Russians turned. In 1794, on the conclusion between Spain and Great Britain of the treaty for the abandonment of Nootka, Baránoff had urged that the spot be seized by Russia. But now (1805) a plea affecting California was to be preferred by a dignitary much higher.

Nikolai Petrovich Rezánoff (erstwhile protégé of Catherine II) was chamberlain to the Czar. His wife, a daughter of Shelikof, had but recently died, and, as a resource in bereavement, the chamberlain, with an ardor that recked neither of scruple nor self, had espoused patriotism. His most cherished plan was the securing for Russia of trade concessions from Japan, and in 1803–04 he was sent as ambassador extraordinary to the Mikado. Meeting with no better success for Russia than Sebastián Vizcaino had met with for Spain, he was eager

to destroy settlements, to drive the Japanese from Sakhalin Island, to frighten them away from the whole coast, and break up their fisheries, and to deprive 200,000 people of food, which will force them all the more to open their ports. . . . It may [he proceeded] be your pleasure, most gracious Sire, to punish me as a criminal for proceeding to active measures without waiting for orders, but I would be guilty of the greater offense of neglecting your interest if I hesitated at a decisive moment to sacrifice myself to your glory. I would be ashamed to limit my undertaking to a simple voyage around the world, a feat which is accomplished every year by merchant vessels.[20]

Besides credentials to Japan, the Chamberlain bore commission as royal inspector of Northwestern establishments and plenipotentiary of the Russian-American Company, and, after the failure of his diplomatic enterprise he was brought by the ship Nadeshda (A. J. von Krusenstern, commander) to Kamtchatka. Thence, with a suite comprising the naturalist G. H. von Langsdorff, two naval lieutenants, Nicholas A. Schwostoff and Gavril I. Davidoff, and others, he crossed to the Aleutian Islands, reaching Unalaska in July, 1805.

Rezánoff was at New Archangel by September, and here the first thing to confront him was Baránoff's problem, — food for the Russian settlements. Purchasing from J. De Wolf (slave-merchant of Bristol, Rhode Island) the Juno, copper-bottomed, fast, and laden with a cargo of Yankee merchandise, he at the same time gave orders for the construction of a vessel to be called the Awos. "In order to get provisions for this country," he wrote to the directors of the Russian-American Company on February 15, 1806, "it is necessary that I should go to California, and I hope to weigh anchor in the Juno on the 20th of this month. The equinoctials threaten us with gales, but to stay here will be to risk starvation." He would go first to Prince of Wales or Queen Charlotte Island to purchase sea-otter; but this only in passing, for "both time and circumstances compel us to hurry to California." In May he would return to Sitka, and go with the Juno and the Awos to Alexander Island for astronomical observations. Thence he would send the Awos to Russia with dispatches. The Juno he would send back to New Archangel, preparatory to taking her "to California for the winter, where I intend to remain and go to Manila on a Spanish vessel, and from there to Batavia and Bengal, in order to make a first experiment in trading with the Indies through Okhotsk." [21]

Impatient of rivalry, Rezánoff counseled the building of a war-brig to drive the Bostonians from California waters. From the latter, he said, Spaniards in California bought surreptitiously every trifle, and, having neither factories nor trade, paid for them in otter-skins. What was sold to the Spaniards by the Bostonians, — cloth, linen, iron-ware, — ought to be supplied by the Russians from factories in Siberia, in exchange for breadstuffs. Yet, if the Bostonians were to be tolerated, it should be on condition of their dealing with the Russians exclusively, bringing them flour, groats, butter, oil, tallow, vinegar, pitch, and rum. Besides, it might be practicable to found a settlement on the Columbia

from which we could gradually advance toward the south to the port of San Francisco, which forms the boundary line of California. If we could but obtain the means for the beginning of this plan, I think I may say that at the Columbia we could assemble population from various localities, and in the course of ten years become strong enough to make use of any favorable turn in European politics to include the coast of California in the Russian possessions. The Spaniards are very weak in this country, and if in 1798, when war was declared by the Spanish Court, our company had possessed adequate means, it would have been easy to seize a part of California north from the 34th degree (latitude of the mission of Santa Bárbara) and to appropriate this part forever, since the geographical position of Mexico would have prevented her from sending any assistance overland. The Spaniards, on account of their shiftlessness, make hardly any use of their lands, and have advanced toward the north only to secure the boundary.[22]

As already stated, patriotism with Rezánoff had become a passion. He disclosed his heart to the acting chamberlain (A. A. Vitovoff) on February 16, 1806.

No personal considerations have entered into my unrestrained revelations, but only the thought of glory and of the common welfare. . . . A man robbed of his tranquillity of soul by a merciless fate does not care for himself, and much less for honors and praise, as they are all insufficient to fill the void in his being which only death can bridge by uniting him again with the one whom he has lost. . . . The moral sufferings, the voyage, and troubles have undermined my physical strength; various diseases have developed themselves; my children in the meantime tell me that I have abandoned them. In my thoughts I am often at St. Petersburg, embracing them and the dust of my friend who lies buried there. The welfare of my fellow beings alone causes me to brave the seas and intrust my orphans to Providence, and I have often shed bitter tears when Nature awakened in me the parental yearnings.[23]

Quitting Sitka on March 8, but driven from the mouth of the Columbia River by the surge of its discharging waters, the Juno on the morning of April 5 — harassed by scurvy but with Rezánoff, Langsdorff, and Lieutenant Davidoff on board — swept in defiance of challenge past San Joaquín Battery, through the Golden Gate, into the Bay of San Francisco. "With pale and emaciated faces," Rezánoff afterwards wrote to the Russian Minister of Commerce, "we reached San Francisco Bay, and anchored outside because of the fog. . . . As a refusal of permission to enter meant to perish at sea, I resolved, at the risk of two or three cannon-balls, to run straight for the fort at the entrance."

The Nadeshda and consort, the Neva, had, under advices from Madrid, long been expected at San Francisco, and, the fact once established that the Juno was Russian, Rezánoff and his party were "overwhelmed with civilities." Comandante José Argüello was absent from home, and to an inquiry regarding the ships, politely put by Luis Argüello, his son, the adroit reply was made that they had returned to Russia, but that Rezánoff "had been intrusted by the Czar with command over all his American possessions, and in this capacity had resolved to visit the Governor of New California to consult him with regard to mutual interests." Monterey was his destination, but he had stopped at San Francisco because of contrary winds. Rezánoff would write to Governor Arrillaga of his purpose to visit him. A letter was sent, but the Governor, wary of the Chamberlain's object, replied that he would do himself the honor of meeting so distinguished a guest at the port of his arrival.

"While awaiting the Governor," Rezánoff explained to the Minister of Commerce, "we visited every day at the house of the hospitable Argüello, and soon became inti-

mate there. Among the beautiful sisters of Luis Argüello, Doña Concepción has the name of being the beauty
of California, and your Excellency will agree with me
when I say that we were sufficiently rewarded for our sufferings, and passed our time very pleasantly." Arrillaga,
a gray-haired man of fifty-six, reached San Francisco on
April 17, and on the 18th there arrived the comandante, José
Argüello, who at once invited Rezánoff to meet the Governor at his house at dinner. The meeting took place, and
as Arrillaga spoke French the Chamberlain made known
the true object of his presence. "I frankly tell you," he
said, "that we need bread, which we can get from Canton;
but as California is nearer to us, and has produce which
it cannot sell, I have come here to negotiate with you a
preliminary agreement to be sent to our respective courts."
This proposal the Governor asked time to consider.[24]

As for Doña Concepción (about to enter our narrative),
her mother was niece to José Joaquín Moraga, Anza's
lieutenant in the founding of San Francisco. She herself
was fourteen years old, and, as described by the intelligent
Langsdorff, "was lively and animated, had sparkling, love-
inspiring eyes, beautiful teeth, pleasing and expressive
features, a fine form and a thousand other charms, yet was
perfectly simple and artless, —

> the heavenly dawn into one drop of dew, —

a beauty of a type to be found, though not frequently,
in Italy, Spain, and Portugal."[25] What California had
been to Doña Eulalia de Callis, that it was to Doña Concepción, — and she pined for adventure.

"The day following my interview with Governor Arrillaga," Rezánoff observed in his communication to the Minister of Commerce, "I learned from a devoted friend in the
house of Argüello, word for word what had been said after

my departure. . . . From day to day, though by means imperceptible to the Governor, my relations with the house of Argüello became more intimate. . . . 'You have accustomed us to your company,' said Don José de Arrillaga, 'and I can assure you that the good family of my friend Argüello prize highly the satisfaction of seeing you at their house, and sincerely admire you.' "

But what regarding a sale to the Russians of breadstuffs? Here the Governor kept silence. Rezánoff had been invited to dine with the padres, whose "desire for trade was very noticeable"; presents, judiciously distributed, had attracted padres from distant missions;[26] beyond these things nothing had been gained.

Seeing [wrote the Chamberlain to his minister] that my situation was not improving, expecting every day that some misunderstanding would arise, and having but little confidence in my own [ship's] people, I resolved to change my politeness for a serious tone. Finally, I imperceptibly created in Doña Concepcion an impatience to hear something serious from me . . . which caused me to ask for her hand, to which she consented. My proposal created consternation in her parents, who had been reared in fanaticism. The difference in religion and the prospective separation from their daughter made it a terrible blow for them. They ran to the missionaries, who did not know what to do; they hustled poor Concepcion to church, confessed her, and urged her to refuse me, but her resolution finally overcame them all. The holy fathers appealed to the decision of the throne of Rome, and if I could not accomplish my nuptials, I had at least the preliminary act performed, the marriage contract drawn up, and forced them to betroth us.[27]

Heedless of designs upon India, Rezánoff now conceived the project of going to Madrid as Russian envoy; of effecting a treaty of amity and commerce with Spain; and (having returned to San Francisco by way of Mexico) of marrying his betrothed. But this for the future. For the present, the cause of the Chamberlain was won. On May 21 the Juno, laden with flour, peas, beans, and maize, and with Rezánoff on board, sailed for Sitka amid the thunders in farewell of the battery of San Joaquín.[28]

But the Chamberlain, — did he return to wed the *Señorita?* In September, 1806, he crossed to Kamtchatka, whence the same month he set forth overland for St. Petersburg. Ill when starting, he was attacked by fever, met a fall from his horse, and on March 1, 1807, died at Krasnoyarsk, where his tomb, fashioned like an altar but void of inscription, was visited by Langsdorff in 1807. It is the opinion of the latter that to gain the vital object of his visit to California, Rezánoff would unhesitatingly have "sacrificed himself" in marriage to the daughter of Argüello.[29] Whether later he would have performed with her his nuptial contract (with naught for Russia to be gained thereby) is open to question. Concepción, be it said, doubted her suitor never. For her the Chamberlain's death, the circumstances of which she learned from Sir George Simpson at Santa Bárbara in 1842, explained all. She remained unwedded, passing the earlier years of her bereavement partly in Mexico and partly at La Soledad Mission as a member of the Third Order of Franciscans. In 1851, she, as Sister María Dominica, entered the Dominican Convent of Santa Catarina at Monterey, and in 1854 followed the convent to Benicia. Here, on December 23, 1857, at the age of sixty-six years, she died. She was buried in the convent cemetery under a brown stone cross bearing the inscription: "Sister María Dominica O. S. D. [Order of Sant Dominic]." The subjoined is from the records of the institution: —

In the convent of Sta. Catarina of Siena at Benicia, California, died Sister María Dominica Argüello, December 23, 1857. She was buried on Christmas Eve, dressed in her white habit as a nun.

She was carried on a bier into the chapel of the convent. First came the cross-bearers bearing the cross; then the young girls of the convent dressed in black; then the novices in white, with white veils, carrying lighted tapers; then the professed nuns, with black veils and lighted tapers, signifying that she had gone from darkness up to light and life. After the solemn requiem service was ended, the last Benediction of the Catholic Church, *Requiescat in Pace*, was pronounced over her mortal remains, and a tired soul was dismissed out of all the storms of life into the divine tranquillity of death. The next morning was Christmas Day. *"Glory be to God on high, and on earth Peace to men of good will."*[30]

Rezánoff's sojourn at San Francisco involved more than the obtaining of a single shipload of provisions. There came of it the founding, within California limits as at present defined, of the Russian fort and settlement of Ross. "Russia would not take California as a gift. It would cost too much to maintain it. Besides, Russia has an inexhaustible treasure in furs." Thus with facile tongue had the Chamberlain addressed Arrillaga at their first interview. "But," observed the former afterwards, "he [Arrillaga] frankly confessed to me that his court feared Russia above all other powers." And well it might. From Sitka the Chamberlain thus exhorted his government: —

Our American possessions will know no more of famine; Kamtchatka and Okhotsk can be supplied with bread. . . . When our trade with California is fully organized, we can settle Chinese laborers there, etc. They [the Spaniards] only turned their attention to California after 1760, and by the enterprise of the missionaries alone this fine body of land was incorporated. Even now there is still an unoccupied interval fully as rich and very necessary to us, and if we let it escape us, what will posterity say? I at least shall not be arraigned before it in judgment.[31]

In the autumn of 1808, Ivan Alexándrovich Kuskof was sent by Baránoff to "New Albion" for otter, and to select a site for a Russian settlement. The expedition consisted of two ships, the Nikolai, destined for the Columbia River but wrecked in passage, and the Kadiak, which with Kuskof on board touched at Trinidad Bay, but in January, 1809, entered Bodega Bay, and there tarried until late in August of the same year. A favorable report was made by Kuskof concerning Bodega, and the Russian-American Company solicited from the Czar a treaty with Spain permitting trade with California. At the same time the Czar was asked to afford "highest protection" against opposition by Americans to any settlement that might be made on the Columbia. The "gradual advance southward to the port of San Francisco as the boundary line of California," which Rezánoff had advocated in 1806, was thus put in course of execution.[32]

"Highest protection," when needed as against opposition by Americans, was promised by the Czar, but the projected Columbia River settlement was never made. As for the post on Bodega Bay, it was forecast by order of the company in a proclamation announcing to "our friends and neighbors, the noble and brave Spaniards, inhabitants of the Californias," the sending of a ship for trade. But attempts to move southward from Sitka were unsuccessful till March 4, 1811, when Kuskof again reached Bodega. The voyage was repeated early in 1812 (this time in force), and on September 10, at a point 18 miles north of Bodega, on a bluff 100 feet above the sea, Ross, a fortification of ten guns, was dedicated by ninety-five Russians assisted by a party of Aleutian Islanders in forty bidarkas.[33]

As already seen, American craft, lured to Northwest waters by the fur-trade, found it their best course to secure skins either by exchanging for them contraband goods with the California padres, or by hunting sea-otter, on shares with the Russians, off the California coast. But more. When Louisiana was purchased by the United States from France in 1803, overtures were made to Spain for the purchase of the Floridas. The overtures were rejected, but Americans had begun to hover upon the Florida-Texas-New-Mexico border, and by 1805 a United States Government expedition — that of Lewis and Clarke — had actually penetrated to the Pacific at the mouth of the Columbia River, a point, according to Spanish claims, within the limits of California. Encroached upon by Americans landward, the encroachments seaward became yet more significant, and the royal and viceregal decrees of 1776–1800 were vigorously reaffirmed.

In 1802 Charles IV notified the American Government that vessels caught smuggling on the California coast would be confiscated.[34] In 1806 Felipe de Goycoechea, as Governor of Baja California, urged that the naval station at San Blas be transferred to the peninsula, the better to check American designs "in the Gulfs of California and of Spain"; and the same year Viceroy Iturrigaray warned Arrillaga of possible warlike demonstrations by the United States because of the failure of the negotiations for Florida.[35] But it was Arrillaga himself who depicted the situation most forcibly. The United States, he said to Rezánoff in 1806, already possessed New Orleans; and Pensacola being near New Mexico, even Santa Fé was beginning to use American goods.

Having [he observed] personally witnessed in our own waters the enterprise of this Republic, I do not wonder at their success. They flourish in trade and know its value. And who at present does not, except ourselves, who pay for our neglect with our purses? . . . The American States sometimes send out ten or fifteen regular robbers, who, on account of our small force, are able to disturb our peace and corrupt our honesty.[36]

Among American ships active in partnership with Bará-noff between 1809 and 1813 there were, besides the O'Cain and Albatross, owned by the Winships, the Mercury, the Catherine, and the Amethyst, owned by Benjamin W. Lamb and others of Boston. The Mercury was navigated by the Bostonian George Washington Eayrs, and her story (from documents here first used) illustrates the times. In February, 1806, at Tepic, José Sevilla, a saddler of Monterey seeking government employment, petitioned Viceroy Iturrigaray to be made coast-guard in California. It was, he alleged, the practice of English [American] vessels to anchor at the Santa Catarina Islands ten leagues from the coast, and there exchange China and East India goods for otter-skins and cattle. The trade, he said, was one at which even the officials themselves connived, and, should he be appointed coast-guard, he asked that the military and naval commanders be instructed not to injure him.

Whether Don José was granted an appointment, we are not told, but between 1808 and 1813 the Mercury appeared on the California coast, bearing Mr. George Washington Eayrs.

Writing on February 7, 1814, Eayrs said:—

I left China in the year 1808, with the small Amt of Cargo about five thousand Dolls, my first Business was Hunting Furs, This Business I entered into with the Russian Governor & continued several years, in which time I was in the Winter season as far South as California for supplies and the purpose of taking Seal Skins, I received several Letters, from the head People & Pardres of California intreating me to bring them many Articles that they was in distress for & could not obtain from the Continent [!] . . . The Hunting and Sealing Business, I continued in untill two Years since when I obtained a large Amount of Furs of the Russian Governor. . . . I entered into a Contract with the Russian Governor, to continue in the Hunting Business; while imployed in this Business, I received Letters from Cape Sⁿ Lucas, intreating me to bring them many Articles, that they was Naked, & was in great want.

As specimens of the letters mentioned above as received from the "Pardres of California," the Eayrs papers supply the following: —

FRIEND DON JORGE: It is necessary that early in the morning a boat be landed to enable me to embark and purchase that of which I have spoken to you. So, as soon as a fire on shore is seen, despatch the boat; since thus I must manage in order to act with safety.

FR. PEDRO MARÍA DE ZARATE.

Sⁱⁱᵒ. ROSARIO [Lower California], April 19, 1812.

SEÑOR COM^dte AND FRIEND DON JORGE: To-day there goes to you the padre of San Fernando who was unable to go last week because of illness. Trade with him, and to-morrow (God willing) I will come to your *Fragata* to dine, and we two will trade on our own account. I am now sending the corporal with a little vegetable stuff for you and the other two comandantes, and also some eggs, the whole a present, I wishing only the honor of serving them. There will be sent likewise the otter-skins which on my coming we will examine. Also be pleased to receive a small pig for yourself, and another for the two comandantes, — a present. *Á Dios* till to-morrow (Monday) at noon.

I remain your friend,

FR. JOSÉ CAULAS.

FRIEND DON JORGE: Greeting. I expect you to dine with me at the *casa del rancho.* Come with this *vaquero* and we will talk of what is interesting in the news from Europe and the whole world. We will also trade, unless you bring things as dear as usual. The boy says that you asked him why I was out of humor with you, and I say I am out of humor with nobody. *Á Dios;* since I do not know what you bring, I ask nothing; and since you say nothing, I get nothing.

Thy friend Q. B. T. M.

FR. LUIS [MARTÍNEZ ?]

Just what the commodities were for which the California padres were thus willing to become smugglers, it would be interesting to know, and here again the Eayrs papers prove serviceable. We find mentioned: hardware, crockery, fish-hooks, gunpowder, cotton cloth and blankets for covering the prevalent "nakedness," shoes, etc.; and besides these things others, to wit: camel's-hair shawls; Chinese silk, *color de rosa;* white ladies' cloth with embroidered edge; large towels (*perfiladas*) for women; fine men's kerchiefs of different colors; fine white thread; blue twisted silk; twisted white silk; cochineal floss; black floss; black handkerchiefs; decorated water-jars; gilded crystal stands, each with twelve small crystal bottles decorated with *flores de oro;* flowered cups for broth; porcelain plates; platters flowered in green and red, with tureens to match; shaving-basins; black mantillas; Brittany linens; peppers; nutmegs.

But the interesting transactions between Mr. Eayrs and the "Pardres of California" were destined to come to an end. The smuggling points of the coast, from Cape San Lucas to Monterey, included San Quentín, San Juan Capistrano, San Pedro, San Luis Obispo, and Santa Cruz; but the chief of them was El Refugio, about fifteen miles below Santa Bárbara, a rancho owned by the descendants of José Francisco Ortega, whom Serra had wished Bucarely to make governor. Here on June 3, 1813, the Mercury, as she lay at anchor about a mile from shore, was surprised by a boat from the Lima coast-guard ship La Flora, under Captain Don Nicolás Noe, and seized as a prize. Eayrs himself was on board with a crew of fifteen men, an Indian boy, "bought in Oregon," and "a young female which he had had several years and whom he esteemed equal the same as if lawfully married to him, and a Daughter only twenty-five days old when the Ship was taken." All were made prisoners, and the comandante at Santa

Bárbara, José Argüello (Eayrs spells it Arwayus), took possession of Eayrs's papers, and of the ship and cargo subject to condemnation proceedings in Mexico.

The period was that of war between the United States and England, and, to lessen chance of trouble from the seizure, orders were given that Eayrs and his family should be well treated. So far as the family were concerned, José de la Guerra certified in 1816 that he had taken charge of them in 1814; that the young woman (known in her Gentile state as Pequi [Peggy]) had been baptized as María Antonia de la Ascensión Stuard, he acting as godfather; and that she had been one of his family, till at length she had gone to San Blás. Eayrs himself was sent first to San Diego, and then to Tepic. In 1814 and 1815 he addressed letters to the Viceroy, to the comandante-general of Nueva Galicia, and to the comandante at San Blas, lamenting eloquently in bad English a poverty due to delay in the sale of the Mercury, which, though appraised by the government at 23,310 *pesos*, had been allowed to depreciate to a fraction of her value.

But in the entire case of the Mercury the significant point is the open recognition by California officials of the fact that the province, denied subsistence under Spanish commercial regulations, must countenance smuggling or perish.

In general all the officials resident on this coast [said Eayrs in a letter translated for him into Spanish] have encouraged my trade, and at their request I have given them agricultural tools and other things that they needed. I have provided the priests with what they required for instructing the natives and for the ceremonies of religion. . . . They have paid me with provisions and some few otter-skins. I have clothed many naked, and they have given me in return products of the soil, as the officers of this district can inform your Excellency. . . .

My dealings have not been clandestine, but with the full and tacit consent of the governors. Let Fray Marcos Amistoy at Santa Bárbara be questioned in *verbo sacerdotis, tacto pectore,* concerning these transactions.

And on November 12, 1819, Argüello wrote to Viceroy Calleja: —

The padres are concerned in illicit trade from a grave and general necessity of clothing and other materials which they have experienced in the past, and experience more and more from day to day in the jurisdiction of this government. A rule of the canonical law says: *Hace lícito la necesidad lo que no es lícito por la ley* [Necessity makes lawful that which by the law is illicit].[37]

The case of the Mercury was not disposed of until after 1819. Meanwhile, on July 13, 1812, Tapis had been succeeded as Father-President by José Señán, and, on July 24, 1814, Governor Arrillaga (sixty-four years old) had died at La Soledad. Under Arrillaga the private rancho — a species of holding instituted in 1784 by Fages, and approved in 1793 by Don José himself — assumed importance. No grants had as yet been made in the districts of San Diego and San Francisco; and of six or seven made within the Monterey district, at least five had been abandoned. But in the district of Santa Bárbara (especially near Los Ángeles) former grants — San Rafael, Los Nietos, San Pedro, Portezuelo, Encino, and possibly El Refugio — were supplemented by Rancho de Félix, Las Vírgenes, El Conejo, and Santiago de Santa Ana.[38]

Multiplication of ranchos and increase of horses led to the expedient of killing the surplus animals. As early as 1784 it had been found necessary to reduce by slaughter surplus cattle at the San Francisco presidio.[39] But horses (mares more especially) were less valuable than cattle, and having increased to vast herds which consumed the mission pasture, and in the San Joaquín Valley roamed hither and yon in squadrons devastating though picturesque, it was ordered in 1805, at the instance of President Tapis, that their number be reduced; and between 1805 and 1810 they were slaughtered by tens of thousands.[40] Nor was the live-stock of the province reduced alone by voluntary means. In 1805, in the single district of Monterey, over four hundred head were destroyed by wolves and bears, and by the accident of miring at the lagoons.[41]

But the harm wrought by wild beasts was as naught to that wrought by *temblores*, or earthquakes. In 1808 San Francisco was rudely shaken, and between December, 1812, and February, 1813, a series of violent shocks devastated Southern California.

These quakes [President Señán wrote on April 9] will form an epoch in history for their great destructiveness. . . . There must be built anew the churches of San Fernando and Santa Bárbara. . . . The San Gabriel Mission suffered somewhat, as did that of San Buena Ventura. At the latter the tower is ready to fall and the chancel front is cracked from the ceiling to the ground. . . . At Purísima the quake was so violent that it caused the bells to swing till they gave forth their chimes. In a few brief moments the building was reduced to fragments and ruins, presenting the spectacle of Jerusalem destroyed. At San Juan Capistrano, California's most famous temple was ruined and forty neophytes killed. Had the catastrophe occurred at High Mass and not when it did (at early Mass), scarcely a neophyte would be left. As it was, six only escaped. No whites were injured. The *celebrador* [priest] saved himself by fleeing through the private door leading to the sacristy.[42]

Arrillaga was, as intimated, a conserver of the equilibrium between State Secular and State Sacerdotal attained under Borica. So pronounced, indeed, was his conserving, that it amounted almost to sacerdotalism. Through him, in 1802, Lasuén successfully withstood a belated attempt from Mexico to introduce into the Californias the Neve-Croix type of Mission discredited on the Colorado.[43] Nor

in opposing secular designs was the Governor merely passive. In 1800 a band of twenty foundlings, ten boys and
ten girls, reached Monterey, and the girls, though "fond of
cigars," turned out well.[44] But toward colonists of any
kind the Governor was little favorable. For such as were
of the convict class, he deemed California too good; and for
such as were of the respectable class, it was, he deemed,
not good enough.[45] Padres, in his opinion, should be
treated with consideration. If they rode abroad attended
by mounted Indians, it was because the soldiers had
grown negligent of their comfort. Let the padres be
waited upon by the soldiers. "It would be an attention,
an act of civility, of good breeding and of respect." If
padres chose for religious ends to remain at Gentile
rancherías overnight, let the escort remain with them.[46]

Indeed, the standard of military subordination under
Salvatierra and Serra was now somewhat restored; for
when at San Antonio de Padua a corporal (José Castro)
and soldier misconducted themselves, they on complaint
of Padre Marcelino Cipres were transferred.[47] Concerning manufactures, Arrillaga was pessimistic, and education
he neglected.[48] His incumbency was marked on September
17, 1804, by the founding, at the base of the Santa Inés
Mountains, of a new mission, — companion to La Purísima, and nineteenth of the list, — the mission of Santa
Inés or Saint Agnes.[49]

CHAPTER XI

THE PROBLEM OF SUBSISTENCE (*continued*)

FOR nearly three hundred years prior to 1810 semi-tropical North America and all of South America, with the exception of Brazil, had been under the dominion of Spain. The principal South American districts on the Pacific Coast were Peru and Chile, and on the Atlantic the valley of the Río de la Plata, where, since 1535, there had risen near the sea a city of forty thousand inhabitants, called, because of its grateful breezes, the city of Buenos Ayres. Throughout Spanish South America discontent with colonial methods (exclusion from official station of all natives even though of Spanish parentage, and restrictions on trade) had been augmenting; and when, in June, 1808, the legitimate sovereign of Spain, Ferdinand VII (son of Charles IV), was displaced by Joseph Bonaparte, the act was made by the colonies occasion for revolt. Of this revolt one of the most active centres was Buenos Ayres. The city was not unlike a city of the ancient Levant, cosmopolitan, commercial, intensely independent, — a resort for freebooters, French, English, and American, — and among its insurgent activities was the commissioning, between 1816 and 1819, of privateering craft to seize the ports of Peru and Chile, and to foment revolution in New Spain itself.

On August 30, 1815, José Argüello (Acting Governor of Alta California) was succeeded by Lieutenant-Colonel Pablo Vicente de Sola of Mondragón, Guipúzcoa. California was loyal to Ferdinand VII, — that ruler having been acclaimed at each presidio as late as March, 1809, — but it was loyal more especially to Spain. Mexico since 1810 had been agitated from causes the same as those affecting Peru and Buenos Ayres, but California had remained tranquil even to monotony. For Sola, therefore, military problems, should they arise, would be extraneous in character.

In April, 1816, word reached Mazatlán of the capture of Spanish vessels by the privateers of Buenos Ayres, and of a blockade by the latter of the ports of Valparaíso, Callao, and Guayaquil.[1] This word was promptly communicated to José Argüello, at Loreto, and by him to Sola, who received it in June. Presidial comandantes were exhorted to gather bows and arrows, and, if they knew the art, to prepare against the enemy *balsas rosas* (red-hot balls); while padres were instructed to hold themselves alert to furnish *vaqueros* armed with *reatas* (lassoes), to pack and conceal Mission silver, and to drive Mission livestock to the interior.[2]

It was not until 1818 that the dreaded insurgents actually appeared. As early as October 6, warning of their approach was given at Santa Bárbara by the Clarion, an American brig, and on November 20 the Argentina, of perhaps thirty-eight guns (Captain Hippolyte Bouchard), and the Santa Rosa of perhaps twenty-six guns (Lieutenant Pedro Covale), were sighted from Point Pinos. What ensued is worthy the recording genius of the authors of the "Pirates of Penzance."

On the morning of the 21st, the Santa Rosa, which had been denied permission to land, sought to force a landing by opening fire. The fire was promptly returned by a shore battery of eight guns under Manuel Gómez and José Estrada. After some time, during which the Spaniards, at least in imagination, wrought upon the enemy havoc with their shot, the Santa Rosa struck her flag, sent ashore an officer and two men, and the conflict subsided. Soon, however, the Argentina approached and dropped anchor. Bouchard, commander of the expedition, thus being arrived, he made known his presence and authority by sending to Sola a flag of truce demanding a surrender of the province. The demand was rejected with hauteur, and hereupon, as though the stage lacked a prompter, again ensued a pause. It lasted until the next morning at eight o'clock, when Bouchard sent ashore nine boats carrying a body of men and four field-guns. Against this force (some three hundred) the presidial troops available to contest a landing (twenty-five men) could effect nothing, and a retreat was executed, first to the presidio and then to the *Rancho del Rey*. From Monterey, where the presidio was set on fire, and where the fort and *casa real*, with its vegetable garden and orchard, were partially destroyed, the invaders set sail on November 27 for the south.

It was presumed that Santa Bárbara, where José de la Guerra held command, would be the next point of attack, and families and goods were dispatched inland to Santa Inés. But near by lay the rancho of Refugio, — rich, it was rumored, through smuggling, — and here the insurgents,

> trying their hand at a burglaree,

landed on December 2. Against them — from Santa Inés, Purísima, and San Luis Obispo — the padres, inflamed by prayers, fastings, and flagellations, mustered with their neophytes the Canaleños.[3] But, although supported by a detachment of troops from Santa Bárbara under Sergeant Carlos Antonio Carrillo, naught was accomplished save the capture of three of the enemy who had ventured apart from the main body; and the rancho having been burned and plundered, the vessels quitted Refugio, and on December 6 cast anchor before Santa Bárbara itself.

To Guerra, Bouchard offered terms. He would leave the coast upon an exchange of prisoners. And now of a surety, facts conspired in aid of some composer of *opéra comique;* for when, as a sequel to Bouchard's offer, Guerra assembled his captives (Lieutenant William Taylor of Boston, Martín Romero of Paraguay, and Mateo José Pascual, negro without domicile), the insurgents brought forward in counterpoise a drunken settler of Monterey by name Molina. The exchange effected, — whereat Governor Sola was much scandalized, — the Argentina and Santa Rosa duly sailed away. On December 14 and 15, the vessels stopped at San Juan Capistrano, but were guilty of no serious depredations; and although at San Diego the comandante awaited them with the "red hot balls" recommended by Sola in 1816, they inconsiderately passed him by, fading in mystery out of sight in the direction of Acapulco.[4]

Manuel Gómez and José Estrada were both made lieutenants for gallantry, while Sola himself was made a colonel. But what of the padres? Had they not mustered their lariated *vaqueros* and archered neophytes, and stood ready themselves at the sound of the *Kyrie Eleïson* to fall fiercely upon the invader, — a foe formidable enough to be stigmatized by Señán as "heretic, schismatic, excommunicate, heathen, and Moor"? Yet was it not true that no mention at all of these things had been made by Sola? The affront was one not meekly to be borne, and on June 19, 1819, Fray Antonio Ripoll of Santa Bárbara appealed to Sola, a course which elicited from that officer, and from the Viceroy, thanks grateful though belated.[5]

The Mexican revolt, by depleting the viceregal resources and barring routes of exit from the country, had stopped the annual supplies for the missions. Writing to President Tapis in February, 1811, the Guardian of San Fernando observed: —

The insurrection began last September in the pueblos of Dolores and San Miguel el Grande. The story would be long were I to relate each event, but the newspapers, which I suppose you read, as they are sent to the various missions, will instruct you fully, etc. . . . We have recovered [from the insurgents] the port of San Blas and the *fragata* Princesa, but it has been impossible to send either the supplies or five or six padres whom I had meant to send this year. We must see how . . . the spirit of agitation [*vertigo*] that the devil has awakened in this unfortunate kingdom will end. We must see what his Excellency [the Viceroy] will resolve, for he will necessarily take some step, either through Acapulco (also cut off) or through San Blas. . . . I have not sent this letter because of the roads. . . . The supplies for this year have not yet left Mexico, nor can the padres be sent while the roads are obstructed.[6]

Hemp, important as an article of California produce, could no longer be taken to San Blas to be bartered for manufactured goods; and, by the seizure of the Peruvian ports in 1816 by the Buenos Ayres privateers, the exchange of tallow for cloth — an exchange effected annually through carriers from Lima — was brought to an end.[7] Comandantes complained loudly to Arrillaga of lack of shirts and of food for their men; and Comandante Luis Argüello at San Francisco begged of Sola clothing for his own family. Sola himself in 1816 pictured the state of the province as deplorable through "ruined fortifications, crumbling esplanades, and dismounted guns." He pointed out how worse than death for him it would be to fail in this remote land after he had given to the world proofs of his quality in conflicts from the beginning of the revolutionary movement. "To see," he said, "the good troops of California going through their evolutions entirely naked, and their families in like case, pierced him to the heart."

So unremitting was the distress, that in 1817 Sola parted with needed clothing of his own to cover the nakedness of troops compelled to "pursue Gentile Indians in their wild retreats"; [8] and the same year a Yankee trader, James Smith Wilcox, — lean, lank, hatted in beaver and coated in swallow-tails, yet (*pace* Rezánoff) aspirant for the hand of Doña Concepción, — made it an excuse for smuggling that he had thereby served "to clothe the naked soldiers of the King of Spain," when, for lack of raiment, they could not attend Mass, and when the most revered fathers had neither vestments nor vessels fit for the churches, nor implements wherewith to till the soil.[9]

A climax was reached in 1819, the year following the attack by Bouchard. In January, Guardian López of San Fernando, lamenting the failure of *memorias*, told the Viceroy that the missionaries of Alta California had been forced to celebrate the *tremendo sacrificio* of the Mass with candles of mere tallow; and that so great was the discontent among neophytes, settlers, and soldiers, that it was only in default of a single insurgent spirit that the province had not become revolutionary along with the others.[10] Thanks to López, supplies to the value of 36,000 *pesos* were soon consigned to José de la Guerra, agent for California in Mexico.

After 1812, want to a great extent was relieved from Ross. In raising grain the Russians proved little adept, but resorting for it, as they did, to San Francisco, they left in exchange valuable merchandise. Occasionally (as in 1818) a Manila ship, driven into Monterey by scurvy, furnished supplies; or an American smuggler, like the Mercury, was laid under tribute; but the principal dependence was Ross. Brought by the diplomacy of Rezánoff to one sale of breadstuffs to the Russians, Arrillaga had found

it easy to consent to further transactions; and although
Lieutenant Gabriel Moraga had kept upon Ross a close
watch, visiting it on the eve of its dedication and again in
1813, it was with undoubted warrant that Tikhemeneff
wrote in his "Historical Review of the Russian American
Company ": "The Russian colonies lost a true friend by
the death of Arrillaga."

Nor at first did traffic with the Russians provoke censure
from Madrid. The reaction in Spain under Charles IV
(reflected in Alta California by Borica and Arrillaga) continued under Ferdinand VII to the time of the displacement of the latter by Joseph Bonaparte, when — the
leaven of the American and French Revolutions asserting
itself — there developed a counter-reaction entailing a
regency. "The kingdoms, provinces, and islands of the
dominions of America," so it was resolved in 1809, "shall
have national representation, and, through deputies sent
to the Spanish peninsula,[11] shall constitute part of the supreme council of the monarchy." And on March 12, 1812, at
Cádiz, there was adopted for the entire *Monarquía Español*
a constitution redolent of fraternalism, anti-clericalism,
and popular sovereignty. News of the founding of Ross,
therefore, reached the regency at a juncture singularly
favorable for the Russians, as witness a dispatch to the
Viceroy of date, February 4, 1814: —

I [Secretary José Lurando] have informed the *Regencia del
Reyno* of your Excellency's secret dispatch No. 7, wherein I am
notified that the Russians have formed an establishment near
the port of Bodega on the coast of Alta California. By the report
which your Excellency incloses from Don Francisco Xavier [*sic*]
de Arrillaga, it cannot be absolutely determined that the establishment is one formed with design. It is formed perhaps from
necessity. That is to say, if the Russian vessel be in bad condition
as reported, it is not strange that they should seek to repair it;
or, if totally useless, that it should have put them under the neces-

sity of remaining in the locality to which they have come. The circumstance that the aforesaid Russians are in a very necessitous condition indicates perhaps the best method of getting rid of the establishment, — withholding provisions except upon their coming to the presidio; in which case they may be deprived of their arms, munitions, and artillery, in order that these things may be kept on deposit and be restored to them when they embark to return to their country.

But this ministry has information that the Russians desire to open traffic between the establishments which they have in Unalaska and the Spanish presidios of Alta California. There are certain claims so absolutely just and mutually convenient as not to be denied when based upon intimate relations of friendship. Considered from a true point of view, it will be found that said establishments, both Russian and Spanish, separated as they are from the commerce of the rest of mortal kind, are almost compelled to help each other; that the traffic which they would conduct *inter se* is the perfectly spontaneous kind which a common humanity points out to men even less civilized; that to attempt to prohibit this entirely is not only impossible but highly inhuman; and, finally, that, limited to what may be called a natural exchange, and one exclusively with the presidios of Alta California, it may be considered that the prohibition of the laws is not violated thereby.

Thus regarded, and with the noble object of diverting the Russians from projects of settlements which they have conceived, it seems to S. A. very fitting that your Excellency direct that the *vista gorda* [broad view] be taken; but that the respective authorities be very alert not to permit traffic to be extended to any point other than the missions of Alta California, — not to those of la Baja; and that it be limited to the exchange of effects adapted to the agriculture and industry of both the Spanish and Russian settlements; since, in other respects, S. A. can enjoin upon your Excellency nothing less than this, that what the laws determine in the particular case be observed and carried out. The zeal, prudence, and shrewd judgment of your Excellency are relied upon to conduct this affair with the delicacy required, in order to secure the removal of the Russian settlement without compromising the friendship of the two nations,[12] etc.

But in March, 1814, Ferdinand (restored) repudiated Liberalism and all its works, including the Constitution of 1812; and although in 1816 he directed Viceroy Calleja to take what course he chose with the Russians in California, provided no harm were suffered to befall "the territory of the Crown,"[13] Calleja deemed it wise to be cautious. Early in 1815, José Argüello notified Kuskof that orders from Mexico required that the Russian post be abandoned.[14]

Kuskof came personally to San Francisco in August, 1815, to assure Argüello that Russia made no claim to territory south of Fuca Strait; and in 1816, in October, a conference concerning Ross was held at San Francisco between Kuskof and Sola on board the Russian exploring vessel Rurik, under Lieutenant Otto von Kotzebue.[15] Yet Calleja not only directed Sola to discontinue relations with Kuskof, but to "eject the Russians from the port of Bodega."[16] Henceforth the Governor was insistent that there be an abandonment of Ross. To Lieutenant Padushkin (emissary from Baránoff), to Baránoff's successor Hagemeister, to Lieutenant Golovnin, and to other emissaries, his answer was ever the same: ground of complaint could only be removed by a withdrawal of the Bodega establishment beyond the Spanish boundaries, — to wit, beyond the Strait of Fuca. Otherwise the King of Spain could not consent to a proposal for placing the products of California at the disposal of the Russians.[17] And to these terms the Russian-American Company at length was constrained to yield. In 1820 it announced to the Czar that it "would willingly abandon its settlement, which fills the Spaniards with fear, and nevermore think of choosing another site on the coast of Albion, if it could by this sacrifice but gain the privilege of permanent trade with New California."[18]

The Bodega Bay controversy, now, in its acute phase, at

an end, served colorably to reëstablish the northern line of
Alta California (limited to San Francisco Bay by the
Nootka Convention) at Fuca Strait. The Spanish claim
to jurisdiction north of the bay had been strengthened
by the founding on December 14, 1817, of the *asistencia*
of San Rafael Arcángel, a retreat to which Indians from
San Francisco Mission might be assigned for reasons of
health.[19] And in 1819 there arrived from Mexico, for use,
if need were, against the Russians, a reinforcement of two
hundred men. Half of them (cavalry from Mazatlán under
Captain Pablo de la Portilla) were excellent material; but
the other half (infantry recruited at San Blas) were a gang
of wretches, mixed in race, short in stature, venomous in
temper, *sin disciplina y sin religión*, drunkards, gamblers,
and thieves, — in a word, the Cholos.[20]

As early as the time of Borica and Lasuén, a tendency
to flee the missions began to be manifested on the part of
neophytes; a tendency that led to the charges of cruelty
preferred by Father Fernández. Dissatisfaction, however,
did not fail of expression more drastic. At San Miguel, in
1801, Padres Baltasar Carnicier, Andriano Martínez, and
Francisco Pujol were each seized by violent illness, of which
Pujol died; and afterwards certain of the Miguelinos
boasted of having administered poison.[21] The same year,
at Santa Bárbara, a female *shaman* (wizard) declared that
it had been revealed to her that a pulmonary disease fatal
among the neophytes was a penalty inflicted by *Chupu*,
the god of the Channel coast, vengeful at the defection of
his worshipers.[22] In 1805 President Tapis ascribed neophyte restiveness to the withdrawal to Mexico in 1803 of
the Catalan Volunteers, a body of seventy men of whom
the Indians stood much in awe. He said: "At San Gabriel
forty neophytes have fled toward the Colorado; at Santa

Bárbara two hundred; and at all the missions there are neophytes mal-inclined, uneasy, and disposed to fight, — evils which can only be corrected and prevented by an increase of troops and by repeated expeditions."[23]

The resort of the fugitives was the great valley or plain of the Tulares between the Coast Range and that of the Sierra Nevada, — a spot of intricate marsh covered with tall reeds, home of the Mariposa tribes, and a way-station to the Colorado. Into this valley, "where the sun rose and set as on the high sea," Fages, it will be remembered, had penetrated in 1772, and Garcés and a portion of Moraga's force in 1776. Throughout 1806 local troops in search of fugitives, under Moraga and other commanders, ranged the Tulare region from Tejón Pass to the latitude of San Francisco. Incidentally the object was exploration, the selection of sites for missions, and the effecting of baptisms. Kings' River (Río de los Santos Reyes) had been discovered and named in 1805, and now the Merced and the Mariposa were discovered.[24] Several mission sites were chosen, and a few Gentiles (192 out of an estimated total of 5300) were baptized.[25]

But neophyte restiveness did not abate. In 1811, at San Diego, a neophyte cook sought to poison Padre José Pedro Panto;[26] and in 1812 Andrés Quintana, padre at Santa Cruz, was murdered by neophytes, who lured him from his room at night on the pretext that his ministrations were required for a dying man.[27] Fear, too, of the Gentile Indians as corrupters of neophytes prevailed, and as early as 1810 Moraga fought a spirited engagement with bands opposite San Francisco.

Señán, as president of missions, was succeeded in 1815 by Mariano Payéras, and it was the opinion of the latter that the time had come for heeding the *Reglamento* provision for founding establishments east of the Coast Range,

— missions not merely, but strong presidios. Said Payéras in his biennial report for 1817–18: —

The object of our ministry being the propagation of the Faith among the Gentiles, and [Gentiles] no longer existing among the coast mountains, the padres of various missions have attempted to baptize those living in the district called the Tulares. They, however, have never succeeded. The Tulare Indians are inconstant. To-day they come, to-morrow they are gone, — not on foot, as they came, but on horseback. With such guests, no horse is safe in the northern valley. And the worst of it is that having crossed the Tulare Valley and the mountains that surround it, they kill the horses and eat them. The government has not been neglectful in pursuing such deadly enemies, but little has been effected, because great lagoons surrounded by green tules furnish them shelter from our horsemen. For this reason, the padres and more intelligent officers think it needful to form in the valley of the Tulares a new chain of missions with presidios. . . . If this be not done, the time will come when the existence of the province will be threatened, and a region that up to a recent time has been the centre of tranquillity will be changed into an Apachería.[28]

And in July, 1819, Payéras wrote to the padres: —

The Governor of this province, Don Pablo Vicente de Sola, advises me that he has been informed from the South of the scandalous abuse at certain missions [San Fernando and San Gabriel] of neophyte equestrianism. Neophytes take with brazenness, and in broad daylight, horses even though tied. They load them with women in the public roads. I am reminded by the Governor of the many royal *cédulas* forbidding Indians to ride, and that even your reverences cannot give them permission to own or use a horse, if Law 33 of Book vi, Title 1, of the *Recopilación* is observed. . . . In the Tulares (I am told by the Governor) both Christians and Gentiles make their journeys on horseback. Even the women are learning to ride. Fairs are held at which horses stolen from the missions are put up for sale.[29]

Neophytes, Payéras avowed, were losing respect for the padres. The Tulare *rancherías* of Telame (east of Tulare

Lake), some four thousand strong, were "a republic of hell and a diabolical union of apostates." If something were not done, the occupation of the missionaries in California would be at an end.[30] By Sola, therefore, the work of beating the Tulares was prosecuted as vigorously as it had been by Arrillaga.

But it was not alone among neophytes that respect for the padres was declining; it was declining among Mexicans themselves. As early as 1808, Viceroy Marino, reviving the idea (emphasized by Gálvez, by Caballero de Croix, by Neve, and by Fages) of reduction of the Indian to civil status, had informed the Guardian of San Fernando that neophytes must be instructed in the principles of social living; must be transformed from barbarians to men. Later (1810) there had come the Mexican revolt against Spain, with stoppage of missionary stipends and traveling expenses, and still later (1817) an impost on Mission goods levied by Sola despite hints of excommunication from the comisario-prefecto, Vicente Francisco de Sarría.[31] But it was the Spanish Constitution of 1812 that was most disturbing. By the principles of this instrument men everywhere were politically equal and entitled to a voice in the government. Accordingly, in 1813 (September 13) the Spanish Cortes had issued a decree requiring the immediate secularization of all missions of ten years' standing.[32]

It was believed, both in Spain and Mexico, that "reduction" in Alta California was impeded because of gain to the padres personally by the Mission system. Padre Concepción had pronounced the Alta California establishments richer than they would acknowledge; and though it had been disproved that they had riches at all, the charge had not been quieted.

Your Reverences [Guardian José Gasol wrote in warning to his California flock in 1806], the office that you exercise does not excuse you from the extreme poverty that we profess. Consequently, the use of silver watches and other valuable jewelry is prohibited. . . . I advise that those who have silver watches, or other jewelry of value for personal use, send them immediately to the Father-President, and he to the *síndico* of Tepic or of Guadalajara, so that, having been sold, the money may be used to aid the respective missions.[33]

And in 1817, Prefect Sarría wrote: —

You should realize that it is edifying for a missionary to appear in the greatest simplicity. *Así se tapa la boca al mundo* [so is the mouth of the world stopped], and so it [the world] is caused to understand that the interest we take in the things of the Mission is not personal, but that of Our Saviour Jesus Christ in the poverty-stricken, as are the neophytes. It sounded ill to me, as to others, to learn that carriages [*volantas*] had arrived (that is, if they are for us), and I wish that you would abstain absolutely from taking them. I might go into detail concerning fine hats, costly chests, etc., but enough.[34]

Discouraged by what was deemed recreancy to sacerdotal vows in Alta California, but more by lack there of padres to take the places of such as had retired or were become superannuated, the College of San Fernando, on December 19, 1816, formally petitioned Viceroy Apodaca to be permitted to cede to the recently founded College of San José de García of the Villa de Orizaba the nine establishments southward of and including La Purísima. The Guardian recalled the services of the Fernandinos against the Buenos Ayres privateers, and the desired permission was obtained, but it was not acted upon. The nine southern missions were the flower of the entire California sisterhood, and Payéras, who became prefect in 1819, opposed with success the cession of them to a new college with a name to win.[35]

Meanwhile, in California, the decree by the Spanish Cortes of 1813 was suffered to remain inoperative. On

May 20, 1814, Naval Lieutenant Pablo de Paula Tamariz submitted to the Viceroy a report characterizing the Alta California Mission as a sacerdotal monopoly; and, to consider this report, the King on July 5 ordered the assembling in Mexico City of a *junta* "composed of five or seven persons of prominence versed in business and familiar with the country." This body, which was known as the *Primera Junta de California*, and which met on July 5, 1817, advised the King to be circumspect, but he was to demand of the Alta California padres, "why, after forty years, the establishments in their charge had not been consigned to the ordinary ecclesiastical jurisdiction, according to the Laws of the Indies."[36] In 1820, on April 21, the decree of 1813 was confirmed by Ferdinand, and it was officially proclaimed in New Spain by Viceroy Benadito on January 20, 1821.

Spain and Mexico were urgent for Secularization, and in 1818 Payéras had written to the Bishop of Sonora that as president of the Alta California missions he was ready for the change. "We, Señor," he said, "do not seek our own welfare in this world, being men dead to it. We live herein only because of necessity. Our one desire is to obtain souls for Jesus Christ. The day these missions are lawfully declared civil communities, we shall welcome dismissal from charge of them to a new apostolic field."[37] And in 1821, on July 7, Payéras as prefect wrote thus to Sola: —

Through my Holy College of San Fernando I have just received a proclamation [from the Viceroy] in which the King, our master, reaffirms the decree of the General and Extraordinary Cortes issued in Cádiz, September 13, 1813 — a decree providing in Article 6 the following: "The missionary priests will retire immediately from the government and administration of the haciendas of the Indians. Upon the Indians it will devolve to arrange, by means of their *ayuntamientos* [town councils], with the aid of the *jefe superior político* [superior political officer], that there be named among them such as are the best fitted for administration, and by these the Indian lands will be reduced to private property and distributed. . . . We desire to carry out exactly the said royal order," etc.[38]

But while Payéras spoke thus to bishop and governor, it was far from his meaning that the Alta California neophyte was ripe for citizenship, or the Alta California missions for a pueblo status. Nor did he fear that citizenship or a pueblo status were things in fact impending. There were no curates with whom the Bishop of Sonora might replace the missionaries, and the latter could not be compelled to serve as curates against their will. On July 8, 1821, the day following his declaration of submission to the secularization decree, Payéras addressed to the padres a cordillera letter inclosing a confidential note, in cryptic phrase of Spanish and Latin, which the recipients were bidden either not to read or, having read, to keep secret. Indignation was expressed toward such in Mexico as had wrought evil for the missionaries. At the same time the padres were exhorted to keep everything in such order that, at the first summons of the leaders clerical and political, they in *vox sonora* could respond: "*Domine, ecce adsum*"; — all, of course, provided the Señor Bishop should be found to have *clérigos* (curates) with whom to replace the padres, — "*grande cosa*"![39]

Be it added that in December the Bishop of Sonora, Sinaloa, and the Californias "took satisfaction" in notifying the prefect that the decree of 1813 had not been enforced in America, and that Payéras and his colleagues in Alta California might therefore continue to develop their "pious and most Christian desires."[40]

Last of the governors of Alta California under Spain, Sola was the first of its governors under Mexico. In his

Hispanic character he belonged rather to the secularists —
Neve and Fages — than to the sacerdotalists — Borica
and Arrillaga. Under him, State Secular, which in 1779
could claim a white population of about 500 persons, and
in 1783 of not over 1000, could in 1820 claim 3270, of
whom about 700 were soldiers. He realized the need of
Spanish colonists, and urged strongly their introduction
to the number of one thousand. With him, as with Borica,
education was important, and he not only reëstablished
primary schools at the presidios and pueblos, but advocated for Monterey a school for neophyte boys, like the
Colegio de Indio in Mexico, and at each mission a girls'
school where Indian girls might be placed at the age of
three for tuition in domestic work, and for the preservation
of their chastity. He interested himself in promoting
blanket-weaving and tanning, — industries which, with
blacksmithing, were nearly all that survived from the
Borica period. Mining, which Arrillaga had pronounced
delusive, "even though one went thirty, forty, or fifty
leagues inland," he thought possibly worth while in view
of the fact that "the greater part of the mountains gave
indications of various metals," and that "eight or nine
marcos of silver" had already been obtained.[41]

To Sola, as to Neve, the Mission in Alta California was
little else than an expensive failure. True it was that by
the founding of San Rafael, the number of establishments
had been advanced to twenty; that by baptisms the number of neophytes had been increased to 20,500 — a gain
since 1800 of 7000.; that livestock (cattle, horses, mules and
sheep) had reached the total of 349,882 head, — a gain of
162,882; and the agricultural products (wheat, barley,
corn, beans, and peas) a total of 113,625 bushels, — a gain
annually of 57,625. Yet, whereas at the end of 1800 the
death-rate had been 50 per cent of baptisms, in 1810 it had

been 72 per cent, and now it was 86 per cent. In 1810, President Payéras had declared that at Purísima nearly all Indian mothers gave birth to dead infants; and in 1815 it had been reported that throughout the province the proportion of deaths to births had for many years been as three to two.[42] Sola pronounced the Indian "lazy, indolent, and disregardful of all authority, costing for half a century millions of *pesos*, without having made in that time any recompense to the body politic." "Settling at the missions," said the Governor, "the Indians become spoiled. Instructed in agriculture and other branches, they are able but half to cover their bodies."[43]

But Spanish rule for California was at an end. In February, 1821, Agustín de Iturbide, a dashing royalist cavalry officer (seduced from his allegiance) proclaimed independence for Mexico; and in August and September he received the submission of the Viceroy (Juan O'Donojú) and his capital.

CHAPTER XII

DOWN to 1821 Alta California had been a world-factor. Cortés groping toward Anian in 1535 had touched California at the nether verge. Searching for Anian in 1542 (but more especially for the Seven Cities that lined its course), Cabrillo and Ferrelo had fared from San Diego to Cape Mendocino. In 1602 Vizcaino, searching for Anian, but now (the age of fable waning) with intent of forestalling France and England, and of providing a station for galleons, had taken possession of the Puerto de Monterey. And in 1769, after a quest long and fruitless for Rica de Oro and Rica de Plata, José de Gálvez, under a discerning policy at Madrid, had availed himself of the instrumentality of the Mission to dot the coast of the Pacific from San Diego to San Francisco with establishments, centres of propaganda for Spanish fealty and the Catholic faith.

But if down to 1821 Alta California had been a world-factor, what of change was wrought by the Revolution?

There are two forces to the appeal of which the man of Latin extraction may be expected to respond, — Tradition and Personality. When, therefore, as in the case of the separation of Mexico from Spain, Tradition is broken (Tradition as ample as ancient) and there arises no figure strong enough to replace it by Personality, that which ensues is that which since the Independencia has ensued in Latin America everywhere — derangement and vertigo. This it was that from 1821 to 1846 ensued in Alta California. This of change it was that the Revolution wrought.

The Mexican governors of Alta California were eleven: Pablo Vicente de Sola (holding over), Luis Antonio Argüello, José María de Echeandía, Manuel Victoria, Pío Pico (twice), José Figueroa, José Castro, Mariano Chico, Nicolás Gutiérrez (twice), Juan Bautista Alvarado, and Manuel Micheltorena. These men, by birth, training, and the conditions locally of the time, failed of equality with their predecessors the Spanish governors, and this despite the circumstance that the prestige and dignity of the latter were kept from becoming in any wise Homeric by incidents such as the quarrel between Rivera y Moncada and Anza, the domestic embroilment of Fages, and the operations against Bouchard.

From José María de Echeandía to Pío Pico in his second term (1825–45) there was no governorship, save Castro's, three months in duration, and the first of Gutiérrez's, four months, not beset by conspiracy and revolt. Against Echeandía the revolt was by the soldiers for lack of pay. Against Victoria, — a miniature Charles I seeking to rule without a parliament,—it was by the people. Against Pico it was double: by Echeandía and by Captain Agustín V. Zamorano, — each on his own account and each against the other. Against Figueroa it was by Los Ángeles. Against Chico it was by Monterey. Against Gutiérrez it was by Alvarado in opposition to military rule. Against Alvarado (himself a local Díaz) it was chronic and complex, to wit: by the South against the North; by the North (at Monterey) in favor of Mexican placemen; by the South in behalf of a "pretender" — Carlos Carrillo. Finally, against Micheltorena it was by the people over a Cholo soldiery; and against Pico (second occasion), it was by José Castro, a rival patriot.

On the capitulation of Viceroy O'Donojú in the summer of 1821, a *junta gubernativa* was assembled in Mexico. According to a plan promulgated by Iturbide in February at Iguala, New Spain was to be an empire, with Ferdinand VII of Old Spain, or one of his family, as emperor; but executive power might temporarily be lodged in a regency of five members, and soon a regency was installed with Iturbide as president.[1] José Manuel Herrera was made Secretary of Relations, and José Antonio de Andrade political and military governor of Guadalajara. As for the intendencias, they already had been resolved into five captaincies-general, one (Nueva Galicia) under Pedro Celestino Negrete, and another (the Provincias Internas de Oriente y Occidente, embracing the two Californias) under Anastasio de Bustamente.

But in naught of this had the Californias been consulted. What would be their attitude toward Mexican independence? The people (soldiers and colonists) would, it was assumed, be favorable; the padres as stanch Spaniards would, it was known, be unfavorable; while as for the Governor, Pablo Vicente de Sola, all was conjecture. The matter for Mexico was one of disquietude and anxious interest. As early as October, 1821, Andrade informed Iturbide that "to demarcate, organize, and consolidate the *nuevo imperio* would be a task arduous and difficult." He had noted with apprehension the danger that menaced "our new possessions of Alta California." The military force there was weak and for eleven years had gone unsuccored, and this despite the fact that the Russians had established themselves at Bodega, and that trading-stations on the Pacific were coveted by the North Americans.[2] Andrade thought that, pursuant to an understanding of the period of the Buenos Ayres privateers, there was grave chance that Spain, impotent otherwise against Mexico, would cede the Californias to Russia.[3]

In January, 1822, the San Blas comandante addressed to

General Negrete the query, whether it were not the part of wisdom to send north in the San Carlos a force of 150 men.[4] The views of the comandante were approved, and on February 8, Iturbide, in the name of the Regency, gave orders that a division of troops be sent to the Californias, "to occupy the country, administer the oath of independence, raise the flag of the empire, depose Sola, and disavow any treaties made by him with the Russians." But Iturbide had failed to count the cost, and having been advised by Negrete that instead of an armed force an agent with dispatches might be sufficient, the suggestion was adopted, and Negrete was asked to name for the undertaking some one á propósito.

Choice fell upon a canon of the Cathedral of Durango, a man jovial, bibulous, and addicted to cards, — Agustín Fernández de San Vicente. His appointment bore date April 10, 1822, and his instructions — drawn with the approval of the four secretaries of state, the captains-general of Nueva Galicia and the Provincias Internas, the padre provincial of the Dominicans, and the guardian of the College of San Fernando — were as follows: He was to go to Loreto with dispatches for the governor of the peninsula (José Argüello) and with pastoral letters for the padres, and not depart until fully informed as to the trend of opinion regarding Mexican independence. At Monterey (whither he was to go next) he was to do as he had done at Loreto. At both Loreto and Monterey he was to inquire concerning the prosperity or decadence of the Californias, and with regard to peril from the Russian and American establishments. He was to ascertain in particular whether Americans had descended the Columbia River and "located themselves on the borders of San Francisco," and whether the Russian force at Bodega was of respectable size. As for the United States, it was to be borne in mind that by treaty her limits were to transcend 42 degrees.[6] On April 2 the above instructions were enlarged. San Vicente was authorized to name, for Baja and Alta California respectively, an acting governor; care being exercised to select an individual well disposed to "our system of independence," and beloved and esteemed by the inhabitants of his province.[7]

With copies of twenty-five government decrees in his pocket, the genial San Vicente prepared to set sail. On May 19, however, Iturbide, by action of the soldiery and rabble, was himself raised to the position of Emperor of Mexico. His agent, therefore, when on June 12 he embarked for the Californias, did so under orders of June 9 (issued to Naval Lieutenant José María Narváez) to make known everywhere the accession to the Mexican throne of his imperial majesty Don Agustín I.[8]

Meanwhile, in March, Sola, advised of the installation of the regency, had convened in council the *comisario-prefecto*, the president of missions, the comandantes of the presidios, and the captains of the Mazatlán and San Blas companies, by whom on April 11 allegiance was sworn to the Mexican Empire.[9] Alta California, moreover, being one of the Provincias Internas, and as such entitled to representation in the Cortes of the Empire, it was decided on April 12 to hold, under the forms of the Spanish Constitution of 1812, an election for *diputado* (delegate).

The province, so Sola directed, was to be divided into five *partidos*, — the first to consist of the presidial district of San Francisco, together with the pueblo San José and the *villa* Branciforte; the second, of the presidial district of Monterey; the third, of that of Santa Bárbara; the fourth, of the pueblo of Los Ángeles and the missions of San Gabriel and San Juan Capistrano; and the fifth, of the presidial district of San Diego. By each mission and pueblo and by the *villa* Branciforte there was to be chosen an elector *de partido*, the mission electors to consist of the neophyte *alcaldes* and *regidores*. Men favorable to the Independencia alone were to be accepted as candidates, and priests and soldiers were excluded from candidacy by their cloth. On a day to be fixed by the *jefes de partido*, the electors *de partido* were to meet at the respective *partido* capitals and cast their votes for electors *de provincia* (provincial electors); and by the latter (convened at Monterey) the *diputado* was to be chosen. Sola proved to be the individual upon whom the honor fell, and on May 21, his election was duly certified by José M. Estudillo, secretary of the Council of State.[10]

San Vicente reached Monterey on September 26. He came from Loreto, where, in the absence of the regular comandante, José María Ruiz, he on June 27 had replaced Governor José Argüello (who voluntarily had resigned) by Fernando de la Torba, and where on July 9 news had been received of the acceptance of Mexican independence in Alta California.

The impact of republican ideas had been too widely and sensibly felt for San Vicente to be other than a discreet envoy. At Monterey he substituted the eagle of the Mexican Empire for the lion of Castile, and he proclaimed with ardor Iturbide as Agustín I; but otherwise imperially he did little. In November he saw to it that the Council of State named as *jefe político* (civil governor) the comandante at San Francisco, Luis Argüello. Under the old régime, the position would have gone to the senior comandante, José de la Guerra of Santa Bárbara; but that it did not go to him now was one proof more that the old régime had passed. Argüello, unlike Guerra, was not a Spaniard. Liberalism with him, moreover, was an incident of birth. His sister Doña Concepción had been affianced to Rezánoff, and his father, Don José, had connived at Russian trade.

But San Vicente did more than select a governor. He established, under the Spanish Constitution of 1812, — an instrument recognized in the plan of Iguala, — a *diputación* or legislative body of six *vocales* (members) and a president, — one *vocal* for each presidio and pueblo district. He withdrew, by abolition of the office of *comisionado*, control by the governor over *alcaldes* and *ayuntamientos* in the pueblos of Los Ángeles and San José. Lastly he relaxed the bonds of neophytes. They were declared possessed of citizenship, and, where capable, might live apart from a mission, subject to the judge of the vicinage. Stocks, fetters, and imprisonment were permitted as formerly,[11] but lashes on the bare back were forbidden. Under Luis Argüello, inhibition of commerce straightway ceased. A contract (January 1, 1823) was put in effect whereby the English house of McCulloch, Hartnell & Company was to take for a term of three years, at a stipulated price, all the hides and tallow of the province;[12] and on December 1 an agreement was made with the Russian-American Company for the hunting of otter on shares.[13]

So very widely and sensibly, however, had the impact of republican ideas been felt, that the imperial name and trappings even were become distasteful. In Mexico on April 8, 1823, a National Congress was assembled and Iturbide was proclaimed an exile. Federalism *versus* Centralism now was the dominant thought, and on November 19, 1823, and January 31, 1824, there were passed in Mexico provisional acts which, on October 4 of the same year, were followed by the adoption of a federal instrument based on the Constitution of the United States and designed to be permanent.[14] The National Congress had been recognized by Argüello's government in November, 1823, and, pending the arrival from Mexico of news of some plan of federation including Alta California, a local plan of government had been adopted on January 17, 1824.[15] In 1825 (March) the news awaited from Mexico was received, and in May the federal instrument—whereby Alta and Baja California were created territories entitled severally or jointly to a governor, and severally to a legislature and delegate [16]—was ratified at the presidios and pueblos. This instrument, on August 18, 1824, and April 14, 1828, was supplemented by decrees favorable to colonization and naturalization,[17] and as thus supplemented remained to 1836 the most significant expression of the spirit of the Mexican people as newly enfranchised.

Argüello's rule—the succession having been declined by General Juan José Miñón—was terminated by the arrival at San Diego in October, 1825, of Colonel José María Echeandía, a man of scholastic bent and training and of Castilian lisp.

Under Echeandía complications arose from two causes: the appointment by the Mexican Government of José María Herrera as *comisario* or financial agent in the Californias, subordinate to a *comisario-general* of the West at Arizpe; and the arrival at Monterey along with Herrera in July, 1825, of a company of eighteen Mexican convicts. Herrera as *comisario* was independent of Echeandía as governor. In 1825 he renewed for five years the contract with the Russians for hunting otter from Cape San Lucas to the port of San Francisco; and in 1827 he addressed to the *comisario-general* a sweeping indictment of the Spanish padres, of José de la Guerra, and finally of Echeandía himself. His suspension from office was soon effected by the Governor on the charge of peculation.[18] As for the convicts, they by nature were intractable. When therefore in 1829 a revolt of the troops (induced by destitution) occurred, it was opportunity for Herrera and for the convicts alike. The latter, through one of their number, Joaquín Solís, took the initiative, but the ending was farcical, for the rebels, after running from the foe on every field, — Santa Bárbara, Cieneguita, and Dos Pueblos, — were all graciously pardoned except the leaders. These (Herrera and Solís among them) were sent to Mexico, where they too, Solís no less than Herrera, were promptly set at liberty.[19]

Noteworthy, also, under Echeandía, were the occurrences following: The surrender to Argüello at Monterey in May, 1825, of the Spanish warships Asia and Constante; the visit the same month to Santa Bárbara of the revolted Spanish warship Aquiles; the completion in December, 1825, or January, 1826, by Captain José Romero, of a trip from Tuçón to San Diego and back over the Anza route; the visit to San Francisco and Monterey, in 1826 and 1827, of the English ship Blossom, under Captain Frederick William Beechey;[20] the convening at Monterey in 1827 of the first territorial *diputación* of six *vocales* under the Federal Constitution — a *diputación* which voted ineffectually to change the name of California to Montezuma;[21] the visit in 1827 and 1828 of the French ship Le Héros under Auguste Duhaut-Cilly;[22] the arrival from Mexico, in 1828 and 1829, of copies of laws ordering the expulsion of Spaniards from Mexican territory; the receipt in 1827 and 1829 of orders to establish a fort and military colony on " Carmelite " (Richardson's) Bay against the Russians; and the arrival in 1830, despite protests, of 130 Mexican convicts.

The journey of Romero coastward from Tuçón, and the orders from Mexico to establish a fort and military colony on Carmelite Bay, bespeak attention.

In October, 1822, San Vicente, accompanied by Payéras, had made a visit to Ross, and, impressed with the need of an overland route from Sonora, had directed that the course of Anza be reopened.[23] On June 8, 1823, Captain Romero, with ten men and Padre Félix Caballero (a Dominican of the peninsula), set forth down the Gila from Tuçón, reaching the Colorado on the 29th. The Cajuenches, whom Anza had used as guides, conducted the party to the mouth of the stream. Here rafts were constructed, and the men with their arms, baggage, and clothing were embarked under the guidance of the Indians. But mid-stream the wily natives deftly overturned the rafts, and Romero, Padre Félix, and the ten men with their effects were thrown into the water. "We extricated ourselves," Romero wrote to Governor Narbona of Sonora, on July 6, "with a thousand labors, and on foot, without accoutrements, clothing, or shoes, have managed to reach Santa Catalina Mártir."

From Santa Catalina, Romero with his escort proceeded to San Diego, to seek from Portilla, stationed there with the Mazatlán Company, help against the Cajuenches; but, wrote the comandante at Loreto, such a move is to be deprecated as "we seem to be menaced by the Russians on the north." The result was that in December, 1825, Romero, under orders from José Figueroa, and escorted by Lieutenant Romualdo Pacheco, reached the Colorado without having been able to reopen the route of Anza, and that from the river in question he made his way back to Tuçón.[24]

In regard to the fort and military colony against the Russians, nothing was done by Echeandía, although his orders were explicit.

The Mexican Government [he was assured] could not view with indifference the way in which the Russians, having possessed themselves of the port of Bodega, were encroaching by way of the interior upon San Francisco, manifesting an intention to appropriate the Río de San Juan Bautista, alias del Sacramento, and to plant themselves at the point called on the old maps La Junta de Evengelistas. . . . Wherefore he was to select two or three men to choose a site for a fort to command the principal river emptying into the Puerto de Sanfrancisco. This fort he was to construct without loss of an instant, and, near it, gather a population for a military colony, — not less than five hundred persons. For four years military discipline was to be maintained there; the President of the Republic during that interval suspending elections, as, by his extraordinary powers under the Constitution, he might lawfully do. The settlement was to be protected by a moat and counter-moat, and the *entradas* with drawbridge and other works.[25]

But the most important occurrence under Echeandía was in the domain sacerdotal, namely, the formulation in 1828 of a plan of Secularization for the missions, and the publication on January 6, 1831, of a *bando* for putting the plan into effect.

The Spanish Government had long made it plain that instruction of the Indians in civil polity, with a view to a conversion of the missions into pueblos, was of the first importance. For Mexico, therefore, the question of the maintenance of the Mission arose at once; and, with the adoption in 1823 of a Mexican law forecasting Federalism, it became insistent. Said Lucas Alamán, Mexican Secretary of Relations, in a report to Congress, dated November 8, 1823: —

It is necessary to consider other interests than those of the missionaries in the vast and fertile peninsula of Californias. . . . If the Mission system is that best suited to draw savages from barbarism, it can do no more than establish the first principles of society; it cannot lead men to their highest perfection. Nothing is better to accomplish this than to bind individuals to society by the powerful bond of property. The government believes that the distribution of lands to the converted Indians, lending them from the Mission fund the means for cultivation, and the establishment of foreign colonies, which perhaps might be Asiatic, would give a great impulse to that important province.[26]

But in this connection, what of the report of Tamariz, upon which in 1817 Viceroy Apodaca had convened a *Junta de California*? This report the Mexican Government now set itself to examine. "I wish," wrote General Juan José Minión to the Secretary of War and Marine, "to inform myself regarding an *expediente* in the office of the Secretary of Relations that treats of a reform in the government of the peninsula of California, and that contains a memorial by Comisario-General Don Francisco de Paula Tamariz," etc. The request was followed by the creation in 1824 or 1825 of a California promotion committee (*Junta de Fomento de Californias*) of which Tamariz himself was a member and leading spirit. To the first President of the Mexican Republic, Guadalupe Victoria, the *Junta de Fomento* said: —

The *junta* is not ignorant that from the Spanish system of discoveries and spiritual conquests has resulted all the progress made in the Jesuit missions of Old California and in those founded later in New California by the Fernandinos. . . . Still, the *junta* has not been able to reconcile the principles of such a system with those of our independence and political constitution, nor with the true spirit of the Gospel. Religion under that system could not advance beyond domination. It could be promoted only under the protection of guards and presidios. The gentiles must renounce all the rights of their natural independence to be catechumens from the moment of baptism; they must be subject to laws almost monastic, while their teachers deemed themselves freed from the laws which forbade their engaging in temporal business; and the neophytes must continue this without hope of ever possessing fully the civil rights of society. . . . The present condition of the missions does not correspond to the great progress which they made in the beginning.[27]

Such were the views of republican Mexico. In Alta California, however, there was an element — the Spanish friars — which, because of the dependent condition of the Indian, was not favorable to Secularization; and which, because of the pleas for Secularization above set forth, was not favorable to the Republic. In 1823, on April 28 and August 24, respectively, Prefect Payéras and ex-President Señán, both men of poise, had died; and Señán had been succeeded as prefect and president by Vicente Sarría, a prelate of energetic qualities. But in April, 1825, Sarría resigned the presidency of missions to Narciso Durán, from whom in 1827 it was transferred to José Sánchez, who held it, contemporaneously with Sarría's prefecture, to the advent of Governor Victoria. It accordingly was with Payéras, Señán, Sarría, Durán, and Sánchez that Echeandía, in the matter of Secularization, was called upon to deal.

The political phase presented itself first.

Since 1810, the year of the Mexican revolt, the padres in Alta California had submitted to exactions for the support of the state, — exactions which though inevitable were contrary to precedent. These exactions, so long as the Spanish royalist régime lasted, had been so made as not to compromise the dignity of the priestly office; but now that the Mexican or republican régime prevailed, the dignity of the priestly office was well-nigh sacrificed. The state was poor, — poorer than ever, — and to support it the padres were not only compelled to pay the usual trade duties and forced loans, but a secular tithe besides; and when they complained that the pueblos paid nothing, they were charged with insolence and presumption.

One day Padre José Barona of San Juan Capistrano, on setting out for San Diego, was assailed by the mission guard and so treated that his horse was caused to throw him, — an affront characterized by Padre Gerónimo Boscana as "the most scandalous ever perpetrated in California."[28] Nor was the situation without effect upon the neophyte. Indian labor at the presidios was no longer recompensed by bountiful *memorias* from San Blas. The soldiers in consequence were disliked, and on February 21, 1824, a revolt of neophytes broke forth at Santa Inés. Spreading rapidly to Purísima and Santa Bárbara, it resulted in the death of several white men and a number of Indians, and, after an expedition to the Tulares, was only quieted by a general pardon secured from Argüello by Padre Antonio Ripoll.[29]

But where the Mexican Republic came most sorely in conflict with the Spanish element — the padres — was with regard to an oath of allegiance. In 1822, Payéras, Señán, and Sarría had sworn to the Independencia, under promise by the Regency to summon to the throne of Mexico Ferdinand VII, or one of his brothers. Nor when the summons failed had any difficulty been made by Payéras over words of fealty to Iturbide as Agustín I. Orders to swear to the Federal Constitution of October 4, 1824, however, were for the most part disregarded. Early in 1825, Sarría and Durán each refused to take the oath, and in October Sarría, by command of the Mexican Government, was put under constructive arrest preparatory to being sent to Mexico, — a step never carried out.[30]

At one time or another in Alta California there were Franciscans — Serra, Lasuén, Tapis, Payéras, Señán — conspicuous for virtue and capacity; but there were others more conspicuous still for idiosyncrasy. Of the latter (stirred by the question of allegiance to the Republic) were Antonio Ripoll of Santa Bárbara and Luis Martínez of San Luis Obispo. In 1818, during the invasion of Bouchard, padres of the type of Payéras and Señán had yielded to excitement, the former (Patrick Henry-like) exclaiming: "*Viva Dios, viva la religión, viva el Rey, viva la patria, y ó vencer ó morir en tan preciosa defensa!*" Not surprising, therefore, is it that Ripoll and Martínez had donned garb of war and proffered advice in tactics. But ardor once roused was not easily repressed. Ripoll, rather than swear allegiance, took with him José Altimíra (founder of San Francisco Solano), stole on board an American brig, the Harbinger, lying at Santa Bárbara, and sailed for Spain.

As for Martínez, his fate was exile. Having exhibited sympathy for the rebel cause in the Solís-Herrera revolt of 1829, he was arrested in February, 1830, by order of Echeandía, tried by court martial, found guilty of conspiracy, and on March 20 sent to Spain by the English ship Thomas Nowlan.[31] Short in stature, swarthy of countenance, knowing in trade, generous of larder, fancier of cattle, horses, and mules, prone to vanity in respect of bebraceleted and beribboned neophyte attendants, yet in naught a scandal to St. Francis, — it is with reluctance, Padre Martínez, that thou art dismissed from our pages to Briebes in Asturias, thy native town.[32]

In 1829 the number of padres in Alta California who remained incorrigible was fourteen. Among those who had taken the oath the one most compliant, and hence highest in favor in Mexico and with Echeandía, was Antonio Peyri. With him, together with three others of the compliant, the Governor in 1826 took counsel and matured a plan of emancipation for deserving neophytes. All not minors, nor likely to become a public charge, might, by consent of their presidial comandante, have the liberty of *gente de razón.* Corporal punishment, moreover, might be exercised only upon males who were minors and unmarried, and was to be limited to fifteen lashes a week.[33]

Emancipation, it is needless to say, was but preliminary to Secularization. In the summer of 1830, a secularization plan was submitted by Echeandía to the territorial *diputación*, and after slight amendment was approved. The various missions one by one (beginning with those nearest the four presidios, two pueblos and one *villa*) were to be converted into pueblos. Each pueblo was to consist of the neophytes who had belonged to it as a mission, and of such Mexicans as it might attract. Land to the extent of a house-lot (*solar*) and a field (*suerte*) was to be assigned to each family (neophyte or immigrant) in severalty, and land to the extent of one square league for each 500 head of livestock was to be assigned in common. The livestock of each family was to be made up by an allotment in severalty of sheep, swine, cows, bulls, horses and stallions from the flocks and herds of the former mission; but of the land assigned in severalty none was to be sold within five years, nor was it to be mortgaged by a holder or by his heirs. The former missionaries might remain as curates of the newly formed pueblos, or they might form mission establishments in the Tulares. For the use of the curates the mission church with its appurtenances was to be assigned, but the rest of the mission buildings were to be converted into prisons, barracks, school-houses, hospitals, and quarters for the *ayuntamientos*, — the whole scheme of public improvement to be supported by the income from mission property not otherwise employed.[34]

Secularization for the missions of Alta California was also forecast by the virtual dissolution of the Franciscan College of San Fernando. This ancient institution — mother of Alta California missionaries, and so in an important sense mother of Alta California itself — was described in 1824 by José Gasol, the guardian, as on the verge of extinction; and in 1828 it had passed into the hands of a *vicario de casa,* under whom the inmates were three padres, two invalid Spaniards, and a few servants.

Meanwhile, as for Echeandía's plan, it was thwarted by a change of political equilibrium in Mexico. The first president, Guadalupe Victoria, had been succeeded in 1829 by Vicente Guerrero. Both Victoria and Guerrero were representatives of Liberalism, as opposed to Conservatism in the guise of Centralism; but Conservatism had for some time been gaining, and in 1830, under Anastasio Bustamente, it triumphed. The result for Alta California was that on March 8, 1830, Echeandía was supplanted by Lieutenant-Colonel Manuel Victoria, half Indian, friend of the padres (especially of Sarría whom he openly praised), and foe to Secularization. To take office, Victoria was compelled to proceed first to Santa Bárbara and then to Monterey, reaching the capital on January 29, 1831. But on January 6, a decree of Secularization (instigated, it was thought, by José María Padrés, newly come from Loreto as adjutant-inspector) was issued, to take immediate effect.[35] The response of Victoria to this *coup* was a sharp order interdicting all action; and interdicted Secularization accordingly remained throughout Victoria's term. In yet another way, during 1831, was Secularization given pause. Alta California's *diputado* in the Mexican Congress, Carlos Carrillo, secured by the old arguments in favor of the maintenance of the Mission the rejection of a plan for confiscating the estates of the Pious Fund.

The rule of Victoria was destined to be brief. Acquainted only with military methods, and arbitrary by nature, his course begat opposition on every hand. He refused to convene the *diputación,* or legislative body, because of its known bias toward Liberalism, including Secularization; and his administration of justice, though marked by the un-Mexican virtue of promptitude, was startling in its employment of the penalties of death and exile. Victims of the latter penalty were José Antonio Carrillo, Abel Stearns (from Massachusetts), and J. M. Padrés, the republican adjutant.[36] The inevitable revolt, heralded by manifesto on November 29, was directed politically by Echeandía, Pío Pico, senior *vocal* of the *diputación*, Juan Bandini, alternate delegate to Congress, José Carrillo, and Abel Stearns; while Pablo de Portilla, comandante at San Diego, was induced to lead in the field.[37]

Warned of trouble, Victoria started south almost alone; but finding at Santa Bárbara a squad under Captain Romualdo Pacheco, he put himself at their head, and with, in all, about thirty men advanced toward Los Ángeles. Between the pueblo and the mission of San Fernando, he, on December 5, came upon Portilla with about 150 men posted on an acclivity. A short parley ensued, at the end of which Pacheco, incensed at a gibe by the Governor at his valor, charged toward the enemy. The latter promptly fled — all save a party headed by José María Ávila, ex-*alcalde* of Los Ángeles, who in turn charged upon Pacheco. Like two jousting knights, though with deadlier intent, Pacheco and Ávila were carried past each other in the lists, delivering cut and thrust with sword and lance. Turning in his saddle, Ávila drew a pistol, shot Pacheco through the heart, and rushed upon Victoria. A *mêlée* ensued, and the Governor was hurled from his horse by a thrust of Ávila's lance. As for Ávila, he was seized by the fallen Victoria, who unhorsed him and transfixed him with his sword.[38]

Between men of Spanish extraction in Alta California, actual warfare had taken place for the first time; — fighting in which red blood had been shed. The field was circumscribed and the combatants were few, but the *gaudium certaminis*, the joy of battle, had been there, and the ridiculous fiascos — the *opéra bouffe* sallies — of other years were atoned for. Honors too had not been unequal, for if Ávila had fallen on the side of Portilla and civil rule, Pacheco had fallen on the side of Victoria and militarism. The wounded governor was carried to San Gabriel Mission, where, under the hands of Dr. Charles Anderson, he gained strength, but only to yield himself to Echeandía with a request to be sent to Mexico, a destination whither on January 17, 1832, he was dispatched in the American ship Pocahontas.[39]

Secularization in Alta California was destined to come ere long. The fact was made evident in connection with the founding in 1832, under Argüello, of the twenty-first and last California establishment — the mission of San Francisco Solano. At a conference in 1822 between San Vicente (the *canónigo*), Argüello and Payéras, it had been decided to transfer the mission of San Francisco, with its erstwhile *asistencia* San Rafael, to the Gentile country north of San Pablo Bay. Argüello having secured from the *diputación*, through José Altimíra, padre at San Francisco, approval for the transfer, submitted the matter to the authorities in Mexico, and sent a party to choose a mission site. Sonoma was selected, and dedicatory ceremonies were held in 1823 on July 4. But neither Señán nor Sarría could be induced to sanction the suppression of San Rafael. To the prelate alone, they contended, and in no sense to the *diputación*, pertained the right "to recommend the founding, suppressing, or moving of establishments." Argüello's reply — a reply itself declaratory of Secularization — was that, State Sacerdotal having in fifty years failed to do aught in the north for the Gen-

tiles, the task now would be undertaken by State Secular.
A compromise was effected. Neither San Francisco nor
San Rafael was suppressed, but San Francisco Solano,
with Altimíra in charge, was given existence as an independent mission.[40]

CHAPTER XIII

FEDERALISM AND CENTRALISM

I

Figueroa

THE manifesto against Governor Victoria — drafted by Juan Bandini and known as the Plan of San Diego — sought two objects: (1) The removal of the Governor, and (2) the separation of the political and military commands.[1]

By a Mexican law of May 6, 1822, it was provided that in case of the death, absence, or disability of a *jefe político*, the position should be assumed by the senior *vocal* of the *diputación*. Accordingly, on January 11, 1832, Pío Pico, as senior *vocal*, was chosen by the *diputación*, *jefe político* for Alta California, and Echeandía was so notified. But the ex-Governor, after some wavering, refused to recognize Pico, preferring to keep in his own hands what of political power had been placed there by the Revolution.

On January 24, the comandante at Monterey, Agustín V. Zamorano, began a movement against both Pico and Echeandía, — a movement culminating, on February 1, in a manifesto at the hands of a *junta*, prominent in which was William E. P. Hartnell of McCulloch, Hartnell & Company, against the Plan of San Diego as the work of plotters and rebels.[2] Echeandía's course on Secularization had won for him the friendship of the neophytes, and in March and April they in great force mustered to his aid near San Gabriel. Zamorano thereupon consented to a conference, and on May 9 it was agreed between the rival comandantes that, pending the appointment of a governor by Mexico, Alta California should remain divided into two parts, — one from San Gabriel southward under Echeandía; the other from San Fernando northward under Zamorano. The district between these points (that of the pueblo of Los Ángeles) was left in a condition of guaranteed neutrality. Echeandía was to advance no armed force to the northward of San Juan Capistrano, and Zamorano none to the southward of San Buenaventura. As in other Alta California revolutionary movements, so in this, no blood was shed, but zest was imparted by the sending of a band of convicts south from Monterey against Echeandía — a band that, soon dispersing, excited terror until captured.

A strong hand was needed, and it was possessed by Brigadier-General José Figueroa. The Californias were not unknown to Figueroa, for in 1824, he, as comandante in Sonora, had been sent to the Colorado to meet the Mazatlán Company, then (supposedly) on the way home from San Diego under Romero.[3] The General was of Aztec blood, hence swarthy in color; and besides being a man of courage, was of popular address. Made *jefe político* on May 9, 1832, he set sail from San Blas on July 7, in the brig Catalina, with a force of seventy-two Cholos of the Acapulco convict class, and reached Cape San Lucas on the 30th. Here, on a return trip of the brig, he was joined by ten Zacatecan friars and by Lieutenant Nicolás Gutiérrez, bearer of 20,000 *pesos* in coin. But the Cholos, tempted beyond endurance by the money, mutinied and put back to San Blas. It was not until December 17 that Figueroa, with some thirty soldiers and his band of friars, was able to quit the peninsula for Monterey, where he arrived on January 14, 1833.[4]

The duties of the new Governor, as signified in his instructions, were the fortification and colonization of Alta California northward toward the Russians; precautionary measures against Anglo-Americans; and a cautious Mission policy.[5] Between April, 1833, and January, 1834, Lieutenant Mariano Guadalupe Vallejo, with a few settlers, and a few neophytes from the mission of San Francisco Solano, occupied the sites Petaluma and Santa Rosa;[6] but attention was diverted by news of the approach from Mexico of a large colony — 204 individuals led by José María Padrés and José María Híjar. The object of the colony was to realize the instructions, given to Echeandía in 1828, to plant on Carmelite Bay a strong barrier against the Russians. But under the changes in Mexico there was involved with this object much that was personal.

Bandini had prayed that in Alta California the political and military commands might be separated, and to this end, in the spring of 1833, two sets of occurrences took place in remarkable conjunction: (1) Padrés became friends with Bandini (now California congressman), and with Gómez Farías, Vice-President under Bustamente's successor, Antonio López de Santa Anna. (2) Figueroa, because of ill health, resigned; Padrés on July 12 was dispatched to Alta California to assume the *comandancia*; and on July 15 Híjar was created *jefe político*.[7]

Already two organizations had been effected: a colonization company, of which Híjar was made director on July 16, and a mercantile company (*compañía cosmopolitana*), of which Bandini was chosen vice-president. Withal, on November 26, by a decree of the Mexican Congress, the governmental side of the Padrés-Bandini-Híjar combination was empowered "to adopt all measures to insure the colonization and make effective the secularization of the missions of Alta and Baja California, . . . using for that purpose in the most convenient manner the estates

of the Pious Fund of these territories, in order to furnish
resources to the commission and families now in this capital and intending to go there." [8] And on April 23, 1834,
Híjar, as *jefe político* and director of colonization, was
instructed to take possession of all the property belonging
to the missions of both Californias. [9]

It was early in 1834 that Figueroa heard of the coming
of Híjar and Padrés. Nor was he pleased. The separation
of the commands was to his distaste as a move by Californians toward "home rule"; [10] and on July 18, he wrote
to Mexico that his health, upon the precariousness of
which his resignation had been predicated, was improved.
This news, adverse to the interests of the combination,
was soon followed by other news. Santa Anna, who, with
a view to studying the probable next leap of that lithe
lion the Mexican populace, had withheld himself from the
presidential seat, now, perceiving that Federalism under
Farías was verging on Radicalism, assumed office on
July 25. A first step was to dispatch across the desert to
Figueroa orders to continue administering the *jefatura*.
When, therefore, the colony, half under Padrés, and half
under Híjar and Bandini, reached Monterey, — the Padrés division by sea on September 25, and the Híjar-Ban-
dini division overland from San Diego on October 14, —
they were met by the Governor with the instructions from
Santa Anna.

Colonization for Alta California (occupation by substantial settlers — farmers, tailors, carpenters, shoemakers,
blacksmiths, saddlers, and teachers — such as the Híjar
colony contained) was a thing the need of which had
been proclaimed from the days of Neve to those of Sola.
Accordingly in the winter of 1835 the colonists for the
most part were gathered under an *alcalde* at and near San
Francisco Solano (Sonoma), the point where settlers were

required as against the Russians. Híjar himself was permitted by the *diputación* to retain of his varied titles that only of director of colonization; while as for Padrés, he was forced to choose between his military office of adjutant-inspector and the civil office (which was his) of sub-director of colonization under Híjar, — a dilemma which he resolved in favor of the civil post.[11]

But Padrés, Híjar, and their associates were not to be shaken off so easily. The Solís revolt against Echeandía, although perhaps not instigated by José María Herrera, was an opportune occurrence for him. In March, 1835, a revolt at Los Ángeles came opportunely for Padrés and Híjar. In 1834, Santa Anna, who for a year had been dallying with the Centralists, had convoked a new Congress. The elections had gone for the Centralists (the clergy and army) overwhelmingly, and the Los Ángeles movement was probably little other than a reflection of Mexican conditions. Be that as it may, the promoters of the revolt were two men — Antonio Apalátegui, a Spaniard from Sonora, and Francisco Torres, a Híjar colonist. A *pronunciamiento* was issued by Apalátegui, declaring it to be the purpose of the rebellionists to restore to the very reverend missionary fathers exclusive charge of temporalties, and to separate the military and political commands, — a separation which was not to affect Híjar in his position as director of colonization. The *pronunciamiento* contained a sop to Herrera in the declaration that Figueroa (like Echeandía) "disposed of the soldiers' pay at his own will, without knowledge of the chief of revenue." [12]

For the conspirators, however, Figueroa was prepared. Híjar and Padrés were in arrest, by March 26; and by May 8, they had been joined at San Pedro by Apalátegui and Torres, — all bound as exiles for San Blas.[13]

The overthrow of Governor Victoria had given Echeandía opportunity to proceed so far with Secularization as
to appoint *comisionados*, or receivers, at certain southern
missions, — missions beyond Zamorano's jurisdiction,
namely, San Luis Rey, San Juan Capistrano, San Gabriel,
and San Diego.[14] The government's instructions to Figueroa counseled caution, but were yet sufficiently radical.
Article 4 recommended a distribution of lands to deserving
neophytes, in order that "the influence of the missionaries [might] be lessened until only the spiritual administration was retained by them." Furthermore, it was
decreed on August 17: (1) That Secularization in Alta
California should take place at once; (2) that the secularized missions should be made each a parish under a
secular priest; and (3) that the cost of the change should
be met by the income of the Pious Fund.

The task of Secularization was assumed by Figueroa
under rules issued on July 15, 1833, called *Prevenciones
de Emancipación;* rules not differing materially from the
Plan of Echeandía. *Comisionados*, aided by the padres,
were to gather into pueblos along the *camino real*
(king's highway) such Indians as had been Christianized for more than twelve years; such as were married or
were widowers with children; and such as knew how to cultivate the soil or ply a trade and were "addicted" to work.
The pueblos, for the present, were to be attached to the
nearest municipality or presidio, but were to be initiated
in self-government through officers appointed annually
from among themselves. For the support of churches,
schools, etc., landed estates (*propios y arbitrios*) were to be
formed. Finally, neophytes who should prove neglectful of their new opportunities were to be returned to the
establishment of which they formerly had been inmates.[15]

Of the success of the *Prevenciones*, we know chiefly

that in 1833 San Juan Capistrano was converted into a pueblo, and that pueblo beginnings were made at San Diego and San Luis Rey.[16] Criticism, however, was not lacking. Said President Durán: "The free Gentile Indians of the pueblo of Los Ángeles are more wretched in estate and more severely chastised for offenses than are the Indians of the missions." Said President Diego, of the Zacatecans: "The Spanish Government that framed the law of 1813, what could it know of California conditions? Under emancipation the Indian will revert to nakedness and barbarism. It is only by force that he can be made to perform religious duties." Said Durán again: "The Indian by nature is apathetic and indolent, so much so that the Spanish rule of a ten years' *neofitia* is for him wholly inadequate." But by this time (October) the law of August 17, 1833, was in force, and Secularization was pressed forward as fast as possible.

On August 9, 1834, it was provided by a *Reglamento Provisional* that house-lots, pasture-lands, and livestock should be assigned to heads of families, and to all males over twenty years of age, much upon the basis of the Plan of Echeandía and of the *Prevenciones*. But it also was provided, that in addition to a *comisionado* or general superintendent of Secularization, a major-domo, or head steward, should be appointed in each mission for the care of all undistributed Mission property; that henceforth the missionaries should be prohibited from slaughtering cattle for hides and tallow; that "nunneries," where for the good of their morals neophyte children were kept apart from their parents, should be abolished; and that isolated *rancherías* having twenty-five families should be permitted to form, if they wished, separate pueblos.[17]

The *diputación* had reckoned that before the end of

October, 1834, every Alta California mission would have become a civil community. In fact, only nine missions had been secularized by the end of the year: San Luis Rey, San Juan Capistrano, San Gabriel, San Fernando, Santa Bárbara, Purísima, Santa Cruz, San Francisco, and San Rafael. By the end of 1835 there were added: San Diego, San Luis Obispo, San Antonio, Soledad, San Juan Bautista, and San Francisco Solano — a grand total of fifteen. As for San Buenaventura, Santa Inés, San Miguel, Santa Clara, and San José, the records for 1834–35 show no change.

Figueroa, a victim of vertigo and of the fogs of Monterey, died on September 29, 1835, and his funeral was celebrated to the noise of cannon. Against his own judgment, but in deference to California opinion as voiced by Bandini, he, at the last, had separated the political and military commands, conferring on José Castro, senior *vocal* of the *diputación*, the *ad-interim jefatura*, and on Lieutenant-Colonel Nicolás Gutiérrez the *ad-interim comandancia*. In January, 1836, however, in obedience to an order from Mexico dated a year before, the two offices were again combined through a transfer of the *jefatura* by Castro.

The only occurrence of note under Gutiérrez was the formal recognition, on January 4, of Los Ángeles as capital of Alta California. In 1825, Echeandía, as governor of both Californias, had fixed upon San Diego as a place of residence, and the South ever since had contended with the North for the seat of government. In 1835 (May 23) the efforts of southern politicians — the Bandinis and Carrillos — had been rewarded by a decree of the Mexican Congress declaring that "the pueblo of Los Ángeles in Alta California, hereby created a city, shall be the capital of that territory." This decree Gutiérrez as governor made public by proclamation.[18]

But what meanwhile of Mexico? First, Liberal or Federalist, — the views of Presidents Victoria and Guerrero reflected in Alta California by Echeandía; next, Conservative or Centralist, — the views of Vice-President Bustamente reflected by Governor Victoria; again Liberal (this time Federalist radically), — the views of Vice-President Farías moderately reflected by Figueroa, and emphatically by Padrés and Bandini, — Mexico now (the autumn of 1835) repudiated Federalism altogether, and repealed the Constitution of 1824.

As governor of Alta California, Colonel Mariano Chico, a Mexican congressman, was chosen, and he received his commission on December 16, 1835, the day following the promulgation by the Mexican Congress of certain "Bases" preliminary to a new constitution. Chico was a second Victoria, captious, tactless, and void of balance, and his administration, like that of his prototype, was incisive and short. He began it in May with addresses eulogistic of Centralism, and by exacting an oath to the "Bases." He continued it by reviving Victoria's quarrel with Abel Stearns, whom he ordered to quit the country.[19] He further continued it by repairing to Los Ángeles and arresting a number of citizens for participation in the lynching of a murderer and his paramour. Again he continued it by ordering the arrest of President Durán for refusing as a Spaniard to swear to the "Bases." On July 31 he brought it to a close by fleeing to Mexico, — an act the sequel to a complicated politico-social imbroglio at Monterey, due to the parading by Chico of his mistress, Doña Cruz, and her friend (even less savory of reputation) Doña Ildefonsa, wife of Herrera, at a public entertainment.

II

Alvarado

Mexico from the first had made Alta California an asylum for Mexican officials, and the fact was resented. Those by whom it was resented most were the young Californians, — the "young Italy" of the land, — and chief among such was Juan Bautista Alvarado.

Born at Monterey on February 14, 1809, Alvarado in 1836 was twenty-seven years old, having held the position of customs-inspector and secretary of the *diputación*, and being now *diputación* president. A protégé of Sola, he had been taught penmanship and arithmetic, and his school companions had been his uncle Mariano Guadalupe Vallejo and José Castro. The few books accessible to him — "Don Quixote," the "Laws of the Indies," a dictionary of geography, "Lives of Celebrated Spaniards," and Venegas's "California" — perchance, despite clerical vigilance, *Gil Blas* and the *Julie* of Jean Jacques — he had read with zest, but his principal study had been life and the ways of men. His acquirements were to be tested against Gutiérrez, to whom the fleeing Chico had confided the *ad-interim jefatura* and *comandancia*.

That once again the political and military commands were combined in the same individual, and he not only a Mexican but a Mexican of Spanish birth, was more than young California was able to bear, and it straightway proceeded to rebel. Alvarado — aided by his friend Castro, and watched sympathetically at a distance by his uncle Guadalupe — led. He gathered recruits, formidable among whom were a hired band of sailors and American backwoodsmen under a Tennesseean, Isaac Graham; and on November 3, 1836, the castillo of Monterey was taken without resistance. Designs were then matured against the presidio, which capitulated on November 5. The capitulation was followed by the deportation to Cape San Lucas of Gutiérrez and others, among them José María Herrera, who as sub-*comisario* had returned to old scenes along with Padrés.[20]

Through its *diputación*, headed by José Castro, Alta California, on November 6, had set up an independent government, — one with the motto *Federación ó Muerte ;* one based on the declaration that the land "was free and would hold aloof from Mexico until no longer oppressed by the present dominant faction called central government." [21] On November 7 Vallejo was made comandante-general of the newly created state, and on December 7 Alvarado was made governor, or, more accurately, autocratic president. On December 9 the *diputación*, or State Congress, passed a decree dividing the land into two cantons, that of Monterey and that of Los Ángeles. In each there was to be a *jefe político*, — at Monterey the Governor himself, and at Los Ángeles some one to be appointed by the Governor from a *terna* (trio) elected by the Angelinos.[22]

A political chief for the South was a confession of peril to the supremacy of Alvarado from southern discontent at the persistent refusal of the North to recognize Los Ángeles as the territorial capital; and no sooner was Alvarado installed than the South, through Los Ángeles, published a determined caveat to the proceeding.[23] It was admitted that Alvarado had delivered the land from Mexican placemen (a thing laudable enough), but he had also separated it from Mexico, styling it an *Estado libre y soberano*. Moreover, he had been aided by Anglo-Americans, at whose hands might be expected for California the fate of Texas. Finally, he had so far impugned the national religious faith as to promise to molest no one in his private religious opinions.[24]

Backed by a force of eighty men, — native sons under José Castro and Americans under Isaac Graham, — Alvarado on January 23, 1837, appeared in Los Ángeles. He dictated a compact extolling Federalism, but insisting henceforth on none but natives (*hijos del país*) for California rulers, and providing for summoning a new *diputación*. The latter, which met at Santa Bárbara on April 11, approved Alvarado's programme, so modified as to embody stipulations for the maintenance of the full supremacy of the Catholic faith, for an undivided *jefatura*, and for the preservation of California as an integral part of the Mexican Republic;[25] and on May 1 the approval by the *diputación* was in turn, though reluctantly, accepted by the *Ayuntamiento* of Los Ángeles.

The South having been placated, Alvarado returned to Monterey. Here, on May 30, he found himself confronted by three new demonstrations against his authority, — the first at Los Ángeles under Juan Bandini; the second at San Diego and San Luis Rey under Captain Andrés Castillero; and the third at Monterey itself, under Ángel Ramírez and Cosme Peña. The Ramírez-Peña revolt proved trifling. With the Bandini-Castillero affair (for the two movements speedily become one) it was otherwise.

On the night of May 26, 1837, Juan Bandini had made himself master of Los Ángeles. On June 12, Andrés Castillero, one of Gutiérrez's companions at the fall of Monterey, had appeared at San Diego with the Mexican Laws of 1836 (the so-called Seven Laws, sequel to the "Bases" of 1835), and having received thereto, despite the Centralism which they established, the enthusiastic subscription of the Diegueños and Angelinos, had joined Bandini, who, with the South in arms under Pablo de Portilla, had taken post at San Fernando. Alvarado was foiled, but stooped to conquer. He induced Castillero to become his representative to Mexico, once again under Bustamente as president, and on July 9, pronounced for the Centralist system: *"Viva la Nación! Viva la Constitución del año de '36! Viva el Congreso que la sancionó! Viva la Libertad! Viva la Unión!"* [26]

The South of a surety was circumvented now, and from the sorrow of campaigning the soul of Alvarado might find surcease. Not so. Forestalling Castillero, Congressman José Antonio Carrillo secured from the Mexican Government the appointment of his brother Carlos as Acting Governor of Alta California, an appointment carrying with it the power to fix the capital provisionally where circumstances might require. It was fixed on December 1 at Los Ángeles, and there on the 6th Carrillo was duly inaugurated. But Alvarado refused to recognize Carrillo's claim, and the latter, sustained by the South, resolved in February, 1838, to fight. He mustered a force under Juan Castañada, and to oppose it Alvarado sent a force under Castro. The two armies, about one hundred men each, met near San Buenaventura, and on March 27–28 fought the kind of action that Carrillo had intended — one loud with cannon, thick with smoke, and devoid of casualties. Castañada none the less was worsted, for his force was dispersed and he himself taken prisoner. A further hostile demonstration by Carrillo at Las Flores in April was followed by a conference between Carrillo and Alvarado at San Fernando.[27] But on May 20 the Governor, suspecting treachery, arrested José Antonio Carrillo, Pío Pico, and other Southerners, and sent them to Sonoma to be watched by Vallejo. Don Carlos himself was arrested, but was permitted to depart on parole to his home in Santa Bárbara.

A third time was Alvarado greeted by the hope that the hour of respite had come.[28] But in August word was received that Don Carlos had violated his parole and fled by boat to Lower California. Deliverance, nevertheless, was at hand. On August 13, a vessel from Mexico brought news that Castillero's mission had succeeded, and that both Alvarado and Vallejo were to be provisionally confirmed in the respective positions which they had held so long.

Alvarado, his right to rule recognized, and his heart blessed in 1839 by a suitable marriage, gave attention to what was the most important phase of the Mexican régime in Alta California — Secularization. But, first, there was to be put into effect the new system of Centralism, which the arms of Santa Anna and the policy of Bustamente had established.

By the Constitution of 1836 — the Constitution of the Seven Laws — the Constitution to which Alvarado with *vivas* had bidden Californians subscribe — the two Californias, Alta and Baja, were converted from two territories into a single department, entitled to a governor, an assembly, and one congressional delegate. The department was required to be subdivided into districts and *partidos* under prefects and sub-prefects, the former to be appointed by the Governor and approved in Mexico; and the latter to be appointed by the prefects and approved by the Governor. On February 27, 1839, three prefectures were designated, — two for Alta, and one for Baja California; the respective capitals being at San Juan de Castro (late mission of San Juan Bautista), Los Ángeles, and La Paz. The two Alta California prefectures were divided each into two *partidos*, with head towns (*cabeceras*) at San Juan de Castro, San Francisco, Los Ángeles, and Santa Bárbara. No *partido* division was as yet attempted for Baja California.[29]

So far as *ayuntamientos* were concerned, they were permitted by the new laws only to the larger towns, the smaller being placed under the authority of justices of the peace.[30] Centralist in design, the new laws wrought a triumph for that Federalist principle of home rule through the assertion of which Alvarado had gained power, for henceforth the Alta California governors were to be appointed from a *terna* of names to be submitted by the assembly to the Mexican Government. And on August 7, 1839, Alvarado himself was chosen governor by President Bustamente from a *terna* embracing the names of Juan B. Alvarado, José Castro, and Pío Pico.

The conditions of Secularization, as they presented themselves to Alvarado, may be summarized thus: Sixteen establishments in the hands of *comisionados;* further Secularization forbidden by law in 1835 pending the appointment of curates; three missions — Santa Inés, San Buenaventura, and San Miguel — delivered to *comisionados* by Chico, despite the law; and two — San José and Santa Clara — so delivered by the *diputación* under Alvarado. The Mission property, by virtue of the curacy law and of civil strife, was being neglected, wasted, stolen, and destroyed. To stop spoliation was the first and paramount duty of a governor, and Alvarado promptly addressed his efforts to the task. It was in his favor that, Spain having recognized the independence of Mexico in 1836, President Durán and the Fernandinos had in 1837 taken the long-deferred oath to support the Mexican Government.

On January 17, 1839, the Governor issued a *Reglamento Provisional* requiring *comisionados* to present accounts in full to December 31, 1838; to submit a statement of Mission debts and credits; to take a classified census of inhabitants; to make monthly reports of expenditures; to pay no claims except upon government order; to prevent the unnecessary slaughter of cattle and the barter of horses and mules, with New Mexicans, for woolens.[31] At the same time the appointment of an inspector of Mission administration was announced — William E. P. Hartnell. The duties and powers of the latter, which Durán approved, included the enforcement of accounting and economy, and the suspending of *comisionados* from office.[32] By October 12, 1839, Hartnell had visited every mission from San Diego to Sonoma; and on March 1, 1840, Alvarado issued a *Reglamento de Misiones*, a feature of which was the substitution of moderately paid major-domos or stewards for excessively paid *comisionados*.[33] Hartnell made a second inspection tour under the *Reglamento* in 1840, but at Sonoma his authority was defied by Vallejo, and at San Luis Rey he was resisted by Pío Pico, and on September 7, he resigned.

The situation, as disclosed by Hartnell's tours, was one of ruin at nearly every mission. At San Luis Rey, San Juan Capistrano, and San Gabriel — establishments which in 1833 were yet the abode of thousands of neophytes, and where crops and livestock were yet abundant — there were left in 1839 and 1840 but a few hundred neophytes, neither well cared for nor well treated; and crops and stock were given over to peculation or neglect. But the most significant fact disclosed was, that in order to control the neophytes yet remaining, the old method of the padres, the method of the Mission of Córdova, of Las Casas, and of Junípero Serra alone was practicable. Despite the humanitarianism of republican Mexico, — a humanitarianism which, harking back to Borica and Neve, shrank from the flogging of recalcitrant neophytes, — it was found by Alvarado imperative to provide in his *Reglamentos* that the neophyte be made to work for the community and be "chastised moderately for his faults"; that there be enforced upon him morality and an attendance on religious duties; finally, that no *gente de razón* be allowed to settle among neophytes gathered in community. As for separate pueblos of Indians, such as had been set up by Figueroa at San Diego (Dieguito and San Pascual) and at San Luis Rey (Las Flores), they were already disintegrating. Even San Juan Capistrano, the most promising of them all, a pueblo with which special pains had been taken by both Figueroa and Alvarado, had been a failure, and as a distinctively Indian town was dissolved.[34]

The rule of Alvarado, a rule noteworthy for many things, was brought to an end by the appointment as governor on January 22, 1842, of Manuel Micheltorena.

CHAPTER XIV

ANGLO–AMERICANS

THE retirement of Alvarado from the Alta California governorship was effected chiefly by his kinsman and schoolmate Mariano Guadalupe Vallejo, the *comandante-militar*. First, however, with regard to those Anglo-Americans against whom Figueroa had been warned.

Under Spain, English and American residents in Alta California had been few; but in 1822 and the years immediately following, the number of residents English and American (English especially) fast increased. In June, 1822, there came the Englishmen Hugh McCulloch and William E. P. Hartnell (McCulloch, Hartnell & Company), and, the same year, William A. Richardson; while in 1824 came the highly influential Scotsman, David Spence. The men named were of substantial character, mercantile in their aims, and interested in the maintenance of a stable Mexican government. Of like qualities and pursuits were certain Americans, prominent among whom were John R. Cooper who came in 1823, W. G. Dana and Henry O. Fitch who came in 1826, John C. Jones and Alfred Robinson in 1829, Abel Stearns in 1830, John Warner in 1831, Thomas O. Larkin (afterwards United States Consul at Monterey) in 1832, and Jacob P. Leese in 1833.

But between 1830 and 1840 Anglo-Americans of a different type presented themselves. To the southwest of the Missouri River lay the ancient Mexican town of Santa Fé. Here trappers and traders — Yankee, English, and

French-Canadian — met to effect exchanges and to organize expeditions; and hither adventurers and refugees repaired, some of them finding their way into California. Of such was Isaac Graham, who in 1836 had led an effective contingent for Alvarado against Gutiérrez. Graham's vocation in 1840 was that of distiller near Monterey, and his cabin was headquarters for men of roistering temper, — woodsawyers, ex-sailors, and the like; men without passports, yet who were not permitted to forget that Mexico was a land where foreigners were required by law to give an account of themselves. In April, 1840, a Grahamite who thought himself in extremity, confessed to Padre Suárez del Real of San Carlos that an uprising of American settlers was in contemplation. Suárez notified Alvarado, who in turn notified José Castro, prefect of the northern district.[1]

The alarm was great. In a total population of two thousand adult males, the number of foreigners was between four and five hundred.[2] Texas had achieved independence through its American element in 1836. If the Grahamites were tolerated further, might not independence be the destiny of Alta California? Such evidently was the conclusion, for Castro having by threats secured from one of Graham's associates, William R. Garner, a declaration that an uprising was imminent, and that Graham and an Englishman, Albert Morris, were its promoters, laid plans with secrecy, and between April 7 and May 8 arrested in the North, and at Santa Bárbara and Los Ángeles, not less than one hundred and twenty men. None were molested who had passports, or who were married to native women, or who were honest and regular in their mode of life.[3]

Forty-six of the prisoners, shackled, and guarded by Castro, were sent to San Blas, to be dealt with by the

Mexican Government.[4] On April 18, however, Thomas
J. Farnham — an American traveler from the Hawaiian
Islands — had reached Monterey. Warmly espousing the
cause of the prisoners, he gave them all possible aid and
followed them to Tepic, their ultimate destination. Here
he enlisted in their behalf the services of the British Consul, Mr. Eustace Barron. An earnest correspondence was
begun with the Mexican officials and with the British and
American ministers,[5] and though some twenty-six of the
accused were banished from Mexican territory, about
twenty (Graham and Morris among them) were purged
of conspiracy, awarded compensation, and in July, 1841,
restored to Alta California. As for Castro, he was tried
for cruelty, but was acquitted, and reached Monterey in
September.[6]

But there were Anglo-Americans other than those led
by Graham. On July 3, 1839, Johann August Sutter, a
native of Baden who had acquired citizenship in Switzerland, arrived at Monterey. His journey had involved a
trip to Santa Fé, a trip by the Oregon Trail to Vancouver,
and a voyage to Honolulu. Sutter was magnetic and tact-
ful, spoke (besides German) English, French, and Spanish,
and bore letters of introduction from officials of the Hudson's Bay and Russian-American companies, and from
Honolulu merchants. At Monterey, David Spence presented him to Alvarado, who, charmed with his bearing,
urged him to announce an intention of becoming a Mexican
citizen, and to select in the interior a tract of land, title
to which under Mexican law might be perfected within a
year. He was furnished with letters to Vallejo, upon whom
he called at Sonoma, and he paid a visit to Ross, the rock-
bound site of which, "dashed upon by the sea," impressed
him. Early in August he set out with a pinnace and two
hired schooners for the Sacramento River, landing after

eight days on the south bank of its tributary, the American. He had with him eight Kanakas, three white men, an Indian, and a bull-dog. Two temporary structures of poles and grass were built on high ground, and the settlement thus begun he christened New Hèlvetia.[7]

Sutter, by the summer of 1840, had ingratiated himself with the Western trappers, and shown resourcefulness with the Indians. In August, therefore, on completing his citizenship, he was made by Alvarado a Mexican official, a representative of the government on the frontiers of the Río Sacramento. Meanwhile Ross, — the settlement which Sutter had visited and admired, the settlement which as a Rezánoff legacy had disquieted Sola, and against which Echeandía had been ordered to plant a *villa*, — this settlement the Russian-American Company had definitely decided to abandon.[8] Between 1830 and 1839, Baron Wrangell, as Governor of Russian America, had made a resolute effort to secure from Mexico land southward of Ross to San Francisco, and eastward to the Sacramento, but without avail, and Ross by itself was not worth keeping. An offer of the buildings and livestock of the establishment was made to Vallejo in 1840 for 30,000 *pesos*. It was declined, and on December 13 the same offer was made to Sutter and accepted. And not only did Sutter buy the Russian movables, — he obtained a quit-claim to such title (or lack of title) as the Russians possessed to the land.[9]

Enriched by his Russian purchase, which included wooden buildings and some brass ordnance, Sutter in 1841 began the erection at New Helvetia of a fort of his own, a structure embracing an area of 150 by 500 feet. The fort in its finished condition, in 1845, is described as protected by adobe walls, eighteen feet high, with bastioned corners. As early as 1842 it boasted an armament of twelve guns. Indeed, by the year named, Sutter at New Helvetia was a veritable lord of the marches. His domains were eleven square leagues in extent. He owned 4200 cattle, 2000 horses, and 1900 sheep, and he trafficked profitably in beaver-skins. He commanded the routes westward from the United States and southward from Oregon. His trappers, ever welcome and quartered without price, were his willing retainers; while his Indians, taught blanket-weaving and hat-making, and organized in military companies, obeyed him like slaves. It is worthy of note that at the time of the Graham affair no question was raised regarding the strangers without passports — the sojourners at New Helvetia.

Grahamites and Sutterites combined, however, were not the only Anglo-Americans. There were others still, and by the autumn of 1841 they began to appear near Sonoma. In 1805, on November 7, Lewis and Clark had reached the mouth of the Columbia.[10] In 1811, Astoria had been founded. Taken by the British during the War of 1812, the post had been restored to the United States in 1818. In 1822, the Ashley Fur Company had been organized, and in 1826, Jedediah S. Smith had reached Alta California (at San Diego) from Salt Lake by a route to the Colorado and through the Mojave country. Smith in 1828 had been followed by Sylvester and James O. Pattie, whose destination had also proved to be San Diego, and in 1833, Joseph Walker, commissioned by Captain Bonneville, had reached Monterey.[11]

As for Jedediah Smith, the Patties, and others, they had either been banished eastward over the Rockies by Echeandía, or imprisoned. But could such a course be taken with the Americans who were approaching in 1841? It was the Bartleson-Bidwell Company — first overland emigrants from the Missouri — who were in question.

Sixty-nine strong, they on May 19 had quitted camp on the Kansas River, — part of them for Oregon, the remainder for California. Sixty-nine strong, they had reached the vicinity of Great Salt Lake by way of the Platte, — South and North Forks, — South Pass, Green River, and Bear Valley. Thence, by way of the desert, Mary [Humboldt] River, Walker River, Sonora Pass, the Stanislaus River, they on November 4, to the number of thirty-two, had arrived at the rancho of Dr. John Marsh, near the foot of Monte Diablo.[12]

The retirement of Alvarado from the Alta California governorship in 1842 was due, it has been said, to Vallejo. Soldier-bred, a disciplinarian and a warm patriot, the presence of foreigners in Alta California — of Americans especially — was distasteful to the latter as a menace to the country. Graham at Monterey, Sutter on the Sacramento, the Bartleson emigrants at Marsh's rancho, what did they one and all portend but evil?[13]

Complicating the situation was Alvarado himself. Wearied by his wars with the South, he for the most part had declined into sloth. In the words of Sir George Simpson, "from a spare Cassius-like conspirator, the Governor had become a plump and paunchy lover of singing, dancing, and feasting." In December, 1841, the apprehensions of Vallejo were suddenly confirmed. Northwest America, including what is now Washington, Oregon, and Montana, was the field of the Hudson's Bay Company. Relations between the latter and Alta California were friendly, even cordial. The Company never encroached, and early in 1841 an agreement was made with Alvarado whereby its trappers might operate along the Sacramento. To this agreement Sutter objected, on November 8, in an angry letter which early came to the hands of Vallejo.

Very curious Rapports [wrote the lord of New Helvetia] come to me from belaw, but the poor wretches don't know what they do. I explained now Mr. Spence to explain these ignorant people, what would be the consequence if they do injure me, the first french freggate who came here will do me justice. The people don't know me yet, but soon they will find out what I am able to do. It is to late now to drive me aut of the country the first step they do against me is that I will make a Declaration of Independence and proclaim California for a Republique independent from Mexico. I am strong now, one of my best friends a German Gentleman came from the Columbia River with plenty people, another party is close by from Missouri. One of the party arrived here, some of my friends and acquaintances are among them, they are about 40 or 50 men of Respectability and property, they came in the intention to settle here. I am strong enough to hold me till the courriers go to the Waillamet for raise about 60 a 70 good men, an another party I would dispatche to the mountains and call the Hunters and Shawnees and Delawares with which I am very well acquainted, the same party have to go to Missouri and raise about 2 or 300 men more. That is my intention sir, if they lete me not alone, if they will give me satisfaction, and pay the expenses what I had to do for my security here, I will be a faithful Mexican, but when this Rascle of Castro should come here, a very warm and hearty welcome is prepared for him. 10 guns are well mounted for protect the fortress, and two field pieces, I have also about 50 faithful Indians which shot their musquet very quick. The whole day and night, we are under arms and you know that foreigners are very expensive, and for this trouble, I will be payed when a french Fregatte come here. I wish you tell the Comandante General Vallejo that I wish to be his friend, and that I am very much obliged for his kindness when my people passed Sonoma. But all is out question so long they let me alone and trouble me not, but I want security from the Government for that.[14]

Sutter, as Vallejo explained to Mexico, assumed the title of *Gobernador de Fortaleza de Nueva Helvecia*, made war on the neighboring Indians, and sold to service such of the Indian children as his wars reduced to orphanage. "I inclose his original letter," he concluded, "*cuerpo de delito infragable.*" [15] But on December 9 the comandante was called upon to face the Bartleson Company. Informed by Marsh of the indispensability of passports, they had repaired to San José, where Vallejo met them, and from necessity issued to them temporary papers. "If," wrote the latter on the 11th, "there be realized the invasion that on all sides is threatened, the only certainty is that the Californians will die. I dare not assure myself that California will be saved."[16]

On December 11, 1841, it devolved upon Vallejo to report to Mexico the survey of San Francisco Bay and of the Sacramento and San Joaquín Rivers by a North American squadron under Captain Charles Wilkes,[17] and on the 12th to announce the sale to Sutter of Ross. The sale, he said, was a matter of no great satisfaction, for the Mexican flag had not been raised; and was there not fair chance that "the Russian eagle would be replaced by the Cruz Britanica"? He pointed out that the Hudson's Bay Company already "had foot" in California. They had established a house in the port of San Francisco, and they had secured territory on the Sacramento for the purposes of a colony.

What was needed, Vallejo urged, was two hundred soldiers assured of their pay; fewer civil officials; a reliable mail-service; reconstruction of the fort at San Francisco; the erection there of a wharf and custom-house; and colonization by Mexicans. Was not the land capable of every product, and yet did not the Californians purchase brandy from Catalonia, tobacco from Virginia, vinegar from Marseilles, cloth from Boston, manufactured goods from everywhere; even things the most common and trivial, as, for example, brooms from the Sandwich Islands? But above all else what was needed was a *jefe*, free from the bonds of consanguinity, to rule freely, firmly, and impartially, —

an end easily to be attained, provided such *jefe* were invested with both civil and military authority.[18]

These representations were emphasized by the arrival in the South of a party of twenty-five Americans from Santa Fé, — the Workman-Rowland party, so called; and on February 22, the Mexican Government notified Vallejo that there had been appointed to succeed Alvarado as *jefe político*, and himself as *comandante-militar*, a governor in whom the two offices were combined, namely, Manuel Micheltorena, general of brigade.[19]

The new Governor reached Los Ángeles late in September, 1842, attended by a force of about three hundred recruits, largely convicts. Setting out after a short interval for Monterey, he was met on the night of October 24, at his stopping-place near San Fernando Mission, by a letter from Alvarado, dated midnight of the 19th, stating that Monterey had just been surrendered to a squadron of United States ships, commanded by Commodore Thomas ap Catesby Jones. It had been Jones's surmise, first, that war had been declared between the United States and Mexico over Texas; and, second, that England had sent a squadron to seize California. On October 20, therefore, he had landed 150 marines, and raised over Monterey the American flag; but having on the 21st learned from Mexican newspapers that war had not been declared, he the same day had restored the Mexican colors, withdrawn his men, and fired a salute in apology.[20]

So far as Monterey was concerned, the incident was at an end; but Micheltorena invited Jones to meet him in personal conference at Los Ángeles, and on January 17, 1843, the commodorè arrived at San Pedro Harbor. He was met by a squad of twenty-five lancers, and after a champagne dinner at the port, was conveyed in an "oak ark-barouche" to the southern capital. The party were entertained at the house of Abel Stearns. Here Jones met the beautiful Mexican wife of his host, and was presented to Micheltorena, who, with fifteen or twenty richly uniformed aides, awaited his coming. For an hour all was nod of plume and shimmer of gold and silver braid, when, the reception over and a ball arranged for the next evening, Jones, intrusted with the password, was ushered to his quarters.[21]

The business of Micheltorena, as it proved, was to present to the American commodore demands for indemnity — demands which it was known could not be entertained, but which later might not be without a tactical value.

But to recur to Mexico. As early as January 9, 1842, F. de Arrángoiz, the Mexican Consul at New Orleans, wrote to the Minister of Relations that the American Government had expressed a determination to acquire territory for a naval station between the Columbia River and Guayaquil. The consul advised that Americans be denied admission to California, and that all such as were domiciled without passports be expelled. On May 7, the same official announced that it was stated in the New Orleans papers that thirty American emigrants (the Bartleson Company), who had reached California without passports, had at first been put under arrest, but later had been liberated by order of the Governor and had had passports given them. Finally, on June 24, he wrote that at the end of May there had left Independence (Missouri) about one hundred individuals who said they were going to settle in Oregon, but who probably were destined for California.[22]

Arrángoiz's advice to deny to Americans admission to California could no longer be disregarded. Accordingly, on July 4, President Santa Anna issued instructions to Micheltorena, that from and after a date to be fixed by him "no individuals belonging to the United States were to be admitted to his department." [23]

The news from Arrángoiz had been disquieting enough, but on October 2, news more disquieting still was received from Juan N. Almonte, Mexican representative at Washington.

There can be no doubt [Almonte asserted], that of the thousand families that this year have emigrated from the States of Arkansas and Missouri, and the Territories of Tova [Iowa?] and Wisconseis in the direction of Oregon, more than a third part have gone with the intention of establishing themselves in Alta California. . . . I infer that the objects of these emigrants are not pure, and that there is involved a project that time will disclose. This I communicate to the end that the comandante-general of the department may be forewarned, not losing sight of the fact that this scheme of emigration may be in consonance with plans that the Texans some time since entertained concerning that beautiful land.

As a result of Almonte's letter, the order excluding Americans from California was reinforced by a second order, dated October 7, which was directed to be communicated to Micheltorena.[24]

A rumor that exclusion measures had been adopted reached the American Minister in Mexico, Waddy S. Thompson, on December 23; but although Thompson made a peremptory demand for revocation, no reply was elicited other than that the measures complained of were not directed against Americans *pacíficos y honrados*, but against those *inicuos, turbulentos*, and "unworthy the generous hospitality of the Mexican nation."[25] It is probable that Thompson's protest came early enough to enable the Mexican Government to recall the obnoxious instructions before Micheltorena received them.[26]

At all events, emigration to the Northwest flowed on unchecked. In 1843, it amounted to eight hundred persons. Of these the Hastings company (some thirty-six strong) and the Chiles-Walker company (about fifty) entered California, the first in one division, from Oregon, and the second in two divisions, one by way of Fort Boisé and New Helvetia,[27] and the other, by way of Owens River and Lake, the Tulares, and Gilroy's rancho.[28] In 1844, three companies came: one (twenty-five strong) under Lieutenant John C. Frémont by way of the Carson River;[29] a Kelsey contingent (thirty-six strong) by a route not definitely known; and the Stevens party (over fifty strong) by way of Truckee and Bear Rivers — line of the modern railway.[30] The companies of 1845 were six or seven in number, and their total membership was perhaps two hundred and fifty. One of them under Green McMahon — a party of which James W. Marshall, the discoverer of gold in California, was a member — came from Oregon. Of the others the best known were the Sublette, the Grigsby (wherein William B. Ide was enrolled), the Frémont-Walker party, and that of Lansford W. Hastings. Aside from the Oregon party, all entered California by the routes of the Sacramento or lower San Joaquín Valley, except the Walker party, which came by Owens River and Lake.

The Oregon Trail had now become a highway. From Independence (suburb of the present Kansas City) to the South Fork of the Platte River (Leroy, Nebraska, — 296 miles) the course was over undulous or rolling prairie sown with wild flowers, well supplied with game — elk, antelope, wild turkeys — and with wood, water, and grass. Its drawbacks were sultry heat, rattling thunder-storms, an occasional cyclone, a cattle stampede, and possible Indians. Along the South Fork — a stream broad and sluggish — the country was sandy, but it was the country of the buffalo, — buffalo by tens of thousands, buffalo as far as the eye could reach, buffalo for days together, buffalo in a herd which, pressing headlong, must at times be split by rifle volleys to save caravans from being trampled out of existence. To the North Fork of the Platte transition was made by Ash Hollow, and here the course increased in ruggedness, disclosing Court-House Rock, Chimney Rock, Scott's Bluffs, and, at a distance from Independence of 616 miles, the low walls of Fort Laramie. Thence the course led to Fort Bridger (southern Wyoming, 1070 miles), a stretch full of the picturesque — Independence Rock and Sweetwater Gap, South Pass marking the summit of the Rocky Mountains, and (beyond the divide) Green River, with anon in the distance the snow-capped peaks of the Wind River Range. Soda Springs on Bear River (1206 miles) came next, and here, or at Fort Hall, eighty miles distant, there disengaged itself from the Oregon Trail the trail for California.[31]

Of the California Trail the first and second stages — Fort Hall southwest to the head of Humboldt River (300 miles) and Humboldt River to its sink (about 350 miles) — were well defined. The first stage, skirting as it did the Salt Lake Desert, was arid, alkaline, and visited by thirst; while the second stage, semi-arid and short of game, was fatiguing from its monotony. As for the third stage, — the sink of the Humboldt to the Sacramento Valley, — it was the worst of the entire journey from Independence. At Humboldt Sink, the emigrant, as a test of his faith, found confronting him a stupendous barrier, that of the Sierra Nevada. Over it, starving and dogged by peril of snow-storms, he might struggle by Walker and Stanislaus Rivers, as did the Bartleson-Bidwell party of 1841; or by Owens River and Walker Pass, as did the Walker-Chiles

party of 1843; or by the route, harder than any other, of
Carson River, as did the Frémont party of 1844. It was
not until the arrival of the Elisha Stevens company in 1844,
late in December, that it was demonstrated that the route
the most practicable was that of the Truckee and Bear
Rivers.[32]

It will be remembered that in 1794 the northern boundary
of Alta California had been forced by the British southward to Fuca Strait, and that in 1812 the Russians had
sought to establish it at Bodega Bay. Now, by the American occupation of Oregon (coupled with the evacuation of
Ross), it was projected again northward to a point below
the valley of the Willamette.

Micheltorena, saved by the timely course of Waddy
Thompson from collision with intruding Americans, was
yet full of trouble. On June 12, 1843, Mexico had adopted
a Centralist Constitution more radical than the instrument of 1836. On November 1, Alta California cast a
unanimous vote for Santa Anna as president, and on
February 10, 1844, submitted a *terna* of names (the name
of Micheltorena first) for governor. But the old question of headship between Monterey and Los Ángeles remained undetermined, and Pío Pico, emulative of Bandini, plotted industriously to secure from the departmental assembly recognition for Los Ángeles. So menacing,
moreover, was deemed to be the attitude of the United
States, as shown by the seizure of Monterey by Jones, that
despair became enthroned in the Governor's heart. "The
latter country," he declared, was "extremely desirous of
an accession of eight hundred and more leagues of coast
of the highest fertility, of every climate, and of every
product. To be sure there was no gold, but there were
silver-quartz, limestone, salt, sulphur, and fur-bearing

animals." If clothing and money for his troops were not supplied, he could die, but that would not restore a province worth four times Texas, the most precious part of the Mexican Republic.[33]

Awaiting him, however, was trouble more immediate. His soldiers — ex-convicts at the best, and unpaid and unclothed — filled Monterey (as already they had filled Los Ángeles) with consternation by their thievery. Like the classic rogues in "Erminie," whom in respect to rags and tatters they resembled, they stole not alone from hunger, but from constitutional inability to withstand temptation. Pots, kettles, shirts, kerchiefs, chickens entangled by hook and line, — there was nothing that they did not steal. From the house of Mrs. Ord, daughter of José de la Guerra, they once, during a few moments' absence of the cook, filched an entire meal. Valuables they stole when possible. At a dance given in Los Ángeles by Don Vicente Sánchez, twelve Cholos employed as guards carried off a chest of jewelry; and it was by no means unusual for them to force pedestrians to stand and deliver at the point of the sword.[34]

The result of this insubordination was a revolt, led by Alvarado and José Castro. On November 22, 1844, Micheltorena left Monterey with 150 men, and within a few days was met by the rebellionists, 220 strong, near San José. After the feints and flourishes inevitable upon such occasions, there was concluded, on December 1, the treaty of Santa Terésa, whereby cause of complaint was removed through an agreement by the Governor to send his Cholos to San Blas.[35]

But the end was not yet. On the appointment of Micheltorena as governor, Vallejo had been made comandante of the northern frontier from Sonoma to Santa Inés, a district including the Sacramento. This had been galling to Sutter, richer and prouder than ever; but (from desire of more land) he had taken pains to cultivate the new Governor and to become to him *persona grata* from the start. While on a trip to Monterey with John Bidwell, in October, 1844, Sutter had heard of the conspiracy on the part of Castro and Alvarado against Micheltorena, and had promised to aid the latter with a force of back-woodsmen and Indians. The campaign of Santa Terésa had put the Governor at a disadvantage, but the treaty could be violated. The signal was to be the appearance of the New Helvetian in the field, backed by his Indians and an American rifle corps.[36]

On January 1, 1845, Sutter, with Indians to the number of about one hundred, with Dr. John Marsh, and with one hundred riflemen under Captains John Gantt and Isaac Graham, — the latter lusting for the blood of Alvarado, — marched southward. Micheltorena — his treaty with Alvarado and Castro canceled by proclamation — joined Sutter at Salinas on the 9th. Meanwhile, the conspirators, surprised, but with a small force, started for Los Ángeles. Here Alvarado put Micheltorena in the wrong by a well-worded appeal to the assembly,[37] and on February 14 and 15, after a refusal by the Governor (then with Sutter at Santa Bárbara) to listen to argument, he declared him deprived of office and superseded, provisionally, by the senior *vocal*, Pío Pico.[38]

The opposing armies, each four hundred strong, met, February 20, at Cahuenga, and artillery shots were exchanged at long range. The next day, at the Verdugo Rancho, the armies met again, and at a range equally long exchanged more shots. But on the side of Alvarado there was a contingent of American backwoodsmen under William Workman and B. D. Wilson, and these, communicating with the Gantt-Graham contingent on the side of

Micheltorena and Sutter, resolved not to contend against one another. Shorn of his principal strength, Micheltorena promptly capitulated. Late in March, in accordance with a treaty signed on the 22d of February at San Fernando, whereby Pío Pico was recognized as governor and José Castro as comandante-general, the Governor and his troops were deported from Monterey to San Blas. As for Sutter, not only had his prestige suffered a hard blow, but he was in personal peril. "Sutter," wrote John C. Jones to Thomas Larkin, "has fallen, and I think, like Lucifer, never to rise again." [39]

Micheltorena was a Centralist and pro-Cleric, a brother in spirit to Victoria and Chico, — in brief, a reactionary; and Manuel Castañares, the representative of Alta California in the Mexican Congress, was of the same faith. Fervently had the latter set forth the needs of his department: the danger from Americans, the wretched plight of the Governor with his poverty-stricken force, the likelihood of revolution. [40] When, therefore, Micheltorena was overthrown, and news of the fact reached Mexico, it was deemed prudent to dispatch north a *comisionado* to placate sentiment, and at the same time, in view of possible complications with the United States, to occupy the country with a military force of six hundred picked men. For *comisionado*, there was chosen our acquaintance of other days, José María Híjar, and for military commander the accomplished soldier (fated never to reach his destination), Colonel Ignacio Iniestra. [41]

Híjar reached Santa Bárbara on June 8. Thence he proceeded to Los Ángeles, where, in December, after some mild official deliverances, he died. As a result of Híjar's coming, the Alta California assembly submitted to Mexico, on June 27, a *quinterna* of candidates for governor, Pío Pico being named first and Juan Bandini second; and

on August 1 the department cast its vote for José Joaquín de Herrera as President of the Mexican Republic,
— Santa Anna having on June 3 been forced into exile
through a Federalist revolt provoked by heavy taxation.

"Ye gods," John C. Jones wrote to Larkin on March 21,
1845, "the idea of Pío Pico with the title of 'Excellency'!"
But Pío Pico — a man of moderation — it now was; and
with him (and with the selection by him of Juan Bandini
as secretary) power came to the South, for at length Los
Ángeles was recognized by the North as the departmental
capital.[43]

The first thing of importance under Pío Pico was to
complete the secularization of the missions. In 1836, on
September 19, the Californias had been made by Mexico
an independent diocese, to the bishop whereof the Pious
Fund was to be intrusted.[44] On April 27, 1840, Fray
Francisco García Diego, president of the Zacatecans in
Alta California, was approved as bishop, and by January 11, 1842, he had established his episcopal residence at
Santa Bárbara, where, for nominal pay but from a throne
canopied in crimson and gold, he was prepared to dispense
ecclesiastical justice.[45]

With the Pious Fund of the Californias controlled by
a California ecclesiastic, the opportunity for a pro-clerical
governor to oust the wasteful *comisionados* from the missions was too valuable to be lost, and on March 29, 1843,
Micheltorena issued a decree restoring to Mission management (temporal as well as spiritual) the twelve establishments — San Diego, San Fernando, San Luis Rey, San
Juan Capistrano, San Gabriel, San Buenaventura, Santa
Bárbara, Purísima, Santa Inés, Santa Clara, San Antonio,
and San José. The restoration was on condition that one

eighth of the total annual produce of each mission be paid
into the public treasury, and was carried out (in so far as
carried out at all) under Joaquín Jimeno and Narciso
Durán, respectively, president and prefect of the Fernandinos, and under José María de Jesús Gonzales, president
of the Zacatecans.[46]

It was not long that Bishop Francisco was able to maintain himself by virtue of the Pious Fund. On February 8,
1842, at the behest of Santa Anna, the Mexican Congress passed a decree restoring the administration of the
fund to the supreme government; and this decree, on
October 24, was followed by one directing a sale of the
Pious Fund estates, and the covering of the entire proceeds into the national treasury as a loan.[47] Thus practically had come to an end a fund which, established by
Salvatierra in 1697, had under Ugarte and his successors
supplied the missions, first of Baja and then of Alta California, with money for stipends, foundations, and subsistence down to 1810, — a fund which, though since 1810
diverted in Mexico as to its proceeds, had until 1842
been kept well intact as to its principal.[48]

In February, 1844, the missions subject to the Franciscans were thus described by Durán: "Three (San Miguel,
San Luis Obispo, and San Diego) as *in toto* abandoned;
two (Santa Inés and San Buenaventura) as moderately
equipped"; and the remaining nine as "destroyed, and
their neophytes demoralized." It no doubt was the condition of the missions as thus described that led the departmental assembly in August to pass a vote ordering a sale,
an hypothecation, or a leasing of the mission properties,
to provide means for defense, in case of aggression by the
United States.[49]

No action under the vote of the assembly proved to
be necessary in 1844, but in 1845 (October 28) there was

issued by Pío Pico a *Reglamento* (based on a departmental
decree of May 28 framed largely in accordance with the
views of Prefect Durán) under which the then abandoned
establishments (Zacatecan and Fernandino) San Rafael,
Dolores(San Francisco), Soledad, San Miguel, and Purísima
were to be sold at public auction. The establishments yet
occupied (mission pueblos), San Luis Obispo, Carmelo (San
Carlos), San Juan Bautista, and San Juan Capistrano,
were also to be sold, but with a reservation in each instance of church and parsonage. The ten other establishments were to be rented to the highest bidder for a term
of nine years. Where there were Indians (ex-neophytes),
they were to be free to go or remain as they listed, and
if remaining to receive title to their lands. Each mission
pueblo was to be self-governed under four Indian *celadores*
(watchmen) chosen monthly and subject to the justices
of the peace of the locality. In case of sale, the proceeds after payment of debts were to be for the support
of public worship.[50]

By July 7, 1846, — date of the formal cessation of Mexican rule in Alta California, — there had been sold by Pío
Pico, under the decree of May 28, 1845, and a further
decree of March 30, 1846, all of the missions save San
Francisco, San Carlos, Santa Cruz, San Antonio, and San
Francisco Solano. The sales were to individual purchasers,
and for the most part were in contravention of an order
by the Mexican Government (reflecting Centralism) that
Micheltorena's re-transfer to the padres should not be
disturbed.[51]

With the Pious Fund virtually confiscated in Mexico,
and with the mission establishments sold and their neophytes dispersed in Alta California, both Bishop Francisco
García Diego and Prefect Narciso Durán — chagrined,
disappointed, and disheartened — laid down the burden of

existence, the one in May, and the other in June, 1846. The Alta California Mission, the work of Córdova and Las Casas, the work of Kino, of Salvatierra, and of Ugarte, the work of Junípero Serra and of Francisco Palou, was dead.

The object of the Mission, under the Laws of the Indies, was everywhere to secularize the Indian; to municipalize him by reducing him to a condition of pueblo life, of civic autonomy. But no pueblo the result of Secularization long survived. The shortest lived were the pueblos purely Indian, — San Dieguito, San Pascual, and Las Flores. In the mission pueblos, ex-neophytes were not as such permitted to vote; local officers (*alcalde, regidores*, and *síndico*) being chosen by the *gente de razón* and *emancipados;* yet even so, none lasted.[52] Vallejo at Sonoma, by availing himself of the municipal organization of the Híjar colonists, did succeed in replacing a mission (San Francisco Solano) by an enduring pueblo, but the instance is unique.

Nor may surprise be felt. Even with the *gente de razón*, it was by the slowest degrees that pueblo life in Alta California was established. Felipe de Neve founded San José and Los Ángeles, and Borica the *villa* Branciforte, yet throughout the Spanish régime civil rule in these communities was merely nominal. The rule actually exercised was that of the Governor's *comisionado* — military rule. Arrillaga, it will be remembered, deemed it farcical and supererogatory for him to qualify as *jefe político.* Under Mexico the *comisionados* were withdrawn, but the pueblos did not improve. As late as 1846, San José was described as "a village of 600 to 800 inhabitants in a fine valley [Santa Clara] of adobe buildings and very irregular streets, with thousands of ground squirrels burrowing in the plaza, and

men and women of all classes engaged in gambling";
while Los Ángeles, with a population of perhaps 1250, and
not without indication of public improvements, was nevertheless (for its gambling, murders, and lewdness) of repute
so evil as to be portrayed to Sir George Simpson as a "den
of thieves, — the noted abode of the lowest drunkards
and gamblers of the country." It was no better with Branciforte. Its *comisionado* was gone, and by union with the
ex-mission of San José it had risen in population to 470
souls; but morally it was profligate, and politically it
remained subject to Monterey, where it had been placed
in 1835.

The establishments best fitted for municipalization
were the presidios. As fortresses they had fallen to de-
cay, but otherwise they were improved. They were seaports, and as such gathered to themselves inhabitants and
developed activity. San Diego, which in 1827 is described
by the traveler Duhaut-Cilly as "without doubt the best
port geographically in all California," had in 1835 been
made a municipality by the introduction of an *ayuntamiento*, and in 1840 consisted of fifty adobe structures.
Santa Bárbara, which in 1827 had been "a closed square
surrounded with houses of a single story," — some "sixty
to eighty of them, each with its little garden," — had
become a municipality in 1834, and in 1842 consisted
of perhaps 900 inhabitants — their houses "whitewashed
adobes with painted balconies and verandas." Monterey,
which in 1825 had been a presidial quadrangle with forty
houses outside the walls, had in 1826 been made a municipality by the election of a full *ayuntamiento*, and in 1841
consisted of a population of about 500, housed, except
when on horseback, which was "almost always," in the
usual adobes. Finally, San Francisco, which in 1825 had
as a presidio consisted of "120 houses and a church,"

had become a municipality in 1835, and by 1846 — counting the fifty souls of the new village of Yerba Buena, added in 1840 — possessed a total of about 300.[53]

In promoting municipalization, Governor Figueroa was foremost. He introduced *ayuntamientos* at San Diego and San Francisco, and perfected them at Santa Bárbara and Monterey.[54] Under Alvarado the movement, though progressive, was conducted on lines less liberal. In 1837, under the Centralist Constitution of 1836, prefectures, *partidos*, and justices of the peace were introduced. *Ayuntamientos* were restricted to the capital, to communities where they had existed prescriptively, to seaports of a population of 4000, and to pueblos of a population of 8000. Places deprived of *ayuntamientos* were to be governed by justices of the peace, who were to be proposed by the sub-prefects, nominated by the prefects, and approved by the governor. The first effect of this system, so far as Alta California was concerned, was to abolish *ayuntamientos* at all points except Los Ángeles (the capital), and San José, Monterey, and Branciforte, — places entitled to them by prescription. Its second effect was to systematize the judiciary.

Judicial recourse under Spain (*vide* chapter VII) was first to the presidial comandante, or pueblo *comisionado*, and then to the governor. It remained unchanged under Mexico save as change was effected by the removal of the *comisionados*. California by 1828 had been brought within the jurisdiction of a circuit court for Sinaloa and Sonora; and by 1830 in that of a district court nominally within Alta California borders.[55] In 1831 the President of the Mexican Republic advised that the system of *alcalde* rule, which on the removal of the *comisionados* had become completely established, should be superseded by that of *jueces de letras* or district judges; but Victoria declared that the distances were such that one judge would be insufficient.

He furthermore declared that so ignorant and seditious
was the Alta California population, that they could be
ruled only by a system purely military; the Governor himself having been compelled to suspend the territorial
diputación.[56]

A supreme court for the territory was prescribed by law
in 1837 (a tribunal of four members with a *fiscal* and *procurador*), but it could not be organized until 1842.[57] Even
then it was little in session, owing to the disinclination of
the Southerners, who controlled it, to meet at Monterey.
Micheltorena, who abolished the prefectures to save expense, reorganized this court; but under Pío Pico, by whom
the prefectures were restored, it was superseded by a court
to consist of two justices and a *fiscal*, — a body which came
into existence not at all.[58]

American emigration to Alta California came for the
most part by the Oregon Trail, but in some part it came
by way of Santa Fé, New Mexico. This fact now assumes
a degree of importance in connection with measures taken
by Pío Pico against New Mexican horse-thieves.

Aside from John A. Sutter, the Alta Californian most
successful in managing the Indians was Mariano Guadalupe Vallejo. The tribes of the North were less docile than
those of the central region, and an officer like Vallejo —
one regardful of ceremony and the high proprieties, yet
upon occasion willing and able to strike home — appealed
to the Indian heart. But if between 1834 and 1846 order
among the Indians was preserved near Sonoma, such was
not the case to the southward. How, under the Mission,
Indians, both neophyte and Gentile, had learned to ride,
and how, by a diminution of military force, coupled with
a failure to plant a presidio in the Tulares, the thing
feared by Rivera y Moncada had resulted, and the south-

ern neophyte, seduced by the Colorado tribes, had waxed insolent, — all this we have seen in chapter XI. But with regard to the particular phase assumed by the insolence of the Indians, it remains to be said that it was horse-stealing. "Crossing the Tulare Valley and the mountains that surround it," Payéras wrote in 1818, "they [the Indians] kill the horses and eat them." And Payéras's testimony is confirmed by that of John Bidwell. "We came," he says (recalling the days of 1841), "to a place in the Sierra Nevada where there was a great quantity of horse-bones, and we did not know what it meant; we thought that an army must have perished there. They were of course horses that the Indians had driven in there and slaughtered."

But horse-stealing was not practiced by Indians alone; it was resorted to by Mexican traders. Since 1824 caravans of wagons had made annual trips from Independence, Missouri, to Santa Fé, with stocks of cottons and calicoes, and the route pursued had become famous as the Santa Fé Trail.[59] The trail, however, did not altogether terminate at Santa Fé. As early as 1828 an American trapper of that town — Sylvester Pattie — had worked his way, by the course of the Gila River and Colorado Desert, into Baja and Alta California; and between 1829 and 1833 the trappers William Wolfskill, David E. Jackson, and Ewing Young had reached Alta California, the first by way of Taos and the Mojave River to Los Ángeles, and the others more directly by way of the Gila. Wolfskill was accompanied by a few New Mexicans, and it being discovered that in exchange for *serapes* and blankets large, well-formed, serviceable mules could be obtained, a brisk trade was begun between Santa Fé and Los Ángeles.[60] In this trade the caravans were composed of pack-animals, and during the thirteen or fourteen years, 1833–1846, that the trade flourished, those engaged in it (including bands of Canadians and Americans) proved to be even more expert as horse- and mule-thieves than as merchants.

A favorite field of operations between 1838 and 1841 was the line of ranchos from San José pueblo to San Juan Bautista Mission, and another favorite field the Los Ángeles-Santa Bárbara district as far north as San Luis Obispo.[61] Raids were now at times attended by arson, by ravishing, and by killing, and culprits when taken were given short shrift. Knowing their peril, a band of thieves — Indians, Mexicans, Americans — would descend upon a Tulare rancho, stampede its horses, and push thundering across the valley for the Puerto del Cajón, beyond which they were comparatively safe. Pursuit was a task not coveted, and men were secured for it only at good wages, and then with difficulty. Especially was this true at Los Ángeles, for in the South the marauders were often Americans expert with the rifle.

In April, 1840, a daring theft of horses was made from San Luis Obispo Mission, and on May 30 Juan B. Leandro, informing the prefect of the results of a pursuit, stated that the thieves, though overtaken on the 25th at the Wells of Ramón, about one hundred leagues distant in the desert, had fled, leaving some baggage, a few horses tied, and about 1500 slaughtered. The pursuers had seen other bands of thieves with more than 1000 horses that had been stolen in small lots. "The robbers composing the rear-guard," Leandro naïvely observed, "were about twenty citizens of the United States."[62]

Resolving to put a stop to depredations, Pío Pico, on the surrender of Micheltorena in 1845, made a compact with Captain John Gantt and Dr. John Marsh to attack the *rancherías* of the lower San Joaquín and of the Merced Rivers, and deliver the captives to "Señor Sutter."[63] On his own part he organized (with what result does not appear) a movement in the South.

As already intimated, the Santa Fé Trail west of Santa Fé was but a trail of the footman and pack-mule.[64] There were two branches, — a southern branch (the general course of Anza) and a northern one, the course in part of Garcés; a course exploited in opposition to that of Anza by Governor Antonio Crespo of Sonora. In 1845, as in all the years from Anza's expedition to the expedition of José Romero, the desert awaited its master.

CHAPTER XV

WAR WITH THE UNITED STATES

"As military men, the Californians have been underrated." Lieutenant
J. B. Montgomery to Lieutenant-Colonel P. St. George Cook, January 18,
1847.

I

WHALING and the port of San Francisco were
what first drew to California the attention of the
United States Government. But a word with regard to
"hides and tallow."

Under Spain the hide and tallow trade had been confined
to government vessels like the Flora, the ship that brought
such disaster to Mr. George Washington Eayrs. But
under Mexico, with its policy of open ports, the trade became extended to the Bostonians John R. Cooper, William A. Gale, Nathan Spear, and Bryant & Sturgis, and to
the Englishmen David Spence, and McCulloch, Hartnell
& Company. In 1826 there were in California not less than
200,000 head of cattle. At the private ranchos, slaughter
(*matanza*) took place yearly, and at the missions weekly.
The hides, when not sold green, were staked out to dry;
while the tallow was "tried" and run into bags of bullock-
skin (*botas*), each with a capacity of an *arroba*, — twenty-
five pounds. An agent or supercargo (we are told by
Thomas O. Larkin) would fit up a store on board ship
with shelves, show-cases and drawers, and from it dispense
tea or shot, from a pound to a box or bag; and silk or calico,
from a yard to a bale. Men, however, like William H.
Davis (agent for Nathan Spear), or Alfred Robinson

(agent for Bryant & Sturgis), were too energetic to wait the coming of buyers to the ship. They either brought them in the ship's boats, or personally visited the ranchos and missions, penetrating to the remotest establishments around the bays of San Francisco and San Pedro.[1]

The ports of California were "open," but the term was relative. At first it applied to all ports, and the duties were moderate, averaging about 25 per cent. Later, foreign vessels were permitted to trade at presidial ports only, the way-places Santa Cruz, San Luis, Refugio, San Juan Capistrano, being closed, except to such as might enter them by favor; and the duties were increased to an average of 42.5 per cent. Still later (January, 1828) all way-ports were closed to foreign vessels, except San Pedro, and in July it also was closed. This was followed by the closing to foreigners of every port of Lower and Upper California, except Loreto and Monterey; although in Upper California San Diego was kept open by special license. Monterey itself was not granted a customs building till 1837.

As a result of the conditions named, smuggling recurred, and the Sandwich Islands were built up at California's expense. Martínez had pointed out to the Viceroy as early as 1788 that foreigners, by using Hawaii as a haven of refuge and a source of food, were to menace Spanish supremacy, and his words were significant. In 1820, seven American missionaries from New England had landed at the Islands. They, who of course were Protestant, were followed in 1827 by two Catholic padres, Alexis Bachelot and Patrick Short. In 1831, the padres were banished by order of the Hawaiian native government; and in 1843, "Mr. Coan," pastor of the Protestant congregation at Honolulu, wrote: "The power and grace of our God have hitherto preserved us from these 'ravening wolves.' Adored be his name!"[2]

But be the attitude of the New Englanders what it might, prosperity grew under their sway. A whaler (the Mary) arrived the first year. In 1827 the ship-yard and wharf of Robinson & Company were built. In 1836 a newspaper in English, the "Sandwich Island Gazette," was established, with an American editor. Indeed, so far as trade and ideas were concerned, Honolulu by 1836 was a distant suburb of Boston. People after siesta read the "Transcript" and Dr. Lyman Beecher's lectures. At Monterey whalers were allowed to purchase provisions by selling a limited quantity (four hundred dollars worth) of manufactures. At Honolulu they might purchase provisions by selling any quantities of manufactures. It was estimated in 1844 that the annual whaling-trade at the Islands was worth at least two hundred and fifty thousand dollars. Said the "California Star" in 1848, "If we allow a fair proportion of the trade with whalers, merchantmen, and men-of-war to be transferred [from Honolulu] to the coast, it will make an immediate change of about half a million a year."

But what of smuggling? By the more timid it was conducted through the method, time-honored and genteel, of the *douceur* or "gratification." The bolder traders — those with a taste for adventure — preferred to "transship" the valuable part of a cargo at one of the Santa Bárbara Channel Islands or at some retired nook of the mainland coast, and, having paid duties on the remainder, to return to the rendezvous, reship, and proceed with the voyage. The Sandwich Island traders, Master John Lawler of the Karimoko, and Captain John Bradshaw of the Franklin, were guilty of transshipment practices in more than an ordinary degree. Lawler made his rendezvous at the Island of Catalina, while Bradshaw's favorite resorts were in Lower California. The latter was arrested in 1828 at San Diego, but, like his predecessor of the Lelia Byrd, managed to get aboard his vessel and run the gauntlet of the defenses, the whole ship's company deriding the Mexican flag, as, pursued by forty cannon-shot, they sped past it seaward.

We are indebted to the trade in hides and tallow for "Two Years Before the Mast," by Richard H. Dana, Jr., of Boston, who first in the Pilgrim and then in the Alert traversed the California coast in 1834–36. Of San Juan Capistrano, Dana says: —

The country here for several miles is high table-land running boldly to the shore and breaking off in a steep cliff at the foot of which the waters of the Pacific are constantly dashing. . . . The rocks were as large as those of Nahant or Newport, but to my eye more grand and broken. Besides, there was a grandeur in everything around, which gave a solemnity to the scene, a silence and solitariness which affected every part! Not a human being but ourselves for miles, and no sound heard but the pulsations of the great Pacific. . . . Reaching the brow of the hill . . . we found several piles of hides, and Indians sitting around them. One or two carts were coming slowly from the Mission, and the Captain told us to begin and throw the hides down. This, then, was the way they were to be got down, — thrown down one at a time, a distance of four hundred feet. . . . Standing on the edge of the hill and looking down the perpendicular height, the sailors

> That walked upon the beach,
> Appeared like mice; and our tall anchoring bark
> Diminished to her cock; her cock a buoy
> Almost too small for sight.

But it is not alone "Two Years Before the Mast" that we owe to the hide and tallow trade. Indirectly we owe to it Alfred Robinson's "Life in California." Dana's book, though charming, lacked in appreciation of the Californians; and to present in this respect a truer picture, Robinson, in 1846, wrote his book, — one hardly less charming than its predecessor.

II

As has been remarked in chapter xiv, San Francisco in 1846 contained about three hundred *gente de razón*.[3] Of this population by far the most active portion was that identified with Yerba Buena, the anchorage to the south of Telegraph Hill. In 1842 the settlement consisted of but ten or a dozen houses, all near the waterside (Montgomery Street);[4] and the principal residents were William A. Richardson, William Hinckley, Nathan Spear, Jacob P. Leese, Jean Jacques Vioget, and William G. Rae. Rae was local factor of the Hudson's Bay Company. Alvarado had conceded a franchise for the Company to Chief Factor James Douglas in 1841, and its actual presence in 1842 gave rise to a solicitude regarding California that was general. The feeling was entertained not only by Californians, but by England, France, and the United States.

Sir George Simpson, governor-in-chief of the Hudson's Bay Company, and John McLoughlin, the company's chief factor on the Pacific Coast, visited San Francisco, Monterey, and Santa Bárbara in January, 1842. Lord Palmerston, British Foreign Secretary, had just quitted office, and officials everywhere were under the influence of his assertive temper. In 1841 James Douglas had noted in his journal: "We have . . . objects [in entering California] of a political nature."[5] It appears that such objects were not alien to the mind of Sir George Simpson. Addressing Sir John Petty, governor of the Hudson's Bay Company, on March 10, 1842, the former said: —

This sale [of Ross to Sutter] was effected previously to my arrival, otherwise it is probable I should have made a purchase of the establishment for the Hudson's Bay Company with a view to the possibility of some claim being based thereon by Great Britain at a future period. . . . The Governor [Alvarado], who

seven years ago was appraiser of custom-house goods, is an ignorant, dissipated man, quite devoid of respectability and character; and the commander of the forces [Vallejo], the next in rank
and standing, who was a few years back a lieutenant in the army,
has no pretension to character or respectability, and, like most
others in the country, betrays a gross want of honesty and
veracity, while much jealousy and ill-will exists between these
great men, who are total strangers to every feeling of honor,
honesty or patriotism, and, I believe, are ready to sell themselves
and their country at a moment's notice, to the highest bidder.
. . . Many of the British residents are much respected, and the
feeling of the different classes of the natives is favorable to Great
Britain, while they look upon the United States, and her citizens, with much jealousy and alarm. . . . I have reason to
believe they would require very little encouragement to declare
their independence of Mexico, and place themselves under the
protection of Great Britain.[6]

A circumstance tending at this time to invoke Palmer-
stonian methods was the Graham affair. Barron, the British
vice-consul at Tepic (instigated by the American Thomas
J. Farnham), had been active in behalf of the Grahamites
through representations to Minister Pakenham in Mexico;
and on August 30, 1841, the latter had written to Palmerston that it was by "all means desirable, in a political point
of view, that California, once ceasing to belong to Mexico
should not fall into the hands of any power but England."
It was to be regretted, he said, that "advantage should
not be taken of the arrangement some time since concluded by the Mexican Government with their creditors in
Europe, to establish an English population in the magnificent Territory of Upper California." Especially was this
to be regretted, as there was "reason to believe that daring
and adventurous speculators in the United States had
already turned their thoughts in that direction [i. e., control of California]."[7]

But Palmerston could no longer be approached, and the

pacific Lord Aberdeen, his successor, dismissed the Pakenham suggestions with promptness. In 1842, however, the
British Minister appointed a vice-consul at Monterey,
James A. Forbes, and it soon became evident that the
opinion of Simpson and Barron that California was inclined toward a British protectorate was not without
foundation. In September, Forbes was waited upon by
a body of native Californians, and the question was put to
him: "Whether this country can be received under the
protection of Great Britain, in a similar manner to that
of the Ionian Isles, but to remain for the present under the
direct government of one of its natives, though under
the same form as the government of that Republic."[8]

To this question, submitted by Forbes through Barron,
the British Secretary replied, on December 31, 1844, that
while Great Britain could not interfere as between California and Mexico, still she "would view with much dissatisfaction the establishment of a protectoral power over
California by any other foreign state."[9] Aberdeen's change
of attitude had been caused by fear of expansion of the
United States through the annexation of Texas.[10] What
Great Britain now looked forward to with satisfaction
was a Texas and a California both independent of Mexico,
and both at the same time independent of the United
States.

So far as France was concerned, solicitude for California was that rather of the reflective observer than the
politician. Pérouse in 1786 and Duhaut-Cilly in 1827 had
each reported intelligently upon the country; and in
August, 1839, Captain Cyrille Pierre Théodore Laplace
had visited Ross, San Francisco, and Monterey, in the
Artémise. His description of the California women —
*jolies, gracieuses, bien faites, de grands yeux noirs au
regard expressif, de belles dents bien blanches, une longue*

*chevelure couleur de jais digne de leur descendance anda-
louse* — recalls the word-portrait of Doña Concepción
by Langsdorff. What political element the French position involved was emphasized by the visit of M. Eugène
Duflot de Mofras in 1841. He came from Mexico, where
he was attaché, by way of the coast states, and, having
stopped at Monterey and San Francisco, passed to Fort
Vancouver, whence he returned to San Francisco in the
same ship with Sir George Simpson and John McLoughlin.
In Mofras's opinion, it was the fate of California "to be
conquered by Great Britain or the United States, unless it
placed itself under the protection of some European monarchy — preferably France. . . . All the people," he said,
"were by religion, manners, language, and origin naturally
antipathetic to the English and to the Americans." [11]

Between Mofras and Vallejo (precisians and martinets)
no love was lost, and the anxieties of the latter regarding the Anglo-Americans, the Hudson's Bay Company, and
Sutter were increased by anxiety regarding the possible
intentions of His Majesty, Louis Philippe. "There is no
doubt," wrote Vallejo to Alvarado in July, "that France
is intriguing to become mistress of California"; [12] and,
to confirm the suspicion, the French Government, on
November 18, 1847, appointed a vice-consul of its own
at Monterey, M. Louis Gasquet.

It was the United States, however, as Sir George Simpson pointed out, toward which California had come to feel
alarm genuine and immediate. So long as the country was
known at a distance, — known, that is, through a few serviceable representatives like Stearns, Robinson, and Larkin,
and (be it said) like Mr. George Washington Eayrs, — she
was respected and even admired. Tired of Mexico, — her
Victorias, her Chicos, her Cholos, and her tariff, — and

eager for a rule of "native sons," the American theory of government appealed to the California leaders, padres no less than politicians. "When will your government come and take possession of this country?" asked the padres of Alfred Robinson; while as for the politicians, one at least (Alvarado) exalted Washington. During the contest with Gutiérrez, Don Juan Bautista had thought of qualified independence for the land under some protectorate foreign yet benign, — possibly that of the United States.

But the United States was a power whereof the Californians were destined to gain a nearer view. In 1826 and 1827 Captain Frederick William Beechey (H. M. S. Blossom) had visited California while awaiting the arrival of Sir John Franklin from the Arctic regions, and in 1831 had published an account of his voyage. It was evident, Beechey wrote, that California must awaken from the lethargy by which it was possessed "under the present authorities or fall into other hands. . . ." It was of "too much importance to be permitted to remain longer in its present neglected state."[13] But before the coming of Beechey, California had been visited by an American skipper, Captain Benjamin Morrell, Jr., of the Tartar, and in 1832 Morrell likewise had published a book. "These beautiful regions [were they but the property of the United States] would not," he said, "be permitted to remain neglected." "The eastern and middle states would pour into them their thousands of emigrants, until magnificent cities would rise on the shores of every inlet along the coast, while the wilderness of the interior would be made to blossom like the rose."[14]

The observations of Morrell show that even thus early the United States was not indifferent to California's future; and in 1835 President Andrew Jackson, mindful of whaling interests on the Northwest Coast, authorized the American chargé in Mexico, an old comrade in arms, Colonel Anthony Butler, to purchase "the whole bay of San Francisco." It was suggested that a line be run northward along the east bank of the Río Bravo del Norte to the thirty-seventh parallel, and then west to the Pacific. Monterey might be excluded from the purchase, as it was not the desire of the United States "to interfere with the actual settlements of Mexico on the Pacific Coast."

But the inception of the movement for the acquisition of California lies further back. In 1819 Spain had ceded to the United States all her North American territory west of the Mississippi River to the northward of the forty-second parallel, — to the northward, that is, of Texas, New Mexico, and California. President John Quincy Adams contemplated acquiring Texas in 1825, but quitted office without actual overtures, and in 1829 Adams was succeeded by Jackson, who offered five million dollars. The offer was made through Butler, but failed, and in 1835 the chargé came to Washington. While there he submitted a new plan of operations. Texas was to be secured by bribing Hernández, Santa Anna's confessor. "Five hundred thousand, judiciously applied," Hernández had assured Butler, "would conclude the matter." The treaty, Butler said, "would be the first of a series which must at last give us dominion over the whole of that tract of territory known as New Mexico, and the higher and lower California, an empire in itself, a paradise in climate, . . . rich in minerals, and affording a water route to the Pacific through the Arkansas and Colorado Rivers."[15]

Naught came of the plan, and in 1841 John Tyler became President, with Daniel Webster as Secretary of State, and Waddy Thompson as Minister to Mexico. In 1842, on April 29, Thompson informed Webster that he

was convinced that Mexico would cede Texas and the
Californias in payment of claims by American merchants.

> As to Texas [he said], I regard it as of but little value compared
> with California, the richest, the most beautiful, and the healthi-
> est country in the world. Our Atlantic border secures us a com-
> mercial ascendency on the Pacific. The harbor of San Francisco
> is capacious enough to receive the navies of the world. In addi-
> tion to which California is destined to be the granary of the
> Pacific. It is a country in which slavery is not necessary, and
> therefore, if that is made an objection, let there be another com-
> promise. France and England both have had their eyes upon it.
> The latter has yet. I am profoundly satisfied that in its bearing
> upon all the interests of our country, the importance of the
> acquisition of California cannot be over-estimated.[16]

The proposition of Thompson was accepted by Webster
to the extent of authorizing negotiations for "a good harbor on the Pacific." Great Britain was consulted, and
Lord Aberdeen (his original attitude as yet unchanged)
gave assurance that "the Queen's Government . . . had
not the slightest objection to an acquisition of territory
[by the United States] in that direction."[17] Then (October, 1842) came the seizure of Monterey by Commodore
Jones and negotiations ceased.

They were resumed in 1845 under James K. Polk.
Texas had been annexed on March 1, and it now was
intended (so Polk himself declared[18]) to enter if possible
into diplomatic relations with Mexico, and secure California by purchase. The Mexican Government was responsible in various amounts to American merchants; let
these amounts be liquidated by a cession of territory. To
manage the affair, representatives were required at two
points, — Mexico City and Monterey. John Slidell accordingly was dispatched as plenipotentiary to the one,
while at the other Thomas O. Larkin, who had served as

United States Consul since April 2, 1844, was made "confidential agent." On July 10, 1845, Larkin had warned the American Government of the maintenance by France and England of consulates in California, and of the fact (so believed) that Mr. Rae had in 1844 furnished the Californians with arms and money to enable them to expel the Mexicans from the country; and it was because of this warning that the confidential agency was created.

You should exert the greatest vigilance [the consul was instructed on October 17] in discovering and defeating any attempts which may be made by foreign governments to acquire a control over that country. In the contest between Mexico and California we can take no part, unless the former should commence hostilities against the United States ; but should California assert and maintain her independence, we shall render her all the kind offices in our power as a Sister Republic. . . . The President could not view with indifference the transfer of California to Great Britain or any other European power. . . . On all proper occasions you should not fail prudently to warn the government and people of California of the danger of such an interference [by Great Britain or France] to their peace and prosperity, — to inspire them with a jealousy of European dominion, and to arouse in their bosoms that love of liberty and independence so natural to the American Continent. . . . If the people should desire to unite their destiny with ours, they would be received as brethren. . . . The President has thought proper to appoint you a confidential agent in California; and you may consider the present dispatch as your authority for acting in that character.[19]

Thus in 1845 the United States placed herself toward California in the exact position in which Great Britain had placed herself in 1844. That is to say, she would welcome independence with a view to acquisition. Further than this there was to be a difference. Great Britain as a suitor was to be observant and passive. The United States was to be observant and active.

But to complicate matters for the latter, there arose just here the fact of the "nearer view." Graham and his followers had ridiculed California officials and defied California laws. The land, moreover, was fast filling with American settlers of whom the greater part, though not like the Grahamites, were yet little tolerant of what to them were institutions paternal and antiquated. For Larkin, therefore, to inspire among Californians a wish to "unite their destiny" with that of his countrymen was a task not without difficulty. Leading men (José Castro, more especially) gave the new agent to understand that they might not object to the United States, provided, in the event of a transfer of allegiance, they could be assured of their positions and salaries.[20] On April 27, Larkin wrote to Jacob P. Leese at Sonoma, Abel Stearns at Los Ángeles, and John Warner at San Diego (all Mexican citizens, but all former Americans and all friendly to the United States), urging them to foster pro-American opinion in their respective localities. He then procured a translation of his official instructions into Spanish, and, adroitly modifying the document, showed it as "my opinion" to "different Californians in authority." And not only so, but at a General Council of Pueblos called to meet at Santa Bárbara on June 15, 1846, to consider the state of the country, he used every effort to secure the attendance of Leese, Vallejo, and Stearns. It was Larkin's opinion at this time that one thousand emigrants would arrive at New Helvetia in October. Should this prove true, and should the number for 1847 be commensurate with that for 1846 the destinies of California would, he declared, be decided by 1848.[21]

James K. Polk had planned to obtain California by purchase, but in the event that Mexico would not sell, what had he planned to do then? Did he purpose to force

Mexico into war, or were his concentration of troops on the Texas border and his increase of naval force in the Pacific (both effected in 1845) merely precautionary measures against hostilities by Mexico; hostilities which Mexico had threatened should the United States annex Texas? To these questions conflicting answers were (and are) possible;[22] but what concerns us here is the fact of the arrival in California of John C. Frémont.

III

Thirty-two years old, son of a French father and Virginia mother, Frémont was son-in-law to Thomas H. Benton (United States Senator from Missouri) and brevet-captain of topographical engineers in the United States Army.[23] He had entered California in 1844, performing the feat of crossing the Sierra Nevada, amid cold and snow, by way of Carson River and Johnson's Pass. The expedition of 1844 was his second to the West, the first (1842) having taken him to the summit of the Wind River Chain of the Rocky Mountains, at a point known since as Frémont's Peak. With twenty-five men our explorer had gone from the Dalles (Oregon) south to Klamath Lake, thence southeast past Pyramid Lake (Nevada), which he named, to Salmon Trout (Truckee) River, and thence to Carson River, whence he had turned west. The objects of his search had been, first, Mary's (Humboldt) Lake, and next, "the San Buenaventura River, reputed to flow from the Rocky Mountains to the bay of San Francisco." After a fortnight at New Helvetia, the party, reduced to nineteen, had ascended the San Joaquín to Kings River, traversed Tehachapi Pass, found the Santa Fé Trail, and passed by it to Utah Lake.

The tours of 1842 and 1844, described in a lucid report to the government,[24] brought to Frémont reputation at home and abroad; but the present tour, that of 1845-46, was to bring him notoriety. Entering California by way of Walker Lake and the Truckee, he reached Sutter's Fort on December 10, 1845, and turned southward to meet a division of his party under Joseph Walker, who had entered by way of Owens River and Lake, and were encamped at "the forks of the main river flowing into Tulares Lake." But by the expression, "forks of the main river," Walker understood the Kern River Forks, and Frémont those of Kings River; and the two divisions (in all about sixty men) remained separated until February 15, when they were united at the Laguna Farm, some twelve miles south of San José.[25]

In 1844 the California authorities had been curious to know Frémont's business, for hardly had he gone south ere an officer had appeared at Sutter's Fort. Now, January 29, 1846, Prefect Manuel Castro sent to Consul Larkin, whom the captain had visited on the 27th at Monterey, a note of inquiry. With what object, he asked, had United States troops entered the department? Frémont's reply, addressed to José Castro as comandante-general, was that the party had come by order of the United States Government to survey a route to the Pacific; that the men (fifty in number) were not soldiers, — that they had been left on the departmental frontier; and that when recruited from their journey they would proceed thence northward to Oregon.[26] But in February, after the reunion of his command, our captain started for the coast by way of Los Gatos and the Santa Cruz Mountains. His appearance with his men in the Santa Clara Valley roused apprehension, and on making camp in the Salinas Valley, at Hartnell's Rancho, he was met, March 5, by an order from José Castro "to retire beyond the limits of the department," as he had "entered the settlements, a thing

prohibited by law." Later a similar order was received
from Prefect Manuel Castro,[27] and Frémont, orally refusing compliance, retired to Gavilán (Hawk) Peak, where
he erected fortifications and raised the United States flag.

Whatever Frémont's motive in approaching the coast
(and there is no indication that he meant to provoke
enmity),[28] his withdrawal within fortifications, without
explanation, was a blunder. Castro menaced him with a
force of two hundred men, and Larkin warned him against
"treachery" and "the vengeance of the common people."
Accordingly, on the 9th, having written to the consul that
he was preparing in the case of attack "to fight to extremity and accept no quarter," he quitted his defenses, proceeded by slow marches to Sutter's Fort, thence to Lassen's
Rancho, and by May was at the north end of Klamath
Lake on the way to Oregon. While here (May 8) he was
overtaken by couriers with the news that behind him was
a United States naval officer with "dispatches" — Lieutenant Archibald H. Gillespie. Hastening south, attended
by the pick of his followers (Kit Carson, Richard Owens,
Alexis Godey, Basil Lajeunesse and four Delaware braves),
— men, their leader said, worthy to be made marshals for
cool courage, — Frémont, after a ride of twenty-five miles,
met the lieutenant, obtained his "dispatches," and went
to bed. That night his camp was surprised by Indians,
who killed Lajeunesse and one of the Delawares; but by
May 24 the party were again in the Sacramento Valley.

Americans, as would-be settlers in California, were
without status. Passports, it is true, had been given them
by Vallejo, Castro, or Sutter (the latter upon his own responsibility), but the holders, not being Mexican citizens,
were disqualified from owning or occupying land. Aware
of the situation, the Mexican Government on July 10,

1845, had instructed the Governor of Alta California "to prevent the introduction of families from the Missouri and Columbia Rivers, as otherwise the general order of the department would be subverted, foreign relations complicated, and embarrassment created."[29] These instructions it was that had pointed the pens of the two Castros in their curt missives to Frémont. "The undersigned," wrote Manuel Castro to Larkin, on March 8, 1846, "when he ordered Captain Frémont to withdraw, based his action on repeated orders and decrees of the supreme government of the Mexican Republic, which prohibit the introduction not only of troops belonging to any power, but even of foreigners who do not come provided with passports."[30] And on April 30, Sub-Prefect Francisco Guerrero sent word to Larkin that "a multitude of foreigners [having] come into California and bought fixed property [land], a right of naturalized foreigners only, he was under necessity of notifying the authorities in each town to inform such purchasers that the transactions were invalid and they themselves subject to be expelled whenever the government might find it convenient." [31]

But noticeable as was the effect of the instructions from Mexico upon the California officials, the effect upon the settlers themselves was more noticeable still. Warnings such as those from Castro and Guerrero recalled the summary eviction of the Grahamites, and alarm became widespread. It was reported, and everywhere believed, that José Castro had threatened to drive all foreigners from the country. Larkin, in April, wrote of "rumors that Castro was collecting people to force settlers from the Sacramento." As early, indeed, as November 4, 1845, the consul had officially declared: "There is a strong jealousy springing up in this country against Americans. . . . I shall be in continual expectation of hearing of some outbreak from one or the other, in one or two years, perhaps in less time." [32]

Frémont (a United States Army officer), returning from the borders of Oregon with Gillespie (an officer of the Navy), was to the fears of the settlers as a spark to powder. Had he not withdrawn to avoid a conflict? Had not Gillespie followed him with dispatches, and had he not, on being overtaken, returned? What could it mean but that the cause of the settlers was to be championed from Washington? That Frémont was in fact directed, or authorized, to incite, encourage, or countenance disorder in California is not, I think, to be believed. The statement almost refutes itself. Gillespie, at the same time that he brought dispatches to Frémont, brought to Larkin the instructions creating the confidential agency, instructions which forbade interference in California affairs. Is it likely that what was forbidden to the agent was permitted to the officer? [33] But concerning the instructions, the settlers knew as little as concerning the "dispatches," and they were controlled by their imaginings.

About June 5, 1846, General José Castro obtained from Vallejo, comandante of the northern frontier, 170 horses. They were put in charge of Lieutenants Francisco Arce and José María Alviso, who were to conduct them across the Sacramento, by way of Knight's Landing, to the general at Santa Clara. Rumor declared that the horses were to be used in operations to free the land of foreigners and to establish a fort on Bear River. This rumor Knight carried to Frémont's camp at the junction of the rivers Bear and Feather, and on June 9 some dozen men from near the camp started in pursuit of Arce. The band, commanded by Ezekiel Merritt (phenomenal as a tobacco-chewer), surprised Arce at dawn of the 10th, seized the horses, and telling the lieutenant that if Castro wanted them he might come and take them, rejoined Frémont, now on Bear River, on the morning of the 11th.[34] The same day it was decided to capture Sonoma, where, under Vallejo, nine small cannon and two hundred muskets constituted a kind of presidio. Twenty in number, the band at once set forth (Merritt in command), and having passed through Napa Valley, where by help of Dr. Robert Semple and John Grigsby its number was recruited to thirty-two or thirty-three, appeared on June 14 at dawn before Vallejo's house.

Merritt and Semple, with perhaps others, entered, and Jacob P. Leese (Vallejo's son-in-law) was chosen interpreter. Leese was surprised at the "rough looks" of the Americans. Semple he describes as "six feet six inches tall and about fifteen inches in diameter, dressed in greasy buckskin from neck to foot, and with a fox-skin cap." The object of the revolt, Semple said, was "to make California a free and independent government; arms and horses were needed, and these Vallejo could supply." A capitulation, embracing Vallejo, his brother Don Salvador, and his secretary Victor Prudon, was drafted and signed, and, stimulated by liberal refreshment, the Americans withdrew. In so doing, however, they insisted on sending the capitulators to Frémont as prisoners.

Merritt by this time had been superseded in command by Grigsby, but the latter resigning, William B. Ide was chosen in his stead. By him the prisoners were dispatched inland, under Merritt, Semple, Grigsby, and others. No vigilance was exercised, and rescue would in all probability have been effected at the stopping-place for the night, Vaca's rancho, had not Vallejo refused to coöperate. Frémont, after some search, was found (June 15) on American River, and, though disclaiming any part in the Sonoma affair, gave orders for the arrest of Leese, who still was in attendance as interpreter, and for the confinement of all the prisoners in Sutter's Fort. "We pass^d the next day," writes Leese, "in the most aughful manner a reflecting on the cituation of our familys and property in the hands of such a desperate set of men."[35]

But the news had spread. On the 15th, José J. Estudillo wrote from San Leandro to José Dolores Pacheco, justice of the peace, at San José: —

Just this moment [eleven o'clock at night] I have learned from the citizen Rafael Feliz, who was sent post haste by Don Jesus Vallejo on behalf of his brother Don Guadalupe, that yesterday Don Guadalupe and Don Salvador Vallejo, Don Victor Prudon, and Don Luis Leis [Leese] were surprised in their houses by the American foreigners, and were taken prisoners toward Feather River, the same Feliz having seen them pass the rancho of Cayetano Suarez, guarded by twelve foreigners including Merritt as Captain.[36]

At Sonoma, meanwhile, quiet prevailed. A flag (the "Bear Flag") had been raised, and Ide was inditing a proclamation.[37]

From the capture of Sonoma two things resulted: (1) The plan of Larkin — that of the Polk administration, that of securing California by quiet and unobtrusive means, a plan the consummation of which would have brought to Larkin personally much distinction — was shattered;[38] (2) Englishmen in California were stirred with renewed expectation of a British protectorate. The Vallejo circle, personal and political, had been favorable to the United States. The effect upon it of the harsh treatment of Vallejo himself (Frémont consenting) may be surmised. At the time of the activities on Gavilán, Larkin, apprehensive of bloodshed, had sent to United States Consul John Parrott, at Mazatlán, for a warship, and on

April 22 the Portsmouth, John B. Montgomery commander, had cast anchor at Monterey. Just before leaving Sonoma, Vallejo had contrived to send to Montgomery, then at Sauzalito, a messenger, José de la Rosa, asking protection for his family. Lieutenant John Misroon was commissioned to visit Sonoma, where, on June 16–17, he found the Bear Flag flying, Ide's proclamation ready, and Vallejo's household alarmed and indignant.

But alarm and indignation in the Vallejo circle were not confined to the Vallejo family. On the 17th of June, — the day of Misroon's departure, — José Castro, in a proclamation from Santa Clara, spoke of the children of Don Guadalupe as "snatched from the bosom of their father, who is prisoner among foreigners": and adjured his "fellow countrymen" to "rise *en masse*, irresistible and just." His own force he recruited to 160 men under J. A. Carrillo, Joaquín de la Torre, and Manuel Castro, and on the 23d sent Torre with fifty or sixty men across from San Pablo to Point Quentín, to reconnoitre the position of Ide, which within a day or two he meant to attack with his entire command. It so happened that on June 18 or 19 two men, Cowie and Fowler, had been sent by Ide to the Fitch Rancho on Russian River for powder. The men were captured by a band of Californians under Juan Padilla (a Mexican barber) and Ramón Carrillo, and put to death with torture and mutilation. William L. Todd and other Americans were captured about this time, and on the 23d, the day that Torre crossed to the Sonoma side of the bay, Lieutenant Henry L. Ford of the Bear party, with some eighteen volunteers, set forth to effect a rescue. At Olompali, between San Rafael and Petaluma, he came upon Torre's men, with those of Padilla, breakfasting at the Camilo Rancho. The Americans were attacked by the enemy, but having posted themselves behind trees, so handled their rifles as to kill one Californian (Lieutenant Manuel Cantua) and wound several others.

The Bear party had anticipated a demonstration by Castro north of the bay, and, on the same 23d of June, Frémont (regardless of circumspection[39]) left American River with ninety men for Sonoma. From this point, which he reached on the 25th, he set out with 130 men for San Rafael Mission. While here (June 28) a boat with four strangers was seen approaching from San Pablo. This boat Kit Carson with a squad was sent to intercept. It landed at Point San Pedro, and, three of the strangers having debarked, Carson and his men left their horses, advanced, took careful aim, and shot them down. The victims proved to be Francisco and Ramón de Haro of San Francisco, and José de los Reyes Berreyesa, an aged ranchero of Santa Clara. An eye-witness of the affair, Jasper O'Farrell, stated in 1856 that Carson asked Frémont whether he should make prisoners of the strangers, and that the lieutenant, waving his hand, replied, "I have no room for prisoners." The tragedy is explained by Senator Benton in a letter. "In return," he says, "for the murder of Cowie and Fowler, three of De la Torre's men, being taken, were instantly shot." It was Joaquín de la Torre whom Frémont and the "Bears" in reality sought, but the former was wily, and by dispatches written to be intercepted sent his adversaries, alarmed, to their base; while he, with seventy-five or eighty Californians, made good a retreat to the south of the bay by way of Sauzalito. Frémont thereupon (July 1) crossed, by help of Captain W. D. Phelps of the Moscow, to the Castillo of San Joaquín, and spiked each of its unresisting ten guns.

Expectations of a British protectorate as a result of the capture of Sonoma rested upon three facts: First, that on

January 28, 1846, Consul Forbes had formally protested
against the presence of Frémont in California; second, that
the same year, early in June, H. M. S. Juno, under Captain Blake (Pacific fleet of Admiral Sir George Seymour),
had arrived at Monterey, conveying the Irish priest and
missionary Eugene McNamara; and third, that on June 17
the Juno, with McNamara and Consul Forbes both on
board, sailed for Santa Bárbara. "It is the duty of the
undersigned," so Forbes's protest ran, "to state clearly and
distinctly to this Departmental Government that while
Great Britain does not pretend to interfere in the political
affairs of California, she would view with much dissatisfaction the establishment of a protectorate power over
this country by any other foreign nation."[40]

The visit of the Juno to Santa Bárbara — a visit to obtain from Governor Pico approval of a grant to McNamara
of land for a colony [41] — served to give emphasis to this
protest, for both Blake and Forbes warned Pico against
a protectorate.[42] Whether the protest and warning were
warranted, depended on whether Aberdeen intended to
abide by his instructions to Forbes of December 31, 1844.
As it chanced, circumstances for Great Britain had
changed; and the Foreign Office, reverting to the position
assumed when it had assured Webster that, so far as California was concerned, "the Queen's Government . . . had
not the slightest objection to an acquisition by the United
States of territory in that direction," dismissed Forbes
with the curt observation, "Her Majesty's Government do
not approve of his late proceeding."

IV

Embarrassment from the Sonoma affair was forestalled
by an event long looked for: war between the United
States and Mexico.

The American force at this time in the Pacific — two ships (the Savannah and Congress), four sloops (the Warren, Portsmouth, Cyane, and Levant) and a schooner (the Shark) — was commanded by Commodore John D. Sloat. Under instructions from Secretary George Bancroft, issued June 24, 1845, and reiterated at intervals to May 13, 1846, Sloat in the event of war was to "possess himself of the port of San Francisco" and of such other California ports as might be open to seizure, "preserving if possible the most friendly relations with the inhabitants." News of war reached Sloat at Mazatlán in 1846 on May 17, but the commodore, though sending the sloop Cyane under Captain William Mervine to Monterey with a confidential message for Larkin, was disposed to await a formal declaration of hostilities before proceeding north himself. On June 7, however, word was received of an attack upon General Taylor and of a blockade of Vera Cruz, and on the 8th Sloat set sail, reaching Monterey with his flagship (the Savannah) on July 2. Here under the influence of Larkin (loath to resign the old plan) the commodore delayed five days, but at length, on the 7th, he disembarked 250 men, who raised over the custom-house the American flag, fired a salute, and posted a proclamation declaring California annexed to the United States.[43] On July 9, by order of Lieutenant Montgomery of the Portsmouth, the flag was raised by Lieutenant Joseph W. Revere over San Francisco and Sonoma, and on the 11th, by Revere's messenger, Edward M. Kern, over Sutter's Fort.

Under the treaty of February 22, 1845, with Micheltorena, the civil and military commands in California were disjoined, and, as of yore, the disadvantages of the arrangement were manifest. Pico was governor, but José

Castro was comandante-general. The one, moreover, represented the South and the other the North. Trouble with the United States (a military matter) was apprehended, wherefore Castro, arrogating supreme authority, refused to divide with Pico — a mere civil functionary — the departmental revenues in the proportion (lately decreed in Mexico) of two to one in favor of the latter.

By the date of the seizure of Monterey, the situation between Pico and Castro was Brutus and Cassius-like in the extreme. On March 17, the comandante-general had reported to the assembly the affair with Frémont, announcing an intention to defend the country alone, if the Governor, in a rôle suitably subordinate, should not come to his aid; moreover, that the defense might be the more effective, Castro early in April had sent Andrés Castillero (discoverer of the Almadén quicksilver mine) to Mexico for munitions, and had summoned a military *junta* at Monterey. This *junta*, which had met in April, had on April 30 been violently assailed by Pico, who on May 13 had summoned the General Council of Pueblos, already mentioned, for "determining all that [might] be deemed best [in order] to avoid the fatal events impending at home and abroad." To Castro a General Council was "abominable"; was the "product of the insane hydra of discord"; was "execrable profanation"; was "unheard-of disloyalty"; was "perjury"; and on June 8 he had proclaimed martial law. Thereupon (June 16) the Governor had quitted Los Ángeles with a military force, and by the 21st had been at Santa Bárbara on his way north to exact submission. Here on June 23 he had heard of the capture of Sonoma, and from here, after much parley with Manuel Castro, he had consented to march to Santa Margarita Rancho, near San Luis Obispo, to meet the comandante-general, not to exact of him submission, but to concert with him measures for defense against the Americans. At the rancho (reached July 11) Pico, through a message from Castro, had first learned of the action of Sloat.

Operations by the United States for the reduction of California present an earlier and a later phase, — the earlier (July 7 to September 24, 1846), when American dominion was acknowledged, and the later (September 24, 1846, to January 13, 1847) when such dominion was disputed. It is to the later phase more especially that significance attaches, for the occurrences constituting it inspired in the conquerors what before they had little possessed, to wit, respect for the conquered.

Possessed of Monterey, Commodore Sloat invited Comandante-General Castro to meet him at the port and sign articles of capitulation. Two days later the commodore wrote to Frémont, asking him to hasten to Monterey with at least one hundred men. Castro, who was at San Juan Bautista, promptly notified Sloat that the Governor and assembly were the proper authorities to whom to apply for a capitulation, it being his duty to defend the country at all sacrifice. About July 10, Castro withdrew southward, and on the 17th, Frémont, from New Helvetia, took possession of San Juan, which he occupied jointly with a party of dragoons sent by Sloat under Purser Daingerfield Fauntleroy to hoist at that point the American flag. Meanwhile as for Ide and the Bear party, their importance had vastly diminished. "I presume," wrote Larkin to Ide on the historic 7th, "you will be inclined to desist from any contemplated movements against the natives, and remain passive for the present." Indeed, on the 4th, the Ide party, with Ide a private member, had resolved itself into an organization of three companies under John Grigsby, Henry L. Ford, and Granville P. Swift, an organization which, for the most part joining

Frémont at Sutter's Fort, had come with him to San Juan Bautista as the California Battalion — 160 men.

The battalion entered Monterey on July 19, and here, legitimately, we obtain that element of the picturesque, a desire for which, in connection with Frémont, possesses the minds of the most sedate. "They were a curious set," wrote Lieutenant Frederick Walpole of Admiral Seymour's flagship, the Collingwood [44] —

A vast cloud of dust appeared at first, and thence in long file emerged this wildest wild party. Frémont rode ahead, a spare, active-looking man, with such an eye! He was dressed in a blouse and leggings, and wore a felt hat. After him came five Delaware Indians, who were his body guard; they had charge of two baggage horses. The rest, many of them blacker than the Indians, rode two and two, the rifle held by one hand across the pommel of the saddle. . . . The dress of these men was principally a long, loose coat of deer-skin, tied with thongs, in front; trousers of the same. The saddles were of various fashions, though these and a large drove of horses and a brass field-gun were things they had picked up in California. . . . They are allowed no liquor . . . and the discipline is very strict. . . . One man, a doctor [Semple], was six feet six high, and an odd-looking fellow. May I never come under his hands.

William Peel, a son of Sir Robert, was an officer of the Collingwood, and it is related by W. F. Swasey that Dr. Semple astonished him by his familiarity with English politics and history. Peel was yet more astonished, Swasey relates, by the accuracy with which Frémont's men were able to bring down with their rifles, at 160 yards, Mexican silver dollars provided by the Englishmen as targets.

At Monterey Frémont met Sloat. Apprehensive lest his course, like that of Jones in 1842, had been precipitate, the commodore could be induced to go in the way of conquest no further than he had gone already. On July 23, however, Commodore Robert F. Stockton, who had arrived from Norfolk on the 15th, was made by Sloat commander-in-chief of all forces and operations on land. By Stockton (a militant character) Frémont's contingent was accepted as a battalion of volunteers, with Frémont himself as major and Gillespie as captain. On the 29th, Sloat sailed for home, and Stockton, now in supreme command, issued a proclamation. It announced that the commodore

could not confine [his] operations to the quiet and undisturbed possession of the defenseless ports of Monterey and San Francisco, . . . but [would] immediately march against [the] boasting and abusive chiefs who had not only violated every principle of national hospitality and good faith toward Captain Frémont and his surveying party, but who unless driven out [would], with the aid of the hostile Indians, keep this beautiful country in a constant state of revolution and blood.[45]

By July 24, Pico and Castro (reconciled) were at Los Ángeles, the capital of the department; Castro making headquarters at Campo de la Mesa. Frémont with his battalion reached San Diego by sea on the 29th, raising there the American flag; and on August 6, Stockton, accompanied by Larkin as conciliator, but with 360 men, reached San Pedro. Here the commodore was met by messengers from Castro (Pablo de la Guerra and José M. Flóres) empowered to arrange for "a suspension of hostilities." This proposition Stockton declined. "I cannot," he wrote, "check any operations to negotiate on any other principle than that California will declare her independence, under the protection of the flag of the United States. If, therefore, you will agree to hoist the American flag in California, I will stop my forces and negotiate the treaty."

Castro on August 9 notified Pico that, being unable to muster more than "one hundred men, badly armed and worse supplied," he was resolved to quit the country. On the 10th, Pico reported Castro's message to the assembly, which adjourned without date, and Castro and Pico together (each the author of a farewell address) took the road for Sonora. The former reached Altar by way of the Colorado in September, and in 1848 returned to California. The latter for a time secreted himself near his rancho, but in September escaped into Lower California, whence he passed to the mainland, returning to California the same year with Castro.

Stockton, joined by Frémont, entered Los Ángeles on August 13. The flag was raised; Juan Bandini and Santiago Argüello declared themselves for the new régime; and the conquest of California was deemed complete. So complete, indeed, was it deemed, that the commodore, having on the 17th proclaimed the country a territory of the United States, and having on September 2 created Frémont military commandant (news whereof he dispatched to Washington by Kit Carson), reëmbarked his men and sailed for the North. Frémont himself left Los Ángeles on September 8, reached Santa Bárbara on the 13th, where he garrisoned the presidio with nine men under Lieutenant Theodore Talbot, and by the end of the month was in the Sacramento Valley. News awaited him: The Vallejos, Prudon, and Leese had been liberated from durance at Sutter's Fort; Dr. Robert Semple, seconded by Rev. Walter Colton, chaplain of the Congress, had on August 15 issued the "Californian," the first American Pacific Coast newspaper; and the Walla Wallas (baseless tale) were menacing the northern frontier with 900 warriors.

California was conquered, but refused to be so regarded. On leaving Los Ángeles, Stockton had appointed Lieutenant Archibald Gillespie, a man of Frémont ideas, southern commandant, with fifty men, and with orders to maintain martial law, but to exercise discretion in granting permits to proper persons to be out before sunrise and carry weapons. Gillespie, whose opinion of Californians was not favorable, made the error of construing his orders strictly, and of harassing, by acts of interference and exaction, the Angelinos, among whom, as in the days of Figueroa, there was a turbulent Mexican element. The result was that on September 24 certain demonstrations by Sérbulo Varela became magnified into an insurrection. Castro's old officers, José María Flóres, José Antonio Carrillo, and Andrés Pico, took command, the town was invested, and Gillespie was powerless.[46]

Once ignited, the spirit of revolt leaped wildly throughout the South. The struggle was one not so much of cavalry against infantry, of lance against musket, as of lightness and mobility against weight and mass; of the dynamics of war against the statics. And what was more, neither combatant at first comprehended the military efficiency of the other. To the Californians Frémont's "Bears" were bears indeed; and Stockton's sailors and marines clowns; while, to the Americans, Carrillo's and Torre's horsemen, ubiquitous on the hills, were guerillas who never could be brought to bay.

The first fight occurred at the Chino Rancho, a point about twenty-five miles to the eastward of Los Ángeles. Benjamin D. Wilson, an early resident, had been given command of twenty Americans (flouters of Californian courage) with whom to guard the frontier along the Colorado against Castro. Satisfied that for the present Castro was harmless, Wilson went hunting. On returning, he was told of the rising at Los Ángeles, and was invited to establish himself at the Chino Rancho owned by Isaac Williams, where he was assured there was a supply of powder. No sooner was the rancho gained (September 26) than two bodies of Californians, one under Varela, Diego Sepúlveda, and Ramón Carrillo, and the other under José del Carmen Lugo, — in all some sixty-five or seventy men, — appeared and demanded a surrender. The house — an adobe of three sides, with but few openings, and with an asphaltum roof — was shielded by a ditch and some adobe corrals. On the morning of the 27th, Varela's and Lugo's horsemen charged these obstructions, losing in the movement one killed (Carlos Ballesteros) and two or three wounded. But the building now furnished cover, and the assailants were enabled to fire the roof with dried grass. Williams, who was brother-in-law to Lugo, presented himself amid the smoke, with his children, and begged for quarter. Varela repeated the demand for surrender, but promised the inmates protection as prisoners of war. The terms were accepted, the garrison, some of whom had suffered wounds, marched forth, and despite the wish of Sepúlveda to shoot them in revenge for the death of Ballesteros, were taken to Los Ángeles and given in charge of Flóres.[47]

Back from Chino, Valera and Lugo found the tricolor afloat over the plaza, and Gillespie surrounded on Fort Hill. Flóres, however, at the intercession of Eulogio Celis and Francisco Figueroa of Los Ángeles, offered, through Wilson, to permit the American commander to march with the honors of war to San Pedro, there to take passage for Monterey by the transport Vandalia. Gillespie departed on September 30, but did not embark till October 4. By the articles of capitulation, which bore date the 29th, and are here first used,[48] he was to consume at the port "only so much time as was indispensable to embarkation"; and, for observing the stipulation, he was placed "on his word of honor." "Devoid of shame, good faith, and word of honor" (records Flóres), Gillespie "prolonged his stay to give time for the arrival of a warship."

But what of events at Santa Bárbara and San Diego? At the former, Talbot and his squad avoided capture by flight to the mountains. The chaparral was set on fire to drive them out; but they made their way northward and reached Monterey in November. At San Diego it was much the same. Gillespie had garrisoned the port with a dozen men under Ezekiel Merritt, and these, on the approach from Los Ángeles of fifty men under Manuel Garfías, betook themselves, not to the mountains but to a whale-ship, a cover whence they dared not emerge for twenty days.

That Gillespie protracted his embarkation in expectation of a warship is more than probable. On September 24 he had dispatched to Stockton by an expert rider (Juan Flaco, "Lean John"), a plea for help. The messenger was instructed to make desperate speed, and he obeyed. Provided with cigarettes concealed in his hair, the wrappers inscribed "Believe the bearer," he set out, pursued by Mexicans, who shot his horse. He reached successively Santa Bárbara and Monterey, where he was aided, at the one place by Talbot, and at the other by Larkin, and arrived at Yerba Buena on the evening of the 29th, — five hundred miles in five days, — a feat paralleled in earlier times by Santa Anna's messenger to Figueroa, and in later by Frémont personally.[49] On receipt of "Lean John's" message, Mervine was at once sent south in the Savannah with 350 men, and Frémont in a transport, the Sterling, with 160 men; Stockton following in the Congress.[50] These vessels met the Vandalia, with Gillespie on board, and Frémont, ascertaining that no horses could be obtained at Santa Bárbara, debarked at Monterey to proceed by land; while Mervine with Gillespie in his wake made all haste for San Pedro, where he arrived on October 6. The day following, the two commands started together for Los Ángeles. The night was passed at Domínguez Rancho, and on the 8th Mervine resumed the advance; his centre composed of seamen and marines in hollow formation, and his flanks covered by Gillespie's squad as skirmishers.

The Californian force consisted of some sixty horsemen, with a field-piece, under José Antonio Carrillo. The Americans once within range, the gun was discharged (by a cigarette, it is said) then dragged by *reatas* to a safe distance and reloaded. Four of Mervine's force had in this way been killed and six wounded, when at the end of an hour the captain withdrew to San Pedro and reëmbarked, leaving to the enemy some baggage and a flag.

Within thirty days two considerable actions had been fought, and in both the Americans had been worsted. The unsuccessful combatants were settlers, sailors, and marines. It remained to be proved what would be the fate of an American force more regularly constituted for military, or at least land, operations.

By the Californians the interval was utilized in reëstablishing civil government, and by Stockton in occupying San Diego. On October 20, the departmental assembly elected José María Flóres acting governor and comandante-general, and named Manuel Castro northern comandante, with Francisco Rico as subordinate.

I have resolved [wrote Flóres to Mexico on October 24] either to oppose the enemy in guerilla warfare, or to risk all on a single battle as may seem best, since up to to-day the land forces of Captain Frémont have not arrived, and there are in view only those which, since the action of the 8th, have remained on board the warships at San Pedro and San Diego, with the hope of the arrival of Frémont, who on the 10th of this month was on the Sacramento, 150 leagues from this capital. . . . The army of invasion is composed of 400 riflemen (hunters), under Captain

Frémont, and three warships capable of landing 1200 men. Besides, there are thirty whale-ships the crews of which are volunteers for the United States. Furthermore, I have reliable news of the impending arrival at the Sacramento River of 3000 male immigrants. . . . From the port of San Diego to the point of San Luis Obispo there are 400 or 500 natives poorly armed; a third part without firearms, and the remainder with four or five rounds each. Even meat for subsistence can no longer be obtained. The skeleton of the missions, the one resource upon which we ought to be able to count, these [sic] the Governor of the department sold for his own benefit on the eve of his flight from this capital.

It was October 23 when Stockton himself reached San Pedro, and he was at San Diego by November. Both points he found closely invested, the hills being "horse-covered," and he was planning with Gillespie an attack toward the north when an important letter was handed to him. It was from an officer of the United States Army, — General Stephen W. Kearny.

Whether Polk's military and naval activity in 1845 was or was not purely precautionary, one thing is certain: if war with Mexico was to ensue, it was Polk's resolve that the acquisition of California should be its principal fruit. When, therefore, Kearny, in August, 1846, had subjugated New Mexico, the successful general was ordered to proceed from Santa Fé to California. He set out on September 25 with 300 men of the First Dragoons, and on October 6, just below Socorro, met Kit Carson. Learning that California was already subdued, he took charge of Stockton's dispatches and compelled Carson to return as scout to his own command, a force which he now reduced to 100 men by sending 200 back to Santa Fé. With him he kept Captain Henry S. Turner, Captain Abraham R. Johnston, Major Thomas Swords, Lieutenant William H. Emory, Lieutenant Davidson with

two mountain howitzers, William H. Warner (topograph-
ist), Assistant Surgeon John R. Griffin, and Antonio
Robidoux (guide). Mules served both as pack-animals
and mounts, and the route was by the Gila to the Colorado junction, which was reached November 22. The
Colorado Desert, pronounced by Emory the worst stage of
the journey, was crossed southward of the Anza Trail, and
on December 2 the command was at Warner's Rancho.
From here Kearny, as already seen, apprised Stockton
of his presence.

To meet the general and conduct him to San Diego, the
commodore on December 3 sent Gillespie with thirty-
nine men, among them ten carbineers from the Congress,
with Acting Lieutenant Beale and Passed Midshipman
Duncan, and twenty-five of the California Battalion under
Captain Samuel Gibson. Andrés Pico had for some time
been watching the Americans from near San Luis Rey
Mission, and by the 5th (when Gillespie met Kearny) was
encamped at the Indian pueblo of San Pascual. At
Stockton's suggestion and with the strong approval of Kit
Carson, it was decided by Kearny and Gillespie to attack
him. The night of the 5th was cold and rainy, and a
reconnoissance proved the Californians to be unsuspect-
ing. In the early dawn of the 6th, Captain Johnston of the
vanguard charged with twenty men down hill upon the
village. The onset was met by Pico's force with pistol and
lance, and Johnston fell, shot through the head. Kearny
and Gillespie now approached, and the Californians, re-
treating, drew after them the Americans in hot pursuit
but much scattered. Suddenly the fleeing squadron — some
eighty men — stopped, turned, closed its ranks and rushed
upon the foe. Poorly mounted and with empty weapons,
the Americans were entrapped. The lance deftly wielded
made sabre and clubbed musket vain things, and the con-

flict though short was deadly. Ere the rear guard could arrive with the howitzers, Moore with sixteen others was killed, and Kearny, Warner, Gillespie, — the latter resisting dexterously with his sword, — Gibson, and Robidoux, with fourteen others, were badly wounded. For the Californians San Pascual was the fight *par excellence* of the war. In no other were their peculiar tactics so advantageously exercised, — the retreat, the pause, the *volte-face*, the couched lance, the rattling spur, the rush, the shock, the carnage, and again the retreat.

On the night of the 6th, Alexis Godey with one or two companions was sent to Stockton for help, and on the 7th Kearny (able to be in the saddle) camped on a hill near the rancho of San Bernardo. But Godey did not return, and on the night of the 8th Kit Carson, Lieutenant Beale, and an Indian set out to find Stockton. On the 11th a reinforcement of 200 marines appeared, and by the 12th the entire Kearny-Gillespie force was at San Diego.[51]

Under Governor Flóres, fortune favored the insurrectionists, but revolt was brewing. The Governor was unpopular for divers acts, but his crowning error was a decision to send the Chino captives to Mexico. So considerable (as the husbands of native women) was the influence of the captives, that Flóres himself was put under arrest by connivance of his subordinate Francisco Rico. Tried by the assembly, he was acquitted of intentional wrong and reinstated in authority, Rico being imprisoned in his stead. But mention of Rico carries us to the North, whence the latter had just returned, and where, early in October, we left Frémont preparing to move south to coöperate with Stockton.

At Monterey, between October 28 and November 17, Frémont recruited by help of Edwin Bryant and W. F.

Swasey 428 men, some of them Walla Walla and California Indians. Horses he took wherever they could be found, giving receipts to be honored by the United States after the war. On the 29th he started south by way of the Salinas Valley, and on December 14 reached San Luis Obispo. Here Jesús Pico lived. He was cousin to Don Pío, the self-expatriated governor, and to Andrés Pico, the hero of San Pascual, but had broken his parole, and feeling was strong against him. When discovered (at Wilson's rancho), he was tried by court martial and sentenced to be shot.

On the morning appointed for the execution [writes Swasey, who was present] the battalion was ordered to parade. I, accompanied by Owens and some few other officers, entering Frémont's room, found him surrounded by Pico's family bathed in tears, the little hands of the children outstretched toward him, beseeching mercy. Captain Owens, myself, and some others immediately added our intercessions . . . alleging Pico's crime to have been committed more through ignorance of the laws of war than from deliberate dishonor. After a moment of hesitation, Frémont turned toward the prisoner. "I had," he said, "rather meet a thousand in the field to-morrow. I pardon you. You are free!"

Frémont himself writes: —

I pointed through the window to the troops paraded in the square. . . . You were about to die, but your wife has saved you. Go thank her! He fell on his knees, made on his fingers the sign of the cross, and said: "I was to die — I had lost the life God gave me — you have given me another life. I devote the new life to you"; a pledge not broken.[52]

From San Luis the battalion, amid fierce winds and torrential rains, crossed the Santa Inés Mountains to Santa Bárbara, where it remained a week. On January 3, 1847, it resumed its march, and, closely surveyed by horsemen from the hills, entered the plain of San Fernando on the 11th. But again our attention must revert to the North.

Early in November, near San Luis Obispo, Manuel
Castro, together with Rico, Joaquín de la Torre, and José
Antonio Chavez, raised a force of 100 men. On the 15th,
Chavez captured Thomas O. Larkin at Joaquín Gómez's
rancho of Los Verjeles, where the consul had stopped
for the night on his way to Yerba Buena; and on the 16th,
an American force under Captains Charles Burroughs and
Bluford K. Thompson (newly arrived immigrants) was
repulsed with spirit. The fight was begun by Torre, who
attacked a scouting party of eight or ten men sent by Burroughs from San Juan Bautista. Driven to the shelter of a
grove on the Natividad Rancho, the party wounded a number of their assailants but lost their leader, George Foster.
News of the plight of the scouts was brought to Burroughs
by Walla Wallas, and the whole American force, about
fifty mounted men, advanced. They encountered Castro's
force, the main body of which had come to Torre's support, exchanged shots with them, and delivered a charge.
The foe feigned flight (tactics of San Pascual),[53] then turned
and in a short *mêlée* killed five Americans, including Burroughs, and wounded as many more. The conflict at
Natividad and a brush with a combative ranchero (Francisco Sánchez) by Captain Ward Marston of the marines,
near Santa Clara, on January 2, 1847, — a brush followed
by Sánchez's capitulation, — were the last acts of the war
with the United States, north of Tehachapi.

In the South, Stockton had begun a movement for the
recovery of Los Ángeles. Accompanied by Kearny and
Gillespie, he left San Bernardo on January 1, 1847, with
600 men, and near San Luis Rey was met by a proposal
from General Flóres for a truce, pending confirmation of
rumors of peace between the United States and Mexico.
The proposal was rejected, but at San Juan Capistrano the
commodore issued to all Californians, except Flóres, who,

like Jesús Pico, had broken his parole, a proclamation of amnesty. It had been intended to intercept Stockton at La Jabonería near the first ford of the San Gabriel River, — a spot covered with willows and adapted to ambuscade, — but the plan being revealed, the American force was directed to Paso de Bartolo, a ford higher up. Here Flóres confronted it with nearly 500 men: the main body — 200 men with two pieces of artillery — being posted opposite the ford, on a bluff fifty feet high and back from the stream some six hundred yards; and the flanks being protected by squadrons of cavalry under Andrés Pico and José Antonio Carrillo.

Stockton's advance through the water was contested by Flóres with round-shot and grape; but, owing to worthless powder, the guns wrought no execution, and a cavalry charge was ordered. The order was not vigorously obeyed, and the Americans having now passed the river, a shot from a field gun aimed by the commodore himself shattered the best gun of the Californians, who, retiring forthwith, pitched their camp on the circumjacent hills. On January 9, the march for Los Ángeles was resumed. It was contested, near the Cañada de los Alisos, by artillery and cavalry, but was not checked; and on the 10th, the Americans entered the town with flags displayed and bands playing. Gillespie raised again the banner which four months before he had lowered in capitulation.[54]

Frémont at San Fernando learned of the fall of Los Ángeles on January 10, and the same day sent his faithful adherent, Jesús Pico, to counsel general submission. The counsel was heeded, and on the 13th commissioners from both sides signed a treaty at Cahuenga. The Californians "surrendered their artillery and public arms," and promised "not again to serve during the war." In return, they were "guaranteed life and property," were acquitted of obligation to take an oath of allegiance, might "leave the country without let or hindrance," and were granted "equal rights and privileges as enjoyed by the citizens of the United States of America." On the 14th, Frémont with his battalion entered the city, and on the 15th, Stockton reported to Washington that he had approved Frémont's course.

It remains to be observed that Flóres had already liberated from confinement Thomas O. Larkin, who had been brought by his captors to Los Ángeles for safe-keeping; [55] had transferred the command to Andrés Pico; and, emulous of the example of his predecessor Don Pío, had figuratively fallen upon his sword by quitting California for Sonora in company with Manuel Castro.

CHAPTER XVI

MISSION, PRESIDIO, PUEBLO, AND PRIVATE RANCHO

Mission

MISSION, presidio, pueblo, and private rancho, each was characterized by its own architecture, its own domestic routine, its own traffic, and its own social life. In the case of the Mission, architecture has proved the most enduring memorial.

The Mission style [writes Mr. Hector Alliot] is first cousin to the Spanish Colonial in Mexico, young, powerful, and distinctive if somewhat unpolished. According to all recognized canons, it embraces essential features of novelty. . . . The thick walls with restraining buttresses, the construction about a court, the arched corridors, the patio, tiled roofs, domed towers, and pierced belfries should alone be sufficient to establish a style; but there are besides two features entirely original, — the terraced bell-tower and the serrated ascent of the curved arch surmounted by the cross.

It has been observed in chapter V that the principal buildings of San Carlos Mission in 1771 were a church, a priest's dwelling, a storehouse and a guard-house, all of wood; all, that is, of posts of pine or cypress set close together and plastered within and without with clay. These "buildings," the guard-house excepted, were but sections of a low earth-roofed structure, fifty yards long and seven wide, constituting one side of a quadrangle (70 by 43 yards) inclosed by a stockade with a single entrance secured by a strong gate.

Down to 1780, California mission buildings everywhere

much resembled those at San Carlos, excepting that where
wood was scarce, as at San Diego, adobes or sun-dried brick
were used. Indeed from 1778, adobes — a material widely
accessible and entirely non-combustible — came into use
more and more. By 1780, there was an adobe church at
San Diego; and by 1783 there were two priests' dwellings, a guard-house, granary, storehouse, infirmary, nunnery, wood-shed, larder, kitchen and oven; the whole
forming three sides of a quadrangle, the fourth side of
which was protected to a height of three *varas* (nearly
three yards) by an adobe wall. By 1782 an adobe church
had been built at San Francisco, and by 1784 one at Santa
Clara. But it was soon learned that adobe walls and earth
roofs crumbled, and that roofs of tules succumbed to fire;
and by 1790 the wood-adobe type of construction — a type
involving an earth or tule roof — began to yield to an
adobe-brick or adobe-stone type with roof of tiles. At Santa
Cruz, in 1793–94, a church was built the front and walls of
which, to a height of three feet, were of stone; and at San
Juan Capistrano, in 1797, there was begun a stone edifice
(arched and towered), the noblest to be built in Alta California, one the ruined fragments of which —

the chapter-room, the cloister-porch —

impart to-day to a quiet landscape an incomparable
melancholy.

Church building had either reached or was fast approaching finality, when, in 1812–13, the earthquake
shocks occurred which are described in chapter X; shocks
so destructive at the South that nearly every establishment (San Gabriel, San Juan Capistrano, Santa Bárbara,
San Buenaventura, Purísima, and Santa Inés) was required to be reared anew. As late as 1818 and 1820, —
as late as the end of the Spanish régime, — dedications

were taking place. But how at any period Indians super-
intended by a few guardsmen, the latter in turn superin-
tended by two padres, could have achieved the beauty of
bell-accentuated San Gabriel, the strength of domed Santa
Bárbara, the grace (flowing yet varied) of San Luis, and
the stateliness, wide-flung, of Capistrano, has remained
a mystery.

So far as artisans were concerned, they were few from
the first. San Carlos was reared by four Indians and three
sailors. San Diego de Alcalá (second structure) was undertaken by neophytes and twenty sailors. Rivera's recruits
for Los Ángeles numbered one mason, one carpenter, and
one blacksmith. Borica, even, brought to Alta California
but six masons, two carpenters, and three blacksmiths;
and of these nearly all returned to Mexico in five years;
wherefore in 1797 it became necessary to import a
master-mason from Culiacán to superintend the stone-
work of San Juan Capistrano.

For San Gabriel, Santa Bárbara, San Luis, and San Juan
it must be that we are indebted to the padres themselves.
Santa Clara (best of the earlier structures) was designed,
we know, by one of its priests, Joseph Antonio de Jesús
María de Murguía of Domaiquía, Álava, a priest who as
a layman had in 1748 laid the first masonry in Serra's old
district of Sierra Gorda. As for San Luis Rey, twin edifice with Santa Bárbara in features distinctively Mission,
its designer was its priest Antonio Peyri of Parrera, Catalonia. To what extent Muraguía and Peyri worked from
plans or pictured representations, Spanish or Mexican, we
do not know; but whatever their models they were not
slavish in imitation. Alta California was a land of out-of-
doors, — a land of earthquakes and of peril from primitive
men; and by these facts Mission architecture was conditioned. Spaces generous and unpreëmpted, coupled with

lack of connoisseurs, dictated dependence on mass and line. Peril from primitive men prescribed a construction fort-like and corridored about a fountain; while, as against the earthquake, walls were made thick, and the buttressing was heavy.[1]

But, in the case of the Mission, domestic routine concerns us even more than architecture. Within the mission quadrangle, or partly within it and partly without, were huts for the neophytes, huts originally of reeds, but since 1790 (notably at Santa Bárbara) of whitewashed and tiled adobes. At sunrise a bell was struck, and from their huts the neophyte population gathered to hear morning prayers (*oraciones*), and to be instructed in Christian doctrine. Then came breakfast (*desayuno*) — a meal of maize-gruel called *atole;* the married partaking of it in their own abodes, and the unmarried in a common quarter, the *pozolera*. Tasks, which came next, were assigned with regard to individual capacity. The males were sent, some to the mountains to hunt; some to the fields to sow or reap grain; some to the shops where the trades — masonry, carpentry, shoemaking, blacksmithing, tanning, soap-boiling, etc. — were taught; and some, mayhap, to the neighboring presidio, to work under contract on the walls or fortifications. The duties of the females were cooking, spinning, knitting, and embroidering. A second meal (*comida*) consisting of *pozole* — meat cooked with corn or beans — was served at midday. In the afternoon, boys and catechumens were instructed in Christianity, and *cena* (a meal of *atole*) was served at seven in the evening. On festival days, attendance upon Mass and religious instruction was exacted with rigor, each catechumen, as his name was called, being required to advance and kiss the hand of the father missionary.[2] Whatever the exercise, — religious, agricultural, or industrial, — the padres were assisted by an overseer, nominally an *alcalde* elected by the Indians, but in fact and of necessity an appointee, more or less trustworthy, of the padres themselves. The nunnery, wherein widows and unmarried girls were restrained at night (and for bachelors there was a like institution), was guarded jealously by a native duenna, vigilant and grim, who kept the key.

The life of a neophyte was one of regular labor (a new thing), but it was not without its recreations. There were games of hoop and ball, and there were dances. For the latter a fire was built, and about it the participants, stripped to the loins, streaked with paint and crowned with feathers, executed to the sound of a drum, horn, and rude castanets a slow movement at once rhythmic and weird.[3] Music, in the rationalized sense, was a means much relied upon by Catholic missionaries everywhere to promote the faith, and it was so in California. At San Gabriel, Indian boys with passable voices chanted at the celebration of the Mass, while such as were apt in the use of instruments essayed the flute, guitar, violin, drum, triangle, or cymbals.[4]

The *gente de razón* who dwelt at the missions were few, and social life for the padres came largely through traffic. How exultantly the visits of Mr. George Washington Eayrs were received has been told already. But dinners aboard ship and at the "ranch house" — dinners seasoned no less by gossip than by wine — present the social side of traffic in its initial stage. After the bargain had been struck, after the goods had been secured, then came forward the rancheros, eager to possess themselves of the wares and merchandise of the luxurious East. A trader of the Eayrs type was Captain William Heath Davis of

Boston. He carried to China sandal-wood from the Sandwich Islands, taking in return silks, teas, and lacquered articles; and his favorite California port was El Refugio, near Santa Bárbara. Here in 1816 he was officially waited upon by Comandante Don Ignacio Martínez, with an aide and two soldiers; but so royal was his treatment of his guest, so artfully did he ply him with wine and gifts, that not a single embarrassing question was propounded. Martínez's daughter — she who became Señora Estudillo — was then but eleven years old, and it is related by her that when, on returning from his visit, her father displayed *serapes*, shawls, fancy silk handkerchiefs, satin shoes, sewing-silk of all colors, and gleaming lacquers, the family were captivated. Never in all their lives had they seen anything so beautiful and so rich.

But in the social intercourse of the padres, large as was the element contributed by traffic, there was another element still. It was that which arose from the part performed by the missions as houses of entertainment for the traveler. Up and down the coast went the horseman, nor ever was he anxious as against the night. Each day at sunrise he quitted one consecrated portal, to be enfolded beneath another at sunset. From San Diego to San Luis, from San Luis to San Juan Capistrano, from San Juan Capistrano to San Gabriel, the sea was his guide. From San Fernando the mountains led him to San Buenaventura. Here, sea and mountain at feud, San Buenaventura confided him to Santa Bárbara, Santa Bárbara to Santa Inés, and Santa Inés to La Purísima, whence, under escort of wide valleys, his course was sure. Nor anywhere for lodging, for meat or drink, for peaches or pomegranates, for relays of horses or for *vaqueros*, was there cost to him of aught. The traveler brought to the padres news, which was life, and news acquitted him.

Presidio and Pueblo

The architecture of the California presidios displayed itself in the barracks of quadrangles and in the walls of certain outlying defenses. At San Diego and Monterey in 1769 the presidial inclosure was also the inclosure of the mission. At San Francisco (1776), where mission and presidio were separate, the space for the latter was 92 yards square, and the walls were of palisades. At Santa Bárbara in 1782 the walls were of palisades, and the inclosure was a square of 60 *varas*. By the energy of Neve, in 1778, the palisades of San Francisco were replaced by adobes, and Monterey was provided with barracks 136 by 18 feet, and with a wall of stone 537 yards in girth, 12 feet high and 4 feet thick.[5] In 1793, Vancouver deemed Santa Bárbara Presidio, with its red tiles, the best of the Spanish establishments, and that of San Diego the worst.

Defenses proper — batteries — were erected, one of logs, in 1793, at Monterey, with eleven guns; one of adobes, in 1794, at San Francisco (battery of San Joaquín), with eight guns; one of adobes, in 1797, at San Diego on Point Guijarros, with eight guns; and one of fascines, in 1797, at Yerba Buena (Black Point), with five guns. In 1816, San Joaquín was rebuilt, and in 1820, it mounted twenty guns, three of them 24-pounders; while at Monterey in 1830 the armament consisted of twenty guns behind a breastwork of adobes. By 1835, the presidio and fort at San Diego had both been abandoned.

In respect to dwellings, presidio and pueblo were architecturally alike: single-story adobes, with whitewashed walls and roofs of asphaltum, or red tiles, but with small barred windows and without gardens. A few dwellings (notably the Guerra house at Santa Bárbara) were more pretentious. They were built after the Moorish fashion,

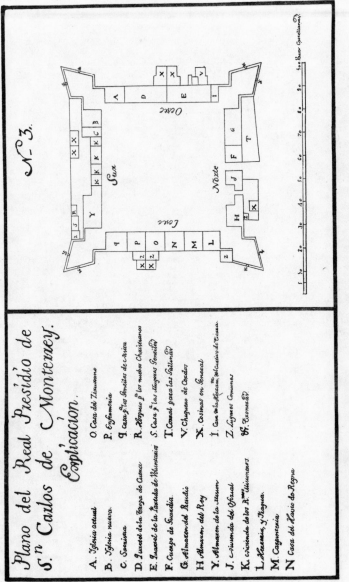

Plano del Real Presidio de
S.ⁿ Carlos de Monterrey.

Explicacion.

N.º 3.

A. Yglesia actual
B. Yglesia nueva.
C. Sacristia
D. Quartel de la tropa de Cuera
E. Quartel de la tropa de Voluntaria
F. Cuerpo de Guardia.
G. Almazen del Rey
H. Almazen del Rey
Y. Almazen de la Mision
J. Vivienda del Oficial
K. vivienda de los R.R.ᵈᵒˢ Misioneros
L. Herreria, y Fragua.
M. Carpinteria
N. Casa del Dueño de Regua

O. Casa del Tamborero
P. Enfermeria
q. Casa p.ᵃ los Soldados de Cuera
R. Hospem p.ᵃ los nuebos Christianos
S. Casa p.ᵃ las Mugeres Gentiles
T. Corral para las Gallinas
V. Chiquero de Cerdos
X. Cozinas en General
Y. Casa p.ᵃ Almazen Probisional de Tierra.
Z. Lugares Comunes
&. Hornos &.ᵃ

Sur

Oeste

Leste

Norte

MONTEREY PRESIDIO AS PLANNED, APPROXIMATELY 1771. (Hitherto unreproduced.)

round a court containing a garden and fountain, and were furnished with tables and mirrors from the United States, Mexico, and China.

The men of California were tall and vigorous, and withal they were picturesque. They wore dark-colored, low-browed, broad-brimmed hat; short jacket; open-necked shirt; rich waistcoat, knee-breeches and white stockings, or trousers slashed below the knee and gilt-laced; deer-skin leggings and shoes; a red sash, and a *serape*. The women were not tall, but, as we know, they had glossy black hair, lustrous black eyes, and the whitest of teeth. Their habit was a gown of silk, crêpe, or calico, loose and short-sleeved; bright-colored belt; satin or kid shoes; necklace and ear-rings; with hair, if unmarried, in long braids, and if married, on a high comb. Within doors the head-drape was the *rebozo;* out of doors it was the mantilla. Beef, red beans, and tortillas constituted the food of the humbler class, a fare to which folk of greater means added chocolate, milk or coffee, but not usually wine, as it was costly. Moreover, at meals, families, except at the best houses, remained standing.

Children were numerous, — thirteen to twenty per wedded pair, — and the deference paid to parents was profound. No son, even if fifty or sixty years old, dared to smoke or wear his hat in his father's presence, and fathers not infrequently chastised a grown son with the lash.[6] At the Guerra home the régime was patriarchal. Rising at dawn, the household repaired to the dining-room, where they partook of coffee, the father at the head of the board (standing), with sons and daughters on either hand. Breakfast, a hearty meal, was taken at eight or nine o'clock. At noon luncheon was served; at four o'clock, tea; and at eight or nine, supper. After supper there were prayers.

These concluded, the sons and daughters withdrew, each bending the knee to the father and kissing his hand.[7]

Objects of pride with the California housewife were the family garments stitched and embroidered to a nicety; but objects of supreme pride were the beds. Not less than luxurious must they be, with ticks filled with down, silken counterpanes, and satin pillow-covers edged with lace or embroidery.

Society at the presidio was dependent somewhat upon traffic, but at the pueblo it was so dependent scarcely at all. The supply-ships with officers from San Blas came annually to San Diego and Monterey; and after 1806, the Russian ships (also with officers) came from New Archangel and Ross to San Francisco. But it was the vessels of the exploring expeditions sent out by England, Spain, and France — the vessels of Vancouver, Pérouse, Malaspina, Duhaut-Cilly, Beechey, Petit-Thouars, and Laplace — that, with their lighthearted midshipmen, their bands of stirring music, and their hospitality, contributed to society most.

Nor were the Californians insensible to amenities on the part of vessels from the United States. At Monterey, in 1842, Commodore Jones emphasized apologies for untimely calls by an entertainment. At San Francisco, in 1846, on the evening of September 8, the American vice-consul, William A. Leidesdorff, gave a grand ball in the large hall of his residence, one hundred Californian and American ladies attending. And, at Monterey, in 1847, on April 9, the United States naval officers gave in the barracks a ball still grander. Present were Commodore Biddle and suite, General Kearny and staff, ex-Governor J. B. Alvarado, ex-Comandante-General M. G. Vallejo, the French Vice-Consul (Gasquet), the English Vice-Consul

(Forbes), and many besides. "The ladies," observes the "Californian," "turned out *en masse*, and if we can judge from the evidence of our eyes, the ladies of California are fairly determined to conquer the conquerors of their country, and then of course *to the victors belong the spoils.*" "For a month," the same journal remarks, "the question among the ladies has been: 'Shall they or shall they not adopt the use of bonnets?' From present indications the ayes have it. Who will supply them?"

The presidio was more sedate than the pueblo, a condition which its social life, as a rule, reflected. Once, however, the presidio of San Diego was startled by a flagrant breach of decorum,—an international elopement. Henry D. Fitch was a New Bedford sailor, young, and in command of the Maria Esther. Stopping at San Diego in 1826, he fell a victim to the charms of Doña Josefa, daughter of Joaquín Carrillo. He was Protestant, she Catholic, and again there arose the dilemma which in other years had embarrassed Rezánoff. "Why don't you carry me off, Don Enrique?" the lady is said to have finally inquired. And carry her off Don Enrique did; or rather Pío Pico, cousin to the lady, did for him; for at night the latter bore her a-gallop on his best steed to the seashore, where she was met by a boat, taken on board the Vulture, — a ship navigated by Fitch's friend, Captain Richard Barry, — and on July 3, 1829, was married at Valparaíso. In 1830, at Monterey, Padre Sánchez procured Fitch's arrest, and for a time there was danger that the marriage might be pronounced a nullity. So radical a step was not taken; but in December Sánchez condemned the culprit "to give as a penance, and as a reparation, a bell of at least fifty pounds in weight for the church at Los Ángeles, which barely has a borrowed one."

Many were the forms of social pleasure prized in California (picnics among them), but the form prized most was the dance — the folk-dance. For the scene, a hall within doors or a bower without; for participants, cavaliers with braided hair, and ladies with hair flowing; for instruments, the violin and guitar; for figures, *la jota* (performed by four to sixteen couples, singly or in chain), *la zorrita* (couples), *el caballo*, *el jarabe*, and *el fandango*. Says Alfred Robinson of a dance which he witnessed at the Bandini home in San Diego: —

The female was erect with her head a little inclined to the right shoulder, as she modestly cast her eyes to the floor, whilst her hands gracefully held the skirts of her dress, suspending it above the ankle to expose to the company the execution of her feet. Her partner . . . was under full speed of locomotion, and rattled away with his feet with wonderful dexterity. His arms were thrown carelessly behind his back, and secured, as they crossed, the points of his serape, that still held its place upon his shoulders. Neither had he doffed his sombrero, but just as he stood when gazing from the crowd he had placed himself upon the floor.

A popular *jota* began: —

A mouse I had, with thirty mice.

Extremely popular was *la zorrita* (the little fox), nor is it forgotten at San Gabriel to this day.

The little fox went to the hills,
And because she went on a lark, a lark,
She came back shorn.

It is related by Thomas Savage that, conversing with Doña Eulalia Pérez, a famous Californian dancer of old days, she thus apostrophized him in farewell: —

O Thomas dear, would I explain
To thee my pain!

.   .   .   .   .   .

With greatest gladness,
And sweetest calmness,
To give to thee my soul and love,
Is my intent.

As for *el caballo*, —

Cuando el caballo entró en Cádiz,

— it was performed by couples with gestures significant of the gallop. *El fandango*, too, was performed by couples, the features being a flourish of castanets, songs, and amorous compliments.

> Do not say to me "Nay"!
>
> . . . . .
> Do not kill me with harshness;
> Do not treat me with cruelty;
> Do not deny me your lealty;
> Do not despise my love,
> No, for I 'm yours alone;
> Do not say to me "Nay"!

When a lady danced with unusual spirit and grace, male spectators were wont to show appreciation by throwing coins at her feet and piling their sombreros one after another upon her head.[8]

Then there was Carnival: —

> Follow me, follow me, nobody ask;
> Crazy is Carnival under the mask.

Throughout this season, at the dance or frolic, it was customary for friends to break upon each other's heads egg-shells (*cascarones*) filled with spangles or scented water. The cavalier who could oftenest thus cause a lady to "float in lavender and cologne" was accounted best; and *vice versa*. William H. Davis relates that calling one day upon Doña Encarnación Briones at North Beach, he failed to catch her off guard, he being so caught by her several times. As he was leaving, she archly remarked: "*Usted vinó á trasquilar, pero fué trasquilado*" (You came to shear, but you were shorn).[9] "The wit of a Californian lady," Davis perhaps was reminded, "glances here and there like the sun-rays through the fluttering leaves of a wind-stirred forest."

Nor was the drama a pastime unknown to Californians.

In the church on Christmas Eve [writes Walter Colton] the Virgin Mother bends before the altar over her new-born babe. A company of shepherds enter. In their wake follows a hermit with long white beard, tattered missal, and sin-chastening lash. Near him figures a wild hunter in the skins of the forest. Last of all comes the Evil One with horned frontlet, disguised hoof and robe of crimson flame. Approaching the manger, the shepherds, led by Gabriel, kneel and to the notes of the harp chant a hymn of praise. The hermit and hunter are not among them; they have been beguiled by the Tempter and are lingering at a game of dice. The Tempter, emboldened, shows himself among the shepherds; but here he encounters Gabriel, who knows him of old. He quails under the eye of the angel and flees his presence. Hermit and hunter, disenthralled, make their homage penitential.[10]

A masque, *El Diablo en la Pastorela*, composed by Padre Florencio of La Soledad, was rendered on Christmas Night, 1837, with much *éclat* at the house of Pío Pico in San Diego; and the year before, at Monterey, Governor Chico was regaled by the feats of a troupe of Mexican acrobats.

Probably the most elaborate function, ceremonial and social, ever celebrated in Hispanic California was the inauguration of Governor Pablo Vicente de Sola at Monterey in 1816. It opened in the plaza with a military display under the flag of Castile. Next came a reception at the *casa real*. Twenty beautiful *señoritas* advanced, and, kissing the hand of the Governor in the name of their respective families, — Estudillo, Vallejo, Estrada, and others, — received in return boxes of sweetmeats from Mexico. A collation followed, the tables graced with roses, and laden with oranges, pomegranates, figs, olives, dates, cordials and wines. After a feast in the plaza by the populace, space was cleared, and bulls and grizzly bears were set upon

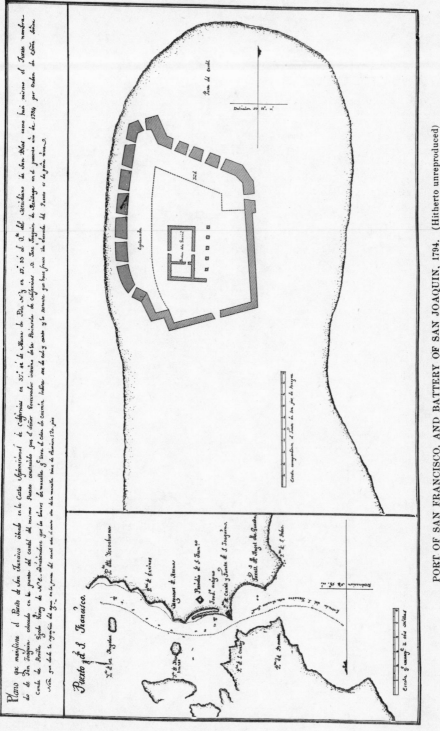

PORT OF SAN FRANCISCO, AND BATTERY OF SAN JOAQUIN, 1794. (Hitherto unreproduced)

one another. Two days later, Sola and his suite — cuirassed cavaliers with shields and lances, and ladies on palfreys, a cavalcade out of the "Faery Queen" itself — set forth to San Carlos Mission. The way led through a wood past stations of the Cross. Suddenly there appeared a band of monks attended by Indian acolytes. Behind came padres from all California, bearing upon a platform an effigy of Christ crucified, and followed by Indians to the number of many hundred. Sola and his officers alighted, kissed the feet of the Christ, and, amid the odor of incense from censers swung by the acolytes, entered the mission. To crown all, Padre Amorós of San Carlos preached, and the Indians presented a sham battle.[11]

Fights between bulls and bears were not uncommon at presidios, and they occasionally were tolerated at a mission; but the audience to whom they appealed with peculiar force was that of one of the two pueblos, San José or Los Ángeles. Around the sides of the plaza a strong wooden barrier was erected, and behind it a high platform for spectators. Bull and bear were then introduced, a hind foot of the bear attached by a long *reata* to a fore foot of the bull. After a vain attempt to escape on the part of the bull, there was a close struggle, the bear it is said usually proving victor. Bulls sometimes were baited by *toreadors*; but more popular at the pueblos than such sport were cock-fighting, horse-racing, and gambling; the latter pursued at the very doors of the sanctuary, and not seldom culminating in a duel with swords.

With regard to education, it proverbially was the thing about which the Californian, priest or layman, troubled himself least. For girls it was said to consist of dancing, music, religion, and amiability. "In 1840," observes Prudencia Higuera, "I went to school in an adobe near where the town of San Pablo now stands. A Spanish gentleman was the teacher, and he told us many new things, for which we remember him with great respect. But when he said the earth was round, we all laughed out loud, and were much ashamed." The more enlightened Californians, when possible, sent their children abroad. Sons of Hartnell, Pacheco, and Spence were educated in the Sandwich Islands. The Suñols sent sons to Paris. Vallejo sent a son to Valparaíso, and other children to the United States.[12]

Private Rancho

By the Laws of the Indies, the settlement of new countries was to be effected by companies of not less than thirty under an *impresario*, or by private companies of not less than ten. Such companies were to establish pueblos, and it was in accordance with the laws in question that Neve founded San José in 1777 and Los Ángeles in 1781. The ultimate conversion of missions into pueblos was assumed. Indeed, the governmental or secular idea of "reduction" involved no segregation of neophytes apart from their abodes. For the native, the pueblo form of organization was to be both first and final. Presidios, too, it was assumed, would become towns by attracting around them a population which sooner or later could be subjected to the laws governing the pueblo.

The first specific legislation affecting California pueblos and presidios was Bucarely's Instructions of August 17, 1773, to Rivera y Moncada. By these not only might the comandante-general designate common lands (*tierras de comunidad*), he might distribute lands in private to such Indians as would dedicate themselves to agriculture and stock-raising, and he might distribute lands among the other *pobladores* according to merit. But in each instance all recipients of lands in private must live "in the town (pueblo) and not dispersed."[13] On October 22, 1791, Pedro

de Nava, comandante of the Provincias Internas de Occidente, specifically authorized presidial comandantes to
grant house-lots and lands to soldiers and citizens, but
only within a district (pueblo limit) of four common
leagues, measured from the centre of the presidio square;
and only to such soldiers and citizens as should desire fixed
places of residence.[14] For California, then, the private
rancho — land to be owned and occupied by an individual
apart from the community — was at first not contemplated. It was an estate not readily subjected to supervision.
In a word, it was alien to the paternalistic spirit of Spanish
rule.

Still, circumstances arose under which the private
rancho was deemed a necessity, and in 1775 Rivera made
such a grant to Manuel Butrón. The land was soon abandoned, and in 1784 Fages, who had been making grants
of the kind provisionally, sought counsel of Comandante-
General Ugarte. By advice of Asesor Navarro, Ugarte
empowered Fages in 1786 to make non-pueblo grants, provided they did not exceed three leagues in extent, were
beyond the limits of existing pueblos, did not conflict with
missions or *rancherías*, were equipped by the grantee with
a stone house, and were stocked by him with at least two
thousand head of animals. It was under this authorization
that the private ranchos enumerated in chapter x — San
Rafael, Los Nietos, San Pedro, and others near Los Ángeles — derived quasi-validity. But though countenanced
by the secular power, the private rancho met determined
opposition from the missionaries. They regarded it as terri-
torially an infringement upon the Mission, and they deemed
it conducive to neophyte insubordination. Under the
Spanish régime the number of such holdings was small, not
more than twenty.[15] With the coming of Secularization,
and the enactment of the naturalization and colonization

laws of 1824 and 1828, whereby a single colonist might own
not to exceed eleven square leagues, but might own that
amount absolutely in fee, the number rapidly increased.
By 1830 it was fifty, and by 1840 it was approximately six
hundred.

That under Nava's order many (or any) California
ranchos were dignified with stone houses is not probable.
The houses were of palisades, or adobes, with roofs of tules
or tiles, and with ox-hide or wooden doors. They might be
of two rooms, one for living and one for sleeping, with a few
vaqueros and Indian servants; or they might be of many
rooms about a court, with *vaqueros* and Indian servants
by the score.[16] In either case, the exterior — save for corrals and a vegetable patch — was absolutely bare, there
being neither barns, stables, nor gardens.

Prior to 1824, a Californian wishing to become a ranchero, would apply to the *alcalde* of his district for land.
The latter, taking with him two witnesses, would erect a
mound or pile of stones as a point of starting, then with
a *reata* fifty feet in length would measure the tract —
five to twenty or even thirty leagues — at a smart gallop.
In a few years the owner, or (prior to 1821) royal tenant,
could boast of 2000 to 10,000 head of cattle, 1500 to 2000
horses and mules, and 10,000 to 20,000 sheep. Of these the
cattle and mules were the most readily exchanged for commodities, although the horses were indispensable. During
the period of the fur-trade (1771–1816), and before that
of the tallow-trade with Lima (1813–18), the ranchero
possessed almost no exchangeable or convertible property;
his cattle and sheep were of use merely to subsist and clothe
himself and retainers. The period of his prosperity was
from 1828 to 1846. Then, as noted in chapter xv, he found
a ready American and English market for hides and
tallow.

The *matanza*, or slaughter, involved as a preliminary the grand *rodeo* or " round-up," and the *rodeo* involved trained horses, and men skilled as wielders of the *reata*, and not unused to the trick of throwing an unruly bull by a twist of the tail. Previous to the grand *rodeo* (held in March or April), *rodeos* were held for the purpose of accustoming cattle to rendezvous at a particular spot. At the grand *rodeo*, stock was counted, or rather estimated; the portion belonging to the ranchero was separated from that belonging to his neighbors; and calves (500 to 3000 head) were branded. It was thus determined what proportion of a herd might properly be slaughtered. The slaughtering itself came later. A band of *vaqueros* armed with knives rode over the fields, selected each an animal, deftly severed a nerve in the nape of the neck, and it fell dead. Or — a more common procedure — the cattle were dispatched after having been corralled and bound with *reatas*. In either event *peladores* (flayers) stripped off the hides, and the meat was cut up by *tasajeros*, or butchers. The *matanza* necessarily caused much offal, and scores of dogs were kept for consuming it. A ranchero riding to town was, it is averred, not infrequently attended by a train of dogs half a mile long. Horses when in excess were destroyed by being driven over a precipice; or by being thrust into corrals, whence, as they were liberated one at a time, they were pierced with the lance. Moreover, as the pueblo possessed its *alcalde*, so the country possessed its high functionary, the *juez de campo*, or judge of the plain, an officer supreme at the *rodeo*.[17]

In agriculture the ranchero was neither interested nor versed. He raised grain (barley and wheat) in quantity barely sufficient for his own need, cultivating it with ludicrous plow and harrow, reaping it with the sickle, threshing it under the feet of mares, and winnowing it in the wind.

Save for the block-wheeled ox-cart, low, crude, and creaking, and the *volanta* of the padre, there were no vehicles; nor was the ranchero, though a cattle-owner, enough of a domesticator of cattle to provide himself to any extent with milk, butter, and cheese.

The better-class ranchero was wont to awaken early, partake of chocolate, rise, order a favorite horse, and ride over his land. Between eight and nine o'clock he breakfasted on *carne asada* (broiled meat), eggs, beans, tortillas, and (occasionally) coffee. Dinner, which was like breakfast, was served at noon or at one o'clock. Then the ranchero rode forth again; this time perchance to the estate of a neighbor; and at eight o'clock he went to bed. His dress differed not materially from that of his fellow countryman of the presidio or pueblo. Both were cavaliers, but the ranchero was cavalier *par excellence*. His pride was his horse, his saddle, his bridle, and his spurs. The horse (of Andalusian descent) was beautiful and strong. White, dapple-gray, or chestnut in color, he was full-chested, thin-flanked, round in the barrel, clean-limbed, with unusually small head, feet, and ears, large full eyes, expanded nostrils, and full flowing mane and tail.[18] The saddle — huge and apparently clumsy — consisted of a "tree," high fore and aft, beneath which were spread two or three broad and low-hanging aprons of leather, the outer one (or two) stamped in figures and embroidered in red, green, gold, or silver. The bridle was of horse-hair and was adorned with silver buckles and buttons; the stirrups were of oak shielded in front with long leather coverings; and the spurs bore rowels of four or six points.

To promote good-fellowship or greet his lady, the ranchero while mounted would sing and play the guitar, his steed stepping in time to the tune:[19] —

Ah for the red spring rose,
  Down in the garden growing,
Fading as fast as it blows,
  Who shall arrest its going?
Peep from thy window and tell,
  Fairest of flowers, Isabel.

Or for a wager, he would pick up at full dash a coin or a kerchief from the ground; nor was a pause needful even to light a cigarette. It was, however, in throwing the lasso (instrument of twisted hide or horse-hair) that the ranchero found the diversion most congenial to him. Sometimes his quarry was the grizzly bear, an animal which, despite its great strength, could be reduced by the *reata* to helplessness.

Our leader [says Colton, describing a hunt in which he had participated] dashed up to [a] tree, which was instantly surrounded by the whole troop. "Give us pistols," exclaimed the *señoritas*, as bravely in for the sport as the rest. Click, crack! and a storm of balls went through the tree-top. Down came old Bruin with one bound into the midst, full of wrath and revenge. The horses instinctively wheeled into a circle, and as Bruin sprung for a death-grapple, the lasso of our *baccaros*, thrown with unerring aim, brought him up all standing. He now turned upon the horse of his new assailant; but that sagacious animal evaded each plunge, and seemed to play in transport about his antagonist. The pistols were out again, and a fresh volley fell thick as hail around the bear. In the smoke and confusion no one could tell where his next spring might be; but the horse of the *baccaro* knew his duty and kept the lasso taut. Bruin was wounded, but resolute and undaunted; the fire rolled from his red eyes like a flash of lightning out of a forked cloud. Foiled in his plunges at the horse, he seized the lasso in his paws, and in a moment more would have been at his side, but the horse sprang and tripped him, rolling him over and over till he lost his desperate hold on the lasso. The pistols were reloaded, and *señoritas* and *caballeros* all dashed up for another shower of fire and lead. As the smoke cleared, Bruin was found with the lasso slack, a sure evidence that the horse who managed it knew his antagonist was dead.

Instead of the bear it might be the elk that the hunter sought, an animal not deficient in prowess, yet capable of being dragged alive into a settlement by the *reatas* of two rancheros. Or the object of pursuit might be a wild horse of the Tulares. In this event, the saddle would be discarded, and a section of lasso be wound loosely about the ranchero's horse, just behind the forelegs. To the rope the rider would attach his *reata;* beneath it he would slip his knees; and thus disencumbered yet secured, would brave the dangers of trampling or a stampede.

Cattle on a rancho were virtually wild, and to proceed among them on foot (a thing which the ranchero or *vaquero* himself never did) was fraught with peril. Parties from vessels at times had narrow escapes from bulls "clothed with all the terrors of the Apocalyptic beast"; and John Bidwell, who deemed bulls more to be dreaded by the footman than grizzly bears, tells of dodging into gulches and behind trees, to avoid them, in 1841. To none, however, it is safe to say, did there befall adventure more remarkable than to J. Ross Browne in the Salinas River Valley, some thirty miles north of Soledad Mission.

Thrown from his mule, Browne was proceeding wearily on foot, when he discovered that a large band of Spanish cattle was beginning to close in toward the line of his route.

A fierce-looking bull [he writes] led the way, followed by a lowing regiment of stags, steers and cows, crowding one upon the other in their furious charge. As they advanced, the leader occasionally stopped to tear up the earth and shake his horns; but the mass kept crowding on, their tails switching high in the air, and uttering the most fearful bellowing, while they tossed their horns and stared wildly, as if in mingled rage and astonishment. . . . The nearest tree was half a mile to the left, on the margin of a dry creek. . . . Scarcely conscious of the act, I ran [for it] with all my might. . . . The thundering of heavy hoofs after me, and the furious bellowing that resounded over

the plain, spread a contagion among the grazing herds on the
way, and with one accord they joined in the chase. It is in no
spirit of boastfulness that I assert the fact, but I certainly made
that half-mile in as few minutes as ever the same distance was
made by mortal man. When I reached the trees, I looked back.
The advance body of the cattle were within a hundred yards,
bearing down in a whirlwind of dust. I lost no time in making
my retreat secure. As the enemy rushed in, tearing up the earth
and glaring at me with their fierce, wild eyes, I had gained the
fork of the tree, about six feet from the ground, and felt very
thankful that I was beyond their reach. . . .

While in this position, with the prospect of a dreary night
before me, and suffering [from thirst] the keenest physical anguish, a very singular circumstance occurred to relieve me of
further apprehension respecting the cattle, though it suggested
a new danger for which I was equally unprepared. A fine young
bull had descended the bed of the creek in search of a water-
hole. While pushing his way through the bushes he was suddenly attacked by a grizzly bear. The struggle was terrific. I
could see the tops of the bushes sway violently to and fro, and
hear the heavy crash of drift-wood as the two powerful animals
writhed in their fierce embrace. A cloud of dust rose from the
spot. It was not distant over a hundred yards from the tree in
which I had taken refuge. Scarcely two minutes elapsed before
the bull broke through the bushes. His head was covered with
blood, and great flakes of flesh hung from his fore-shoulders; but,
instead of manifesting signs of defeat, he seemed literally to glow
with defiant rage. Instinct had taught him to seek an open space.
. . . But scarcely had I time to glance at him when a huge bear,
the largest and most formidable I ever saw in a wild state, broke
through the opening.

A trial of brute force that baffles description now ensued.
Badly as I had been treated by the cattle, my sympathies were
greatly in favor of the bull, which seemed to me to be much the
nobler animal of the two. He did not wait to meet the charge,
but, lowering his head, boldly rushed upon his savage adversary.
The grizzly was active and wary. He no sooner got within reach
of the bull's horns than he seized them in his powerful grasp,
keeping the head to the ground by main strength and the tremendous weight of his body, while he bit at the nose with his

teeth, and raked strips of flesh from the shoulders with his hind paws. The two animals must have been of very nearly equal weight. On the one side there was the advantage of superior agility and two sets of weapons — the teeth and claws; but on the other, greater powers of endurance and more inflexible courage. . . .

In the death-struggle that ensued [Browne continues] both animals seemed animated by a supernatural strength. The grizzly struck out wildly, but with such destructive energy that the bull, upon drawing back his head, presented a horrible and ghastly spectacle; his tongue, a mangled mass of shreds, hanging from his mouth, his eyes torn completely from their sockets, and his whole face stripped to the bone. On the other hand, the bear was ripped completely open, and writhing in his last agonies. Here it was that indomitable courage prevailed; for, blinded and maimed as he was, the bull, after a momentary pause to regain his wind, dashed wildly at his adversary again, determined to be victorious even in death. A terrific roar escaped from the dying grizzly. With a last frantic effort he sought to make his escape, scrambling over and over in the dust. But his strength was gone. A few more thrusts from the savage victor, and he lay stretched upon the sand, his muscles quivering convulsively, his huge body a resistless mass. A clutching motion of the claws — a groan — a gurgle of the throat, and he was dead.

The bull now raised his bloody crest, uttered a deep bellowing sound, shook his horns triumphantly, and slowly walked off, not, however, without turning every few steps to renew the struggle if necessary. But his last battle was fought. As the blood streamed from his wounds a death-chill came over him. He stood for some time, unyielding to the last, bracing himself up, his legs apart, his head gradually drooping; then dropped on his fore-knees and lay down; soon his head rested on the ground; his body became motionless; a groan, a few convulsive respirations, and he too, the noble victor, was dead.[20]

As has been said, the private rancho was an object of dislike to the padres, because of its effect upon the Indian. President José Señán wrote to Viceroy Branciforte in 1796:

Under no pretext, it seems to me, should retired soldiers or others be permitted to establish themselves in places solitary and withdrawn from men. The evils to which those thus dwelling in solitude are subject cannot easily be computed. They live exposed to the ridicule of the Gentiles; exposed to the committing of many excesses without correction or punishment, without King to command, or Pope to excommunicate. . . . It is no small part of the task of the padres to keep their neophytes congregated in the missions, and to subdue in them their instinct for the wild. But if *gente de razón* adopt the same mode of life, to what purpose their efforts? [21]

Rancheros deserving of censure, civil and ecclesiastical, there undoubtedly were, but there also were those who were ornaments to their class. One of the stateliest men of his time (1775–1860) was a ranchero, Antonio María Lugo. Tall, proud, the owner of countless acres, he might have been seen upon the Los Ángeles streets, shoulder draped in Saltillo *serape*, and sword beneath his arm.

In the style of their dwellings, presidio and pueblo were alike. In respect to birth, bridal, and burial, the likeness extended to the private rancho. Scarcely was a child born ere it was hurried to the priest for christening and baptism. When eight or ten, it often was betrothed; and when thirteen or fourteen, if a girl, married. Fathers made the contract, and the wedding festivities were elaborate. Says Colton: —

The bridegroom must present [the bride] with at least six entire changes of raiment, nor forget, through any sentiment of delicacy, even the chemise. Such an oversight might frustrate all his hopes, as it would be construed into a personal indifference, — the last kind of indifference which a California lady will forgive. He therefore hunts this article with as much solicitude as the Peri the gift that was to unlock Paradise. Having found six which are neither too full nor too slender, he packs them in rose-leaves which seem to flutter like his own heart, and sends them to the lady as his last bridal present. . . .

Two fine horses procured for the occasion are led to the door, saddled, bridled, and pillioned. The bridegroom takes up before him the godmother, and the godfather the bride, and thus they gallop away to church. The priest, in his rich robes, receives them at the altar, where they kneel, partake of the sacrament, and are married. This over, they start on their return, — but now the gentlemen change partners. The bridegroom, still on the pillion, takes up before him his bride. With his right arm he steadies her on the saddle, and in his left hand holds the reins. They return to the house of the parents of the bride, where they are generally received with a discharge of musketry. Two persons, stationed at some convenient place, now rush out and seize him by his legs, and, before he has time to dismount, deprive him of his spurs, which he is obliged to redeem with a bottle of brandy.

The married couple then enter the house, where the near relatives are all waiting in tears to receive them. They kneel down before the parents of the lady, and crave a blessing, which is bestowed with patriarchal solemnity. On rising, the bridegroom makes a signal for the guests to come in, and another for the guitar and harp to strike up. Then commences the dancing, which continues often for three days, with only brief intervals for refreshment, but none for slumber; the wedded pair must be on their feet; their dilemma furnishes food for good-humored gibes and merriment.[22]

Nor was burial itself always a scene entirely sad. If the dead were a little child, it was deemed to have passed in angelic form straight to Abraham's bosom. "Its coffin, draped in white and garlanded with flowers, was borne amid voices of gladness. The untimely blight and the darkness of the grave were all forgotten."

With the American occupation of California, Hispanic institutions fell at a blow. In 1849 the people adopted an American constitution. By this instrument it was provided that all laws in force should remain in force until altered or repealed by the legislature. The first legislature

(1850) passed on April 20 an act repealing every Spanish law but one, and that, it is interesting to note, a law pertaining to the private rancho, — the law providing for a *juez de campo*, a judge of the plain.[23] As for California life, — the life led under Serra and Fages, and their successors, — it has declined rapidly. Something of it lingers in San Diego and San Gabriel, in Guahome and Camulos Ranchos, in Los Ángeles, Santa Bárbara, and San Luis Obispo, and most of all in Monterey; but it lingers in nooks and corners only.

One day in Venice Mr. William D. Howells saw from a balcony on the Grand Canal a boat bearing a strange figure. It was a man clad *cap-à-pie* in a suit of gleaming mail, with visor down and shoulders swept by heavy raven plumes. What Mr. Howells saw was ancient Venice come back. One day in Monterey the writer saw from the street a figure not so strange as the armored Venetian, but yet strange. It was a man in jacket, slashed trousers, and sombrero. He bestrode with Spanish grace a steed that for mettle and trappings might well have been Andalusian. The day was not a festival. The rider seemingly was without intent. He was simply old California — California under Spain and Mexico — come back.

NOTES

WITH LISTS OF SOURCES

M. A. = Mexican Archives; S. A. = Spanish Archives; B. A. = British Archives; A. A. = American Archives; B. C. = Bancroft Collection. Under M. A., "Cor. de Virreyes, ser. II, t. 2/12, No. 376, f. 74," would signify: Correspondence of the Viceroys, second series, serial volume 2, volume 12, document No. 376, page 74. In making the card index to California material in the Mexican Archives, Dr. Bolton was compelled to create his own system of designation, there being none in existence. With regard, therefore, to the correspondence of the Viceroys he numbered the volumes both consecutively from first to last, and by series. Under S. A., Est. (*estante*) = section; caj. (*cajón*) = shelf; and leg. (*legajo*) = bundle or package. Under B. C., designations such as "Prov. [or Dept.] St. Pap. [or Rec.]" = Provincial [or Departmental] State Papers [or Records]. The abbreviation Mil. = Military; and Leg. Rec. = Legislative Records. Under B. A., F. O. = Foreign Office.

NOTES

CHAPTER I

DISCOVERY

New Chapter Sources. — *Application of the name California:* — Letter, Marqués del Valle to Cristóbal Oñate, Santa Cruz, May 14, 1535; Depositions relative to the discoveries of Francisco de Ulloa, Mexico, May 29, 1540; Map of the World, by Alonzo de Santz Cruz, 1542, — E. W. Dahlgren, Stockholm, 1892 (S. A.); *Informe de Gonzalo de Francia*, boatswain Vizcaino expedition, 1629; Tattonus Map of California, Benjamin Wright, 1600 (Library of Congress). *Derivation of name:* — "M. L." of Fresno, San Francisco *Chronicle*, June, 1893; *The Origin and Meaning of the Name California*, by Dr. George Davidson, Geographical Society of the Pacific, San Francisco, 1910. (Specific citations below.)

1. By *Marco Polo's Book* (A. D. 1477) it became known that the Asiatic coast was heavily fringed with islands. There was "Chipango [Japan], an island toward the east in the high seas 1500 [!] miles distant from the continent — a very great island." And "the sea in which lay the islands of those parts was called the sea of Chin [China]." And "with regard to that eastern sea of Chin, according to what was said by the experienced pilots and mariners of those parts, there were 7459 islands [Philippines and Moluccas] in the waters frequented by the said mariners." — "In those islands grew pepper as white as snow, as well as the black in great quantities. In fact the riches of those islands was something wonderful, whether in gold or precious stones, or in all manner of spicery; but they lay so far off from the mainland that it was hard to get to them." — "Moreover, Messer Marco Polo never was there." (*The Book of Ser Marco Polo* (Yule), 3d ed., 2 vols., 1903, vol. ii, pp. 253, 264.) See also map of Toscanelli (thought to have been used by Columbus) as reproduced in Sir A. Helps's *The Spanish Conquest in America*, London, 4 vols., 1900, vol. i, p. 58.

In Spain, for over two hundred and fifty years, North America (Asiatic Archipelago that it was presumed to be) was known rather as "the Indies" (Columbus's own designation) than as America. With South America the case was different. Looking, as the post-Columbian navigators were, for an Asiatic continent to the westward and southward of the islands, they deemed the conditions fulfilled by South America (described by Amerigo Vespucci in 1504), and this region was charted as continental from as early a date as 1507. Indeed, where the early navigators erred was not in their hypothesis as to the Asiatic coast-line, which was singularly correct, but in their confounding of North America — insular and peninsular — with insular Asia.

2. Map III (two plates, head of chapter I) portrays North America as a group of islands. The earliest maps representing California as apart from the continent are the "Herrera" (Kaspar van Baerle) map of 1622, the "Purchas" (Briggs) map of 1625, the "Prospect" (Speed) map of 1626, and the "World Encompassed" (Drake) map of 1628. (See chap. II of text, n. 27.) It moreover is in connection with insularity that there arises the question of the name California.

THE NAME CALIFORNIA

Bestowing of the name. — By " California " (a name first used in a book published in Spain in 1510 — *Las Sergas de Esplandián*) there was implied insularity coupled with riches. " 'Know,' the *Sergas* says, 'that on the right hand of the Indies there is an island called California, very close to the side of the Terrestrial Paradise; and it was peopled by black women, without any man among them, for they lived in the fashion of Amazons. They were of strong and hardy bodies, of ardent courage and great force. Their island was the strongest in all the world, with its steep cliffs and rock shores. Their arms were of gold, and so was the harness of the wild beasts they tamed to ride; for in the whole island there was no metal but gold.' " (Edward Everett Hale, *Proceedings American Antiquarian Society*, April 30, 1862, p. 45; *Atlantic Monthly*, vol. xiii, p. 265.)

With the *Sergas*, moreover, Cortés and his followers (the discoverers of Lower California, 1533–1535) had ample opportunity to be acquainted. Hardly less than the *Amadis de Gaul* was it a favorite in sixteenth-century Spain. Cervantes, writing in 1605, brands the *Sergas* as among the tales which had turned the head of Don Quixote. And in the Indies so much were books of its class prized, that in 1543 Charles V forbade their importation, describing them as *libros de romance que traten de materias profanas y fabulosas y historias fingidas*. (*Recopilación de Leyes de las Indias*, lib. i, tit. xxiv, ley 4.)

But Cortés and his followers — discoverers of California though they were, and familiar with the *Sergas* though they may have been — did not, it would seem, give to the land its name. Having sighted California on May 1, " day of the two apostles," says Cortés, and "because in the part sighted there were the highest sierras of this land, there was given to them the name 'Sierras de San Felipe.' . . . This same day," he continues, "we discovered an island near the land, and we called it Isla de Santiago [Cerralvo]. And soon we saw two others, one of which was called Isla de San

Miguel, and the other, Isla de San Cristóval [*Perlas* of Cortés's map, *post,* IV]. And reaching this port and bay of Santa Cruz, the day of Santa Cruz, May 3, it therefore was given that name." (Marqués del Valle to Cristóbal de Oñate at Compostela, from the port and bay of Santa Cruz, 14th of May, 1535, — S. A., Madrid, Academia de la Historia, Colección de Muñoz, tom. 80, fol. 137; *Congreso Internacional de Americanistas* (" Actas 4ª Reunión," Madrid, 1881), Madrid, 1883; vol. ii, p. 332.)

Furthermore, in 1537 [?] Cortés deposited with the government a map bearing at the point of his landing the name Santa Cruz (*post,* IV), and in 1540 Lower California was repeatedly referred to by him as *la tierra de Santa Cruz.* "I arrived," he says, "at the land of Santa Cruz and was in it . . . and being in the said land of Santa Cruz, I had complete knowledge of the land." (Memorial que dió al Rey el Marqués del Valle en Madrid, *Documentos Inéditos de las Indias,* vol. iv, p. 211.) And the companions of Cortés, when officially catechized as to the country, its name, etc., testified: one, that it was called Tarsis; another, that it had no name, but that the bay was called Santa Cruz; and some, that they could remember no name. (" Probanza," Pacheco y Cárdenas, *Docs.,* vol. xvi, pp. 12, 22, 27.)

The first time (so far as known) that the name of California was applied to any actual body of land was in 1539. In that year Francisco de Ulloa, one of the lieutenants of Cortés (a man who had been with the Spanish leader to Santa Cruz in 1535), made, under orders from his superior, a second voyage thither, taking with him as diarist Francisco Preciado. The latter employs the name California at various times and each time in the same sense. He says: (1) "On November 10 we found ourselves 54 leagues distant from California a little more or less always in the southwest, seeing in the night three or four fires "; (2) and (3): " In the meanwhile our Chichimeco interpreter, borne in the isle of California, was come unto us," etc. "The captain commanded the Indian our Chichimeco to speake unto them [Indians of the northeast coast of Lower California], but they could not understand him, so that we assuredly believe that they understand not the language of the isle of California." (Ramusio, *Viaggi,* 1565, vol. iii, pp. 343, 347; Hakluyt, *Voyages,* 1600, vol. iii, pp. 406, 412.)

In 1539, therefore (and to Preciado), "California " was an island; one so situated that on November 10, Ulloa was distant therefrom some 54 leagues. That at this time California signified Cortés's "land of Santa Cruz " (Lower California) may well seem improbable, for the allusions by Preciado to California are to it as insular unequivocally and *per se,* whereas his allusions to Lower California are to it, first, as almost certainly non-insular, and, second (whether insular or not), as not California, but " Santa Cruz." "Wee began," says Preciado, "to be of divers opinions, some thinking that this coast of Santa Cruz was a firme land . . . others the contrary," etc. (Hakluyt, 1600, vol. iii, p. 399.) And (after rounding the head of the gulf): " Here from this day forward wee began to bee afraid, considering that we were to return to the port of Santa Cruz; for it was supposed, that all along this mighty gulfe from the entrance in at Culiacan until the returning backe unto the said haven was all firme land, and also because wee had the firme land alwayes on our right hand and it goeth round circle-wise unto the sayd haven." (*Ibid.*, p. 402.)

But if California was not the Lower California of to-day, but so distinct and apart from it as to be an actual island, — an island so actual as to have supplied Ulloa with his interpreter, — what island was it?

It may have been Cerralvo (the Santiago of Cortés), or Espiritu Santo (so named by Francisco de Ortega in 1632), both at the mouth of the Bay of Santa Cruz, now La Paz. Cerralvo Island especially is so situated as to answer to that "California" from which on November 10, 1539, Ulloa was distant 54 leagues, — a California placed even by Bancroft (*History of California*, vol. i, p. 65, n. 2) "at or near Santa Cruz." But not only by their situation do these islands to-day answer to Preciado's California of 1539; they in 1539 — by their real pearls (maps, *post*, IV, V, VI) and reputed Amazons — answered to the California of the *Sergas de Esplandián* of 1510. Said Cortés, writing to the Emperor Charles V, on October 15, 1524: "He [one of my captains] brought me an account of the chiefs of the province of Ceguatán, who affirm that there is an island inhabited only by women without any men, and that at given times men from the mainland visit them. . . . This island is ten days' journey from the province, and many of them went thither and saw it, and told me also that it is very rich in pearls and gold." (H. Cortés, *Historia de Nueva España*, Lorenzana, 1770, p. 349.) Again (a bit of evidence quite new), Gonzalo de Francia, boatswain of the ship which, under Sebastián Vizcaino, visited Santa Cruz Bay in 1597, wrote to the King on May 27, 1629: "We came upon *un puerto grande* which was called *el puerto de la Paz* . . . and an island at the mouth which was called Island of Women, who were without men, none passing over to them except in summer on rafts made of reeds." (S. A., Madrid, Dirección de Hidrografía, Colección Navarrete, t. 19, no. 15.) Finally (a bit of evidence quite as new as the last), Pedro de Valencia, *escribano público* of Ulloa's armada, submitted to Cortés in 1540 (May 29) a report which described the Indian interpreter with the armada, who could not be understood by the natives of northeastern Lower California, "as from the port and bay of Santa Cruz" [*el yndio que llevábamos del puerto y baya de Santa Cruz*], an indication that Preciado's "isle of California" was within Santa Cruz (La Paz) Bay limits. (*Testimonio de los descubrimientos que hizó el Capitán Francisco de Ulloa, por orden de Hernán Cortés en la costa Norte de Nueva España, con una relación de su viaje desde Acapulco hasta la Isla de los Cedros, Méjico, 29 de Mayo, 1540*, S. A. (Sevilla), Arch. Genl. de Indias, est. i, caj. i, leg. 1-20.)

When and by whom, on the foregoing hypothesis, the name California was transferred from Cerralvo, or Espiritu Santo Island, to the mainland, is a question to which no definite answer is possible. It may have been in 1541 by Hernando de Alarcón, who in that year made thither an expedition, for on Alarcón's map, drawn by Castillo (*post*, v), the mainland is for the first time shown under the designation California.

But the hypothesis presented is not without a competing one. Preciado (Ulloa's diarist) discriminates between the "isle of California" and the "land of Santa Cruz." Yet it is not impossible that by California he means a portion of Lower California itself, to wit, the portion below Santa Cruz Bay — a portion which, though not charted as insular by Cortés, may in the mind of the lay Spaniard have been identified with the famed Amazonian isle "ten days' journey from Ceguatán." At any rate, as early as 1542 the cosmographer royal of Charles V (Alonzo de Santa Cruz) published a map (*post*, VII) which shows California as in the lower part insular, and in the upper part peninsular. The lower part bears the legend: *Ysla que descubrió el Marqués del Valle;* and the upper, *Tierra que enbió á descubrir Don Antonio de Mendoça* ("Map of the World by Alonzo de Santa Cruz, 1542," E. W. Dahlgren, Stockholm, 1892). "This map," says Dahlgren, "is almost identical with the great official Spanish Map (now lost) by Alonzo de Chaves, royal cosmographer to Charles V, issued in 1536 to correct the cartography of the world to date. It may be taken as embodying geographical ideas to 1539."

Derivation of the name. — M. Venegas (*Noticia de la California*, tom. i, pte. i, sec. 1, p. 3) mentions as a derivation for the name California, *calida fornax*, hot furnace, from the heat of California, but does not think the Spanish adventurers "could boast of so much literature." His own suggestion is that the derivation is from some Indian word misunderstood by the Spaniards. This suggestion gains weight from the contention of Upper Californians (Vallejo, Alvarado, and others) that the derivation is *kali forno*, an Indian phrase of Lower California signifying " high hill," " sandy coast," or "native land." The suggestion is countenanced by Bancroft (H. H.), who states that an old Indian of Sinaloa (Mexico) called the peninsula (A. D. 1878) *Tchalifalni-al* — "the sandy land beyond the water." On the other hand, the *calida fornax* derivation (rejected by Venegas because too "literary" for the *conquistadores*, and by Bancroft because the peninsula though hot was not so compared with other regions to which the *conquistadores* were accustomed) emerges rehabilitated at the hands of Jules Marcou, who ascribes it to Cortés, "to whom [he says] is due the appropriate classification of the Mexican regions into *tierra fria, tierra templada, tierra caliente*, and *tierra california*." To such as find Marcou's derivation faulty, yet cling to the phrase *calida fornax*, there is left the chance that the phrase relates not to the climate, but to the hot baths (*temescales*) which were wont to be taken by the Indians. (J. Marcou, *Notes;* Washington, 1878.) For derivations almost certainly fanciful, see J. Archibald, "Why California?" in *Overland Monthly*, vol. ii, p. 437.

In 1910 (the year just past), Dr. George Davidson, President of the Geographical Society of the Pacific, published a monograph entitled *The Origin and Meaning of the Name California.* The publication mentions the first uses of the name California, and gives a list of the early maps on which the name appears. The *Sergas de Esplandián* is accepted as the source of the name, and the etymology is dealt with as follows: California; from κάλλος, beauty (or κάλλι-, beautiful), and ὄρνις (ornis), a bird. "In this island are many griffins . . . which can be found in no other part of the world. The queen took five hundred of these griffins to assist in the capture of Constantinople."

Professor Davidson alludes to a derivation by "M. L." of Fresno, printed in the San Francisco *Chronicle* for June, 1893. He says: "A late writer, M. L. of Fresno, who appears to be well posted on the subject, and who has evidently examined the geology of Lower California, expresses the opinion that the name came from the Indians. In approaching Loreto (on the eastern coast of the peninsula in latitude 26° 10′) he saw snow-white heaps upon a knoll, and asked the guide, ' *Qué cosa es?* ' ' *Cal y forno,*' answered the Indian; when he knew at once he had the true meaning and origin of the name California, because these white heaps were lime-kilns; *cal* meaning lime, and *forno* an oven or kiln. He believed that Ulloa, remembering Montalvo's California, accepted the name for the country. (*Transactions and Proceedings of the Geographical Society of the Pacific,* 1910, vol. vi, part 1, pp. 34, 38.)

3. See chart I (head of chapter II) showing "Anian" and route of Magellan.

4. H. Cortés, *Historia de Nueva España,* Lorenzana, 1770, p. 382. Translations: M. Venegas, *History of California,* 2 vols., vol. i, p. 127; G. Folsom, *Dispatches of Hernando Cortés,* 1834, pp. 417–18; F. A. MacNutt, *The Letters of Cortes to Charles V,* 1908, 2 vols., vol. ii, pp. 207–209; H. H. Bancroft, *North Mexican States and Texas,* vol. i, p. 5, n. 4. In June, 1523, Cortés had been ordered by the King to hasten the search for a strait (Pacheco y Cárdenas, *Docs.,* vol. xxiii, p. 366); and in 1525 Estevan Gómez actually made a search, coasting from Nova Scotia to Florida. (W. Lowery, *The Spanish Settlements in the United States,* 1901, p. 169, notes.)

5. *Y adelante la California adonde llegó el primer Marqués del Valle que le pusó este nombre.* (Antonio de Herrera, *Historia General,* 1601, dec. viii, lib. 6, cap. 14; B. Díaz, *Historia Verdadera de la Conquista de la Nueva España,* 1632, cap. 200.)

6. Hitherto the only available account of Ulloa's voyage has been that of Preciado. The account submitted by Pedro de Valencia agrees generally with Preciado's, but it is worthy of note that, although Preciado is mentioned therein as a Franciscan padre, and the name Santa Cruz is used to designate Lower California, the name California is not used at all.

7. "But because your Lordship comanded mee that I should bring you

the secret of that gulfe [California], I resolved that although I had knowen I should have lost the shippes, I would not have ceased for anything to have seen the heád thereof. . . . And it pleased God that after this sort we came to the very bottom of the Bay; where wee found a very mightie river [Colorado], which ranne with so great fury of a streame, that we could hardly saile against it." (Hakluyt, 1600, vol. iii, p. 425.)

8. Diary of Cabrillo and Ferrelo, Pacheco y Cárdenas, *Docs.*, vol. xiv, p. 165; *Florida Coll. Docs.*, vol. i, p. 173. Translation, R. S. Evans, *Report of U. S. Geological Survey* (Wheeler), vol. vii, p. 293.

9. According to physiographists, the Golden Gate originally was the outlet for the combined waters of the Sacramento and San Joaquín Rivers. By a subsidence of the bed of these streams, the sea was admitted through the Golden Gate, thus forming San Francisco Bay.

10. See map i (relief map of California), head of chapter i.

11. "It is held by geologists that the Sierra Nevada originated at the close of the Jurassic period, and that through the Cretaceous, Eocene, and Neocene periods it was worn down to a region of low relief. There may have been disturbances, but during this long period the range was certainly much lower than now, and the Great Valley of the San Joaquin occupied by a body of brackish or salt water. At the close of the Neocene, which was the time of the accumulation of the great deposits of auriferous gravels, there was a removal of faulting along the eastern side of the range, and this disturbance was accompanied by volcanic outbursts. The mountain range began to rise toward its present position, and these movements with relation to the depressed areas of the Great Basin have not yet ceased. With reference to the depressed valley known as Owens Valley, the crest of the Sierra is probably higher now than it has been; but during the glacial period it is likely that this region as a whole was higher than now." (H. W. Fairbanks, 1910, University of California.)

12. "The prevailing easterly drift of the atmosphere in temperate latitudes, causing the well-known winds from the west, is one of the prime factors in modifying the climate of the coast of California. This coast-line, stretching for 10 degrees of latitude, is subjected to a steady indraft from the west. In this movement, together with the fact that to the west is the Pacific Ocean, lies the secret of the difference in temperature between the Atlantic and the Pacific coasts at places of like latitude. For some years there has been an impression that the milder climate of the Pacific Coast was due to a warming influence of the Kuro Siwo, or Japan Current. No reliable data exist to support such a belief, and it is quite unlikely that the Japan Current plays any important part in modifying the climate of the Pacific Coast. The active factors are, as said above, the prevailing easterly drift of the atmosphere and the proximity of the mass of water, a great natural conservator of heat. One of the most noticeable differences between the climate of the Atlantic and Pacific seaboards is found in the trend of

NOTES

the isotherms, those of the Atlantic Coast corresponding more or less with the parallels of latitude, while on the Pacific Coast the isotherms run more nearly like meridians. Too much emphasis cannot be laid upon the effect of these two factors, the easterly drift of the air and the proximity of the ocean in modifying climate. It is probable that if one of these conditions could be reversed, and the general movement of the air in these latitudes be from east to west, marked differences in climate conditions would result, and the Pacific Coast might then have a rigorous climate." ("Climatology of California," U. S. Dept. of Agriculture, *Bulletin L*, 1903, p. 15.)

13. John Muir, *The Mountains of California*, 1903 ; C. F. Lummis, *Encyclopedia Americana*, 1903, article " California."

14. See map II (Indian Linguistic Families), head of chapter I.

15. "From the time of the first settlement of California, its Indians have been described as both more primitive and more peaceful than the majority of the natives of North America. On the whole this opinion is undoubtedly true." "The picturesqueness and dignity of other Indians are lacking." — "Throughout the greater part of the State the civilization of the Indians is very much alike." — "The exceptions are Southern California and the northwesternmost part of the State." — "More than two thirds of the State, including all the central part, show a fundamental ethnical similarity, whose distinguishing characteristics furthermore are not found outside of the State." — "Structures of brush or tule were common." — "The shape of the houses was conical or domed." — "Basketry alone [among the arts] had reached a considerable development. Pottery was virtually unknown." — "Beyond the family, the only bases of organization were the village and the language." Religion was manifested not as symbolism and ritualism but as "individual shamanistic effort." The above characteristics of culture "pertain to all the Indians between Point Conception and Cape Mendocino, and between this stretch of coast and the Sierra Nevada, extending from north to south, from Mount Shasta to the Tehachapi Range." (A. L. Kroeber, *Types of Indian Culture in California*, 1904, University of California Pubs., vol. ii, no. 3; F. W. Hodge, *Handbook of American Indians North of Mexico*, Washington, 1907, part i, p. 190.)

The Indian substitute for the deity is the culture hero. But among the California Indians "the conception of a culture hero is wanting. Instead of a human divinity there is almost everywhere a true creator, a god who makes. Sometimes he is a person, sometimes an animal. . . . Often he makes the world from primitive water. Generally he makes also mountains and rivers. Usually he creates food. Almost always he creates men, and frequently divides them by languages and localities." But "the exceptional tendency of the California Indian to form real creation myths is seemingly not the result of a higher intellectuality which seeks and finds explanations, and to which other Indians have not attained. The tendency is probably due rather to a lack on the part of the Californian of the mythological specialization which characterizes other American Indians." (Kroeber, *supra*.)

Sta. Bárbara Channel Tribes, University of California Pubs., vol. iv, no. 3, p. 152. *California Tribes as Differentiated by Basketry, Ibid.*, vol. ii, no. 4, p. 151. Minute descriptions of the California Indians are to be found in B. C., *Arch. of Sta. Bárbara*, vol. vii, pp. 150–214. Extracts have been published under the title *A Mission Record of the California Indians*, A. L. Kroeber, University of California Pubs. in American Archæology and Ethnology, 1908, vol. viii, no. 1. For further description of the California Indians, see Powers, *Tribes of California;* Fages, *Noticias del Puerto de Monterey y Diario Histórico de los Viages Hechos al Norte de California*, 1775 (M. A., *Misiones*, vol. iv).

CHAPTER II

OCCUPATION OF MONTEREY

MATERIAL for the present chapter hitherto unused has been found in portions of the correspondence of Philip II and Philip III with Miguel López de Legazpi, Viceroy Luis de Velasco, the Audiencia of Manila, Andrés de Urdaneta, Santiago de Vera, Hernando de los Ríos Coronel, Viceroy Marqués de Montesclaros, Viceroy Pedro de Moya y Contreras, and others, as printed in *The Philippine Islands*, edited by Blair and Robertson. Much also, especially as relating to the islands of Rica de Oro and Rica de Plata, and to the voyage of Pedro de Unamunu (neglected subjects in their bearing upon the history of California), has been found in the Spanish Archives at Sevilla. The same archives have proved rich in material on Sebastián Vizcaino. Some of it is in print in *Documentos Referentes al Reconocimiento de las Costas de las Californias desde el Cabo de San Lucas al de Mendocino, Recopilados en el Archivo de Indias*, por D. Francisco Carrasco y Guisasola, coronel y capitán de fragata, Madrid, Dirección de Hidrografía, 1882. Other printed material of value for the chapter is the *Sucesos* of Antonio de Morga, 1609; *Transactions of the Royal Society*, London, 1674; *En Studie i Historisk Geografi*, by E. W. Dahlgren, Stockholm, 1893 and 1900; *Tasman's Journal* (Heeres), Amsterdam, 1898; and *Ein Unentdecktes Goldland*, by O. Nachod, Tokyo, 1899. (Specific citations below.)

1. In *Periplus*, Nordenskiöld states that the first dated map bearing the name Anian is the Zalterius map, Venice, 1566. It possibly (he says) is on an older map in the Correr Collection, Venice, Museo Civico.

2. Blair and Robertson, "Life and Voyage of Magellan" (*The Philippine Islands*, 55 vols., 1903–1909, vol. i, p. 250). "Expedition of García de Loaysa," "Voyage of Alvaro de Saavedra," and "Expedition of Ruy López de Villalobos," *Ibid.*, vol. ii, pp. 25–73.

3. H. C. Lea, *The Moriscos of Spain*, 1901, pp. 6, 394; M. A. S. Hume, *The Spanish People*, 1901, ch. xi.

4. A. Helps, *The Spanish Conquest* (Oppenheim, 1902, vol. i, p. 334, n. 3; vol. ii, p. 44, n.). Las Casas points out that between 1514 and 1519 a million of gold (£300,000, or £3,000,000 present value) had been taken from the Indians, but that only 3000 *castellanos* had been sent to the King in that time.

5. W. Cunningham, *Western Civilization in its Economic Aspects*, 1900, vol. ii, p. 192.

6. B. and R., "Expedition of Miguel López de Legazpi" (*Philippine Islands*, vol. ii, p. 77, vol. iii, p. 44); J. A. Robertson, *Legazpi and Philippine Colonization*, 1909.

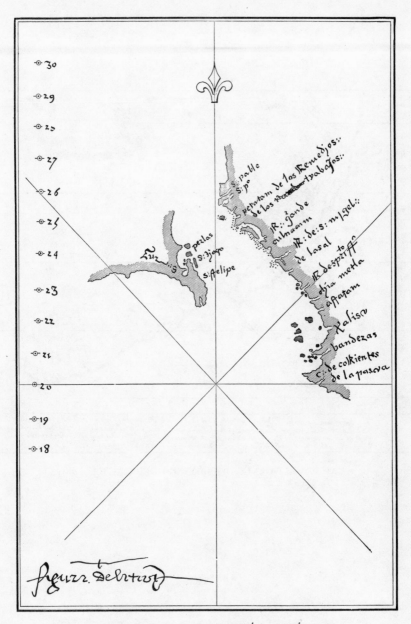

MAP IV. CALIFORNIA. BY HERNÁN CORTÉS, 1535

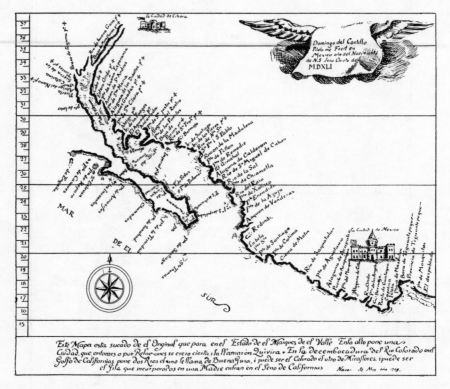

MAP V. CALIFORNIA. BY DOMINGO DEL CASTILLO, 1541

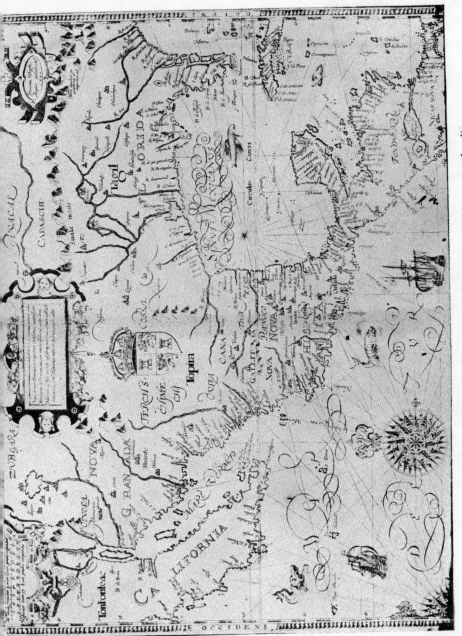

MAP VI. TATTONUS MAP OF CALIFORNIA, 1600. (Hitherto unreproduced)

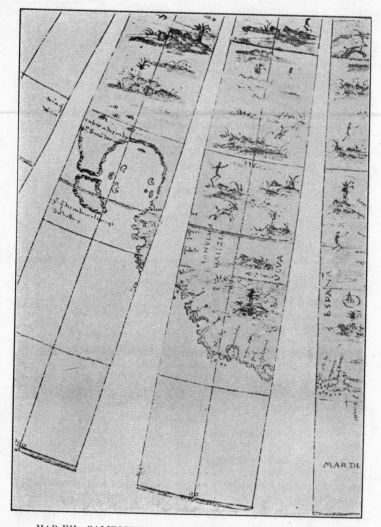

MAP VII. CALIFORNIA. BY ALONZO DE SANTA CRUZ, 1542

Y[sl]a que descubrió el marqués del Valle.
Tierra que enbió á descubrir don Antonio de Mendoça

7. Antonio de Morga, *Sucesos de las Islas Filipinas*, 1609 (Hon. H. E. J. Stanley, 1868), p. 336; B. and R., *Philippine Islands*, vol. ii, pp. 142, 198, 223, 236, vol. iii, pp. 57, 76, vol. vi, p. 150.

8. La Navidad (latitude 19° 13′ N.) was at first the principal port on the Pacific, but after 1550 Acapulco rapidly took precedence.

9. Felipe II to Viceroy Luis de Velasco, September 24, 1559: Two ships to be sent for the discovery of the western islands toward the Moluccas; these ships to return to Nueva España, " so that it may be known whether the return voyage is assured " (B. and R., *Philippine Islands*, vol. ii, p. 78); Legazpi, report of ship sent to discover return route (*Ibid.*, pp. 175, 239). Bancroft (*North Mexican States and Texas*, vol. i, p. 139, n. 10) notes that Burney (*Chronological History of the Discoveries in the South Sea*, London, 1803, vol. i, p. 271) mentions a voyage to the Philippine Islands in 1566 by the San Gerónimo and return voyages to New Spain in 1567 by the San Juan and two other ships. In B. and R., *Philippine Islands* (vol. iii, p. 129), may be found a document noting in detail the voyages immediately following that of Legazpi. On June 1, 1565, Urdaneta sailed for New Spain, reaching Acapulco early in October. A return vessel reached the Philippines, October 15, 1566. On November 16, 1567, a Philippine ship reached New Spain, etc. Perhaps the earliest date of regular systematic trade was 1573, for on December 5 Viceroy Martín Enríquez wrote to Philip of the arrangement for that year as " an initial attempt " (*Ibid.*, p. 214). See also Bancroft, *History of Mexico*, vol. ii, p. 600, and notes.

10. The San Lucas (under Alonso de Arellano) deserted her consorts, and, returning to New Spain by the course of the Japan Current, actually anticipated the arrival of Urdaneta at Acapulco by three months. The object was reward for the discovery of a return route. But Arellano was sent back from Spain to Mexico to be punished for disobedience. (Morga, *Sucesos*, B. and R., *Philippine Islands*, vol. xv, p. 47; Bancroft, *North Mexican States and Texas*, vol. i, p. 139, n. 9.)

11. F. Gali (Ramusio, *Viaggi*, 1565, vol. iii, p. 343; Hakluyt, vol. iii, pp. 446–447). For the orders to Gali, see B. and R., *Philippine Islands*, vol. vi, pp. 69, 307. Between 1580 and 1583 Gonzalo Ronquillo, Governor of the Philippine Islands, tried to find a southern route to Nueva España, but his captain Juan Ronquillo de Castillo only succeeded in reaching Nueva Guinea (Morga, *Sucesos*, B. and R., *Philippine Islands*, vol. xv, p. 56). As to the naming of Cape Mendocino, all is conjecture. Torquemada (*Monarquía Indiana*, vol. i, p. 693) ascribes it to Urdaneta (or Arellano). Hittell (*History of California*, vol. i, p. 76) ascribes it to Cabrillo. Bancroft discusses the subject: *North Mexican States and Texas*, vol. i, p. 139, n. 9; *History of California*, vol. i, p. 94.

12. See chart i (head of chapter ii). A description of the Acapulco-Manila and Manila-Acapulco routes is given in detail in Morga's *Sucesos* (B. and R. *Philippine Islands*, vol. xvi, pp. 200–209). From Acapulco, galleons began

their voyages between February 28 and March 20, and from Manila, on or after June 20. The route from Acapulco was invariable: southwest to 13° or 14°, then straight west to Guam in the Ladrones, where from the year 1668 Spain maintained a beacon station; but from Manila the route varied with conditions of wind and weather. According to Morga (1609), the California landfall was (then) usually made just below Cape Mendocino, between 40° and 36°. According to a Spanish chart of 1742 (chart I, head of chapter II), it (then) was made below 36°. Urdaneta (*Documentos Inéditos de Ultramar*, tom. ii, pp. 427–456) reached latitude 39° 30', Arellano 43° (*Ibid.*, tom. iii, pp. 1–76), and Gali, by his own reckoning (Hakluyt, *Voyages*, vol. iii, pp. 442–447), sighted California in 37° 30'. The route down the coast of New Spain to Acapulco is described by Cabrera Bueno (native of the island of Teneriffe and *piloto-mayor* of the Philippine voyages) in *Navegación Especulativa y Práctica*, Manila, 1734. See F. Palou, *Noticias de California* (J. T. Doyle, 1874), vol. ii, pp. 201–203, n.

13. G. Careri, "A Voyage Round the World," 1693–1699 (Churchill, *Voyages*, 1704, vol. iv, p. 486); Dr. P. C. Sebastián, *Peregrinación del Mundo*, 1688, p. 268; E. G. Bourne, Introduction to Blair and Robertson, *Philippine Islands*, vol. i, p. 65. Storms off Cape Mendocino in 1603 vividly described by Morga in the *Sucesos* (B. and R., *Philippine Islands*, vol. xvi, p. 28).

CERMEÑO'S SAN FRANCISCO BAY

14. Cermeño's *piloto-mayor*, Francisco Bolaños, afterwards served under Vizcaino. Some of the crew of the San Agustín, therefore, were saved. But no writer down to a date subsequent to the publication of the Bancroft Pacific Coast histories seems to have been possessed of any details of the matter. Bancroft (*North Mexican States and Texas*, vol. i, p. 147) says: "Whether the ship escaped after being lightened of her cargo, or was accompanied by a tender on which the crew escaped, is not recorded. . . . It is not impossible that some additional results of the expedition were intentionally kept secret by the government; at any rate no record has ever come to light in the archives." Again (*History of California*, vol. i, p. 96): "It is possible that the San Augustin was accompanied by another vessel on which the officers and men escaped; but much more probable, I think, that the expression 'was lost' in the record is an error, and that the ship escaped with a loss of her cargo."

The following are the facts: On May 31, 1591, Viceroy Luis de Velasco wrote to Philip II that the frequent disasters befalling the Philippine ships made it very necessary to discover *los puertos de la tierra firme*, and to survey them and know their locations. Accordingly, on January 17, 1593, Philip gave orders to Velasco to institute " a survey of the harbors to be found on the voyage to and from the Philippine Islands." On April 6, 1594, Velasco reported to the King that he had directed a survey to be made by Sebastián Rodríguez Cermeño, " a man of experience in his calling, one who could be depended upon and who had means of his own — although he was a Portuguese, there being no Spaniards of his profession whose services were available." On February 1, 1596, the royal officers at Acapulco wrote to Viceroy Conde de Monterey that on Wednesday, January 31, there had entered the port a *viroco* (a small open vessel propelled by square sails and by sweeps) having on board Juan de Morgana, navigating officer, four Spanish sailors, five Indians, and a negro. These reported the loss of the San Agustín "on a coast where she struck and went to pieces," and the drowning of a barefooted friar and one other. Some seventy men had escaped in the *viroco*, all but themselves having landed at La Navidad. The La Navidad party in due time reached Mexico City. The story of their journey became exaggerated, and when, on October 9, 1772, Miguel Costansó wrote to the royal secretary a letter describing the re-discovery of the San Francisco Bay of Cermeño (Francis Drake's Bay), he said: "Some mariners of its [the San Agustín's] crew with the pilot saved themselves, who, traversing the immense country which intervenes between said port [Drake's Bay] and New Biscay, arrived at the end of many days at Sombrerete [near Zacatecas], a mining-camp of that government bordering upon New Galicia." (*Documentos*, por D. Francisco Carrasco y Guisasola, Madrid, Dirección de Hidrografía, 1882, nos. 3, 6, 10; Publications of the Historical Society of Southern California, *Documents from the Sutro Collection*, 1891, nos. 3, 4, 5; *Out West*, Jan., 1902, p. 58.)

Cermeño's *Derrotero y Relación*, dated Mexico, April 24, 1596, is in the Archivo de Indias at Sevilla (Simancas, Secular, Aud. de Méjico, est. lviii, caj. iii, leg. 16). Cermeño says: "We left the port of Cavite, Philippine Islands, on July 5, . . . and sighted New Spain at Cape Mendocino on November 4. . . . We left the bay and port of San Francisco, which is called by another name, a large bay where we were wrecked the morning of Friday, December 8. The bay is in 38 2/3°, and the islets in the mouth are in 38½°, the distance between the two points of the bay being 25 leagues. . . . On Sunday we discovered a very large bay and we named it San Pedro. It is 15 leagues from point to point and the latitude is 37°." (Very probably Monterey Bay.)

15. G. Davidson, *Identification of Sir Francis Drake's Anchorage in 1579* (California Historical Society Publication); *The Discovery of San Francisco Bay*, 1907, pp. 13–23.

16. Memorial by citizens of the Philippine Islands, B. and R., *Philippine Islands*, vol. vi, p. 226.

17. Letter, Manila Audiencia to Felipe II, June 25, 1588, B. and R., *Philippine Islands*, vol. vi, p. 311; Vera to Felipe II, June 26, 1588, *Ibid.*, vol. vii, p. 52; Salazar to Felipe II, June 27, 1588, *Ibid.*, vol. vii, pp. 66, 68; "Viceroy of India," a letter, *Ibid.*, vol. vii, p. 81.

18. As early as 1556, Spanish-American treasure was carried to Spain by

a fleet of fourteen vessels; but the fleet system in the Atlantic was not legally established until 1561. (*Recopilación de Leyes*, lib. ix, tit. 30, ley 1. See Bourne, *Spain in America*, 1904, p. 284.)

19. Letter, Vera to Felipe II, June 26, 1588, B. and R., *Philippine Islands*, vol. vii, p. 53.

20. B. and R., *Philippine Islands*, vol. ix, p. 307.

21. S. A., Madrid, Dirección de Hidrografía, Navarrete, t. xix, nos. 4, 5.

22. Monterey hesitated to confirm his predecessor's contract because, first, the instrument "had reference to the pearl-fishery only, and not at all to the entry and pacification of the land"; and to the circumstance, second, that Vizcaino, "as leader and chief," was "obscure," and apparently not possessed of the "resolution and capacity necessary for so great an enterprise" as entry and pacification would involve. (Monterey to Felipe II, February 29, 1596, Pub. Hist. Soc. of South. Calif., *Sutro Collection*, no. 8.) There was much vacillation on the part of the Viceroy and of the Spanish Government (docs. 8 and 11), but Vizcaino finally was allowed to proceed. (Cf. *Documentos*, por Carrasco y Guisasola, *supra*, 14.)

23. Sutro, 9 and 10. On the bestowing of the name La Paz the testimony is direct. Says Gonzalo de Francia, *contramaestre* (boatswain) of Vizcaino's flagship, May 27, 1629: . . . *Un puerto grande que el pusieron el puerto de la Paz porque allí nos salieron los indios de paz*. (S. A., Madrid, Dir. de Hid., Navarrete, tom. xix, no. 15.)

24. Letter, Vizcaino to Felipe II, 1597; Letter, Monterey to Felipe II, November 26, 1597, in Pub. Hist. Soc. of South. Calif., Sutro, 10 and 12.

25. M. Venegas, *Noticia de la California*, 1757, 3 vols., vol. i, p. 189; Translation, 1759, 2 vols., vol. i, p. 168; *Cédula*, August 19, 1606, B. and R., *Philippine Islands*, vol. xiv, pp. 182–183.

On May 31, 1602, Viceroy Monterey wrote to the King that he had not been able, as ordered on September 7, 1599, to send an expedition to survey the ports and bays of the South Sea. It had been ascertained that there would be needed two vessels and a *lancha* and sixty mariners. As there was at Acapulco no vessel fit for the voyage, he had ordered that the ports of Guatemala be searched, and for this task he had named Captain Toribio Gómez, lately from Castile, a seaman of sixteen years' service in the royal armadas. Gómez, with another captain of distinction, had sailed in July of the past year, intending to be back by November, when the *lancha* was to be ready. Meantime he had chosen for the chief command Sebastián Vizcaino, as more familiar with that coast than any other man in the kingdom, — a person of diligence and reliability and of moderate talent. He had chosen as officers Captain Peguero and Lieutenant Alarcón, who had served in Flanders and Brittany, and as cosmographer Gerónimo Martín (Palacios), who bore the title " cosmographer" from the Casa de Contratación at Sevilla, and who had served twenty years in the royal fleets and armadas. But Toribio had been delayed, etc. The expedition had sailed from Acapulco about

May 5. It was hoped that there would be discovered "some good port and harbor where the ships from China might recruit." Vizcaino, on penalty of his life, was to make no stop in the Ensenada de las Californias. Instructions in detail, dated March 18, were annexed. (Carrasco y Guisasola, *Docs.*, nos. 18, 19, 20.) From Tezcuco, on March 26, 1603, Monterey wrote to the King that Vizcaino had returned. He had discovered "three very good ports, — San Diego in 33°, another adjacent to it of less consequence [San Pedro?], and a third, greater and better adapted to the ships from China, called Monterey, in 37°." The Viceroy wrote again, on May 28, transmitting *relaciones* of the voyage and a map and table of reckonings. On November 22 (from Otumba) he wrote, stating that in view of the great services performed by Vizcaino he had made him "general of the ships this year making the voyage to the Philippines," so that on returning he might examine more closely the port or ports he had discovered, and entering them might procure wood and water and whatever else the ships required. The various captains also were recommended for honors. On July 10, 1604, Viceroy Montesclaros was charged by the King to put the recommendations into effect. (Carrasco y Guisasola, *Docs.*, nos. 23, 25, 26.)

26. Letters by Vizcaino: Acapulco, May 5, 1602, Monterey, December 28, 1602, Mexico, May 22, 1603, Sutro, 13, 14, 15. (Cf. Carrasco y Guisasola, *Docs.*) *Viage y Derrotero* [with 34 charts] *de las naos que fueron al Descubrimiento del Puerto de Acapulco á cargo del G^{rl} Sebastián Vizcaino Año de 1602*, by Martín Palacios, cosmógrafo-mayor, S. A., Sevilla, Arch. Genl. de Indias, Simancas, Sec., Aud. de Méjico, Año de 1602, est. lx, caj. 4, leg. 37; copy, Acad. de la Hist., Madrid, Col. Muñoz, tom. xxxiv, fols. 139–190; copy, S. A., Madrid, Direc. de Hid., Navarrete, tom. xix, no. 9; copy in part (10 maps), Library of Congress, Washington, Lowery Coll., Calif., 1588–1800, Am. S. 1517, Ac. 854. Palacios's *Derrotero*, accompanied by an anonymous *relación*, is printed in Carrasco y Guisasola, *Docs.*, as no. 28. *Derrotero cierto y verdadero desde el Cavo Mendosino hasta el Puerto de Acapulco. . . . Hecho por el P. Fr. Antonio de la Ascensión . . . que fué por Segundo Cosmógrafo del dicho descubrimiento;* copy, S. A., Salamanca, Colegio Mayor de Cuentas, MSS., no. 354; copy, British Museum, Add. MSS. 17583, ff. 206–217v. *Relación* by Ascensión (early copy), with appendix in Ascensión's own hand, 16 chapters, Ayer Coll., Newberry Library, Chicago. See J. Torquemada, *Monarquía Indiana*, lib. v (embodying Ascensión's *Relación*); and for translation of Torquemada, Venegas, London, 1759, vol. ii, p. 229. *Derrotero cierto y verdadero, etc., hecho por Francisco Bolaños piloto, y reformado por Fr. Antonio de la Ascensión*, 1603 (S. A., Madrid, Bib. Nac. MSS. 3203).

On Palacios's chart, sections 49–50 (chart II, two plates, pp. 22–23 of text), the concave trend of the coast-line called *ensenada grande* (at the bottom of which lies the "Golden Gate") is unbroken, showing the failure of Vizcaino to suspect the existence of the present Bay of San Francisco. Chart-sections 37–53 show the following present-day nomenclature: Islas de Todos Santos, Puerto Bueno de San Diego, Islas de Santa Catalina, Santa Bárbara y San Nicolás, Punta de Limpia Concepción, Punta de Pinos, Puerto de Monterey, Puerto de Año Nuevo, Puerto de Los Reyes, Cabo de Mendocino. Under a nomenclature different from the present are shown: Enseñada de San Andrés (San Pedro Bay), Islas Gente Barbada, San Ambrosio y San Cleto(Islands Santa Cruz, Santa Rosa, and San Miguel), Enseñada del Roque (Carmelo Bay), Los Frailes (Farallones). As for the name Puerto de Don Gaspar (mentioned in Palacios's *Derrotero* as an *alias* for the name Puerto de los Reyes), it was a further tribute to the Viceroy, Don Gaspar de Zúñiga y Azevedo. In *relaciones* of dates October 12, 1620, and March 22, 1632, Ascensión mentions Santa Catalina Island and Carmelo River as having received their present names under Vizcaino.

27. Torquemada (*Monarquía Indiana*, vol. i, p. 725) observes: "Had only fourteen persons been able to do duty at Cape Blanco, the General intended to have entered the strait called Anian . . . and thence if possible to have reached the North Sea, and after visiting Newfoundland to sail directly for Old Spain. This," he naïvely continues, "would have been making the tour of the world, Cape Mendocino being the antipodes to old Castile and particularly to the cities of Salamanca, Valladolid, and Burgos." In allusion to Aguilar's river, Torquemada (vol. i, pp. 719, 725) says: "It is understood that this river is the one that leads to a great city discovered by the Dutch, and that this is the strait of Anian, etc., and that it is of this place that the relation treats which His Majesty read and by which he was moved to the exploration." (See also Bancroft, *Northwest Coast*, vol. i, p. 88.)

One of Ascensión's accounts, dated October 12, 1620, was sent to the King (Philip III) in December (*Documentos*, Pacheco y Cárdenas, vol. viii, p. 539). Another account (dated at the Carmelite Convent of Valladolid de Michoacán, May 20, 1629) is that from which quotation is made in the text. It is preserved in S. A., Madrid, Direc. de Hid., Navarrete Col., tom. xix, no. 12, and was prepared in response to an order of Philip IV, August 2, 1628. In it Ascensión mentions his *Relación* of the Vizcaino voyage of 1602, and a *Breve Relación* for the King, — the latter document evidently that of October 12, 1620. On June 8, 1629, and March 22, 1632, Ascensión made further reports: that of 1629, emphasizing the points of the report of May 20 of the same year, and that of 1632 recommending the port of Monterey because of its nearness to the Strait of Anian, *en que puerto y paraje está el gran ciudad de Quivira* (Navarrete Col., tom. xix, nos. 16, 21). Between 1629 and 1636 the *relaciones* of Ascensión were subjected to much critical comment by royal officials (Navarrete Col., tom. xix, nos. 17, 19, 20, etc.), and in 1636 (Sept. 17), the question of the insularity of California was elaborately argued by Alonso Botello y Serrano, and Pedro Porter y Casanate. *Unos* (it was declared) *hacen Ysla la California; otros, tierra firme. Unos ponen Estrecho de Anian, otros no*, etc., etc.

It is worthy of note that the German cosmographer Eusebio Francisco Kino, in his long-lost and newly discovered (1908) manuscript on California and Pimería (see chapter IV of Notes), ascribes the prevalence of the conception of California as insular not to Ascensión but to Francis Drake. "The said Drake," he writes, "on his return to his country misled all Europe, — almost all the cosmographers and geographers of Italy, Germany, and France, etc. He delineated California as an Island" (M. A., *Favores Celestiales*, part ii, book iv, chap. 1). The Drake voyage, from what we know of it through the cartography of the years 1582–1593, is chargeable with no such revolution as that stated by Kino; but its influence was toward insularity for California, as is shown not only by the Lok map of 1582, but by the Molineaux globe of 1592, on which the course of Drake is indicated (J. Winsor, *The Kohl Collection of Maps*, reëdited by Phillips, Wash., 1904, sec. 281. See also Mercator-Hondius Atlas, 1613, *Ibid.*, sec. 284). Kino's idea of the effect of the Drake voyage may have been derived from the Herrera map of 1622, or the Briggs map of 1625, or the Hondius map of 1628 (*post*, VIII, IX, X), all of which represent California as insular (*Ibid.*, secs. 91, 284). The *Arcano del Mare* of Robert Dudley, 1630 (a work executed under the influence of Drake's voyage), says in its last paragraph: "The Vermilion Sea begins at the Cape Santa Clara of California [*Cabo Santa Clara della California*], as shown elsewhere, and passes by the island which is named de' Giganti, and is in the Northern Sea, in 43° of latitude, through the kingdom of Coromedo; and this determines that California may be an island off Western America, and not *terra firma* as Giovanni Jansonio states on his chart."

28. *Cédula*, Venegas, *Noticia*, vol. i, p. 200; Translation, vol. i, p. 178; newly translated, B. and R., *Philippine Islands*, vol. xiv, p. 182.

29. Letter, Aguirre, Pub. Hist. Soc. South. Calif. (Sutro, 1); Letter, Viceroy Marqués de Villamanrique to Felipe II, May 10, 1585 (*Ibid.* 2); S. A., Sevilla, Arch. Genl. de Indias, Audiencia de Méjico, Años 1607 á 1609, est. lviii, caj. 3, leg. 16. It is the shrewd surmise of the Swedish writer E. W. Dahlgren (*En Studie i Historisk Geografi*, vol. xiii, Ymer. Tidskrift Utgifven af Svenska Sällskapet för Antropologi och Geografi, 1893) that Aguirre's " isles of the Armenian" were no other than Los Dos Hermanos named by Mercator, map of 1569.

30. Viceroy Marqués de Villamanrique to King, Dec. 10, 1587: Gali had been sent by the Archbishop, Governor of the Philippines, to make discoveries, but Doctor Santiago de Vera, President of the Philippine Audiencia, had intervened, and Pedro de Unamunu had been sent instead. (S. A., Sevilla, Arch. Genl. de Indias, Sim., Sec., Aud. de Méj., est. lviii, caj. 3, leg. 10.) On November 29, 1588, Villamanrique to the King: Gali, returning from an expedition to survey *la tierra firme* of Japan and los Yslas de Armenico, on which he had been sent by the Archbishop, had died, and Unamunu had made the voyage to Acapulco in his stead. (*Ibid.*)

31. Unamunu's account is of such interest that the whole deserves to be reproduced in translation.

32. *Cédula*, Sept. 27, 1608, recites the substance of the letter by Montesclaros (B. and R., *Philippine Islands*, vol. xiv, p. 270; S. A., Sevilla, Arch. Genl. de Indias, Sim., Sec., Aud. de Méj., est. lviii, caj. 3, leg. 16). On tempests off the coast of Japan and loss of Spanish vessels in 1576 and 1609, see letter by Antonio de Morga to Felipe II, June 30, 1597, and *Relación*, 1609–10, by Padre Gregorio López (B. and R., *Philippine Islands*, vol. x, p. 26, and vol. xvii, p. 132).

33. *Cédula*, Sept. 18, 1607, directs that 20,000 ducats appropriated for settlement of Monterey be used in promoting colonization of Rica de Plata. *Cédula*, May 3, 1609: this supplementary document directs that unless Vizcaino has undertaken his voyage, the matter be withdrawn from his hands and placed in those of the Governor of the Philippines (B. and R., *Philippine Islands*, vol. xiv, pp. 270, 275). The cause of the change of plan was a series of letters from Hernando de los Ríos Coronel, contending that an expedition from Manila would be less expensive, could be made at a better season, and above all could be so made as to use Japan, where conditions were now favorable to foreigners, as a base of operations. (Coronel letters, *Consulta del Consejo de Indias*, and *Cédula*, A. D. 1610, Sevilla, Arch. Genl. de Indias, Secretaría de N. E., Secular., Aud. de Filipinas, est. lxix, caj. 1, leg. 6.) In 1602, Feb. 16, the King had approved and sent to Pedro de Acuña, Governor of the Philippines, a letter written by Hernando de los Ríos Coronel, counseling that for the discovery of the Straits of Anian it would be well to "take possession of la Isla de Armino, in order to make of it a station for the galleon." (S. A., Madrid, Direc. Filipinas, tom. iii, p. 62–d2a.)

34. On April 7, 1611, Viceroy Velasco informed the King that according to royal order, Sebastián Vizcaino had set out on an embassy to Japan. He was not to touch at the Philippines. His ship's company comprised 50 persons, 40 *arcabuses* and *moxquetes*, two pieces of artillery, and some little merchandise, the whole voyage to cost not to exceed 20,000 ducats (S. A., Sevilla, Arch. Genl. de Indias, Sim., Sec., Aud. de Méj., Años 1610 á 1617, est. lviii, caj. 3, leg. 17). On Dec. 2, 1613, the King issued a decree stating that Don Juan de Silva, Governor of the Philippines, had written that certain religious had declared that Vizcaino had taken to Japan a cargo of merchandise, and that he had engaged in trade and given the Japanese license to build ships for New Spain, etc., — all contrary to his instructions; wherefore let the said matter be investigated. (S. A., Sevilla, Arch. Genl. de Indias, Aud. de Méj., Registros de Oficio, tom. vi, fol. 91 vᵗᵒ, est. lxxxvii, caj. 5, leg. 2.)

35. Vizcaino, *Relación del Viage hecho para el Descubrimiento de las Islas llamadas Ricas de Oro y Plata*, 1611–14 (Pacheco y Cárdenas, *Docs.*, vol. viii, pp. 101–199); "Reforms needed in the Philippines," Hernando de los Ríos Coronel (B. and R., *Philippine Islands*, vol. xviii, p. 326). Says Ríos: "I

believe that a decree [the decree of Feb. 16, 1602, cited above] was sent to the Governor in a former year to explore it [Rica de Plata]; but that must be ordered again. A man of experience should be sent, so that he may display the prudence and make the exploration requisite, in accordance with the art and science of hydrography." Vizcaino is reported by Venegas and others to have died at the end of his second voyage to California; but the *Relación* cited above negatives this statement.

Apropos of the Rica de Oro and Rica de Plata expedition, Bancroft (*North Mexican States and Texas*, vol. i, p. 162), following the *Relación*, says: " Vizcaino actually sailed from Acapulco in March, 1611, on the San Francisco. But meanwhile reports of certain Islas Ricas de Oro y Plata in the far west seem to have rendered the occupation of the northwest coast for the time a secondary consideration; and the General went as ambassador to Japan to seek license for further explorations in that region. Probably it was still intended to take steps on his return for the occupation of Monterey; but his experience in Japan was so disastrous, the complicated details having no bearing on the present subject, that Vizcaino was obliged in poor health to give up all his projects and to return as a passenger on his own ship in 1613. The return was by the usual northern route, the California coast was sighted in December, and finally the San Francisco arrived at Zacatula in January, 1614. This seems to have been the end of Vizcaino's career as an explorer." There is here a failure to perceive that the Rica de Oro and Rica de Plata expedition was planned by Spain, not in temporary suspension of the Monterey project while search was made for fabulous isles of treasure near Japan, but with a view to finding a port which should render occupation of Monterey, and hence of Alta California, unnecessary.

GOLD AND SILVER ISLANDS

The actual existence of North Pacific islands which served to suggest to early Spanish navigators the mythical " Isles of the Armenian " is a question not without interest. Such islands were mentioned first by Villalobos in 1543. (Gastaldi maps, 1550, and Mercator map, 1569; latter containing Los Dos Hermanos.) As for Rica de Oro and Rica de Plata, into which the Isles of the Armenian seem early to have been resolved, they appear first in 1586, when Pedro de Unamunu was sent to search for them together with the Isles of the Armenian. Unamunu knew the Orient, and according to the folklore of Japan there lay east-northwest from the province of Osui, between 37° and 39° N. L., two islands, Kinsima (Gold) and Ginsima (Silver). (E. de Kaempfer, *De Beschryving van Japan*, Amsterdam, 1729, p. 49.) At no time was the location of these islands precise, the variation in respect to latitude being from 29° 30′ (Delisle, 1723) to 31° 10′ (Stockholmskartan); and in respect to longitude from 152° 20′ (John Meares, 1788) to 158° 10′ (Stockholmskartan). By an error of reckoning, Meares placed the actual island Lot's Wife in longitude 154° 44′, a position nearly the same as that in which he placed Rica de Oro, and it has ensued that the two ever since have been regarded as one and the same.

The failure of Vizcaino to discover Rica de Oro and Rica de Plata in 1611 quieted the Spanish mind until 1729. In that year it was reported that a Jesuit padre on the way from China to New Spain had actually seen these islands, and in 1730 the Spanish Government sought earnestly to discover whether anything about them were known by navigators; the idea still being entertained that in one or other a port of refuge for the galleon might be found. Satisfactory information was not obtained, and on December 12, 1741, it was ordered by the King that no galleon should depart from its course to search for them. (Burney, *Chron. Hist.*, vol. ii; S. A., Sevilla, Arch. Genl. de Indias, Secretaría de N. E., Secular., Aud. de Filipinas, Años 1740–1742, est. lxviii, caj. 3, leg. 31.) In 1639 and 1643 search for the gold and silver islands of the Pacific was made by the Dutch under Abel Tasman (*Tasman's Journal*, Amsterdam, 1898), and Mattys Quast (*Transactions of the Royal Society*, London, Dec. 14, 1674). In 1798 the French commander Comte de la Pérouse made a like search (*Voyage autour du Monde*, vol. iii, p. 210). And all this while a group of islands convenient for the purposes of the Spanish galleon actually did exist, as was pointed out in 1777 by Captain James Cook. " If," he said, " the Sandwich Islands had been discovered at an early period by the Spaniards, they would doubtless have availed themselves of so excellent a station, and have made use of Atooi, or some other of the islands, as a place of refreshment for the ships that sail annually between Manila and Acapulco. They lie almost midway between the last mentioned place and Guam, one of the Ladrones, which is at present their only port in traversing this vast ocean; and it would not have been a week's sail out of their ordinary route to have touched at them." (*Voyage*, vol. ii, p. 192.) On the whole subject see O. Nachod, *Ein Unentdecktes Goldland*, Tokyo, 1899.

36. S. A., Madrid, Dirección de Hidrografía, Navarrete Coll., tom. xix, nos. 12, 17, 19.

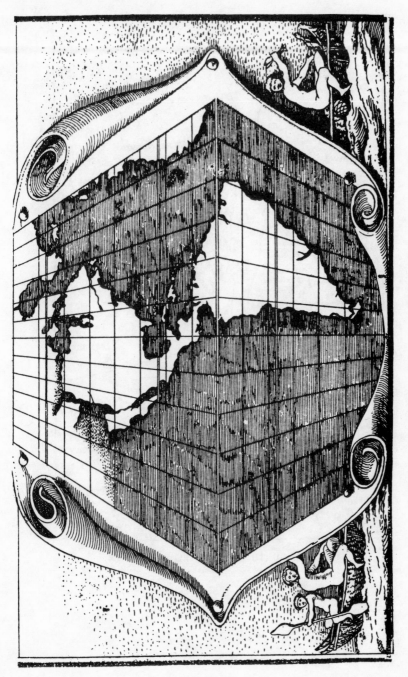

MAP VIII. THE WORLD. BY KASPAR VAN BAERLE, 1622

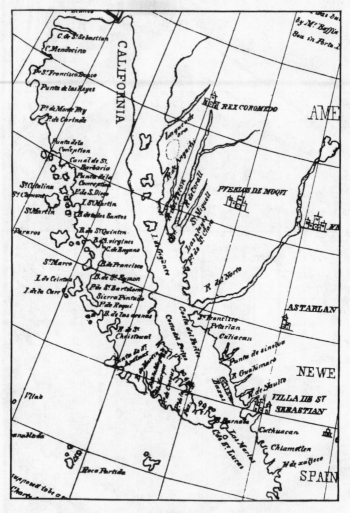

MAP IX. NORTH AMERICA. BY BRIGGS, 1625

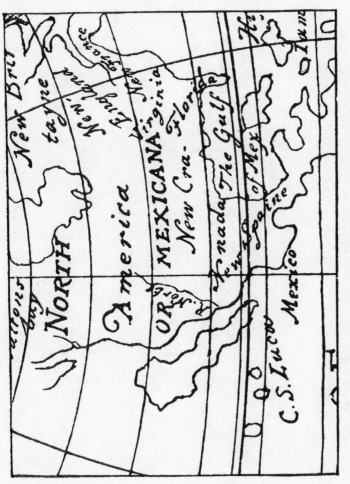

MAP X. DRAKE "WORLD ENCOMPASSED" MAP. BY HONDIUS, 1628

CHAPTER III

THE MISSION

New Chapter Sources: — Indian segregation (Mission and *Custodia* plans), letters of Antonio de los Reyes, Rafael Verger (Guardian of the College of San Fernando) and "A Minister of St. Francis." (M. A.) (Specific citations below.)

1. "The acquisitions which have been made slowly by means of the missionaries have always resulted better than those secured by force of arms."

2. W. Dampier, *New Voyage round the World*, 1699–1709; W. Rogers, *Cruising Voyage round the World*, 1718. Alexander Selkirk, the original of Defoe's Robinson Crusoe, was rescued from the island of Juan Fernández, three hundred miles off the coast of Chile, by Captain Woods Rogers on February 1, 1709. He is described as "a man in goat-skins who looked wilder than the first owners of them."

3. The Kino explorations are treated in chapter iv.

4. G. Shelvocke, *Voyage round the World*, 1719–1722, 1726. In October, 1719, Simon Hatley, mate of Captain Shelvocke's ship the Speedwell, observing "in one of his melancholy fits" that the ship was followed by an albatross, imagined from its color that it might be of ill omen, and so shot it, — an incident developed by Samuel Taylor Coleridge into the poem "The Rime of the Ancient Mariner."

> "And a good south wind sprung up behind;
> The Albatross did follow,
>
> .   .   .   .
>
> — all averred I had killed the bird
> That made the breeze to blow."

5. R. Walter, *Voyage round the World* [George Anson], 1748.

6. A. Dobbs, *An Account of the Countries adjoining to Hudson's Bay*, etc., 1744; H. Ellis, *Voyage to Hudson's Bay*, 1748; J. Winsor, *Narrative and Critical History of America*, vol. viii, p. 1, *et seq.*; G. Bryce, *The Remarkable History of the Hudson's Bay Company*, 1900, ch. 8: "Dream of a Northwest Passage."

7. B. C., P. Tikhmeneff, *Report on Colonies*, part i; W. Coxe, *Account of the Russian Discoveries between Asia and America*, 1780. Authorities summarized by Bancroft: *History of Alaska*, chaps. i–viii; p. 217, n. 43; *History of the Northwest Coast*, vol. i, pp. 149–150, n. 20; *History of California*, vol. i, p. 112; vol. ii, p. 58; G. Davidson, *Tracks and Landfalls of Bering and Chirikof on the Northwest Coast of North America, June to October, 1741*, 1901.

8. B. and R., *Philippine Islands*, vol. i, pp. 100–101. As late as 1546 it was resolved by a synod of prelates in Mexico that " the final and only reason why the Apostolic See had given supreme jurisdiction in the Indies to the kings of Castile and León was that the Gospel might be preached and the Indians converted. It was not to make those kings greater lords and richer princes than they were." (Sir A. Helps, *The Spanish Conquest in America*, vol. iv, p. 209; F. A. MacNutt, *Bartholomew de Las Casas*, 1909, p. 273.)

9. *Recopilación de Leyes de los Reynos de las Indias*, 1681, lib. vi, tit. x, ley 1. The original will is kept in the monastery of La Rabida. It was displayed at the Columbian Exposition in Chicago in 1893. The text in Spanish and English may be found printed in *The American Anthropologist*, 1894, p. 194.

10. Sir A. Helps, *The Spanish Conquest*, vol. i, pp. 138–139, and notes; E. G. Bourne, *Spain in America*, 1904, pp. 207–210, and citations.

11. B. Las Casas, *Historia General de las Indias*, 1875, vol. iii, p. 71.

12. The *encomienda* of Ovando was an amplification of the *repartimiento* of Columbus. By the former a given plantation with its cacique and band was assigned to a given Spaniard as overlord. By the latter it was not so much the plantation that was assigned as the cacique and band upon it. In the *encomienda*, in other words, the emphasis was placed upon persons, and its tendency therefore was toward slavery. (Sir A. Helps, *The Spanish Conquest*, vol. i, pp. 103, 123, 139, vol. iii, pp. 79, 92, vol. iv, p. 237; W. Lowery, *Spanish Settlements in the United States*, 1901, p. 109; E. Armstrong, *The Emperor Charles V*, 1902, vol. ii, p. 99; E. G. Bourne, *Spain in America*, 1904, p. 255. See also Bancroft, *History of Central America*, vol. i, p. 262, n. 7; F. A. MacNutt, *The Letters of Cortés to Charles V*, 1908, 2 vols., vol. ii, appendix to fourth letter.)

13. F. A. Lorenzana, *Historia de Nueva España por Hernan Cortés*, 1770. Translations of passage: Helps, vol. iii, p. 20; Lowery, p. 86. On morals of the secular clergy, H. C. Lea, *Sacerdotal Celibacy in the Christian Church*, p. 564; — says Mr. Lea: "A majority of the ecclesiastics seeking the colonies of Spanish America were of the worst description "; Lowery, p. 87 ; MacNutt, *Letters of Cortés*, vol. ii, pp. 214–215.

14. Sir A. Helps, vol. i, p. 185.

15. "By night sweet odors, varying with every hour of the watch, were wafted from the shore . . . and the forest trees, brought together by the serpent tracery of myriads of strange parasitical plants, might well seem to the fancy like some great design of building, over which the lofty palms, a forest upon a forest, appeared to present a new order of architecture. In the background rose the mist, like incense. These, however, were but the evening fancies of the mariner who had before him fondly in his mind the wreathed pillars of the Cathedral of Burgos, or the thousand-columned Christian mosque of Córdova, or the perfect fane of Seville; and when the moon rose, or the innumerable swarms of luminous insects swept across the

picture, it was but a tangled forest after all, wherein the shaping hand of man had made no memorial to his Creator." (Sir A. Helps, vol. ii, p. 95.)

16. Sir A. Helps, vol. i, p. 356, note by editor.

17. MacNutt, *Bartholomew de Las Casas*, chaps. 11, 12.

18. S. A., Madrid, *Muñoz MSS.*, tom. 79; cited by Helps.

19. MacNutt, *Bartholomew de Las Casas*, p. 191. By a law of the Indies, promulgated in 1523, and again in 1618, it was forbidden to convert the Indians to Christianity by force. (W. Roscher, *The Spanish Colonial System* (Bourne), p. 9; *Recopilación*, lib. vi.)

20. A. Remesal, *Historia de Chiapa y Guatemala*, 1619, lib. iii, cap. 2, par. 3; Sir A. Helps, *The Spanish Conquest*, vol. iii, book xv, chaps. 6, 7.

It is related by Remesal (lib. iii, cap. 2, par. 1, p. 124) that a potent means for the conversion of the people of the Tierra de Guerra was found in music. The great doctrines of salvation were translated in Quichi verse; the verse was then set to simple music and sung to the accompaniment of Indian wind-instruments. Upon this story in some of its details Bancroft (*History of Central America*, vol. ii, p. 350, n.) casts not unreasonable doubt. It, however, is probable that music played a part in the subjugation of Tuzulatlán. Remesal states (lib. iv, cap. x, p. 190) that Luis Cáncer, having returned in 1542 to Vera Paz, procured for the delectation of converts some Mexican Indians who knew how to sing and play church music (Lowery, *Spanish Settlements*, p. 414). It was even commanded by the King (Remesal, lib. iii, cap. 21, p. 155) that "some Indians who knew how to play loud wind-instruments, clarions, sackbuts, flutes, and also some singers of church music out of those in the monasteries of the Franciscans in New Spain," be permitted to be taken by Las Casas into the province (Helps, vol. iii, p. 255). Indeed, wherever the Spanish missionary went, music, with its proverbial power to soothe the breast of the savage, was a means of conversion not neglected. It was made use of in Mexico, in the Philippines (A. de Morga, *Sucesos*, B. and R., *Philippine Islands*, vol. xvi, p. 152), and (as related in the text, chapter XVI) it was employed in California.

21. (I) "For which I say and promise you and give my word in the name and on behalf of his Majesty, in virtue of the royal powers delegated to me, that you or any of your monks, being at present Father Bartholomew de Las Casas, Rodrigo de la Drada, and Pedro de Angulo, bringing and securing by your teaching and persuasion whatsoever provinces with the Indians within them (all or in part I hold from his Majesty) into conditions of peace, so that they recognize the lordship of his Majesty and agree to pay him a moderate tribute, according to their possibility of personal service and poor possessions, such as they can conveniently give, whether in gold, if there be any in the land, or in cotton, maize, or in whatsoever other things they possess or are accustomed to cultivate or traffic with among themselves, — that I, in virtue of the powers I hold from his Majesty and in his royal name, will place all those provinces and the Indians in them so agreeing under his

Majesty in chief that they may serve him as his vassals, and will not give them to any Spaniard in *encomienda*, now or at any future time." (Remesal, lib. iii, cap. 9, p. 122; translated, Helps, vol. iii, p. 233.)

(II) "And I shall order that no Spaniard molest them, nor approach them, nor their lands, under serious penalty for five years. As for myself, I shall go when you think it convenient [fitting], and when you can go with me." (*Ibid.*, p. 123; F. A. MacNutt, *Bartholomew de Las Casas*, chap. xiv.)

22. The first of the two letters constituting "The New Laws" (a letter signed jointly by Charles V and his mother Doña Joanna, daughter of the venerated Isabella) was dated from Barcelona, November 20, 1542. The second was dated from Valladolid, June 4, 1543. They were printed together at Alcalá de Henares, July 8, 1543, and were sold at the price of 4 *maravedis* for each sheet. A translation of the Laws into English was made in 1893 by the late Henry Stevens (of Vermont) and Fred W. Lucas (of London), and the same year the translation (together with a facsimile of the originals and an historical introduction by Mr. Lucas) was issued (privately) from the Chiswick Press in an edition of 88 copies. One copy is owned by the University of California.

"The New Laws" were distinctly an advance upon any which had preceded them, in two clauses: (I) that "after the death of the conquerors of the Indies, the *repartimientos* of Indians which had been given to them in *encomienda*, in the name of his Majesty, should not pass in succession to their wives or children, but, as in stipulation 1 between Las Casas and the lieutenant-governor of Guatemala, should be placed immediately under the King, the said wives and children receiving a certain portion of the usufruct for their sustenance"; (II) that "the bishops, monastic bodies, governors, presidents, auditors, corregidors, and other officers of his Majesty, both past and present, who held *repartimientos*, should be obliged to renounce them." (Helps, *The Spanish Conquest*, vol. iv, p. 104; MacNutt, *Bartholomew de Las Casas*, p. 204.) On the enforced partial abrogation of "The New Laws," see Helps, vol. iv, pp. 237, 253; E. G. Bourne, *Spain in America*, p. 255.

For the laws cited in the text other than "The New Laws," see *Recopilación de Leyes*, as follows: Indians to live under own magistrates (lib. vi, tit. iii, ley 15); Indians not to be slaves, — text of decree by Ferdinand and Isabella (lib. vi, tit. ii, ley 1); Indians not to live outside village (lib. vi, tit. iii, ley 19); no lay Spaniard, negro, *mestizo*, or mulatto to live in an Indian village (lib. vi, tit. iii, ley 22); no Spaniard to tarry more than a night (lib. vi, tit. iii, ley 23); but Spaniards who were ill or who were merchants might tarry not more than three days (lib. vi, tit. iii, ley 24). Infraction of original act forbidden under penalty of fine of 50 *pesos* in gold. An *encomendero*, even, was not permitted to own a house in an Indian village, or to remain there more than one night. His relatives and slaves might not enter at all (lib. vi, tit. ix, ley 14). Indians to be instructed in the Catholic faith (lib. vi, tit. iii, ley 1). Useful summaries of Spanish legislation for protection of the Indians: J. G. Bourke, Capt. U. S. A., "The Laws of Spain in their Application to the American Indians," *American Anthropologist*, 1894, vol. vii, p. 193; W. Roscher, *The Spanish Colonial System* (Bourne), 1904.

23. Says Mr. Edward Armstrong, apropos of the fierce struggle in New Spain between the passions of Avarice and religious Propagandism — that struggle whereby the system of the Mission was evolved (*The Emperor Charles V*, 2 vols., 1902, vol. ii, pp. 101, 105): "The Spanish missionary was pitted against the Spanish conqueror and proved a foeman worthy of his steel. . . . Charles [the Emperor] it must be admitted was on the side of the missionary." The steps by which, through Charles, the essential idea of the Mission (Indian segregation under sacerdotal protection) came to be embodied in law were the following: (1) Laws of Burgos (1512, Ferdinand), sanctioning enforced association of Indians with Spaniards (Las Casas, *Historia*, tom. i, lib. iii, cap. 7, 9); (2) Laws of Las Casas (1515, Ximénes Regent for Charles V), providing for settlements of Indians in villages under a *clérigo* (secular priest) or *religioso* (friar), and, for civil ends, under a cacique and Spanish administrator, the latter to be married and not to live in the settlement (*Docs. Inéd. de Ultramar*, vol. iv, pp. 109–128); 3 *cédulas* (1526, Charles V), ordering resumption of plan for settling Indians " in villages by themselves with their own priests," the first village, 1517, having been broken up by smallpox (R. de la Sagra, *Historia . . . de la Isla de Cuba*, vol. ii, *apéndice; Docs. Inéd. de Ultramar*, vol. iv, pp. 109–128). In a report on village settlements by Governor Guzmán (Sagra, vol. ii, *apéndice*), the Governor calls such settlements the King's " project for peaceful colonization."

24. Segregation, according to the governmental or secular conception, was known as the *Custodia* plan, operations being conducted from an *hospicio* or "home," whence the missionaries issued, and whither they returned. On June 20, 1783, it was pointed out by Antonio de los Reyes, Bishop of Sonora, a secular minister, that in 1538 and 1618 (laws 19 and 20 of the *Recopilación*, lib. vi, tit. i) it was provided that the Indians were to be " *puestos en policía* and taught to apply themselves to useful and profitable work." Earlier (Sept. 16, 1776) the Bishop had cited a Bull of Innocent XI, of date Oct. 16, 1686, directing the reduction of mission Indians to *pueblos formales*. The same bishop cited the course of Cortés as demonstrating the sufficiency of the *Custodia* plan of segregation. (M. A., Arch. Genl., *Misiones*, xiv.)

25. On the part of the missionaries of upper Sonora (Pimería) and of the Californias, 1771, 1772, pleas were urgent for segregation, according to the Mission plan, as a present and pressing necessity; yet what was asked was recognized as contravening old customs and opinion. Said Rafael Verger, Guardian of the missionary college of San Fernando, to his superior on Nov. 15, 1772: " It is true, most excellent Señor, that law 6 of book i, title 13 of the *Recopilación*, prohibits these and other things [temporal control] to *curas*,

doctrineros, clérigos y religiosos. But such are pastors of civilized Indians and lack the title of tutors and guardians." Much reliance was placed by the missionaries upon decrees issued in 1719 by Baltasar de Zúñiga, Marqués de Valero, and in 1740 by Pedro de Castro y Figueroa Salazar. (M. A., Museo, *Trasuntos.* Cf. chapter VI of text, n. 15, 16; chapter VIII of text, n. 24.) It is stated by a "minister of St. Francis" (cited chapter VIII of text, n. 9) that the first Mexican mission, in the missionary sense of the term, was the *villa* of Sinaloa, founded in 1611.

26. The *Patronato Real* was the right of church regulation, on the part of the Crown, under Bulls by Alexander VI, 1493 (*Docs. Inéd. de las Indias,* vol. xxxiv, p. 14, — translated, J. Fiske, *Discovery of America,* app. B), and Julius II, 1508 (A. J. de Ribadeneyra, *Regio Patronato,* pp. 408–409); and under a *cédula,* 1574, by Philip II (translated, B. Moses, *South America on the Eve of Emancipation,* 1908, p. 123). The Crown might nominate and license bishops and all subordinate ecclesiastics; reprimand and remove the same, fix the salaries of benefices; collect tithes; take cognizance of ecclesiastical causes; inspect papal Bulls; grant permission for erecting churches and hospitals. Finally, the Crown might license friars; permit the erection of monasteries; and pass upon all patents, or general orders to religious houses by their superiors, naught being exempt from review save rules of such houses for their internal government. (J. C. Icazbalceta, *Zumárraga,* p. 127; Montemayor, *Sumarios,* pp. 36–38; A. J. de Ribadeneyra, *Manual Compendio de el Regio Patronato,* pp. 51–68; Sarsfield, *Derecho Público Eclesiástico,* 1889.) Subject discussed: Bancroft, *History of Mexico,* vol. iii, p. 684; W. Lowery, *Spanish Settlements,* p. 381; B. Moses, *South America on the Eve of Emancipation,* ch. 6.

27. Helps, vol. iv, pp. 272, *et seq.,* "The Missions of Paraguay"; W. Roscher, *The Spanish Colonial System* (Bourne), p. 15. It may be observed that the great Jesuit establishment in Canada — the mission to the Hurons — was much less specialized than the Paraguayan or Mexican establishment. The proud, intractable character of the northern Indian nations made Mission control more difficult. Still, with the Hurons, had it not been for the struggle forced upon them by the Iroquois, the Mission might have succeeded. If so, the model, we are told, would have been that of Paraguay. "Que si celuy qui a escrit cette lettre a leu la Relation de ce qui se passe au Paraguais, qu'il a veu ce qui se fera un jour en la Nouvelle France." (Le Jeune, *Relation,* 1637.) Regarding the *Patronato Real,* and the Spanish Mission in Paraguay and in California, see R. Altamíra y Crevea, *Historia de España,* 1906, tom. iii, pp. 417, 346.

CHAPTER IV

CALIFORNIA NO ES YSLA

THE principal authority for the present chapter is an unpublished manuscript, the *Favores Celestiales* of Eusebio Francisco Kino. This book (lost since 1767, the year of the composition by Alegre of the *Historia de la Compañía de Jesús en Nueva España*) was found in 1908 by Dr. Herbert E. Bolton of the University of Texas (now at Leland Stanford Jr. University), in the Archives of Mexico. As described by Dr. Bolton, the book in the original manuscript contains 433 folio pages (about 150,000 words) and covers the period of Kino's entire service as rector of Jesuit missions in Pimería Alta, 1687–1710. Not all of the record is new. The *Apostólicos Afanes*, by Padre José Ortega, 1754, is based upon it and constitutes a summary of it. Portions more or less complete are to be found in various MS. collections and in print, — the Boturini Collection (Real Academia de la Historia, Madrid); *Documentos para la Historia de Méjico*, etc.

The Peabody Museum (Hemenway Collection), Harvard, contains a volume of transcripts (426 pages) from the Biblioteca Nacional of Mexico, which includes the *Luz de Tierra Yncógnita* (1720) of Kino's friend and companion Manje, and the latter's *Relación diaria de la entrada al norueste . . . de Septiembre hasta 18 de Octubre* [1698], *y Descubrimiento del desemboque del río grande á la mar de la California y del Puerto de Sta. Clara* — dated Nuestra Señora de los Dolores, Dec. 8, 1698. A further source is the manuscript volume: *Establecimiento y progresos de las Misiones de la Antigua California y Memorias piadosas de la Nación Indiana por un Religioso de la Provincia del Santo Evangelio de México, Años 1790, 1791* (Edward E. Ayer Collection, Newberry Library, Chicago). The *Establecimiento* sustains to the history of Lower California a relation equivalent to that of the *Noticias* of Palou to the history of California Alta. (Specific citations below.)

1. Kino, sketch of life, *Favores Celestiales*, part i, book iv, chap. 1; *Apostólicos Afanes*, 1754, par. 230, 328. The more important *entradas* by Kino are delineated on general map of the Southwest (pocket).

2. *Favores Celestiales*, part i, book i, chaps. 1–3.

3. Salvatierra, sketch of life, Alegre, *Historia de la Compañía de Jesús*, vol. iii, 96; *Favores Celestiales*, part i, book ii, chaps. 1–3.

4. *Favores Celestiales*, part ii, book iv, chap. 1.

5. *Ibid.*, part i, book ii, chap. 3.

6. *Ibid.*, part i, book ii, chap. 5. Bancroft, following Manje's *Informe*, dates this *entrada* February, 1694.

7. *Favores Celestiales*, part i, book ii, chap. 6. Bancroft dates this *entrada* also 1694. For dimensions of the boat, *Favores Celestiales*, part ii, book i, chap. 2. Description of boat by Manje, *Docs. para la Historia de Méjico*, série iv, tom. i, p. 243.

8. *Favores Celestiales*, part i, book ii, chap. 7.

9. *Ibid.*, part i, book ii, chap. 8. Kino here says nothing about Mass in the Casa Grande itself. His words are: "The First Ranchería of El Tusonim we named La Encarnación, as we arrived there to say Mass on the First Sunday in Advent." Manje states that Mass was said *dentro de las cuales* (*casas grandes*). He may have had reference to the locality in general. (Cf. E. Coues, *The Trail of a Spanish Pioneer*, 1900, vol. ii, pp. 537–538.) To Kino the *casas grandes* were "certainly the seven cities mentioned by the holy man, Fray Marcos de Niza." Regarding the visit to Mexico, *Favores Celestiales*, part i, book v, chap. 1.

10. M. Venegas, *Noticia de la California*, Mexico, 1757, 3 vols., vol. ii, p. 14; Translation (London, 1759, 2 vols.), vol. i, p. 224. Decree translated in full, *Proceedings Mexican and American Claims Commission*, Claim no. 493, transcript, Washington, 1902, p. 401.

11. See note 35 *post*.

12. Translated, *Proceedings Mexican and American Claims Commission*, Claim no. 493, transcript, p. 405. See also Salvatierra to Ugarte, Nov. 27, 1697, S. A., Madrid, Real Acad. Historia, Boturini Coll., tom. i; *Docs. para la Historia de Méjico*, série ii, tom. i, p. 103.

13. *Proceedings Mexican and American Claims Commission*, Claim no. 493, transcript, p. 418.

14. Cf. chapter vi.

15. Venegas, *Noticia*, vol. ii, p. 69; Translation, vol. i, p. 277. See also *Noticia*, vol. ii, pp. 264, 274, 278, 281; Translation (here incomplete and weak), vol. i, pp. 452, 455.

16. J. M. Salvatierra, "Informe Sobre puntos de las Cédulas Reales, 25 de Mayo, 1705," Venegas, *Noticia*, vol. ii, p. 153; Bancroft, *North Mexican States and Texas*, vol. i, pp. 418, 437.

17. Letter, Kino to Visitador Horacio Polici, Oct. 18, 1698 (M. A., Arch. Genl., *Historia*, 16; *Favores Celestiales*, part i, book vi, chap. 4). Bancroft is perhaps correct in his statement (*North Mexican States*, vol. i, p. 266, n. 53) that as yet Kino had discovered no convergence of the Pimería and peninsular coasts at the mouth of the Colorado; for in the *diario* none such is mentioned. It was later, in retrospect, that Kino stated: "In the year 1698, on a very high Hill [Santa Clara], I descried most plainly the juncture of these lands of New Spain and of California."

18. *Favores Celestiales*, part i, book vi, chap. 5.

19. *Ibid.*, part i, book vi, chap. 6.

20. In 1699 (November) "the Señor lieutenant [Manje] and I passed on to San Raphael of the other Actum and to San Marzelo del Sonoydag, 20 leagues journey, to inform ourselves better in regard to the passage by land to California . . . and we informed ourselves very well in regard to the blue shells of the opposite coast, and to the passage by land to California." (*Favores Celestiales*, part i, book vii, chap. 4.)

21. *Ibid.*, part ii, book i, chaps. 4, 6.

22. *Favores Celestiales*, part ii, book i, chaps. 9, 10.

23. *Ibid.*, part ii, book i, chaps. 12–14; book ii, chaps. 1–6.

24. *Ibid.*, part ii, book ii, chaps. 7, 8. The view from the ridge had not satisfied Manje. He states: " We remained in the same doubt as when on the beach." (*Docs. para la Historia de Méjico*, série iv, vol. i, p. 334.)

25. *Favores Celestiales*, part ii, book ii, chap. 11.

26. *Ibid.*, part ii, book ii, chap. 12. Manje himself states that, although the sea seemed to narrow, it might turn and widen again as that of Gibraltar in Spain into the Mediterranean. There might be a connection with the South Sea on the westward, for the sea extended also in that direction (*Ibid.*, p. 332). A letter for Piccolo was intrusted to the Indians, but it never reached him (*Ibid.*, p. 333).

27. *Favores Celestiales*, part ii, book iii, chaps. 2–5. It is of interest to note that Kino fixes the south line of Alta California at the Meridian, " because its Meridian passes through the midst of its Head of the Sea of California." (*Ibid.*, part ii, book iv, chap. 3.)

28. *Ibid.*, part ii, book iv, chaps. 2–5.

29. *Ibid.*, part ii, book iv, chap. 12.

30. *Ibid.*, chap. 13.

31. *Ibid.*, chap. 11.

32. If, as is probable, Kino was at La Libertad, or between it and Tepoca, he might have been looking southwest between the islands Angel de la Guarda and Tiburón. His companion was Padre Gerónimo Minutuli, and on June 7 the latter wrote that a passage into California by the newly found island and cape ought not to be very difficult. On Nov. 4, Kino, replying to an appeal for help from Ugarte at Loreto, wrote that the bark which he (Kino) had partially constructed at Dolores and at Caborca was yet available. All that was needed (now that the passage by way of the island and cape was known) was a couple of ship's boys or Chinamen *para la dirección del barquillo, ó lancha, ó canoa grande.* (*Favores Celestiales*, part iv, book iii, chap. 3; book iv, chap. 3.)

33. By special order of Fuens-Zaldana, diaries of the autumn *entrada* of 1706 were kept by Ramírez and Ojuela. Durán was also ordered to keep a diary. All were to be sent to the Viceroy. Kino embodies Ramírez's and Ojuela's accounts in his history, but gives none of his own. Describing the view from Santa Clara, Ramírez says that while sea was visible as far as the eye could reach on the South, none was visible on the East, nor on the West as extending to the North or Northwest. On the contrary, what was plainly visible was the " Continuation of our land with that of the West, which was sand dunes and hillocks for more than 40, 50 or 60 leagues." (*Favores Celestiales*, part iv, lib. v, chap. 6.)

34. The most important of these decrees may be found in substance in Venegas, vol. ii, pp. 63, 139, 169; Translation, vol. i, pp. 272, 340, 369; translated excerpts, *Proceedings Mexican and American Claims Commission*,

Claim no. 493, p. 406. *Cédula* of 1719 inclosing one of 1716 (June 29), urging attention to earlier decrees; translated, *Proceedings Mexican and American Claims Commission*, p. 434. See also B. C., *Baja California Cédulas*, pp. 82, 98.

PIOUS FUND

35. Prior to 1716, the fund consisted of bequests, the capital of which was kept by the various donors under their own control, the interest being paid annually to the California Mission. But the sum for the support of one establishment having been lost by the failure of the donor in trust (Juan Bautista López), it was deemed needful that the moneys be invested in lands to be controlled by the Mission itself. Originally the Society of Jesus could not own temporalties, but upon petition of Salvatierra in 1717 it was given the power. Hereupon the Mission purchased an extensive tract from Captain Manuel Fernández de Azunio, but for what price is not known. It also loaned 54,000 *pesos* upon the security of the Jesuit College of San Ildefonso at Puebla.

Early in the eighteenth century, the Marqués de Villapuente had given to the California Mission the hacienda of Arroyozarco in the State of Mexico. In 1726 and 1735 the Marqués de Villapuente, the Marquesa de Torres de San Roda, and Doña Rosa de la Peña gave the hacienda San Pedro de Ybarra in the State of Guanajuato, together with lands in the Reyno de León (later Tamaulipas), called the hacienda San Agustín de los Amoles, and lands in the State of San Luis Potosí, called San Ignacio del Buey and San Francisco Xavier de la Baya. A further gift by Doña Josefa Paula de Argüelles comprised the haciendas of Maguey, Torreón Buey in Zacatecas, and of Cienéga del Pastor within the pueblos of Atotonilco el Alto y la Barca, whereof at the end of long litigation there was decreed to the California Mission the $4\frac{1}{2} = 2\text{-}9$ part of Cienéga in the State of Jalisco. (M. A., Arch. Gen., *Gobernación*, "Junta de Califs. 1824.")

According to Palou, the history of the Fund, and its condition in 1767 on the expulsion of the Jesuits, were as follows: —

LIST OF THE PIOUS WORKS FOUNDED BY VARIOUS PERSONS FOR THE SPIRITUAL CONQUEST OF CALIFORNIA

Year		Pesos.
1698.	Don Juan Caballero founded the first mission, and for that purpose gave the sum of	10,000.00
1699.	The same founded the second mission	10,000.00
1700.	Don Nicolás Arteaga founded the third mission with the same amount	10,000.00
1702.	Various persons, through Father José Vidal, Jesuit, founded the fourth mission	7,000.00
1704.	The Marqués de Villapuente founded the fifth mission with the same amount	10,000.00
1709.	The same founded the sixth mission	10,000.00
1713.	The same founded the seventh mission	10,000.00

1718. His Excellency, Don Juan Ruiz de Velasco, founded   *Pesos*
the eighth mission   10,000.00
1719. The Marqués de Villapuente founded the ninth
mission   10,000.00
1725. Father Juan María Luyando, Jesuit, founded the
tenth mission   10,000.00
1731. Doña María Rosa de la Peña endowed one of the
missions through the Marqués de Villapuente   10,000.00
1746. The Marqués de Villapuente founded the eleventh
mission   10,000.00
1747. Her Excellency Doña María de Borja, Duchess of
Gandia, in her testament bequeathed for the missions of California (and it is shown that it was re-
ceived)   62,000.00

    Total of Alms   179,000.00

FUNDS AND PROPERTIES WHICH EXISTED AT THE TIME OF THE EXPULSION OF THE JESUIT FATHERS

In money which was found in the *procuraduría-general* of   *Pesos*
California at the time of the expulsion   92,000.00
Goods found in the warehouse of said *procuraduría*, esti-
mated by commercial men of Spain and Mexico   27,255.06
Merchandise which was found in the warehouse of Loreto,
according to the prices charged and for which it was sold   79,377.03

    Total amount of funds   199,033.01
                [198,632.09]

LOANS MADE BY THE PROCURADURÍA-GENERAL OF CALIFORNIA FROM THE FUNDS OF THE MISSIONS AS IS EVIDENCED BY THE RESPECTIVE DOCUMENTS

To the College of San Ildefonso of Puebla at three and one   *Pesos*
half per cent   22,000.00
To the College of San Ignacio of Puebla with revenues of
four per cent   5,000.00
To the College of San Pedro y San Pablo of Mexico without
indication of the percentage   29,100.00
To the College of San Ildefonso of Puebla at three per cent   23,000.00
To the College of San Gerónimo of Mexico at three per cent   38,500.00
To the College of San Ildefonso of Puebla at three per cent   9,000.00

    Total investments   126,600.00

GENERAL SUMMARY

Total of alms given   179,000.00
Total of goods on hand   199,033.01
                [198,632.09]
Total invested or loaned   126,600.00

    Total amount of the Fund   504,633.01
                [504,232.09]

"Besides this capital there are the plantations called *Ibarra*, whose administrator told me that in ordinary years they produced twenty thousand dollars income clear, to which amount must be added the revenues from the haciendas of Arroyo-Sarco. Thus far the paper."

"From what is said I infer that at the expulsion of the Jesuit Fathers there existed only the said haciendas besides the goods and the investments, which amounted to 325,633 *pesos* and one *real*." (F. Palou, *Noticias*, tom. i, chap. 28, pp. 183–195.)

36. *Cédula* of 1703 (September 28); translated in full, *Proceedings Mexican and American Claims Commission*, Claim no. 493, p. 442.

37. Venegas, *Noticia*, vol. ii, p. 285.

38. *Ibid.*, p. 342; *Docs. para la Historia de Méj.*, série ii, tom. iv, pp. 26, 98.

39. Venegas, *Noticia*, vol. ii, p. 493; Translation, vol. ii, p. 158.

40. *Ibid.*, p. 502; Translation, vol. ii, p. 164. In translation the decree is much abbreviated. On Sept. 15, 1706, Lieutenant Manje wrote to Kino that he had already penned "a hundred sheets" advocating the establishment of a *villa* on the Colorado as an *escala y ante mural y refugio* for the Sobas, Pimas, Sobaipuris, Cocomoricopas, and Yumas, and for the reduction of the Moquis, Apaches, and nations of the north and northeast and northwest up to the Mar del Sur, and as a *refugio de las Navegantes de China*. (*Favores Celestiales*, part iv, book iv, chap. 3.)

41. *Noticia*, vol. iii, p. 140; Translation, vol. ii, p. 308. In 1765 Wenceslao Link (a Bohemian Jesuit) explored the northern peninsula well toward the Colorado. (*Diario*, 1766, B. C.)

42. *Noticia*, vol. iii, p. 1; Translation, vol. ii, p. 213.

43. Chihuahua, Arch. de Secretaría, Siglo xviii, leg. S.; Sedelmair, "Relación," 1746, *Doc. para la Hist. de Méj.*, série iii, tom. iv.

44. J. Baegert, *Nachrichten von der Amerikanischen Halbinsel California*, 1773.

45. P. Fages, *Informe del Estado de las Misiones de Baja California*, 1786 (B. C., *St. Pap. Miss. and Col.*, vol. i, p. 9). See also Viceroy to King, 1784 (M. A., Arch. Genl., *Historia*, 42; translated, *Proceedings Mexican and American Claims Commission*, p. 422, sec. 33).

46. J. Gálvez, *Informe* (Dec. 31, 1771), gives total population of the peninsula in 1769, Spaniards, Indians, and others, as 7888. Palou gives total registered population in 1772, " a large part wandering in the mountains," as 5074 in thirteen establishments.

47. Decree of Expulsion, Feb. 27, 1767; translated, *Proceedings Mexican and American Claims Commission*, p. 410.

CHAPTER V

REOCCUPATION OF MONTEREY, AND DISCOVERY OF THE BAY OF SAN FRANCISCO

HITHERTO the principal available sources for the Gálvez (Portolá) expedition have been the following: *Diario* of Portolá, early copy (B. C.) ; *Diario Histórico* of Pedro Fages, — an abbreviated French rendering of the original (*Annales des Voyages*, vol. ci); *Diario Histórico* of Miguel Costansó (Mexico, 1770), — Translations by William Revely (London, 1790), and by Charles F. Lummis (*Land of Sunshine*, 1901); *Noticias de la Nueva California*, by Francisco Palou (J. T. Doyle, 4 vols., San Francisco, 1874); *Diario* of Juan Crespi (Palou, *Noticias*, vol. ii), — translated as to portion San Diego to Monterey by Frank de Thoma (Los Ángeles *Times*, 1898); *Diario* of Junípero Serra (Edward E. Ayer Collection, Newberry Library, Chicago, holograph), — Translation by Charles F. Lummis (*Out West*); Letters of José de Gálvez to Fermín Francisco Lasuén and to Pedro Fages and Miguel Costansó, 1768 (B. C., *Archives of Santa Bárbara*, vol. i); *Instrucciones* of Gálvez to Vicente Vila and Pedro Fages (B. C., *Provincial State Papers*, vol. i); " Manifest " of the San Carlos (B. C., *Ibid.*); " Extracto de Noticias del Puerto de Monterey," Mexico, 1770 (Palou, *Noticias*, vol. ii), — translated (*Land of Sunshine*, 1901); *Informe General de Gálvez*, Dec. 31, 1771 (Mexico, 1867); Palou, *Vida de Serra* (Mexico, 1787); *Informe de Revilla Gigedo*, 1793 (M. A.), — Translation (*Land of Sunshine*, 1899); *Identification of Sir Francis Drake's Anchorage on the Coast of California in the Year 1579*, by George Davidson, California Historical Society Publication, pamphlet.

To the above there may now be added: *Instrucción que deberá observar el Capitán de Dragones, D. Gaspar de Portolá, en la expedición y viaje por tierra á los puertos de San Diego y Monterrey*, Cabo de San Lucas, 20 Febrero, 1769; *Instrucción que ha de tener presente Dⁿ Fernando de Rivera y Moncada para la proxima entrada por tierra á Monterrey*, Puerto de la Paz, 4 Abril, 1769 (S. A., Sevilla); *Diarios de los Viajes que el R. P. Fr. Juan Crespi y otros Misioneros del Colegio de San Fernando hicieron en la California, escritos por el mismo;* in six parts (each part by a separate missionary and with a prologue by Crespi), constituting the basis of Palou's *Noticias*, but with variations from the latter in substance and expression (Lenox Library, N. Y., Ramírez Coll.); Palou, *Noticias*, MS. copy, 2 vols. (Ayer Collection, Newberry Library); *Diario Histórico* of Pedro Fages (M. A., and Lenox Library, New York); *Diario del Viaje de Tierra hecho al Norte de la California*, by Miguel Costansó, San Diego, Feb. 7, 1770 (S. A., Madrid, and Sutro Library, San Francisco); *Diario de Navegación del Paquebot San Carlos . . . de la Paz al Puerto de San Diego*, by Vicente Vila (S. A., Madrid); *Relación*

Diaria de la Navegación del Paquebot San Carlos desde 11 de Enero al 1° de Mayo de 1769 á San Diego y Monterey, by Vicente Vila (S. A., Madrid); *Listas de Carga del Navío San Antonio, alias El Príncipe* (S. A., Sevilla); correspondence (during expedition) of Portolá, Fages, Costansó, Rivera y Moncada, and Crespi, with Viceroy Don Carlos Francisco de Croix (S. A., Sevilla, and M. A.); letter, Serra to Gálvez, Monterey, July 2, 1770 (S. A., Sevilla); general correspondence (preliminary to expedition) of Gálvez (35 letters) and of Viceroy Croix (M. A.); special correspondence of Rafael Verger, Guardian of the College of San Fernando, with *comisarios-generales* of the Indies (M. A., 15 letters, 1771–72), of four of which, dated June 30, Aug. 3, Aug. 27, and Aug. 28, 1771, originals are to be found in Boston Public Library. Of the Portolá diary and of the "Extracto de Noticias," the Spanish texts with translations have been published (1909) by the Academy of Pacific Coast History, vol. i, nos. 2 and 3, — Bancroft Library, Berkeley, California.

The later sources, besides contributing much of detail on all points, reveal for the first time the attitude of the College of San Fernando toward Gálvez and Alta California. (Specific citations below.)

1. A thousand Franciscans emigrated to Barbary at the close of the fifteenth century rather than submit to the rule of chastity. (H. C. Lea, *An Historical Sketch of Sacerdotal Celibacy in the Christian Church,* 1867, pp. 292–293; Mariana, *Historia de España,* vol. vi, p. 387.)

2. Sir A. Helps, *The Spanish Conquest in America,* 1900, vol. i, p. 179. "The Fathers [Jeronimite] asked the opinion of the official persons, and also of the Franciscans and Dominicans, touching the liberty of the Indians. It was very clear beforehand what the answers would be. The official persons and the Franciscans pronounced against the Indians, and the Dominicans in their favor." (*Ibid.* 359.) "There does not appear sufficient ground for the statement that the Franciscans were always opposed to the Dominicans on the question of the liberty of the Indian. At any rate, at this early period [1532] we find both Orders protesting in favor of the Indians." (*Ibid.,* vol. iii, p. 160, n. 1.)

3. Three Franciscans (Flemings) had reached Mexico as early as 1522. (Bancroft, *History of Mexico,* vol. ii, p. 160, etc.)

4. A "college" was a convent the inmates of which were trained for missionary work among the heathen. It differed from a convent *per se* in being independent of any other house or province. It possessed a "novitiate" (seminary) of its own for recruiting and instructing novices, a privilege accorded otherwise only to a province. The head of a college was called a guardian. He was elected (in an institution of full membership) by twelve councillors or voters, and the only officer to whom he was subject was a commissary-general in Spain, represented by a sub-commissary in Mexico or in one of the provinces. The conventual hierarchy was as follows: (1)

President (head of a group of two or more friars); (2) Guardian; (3) *Custodio* (director of a number of convents); (4) Provincial (head of a province, — a group of convents, usually not less than seven).

5. San Fernando, at first an *hospicio,* " home," was created a college on October 15, 1734, by a *cédula* issued by Philip V, in conformity with a Bull promulgated by Pope Innocent XI in 1682. The oldest Franciscan college in Mexico was that of Santa Cruz de Querétaro, founded in 1683. (Guardian Fray Rafael Verger to Manuel Lanz de Casafonda, *comisario-general de las Indias,* " Carta Segunda," par. 37, August 3, 1771, M. A., Museo Nacional, *Trasuntos.*) In 1771 the membership of San Fernando was as follows: Priests, 43; choristers, 7; laics (novices included), 22; lay brothers, 2 — 74 in all. (" Paper presented to Fourth Mexican Council," par. 17, August 26, 1771, by Fray Rafael Verger, *ut sup.*)

Because of the rumored differences between the Franciscans of Jalisco and Querétaro, an order had been procured from the Viceroy sending the Jaliscans to California and the Fernandinos with the Querétarans to Sonora. A vigorous protest from Palou, Crespi, Lasuén, and the other Fernandinos (four letters, Oct. 12–25, 1767, to the College of San Fernando) resulted in a resumption of the original plan. (M. A., Arch. Genl., *Documentos Relativos á las Misiones de Californias,* Qto i; Palou, *Noticias,* vol. i, p. 8, etc.)

6. Palou had been president of the Sierra Gorda missions. He was pronounced by Verger *mui capaz, verídico, y práctico en la reducción de Indios.* As for Serra, he was born at Petra, Mallorca, on November 24, 1713, and educated at the University of Mallorca, where later he became a professor of distinction, — *mui aplaudido en su empleo,* says Verger, *para su literatura y bellas prendas.* " But," continues the Guardian, " it will be necessary to moderate somewhat *su ardiente zelo.*" (" Carta Segunda," par. 1, M. A., Museo, *Trasuntos,* f. 128; Palou, *Vida de Serra,* p. 1.)

7. M. Ribero to Croix, March 23, 1768 (M. A., Arch. Genl., *Historia,* 14, f. 328).

8. Gálvez was born at Velez-Malaga in October, 1729. His parents were poor, but managed to send him to the University of Alcalá, where he graduated with the degree of doctor. He distinguished himself as an advocate, and, loving French society, made the acquaintance of one of the secretaries of the Marquis de Duras, the French ambassador. By the latter Gálvez was appointed advocate to the embassy, and in this capacity came to the notice of the Marqués de Grimaldi, who made him his private secretary. From this post the King (Charles III) advanced him to membership in the Council of the Indies. (*Biographie Universelle* (Michaud), Paris, 1856.)

9. *Plan para la Erección de un Govierno y Comandancia G^{ral} que comprehenda la Peninsula de Californias y las Provincias de Sinaloa, Sonora, y Nueva Viscaya,* Jan. 23, 1768 (M. A., Arch. Genl., *Provincias Internas,* 154; copy, Harvard Library, Sparks Collection, 98, with letter of approval

by the Archbishop of Mexico, Jan. 28, 1768, *Papeles Varios de America*, iii; translated, Appendix A of this volume).

10. *Los Rusos han hecho en varias veces diferentes tentativas para facilitarse una comunicación con la América, y ultimamente, lo han conseguido intentando la navegación por el Norte de la Mar del Sur. Se asegura que lo han logrado y que han llegado á tierra firme sin determinar en que grado, habiendo efectuado un desembarco en parage al parecer poblado de Salvages, con los quales pelearon con muerte de 300 Rusos.* Marqués de Grimaldi (First Secretary of State) to Croix, Jan. 23, 1768 (M. A., Arch. Genl., *Real Cédulas y Ordenes*, 92, f. 58). On Russian aggression, see also Costansó, *Diario Histórico;* translated, *Land of Sunshine*, vol. xiv, pp. 486–490.

The *junta* referred to in the Croix-Gálvez dispatch of Jan. 23, 1768, as having decided to send Gálvez to Sonora, Sinaloa, Nueva Vizcaya, and the Californias, was held in the City of Mexico on Jan. 21, 1768. Its determination was that *sobre este punto la nueva adquisizion de la rica peninsula de Californias, y los demas territorios que en la Sonora y Nueva Vizcaya poseian las Misiones de los regulares de la Compañia, es oy incomparablemente maior la conveniencia, y mucho mas urgente la nezesidad de que el Señor Visitador pase á las expresadas Provincias y arregle sus Pueblos, govierno y demas puntos que son indispensables*, etc., and that he *disponga su Viage á las zitadas Provincias de Californias, Sonora, y Nueva Vizcaya para mediados de Abril de este presente año, llevando la plena comision y ampleas facultades*, etc. (Harvard Library, Sparks Coll. 98, *Papeles Varios*, iii.) On Jan. 26, 1768, Viceroy Croix reported to the King that the *junta* had been held and that Gálvez had volunteered to go to the Californias and to the other Northern provinces. The Viceroy asked that the King "from his generous heart" condescend *aumentar al Visitador el sueldo.* (*Ibid.*) Croix to Julian de Arriaga, Minister of Marine and of the Indies, May 28, 1768, stating resolution to send an expedition to Monterey. (M. A., Arch. Genl., *Correspondencia de los Virreyes*, vol. xii, no. 376, f. 74, série ii (Croix), tom. ii.) Acknowledgment by Arriaga, Oct. 18, 1768, stating that "pending outcome of an expedition so important, the King would await with impatience news of the successive steps." (M. A., Arch. Genl., *R. Céd. y Ord.* 93, f. 163.)

As noted by Gálvez in his *Informe General* of 1771 (Dec. 31), the steps in the matter of the expedition to Monterey were the following: (1) An offer by the *visitador* in 1765 to go to Nueva Vizcaya and other provinces, in order to establish *poblaciones* for the raising of funds to maintain forces in Sonora in the perpetual struggle waged with the Indians; (2) a reply by Arriaga in 1767 (July 20), directing the calling of a *junta;* (3) a *junta* (1768, prior to March 2) at the capital, composed of the Archbishop and various ministers, approving Gálvez's offer, and indicating the peninsula of California as in need of visitation because of the recent expulsion of the Jesuits; (4) approval by the King in a royal order of Sept. 20, 1768; (5) urgent order by the King, Jan. 23, 1768, to Viceroy Croix, directing measures for defense of the California peninsula as against the Russians; (6) receipt of this order by Gálvez before his arrival at San Blas, whither, on April 9, he had set out from the capital, and where (Costansó, *Diario*; translated, *Land of Sunshine*, vol. xiv, p. 489) he held a *junta* on May 16. Of the dispatches referred to by the *visitador*, only those of Jan. 23, 1768, and later, have been found in the Mexican Archives, and indeed it is they only that directly affected the Monterey expedition. (*Informe General de Gálvez*, Mexico, 1867; pp. 139–141.)

11. Letter to Serra from Santa Ana, July 12, 1768, announcing arrival *en el dia 5 del corriente.* (M. A., Museo, *Documentos Relativos á las Misiones de Californias*, Qto i.) The *visitador* set sail from San Blas on May 24 in the sloop Sinaloa. On the eighth day out, he was forced by contrary winds into a bay of Isabella Island, where he was held four days. On June 5, in a calm, the Sinaloa was rowed to the Tres Marías Islands, which for six days Gálvez carefully explored. Setting sail on the 13th, he was forced to Mazatlán. Here he remained until July 2, when, with a wind *fresco y favorable*, he started for the peninsula. (Croix to Arriaga, July 30, 1768, M. A., Arch. Genl., *Cor. de Virr.*, vol. xii, no. 515, f. 281, sér. ii (Croix), tom. ii.) As consorts of the Sinaloa from San Blas, were the brigantine Concepción and the bark Pisón. The Concepción reached Cerralvo Inlet on June 14, having lost sight of the Sinaloa and Pisón on the night of May 28. From the beach of *la enseñada de Cerralvo*, the cargo of the Concepción was transferred to Osio's hacienda, and from this beach, on June 19, Rivera y Moncada was notified of the hourly anticipated arrival of Gálvez. (M. A., Arch. Genl., *Californias*, 76.)

12. Portolá, in a report to Croix, of date Dec. 28, 1767, describes the peninsula as pure sand sown with thorns and thistles. On a journey from Santiago to La Pasión (ten long days), he had met with naught, *ni rancho, ni casa; ni aun el menor abrigo*, save the mining-camp of Osio. In this land, he continues, one need rather be *vaquero* than *soldado*. (M. A., Arch. Genl., *Californias*, 76, no. 1.)

13. On March 5, 1768, Portolá had been instructed by the Viceroy to intrust to the Franciscans in the peninsula only that which pertained to the *sagrada y espiritual* of the missions, and on April 9 he had reported having placed in the missions, as *administradores*, soldiers "that were very loyal" (M. A., Arch. Genl., *Californias*, 76, nos. 3, 10). Verger, writing to Casafonda on August 3, 1771, states (citing Palou) that the Spiritualties were intrusted to the Franciscans on April 9, 1768, and the Temporalties on August 12. Gálvez's own letters to Serra on the subject bear date Aug. 13. He says: "*Comisarios* are born to obey and not govern, except it may be their own mounts." (M. A., Museo, *Docs. Rel. á las Mis. de Califs.*, Qto i.) The *visitador* used the *omnímoda facultad* (which he held) from alarm at the waste practiced by the *administradores*, who, within six months of their appointment, had killed at one mission 600 cattle, at another 400,

and at another 300. (M. A., Museo, *Trasuntos,* "Carta Segunda," pars. 2, 3.)

14. Gálvez, writing on Oct. 31 from Santa Ana, speaks of the horror with which, on first "placing eyes upon the peninsula, and foot in it," he was inspired "by the universal ruin that impended." On Nov. 23, in a letter to Padre Basterra at Santa Gertrudis, he describes the natives as "wandering in the mountains like wild beasts seeking pasture," — beings for the redemption of whom settled habitations (*domicilios fixos*) are indispensable. "The total nakedness," he continues, "in which the men and women have lived, does not permit to be borne in them that modesty [*pudor*] which is the first incentive to every action and virtue in rational creatures. . . . It is needful that they be clothed, even though poorly. . . . In a word, *la California conquistada* must have no native not reduced *á Población y Civilidad*, and who is not fed and clothed!" Transfer of natives from the North, and land ownership: Letter, Gálvez to Serra, from Santa Ana, on Oct. 10, 1768 (M. A., Museo, *Docs. Rel. á las Mis. de Califs.*, Qto i); Gálvez to Lasuén, Nov. 23, 1768 (B. C., *Arch. Sta. Bárb.*, vol. i, pp. 22–28; Palou, *Noticias,* vol. i, pp. 25–29, 31, 55); Gálvez, Orders, Nov. 19 and 23, 1768 (*Informe General,* 1771); Bancroft, *North Mexican States and Texas,* vol. i, pp. 486–87, nn. 41, 42, 43.

15. Gálvez to Serra, Nov. 23, 1768 (M. A., Museo, *Docs. Rel. á las Mis. de Califs.*, Qto i).

16. Gálvez, *Decreto de Colonización en Baja California,* 1768 (B. C., *Prov. St. Pap.*, vol. i, pp. 61–66).

17. Palou, *Vida de Serra,* pp. 44, 261. In imitation of Saint Francis, Serra was wont to beat his shoulders with a chain; and, while holding aloft a crucifix in his left hand, to beat his breast with a stone. He also used fire.

18. Gálvez to Serra, Oct. 7, 1768, letter expressing wish that if not too severe a tax upon his energies, Serra might come to Santa Ana for a conference upon certain points which he holds pending. Same to Same, Oct. 22: Is as glad to hear that Serra will come as that the Lauretana, which had gone aground, is saved. (*Docs. Rel. á las Mis. de Califs.*, Qto i.)

19. San Carlos, 62 men, Crespi, *Diario* (Palou, *Noticias,* vol. ii, p. 13); "Manifest" of San Carlos (*Prov. St. Pap.*, vol. i, pp. 13–21).

San Antonio, 28 men, Costansó, *Diario Histórico;* Translation, *Land of Sunshine,* vol. xiv, p. 494.

First land division, 31 men, Crespi, *Diario* (Palou, *Noticias,* vol. ii, pp. 21, 40). (Indian auxiliaries), 42 men, Crespi to Guardian Juan Andrés, June 22, 1769 (M. A., Museo, *Docs. Rel. á las Mis. de Califs.*, Qto i).

Second land division, 19 men, Portolá tó Viceroy, July 4, 1769 (M. A., Arch. Genl., *Californias,* 76; Palou, *Noticias,* vol. ii, p. 35). (Indian auxiliaries), 44 men, — making, for both divisions, a total of 226 men.

Says Mr. Zoeth S. Eldredge (*The March of Portolá,* p. 30): "Among the rank and file were men whose names are not less known: Pedro Amador, who gave his name to Amador County; Juan Bautista Alvarado, grandfather of Governor Alvarado; José Raimundo Carrillo, later *alférez* (lieutenant) and captain, comandante of the presidio of Monterey, of Santa Bárbara, and of San Diego, and founder of the great Carrillo family; José Antonio Yorba, sergeant of Catalonian volunteers, founder of the family of that name and grantee of the Rancho Santiago de Santa Ana; Pablo de Cota, José Ignacio Oliveras, José María Soberanes, and others."

20. M. A., Museo, *Docs. Rel. á las Mis. de Califs.*, Qto i.

21. *Ibid.*

22. *Ibid.*

23. *Ibid.*

24. Full list of articles taken from all the missions, attested by Palou, May 8, 1773 (M. A., Arch. Genl., *Prov. Int.* 211); summary by Bancroft (*History of California*, vol. i, p. 119, n. 9). In 1774 Francisco de Estavillo, *procurador-general* of the Dominicans for California, petitioned for a return of the *ornamentos* and *vasos sagrados* sent north by order of Gálvez; but the petition was denied by Fiscal Areche on the ground that the articles taken were either from an excess quantity in establishments yet existing, or from suppressed establishments. (M. A., Arch. Genl., *Prov. Int.* 211.)

On despoliation of the peninsula, see note 34, *post*. As to three Northern missions, Gálvez (M. A., Museo, *Docs. Rel. á las Mis. de Califs.*, Qto i). The plan at this juncture seems to have been for three establishments in what, later, was Alta California; and for two establishments auxiliary to these in the northern part of the peninsula. (Gálvez to Palou, Aug. 12, 1768, *Ibid.*)

25. As intimated, Gálvez named the intermediate mission San Buenaventura, because of the special favor with which that saint was regarded by Saint Francis. The story is that the latter, one day, meeting the Tuscan Giovanni de Fidanza, exclaimed, in prophetic vision of his future greatness, " O buona ventura"! — whence the appellation.

26. Gálvez to Palou, two letters, Oct. 7, 1768 (M. A., Museo, *Docs. Rel. á las Mis. de Califs.*, Qto i).

27. Gálvez to Serra, Dec. 28, 1768 (*Ibid.*).

28. " Manifest " of the San Carlos (B. C., *Prov. St. Pap.*, vol. i, pp. 13–21); Palou, *Noticias*, vol. ii, p. 13 ; Costansó, *Diario Histórico*, — Translation, *Land of Sunshine*, vol. xiv, pp. 490–491; Serra, *Diario*, — Translation, *Out West*, vol. xvi, p. 294.

29. M. A., Museo, *Docs. Rel. á las Mis. de Califs.*, Qto i. "On the 6th of January of this same year [1769], finding myself in the Port of La Paz, with his Eminence the Señor Inspector, I blessed the Packet named the San Carlos, saying the Mass aboard her, and blessed the standards; the Litany was sung, and other devotions to Our Lady. And his Eminence made a fervent exhortation with which he kindled the spirits of those who were to

go in that vessel to said Ports of San Diego and Monterey. These embarked on the 9th, at night, and on the 10th set sail." (Serra, *Diario*; Translation, *Out West*, vol. xvi, p. 294.)

30. M. A., Museo, *Docs. Rel. á las Mis. de Califs.*, Qto i.

31. Vila, *Diario de Navegación del Paquebot San Carlos* (S. A., Madrid, Dirección Hidrografía, *California, Historia y Viages*, t. i, caj. 7°, 63ª).

32. M. A., Museo, *Docs. Rel. á las Mis. de Califs.*, Qto i.

33. M. A., Museo, *Docs. Rel. á las Mis. de Califs.*, Qto i. Writing to Palou on Nov. 23, 1768, Gálvez asked prayers that (for the safety of the ships) the north winds might be put to sleep — *adormezca los Nortes*. (B. C., *Arch. de Sta. Bárb.*, vol. xi, p. 370.)

34. Palou, Jan. 7, 1772, list of mules and horses taken by Rivera y Moncada from the various missions of the peninsula, with Rivera's corrections (M. A., Arch. Genl., *Prov. Int.* 211). This list was made apropos of an order by Gálvez for a restoration of the animals. According to Bancroft (*North Mexican States and Texas*, vol. i, p. 491), Gálvez and Serra being in accord, there was no one to make objection to the despoiling of the peninsular missions for the benefit of those to be planted to the northward. On the contrary, on July 26, 1770, the *discretario* of the College of San Fernando addressed to Viceroy Croix a drastic criticism of the entire proceeding. Speaking of the spoliation wrought by Portolá's *administradores*, he said that it was great, but not nearly so great as that wrought by Gálvez for the Monterey expedition. Some 500 head of stock, in all, had been taken, and if not restored, the peninsular Indians could not be fed. (M. A., Museo, *Docs. Rel. á las Mis. de Califs.*, Qto ii). According to Serra, not a mule had been replaced up to April 22, 1773 (B. C., *Prov. St. Pap.*, vol. i, p. 91). It is the explanation of Palou that compensation was made by the government through the *almacén* (royal warehouse) at Loreto, and from the money left by the Jesuits (*Noticias*, vol. i, p. 232). Bitterly opposed as was the College of San Fernando to the spoliation by Gálvez, it yet dared not interfere in the matter even in restraint of its own sons Serra and Palou.

35. M. A., Museo, *Docs. Rel. á las Mis. de Califs.*, Qto i. Gálvez, in a letter to Serra of date March 28, 1769, makes mention of a *segunda or[n], positiva que dirigí al Capitán con la noticia del despacho del ultimo Paquebot desde el cabo.* (*Ibid.*)

36. Cáñizares, *pilotín* (master's mate) of the San Carlos, was detached for land duty

37. Portolá's birthplace was Balaguer, and his rank noble. He had seen service in Italy and Portugal. (Pub. Acad. Pacific Coast Hist.,vol. i, no. 3, p. 6.)

38. J. Crespi, *Diario*, in Palou, *Noticias*, vol. ii, pp. 6–39; Crespi to Juan Andrés, Guard. San Fernando, San Diego, June 22, 1769 (M. A., Museo, *Docs. Rel. á las Mis. de Califs.*, Qto i); Portolá, *Diario* (B. C., Pinart, *Papeles Varios*); Portolá to Croix, San Diego, July 4, 1769 (M. A., Arch.

Genl., *Californias*, 76); M. Costansó, *Diario Histórico*, — Translation, *Land of Sunshine*, vol. xiv, pp. 490–491; Serra, *Diario*, — Translation, *Out West*, vol. xvi, p. 294; Fages and Costansó, Jan. 4, 1769 (M. A., Arch. Genl., *Californias*, 66).

39. Palou,*Vida de Serra*, p. 20. Padre Navarrete, who made the journey from Vera Cruz to the capital in 1646, wrote: "We passed through places infested with mosquitoes or gnats that sting cruelly." (Churchill, *Collection of Voyages*, vol. i, p. 208.)

40. M. A., Museo, *Docs. Rel. á las Mis. de Califs.*, Qto i.

41. The orders issued by Gálvez (March and April, 1769), covering the points indicated in the text, were nineteen in number. Rules were framed for compensation to be paid the Indians for their labor; for a distribution of house-lots (*solares*) and fields (*suertes*), and for a demarcation of commons (*ejidos*), — all to be recorded in a *Libro de Población*. It was provided (and herein a germ of conflict between State Sacerdotal and State Secular in the peninsula), that at Loreto the temporalties in charge of the padre (Palou) were to consist only of the Rancho San Juan and the *huerta* (garden) attached to the mission. Grain from the royal warehouse (*almacén*) was to be given to the mission in exchange for garden vegetables and garden fruit, and meat was to be supplied to the *jefe del Govierno* and royal commissary by the mission at a stipulated price. "Instruction to Felipe Neve" (addenda), 1774, no. 22 (M. A., Arch. Genl., *Prov. Int.* 166). By the College of San Fernando much of the foregoing, together with other portions of the policy of the *visitador* in the Californias, was disapproved. See this chapter, notes 24, 34, 78, 80, with citations.

42. Gálvez to Serra (two letters), La Paz, March 28, 1769 (M. A., Museo, *Docs. Rel. á las Mis. de Califs.*, Qto i). The parting words of Serra to Palou were pathetic: *Á Dios hasta Monterey, donde espero juntaremos, para trabajar en aquella Viña del Señor. Mucho me alegré de esto; pero mi despedida fué hasta la eternidad*, — Good-bye until Monterey, where I hope we shall meet to work together in the Lord's vineyard. At this I was much rejoiced, but my farewell was until eternity. (Palou, *Vida de Serra*, p. 68.)

43. Addenda to "Instructions to Felipe Neve," pars. 5, 13, 17 (M. A., Arch. Genl., *Prov. Int.* 166).

44. Crespi, *Diario*, Palou, *Noticias*, vol. ii, p. 26.

45. The selection of Joseph as patron saint was determined by the circumstance that prayers to him had been followed by relief from a locust plague. On September 15, 1768, the *visitador* had explained to Serra (in apology for not naming the Monterey presidio for Saint Joseph) that the latter would not be offended, as he was very humble, and devoted especially to poor artisans; and as already two churches were named for him in the peninsula. (M. A., Museo, *Docs. Rel. á las Mis. de Califs.*, Qto i.)

46. Vila, *Relación Diaria*, S. A., Madrid, Direc. Hid., *Costa No. de America*, t. i, pp. 276–282, C 2ª; Vila, *Diario de Navegación* [Log], *Ibid.*; California,

Historia y Viages, t. i, 7, 63ª. For the course of the San Carlos, see general map (pocket).

47. Serra, *Diario*, Ayer Coll., Newberry Library; Translation, *Out West*, vol. xvi.

48. Crespi, *Diario*, in Palou, *Noticias*, vol. ii, pp. 38–100; Portolá, *Diario* (B. C., Pinart, *Papeles Varios*); Costansó, *Diario Histórico*, — Translation, *Land of Sunshine*, vol. xiv. Says the latter (p. 494): "And this whole [sea] expedition, which had been composed of more than ninety men, saw itself reduced to only eight soldiers and as many marines in a state to attend to the safeguarding of the Barks, the working of the Launches, Custody of the Camp and service of the Sick." In his *Relación Diaria*, Vila states that up to March 29 there had died of his own crew sixteen men, and of the crew of the San Antonio nine. Of Fages's men six only were effective. Neither in the B. C. nor M. A. has anything been found relative to the number of the crew of the San Antonio. But it must have been approximately twenty-eight, taking the total of both ships at ninety.

49. M. A., Museo, *Docs. Rel. á las Mis. de Califs.*, Qto i.

50. M. A., Arch. Genl., *Californias*, 76.

51. "Instrucciones á Portolá y á Rivera y Moncada," Feb. 20 and April 4, 1769 (S. A., Sevilla, Audiencia de Guadalajara, est. 104, caj. 3, leg. 3); "Instrucciones á Vila" (B. C., *Prov. St. Pap.*, vol. i, pp. 22–31); "Instrucciones á Fages" (*Ibid.*, pp. 31–43); summary of foregoing instructions, Bancroft, *History of California*, vol. i, pp. 129, n. 7, 131, n. 11.

52. Portolá to Croix, San Diego, July 4, 1769 (M. A., Arch. Genl., *Californias*, 76); Croix to Portolá in approval, Aug. 12, 1769 (*Ibid.*); Crespi, *Diario* (Palou, *Noticias*, vol. ii, pp. 99, etc.).

53. Palou, *Noticias*, vol. ii, pp. 99, 248; *Vida de Serra*, p. 82.

54. The San José or Saint Joseph (*alias* el Descubridor) was dispatched from San Blas for La Paz, early in 1768, under Capitán and Piloto Don Domingo Antonio Calegari. (M. A., Arch. Genl., *Historia*, 329; Palou, *Noticias*, vol. ii, p. 33.)

55. Crespi, *Diario*, in Palou, *Noticias*, vol. ii, p. 252; R. Verger to Casafonda, "Carta Segunda" (M. A., Museo, *Trasuntos*, f. 128). Upon this occasion the blacksmith of the camp distinguished himself by his bravery, receiving a wound from an arrow. His name was Juan Joseph Chacón. (Fages to Gálvez, Feb. 8, 1770, M. A., Arch. Genl., *Californias*, 66.)

56. A copy may be found in the B. C.

57. Crespi, *Diario* (Palou, *Noticias*, vol. ii, pp. 100–175); Portolá, *Diario* (B. C., Pinart, *Papeles Varios*), — Spanish text, with translation, Publications Academy Pacific Coast History, vol. i, no. 3; Fages, *Diario* (M. A., Museo, *Docs. Rel. á las Mis. de Califs.* iv).

58. Costansó, *Diario Histórico*, Mexico, 1770; Translation, *Land of Sunshine*, vols. xiv, xv, 1901.

59. Fages: "All the country about San Gabriel Mission invites to oc-

cupation by families of Spaniards, among whom, with no prejudice to the mission, there might be allotted fertile lands with *sitios* suitable for every kind of livestock . . . there being begun in them [the settlers] hopes of a *población bien importante.*" (*Diario,* M. A., Museo, *Docs. Rel. á las Mis. de Califs.* iv.)

60. Costansó, *Diario* (S. A., Madrid, Direc. Hid., *Reino de Méjico,* t. i, 62ª, 141 á 209). As carefully worked out by Mr. Z. S. Eldredge, the route was as follows: July 24, Sierra San Onofre; 25, San Juan Capistrano, where Santa Catalina Island sighted; 28, Santa Ana River (Río Jesús de los Temblores); 30–31, San Gabriel Valley (San Miguel); Aug. 1, site of Los Ángeles (Río de Nuestra Señora de Los Ángeles de Porciúncula); 4–9, San Fernando Valley (Valle de Santa Catalina de las Encinas); 12, Santa Clara River, *via* Santa Susana Mountains; 14, San Buenaventura (la Asunción); 18, Santa Bárbara (Laguna de la Concepción); 28, Point Conception; 30, Santa Inéz River (Río de Santa Rosa); Sept. 1, Guadalupe Lake (Laguna Larga); 3–4, San Luis Cañon, Bald Knob (Point Buchón); San Luis Obispo; Morro Bay (Estero de San Serafín), *via* Cañada de los Osos; 13, Sierra de Santa Lucía; 16–20, San Caproforo Cañon — Mount Mars; 26, Salinas River (Río de San Elizarto), *via* Arroyo Seco (Cañada del Palo Caido, — Fallen Tree); 30, the Sea; Oct. 1, Point Pinos.

61. Portolá to Croix, San Diego, Feb. 11, 1770 (M. A., Arch. Genl., *Californias,* 76).

62. *Ibid.*

63. Crespi, *Diario,* in Palou, *Noticias,* vol. ii, p. 183; Translation, F. de Thoma, Los Ángeles *Times,* 1898. Of these trees Fages writes in his *Diario:* "Here are trees of girth so great that eight men placed side by side with extended arms are unable to embrace them."

64. *Ibid.*; Crespi to Guardian Juan Andrés, San Diego, Feb. 8, 1770, and to Gálvez, Feb. 9, 1770 (M. A., Museo, *Docs. Rel. á las Mis. de Califs.,* Qto ii, and Arch. Genl., *Californias,* 66); Portolá to Croix, San Diego, Feb. 11, 1770 (M. A., Arch. Genl., *Californias,* 76). On identity of the bay under Point Reyes with the San Francisco Bay of Cermeño, Palou, *Noticias,* vol. ii, pp. 198–208, vol. iv, pp. 221, 288–294. On the identity of the San Francisco Bay of Cermeño with Francis Drake's Bay, G. Davidson, *Identification of Sir Francis Drake's Anchorage* (Calif. Hist. Soc. Pub.), pamphlet; and *The Discovery of San Francisco Bay,* 1907. For route of Portolá, see general map (pocket).

65. Crespi, *Diario,* in Palou, *Noticias,* vol. ii, p. 200; Translation, F. de Thoma, Los Ángeles *Times,* 1898.

66. See note 65, chapter vi, Golden Gate.

67. Portolá to Croix, San Diego, Feb. 11, 1770 (M. A., Arch. Genl., *Californias,* 76); Crespi, *Diario,* in Palou, *Noticias,* vol. ii, p. 213; Same to Guardian Andrés and José de Gálvez, San Diego, Feb. 8 and 9, 1770 (M. A., Museo, *Docs. Rel. á las Mis. de Califs.,* Qto ii, and Arch. Genl., *Californias,* 66).

68. Portolá to Viceroy, Feb. 11, 1770 (M. A., Arch. Genl., *Californias*, 76). With regard to the number of sick or dead, at specific dates, the accounts conflict. In the text, reliance is placed upon the official letters of Portolá.

69. Portolá to Croix, Feb. 11, 1770, and "Noticia total de Grano y Arina," San Diego, Jan. 28, 1770 (M. A., Arch. Genl., *Californias*, 76); Costansó and Fages to Gálvez and Croix, five letters, San Diego, Feb. 3, 7, 1770 (M. A., Arch. Genl., *Californias*, 66). In one letter to Gálvez, Costansó and Fages mention "hot disputes" on this expedition — *contestaciones y disputas . . . agriarse el genio y humor de algunos de los altercantes*, etc. Writing to Gálvez from San Diego Feb. 8, 1770, Fages states that "there are left 60 men to be fed, including 4 padres and 8 seamen with Vila." From this force "28 men are to go to Velicatá to lighten the burden on the commissary." (*Ibid.*; Palou, *Noticias*, vol. ii, pp. 254–55, 257; *Vida de Serra*, pp. 90, 93–99.)

70. Portolá to Croix, San Diego, April 17, 1770 (M. A., Arch. Genl., *Californias*, 76).

71. Palou, *Noticias*, vol. ii, p. 264.

72. Portolá to Croix, Monterey, June 15, 1770, official report of occupation of the port, with attestation by Pedro Fages, Juan Pérez, and Miguel del Pino. (M. A., Arch. Genl., *Californias*, 76; Crespi, *Diario*, in Palou, *Noticias*, vol. ii, p. 269; Palou, *Vida de Serra*, p. 101, with letter by Serra describing ceremonies.)

73. J. Gálvez to Fages and Costansó, Cape San Lucas, Feb. 14, 1769 (B. C., *Prov. St. Pap.*, vol. i, p. 46); Serra to Gálvez, Monterey, July 2, 1770 (S. A., Sevilla, Aud. de Guad., est. 104, caj. 3, leg. 3); J. Velásquez, *Diario* (M. A., Arch. Genl., *Californias*, 76); Portolá to Croix, San Blas, Aug. 1, 1770, and Portolá to Croix, Guadalajara, Aug. 28, 1770 (*Ibid.*). In a letter of July 1, 1770, to Croix, Fages states that there remain at Monterey 12 volunteers, 6 cuirassiers, 5 seamen, and Prat the surgeon. (M. A., Arch. Genl., *Californias*, 66.)

74. "The corners of the principal front of the Cathedral are formed by two strong towers. . . . One [tower] has many celebrated bells, among them one weighing 100 *quintales*. . . . These bells are not rung except on occasions of joy and thanksgiving. . . . All the churches will answer this well-known chime immediately." (J. M. de San Vicente, *City of Mexico, its Cathedral and Palace*, Cádiz, — B. C., *Papeles Varios*, México, vol. v, no. 2; Palou, *Noticias*, vol. ii, pp. 269–282, vol. i, p. 101; *Vida de Serra*, pp. 104, 107–109.)

75. F. Trillo y Vermudez to Croix, San Blas, Oct. 17, 1769 (M. A., Arch. Genl., *Historia*, 329); Croix to the King, Dec. 20 and 31, 1769, — *visitador* persuaded to return to the capital (M. A., Arch. Genl., *Cor. de Virreyes*, vol. xv (serial vol. v), nos. 1259, 1260, fol. 50, 51); Falenback to Croix, Guadalajara, Aug. 23, 1769, — concerning *actividad y infatigable trabajo* of

Gálvez *in servicio de el Real y de el público,* etc. (M. A., Arch. Genl., *Historia,* 329).

76. M. A., Museo, *Docs. Rel. á las Mis. de Califs.,* Qto i.

77. *Ibid.*

78. *Ibid.,* vol. ii. The project of mission establishments, as far north as San Diego and Monterey, was at this juncture that of the government and of ardent individual missionaries, — the government to thwart Russia, and the missionaries to multiply conversions. As for the missionary colleges, they were for a conservative course. San Fernando was as bitter against the planting of establishments in Northern California as against the despoiling of the peninsula and the Gálvez rules for Loreto. Said Verger to Casafonda on June 30, 1771: "In no manner has this college approved the founding at one time so many and such missions. If missionaries have been sent, it has been perforce and because we have not been able to resist him that commands us with power absolute, admitting neither supplication nor argument. . . . Unless God our Master works with miracles and prodigies, a happy issue cannot be expected. (" Carta Primera," M. A., Museo, *Trasuntos,* f. 127.) It is declared (1) that Monterey is 790 leagues distant; (2) that navigation is perilous, and lives and ships would be lost; (3) that many soldiers would be needed; (4) that the Indians, as confessed by Serra, are great thieves; (5) that the Indian tongues are not understood; (6) that Indian docility, so much dwelt upon by Crespi and Serra, is a sham, as witness that attack on San Diego on August 15, 1769. (" Carta Segunda," M. A., Museo,, *Trasuntos,* f. 128, *passim.*) Commenting on the urgency of the *visitador's* letters, Verger, on August 3, 1771, thus addressed Casafonda: "Hardly had the [forty-five] padres reached this college, when the *visitador* and (in consequence) the Viceroy desired them to start for California. It was necessary to moderate this ardor, as already the padres had been ninety-nine days on the way from Spain, and half of them were ill and all debilitated." Furthermore, when of the forty-five "we would permit but thirty to go to the Californias, the *visitador* vented upon us the calumny, that we were excusing ourselves from the exercise of the ministry pertinent to a Seminary or College *de Propaganda Fide,* and this after the King had paid for the transportation of the missionaries hither." (" Carta Segunda," M. A., Museo, *Trasuntos,* f. 128, par. 38, 39.)

79. Gálvez to Serra, Sta. Ana, Oct. 10, 1768; and Gálvez, decree, La Paz, Nov. 19, 1768. The decree recites the discovery of various amounts of gold dust, and of gold and silver bullion, accumulated by the Jesuits, and not accounted for to the royal treasury as required by law. It recites, further, as fact, the maintenance of the missions by the *trabajo* (labor) and *sudor* (sweat) *de los miserables Indios,* at the same time that the Indians are neither fed nor clothed. Wherefore it is ordered that the gold and silver aforesaid (7650 *pesos*) be converted to the use of the Indians, and that *sínodos* (salaries) of padres, etc., be paid from the Pious Fund. (M. A., Museo,

Docs. Rel. á las Mis. de Califs., Qto i.) It is worthy of note that in effecting the Santa Expedición (and up to May 22, 1773) there was expended from the "Pious Fund," by order of the Viceroy, 136,184 *pesos*, 3 *tomines*, 9½ *granos*. (Viceroy to Arriaga, 27 Dec., 1774, — M. A., Arch. Genl., *Cor. de los Virreyes*, vol. lxii, no. 1681, sér. ii (Bucarely), vol. xlv.)

80. Croix to Palou, Nov. 12, 1770, three letters (M. A., Museo, *Docs. Rel. á las Mis. de Califs.*, Qto ii). The *sínodos* and foundation-fund assignments met with ridicule at San Fernando. It was stated to the Viceroy by the Discretario, that in the Sierra Gorda the *sínodos* were 300 and 450 *pesos*, according to the remoteness of the mission; and (" Carta Segunda," pars. 12, 13) it was pointed out by Verger to Casafonda that the Jesuits had been allowed 500 *pesos*, while to missionaries in Texas 450 were allowed. Strange that the *visitador*, who assumed the omnipotence of God, could do no better for California padres than 275 *pesos*. As for the 1000 *pesos* for founding a California mission (at Monterey, for example), the idea was worthy of laughter (*digna de risa*), and more a Don Quixote matter than a serious proposition. Monterey was 800 leagues from the capital, and thither must be taken implements for farming, — plough-shares, axes, hoes; a complete carpenter's outfit, saws, little and big, augers, adzes, planes, chisels, compasses, hammers; the tools of masons; cooking-utensils. A house, church, and granary would be necessary; and there must be livestock (not for a family but for a pueblo), — mules, horses, oxen. Then the Indians were to be taught to work, and at the same time instructed and fed, — all with 1000 *pesos!* "What solemn nonsense!"

In a caustic supplement to his " Carta Segunda," Verger notes that the projectors of the scheme for the conquest of California were actuated by a wish to be " honored for seeming great deeds, like a Hernán Cortéz." But so niggardly were they with supplies that three hens with their broods had been deemed sufficient for the three missions, San Antonio, San Gabriel, and San Buenaventura; and for the missions together, one rooster.

81. Serra and Fages, June 9, 1771, assignment of padres to San Antonio, San Gabriel, San Luis Obispo, San Carlos (M. A., Arch. Genl., *Californias*, 66). Founding of San Gabriel, Verger, *Informe* no. 4, 1772 (M. A., Museo, *Docs. Rel. á las Mis. de Califs.*, Qto ii) ; Palou, *Noticias*, vol. ii, p. 290; vol. iii, pp. 229–252.

CHAPTER VI

SAN FRANCISCO FOUNDED

NEW CHAPTER SOURCES: 1891. *Diarios* of Crespi and Peña, 1774; Letter of Serra to Bucarely, Sept. 9, 1774. (Publications of the Historical Society of Southern California, *Sutro Documents*, nos. 16, 18, 19, — Spanish texts with translations.)

1899. "Espedición y Registro de las Cercanías del Puerto de San Francisco," *Noticias* of Palou (manuscript translation by F. de Thoma, A. S. Macdonald Collection, Oakland, California).

1900. *Diario* of Garcés, 1775–76 (Translation by Dr. Elliott Coues, New York, *On the Trail of a Spanish Pioneer*); covers also the earlier *entradas* of Garcés, the still earlier *entradas* of Kino, and collateral matters.

1907–1909. *Diario* of Juan Bautista de Anza, 1774: one version, S. A., Sevilla; three versions, M. A.; one version, Ayer Coll., Newberry Library. Anza *diario*, 1775–76, M. A.; *Diario* (*borrador*) of Pedro Font, 1775–76, M. A. (manuscript translations, Zoeth S. Eldredge Collection, San Francisco) ; summary of Anza *diarios* by Z. S. Eldredge, *Journal of American History*, 1908–09.

1908–09. *Diario* (*borrador*) of Pedro Font, 1775–76 (Bancroft Library, Cowan Collection); *Diario* (complete) of Pedro Font, 1775–76 (John Carter Brown Library, Providence, R. I.; copy in Public Library, Los Ángeles, California).

1908–1910. Verger-Casafonda, and Verger-Vega, correspondence, 1771–72; dispatches of Bucarely to the King, 1770–76; Armona letters, 1770; Fages's *Diarios* of 1770 and 1772, Fages's letters of 1771, and Tulare report of 1773; Anza, Sr., correspondence, royal decree, etc., 1737–38; Anza, Jr., correspondence, 1772–76; Garcés's *Diario* of 1771, and correspondence of 1772–76; *Diario* of Juan Díaz, 1774; Costansó letters, 1772; Rivera y Moncada correspondence, 1773–76; Fuster on the affair of the neophyte Carlos, 1775; Escalante and Domínguez reports, 1776 (M. A.).

Facts and deductions: (1) Early application of the name San Francisco to the *estero* or present San Francisco Bay; (2) effort by Juan Bautista de Anza, Sr., to promote exploration westward, 1737–38; (3) outfitting and officering of first expedition of Juan Bautista de Anza, Jr.; (4) probable identification of San Carlos Pass (Z. S. Eldredge); (5) an expedition of Fages to San Francisco Bay, 1770; (6) Tulare Valley as seen by Fages, 1772. (Specific citations below.)

1. "Where I am on the Colorado, no troop of his Majesty has passed until to-day."

2. From Mexico on Sept. 15, 1771, Gálvez announced to Palou his im-

pending *viage á España,* and asked that there be procured for him some *perlas esquisitas* as a gift *á la Princesa, Nuestra Señora.* (M. A., Museo, *Docs. Rel. á las Mis. de Califs.,* Qto ii.)

3. Croix in 1783 was made Viceroy of Peru.

4. R. Verger to Viceroy Bucarely (Palou, *Noticias,* vol. i, p. 129).

5. Verger to Casafonda, " Carta Sexta," Jan. 23, 1772, stating that opposition to Dominicans was by Gálvez and Croix only, not by the Franciscan body. (M. A., Museo, *Trasuntos.*) At the same time it was not advisable to mingle the Orders in one college. (Same to same, Feb. 8, 1772, *Ibid.*)

6. M. A., Arch. Genl., *Real Céd. y Ord.* 96, f. 202; 97, f. 240; Verger to Comisario-General Manuel de la Vega, March 23, 1772, June 26, 1773 (M. A., Museo, *Trasuntos*).

7. Palou, *Noticias,* vol. i, p. 204, etc.

8. *Ibid.,* p. 259. A strong reason for admitting the Dominicans to California was that they might extend their occupation northeastward to the Gila-Colorado junction. Thus Bucarely in a letter to the King, October 27, 1772, expresses doubt whether it be wise to await the establishment of missions on the Colorado by the Dominicans before sending Anza thither, as a military expedition would be an obstacle to the conversion of the Gentiles. (M. A., Arch. Genl., *Cor. de Virreyes,* vol. xxxi, ser. ii (Bucarely), vol. xiv, no. 613, f. 35; *Ibid.,* June 26, 1774, vol. iv, serial vol. xxxviii, no. 1421, f. 1.) Cf. chapter vii of text, n. 52; chapter x, n. 10.

9. Armona had been appointed *Governador Yntendente y Comandante de Californias* in March or April, 1769. He had set forth from the capital for the peninsula on April 10, and had reached Loreto on June 12. Meanwhile Gálvez at Álamos, having been notified of the departure of Armona, had (June, 1769) written to Croix, stating that he had notified the Governor to visit him for instructions *viva voz,* and that it was his wish that the latter be granted a salary of 4000 *pesos* to enable him to live *con el lustre correspondiente* to his position (M. A., Arch. Genl., *Californias,* 67, nos. 5, 10, of no. 331). Reply had been made from Guadalajara, on July 4, that the total income for the peninsula was but 34,500 *pesos,* and that the cost of manning the presidio, packet-boats, etc., was 26,730 *pesos,* — a cost irrespective of the proposed salary for the Governor and of maintenance for the two *Reales* Sta. Ana and Loreto. (*Ibid.*) In 1770, June 19, Armona had written enthusiastically to Palou and Antonio López de Toledo (commissary) at Loreto, regarding supplies for San Diego; but by August of the same year he evidently had become disgusted with the narrow resources of his district. Thus on the 14th he had warned Serra to "go very slow" in his demands for guards for new establishments, as there were only 20 men at San Diego, and about the same at Monterey, without sufficient horses and *cuera.* The Indians now were "complacent" over their gifts, but so brutal and independent were they by nature, that it would not be long ere the Father-President "would have to offer to God the blood of arrows and the bitter-

ness of calumny." And the same day prediction had been freely made by the Governor to Palou that unless the peninsula were speedily succored there would supervene "a civil war a thousand times worse than that in Sonora" (M. A., Arch. Genl., *Californias*, 67, 76). On Nov. 12, 1770, Armona had been notified of the appointment of a successor, Felipe Barri. It is the comment of Verger on the retirement of Armona, that it was because he did not approve the decrees of Gálvez: *y este es un crimen lesae Majestatis.* ("Carta Segunda," M. A., Museo, *Trasuntos.*)

10. Letter Aug. 14, 1770.

11. States to Fages that 10 religious are being sent to erect four *doctrinas*, besides that of San Buenaventura, at fitting intervals between San Diego and Monterey, and that it is desired that as soon as possible he survey by land or sea the port of San Francisco, *y que no quede expuesto tan importante parage á ocupación ajena* (M. A., Arch. Genl., *Californias*, 66; B. C., *Prov. St. Pap.*, vol. i, p. 70). Apropos of the wish at the capital that the port of San Francisco be surveyed for a mission site, Fages on Nov. 21 set out from Monterey with 6 soldiers, and on the 26th came to the *cabeza* (head) *del Estero del Puerto de San Francisco*, hard by a river that held some *pozos* (pools) *de agua dulce.* On the 28th four soldiers explored further, and reported that "having gained a high hill, they had not been able to see the end of the *estero*, but had seen many cleft tracks left, it was thought, by *cíbolos* (bison)." They also had seen "*la Boca* (mouth) *del Estero* which they believed was that which entered by the *Bahía del Puerto de San Francisco.*" On the 29th, "It was decided to return, as they could not (except by spending many days) pass to the other side *de la Punta de los Reyes.*" (*Diario de Salida al Puerto de San Francisco*, 1770, M. A., Arch. Genl., *Cor. de Virreyes*, vol. xiv, ser. ii (Croix), vol. iv, no. 1176, f. 385; Letters, Fages to Croix, June 20, 1771, M. A., Arch. Genl., *Californias*, 66.)

On June 18, 1771, Serra, writing to Croix from San Carlos, announces the arrival on May 21 of the 10 religious, and acknowledges receipt of the *ornamento especial* sent by the Viceroy, which he has taken prompt occasion "to display [*lucir*] on the celebration of Corpus by the 12 priests now at the mission." Serra reports a failure as yet to found Santa Clara or San Francisco, because of Fages's insistence that there are not sufficient men for guards, and that the port of San Francisco must be fully surveyed. "But," he continues, "I wish first to see placed there the mission of my most beloved Padre Serafico, and, so far as I am concerned, this by the favor of God shall not be delayed." (*Ibid.*)

12. As for Rivera personally, he by July 3, 1770, had returned to San Diego, where he had remained till April 23, 1771. He then, by permission of the Viceroy, had retired to Loreto.

13. In one of his letters of June 20, 1771, Fages states to Croix that he has assigned 15 soldiers *de cuera* for the founding of San Buenaventura (M. A., Arch. Genl., *Californias*, 66). In a second letter to Croix he reports a dis-

cussion with Serra regarding the planting of a mission at San Francisco, but says that up to date he has not been able to effect anything *por faltarme soldados para la escolta;* as soon as he obtains soldiers, the Viceroy may be assured that he will found the mission. (*Ibid.*) On July 17, Fages reminds Croix that on Nov. 12, 1770, he had been promised 12 men from Guaymas, and that the men, recruited by Rivera in the peninsula, together with the escort at Velicatá, amount to about 21. As soon as these reach San Diego, he will found San Gabriel and San Buenaventura. Santa Clara shall come third. The day following (July 18), Fages announces the arrival of the 21 men, who bring word of the presence in the peninsula of the 12 from Guaymas. San Gabriel, San Buenaventura, and San Luis Obispo shall therefore be founded. (*Ibid.*) Barri's appointment was made known to Armona by a communication from the Viceroy, dated Nov. 12, 1770 (M. A., Arch. Genl., *Californias,* 76). On Oct. 24, 1771, Barri reported to the Viceroy that the troops available for both Californias were in all 82 cuirassiers, of whom 51 were at San Diego and Monterey, 12 at Velicatá, 9 at various other missions, and 10 at Loreto, ill and unarmed. To enable Fages to proceed with the work of founding missions in Alta California, and to enable Rivera to found the five establishments planned for the peninsula north of Santa María, there were needed 40 men additional. (M. A., Arch. Genl., *Californias,* 13. See also M. A., Arch. Genl., *Cor. de Virreyes,* ser. ii, vol. iv, no. 1176, f. 381.)

14. On July 22, 1772, Guardian Verger, in his fourth *Informe sobre las Misiones* to Viceroy Bucarely, makes relation in detail. The Indians, at first hostile, were led to throw down their bows and arrows by a likeness of the Holy Virgin which was shown them. They even assisted in the building of the mission houses. But soon Fages appeared, and, dismayed at the number of Gentiles crowding about, and the small guard with which to control them (10 men), gave orders for the admittance to the mission of only 4 or 5 Indians at a time. The padres had been admitting 40 or 50 at a time (unarmed), and the effect of the new order, when put in execution, was to anger the Indians, who, armed with clubs, rushed to the camp and began to plunder. For a time the mission was in a state of siege, but after some hostile interchanges the Indians offered peace. The declaration of Fages upon the whole affair was, that he could not now found San Buenaventura nor San Luis Obispo, because there was need of all his men to reinforce San Gabriel, San Antonio de Padua, and Carmelo, where he feared that already something might have happened. (M. A., Museo, *Docs. Rel. á las Mis. de Califs.,* Qto ii.)

15. *Vida de Serra,* pp. 58, 132–33, 146.

16. July 10, 1770, "Memorial of 15 points." No. 10 reads thus: "That neither the governor, nor royal commissary, be permitted to meddle in the temporalties intrusted by your Highness to the padres, since Antonio Josef López de Toledo was possessed of the idea that all there was in the

missions was at his disposal, and that *los Padres eran como subalternos suos*. (M. A., Museo, *Docs. Rel. á las Mis. de Califs.*, Qto ii; Palou, *Noticias*, vol. i, pp. 84–89.) Cf. chapter v, n. 41.

17. R. Verger to Viceroy Bucarely, Nov. 15, 1772: *Primer Informe ó Methodo nuebo de Misiones para su Gobierno espiritual y temporal*. Paragraph 19 states that, as early as 1719, Viceroy Baltasar de Zúñiga had decreed that the captains, governors, and other officers of the province of the Tejos (Texans) were to assist the padres of the colleges of Querétaro and Zacatecas by providing guards, and in every other way, as the padres should demand; and that in 1740 Viceroy Salazar had ordered the same thing under penalty of 200 *pesos*. Paragraph 5 states that in the Sierra Gorda, during the period of control of the temporalties by *caudillos, capitanes, y thenientes*, the Indians were made house-servants, *vaqueros*, etc., without pay, and that the secular officers appropriated the mission lands to their own uses, etc., with the result that the neophytes either fled to the hills or became *broncos* (morose) and discontented. The same was true of the peninsular California Indians under Portolá's *comisionados*. Paragraph 6: "No others than the missionaries are able to administer the temporalties and fill, in the name of his Majesty (whom God guard), the office of tutors and guardians of these new and helpless vassals. [Palou] writes that, unless the governor of the Californias [Barri] be given to understand that the government of the missions is exclusively for the padres, these establishments will be lost. 'The Governor and Fages,' he says, 'are already united and at one, intending to limit us to saying Mass and preaching.' If so, we may as well retire to our college, and the King be saved useless expense in seeking to spread the Catholic faith and to extend his dominion." Paragraph 7: "In the peninsula, Gálvez reserved only *causas de sangre* [causes of blood] to the Governor, and he gave the baton of local command to the Indian governors." In the Sierra Gorda, after the padres assumed the temporalties, "the Indians began to be tractable and docile. They were able to build churches of lime and stone, with arches adorned with their corresponding altars, *ornamentos*, and sacred vessels, — indeed to such perfection of civil life were they brought that, by the end of 1770, they were transferred to Archbishop Lorenzana, to be erected into curacies.

"There be some that scruple [*escrupulizan algunos*] that the religious interpose in the temporal affairs of the Indians, *y que los castiguen con azotes* [and that they punish them with stripes] when they absent themselves from the catechism and other services of the missions; . . . but in all this the missionaries do not proceed of their own authority, but *en nombre del Rey*, who makes of them tutors and guardians of the neophytes and Gentiles; hence vain is the fear that the royal jurisdiction will be prejudiced. (M. A., Museo, *Trasuntos*.) In 1771, in his "Carta Segunda," Verger had observed to Casafonda, that to some it doubtless seemed improper that the missionaries should control the temporalties of *Indios recién conquistados*, and that among objectors, at first, were the *visitador* and Viceroy. (*Ibid.*, f. 128.) See n. 18; see also chapter iii, n. 25.

18. M. A., Arch. Genl., *Cor. de Virreyes*, vol. xl, ser. ii, vol. xxiii, no. 1019, f. 90; Palou, *Noticias*, vol. iii, pp. 35–66, par. 6, 8–9, 22, 26. In asking authority to transfer soldiers (par. 8), Serra alleged their *mal ejemplo*, *máxime en puntos de incontinencia*. Regarding reprehensible conduct of soldiers at San Gabriel, see Serra, "Representación de 21 de Mayo, 1773." They were wont, it seems, for their diversion to capture Indian women by use of the lasso. (*Cor. de Virreyes*, vol. and ser. *supra*, f. 158; B. C., *Prov. St. Pap.*, vol. i, p. 122; Palou, *Noticias*, vol. iii, p. 47; *Vida de Serra*, pp. 130–32.) Said Verger to Bucarely in his *Informe* of Nov. 15, 1772: "The padres do not assume to control the officers nor the soldiers, if the latter do not destroy by their ill living that which appertains to the apostolical preaching and paternal admonition of the former." "The tumults," says Father Luis Jayme of San Diego, "which have arisen in certain *rancherías* have been caused by the soldiers seizing the Indian women."

19. "Representación de 22 de Abril, 1773" (M. A., Arch. Genl., *Cor. de Virreyes*, vol. xl, ser. ii, vol. xxiii, no. 1019, f. 158; B. C., *Prov. St. Pap.*, vol. i, p. 91). "Representación de 13 de Marzo, 1773" (M. A., Arch. Genl., *Cor. de Virreyes*, vol. xl, ser. ii, vol. xxiii, no. 1019, f. 90; Palou, *Noticias*, vol. iii, p. 41, par. 5).

20. Palou, in an *Informe* to the College of San Fernando, Feb. 12, 1772, had dwelt on the right of the missionaries, *civilizar, educar, y corregir* the natives (Palou, *Noticias*, vol. i, p. 190), and the decision of the *junta* of May 9, 1773, was: *Se declaró así deberlo ejecutar en todo lo económico á que un padre de familia se maneja con el cuidado de su casa, educación y corrección de sus hijos*, etc. (*Ibid.*, vol. iii, p. 78). In his "Representación of March 13," par. 9, Serra had referred to the above as *costumbre inmemorial del reino desde su conquista* (*Ibid.*, pp. 47–48). The rule was indeed time-honored. Under Isabella and Charles V, the Indians were declared by law minors for life, — *no pueden tratar y contratar* (not competent to trade or contract) for more than five *pesos* (*Recopilación*, vi, tit. 10). This law was not abrogated till 1810. For instructions by Bucarely tending toward a modification of the power of State Sacerdotal, with respect to the Indians, see chapter vii of text, n. 21.

21. "Representación de 22 de Abril, 1773" (M. A., Arch. Genl., *Cor. de Virreyes*, vol. xl, sér. ii, vol. xxiii, no. 1019, f. 158). It is evident from the letter of Governor Armona to Palou and Toledo, June 19, 1770, that it was at first designed to forward supplies chiefly by land, establishing *una comunicación frecuente* between San Diego and Velicatá, *y á Monterey y puerto de San Francisco*. Serra's opposition to this was for the reason assigned; but it-was also for a further reason. In journeying to and fro along the Santa Bárbara Channel, the soldiers were wont to debauch the native women. Said the Father-President: "It would be a miracle if so many Indian women,

as were to be encountered along this channel, did not corrupt the soldiers; and it would be equally a miracle if thus the Indian men were not converted from quietude and docility into tigers." (B. C., *Arch. Sta. Bárbara*, vol. i, p. 240; Palou, *Vida de Serra*, pp. 145, 152–153, 155.) The views of Serra were (later) shared by Garcés. On April 12, 1776, Garcés wrote: "Arrived at a *ranchería* [on the Channel] where the young women were in hiding on account of some experiences they had had on the passing of the soldiers." (*Diario*, E. Coues, *On the Trail of a Spanish Pioneer*, 1900, 2 vols., vol. i, p. 266.)

22. The plan of Echeveste made no provision for a lieutenant, but Ortega was made lieutenant and stationed at San Diego. (Palou, *Noticias*, vol. iii, p. 144.) Serra had asked that Ortega be made comandante to succeed Fages. (*Ibid.*, p. 43.)

23. Palou, *Noticias*, vol. iii, pp. 84–106. By a provision that payment to officers and men (governor and commissary excepted) be made in goods at an advance, in Lower California, of 100 per cent on original cost, and in Alta California of 150 per cent, a saving of 27,168 *pesos* was effected, which wrought a reduction in the total cost to the government. This total, according to Bancroft (*Hist. of California*, vol. i, pp. 211–214), was 90,476 *pesos*, and according to Revilla Gigedo (*Informe* of 1793; Translation, *Land of Sunshine*, vol. xi, p. 37), 92,476 *pesos*.

24. Anza, J. B., to Viceroy Juan Antonio (M. A., Arch. Genl., *Prov. Int.* 245).

25. Anza Sr.'s request was first referred to the Audiencia of Guadalajara, and on April 11, 1737, a report by Juan de Oliván Rebolledo (*oydor*) was returned, reciting: That in 1715 the Jesuit padre Agustín de Campos had written to the Viceroy Duque de Linares, asking that the *comisario-general* of the Franciscans consent to allow him to pass from Pimería Baja (under Jesuit control) to Pimería Alta (under Franciscan control), there to preach *la ley Santa de Dios* to the Indians of the Sierra Azul and kingdom of Moqui. Consent was refused, but later, the Bishop of Durango having been consulted by the King, there was issued (1732) a *cédula* sending forth to Pimería Alta three or four Jesuits, under escort of Juan Bautista de Anza, who at the same time was *á descubrir las tierras* (from Fronteras) *al Rio Colorado* and to the Red Sea, and to determine whether California was an island. (M. A., Arch. Genl., *Historia*, 396.) The *junta* was to consult the Bishop of Durango and the prelate of the missions. (*Cédula* of 1738, *Ibid.*)

26. F. Garcés, *Diario*, August 8 to October 27, 1771 (M. A., Arch. Genl., *Historia*, 396); Juan D. Arricivita, *Crónica Seráfica y Apostólica del Colegio de Propaganda Fide de la Santa Cruz de Querétaro*, Mexico, 1792, chap. xvii, pp. 418–426, — translated in part, E. Coues, *Trail of a Spanish Pioneer*, vol. i, pp. 30–38.

27. Mr. James B. Ainza of San Francisco, who claims descent from Juan Bautista de Anza, states (San Mateo *Leader*, Oct., 1909) that his ancestor

was born at Arizpe in 1715, and was educated at the College of San Ildefonso, Mexico City.

28. Dr. H. E. Bolton, of Leland Stanford University, is engaged upon a study of this *entrada* of Garcés.

29. Anza to Bucarely, letter May 2, 1772 (M. A., Arch. Genl., *Historia*, 396).

30. M. Costansó to the Sr. Fiscal (Areche), Sept. 5, 1772. There were, said Costansó, three points to be considered: (1) The distance to be traversed; (2) the likelihood that the Pimas of the Gila and Colorado had news of the Monterey establishments; (3) the attainability and utility of communication with these establishments by way of Sonora. There would be difficulty in crossing the mountains, but passes used by the Indians no doubt existed. It was to be borne in mind that Northern California was poor in products, and that if succored from Loreto, it must, as far even as San Diego, be by a rough road (*áspero camino*) of 300 leagues; and if by sea from San Blas, over a course long and difficult, and in ships so small as not to be fitted to carry families for settling the land. If succored from Sonora, not only might every kind of grain and fruit be obtained, but this by a way not immoderate for length, and that would admit of the passage of families. (M. A., Arch. Genl., *Historia*, 396.)

31. The *fiscal* having on Oct. 12, 1772, reported favorably on Anza's project, Bucarely, on Oct. 13, called a *junta* for the 17th. By this body it was decided to ask the opinion of the Governor of Sonora. His reply (M. Santre to Bucarely) bore date Jan. 27, 1773. (*Ibid.*)

32. The influence of Serra in securing a determination of the matter is mentioned by Palou (*Noticias*, vol. iii, p. 155). Direct evidence of it is furnished by Arriaga in a dispatch to the Viceroy, dated March 9, 1774, which refers to a letter from Bucarely of date Sept. 26, 1773, wherein the latter had said that *haviendo oydo al Presidente de las Misiones de San Diego y Monterey, Fr. Junípero Serra, que apoyó el pensamiento de Anza, convocó V. E. á Junta de Guerra*, etc. (M. A., Arch. Genl., *Californias*, 72). At about the time of Serra's conferences with the Viceroy, Anza (March 7, 1773), replying to queries, wrote praising the padres as pioneers. A poor missionary on a poor horse was able to demonstrate that the Indians, if only well treated, were prone to be friendly. And he (Anza) had faith in Padre Garcés, whose reports regarding the Colorado River were most thorough of all. As to whether missions by the Dominicans on the further (California) side of the Colorado might be serviceable, he could not determine; but he thought that it might be necessary to erect missions on the Sonora side. If so, soldiers could be taken from the presidios San Miguel (Horcasitas) and Buenavista, which now were in a condition of tranquillity (M. A., Arch. Genl., *Historia*, 396). A little later (May 8), Garcés wrote to the Viceroy. He did not think Anza's expedition would be prejudicial to the Dominican missions, as they were far distant and among natives who were enemies to

the Yumas, through whose country Anza would pass. Communication, he thought, could be maintained by the existing presidios, Altar, San Miguel, and Buenavista. (*Ibid.*)

It is stated by Palou (*Noticias*, vol. iii, p. 154) that Anza had applied to Gálvez for permission to join the *Santa Expedición* of 1769 with a force from Tubac, but had been refused. In none of the correspondence in the Mexican Archives have I found allusion to such a request, save the following by Garcés in his letter of May 8: *Atendiendo tambien á que dicho capitán (segun me dijó) havía procurado hacer este gran servicio en tiempo de los Padres Jesuitas por cuio Visitador no tubó efecto*, etc.

33. J. B. Anza, *Diario de la Expedición que practicó por Tierra, el año de '74, el Teniente Coronel Don Juan Bautista de Anza á los Nuevos Establecimientos de la California* (M. A., Arch. Genl., *Historia*, 396); a careful rendering of the substance of the Diary by Zoeth S. Eldredge (*Journal of American History*, 1908–1909). On supplies, etc., at Altar. Anza to Bucarely, Jan. 18, 1774 (M. A., Arch. Genl., *Cor. de Virreyes*, vol. liv, sér. ii, vol. xxxvii, no. 1389). See also Palou, *Noticias*, vol. iii, pp. 152–160. For route, see general map (pocket).

34. Anza, *Diario;* F. Garcés, *Diario de la Entrada que se practicó á fin de abrir camino por los Ríos Gila y Colorado, para los Establecimientos de San Diego y Monterey* (M. A., Arch. Genl., *Historia*, 52; J. C. Arricivita, *Crónica Seráfica*, lib. iv, cap. i, pp. 450–56). Garcés says (Feb. 7) that he first met Palma on Aug. 24, 1771, on the occasion of his *entrada* of that year among the Yumas. The meeting is described in Garcés's Diary for 1771 (M. A., Arch. Genl., *Historia*, 396; Arricivita, *Crónica Seráfica, supra*).

35. Anza to Bucarely, Sitio de San Dionisio, Feb. 9, 1774. Díaz in 1540 had crossed the stream into the peninsula with royal troops. As to the crossing in 1774, Bernardo de Urrea to Bucarely, Altar, Feb. 22, and Governor Francisco Antonio Crespo to the same, Horcasitas, Feb. 25 (M. A., Arch. Genl., *Cor. de Virreyes*, vol. liv, sér. ii, vol. xxxvii, no. 1389).

Anza and Garcés both mention the striking scenery of the region (that of Fort Yuma). Pilot Knob and Chimney Rock are mentioned by Garcés as having been noted by him in 1771. Now (1774) they were named Cabeza del Gigante (Giant's Head) and la Campaña (the Bell), respectively. (Garcés, *Diario*, Feb. 9; Anza, *Diario*, Feb. 9.) In 1702, when in this locality on the way to the Quiquimas with Padre Gonzáles, Kino described "some very mighty rocks which seemed to have been made by hand with very great art."

36. From Santa Olaya, Anza, on Feb. 28, wrote to the Viceroy. He spoke of the *leguas de Medaños ó Arenales intrancitables* (impassable sand hills), to avoid which as much as possible he had descended the Colorado; of having left the poorest of his animals and seven of his own men with Palma; and of having no fear of the Cojats (M. A., Arch. Genl., *Cor. de Virreyes*, vol. lv, sér. ii, vol. xxxviii, no. 1421).

37. Anza, *Diario;* Garcés, *Diario*, Feb. 12. Of the Cajuenches, Garcés

says: *Esta nación tiene varios nombres : los Pimas la llaman Cojat, y á los que vivan en la sierra, llaman los de los Zapatos de mezcal ó, mas propriamente, Guarachas.* "But the Yumas call them Axagueches, and they say that this nation is the one that extends to San Diego."

38. Anza and Garcés, *Diarios.*

39. Anza, *Diario;* Garcés, *Diario;* Juan Díaz, *Diario en el viage para abrir camino de la Provincia de la Sonora á la California Septentrional y puerto de Monterey,* etc., 1774 (M. A., Arch. Genl., *Historia,* 396). Garcés points out that San Jacome had been abandoned, as he discovered later, because of a failure of water.

40. It has been shown by Mr. Zoeth S. Eldredge, in his rendering of Anza's Diary of 1774, that the statement by Bancroft (*History of California,* vol. i, p. 223) that Anza crossed by the San Gorgonio Pass (route of the Southern Pacific Railroad) is probably erroneous (*Journal of American History,*1908).

41. Both Anza and Garcés wax enthusiastic over the beauty of the region about San Jacinto Lake. Nor were they unmindful of the mineral deposits of the country, for both mention a specimen of silver ore (*metal de plata*) which had been found (*Diarios,* March 16, 18).

As traced by Mr. Eldredge, the route of Anza was as follows: San Felipe River, Coyote Cañon, Horse Cañon, Vandeventer Flat, San Carlos Pass, Hemet Reservoir (Laguna del Príncipe), San Jacinto (San José) River, and San Jacinto Lake (Laguna de San Antonio de Bucareli). In June, 1910, the writer personally verified this route, and it corresponds closely with Anza's description of the route actually taken. San Carlos Pass to-day is a wild region of crags and boulders ("scrap-heap of the world," Font called it), covered thickly with live-oak, red-shank, sage-brush, willow and chimisal, and abounding in rattlesnakes. Vandeventer Flat lies at the foot of Santa Rosa Mountain, a peak of some 8000 feet; Lookout Mountain being considerably to the west of it. Hemet Valley is a long stretch of luxuriant pastures between parallel ridges of mountains, the easterly ridge containing the abandoned silver mine " Garnet Queen." Hemet Reservoir, much shrunken from Anza's Laguna del Príncipe (if such it be), supplies water by a pipe-line to the valley of the San Jacinto River, a stream dry in summer; and San Jacinto Lake (Anza's Laguna de Bucarely) is now locally known as Lake View. Of the gorge of the North Fork of the San Jacinto — a dashing cascaded stream — the Spaniards said not too much when they called it Cañada de Paraíso. For route, see general map (pocket).

42. No instrument for taking altitudes was carried on this expedition, and when San Gabriel was reached, and news received of the presence of the Santiago (with Serra on board) at San Diego, Padre Díaz went to the port to ascertain if an instrument might not be borrowed. An astrolabe was obtained at San Diego Mission, and Díaz, having been instructed in its use, awaited at San Gabriel the return of Anza from Monterey. Henceforth the altitudes were regularly taken (Anza, *Diario,* April 10, May 2, 27). A map

of the return route was made by Díaz, but it has not been found. See, further, Garcés to Viceroy Bucarely, April 27, 1774, "from the beautiful *Playa* of the Junction of the Rivers."

43. Anza, *Diario.* Garcés's Diary ends April 26, 1774, at the Gila-Colorado junction. From San Gabriel, April 10, Anza had written to Bucarely describing his journey to that point (M. A., Arch. Genl., *Cor. de Virreyes*, vol. lv, sér. ii, vol. xxxviii, no. 1421).

44. Palou, *Vida de Serra,* pp. 88–89.

45. P. Fages, *Salida que hizó el theniente de Voluntarios de Cataluña con seis soldados y un Harriero* (M. A., Arch. Genl., *Cor. de Virreyes*, Croix, 1770–71, vol. xiv, serial vol. iv, no. 1176). Printed in full as Appendix B.

P. Fages, *Diario . . . en Busca del Puerto de San Francisco*, March 20 to April 5, 1772. Besides Fages and Crespi, the expedition consisted of 14 soldiers and an Indian servant. On March 26, some very large animals were seen — bears and (from the description) mountain sheep. On the 27th, they saw the "great mouth of the *Estero de San Francisco paralelo á la Enseñada de la Punta de Reyes,* in front of which were *los siete farallones que, el Año de 1769, vimos quando acampamos serca á ella.* Within the *estero* there were seen (the standpoint was the Berkeley side of the bay) five islands, three of which formed a triangle opposite the mouth. On the 29th, San Pablo Bay (*una Baía Grande Redonda*) was observed, and on the 30th, *el Río Grande de Nuestro P. San Francisco* — the San Joaquín. (M. A., Arch. Genl., *Californias,* 66; J. Crespi, *Diario;* Palou, *Noticias,* vol. iii, p. 3; Crespi to Palou, May 21, 1772, Ayer Coll., Newberry Library, — translated, *Out West,* vol. xvi, p. 56.)

46. *que ya llamamos de S^n $Fran^{co}$.*

47. Costansó to Melchior de Paramas, secretary to Viceroy, Oct. 9, 1772 (Ayer Coll.; translated, *Out West,* vol. xvi, pp. 58–59). Map reproduced in *Identification of Sir Francis Drake's Anchorage,* by George Davidson, appendix, no. 15, Pub. Calif. Hist. Soc., pamphlet. (See chart iv, chapter vi, of text.) Costansó's statement and map are at variance with Bancroft's assertions (*History of California,* vol. i, pp. 159, 232) that "it must be borne in mind that the inner bay was not named during this trip [that of Portolá in 1769], nor for some years later"; and (*Ibid.,* p. 245) that "from 1775 the newly found and grand bay bears the name San Francisco, which has before belonged to the little harbor under Point Reyes."

48. On hearing from the deer-hunters of the existence of the *brazo de mar ó estero,* Costansó had said: "We were more and more confirmed in our opinion that we were in the puerto de San Francisco and that this [the *estero*] was that spoken of by the *piloto* Cabrera Bueno in the following words: 'By the gorge [*barranca*] enters an *estero* of salt water without surf. Within we met friendly Indians and easily obtained fresh water and firewood.'" (*Diario,* S. A., Madrid, Direc. de Hid., *Reino de Méjico,* tom. i, C 2^2.)

49. The advisability of a speedy occupation of the shores of the *estero* had indeed been urged by Guardian Verger upon Comisario-General Casafonda shortly after the Fages-Crespi survey. Said Verger in a letter of date Dec. 22, 1772: "Cabrera Bueno locates the Port of San Francisco between Mussel Point and that of Reyes [rather a broad rendering of the Manila pilot's description]. What is to be seen between these two points is *una grande Enseñada*, and we judge that, upon the north side, it affords some protection from the northwest winds, which prevail in these seas almost the entire year, and at that protected spot would be called Puerto de San Francisco, as in the case of the port of Monterey. At the bottom of said *Enseñada* the land opens to the width of a league, and by this opening the sea enters, forming *un brazo ó estero*," etc. "In the named mouth, or opening, there is seen a *farallón* . . . and three Islands, but the entrance does not seem to be obstructed; and, from the fact of whales having entered, there seems to be some depth. . . . But," continues Verger, "if the entrance gives passage to ships, as is very probable, its occupation is highly necessary, for its shores abound in scrub-oak and live-oak for a shipyard. Moreover, the river that empties into the round bay is so copious that some of the explorers say the Ebro is not half so great. This indicates that it may rise in the interior sierras, and come from the East, joining with New Mexico. It also may approach the Colorado. . . . Great prejudice to the Crown of Spain must be feared should some foreign nation establish itself in this port." (M. A., Museo, *Trasuntos*.) The foregoing is Verger's " Carta Octava," to Casafonda, and the difference in tone between it and his " Carta Segunda," wherein the possibility of establishments in Northern California is ridiculed, is noteworthy.

In two dispatches, of dates June 26, and Nov. 26, 1774, the success of Anza was made known by the Viceroy to the King. The question of missions on the Colorado was broached, the importance of a continued good understanding with Palma emphasized, and the relative value of sea route and land routes to Monterey considered. (M. A., Arch. Genl., *Cor. de Virreyes*, vol. lv, sér. ii, vol. xxxviii, no. 1421; *Ibid.*, vol. xli, serial vol. xliv, no. 1609.)

50. Palou to College of San Fernando, April 22, 1774 (M. A., Museo, *Docs. Rel. á las Mis. de Califs.*, Qto ii).

51. Bucarely, Aug. 14, 1773 (M. A., Arch. Genl., *Misiones*, 13); *Instrucción al Comandante de San Diego y Monterey* (B. C., *Mayer MSS.* par. 18). Viceroy to Rivera y Moncada, Sept. 19, 1773; Rivera y Moncada to Viceroy, Oct. 12, 1773 (M. A., Arch. Genl., *Cor. de Virreyes*, vol. xxxi, sér. ii, vol. xiv, f. 143); Viceroy to King, May 27, 1774 (*Ibid.*, serial vol. xxxvii, vol. liv, no. 1389); Rivera y Moncada to Viceroy, June 16, Oct. 8, 1774 (M. A., Arch. Genl., *Californias*, 35). At the time of his appointment as comandante, Rivera had served thirty-two years, his term having begun in 1742.

52. M. A., Arch. Genl., *R. Céd. y Ord.* 104, f. 101.

53. Anza-Bucarely correspondence, and determinations of *junta* (M. A., Arch. Genl., *Prov. Int.* 134); *Testimonio del expediente formado*, etc., *para la Segunda Expedición que deve hacer Don Juan Bautista de Anza, capitán del Presidio de San Ignacio de Tubac, desde él á Monterey*, etc. (*Ibid., Californias*, 72). For the expedition the following were the estimates: (1) *Preparatory to assembling at Tubac:* 30 suits of clothing for men and women, — shirts, drawers, trousers, vests, skirts,· capes, jackets, hose, boots, shoes, *rebozos*, sombreros; clothing for 90 boys and 90 girls; arms, — 20 firelocks, 20 swords, 20 lances, 22 cuirasses, 20 cartridge-boxes with 14 charges, and 30 belts with the name "San Carlos de Monterey"; mounts for men, — 60 horses (two per man), 20 saddles, 20 pairs of spurs, 20 bridles, 20 pairs of cushions; mounts for women, — 60 mares, 30 saddles, 30 bridles; baggage, etc., — 20 mules, 20 outfittings for same, 30 shammy-skin bags; (2) *Seventy days' march to Monterey for 122 individuals:* 1 banner with the royal escutcheon, 11 camp-tents, tools, dishes, money-box with duplicate keys, registry-books; beef-cattle and other provisions, — 100 cows (one per day), flour, 6 boxes of chocolate, 3 demijohns of brandy, ham, sausages, and spices; a table for the comandante and for the saying of Mass; means of transport, — 4 relays of 132 mules, 100 outfittings for same, 20 drivers; provisions for the New Establishments, — 200 head of livestock (bulls and cows); articles for the Indians, — 6 boxes of beads, nearly all red (no black ones), tobacco, and (for Palma) 1 blue woolen cloak trimmed with gold braid, 1 waistcoat and pair of shammy-skin trousers, 2 shirts, 1 cap with escutcheon like that of the dragoons. *Signed :* Juan José de Echeveste, Dec. 5, 1774.

54. In his letters to the King of June 26, and Nov. 26, 1774 (note 49, *ante*), the Viceroy had spoken of the first expedition of Anza as a piece of good fortune reserved for the happy reign of "your Majesty"; for while the idea had been conceived by Anza the father, the execution had been left for Anza the son. Upon the latter, accordingly, it had been deemed fitting that the rank of lieutenant-colonel be conferred. The route to Monterey opened by Anza was styled *camino glorioso*, and the task achieved *prodigiosa operación*.

55. J. B. Anza, *Diario de la Ruta y Operaciones que yo, el Intrascripto Theniente Coronel y Capitán del Real Presidio de Tubac*, etc., *practicé segunda vez . . . á la California Septentrional . . . como consta de Superior Decreto de 24 de Nov. del Año de 1774*, etc. (M. A., Arch. Genl., *Historia*, 396); P. Font, *Diario, borrador* (M. A., Arch. Genl., *Historia*, 24); P. Font, *Diario*, complete (John Carter Brown Library); F. Garcés, *Diario* (M. A., Arch. Genl., *Historia*, 24), — Translation, E. Coues, *On the Trail of a Spanish Pioneer ;* Palou, *Noticias*, vol. iv, pp. 133–160.

56. Palou to Viceroy, Nov. 11, 1776 (M. A., Arch. Genl., *Prov. Int.* 23).

57. Anza, when within two days of San Gabriel on his first expedition, carved in the bark of a huge alder tree the symbol I H S. On the second

expedition, he carved beneath this symbol: *Año 1776 : Vinó la Expedición de San Francisco.* (Font, *Diario*, Jan. 2, 1776.) For route, see general map (pocket).

58. Anza, *Diario*, Jan. 1, 1776. The attack was one of determined ferocity. The few inmates of the mission — three soldiers, two padres (Jayme and Vicente Fuster), two blacksmiths, two boys (a son and nephew of Lieutenant Ortega), eleven in all — were awakened at about one o'clock at night by yells and commotion. Fuster and the men were driven from one cover to another, making a final stand in an adobe magazine, whence with musketry they kept their assailants at bay. As for Jayme, he was found dead in the dry bed of a creek, his body disfigured by blows. (Fuster to Serra, Nov. 28, 1775, M. A., Museo, *Docs. Rel. á las Mis. de Califs.*, Qto ii; J. F. Ortega, *Informe*, Nov. 30, 1775 (B. C.); Palou, *Noticias*, vol. iv, pp. 118–127.)

59. Fuster to Serra, Nov. 28, 1775 (M. A., Museo, *Docs. Rel. á las Mis. de Califs.*, Qto ii); F. F. Lasuén, to Guardian Pangua, Aug. 17, 1775 (*Ibid.*). Lasuén to Juan Prestamero, Jan. 28, 1776, telling of cessation of work on San Juan Capistrano at news of massacre, and of burying the bells of the proposed mission to save them. If work is not to be resumed, Lasuén wishes to retire to his college. (*Ibid.*)

60. Rivera y Moncada, writing to Padre Fuster, March 27, 1776, states that news of the San Diego affair was brought to him at Monterey on the evening of December 13, 1775, between seven and eight o'clock, by a squad of six soldiers commanded by Lieutenant Ortega. (M. A., Museo, *Docs. Rel. á las Mis. de Califs.*, Qto ii.)

61. Font, *Diario* (complete).

62. Anza, *Diario*, Jan., Feb., March, 1776; Palou, *Noticias*, vol. iv, p. 139, etc.

63. Palou, *Diario* (*Noticias*, vol. iii, p. 261); translated by Frank de Thoma, MS. 1899, Macdonald Coll. According to Palou, Rivera y Moncada on this occasion closely reconnoitred the estuary, pronouncing the mouth half a league wide, and stating that within was an island, and behind the island a very large bay of smooth water. Horses, Palou thought, if guided by skiffs, might be swum across the mouth of the estuary. Indeed, when seen near by, the mouth was only one quarter of a league in width. "Considering," he said, "that the cliff of the strait, or mouth, of the estuary of San Francisco is the extreme point of the land, and that up to the present day no Spaniard or any other Christian has set his foot upon it, it seemed proper to the commander and to me to plant the standard of the Holy Cross on its summit." Much notice, moreover, was taken of the redwoods. "In a *cañada* having a dense growth of timber, we came to a gigantic tree, the inside burned out, and the hollow trunk resembling a cave. One of the soldiers, mounted on horseback, rode into it, saying, 'Now I have a house if it should rain.'"

64. Palou, *Vida de Serra*, p. 202. The instructions were, that he *pasase*

*al Puerto de San Francisco de ver si tenía entrada por la canal ó garganta
que de tierra se había visto.*

65. The name Golden Gate was originated by John C. Frémont. On his map of California and Oregon, published in 1848, the Greek form "Chrysopylæ" was used. In his *Geographical Memoir*, published at the same time, Frémont stated that Chrysopylæ (Golden Gate) had been applied to the entrance of San Francisco Bay for reasons (advantages of the bay for commerce) similar to those for which Chrysoceros (Golden Horn) had been applied to the harbor of Byzantium, now Constantinople. (30th Cong., 1st Sess., *Senate Docs., Mis.*, no. 143, p. 32.)

66. Log of the San Carlos (summary), report of Ayala, report of Cañizares, and map of the port of San Francisco from Archivo General de las Indias, Sevilla, edited by Z. S. Eldredge and E. J. Molera, *March of Portolá*, etc., San Francisco, 1909; Palou, *Noticias*, vol. iv, pp. 72–74, 102–103. Bucarely to King, Nov. 26, 1775, announces return of Ayala to San Blas, after having visited *el Puerto de San Francisco*. The diaries of Ayala and of his *piloto* Cañizares are highly commended for their information. By Cañizares and Juan Bautista Aguirre, the estuary was thoroughly explored, with the result that it was affirmed to be "not one port, but many with a single entrance." (M. A., Arch. Genl., *Cor. de Virreyes*, sér. i, vol. ii, no. 2032, f. 221.)

67. Palou, *Noticias*, vol. iv, pp. 100–102.

68. See chart v (Ayala), pp. 109–110 of text. Anza, *Diario*. Anza's first sight of the estuary was obtained on March 25, and it is worthy of note that he speaks of it as coming or extending from the Port of San Francisco, — *el Estero que sale del Puerto*, etc. According to Palou, Mission Bay received its name Los Dolores, from the circumstance that Aguirre had observed three Indians weeping on its shores. (*Noticias*, pp. 103, 142–43; but see Font, *Diario*.)

69. Anza, *Diario;* Font, *Diario ;* Palou, *Noticias*, vol. iv, pp. 144–160.

70. For sketch, see text, p. 111.

71. Rivera, on March 27, had presented to Fuster a paper containing a formal statement of his reasons for his conduct in seizing Carlos. The paper was attested by Raphael de Pedro y Gil and Hermenegildo Sal. It charged Carlos, Carlos's brother Francisco, and another neophyte, Rafael, with having planned and brought about *la perdición, ruina, y destrucción* of the mission, and the deaths of Jayme and of the blacksmith and carpenter, — crimes for which right of asylum "could not be pleaded." Under Bulls by Popes Gregory XIV, Benedict XIII, Clement XII, and Benedict XIV, murderers, robbers, mutilators, forgers, heretics, traitors, etc., were denied the privilege of asylum. Besides, the place where Carlos had taken refuge was not a church but a storehouse (*almacén*). (M. A., Museo, *Docs. Rel. á las Mis. de Califs.*, Qto ii.) On April 3, Fuster wrote in great detail about the matter to Guardian Franc⁰ Pangua, of the College of San Fernando. Find-

ing Carlos in the church on March 27, he had informed Rivera, but, the case being one upon which he was in doubt, he had asked time to present it to the Bishop at Durango. This not being acceptable, he had consulted Lasuén and Amurrio (who were waiting to take charge of San Juan Capistrano). Rivera, pursuing the matter, had demanded a prompt answer. A paper had been given him, but he, declaring the whole affair an Indian trick, had run out a cannon and ordered the troop under arms. Fuster thereupon had rung the bell for prayer. Just as prayer was begun, Rivera had come with sword, staff, and a lighted candle. He had surrounded the building with soldiers, had entered with the candle in his hand, and with help from the soldiers had seized and bound Carlos. Thereupon he (Fuster) had called upon all to witness that, by decree of three Supreme Pontiffs, excommunication was *ipso facto* incurred by *los jueces seculares* who took from a church a refugee, without license from the Bishop. The Church of God, he had said, was not guarded after the manner of a castle. Rivera at the doorway had protested that "naught was intended by him against our Mother the Church." Fuster, then, in the presence of the *pobres Indios escandalizados*, had closed the church. (*Ibid.*) For his conduct, Rivera on May 13, at San Diego, offered to Fuster a bantering apology. His temper, he said, was not stern, but, if crossed, it seemed so, —well, he relished jokes and a laugh. He was charged with having ordered his men to arms, but had not Cortés, upon a time, done this in the case of the Toltecs, saying, "It was a token of a *fiesta*, or holiday, for Spaniards to go armed"? (*Ibid.*)

As for Bucarely, he virtually was on the side of the padres, for on April 13, he had written to Serra that he had ordered Rivera to use measures of conciliation with the Indians. The words of the Viceroy were urgently commended to Rivera by Serra in a letter from San Diego, dated Oct. 5, 1776. The advice of the latter was to capture the leaders, assemble the Indians, explain the power of the King, then show mercy. "Thus will be exemplified the law which we enjoin upon them, to return good for ill and forgive their enemies." (M. A., Museo, *Docs. Rel. á las Mis. de Califs.*, Qto ii.) The outcome was a release of all prisoners (Carlos presumably included) in 1777, after the delivery to them of such a harangue as Serra had counseled. (B. C., *Prov. Rec.*, vol. i, p. 60.)

72. Anza, *Diario;* Font, *Diario.*

73. Garcés, *Diario*, translated by E. Coues; Garcés to Bucarely, Jan. 12, 1776, from Yuma, stating that he has been down the Colorado, having passed among the Cajuenches, Jallicuamais or Quiquimas, and Culapas, to the beaches of the sea, the waters whereof he has seen and enjoyed, especially in their flux and reflux. "All the nations await with joyful expectation the coming of the padres." (M. A., Arch. Genl., *Historia*, 52.)

74. The following is the description of the Tulare Valley by Fages: "The San Francisco [San Joaquín], which discharges into the estuary of that name, is more than 120 leagues in length by (in places) 15 or 20 in width, and it

winds through a plain which is a labyrinth of lagoons and tulares. The plain is thickly peopled, having many and large *rancherias ;* and it abounds in grain, deer, bear, geese, ducks, cranes, indeed every kind of animal, terrestrial and aërial. In the *rancherias,* in winter, the Indians live in large halls, the families separated from each other; and outside are their houses, spherical in form, where their grains and utensils are kept. The people are good-looking, excellently formed, frank and liberal. Theft does not seem to be practiced, and they use large stones for grinding. . . . The past year [1772], going in pursuit of deserters, I passed to the eastward of San Diego 50 leagues. Lack of water forced us to the Sierra, and we descended to the plain opposite to the mission of San Gabriel. We then followed the edge of the plain toward the north, about 25 leagues, to the pass of Buenavista. For most of the 25 leagues we traveled among date-palms; and to the east and south the land was more and more a land of palms, but seemed very scarce of water. Over all the plain we saw not a little smoke." (San Carlos, Nov. 27, 1773, M. A., Arch. Genl., *Californias,* 66.)

Fages's survey of the Tulares was from the vicinity of Buena Vista Lake. He describes the spot as seven leagues (18.41 miles) to the north of Buena-vista Pass (Tehachapi?). Most of his journey, however, was to the south of Tehachapi, and in the desert.

75. Palou, *Noticias,* vol. iii, pp. 41, 69, 78.

76. Crespo to Bucarely, Altar, Dec. 15, 1774 (M. A., Arch. Genl., *Historia,* 25). In an elaborate report to Bucarely, by Padre Díaz, from Ures on March 21, 1775, a route westward from New Mexico is advised, and the hope expressed that Crespo may be commissioned to explore it. (M.A., Arch. Genl., *Prov. Int.* 88.)

77. S. V. Escalante y F. A. Domínguez, " Diario . . . para descubrir el Camino desde . . . Santa Fé del Nuevo Mexico al de Monterey " (*Docs. para la Historia de Méjico,* sér. ii, tom. i, pp. 375–558); Coues, *Trail of a Spanish Pioneer,* vol. ii, p. 469; Bancroft, *History of Utah,* pp. 7–18.

S. V. Escalante to Pedro Fermín de Mendinueta (Governor of New Mex-ico), Guadalupe de Zuñi, Oct. 28, 1775, states that at the end of June, 1775, he made a tour of exploration toward Monterey, but not being able to cross the Río Grande de los Cominas (the Colorado), he for eight days examined the situation, defenses, water-supply, and means of subsistence of the Moqui pueblos. Forty-six leagues (120.98 miles) to the west of Zuñi he found seven pueblos distributed on three plateaus. On the first were Tanos (Teguas), 110 families; a new foundation by the Moquis of Gualpi, 15 families; and a third pueblo of 200 families. On the second plateau were the fourth pueblo (Mesaznabi), 50 families; the fifth (Xipaolabi), 14 families; and the sixth (Xongopabi), — better situated than any of the others, — 60 families. Two and one half leagues away lay the third plateau, and here was situated the pueblo (Oraibe), the best-constructed and best-known Moqui town in the Provincias Internas. It contained eleven sections with regular streets, and a population of about 800 families. On this third plateau were six great cisterns, in which, when it snowed or rained, quantities of water were gathered. To the east of Moqui were the Navajóes; to the west and northwest the Cominas; to the north the Iutas, with the Apaches of the Gila; and to the southwest the Mezcaleros, or, in Moqui speech, Ióchies and Tasabuez. The Moquis were much civilized, and diligent in weaving and cultivating the soil. They raised abundant harvests of maize, frixol, and chile, and grew some cotton. . . . The Moquis had proved obstinate and should be reduced by force. . . . They could be overcome by cutting them off from their watering places. . . . A presidio would be needed to keep them in subjection. Captain D. Francisco Antonio Crespo advised a Monterey connection *via* the Colorado, the Galchedunes, the Cominas, and Moqui, but this would be over an intolerable course. He (Escalante) would advise a course *via* the Iutas Payuchis, who, according to the map of the engineer Lafora, were in the same latitude as Monterey. [The Lafora map has been found in the Mexican Archives by Dr. H. E. Bolton.] (M. A., Arch. Genl., *Historia*, 25.)

Escalante y Domínguez to Governor Pedro Fermín de Mendinueta, Zuñi, Nov. 25, 1776. This communication states that the party of July 29, 1776, taking a course north-northwest, came at length to the Yutas, and afterwards to the Comanches Yamparicas and the great river which divides the Yuta and Comanche nations. Pressing further to the north and northeast, they attained latitude 41° 19', their highest point; then, passing the river, they kept west-southwest until, at 316 leagues from Sta. Fé, they reached the great valley and laguna of the Tympanogotzis, to which they gave the name of Nuestra de la Merced [Utah Lake]. "The valley," declares the two padres, "is bounded on the west by a *dilatada sierra* that runs to the northeast. It is so extensive and so fertile that there might be planted in it, and subsisted from it, a province like New Mexico." From Lake Merced the party set out in a southwesterly direction for Monterey; but having given largely of their provisions to the Yutas, and having encountered snow and cold almost intolerable, they (despite good fortune in killing two bison) turned backward from latitude 38° — by the Río Grande de Cojnina," for Moqui and Zuñi. The opinion is expressed that, to reach Monterey, from Lake Merced, would be a task easily accomplished even by a small party. (M. A., Arch. Genl., *Historia*, 52.) On the same date as the above, Domínguez wrote to the provincial of the Franciscans of New Mexico, Fray Isidro Murillo. Both communications stated that the Yutas and Comanches had heard naught of the Monterey settlements, and that at none of the Moqui pueblos were any willing to receive the Gospel. (*Ibid.*)

78. It will be remembered that as early as May 21, 1774, Garcés had been seeking to open communication with New Mexico, by means of a letter passed thither by the hands of the Moquis. What became of this letter we are not informed; but in 1776, having reached Moqui himself, he successfully dispatched thence a letter to the minister at Zuñi. (E. Coues, *Trail of a Spanish Pioneer*, vol. ii, p. 380, n. 17.) For route, see general map (pocket).

79. Garcés, *Diario;* Translation, E. Coues, vol. ii, p. 438.

80. Palou, *Noticias,* vol. iv, pp. 162–182. Fuster to Guardian Pangua, Sept. 29, 1776, — letter from San Gabriel describing arrival of the San Carlos and Príncipe at Monterey, June 3, 1776, and departure therefrom, on the 17th, of Anza's people for the founding of San Francisco. (Moraga, *Informe* of 1777, B. C.) For list of the founders see Appendix D.

81. Bucarely to King, Aug. 27, 1776. (M. A., Arch. Genl., *Cor. de Virreyes,* vol. lxxxii, sér. ii, vol. lxv, no. 2429.) From the affair of Carlos, it becomes apparent that the relation of State Secular to State Sacerdotal in Alta California was quite as strained under Rivera y Moncada as it had been under Fages. Indeed, the complaints of padres against Rivera were constant. See letters: Oct. 2, 1776, Lasuén to Pangua, on insolence of Rivera to padres, and insubordination of Ignacio Vallejo. (M. A., Museo, *Doc. Rel. á las Mis. de Califs.,* Qto ii.)

82. Palou, *Noticias,* vol. iv, secs. xiii, xxi; *Vida de Serra,* pp. 207–214, 224.

CHAPTER VII

THE PROVINCIAS INTERNAS

NEW CHAPTER SOURCES: Lacy-Grimaldi correspondence in full, 1773–74; Pérez, *Diario*, 1774 (M. A.); Crespi and Peña, *Diarios*, 1774, with translations in Sutro volume of Publications of the Historical Society of Southern California; Bucarely correspondence on Pérez expedition, 1774–76; settlers and ship's company, Santiago, 1774 ; Heceta, *Diario ;* Campa's account of discovery of Trinidad Bay, 1775 ; Bucarely correspondence on Heceta-Quadra expedition, 1774–76; Bucarely correspondence on Byng-Cook expeditions, 1776; on ships to be built at Lima, 1776, and on Arteaga expedition, 1779; Arteaga, Maurelle, and Quadra, *Diarios;* Bucarely on removal of Barri; Instructions to Neve, as governor of Alta California, Dec. 25, 1776 (M. A.); Instructions to Caballero de Croix, 1776 (Harvard University, Sparks Collection); Garcés, *Diario* (M. A.),— Translation, Coues, *On the Trail of a Spanish Pioneer;* Font, *Diario*, complete (John Carter Brown Library); Anza-Crespo-Díaz-Oconor correspondence, and Palma petition for Gila-Colorado presidios, 1775–76; Vicente de Mora, *Diario* of peninsular trip, 1774–75 (M. A.); Morfi's report to Bucarely, 1777 (Ayer Collection, Newberry Library); Barbastro and Neve on massacre by Yumas (M. A.); Croix, report to King, 1781 (S. A.); Letter, Serra to Bucarely, 1778; Report of Treasury Department on California, 1777 (M. A.). (Specific citations below.)

1. M. A., Arch. Genl., *R. Céd. y Ord.* 102, f. 168. Concerning the Laws of the Indies on navigating the Pacific, see chapter IX of text, n. 8.

2. Lacy to Grimaldi, Feb. 7, 1773 (*Ibid.*, 102, f. 178).

3. Lacy to Grimaldi, May 7 and 11, 1773 (M. A., Arch. Genl., *R. Céd. y Ord.* 103, f. 238; *Ibid.*, *Historia*, 61, "Viajes y Descubrimientos," i; summary, B. C., Pinart *Papeles ;* Bancroft, *History of the Northwest Coast*, vol. i, p. 150, n. 20).

4. The maps presumably were G. H. Muller's, Amsterdam, 1766, and J. von Staehling's in *The New Northern Archipelago;* Translation from German edition, London, 1774. (Staehling map, Macdonald Coll., Oakland.) On Dec. 27, 1773, Viceroy Bucarely wrote to the King that hardly had there been time to make "a copy of the new map published in Russia this year, which, because it differed from that of 1758, it had seemed to him necessary for Pérez to take with him." (M. A., Arch. Genl., *Cor. de Virreyes*, ser. i, vol. ii, no. 1224, 60, f. 58.)

5. J. Pérez, *Diario* (M. A., Arch. Genl., *Historia*, 62) ; Pérez and Martínez, *Diario* (M. A., Arch. Genl., *Historia*, 61).

J. Pérez, "Relación del Viaje" (B. C., *Viajes al Norte* — copied from the Spanish Archives — no. 1; Bancroft, *History of the Northwest Coast*, vol. i,

p. 151, n. 23). Crespi, *Diario* (Palou, *Noticias*, vol. iii, p. 164); Peña and Crespi, *Diarios*, with translations (Sutro vol., Publications of the Historical Society of Southern California, p. 83 etc.). Bucarely to King, series of nine letters on Pérez expedition, July 27, 1773, to Sept. 28, 1774 (M. A., Arch. Genl., *Cor. de Virreyes*, sér. i, vol. xi, no. 1086, 57, f. 54 ; *Ibid.*, no. 1104, 58, f. 55; *Ibid.*, no. 1182, 59, f. 56; *Ibid.*, no. 1562, 80, f. 110; *Ibid.*, no. 1608, 94, f. 123; *Ibid.*, no. 1259, 62, f. 60; *Ibid.*, no. 1224, 60, f. 58; *Ibid.*, no. 1048, 56, f. 50; *Cor. de Virreyes*, 1774, vol. lviii, serial vol. xli, no. 1519, f. 1). *Instrucción que debe observar el Alférez . . . Juan Pérez*, Dec. 24, 1773 (M. A., Arch. Genl., *Historia*, 61, "Viajes y Descubrimientos," i). List of settlers and ship's company in detail, with two short notes by Serra to Bucarely, Jan. 7 and 27, 1774. (*Ibid.*)

6. Bucarely to King, reciting order of 24th of Aug., 1773 (M. A., Arch. Genl., *Cor. de Virreyes*, sér. i, vol. ii, no. 1182, 59, f. 56; *Ibid.*, no. 1608, 94, f. 123).

7. B. Heceta, *Diario* (M. A., Arch. Genl., *Historia*, 24, 324).

B. Heceta (B. C., *Viajes al Norte*, nos. 2, 3; Bancroft, *History of the Northwest Coast*, vol. i, p. 159, n. 36; Palou, *Noticias*, vol. iv, p. 75). Heceta, *Diario;* translation by Greenhow of part relating to discovery of the Columbia (*Oregon and California*, 1845, Appendix E). Miguel de la Campa to Guardian Pangua, Carmelo, Oct. 12, 1775, brief report of discovery of bay to which the name Trinidad was given (M. A., Museo, *Docs. Rel. á las Mis. de Califs.*, Qto ii).

8. Bucarely to King, series of eight letters on Heceta-Quadra expedition, Dec. 27, 1774, to Nov. 26, 1776 (M. A., Arch. Genl., *Cor. de Virreyes*, sér. i, vol. ii, no. 1815, 109, f. 189; *Ibid.*, no. 2032, 133, f. 221; *Ibid.*, no. 2033, 134, f. 223; *Ibid.*, no. 2034, 135, f. 224; *Ibid.*, no. 2073, 124, f. 231; *Ibid.*, no. 2031, 132, f. 220; *Cor. de Virreyes*, 1775, vol. lxv, serial vol. xlviii, no. 1752, f. 1; *Ibid.*, no. 1753). On March 27, 1775, Bucarely advises the King that three days out from San Blas the commander of the San Carlos, Miguel Manrique, had become insane, and that Ayala had been substituted in the command. On Dec. 27, 1775, Bucarely expresses the opinion that " if not wholly disproved by this voyage, it at least has been reduced to a very slender possibility that there leads westward any pass from Hudson's Bay." He furthermore approves a recommendation by Heceta that the port of Trinidad be fortified. On Nov. 26, 1776, Bucarely writes in the strongest terms of the courage and resourcefulness of Bodega y Quadra, and recommends him for promotion. In a letter of Aug. 27, 1775, the Viceroy reports the cost of Pérez's expedition as 15,455 *pesos*, and that of Heceta and Quadra as 11,215 *pesos.* (M. A., Arch. Genl., *Cor. de Virreyes*, Bucarely, 1775, vol. lxx, serial vol. liii, no. 1939, f. 8.)

9. Gálvez to Bucarely, Jan. 9, 1777 (M. A., Arch. Genl., *R. Céd. y Ord.* 110, f. 30).

10. By this time, fear of the English by way of a passage from Hudson's

Bay had practically ceased. Bucarely to King, Sept. 28, 1774 (M. A., Arch. Genl., *Cor. de Virreyes*, sér. i, vol. xi, no. 1562, 80, f. 110).

11. On March 23, 1776 (M. A., Arch. Genl., *R. Céd. y Ord.* 107, f. 198), the King had written to the Viceroy that Captain Cook, under pretext of restoring to the islands of Otaheyti an Indian taken thence on a previous voyage, was to visit the South Sea, but that his real object was to cruise for " our fleet, reconnoitre well the Ladrone Islands, and, passing thence to California, to open commerce with New Mexico and try to find the famous N.W. Passage, in order to gain the reward offered by the House of Commons." Against such attempts the *comandantes de la costa de California* were to be vigilant. Replying to the above on June 26, 1776, Bucarely reviewed the entire California situation: English voyages (from Anson's day) around Cape Horn; Byng's contemplated adventure *via* the North Pole; the proposed occupation of Trinidad Bay against Russia; the question of succor to the missions of Monterey by the San Blas transports or by the Anza route overland from Sonora. The conclusion was that the King should advise distinctly whether he (Bucarely) was to oppose Captain Cook " with force" from the moment he passed Cape Horn, or (the only thing really practicable) to withhold from him supplies and refreshment (M. A., Arch. Genl., *Cor. de Virreyes*, sér. i, vol. xii, no. 2296, 158, f. 21). Directions were sent to the Viceroy, Oct. 18, 1776, to proceed according to the provisions of the Laws of the Indies, whereby " there were to be admitted to California waters only the yearly Manila galleon and the San Blas transports," — a course which would involve the "detaining, seizing, and confiscating" of the interloping ships. (M. A., Arch. Genl., *R. Céd. y Ord.*, 109, f. 102; M. A., Arch. Genl., *Cor. de Virreyes*, no. 2534, 169, f. 41; *Ibid.*, vol. xiii, no. 2702, 187, f. 3; Captain J. Cook, A *Voyage to the Pacific Ocean*, 1785, 3 vols.; secret instructions, in vol. i, pp. xxxii–xxxv.)

12. Bucarely to King, Aug. 27, 1776, reports careening of the Santiago, and need of a vessel to go to Peru to carry the *visitador* for that viceroyalty. (M. A., Arch. Genl., *Cor. de Virreyes*, Bucarely, 1776, vol. lxxxii, serial vol. lxv, no. 2427, f. 5.) Bucarely to King, Sept. 26, 1776, suggests that the Viceroy at Lima (Peru) be instructed to build at Guayaquil two *fragatas* of twenty guns, drawing only twelve feet of water, for San Blas use. (*Ibid.*, vol. lxxxiii, serial vol. lxvi, no. 2507, f. 42.) Beginning Nov. 18, 1776, there was held at Tepic a *junta* of naval officers: Heceta, Quadra, Fernando Quirós, Diego Choquet de Islas, Ignacio Arteaga, Francisco Hijosa, Juan Manuel de Ayala, José de Cañizares, Francisco Antonio Maurelle, Francisco Álvarez Castro, and Juan Bautista de Aguirre. It was decided by this body of capable officers that the Santiago should proceed to Lima with the *visitador*, and that at Lima or Callao there should be constructed two ships fitted for northern explorations and effectively armed. (*Ibid.*, vol. lxxxvi, serial vol. lxix, no. lacking, f. 149.) On March 18, 1778, the King consented to a postponement of the expedition until 1779. (M. A., Arch. Genl., *R. Céd. y Ord.* 113, f. 251.)

13. Arteaga, Maurelle, and Quadra, *Diarios* (M. A., Arch. Genl., *Historia,* 63, 64); *Viajes al Norte,* nos. 4, 5, 6½ (B. C.); Bancroft, *History of the Northwest Coast,* vol. i, p. 173, n. 8. Bucarely to the King, Feb. 24, 1779, stating condition and outfit of the two vessels and fact of their sailing (M. A., Arch. Genl., *Cor. de Virreyes,* Bucarely, 1777, vol. cxvi, serial vol. xcix, no. 4261). Report of voyage, Viceroy Mayorga to the King, Dec. 27, 1779 (*Ibid., Cor. de Virreyes,* vol. cxxv, serial vol. iv, no. 187, f. 294; Palou, *Noticias,* vol. iv, p. 211).

14. Bancroft finds the name used in royal *cédulas,* as an official designation in 1712–13 (*History of North Mexican States and Texas,* vol. i, p. 636, n. 2).

15. In 1729 the number of presidios for New Spain was fixed at twenty — that of Santa Fé being the most remote. In 1766 the Marqués de Rubí inspected by royal order the presidios of Nueva Vizcaya, Sonora, Coahuila, and New Mexico. Of those constituting the New Mexico-Sonora [Arizona] group, Fronteras had been founded between 1680 and 1690, Terrente and Pitic in 1741, Horcasitas between 1746 and 1750, Tubac in 1752, and Altar in 1753–54. Of the Nueva Vizcaya-New Mexico group, Santa Fé had been founded in 1630, Janos between 1680 and 1690, and Paso del Norte in 1682. The two California presidios, Loreto and Cabo San Lucas, had been founded, the one in 1697 and the other in 1735.

16. M. A., Arch. Genl., *Prov. Int.* 154.

17. *Ibid.*

18. Beleña, *Recopilación de Leyes,* i, pt. iii, pp. 290–291. Location of capital confirmed by King, Feb. 12, 1782 [83]. (B. C., *Prov. St. Pap.,* vol. ii, p. 89; iii, p. 182.) On June 22, 1771, Viceroy Croix had written to Minister Arriaga that Arizpe would be a better location for the capital than Caborca. The latter had almost been destroyed by the Apaches. A *jefe superior* was needed in Sonora to aid the Californias, wherein the conquest had now been extended to Monterey. (Harvard Library, Sparks Coll. 98, *Papeles Varios de America,* iii.)

19. Cf. chapters III of text, n. 26, and VIII, n. 15.

20. B. C., *Documents for the History of Chihuahua,* p. 7. In 1794 the practices introduced by Croix were ordered by the King to be discontinued. (*Ibid.,* p. 14.)

Croix's instructions, which bore date, San Ildefonso, Aug. 22, 1776, were addressed to him as *Don Teodoro de Croix, Caballero del Orden Teutonico, Brigadier de mis Exércitos, segundo Teniente de la Compañia Flamenca de mis Rs Guardias de Corps, Governador y Comandante-General en gefe de las Provincias de Sinaloa, Sonora, Californias y Nueva Vizcaya.* It was stated that as early as 1752 it had been proposed to erect a *comandancia-general* for the interior provinces, and that in July, 1769, it had been resolved to do so. Besides the Californias and other provinces named by Gálvez, there were placed under Croix's command the *gobiernos subalternos* of Coahuila, Texas, and New Mexico, with their presidios, and all other presidios situated (under the *Reglamento para Presidios* of Sept. 10, 1772) *en el cordón ó Línea* from the Gulf of the Californias to the bay of Espiritu Santo [Texas, San Antonio River]. (H. E. Bolton, " Spanish Abandonment and Reoccupation of East Texas," *Quarterly of Texas State Hist. Assoc.*, vol. ix, no. 2.) The comandante-general was to be dependent directly upon the King and upon such orders as should reach him *por via reservada de Indias*, but he was to report all matters of consequence to the Viceroy, so that the latter might be informed and lend necessary aid. He was made superintendent of the *Real Hacienda* [Treasury] in the Provincias, and invested with the power of the *Patronato Real*. His capital was fixed at Arizpe in Sonora, as a point "near the frontier of that province, and central as between Nueva Vizcaya and the Californias," — a point, moreover, where he "straightway could be lodged *en la suntuosa casa* used by the *antiguos misioneros*." He was ordered to establish a mint at his capital, and his salary was fixed at 20,000 *pesos* annually. He was to permit judicial appeals to the Audiencia of Guadalajara, but in matters military (*del fuero militar*) and of the *Real Hacienda* he was to act independently, reporting his acts to the King for approval. His personal guard was to consist of an officer and twenty men. In the interior provinces the missionaries were the principal *operarios* for winning the natives to the *Fé Católica*, and their requests should have prompt attention. It should be his especial care to establish, on the *línea de Presidios*, pueblos of Spaniards and of *Indios reducidos*, according to tit. 5, lib. 4, of the *Recopilación de Indias*.

With regard especially to Northern California, Croix was to be diligent in a high degree. He was to "conserve, foment and advance the *nuevas conquistas y Reducciones* effected [there], and also the presidios established in the ports of San Diego and Monterey." He was ordered to "visit and become acquainted with that province as soon as practicable." He was to take steps to assure communication by land between California and Sonora, availing himself of the *noticias, informes, y derroteros* of Don Juan Bautista de Anza. He was also to open communication between the presidio of Monterey and that of Santa Fé in New Mexico. Supplies and families of Spanish settlers for the Californias were to be brought from Sonora and Sinaloa. The naval and supply station of San Blas was to be maintained, and the Viceroy, as heretofore, was to send *memorias*. To the end of good government, the comandante-general was forbidden to accept gifts; and on his travels he was not to be received by pueblos or presidios with *fiestas* or other demonstrations, and his personal household was to be kept at a minimum. (Harvard Library, Sparks Coll. 98, *Papeles Varios de America*, iii.)

21. Instructions to Felipe de Neve, Sept. 30, 1774 (M. A., Arch. Genl., *Prov. Int.* 166, no. 22, par. 25). On Dec. 27, 1774, Bucarely stated to the King that the cause for the change of governors was *discordia . . . entre* [Barri] *y los P. P. Misioneros sobre puntos de jurisdicción* (M. A., Arch.

Genl., *Cor. de Virreyes*, Bucarely, 1774, vol. lxii, serial vol. xlv, no. 1643). The whole matter is set forth by Palou, *Noticias*, vol. iv, pp. 3 *et seq.*

The Barri-Mora conflict drew from the Viceroy an intimation that the power of the padres over the soldiery, and in other temporal respects, was limited. In his instructions to Neve, Bucarely stated that because of the privilege of chastising neophytes accorded to the padres on May 6 [9], 1773 (chapter VI of text, n. 20), it did not follow that the Governor was precluded from *la jurisdicción ordinaria . . . inseparable del empleo de gobernador*. Padres were not to use soldiers, without license of the Governor, except in an urgent and rare case. The power of dispatching boats pertained peculiarly to the Governor. (M. A., Arch. Genl., *Prov. Int.* 166, secs. 13, 14, 15.)

22. M. A., Arch. Genl., *Cor. de Virreyes*, Bucarely, 1776, vol. lxxxi, serial vol. lxiv, no. 2374; *Ibid.*, vol. lxxxii, serial vol. lxv, no. 2429; *Ibid.*, vol. lxxxvi, serial vol. lxix, no. 2636.

23. M. A., Arch. Genl., *Californias*, xiii, no. 32. Neve was to observe and enforce the instructions issued to Rivera y Moncada. In August, 1776, Bucarely had instructed Neve, on arriving at Monterey, to obtain supplies from the Gila and Colorado region, where in May and June there was abundant wheat, and in November and December, corn and beans. (B. C., *Prov. St. Pap.*, vol. i, p. 205.)

24. B. C., *Prov. Rec.*, vol. i, p. 66.

25. B. C., *Prov. St. Pap.*, vol. i, p. 252.

26. Neve to Bucarely, April 15, 1778 (B. C., *Prov. Rec.*, vol. i, p. 8, — translated by J. W. Dwinelle, *Colonial History of San Francisco*, 1863, Ad. v; Palou, *Noticias*, vol. iv, p. 203).

27. Croix to Rivera y Moncada, Arizpe, Dec. 27, 1779 (M. A., Arch. Genl., *Prov. Int.* 122; B. C., *Prov. St. Pap.*, vol. ii, p. 58).

28. Croix to Neve, Dec. 18, 1780 (B. C., *Prov. St. Pap.*, vol. ii, pp. 117–125); Croix to [King], about August, 1781, stating that he has sent to California 59 soldiers, 16 settlers, 65 women, and 89 children — 170 souls (S. A., Madrid, Dirección Hidrografía, *Virreinato de Méjico*, t. i, 9°, Doc. A. 3ª).

29. Neve to Croix, July 14, 1781 (B. C., *Prov. Rec.*, vol. ii, pp. 87–88).

30. *Recopilación de Leyes*, lib. iv, tit. v, ley vi. Towns may be founded by not less than thirty settlers who are to possess, each, a house, ten breeding cows, four oxen, or two oxen and two steers, one brood mare, one breeding sow, twenty breeding ewes of Castilian breed, six hens and one cock. . . . Such towns shall be granted, for occupancy, "four leagues of extent and territory in a square or prolonged form according to the character of the land, etc., with the condition that the limits of said territory shall be distant at least five leagues from any city, town, or village of Spaniards previously founded; and that there shall be no prejudice to any Indian town or private person"; translated, *Colonial History of San Francisco*, Ad. i.

31. *Instrucción para la Fundación de Los Ángeles*, 26 de Agosto, 1781 (B. C., *St. Pap. Miss. and Col.*, vol. i, p. 97; translated in part by Bancroft, *History of California*, vol. i, p. 345, n. 23).

32. B. C., *St. Pap. Miss. and Col.*, vol. i, pp. 105-119; Neve, *Reglamento y Instrucción*, 1781, sec. xiv; Arrillaga, *Recopilación*, 1828, 121-175, — Translation, C. F. Lummis, *Land of Sunshine*, 1897, vol. vi, nos. 2-6.

33. For explanatory definitions of the terms, *solares, suertes, ejidos*, etc., see Dwinelle, *Colonial History of San Francisco*, pp. 7-13.

34. Neve, *Reglamento*, sec. xiv, *supra*, n. 32. On *alcaldes*, etc., see text, chapter iii.

35. Los Ángeles, *padrón*, 1781, in Bancroft, *History of California*, vol. i, p. 345, n. 24.

36. B. C., *Prov. Rec.*, vol. iii, pp. 154-156; *St. Pap. Miss. and Col.*, vol. i, p. 30. Plat of town of San José (B. C., *St. Pap. Miss. and Col.*, vol. i, p. 243). Plats of Los Ángeles (*Prov. St. Pap.*, vol. iii, p. 55; *Prov. St. Pap.* (Benicia), vol. ii, p. 2; *St. Pap. Miss. and Col.*, vol. i, pp. 103, 307). Approval of design for founding Los Ángeles, Gálvez to Viceroy, Feb. 8, 1782 (M. A., Arch. Genl., *R. Cédulas*, 1782, 122, f. 55).

37. Serra to Bucarely, June 30, 1778 (Harvard Library, Sparks Coll. 98, *Papeles Varios de America*, v); Neve to Croix, Aug. 10, 1778 (B. C., *Prov. Rec.*, vol. i, p. 91); Neve to Fages, Sept. 7, 1782 (*Prov. St. Pap.*, vol. iii, p. 145).

38. At the time of the organization of the Provincias, there had been expressly reserved to the Viceroy the control of *memorias* (mission supplies), — a reservation construed by the missionaries as involving control of Mission, as distinguished from military, affairs (Bucarely to Neve, June 3, 1777). Concerning supplies and effects, Neve is not to communicate with the comandante-general, but with the Viceroy as heretofore (B. C., *Prov. Rec.*, vol. i, p. 66). In 1788 the Conde de Gálvez instructed Comandante-General Ugarte y Loyola that the latter had "full powers, though subordinate to the Viceroy, to whom he must report." The latter had "no part in financial administration. It was his business to fight and exterminate or subdue the wild Indians." (B. C., *Mayer MSS*.) On July 10, 1788, Viceroy Flórez wrote Governor Fages that it had been determined by the King himself that the superior government and not the comandante-general of the Provincias Internas was to pay the missionaries within the limits of the *comandancia*. (B. C., *Prov. St. Pap.*, vol. viii, p. 3.)

Facultad de Confirmar (B. C., *Arch. de Sta. Bárb.*, vol. xii, p. 270). What Serra was not willing to recognize was the fact that, in the case of the Provincias Internas, the *Patronato Real* had been attached to the *comandancia-general*; the *Patronato* itself being vested in the comandante-general, and the *vice-patronato* in each of the governors under him; and this not alone with regard to the secular clergy but also the regulars (cf. n. 21, *supra*).

39. Croix to Neve, July 19, 1779 (B. C., *Prov. St. Pap.*, vol. ii, p. 47; *St. Pap. Miss. and Col.*, vol. i, p. 28).

40. *Reglamento, supra*, n. 32. Approved by the King (M. A., Arch. Genl., *R. Cédulas*, 1781, 121, f. 266; *Ibid.*, 122, f. 55).

41. Garcés, *Diario*, 1775–76; Translation, E. Coues, *On the Trail of a Spanish Pioneer*, vol. ii, p. 455; Anza to Bucarely, Mexico, Nov. 20, 1776 (M. A., Arch. Genl., *Prov. Int.* 23). Anza wrote: *La trasladación de los dos Presidios . . . á los Rios Colorado y Gila . . . son* [sic] *indispensables para sobstener y asegurar los Misiones.*

42. Pretensions and activity of the Dominicans: Vicente de Mora, *Diario*, 1774 (M. A., Arch. Genl., *Cor. de Virreyes*, vol. lv, sér. ii, vol. xxxviii, no. 1422, f. 7); Velásquez, *Diario*, 1775 (M. A., Arch. Genl., *Historia*, 52). Cf. chapter vi, n. 8; chapter x, n. 10.

43. J. Díaz, to Bucarely, San Miguel de los Ures, March 21, 1775 (M. A., Arch. Genl., *Prov. Int.* 88, no. 55). In this communication Garcés seems to have joined, but it is distinctively a Díaz production.

44. Crespo to Bucarely, Altar, Dec. 15, 1774 (M. A., Arch. Genl., *Historia*, 25, f. 252); Oconor to Crespo, Tubac, Nov. 25, 1774 (*Ibid.*); Oconor to Mendinueta, Sta. Fé, Nov. 9, 1775 (M. A., Arch. Genl., *Prov. Int.* 169).

45. *Ibid.*

46. B. C., *Reglamento para los Presidios*, etc., *Cédula de 10 de Septiembre de 1772.* Díaz to Bucarely, *supra*, n. 43. Bucarely to the King, letters, May 27, Oct. 27, 1775, reporting request by Díaz and Garcés to change location of presidios from sites as recommended by Inspector Marqués de Rubí. (M. A., Arch. Genl., *Prov. Int.* 23.) Approval by the King of request of padres, Feb. 14, 1776. (*Ibid.*) On objection by Anza, the presidio of Altar was not changed. Reporting on presidios in 1781, Comandante-General Croix digests the recommendations of all previous reports, and designates the following as a correct presidial line: —

San Miguel de Babispe	23 leagues	SO
Fronteras	29 "	O
Santa Cruz	25 "	NO
Nuevo de Buenavista	21 "	NO¼ O
Tupson	26 "	NO
Total of the line	124 "	

— (S. A., Madrid, Direc. Hid., *Virreinato de Méjico*, t. i, 9º, Doc. A 3ª).

47. Rivalry much the same as later between the " Santa Fé " and the "Southern Pacific."

48. Morfi to Bucarely, *Informe*, 1777 (Ayer Collection, Newberry Library).

49. Bucarely to King, Aug. 27, 1776, announcing determination of Palma to accompany Anza to Mexico (M. A., Arch. Genl., *Cor. de Virreyes*, Bucarely, 1776, vol. lxxxii, serial vol. lxv, no. 2429, f. 10). Palma to Bucarely, Nov. 11, 1776, — a letter composed by Anza and signed by Palma with three X marks. This communication sets forth the life-history and creed of the Yuma chief, as interpreted by a Spanish mind. It is not so distinctively Indian as the autobiography of the Sac and Fox chief, Black Hawk, recorded

in 1833 by Antoine Le Claire, Indian agent at Rock Island, Ill., but it is not without interest. It states that its author reigns by right of descent, does not favor polygamy, and worships God, *criador de todos*, whom he calls *Duchi y Pá;* that he came to love Anza because the Spaniards were friends of his allies the Papagos; that Anza had from the first diligently instructed him in religion; that he had aided Anza in effecting a crossing of the Colorado, and that the latter thereupon had named him Salvador [Saviour] Palma, a name he had assumed instead of that given him in his own land, which was Olley-quotequiebe; that he had always kept faith with the Spaniards; that his people number 3000, and that he will be able to reduce neighboring vassal tribes to the Catholic faith and the royal dominion; finally, that he will keep open the way from Sonora and New Mexico to California (M.A., Arch. Genl., *Prov. Int.* 23, no. 7). On Palma's stay in Mexico City, see *Diario Curioso de México de D. José Gómez, Cabo de Alabarderos* (*Docs. para la Historia de México*, 1st ser., vol. i, Mexico, 1854, cited by Coues, *Trail of a Spanish Pioneer*, vol. ii, p. 503, n. 49).

50. M. A., Arch. Genl., *Prov. Int.* 23; *Ibid., R. Céd. y Ord.* 110, f. 193. In the dispatch of Feb. 14, 1777, the King (by Gálvez) gave orders that Palma's request for missions should be granted, after he had been sufficiently instructed "in our sacred religion." The matter of instruction had been dwelt upon in a report to Bucarely by the *fiscal,* dated Nov. 18, 1776, covering Palma's petition of Nov. 11 (M. A., Arch. Genl., *Prov. Int.* 23).

51. J. C. Arricivita, *Crónica Seráfica . . . del Colegio . . . de la Santa Cruz de Querétaro,* pp. 489 *et seq.*

52. It is stated by Croix in his report of 1781 that from 1745 to 1780 comandantes, inspectors, and padres, excepting Ugarte and Rocha, have favored the occupation of the Gila tributary San Pedro, and of the Gila itself. Nobody, however, has from actual personal examination been able to select just the right situations. "We, therefore," proceeds the report, "content ourselves with two pueblos of Spaniards among the Yumas, because these fortunate Indians have embraced [our] religion and vassalage voluntarily. We are postponing the reduction of the Pimas Gileños, of the Cocomari-copas, and of other nations, until such opportune time as God may appoint, and we are rectifying the Apache frontier by removing Horcasitas to Pitic, and by leaving Buenavista where it is." The report then continues: "It not being possible to transfer the [two] presidios to the Colorado, I determined to found two pueblos of Spaniards in the territory of the Yumas. For their security I destined a troop composed of a subaltern, a sergeant, two corporals, and eighteen men from each of the presidios, Altar, Horcasitas, and Buenavista, whose families, with twenty others, will constitute a population augmented by such Gentile Indians as may wish to join. I conferred the political and military command on Lieutenant D. Santiago Islas, and for the spiritual there were named the padres Fr. Francisco Garcés and Fr. Juan Díaz, with a *sínodo* of 400 *pesos* each. . . . The recruiting of families was

happily effected in Pimería Alta, and already they are at their destination with the troop and comandante. They were well received by the Yumas. The family of Captain Salvador Palma, with others of his nation, are now working with ardor in the formation of the pueblo. The troop and settlers have chosen an *habilitado-general*. . . . Doubtless results will be happy, for a union with the Spanish pueblos will foster the docility of the Indians, protect the communication with la Nueva California, render Sonora secure, and eventually New Mexico. These establishments, had the presidios been transferred, would have cost annually 18,998 *pesos, 6 reales ;* but as it is, they will cost only the subsistence of the settlers' families (47 *pesos* for each annually), a sum which as the families become self-supporting will be extinguished. . . . If the Yumas but keep loyal, the banks of the Colorado will soon be covered with fields, cattle, and towns of faithful vassals, whose resources, augmenting those of Sonora, will make for reciprocal defense; as also for the defense of the Californias, to whose jurisdiction [those towns] should belong, by reason of being on the further side of the river marking the limits of Sonora, and at a less distance from Monterey."

By the foregoing there were put in effect almost the exact recommendations of the Franciscan father, signing himself "The most unworthy minister of the Order St. Francis," whose " Brief Reflections " in favor of *custodias* are cited at length in chapter viii of the text, note 9.

53. The news, as first carried to Croix, was that Rivera y Moncada had repulsed the Yuma attack. Says the comandante-general : "Moncada arrived happily at the Colorado, where he intended to winter. I am without other news than that the Apaches made an assault upon him of four hours without inflicting loss. The families of the settlers were already gone, and the expedition was beyond danger. In everything Rivera has conducted himself with his customary zeal, sexagenarian though he be." (S. A., Madrid, Direc. de Hid., *Virreinato de Méjico,* t. i, 9°, Doc. A 3ª.)

54. Arricivita, *Crónica Seráfica,* pp. 504–509. Dr. Elliott Coues, commenting on the massacre, says that he does not know where to find an exact parallel to it in Indian annals.

55. P. Font, *Diario,* complete (John Carter Brown Library); M. A., Arch. Genl., *Historia,* 24, — translated in part, Coues, *On the Trail of a Spanish Pioneer,* vol. i, p. 172, n. 15.

56. Arricivita, *Crónica Seráfica,* pp. 497–504: It is not to be overlooked that by his instructions (*ante,* n. 20) it was enjoined upon Croix to establish pueblo-missions, — missions composed of "Spaniards and of *Indios reducidos.*"

57. Tubutama, Sept. 25, 1781 (M. A., Arch. Genl., *Historia,* 24, f. 66). The four murdered padres were buried in one coffin in the church at Tubutama.

58. Arricivita,*Crónica Seráfica,* etc., pp. 510 *et seq.* ; Council of War, report by Antonio Bonilla, Arizpe, Sept. 10, 1781 (B. C., *St. Pap.* (Sacramento),

vol. vi, p. 124); Neve to Croix, Nov. 18, 1781 (*Prov. St. Pap.*, vol. ii, p. 69); Same to Same, March 10, 1782 (*Prov. Rec.*, vol. i, p. 76); Fages to Fray Agustín Morfi, Pitic, Feb. 12, 1782 (M. A., Arch. Genl., *Historia*, 24, f. 66); Examination of survivors of massacre (B. C., *Prov. St. Pap.*, vol. iii, pp. 319–32; Palou, *Noticias*, vol. iv, p. 228).

59. Correspondence, Neve-Croix (B. C., *Prov. St. Pap.*, vol. iii, pp. 236–39, 182–83, 185, 198–207; *Prov. Rec.*, vol. ii, pp. 47, 53, 57, 65–66; *Crónica Seráfica*, p. 514). The fact is strongly emphasized by Arricivita that the pueblo plan was contrary to the Laws of the Indies, because natives and Spaniards were permitted to dwell together.

60. June 3, 1777 (B. C., *Prov. Rec.*, vol. i, p. 70).

61. Neve . . . *al Comandante del Presidio de Sta. Bárbara* (B. C.).

62. Pangua-Mayorga Correspondence (B. C., *Arch. Sta. Bárb.*, vol. i, pp. 231–46; vi, 266–71). On Jan. 8, 1783, Guardian Pangua instructed President Serra not to consent to founding of presidio and missions on Sta. Bárbara Channel as by plan of Neve (B. C., *Arch. Sta. Bárb.*, vol. xii, p. 158). Presidio Sta. Bárbara founded: Neve to Croix, April 24, 1782 (B. C., *Prov. Rec.*, vol. ii, pp. 61–62); Serra, April 29, 1782 (*Arch. Sta. Bárb.*, vol. ix, pp. 293–94); Croix to Neve in approval, July 22, 1782 (*Prov. St. Pap.*, vol. iii, p. 232); Palou, *Noticias*, vol. iv, p. 235.

63. By the *Reglamento* of Neve there was prescribed for Alta California the following force: An *ayudante* (adjutant)-inspector, four *habilitados* (paymasters, chosen, one for each presidio by the company from its own subalterns), four lieutenants, six sergeants, sixteen corporals, 172 soldiers, a surgeon, and five master-mechanics.

As reported in 1777 for the use of Comandante-General Croix (M. A., Arch. Genl., *Californias*, 39), the California governmental establishment, under the *Reglamento* of Echeveste, was the following: —

ALTA CALIFORNIA

Monterey Presidio

Governor (4000 *pesos*), one sergeant, two corporals, two carpenters, two farriers, four muleteers, a storekeeper, 22 soldiers.

Monterey Missions

San Carlos, San Luis Obispo, and San Antonio de Padua, one corporal and five soldiers each.

San Diego Presidio

Lieutenant (700 *pesos*); thirteen officers and mechanics, with a commissary storekeeper and 47 soldiers.

BAJA CALIFORNIA

Loreto Presidio

Comandante (3000 *pesos*), lieutenant (500), *alférez* [sub-lieutenant], two sergeants, three corporals, a commissary, 39 soldiers.

San Diego Missions

San Diego de Alcalá and San Gabriel Arcángel, one corporal and five soldiers each.

San Francisco Presidio

Lieutenant (700 *pesos*), a sergeant, eight colonist families from Sonora, 29 soldiers.

Total of 166 officers and men, including eight heads of colonist families at San Francisco, at a cost of 63,222 *pesos*.

Total of 47 officers and men, at a cost of 31,287 *pesos*.

(Cf. estimated expenditures by Echeveste, chapter VI.)

64. In later years, when the pueblos had become degenerate, Governor Arrillaga wrote to Viceroy Iturrigaray, contending that the *gobernador* of Alta California had no political (civil) jurisdiction. "All," he said, "is military. It [the province] is composed of four presidios, three pueblos, and missions without *gente de razón*. In the latter the Indian who acts as governor, or *alcalde*, is subject *en lo civil* to the padre, and *en lo criminal* to the corporals [of the guard], by whom causes are remitted to this *superioridad*. The pueblos (little they merit the name) are composed of invalids and of a small number of citizens, who, though they have an *alcalde*, are ruled by the *gobernador* through a sergeant-*comisionado* who administers justice. Everything is done in a military way, and the *gobernador* intervenes in nothing except to refer some criminal proceeding to your Excellency. It is only with respect to the *Patronato Real* that a *gobernador* might exercise some authority, but there is so little occasion even for this that it does not deserve mention. If the *gobernador* should wish to act in civil matters, there is nobody with whom he could consult in seven hundred leagues. The presidial comandantes hold under their jurisdiction all the missions, and administer justice *militarmente* according to the *Reglamento*." (Loreto, Dec. 20, 1804, M. A., Arch. Genl., *Californias*, Segunda Parte, L. 18, no. 7102.)

The above was elicited by an order from the Viceroy directing Arrillaga to apply to the *Cámara de Indias* for authority as *jefe político*.

65. J. R. Robertson, *From Alcalde to Mayor*, MS. (Academy of Pacific Coast History, Bancroft Library, Berkeley, California.)

66. *Ayuntamientos* (town councils) were created in 1613 by Philip III (*Recopilación*, lib. iv, tit. 9, ley 10). They were at first popularly elective, but later were renewed by coöptation. Under the Spanish Constitution of 1812 — to be spoken of in chapter XII — *ayuntamientos* were permitted to pueblos of 1000 inhabitants. Small pueblos could unite or be joined to larger ones (Article 310).

67. Capital cases (other than those cognizable by court-martial) were, it would seem, referred by the Governor to the *Audiencia*.

CHAPTER VIII

STATE SECULAR *VS.* STATE SACERDOTAL

NEW CHAPTER SOURCES: Letters of Palou to Guardian Sancho of the College of San Fernando, and to José de Gálvez (Sept. and Nov. 1784), describing the last hours of Junípero Serra, — letters upon which Palou based in part his *Vida de Serra;* the *Intendencia*, its nature and history, as described by Viceroy Croix and by Gálvez (Ayer Coll., Newberry Library); plan of the *Custodia* by Bishop Reyes, and correspondence relative to putting the plan into effect, 1776, 1783, 1784; royal letter on the question of one padre at a mission (1784); Guardian Sancho on the conflict between the *Reglamento* and plan of the *Custodia*, 1785; Palou's letter (Alta California under Fages) to Manuel María Truxillo, 1787; proceedings of Doña Eulalia de Callis for divorce (1785), and Fages's letter thereon, 1787; the *Patronato Real* as discussed by Asesor Galindo Navarro, 1791. (M. A., except *Intendencia* dispatch.)

1. Palou to Guardian Juan Sancho, Sept. 7, 1784 (M. A., Museo, *Docs. Rel. á las Mis. de Califs.*, Qto iii); Same to Gálvez, Sept. 6, 1784 (*Ibid.*). On Sept. 13, 1784, Palou notifies Guardian Sancho of willingness to go to Madrid to oppose the transfer of the Alta California missions to the Dominicans, — missions "watered by the blood of Luis Jayme." The transfer (termed by Palou a second expulsion for the California Franciscans) was deemed a part of the plan of Bishop Reyes of Sonora, as related in text. So confident was Palou that a transfer would be effected that he instructed the padres in the South to make ready their inventories. (*Ibid.*) Reyes had advised the step in a letter to Comandante-General Neve, Dec. 13, 1783. (L. Sales, *Noticias de la Provincia de Californias*, 1794, pp. 71–75.)

2. Letter of Sept. 6, 1784, n. 1, *supra;* Palou, *Vida de Serra*, pp. 261–305. On Feb. 6, 1785, Guardian Sancho wrote to Palou acknowledging receipt of the news of Serra's death. (M. A., Museo, *Docs. Rel. á las Mis. de Califs.*, Qto iii.)

3. Manuel de la Vega (*comisario-general*) to Guardian Sancho, Oct. 20, 1784, stating that Palou, Oct. 5, has been granted permission by the King to retire to his college, but intimating that in the first instance applications for retirement should be made to him (M. A., Museo, *Docs. Rel. á las Mis. de Califs.*, 8vo i). The permission was forwarded to Monterey by the Audiencia of Mexico, Feb. 18, 1785 (M. A., Arch. Genl., *R. Audiencia, 1785*, 1, 136). Palou's departure was postponed, because if taken at once certain missions would be left *en solo ministro* (M. A., Museo, *Docs. Rel. á las Mis. de Califs.*, Qto iii).

4. Palou left Monterey about Dec. 7, 1785. He was heartily congratu-

lated on his retirement by Gálvez and by Fages (M. A., Museo, *Docs. Rel. á las Mis. de Califs.*, Qto iii). In his letter to Sancho, Sept. 13, 1784, he expresses a wish for a portrait of Serra and (in commemoration of Serra's last sacrament) that the posture be that of the Father-President "on his knees before the altar surrounded by Indians and by cuirassed soldiers, all bearing candles" (*Ibid.*). In his letter of Feb. 6, 1785, Sancho informs Palou that Serra's portrait is being painted at Verger's expense (*Ibid.*). The place of deposit and authenticity of various portraits of Serra are minutely discussed by Mr. George Watson Cole, *Missions and Mission Pictures*, Pub. Calif. Library Assoc., no. 11.

THE INTENDENCIA

5. The dispatch regarding *Intendencias* has not been found in the Mexican Archives. An intimation of its contents is made by Gálvez in the "joint dispatch" (M. A., Arch. Genl., *Prov. Int.* 154), and in his *Informe General* of Dec. 31, 1771, Mexico, 1867. Fortunately, however, the Ayer Collection (Newberry Library, Chicago) contains a complete copy of the missing paper. The instrument bears date Jan. 15, 1768 (eight days prior to the dispatch relative to a *comandancia-general*), and its main recitals are the following: At the beginning of the eighteenth century, Spain itself was the prey of "governors and subaltern judges, who, being temporary, regarded only their personal interest and enriched themselves at the expense of the state." This ruinous arrangement, uprooted at home by Philip V, obtains to-day in her rich and widespread dominions of America. Indeed, these dominions have "reached a point of decadence where they are menaced with total ruin, and it is necessary to apply the remedy which has cured the ills of the parent."

In "discharging his vast duties as captain-general, political governor, and general superintendent of the royal treasury, the Viceroy has hitherto possessed no other aid than that of the *alcaldes mayores*." These officials "for the most part are regarded as tyrants, which in fact they are, for their term is but five years, and within it they seek to make themselves rich." In the principal localities there should be placed *Intendentes* as in Spain, men compensated by fixed salaries, thus ridding New Spain of more than 150 officials who each year filch from 500,000 to 600,000 *pesos*. This is the more necessary as the *alcaldes mayores* are accustomed to appoint lieutenants who pay to their superiors excessive annuities. The number of *Intendencias* should be eleven, — one, general in character, for the capital of Mexico, and the others for the provinces, all subject to the Viceroy. The *Intendencias de Provincia* should be located one in each of the localities — Puebla, Oaxaca, Mérida or Campeche, Valladolid de Michoacán, Guanaxuato, San Luis Potosí, Guadalaxara, Durango, Sonora, and Californias. For the *Intendentes* of Guadalaxara, Durango, Sonora, and Californias, the salaries should be 8000 *pesos;* for those of the remaining localities, 6000 *pesos;* and for the *Inten-*

dente-General, 12,000 *pesos*. Besides *Intendentes*, "there should exist in the various capitals *corregidores*, or political governors, as in Spain, with power to name *subdelegados* in the more considerable pueblos." "The two *Intendencias* of Sonora y Californias, which, together with that of Durango, are to be immediately subject to a *comandancia-general*, as proposed in a separate report, will produce copious additions to the royal treasury by the incomparable wealth of these great provinces. Under an authorized *comandancia*, the *Intendencias* last named will curtail the considerable expenses now incident to their eight presidios, and will render it possible to convert the missions into curacies."

The foregoing dispatch was approved on January 16, 1768, by the Bishop of Puebla, and on the 21st by the Archbishop of Mexico. The latter said: "The main subsistence of the *alcaldes mayores* is derived from the *repartimientos* of clothing, mules, and other commodities which they make (they and their lieutenants) to the Indians at a high price. . . . These *repartimientos* were necessary at the beginning of the conquest, but now the Indians weave their own clothing and raise their own livestock. . . . In Spain, an *alcalde mayor* ordinarily is an educated man ; here, not. . . . In Spain, recourse to superiors is easy ; here, it is a matter of 100 or 200 leagues to the Royal Audiencias. In Spain, peace and order prevail in the pueblos, etc.; here, it is constantly necessary to appeal to the strong hand."

On March 29, 1778, there was created by order of the Minister for the Indies (José de Gálvez) the *Intendencia* of Buenos Ayres, the first *Intendencia* in the two Americas. The order reads : *Consiguientemente y haviendo manifestado la esperiencia, las ventajas q, ha conseguido la Real Hacienda en la mejor Administración de las rentas y Trop^s en la seguridad y subcistencias con el Establecim^{to} de las Yntendencias en los reyños de Castilla, y lo mismo con la que se halla establecida en la Ysla de Cuba, se ha servido el Rey crear una Yntendencia de Exército y R^l Hac^{da} para el nuevo Virreynato de Buenos Ayres, con el importante objecto de ponerse en sus devidos valores las rentas de todas sus Provincias y Territorios, y de fomentar sus Poblaciones, Agricultura y Comercio, á nombre de S. M. para este Empleo al Yntendente D^n Manuel Frez que lo fué en la expedición Militar destinado á la América Meridional.*

So far as North America was concerned, the plan of *Intendencias* was not put in operation till 1786, when, by a decree (*orden*) dated Sept. 4, *Intendentes* were placed in "Mexico [City], Puebla, Vera Cruz, Mérida, Oaxaca, Valladolid, Guanajuato, San Luis Potosí, Guadalaxara, Zacatecas, and (for Sonora and Sinaloa) Durango and Arizpe." None was appointed for the Californias.

6. Feb. 22, 1769, "The reduction of the natives *en policía* [to civil status] is a thing so important as to admit neither of excuse nor delay." (M. A., Museo, *Docs. Rel. á las Mis. de Califs.*, Qto i.)

7. M. A., Museo, *Docs. Rel. á las Mis. de Califs.*, Qto ii.

8. *Informe*, no. 4 (M. A., Museo, *Trasuntos*).

9. M. A., Arch. Genl., *Misiones*, 14. In support of his plan of the *Custodia*, — a plan the complement (ecclesiastically) of the *Intendencia* system of secular control, — Reyes was successful in marshaling a powerful *junta*, headed by the Franciscan *comisario-general* of the Indies, Manuel de la Vega. The conclusive argument for the plan was the great distance between missions and their colleges or provincials, and the varying sets of rules governing missions.

THE CUSTODIA

Much light is shed upon the *Custodia* by the following interesting paper, which, though without date, evidently was written some time in 1779, and is signed "The most unworthy minister of the Order of Saint Francis ": —

"The history of the Indies shows a rapid spiritual and temporal conquest by the Spaniards during the first twenty years. Since this epoch there has been little advance, and now we are unable to support our pueblos and *provincias internas*. Yet we are not to think that the valor, zeal, and spirit of Spaniards have failed. We simply have changed our method. Formerly the missionaries entered the country of the Indians, formed *villas* and *pueblos unidos*. Fifty or one hundred families cultivated the soil, worked the mines, and bred livestock. The missionaries established themselves along with the Spaniards, built small convents where they observed their sacred law, lived in community, and at opportune times visited the mountains, prevailing upon the Indians by exhortation to become reduced to pueblos and to the *doctrina*. As the towns grew and the Indians became converted, more missionaries were obtained. In this way were established all the cities, *villas*, pueblos, and convents of New Spain.

"At the beginning of the past century [seventeenth], there was established the existing government of missions and presidios. The first of these in New Spain was the *Villa* of Sinaloa, founded in 1611. Its missionaries and soldiers were the first that opened the royal exchequer to cover *sínodos* [salaries] and *situados* [allowances]. They altered the fixed plan of our ancestors and started the abuses and errors now practiced. The missionaries became convinced that to reduce the Indians to pueblos, and to convert them, it was needful to assist them in all temporal respects. Thus the missionaries became charged with the obligation of feeding, clothing, and housing the Indians. It was at the beginning of the last century that there was introduced the abuse of furnishing to the Indians pick-axes, axes, hoes, etc., for building houses and cultivating the soil; and it is to be noted that from this epoch expenses have vastly increased, and that we have lost whole provinces, with many ancient towns, notably in Texas, Coahuila, Nueva Vizcaya, Nuevo México, and Sonora.

"In the provinces named we come upon ruins of Spanish and Indian pueblos. If we ask of the missionaries the cause of these ruins, of the decadence of the missions, of the repugnance of the Gentiles to gather in *doctrinas*, and of the innumerable apostates fugitive in the mountains, they attribute all to the natural inconstancy of the Indians and their impatience of subordination and labor. But it is my conviction, after many years' experience in missions, that the true causes are the following: (1) The confiding to a single missionary of two, three, or more widely separated pueblos, with the result that the Indians fail of instruction in religion and in Christian obligations, becoming in some cases worse than Gentiles; (2) the exempting of the Indians from tithes, whereby there is imposed upon the missionary the burden of countless personal community services; also the punishing of Indians with lashes for small faults, which in the case of the old and married produces shame and *saxza* of mind, so that at times the victims die of chagrin and melancholy, or desert to the mountains, or, if women, are rejected by their husbands; (3) the confiding (upon secularization) of a large district to a single curate, with the result of much apostasy, as upon the four rivers, Sinaloa, Fuerte, Mayo, and Hiaqui, and in the Sierra Gorda; (4) the levying of contributions by curates; (5) the maintaining of dispersed ranchos of Spaniards, mulattoes, and other castes, who by their isolation become a prey to Gentile Indians; (6) the keeping of lands in common, whence it results that the most powerful appropriate them in order to form haciendas fifteen, twenty, and thirty leagues in extent; (7) unlimited authority on the part of *alcaldes mayores;* lack in Spanish pueblos of subordinate judicial officers; helplessness in Indian pueblos on the part of ordinary *alcaldes* against the *alcaldes mayores;* (8) failure to observe the printed *Reglamento de Presidios* requiring the presidios to be so aligned as to protect the frontier of the internal provinces.

"All of the above evils may be corrected under the plan of four Franciscan *custodias* resolved upon by the supreme government; but the following safeguards should be instituted: (1) The *comisario-general* of the Indies should choose the first *custodios* and missionaries, but by and with the advice of Padre Reyes; (2) a *junta* of the most distinguished subjects of the Provincias should be assembled to fix the limits of *custodia* districts, assigning to each a portion of the infidel frontier.

"It is especially necessary to give attention to California, where the missions [those of Baja California] are almost entirely ruined. Navigation and commerce with the four rivers and missions of the coasts of Cinaloa, Ostimuri, Pimería Alta and Baja should be encouraged, as these provinces are near the interior [gulf] coast of California, and extend well toward the Colorado River. The *Custodia* of California should place missionaries in the pueblos nearest the sea in the aforesaid provinces, so that small boats may be built and mutual succor given. In this way, in time, there would be occupied the islands, María, Tiburón, and others. . . . In all the Provincias there are no schools for the instruction of the youth. It should be ordered that in every *hospicio* there be at once placed primary teachers, and later teachers of a grade more advanced. Uniformity among missionaries should be enforced to the extent that they wear robes of the same color, length, and cut, and there should be adopted a uniform set of ordinances. . . . In all the Provincias the Indians should retain their natural liberty without obligation to perform community labor, or render personal service to missionaries or secular judges. . . . There should be put in effect the instruction of Visitador-General Gálvez, that lands be granted to the Indians in severalty — one irrigated plot and one range plot; and that, without prejudice to the Indians, the same favor be granted to Spaniards, mulattoes, and the other castes. To the padre missionary there should belong only the *huerta* [garden] of the mission; all the mountains and uncultivated lands remaining the common property of the pueblos. The Indians should be compelled to assemble in pueblos of fifty or more families, as likewise the Spaniards, mulattoes, and other castes, thus lessening the danger of Gentile raids. In every pueblo of fifty families there should reside one missionary priest; in every pueblo of a hundred families, two missionary priests; and so forth. In all frontier pueblos and missions there should reside two missionary priests of experience and proved fidelity, and to these there should be given liberal alms. The Indians should pay tithes, but all brotherhoods and almoners, even though of the mendicant orders, should be prohibited. In every mission there should be elected annually two *alcaldes*, two *regidores*, and a *sindico-procurador*. In pueblos where Spaniards and Indians live together, the offices should be divided, but the *sindico-procurador* should be a Spaniard. Inasmuch as large settlements of Spaniards have ever been the safeguard of our American colonies, and the means of controlling the fickleness of the natives, let there be conceded by his Majesty the privileges of one or two cities and of four or six *villas* in the provinces of California, Sonora, Nueva Vizcaya, and Nuevo México. The foregoing suggestions having been observed, the *milicia* could be so handled as to afford a good defense, even though all the presidios were suppressed, establishments which (besides being useless as now distributed) are a burden on the royal treasury of a million and more than 200,000 *pesos* annually." (S. A., Madrid, Bib. Nac. MS., no. 2550.)

10. M. A., Arch. Genl., *Misiones*, 14. The protest (Sec. 24) points out that the *Custodia* plan as advocated by Reyes squarely contradicts statements of the prelate made in his *Informe* of 1772.

11. Reyes's plea for *custodias* was sent to Gálvez on Sept. 9, 1776. On May 20, 1782, there was issued a royal decree establishing the system. On Feb. 11, 1783, the protest by the colleges was signed. The reply of the Bishop bore date June 20, 1783, and on Jan. 14, 1784, the protest was disallowed under the *rúbrica* of Gálvez (M. A., Arch. Genl., *Misiones*, 14). In 1783 (Jan. 8), Guardian Pangua instructed Serra (should he receive orders to establish the *Custodia* in Alta California) to temporize; and on Feb. 3, Pangua addressed a letter to Guardian Pérez of Santa Cruz (Querétaro) and one to the

Guardian of the Guadalupe College (Zacatecas) couched in terms afterward employed in the protest. In 1785 (April 12), Guardian Sancho instructed Lasuén (president of the Monterey establishments) that there remained naught to be done but, *punto en boca* [stitch in lip], to obey the royal orders (B. C., *Arch. Sta. Bárb.*, vol. xii, pp. 158, 200, 214–15). Meantime in Sonora Bishop Reyes found himself thwarted. On July 24, 1784, he wrote to Neve (comandante-general after Croix) that upon him, "in whom, for the Provincias Internas, there resided *todas las Vice-Regias Facultades*, it depended to establish and confirm the *Custodia*, already erected, of San Carlos de Sonora." "License, it was reported, had been given for many *religiosos* to withdraw from their missions, and if they withdrew, the *Custodia* must perish from *insubsistencia*." This letter on Oct. 1 was followed by one to the Viceroy, stating that Neve had just died. The Viceroy in 1785 addressed to each of the colleges — San Fernando, Santa Cruz, and Guadalupe — an injunction of obedience, an injunction reflected in the *punto en boca* order of Pangua to Lasuén (M. A., Arch. Genl., *Mis.* 14). As late as 1787 (March 20), a royal *cédula* required missionaries for the California establishments to be taken from Michoacán if they could not be supplied by the College of San Fernando (B. C., *Arch. Sta. Bárb.*, vol. **x**, p. 287). In 1784 (Nov. 9) Palou had sent to Bishop Reyes a plan of the Californias, showing by the sparseness of population, the vastness of the distance, and the roughness of the roads, how impossible it would be to collect there in support of the *Custodia una tortilla de limosna*. (M. A., Museo, *Docs. Rel. á las Mis. de Califs.*, Qto iii.) The *Custodia* in Sonora, J. D. Arricivita, *Crónica Seráfica*, pp. 564–75.

12. M. A., Museo, *Docs. Rel. á las Mis. de Califs.*, Qto ii; B. C., *Arch. Sta. Bárb.*, vol. x, p. 99. Lasuén makes the point that by the same laws appealed to by Neve, *alcalde* elections are required to take place *en presencia de los curas* [secular priests], and that the missionaries do not presume to be such. In other words, it is not contemplated by the Laws of the Indies that neophytes will be competent to choose *alcaldes* until they have so far progressed as to be free of missionary jurisdiction. On Dec. 9, 1782, Fages instructed Palou that the Indians at his mission must, on Jan. 1, 1783, proceed to an election of *alcaldes*. (B. C., *Prov. Rec.*, vol. iii, pp. 71, 170.)

13. Neve to Fages, Sept. 7, 1782, "Instrucción" (B. C., *Prov. St. Pap.*, vol. iii, p. 127; *St. Pap. Sac.*, vol. i, p. 72). Stopping of the galleon at San Francisco or Monterey, see chapter x.

14. Fages to Palou, Jan. 2, 1787. Official communications may be franked but not *correspondencia* by the padres *entre si*. (*Ibid.*)

15. Croix to Mayorga, Sept. 27, 1781 (M. A., Arch. Genl., *Californias*, 33). Communication emphasizes point that departure of padres without a government license, and unlicensed change of padres from one station to another, are acts contravening the *Patronato Real*. Replies by Serra to letters from Croix covering same point, April 26 and 28, 1782. The Father-President argues that the *Patronato Real*, in the matters mentioned, applies not to

missions, but to *beneficios eclesiásticos formales y formados como son los curatos.* (*Ibid.*, 2, Segunda Parte.)

16. Yet what were the padres to do? Their work as missionaries often compelled them to pay visits to distant *rancherías*, absenting themselves for a night. Moreover, the mission herds and flocks (nearly 13,000 head) made *vaqueros* necessary. If soldiers might not be used as escorts, nor even dispatched as messengers, and if *vaqueros* there were none, neophytes must be employed instead, — contrary as the practice was to the law of 1568, which forbade Indians to ride, save by special license of a governor. Lasuén to Croix, Oct. 20, 1787. (M. A., Arch. Genl., *Californias*, 12.)

17. This rule was laid down by Neve in his instructions to Soler, July 12, 1782. It provided that absconders should be tempted back by promises communicated to them by other Indians that they would not be punished. "On kind treatment depended the good order of the peninsula" (B. C., *Prov. St. Pap.*, vol. iii, p. 113, secs. 33 and 34). Neve's own instructions from the Viceroy (chapter VII of text, n. 21) were to same effect. Fages thereon, letter to J. A. Romeu, Feb. 26, 1791 (*Ibid.*, vol. x, p. 151, par. 8).

18. Dec. 7, 1785 (B. C., *Prov. Rec.*, vol. iii, p. 60).

19. The government (wrote Father Cambón of San Francisco, early in 1783) favored not the padres, who prior to the coming of Neve had freely visited the presidios in all weathers to hear confessions and say Mass. Why, therefore, should the padres favor the government? And, the summer preceding, Father Lasuén had written to the Guardian of San Fernando: "The same author of the *Reglamento* who would consign an uncompanioned padre, surrounded by Gentiles and attended by neophytes little reliable, to illness without succor, and death without the sacraments, this same Felipe de Neve has just now been accorded a personal adjutant [Nicolás Soler] at a salary of 2000 *pesos*. Adjutants I am bound to suppose necessary, but what I cannot understand is, how there is to be ascribed to a king, so provident and liberal for the temporal good of his possessions, a conception so narrow and limited for their spiritual good; the latter good being, in the royal mind, the principal one, and the former the accessory." (July 8, 1782, M. A., Museo, *Docs. Rel. á las Mis. de Califs.*, Qto ii.)

20. In a letter from Madrid to the College of San Fernando, dated Feb. 12, 1784, it is stated by Antonio Ventura de Taranco that the King has received the complaint of the padres that the order (by Neve) reducing the quota at a mission contravened the royal *cédulas* of Nov. 3, 1744, Dec. 4, 1747, and Sept. 10, 1772, and that he would take the matter under consideration (M. A., Museo, *Docs. Rel. á las Mis. de Califs.*, Qto iii). That the order was reactionary is plain. It was a settled policy that missionaries should not be solitary. Bishop Reyes, in his plea for the *Custodia*, argued that by the plan of the Mission (as carried out in Sonora) establishments had but one padre, whereas by the *Custodia* plan there would be an *hospicio* with many padres. Writing on August 20, 1785, Guardian Sancho points

out that at the same time the *Reglamento* required one padre in California, the *estatutos* for the *Custodia* (par. 6, no. 3) required *que ningún Misionero pueda vivir solo en las Misiones ó nuevas conversiones.* (M. A., Museo, *Docs. Rel. á las Mis. de Califs.*, Qto ii.)

21. Palou speaks of having seen the *Reglamento* in September, 1784. Guardian Sancho names December as the month of promulgation in the Californias.

22. *Expediente formado sobre resiprocas quexas del Governador Don Pedro Fages y Religiosos de aquellas Misiones, 1787.* (M. A., Arch. Genl., *Californias*, 12.)

23. *Ibid.*

24. Discussing the *Patronato Real*, Lasuén observed (as had Serra) that it was largely without pertinence in frontier regions like the Californias. Still the padres did not dispute the Governor's authority as *vice-patrono*. Apropos of the *Patronato*, Comandante-General Pedro de Nava in 1791 (Oct. 11) issued to the College of San Fernando elaborate instructions, prepared by Asesor [Solicitor-General] Galindo Navarro. The document traces the history of the power (chapter III of the text, n. 26), citing specifically the *Recopilación*, ley 1, tit. 2, lib. 1; ley 1, tit. 6, lib. 1. *Curatos* and *doctrinas* (villages of converts) are first considered, and then missions. The latter, it is stated, are conducted by *religiosos que se destinan á tierras y paises de infieles y gentiles, antigua ó nuevemente descubiertos con el santo fin de predicar el Evangelio, instruir en el Doctrina Christiana, reducir á pueblos, y convertir á Nuestra Santa Fé Católica á sus naturales y habitantes.* These are the true missions treated of in leyes 36, 37, and 38 (lib. i, tit. 6). When missions in *nuevos descubrimientos* are to be erected, the following is the course to be pursued: (1) The governor of the province and the *ordinario* (bishop) are to be consulted, and the number and qualifications of padres are to be specified; (2) removals of padres by provincials are to be made only for just and necessary causes; and (3) viceroys, *audiencias, justicias,* archbishops and bishops are to help and honor mission undertakings. But (it is stated) a great abuse, *antiguo y contrario á las citadas leyes,* prevails in the Provincias Internas. More than a century has elapsed since missions there became *verdaderas doctrinas y beneficios curados,* subject to leyes 24 and 41, tit. 6, lib. 1, of the *Recopilación,* yet they continue to be classed as *nuevas conversiones.* It is only in Nueva California that true missions now exist. (M. A., Museo, *Docs. Rel. á las Califs.*, Qto iii.)

25. Goycochea (comandante at Santa Bárbara) to Fages, Nov. 19, 1786 (B. C., *Prov. St. Pap.*, vol. vi, p. 57); Fages to Vicente Félix (*Prov. St. Pap.*, vol. vii, p. 145). Visiting of *rancherías*, except by license, forbidden. Indian women at pueblos not to be allowed in houses. Punishment of an Indian to be conducted in presence of the head man of his *ranchería*, and to consist of fifteen or twenty lashes applied humanely. Whites to be punished for misdemeanors against Indians. It is significant that while at the pueblos a

comisionado was needed to oversee Spanish *alcaldes*, such oversight by the padres in the case of Indian *alcaldes* was (at first) not permitted. On necessity for *comisionados*, Fages to Romeu, Feb. 26, 1791 (*Ibid.*, vol. x, p. 151, pars. 5, 6, of doc.).

26. B. C., *Arch. Sta. Bárb.*, vol. viii, pp. 133–34; xii, pp. 24–25.

27. B. C., *Prov. St. Pap.*, vol. vi, pp. 51, 58; vii, pp. 43, 58–59. Fages to Palou, Jan. 2, 1787, describes the founding of Sta. Bárbara Mission as effected Dec. 16. (M. A., Museo, *Docs. Rel. á las Mis. de Califs.*, Qto iii. See *Prov. Rec.*, vol. i, pp. 192–93; *Prov. St. Pap.*, vol. vi, pp. 112–13.) Six new missionaries had arrived from Spain. Writing on June 22, 1787, to the Guardian of San Fernando, the Secretary-General for the Indies said that until the appointment of a successor to José de Gálvez, who had died at Aranjuez on the night of June 17, passes to missionaries could not be given. (M. A., Museo, *Docs. Rel. á las Mis. de Califs.*, Qto iii.)

28. B. C., *Prov. St. Pap.*, vol. v, p. 9.

29. M. A., Museo, *Docs. Rel. á las Mis. de Califs.*, Qto iii.

30. Correspondence, Fages, Ugarte y Loyola, Revilla Gigedo, 1789–1790. Fages's letter asking to be relieved bore date Dec. 4, 1789. Romeu appointed May 18, 1790. (M. A., Arch. Genl., *Californias*, 70; B. C., *Prov. St. Pap.* (Benicia), vol. i, pp. 8–10. See also *Prov. St. Pap.*, vol. ix, pp. 308, 346–47; x, pp. 139, 144–45.)

31. B. C., *Prov. St. Pap.* (Benicia), vol. i, pp. 8–10; x, pp. 150–51.

32. B. C., *Prov. Rec.*, vol. iii, pp. 127, 144; ii, pp. 105–06, 111; *Prov. St. Pap.*, vol. v, pp. 254–55.

33. *Instancia de Doña Eulalia Callis, muger de Don Pedro Fages, gobernador de Californias, sobre que se le oyga en justicia y redima de la opresion que padece, 1785.* (M. A., Arch. Genl., *Prov. Int.* 120.)

34. M. A., Museo, *Docs. Rel. á las Mis. de Califs.*, Qto iii.

CHAPTER IX

DOMESTIC EQUILIBRIUM

New Chapter Sources: *Informe*, J. B. Matute to comandante at San Blas, Nov. 7, 1793, covering expedition by sea to the port of Bodega; *informe* by Pedro Callejas, Guardian of San Fernando, Oct. 23, 1797, on provision of *Reglamento* reducing quota of padres at missions; letter, R. Verger, Guardian of San Fernando, to M. L. Casafonda, Comisario-General of the Indies, June 30, 1771, stating that the missions of the peninsula never would become pueblos; *expediente* on the charges preferred by Padre Antonio de la Concepción — a collection containing (besides documents hitherto available) Borica's *informe*, Dec. 31, 1798, and *Resumen y Notas de los estados de Misiones*, July 8, 1797; Lasuén's request for Concepción's deportation, Aug. 19, 1797; Borica's reply, Dec. 13, 1797; Buenaventura Sitjar's letter to Lasuén, Jan. 31, 1799, describing Concepción's conduct at San Miguel; *informe* by Miguel Lull, Guardian of San Fernando, Oct. 9, 1799; *informes* by padres at Purísima and San Buenaventura, 1800, and by R. Carrillo, comandante at Santa Bárbara, 1802; letter by Guardian and *discretos* of San Fernando to Viceroy, March 23, 1805; letters of *fiscal* to College of San Fernando and to Governor Arrillaga, April 19, 1805; medical report and orders for Concepción's return to Spain, 1801–1805. (M. A.) Mention should also be made of documents in the Spanish Archives pertaining to the Nootka Sound affair. See *The Nootka Sound Controversy*, W. R. Manning, Washington, 1905. (Specific citations below.)

1. Order dated Nov. 23–24, 1792, carried into effect 1793 (*Instrucciones de los Virreyes*, secs. 291–293).

2. Captain J. Cook, *A Voyage to the Pacific*, 3 vols., vol. ii, pp. 295–96, vol. iii, pp. 434–35.

3. W. Coxe, *Russian Discoveries*, pp. 209, 210, 234–35, 248.

4. R. Greenhow, *Oregon and California*, chap. 7; H. H. Bancroft, *Northwest Coast*, vol. i, chap. 6.

5. Comte de la Pérouse, *Voyage autour du Monde*, Paris, 1798, 4 vols., vol. ii, pp. 309–317. Captain Cook regarded the fur trade as of problematical outcome even for England, unless an interoceanic passage were discovered.

6. M. A., Arch. Genl., *Historia*, 396.

7. S. A., Arch. Gen. de Indias, Sevilla, 90–3–18, cited in *The Nootka Sound Controversy*, W. R. Manning.

8. W. R. Manning, *The Nootka Sound Controversy*, chap. 13. See also Greenhow, pp. 191, 210; Bancroft, *Northwest Coast*, vol. i, chap. 7; Conde de Revilla Gigedo, *Informe*, April, 1793, — Translation, *Land of Sunshine*, vol. xi, p. 168.

Assertion by Spain of exclusive sovereignty in the Pacific: Laws of Philip II, based on grant by Pope Alexander VI and successors. By these laws all intercourse with foreigners, except by express permission, was forbidden under penalty of death and confiscation. Said Antonio de Morga in his *Sucesos*, 1609: "The crown and sceptre of Spain have extended themselves wherever the sun sheds its light, from its rising to its setting, with the glory and splendor of their power and majesty " (B. and R., *Philippine Islands*, vol. xv, p. 37). In accordance with this idea, the Manila galleon, upon reaching that part of the North Pacific where direction was changed to the south, was said to have entered the "Gulf of New Spain." Said Montesclaros, Viceroy of Peru, addressing the King in 1612: "They [the Dutch] content themselves with going in the Pacific where they are received, and with receiving what they are given, without caring much whether others enter that district, while your Majesty desires, as is right, to be absolute and sole ruler, and to shut the gate to all who do not enter under the name and title of vassals." (*Ibid.*, xvii, p. 228.) In 1692 a strong royal order was issued against foreigners in the Pacific. (Manning, p. 357.) In 1788, when the American ship Columbia entered the Pacific, she stopped at a port in the island of Juan Fernández. Here she was permitted to refit and continue her voyage to Nootka Sound. For granting the permission the governor of the islands (Blas Gonzáles) was cashiered by the Captain-General of Chile, who in turn was sustained by the Viceroy of Peru. (Manning, pp. 309–10.) In point of usage and treaties, Spain's pretension as to the Pacific was strong — treaties of 1670 and 1783. (*Ibid.*, p. 358; also Pizarro y Mangino, *Compendio Histórico*, etc., *para excluir á todas las Naciones de la Navegación de las Mares de Indias*, etc., Ayer Coll., Newberry Library.) "The Nootka Convention," observes Dr. Manning, "was the first express renunciation of Spain's ancient claim to exclusive sovereignty over the American shores of the Pacific Ocean and the South Seas." (*The Nootka Sound Controversy*, p. 462.)

9. W. R. Manning, *The Nootka Sound Controversy*, p. 442.

10. *Ibid.*, pp. 442–45; Flórez-Revilla-Gigedo correspondence, Aug. 27– Sept. 30, 1789 (M. A., Arch. Genl., *Historia*, 65); Same, with full correspondence on seizure of British vessels (S. A., as cited by Manning in *The Nootka Sound Controversy*, chap. 6). See also H. H. Bancroft, *Northwest Coast*, vol. i, chap. 7.

Martínez's diary for 1789 has been lost. Bancroft (*Northwest Coast*, vol. i, p. 212) reports it not found; and Manning (p. 342, n. *a*) reports it missing from S. A. at Sevilla. There exists in the M. A. a letter from Martínez to Flórez, dated Dec. 6, 1789, reporting his arrival at San Blas *en devido cumplimiento de la Sup^{or} Orden de V. E. de 25 de Febrero*. Revilla Gigedo was surprised at the return of Martínez, but later (Feb. 26, 1790) it came to his knowledge that on October 13, 1789, an order for Martínez's transfer to Spain had been issued from Madrid, because of failure to provide support for his family. (M. A., Arch. Genl., *Historia*, 65.)

11. Fidalgo and Elisa, B. C., *Viajes al Norte de Californias*, nos. 8, 10, 7; M. A., Arch. Genl., *Historia*, 68, 69, 71; Malaspina, M. A., Arch. Genl., *Historia*, 397; *J. Caamaño* . . . " á comprobar la Relación de Fonte," M. A., Arch. Genl., *Historia*, 69, 71.

12. G. Vancouver, *A Voyage of Discovery to the North Pacific Ocean* . . . *in the years 1790–95*, 3 vols., 1798, vol. i, p. 388; Greenhow, *Oregon and California*, pp. 239–46; Revilla Gigedo, *Informe*, April, 1793, — Translation, *Land of Sunshine*, vol. xi, pp. 168–73.

13. Revilla Gigedo, *Informe*, April, 1793; Translation, *Land of Sunshine*, vol. xi, p. 169. The instructions from Spain were that the boundary line between California and the free territory on the north be fixed at 48°, Nootka being divided between Spain and England.

14. Bancroft, *Northwest Coast*, vol. i, pp. 302–303; Manning, *The Nootka Sound Controversy*, pp. 467–71.

15. Basadre y Vega to Viceroy Gálvez, Dec. 20, 1786 (M. A., Arch. Genl., *Historia*, 396).

16. Pérouse, *Voyage autour du Monde*, tom. ii, pp. 288–89.

17. B. C., *Prov. St. Pap. Mil.* (Benicia), vol. xx, p. 3; *St. Pap.* (Sacramento), vol. i, p. 115; vol. v, p. 6.

18. Arrillaga to Viceroy, acknowledging receipt of instructions, July 16, 1793 (B. C., *Prov. St. Pap. Mil.* (Benicia), vol. xix, pp. 1–2).

19. *Ibid.*

20. Arrillaga to Viceroy, Aug. 20, 1793: mentions instructions to occupy Bodega, as of date March 30, and reports as to land expedition thither (B. C., *Prov. St. Pap.*, vol. xxi, p. 113). J. B. Matute to comandante at San Blas, Nov. 7, 1793: full report of expedition by sea (M. A., Arch. Genl., *Historia*, 71). Interest attaches to this report as covering facts upon which Bancroft found no information. Bodega project abandoned, Viceroy to Arrillaga, June 9, 1794. (*Ibid.* See also B. C., *Prov. St. Pap.*, vol. xi, p. 175.)

21. Borica to Francisco Joaquín Valdéz (B. C., *Prov. St. Pap.*, vol. xxi, p. 198). Other letters (May 16, 17, 21, and June 15, 1794) to his brother-in-law, to his mother-in-law, Doña Juniata, to Arrillaga, and to Valdéz. To Arrillaga he is very jocose, describing the *habilitado* at Loreto as what he himself would be as prior of Santo Domingo, and observing that his "jewel of a treasurer has gone on sprees which interfere with work." (*Ibid.*, pp. 201–205.)

22. Borica to Antonio Cordero (*Ibid.*, p. 209). Other letters, — to Manuel de Cárcaba, "My Lord Fox," Savino de la Pedruzea, Antonio Grajera, to his sister (Bernarda), and to Francisco Hijosa, — Nov. 13, 1794 to Sept. 13, 1795. From Cárcaba he asks five or six pairs of gloves, — buckskin, chamois, rabbit-skin, — as at Monterey it is quite cold. To the same he expresses hope that they both may be made generals when the Prince of Asturias marries. To Hijosa he sends seal-skins for gifts to Cárcaba and Lanza. (*Ibid.*, pp. 210–228.)

23. In 1776 (Oct. 23), Bucarely, pursuant to instructions (chapter VII of text, nn. 11, 12) had ordered Neve to see that Captain Cook's vessels were refused admission to California ports (B. C., *Prov. St. Pap.*, vol. i, p. 213). In 1780 (Aug. 25) Croix had advised Neve of the supposed approach of a part of Admiral Hughes's fleet to the South Sea, with the object of destroying commerce and ransacking the meridional coasts of the Spanish dominions, etc. (*Ibid.*, vol. ii, p. 112.) In 1789 (May 13) Fages had warned Argüello, at San Francisco, to capture the Columbia with "skill and caution" should she appear (B. C., *Miss. and Col.*, vol. i, pp. 53–54). The Columbia and her commander were as courteously treated by Martínez at Nootka as they had been by Gonzáles at the Juan Fernández Islands. (Letters of Martínez, (M. A., Arch. Genl., *Historia*, 65.)

24. Stringent orders by Viceroy to Arrillaga, August, 1793, to expel foreign ships from California ports "without pretext or excuse," save in most urgent cases of distress (B. C., *Prov. St. Pap.*, vol. xi, p. 96). In 1795 orders were issued by Borica that all ships which approached California ports under Spanish colors were on landing to be searched, in order to determine whether Spanish or not. (*Ibid.*, vol. xiii, p. 16; vol. xiv, p. 29.)

25. Viceroy Miguel José de Azanza to Borica, Dec. 21, 1799, Feb. 8, 1800, regarding Kamtchatka. (B. C., *Prov. St. Pap.* (Sacramento), vol. ix, p. 54; *Prov. Rec.*, vol. x, p. 5.) Fear of the United States was not a new emotion in Spain. In 1783 the Conde de Aranda (just returned from signing, at Paris, the treaty preliminary to the recognition by Great Britain of American independence) had proposed an independent Mexico and Peru as an offset to independent America, — a land which otherwise might be expected to encroach on New Spain. Furthermore, in 1787 there had arrived at Vera Cruz, as viceroy of Mexico, Manuel Antonio Flórez, vice-admiral of the royal navy, and on Dec. 23, 1788, Flórez, citing the Nootka voyages of the Columbia, had thus written to his government: "We ought not to be surprised that the English colonies of America, being now an independent Republic, should carry out the design of finding a safe port on the Pacific and of attempting to sustain it by crossing the immense country of the continent above our possessions of Texas, New Mexico, and California." (Flórez to Valdéz, S. A., Arch. Genl. de Indias, Sevilla, 90–3–18, cited by Manning.)

26. Costansó, *Informe*, Oct. 17, 1794 (B. C., Pinart Collection, *Papeles Varios*, p. 193). On July 25, 1795, Viceroy Branciforte advised Borica of the sending of aid sufficient to man the three batteries at San Francisco, Monterey, and San Diego. (B. C., *Prov. St. Pap.*, vol. xiii, p. 51.)

27. The total military force of Alta California after 1796–97 was 280 men of the presidial companies, and 90 Catalan volunteers and artillerymen. In 1794, Costansó placed the total at 218. In 1795, Branciforte placed it at 225. Arrillaga desired 271, and Borica 335 men. Córdoba sent to Mexico plans for fortifications (Córdoba, *Informe*, 1796). Borica to Viceroy (B. C., *St. Pap.* (Sacramento), vol. iv, pp. 56–57).

28. Plan of Pitic (B. C., *Miss. and Col.*, vol. i, p. 343; translated, J. W. Dwinelle, *The Colonial History of San Francisco*, 1863, Add. no. vii). Commentary on Plan of Pitic (*Ibid.*, pp. 30–33).

29. *Informe*, May 11, 1796 (B. C., *Arch. Sta. Bárb.*, vol. ii, p. 73).

30. *Informe*, May 14, 1796 (M. A., Museo, *Docs. Rel. á las Mis. de Califs.*, Qto ii; B. C., *Arch. Sta. Bárb.*, vol. ii, p. 42).

31. B. C., *St. Pap.*, vol. xiii, p. 183.

32. Córdoba to Borica, July 20, 1796 (B. C., *Miss. and Col.*, vol. i, p. 576).

33. Branciforte to Borica, instructions as to founding of *villa*, Jan. 25, 1797 (B. C., *Miss. and Col.*, vol. i, p. 78). List of colonists, Jan. 23, 1797 (B. C., *Prov. St. Pap.*, vol. xv, p. 223).

34. Instructions, Borica to Moraga, July 17, 1797 (B. C., *Miss. and Col.*, vol. i, p. 360).

35. Borica to *comisionado* at Branciforte, Jan. 25, Oct. 29, Dec. 5, 1798 (B. C., *Arch. Sta. Cruz*, p. 71; *Prov. St. Pap.*, vol. xxi, p. 50). Borica to *alcalde* of San José, March 27, April 8, 1799; same to *comisionado* of San José, April 20, 1799 (B. C., *Prov. Rec.*, vol. iv, pp. 291, 293, 294).

36. B. C., *Prov. Rec.*, vol. iv, p. 56; *Prov. St. Pap.*, vol. xxi, p. 271.

37. B. C., *Prov. Rec.*, vol. vi, p. 55; *Prov. St. Pap.*, vol. xvii, p. 19.

38. M. A., Arch. Genl., *Prov. Int.* 5, exped. 11.

39. Branciforte to Guardian of San Fernando, Aug. 19, 1796, stating that it would be impracticable to conform to the *Reglamento* with respect to foundations toward the east, as there were no fit lands, and it would not be prudent to expose missionaries or guard to the *genio feroz* of the Gentiles there. (M. A., Museo, *Docs. Rel. á las Mis. de Califs.*, Qto iii.)

40.

POPULATION OF ALTA CALIFORNIA

	A. D. 1783	A. D. 1790	A. D. 1795	A. D. 1797	A. D. 1800
Neophytes	4027	7353			13,500
Spaniards		970		1200	1200
Neophytes and Spaniards			11,226	12,921	

— (B. C., *St. Pap. Mis.*, vol. i, p. 5; M. A., Arch. Genl., *Californias*, 74.)

According to figures submitted by Borica on July 24, 1797, the total of Spaniards was 832; of Indians, 11,060; of *mestizos*, 464; of mixed color, 385; of slaves, 1. The grand total of population was 12,748 (M. A., Arch. Genl., *Californias*, 74). At the end of 1804 the grand total of neophytes was reported as 19,099 (M. A., *Docs. Rel. á las Mis. de Califs.*, Qto i).

In 1800, the total livestock was 187,000 head: 88,000 sheep, 74,000 cattle, 24,000 horses, 1000 mules, etc.

41. On Sept. 10, 1790, Fages computed as needful for the instruction of neophytes in each of the presidial districts of Alta California: 2 carpenters, 2 smiths, 1 armorer, 1 mason, 1 weaver, 1 master-mechanic, 1 tanner, 1 stone-cutter, 1 tailor, 1 potter. In 1790 there were the following craftsmen

in Los Ángeles: 3 ploughmen, 1 builder, 1 tailor, 2 shoemakers, 1 master-mechanic, 1 smith, 1 *jomateros*, 6 herdsmen, 2 muleteers, 7 pickmen. In 1790 in Alta California as a whole there were: 2 silversmiths, 5 miners, 38 plough-men, 19 owners of ranchos, 2 master-mechanics or builders, 5 carpenters, 3 smiths, 6 tailors, 2 masons, 8 shoemakers, 1 doctor, 123 herdsmen and mule-teers. In 1797, Borica reported the principal branch of mission industry to be the weaving of woolen cloth. At San Luis Obispo, San Gabriel, San Francisco, and San Juan Capistrano some cotton cloth was woven, but as the raw material must be obtained from San Blas, it was difficult to continue the work. At all the missions hides were cured and deer-skins collected. Some Indians of San Carlos were being taught carpentry and masonry. At San Francisco two or three were being taught blacksmithing, and at Santa Clara, tanning. There was a mill at San Luis Obispo and another at Santa Cruz. (*Resumen y Notas de los Estados de Misiones*, July 8, 1897, — M. A., Arch. Genl., *Prov. Int.* 216.)

42. Borica to Father José Lorente, Feb. 1, 1795: Guards will be furnished to padres, even though forbidden by orders, strictly construed (B. C., *Prov. St. Pap.*, vol. xxi); Branciforte to Guardian of San Fernando, Nov. 7, 1795 (M. A., Museo, *Docs. Rel. á las Mis. de Califs.*, Qto iii).

43. Borica to Lasuén, Sept. 22, 1796 (B. C., *Prov. Rec.*, vol. vi, p. 173). Borica to same, Dec. 2, 1796 (*Ibid.*, p. 178). Lasuén to padres from Soledad to San Diego, circular directing elections *pro forma* and as a means merely for neophyte enlightenment for the future. "There can be no regular civil government as by Laws of Indies till the missions become pueblos or *doctrinas*." (B. C., *Arch. Sta. Bárb.*, vol. xi, p. 138.) Viceroy to Lasuén, Dec. 20, 1797, calls attention to requirement of *Reglamento* as to *alcaldes*, and explains that elections are for the political advancement of Indians as contemplated by law 20, tit. i, lib. vi of the *Recopilación*. (*Ibid.*, vol. x, p. 90.) Cf. chapter viii of text, nn. 6, 12, 24.

44. As stated in chapter viii, note 20, the provision of the *Reglamento* for reducing the quota of padres from two to one at a mission was contravened by the royal order of May 20, 1782, approving the *estatutos* of Comisario-General Manuel de la Vega, which provided that *ningún Misionero pueda recidir, ni vivir solo en los Pueblos, Misiones y nuevas conversiones*. On Feb. 3, 1797, Branciforte wrote to the Guardian of San Fernando, stating that he could not find the *cédula* in his *secretaría de cámara*, and asking for a copy. On Oct. 23, 1797, a full exposition of the law was made by the Guardian (Pedro Callejas). He showed that by law 24, 7, part 1 (?) of the *Recopilación*, it was decreed that no religious ought to be allowed to die alone in *villa* or *castillo*, or to be placed alone in a parochial church, but with breth-ren, so that he might be aided "to contend with the world, the flesh, and the devil." In confirmation of the old law there were *cédulas* by Felipe V and Fernando VI, of dates Nov. 13, 1744, and Dec. 4, 1747. (M. A., Museo, *Docs. Rel. á las Mis. de Califs.*, Qto iii.)

As for chaplain duty at the presidios (an old question), reports to Borica by the comandantes of the four presidios show that it was reasonably well performed everywhere save at San Francisco. (M. A., Arch. Genl., *Californias*, 12.)

45. June 30, 1771 (M. A., Museo, *Trasuntos*).

46. To Pedro de Alberni, August 3, 1796 (B. C., *Prov. St. Pap. Mil.* (Benicia), vol. xxiv, pp. 7-8).

The backward condition mentioned to Alberni was ascribed by Borica to four distinct causes: (1) Loss of freedom, the Indians being a race unable to endure subjection of any kind, industrial or political; (2) insufficient food, the missions not raising enough grain; (3) filth of body and abodes; (4) corralling of Indian girls and women at night in straitened and ill-ventilated quarters, — *monjas*, so-called, or nunneries. The Governor had inspected some at a time when they were empty, and "so pestiferous were they that he had not been able to endure them for a single minute." Indian mortality was great. From 1769 to 1797, baptisms had been 21,653 and deaths 10,437. If gain was to be made, the Indians must be given more freedom, fed on warm meals, punished more moderately, compelled to bathe often, and to keep their huts clean. The girls and women must be provided at night with spacious quarters. There soon would be no Indians on the existing plan of treatment. (*Resumen y Notas de los Estados de Misiones*, July 8, 1897, — M. A., Arch. Genl., *Prov. Int.* 216.) Replying to Borica, Lasuén asserted that the mission Indians were fatter and better than the Gentiles. The *monjas* were kept as clean and well ventilated as possible, and it was not the inmates that died, but those that betook themselves to the mountains. (Lasuén to Guardian of San Fernando, Nov. 12, 1800, June 19, 1801, — *Ibid.*, secs. 27, 28, 31.)

The object of the *monjas*, it may be explained, was the preservation of morality. As for Indian mortality at this period, the following table was submitted in 1796 for the period 1792–96: —

At San Francisco,	15.75 per cent
Sta. Clara,	12.62
Sta. Cruz,	11.75
San Carlos,	7.87
La Soledad,	6.83
San Antonio,	4.12
San Luis Obispo,	5.50
La Purísima,	5.50
Sta. Bárbara,	8.45
San Buenaventura,	7.50
San Gabriel,	6.87
San Juan Capistrano,	5.75
San Diego,	6.25

In Europe the mortality (in villages) was stated to be 2.5 per cent; and in towns of moderate size, 4 per cent. In Spain as a whole it was a little over 3 per cent. (B. C., *Misiones*, i.)

47. On Sept. 27, 1793, Guardian Pangua of San Fernando reported to Viceroy Revilla Gigedo that the Alta California missions were in no condition to be secularized. "These new Christians," he said, "like tender plants not yet well rooted, easily wither, reverting to their old Gentile liberty and indolent savage life." He even remarked that the Sierra Gorda establishments had deteriorated since secularization (M. A., Arch. Genl., *Prov. Int.* 5). On Dec. 27, 1793, the Viceroy wrote to the government at Madrid: "I am not well satisfied with the missions that have been secularized, nor will I take this step [Secularization], unless success is assured. *Clérigos* [curates] can do no more than *religiosos* [friars]." (B. C., *Miss. and Col.*, vol. i, p. 25, sec. 423.)

48. In 1785, 1788, and 1791, Fages had complained of punishment of neophytes by various padres. (B. C., *Prov. Rec.*, vol. iii, pp. 51, 67; *Prov. St. Pap.*, vol. x, p. 167.)

49. M. A., Museo, *Trasuntos*. Serra cites also the example of San Francisco Solano in Peru, who, though gifted by God with the power of taming the ferocity of the most barbarous by his presence and sweet words, nevertheless corrected disobedience even on the part of *alcaldes* by the lash. (B. C., *Arch. Sta. Bárb.*, vol. x, p. 99.)

50. Neve, instructions to his successor, Sept. 7, 1782. For cattle-stealing he has been compelled to punish both neophytes and Gentiles, by eight or ten days in the stocks, or twenty or twenty-five lashes (B. C., *Prov. St. Pap.* (Sacramento), vol. i, p. 72). Borica to Padre Mariano Apolinario, Sept. 26, 1796 (B. C., *Prov. Rec.*, vol. vi, p. 174 *et seq.*). In 1787, Fages had ordered fifteen or twenty lashes for cattle-stealing (*Prov. St. Pap.*, vol. vii, p. 145). Gasol, Guardian of San Fernando, forbade more than twenty-five lashes for neophytes. (B. C., *Patentes Eclesiásticas*, part ii, sec. 8.)

51. B. C., *Prov. St. Pap.*, vol. xiii, p. 147. Borica to Lasuén, Sept. 15 and Oct. 3, 1796 (B. C., *Prov. Rec.*, vol. vi, pp. 172, 176). For securing the return of runaways, the padres at San Francisco were in the habit of sending out neophyte bands. Against this practice Borica issued orders to Alberni (B. C., *Prov. St. Pap.*, vol. xxiv, p. 8; *Prov. Rec.*, vol. v, p. 91). On July 1, 1798, Borica wrote to the Viceroy that since October, 1796, the rigor with which the Indians of San Francisco had been treated had ceased. "I do not attribute," he said, "the merit of this change to myself. . . . The true author is Father José María Fernández." (B. C., *Prov. Rec.*, vol. vi, p. 97.)

52. Grajera, comandante at San Diego, was ill; his report was sent in 1799.

53. The history of Father Concepción, as above set forth, is based upon the complete *expediente* in the Mexican Archives, entitled "Expediente

s^{re} denuncia que hizó el Padre Ant. de la Concep^{n} acerca de los Desordenes de las Misiones de Californias y mal trato q en ella se da á los neofitos" (Arch. Genl., *Prov. Int.* 216). The document entitled "La restitución á España del Misionero Fr. Antonia de la Concepción pr causa de sus enfermedades" has also been used. (M. A., Arch. Genl., *Californias*, 59.) Bancroft lacked many of the documents contained in the *expediente*. He lacked also the document pertaining to the restitution.

54. See chapter x, n. 10, where the matter is considered in connection with Arrillaga.

55. On the subject of secular education under Borica, see Bancroft, *History of California*, vol. i, pp. 642–644, and notes. In 1796, Salazar urged that instruction in *primeras letras* be given in all the missions.

56. The separation was effected August 29, 1804.

CHAPTER X

THE PROBLEM OF SUBSISTENCE

New Chapter Sources: B. C., Russian-American Series, MS. (Translation by Ivan Petróff) reëxamined; Mary Graham, *Our Centennial* — "Concepción Argüello," San Francisco, 1876; *The Mercury Case*, original manuscript, — Los Ángeles Public Library. (Specific citations below.)

1. Fages to Croix, June 26, 1772. States non-arrival of ship at Monterey, and scarcity. Reports having given orders for the formation of two parties to kill bears and that already some thirty have been killed. Replying to above on Oct. 14, Croix complains of lack of information concerning presidio and missions; alludes to suspicion of their abandonment; asks regarding discovery of port of San Francisco. (M. A., Arch. Genl., *Californias*, 66.)

2. May 21, 1772, Ayer Coll.; Translation, *Out West*, vol. xvi, p. 56.

3. Nov. 26, 1773 (M. A., Museo, *Docs. Rel. á las Mis. de Califs.*, Qto ii). A cause of failure by transports to reach Monterey, and sometimes San Diego, was the conviction, then strong in Mexico, that these points could better be reached overland from the peninsula (chapter vi, n. 21). On Dec. 2, 1772, the Viceroy reprimanded Fages for allowing the San Antonio to protract her voyage to Monterey. Her cargo should have been sent by land (B. C., *Prov. St. Pap.*, vol. i, p. 77). But in 1774, when Serra went north in the Santiago, the Viceroy became vexed that Pérez was induced to stop at San Diego. (M. A., Arch. Genl., *Cor. de Virreyes*, sér. ii, 38/55, no. 1421; *Ibid.*, Bucarely, 1774, 41/58, no. 1519.)

4. Cf. chapter ix, n. 8, 24. Arrillaga on Spain's attitude toward commerce: "Trade has been entirely neglected by us, but now the government is beginning to open its eyes with regard to these [California] ports. . . . The class of people engaged in [trade] is now so much respected that the King, in opposition to the rules of the Court, has given to many of them the title of *marqués*, which has never happened in Spain before. Yet when it was wished to advance our [California] trade, some private persons, who had from olden times been sending an occasional galleon from Manila to Acapulco, protested against it as an infringement upon their rights. . . . The Manilans ship on their galleon some Chinese goods. . . . We do business with some Mexicans, who, with the help of the two men-of-war annually dispatched along our coasts from San Blas, send us some goods at excessive prices, and we have to pay the *piasters* in advance in order to obtain the following year the necessaries of life." (N. P. Rezánoff to Russian Minister of Commerce, New Archangel, June 17, 1806.) See P. Tikhmeneff, *Historical Review of the Russian-American Company*, St. Petersburg, 1861 (B. C., Translation, Ivan Petróff), part ii, pp. 828–832.

5. M. A., Arch. Genl., *Cor. de Virreyes*, Bucarely, Sept. 26, 1774; *Ibid.*, 1774, 41/58, no. 1519; *Ibid.*, 1776, 67/84, no. 2542.

6. Neve to Fages, Sept.7, 1782, par. 17 (B. C., *Prov. St. Pap.* (Sacramento), vol. i, p. 72); Fages to Romeu, Feb. 26, 1791, par. 16 (B. C., *Prov. St. Pap.*, vol. x, p. 151). Prior to 1801 the stopping of the galleon at San Francisco or Monterey seems to have been dispensed with. (See Tagle's petition as cited at p. 189 of text, and Arrillaga as quoted in n. 4, *supra*.)

7. Viceroy to King, Oct. 27, 1785, inclosing *expediente* on advisability of concession and recommending it. (*Cor. de Virreyes*, Conde de Gálvez, 1785, 1, 138, no. 250.) Fages to Romeu, Feb. 26, 1791, pars. 16, 17, 18, on evils of free commerce (B. C., *Prov. St. Pap.*, vol. x, p. 151). See Bancroft, *History of California*, vol. i, p. 625, n. 2.

8. May 24, 1797 (B. C., *Prov. St. Pap.* (Sacramento), vol. ix, p. 22); Nov. 16, 1797 (B. C., *Prov. Rec.*, vol. vi, p. 61).

9. Beltrán, *Informe*, March 7, 1796 (B. C., *Prov. St. Pap.*, vol. xiv, p. 140). Borica to Viceroy, Sept. 11, 1796. It was the recommendation of the latter that Alta California be defined to extend from San Diego Presidio to that of San Francisco, "the last point that we can possess with exclusive dominion on the Northwest Coast, according to the agreement with the Court of London made in the year 1790" (B. C., *Prov. St. Pap.* (Sacramento), vol. iv, p. 49). Viceroy Iturrigaray to Governor of Californias, Aug. 29, 1804, citing royal order concerning division (B. C., *Prov. St. Pap.*, vol. xviii, p. 175; *Instrucciones de los Virreyes*, Mexico, 1867, secs. 290, 291, 293). The dividing line was declared coincident with "the stream and *ranchería* of Rosario at Barrabas."

10. From 1781 (year of the massacre on the Colorado) to 1796, the question of a Sonora-California or New Mexico-California connection had been given but little attention. In 1785 a proposal by Fages to open communication with New Mexico was forbidden by Viceroy Conde de Gálvez, on the ground of Indian hostility (B. C., *Mayer MSS.*, no. 8; *Prov. St. Pap.*, vol. xviii, p. 34). But in 1796, Aug. 20, Viceroy Branciforte wrote to Governor Borica, favoring a new attempt to found a mission on the Colorado, as suggested by the latter (B. C., *Prov. St. Pap.* (Sacramento), vol. v, p. 27), and on Sept. 11, 1796, Borica revived the plan (cf. chapter vi, n. 8; chapter vii, n. 52), whereby the Dominicans of the peninsula were to push on to the river. Let them (he said) occupy Tucsón with a view to a connection between California and New Mexico (*Ibid.*, vol. iv, p. 49). On Oct. 5, 1796, Borica wrote to the Viceroy as per the present chapter, and it was this letter that drew forth objection from Lasuén (B. C., *Arch. Sta. Bárb.*, vol. x, p. 73 *et seq.*).

Meanwhile (June, 1796), Arrillaga, lieutenant-governor of the Californias at Loreto, had begun (in the interest of the Dominicans) a survey of the peninsula to the northeast. Already there had been established the Dominican missions S^mo Rosario, San Pedro, Santo Domingo, San Vicente,

Santo Tomás, and San Miguel, the last only a day's journey south of San Diego; and Arrillaga's tour was for determining the practicability of a mission and presidio near the gulf on the northeast. It resulted in the founding (Nov. 12, 1797) of the mission Santa Catarina, and in a recommendation for the founding of a presidio of one hundred men either at Santa Olaya or at the mouth of the Colorado (B. C., *Prov. St. Pap.*, vol. xvi, p. 136). On Dec. 22, 1797, Borica sent Arrillaga's recommendation to the Viceroy, but advised conciliation of the Indians in order to remove the hostile feeling engendered in 1781 (B. C., *Prov. Rec.*, vol. vi, p. 65).

Pedro de Nava's *informe* bore date Chihuahua, July 20, 1801. It reviewed the communications of Borica and Arrillaga, stating objections. A New Mexico-California connection was desirable for California but not urgent. New Mexicans might be harmed by trading westward. At present Chihuahua fully met all needs, and Indians were too warlike. The *gente de razón* reported idle by Concha were required to repopulate the four abandoned pueblos on the *Camino Real* between Paso del Norte and Santa Fé. (B. C., *Prov. St. Pap.*, vol. xviii, p. 34.)

11. Borica in his report on commerce alludes to "the cattle ranches of Monterey, San Diego, and the newly established one in San Francisco, which are administered on the King's account."

12. Revilla Gigedo, *Informe sobre las Islas de la Mesa ó Sanduich*, Dec. 27, 1789 (M. A., Arch. Genl., *Cor. de Virreyes*, Revilla Gigedo, 1789, no. 199).

13. Jan. 28, 1797 (B. C., *Arch. Sta. Bárb.*, vol. vi, p. 185). Gálvez had said: "The idea came to me of proposing to H. M. that he order a fraternity to be founded under his immediate and supreme protection, with the jurisdiction and title of *Propaganda Fide*," etc. (*Informe*, 1771, Mexico, 1867, p. 147).

14. April 7, 1801 (B. C., *Prov. St. Pap.*, vol. xviii, p. 107). Colonial projects other than those mentioned in the text were not lacking. In 1792, Alejandro Jordán proposed to found a colony in California to supply San Blas with products, but the offer was declined by the King in 1794, for the reason that free trade by the transports would be sufficient. (Arrillaga to Viceroy, Nov. 8, 1792, etc.; Bancroft, *History of California*, vol. i, p. 503, n. 8.)

15. The leading authorities are R. Greenhow, *Oregon and California*, Boston, 1844; W. Sturgis, "Northwest Fur Trade," Hunt's *Mercantile Magazine*, vol. xiv; Russian-American Series (MS., in B. C.), translated from the Russian by Ivan Petróff; Bancroft, *History of the Northwest Coast*, vol. i, chaps. 10, 11; Same, *History of Alaska*, chap. 11.

16. As carried on under Vicente Basadre for the Spanish Government (cf. chapter ix, n. 5), the otter-skin trade was in the hands exclusively of the padres and Indians. (Fages, *Bando*, Aug. 29, 1786, — B. C., *Prov. St. Pap.*, vol. vi, p. 140; *Arch. Sta. Bárb.*, vol. i, p. 283; vol. x, p. 8; Fages, *Bando*,

Sept. 15 and 20, 1787, — B. C., *Arch. Sta. Bárb.*, vol. xii, p. 3; *Prov. Rec.*, vol. i, p. 35.) In 1788, Father Cambón welcomed the decrees of Fages as giving to the neophytes opportunity to trade and barter in merchandise of their own land — something hitherto monopolized by the soldiery (M. A., Museo, *Docs. Rel. á las Mis. de Californias*, Qto iii). In 1790, when the trade as a government monopoly ceased, the padres were deprived of a market, save as they were able to sell a few skins through the medium of the transports, or save as they sold them to American smuggling vessels. In Jan., 1791, the Guardian of San Fernando gave orders that skins were to be sent to Mexico, and Lasuén's instructions to the padres were to send them so packed that the college *síndico* "alone should know what was being sent" (B. C., *Arch. Sta. Bárb.*, vol. ix, p. 314). In 1805, the Russians thought of California as a source of bread-supply, and also, perhaps, of furs, "if not with permission of the Viceroy, at least in a private manner with the missionaries. . . . The missionaries, as far as known, were the chief agents in the contraband trade." (Tikhmeneff, *Historical Review of the Russian-American Company*, St. Petersburg, 1861, in B. C.; Translation (MS.), Ivan Petróff.) In 1806, José Gasol, Guardian of San Fernando, warned the Alta California padres not to provoke the accusation that " some of their number were trading with foreigners." (B. C., *Patentes Eclesiásticas*, p. 3.)

17. M. Rodríguez, *Informe*, April 10, 1803 (B. C., *Prov. St. Pap.*, vol. xviii, p. 252). R. J. Cleveland, *A Narrative of Voyages*, etc., 2 vols., 1842, vol. i, pp. 210–16.

18. Tikhmeneff, *Historical Review of the Russian-American Company*, St. Petersburg, 1861 (B. C.); Translation, Ivan Petróff, part ii, p. 766, etc.

19. K. Khlebnikoff, *Alexander Baránoff*, St. Petersburg, 1835 (B. C.); Translation, Ivan Petróff.

20. Tikhmeneff, part ii, p. 710. Rezánoff's instructions to Schwostoff, says Tikhmeneff, were to go to the south end of Saghalien Island, destroy the Japanese settlements, making prisoners of all the able-bodied men, especially the mechanics and tradesmen. The old and sick were to be set at liberty, never to visit Saghalien again, except to trade with the Russians. Schwostoff was to gather all the Japanese idols and a few priests, to be sent to an island in Sitka Bay, called Japanese Island to this day. . . . No reply by the Czar was made to Rezánoff's letter (quoted in text), and the Chamberlain tried to revoke his orders to Schwostoff, but the latter insisted on carrying them out. With the Juno, tended by the Awos under Davidoff, he went to Aniva [?], burned villages, destroyed Japanese vessels, appropriating cargoes and carrying on piracy for a whole summer to "coax" the Japanese into friendship. The vessels returned to Okhotsk, where the goods were seized and men arrested. (*Ibid.*, part i, pp. 176–78.)

21. Tikhmeneff, part ii, p. 766, etc. It is noteworthy that it was Rezánoff's opinion that the Russian missionaries (of whom there were a number

in the Northwest) might with profit imitate the Jesuits of Paraguay, "entering into the extensive views of the government."

22. Tikhmeneff, part ii, p. 769, etc.

23. Tikhmeneff, part ii, p. 799.

24. Tikhmeneff, part ii, pp. 801–828.

25. G. H. Langsdorff, *Voyages*, London, 1814, vol. ii, p. 153.

26. Langsdorff notes that the padres were "much pleased" with the following articles exhibited from the stores on board the Juno: linen cloths, Russian ticking, English woolen cloth. Articles inquired for were: tools for mechanical trades, implements for husbandry, household utensils, shears for shearing sheep, axes, large saws for sawing-out planks, iron cooking-vessels, casks, bottles, glasses, fine pocket- and neck-handkerchiefs, leather, particularly calf-skins, and sole-leather. (*Ibid.*, p. 173.) The ladies at the presidio inquired, he says, for cotton and muslin, shawls, striped ribands, etc. (*Ibid.*, p. 174.)

27. Tikhmeneff, part ii, pp. 808–28.

28. Langsdorff, part ii, p. 217. "The whole family of Argüello and several other friends and acquaintances had collected themselves at the fort, and wafted us an adieu with their hats and pocket-handkerchiefs."

29. *Ibid.*, pp. 183, 385.

30. Mary Graham, *Our Centennial*, San Francisco, 1876.

31. Tikhmeneff, part ii, pp. 808–28. Apropos of Chinese laborers, it is interesting to note that in 1788, Meares shipped, by the Iphigenia, Chinese smiths and carpenters to Nootka Sound, "because of their reputed hardiness, industry, and ingenuity, simple manner of life, and low wages. . . . If hereafter," Meares records, "trading-posts should be established on the American coast, a colony of these men would be a very important acquisition." (W. R. Manning, *The Nootka Sound Controversy*, p. 289.)

32. Rezánoff intended first to establish a settlement on the Strait of Juan de Fuca at Port Discovery; then settlements at Havre de Grey and on the Columbia River. "The advantageous position of the port of San Francisco was sure to attract the commerce of all nations" (Tikhmeneff, pt. i, p. 175). In 1813, Viceroy Calleja claimed a recognition by Russia (*vide* treaty, 8th of July, 1812) of Juan de Fuca Strait as the northern limit of Alta California (B. C., *Prov. St. Pap.*, vol. xix, p. 33).

33. Bancroft, *History of California*, vol. ii, pp. 298–99, and notes.

34. B. C., *Prov. St. Pap.* (Sacramento), vol. v, p. 59.

35. B. C., *Prov. St. Pap.*, vol. xix, p. 14.

36. *Ibid.*, p. 73. Arrillaga to Viceroy, Jan. 2, 1806, reporting statement by "Don José Ocain" that an individual from Philadelphia had asked Congress for 40,000 men with whom to take possession of New Spain. (B. C., *Prov. Rec.*, vol. ix, p. 70.)

37. *The Mercury Case*, MS., Los Ángeles Public Library.

38. The private rancho is considered in chapter xvi.

39. B. C., *Prov. Rec.*, vol. i, pp. 173, 181.

40. B. C., *Arch. Sta. Bárb.*, vol. vi, p. 35. Macario de Castro to Arrillaga, San José, March 24 and June 5, 1805, on necessity of killing mares (B. C., *Prov. St. Pap.*, vol. xix, p. 77). Petition of Russian-American Company stating that immense herds of wild cattle and horses range as far north as the Columbia River, and that an annual slaughter of 10,000 to 30,000 head has been ordered. (Potechin, *Selenie Ross*, 2, 3; Langsdorff, *Voyages*, vol. ii, p. 170.)

41. B. C., *Prov. St. Pap. Mil.* (Benicia), vol. xxxiii, p. 19. Depredations in 1801 (B. C., *Prov. Rec.*, vol. xi, p. 159).

42. B. C., *Arch. Sta. Bárb.*, vol. xii, p. 89.

43. Lasuén to Guardian of San Fernando, June 16, 1802: cites failure on the Colorado; makes mention of preference by Santa Bárbara Channel Indians for the Mission plan, when "some years ago" given a choice between it and *rancheria* plan (M. A., Museo, *Docs. Rel. á las Mis. de Califs.*, Qto iii).

44. M. A., Arch. Genl., *Californias*, 41; *Cor. de Virreyes* (Azanza, 1800), sér. ii, 8/199, no. 806; B. C., *Prov. Rec.*, vol. ix, p. 86.

45. Arrillaga to Viceroy, *Informe*, July 15, 1806 (*Prov. Rec.*, vol. ix, p. 86).

46. B. C., *Prov. St. Pap.*, vol. xix, p. 343.

47. Bancroft, *History of California*, vol. ii, p. 162, n. 8. On transfer of corporal and soldier, B. C., *Arch. Arzobispado*, vol. ii, p. 6. On one occasion the Governor asserted himself roundly, to wit, when in 1810 Guardian Gasol empowered a padre to take a judicial declaration (B. C., Gasol, *Patentes*, 1806; *Prov. Rec.*, vol. xii, p. 102).

48. The need of education was recognized (*Informe*, note 45, *ante*).

49. B. C., Santa Inés, *Lib. de Misión*, p. 3; *Arch. Sta. Bárb.*, vol. viii, p. 151; *Prov. St. Pap.*, vol. xviii, p. 359.

CHAPTER XI

THE PROBLEM OF SUBSISTENCE (*continued*)

1. SOLA to Viceroy, July 3, 1816, acknowledging receipt of news of the insurgent ships from Don Bernardo Bonavía, comandante-general of the Provincias Internas. Annexed to Bonavía's letter were communications from Paita, stating that there had reached that port a ship of the Royal Philippine Company (the San Fernando) with news of "an insurgent expedition from Buenos Ayres commanded by General Braun of the Anglo-American nation. It was the object of these *piratas infames* to harry all the coast and then take refuge in the United States." (M. A., Arch. Genl., *Prov. Int.* 23.)

2. B. C., *Arch. Arzob.*, vol. iii, part i, p. 55; *Prov. St. Pap.*, vol. xx, pp. 104, 111; *Arch. Sta. Bárb.*, vol. xii, p. 358.

3. B. C., *Arch. Arzob.*, vol. iii, part ii, pp. 2–24, 41. Writing to Guerra on Dec. 11, 1818, Padre Luis Martínez of San Luis Obispo ventured upon some jocose counsel. "Remember," he said, "the tactics of the Galicians. In the front rank they placed women, and when the French, who always paid homage to women, advanced, they [the French] quickly abandoned warfare for gallantry. If you wish to conquer the insurgents, you must do the same." (B. C., Guerra, *Docs. para la Historia de Calif.*, vol. iii, p. 9.)

4. Sola, *Informe*, Dec. 12, 1818; Bustamente, *Historical Picture*, vol. v, p. 62; Payéras, *Informe*, 1817–18 (B. C., *Arch. Sta. Bárb.*, vol. xii, p. 100); Gonzáles, *Experiences*, p. 6. Joseph Chapman, an American impressed by Bouchard at the Sandwich Islands, deserted at Monterey, and became an early foreign settler in California. (Cf. chapter XIV, n. 28.)

5. Antonio Ripoll to Governor Sola. The taste for war inspired in Padre Ripoll by the insurgent demonstration induced the padre to undertake a systematic organization of the neophytes of the mission of Santa Bárbara. In 1820 (April 29) he wrote thus to Sola. Noticing that the Indians were filled with enthusiasm to defend their "king, their country, and their religion," he was forming a company of 100 men — *compañia de Urbanos Realistas de Santa Bárbara*. Their arms were to be good bows and arrows. Besides, he was forming a company of axemen (*macheteros*), fifty strong, and a squadron of lancers, thirty strong. "Thus will the insolent insurgents or pirates, who shall venture to attack us, be warned." (B. C., *Arch. Arzob.*, vol. iv, part i, p. 17.)

6. B. C., *Arch. Sta. Bárb.*, vol. vi, p. 215.

7. B. C., *Prov. Rec.*, vol. ix, p. 161. The Lima ships came again in 1817.

8. B. C., *Prov. St. Pap.*, vol. xix, pp. 341, 344; vol. xx, pp. 103, 148; Sola to Viceroy, July 3, 1816 (M. A., Arch. Genl., *Prov. Int.* 23, no. 52).

9. B. C., *Prov. St. Pap.*, vol. xx, p. 168. Wilcox (known to the Spaniards as Don Santiago) wooed Concepción with the plea that by marrying him she would win a convert to the Catholic faith. The lady's reply was: "I did think something of saving his soul, but his Divine Majesty took from me the foolish fear of its loss, for I remembered that Concepción was not necessary to him if his conscience was sincere. . . . The poor fellow, I pity him and am grateful to him," etc. (B. C., Guerra, *Docs. para la Historia de Calif.*, vol. vi, p. 132.)

10. B. C., *Arch. Sta. Bárb.*, vol. iii, p. 104.

11. B. C., *Prov. Rec.*, vol. ix, p. 116. In 1801, Dec. 12, the King had granted to New California the privilege of naming a delegate from the presidios. (*Ibid.*, p. 13.)

12. M. A., Arch. Genl., *Prov. Int.* 23, no. 1.

13. *Ibid.*

14. B. C., *Prov. St. Pap.*, vol. xix, p. 33.

15. B. C., *Conferencia celebrada en el Presidio de San Francisco*, etc., October, 1816.

16. B. C., *Prov. St. Pap.*, vol. xx, p. 5; vol. xxii, p. 28.

17. B. C., Vallejo, *Historia de California*, vol. iv, p. 209.

18. B. C., P. Tikhmeneff, *Historical Review of the Russian-American Company*, part i, p. 221.

19. B. C., Sarría, *Informe*, Nov., 1817, p. 73; *Libro de Misión*, p. 5. See *Arch. Sta. Bárb.*, vol. iii, p. 142; vol. iv, p. 157; vol. xii, p. 125; Payéras, memorandum, *Docs. para la Hist. de Calif.*, vol. iv, p. 344.

20. B. C., *Arch. Arzob.*, vol. iii, part ii, pp. 90, 96. Payéras made protest against any commingling of the Cholos with the Indians.

21. B. C., *Prov. St. Pap.*, vol. xviii, pp. 200, 202.

22. E. Tapis, to Arrillaga, March 1, 1805. "The story goes that after a fit of frenzy the woman said that Chupu had appeared, assuring her that the Gentiles and Christians would perish of the epidemic, if they did not offer Chupu alms, and did not bathe their heads with a certain water. The news of the revelation flew throughout the huts of the mission at midnight, and nearly all of the neophytes, including the *alcalde*, went to the woman's house to offer beads and seeds, and to witness renunciation by the Christians. Though the tale was spread throughout the Channel *rancherías* and into the mountains, the missionaries remained ignorant of it, for Chupu had said that whoever should tell the padres would die immediately. But after three days a neophyte woman, casting aside fear, related the whole story. If the frenzied woman had added to her tale that, for the epidemic to cease, it was necessary to kill the padres, the two soldiers of the guard, the *alcaldes* and others, as much credit would have been given to this as to the first part of her account." (B. C., *Arch. Sta. Bárb.*, vol. vi, p. 32.)

23. Tapis to Arrillaga, Feb. 21, 1805. "The guards of the seventeen missions are reduced to two or three each. The missions, excepting Santa Inés,

which is entitled to ten men, can have, each, but six men, including the corporal. (B. C., *Arch. Sta. Bárb.*, vol. xii, p. 75.)

24. P. Muñoz, *Diario de la Expedición hecha por Don Gabriel Moraga á los Nuevos Descubrimientos del Tular*, Sept. 21 to Nov. 2, 1806 (B. C., *Arch. Sta. Bárb.*, vol. iv, p. 27). "We found, after having traveled five leagues, the *Río de los Santos Reyes*, which had been discovered in the previous year, 1805."

25. B. C., E. Tapis, *Informe*, 1805-06, p. 81.

26. The trial of the cook (Nazarío by name) makes an interesting record. The crime was not denied. Nazarío confessed, and his words were taken down. He was angry, he said, with the padre because on Dec. 15 he had given him fifty lashes, and on the night of the same day twenty-four lashes, on the morning of the 16th twenty-seven lashes, and on the afternoon of the 16th twenty-five lashes. "I was so tormented with the many lashings that I received that, as I could take no other revenge, I resolved on the night of the 16th to put poison in the padre's soup to see if I and the other Indians of the mission could not thus be delivered. This padre is unbearable. Sometimes I did not save food for the family of the sergeant, either because there wasn't enough, or I forgot. For the omission I was given fifty lashes. When I was being punished, and he did not do it himself, he would get some servant to sing *merienda, merienda* [food, food]. None of the mission Indians like him, much less the Gentiles." The prosecutor in summing up said: "It is proved by the culprit's declaration that in two days he received more than two hundred lashes and this without serious cause." His sentence was eight months' detention at the San Diego Presidio. (B. C., *Prov. St. Pap.* (Benicia), vol. xlix, p. 4.)

27. B. C., *Arch. Obispado: Monterey y Los Ángeles*, p. 86; *Arch. Sta. Bárb.*, vol. xii, p. 93. Quintana was accused of inflicting cruel punishments. It was alleged by the Indians that he had ordered an iron strap made with which to punish for fornication and theft. Sola defended the padre against these charges. (B. C., *Prov. Rec.*, vol. ix, p. 139.)

In 1877 Mr. Bancroft obtained from an Indian, Lorenzo Asisara, the story of the Quintana murder as related to Asisara by the latter's father, a neophyte of Santa Cruz. Quintana, it would seem, was seized, gagged, and strangled. Fear of his iron strap was intense. (J. D. Amador, *Memorias*, p. 58.)

28. B. C., *Arch. Sta. Bárb.*, vol. xii, p. 101.

29. B. C., *Arch. Sta. Bárb.*, vol. vi, p. 102.

30. B. C., Guerra, *Docs. para la Hist. de Calif.*, vol. v, p. 31. And yet again, Payéras, Petition to Sola, Sept. 17, 1819: "Apostates are increasing and the haughty and wandering spirit is growing astonishingly. . . . The cause of this is that expeditions have ceased. . . . The missions can be attacked, when least expected, by strong bodies composed of Christians and Gentiles, who with the greatest insolence deride the soldiers and challenge them to fight." (B. C., *Arch. Arzob.*, vol. iii, part ii, p. 90.)

31. By 1820, State Secular was indebted to the missionaries in the sum of 400,000 *pesos*. Sola to Sarría, May 29, 1821 (B. C., *Prov. St. Pap.* (Sacramento), vol. xviii, p. 44).

The *Comisario-Prefecto* was the immediate local representative of the *Comisario-General* of the Indies in Madrid. The appointment for Alta California would seem to have followed upon Borica's suggestion that the presidents of missions be made subject to local prelates or inspectors. Regarding the threatened excommunication, see B. C., *Protesta de los Padres contra Gabelas*, 1817, by Sarría, Amorós, Durán, Viader, and Marquínez.

32. B. C., *Decreto de las Cortes de 13 de Septiembre de 1813;* Translations, Jones, *Land Report*, no. 8; Dwinelle, *Colonial History of San Francisco*, 39.

33. B. C., Gasol, *Patentes*, 1806, sec. 10. At the same time the padres were warned not to employ female servants, but to depend entirely on men or boys.

34. B. C., *Arch. Sta. Bárb.*, vol. vi, p. 63. In 1820, Guardian Baldomero López wrote to the president of the missions: "To such a height has rumor mounted in this capital [Mexico] that the missionaries of Alta California are said to go about in vehicles of two wheels and carriages of four wheels. . . . I do not doubt it will be said that the poor missionary fathers of New California do not suffer the hardships which they proclaim, but enjoy themselves to an extent such that they ride in carts and carriages, a thing becoming the rich and powerful but not the poor."

35. The petition was preceded by a letter to the Viceroy, from Sola, of date August 21, 1816, representing need for padres (M. A., Arch. Genl., *Historia*, 287). Protest by Payéras (B. C., *Arch. Arzob.*, vol. iv, part i, p. 25).

36. *Expediente . . . la primera Junta de California, celebrada ante el Exmo Sor Virrey Don Juan Ruiz de Apodaca, en 5 de Julio de 1817* (M. A., Arch. Genl., *Gobernación*, "Indios Barbaros," 1).

37. B. C., *Arch. Sta. Bárb.*, vol. iii, p. 219.

38. B. C., *Arch. Arzob.*, vol. iv, part i, p. 66. *Cédulas Reales* (1818), 218; (1820) 223 (M. A., Arch. Genl.).

39. B. C., *Arch. Arzob.*, vol. iv, part i, p. 68.

40. *Ibid.*, p. 23. On July 16, 1821, Payéras assured the Bishop of Sonora that it was the wish of the Alta California missionaries to fulfill the requirements of Article 3 of the Decree of 1813, and "dedicate themselves to spreading religion in places yet unreduced" — places, so far as Alta California was concerned, lying east and north of the existing mission chain (*Ibid.*, p. 73). On Aug. 25, José María Estudillo of San Diego wrote to Sola, expressing the opinion that the Decree of 1813 would not be carried out in Alta California, because of the peculiar condition of the missions there (B. C., *Prov. St. Pap.*, vol. xx, p. 291).

41. Arrillaga, *Informe*, 1806 (B. C., *Prov. Rec.*, vol. ix, p. 86); Sola,

Informe, 1817 (B. C., *Prov. Rec.*, vol. viii, p. 155); Sola, *Tour of Inspection*, 1818 (B. C., *Prov. Rec.*, vol. viii, p. 176).

42. The death-rate of 1820 was 42 per cent of the population as a whole. In 1810 it had been 45 per cent of the original population plus baptisms.

43. Sola, 1817, 1818, note 41, *ante*. Sola sought to enforce the Spanish laws against selling or giving wine to the Indians. These laws were given by Philip III, 1594; Philip IV, 1637. (*Recopilación*, law 36, lib. 6, tit. 1; also law 7, lib. 6, tit. 13, B. C., *Arch. Sta. Bárb.*, vol. vi, p. 104.)

B. C., *Legislative Rec.*, vol. i, p. 104). These regulations Echeandía pronounced in conformity with Article 16 of the Federal Constitution, and an order of the government of July 19, 1824.

22. A. Duhaut-Cilly, *Voyage autour du Monde*, 1826–29, Paris, 1835 ; Italian edition, Turin, 1841, 2 vols.

23. As early as September, 1822, orders for a survey westward from Tuçón to the peninsula had, at the solicitation of Sola, been issued by Lieutenant-Colonel Antonio Narbona, comandante in Sonora.

24. Narbona's instructions to Romero contemplated the selection of a presidio site at the mouth of the Colorado; the gathering of skulls and skins of animals; of skulls of Gentile Indians; of minerals, etc. The Casa Grande was to be visited, and it was to be ascertained whether the North Americans had established relations with the natives. (*Informe* (Narbona), with Romero's diary and Romero's and Caballero's letters, M. A., Arch. Genl., *Relaciones*, vol. i, Carpt[a] no. 189.)

25. M. A., Arch. Genl., *Fomento, Baldíos*, leg. 2, exped. 52.

26. B. C., Mexico, *Mem. Relaciones*, 1823, pp. 31–33 (Bancroft's translation).

27. B. C., *Junta de Fomento de Californias*, Mexico, 1827.

28. B. C., *Arch. Arzob.*, vol. iv[2], p. 6.

29. B. C., Ripoll to Sarría, May 5, 1824 (*Arch. Arzob.*, vol. iv[2], p. 95).

30. Sarría to Argüello, April 14, 1825; explanation that oath to the Constitution would be a violation of oath of allegiance to the Spanish King (B. C., *Arch. Arzob.*, vol. iii[2], p. 127). Order for arrest of Sarría, Mexico, June 29, 1825 (B. C., *Sup. Gov. St. Pap.*, vol. iii, p. 4). Oath as taken or refused by each padre, 1826 (M. A., Arch. Genl., *Californias*, " Misiones," 18, exped. 24). In California there was strong opposition to expulsion of the padres. The *ayuntamientos* of San José and Monterey petitioned the Mexican Government against it.

31. Echeandía to Minister of Relations, Jan. 29, 1828: reports flight of Ripoll and Altimíra on Jan. 25, and asks whether, in order to avoid another like scandal, he shall not grant license of departure to such other padres as have refused to swear to the Constitution. The Minister of Justice, March 19, 1828, recommends that, in view of arrangements already made by the College of Zacatecas to supply missionaries to Alta California, and in view of the law for the expulsion of Spaniards, the incorrigibles be given license to depart. The Harbinger will be seized at whatever Mexican port she may stop. As she is an Anglo-American vessel, representation will be made to the United States (M. A., Arch. Genl., *Californias*, " Misiones," 18, exped. 26).

32. With regard to Ripoll and Altimíra, see A. Ord, *Ocurrencias en California* (B. C.). With regard to Martínez, see Ord, and E. de la Torre, *Reminscencias* (B. C.). See also *Proceso contra Solís* (*ante*, n. 19), Sarría, *Defensa del Padre Luis Martínez*, 1830 (B. C.), and Martínez, *Letters to*

José de la Guerra (B. C., Guerra, *Docs. para la Historia de Calif.*, vol. iii, pp. 12, 13).

33. Echeandía, April 28, 1826 (B. C., *Dept. St. Pap.*, vol. i, p. 130); Same, emancipation decree, July 25, 1826 (B. C., *Arch. Arzob.*, vol. v, p. 104; M. A., Arch. Genl., *Californias*, "Misiones," 18, exped. 24; summary by Bancroft, *History of California*, vol. iii, pp. 102–03).

34. Secularization plan, 1829–30 (B. C., *Leg. Rec.*, vol. i, p. 135; summary by Bancroft, *History of California*, vol. iii, p. 302, n. 2). Education was to be a fundamental feature. See Secularization Chart (pocket).

35. *Decreto de Secularización*, Jan. 6, 1831 (B. C., *Arch. Sta. Bárbara*, vol. ix, p. 420; summary by Bancroft, *History of California*, vol. iii, p. 305, n. 6). Supplementary *Reglamento*, Nov. 18, 1832 (B. C., *Miss. and Col.*, vol. ii, p. 63; summary by Bancroft, *History of California*, vol. iii, p. 314, n. 23).

36. On Oct. 17, 1829 (in accordance with a decree of Aug. 29), the first *asesor* (solicitor-general) for Alta California was appointed, in the person of the *licenciado*, Rafael Gómez of Jalisco. The position was resigned by Gómez in 1834, and Cosme Peña was named (M. A., Arch. Genl., *Justicia*, 104). Cf. chapter xiv, on California judicial system under Mexican régime.

On Oct. 6, 1829, Echeandía reported the arrival at Monterey of "Don Abel Stearns with four others, and one woman, bearing a passport from the supreme government."

37. First steps toward resistance: Pío Pico, *Narración Histórica*, p. 24 (B. C.); summary by Bancroft, *History of California*, vol. iii, p. 200, n. 36; *Pronunciamiento* (translated by Bancroft, *Ibid.*, p. 202, n. 39); Victoria to Mexico, dispatches (L. Alamán, *Sucesos de California*, 1831, B. C., *Sup. Gov. St. Pap.*, vol. viii, p. 13).

38. Pío Pico, *Historia de California*, pp. 35–40 (B. C.); J. Ávila, *Notas*, pp. 11–15 (B. C.).

39. M. Vallejo and S. Argüello, *Expediente vs. Victoria*, Feb. 17, 1832 (B. C., *Leg. Rec.*, vol. i, p. 298).

40. M. A., Arch. Genl., *Californias*, "Misiones," 44, exped. 8. See also Bancroft, *History of California*, vol. ii, pp. 496–506, and notes.

Brief, ex. 2; Dwinelle, *Colonial History of San Francisco*, Add. 3, — summary by Bancroft, *History of California*, vol. iii, p. 342, n. 4.

18. Arrillaga, *Recopilación*, 1835, p. 189.

19. M. A., Arch. Genl., *Gobernación*, "Congreso Genl.," leg. 12.

20. Alvarado to Vallejo, "Carta Confidencial," Nov. 7, 1836 (B. C.,*Vallejo Docs.*, vol. iii, no. 262); *Honolulu Gazette*, Dec. 2, 1837, — impartial as to Isaac Graham.

21. "Plan de Independencia" for California, Nov. 7, 1836 (B. C., *Bandini Docs.*, no. 41; summary by Bancroft, *History of California*, vol. iii, p. 470, n. 28).

22. J. Castro, *Decretos*, Dec. 7 and 9, 1836, nos. 5, 7, 8, 9 (B. C.).

23. B. C., *Arch. Los Ángeles*, vol. i, p. 106; vol. iv, p. 238.

24. "Plan de Independencia," *supra*, n. 21. Alvarado later confessed to a design to place Alta California under foreign protection. (Alvarado, *Historia de California*, vol. iii, pp. 199, 205, B. C.; Vallejo, *Historia de California*, vol. iii, p. 245 B. C., Cf. text, chapter xv.)

25. *Plan de Gobierno*, Sta. Bárbara, April 11, 1837; summary by Bancroft, *History of California*, vol. iii, p. 507, n. 47.

26. B. C., *Vallejo Docs.*, vol. iv, no. 276; translated by Bancroft, *History of California*, vol. iii, p. 529, n. 24.

27. "Tratado de Las Flores," April 23, 1838 (B. C., *Vallejo Docs.*, vol. xxxii, no. 130; translated by Bancroft, *Hist. of Calif.*, vol. iii, p. 562, n. 36).

28. Like California wars in general, this war had been bloodless. So much impressed with the humor of this circumstance was Lieutenant Juan Rocha, of the Los Ángeles force, that he is said to have observed that in future he should take with him his barber to bleed him, as thus only would blood ever be seen.

A plot to assassinate Alvarado when in Los Ángeles in 1837 was disclosed to him by a woman, heavily veiled, whom the Governor believed to be Doña Concepción, the erstwhile fiancée of Rezánoff.

29. Prefectures: Arrillaga, *Recopilación*, 1837, p. 202; translated, F. Hall, *History of San José*, 1871, p. 489.

30. Arrillaga, *Recopilación*, 1835, p. 583; translated, *Hartman's Brief*, ex. 6; Halleck, *Report on Land Titles*, p. 154.

31. B. C., *Arch. Sta. Bárb.*, vol. x, p. 205; translated by Dwinelle, *Colonial History of San Francisco*, Add. xxxvii; summary by Bancroft, *History of California*, vol. iv, p. 55, n. 21.

32. *Instrucciones;* translated, Halleck, *Report on Land Titles*, p. 156; summary by Bancroft, *History of California*, vol. iv, p. 56, n. 23.

33. B. C.,*Vallejo Docs.*, vol. xxxiii, p. 30; translated by Dwinelle, *Colonial History of San Francisco*, Add. xxxix; summary by Bancroft, *History of California*, vol. iv, p. 59, n. 28.

34. Dissolution of pueblo at San Juan Capistrano and gradual extinction of pueblos Las Flores, San Dieguito, and San Pascual. (Bancroft, *History of California*, vol. iii, p. 626; vol. iv, pp. 196, 625, with citations.)

CHAPTER XIV

ANGLO-AMERICANS

NEW CHAPTER SOURCES: Castro letters and diplomatic correspondence in Isaac Graham affair; protest by Viceroy Iturrigaray against occupation by Americans of the region at the mouth of the Columbia River; Vallejo list of the Bartleson-Bidwell Company, Castro-Alvarado letter to Mexican Minister of Relations, 1844; *informes* with regard to Pious Fund, 1793, 1823; Arrángoiz correspondence relative to "Anglo-Americans." (M. A.) (Specific citations below.)

1. M. A., Arch. Genl., *Justicia*, 1, 1840. Castro to Alvarado, April 8, 1840; Alvarado to Minister of Interior, April 22, 1840 (B. C., *Dept. Rec.*, vol. xi, p. 67).

2. Vallejo to Minister of War, Dec. 11, 1841: gives white population of Alta California as 6000, Indians 15,000 (M. A., *Californias*, 1841, leg. 2).

3. Bancroft (*History of California*, vol. iv, p. 5, n. 4) states that no explanation is anywhere given of the manner in which Garner's confession was obtained. Castro in his letter of April 8 (not cited by Bancroft) says: *Habiendo comparecido le hice entender que el Gobierno tenia fundados avisos de la intentona de varios estrangeros que maquinavan una desastrosa revolución y que ya se tomban medidas muy energicas para aprehender á los malvados. Sobresaltado de temor, el dicho individuo me contestó al momento dicendo: " que si se le ofrecia seguridad de su vida y de sus propriedades descubriria esta funcion y los cabecillas de ella."* Le aseguré de mil maneras esto, infundiendole *confianza, y declaró que los cazadores G^{rl} Graham y Alverto Morris y otros heran los principales caudillos.*

On the arrests, see Bancroft, pp. 11–15 and notes. Castro, in a letter to Alvarado of April 15 (not cited by Bancroft), quotes a letter from José M. Covarrubias, captain of auxiliaries, stating that the latter on the 7th went to the pueblo de Alvarado, arrested the foreigners there, dispatched a force over the Sierra de Sanfrancisquito, which arrested " Juan Copinger" and his companions, and was now sending a party to the port of San Francisco to make arrests, and would send a force to the Contracosta of San Pablo and valley of San José.

4. Bancroft (*History of California*, vol. iv, p. 18) gives a list of 47 names. An official list, certified at Monterey on April 22 by Juan Miguel Ctnzar, gives 46 names, and of these only 23 are found in Bancroft's list. It would appear that the other 23 were names of men from the South who were substituted for 23 apprehended in the North. (M. A., Arch. Genl., *Californias*, 1840.)

5. The course of events at Tepic was as follows: (1) Delivery by Castro of

tion and envy of European nations, and that the Anglo-American Commercial Company (that exists in the Sandwich Islands) has, in conjunction with the settlers on the Columbia, already projected a railway; that when the Spanish Cortes was considering the question of Mexican independence, the Russian minister had said that if there was exacted indemnification from Mexico, he was authorized to purchase Alta California up to 37° as a granary for Russia ; that even to-day the Russians hold Ross; that Mexican colonies should be planted toward the Columbia.

14. M. A., Arch. Genl., *Californias*, 1841, leg. 2; B. C., *Vallejo Docs.*, vol. x, 332.

15. M. A., *Californias*, 67.

16. *Ibid.*, 61. Bancroft prints a list of the Bartleson-Bidwell Company. It agrees with a list made by Vallejo, excepting that on Vallejo's list there appears the name U. W. Davison, — a name not given by Bancroft. (M. A., Arch. Genl., *Californias*, 1841.)

17. *Ibid.*, 64; *United States Exploring Expedition, 1838–1842*, Philadelphia, 1844–58, 20 vols.; vol. v, on California.

18. *Ibid.*, 68.

19. A change was vigorously opposed by Alvarado, who sent Manuel Castañares to Mexico to work against it. (Bancroft, *History of California*, vol. iv, chap. 11.) Alvarado minimized the danger from foreigners.

20. Message of President of United States to House of Representatives, on conduct of Jones, Feb. 22, 1843 (27th Cong., 3d Sess., *House Ex. Doc.* 166; M. A., Arch. Genl., *Californias*, 1842). Full correspondence, Micheltorena with Mexican Government, letters, Alvarado to Micheltorena, nos. 8, 9, 10, Oct. 19, 20, 21, announcing capitulation; Articles of Capitulation, Oct. 19; proclamation to the inhabitants of the two Californias, Oct. 19; letters, Jones to Micheltorena, announcing "later accounts from Mexico which induce me to believe that amicable relations have been restored between the two nations," Oct. 21, Nov. 1 (M. A., Arch. Genl., *Operaciones Militares*, leg. 2, frac. 1).

Letters, J. N. Almonte (Mexican minister to the United States) to Mexican Government: Letter of March 20, expressing opinion that United States was striving to gain time, so as to avoid necessity of punishing Commodore Jones, and that Mexico should insist on punishment; March 25, asking bill of items as basis of demand for indemnification; April 28, mentions rumor circulated by an officer in the United States squadron that Jones's coach (at San Pedro) was drawn by Mexican soldiers, — item appeared in *National Intelligencer;* letter, F. de Arrángoiz, Mexican consul at New Orleans, Feb. 12, 1843, announcing that Jones had been superseded by Commodore Dallas (M. A., Arch. Genl., *Internacional*, 1843 and 1847).

21. T. ap Catesby Jones, narrative printed in *Southern Vineyard*, Los Ángeles, May 22, 1858 (B. C.).

22. M. A., Arch. Genl., *Relaciones, Reseñas Políticas*, 1841–42; Dispatches, "Californias," nos. 4, 129, 183, 265, 374; replies, nos. 31, 73, 85. In a dispatch by the consul (no. 348, Dec. 1, 1842) it is reported that rumors of an agreement to cede California to the United States in payment of the Mexican debt are current.

23. The order is declared to be based on power given the President under the law of Feb. 22, 1832 (M. A., Arch. Genl., *Californias*, 1843). "About this order and the motive which prompted it," Bancroft says, "there is a mystery that I am unable to penetrate " (*History of California*, vol. iv, p. 380). The dispatches of Arrángoiz would seem to make all clear as to motive.

24. The order was sent also to the governors of Sonora, Sinaloa, Jalisco, and Coahuila, and receipt acknowledged. Almonte's dispatch (the basis for a repetition of the order) was accompanied by a letter written by a friend detailing a conversation with "a Mr. Pearce of Missouri," who said that Americans, being unable to enter California without passports, would go in great numbers to Oregon and "settle *sobre la línea* [on the line]." They would take, Almonte thought, their slaves with them.

25. Letters, Waddy Thompson, United States minister to Mexico, to Mexican Minister of Relations, Dec. 22, 30, 31, 1843, with reply of Minister of Relations, Jan. 3, 1844. (M. A., Arch. Genl., *Californias*, 1843, 1844.)

26. No acknowledgment of receipt of the order by Micheltorena is to be found.

27. See general map (pocket).

28. See general map (pocket). Gilroy was the first foreigner to settle permanently in California. He was a Scotch sailor, left at Monterey in 1814. His true name was John Cameron.

29. See general map (pocket).

30. See general map (pocket).

31. See general map (pocket). The course and distances of the Oregon Trail are set forth generally in Emerson Hough's *The Way to the West*, 1903, pp. 287 *et seq.*, and in R. Parrish's *The Great Plains*, 1907, chap. 5. But see H. M. Chittenden, *The American Fur Trade of the Far West*, 1902, map and text; and for detailed notation of localities, R. G. Thwaites's *Early Western Travels*, 1905, vol. xxx (Palmer's "Journal "), vol. xxvii (De Smet's "Letters").

32. See general map (pocket). T. J. Farnham, "Travels" (*Early Western Travels*, vol. xxviii, p. 113, and notes); J. Bidwell, "First Emigrant Train to California," *Century Magazine*, vol. xix, pp. 106 *et seq.*; Bancroft, *History of California*, vol. iv, chaps. 10, 16, 24.

33. Letter to Minister of War, Feb. 23, 1843 (M. A., Arch. Genl., *Californias*, 1843).

34. B. C., A. F. Coronel, *Cosas de Calif.*, p. 53; J. B. Alvarado, *Historia de California*, vol. v, p. 40; E. de la Torre, *Reminiscencias*, p. 106, relating the outraging in public plaza by the Cholos of an intoxicated Indian woman.

	Pesos
The yearly income of the said fund, taking the average of five years...	55,177.38

Expenses of the missions

34 Dominican Missionaries in charge of 17 missions at 350 *pesos* each, and 250 *pesos* for the dotation of Alampara at the Presidio of Loreto...	12,150.00	
13 Missions of the Fernandinos at 800 *pesos* each.................	10,400.00	22,550.00

Other expenses

Advances made to the haciendas on an average of one year with another..............................	23,000.00	
Aid toward the general expenses.............................	1,000.00	
Rent of Guapango...	150.00	24,150.00
Total...		46,700.00

Comparison

Yearly income...	55,173.37
Yearly expenses..	46,700.00
Balance..	8,473.37

— (*Mexican and American Claims Commission*, Claim no. 493; Transcript, p. 433.)

By the above it appears that at the end of 1792 the Fund was in excellent condition, its total being 828,937 *pesos*, from which there was derived an average annual income of 55,177 *pesos*, — an excess over expenditure of 8473 *pesos*. In 1805, however, the haciendas had become deteriorated, and schemes of promotion were broached, with the alternative of selling the haciendas. Then in 1811 there befell the devastation of the war for independence and a suspension of payment of missionary stipends. During the years 1819–23 the annual income was 13,730 *pesos*, 5665 *pesos*, 737 *pesos*, (no income), and 138 *pesos*.

In 1836 (as noted in the text) the administration of the Fund, which, since the expulsion of the Jesuits, had been in the hands, first of the Spanish, and next, of the Mexican Government, was given to the first bishop of Alta California. In 1842 it again was assumed by the state, the haciendas being sold and the government pledging itself to pay on the proceeds 6 per cent interest from the tobacco revenue. The Bishop of Alta California protested against resumption of state control, and on April 3, 1845, such of the properties as remained unsold (an inconsiderable portion) were restored to him. (Translation of restoration decree, *Mex. and Am. Claims Commission*, Claim no. 493, — Transcript, p. 581; résumé of history of Pious Fund, *Ibid.*, p. 374; *Colección de Leyes y Decretos desde 1° de Enero*, 1834, Edición del Constitucional, no. 20, Mexico, 1851, pp. 100–101; Spanish text of the Bishop's protest, *Mex. and Am. Claims Commission*, Claim no. 493, — Transcript, p. 359.) Cf. *History of the Pious Fund of California*, by John V. Doyle, Papers, California Historical Society, vol. i, part i, 1887.

49. B. C., *Leg. Rec.*, vol. iv, pp. 20, 25; translated, *Hartman's Brief*, ex. 15.

50. Decree, May 28, 1845 (B. C., *Leg. Rec.*, vol. iv, p. 63); Decree, Oct. 28, 1845 (Pico, *Reglamento*) ; translated, *Hartman's Brief*, exs. 17, 18.

51. On sales, see United States *vs.* Workman (U. S. Sup. Court Reps.), 1 Wall. 745. Decree, March 30, 1846 (B. C., *Leg. Rec.*, vol. iv, p. 336; *Hartman's Brief*, ex. 23). For conveyances, see Hartman (Spanish and English). Translation of decree of March 30, 1846 (Bancroft, *History of California*, vol. v, p. 559, no. 5). List of sales (*Ibid.*, p. 561, n. 8). Order of Mexican Government (Montesdeoca order) against interference with Micheltorena's order for restoration of missions to padres (B. C., *St. Pap. Miss. and Col.*, vol. ii, p. 404; translated, Bancroft, vol. v, p. 560, n. 6). In the so-called Mission Cases, decided in the U. S. District Courts for California, in 1859, it was contended (1) that it was not within the power of local authorities to *sell* the public lands, — they could only make grants ; and (2) that the grants (so-called) did not conform to the requirements of law. The decision (which was against the validity of the sales so far as they included the mission buildings and gardens) was placed upon the ground that the Montesdeoca order was still valid.

52. Figueroa, Oct. 15, 1833, elections — only *emancipados* to vote; neophytes are not citizens (B. C., *Dept. St. Pap.* (Ángeles), vol. xi, p. 12). The ideas of San Vicente, emphasized by Echeandía, regarding neophyte citizenship and right to the ballot, were thus modified.

On September 30, 1849, the *alcalde* of San Juan Bautista reported the decline of that mission pueblo, urging changes (B. C., *Unbound Docs.*, p. 183), cited by Robertson, *From Alcalde to Mayor* (MS.). By a decree of Pío Pico (1846) the following are recognized as pueblos: Los Ángeles, Santa Bárbara, San José, Monterey, San Diego, San Francisco, Branciforte, Sonoma, San Juan Bautista, San Juan Capistrano, San Luis Obispo. (Robertson, *supra*.)

53. On condition and appearance of Alta California presidial settlements, see F. W. Beechey, *A Voyage to the Pacific*, London, 1831; R. H. Dana, *Two Years Before the Mast*, New York, 1840; Sir E. Belcher, *Narrative of a Voyage Round the World*, London, 1843; A. du Petit Thouars, *Voyage autour du Monde*, Paris, 1840.

54. Municipal government in Monterey was instituted about 1820, when an *alcalde* was chosen. Beginning with 1827 there was chosen an *ayuntamiento*, or town council, composed of an *alcalde*, two *regidores*, and a *síndico*. At Santa Bárbara the first *ayuntamiento* was elected by order of Echeandía in 1826 (*Dept. St. Pap.*, vol. i, pp. 189–90); but during the Zamorano-Echeandía contest the town was declared by the *diputación* as yet embryonic, and in 1833 Figueroa essayed to perfect its organization. The result was a vote in 1834 by the *diputación* to create an *ayuntamiento*, with *alcalde*, four *regidores*, and *síndico* (*Dept. St. Pap. Mil.* (Benicia), vol. lxxvi, pp. 6–9; *Leg. Rec.*, vol. ii, pp. 51–68, 188–89). At San Francisco the establishment of municipal rule was due directly to Figueroa. On Nov. 3,

1834, the *diputación* voted to create an *ayuntamiento*, with *alcalde*, two *regidores*, and *síndico*, to reside at the presidio and assume the political and judicial functions formerly exercised by the comandante. Judicial administration, as carried on in Alta California prior to 1824, is well indicated in Argüello's *Plan de Gobierno.* Thus, Title IV of the Plan, Art. 1: "For Civil Cases in towns [pueblos] there shall be three resorts [*instancias*], 1st, to *alcalde;* 2d, to comandante; 3d, to governor. Civilians at presidios will apply first to comandante; secondly and finally, to governor. Art. 2: Criminal cases will be tried by a court-martial, whose sentence will be executed without appeal " (*Leg. Rec.*, vol. i, pp. 17–19; translated by Bancroft, *History of California*, vol. ii, p. 511, n. 2). In 1835 (Jan. 12) petitions for land grants were directed to the *alcalde*, "since San Diego is no longer a presidio"; and on Feb. 5 the comandante referred to the *alcalde* petitions for lands, as involving an exercise of powers no longer his (*Arch. S. Diego*, pp. 32 and 35).

55. Echeandía to Minister of Justice, June 25, 1829: reports misdemeanors as determined by *alcaldes*, and more serious causes as referred first to presidial comandantes and then to governor, who consults *asesor-general* of Sonora, from whom matter may go to Minister of War in Mexico (B. C., *Dept. Rec.*, vol. vii, p. 21). Alta California subject to Circuit Court of Sinaloa (B. C., *St. Pap.* (Sacramento), vol. xix, p. 47). It was at Echeandía's request that an *asesoría* for Alta California was established (*vide* chapter XII, n. 36).

56. Victoria to Minister of Justice, Sept. 21, 1831 (M. A., Arch. Genl., *Justicia*, 130).

57. Law of 1837 regarding judiciary (May 22), translated, Hall, *History of San José*, p. 518. During 1839 and 1841 complaints of the failure to organize courts of first instance (courts of record superior to *alcalde* or justice courts) were emphatic. Alvarado to Minister of Interior, March 9, 1839, transmitting report of departmental commission (M. A., Arch. Genl., *Justicia*, 207). In these complaints San José was prominent (*Ibid*).

58. The abolition was the result of a *Junta Consultiva y Económica*, Oct., 1843. The restoration (July 4, 5, 1845) was effected by dividing Alta California into two prefectures as before, but the *partidos* were altered. In the first prefecture (that of Los Ángeles), extending from San Luis Obispo southward, there were three *partidos* — Los Ángeles, Santa Bárbara, and San Diego. In the second prefecture (that of Monterey), extending from San Miguel northward, there were two, — Monterey and Yerba Buena. Moreover, there was to be but one prefect (at Monterey), while *ayuntamientos* were permitted only to Monterey and Los Ángeles. In the remaining *partidos*, affairs were to be managed by a council consisting of a justice of the peace and two citizens under the presidency of a sub-prefect. (B. C., *Leg. Rec.*, vol. iv, p. 79; *Dept. St. Pap.* (San José), vol. v, p. 98.)

59. J. Gregg, *Commerce of the Prairies*, New York, 1845; republished by

Mr. R. G. Thwaites, *Early Western Travels*, vol. xix; Chittenden, *American Fur Trade*, vol. ii, p. 504.

60. J. J. Warner, *Reminiscences*, Pub. Hist. Soc. South. Calif., vol. vii, p. 189.

61. Bancroft, *History of California*, vol. iii, pp. 386, 395, and notes; vol. iv, p. 74, and notes. J. O. Pattie, *Personal Narrative*, Cincinnati, 1831, republished by Thwaites, *Early Western Travels*, vol. xviii. See general map (pocket).

62. B. C., *Dept. St. Pap.* (Ángeles), vol. iv, p. 99.

63. B. C., *Dept. St. Pap.*, vol. vi, pp. 169, 171.

64. "When Jackson's party came from New Mexico to California in 1831," writes Mr. J. J. Warner, "there could not be found in either Tucsón or Altar — although they were both military posts and towns of considerable population — a man who had ever been over the route from those towns to California by the way of the Colorado River, or even to that river, to serve as a guide, . . . and the trail from Tucsón to the Gila River at the Pima villages was too little used and obscure to be easily followed, and from those villages down the Gila River to the Colorado River, and from thence to within less than a hundred miles of San Diego, there was no trail, not even an Indian path." (Pub. Hist. Soc. South. Calif., vol. vii, p. 188.)

CHAPTER XV

WAR WITH THE UNITED STATES

NEW CHAPTER SOURCES: Official letters, Sir George Simpson to Governor of Hudson's Bay Company; consular letters, James A. Forbes (Monterey), and Barron-Aberdeen official correspondence (B. A.); letters of Anthony Butler to President Andrew Jackson, and Thompson-Webster correspondence (A. A.); *Diary of James K. Polk*, Chicago, 1910; official correspondence of Thomas O. Larkin, reëxamined (B. C.); instructions of Secretary George Bancroft to Commodore John D. Sloat (*Nation*), instructions of Bancroft to Commodore Robert F. Stockton (A. A., Navy), and letters and statements of John C. Frémont (*Century Magazine*); Larkin, Sutter, Richardson letters, citations and excerpts by W. R. Kelsey, *The United States Consulate in California*, Pub. Acad. of Pacific Coast History, Berkeley,1910; official letters, Admiral Sir George Seymour (B. A.); Gillespie-Flóres Articles of Capitulation and correspondence, and official reports of Flóres (M. A.); *Diary*, R. C. Duvall of U. S. SS. Savannah; *Californian*, 1846-47 (reëxamined); San Francisco *Star*, 1847. (Specific citations below.)

1. Prudencia Higuera of Martínez, who in 1840, as a child, lived near San Pablo, and whose male relatives exchanged with American captains hides for cloth, axes, shoes, fish-lines, and grindstones, says: "My brother had traded some deer-skins for a gun and four tooth-brushes, the first ones I had ever seen. I remember that we children rubbed them on our teeth till the blood came, and then concluded that after all we liked best the bits of pounded willow-root that we had used for brushes before. After the ships sailed, my mother and sisters began to cut out new dresses, which the Indian women sewed. On one of mine mother put some big brass buttons about an inch across, with eagles on them. How proud I was! I used to rub them hard every day to make them shine, using the tooth-brush and some of the powdered egg-shell, that my sisters and all the Spanish ladies kept in a box to put on their faces on great occasions. Then our neighbors, who were ten or fifteen miles away, came to see all the things we had bought. One of the Moragas heard that we had the grindstones, and sent and bought them with two fine horses. [A] girl offered me a beautiful black colt for six of my buttons, but I continued for a long time to think more of these buttons than of anything else I possessed." (*Century Magazine*, vol. xix, p. 192.)

2. *Missionary Herald*, Boston, 1844. Concerning the American missionaries, Sir George Simpson wrote in 1842: "They [the Sandwich Islanders] are too much under the influence of the Calvinist Missionary Society in the United States . . . and they [the missionaries] have had sufficient in-

fluence to get one of their own number, a narrow-minded, illiterate American [William Richards] installed as Prime Minister or principal Councillor of the King."

3. In 1847 the *Star* gives the population of San Francisco as, whites 375, Indians 34, Sandwich Islanders 40, negroes 10.

4. Same journal states, Sept. 4, 1847, that prior to April, 1847, there were in San Francisco 22 shanties, 31 frame dwellings, 26 adobes, — in all, 79 structures. On Nov. 16, 1846, Larkin observed to Samuel J. Hastings: "It [Monterey] will not increase fast. It will, I think, be a good, moral, gentle town. . . . Yerba Buena, and other places in and about San Francisco, will be the busy, bustling, uproarious places."

5. J. Douglas, *Journal* (B. C.).

6. B. A., Public Record Office, America, 388 (*American Historical Review*, vol. xiv, no. 1, "Documents," Joseph Schafer). But on Nov. 25, 1841, Simpson had written: "Any title the Russian-American Company could give us would be of no avail unless backed by a force of 80 to 100 men. . . . Under these circumstances, I made . . . no offer, nor did I encourage the hope of our becoming purchasers." (*Ibid.*, 399.)

7. B. A., F. O., Mexico, 136 (*American Historical Review*, vol. xiv, no. 4, "English Interest in the Annexation of California," Ephraim D. Adams).

8. *Ibid.*, Barron to Aberdeen, Sept. 9 and Oct. 19, 1843; and Barron to Aberdeen, Jan. 20, 1844 (F. O., Mexico, 179).

9. *Ibid.*, Aberdeen to Barron (F. O., Mexico, 179).

10. *Ibid.*, Aberdeen to Elliott (F. O., Texas, 20); E. D. Adams, *British Interest and Activities in Texas*, Johns Hopkins Press, 1910.

11. Eugène Duflot de Mofras, *Exploration de l'Oregon, des Californies,* etc., Paris, 1844.

12. J. B. Alvarado, *Historia de California*, vol. iii, p. 203. The author here states that in 1827 he had been in negotiation with Don Diego Forbes regarding a protectorate, but that he is glad nothing came of it, because, "I do not think it possible that under the dominion of aristocratic England we could have made the great and admirable progress we have made under the banner that the immortal Abraham Lincoln caused to wave triumphantly over the proud city of Richmond."

13. F. W. Beechey, *Narrative of a Voyage to the Pacific*, 1825–28, 2 vols., London, 1831.

14. B. W. Morrell, *Narrative of Four Voyages*, New York, 1832, p. 210.

15. Butler to Forsyth, June 9, 1835 (24th Cong., 1st Sess., *House Ex. Doc.* 256); Butler to Forsyth, June 17, 1835 (A. A., State); J. S. Reeves, *American Diplomacy under Tyler and Polk*, Johns Hopkins Press, 1907, pp. 69–74.

16. Thompson to Webster, April 29, 1842 (A. A., State); Webster to Thompson, June 27, 1842 (*Letters of Daniel Webster*, Van Tyne, p. 269; Reeves, *American Diplomacy*, pp. 100–103). As early as April 25, 1842, Webster had intimated to Lord Ashburton, then negotiating the Treaty

of Washington, that the United States might yield something in the Oregon matter for the sake of acquiring California (B. A., F. O., America, 379). It is interesting to note that in 1843, Forbes suggested to Barron that Great Britain exchange Oregon for California (*Ibid.*, F. O., 179); and that on August 4 and 14, 1844, Larkin suggested that England be granted eight degrees north of the Columbia River, in exchange for eight degrees of California south of the 42d parallel. A tripartite treaty between Great Britain, Mexico, and the United States was favored by Webster (Niles, *Register*, vol. lxx, p. 257; Tyler, *Letters and Times*, vol. ii, pp. 260–62, vol. iii, p. 206; J. Schouler, *History of the United States*, vol. iv, p. 447). See R. W. Kelsey, *The United States Consulate in California*, p. 49 (Pub. Acad. Pacific Coast History, vol. i, no. 5).

17. Everett to Calhoun, March 28, 1845 (A. A., State).

18. J. K. Polk, *Diary*, Sept. 17, 1845; Reeves, *American Diplomacy*, p. 275.

19. Buchanan to Larkin (*The United States Consulate in California*).

20. Larkin, *Official Correspondence*, July 20, 1846 (B. C.), states that the general (Castro) put a paper in his (the consul's) hands, containing a plan for declaring California independent in 1847 or 1848. The general asked if after so many revolutions he "would find repose and receive a benefit." As early as April 23, 1846, Larkin had told Castro that "by adjusting circumstances he could secure to himself and his friends fame and honor, permanent employ and pay." (*Ibid.*)

21. R. W. Kelsey, *The United States Consulate in California*, chap. 7. T. O. Larkin, *Off. Cor.*, April 17, 1846 (B. C.).

22. The contention of Mr. Reeves, that "the Mexican War was not the result of the annexation of Texas," is broad; but his remark (*American Diplomacy*, p. 90), that Von Holst's *Constitutional History of the United States* (valuable as it is) is little else than a paraphrase of the *Diary* of John Quincy Adams, is not unenlightening.

23. Of Frémont's personal appearance, Professor Josiah Royce writes in the *Atlantic Monthly* for October, 1890: "The charming and courtly manner, the deep and thoughtful eyes, the gracious and self-possessed demeanor," etc.

24. "Report of Exploring Expedition to the Rocky Mountains in the year 1842, and to Oregon and California in the years 1843–44" (28th Cong., 2d Sess., *Sen. Doc.* 174).

25. "Geographical Memoir upon Upper California," 1848 (30th Cong., 1st Sess., *Sen. Doc.* 148).

26. Niles, *Register*, vol. lxxi, p. 188.

27. *Ibid.*, and S. F. *Alta*, June 15, 1866.

28. Kelsey points out (*The United States Consulate in California*, pp. 96–97) that it is not improbable that Frémont was on his way to Santa Bárbara for supplies, as he had arranged for supplies to be delivered at that

point. Frémont himself (*Century Magazine*, vol. xix, p. 921) says: "The Salinas Valley lay outside of the more occupied parts of the country, and I was on my way to a pass opening into the San Joaquín Valley at the head of a western branch of the Salinas River." But see Vice-Consul Forbes to Consul Barron, Jan. 26, 1846 (B. A., F. O., Mexico, 176).

29. M. A., Secretaría de Fomento, *Colonización y Terrenos Baldíos*, leg. 7, ex. 221.

30. *Sawyer Documents* (B. C.).

31. *Ibid.*

32. On Nov. 5, 1845, Sutter wrote to Larkin: "I wish you had not been so much engaged that you could not come up here to assist your respectable countrymen . . . if it would be not in your power, or in the power of a Man of War to protect them, *I will do it*. The snow is on top of the mountains, their animals are worn out . . . they could not leave the country [under orders of expulsion] before the next month of May or June." (*Off. Cor.*) On July 8, 1846, Larkin wrote to Sloat: "From April to June the foreigners in the Sacramento Valley were continually harassed by verbal reports and written proclamations that they must leave California." John Bidwell states that, so far as he knew, there was no disquiet among the settlers, but on this point the testimony of Larkin, who, besides being entirely friendly to the Californians, was taking official cognizance of their conduct, is clearly the best evidence.

FRÉMONT AND SECRETARY BANCROFT

33. Mrs. Frémont (Jessie Benton) contends (*Century Magazine*, vol. xix, p. 923, n. 2) that the instructions to Larkin from the Secretary of State differed from those to Commodore Sloat, the latter instructions being the ones by which Frémont was governed. But an examination of the navy files has brought to light the Bancroft dispatch to Sloat. It bears date Oct. 14, 1846, three days prior to the dispatch to Larkin. "You will communicate," it says, "frequently with our consul at Monterey, and will ascertain as exactly as you can the nature of designs of the English and French in that region, the temper of the inhabitants, their disposition toward the United States, and their relation toward the central governments of Mexico. You will do everything that is proper to conciliate toward our country the most friendly regard of the people of California." (*Nation*, vol. lii, no. 1351.) Many years later (Sept. 3, 1886) Mr. Bancroft (not having before him what he had written in 1846, and depending on memory) wrote to Frémont from Newport, R. I.: "It was made known to you on the authority of the Secretary of the Navy that a great object of the President was to obtain California. If I had been in your place, I should have considered myself bound to do what I saw I could to promote the purpose of the President. You were alone; no Secretary of War to appeal to; he was thousands of miles off; and yet it was officially made known to you that

your country was at war; and it was so made known expressly to guide your conduct," etc. As pointed out by Professor Josiah Royce (*Nation, supra*), not only was Frémont without *official* information that his "country was at war," — he was without any information of it.

34. A curious forecast of the course of the settlers in seizing the horses is contained in a letter from William A. Richardson to Larkin, as early as Dec. 19, 1845. He says: "I arrived here [Santa Clara] last night; everything is in a very disorderly state; they are fortifying in San José; . . . you will hear very soon of a general turn-out; if the party goes over to the north to pass over horses as they say, we shall be ready to oppose them and give them a warm reception if required." (Cited by Kelsey, *The United States Consulate in California*, p. 51, no. 12.)

35. *Bear Flag Papers* (B. C.).

36. M. A., Arch. Genl., *Internacional*, 1842 and 1847; *Mem. de Relaciones*, 1846, Prefectura del 2 Distrito del Dep. de Califs. On June 18, Manuel Castro wrote to the Mexican Minister of Relations: "This prefecture has been informed that this treacherous crime has been committed with the privity or by the order of the [herein-mentioned] Frenot [Frémont], who has camped in Sutter's establishment; also with that of the captain of the U. S. warship Portsmouth, anchored in the port of San Francisco, because the said ship has helped the invaders of Sonoma with a boat-load of provisions."

37. The flag (constructed by William L. Todd of Illinois) was five feet long and nearly a yard wide. Along the lower edge was a stripe of red flannel. In the upper left-hand corner was a red star, five-pointed and fifteen inches in diameter. Facing the star was a bear. Beneath the star and bear was the emblem "California Republic." This flag, which was preserved in the hall of the California Pioneers in San Francisco, was destroyed by the earthquake-fire of 1906. For the Ide proclamation, etc., see Bancroft, *History of California*, vol. x, pp. 150–160.

38. "I had anticipated," wrote Larkin on July 20, 1846, "the pleasure of following up the plans partially laid down in the dispatch to this office of Oct. 17, 1845, and of bringing them to a conclusion in the latter part of 1847 through the will and voice of the Californians." And on Jan. 14, 1847, he wrote: "It has been my object for some years to bring the Californians to look on our countrymen as their best friends. . . . The sudden rising of the party on the Sacramento under the Bear Flag, taking California property to a large amount, and other acts, completely frustrated all hopes I had of the friendship of the natives to my countrymen." (*Off. Cor.*, B. C.)

CONDUCT AND MOTIVES OF JOHN C. FRÉMONT

39. Whether or not Frémont, in furthering the "Bear Flag revolt," was guided by official instructions brought to him by Gillespie, has been much discussed.

(1) No instructions are to be found in the Navy Department. Personal examination of the secret records of the Department was made by the editor of the *Century Magazine* in 1891. (See vol. xix of the *Century*, p. 928.)

(2) The papers brought by Gillespie were: (*a*) letters of introduction to Larkin and Frémont; (*b*) duplicate of Buchanan's dispatch to Larkin creating him confidential agent (destroyed and contents committed to memory); (*c*) letters to Frémont from Senator Thomas H. Benton. (30th Cong., 1st Sess., *House Report*, 817, pp. 12, 13; *Senate Rep.* 75, pp. 373–74; *Century Magazine*, vol. xix, p. 922.)

(3) Frémont in his *Memoirs* (Chicago, 1887, p. 520), and in the last word penned by him relative to his connection with the Bear Party (*Century Magazine*, vol. xix, p. 917), claims to have been guided not by instructions from the responsible head of a department, but by personal and intimate knowledge of the wishes and designs of the government, obtained, first, from Senator Benton, second, from the Benton letters brought by Gillespie, and third, from Gillespie himself. He says (*Century Magazine*, vol. xix, p. 922): "Lieutenant Gillespie brought a letter of introduction from the Secretary of State, Mr. Buchanan, and letters and papers from Senator Benton and family. The letter from the Secretary of State was directed to me in my private or citizen capacity, and though seeming nothing beyond an introduction, it accredited the bearer, and in connection with circumstances and place of delivery it indicated a purpose in sending it. From the letter I learned nothing, but it was intelligibly explained to me by my previous knowledge, by the letter from Senator Benton, and by communications from Lieutenant Gillespie. . . . The letter of Senator Benton, while apparently one only of friendship and family details, was a trumpet giving no uncertain note. Read by the light of many conversations and discussions with himself and other governing men in Washington, it clearly made me know that I was required by the government to find out any foreign schemes in relation to California, and to counteract them so far as was in my power. His letters made me know distinctly that at last the time had come when England must not get a foothold, that we *must be first*. I was to *act* discreetly but positively."

So far as the foregoing is concerned, Frémont, in countenancing and aiding the Bear Party, acted on his own responsibility, but under a strong conviction of duty; one inspired by communications (from persons identified with the government) that war with Mexico was imminent (if not already declared), and that at the first breath of war the government was determined to seize California.

But the foregoing is not all with which we have to reckon. Frémont, besides being unprovided with instructions to interfere in California affairs, possessed what virtually were instructions to the contrary. On June 16, two days after the capture of Sonoma, he wrote to Lieutenant Montgomery:

"The nature of my instructions [as topographical engineer] and the peaceful nature of our operations do not contemplate any active hostility on my part even in the event of war between the two countries [Mexico and the United States]; and therefore, although I am resolved to take such *active* and precautionary measures as I shall judge necessary for our safety, I am not authorized to ask from you any other than such assistance as, without incurring yourself unusual responsibility, you would feel at liberty to afford me." And not only so. On Gillespie's arrival, the dispatch to Larkin (creating the latter confidential agent and directing a policy of conciliation) was communicated to Frémont. In 1884, in a conversation with Professor Josiah Royce (*Atlantic Monthly*, vol. lxvi, p. 556), Frémont, forgetful that it was the dispatch to Larkin which he had seen, denied the existence of any such document, and claimed that he himself had received a dispatch from Secretary Buchanan of a different tenor. But a copy of the dispatch to Larkin being shown to him, and it appearing (*National Intelligencer*, Nov. 12, 1846) that on May 24, 1846, he had written to Senator Benton that though expecting word from Buchanan he had "received nothing," Frémont in 1891 (*Century Magazine*, vol. xix, p. 922) admitted that the dispatch to Larkin was after all what had been communicated to him by Gillespie. His words are: "This officer [Gillespie] informed me also that he was directed by the Secretary of State to acquaint me with his instructions to the consular agent, Mr. Larkin." In furthering the Bear Flag Revolt, then, Frémont, by the documents and by his own admission, was consciously disregarding the official plans of the government.

How far, in view of everything, such disregard of official plans was morally culpable, the reader will decide. To some it will be indubitable that Frémont could not have done as he did without being actuated by unworthy personal motives. To others it will be just as indubitable that in doing as he did his motives were of the best. It is his own explanation (given in vindication of himself in 1891) that "this idea [of conciliation embodied in the instructions to Larkin] was no longer practicable, as war was inevitable and immediate; moreover, it was in conflict with our own [unofficial and inferential] instructions. We dropped this idea from our minds, but falling on others less informed, it came dangerously near losing us California."

40. B. A., F. O., Mexico, 196 (*American Historical Review*, vol. xiv, no. 4, p. 754).

41. To Minister Charles Bankhead, late in 1844, and again to H. M. Consul Mackintosh, in July, 1845, McNamara proposed to plant a colony in California, and submitted to the President of Mexico a request for a grant of lands. The region within which the grant was desired was defined as between the Cosumnes River on the north, the extremity of the Tulares on the south, the San Joaquín River on the west, and the Sierra Nevada on the east. The colony was to consist of 2000 Irish families, and its objects were to "advance the cause of Catholicism," and to check "further usurp-

ations on the part of an irreligious and anti-Catholic nation [the United States]." Mexico favored the plan. Pico and the California Assembly accepted it with modifications, and on July 4 a grant was signed. No attempt was ever made to secure recognition of it. On the part of Great Britain the matter was ignored, although Bankhead reported to Aberdeen, May 3 and July 30, 1845. (B. A., F. O., Mexico, 185, no. 52; 186, no. 74.) Frémont, "California Claims" (30th Cong., 1st Sess., *Senate Rep.* 75), contains documents with translations.

42. Admiral Sir George Seymour, to Minister Bankhead in Mexico, June 13, 1846: "Having, however, detached the Juno last month with instructions to Captain Blake, if the inhabitants of California declared their independence of Mexico, to endeavor to induce their leaders not to place themselves under the control or subjection of any foreign power, I think it my duty to call at Monterey to ascertain if the inhabitants should have come to any resolution which will facilitate the maintenance of their independence." (B. A., F. O., Mexico, 197, Bankhead's no. 91; Admiralty-Secretary, In-Letters, no. 5561, — *American Historical Review*, vol. xiv, no. 4, p. 758.)

43. 29th Cong., 2d Sess., *H. Ex. Doc.* 4, p. 640, etc.

44. Seymour had "called at Monterey" pursuant to his intention as announced in his dispatch to Bankhead (note 42, *supra*). His object, therefore, was to ascertain whether "the inhabitants [had] come to any resolution which [would] facilitate the maintenance of their independence." Finding Sloat in possession, he stated that his object was a mere stop on his way to the Sandwich Islands (B. A., F. O., Mexico, 198).

45. 31st Cong., 1st Sess., *H. Ex. Doc.* 1. Commodore Stockton's orders from the Navy Department (never before published) appear in this volume as Appendix E.

46. M. A., Arch. Genl., *Operaciones Militares*, 1846, frac. 1, leg. 13. R. F. Stockton, "Report of Operations on the Coast of the Pacific" (31st Cong., 1st Sess., *H. Ex. Doc.* 1, Military and Naval Operations, 30th Cong., 2d Sess., *Sen. Ex. Doc.* 31).

47. B. D. Wilson, *Observations on Early Days in California;* S. C. Foster, *Ángeles,* 1847–49; Lugo, *Vida de un Ranchero* (B. C.).

GILLESPIE-FLÓRES ARTICLES OF CAPITULATION

48. Articles of Capitulation (translation): " (1) Captain Gillespie will retire from the plaza of Los Ángeles with all his force within the time necessary to prepare his march to the port of San Pedro; remaining in said port the time indispensable for arranging everything essential to embarkation; under word of honor not to protract the time. (2) He will quit said plaza with all the honors of war, taking his private and personal property. (3) He will take the artillery mounted in this plaza with the customary quantity of ammunition, leaving said artillery in the port of San Pedro, at

the time of embarkation, in charge of an officer of the Mexican forces. (4) All the other stores and effects (property of the United States) shall be delivered by inventory to a Mexican official. (5) All arms taken by the United States forces shall be promptly restored to their owners. (6) Prisoners shall be exchanged grade for grade, and such as by the continuance of hostilities are taken hereafter shall be treated according to the laws of war between civilized nations. (7) All the property and persons of all the foreigners of each nation shall be respected, and no account shall be made of their past conduct.

"Additional. The term fixed for evacuation of the plaza shall be nine o'clock of the morning of the thirtieth instant.

"Further. The forces of Captain Gillespie, in passing to the port of San Pedro, shall not be molested in any manner by the Mexican forces; the intention being that an observation corps shall march at the distance of a league from them.

"Further. The horses and other transportation (taken by Captain Gillespie's forces), that may not belong to any individual under the command of the captain, shall be delivered to the commissioner on the part of the commander of the Mexican forces that shall be named to receive them after arrival at San Pedro.

"These articles and additions have been accepted by said Commissioners of both belligerent forces, giving their word of honor that they be faithfully observed: In testimony whereof they affix their signatures . . . José Mª Segura (Rúbrica), T. Corl y Capn; Leonardo Cota (Rúbrica), Tente de Auxiliares; Edward Gilchrist (Rúbrica), Surgeon California Battalion; Nathaniel M. Pryor (Rúbrica), Lieutenant. These stipulations approved: José M. Flóres, Commander in Chief of the Mexican forces: Approved, Arch. H. Gillespie, Capt. and Military Commandant."

CORRESPONDENCE BETWEEN FLORES AND GILLESPIE, OCT. 2–6, 1843

(Summary): Gillespie to Flóres, San Pedro, Oct. 2: Denies violation of any article of capitulation; states that no commissioner from Flóres has arrived to receive public property; horses loaned as transports have been returned and paid for; arms of particular individuals are to be delivered at time of embarkation; gratified that Flóres "appreciates the high sense of honor of Dr. Gilchrist, as it is quite impossible for an American officer to violate his pledged word of honor in the slightest degree." Same to same, Oct. 3: denies bad faith; "no more time has been employed at this point than is absolutely necessary for the safety of the force under my command at sea." Same to Same, Oct. 3: Embarkation will take place as soon as the ship is ready to receive the troops. Flóres to Gillespie, Palo Verde, Oct. 4: Charges Gillespie with repairing his artillery and erecting intrenchments, and asks: "Do these things belong to preparations necessary for departure? Is this the conduct of troops under capitulation? Ought I to remain a cold spectator of those acts militating against the security of the forces I command?" Gillespie is then informed that his embarkation must be effected "within two hours of this very day." Gillespie to Flóres, Oct. 4: "Although the preparations of the vessel to receive the force under my command are not concluded, I find myself obliged to give way to your pressing demands, and embark the troops, which will take place by sunrise to-morrow morning." (M. A., *Operaciones Militares*, 1846, frac. 1, leg. 13.) See also Flóres to Mexican Government. (*Ibid.*)

49. March, 1847, Los Ángeles to Monterey and back, 800 miles in eight days.

50. On Oct. 5, at a banquet at Yerba Buena, Stockton delivered a speech. "A few nights," he said, "after my arrival [at Monterey] from the south, I was aroused by a courier bringing sad intelligence. Two hundred mounted armed men had made an attack upon our little band in the city [of Los Ángeles], etc. Yes, fellow citizens, those very men who refused the offer of a fair fight under every advantage of numbers, being almost two to one, . . . went like cowards, like miscreants, like assassins in the darkness of midnight, and fell upon our little band of brothers who were left for their protection, etc. We go this time to punish as well as to conquer. . . . Cheer up, then, and let no man think there's danger. What if there be 10,000 men of Sonora! Who cares?" (*Californian*, Oct. 24, 1846.)

51. S. W. Kearny, Reports (30th Cong., 1st Sess., *Sen. Ex. Doc.* 1, p. 513); W. H. Emory, "Notes of a Military Reconnoissance" (30th Cong., 1st Sess., *H. Ex. Doc.* 41, p. 55); P. St. G. Cooke, "Journal of March of Mormon Battalion" (30th Cong., Special Sess., 1849, *Sen. Doc.* 2).

52. W. F. Swasey, *The Early Days and Men of California*, Oakland, 1891, pp. 76, 141; Frémont, *Memoirs*, p. 599.

53. On November 7 the *Californian* had remarked: "We now have some hopes that the Californians will give us an example of their bravery by coming to an open and honorable engagement, instead of making a rush and then flying to the bush to hide themselves for a month or two."

54. R. F. Stockton, Report to Secretary of the Navy (30th Cong., 2d Sess., *Sen. Ex. Doc.* 31); Emory, "Military Reconnoissance." Larkin was regarded as the author of the conflict with the United States. As a prisoner, he was at Natividad, where "a Californian, seeing a relative shot, called out, 'This man caused it all,' and, coming full speed toward him, leveled his gun." Larkin escaped by backing his horse behind that of a Californian. There was talk of sending Larkin to Sonora, but the Californian officers feared that they in turn might be sent "round the Horn" by Stockton. Larkin says: "Altogether there were 900 men in arms on the California side, every man with good horses and a lance, most of them with swords, pistols, rifles, and carbines; with all their countrymen to aid; a perfect knowledge of every hill and valley; and an utter contempt for foreign infantry, especially seamen; yet they did not succeed." ("Journal," *Californian*, Feb. 27, 1847.)

CHAPTER XVI

MISSION, PRESIDIO, PUEBLO, AND PRIVATE RANCHO

1. "ALTHOUGH the mission buildings differ widely in treatment and detail, there is a general family resemblance, as if they had been designed by a single mind ; usually the façade of a central romanesque pedimented gable with pilasters supporting the pediment; with a square tower or belfry pierced with romanesque windows flanking each side, the arched entrance in the centre being usually surmounted by a square projecting cornice. Sometimes one of the towers has been omitted, as at Santa Inéz; sometimes partly missing, as at San Luis Rey, or wholly missing, as at San Gabriel, where the entire façade has been destroyed." (William L. Judson, Pub. Hist. Soc. South. Calif., vol. vii, p. 117.)

2. *Primer Informe ó Methodo Nuebo de Mision para su Gobierno Espiritual y Temporal*, R. Verger (Guardian of San Fernando) to Viceroy Bucarely, Nov. 15, 1772 (M. A., Museo, *Trasuntos*). A detailed account of mission routine in the establishments of Sonora, Nueva Vizcaya y Nueva México (S. A., Madrid, Bib. Nac. MS., no. 2550). See also Doña Eulalia Pérez, *Una Vieja y sus Recuerdos* (B. C.); Esteván de la Torre, *Reminiscensias* (B. C.).

3. "The native instruments of California were a flute of elder wood or deer's horn and the wooden rattle [clap-stick]." In 1811 President Tapis thus described the native music and dance: [At San Antonio] "they still preserve a flute which is played like the *dulce*. It is entirely open from top to bottom, and is five palms in length. Others are not more than about three palms. It produces eight tones [*puntos*] perfectly. They play various tunes [*tocatas*], nearly all in one measure, most of them merry. These flutes have eleven [*sic*] stops; some more, and some less. They have another musical instrument, a string instrument, which consists of a wooden bow to which a string of sinew is bound, producing a note. They use no other instruments. In singing they raise and lower the voice to seconds, thirds, fourths, fifths, and octaves. They never sing in parts, except that when many sing together some go an octave higher than the rest. Of their songs most are merry, but some are somewhat *mistes* in parts. In all these songs they do not make any statement [*proposición*], but only use fluent words, naming birds, places of their country, and so on." [At San Carlos] "they use a split stick like a distaff which serves them to beat the measure for their songs, which, whether happy or sad, are all in the same tone [*tonada*]. For instance, they sing as follows to the lively tunes, in which they mention their seeds or their asanas: '*Bellota-a-a, bellota; mucha semilla-a-a, mucha semilla.*' If the song is one of vengeance or bad wishes, which is very often, and from which many fights result, they sing and dance to the same time, speaking ill of that

nation with which they are on bad terms, thus: '*Manco-o-o, manco,*' or other words or defects which they know concerning the nation or person which they are comparing [*contrapuesta*]." [At Santa Cruz] "their dances are most insipid. They gather in a circle and without moving from the spot bend their bodies. They move their feet and make many contortions to the sound of their disagreeable voices, with which they do not form articulate words." ("A Mission Record of the California Indians, from a manuscript in the Bancroft Library": Univ. of Calif. Pubs. in Am. Arch. and Eth., vol. viii, no. 1.)

4. Says Tapis: "What is truly noteworthy is the admirable time and imperturbable gravity kept by those who sing and dance. . . . In Spanish they sing perfectly and learn easily all that is taught them. They sing a chorus or a mass, even though containing solo parts. They, both men and women, have clear and sonorous voices and an ear for music." (*Ibid.*, from portions omitted by Kroeber.)

5. For plans of presidios at Monterey and San Francisco, see chapter xvi of text, pp. 338, 346.

6. "Usage here allows [even] a mother to chastise her son, so long as he remains unmarried and lives at home, whatever may be his age, and regards a blow inflicted on a parent as a high offense. I sent for the culprit [who had struck his mother]; laid his crime before him, for which he seemed to care but little; and ordered him to take off his jacket. . . . Then putting a *reata* into the hands of his mother, whom Nature had endowed with strong arms, directed her to flog him. Every cut of the *reata* made the fellow jump from the floor. Twelve lashes were enough; the mother did her duty, and, as I had done mine, the parties were dismissed." (W. Colton, *Three Years in California*, 1850.)

7. W. A. Streeter, *Recollections of Santa Bárbara* (B. C.).

8. E. Pérez, *Recuerdos* (B. C.); José del Carmen Lugo, *Vida de un Ranchero* (B. C.).

9. W. H. Davis, *Sixty Years in California*, San Francisco, 1889.

10. *Three Years in California.*

11. J. B. Alvarado, a child of six years, was present on the occasion. His description (possibly somewhat colored by time) is the one used.

12. Manuel Torres, *Peripecias de Vida California* (B. C.).

13. *Mayer MSS.*, no. 18 (B. C.).

14. G. Navarro, *al Com^{te} G^{rl} relati^{vo}, á la distribución de tierras á los Pobladores de California*, Oct. 27, 1785 (B. C., *St. Pap. Miss. and Col.*, vol. i, p. 323). Navarro describes the tenure of the private rancho as a *merced* [license] *y concesión*, and the *pastos de aprovecham^{to}* should, he states, be in common, as prescribed for Hispaniola in *Recopilación*, lib. iv, tit. xvii, ley 5 (*Ibid.*).

15. By 1790 there were in California nineteen private ranchos (Borica, chapter ix of text, n. 41). By 1823 there were not to exceed twenty, to wit:

SANTA BÁRBARA DISTRICT

San Rafael (to Verdugo).
Los Nietos (Sta. Gertrudis) to Nieto.
Portezuelo (to Verdugo).
Simí (San José de García y) to Pico.
Refugio (to Ortega).
San Pedro (to Domínguez).
Conejo (Altagracia) to Polanco.
Santiago de Santa Ana (to Yorba).
Vírgines (to Ortega).
Félix.
San Antonio (to Lugo).
Sauzal Redondo (to Ávila) 1822.

MONTEREY DISTRICT

Pájaro (to Castro).
Potrero (Familia Sagrada) to
  Torre, 1822.
Buenavista (to Soberanes).

SAN FRANCISCO DISTRICT

San Isidro (to Ortega).
San Antonio (to Peralta).
Las Ánimas (to Castro).
Tularcitas (to Higuera).
Llano del Abrevadero (to Higu-
  era) 1822.

In 1907, the General Land Office of the United States Government issued under the direction of I. P. Berthrong, a land-grant map of the State of California, showing the location of Spanish and Mexican grants to the number of 553.

16. Concerning the Vallejo house at Sonoma, Torres says: "I found the *patio* full of servants of both sexes, but in the group the women prevailed. . . . I asked the General's wife in what so many Indians were occupied. 'Each one of my children, boy or girl,' she said, 'has a servant who has no other duty than to care for him or her. I have two servants for myself. Four or five grind the corn for the tortillas, for here we entertain so many guests that three grinders are not enough. Six or seven serve in the kitchen. Five or six are constantly busy washing the clothes of the children and servants. And nearly a dozen are required to attend to the sewing and spinning. As a rule, the Indians are not inclined to learn more than one duty. She who is taught cooking will not hear to washing clothes; and a good washerwoman considers herself insulted if she is compelled to sew or spin. All our servants are very clever. They have no fixed pay; we give them all they need. If sick, we care for them; when their children are born, we act as godparents, and we give their children instruction.'"

17. Sets of instructions for the *juez de campo* are preserved in B. C., *Arch. Sta. Cruz*, p. 94, and *Arch. Monterey County*, vol. ii, pp. 17, 56.

18. The description is by Lieutenant Joseph Warren Revere of the United States Navy. Regarding horses he was an expert, having, as he says, "mounted the noblest of the race in the stables of Mohammed Ali, Viceroy of Egypt, as well as those belonging to other potentates in Syria, Egypt, and Barbary, besides choice specimens of the Persian stock in British India." (*A Tour of Duty in California*, New York and Boston, 1849.)

19. The old Spanish serenades, once sung everywhere in California, are rapidly disappearing. Mr. Charles F. Lummis is doing much to preserve them by phonographic record. Already the Southwest Museum has

500 cylinders of his procuring. Mr. Lummis says: "A poor old washerwoman, proud of her race, was a perfect bonanza of the early California songs; while a rich young matron, a famous toast, equally cherishes this her inheritance. A blind Mexican lad has been one of the stanch props of the work ; and several brave young women, who could ill afford the sacrifice of time, have contributed to science far more in proportion than does many a rich 'patron.' The most extraordinary achievement has been that of Miss Manuela C. García, of Los Ángeles, who has sung the records of no less than 150 songs, with the full words! Few can do that in any language, from sheer memory. Doña Adalaida Kemp, of Ventura, comes next with sixty-four records. Credit and gratitude belong also, in generous measure, to the Misses Luisa and Rosa Villa, Don Rosendo Uruchurtu, Mrs. Tulita Wilcox Miner, Don Francisco Amate, and many others." (*Third Bulletin*, The Southwest Society of the Archæological Institute of America, p. 59.) In illustration of the Spanish-California serenade, the *Bulletin* prints the following: —

SERENADE

La Noche Está Serena

La noche está serena, tranquilo el aquilón;
Tu dulce centinela te guarda el corazón.
Y en alas de los céfiros, quevagan por doquier
Volando van mis súplicas, á tí, bella mujer,
Volando van mis súplicas, á tí, bella mujer.

De un corazón que te ama, recibe el tierno amor;
No aumentes mas la llama, piedad á un trobador.
Y si te mueve á lastima mi eterno padecer,
Como te amo, amame, bellísima mujer!
Como te amo, amame, bellísima mujer!

[So still and calm the night is,
The very wind 's asleep;
Thy heart's so tender sentinel
His watch and ward doth keep.
And on the wings of zephyrs soft
That wander how they will,
To thee, oh woman fair, to thee ⎱
My prayers go fluttering still. ⎰   (*Bis.*)

Oh take the heart's love to thy heart
Of one that doth adore!
Have pity — add not to the flame
That burns thy troubadour!
And if compassion stir thy breast
For my eternal woe,
Oh, as I love thee, loveliest ⎱
Of women, love me so!] ⎰   (*Bis.*)

20. *Crusoe's Island*, etc., New York, 1864, p. 183.
21. M. A., Museo, *Docs. Rel. á las Mis. de Califs.*, Qto iii.

22. Says Guadalupe Vallejo: "One of the customs which we always observed at the wedding was to wind a silken tasseled string or a silken sash, fringed with gold, about the necks of the bride and groom, binding them together as they knelt before the altar. . . . A charming custom among the middle and lower classes was the making of the satin shoes by the groom for the bride. A few weeks before the wedding he asked his betrothed for a measurement of her foot, and made the shoes with his own hands; the groomsman brought them to her on the wedding-day." (*Century Magazine*, vol. xix, p. 189.)

23. "As late as 1870 we find mention of the officer who, next to the *alcalde*, embodied the life of the early Spanish and Mexican civilization: —

"'The municipal law of California contains proof of [Spanish] influences. Tribunals of conciliation, community property, separate property of the wife, domestic relations, descents and distribution, trespass on land, proceedings in action, may be mentioned as examples. . . . To California is granted the distinguished privilege of uniting in her jurisprudence the common law of England and the civil law of Rome, each the product of a great civilization.'" (John J. Boyce of Santa Bárbara, in address before San Francisco Bar Association, Jan. 12, 1895.)

"The memory of the Spanish origins was preserved also in the number of legal questions that were brought up in courts and engaged attention for many years. Most prominent among these questions was that of the titles to the pueblo lots, which arose out of the *alcalde* grants of the transition period. The Spanish local institutions came to have a real significance to the people of the places where these contests occurred. San Francisco was the centre of the controversy, and for many years the titles were indefinite. Never did the welfare of so many people depend on the decision of a judicial tribunal as to the legal existence of a pueblo at that place." (J. R. Robertson, *From Alcalde to Mayor*, MS., B. C.)

APPENDIX

APPENDIX

APPENDIX A

PLAN FOR THE ERECTION OF A GOVERNMENT AND GENERAL COMMANDANCY

Which includes the Peninsula of Californias and the Provinces of Sinaloa, Sonora, and Nueva Viscaya

[Archivo General of Mexico, *Provincias Internas*, 154. This important document (here published for the first time) is the joint work of Visitador José de Gálvez and Viceroy Marqués de Croix. It bears date January 23, 1768. The translation is by Miss Emma Helen Blair, of Madison, Wisconsin.]

IF, since the glorious Conquest which the great Hernan Cortes made of the broad Domains which come under the name of Nueva España, effort had been made by his Successors in this Government to Second and to carry out the lofty designs of that Hero, the Light of the Gospel and the supremacy of the August Kings of España would have reached even to the utmost Bounds, not yet known, of this immense Continent. But as the spirit of activity and of Conquest was extinguished with the life of that inimitable Man, with his death came to an end the rapid advances which he accomplished in this new World; and at last we have not even maintained and conserved the possession which we enjoyed, in undisturbed tranquillity, of the richest territories on the Frontiers of Sonora and Nueva Viscaya.

The more immediate (and perhaps the exact) causes of this failure, and of the veritable ruin which has befallen the unfortunate inhabitants of those Provinces, with grave injury to the State, are, in reality, the utter neglect with which they have been regarded at Mexico in these latter years; the considerable distance at which they are situated, more than Six Hundred Leagues, from this Capital; and the pressing Crowd of more immediate business and cares which engross the entire attention of any Viceroy of Nueva España. For, as he is not supplied with

Subordinates to assist him, it is not possible for him to make active provision, or for the influence of his authority to be felt, at the remote confines of an almost boundless Empire.

This practical knowledge which the present Viceroy has been acquiring, with no less discomfort than hardship, and the favorable opportunity afforded to him by the present expedition to Sonora, have made him reflect very seriously on the means which may be most suitable and efficacious for reëstablishing this great Monarchy in its earlier prosperity, and to put the distant Provinces into condition for maintaining themselves with Vigor, and for enlarging the [Spanish] domination — extending at the same time the Catholic Faith, in acknowledgment and reward for which God is allotting to the Crown of España the Richest Empires of the Universe.

With the view, then, of establishing in the uncultivated Provinces of this [new] world good order and Justice, and the opulence which is natural for them if they are placed under proper management, he proposes, and sends to the Viceroy by this post, another and separate Plan for Intendancies, in imitation of those which exist in the Metropolitan Province. And to the end that Our Sovereign the King may secure the important advantages of quickly aggrandizing the Rich Frontiers of this Empire, he has come to an agreement with the Visitador-General to develop the idea of a General Commandancy, suitably empowered, which shall comprehend under its exclusive administration the aforesaid Provinces of Sonora, Sinaloa, Nueva Viscaya, and the Peninsula of Californias. That region will now begin to recognize the Spanish Power, and to repay part of the great amount that it has cost the Crown and the Nation since its discovery and the foundation of the first Jesuit Missions.

What has most contributed to this idea — which the Viceroy and the Visitador regard as very serviceable, and its execution as quite indispensable — is the previously planned decision which has been reached in Council, and fully approved, that the Visitador shall go to establish Settlements in the said Provinces, and organize the Government of the latter with full powers and Commission from the Viceroy. The object of this action is to facilitate and hasten the erection of such Government and Commandancy upon the footing which is proposed in this Plan, since obstacles can never arise between two faithful Servants of the King who, Moving toward the same end, with upright intentions, always agree in their discussions and unite their efforts, with mutual concessions.

In view of these facts, and with the further incentive of having seen a project which was laid before the Lords Ministers of Madrid in December, 1760, for the creation of a Viceroyalty independent from that of Mexico, and including all the Provinces situated in the great district under the jurisdiction of the Audiencia of Guadalaxara, the Viceroy and the Visitador have concluded that it will be much more advantageous and less expensive to establish an authorized Government and General Commandancy in the three frontier Provinces. For [such a Government], possessing all the powers necessary to maintain them free from the invasions of the Barbarians, and gradually to extend their boundaries, will render them of use to their Sovereign Master; and it will be responsible only to the Chief who represents him in these Domains, and subordinate to him only so far as to report Affairs to him and to request his aid when that may be necessary.

In this manner will be avoided the difficulties, always odious, which usually arise over jurisdiction or limits between coördinate officials when they have similar duties; and by surrendering to the Commandancy of the Frontier Provinces the entire authority — which is indispensable in regions so far distant, in order not to cause failure in opportunities and in the most important projects — the exceedingly important object will be attained of furnishing life and movement to regions so extensive, fruitful and rich by Nature, which can in a few years form a New Empire, equal or even superior to this one of Mexico.

Nor are these advantages and utilities, although great, the only ones which the proposed new Government will yield; for as soon as the activity of a Commandant with authority and energy is felt, many dangers can be averted which now threaten us, by way of the South Sea, from certain foreign Powers who now have an opportunity and the most eager desire to establish some Colony at the Port of Monterrey, or at some other of the many harbors which have already been discovered on the western Coasts of this new World.

In this report is purposely omitted extended discussion of the continual attempts by which France and England have striven, for some two centuries, to find a passage from the Northern to the Southern Sea — especially by their Colonies in this North America — and of the exertions that the Russians are making, through the Sea of Tartary, to penetrate into our Indias. This is partly because Field-Marshal Don Antonio Ricardos departed from here the year before, with the purpose of presenting an elaborate Memorial on these facts, which are more easy to verify in Europe; and partly because the Prime Minister of España knows very well that the English — who now, as a result of the last War, are Masters of Canada and a great part of Luciana [Louisiana] — will spare no expense, diligence, or hardship to push forward the discoveries which the French made through those Colonies, a new Viceroyalty. It has seemed proper to put forth this idea clearly, for the reasons above explained, as well as to avoid so great expenses, when the same results can be obtained by means of the Commandancy which is proposed in this Plan.

Nor is it reckoned expedient that the new Governor and Commander-in-Chief establish his residence in the City of Durango, the Capital of Nueva Viscaya, as was proposed in the year 1760 — not only because that Town is very distant from Sonora, and much farther from the Californias, which at the present time need an active and continual promotion; but because (from the necessity of stationing an Intendant in Durango, if the Separate Plan which is sent be approved), the establishment which is therein proposed would be in any event less advantageous [at Durango]. For the Governors who have hitherto administered Nueva Viscaya have all (excepting the present one) lived in the Town of San Felipe de Chihuahua, which is the Frontier settlement and a very important Mining Centre, where the presence of a Governor who can defend it is certainly needed.

In this connection, likewise, [it may be noted] that for the present the Audiencia of Guadalaxara remains in that Capital, where it was established, with the object of avoiding the great expenses which would assuredly be caused by its transfer; and if in the course of time (which must make known the benefits that the General Commandancy will produce) it shall seem expedient, as it may, to locate the Superior Tribunal of Nueva Galicia, or to erect another, in the Capital which is to be established in Sonora, it would be very easy to carry out that plan then at little expense, and with the knowledge which experience furnishes in all human affairs.

What is judged to be certainly indispensable, and to be immediately effected, is the erection of a central Settlement on the confines of Sonora — either on the shore of the Gila River, or very near it (arrangements being meanwhile made to set up the Government at the Mission of Caborca, as being the station most advanced toward the Frontier), or else at the junction of that River and the Colorado. Then, the Capital of the New Government being located at almost equal distances from the Californias and Nueva Viscaya, its Chief with his administrative measures can proceed to either Province with the same ease — and indeed he ought to travel through them and visit all places, in order that by examining them with his own eyes, and gaining specific knowledge from being actually in the field, he may be enabled to shape his course with good judgment.

No less necessary and useful will be a Mint, which ought to be erected in that same Capital of Sonora, in order that Commerce may have free course, to the benefit of the public and of the Royal Treasury ; and that the poor Vassals who have settled in those remote regions may not be under the painful necessity of transporting all the Gold and Silver to Mexico. [This they have done], with only damages and great expenses which utterly ruin them, or, when not so heavy, deprive them of the profits which the richness of the Ores would allow them if they could sell those metals in the same Region where they dig and Smelt them. And, lest it be feared that the establishment of a Mint in that Province would cause notable diminution in the Output of the Mint at Mexico, that of Sonora could be restricted to the coining of only a Million *pesos* each year; for that sum would be sufficient at present to supply that province with Money and to give a like share to the Californias and Nueva Viscaya — where, in truth, through the lack of Money, the King is suffering a great diminution in his Imposts, and the inhabitants intolerable grievances.

In the Capital which should be founded, a Bishop's See also ought to be erected, setting aside for the support of this New Dignity the Province of Sonora, also Sinaloa (which belongs to the Bishopric of Durango, and is at the considerable distance of more than Two Hundred and Fifty leagues), and the Peninsula of Californias. Although the last-named, as is claimed, is included in the Diocese of Guadalaxara, neither the reverend Bishops nor their Visitadors ever possessed any acquaintance with it; and consequently neither is the See of Nueva Galicia injured by the separation of Californias, nor is the loss which that of Durango will actually experience by cutting off from it Sonora and Sinaloa worthy of consideration, for in those territories there are very few Curates and the tithes are almost nothing. But these will very soon be increased, with the Government and General Commandancy in the undeveloped territories which are assigned to the new Bishopric.

It would be idle to enumerate the great [advantages] which the Bishop's See that is proposed in the Metropolis of Sonora would confer on Religion and the state; for the ardent zeal and Apostolic ministry of a Diocesan Prelate would immensely advance the conversion of the Heathen, hastening their reduction by influences near at hand, and conquering many souls for the Creator, at the same pace with which new Domains are acquired for the Sovereign who is His Immediate Vicar in the world. And it is certain that in no part of America are there so fine opportunities and so abundant a harvest as in the confines of Sonora and in the Missions of Californias; for the Tribes of Indians are exceedingly numerous, and their natural disposition renders them most easily persuaded of the infallible truth of the Catholic faith.

In view of these just considerations, the erection of the new See should not be considered a burden, even though it might be necessary at the beginning to assist the Prelate and his limited Church with some revenue from the Royal Treasury; for such pension would not continue long, when we consider the natural fertility of those lands — which, placed under cultivation, will yield the most abundant produce — and just as certainly would the Royal Estate be repaid [for this outlay] and even much more, on account of the richness of the Mines in those Provinces, which are well understood and known by all.

As to what is proper for the General Commandant, it is proposed that he should be independent of the Audiencia and President of Guadalaxara; and it would be necessary to confer on him the salary of twenty thousand *pesos*, in order that he may have barely means on which to live with any [suitable] display in those remote regions, and to meet the expenses of his journeys from one Province to another, without its being necessary for him to avail himself of the [extra] imposts, [now] condemned, which have been tolerated in the Indias, and which have brought them into the melancholy decadence which they are suffering up to the present time. If perchance this salary, and those of the three Intendants who in another Plan are proposed by the Californias, Sonora, and Durango, shall seem excessive, it will be easy to make it evident by experience that the Treasury will be well indemnified for the amount of all these expenses. For after the second year from the establishment of these positions the amount allotted to them certainly cannot reach even the tenth part of the increase which will appear in one branch of revenue alone, the fifths of the Silver and the Gold which may be dug and smelted in Sonora and Californias. To this must be added the revenue from the Pearls; from that fishery, although it might be very abundant on the Coasts of that Peninsula, nothing has been thus far produced to the Royal Treasury.

The greatest saving of expense which should be reckoned upon to the benefit of His Majesty is in the very large expense-accounts [*situados*] of the many Garrisons [*Presidios*] which exist in the Californias, Sonora, and Nueva Viscaya; for, as the profitable idea of establishing Settlements on the Frontiers of these Provinces has for its aim to guard them from the invasions of the Infidel Indians, it will result in liberation from the useless and insupportable burden of so many Garrisons, which, as events prove, are of little or no use. For, although six of these are maintained in the Province of Sonora alone, it is more often invaded and more devastated, than the others — because those Garrisons are, in effect, really Rancherías, and chiefly serve to enrich the Captains and their outfitters.

It is true that, in order to garrison the Capital that is projected in Sonora and to guard the chain of Settlements on the Frontiers (which should be quasi-Military), two Companies of Dragoons and three of Mountain Fusileers, each of a hundred men, will be needed; but nothing is easier than to fill out this force by adding fifty recruits to the two [companies?] who have gone on the Sonora expedition. Taking for granted that the expense of these Veteran Bodies hardly reaches the third part of that which is caused at present by the Garrisons, it is clear that the Royal Treasury, thus coming out with much profit, would be able to pay the salaries of the Commandancy and intendancies; and the Frontiers of the three Provinces would be really shielded from the incursions of the Barbarians. For the new Towns, protected by the Squads into which the Fusileer Companies should be divided, could immediately be put into condition to defend their respective territories, and in time to aid in extending the [Spanish] domination — in view of which, and with these obligations, the Colonists must be established in the new Settlements, giving to each one the Arms necessary for his defense.

With the five Companies of Veteran Infantry and Cavalry, the Militia which the new Towns ought to form, and those who may be recruited in the Town of San Felipe de Chihuahua and its vicinity, it is estimated that the new General Commandant will be able for the present to maintain the defense of the Provinces embraced in his Government. If afterward he shall need, as is probable, larger forces for the expeditions which he will find expedient to send out for the purpose of advancing the Conversions and discoveries, it should not be difficult to increase the troops, either regular or provincial, when experience makes known the great benefits which are promised by this useful establishment in Provinces which are undoubtedly more abundant and rich in mineral products than any others that have been discovered in this Northern America.

Recently news has come that [the English have gone] as far as the Lake of Bois, from which issues the deep-flowing River of the West, directing its course, as discovered, toward the Sea of that name; and if it empties therein, or reaches the South Sea, or is (as may be the case) the famous Colorado River, which forms the Gulf of Californias, there is no doubt, in whichever of these alternatives, that we already have the English very near to our Settlements in New Mexico, and not very distant from the Western Coast of this Continent of America.

Moreover, the Prime Minister of our Court knows, from the voyages and memoirs that are published in Europe, that the Russians have been gaining an intimate knowledge of the navigation of the Sea of Tartary; and that they are, according to very credible and well-grounded statements, carrying on the Fur Trade on a Continent or Island which, it is estimated, lies at the distance of only eight hundred leagues from the Western Coast of Californias, which runs as far as Capes Mendocino and Blanco.

But, while the attempts of Russia and England need not revive at this time all the suspicions and anxieties that Spain manifested in former days (especially after the Reign of Felipe Second) for discovering and gaining possession, by way of the South Sea, of the alleged passage which the other Nations were seeking by way of the North Sea, it is indubitable that since the year 1749 [sic] — in which Admiral Anson came to the Western Coast of this Kingdom, as far as the entrance to the Port of Acapulco — the English and the Dutch (who afterward brought their ships from Eastern India within sight of Cape San Lucas and the Coasts of New Galicia) have acquired a very detailed knowledge of the Ports and Bays which we hold on the South

Coast, especially in the Peninsula of Californias. With all this no one can regard it as impossible or even very difficult for one of those two Nations or for the Moscovites to establish, when that is least expected, a Colony at the Port of Monterrey, where they would have all desirable facilities and conveniences; and that thus we should come to see our North America invaded and exploited by way of the South Sea as it has been by that of the North.

In these circumstances, it seems as if worldly prudence may counsel, and even carry into effect, that we should take proper precautions in time, putting into practice whatever measures may be feasible to avert the dangers that threaten us. And, as at present the Peninsula of Californias is free from obstruction, it follows that we should and easily could — its population being increased by the aid of the free Commerce which ought to be carried on between that territory and this Kingdom — transport a Colony to the Port of Monterrey with the same vessels that we now have in the South Sea, which have been built for the use of the Sonora expedition. It only remains to establish in this Province the General Commandancy, which very soon can promote and facilitate the Settlement of Monterrey, and of other points on the Western Coast of the same Californias — where there are good Harbors, and the soil is more fertile and productive than that of the North Shore.

A Chief who is on the ground and energetic will secure considerable extensions to the Frontiers of Sonora and Nueva Viscaya, unless he is insufficiently provided with the funds that are necessary in order that the establishment of his Government may produce the utilities and advantages that ought to be expected. These are set forth at length in the project, already cited, which was presented to the Court in the year 1760, with the aim of securing the erection [of such a Government]. If the decision be reached that it is more expedient to maintain on the Frontiers of Chihuahua an Official, subordinate to the Governor, for the defense of that Mining Centre, a suitable person for that employ is Captain Don Lope de Cuellar, who was appointed by the Viceroy in fulfillment of the instructions addressed to him for the expulsion of the regulars belonging to the Company [of Jesus]. As that measure would do away with the office of *corregidor* that was established in that Town, which enjoys very considerable imposts, from the fund that they produce can be drawn the Salary of two thousand *pesos*, which of course will be an addition to his pay sufficient to maintain the said Governor. At the same time he ought to look after the affairs of the Royal Treasury, with rank as Deputy of the Intendant of Nueva Viscaya — who must reside in the Capital City of Durango, and be, like the Intendants of Sonora and Californias, directly subordinate to the General Commandant of the three Provinces, since that Chief is responsible for rendering account to the Viceroy of Nueva España of whatever enterprises he may undertake, and of all occurrences worthy of note in the region under his command.

An examination of this plan will make evident at first view that in it are discussed only the principal points and designs of the idea, and that its sole aim, with nothing else in view, is to promote the public Interests of the King and the State in an establishment which, besides the urgent necessity of effecting it, carries the special recommendation that it will be very advantageous in a short time; for, from now on, the Foundations of the Work are going to be laid with Solidity, Integrity, and Zeal.

At Mexico, the twenty-third of January, [in the year] One Thousand, Seven Hundred, and Sixty-Eight.

DON JOSÉ DE GÁLVEZ.

To THE MARQUÉS DE CROIX.

APPENDIX B

EXPEDITION WHICH WAS MADE BY DON PEDRO FAGES, LIEUTENANT OF THE CATALONIAN VOLUNTEERS, WITH SIX SOLDIERS AND A MULETEER

[Archives of Mexico. Cor. Vir., Sér. iii, T N 4/14, 1176, f. 385 (*Sc.* 385–389). A. Gen. y Púb., Croix, 1770–71, 4/14, copy no. 2. This document (here published for the first time) is a diary kept by Lieutenant Fages on a tour of exploration made by him to San Francisco Bay in 1770. The translation is by Miss Emma Helen Blair, of Madison, Wisconsin]

November 21, 1770.   We set out from Monterrey about 11 o'clock, and immediately went around the head of a large inlet, and took a N. E. course. After a march of three leagues, we halted on the other side of the River Carmelo, a name which was given to it by mistake at the first exploration of Monterrey. All day we traveled through somewhat rolling country, part of it good soil, part sandy.

November 22.   We set out early in the morning, crossed the flats of the aforesaid River, and at four leagues distance we entered the Arroyo, in which no water flowed; it was thickly set with Alders, Live-oaks, and other Trees which we could not identify. We saw many paths made by bears, which we knew by the locks of their hair; only the path which we followed [showed the tracks] of Heathens. We went forward through this Arroyo about a league, and, following in the same direction on the slope of a hill, ascended to the top of it, from which we descried at some distance a spacious Valley; this was four leagues broad in some places, and ran from N.W. to S.E. We descended by the slope of a hill, and after going one eighth of a league came to a narrow Valley which ran from N.E. to S.W., in which we made our camp. It contained a small Arroyo with water, which ended not far away among its own scanty sands; its breadth was 200 Varas, and it received the name la Cañadita ["the little brook"]. This day's march was five leagues. [On the left-hand margin is written: "To la Cañadita, 5 leagues"; on the right-hand margin, "From Monterrey, 8 leagues."]

November 23. We left the Camp at la Cañadita, and after marching half a league reached the large Valley which we saw from the top of the Hill; we crossed it, which cost us three leagues. We saw on the way many herds of Wild Pigs [*Berrendos*], and some of these numbered more than 50; we also saw many Geese, of which we killed four. The Soil of this Valley was very good. From this place we crossed a small valley abounding in patches of reeds, which at the right-hand side had a Pool of fresh water. Very soon afterward we had to cross an Arroyo in which Alders grew thickly, and this one had a large Pool of fresh water. After that, we made our way through a gap in the Mountain range that lay before us; it was overgrown with Oaks, and had many Freshwater Pools, which at the edges were thickly fringed with reeds [*tule*]. At a little distance from them we halted, in the bend of a Hill at the foot of which ran a tiny Rivulet, which hardly supplied drink for our Animals. This day's march was four leagues, in a N.E. Direction.

In the evening of this day a reconnoissance was made in the direction of the N.E., for the distance of some two leagues, climbing up a very rocky Hill; from the top of this was seen an immense number of Ridges which stretched directly across our course, which obliged us to retrace our steps. This place was called los Berrendos. [On the left margin: "To the Pools, 4 leagues"; on the right margin, "From Monterrey, 12 leagues."]

November 24. We left this Camp, and, returning on our path for the distance of a league, which we had marched on the preceding day, we took a N.W. direction, through the Valley which we had crossed the day before, on the right-hand side along the foot of the Hills which shut it in, leaving on the left hand many patches of reeds. We crossed many bear-trails, and at the end of them was a very large Pond. At the upper end of this was a Ranchería of Heathens, in which we saw about fifty Souls.

Two of these Heathens were going with two little Rafts to hunt Ducks in the Pond. With all the efforts that we made, we could not succeed in pacifying them; the only result was, that they uttered loud cries, and two of them hastened over the plain to notify of our passage two very large Rancherías which stood in the middle of it, within our view. In consequence, the people rushed out to gaze on us, at a distance, and were lost in admiration at seeing a soldier, as he marched, kill nine Geese with three shots. We continued our journey, and when we had completed a five leagues' march, we halted on a rising ground close to the same Valley, between two little Springs [*Ojitos*] of excellent water. Camp of los Ojitos. [On the left margin: "To the Camp of los Ojitos, 5 leagues"; on the right margin, "From Monterrey, 17 leagues."]

November 25. We set out from the Camp of los Ojitos and crossed some Hills, not very high, which stood close to the Camp, and went toward the same Valley, to the N.W. All this day's March was over level Ground, of good soil, with many Oaks and some Live-oaks. On the right hand we left an Arroyo which came out of the Ridge, thickly set with Alders, but containing no water. The Ridge which we were leaving to the right was very bare, having many outcroppings of Ore Rock [*Panino*] which showed various sorts of lustre; and some of the Soldiers said that it seemed to have traces of Metals, for which reason I gave orders that some pieces of it be collected. This day we advanced about five leagues; we came to a halt under a Hill on the right hand, which formed a slender Rivulet [*Arroyto*] of excellent water, enough for us and the Animals. [On the left margin: "To the Camp at el Arroyto, 5 leagues"; on the right margin: "From Monterrey, 22 leagues."]

November 26. We started very early in the morning, and continued to follow the same Valley, although now its course was deflected toward the N.N.W. We proceeded some four leagues, over ground thickly set with Oaks, Live-oaks, and other Trees which we could not identify. On the way we descried a very large Ranchería of mountain Heathens, and when we undertook to go near it the people took to flight; nevertheless, we were able to pacify them with the many trinkets that we offered them, and induced them to accept some strings of Glass Beads, and Ribbons. We saw likewise two other Rancherías, but small ones, and some columns of smoke on each side of the Valley. Four Heathens followed us until we made halt at the head of the *Estero* of the Port of San Francisco, alongside a river, [in a place] which had some Pools of excellent fresh water. [On the left margin: "To the Estero of San Francisco, 4 leagues"; on the right margin, "From Monterrey, 26 leagues."]

November 27. We set out in the early morning, crossing the Valley in a N.E. direction, which cost us about two leagues. We went around the heads of many inlets which branch from the large one, and took a Northerly direction; and after going one league we had to pass an Arroyo abounding in Alders and other Trees, which had no water. Near this was a lake of excellent fresh water, the circumference of which was fringed with reeds, rushes, and many grassy places — among which were abundance of Geese, and we succeeded in killing seven of them. We saw close by the Lake many Heathens, of friendly and pleasant manner, to whom we presented some strings of Glass Beads; they returned the favor by giving us some Feathers, and Geese stuffed with Grass, which they use [as decoys] in order to catch enormous numbers of these Birds. At three leagues from this place we passed an Arroyo with considerable water, well covered with Alders, Laurels, and other Trees which we did not recognize, and halted in a level spot close by.

The entire March of this day was six leagues; the Soil was very good, and full of cracks, which made crosses in more than one sense of the word. We passed two Rivulets of very good water, and we marched all Day, leaving at the right hand some Hills — not very high, of good Soil, and here and there the Slopes dotted with many Laurels.

November 28. Four Soldiers went out to explore the Country, and at night they came back, saying that they had gone about seven leagues toward the North. They said that the land was very good, and level; that they had climbed to the top of a Hill, but had not been able to discern the end of an inlet which lay before them and communicated with the one which was at our left hand. They had seen many tracks of cloven feet, which they believed to be those of Mexican Bulls [*Zíbolos: i. e.,* buffaloes]; also that close to the Hills which they left at the right hand were some little springs of Water, and that they had crossed two little streams like it. They added that they had seen the mouth of the *estero* which they believed was the one which had its entrance through the Bay of the Port of San Francisco — which I made certain by having viewed it.

November 29. On this day we determined to return to our starting-point, on seeing that it was impossible for us to pass over to the other side of the Punta de los Reyes without wasting many days' time, also because of the anxiety that I felt about the Camp, the Farm-work, and the care of the Cattle. Retracing the march that we had made on the 27th, we halted in the same place [as then], without anything new occurring. This day's march was the same [as before], six leagues. As we passed along our way, near a little brook about 20 Heathens came out to see us; and some of the women began to entertain us with Dancing and many gestures of joy. One of the Women made us a quite long harangue. We gave them some large Beads, and they returned the compliment with some Feather ornaments. We saw on this day the smoke from many fires.

November 30. We set out at an early hour from the Head of the Inlet, and marched four leagues. We passed along the edge of a small Ranchería, in which there were four Women and three Infants; they were frightened, and gave us two stuffed Geese. We halted at the same place which we occupied and from which we set out on the 26th.

December 1. When we started the Sun was already high, because we had lost some Animals; but we encountered them along the road on which we were returning. This day we marched five leagues, the same as on November 25.

December 2. Early in the morning we set out, in a S.E. direction, and marched five leagues without the least incident. The Land was the same as on November 25; and we halted about half a league from the place where the little springs were, on the Monterrey side, at some little Pools in a small Arroyo.

December 3. We began our march an hour after the Sun rose, because we had lost two Animals, but we found them after we had gone a league. We crossed the Valley, leaving at the left hand the ranchería, Pond, and reedy ground, and at the right the [smaller] rancherías that we had seen on November 24; and they even seemed to us much larger [than before]. After going five leagues we reached the Camp of la Cañadita, at which we came to a halt and pitched our Camp.

December 4. We started early in the morning, climbing up the slope which we had descended on the 22d of November, and went toward the Arroyo, which we crossed on the same day, crossing the flats in it, where we saw many flocks of Geese. We came to the river, which we crossed at the same place as before; and after marching eight leagues we arrived at this Royal Presidio of San Carlos at Monterrey, where we found that nothing new had occurred. This expedition was made in the service of His Majesty, with the object of reconnoitring the country as far as the Port of San Francisco.

PEDRO FAGES.

APPENDIX C

GOVERNORS OF THE CALIFORNIAS

(Spanish Régime 1767–1804)

(Dates of service in the case of each governor are from assumption to surrender of office.)

Gaspar de Portolá,
November 30, 1767, to July 9, 1770.

From May 21, 1769, Portolá's position was in fact that of Comandante-militar for Alta California. From July 9, 1770, to May 25, 1774, the position of Comandante was filled by Pedro Fages; and from May 25, 1774, to February, 1777, by Fernando Rivera y Moncada.

Matías de Armona,
June 12, 1769, to November 9, 1770.

After Armona's appointment, but prior to his arrival on June 12, 1769, Diego (?) González served as lieutenant-governor. From June 24, 1769, to June 13, 1770, Armona was absent in Sonora, and Juan Gutiérrez served as lieutenant, or acting, governor, to October 3, 1769, when he was succeeded by Antonio López de Toledo, who served until June 13, 1770. From November 9, 1770 (date of Armona's retirement) the acting governor was Bernardino Moreno.

Felipe Barri,
March ——, 1770, to March 4, 1775.

Felipe de Neve,
March 4, 1775, to July 12, 1782.

In February, 1777, Neve took up his residence at Monterey in Alta California, and Rivera y Moncada went south to assume the lieutenant-governorship at Loreto. The acting lieutenant-governor, pending Rivera's arrival, was Joaquín Cañete.

Pedro Fages,
July 12, 1782, to April 16, 1791.

On July 18, 1781, Rivera y Moncada was killed on the Colorado, and Joaquín Cañete served as lieutenant-governor till late in November, 1783, when he was succeeded by José Joaquín de Arrillaga.

Antonio Romeu,
April 16, 1791, to April 9, 1792.

José Joaquín de Arrillaga,
April 9, 1792, to May 14, 1794.

During this period, Arrillaga was lieutenant-governor and Comandante of Lower California, and governor of the Californias *ad interim.*

Diego de Borica,
May 14, 1794, to March 8, 1800.

José Joaquín de Arrillaga,
March 8, 1800, to November 16, 1804.

Until March 11, 1802, when he died, Pedro de Alberni, who outlived Arrillaga, was Comandante-militar for Alta California.

GOVERNORS OF ALTA CALIFORNIA

(Spanish Régime 1804–1821)

(The decree making Alta California a separate province bore date August 29, 1804, and reached Arrillaga November 16.)

José Joaquín de Arrillaga,
November 16, 1804, to July 24, 1814.

José Darío Argüello,
July 24, 1814, to August 30, 1815.

Governor *ad interim.*

Pablo Vicente de Sola,
August 30, 1815, to November 10, 1822.

GOVERNORS OF ALTA CALIFORNIA

(Mexican Régime 1821–1847)

Luis Antonio Argüello,
November 10, 1822, to November ——, 1825.

Until April 2, 1823, Argüello's authority was derived from the Spanish Regency. After that date until November 17 it was derived from Iturbide as Agustín I. After November 17 it was derived from the *Congreso Constituyente* [National Congress]. In March, 1823, Iturbide named Naval Captain Bonifacio de Tosta governor of Alta California.

José María Echeandía,
November ——, 1825, to January 31, 1831.

In 1824 José Miñón was appointed governor of Alta California, but he declined the office.

Manuel Victoria,
January 31, 1831, to December 6, 1831.

Antonia García was first appointed as Echeandía's successor, but the appointment was revoked.

José María Echeandía,
November 6, 1831, to January 14, 1833.

De facto *Jefe político* and *jefe militar* in the district south of, but not including, Santa Bárbara.

Pío Pico,
January 27 to February 16, 1832.

Jefe político by appointment of the Diputación.

Agustín V. Zamorano,
February 1, 1832, to January 14, 1833.

De facto *Jefe militar* in the district north of and including Santa Bárbara.

José Figueroa,
January 14, 1833, to September 29, 1835.

Early in 1833 Figueroa asked to be relieved of office. On July 16th, 1833, José María Híjar was appointed *jefe político*, but the appointment was revoked by President Santa Anna on July 25. On July 18, 1834, Figueroa withdrew his request to be relieved.

José Castro,
September 29, 1835, to January 2, 1836.

From October 8, 1835, to January 1, 1836, the position of *jefe militar* was held by Nicolás Gutiérrez.

Nicolás Gutiérrez,
January 2 to May 3, 1836.

Mariano Chico,
May 3 to August 1, 1836.

Nicolás Gutiérrez,
August 1 to November 5, 1836.

José Castro,
November 5 to December 7, 1836.

Castro was *jefe militar* until November 29, when he was succeeded by Mariano Guadalupe Vallejo.

Juan Bautista Alvarado,
December 7, 1836, to December 31, 1842.

Manuel Micheltorena,
December 31, 1842, to February 22, 1845.

Pío Pico,
February 22, 1845, to August 10, 1846.

José María Flóres,
October 31, 1846, to January 11, 1847.

Andrés Pico,
January 11 to January 13, 1847.

Until August 7, 1839, Alvarado was governor *ad interim*. On June 6, 1837, Carlos Carrillo was appointed governor, and on December 6, he assumed office at Los Ángeles, but he was arrested and deposed by Alvarado on May 20, 1838.

By the departmental junta Pío Pico was declared governor *ad interim* on February 15, 1845.

José Castro was *jefe militar* for same period.

APPENDIX D

THE SPANISH FOUNDERS OF SAN FRANCISCO

[From the diary of Fray Pedro Font, A. D. 1776, and here printed (it is believed) for the first time. Original document is in the John Carter Brown Library at Providence, R. I.]

SERGEANT, soldiers, and settlers, with their respective families, whom — by order of his Excellency the Viceroy — Don Juan Bautista de Anza, lieutenant-colonel of cavalry and captain of the Royal Presidio of Tubac, in the province of Sonora, has conducted to the presidio of Monterey in Northern California, for the purpose of turning them over to their comandante, Don Fernando de Rivera y Moncada.

Presidio Soldiers

1. Lieutenant Don Joseph Joachín Moraga came without wife and family because of the illness of his wife, whom he left in Terrente where he lives.

1. Sergeant Juan Pablo Grijalva and his wife María Dolores.

Valencia.
Children:
María Josepha,
5. María del Carmen,
Claudio.

Domingo Alviso
   and his wife,
María Angela Chumasero.
Children:
6. Francisco Xavier,
Juan Ignacio,
María Loreto.

Valero Mesa,
   and his wife,
María Leonor Barboa.

Rosalia Samora,
   wife of Salvador Manuel.

Ygnacio Linares,
   and his wife,
Gertrudis Rivas.
6. Children:
José Ramón,
Salvador Ygnacio,
María Gertrudis,
María Juliana.

Justo Roverto,
   and his wife,
María Loreto Delfina.
4. Children:
Joseph Antonio,
Joseph Matias.

8. Children:
Joseph Joachín,
Joseph Ignacio,
Joseph Dolores.
Joseph Antonio,
Juan,
María Manuela.

Ramón Bajórquez,
and his wife,
María Francisca Rovero.
4. Children:
María Gertrudis,
María Michaela.

Carlos Gallegos,
2. and his wife,
María Josepha Espinosa.

Juan Antonio Amézquita,
and his wife,
Juana Goana.
Children:
Salvador Manuel,
8. María Josepha,
María Dolores,
María Matilde,
María de los Reyes.

Antonio Quiterio Aceves,
and his wife,
María Feliciana Cortés.
Children:
8. Joseph Cipriano,
Juan Gregorio,
Juan Pablo,
Joseph Antonio,
María Petra,
María Gertrudis.

Phelipe Santiago Tapia,
and his wife,
Juan María Cárdenas.
11. Children:
Joseph Bartolomé,
Juan Joseph,
Joseph Cristóval,
Joseph Francisco,
Joseph Victor,

Gabriel Peralta,
and his wife,
Francisca Manuela Valenzuela.
6. Children:
Juan Joseph,
Luis María,
Pedro,
Gertrudis.

Soldiers (Recruits)
Juan Athanasio Vázquez,
and his wife,
Gertrudis Castelo.
Children:
Josepha Tiburcio,
6. Joseph Antonio,
Pedro Joseph,
María Antonio Bajórquez,
wife of Joseph Tiburcio.

Joseph Antonio García,
and his wife,
Petronila Josepha.
7. Children:
Joseph Vicente,
Joseph Francisco,
Juan Guillermo,
María Graciana,
María Josepha.

Lasa Ortiz.
Children:
4. Juan Francisco,
María Francisca.

Ygnacio Soto,
and his wife,
Bárbara Espinosa.
4. Children:
Joseph Antonio,
María Francisca.

Pablo Pinto,
Francisca Xaviera Ruelas.
Children:
6. Juan María,
Joseph Marcelo,
Juana Santos,
Juana.

María Rosa,
María Antonio,
María Manuela,
María Ysidora.

Ygnacia María Gutiérrez,
and his wife,
Ana María Ossuna.
5. Children:
María de los Santos,
María Petra,
Diego Pascual.

Agustín Valenzuela,
and his wife,
3. Petra Ygnacia Ochoa.
Children:
María Zeferina.

Luis Joachín Álvarez de Acenedo,
and his wife,
María Nico.
5. Children:
Francisca María,
Ygnacio María,
María Gertrudis.

Sebastián Antonio López,
and his wife,
Phelipa Neri.
5. Children:
Sebastián,
María Thomasa,
María Justa.

Juan Francisco Vernal,
and his wife,
María Soto.
Children:
9. Joseph Dionisio,
Joseph Joachín,
Joseph Apolinario,
Juan Francisco,
Thomás Januario,
Ana María,
María Theresa.

Juan Salvio Pacheco,
and his wife,
María Carmen del Valle.

Joseph Antonio Sotélo,
and his wife,
3. Peralta.
Children:
Ramón.

Pedro Bajórquez,
and his wife,
3. María Francesca de Lara.
Children:
María Agustina.

Santiago de la Cruz Pico,
and his wife,
María Jacinta Bostida.
Children:
8. Joseph María,
Joseph Dolores,
Joseph Patricio,
Francisco Javier,
María Antonia Thomasa.

Joseph Manuel Valencia,
and his wife,
María de la Luz Muñoz.

María Encarnación.
María Martina.
Vicente Félix (widower).
(His wife died on the way,
on the 24th of November at
dawn.)
Children:
Joseph Francisco,
Joseph Dorotheo,
Joseph de Jesús,
Joseph Antonio Capistrano,
María Loreto,
María Antonia,
María Manuela.

Casimiro Varela,
1. Marida de Juana,
Santos Pinto.

1. Ygnasio Anastasio Higuera —
husband of Michaela Bajórquez.

7. Children:
Miguel,
Francisco.

Joseph Antonio Sánchez,
   and his wife,
María Dolores Morales.
Children:
5. Joseph Antonio,
María Josepha,
Ygnacio Cárdenas
   (his adopted son).

Joachín Ysidro Castro,
   and his wife,
María Martina Botiller.
Children:
Ygnacio Clemente,
11. Joseph Mariano,
Francisco,
Francisco Antonio,
Carlos Antonio,
Ana Josepha.

Nicolás Galindo,
   and his wife,
3. Theresa Pinto.
Children:
Juan Venancio.

Pedro Pérez de la Puente,
Marcos Villela,
3. Dn. Francisco Muñoz.
   (The three are unmarried.)

Christóval Sandoval,
1.   and his wife,
Dolores Ontiveros.

Feliciana Arballa,
   (widow),
3. María Thomasa Gutiérrez,
María Eustaquia.
   (The three are unmarried.)

Bartholomé.
María Gertrudis.
Bárbara.

Manuel Ramírez Arrellano,
   and his wife,
4. María Agueda López de Aro.
Children:
Mariano Mathias Vega
   (his adopted son).

Settlers who were not Soldiers
Joseph Manuel Gonzáles,
   and his wife,
María Michaela Ruez.
Children:
6. Juan Joseph,
Ramón,
Francisco,
María Gregoria.

Nicolás Antonio Berrélleza,
2. María Ysabel Berrelleza.
   (Brother and sister, and unmarried.)

According to this list, there were 193 persons. I do not know if it be complete or lacks some name, since I was not permitted to be informed; yet I was so far favored as to be allowed to see the list, which I copied.

APPENDIX E

SEALED ORDERS ISSUED TO COMMODORE ROBERT F. STOCKTON IN 1845

[These orders have never before appeared in print. The author is indebted for them to the courtesy of the U. S. Navy Department.]

S. O. NAVY DEPARTMENT,
October 17, 1845.

Commodore R. F. Stockton,
    Comdg. U. S. S. Congress,
        Norfolk, Va.

COMMODORE, — So soon as the U. S. frigate, of which you have volunteered to take the command, shall be in all respects ready for sea, and you shall have received Messrs. Ten Eyck and Terrell, the Commissioner and Consul to the Sandwich Islands, you will proceed directly to the Pacific, touching at such ports as you may think proper.

On reaching the Pacific, you will by letter, as often as occasion offers, inform Commodore Sloat of your approach, and will, in the mean time, make the best of your way to the Sandwich Islands.

You will there land Messrs. Ten Eyck and Terrell at the place of their destination. During your presence at the Islands, you will do all in your power to cherish, on the part of their government, good feelings towards the United States. You may find there United States stores of which you will avail yourself.

Having done this duty at the Sandwich Islands, you will next proceed with all dispatch to perform the special duty assigned you by the sealed instructions which you are not to open till you pass the Capes of Virginia.

You will communicate to all the officers under your command the order of this Department that no one be concerned in a duel.

Commending you and your ship's company to the protection of Divine Providence, and wishing you all a pleasant cruise and a safe return to your country and friends, I am,

        Very respectfully,

           GEORGE BANCROFT.

NAVY DEPARTMENT, Octo. 17, 1845.

SEALED ORDERS,
not to be opened till the U. S. Frigate "CONGRESS"
shall be without the Capes of Virginia.

Commodore R. F. Stockton,
    Commanding U. S. Frigate "CONGRESS."
    SIR: So soon as the U. S. Frigate "CONGRESS," under your command, shall be in all respects ready for Sea, you will proceed directly to the Pacific, touching at such ports on your way as you may think necessary. You will find Commodore Sloat as soon as possible and report to him as forming part of the squadron under his command. The dispatches for Commodore Sloat, herewith forwarded to you, you will deliver so soon as you have opportunity.

    When you have finished your duties at the Sandwich Islands, you will sail directly for Monterey, and in person, or by a perfectly trustworthy hand, deliver the enclosed letter to our Consul at that place. You will confer with the Consul, gain all the information you can on Mexican affairs and do all in your power to conciliate the good feeling of the people of that place towards the United States. On leaving Monterey, you will join the squadron of Commodore Sloat.

    Commending you and your ship's company to the protection of Divine Providence, and wishing you all a pleasant cruise and a safe return to your country and your friends, I am,

                    Very respectfully,
                            GEORGE BANCROFT.

INDEX

INDEX

Aberdeen, Lord, 298, 302, 314.
Adams, J. Q., contemplates purchase of California, 301.
Aguirre, Fray Andrés, letter by, on station for galleons, 24; describes "Isles of the Armenian," 24–25.
Agustín I, 232, 241.
Alamán, L., 238.
Alaska, 34.
Alberní, Lt. Col. P., 170, 172.
Alcalde, the, *see* under Local government.
Almonte, J. N., 275.
Altimíra, J., 246.
Alvarado, J. E., governor, 229; early life of, 257; president of *California libre*, 258; conspiracies against, 259; confirmed in governorship, 262–264; resists Micheltorena, 279; contemplates protectorate for California, 487, 495.
America, North, as an archipelago, 3–4.
American Revolution, effect in Spain, 216.
Americans (Anglo-Americans), 265; immigration by, 269, 273, 276; devoid of status in California, 307.
Andrade, J. A. de, 230.
"Anian," strait of, 12, 16, 17–18, 19, 21, 23; Ascensión's opinion regarding, 23; 34; Kino regarding, 55; 59; 86; existence of, disproved, 163; 166; 376, 427–428.
Anza route, attempt to reopen, 237.
Anza, J. B. de, Jr., 90; Sonora to Monterey, 98–102; Monterey to S. F. Bay, 102–110; colloquy with Rivera, 111–112; presidio on the Colorado, 130.
Anza, J. B. de, Sr., 97, 413.
Apaches, the, 10, 96, 434.
Apachería, 41.
Apalátegui, A., revolt under, 252.
Aranda, 64.|
Architecture, of the missions, 332–335, 496; of the presidios, 338.
Arellavo, A. de, seeks route east from Philippines, 15.
Argüello, L., 196, 197, 214; governor, 233; 246.
Argüello, J. D., 126, 134, 196; governor *ad interim*, 210; governor of Lower Calif., 233.
Arrángoiz, F. de, Mexican Consul, 274.
Arrillaga, José J., reviews charges by Padre Concepción, 183; governor, 185, 187; on American traders, 202; death of, 207; friendship of, for Russians, 215–216.
Arteaga, I., northern voyage by, 120.
Ascensión, Fr. Antonio de la, narratives by, of Vizcaino's voyage, 376.

Ashley Fur Company, 269.
Astoria, 269.
Asylum, right of, for criminals in California, 111, 112, 421.
Ávila, J. M., 245.
Ayala, Capt. J. M., enters S. F. Bay with the San Carlos, 109.
Ayuntamientos, *see* under Local government in Hispanic California.

Bachelof, A., 293.
Bancroft, G., Sec. of Navy, 315; defense of Frémont by, 489.
Bandini, J., 248; seizes Los Ángeles, 259.
Baránoff, A., 192.
Barona, Padre J., 240.
Barron, E., British Consul at Tepic, 267.
Bartleson-Bidwell Company, the, 269, 277.
"Bear Flag" Party, the, 311, 317, 490.
Beechey, Capt. F. W., 236, 300.
Behring, V., 34.
Blanco Cape, 65.
Bodega Bay, attempt to settle at, 167; Russians under Kuskof at, 200–201, 216, 231.
Bodega y Quadra, J. F., northern voyage by, 119.
Bonaparte, Joseph, 210, 216.
Bonneville, Capt., 269.
Borica, D. de, governor, 159; reaches peninsula, and Monterey, 168; introduces artisans, 176; on slow progress of the Mission, 177; on cruelty of padres, 178; retires, 184.
Bostonians, as traders and smugglers, 190, 194, 203.
Bouchard, Capt. H., 211.
Boundaries of California, *see* under California.
Branciforte, *villa* of founding of, 171–174; condition of, in 1846, 286.
Brown, John ("Lean John"), 323.
Bryant and Sturgis, 292.
Bucarely, Viceroy Fray A. M., 94.
Buenos Ayres, 210.
Burgos, Laws of, 37–38.
Burroughs, Capt. C., 329.
Bustamente, A. de, 230; president of Mexico, 244.
Byng, Admiral, to seek California by way of Pole, 119.
Byrd, the Lelia, 191.

Cabrera Bueno, manual of navigation by, 81.
Cabrillo, J. R., explores California coast, 6–7.
California, discovery of, by Cortés, 5; as an